AF752233

June 19–23, 2017
Niagara Falls, NY, USA

Association for Computing Machinery

Advancing Computing as a Science & Profession

MobiSys'17

Proceedings of the 15th Annual International Conference on

Mobile Systems, Applications, and Services

Sponsored by:

ACM SIGMOBILE

Supported by:

NSF, Microsoft, Intel, Samsung, IBM Research, Nokia Bell Labs, Huawei, University at Buffalo, & Google

Association for
Computing Machinery

Advancing Computing as a Science & Profession

The Association for Computing Machinery
2 Penn Plaza, Suite 701
New York, New York 10121-0701

Copyright © 2017 by the Association for Computing Machinery, Inc. (ACM). Permission to make digital or hard copies of portions of this work for personal or classroom use is granted without fee provided that copies are not made or distributed for profit or commercial advantage and that copies bear this notice and the full citation on the first page. Copyright for components of this work owned by others than ACM must be honored. Abstracting with credit is permitted. To copy otherwise, to republish, to post on servers or to redistribute to lists, requires prior specific permission and/or a fee. Request permission to republish from: permissions@acm.org or Fax +1 (212) 869-0481.

For other copying of articles that carry a code at the bottom of the first or last page, copying is permitted provided that the per-copy fee indicated in the code is paid through www.copyright.com.

Notice to Past Authors of ACM-Published Articles
ACM intends to create a complete electronic archive of all articles and/or other material previously published by ACM. If you have written a work that has been previously published by ACM in any journal or conference proceedings prior to 1978, or any SIG Newsletter at any time, and you do NOT want this work to appear in the ACM Digital Library, please inform permissions@acm.org, stating the title of the work, the author(s), and where and when published.

ISBN: 978-1-4503-4928-4 (Digital)

ISBN: 978-1-4503-5596-4 (Print)

Additional copies may be ordered prepaid from:

ACM Order Department
PO Box 30777
New York, NY 10087-0777, USA

Phone: 1-800-342-6626 (USA and Canada)
+1-212-626-0500 (Global)
Fax: +1-212-944-1318
E-mail: acmhelp@acm.org
Hours of Operation: 8:30 am – 4:30 pm ET

Printed in the USA

General Chairs' Welcome

It is our great pleasure to welcome you to *the 15th ACM International Conference on Mobile Systems, Applications, and Services (MobiSys'17).* MobiSys is the premier venue for publishing cutting-edge research in mobile systems and applications. This year is its 15th iteration, and we are delighted that the steering committee led by Victor Bahl has decided to bring the conference to Niagara Falls.

The program committee, led by Andrew Campbell and Deepak Ganesan, has come up with an excellent program for this year's conference. They have done a fantastic job in reviewing 190 papers and selecting 34 outstanding papers. We are very thankful to Andrew and Deepak for their exceptional effort in coming with such a wonderful program.

We encourage you to attend the keynote and invited talk presentations. These valuable and insightful talks can and will guide us to a better understanding of the future of mobile. Our keynote speaker is Pattie Maes from MIT Media Lab, and her talk is entitled *"Augmenting the Human Experience."* Norman Abramson from the University of Hawaii has received *SIGMOBILE Outstanding Contribution Award*, and will give his award talk entitled *"ALOHA to the Web."* We also have invited speakers from the government, academia, and industry---Thyagarajan Nandagopal (NSF), Matthai Philipose (Microsoft Research), David Erickson (Cornell), David Chu (Google), Minkyong Kim (Samsung). Lastly, we have a special session on *SIGMOBILE Test of Time Presentation Awards*, and the awardees will recollect and share their experience in writing their papers. We would like to thank all the speakers for giving a talk on these interesting topics.

In addition, we encourage you to attend the poster and demo session. We have selected 15 demos and 34 posters that are outstanding in quality. The poster/demo chairs, Inseok Hwang, Aruna Balasubramanian, Dimitrios Koutsonikolas, and Chunyi Peng, deserve special mention for selecting those excellent posters and demos.

We have multiple workshops on emerging topics, which allow our community to discuss new and exciting directions for future mobile systems. Our workshops chairs, Ben Greenstein and Tam Vu, have done an excellent job in inviting individual workshop chairs and providing all logistical support for them. We thank all the individual workshop chairs for their heroic effort in organizing each workshop.

Putting together *MobiSys'17* was a team effort. First of all, we thank all the authors of papers, posters, and demos for providing the content of the program. We also thank our sponsors, ACM SIGMMOBILE, and our generous supporters, NSF, Microsoft, Intel, Samsung, IBM Research, Nokia Bell Labs, Huawei, Google, and the University at Buffalo. Last but not least, we thank the rest of the organizing team for making MobiSys a very successful event — Karthik Dantu and Lukasz Ziarek (local arrangement chairs), Ardalan Amiri Sani and Robert LiKamWa (web chairs), Hong Lu (registration chair), Aziz Mohaisen and Kyungmin Lee (treasurers), Eduardo Cuervo (publication chair), Mi Zhang (student scholarship chair), and Taeyeon Ki and Sharath Chandrashekhara (app chairs). On behalf of the entire organizing team, we would like to welcome you to Niagara Falls!

Tanzeem Choudhury
MobiSys'17 General Co-Chair
Cornell University

Steve Ko
MobiSys'17 General Co-Chair
University at Buffalo

MobiSys 2017 Program Chairs' Welcome

It is our pleasure and privilege to serve as program chairs for ACM MobiSys 2017 - the 15th ACM International Conference on Mobile Systems, Applications, and Services. We hope you enjoy this technical material behind the conference that attracts a diverse set of attendees from both academia and industry and is a leading venue for publications and idea exchange on mobile systems. ACM MobiSys 2017 has a highly selective, single-track program featuring research related to mobile systems and applications. It is an ideal venue to address research challenges facing the design, development, deployment, use, and fundamental limits of these systems.

Notes on the review process: Since its inception in 2003 MobiSys has had a single-blind review policy where the identity of the reviewers is not revealed to the authors but the reviewers know the names, affiliations and contact information of the authors. Beginning 2017, we modified this policy so that the identity of the authors was not revealed to the reviewers during the initial review of the paper. However, once preliminary outcomes were decided, identities of the authors was revealed to enable referees to ask appropriate questions, making it easier to compare the new results with the author(s) previously published work and to ensure that a true advance was being reported.

Our paper review process this year was highly selective. Out of 188 submissions, the technical program committee accepted only 34 for publication and presentation as full papers, yielding an acceptance rate around 18%. Submitted papers underwent a rigorous, multi-stage review process. First, we checked all submissions for compliance, general quality, and topic match. We administratively rejected those not meeting our submission criteria. We assigned 3 reviewers to papers that survived this stage from the program committee and the external review committee. At the conclusion of this stage, those papers where none of the reviewers were enthusiastic about acceptance were rejected. We then assigned at least 2 additional reviewers from the program committee to papers that survived, thus totaling at least 5 reviews per paper. An online discussion phase then ensued, resulting in the PC recommending 60 papers for discussion at the PC meeting. The PC meeting was held in person in Sonoma CA, USA, the day after ACM HotMobile 2017. At the conclusion of the PC meeting, we accepted 34 papers to the conference. Several accepted papers were assigned shepherds to help ensure that the authors produce a final manuscript that satisfactorily addresses reviewer comments.

The program: Our program this year covers an exciting set of topics including sensing using acoustic, RF, and light signals, novel communication techniques, deep learning on mobiles, mobile performance, security and privacy, and operating systems. It also includes a keynote by Pattie Maes on human augmentation i.e. how systems can actively assist people with memory, learning, decision making, communication and physical skills, a SIGMOBILE Outstanding Contribution Award talk by Norman Abramson, recognized for his pioneering work on the ALOHAnet wireless networking system, five invited talks on trends in deep learning on mobiles, virtual reality, internet of things, biomedical diagnostics using phones, and large-scale wireless testbeds, brief talks by five Test-of-Time award winners, as well as an extensive poster/demo session.

Acknowledgements: Putting together the program for MobiSys 2017 was a team effort. We thank the authors for submitting their best work to MobiSys, and the members of the Technical Program Committee (TPC) and External Program Committee (ERC) for providing detailed and constructive feedback to authors. We were also pleased to see almost full attendance at the TPC meeting, and very grateful to the TPC members for taking time out of their busy schedules to travel to the meeting. We are indebted to Elizabeth Belding, who in her role as General Chair for HotMobile 2017 handled the logistics for the TPC meeting. We are very thankful to the General Chairs, Tanzeem Choudhury and Steve Ko, for their support with logistics and conference organization as well as their ideas and suggestions that helped shape the conference program. We are grateful to many others who helped with various aspects of conference organization including the Steering Committee, Publicity Chairs (Xia Zhou, Lu Su, Christos Efstratiou, Tadashi Okoshi, and JeongGil Ko), Website chairs (Ardalan Amiri Sani and Robert LiKamWa), Publications Chair (Eduardo Cuervo), and others in the organizing committee for their dependability and commitment to making MobiSys 2017 a success.

As the flagship conference in mobile systems, MobiSys provides a unique opportunity to see important research in the field and have stimulating interactions with experts across a range of sub-areas within the field. We hope that you will find this program interesting and thought-provoking and look forward to seeing many of you at the conference.

Andrew Campbell
Technical Program Co-Chair
Dartmouth College

Deepak Ganesan
Technical Program Co-Chair
University of Massachusetts Amherst

Table of Contents

Poster/ Demo Session

SIGMOBILE Oustanding Contribution Award

SESSION PAPER 4: Security and Privacy I

Session Chair: Kyle Jamieson *(Princeton University)*

PAPER SESSION 5: RF Sensing

Session Chair: Lin Zhong *(Rice University)*

PAPER SESSION 6: Offloading and Sharing

Session Chair: Robin Kravets *(University of Illinois at Urbana-Champaign)*

PAPER SESSION 7: Wearables and CPS
Session Chair: Aruna Balasubramanian *(Stony Brook University)*

PAPER SESSION 8: Mobile Performance
Session Chair: Rajesh Krishna Balan *(Singapore Management University)*

SESSION PAPER 9: Security and Privacy II
Session Chair: Ardalan Amiri Sani *(University of California, Irvine)*

MobiSys 2017 Symposium-Conference-Workshop Organization

General Co-Chairs:	Tanzeem Choudhury *(Cornell University, USA)* Steve Ko *(University at Buffalo, USA)*
Technical Program Co-Chairs:	Andrew Campbell *(Dartmouth College, USA)* Deepak Ganesan *(University of Massachusetts, USA)*
Local Arrangements Co-Chairs:	Kurthik Dantu *(University at Buffalo, USA)* Lukasz Ziarek *(University at Buffalo, USA)*
Web Co-Chairs:	Ardalan Amiri Sani *(University of California, Irvine, USA)* Robert LiKamWa *(Arizona State University, USA)*
Registrations Chair:	Hong Lu*(Intel Labs, USA)*
Treasurer:	Aziz Mohaisen *(University at Buffalo, USA)* Kyungmin Lee *(IBM Research, USA)*
Workshop Co-Chairs:	Tam Vu *(University of Colorado, Denver, USA)* Ben Greenstein *(Google, USA)*
Posters/Demos/Videos Co-Chairs:	Inseok Hwang *(George Mason Institute, USA)* Aruna Balasubramanian *(Stony Brook University, USA)* Dimitrios Koutsonikolas *(University at Buffalo, USA)* Chunyi Peng *(The Ohio State University, USA)*
Publication Chair:	Eduardo Cuervo *(Microsoft Research, USA)*
Publicity Co-Chairs:	Xia Zhou *(Dartmouth College, USA)* Lu Su *(Univeristy at Buffalo, USA)* Christos Efstratiou *(University of Kent, UK)* Tadashi Okoshi *(Keio University, Japan)* JeonGil Ko *(Ajou University, South Korea)*
Student Scholarship Chair	Mi Zhang *(Michigan State University, USA)*
Ph.D. Forum Chairs	Shubham Jain *(Rutgers University, USA)* Tianxing Li *(Dartmouth College, USA)* Kevin Boos *(Rice University, USA)*
App Co-Chairs	Taeyeon Ki *(University at Buffalo, USA)* Sharath Chandrashekhara *(University at Buffalo, USA)*

Program Committee: Fadel Adib *(Massachusetts Institute of Technology, USA)*
Ardalan Amiri Sani *(University of California, Irvine, USA)*
Mary Baker *(HP Labs, USA)*
Rajesh Krishna Balan *(Singapore Management University, Singapore)*
Aruna Balasubramanian *(Stony Brook University, USA)*
Elizabeth M. Belding *(University of California, Santa Barbara, USA)*
Geoffrey Challen *(University at Buffalo, USA)*
David Chu *(Google, USA)*
Sarah Clinch *(University of Manchester, UK)*
Mark Corner *(University of Massachusetts Amherst, USA)*
Shyam Gollakota *(University of Washington, USA)*
Y. Charlie Hu *(Purdue University, USA)*
Wenjun Hu *(Yale University, USA)*
Kyle Jamieson *(Princeton University, USA)*
Minkyong Kim *(Samsung, South Korea)*
Robin Kravets *(University of Illinois at Urbana-Champaign, USA)*
Santosh Kumar *(University of Memphis, USA)*
Nicholas Lane *(University College London and Bell Labs,* UK*)*
Qin Lv *(University of Colorado Boulder, USA)*
Z. Morley Mao *(University of Michigan, USA)*
Cecilia Mascolo *(University of Cambridge, UK)*
Luca Mottola *(Politecnico di Milano, Italy)*
Badri Nath *(Rutgers University, USA)*
Chunyi Peng *(Ohio State University, USA)*
Matthai Philipose *(Microsoft Research, USA)*
Oriana Riva *(Microsoft Research, USA)*
Silvia Santini *(TU Dresden, Germany)*
Souvik Sen *(Google, USA)*
Junehwa Song *(KAIST, South Korea)*
Roy Want *(Google, USA)*
Moustafa A. Youssef *(Egypt-Japan University of Science and Technology)*
Pengyu Zhang *(Stanford University, USA)*
Haitao Zheng *(University of California, Santa Barbara, USA)*
Lin Zhong *(Rice University, USA)*
Xia Zhou *(Dartmouth College, USA)*

External Review Committee:

Yuvraj Agarwal *(Carnegie Mellon University, USA)*
Nilanjan Banerjee *(University of Maryland, Baltimore County, USA)*
Suman Banerjee *(University of Wisconsin-Madison, USA)*
Krishna Chintalapudi *(Microsoft Research, USA)*
Dave Choffnes *(Northeastern University, USA)*
Landon Cox *(Duke University, USA)*
Samir Das *(Stony Brook University, USA)*
Ben Greenstein *(Google, USA)*
Marco Gruteser *(Rutgers University, USA)*
Jeremy Gummeson *(Disney Research, USA)*
Polly Huang *(National Taiwan University, Taiwan)*
JeongGil *(Ko Ajou University, South Korea)*
Ravi Kokku *(IBM Research, USA)*
Youngki Lee *(Singapore Management University, Singapore)*
Mo Li *(Nanyang Technological University, Singapore)*
Robert LiKamWa *(Arizona State University, USA)*
Felix Xiaozhu *(Lin Purdue University, USA)*
Hong Lu *(Intel Labs, USA)*
Lama Nachman *(Intel Labs, USA)*
Suman Nath *(Microsoft Research, USA)*
Tadashi Okoshi *(Keio University, Japan)*
Giovanni Pau *(UPMC/LIP6, France)*
Bodhi Priyantha *(Microsoft Research, USA)*
Anthony Rowe *(Carnegie Mellon University, USA)*
Aaron Schulman *(University of California, San Diego, USA)*
Kannan Srinivasan *(Ohio State University, USA)*
Edison Thomaz *(University of Texas at Austin, USA)*
Thiemo Voigt *(SICS, Sweden)*
Tam Vu *(University of Colorado, Denver, USA)*
He Wang *(Purdue University, USA)*
Alec Wolman *(Microsoft Research, USA)*
Jie Xiong *(Singapore Management University, USA)*
Mi Zhang *(Michigan State University, USA)*
Pei Zhang *(Carnegie Mellon University, USA)*

MobiSys'17 Sponsors & Supporters

Sponsors: ACM, SIGMOBILE

Platinum Supporter: NSF

Silver Supporters: Microsoft, Intel, Samsung Digital Appliance, IBM Research, Nokia Bell Labs, Huawei, University at Buffalo School of Engineering and Applied Sciences

Bronze Supporters: CSE50 1967-2017 University at Buffalo, Google

Augmenting the Human Experience

Pattie Maes
MIT Media Lab
Massachusetts Institute of Technology
pattie@media.mit.edu

BIOGRAPHY

Pattie Maes is the Alexander W. Dreyfoos (1954) Professor in MIT's Program in Media Arts and Sciences and associate head of the Program in Media Arts and Sciences. She founded and directs the Media Lab's Fluid Interfaces research group. Previously, she founded and ran the Software Agents group. Prior to joining the Media Lab, Maes was a visiting professor and a research scientist at the MIT Artificial Intelligence Lab. She holds bachelor's and PhD degrees in computer science from the Vrije Universiteit Brussel in Belgium. Her areas of expertise are human-computer interaction and artificial intelligence. Maes is the editor of three books, and is an editorial board member and reviewer for numerous professional journals and conferences. She has received several awards: FastCompany named her one of 50 most influential designers (2011). Newsweek magazine named her one of the "100 Americans to watch for" in the year 2000; TIME Digital selected her as a member of the Cyber-Elite, the top 50 technological pioneers of the high-tech world; the World Economic Forum honored her with the title "Global Leader for Tomorrow"; Ars Electronica awarded her the 1995 World Wide Web category prize; and in 2000 she was recognized with the "Lifetime Achievement Award" by the Massachusetts Interactive Media Council. She also received an honorary doctorate from the Vrije Universiteit Brussel in Belgium. Her 2009 TED talk is among the most watched TED talks ever. In addition to her academic endeavors, Maes has been active as an entrepreneur as cofounder of several venture-backed companies including Firefly Networks (sold to Microsoft) and Open Ratings (sold to Dun & Bradstreet). She remains an advisor and investor to several MIT spinoffs.

Permission to make digital or hard copies of part or all of this work for personal or classroom use is granted without fee provided that copies are not made or distributed for profit or commercial advantage and that copies bear this notice and the full citation on the first page. Copyrights for third-party components of this work must be honored. For all other uses, contact the Owner/Author(s). Copyright is held by the owner/author(s).
MobiSys '17, June 19–23, 2017, Niagara Falls, NY, USA.
ACM ISBN 978-1-4503-4928-4/17/06.
DOI: http://dx.doi.org/10.1145/3081333.3081474

BackDoor: Making Microphones Hear Inaudible Sounds

Nirupam Roy, Haitham Hassanieh, Romit Roy Choudhury

University of Illinois at Urbana-Champaign

ABSTRACT

Consider sounds, say at 40kHz, that are completely outside the human's audible range (20kHz), as well as a microphone's recordable range (24kHz). We show that these high frequency sounds can be designed to become recordable by unmodified microphones, while remaining inaudible to humans. The core idea lies in exploiting non-linearities in microphone hardware. Briefly, we design the sound and play it on a speaker such that, after passing through the microphone's non-linear diaphragm and power-amplifier, the signal creates a "shadow" in the audible frequency range. The shadow can be regulated to carry data bits, thereby enabling an acoustic (but inaudible) communication channel to today's microphones. Other applications include jamming spy microphones in the environment, live watermarking of music in a concert, and even acoustic denial-of-service (DoS) attacks. This paper presents *BackDoor*, a system that develops the technical building blocks for harnessing this opportunity. Reported results achieve upwards of 4kbps for proximate data communication, as well as room-level privacy protection against electronic eavesdropping.

1. INTRODUCTION

This paper shows the possibility of creating sounds that humans cannot hear but microphones can record. This is not because the sound is too soft or just at the periphery of human's frequency range. The sounds we create are actually 40kHz and above, completely outside both human's and microphone's range of operation. However, given microphones possess inherent non-linearities in their diaphragms and power amplifiers, it is possible to design sounds that exploit this property. To elaborate, we shape the frequency and phase of sound signals and play them through ultrasound speakers; when these sounds pass through the non-linear amplifier at the receiver, the high frequency sounds are expected to create a low-frequency "shadow". The "shadow" is within the filtering range of the microphone and thereby gets recorded as normal sounds. Figure 1 illustrates the effect. Importantly, the microphone does not require any modification, enabling billions of phones, laptops, and IoT devices to leverage the capability. This paper presents *BackDoor*, a system that develops the technical building blocks for harnessing this opportunity, leading to new applications in security and communications.

Permission to make digital or hard copies of all or part of this work for personal or classroom use is granted without fee provided that copies are not made or distributed for profit or commercial advantage and that copies bear this notice and the full citation on the first page. Copyrights for components of this work owned by others than the author(s) must be honored. Abstracting with credit is permitted. To copy otherwise, or republish, to post on servers or to redistribute to lists, requires prior specific permission and/or a fee. Request permissions from permissions@acm.org.

MobiSys '17, June 19–23, 2017, Niagara Falls, NY, USA.

© 2017 Copyright held by the owner/author(s). Publication rights licensed to ACM.

ISBN 978-1-4503-4928-4/17/06...$15.00

DOI: http://dx.doi.org/10.1145/3081333.3081366

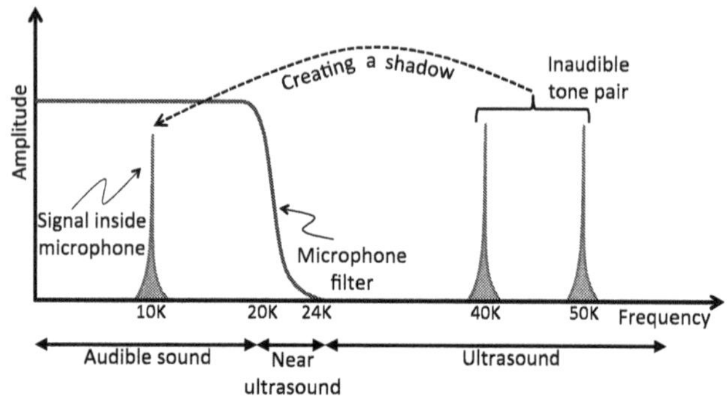

Figure 1: The main idea underlying *BackDoor*.

■ **Security:** Given microphones record these inaudible sounds, it should be possible to silently jam spy microphones from recording. Military and government officials can secure private and confidential meetings from electronic eavesdropping; cinemas and concerts can prevent unauthorized recording of movies and live performances. We also realized the possibility of security threats. Denial-of-service (DoS) attacks on sound devices are typically considered difficult as the jammer can be easily detected. However, *BackDoor* shows that inaudible jammers can disable hearing aids and cellphones without getting detected. For example, during a robbery, the perpetrators can prevent people from making 911 calls by silently jamming all phones' microphones.

■ **Communications:** Ultrasound systems today aim to achieve inaudible data transmissions to the microphone [34]. However, they suffer from limited bandwidth, around 3kHz, since they must remain above human hearing range (20kHz) and below the microphone's cutoff frequency (24kHz). Moreover, FCC imposes strict power restrictions on these bands since they are partly audible to infants and pets [20]. *BackDoor* is free of these limitations. Using an ultrasound-based transmitter, it can utilize the entire microphone spectrum for communication. Thus, IoT devices could find an alternative channel for communication, reducing the growing load on Bluetooth (BLE). Museums and shopping malls could use acoustic beacons to broadcast information about nearby art pieces or products. Various ultrasound ranging schemes, that compute *time of flight* of signals, could benefit from the substantially higher bandwidth in *BackDoor*.

This paper focuses on developing the technical primitives that enable these applications. In the simplest case, *BackDoor* plays two tones at say 40kHz and 50kHz. When these tones arrive together at the microphone's power amplifier, they are amplified as expected, but also multiplied due to fundamental non-linearities in the system. Multiplication of frequencies f_1 and f_2 result in frequency components at $(f_1 - f_2)$ and $(f_1 + f_2)$. Given that $(f_1 - f_2)$ is 10kHz in this case, well within the microphone's range, the signal passes unaltered through the low pass filter (LPF). Human ears, on the other hand, do not exhibit such non-linearities and completely filter out the 40kHz and 50kHz sounds.

While the above is a trivial case of sending a tone, *BackDoor* intends to load data on transmitted carrier signals and demodulate the "shadow" after receiving through the microphone. This entails challenges. *First*, The non-linearities we intend to exploit are not unique to the microphone; they are also present in speakers that transmit the sounds. As a result, the speaker also produces a "shadow" within the audible range, making its output audible to humans. We address this by using multiple speakers and isolating the signals in frequency across the speakers. We show, both analytically and empirically, that none of these isolated sounds create a "shadow" as they pass through the speaker's diaphragm and amplifier. However, once these sounds arrive and combine non-linearly inside the microphone, the "shadow" emerges within the audible range.

Second, for communication applications, standard modulation and coding schemes cannot be used directly. Section 4.1 shows how appropriate frequency-modulation, combined with inverse filtering, resonance alignment, and ringing mitigation are needed to boost achievable data rates. *Finally*, for security applications, jamming requires transmitting noisy signals that cover the entire audible frequency range. With audible jammers, this requires speakers to operate at very high volumes. Section 4.2 describes how *BackDoor* is designed to achieve equally effective jamming, but in complete silence. We leverage the *adaptive gain control* (AGC) in microphones, in conjunction with selective frequency distortion, to improve jamming at modest power levels.

The final *BackDoor* prototype is built on customized ultrasound speakers and evaluated for both communication and security applications across different types of mobile devices. Our results reveal the following:

- 100 different sounds played to 7 individuals confirmed that *BackDoor* was completely inaudible.
- *BackDoor* attained data rates of 4 kbps at a distance of 1 meter, and 2 kbps at 1.5 meters – this is 2× higher in throughput and 5× higher in distance than systems that use the near-ultrasound band.
- *BackDoor* is able to jam and prevent the recording of any conversation within a radius of 3.5 meters (and potentially a room-level coverage with higher power [25]). When 2000 English words were played back to 7 humans and a speech recognition software [2], less than 15% of the words were decoded correctly. Audible jammers, aiming at comparable performance, would need to play white noise at a loudness of 97 dBSPL, considered seriously harmful to human ears [19].

In sum, this paper makes the following contributions:

- *Exploits non-linearities in off-the-shelf microphones to enable a "backdoor" from high to low frequencies.* This backdoor permits playback of high frequency sounds that are inaudible to humans and yet recordable through microphones.
- *Builds enabling primitives for applications in acoustic communication and privacy.* The acoustic radio outperforms today's near-ultrasound systems, while jamming raises the bar against eavesdropping.

The subsequent sections expand on these contributions. We begin with an acoustic primer, followed by intuitions, system design, and evaluation.

2. ACOUSTIC SYSTEMS PRIMER

Common Microphone Systems

Any sound recording system requires two main modules – a transducer and an analog-to-digital converter (ADC). The transducer contains a "diaphragm" that vibrates due to sound pressure, producing a proportional change in voltage. The ADC measures this voltage variation (at a fixed sampling frequency) and stores the samples in memory. These samples represent the recorded sound in the digital domain.

A practical microphone needs two more components between the diaphragm and the ADC, namely a *pre-amplifier* and a *low pass filter*. Figure 2 shows the pipeline. The pre-amplifier's task is to amplify the output of the transducer by a gain of around 10× so that the ADC can measure the signal effectively using its predefined quantization levels. Without this amplification, the signal is too weak (around tens of millivolts).

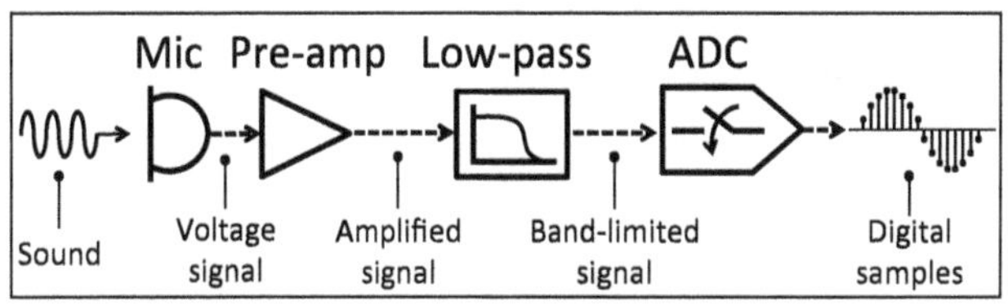

Figure 2: The sound recording signal flow.

As per Nyquist's law, if the ADC's sampling frequency is $f_s Hz$, the sound must be band limited to $\frac{f_s}{2} Hz$ to avoid aliasing and distortions. Since natural sound can spread over a wide band of frequencies, it needs to be low pass filtered (i.e., frequencies greater than $\frac{f_s}{2}$ removed) before the A/D conversion. Since ADCs in today's microphones operate at 48kHz, the low pass filters (LPFs) are designed to cut off signals at 24kHz. Figure 3 shows the effect of the low pass (or anti-aliasing) filter on the recorded sound spectrum.

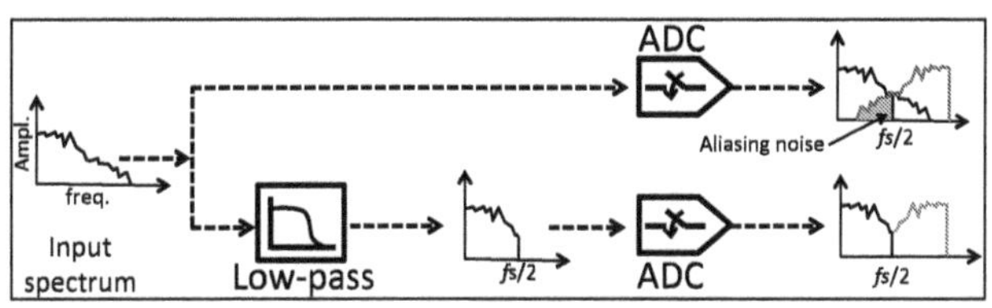

Figure 3: The digital spectrum with and without the (anti-aliasing) low-pass filter.

Sound Playback through Speakers

Sound playback is simply the reverse of recording. Given a digital signal as input, the digital-to-analog converter (DAC) produces the corresponding analog signal and feeds it to the speaker. The speaker's diaphragm oscillates to the applied voltage producing varying sound pressures in the medium, which is then audible to humans.

Linear and Non-linear Behavior

Modules inside a microphone are mostly linear systems, meaning that the output signals are linear combinations of the input. In the case of the pre-amplifier, if the input sound is S, then the output can be represented by

$$S_{out} = A_1 S$$

Here A_1 is a complex gain that can change the phase and/or amplitude of the input frequencies, but does not generate spurious new frequencies. This behavior makes it possible to record an exact (but higher-power) replica of the input sound and playback without distortion.

In practice, however, acoustic amplifiers maintain strong linearity only in the audible frequency range; outside this range, the response exhibits non-linearity. The diaphragm also exhibits similar behavior. Thus, for $f > 25kHz$, the net recorded sound S_{out} may be expressed in terms of the input sound S as follows:

$$S_{out}\Big|_{f>25} = \sum_{i=1}^{\infty} A_i S^i = A_1 S + A_2 S^2 + A_3 S^3 + ...$$

While in theory the non-linear output is an infinite power series, the third and higher order terms are extremely weak and can be ignored. *BackDoor* finds opportunities to exploit the second order term, which can be manipulated by designing the input signal S.

3. CORE INTUITION AND VALIDATION

As mentioned earlier, our core idea is to operate the microphone at high (inaudible) frequencies, thereby invoking the non-linear behavior in the diaphragm and pre-amplifier. This is counter-intuitive because most researchers and engineers strive to avoid non-linearity. In our case, however, we intend to create an inlet into the audible frequency range and non-linearity is essentially the "backdoor". We sketch the basic technique next, followed by some measurements to validate assumptions.

To operate the microphone in its non-linear range, we use an off-the-shelf ultrasound speaker and play a sound S, composed of two inaudible tones $S_1 = 40$ and $S_2 = 50$kHz. Mathematically, $S = Sin(2\pi 40t) + Sin(2\pi 50t)$. After passing through the diaphragm and pre-amplifier of the microphone, the output S_{out} can be modeled as:

$$S_{out} = A_1(S_1 + S_2) + A_2(S_1 + S_2)^2$$

$$= A_1\{Sin(\omega_1 t) + Sin(\omega_2 t)\} \;\; + A_2\{Sin^2(\omega_1 t) +$$

$$Sin^2(\omega_2 t) + 2Sin(\omega_1 t)Sin(\omega_2 t)\}$$

where $\omega_1 = 2\pi 40$ and $\omega_2 = 2\pi 50$.

Now, the first order terms produce frequencies ω_1 and ω_2, which lie outside the microphone's cutoff. The second order terms, however, is a multiplication of signals, resulting in various frequency components, namely, $2\omega_1$, $2\omega_2$, $(\omega_1 - \omega_2)$, and $(\omega_1 + \omega_2)$. Mathematically,

$$A_2(S_1 + S_2)^2 = 1 - \frac{1}{2}Cos(2\omega_1 t) - \frac{1}{2}Cos(2\omega_2 t) +$$

$$Cos((\omega_1 - \omega_2)t) - Cos((\omega_1 + \omega_2)t)$$

With the microphone's cut off at 24kHz, all of the above frequencies in S_{out} get filtered out by the LPF, except $Cos((\omega_1 - \omega_2)t)$, which is essentially a 10kHz tone. The ADC is oblivious of how this 10kHz signal was generated and records it like any other sound signal. We call this the "shadow" signal. The net effect is that a completely inaudible frequency has been recorded by unmodified off-the-shelf microphones.

3.1 Measurements and Validation

For the above idea to work with unmodified off-the-shelf microphones, two assumptions need validation. (1) The diaphragm of the microphone should exhibit some sensitivity at the high-end frequencies (> 30kHz). If the diaphragm does not vibrate at such frequencies, there is no opportunity for non-linear mixing of signals. (2) The second order coefficient A_2 needs to be adequately high to achieve a meaningful signal-to-noise ratio (SNR) for the shadow signal, while the third and fourth order coefficients (A_3, A_4) should be negligibly weak. We verify these next.

(1) Sensitivity to High Frequencies: Figure 4 reports the results when a 60kHz sound was played through an ultrasonic speaker and recorded with a programmable microphone circuit. To verify the presence of a response at this high frequency, we "hacked" the circuit using an FPGA kit, and tapped into the signal before it entered the low pass filter (LPF). Figure 4(a) shows the clear detection of the 60kHz tone, confirming that the diaphragm indeed vibrates to ultrasounds. We also measured the channel frequency response at the output of the pre-amplifier (before the LPF): Figure 4(b) illustrates the results. The take away message is that the analog components indeed operate at a much wider bandwidth; it is the digital domain that restricts the operating range.

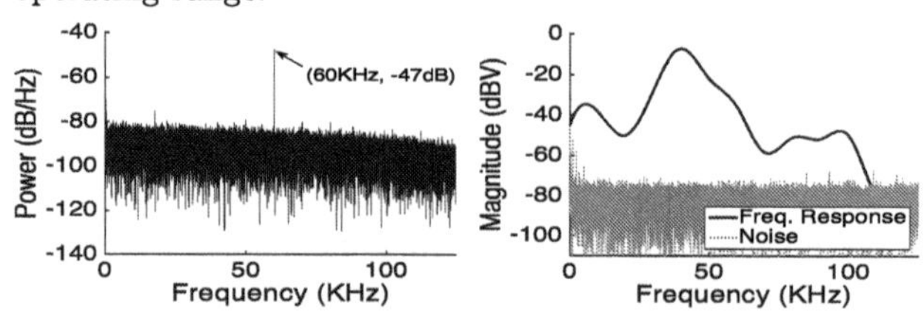

Figure 4: (a) Microphone signals (measured before the LPF) confirm the diaphragm and pre-amplifier's sensitivity to ultrasound frequencies. (b) Full freq. response at the output of the amplifier.

(2) Magnitude of Non-linear Coefficients: Figure 5(a) shows the entire spectrum after the non-linear mixing has occurred, but before the low pass filter (LPF). Except for the shadow at $(\omega_1 - \omega_2)$, we observe that all other frequency spikes are above the LPF's 24kHz cutoff frequency. Similarly, the nonlinear effect on a single frequency – shown in Figure 5(b) – only produces integer multiples of the original frequency, i.e., ω, 2ω, 3ω, and so on. These two types of non-linear distortions are called *intermodulation* and *harmonic* distortions, respectively. Importantly, the shadow signal is still conspicuous above the noise floor, while the third order distortion is marginally above noise. This confirms the core opportunity to leverage the shadow.

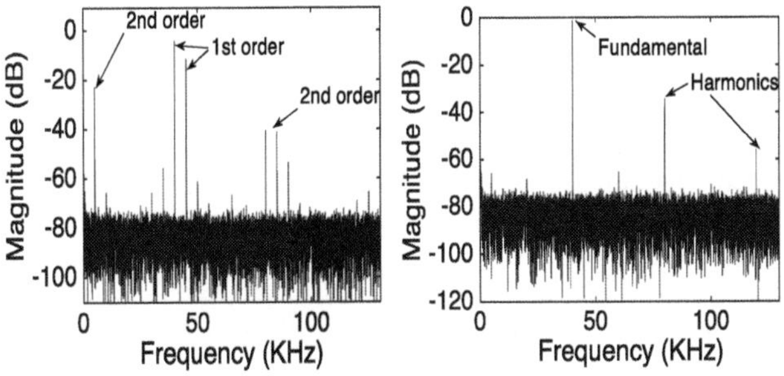

Figure 5: (a)The intermodulation distortion of signal (b) Harmonic distortion.

3.2 Hardware Generalizability

Before concluding this section, we report measurements to confirm that non-linearities are present in different kinds of hardware (not just a specific make or model). To this end, we played high frequency sounds and recorded them across a variety of devices, including smartphones (iPhone 5S, Samsung Galaxy S6), smartwatch (Samsung Gear2), video camera (Canon PowerShot ELPH 300HS), hearing aids (Kirkland Signature 5.0), laptop (MacBook Pro), etc. Figure 6 summarizes the SNR for the shadow signals for each of these devices. The SNR is uniformly conspicuous across all the devices, suggesting potential for widespread applicability.

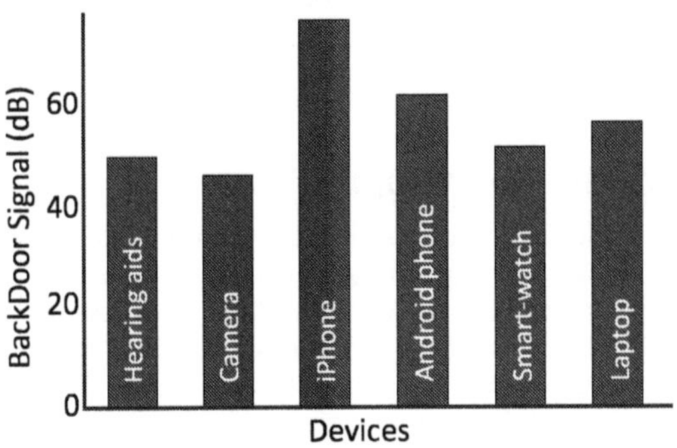

Figure 6: Consistent shadow at 5kHz (in response to 45 and 50kHz ultrasound tones) confirms non-linearity across various microphone platforms.

4. SYSTEM DESIGN

This section details the two technical modules in *BackDoor*: communication and jamming.

4.1 Communication

Thus far, the shadow signal is a trivial tone carrying one-bit of information (presence of absence). While this was useful for explanation, our actual goal is to modulate the high frequency signals at the speaker and demodulate the shadow at the microphone to achieve meaningful data rates. We discuss the challenges and opportunities in developing this communication system.

Failure of Amplitude Modulation (AM)

Our first idea was to modulate a single ultrasound tone, a data carrier, with a message signal $m(t)$. Assuming amplitude modulation [23, 27], this results in $m(t)Sin(\omega_c t)$, where ω_c is a high frequency, ultrasound carrier. Now, if $m(t) = a.Sin(\omega_m t)$, then the speaker should produce this signal:

$$S_{AM} = aSin(\omega_m t)Sin(\omega_c t)$$

Now, when this signal arrives at the microphone and passes through the non-linearities, the squared components of the amplifier's output will be:

$$\begin{aligned} S^2_{out,AM} &= A_2\{aSin(\omega_m t).Sin(\omega_c t)\}^2 \\ &= -A_2\frac{a^2}{4}\{Cos(\omega_c t - \omega_m t) - Cos(\omega_c t + \omega_m t)\}^2 \\ &= -A_2\frac{a^2}{4}Cos(2\omega_m t) + (terms\ with\ frequencies \\ &\qquad above\ \omega_c\ and\ DC) \end{aligned}$$

The result is a signal that contains a $Cos(2\omega_m t)$ component. So long as ω_m, the frequency of the data signal, is less than 10kHz, the corresponding shadow at $2\omega_m$ = 20kHz is within the LPF cutoff. Thus, the received sound data can be band pass filtered in software, and the data signal correctly demodulated.

Importantly, the above phenomenon is reminiscent of *coherent demodulation* in conventional radios, where the receiver would have multiplied the modulated signal ($aSin(\omega_m t)Sin(\omega_c t)$) with the frequency and phase-synchronized carrier signal $Sin(\omega_c t)$. The result would be the $m(t)$ signal in baseband, i.e., the carrier frequency ω_c eliminated. Our case is somewhat similar – the carrier also gets eliminated, and the message signal appears at $2\omega_m$ (instead of ω_m). This is hardly a problem since the signal can be extracted via band pass filtering. Thus, the net benefit is that the microphone's non-linearity naturally demodulates the signal and translates to within the LPF cutoff, requiring no changes to the microphone. Put differently, *non-linearity may be a natural form of self-demodulation and frequency translation*, the root of our opportunity.

Unfortunately, the ultrasound transmitter – a speaker with a diaphragm – also exhibits non-linearity. The above property of self-demodulation triggers in the transmitter side as well, resulting in $m(t)$ becoming audible. Figure 7 shows the output of the speaker as visualized by the oscilloscope; a distinct audible component appears due to amplitude modulation. In fact, any modulation that generates *waveforms with non-constant envelopes* [45] is likely to suffer this problem. This is unacceptable and brings forth the first design question: *how to cope with transmitter-side non-linearity?*

Bypassing Transmitter Non-linearity

The design goal at this point is to modulate the carrier signal with data without affecting the envelope of the transmitted signal. This raises the possibility of *angle modulation* (i.e, modulating the phase or frequency but leaving amplitude untouched). However, we recognized that phase modulation (PM) is also unsuitable in this application because of unpredictable noise from phone movements. In particular, the smaller wavelength of ultrasonic signals are easily affected by phase noise and involves complicated receiver-side schemes during demodulation. Therefore, we choose the other alternative of angle modulation: *frequency modulation* (FM). Of

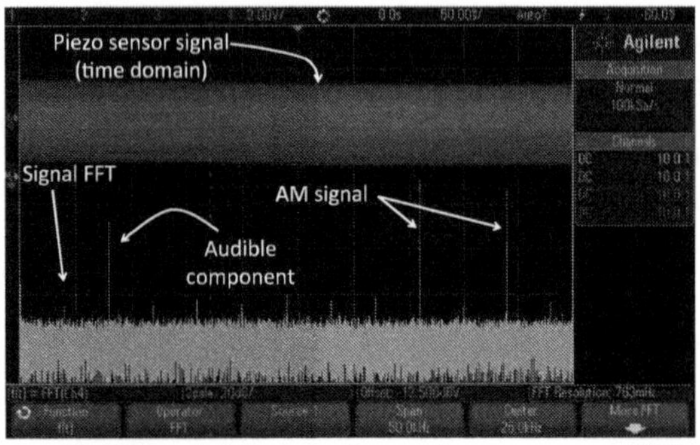

Figure 7: The AM signal produces an audible frequency due to self-demodulation, shown in this oscilloscope screenshot.

course, FM modulation is not without tradeoffs; we discuss them and address the design questions step by step.

FM: No Frequency Translation

FM modulated signals, unlike AM, do not get naturally demodulated or frequency-translated when pass through nonlinear transmitter. Assuming $Cos(\omega_m t)$ as the message signal, we have the input to the speaker as:

$$S_{fm} = Sin(\omega_c t + \beta Sin(\omega_m t))$$

Note that the phase of the FM carrier signal should be the integral of the message signal, hence it is $Sin(\omega_m t)$. Now when S_{fm} gets squared due to non-linearity, the result is of the form $(1+Cos(2\omega_c t+otherTerms))$ i.e., a DC component and another component at $2\omega_c$. Hence, along with the original ω_c frequency the transmitter output contains frequency at $2\omega_c$, both above the audible cut-off. Thus nothing gets recorded by the microphone. The advantage, however, is that the output of the speaker is no longer audible. Moreover, as typically the speaker has a low response at high frequencies near $2\omega_c$, the output signal is dominated by the data signal at ω_c as in original S_{fm}.

Second Carrier for Frequency Translation

To get the message signal recorded, we need to frequency-shift the signal at ω_c to the microphone's audible range, without affecting the signal transmitted from the speaker. To achieve this, *BackDoor* introduces a second ultra-sound signal transmitted from a second speaker collocated with the first speaker. Let us assume this second signal is called the *secondary carrier*, ω_s. Since ω_s does not mix with ω_c at the transmitter, the signal that arrives at the microphone diaphragm is simply of the form:

$$S_{fm}^{Rx} = \Big(A_1 Sin(\omega_c t + \beta Sin \omega_m t) + A_1 Sin(\omega_s t)\Big)$$

Note that the first term from the FM modulated ω_c signal, and the second term from the ω_s secondary carrier. Now, upon arriving on the receiver, the microphone's non-linearity essentially squares this whole signal as $(S_{fm}^{Rx})^2$. Expanding this mathematically results in a set of frequencies centered at $(\omega_c - \omega_s)$, and the others at $(\omega_c + \omega_s)$, $2\omega_c$, and $2\omega_s$. If we design ω_c and ω_s to have a difference less than the LPF cutoff, the microphone can record the signal.

Choosing ω_c and ω_s :

As we considered the requirements of the system, the choice of ω_c and ω_s became clear. First, note that the FM-modulated signal has a bandwidth of, say $2W$, ranging from $(\omega_c - W)$ to $(\omega_c + W)$. Thus, assuming that the microphone's LPF cutoff is 20kHz, we should translate the center frequency to 10kHz; this maximizes W that can be recorded by the microphone. Immediately, we know that $(\omega_c - \omega_s) = 10$kHz.

Second, the microphone's diaphragm exhibits resonance at certain frequencies; ω_c and ω_s should leverage this to improve the strength of the recorded signal. Figure 8 plots the normalized power of the *translated signal* for different values of ω_c and ω_s. Given $(\omega_c - \omega_s) = 10$kHz, the resonance effects demonstrate the maximum response when ω_c is 40kHz, and ω_s is 50kHz.

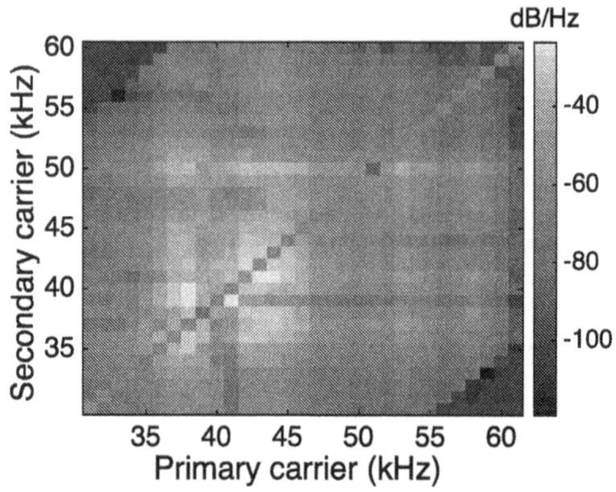

Figure 8: Resonance for various $\omega_c - \omega_s$ values.

Coping with the "Ringing" Effect

The piezo-electric material in the speaker, that actually vibrates to create the sound, behaves as an oscillatory inductive-capacitive circuit. This loosely means that the actual vibration is a weighted sum of input sound samples (from the recent past), and hence, the piezo-electric material has a heavy-tailed impulse response (shown in Figure 9). Mathematically, the output of the speaker can be computed as a convolution between this impulse response and the input signal. Unfortunately, the non-linearity of the speaker impacts this convolution process as well, and generates low frequency components similar to the natural demodulation effect discussed earlier. The result is a "ringing effect", i.e., *the transmitted sound becomes slightly audible even with FM modulation.*

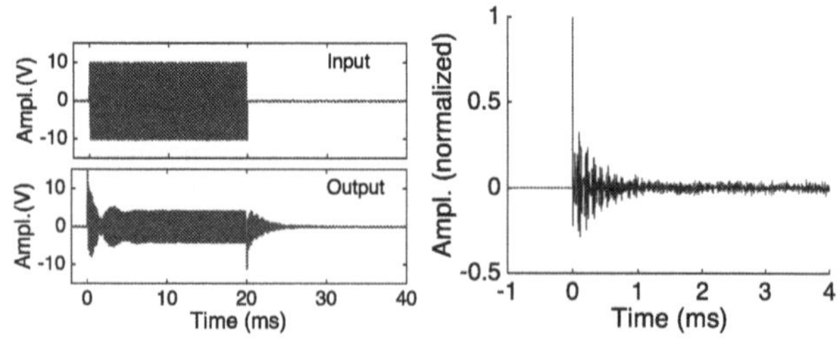

Figure 9: (a) The prolonged oscillation in an ultrasonic transmitter following a 40kHz sine burst input. (b) The impulse response of the ultrasonic transmitter.

To explain the self-demodulation effect, we assume a simplified impulse response 'h':

$$h = \sum_{i=0}^{\infty} k_i \delta(t-i) \approx k_0\delta(t) + k_1\delta(t-1)$$

When an angle modulated (FM/PM) signal 'S' is convolved with 'h', the output 'S_{out}' is:

$$\begin{aligned} S_{out} &= S * h \\ &= sin(\omega_c t + \beta sin(\omega_m t)) * (k_0\delta(t) + k_1\delta(t-1)) \\ &= \quad k_0 sin(\omega_c t + \beta sin(\omega_m t)) \\ & \quad + \quad k_1 sin(\omega_c(t-1) + \beta sin(\omega_m(t-1))) \end{aligned}$$

While S_{out} contains only high frequency components (since convolution is linear), the non-linear counterpart S_{out}^2 mixes the frequencies in a way that has lower frequency components (or shadows):

$$\begin{aligned} S_{out}^2 &= k_0 k_1 cos(\omega_c + 2\beta sin(\frac{\omega_m}{2}) sin(\omega_m t - \frac{\omega_m}{2})) \\ & \quad + (terms\ with\ frequencies\ over\ 2\omega_c\ and\ DC) \end{aligned}$$

Figure 10 shows the spectrum of S_{out} and S_{out}^2, with and without the convolution. Observe the low frequency "shadow" that appear due to the second order term for the convolved signal – this shadow causes the ringing and is noticeable to humans.

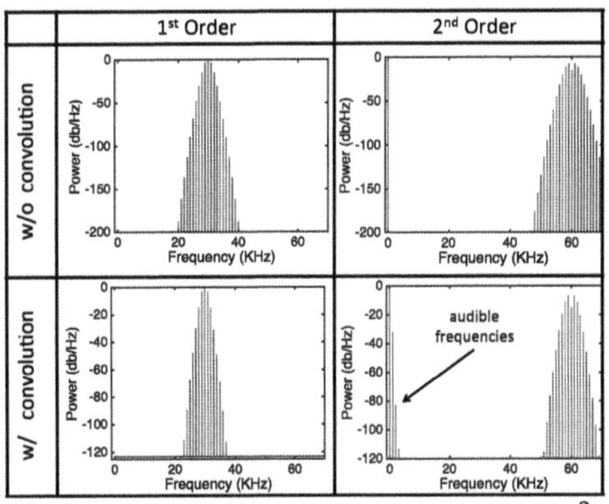

Figure 10: The spectrogram of S_{out} and S_{out}^2, with and without the convolution. The shadow signal appears due to second-order non-linear effects on the convolved signal.

In most speakers, this "shadow" signal is weak; some expensive speakers even design their piezo-electric materials to be linear in a wider operating region precluding this possibility. However, we intend to be functional across all speaker platforms (even the cheapest ones) and aim to be completely free of any ringing whatsoever. Hence, we adopt an inverse filtering approach to remove ringing.

Inverse Filtering to Eliminate Ringing

Our core idea draws inspiration from *pre-coding* in wireless communication, i.e., we modify the input signal S_{fm} so that it remains the same after convolution. In other words, if the modified signal $S_{mod} = h^{-1} * S_{fm}$, then the impact of convolution on S_{mod} results in $h * h^{-1} * S_{fm}$, which is S_{fm} itself. With S_{fm} as the output of the speaker, we do not experience ringing. Of course, we need to compute h^{-1}, i.e., learn the coefficients of the impulse response. For this, we monitor the current passing through the ultrasonic transmitter at different frequencies and calculate the $(k_0, k_1, k_2, ...)$. Fortunately, unlike wireless channels, the response of the transmitter does not vary over time and hence the coefficients of the inverse filter can be pre-calculated. Figure 11(a) shows the frequency response of one of our ultrasound speakers, while Figure 11(b) shows how our inverse filtering scheme curbs the ringing effect.

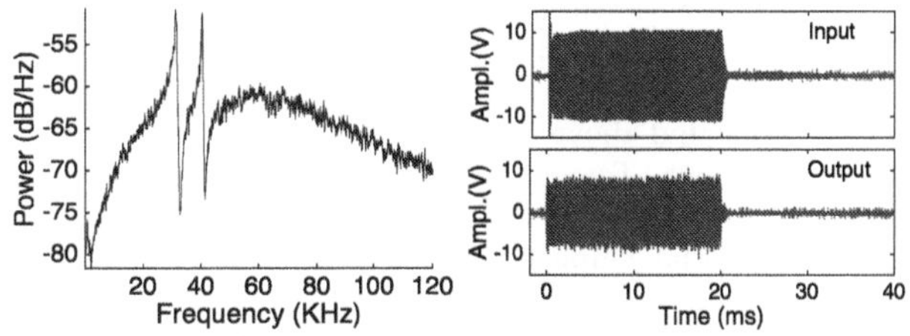

Figure 11: (a) Freq. response of the ultrasonic speaker. (b) Inverse filtering method almost eliminates ringing effect compared to Figure 9

Receiver Design

This completes the transmitter design and the receiver is now an unmodified microphone (from off-the-shelf phones, cameras, laptops, etc.). Of course, to extract the data bits, we need to receive the output signal from the microphone and decode them in software. For example, in smartphones, we have used the native recording app, and operated on the stored signal output. The decoding steps are as follows.

We begin by band pass filtering the signal as per the modulating bandwidth. Then, we need to convert this signal to its baseband version and calculate the instantaneous frequency to recover the modulating signal $m(t)$. This signal contains the negative-side frequencies that overlap with the spectrum-of-interest during the baseband conversion. To remove the negative frequencies, we Hilbert Transform the signal, producing a complex signal [29]. Now, for baseband conversion, we multiply this complex signal with another complex signal $e^{-j2\pi(\omega_s - \omega_c)t}$. Here $(\omega_s - \omega_c)$ is 10kHz, i.e., the shifted carrier frequency. This operation brings the modulated spectrum to baseband, centered around DC. The differentiation of its phase gives the instantaneous frequency [40], which is then simply mapped to data bits. Section 5 will present performance evaluation, but before that, we present the techniques for inaudible voice jamming.

4.2 Jamming

Imagine military applications in which a private conversation needs to be held in an untrusted environment, potentially bugged with spy microphones. We envision turning on one/few *BackDoor* devices in that room. The device will broadcast appropriately designed ultrasound signals that will not interfere with human conversation, but will jam microphones in the vicinity. This section targets 2 jamming techniques towards this goal: (1) passive gain suppression, and (2) active frequency distortion. Together, the techniques mitigate electronic eavesdropping.

(1) Passive Gain Suppression

Our core idea is to leverage the *automatic gain control* (AGC) circuit [31, 38, 44] in the microphone to suppress voice conversations. By transmitting a narrowband ultrasound frequency at high amplitude, we expect to force the microphone to alter its dynamic range, thereby weakening the SNR of the voice signal. We elaborate next, beginning with a brief primer on AGC.

■ **AGC Primer:**

Our acoustic environment has large variations in volume levels ranging from soft whispers to loud bangs. While human ears seamlessly handle this dynamic range, it poses one of the major difficulties in microphones. Specifically, when a microphone is configured at a fixed gain level, it fails to record a soft signal below the minimum quantization limit, while a loud sound above the upper range is clipped, causing severe distortions. To cope, microphones use an Automatic Gain Control (AGC) (as a part of its amplifier circuit) that adjusts the signal amplitude to fit well within the ADC's lower and upper bounds. As a result, the signal covers the entire range of the ADC, offering the best possible signal resolution.

Figure 12 demonstrates the AGC operation in a common MEMS microphone (ADMP401) connected to the line-in port of a Linux laptop running the ALSA sound driver. We simultaneously play 5kHz and 10kHz tones through two different (but collocated) speakers and display the power spectrum of the received sound. Figure 12(a) reports both the signals at around −20dB. However, when we increase the power of the 10kHz signal to reach its AGC threshold (while keeping the 5kHz signal unaltered), Figure 12(b) shows how the microphone reduces the overall gain to accommodate the loud 10kHz signal. This results in a 25dB reduction of the unaltered 5kHz signal.

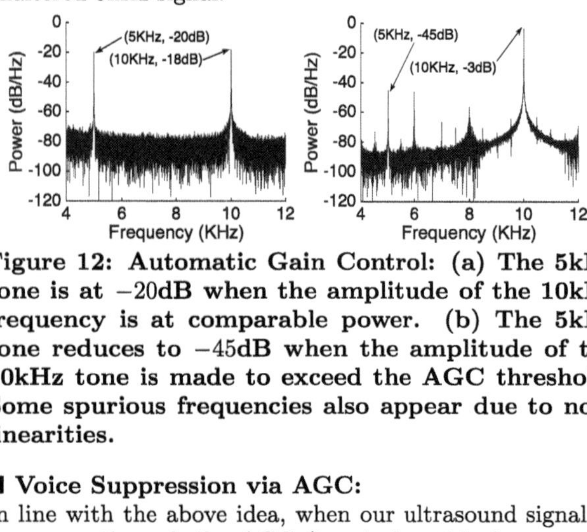

Figure 12: Automatic Gain Control: (a) The 5kHz tone is at −20dB when the amplitude of the 10kHz frequency is at comparable power. (b) The 5kHz tone reduces to −45dB when the amplitude of the 10kHz tone is made to exceed the AGC threshold. Some spurious frequencies also appear due to non-linearities.

■ **Voice Suppression via AGC:**

In line with the above idea, when our ultrasound signal at ω_c passes through the AGC (i.e., before this frequency is removed by the low pass filter), it alters the AGC gain configuration and significantly suppresses the voice signals in the audible frequency. Figure 13 shows the reduction in the received sound power in a *Samsung Galaxy S-6* smartphone when ultrasound tones are played at different frequencies from a piezo-electric speaker. Evident from the plot, the maximum reduction is due to the signal at 40kHz – this is because 40kHz is the resonance frequency of the piezo-electric transducer, and thereby delivers the highest power. In that sense, using the resonance frequency offers double gains, one towards increasing the SNR of our communication signal, and the other for jamming.

This reduction in signal amplitude results in low resolution when sampled with discrete quantization levels at the ADC.

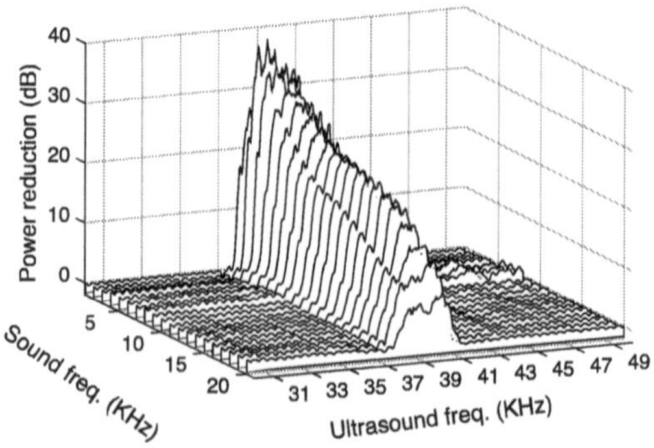

Figure 13: The reduction in sound power due to the AGC: reduction maximum for the 40kHz tone due to the speaker's resonance at this frequency.

In fact, an adequately loud ultrasonic tone can completely prevent the microphone from recording any meaningful voice signal by reducing its amplitude below the minimum quantization level. However, as the electrical noise level is usually higher than the minimum quantization level of the ADC, it is sufficient to reduce the signal power below that noise floor.

Figure 14 shows the reduction in the signal power of a recorded voice segment for 3 different power levels of the 40kHz tone. In practice, an absolute amplitude reduction is difficult unless the speaker uses high power. Importantly, high power speakers are possible with *BackDoor* since the jamming signal is inaudible. *On the other hand, regular white noise audio jammers must operate below strict power levels to not interfere with human conversation/tolerance. This is a key advantage of jamming with BackDoor.* Nonetheless, we still attempt to lower the power requirement by injecting additional frequency distortions at the eavesdropper's microphone.

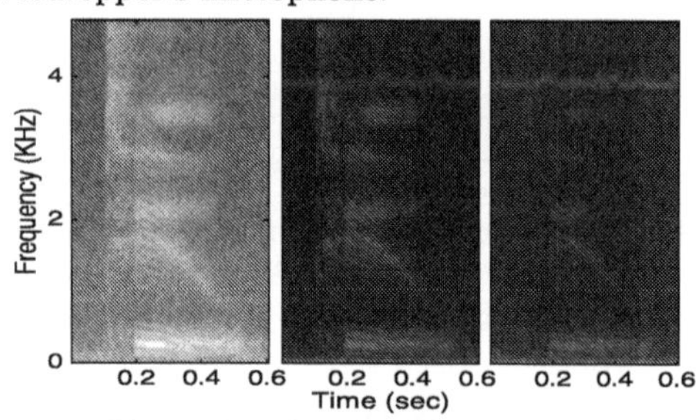

Figure 14: The reduction in signal power of recorded voice segment for 3 power levels (darker is lower power).

(2) Injecting Frequency Distortion

A traditional jamming technique is to add strong white noise to reduce the SNR of the target signal. We first implement a similar technique, but with inaudible band-limited Gaussian noise. Specifically, we modulate the ω_c carrier with white noise, bandpass filtered to allow frequencies between 40kHz to 52kHz only. The 52kHz ω_s carrier shifts this noise to [0, 12]kHz, which is sufficient to affect the voice signal.

To improve, we then shape the white noise signal to boost power in frequencies that are known to be important for voice. Note that these distortions are designed in the ultrasound bands (to maintain inaudibility), and hence they are

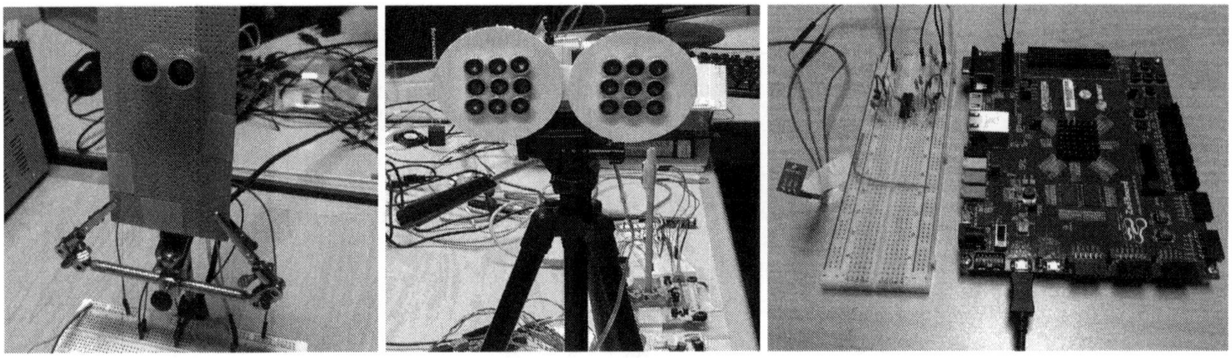

Figure 15: *BackDoor* experimental setup: (a) Two ultrasonic speakers mounted on a circuit board for data communication. (b) A $2Watt$ speaker array system for jamming applications. (c) The FPGA based set up for probing into individual components of the microphone.

played through the ultrasound speakers. Section 5 will report results on word legibility, as a function of the separation between the jammer and the spy microphone.

5. EVALUATION

BackDoor was evaluated on 3 main metrics: (1) human audibility, (2) throughput, packet error rates(PER) and bit error rates (BER) for data communication, and (3) the efficacy of jamming. We summarize the key results here, followed by details.

• Table 1 reports human perception of audibility for *BackDoor* for various frequencies, modulations, and SNR levels. Except for amplitude modulation (AM), all the human volunteers reported complete silence.

• Figure 17 and 18 report the variation of throughput against increasing distance, different phone orientations, and impact of acoustic interference. The results show throughput of 4 kbps at 1 meter away which is 2× to 4× higher than today's mobile ultrasound communication systems.

• Figure 19 compares the jamming radius for *BackDoor* and audible white noise-based jammers. To achieve the same jamming effect (say, < 15% words legible by humans), we find that the audible jammer requires a loudness of 97 dB-SPL which is similar to a jackhammer and can cause severe damage to humans [19]. *BackDoor*, on the other hand, remains completely silent. Conversely, when the white noise sound level is made tolerable, the legibility of the words was 76%.

We elaborate on these results below, starting with details on our implementation platform.

5.1 Implementation

(1) Transmitter Speakers: Figure 15(a) and (b) show two different transmitter prototypes we have developed, the first one for communication and the other for jamming. The communication transmitter consists of two ultrasonic piezoelectric speakers [33]; each transmits a separate frequency as described in Section 4. A programmable waveform generator (*Keysight 33500b series*) drives the speakers with frequency modulated signals. The signals are amplified using an NE5535AP op-amp based non-inverting amplifier, permitting signals up to 150kHz. The jamming transmitter in Figure 15(b) is composed of two speaker arrays, each array with 9 piezoelectric speakers connected in parallel to generate a 2Watt jamming signal. The signals driving these arrays are first amplified using an *LM380* op-amp based power amplifier separately powered from a constant DC-voltage source. Figure 16 shows the circuit diagram of the speaker array.

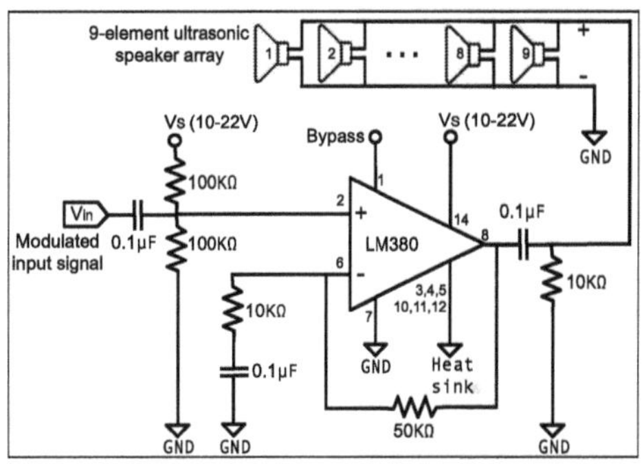

Figure 16: The circuit diagram of the jamming transmitter.

(2) Receiver Microphones: We experiment with two types of receivers. The first is an off-the-shelf *Samsung Galaxy S6* smartphone (released in Aug, 2015) running Android OS 5.1.1. Signals are recorded through a custom Android app using the standard APIs. The second receiver is shown in Figure 15(c) – a more involved setup that was mainly used for micro-benchmarks reported earlier in Sections 3 and 4. This allowed us to tap into different components of the microphone pipeline, and analyze signals in isolation. The system runs on a high bandwidth data acquisition *ZedBoard*, a Xilinx Zynq-7000 SoC based FPGA platform [12], that offers a high-rate internal ADC (up to 1 Msample/sec). A MEMS microphone (*ADMP 401*) is externally connected to this ADC, offering undistorted insights into higher frequency bands of the spectrum.

5.2 Human Audibility Results

We played *BackDoor* signals to a group of 7 users (ages between 27 and 38) seated around a table 1 to 3 meters away from the speakers. Each user reported the perceived loudness of the sound on a scale of 0-10, with 0 being perceived silence. As a baseline, we also played audible sounds and

Reference Mic.	2kHz Tone		5kHz Tone		FM		AM		White Noise	
SNR (dB)	*BackDoor*	Audible	*BackDoor*	Audible	*BackDoor*	Audible	*BackDoor*	Audible	*BackDoor*	Audible
25	0	0.75	0	3.33	0	1.2	0	0.46	0	0.1
30	0	1.5	0	4.08	0	2.3	0.1	1.36	0	0.26
35	0	2	0	4.91	0	3.5	0.1	1.85	0	0.5
40	0	2.67	0	5.42	0	4.2	0.16	2.4	0	0.8
45	0	3.17	0	6.17	0	4.8	0.68	3.06	0	1.24

Table 1: Perceived loudness of *BackDoor* in comparison to audible sounds.

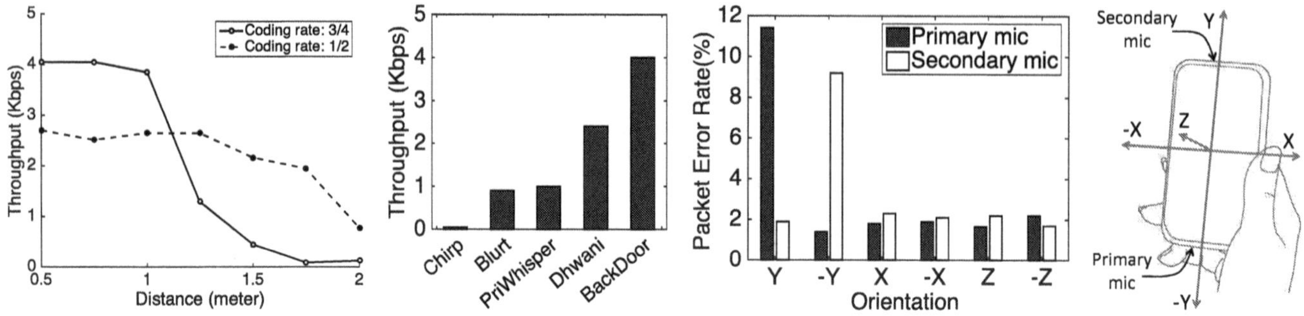

Figure 17: *BackDoor* Communication Results: (a) Throughput vs. Distance, (b) Throughput comparison against related P2P communication schemes. (c) Packet error rate vs. Orientation. (d) Phone orientations.

asked the users to report the loudness levels. A reference microphone is placed at 1m from the speaker to record and compute the SNR (Signal to Noise Ratio) of all the tested sounds. We varied the SNR and equalized them at the microphone for fair comparison between audible and inaudible (*BackDoor*) sounds.

Four types of signals were played: **(1) Single Tone Unmodulated Signals:** In the simplest form, we transmitted multiple pairs of ultrasonic tones (<40, 42> and <40, 45>) that generate a single audible frequency tone in the microphone. As baseline, we separately played a 2kHz and 5kHz audible tone. **(2) Frequency Modulated Signals:** We modulated the frequency of a 40kHz *primary carrier* with a 3kHz signal. We also transmitted a 45kHz *secondary carrier* on the second speaker, producing 3kHz FM signal centered at 5kHz in the microphone. As baseline, we played the equivalent audible FM signal on the same speakers. **(3) Amplitude Modulated Signals:** Similar to FM signals, we created these AM signals by modulating the amplitude of 40kHz signal with a 3kHz tone. **(4) White Noise Signals:** Finally, we generated white Gaussian noise with zero mean and variance proportional to the transmitted power, at a bandwidth of 8kHz, band-limited to [40, 48]kHz. We also transmit a 40kHz tone on the second speaker to frequency shift the white noise to the audible range of the speaker. As baseline, we create audible white noise with the same properties band-limited to [0, 8]kHz and played it on the speakers.

Audibility Vs. SNR

Table 1 summarizes the average of perceived loudness that users reported for both *BackDoor* and audible signals as a function of the SNR measured at the reference microphone. For all types of signals except amplitude modulation (AM), *BackDoor* is completely inaudible to all the users. AM signals are audible due to speaker non-linearity, as described earlier. However, the perceived loudness of *BackDoor* is significantly lower than that of audible signals. Thus, so long we avoid AM, *BackDoor* signals remain inaudible to humans but produce audible signals inside microphones with the same SNR as loud audible signals.

5.3 Communication Results

The *BackDoor* transmitter is the 2-speaker system while the receiver is the Samsung smartphone. The recorded acoustic signal is extracted and processed in MATLAB; we compute bit error rate (BER), packet error rate (PER) and throughput under varying parameters. Overall, 40 hours of acoustic transmission was performed to generate the results.

Throughput

Figure 17(a) reports *BackDoor*'s net end-to-end throughput for increasing separation between the transmitter and the receiver. *BackDoor* can achieve a throughput of 4kbps at 1m, 2kbps at 1.5m and 1kbps at 2m. Figure 17(b) compares *BackDoor*'s performance in terms of throughput and range with state-of-the-art mobile acoustic communication systems (in both commercial products [1, 13] and research [34, 22]). The figure shows that *BackDoor* achieve 2× to 80× higher throughput. This because these systems are constrained to a very narrow communication band whereas *BackDoor* is able to utilize the entire audible bandwidth.

Impact of Phone Orientation

Figure 17(c) shows the *packet error rate* (PER) when data is decoded by the primary and secondary microphones in the phone, placed in 6 different orientations (shown in Figure 17(d)). The aim here is to understand how real-world use of the phone impacts data delivery. To this end, the phone was held at a distance of 1m away from the transmitter, and the orientation changed after each transmission session. The plot shows that except Y and $-Y$, the other orientations are comparable. This is because the $Y/-Y$ orientation align the two receivers and transmitters in almost a straight line, resulting in maximal SNR difference. Hand blockage of the further-away microphone makes the

SNR gap pronounced. It should be possible to compare the SNR at the microphones and select the better microphone for minimized PER (regardless of the orientation).

Impact of Interference

Figure 18(a) reports the bit error rate (BER) variation against 3 different audible interference sources. To elaborate, we played audible interference signals – a presidential speech, an orchestral music, and white noise – from a nearby speaker, while the data transmission was in progress. The intensity of the interference at the microphone was at 70 dBSPL, equaling the level of volume one hears on average in face-to-face conversations. This is certainly much louder than average ambient noise, and hence, this serves as a strict test for *BackDoor*'s resilience to interference. Also, the smartphone receiver was placed 1m away from the speaker, and transmissions were at 2kbps and 4kbps.

Evident from the graph, voice and music has minimal impact on the communication error. On the other hand, white noise can severely degrade performance. Figure 18(b) plots the power spectral density of each interference – the decay beyond 4kHz for voice and music explains the performance plots. Put differently, since *BackDoor* operates around 10kHz frequency, voice and music signals do not affect the band as much as white noise, that remains flat over the entire spectrum.

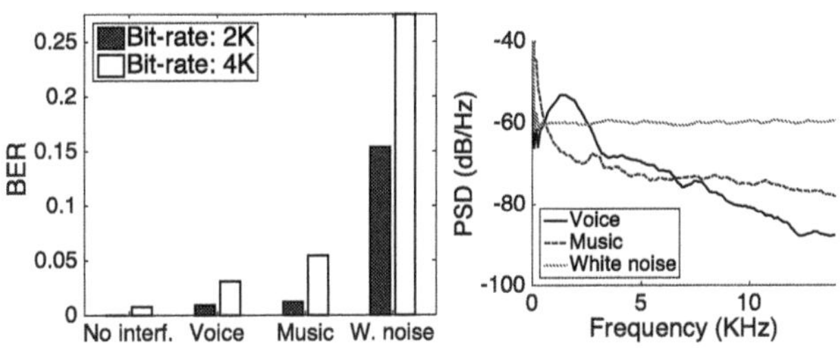

Figure 18: (a) BER vs. Interference. (b) Spectral density of interfering signals.

5.4 Jamming Results

■ **Setup:** Consider the case where Bob is saying a secret to Alice and Eve has planted a microphone in the vicinity, attempting to record Bob's voice. In suspicion, Bob places a *BackDoor* jammer in front of him on the table. We intend to report the efficacy of jamming in such a situation. Specifically, we extract the jammed signal from Eve's microphone and play it to an automatic speech recognizer (ASR), as well as to a group of 7 human users. We define *Legibility* as the percentage of words correctly recognized by each. We plot L_{asr} and L_{human} for increasing jamming radius, i.e., for increasing distance between Alice and Eve's microphone.

We still need to specify another parameter for this experiment – the loudness with which Bob is speaking. Acoustic literature suggests that at social conversations, say between two people standing at arm's length at a corridor, the average loudness is 65 dBSPL (dB of sound pressure level). We design our situation accordingly, i.e., when Bob speaks, his voice at Alice's location 1m away is made to be 70 dB-SPL (i.e., Bob is actually speaking louder than general social conversations).

In the actual experiment, we pretend that a smartphone is a spy microphone. Another smartphone's speaker is a proxy for Bob, and the words played are derived from Google's Trillion Word Corpus [10]; we pick the 2000 most frequent words, prescribed as a good benchmark [35]. As mentioned earlier, the volume of this playback is set to 70 dBSPL at 1m away. Now, the *BackDoor* prototype plays an inaudible jamming signal through its ultrasonic speakers to jam these speech signals.

■ **Baseline:** Our baseline comparison is essentially against *audible* white noise-based jammers in today's markets. Assuming *BackDoor* jams up to a radius of R, we compute the loudness needed by white noise to jam the same radius. All in all, 14 hours of sound was recorded and a total of 25,000 words were tested. The ASR software is the open-source *Sphinx4* library (pre-alpha version) published by CMU [2, 21]. We present the results next.

Audible and Inaudible Jamming Radius

Figure 19(a) plots L_{asr} and L_{human} for increasing jamming radius. Even with a 1W power, a radius of 3.5m (around 11 feet) can be jammed around Bob. We compare against audible noise jammers presented in Figure 19(b). For jamming at the same radius of 3.5m, the loudness necessary for the audible white noise is 97 dBSPL which is the same as a jackhammer and can cause damage to the human ear [19]. Conversely, we find that when the audible white noise is made tolerable (comparable to a white noise smartphone app playing at full volume), the legibility becomes 76%. Thus, *BackDoor* is a clear improvement over audible jammers. More importantly, increasing the power of *BackDoor* jammers can increase the radius proportionally. This can be easily achieved. In fact, current portable Bluetooth speakers already transmit 10× to 20× higher power than *BackDoor* [4, 3]. Audible jammers cannot increase their power to boost the range since they are already intolerable to humans.

Impact of Selective Frequency Distortion

Figure 19(c) shows results when the jamming signal is simply a white noise, without the deliberate distortions of voice-centric frequencies (fricatives, phonemes, and harmonics). Evidently, the performance is substantially weaker, indicating the importance of signal shaping and jamming. Finally, Figure 19(d) shows the confidence scores from ASR for all correctly recognized words. Results show quite low confidence on a large fraction of words, implying that voice fingerprinting and other voice-controlled systems would be easy to DoS-attack with a *BackDoor*-like system.

6. POINTS OF DISCUSSION

Needless to say, there is much room for further work and improvement. We discuss a few points here.

• **Jamming Range:** *BackDoor*'s restriction in the jamming range stems from the attenuation of ultrasound in air and the limited amplitude at which the ultrasound speakers can vibrate, producing low power signals. We have demonstrated a proof-of-concept with 9 speakers that boosts the jamming power level – direct materials cost is around $4. It should be certainly possible to develop a bigger speaker array to significantly increase the power [25]. In some cases (e.g. movie theater) multiple short-range jammers can be used to sufficiently cover the space. The jammers could be wall powered where necessary, and yet, will remain inaudible.

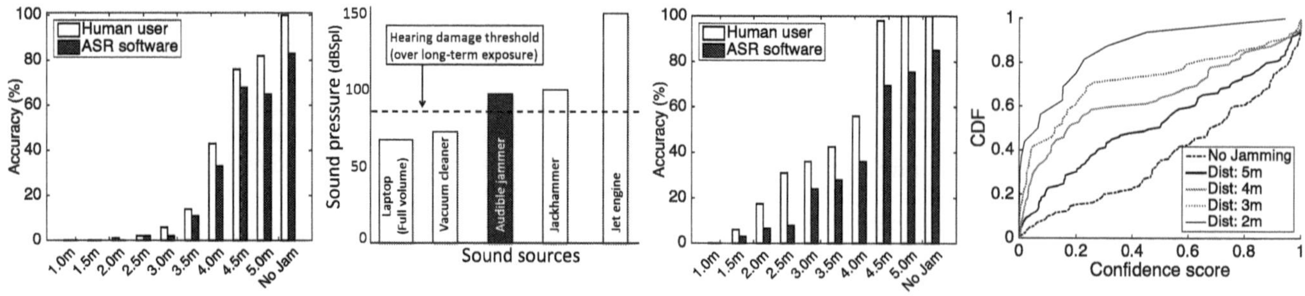

Figure 19: Jamming results: (a) *BackDoor* jams a radius of 3.5m at 2W power. (b) White noise power needed to match *BackDoor* is intolerable. (c) Jamming radius when *BackDoor* uses inaudible white noise, showing importance of selectively jamming voice-centric harmonics. (d) Confidence of speech recognizer.

• **Smarter Spy:** We have assumed a fairly simple attacker planting a single microphone in the vicinity. Multiple microphones, perhaps even with various beamforming capabilities, may be able to extract out the voice from the jamming signal. However, greater sophistication in jamming should be feasible too, such as variation in the jamming signal to prevent channel estimation; even some movements of the speakers. We leave this to future work.

• **Interference with Phone Calls:** Data communication with *BackDoor* can interfere with people talking on the phone nearby. To this end, data communication applications will inherently need to be proximate and at low power. One possibility is an acoustic NFC, but at greater ranges of 1 or 2 feet. Alternatively, the communication could be made spread spectrum so that the interference remains below the noise floor. Our ongoing work is investigating these unresolved issues.

7. RELATED WORK

■ **Literature in Acoustic Non-linearity:** The literature in acoustic signal processing and communication is extremely rich. The notion of exploiting non-linearity was originally studied in the 1957 by Westervelt's seminal theory [43, 42], which later triggered a series of research. The core vision was that non-linearities of the air can naturally self-demodulate signals; when combined with directional propagation of ultrasound signals, it may be possible to deliver audible information over large distances using relatively low power [17, 14, 46]. Recently, there has been a revival of these efforts with *AudioSpotlight* [5], *SoundLazer* [9, 8], and other projects [47, 11, 36]. Our work, however, is opposite of these efforts – we are attempting to retain the inaudible nature of ultrasound while making it recordable inside electronic circuits.

■ **Medical Devices:** Human bones have also been shown to exhibit non-linearities that self-modulate signals, resulting in applications in bone conduction ultrasound hearing aids for severely deaf individuals [28, 15, 16, 37, 32]. Even bone conduction headphones are being considered that exploit similar non-linearities [24].

■ **Assorted Topics Related to *BackDoor*:** A set of recent works bear some degree of relevance to *BackDoor*. *Dhwani* [34] explores in-air sound signals as a short range, ad-hoc data transfer modality. *Chirp* [1] and *Zoosh* [39, 13] have rolled out commercial products using sound for a secure data exchange medium. *GhostTalk* [26] explores various attack scenarios on the consumer electronics using high power electromagnetic interference. Another thread of recent work has looked into watermarking audio-visual media. *Dolphin* [41] enables speaker-microphone communication by embedding data bits on the sound. It adapts the signal parameters in real-time to keep the embedded signal imperceptible to human ears while achieving 500 bps data rate. *Kaleido*[48] proposes a video precoding based solution to prevent videotaping an on-screen show in a theater or on website. It precodes distortions in the video such that it is invisible to humans but severely distorts videotaping (due to specific limitations of the camera). Finally, sound maskers have also been used for protecting private conversation, however, these techniques have been limited to audible frequencies [18, 30, 6, 7]. *BackDoor* differs from the above in the sense that it exploits discrepancies between humans and electronics, ultimately enabling a new capability to the best of our knowledge.

8. CONCLUSION

Device non-linearity has been conventionally viewed as a peril. This paper breaks away from this point of view and discovers various opportunities to harness non-linearity. By carefully designing ultrasound signals, we demonstrate that such signals remain inaudible to humans but are record-able by unmodified off-the-shelf microphones. This translates to new applications including inaudible data communication, privacy, and acoustic watermarking. While our ongoing work is focused on deeper understanding of these capabilities and applications, our longer term goal is focused on generalization to other platforms, such as wireless radios and inertial sensors.

Acknowledgement

We sincerely thank the anonymous reviewers for their valuable feedback. We are grateful to the Joan and Lalit Bahl Fellowship, Qualcomm, IBM, and NSF (award number: 1619313) for partially funding this research.

9. REFERENCES

[1] Chirp technology. http://www.chirp.io. Last accessed 28 November 2016.

[2] Cmu sphinx. http://cmusphinx.sourceforge.net. Last accessed 6 December 2015.

[3] Hight power bluetooth speaker: 12watt. https://www.cnet.com/products/jbl-pulse/specs/. Last accessed 28 November 2016.

[4] Hight power bluetooth speaker: 38watt. http://www.fugoo.com/fugoo-tough-xl/. Last accessed 28 November 2016.

[5] Holosonics webpage. https://holosonics.com. Last accessed 28 November 2016.

[6] Sound masking device. http://www.oeler.com/sound-masking-systems/. Last accessed 28 November 2016.

[7] Sound masking solutions. https://www.speechprivacysystems.com. Last accessed 28 November 2016.

[8] Soundlazer kickstarter. https://www.kickstarter.com/projects/richardhaberkern/soundlazer. Last accessed 28 November 2016.

[9] Soundlazer webpage. http://www.soundlazer.com. Last accessed 28 November 2016.

[10] Top 10000 words from google's trillion word corpus. https://github.com/first20hours/google-10000-english. Last accessed 6 December 2015.

[11] Woody norris ted talk. https://www.ted.com/speakers/woody_norris. Last accessed 28 November 2016.

[12] Zedboard. http://zedboard.org. Last accessed 28 November 2016.

[13] Zoosh technology. http://www.bdti.com/insidedsp/2011/07/28/naratte. Last accessed 28 November 2016.

[14] Bjørnø, L. Parametric acoustic arrays. In *Aspects of Signal Processing*. Springer, 1977, pp. 33–59.

[15] Deatherage, B. H., Jeffress, L. A., and Blodgett, H. C. A note on the audibility of intense ultrasonic sound. *The Journal of the Acoustical Society of America 26*, 4 (1954), 582–582.

[16] Dobie, R. A., and Wiederhold, M. L. Ultrasonic hearing. *Science 255*, 5051 (1992), 1584–1585.

[17] Fox, C., and Akervold, O. Parametric acoustic arrays. *The Journal of the Acoustical Society of America 53*, 1 (1973), 382–382.

[18] Goubran, R., and Botros, R. Adaptive sound masking system and method, June 5 2003. US Patent 20,030,103,632.

[19] Hamby, W. Ultimate sound pressure level decibel table, 2004.

[20] Heffner, H. E., and Heffner, R. S. Hearing ranges of laboratory animals. *Journal of the American Association for Laboratory Animal Science 46*, 1 (2007), 20–22.

[21] Huggins-Daines, D., Kumar, M., Chan, A., Black, A. W., Ravishankar, M., and Rudnicky, A. I. Pocketsphinx: A free, real-time continuous speech recognition system for hand-held devices. In *in Proceedings of ICASSP* (2006).

[22] Iannucci, P. A., Netravali, R., Goyal, A. K., and Balakrishnan, H. Room-area networks. In *Proceedings of the 14th ACM Workshop on Hot Topics in Networks* (2015), ACM, p. 9.

[23] Jacobs, I. M., and Wozencraft, J. Principles of communication engineering.

[24] Kim, S., Hwang, J., Kang, T., Kang, S., and Sohn, S. Generation of audible sound with ultrasonic signals through the human body. In *Consumer Electronics (ISCE), 2012 IEEE 16th International Symposium on* (2012), IEEE, pp. 1–3.

[25] Kumar, S., and Furuhashi, H. Long-range measurement system using ultrasonic range sensor with high-power transmitter array in air. *Ultrasonics 74* (2017), 186–195.

[26] Kune, D. F., Backes, J., Clark, S. S., Kramer, D., Reynolds, M., Fu, K., Kim, Y., and Xu, W. Ghost talk: Mitigating emi signal injection attacks against analog sensors. In *Security and Privacy (SP), 2013 IEEE Symposium on* (2013), IEEE, pp. 145–159.

[27] Lee, E. A., and Messerschmitt, D. G. *Digital communication.* Springer Science & Business Media, 2012.

[28] Lenhardt, M. L., Skellett, R., Wang, P., and Clarke, A. M. Human ultrasonic speech perception. *Science 253*, 5015 (1991), 82–85.

[29] Lyons, R. G. *Understanding Digital Signal Processing, 3/E.* Pearson Education India, 2004.

[30] McCalmont, A. M. Voice privacy system with amplitude masking, Mar. 25 1980. US Patent 4,195,202.

[31] Mercy, D. A review of automatic gain control theory. *Radio and Electronic Engineer 51*, 11.12 (1981), 579–590.

[32] Nakagawa, S., Okamoto, Y., and Fujisaka, Y.-i. Development of a bone-conducted ultrasonic hearing aid for the profoundly sensorineural deaf. *Transactions of Japanese Society for Medical and Biological Engineering 44*, 1 (2006), 184–189.

[33] Nakamura, T. Piezoelectric speaker, June 3 1986. US Patent 4,593,160.

[34] Nandakumar, R., Chintalapudi, K. K., Padmanabhan, V., and Venkatesan, R. Dhwani: secure peer-to-peer acoustic nfc. In *ACM SIGCOMM Computer Communication Review* (2013), vol. 43, ACM, pp. 63–74.

[35] Nation, P., and Waring, R. Vocabulary size, text coverage and word lists. *Vocabulary: Description, acquisition and pedagogy 14* (1997), 6–19.

[36] NORRIS, E. Parametric transducer and related methods, May 6 2014. US Patent 8,718,297.

[37] Okamoto, Y., Nakagawa, S., Fujimoto, K., and Tonoike, M. Intelligibility of bone-conducted ultrasonic speech. *Hearing research 208*, 1 (2005), 107–113.

[38] Pérez, J. P. A., Pueyo, S. C., and López, B. C. Agc fundamentals. In *Automatic Gain Control.* Springer, 2011, pp. 13–28.

[39] Sherif, M. H. *Protocols for secure electronic commerce.* CRC press, 2016.

[40] Tretter, S. A. *Communication System Design Using DSP Algorithms: With Laboratory Experiments for the TMS320C6713TM DSK.* Springer Science & Business Media, 2008.

[41] Wang, Q., Ren, K., Zhou, M., Lei, T., Koutsonikolas, D., and Su, L. Messages behind the sound: real-time hidden acoustic signal capture with smartphones. In *Proceedings of the 22nd Annual*

International Conference on Mobile Computing and Networking (2016), ACM, pp. 29–41.

[42] WESTERVELT, P. J. The theory of steady forces caused by sound waves. *The Journal of the Acoustical Society of America 23*, 3 (1951), 312–315.

[43] WESTERVELT, P. J. Scattering of sound by sound. *The Journal of the Acoustical Society of America 29*, 2 (1957), 199–203.

[44] WHITLOW, D. Design and operation of automatic gain control loops for receivers in modern communications systems. *Microwave Journal 46*, 5 (2003), 254–269.

[45] XIONG, F. *Digital modulation techniques.* Artech House, 2006.

[46] YANG, J., TAN, K.-S., GAN, W.-S., ER, M.-H., AND YAN, Y.-H. Beamwidth control in parametric acoustic array. *Japanese Journal of Applied Physics 44*, 9R (2005), 6817.

[47] YONEYAMA, M., FUJIMOTO, J.-I., KAWAMO, Y., AND SASABE, S. The audio spotlight: An application of nonlinear interaction of sound waves to a new type of loudspeaker design. *The Journal of the Acoustical Society of America 73*, 5 (1983), 1532–1536.

[48] ZHANG, L., BO, C., HOU, J., LI, X.-Y., WANG, Y., LIU, K., AND LIU, Y. Kaleido: You can watch it but cannot record it. In *Proceedings of the 21st Annual International Conference on Mobile Computing and Networking* (2015), ACM, pp. 372–385.

Strata: Fine-Grained Acoustic-based Device-Free Tracking

Sangki Yun[*], Yi-Chao Chen, Huihunag Zheng, Lili Qiu, and Wenguang Mao
The University of Texas at Austin
{sangki, yichao, huihuang, lili, wmao}@cs.utexas.edu

ABSTRACT

Next generation devices, such as virtual reality (VR), augmented reality (AR), and smart appliances, demand a simple and intuitive way for users to interact with them. To address such needs, we develop a novel acoustic based device-free tracking system, called Strata, to enable a user to interact with a nearby device by simply moving his finger. In Strata, a mobile (*e.g.*, smartphone) transmits known audio signals at inaudible frequency, and analyzes the received signal reflected by the moving finger to track the finger location. To explicitly take into account multipath propagation, the mobile estimates the channel impulse response (CIR), which characterizes signal traversal paths with different delays. Each channel tap corresponds to the multipath effects within a certain delay range. The mobile selects the channel tap corresponding to the finger movement and extracts the phase change of the selected tap to accurately estimate the distance change of a finger. Moreover, it estimates the absolute distance of the finger based on the change in CIR using a novel optimization framework. We then combine the absolute and relative distance estimates to accurately track the moving target. We implement our tracking system on Samsung Galaxy S4 mobile phone. Through micro-benchmarks and user studies, we show that our system achieves high tracking accuracy and low latency without extra hardware.

Keywords

Acoustic Tracking; Gesture Recognition; Channel Impulse Response

1. INTRODUCTION

Motivation: Smart appliances, Virtual Reality (VR), and Augmented Reality (AR) are all taking off. The availability of easy-to-use user interface is the key to their success. Smart TVs are still cumbersome to navigate through menus. Many smart appliances require users to manually launch smartphone applications and click through, which is even more cumbersome than actually turning on/off switches. VR and AR are expected to hit $150 billion by 2020. They provide immersive experience, and open the doors to new ways of training, education, meeting, advertising, travel, health care, emergency responses, and scientific experiments. However, the current user interfaces of VR/AR are rather limited. Our vision is to develop a device-free user interface (UI) so that a user can freely move his or her hand to control game consoles, VR, AR, and smart appliances.

Directly tracking hand or finger movement without any device is appealing due to convenience. We have interviewed VR, AR, game developers and users. They all prefer device-free based user interface (UI) (*i.e.*, controlling devices directly using hands without holding anything) since it is cumbersome to hold a device outside the view and it is more natural to play games and interact with VR/AR objects using hands directly.

Challenges: There have been considerable work on enhancing the user interface of VR/AR devices. Google Daydream [8] and HTC VIVE [37] provide controllers for motion tracking. Device-free tracking is more convenient for VR users. Microsoft HoloLens [11] enables vision based device-free gesture tracking using camera and depth sensor fusion. However, it costs more than $3,000 in the market. Vision based tracking incurs significant energy and computational cost [30]. Also, its tracking accuracy highly depends on the background color and lighting condition.

Besides vision techniques, radio and acoustic signals based object tracking has received significant research attention. However, enabling accurate device-free tracking using radio and acoustic signals is particularly challenging. In such a case, reflected signal has to be used for tracking. Reflected signal is much weaker than directly received signal (*e.g.*, in free space, the directly received signal attenuates by $1/d^2$ whereas the reflected signal attenuates by $1/d^4$, where d is the distance between the device and target to be tracked). Moreover, it is more difficult to handle multiple reflection paths in device-free tracking. In device-based tracking, one may rely on finding the first arriving signal since the straight-line path between the sender and receiver is shortest. In comparison, in device-free tracking, the path of interest is not the shortest, which makes it even harder to distinguish which path should be used for tracking.

In particular, there has been considerable amount of work on device-free motion tracking using RF signals (*e.g.*, [13, 2, 41, 32]) and acoustic signals (*e.g.*, [21, 40]). However, they either require specialized hardware, or provide insufficient accuracy. For example, WiDeo [13] is a recent WiFi-based tracking scheme and pushes the tracking accuracy to within a few centimeters, but it requires full-duplex wireless hardware. WiTrack [2] tracks user position with 10-13 cm error by using customized hardware that transmits chirp signal through 1.67 GHz bandwidth. WiDraw [32] achieves 5 cm tracking accuracy with the support of 25 WiFi APs around

[*]Sangki Yun is currently a research staff at Hewlett Packard Labs.

Permission to make digital or hard copies of all or part of this work for personal or classroom use is granted without fee provided that copies are not made or distributed for profit or commercial advantage and that copies bear this notice and the full citation on the first page. Copyrights for components of this work owned by others than ACM must be honored. Abstracting with credit is permitted. To copy otherwise, or republish, to post on servers or to redistribute to lists, requires prior specific permission and/or a fee. Request permissions from permissions@acm.org.
MobiSys'17, June 19-23, 2017, Niagara Falls, NY, USA
© 2017 ACM. ISBN 978-1-4503-4928-4/17/06...$15.00
DOI: http://dx.doi.org/10.1145/3081333.3081356

the user. Therefore, they require complicated hardware while providing insufficient accuracy to enable motion-based UI for VR/AR users. Millimeter-wave based tracking schemes, such as Goolge Soli [17] or mTrack [41] achieve higher accuracy, but require 60 GHz antenna arrays that are not widely available yet. The acoustic based tracking schemes, such as AAMouse [44] or CAT [18], achieve around 1 cm or lower median error on commodity devices. However, they are device based schemes and assume the first arriving signal should be used for tracking, which does not hold for reflected signals. RF-IDraw [38] achieves high tracking accuracy, but it requires the user to hold the RFID tag to be tracked.

Recently, two state-of-the-art acoustic tracking schemes (*i.e.*, FingerIO [21] and LLAP [40]) enable device-free tracking only using the existing speaker and microphones in mobile device. Although they achieve higher accuracy than the other schemes, their tracking accuracy is still limited due to multi-path and other movements. For example, based on our extensive experiment, LLAP [40] achieves 0.7 cm distance estimation error in 1D tracking, but its trajectory error in 2D space increases to 1.9 cm. When there are people moving around the tracking object, the accuracy further degrades. The accuracy of FingerIO is even lower than LLAP.

Therefore, despite significant progress, achieving highly accurate and responsive device-free tracking on commodity hardware remains an open challenge. According to personal communication with game and application developers, sub-centimeter level accuracy and within 16 ms response time are required in order to provide good user experience. This is especially challenging to achieve using a commodity device, such as a smartphone, given its limited processing power and lack of special hardware.

Our approach: Built on the existing work, we develop a new device-free tracking using acoustic signals. In our system, a mobile device (*e.g.*, smartphone) continuously transmits inaudible acoustic signals. The signals are reflected by nearby objects, including a moving finger, and arrive at the microphone on the same mobile. The mobile analyzes the received signal to estimate the channel, based on which it estimates the distance change and absolute distance to locate the finger. Due to the small wave-length of acoustic signals, it is promising to derive the distance change based on the phase. Phase is also more robust to imperfect frequency response of a speaker. However, like many wireless signals, audio signals go through multiple paths to reach the receiver (*e.g.*, due to reflection by different objects). Such multipath propagation poses significant challenges for phase-based tracking. To address the challenge, we estimate channel impulse response (CIR) in the time-domain. The estimate gives the channel coefficient of each channel tap. We then select an appropriate channel tap and use the phase of the selected tap to estimate the distance change of a finger.

To further derive the absolute distance, we develop a novel framework to estimate the absolute distance of the path reflected by the moving finger during a few consecutive intervals such that its changes match with the changes in the CIR during these intervals and the distance changes between the intervals match with the phase measurement. Inferring the absolute distance serves two purposes: (i) it allows us to get the initial absolute distance so that we can translate the subsequent distance change into a new absolute distance, and (ii) it can be used to improve the tracking accuracy and alleviate error accumulation in subsequent intervals by combining it with the relative distance change.

We implement our approach on Samsung Galaxy S4 mobile phone, which has one speaker and two microphones, and enable real-time tracking of the user's moving finger. Using extensive evaluation, we show our system has three distinct features: (i) high accuracy: within 0.3 cm distance tracking error, 1.0 cm 2D tracking error, and 0.6 cm drawing error in a 2D space; (ii) low latency: we can update the position every 12.5ms, and (iii) easy to deploy: with a software app installation, a smartphone can track a nearby finger movement without extra hardware.

Paper outline: The rest of this paper is organized as follows. We describe our approach in Section 2, and evaluate its performance in Section 3. We review related work in Section 4, and conclude in Section 5.

2. OUR APPROACH

In this section, we present a fine-grained acoustic-based device-free tracking.

2.1 Overview

We use the phase change of the acoustic channel to estimate the distance change. This allows us to achieve high accuracy because the acoustic wavelength is very short. For example, the wavelength is 1.9 cm in 18 KHz audio frequency. Only 1 mm movement causes the reflected path length to change by 2 mm, which results in 0.21π phase change, large enough to detect.

However, in practice, due to multi-path propagation (*i.e.*, a signal traverses multiple paths before arriving at the receiver), the impact of a moving target on the overall channel can be very complicated, and varies across environments. In order to address this challenge, we use the phase from the estimated channel impulse response (CIR) rather than the raw received signal. CIR is a characterization of all signal traversal paths with different delays and magnitudes [27]. Specifically, it is a vector of channel taps where each channel tap corresponds to multi-path effects within a specific delay range. By focusing on the phase change of certain channel taps whose delays are close to the target delay range, we can effectively filter out the phase change incurred by the movement of objects outside a certain range as determined by the number of taps being used.

The phase change only gives us the distance change. We need to know the absolute distance at some point in order to translate the distance change into an absolute distance for tracking. Moreover, using the distance change alone incurs error accumulation, since the distance at a given time is estimated as the sum of all previous distance changes plus the initial position, each of which may incur an error. To address both issues, we develop a technique to estimate the absolute distance, which is used to get the initial position and also enhance the tracking accuracy by combining it with the distance change over time.

Putting together, our overall system consists of the following steps, which we will elaborate in this section.

1. Estimate channel impulse response (CIR) (Section 2.3);
2. Identify the channel tap corresponding to the target, and track the phase change of the selected tap in CIR to estimate the distance change (Section 2.4);
3. Estimate the absolute distance based on CIR (Section 2.5);
4. Combine the absolute distance with the relative distance to get a more accurate distance estimate, and track the target's position based on the distance to different landmarks (*e.g.*, microphones) (Section 2.6).

Our system implementation uses 18-22 KHz frequency and 48 KHz sampling rate. We can easily support other bandwidths and sampling rates.

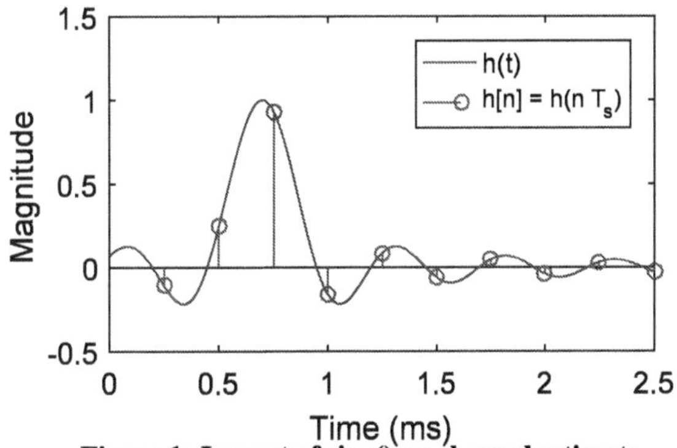

Figure 1: Impact of sinc() on channel estimate.

2.2 Background

A wireless signal, including an audio signal, travels through a straight line from the transmitter to the receiver in free space. In reality, due to obstacles in the environment, a single transmitted signal will reach the receiver via multiple paths (*e.g.*, paths going through different reflectors). Therefore, the received signal is a superposition of multiple signals with different delays. The received signal via multipath is traditionally modeled as the following Linear Time-Invariant (LTI) system [35]. Suppose the channel has L paths and the received signal from path i has delay τ_i and amplitude a_i determined by the travel distance of the path and reflectors. Then, the received signal $y(t)$ is the summation of L signals, as shown below:

$$y(t) = \sum_{i=1}^{L} a_i x(t-\tau_i) = \sum_{i=1}^{L} a_i e^{-j2\pi f_c \tau_i} s(t-\tau_i) = h(t) * x(t), \quad (1)$$

where $s(t)$ and $x(t)$ are the transmitted baseband and passband signals at time t, respectively, and $h(t)$ is the channel impulse response. $h(t) = \sum_{i=1}^{L} a_i e^{-j2\pi f_c \tau_i} \delta(t-\tau_i)$, where $\delta(t)$ is Dirac's delta function [22].

The channel estimate from the received baseband symbols is a discrete output of $h(t)$ sampled every T_s [35], which is

$$h[n] = \sum_{i=1}^{L} a_i e^{-j2\pi f_c \tau_i} \operatorname{sinc}(n - \tau_i W), \quad (2)$$

where $\operatorname{sinc}(t) = \frac{\sin(\pi t)}{\pi t}$. Conventionally, $h[n]$ is called the n-th channel tap, because CIR is regarded as a discrete-time filter in LTI system. Note that sinc function decays over time, so the impact of delayed signal on the measured $h[n]$ is small when the difference between nT_s and τ_i are sufficiently large. However, if they are relatively close, movement is captured in multiple channel taps due to the signal dispersion effect of *sinc* function. This is illustrated in simulation result in Figure 1, where the channel is affected by one reflected signal at 30 cm (*i.e.*, $\tau = 0.697$ ms). From the figure, we can observe that not only the closest channel tap from τ (*i.e.*, $h[3]$), but also the other nearby channels are affected by a single reflected signal.

2.3 Estimating Channel Impulse Response

Single-carrier communication channel: To estimate the channel, we design data communication for acoustic channel. An important design decision is whether we should use single-carrier or multi-carrier (*e.g.*, OFDM) communication. OFDM is widely used in modern wireless communication due to its efficiency and robustness to Inter Symbol Interference (ISI) caused by multipath. However, it yields channel estimation in frequency domain, while channel estimate is often more useful in time domain for tracking and localization purpose [19]. So we need to transform channel coefficients from frequency domain to time domain, but this process requires additional computation due to IFFT. Therefore, we use a single-carrier based communication system to directly estimate the channel in time domain without extra processing.

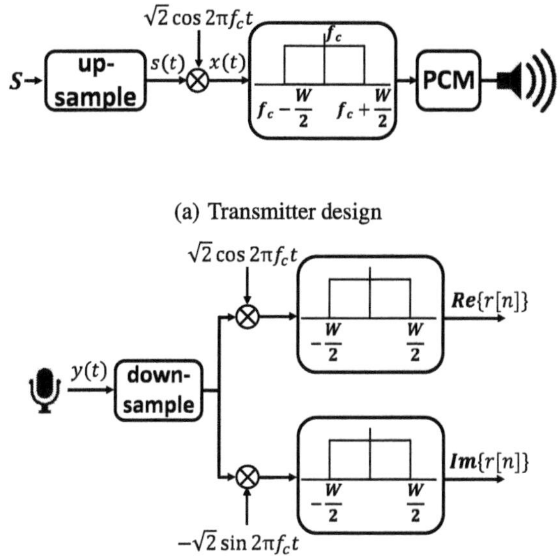

(a) Transmitter design

(b) Receiver design

Figure 2: Transmitter and Receiver system diagram.

Transmission signal design: A transmitter sends a known training sequence for channel estimation. Let $\mathbf{S} = \{s[1], ..., s[K]\}$ denote the training sequence, where K is the length of the sequence. It can be any random bits. We choose 26-bit GSM training sequence because it is known to have good properties for synchronization and channel estimation [25] and widely used in single carrier communication. We modulate $\mathbf{S}$ to BPSK symbols, where bits 0 and 1 are mapped to baseband symbols 1 and -1, respectively.

Figure 2(a) illustrates signal generation and transmission process. To transmit a modulated symbol over the inaudible frequency band, we first need to reduce the signal bandwidth so that it does not exceed the maximum allowed bandwidth of the inaudible band. Let f_s and B denote the sampling rate and the channel bandwidth, respectively. To limit the bandwidth of the transmitted symbol, we upsample the symbol at a rate of $\frac{f_s}{B}$, which is done by zero padding and low-pass filtering to smooth discontinuity [22]. Finally, we upconvert the signal to transmit it over the inaudible band. Let f_c denote the center frequency of the passband. We change the frequency of the signal by multiplying $\sqrt{2}\cos(2\pi f_c t)$ to the baseband signal: $x(t) = \sqrt{2}\cos(2\pi f_c t) s(t)$, where $s(t)$ and $x(t)$ are upsampled baseband and passband signals, respectively. Since BPSK only has real parts, $x(t) = \sqrt{2} e^{-j2\pi f_c t} s(t)$.

To remove noise outside the transmission band, we perform band-pass filtering on $x(t)$ with pass-band from $f_c - \frac{B}{2}$ Hz to $f_c + \frac{B}{2}$ Hz. The generated passband signals are transmitted through the smartphone speaker. Since the transmitted training sequence is always fixed, it can be generated offline and saved as a format of 16-bit Pulse Coded Modulation (PCM) in a Waveform Audio (WAV) file, which can be played by any mobile device that supports it (*e.g.*, smartphone or smart watch).

We refer to the training sequence as a frame. Between frames, we insert a fixed gap (*i.e.*, zero symbols) to avoid inter-frame interference. The gap should be sufficiently long so that the delayed signal from the previous frame does not interfere with the new frame. However, it should be as short as possible to provide low latency. Our study shows 24 zero symbols between frames are sufficient. As a result, a frame has 50 symbols. Given that the baseband symbol interval is $\frac{1}{B} = 0.25$ ms, each frame lasts 12.5 ms. So we update new channel estimate and the target's position every 12.5ms, which is below 16 ms required for providing seamless user experience.

Receiver design: Figure 2(b) illustrates the signal reception and baseband conversion process. The received passband signal $y(t)$ arriving at the microphone is converted into a baseband symbol $r[n]$ using the following down-conversion process: $y(t)$ is multiplied by $\sqrt{2}\cos(2\pi f_c t)$ and $-\sqrt{2}\sin(2\pi f_c t)$ to get the real and imaginary parts of the received baseband symbol, respectively. We perform low-pass filtering and down-sampling to select a signal every symbol interval. This gives us the following baseband signal [1]:

$$\begin{aligned} r[n] &= \sqrt{2}\cos(2\pi f_c t)y(t) - j\sqrt{2}\sin(2\pi f_c t)y(t) \\ &= \sqrt{2}e^{-j2\pi f_c t}y(t), \end{aligned}$$

where t is the time that the n-th baseband symbol is sampled (*i.e.*, $t = n \times T_s$, where T_s is a symbol interval).

Frame detection: After passband-to-baseband signal conversion, the receiver detects the first symbol of the received frame by energy detection and cross-correlation. We first detect the rough beginning of the frame based on energy detection: if the magnitude of three consecutive symbols is higher than the threshold σ, we treat the first symbol as the beginning of the frame symbols. Our implementation uses $\sigma = 0.003$. This value needs to be carefully selected depending on the phone and the volume of the speaker. Then we find more precise starting point based on cross-correlation. Specifically, we find the sample that gives the maximum cross-correlation magnitude between the received and transmitted frames. Note the frame detection procedure is only necessary at the beginning of tracking. Since the frame interval is fixed, once a frame is detected, the subsequent frames can be determined by adding a constant frame interval.

Channel estimation: Next we estimate the channel based on the received frame and the known training sequence. There are several existing channel estimation algorithms in single carrier communication system. We use least-Square (LS) channel estimation since it is cheap to compute on a mobile. We mainly focus on the algorithm implementation, and refer readers to [25] for the fundamental theory behind it.

For LS channel estimation, one needs to decide the reference length P and the memory length L, where L determines the number of channel taps we can estimate and $P + L$ is the training sequence length. Increasing L allows us to estimate more channel taps but reduces the reliability of estimation. Our implementation uses $P = 16$ and $L = 10$, which implies we can track movement up to 50 cm away (see Section 2.4.1). One can easily adapt P according to the environment.

Let $\mathbf{m} = \{m_1, m_2, \ldots, m_{L+P}\}$ denote the training sequence.

[1]Conventionally, $(\cdot)$ and $[\cdot]$ notations are used to represent analog and digital signals, respectively. Here every signal is digital because a mobile app cannot access the analog signal. We use $(\cdot)$ and $[\cdot]$ notations to distinguish upsampled signal with rate f_s from the downsampled signal with rate B.

A circulant training matrix $\mathbf{M} \in \mathbb{R}^{P \times L}$ is:

$$\mathbf{M} = \begin{bmatrix} m_L & m_{L-1} & m_{L-2} & \cdots & m_1 \\ m_{L+1} & m_L & m_{L-1} & \cdots & m_2 \\ \vdots & \vdots & \vdots & \ddots & \vdots \\ m_{L+P} & m_{L+P-1} & m_{L+P-2} & \cdots & m_{P+1} \end{bmatrix}.$$

Let $\mathbf{y} = \{y_1, y_2, \ldots, y_{L+P}\}$ denote the received training sequence. The channel is estimated as

$$\hat{\mathbf{h}} = (\mathbf{M}^H\mathbf{M})^{-1}\mathbf{M}^H\mathbf{y_L}, \tag{3}$$

where $\mathbf{y_L} = \{y_{L+1}, y_{L+2}, \ldots, y_{L+P}\}$.

Given the pre-computed $(\mathbf{M}^H\mathbf{M})^{-1}\mathbf{M}^H$, the computational cost of the channel estimation is only the matrix-to-vector multiplication, which is $O(P \times L)$. Considering $P = 16$ and $L = 10$, the channel estimation complexity is low enough to implement on a mobile.

To further improve the channel estimation accuracy, unlike in the traditional digital communication, which picks one out of every r samples during downsampling, where r is the upsampling rate, we use the average of the first l in the r samples to estimate the channel every sampling interval.

2.4 Tracking Phase Change

2.4.1 Overview

Next we track the phase change based on CIR estimates. We study the impact of the reflected signal using the following experiment. We move a small aluminum ball (< 1 cm diameter) attached to a long and thin wood stick. The person moving the stick is over 1 m away from the ball (outside the range of CIR taps). The ball is initially 30 cm away from the smartphone and moved 20 cm towards the phone. Figure 3 shows the phase of multiple channel taps while the ball is moving towards the smartphone. How to observe the phase of the moving object will be explained in detail in Section 2.4.2. The result shows that the phase rotates in multiple taps, which indicates the path length is changing. This change is caused by the moving ball. As shown in Figure 3, even though only a single small object moves, the phase rotation is observed in multiple taps. We repeat the experiments multiple times, and find that the phase rotation is observed approximately in 3 consecutive taps and the reflected signal with delay τ affects the three $h[n]$ that have the smallest $|\tau - nT_s|$. As a result, $h[n]$ can be approximated as:

$$h[n] \approx \sum_k a_k e^{-j2\pi f_c \tau_k}, \qquad (n - \frac{3}{2})T_s < \tau_k < (n + \frac{3}{2})T_s. \tag{4}$$

In other words, each channel tap $h[n]$ contains the phase and magnitude of the reflected signals whose delays are between $(n - \frac{3}{2})T_s$ and $(n + \frac{3}{2})T_s$. The path length changes with the delay τ_k according to $d_k = \tau_k V_c$, where d_k is the travel distance of the path k and V_c is the propagation speed of the audio (*i.e.*, $V_c \approx 340m/s$). Assuming that the speaker and microphone are closely located, the distance from the microphone to the reflecting object is approximately half of the travel distance. Therefore, $h[n]$ indicates the object's distance from microphone is between $(n - \frac{3}{2})\frac{T_s V_c}{2}$ and $(n + \frac{3}{2})\frac{T_s V_c}{2}$. Given $T_s = 0.25$ ms, $\frac{T_s V_c}{2} = 4.25$ cm and each tap captures objects across 12.75 cm range. This enables us to filter out the movement of objects outside the target range. For example, if we want to track the movement of a finger within 50 cm from the mobile, we can limit the channel taps to the first 10 taps to filter out the movement outside 50 cm. This is because the 10th tap may contain information from objects up to around 12th taps away, which gives $12 * 4.25 = 51$ cm.

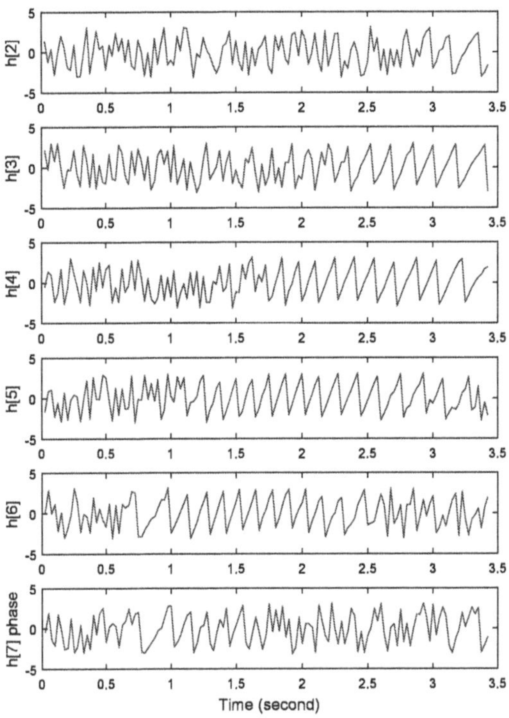

Figure 3: Phase change in multiple channel taps while moving a ball.

Next we track the phase change using the CIR estimate. While the CIR vector captures the channel with different propagation distances, it is challenging to extract the phase change caused by the target movement based on CIR since multiple paths with similar distances are mixed within each channel tap. To address the issue, we decompose the problem into the following two steps: (i) if we know which channel tap is affected by the moving target, how to extract the phase change caused by the target's movement, and (ii) how to determine which channel tap is affected by the target. Below we present our approaches to address both issues.

2.4.2 Estimate Phase Change

We assume the k-th channel tap is affected by the target's movement. In order to observe the phase change of the moving target, we compare the two consecutive channel measurements. Taking difference between the two consecutive channels effectively removes dominant static reflections. Let L_k denote the number of paths observed in $h[k]$. Suppose the L_k-th path is the path reflected from the moving finger, while the other $L_k - 1$ paths remain the same during the two consecutive channel measurement periods $t-1$ and t. Then,

$$h[k]^{t-1} = \sum_{i=1}^{L_k} a_i e^{-j2\pi f_c \tau_i(t-1)},$$

$$h[k]^{t} = \sum_{i=1}^{L_k-1} a_i e^{-j2\pi f_c \tau_i(t)} + a_{L_k} e^{-j2\pi f_c(\tau_{L_k}(t-1)+\tau_d(t))},$$

where $h[k]^t$ is the k-th channel tap estimated from the t-th frame and $\tau_d(t)$ is the delay difference caused by the target movement between the t-th and $(t-1)$-th frame intervals (*i.e.*, $\tau_d(t) = \tau_{L_k}(t) - \tau_{L_k}(t-1)$). By taking their difference, we get

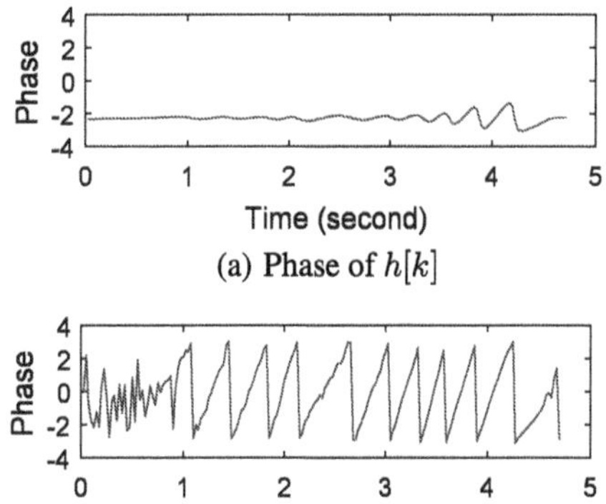

(a) Phase of $h[k]$

(b) Phase of $h_d[k]$

Figure 4: Phase of the channel impulse responses while a finger is moving.

$$h_d[k]^t = a_{L_k}(e^{-j2\pi f_c(\tau_{L_k}(t-1)+\tau_d(t))} - e^{-j2\pi f_c \tau_{L_k}(t-1)}), \quad (5)$$

where $h_d[k]^t = h[k]^t - h[k]^{t-1}$. Equation 5 assumes that a_{L_k} associated with a propagation path is constant over two consecutive measurements due to a very small distance change in a 12.5 ms interval. From the angle of $h_d[k]^t$, we observe the phase rotation caused by the change of $\tau_{L_k}(t)$.

$$\begin{aligned}\angle(h_d[k]^t) &= \angle(e^{-j2\pi f_c(\tau_{L_k}(t-1)+\tau_d(t))} - e^{-j2\pi f_c \tau_{L_k}(t-1)}) \\ &= \angle(e^{-j2\pi f_c \tau_{L_k}(t-1)}(e^{-j2\pi f_c \tau_d(t)} - 1)) \\ &= \angle(e^{-j2\pi f_c \tau_{L_k}(t-1)}) + \frac{\angle(e^{-j2\pi f_c \tau_d(t)})}{2} + \frac{\pi}{2}, \quad (6)\end{aligned}$$

where $\angle(X)$ is the phase of the complex number X. We can prove $\angle(e^{-j2\pi a} - 1) = \frac{\angle(e^{-j2\pi a})}{2} + \frac{\pi}{2}$ geometrically. The proof is omitted in the interest of brevity. Equation 6 assumes $\angle(h_d[k]^t)$ is smaller than π.

Figure 4 (a) and (b) show the phases of $h[k]$ and $h_d[k]$, respectively, while a user is moving his finger towards the speaker and microphone. In the collected trace, we conjecture $h[k]$ includes the finger movement related path between 1.0 second and 4.6 second. In Figure 4(a), the phase is very stable and the change by the finger movement is not clear because the majority portion of $h[k]$ contains signals from the static paths. After removing the impact of the static paths, we can observe clear phase rotation due to the finger movement from $h_d[k]$.

From the phase difference between $h_d[k]^{t+1}$ and $h_d[k]^t$, we get the phase rotation caused by the delay difference $\angle(e^{-j2\pi f_c \tau_d(t)})$, and eventually the travel distance of the finger during the measurement interval using the relation between the phase change. Note that $\tau_d(t) = \tau_{L_k}(t) - \tau_{L_k}(t-1)$. Using Equation 6, we represent the phase difference as

$$\begin{aligned}&\angle(h_d[k]^{t+1}) - \angle(h_d[k]^t) = \angle(e^{-j2\pi f_c \tau_{L_k}(t)}) \\ &-\angle(e^{-j2\pi f_c \tau_{L_k}(t-1)}) + \frac{1}{2}(\angle(e^{-j2\pi f_c \tau_d(t+1)}) - \angle(e^{-j2\pi f_c \tau_d(t)})) \\ &= \angle(e^{-j2\pi f_c \tau_d(t)}) + \frac{1}{2}(\angle(e^{-j2\pi f_c \tau_d(t+1)}) - \angle(e^{-j2\pi f_c \tau_d(t)})).\end{aligned}$$

By solving the above equation, we can calculate $\angle(e^{-j2\pi f_c \tau_d(t)})$. Without prior, we can simply assume $\tau_d(t+1) = \tau_d(t)$. Once we get the phase rotation, we can calculate the distance change based on $d^t = \lambda \times \angle(e^{-j2\pi f_c \tau_d(t)})/2\pi$, where d^t is the distance change of the dynamic path at time t, and λ is the wavelength of the audio signal. This relationship holds as long as the phase change is smaller than π, which holds for our finger movement speed and interval duration.

2.4.3 *Finding Channel Tap Corresponding to the Target*

Section 2.4 assumes we already know which tap to use for tracking the finger movement. This section describes how to find the right tap that includes the path reflected from the finger among multiple possible taps. Note that as mentioned in Section 2.4.1, the phase rotation by the finger movement is observed in multiple taps rather than in a single tap. Therefore, we just need to select one of these taps.

The channel taps can be classified as dynamic taps (*i.e.*, those that includes dynamic paths) and static taps (*i.e.*, those that do not). The right taps should be dynamic taps, since we are interested in tracking finger movement. If all taps are static taps, it means the finger does not move and its position does not need to be updated.

Criterion 1: Compared to the static taps, the dynamic taps have relatively larger variation of the channel over time. Therefore, we develop the following test to identify dynamic paths in the tap k:

$$M_1[k]^t = \frac{|h[k]^t - h[k]^{t-1}|}{|h[k]^t|} > \sigma_l,$$

which compares the normalized difference in the magnitude of two consecutive channels with a threshold σ_l. We use $\sigma_l = 0.05$.

Criterion 2: While the above condition distinguishes between the dynamic and static taps, the noise in the channel estimation might cause the classification error. Therefore, we add another criterion based on the following observation: the phase rotation of static tap k, denoted as $h_d[k]$, is very unstable because all static paths are removed during the differentiation process and the remaining value in $h_d[k]$ may contain random noise. In comparison, if k is a dynamic tap, the phase rotation of $h_d[k]$ is much more stable because $h_d[k]$ includes the dynamic path and its phase change over the measurement interval is stable. This is evident from Figure 3 and 4, which show the phase changes when the dynamic path is not included in the channel tap.

Based on this observation, we develop the following criterion to select the final tap. We measure the stability of phase change, which is defined as the phase change difference over the last three measurements. Specifically, we find the maximum phase change over the three periods: $M_2[k]^t = \max_{i=t-2,t-1,t} f(i)$, where $f(i) = |\angle(e^{-j2\pi f_c \tau_d^k(t)}) - \angle(e^{-j2\pi f_c \tau_d^k(t-1)})|$. We select the tap with the smallest maximum phase change (*i.e.*, the smoothest tap) from all taps that satisfy the criterion 1 as the final tap.

2.5 Estimating Absolute Distance

So far, we have focused on tracking the distance change of the finger by observing the phase. We need an absolute initial distance at some point in order to get the distance over time. Therefore, we develop a method to estimate the absolute distance based on the channel coefficients.

How to accurately estimate the absolute distance based on the channel estimate is an open problem. WiDeo [13] and Chronos[36] cast this problem as non-linear optimization problems, which search for the parameters associated with each channel tap such that the sum across all taps matches the overall channel measurement. This is effective when the channel is sparse. [13, 36] show this approach achieves decimeter-level accuracy in WiFi. We have tried this approach in our context, and found the accuracy is poor when applied to acoustic signals due to many multipaths, which results in many unknowns and a severely under-constrained system.

Basic framework: We develop a new formulation to address the under-constrained problem. It is motivated by the following important observation. We do not need to reconstruct complete channel profile in order to track a moving finger. Instead, we just need to reconstruct the delay and magnitude of the path that is reflected by the finger. Since a finger is small, it is reasonable to assume only one path is reflected by the finger. Therefore, we can take the difference between the two consecutive CIR estimates, which will cancel out all static paths and reduce the unknowns to the number of the parameters associated with the path that is reflected by the finger. Recall Equation 2 models the impact of reflection on the estimated channels. We take the difference between the two consecutive CIR, which removes all static paths and only keeps the path reflected by the moving finger:

$$\begin{aligned} h_d[n] = a(&e^{-j2\pi f_c(\tau+\tau_d)}\operatorname{sinc}(n-(\tau+\tau_d)W) \\ &- e^{-j2\pi f_c\tau}\operatorname{sinc}(n-\tau W)), \end{aligned} \quad (7)$$

where a and τ are the amplitude and delay of the signal reflected from the finger, respectively [2]. Based on the measured $h_d[n]$, our goal is to find τ and a that minimize the difference between the measured and estimated CIR change, where the estimated CIR is derived from the mathematical model using Equation 7.

To further improve the accuracy, we minimize the difference between the measured and estimated CIR change over multiple consecutive CIR measurements. Our implementation considers the past 3 CIR measurements (*i.e.*, the CIR change from $t-2$ to $t-1$ and from $t-1$ to t). We still compute the coordinate every interval except that we use the most recent 3 CIR measurements to construct the optimization problem. Therefore, we can improve the accuracy while maintaining 12.5 ms tracking interval.

Putting together, we solve the following optimization problem:

$$\begin{aligned} \min_{\tau,\tau_d^{est}(i),a} : &\sum_i \sum_{n=1}^{L} \Big[h_d^{t,t+i}[n] - \\ &a(e^{-j2\pi f_c(\tau+\tau_d^{est}(i))}\operatorname{sinc}(n-(\tau+\tau_d^{est}(i))W) \\ &-e^{-j2\pi f_c\tau}\operatorname{sinc}(n-\tau W))\Big]^2 + \alpha\sum_i |\tau_d^{est}(i) - \tau_d(i)| \end{aligned} \quad (8)$$

where $h_d^{t,t+i}[n]$ denotes the measured CIR change in the n-th tap from the t-th measurement to the $t+i$-th measurement, $\tau_d^{est}(i)$ is the inferred delay change from the t-th measurement to the $t+i$-th measurement, and $\tau_d(i)$ is the delay change derived from the phase measurement in Section 2.4. a, τ, and $\tau_d^{est}(i)$ are unknowns. The first term in the objective captures the fitting error between the measured CIR change versus the CIR change derived from the absolute distance based on a, τ and $\tau_d^{est}(i)$, and the second term captures the fitting error between the inferred delay change versus the delay change measured from the phase. α captures the relative weight between the two terms, and set to 100 in our evaluation due to more accurate distance change measurement.

Compared with the channel decomposition in [13, 36], which tries to find τ's and a's associated with all paths in the channel, our scheme finds τ and a associated with the path reflected by the moving finger. This has two benefits: (i) it reduces the number of unknowns and improves the accuracy while reducing computation cost, (ii) it removes all static paths and helps reduce the error.

[2]Note that Equation 5 is based on Equation 4, which is an approximation to Equation 2.

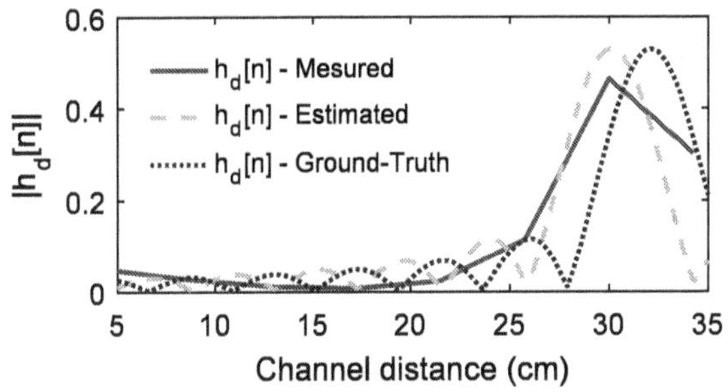

(a) Coarse grained channel

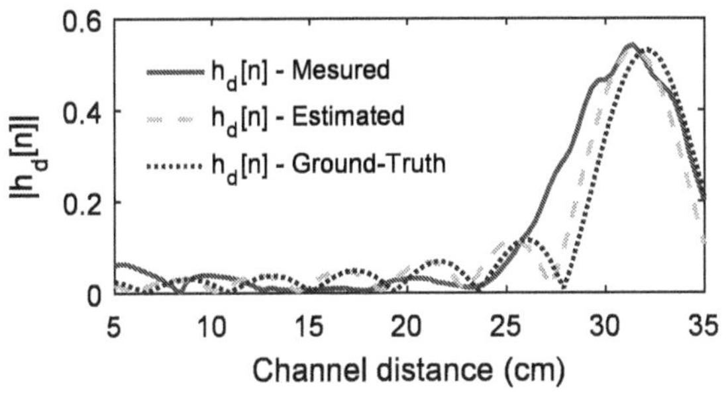

(b) Fine grained channel

Figure 5: Measured, re-generated, and ground-truth channel differences with coarse and fine grained channels based absolute distance estimation.

Moreover, we leverage the information across multiple measurements to further enhance the accuracy. Once we get τ, we can easily calculate the absolute distance as the product of delay (τ) and sound propagation speed.

Enhancement: While the above approach is useful to find the absolute distance, its accuracy is limited by the resolution of the estimated channel. Since the channel bandwidth is limited to 4 KHz, the baseband symbol interval is 0.25 ms, which is translated into the channel resolution of 4.25 cm. When we try to find τ using $h[n]$ sampled every 4.25 cm, the error increases due to the coarse resolution.

To enhance the accuracy, we exploit the over-sampled signals to achieve finer resolution. For the over-sampled signals received between $h[k]$ and $h[k+1]$, we estimate the channel using the same method in Section 2.3. These samples are 0.0208 ms apart (*i.e.*, $\frac{1}{F_s}$ ms), which corresponds to the distance resolution of 3.5 mm. As a result, the resolution of the channel estimation is limited not by the baseband symbol rate but by the sampling rate of the audio signal, which is 12 times higher! With this fine-grained channel estimation, we find τ using the same optimization framework.

Figure 5 shows the impact of coarse-grained and fine-grained channel estimation on the absolute distance estimate. In this experiment, we record the audio signal while a user is moving his finger, and estimate the absolute distance using the measured channels. For ease of interpretation, we represent the x-axis of Figure 5 as the distance corresponding to the delay of the channel. The red lines in the figures show measured channel difference. The green and blue lines correspond to the channel differences by plugging in the estimated and ground-truth delays into Equation 7, respectively. The ground-truth finger distance is 32 cm. As we can see, the channel difference under the coarse channel estimation deviates from the ground-truth, and has 2 cm error. In comparison, the channel difference from the fine grained estimation is close to the ground-truth, and has only 0.4 cm error.

2.6 Tracking the moving finger in 2D space

In Section 2.4 – Section 2.5, we present an approach to estimate the distance to the target. This allows us to track in 1D space, which is already useful for some applications. Next we describe how to track a finger in 2D space by leveraging two microphones on a smartphone (*e.g.*, Samsung S series).

Combine relative and absolute distance: We use both absolute distance and distance change estimated from the phase to track the target. At the beginning, we use the absolute distance to get the initial position of the target. Afterwards, we can get two distance estimates: d_k^p estimated from the phase and d_k^c estimated from the channel difference, where $d_k^p = d_{k-1} + \Delta d_k^p$ and Δd_k^p is computed as a function of the phase change. We then combine the two distance estimates using a weighting factor β: $d_k = (1-\beta)d_k^p + \beta d_k^c$. β is set to 0.1 due to more accurate phase change measurement. In section 3.3.3, we extensively evaluate the various β values.

Estimate coordinate: Given the phone form factor, we know the relative locations of the speaker and microphones. Suppose the speaker is located at the origin $(0, 0)$, and the two microphones are located at $(x_1, 0)$ and $(x_2, 0)$, respectively. We assume they are all aligned in the same Y-axis. The finger should be on the ellipse whose foci are $(x_1, 0)$ and $(x_2, 0)$ and the total distance to the foci are d_1 and d_2, respectively. Using two microphones as landmarks, we can track the finger by finding the intersection of the two ellipses. There are multiple intersections between two ellipses when they overlap, and we select the one closer to the previous position.

3. PERFORMANCE EVALUATION

3.1 Experiment setup

To evaluate performance and conduct user study, we implement an Android app that processes the audio signal and tracks the finger movement in real-time. We use Samsung Galaxy S4 with Android 5.1.1 as a tracking device. It has one rear speaker and two microphones at the top and bottom of the phone with 14 cm separation. The mobile app plays audio file generated as explained in Section 2.3, and analyzes the audio signal received from the microphones to track the finger in real-time. The speaker's volume is set to 80% of the maximum. We use inaudible audio frequency between 18 KHz and 22 KHz for transmission, and set the tracking interval to 12.5 ms. To convert passband to baseband, we implement an infinite-impulse response (IIR) low-pass filter.

To collect the ground-truth of the finger movement, we let the user move the finger on the top of a smart tablet, shown in Figure 6. It collects the touch event of the screen and generates the ground-truth trajectory of the finger movement, which is compared with the position estimated by our approach. This setup is only needed for collecting the ground truth to quantify the accuracy, and our scheme lets users freely draw in the air. In user study, we show simple shapes, such as a triangle, diamond, and circle on the tablet screen, and ask the user to trace the shapes. The average distance of the shapes is 22.3 cm. For data collection and user study, we recruit 5 users: four are men and one is woman. They are college students between 21 to 29. This age-group is among the most active VR/AR users. The data is collected at a student office in the department building surrounded by desks, cubicles, walls and small objects nearby, and people are allowed to move around the tracking device.

Figure 6: Testbed setup for the performance evaluation.

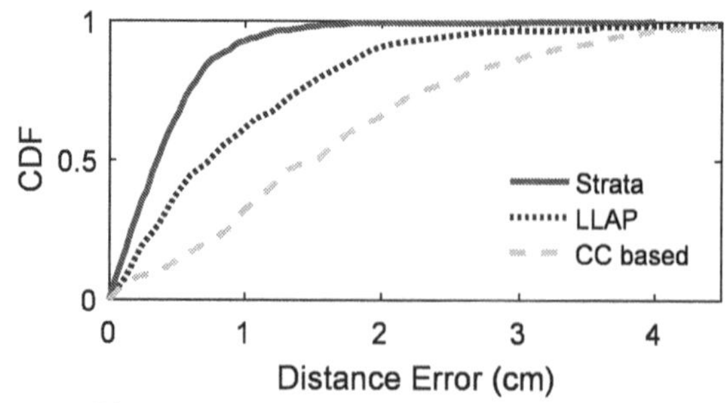

Figure 7: Impact of distance on tracking error.

3.2 Baseline Schemes

We compare our scheme with the following two acoustic signal based device-free tracking schemes:

Low Latency Acoustic Phase (LLAP): LLAP [40] tracks the finger movement by observing the phase change of the reflected signal. In this scheme, the transmitter continuously sends sine waves and the receiver tracks the moving target based on the phase change of the received waves. We implemented LLAP closely following [40]. We generate the transmission signal $\sin(2\pi f_c t)$ using MATLAB, stored as 16-bit PCM-format *WAV* file, and transmitted through the speaker. At the receiver side, the audio signal from the microphone is first multiplied by $\sqrt{2}\cos(2\pi f_c t)$ and $-\sqrt{2}\sin(2\pi f_c t)$, and goes through a low-pass filter to get the real and imaginary parts of the received signal, respectively. The phase of the moving finger is tracked by Local Extreme Value Detection (LEVD) algorithm in [40] that filters out static signals and tracks the phase change by the finger movement. It improves the accuracy of the phase estimation by averaging multiple received signals. We take the phase after averaging all received signals during 12.5 ms so that both Strata and LLAP have the same tracking delay. Also, we used the multiple frequencies to address the multi-path fading as proposed in [40]. We did not implement its absolute distance estimation algorithm in LLAP for initialization. Instead, we used the ground-truth for the initial position estimation.

The main difference between Strata and LLAP is that the former separately measures the phase change of the signals with different delays while the latter measures the phase change caused by all of the surrounding objects. Since multiple body parts may move together while the user moves the finger, using the combined phase change yields less accurate finger tracking. The problem is even worse when there are other moving objects and people nearby, which can be common in practice. Our evaluation results of its 1D distance estimation error is similar to what is presented in [40]. Interestingly, [40] did not evaluate the 2D tracking error.

Cross-correlation based tracking: This scheme tracks a moving object by measuring the change in the cross-correlation of the received signal, called *echo profile* proposed by FingerIO [21]. It transmits an OFDM symbol every interval and locates the moving finger based on the change of the echo profiles of the two consecutive frames. Specifically, every interval it compares the difference between the echo profiles of the two consecutive frames and filters out the points whose differences are smaller than a pre-defined threshold. Among the remaining unfiltered points, it selects the point closest to the beginning of the interval since the direct path is the shortest path. We carefully followed the description of [21] in our implementation, but achieved much lower accuracy than [21] perhaps due to additional optimization used but omitted in [21]. We identified a few ways to improve [21]. First, we use larger bandwidth and longer FFT size for OFDM symbol, both of which help to improve the tracking accuracy. We select FFT size of 256 and 6 KHz bandwidth (16 – 22 KHz) for transmission while the other approaches including ours still use 4 KHz bandwidth. Second, we find the difference between the two consecutive profiles is small as the finger is moving, which makes it challenging to select an appropriate threshold for filtering. Instead, we select the point that has the maximum cross correlation difference. Our results show this helps to improve accuracy and we can now roughly track the position of the moving finger, but sometimes detect a random location due to noise. Therefore, we further filter out the positions that are too far from the previous position. Our evaluation picks the maximum peak that is within $+-$ 10 cm away from the previous position. 10 cm is a loose bound to tolerate the error in estimating the previous position. After getting the distance estimation, we use the same algorithm introduced in Section 2.6 to locate the finger in a 2D plane.

3.3 Experimental Result

3.3.1 Phase based Tracking

Tracking accuracy in 1D: We first evaluate the accuracy of estimating distance change. In this experiment, the user initially places the finger 20 cm away from the mobile phone, and moves 10 cm towards it. We repeat the experiment 200 times for each scheme and collect the CDF of the distance error. As shown in Figure 7, the median errors of Strata, LLAP, and cross-correlation based tracking (*i.e.*, CC based) are 0.3 cm, 0.7 cm, and 1.5 cm, respectively. Their 90th percentile errors are 0.8 cm, 1.8 cm, and 3.2 cm, respectively. The performance of LLAP is similar to the result presented in [40] when the finger is a moving object and the initial distance is 20 cm (*e.g.*, see Figure 11(c) in [40].). Note that in [40], the authors mostly used a hand rather than a finger to evaluate the tracking performance. Figure 7 indicates that Strata can accurately track the movement by observing the phase rotation from CIR. Its median tracking error is less than half of LLAP. Since Strata separately tracks the phase in the CIR vector, it can effectively filter out the measurement noise from the user's body movement. In comparison, LLAP cannot since all signals are mixed up. The accuracy of the cross-correlation based tracking (even after optimization) is lower than both phase-based tracking schemes.

Tracking accuracy in 1D with other moving objects: One advantage of Strata is that it can distinguish movements at different distances. This allows us to easily filter out the interference incurred by the movement of the surrounding objects in the phase tracking. By limiting the channel taps to the first 10, we can ignore the phase change caused by the moving object with the distance larger than 50 cm.

To validate its effectiveness, we perform the distance tracking experiment with a person moving in the background while another

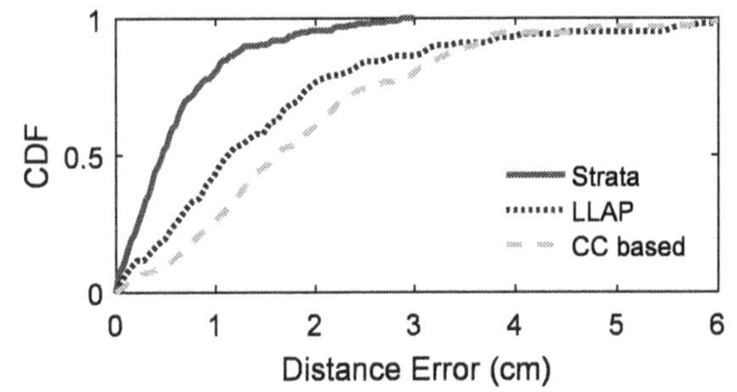

Figure 8: CDF of the distance tracking error with interrupting user.

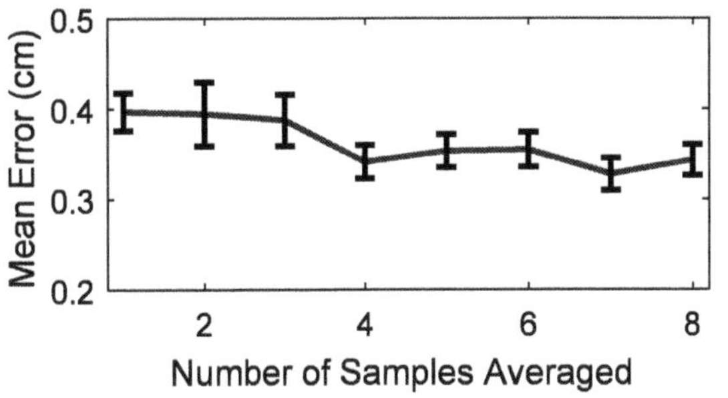

Figure 9: Tracking error with a varying number of samples averaged.

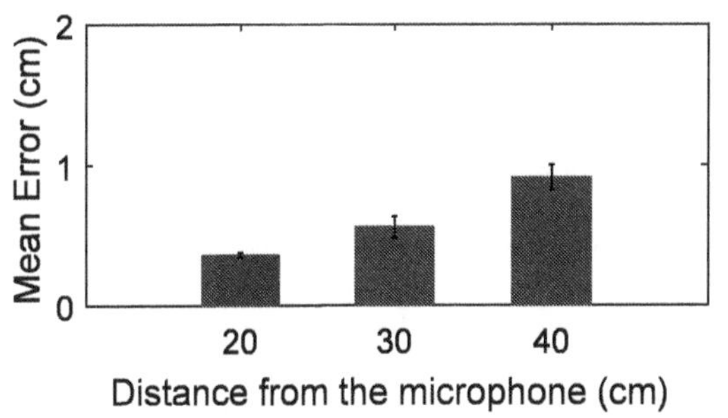

Figure 10: Impact of distance on tracking error.

user is moving his finger. The background user is approximately 60 cm away from the mobile phone. Figure 8 plots CDF of the distance tracking error. In Strata, the tracking accuracy is almost not affected by the background user: the median error increases by only 1 mm over no background moving user.

For the cross-correlation based tracking, we set it to focus on the phase change within the range between 0 to 40 cm. Even if there is a change in echo-profile in the distance of the moving user, we ignore it. As a result, it can effectively avoid the interference and achieves similar median tracking error as before: 1.6 cm. In comparison, LLAP incurs considerable degradation due to the moving user. The median error increases from 0.8 cm to 1.2 cm. Since it does not have a mechanism to distinguish the phase change caused by different objects, the background movement significantly degrades its tracking accuracy. LLAP [40] proposes to combine the phase tracking results of different frequencies to mitigate the multipath fading, but we find it is not sufficient to cancel out the large fading caused by moving people near the object to be tracked.

Varying the number of samples: Figure 9 is the average 1D tracking error with 95% confidence interval when various number of samples are used for averaging downsampled signals as explained in Section 2.3. The result shows that averaging 4 samples reduces the error from 0.39 cm to 0.35 cm compared to simple downsampling. Moreover, it reduces the variance. The 90th percentile error

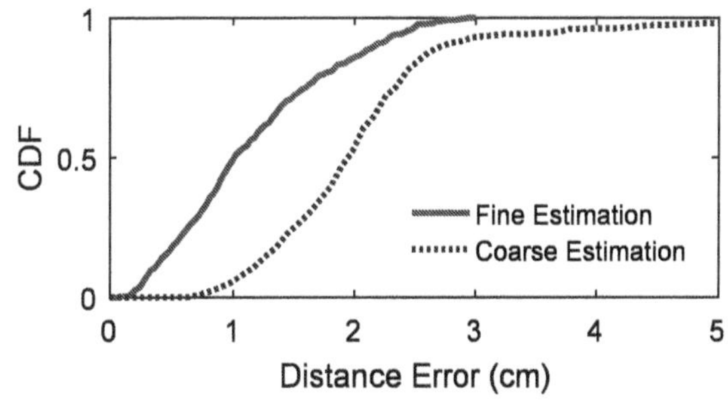

Figure 11: CDF of the absolute distance error.

decreases from 1.1 cm to 0.8 cm. Using more than 4 samples does not lead to significant additional improvement. So we use 4 samples to reduce the computation cost.

Besides the number of samples, there are a few parameters that should to be carefully selected for accurate tracking: 1) the frame detection threshold σ, 2) the dynamic channel tap selection threshold σ_l, and 3) weighting factor β. We extensively address β in the next section, and skip detailed microbenchmark of σ and σ_l. These parameters require calibration on different phones, but are relatively easy to get after a few trials.

Impact of distances: We further vary the distance of the moving target. Specifically, we set the initial distance of the finger from the microphone to 20 cm, 30 cm, and 40 cm, move it 10 cm towards the mobile phone, and measure the distance error. Figure 10 shows the average error with 95% confidence interval. The mean tracking errors are 0.35 cm, 0.55 cm, and 0.9 cm, respectively, as the distance changes from 20 cm to 30 cm to 40 cm. In all cases, the average error is within 1 cm.

3.3.2 *Estimating Absolute Distance*

Strata can not only track the distance change from the phase, but also estimate the absolute distance using the channel difference as explained in Section 2.5. To evaluate the accuracy of the absolute distance estimation, we collected the audio and ground-truth data while users are tracing the shapes on the tablet where initial position of the finger is 20 cm away from the phone. The distance error is measured by calculating the difference between the estimated distance of the finger and microphones versus the ground-truth distance. Figure 11 shows the CDF of the distance error in 200 collected traces. The median and the 90th percentile errors are 1.0 cm and 2.1 cm, respectively. Note that the fine-grained channel estimation significantly improves the accuracy. In terms of the median error, the error reduction from the coarse channel estimation is 48%. We also implement the other schemes that exploits CIR to detect the distance of the target (*i.e.*, WiDeo [13] and Chronos [36]) and evaluate their absolute distance estimation accuracy, but they perform poorly for acoustic signals: their median tracking error is larger than 10 cm, so we do not include the result in Figure 11.

3.3.3 *Combining Relative and Absolute Distance Estimation*

Comparison with the other acoustic tracking schemes: Finally, we evaluate the tracking error in 2D plane. Given the finger's distance from the left and right microphones, Strata and the baseline schemes track the finger position in a 2D plane as explained in Section 2.6. As shown in the previous evaluation results, the phase-based distance tracking is more reliable than the absolute distance estimation. Therefore, we set β of Strata to 0.1 to give a higher weight to the estimate based on phase based tracking. For

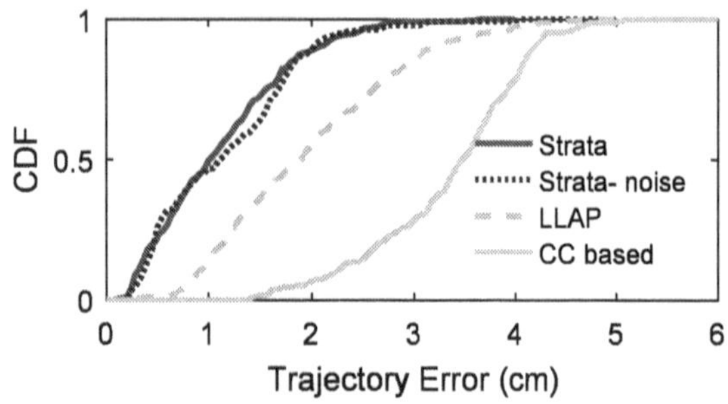

Figure 12: CDF of the trajectory errors with Strata, LLAP, and cross-correlation based tracking.

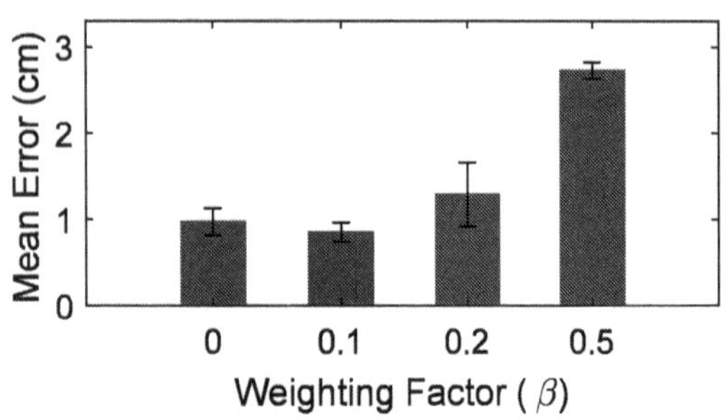

Figure 13: 2D trajectory errors with various weighting factors.

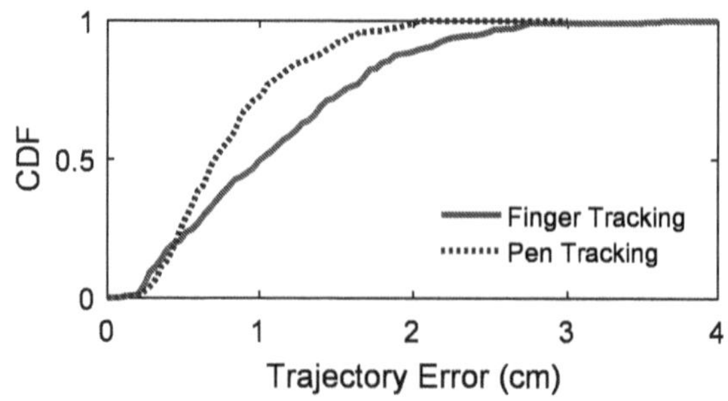

(a) CDF of the 2D trajectory errors.

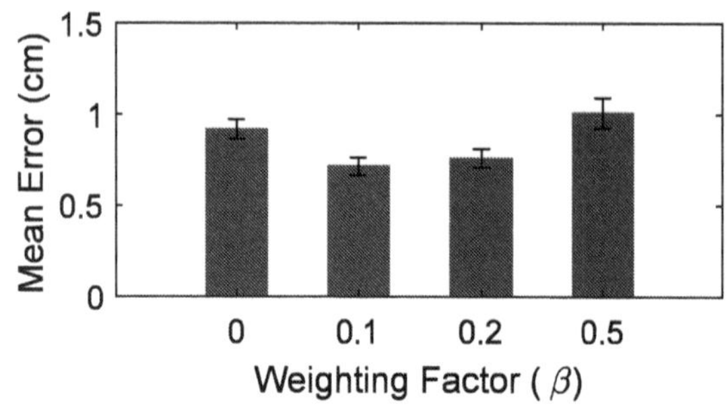

(b) 2D trajectory errors with various weighting factors.

Figure 14: Strata tracking evaluation when pen is tracked instead of finger.

LLAP, we provide the ground-truth initial position and let it track the finger starting from the ground-truth initial position. We collect the finger trajectory tracked by the three schemes as well as the ground-truth trajectory while the users are following the shapes on the tablet screen. The initial distance is 20 cm. The trajectory error is calculated by averaging the difference in the distance between the estimated and ground-truth positions from all samples. Figure 12 shows the CDF of the trajectory errors of the three schemes after repeating the experiment 200 times for each scheme. The median errors of Strata, LLAP, and cross-correlation based tracking are 1.01 cm, 1.9 cm, and 3.47 cm, respectively. The 90th percentile errors are 2.05 cm, 3.19 cm, and 4.18 cm, respectively. Similar to 1D tracking result, Strata yields the tracking error close to half of that in LLAP, and cross-correlation based tracking shows the highest error among them. Note that the trajectory tracking error in 2D is not reported in [40].

Figure 12 also shows the tracking experiment result in noisy environment. Using a PC with an external speaker, we played EDM music [9] near the tracking device with the distance approximately 1m. We played it with median volume in the speaker, where the sound pressure level near the phone was 70 dB. The result shows noise has little impact on the tracking accuracy of Strata. Compared to the other result without artificial noise, the distribution of the tracking error is quite similar. The median error increases by 1 mm, but the 90th percentile error is hardly affected by the noise. Similar findings were reported in several different acoustic signal based tracking schemes (*e.g.*, [44, 40, 33, 18]).

Figure 13 shows the average trajectory error with various weighting factors on the absolute distance estimation (*i.e.*, β). The result shows that when we set β to small values, such as 0.1, it improves the accuracy over the phase-based tracking alone. However, increasing β more than 0.1 tends to increase the error because the absolute distance error is less accurate than the phase based tracking. Note that even when $\beta = 0$, the absolute distance estimate is still useful for getting the initial position.

Tracking pen: So far, we have focused on tracking the finger movement. Our CIR based tracking can effectively nullify the tracking noise from surrounding reflectors when they are sufficiently separated. However, the reflections from the hand and arm movement can affect the finger movement tracking, since the hand and arm are close to the finger and their reflections are observed in the same channel tap of the CIR. To understand the impact of hand and arm movement on the tracking accuracy, we conduct the following experiment. We track a pen attached to a 60 cm thin stick instead of a finger. The user can remotely move it so that his body movement does not affect tracking. We wrap the pen with aluminum foil so that it can generate touch event to the capacitive sensing based touch screen in the tablet, and collect the ground-truth of the pen trajectory using the same method as before.

Figure 14 shows the pen tracking result. Its median and 90th percentile errors are 0.71 cm and 1.44 cm, respectively, which are 0.3 cm and 0.6 cm reduction from the corresponding finger tracking, respectively. The error decreases since the impact of hand and arm movement is removed. Figure 14(b) shows the mean tracking errors with various weighting factors. Interestingly, when $\beta = 0$, the finger and pen tracking have similar tracking errors. In this case, we only use the phase to track the movement. Since the finger and hand have roughly the same movement, phase-based tracking is more robust to the arm and hand movement. In comparison, since the hand and arm have different distances from the finger, their movement has a larger impact on the absolute distance estimation. In Figure 14(b), we observe the mean pen tracking error reduces from 0.92 cm to 0.7 cm by increasing β from 0 to 0.1. Unlike the finger tracking, further increasing β does not degrade the tracking error of a pen. These results confirm our intuition that part of the absolute distance estimation error comes from the hand and arm movement.

User study: We evaluate how accurately users can draw shapes with real-time feedback. We implement a JAVA program that re-

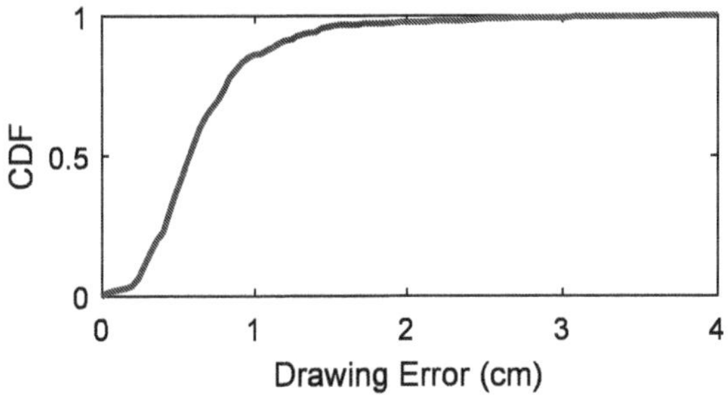

Figure 15: CDF of the drawing error in user study.

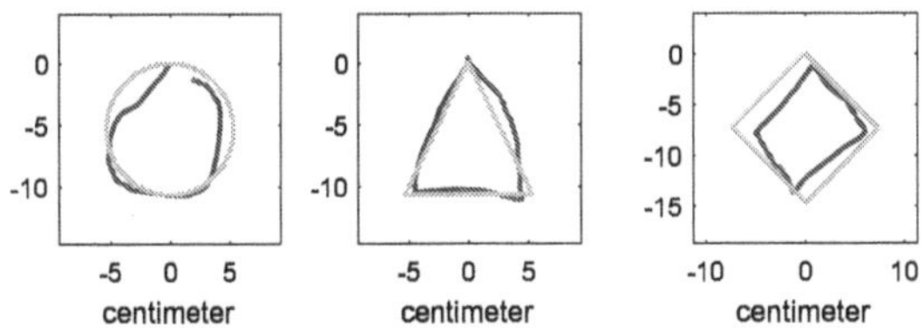

(a) Circle (b) Triangle (c) Diamond

Figure 16: Median drawing error samples drawn by finger tracking.

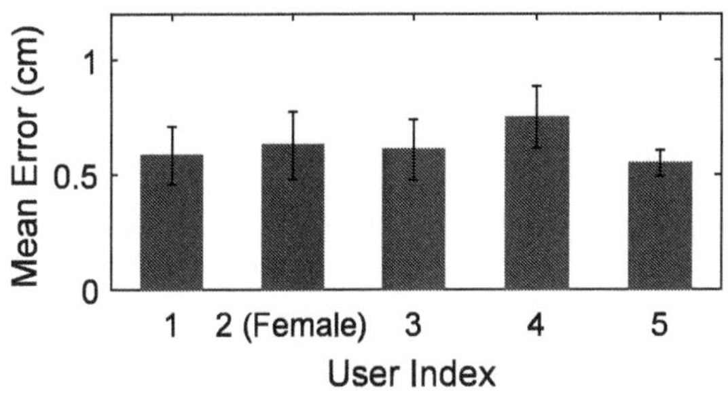

Figure 17: Mean drawing errors of 5 users.

ceives the tracking result from the mobile phone and visualizes a pointer on a PC screen controlled by the finger movement in real-time. Then we asked the user to move the pointer to trace the shapes (*e.g.*, triangle, diamond, and circle) on the screen. The average surface area of them are 31.1 cm. The quality of the drawings is quantified using the drawing error, which is also used in [40]. For each point that Strata estimates using the acoustic signals, we find the closest point on the original shape to compute the distance and compute the distance over all points.

Figure 15 shows the CDF of the drawing errors using 200 trajectories collected from 5 users. The median and 90th percentile drawing errors are 0.57 cm and 1.14 cm, respectively. When the users draw with real-time feedback, they can compensate portion of the tracking error by moving his finger towards the desired position. As a result, the drawing error tends to lower. Figure 16 shows sample drawings of the three shapes under median drawing errors. As we can see, the traced trajectories are close to the original shapes. Figure 17 shows the mean drawing errors of 5 users. The user 2 corresponds to a female user while the other users are male. The result shows that users achieve similar accuracy.

Tracking time: Every 12.5ms, Strata performs low-pass filtering, passband to baseband conversion, channel estimation, and eventually tracks the finger movement. In our Samsung Galaxy S4, the average processing time is 2.5 ms. According to [40], the processing time of LLAP at each interval is 4.3 ms when the same device is used. For the down-conversion, it already takes 3.5 ms. We expect that since LLAP uses multiple sine waves in different bands

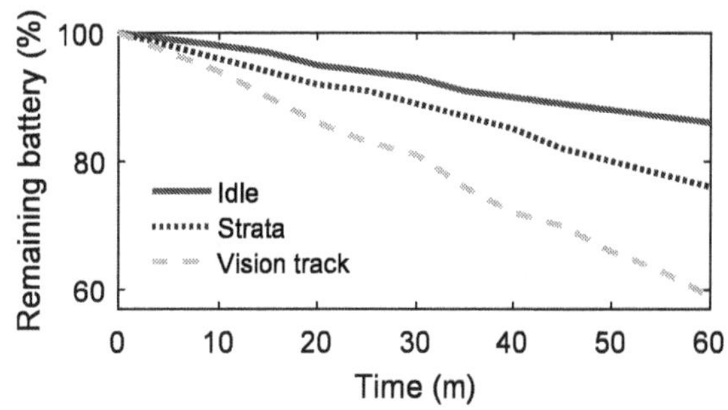

Figure 18: Energy consumption evaluation.

during the down-conversion process, it needs to filter the signal for every band they use to receive the sine waves (9 in our implementation). On the other hand, Strata performs filtering only once for the whole band. As a result, Strata spends less than 1 ms for the down-conversion.

Energy consumption: Finally, we evaluate the energy efficiency of Strata. In this experiment, we first fully charge the battery of the phone, turn on the tracking app and let it track the finger movement, and measure the battery consumption during 1 hour. For comparison, we also evaluate the energy consumption of the vision based tracking scheme. Since there is no particular finger tracking app in the app market, we downloaded a popular camera app in Google Play store, *Face Camera* [10], which tracks human face in camera and adds some visual effects on it. We believe finger tracking and face tracking are not quite different in terms of energy consumption. While running *Face Camera* app, we only use camera based track and do not use other features, such as taking picture or adding visual effect. We also evaluate the energy consumption of the idle phone as baseline. In all of these cases, we keep the screen turned on assuming active use of the device.

Figure 18 shows the energy consumption during one hour. While the phone is not actively running apps, it consumes 14% of its battery in an hour. When the acoustic finger tracking is used, it spends 8% more battery. On the other hand, vision based tracking consumes 27% additional energy, which is 3 times more than the energy consumption of the acoustic tracking. The result demonstrates Strata can achieve energy efficient finger tracking and is more energy efficient than vision based tracking.

4. RELATED WORK

We classify existing work into (i) device-free tracking and (ii) device-based tracking.

4.1 Device-Free Tracking and Gesture Recognition

Vision-based: Vision has been widely used in object tracking and gesture recognition. Among them, Microsoft Kinect [1] has been commercially very successful. It uses depth sensor as well as camera to recognize a user's movement. LeapMotion [16] is another vision based object tracking device on the market. Mirosoft Hololens [11] provides vision and depth sensing based AR capability. While it is expected that it can provide fine grained finger-level gesture recognition based on rich amount of signal resources [34], it requires a high-end device that costs over $3,000.

To increase the user base for VR/AR, Google provides a $10 Google cardboard [6] and many other companies sell VR headsets within $100 (*e.g.*, Samsung Gear), which transforms a smartphone into an AR/VR device. It is expected that smartphone-based VR/AR will likely dominate in the future due to widely available smartphones. Since existing smartphones have limited computation power, energy, and sensing capability (*e.g.*, no depth sensors), audio based tracking used in Strata is more attractive than vision to support smartphone-based VR by using the existing speaker and microphone on the phone and significantly reducing energy consumption. For example, [30] reports acoustic sensing consumes 20% energy compared to vision-based object recognition, and our system is even more energy efficient than vision-based approach as shown in Section 3.3.3.

RF-based: Recently, RF based device-free object tracking schemes in smart home and office environment have received significant attention [2, 32, 13, 41, 17]. WiSee [24] is a pioneering work that uses WiFi signals to recognize 9 gestures in several environments. WiTrack [2] applies Frequency Modulated Continuous Wave (FMCW) to track a user's location with 10-13 cm error in the x and y coordinates, and 21 cm in the z-dimension. It uses customized hardware that can sweep the channel in 1.7 GHz bandwidth. WiDraw [32] estimates angle of arrival (AoA) using CSI, and achieves a median tracking error of 5 cm using 25 WiFi access points (APs). The requirement of such a large number of APs significantly limits the applicability of WiDraw. In comparison, we only require 1 speaker and 2 microphones on one machine to achieve higher accuracy. WiDeo [13] tracks human motion based on reflected WiFi signals with 7 cm tracking error. It implements on WARP using 4 antennas with full-duplex capable transceivers, which is not readily available on the market. VitalRadio [3] also uses specialized hardware to monitor the breathing rate by observing the phase change of the RF signal. mTrack [41] and Soli [17] use 60 GHz signals for gesture recognition. While 60GHz is promising, it requires significant extra hardware for sending, receiving, and processing signals in real-time. [39] proposes Soli gesture recognition scheme with the support of Convolutional Neural Networks (*i.e.*, deep learning), which is too expensive to run on mobile device.

Acoustic-based: Both LLAP [40] and FingerIO [21] track the finger movement using the reflected audio signal from a mobile phone. LLAP develops a phase based tracking while FingerIO uses OFDM symbol based movement detection. Our evaluation in Section 3.2 shows Strata out-performs both schemes because we extract the path associated with the finger movement and track its phase change instead of using the mixed signals. The authors of [7] develop a system, called UltraHaptics, to provide haptic feedback based on acoustic radiation force from a phased array of ultrasonic transducers. This requires customized hardware while Strata supports tracking in software. ApneaApp [20] uses FMCW to track heartbeat by looking at periodic patterns. Gesture recognition performs pattern matching and requires significant training data. In comparison, continuous tracking is more challenging due to the lack of training data or patterns to match against.

4.2 Device-based Tracking and Recognition

IMU-based: IMU sensors have been commonly used for motion tracking. Several works have reported that accelerometer has large error and its error increases rapidly over time due to double integration over time [38, 44]. Gyroscope has pretty good accuracy, but is not easy to use, since users have difficulty in how much to rotate in order to control certain displacement movement [44].

Acoustic-based: Audio is attractive for localization and tracking due to its slow propagation speed, which helps improve the accuracy. One line of research uses acoustic signals to estimate distance. For example, BeepBeep [23] develops a novel approach that allows the sender and receiver with unknown clock offsets to measure the one-way propagation delay. SwordFight [45] addresses several practical challenges in using audio signals for tracking (*e.g.*, quickly detecting the signal, reducing computation overhead, and accounting for measurement error during movement). Another line of research uses acoustic signals for localization. Cricket [31] uses both audio and RF to achieve median error of 12 cm with 6 beacon nodes. Swadloon [12] exploits the Doppler shift of audio signal for fine-grained indoor localization. Its error is around 50 cm. [15] uses chirp-based ranging to achieve localization error within 1 m. AAMouse [44] uses the Doppler shift to estimate the velocity, from which it computes the distance to localize the mobile. Its median error is 1.4 cm. Recently, CAT [18] develops a distributed FMCW and combines it with the Doppler shift estimation to achieve 7 mm error. The third line of audio based approaches target gesture recognition. DoplLink [4] and Spartacus [33] use the Doppler shift of the audio signal between the two mobile phones for gesture recognition. DopLink [4] detects if a device is being pointed by another device. Spartacus [33] uses the Doppler shift to determine the device's moving direction and pairs it with another device moving in the same direction. However, these all require the user to hold the device, which have different applications from Strata that tracks hand movement without device.

RF-based: WiFi has been widely used for localization and tracking (*e.g.*, [5, 26, 28, 36]). Many WiFi based localization uses received signal strength and their accuracy is limited due to obstacles and multipath. More recently, several works use channel state information (CSI), which reports the RSS on each OFDM subcarrier group, to provide accurate location distinction [28]. ArrayTrack [42] and SpotFi [14] further use phase of the received signal to enhance the accuracy. For example, ArrayTrack achieves a median error of 23 cm using 16 antennas. RF-IDraw [38] achieves 3.7 cm tracking error. Tagoram [43] and MobiTagbot [29] achieve higher tracking accuracy than the above RF-based schemes by assuming the RFID tag or reader moves at a constant speed, so they have different applications from Strata.

5. CONCLUSION

This paper develops a novel device-free acoustic tracking system that achieves 1.0 cm median tracking error. Through this process, we gain several important insights: (i) phase-based tracking is effective for acoustic signals due to its small wavelength, but we need to use the channel estimate from an appropriate tap (instead of the overall channel) to achieve high accuracy, (ii) it is hard to estimate the absolute distance by directly decomposing the channel since acoustic channel is not sparse, and our formulation based on the change removes static paths, which significantly reduces the number of unknowns and improves accuracy, and (iii) combining both distance change and absolute distance helps further improve the accuracy. Moving forward, we are interested in further enhancing the accuracy and developing applications on top of device-free tracking.

6. REFERENCES

[1] Microsoft X-box Kinect. http://xbox.com.

[2] F. Adib, Z. Kabelac, D. Katabi, and R. Miller. Witrack: Motion tracking via radio reflections off the body. In *Proc. of NSDI*, 2014.

[3] F. Adib, H. Mao, Z. Kabelac, D. Katabi, and R. C. Miller. Smart homes that monitor breathing and heart rate. In *Proceedings of the CHI Conference on Human Factors in Computing Systems*, pages 837–846. ACM, 2015.

[4] M. T. I. Aumi, S. Gupta, M. Goel, E. Larson, and S. Patel. Doplink: Using the doppler effect for multi-device

interaction. In *Proc. of ACM UbiComp*, pages 583–586, 2013.

[5] P. Bahl and V. N. Padmanabhan. Radar: An in-building RF-based user location and tracking system. In *INFOCOM 2000. Nineteenth Annual Joint Conference of the IEEE Computer and Communications Societies. Proceedings. IEEE*, volume 2, pages 775–784, 2000.

[6] Google Cardboard. https://www.microsoft.com/microsoft-hololens/en-us.

[7] T. Carter, S. A. Seah, B. Long, B. Drinkwater, and S. Subramanian. Ultrahaptics: Multi-point mid-air haptic feedback for touch surfaces. In *Proceedings of UIST*, 2013.

[8] Google Daydream. https://vr.google.com/daydream/.

[9] Edm mix 2017 - best remixes of popular music. https://www.youtube.com/watch?v=IpHXpQ5sWZI&t=1038s.

[10] Face camera - snappy photo. https://play.google.com/store/apps/details?id=com.fotoable.snapfilters.

[11] Microsoft HoloLens. https://www.microsoft.com/microsoft-hololens/en-us.

[12] W. Huang, Y. Xiong, X.-Y. Li, H. Lin, X. Mao, P. Yang, and Y. Liu. Shake and walk: Acoustic direction finding and fine-grained indoor localization using smartphones. In *Proc. of IEEE INFOCOM*, 2014.

[13] K. Joshi, D. Bharadia, M. Kotaru, and S. Katti. Wideo: Fine-grained device-free motion tracing using RF backscatter. In *Proc. of NSDI*, 2015.

[14] M. Kotaru, K. Joshi, D. Bharadia, and S. Katti. Spotfi: Decimeter level localization using wifi. In *ACM SIGCOMM*, volume 45, pages 269–282. ACM, 2015.

[15] P. Lazik and A. Rowe. Indoor pseudo-ranging of mobile devices using ultrasonic chirps. In *Proc. of ACM SenSys*, pages 99–112, 2012.

[16] Leap motion. https://www.leapmotion.com/.

[17] J. Lien, N. Gillian, M. E. Karagozler, P. Amihood, C. Schwesig, E. Olson, H. Raja, and I. Poupyrev. Soli: ubiquitous gesture sensing with millimeter wave radar. In *Proc. of SIGGRAPH*, 2016.

[18] W. Mao, J. He, and L. Qiu. Accurate audio tracker. In *Proceedings of ACM MobiCom*, Oct. 2016.

[19] A. T. Mariakakis, S. Sen, J. Lee, and K.-H. Kim. Sail: Single access point-based indoor localization. In *Proceedings of the 12th annual international conference on Mobile systems, applications, and services*, pages 315–328. ACM, 2014.

[20] R. Nandakumar, S. Gollakota, and N. Watson. Contactless sleep apnea detection on smartphones. In *Proc. of ACM MobiSys*, 2015.

[21] R. Nandakumar, V. Iyer, D. Tan, and S. Gollakota. Fingerio: Using active sonar for fine-grained finger tracking. In *Proceedings of the 2016 CHI Conference on Human Factors in Computing Systems*, pages 1515–1525. ACM, 2016.

[22] A. V. Oppenheim, R. W. Schafer, J. R. Buck, et al. *Discrete-time signal processing*, volume 2. Prentice-hall Englewood Cliffs, 1989.

[23] C. Peng, G. Shen, Y. Zhang, Y. Li, and K. Tan. BeepBeep: a high accuracy acoustic ranging system using COTS mobile devices. In *Proc. of ACM SenSys*, 2007.

[24] Q. Pu, S. Gupta, S. Gollakota, and S. Patel. Whole-home gesture recognition using wireless signals. In *Proc. of ACM MobiCom*, 2013.

[25] M. Pukkila. Channel estimation modeling. *Nokia Research Center*, 2000.

[26] A. Rai, K. K. Chintalapudi, V. N. Padmanabhan, and R. Sen. Zee: zero-effort crowdsourcing for indoor localization. In *Proc. of ACM MobiCom*, 2012.

[27] T. S. Rappaport et al. *Wireless communications: principles and practice*, volume 2. Prentice Hall PTR New Jersey, 1996.

[28] S. Sen, J. Lee, K.-H. Kim, and P. Congdon. Avoiding multipath to revive inbuilding wifi localization. In *Proceeding of the 11th annual international conference on Mobile systems, applications, and services*, pages 249–262. ACM, 2013.

[29] L. Shangguan and K. Jamieson. The design and implementation of a mobile rfid tag sorting robot. In *Proceedings of ACM MobiCom*, pages 31–42. ACM, 2016.

[30] K. G. Shin and Y.-C. Tung. Real-time warning for distracted pedestrians with smartphones, Sept. 25 2015. US Patent App. 14/865,262.

[31] A. Smith, H. Balakrishnan, M. Goraczko, and N. Priyantha. Tracking moving devices with the cricket location system. In *Proc. of ACM MobiSys*, 2005.

[32] L. Sun, S. Sen, D. Koutsonikolas, and K. Kim. Widraw: Enabling hands-free drawing in the air on commodity wifi devices. In *Proc. of ACM MobiCom*, 2015.

[33] Z. Sun, A. Purohit, R. Bose, and P. Zhang. Spartacus: spatially-aware interaction for mobile devices through energy-efficient audio sensing. In *Proc. of ACM Mobisys*, pages 263–276, 2013.

[34] J. Taylor, L. Bordeaux, T. Cashman, B. Corish, C. Keskin, T. Sharp, E. Soto, D. Sweeney, J. Valentin, B. Luff, A. Topalian, E. Wood, S. Khamis, P. Kohli, S. Izadi, R. Banks, A. Fitzgibbon, and J. Shotton. Efficient and precise interactive hand tracking through joint, continuous optimization of pose and correspondences. In *Proc. of SIGGRAPH*, 2016.

[35] D. Tse and P. Viswanath. *Fundamentals of wireless communication*. Cambridge university press, 2005.

[36] D. Vasisht, S. Kumar, and D. Katabi. Decimeter-level localization with a single wifi access point. In *13th USENIX Symposium on Networked Systems Design and Implementation (NSDI 16)*, pages 165–178, 2016.

[37] Vive. http://www.htcvive.com.

[38] J. Wang, D. Vasisht, and D. Katabi. RF-IDraw: virtual touch screen in the air using RF signals. In *Proc. of ACM SIGCOMM*, 2014.

[39] S. Wang, J. Song, J. Lien, I. Poupyrev, and O. Hilliges. Interacting with soli: Exploring fine-grained dynamic gesture recognition in the radio-frequency spectrum. In *Proceedings of the 29th Annual Symposium on User Interface Software and Technology (UIST)*, pages 851–860. ACM, 2016.

[40] W. Wang, A. X. Liu, and K. Sun. Device-free gesture tracking using acoustic signals. In *Proceedings of ACM MobiCom*, pages 82–94. ACM, 2016.

[41] T. Wei and X. Zhang. mTrack: high precision passive tracking using millimeter wave radios. In *Proc. of ACM MobiCom*, 2015.

[42] J. Xiong and K. Jamieson. Arraytrack: A fine-grained indoor location system. In *Proc. of NSDI*, pages 71–84, 2013.

[43] L. Yang, Y. Chen, X.-Y. Li, C. Xiao, M. Li, and Y. Liu. Tagoram: Real-time tracking of mobile RFID tags to high

precision using cots devices. In *Proc. of ACM MobiCom*, 2014.

[44] S. Yun, Y. chao Chen, and L. Qiu. Turning a mobile device into a mouse in the air. In *Proc. of ACM MobiSys*, May 2015.

[45] Z. Zhang, D. Chu, X. Chen, and T. Moscibroda. Swordfight: Enabling a new class of phone-to-phone action games on commodity phones. In *Proc. of ACM MobiSys*, 2012.

SoundSifter: Mitigating Overhearing of Continuous Listening Devices

Md Tamzeed Islam
UNC at Chapel Hill
tamzeed@cs.unc.edu

Bashima Islam
UNC at Chapel Hill
bashima@cs.unc.edu

Shahriar Nirjon
UNC at Chapel Hill
nirjon@cs.unc.edu

ABSTRACT

In this paper, we study the overhearing problem of continuous acoustic sensing devices such as Amazon Echo, Google Home, or such voice-enabled home hubs, and develop a system called *SoundSifter* that mitigates personal or contextual information leakage due to the presence of unwanted sound sources in the acoustic environment. Instead of proposing modifications to existing home hubs, we build an independent embedded system that connects to a home hub via its audio input. Considering the aesthetics of home hubs, we envision SoundSifter as a smart sleeve or a cover for these devices. SoundSifter has hardware and software to capture the audio, isolate signals from distinct sound sources, filter out signals that are from unwanted sources, and process the signals to enforce policies such as personalization before the signals enter into an untrusted system like Amazon Echo or Google Home. We conduct empirical and real-world experiments to demonstrate that SoundSifter runs in real-time, is noise resilient, and supports selective and personalized voice commands that commercial voice-enabled home hubs do not.

1. INTRODUCTION

Having reached the milestone of human-level speech understanding by machines, continuous listening devices are now becoming ubiquitous. Today, it is possible for an embedded device to continuously capture, process, and interpret acoustic signals in real-time. Tech giants like Apple, Microsoft, Google, and Amazon have their own versions of continuous audio sensing and interpretation systems. Apple's Siri [10] and Microsoft's Cortana [16] understand what we say, and act on them to fetch us a web page, schedule a meeting, find the best sushi in town, or tell us a joke. Google and Amazon have gone one step further. Android's 'OK Google' feature [13], Amazon's Echo [2], and Google Home [8] devices do not even require user interactions such as touches or button presses. Although these devices are activated upon a hot-word, in the process, they are continuously listening to everything. It is not hard to imagine that sooner or later someone will be hacking into these cloud-connected systems and will be listening to every conversation we are having at our home, which is one of our most private places.

Permission to make digital or hard copies of all or part of this work for personal or classroom use is granted without fee provided that copies are not made or distributed for profit or commercial advantage and that copies bear this notice and the full citation on the first page. Copyrights for components of this work owned by others than ACM must be honored. Abstracting with credit is permitted. To copy otherwise, or republish, to post on servers or to redistribute to lists, requires prior specific permission and/or a fee. Request permissions from permissions@acm.org.

MobiSys'17, June 19-23, 2017, Niagara Falls, NY, USA
© 2017 ACM. ISBN 978-1-4503-4928-4/17/06... 15.00
DOI: http://dx.doi.org/10.1145/3081333.3081338

Furthermore, there is a recent trend in the IoT world that many third-party, commercial IoT devices are now becoming voice enabled by using the APIs offered by the voice-controlled personal assistant devices like Echo or Google Home. Henceforth, we will refer to these devices interchangeably as smart hubs, home hubs, or simply hubs. For example, many home appliances and web services such as Google Nest thermostats [9], Philips Hue lights [15], Belkin WeMo switches [5], TP-Link smart plugs [19], Uber, and Amazon ordering are now 'Alexa-Enabled' – which means, we can send voice commands to an Amazon Echo device to actuate electrical devices and home appliances. Because it enables actuation and control of real-world entities, a potential danger is that they can be activated by false commands (e.g., sounds from a TV) and/or unauthorized commands (e.g., an outsider commands someone's home hub to control his home appliances, places a large purchase on his Amazon account, or calls a Uber driver). A careful scrutiny of voice commands is therefore a necessity to ensure safety and security.

Unfortunately, none of the existing voice-enabled home hub devices take any of these vulnerabilities into account while processing the audio. They merely apply standard noise-cancellation [22, 50, 52] to suppress non-speech background sounds in order to improve the signal-to-noise ratio. However, this process alone cannot eliminate acoustic signals from unwanted acoustic sources that happen to be present in the environment and overlap in time and/or frequency with a user's voice signals. There is also no support for personalization of speech commands in these devices.

In this paper, we study the 'overhearing' problem of acoustic sensing devices, and develop a system that mitigates personal or contextual information leakage due to the presence of unwanted sound sources in the acoustic environment. Instead of developing a special-purpose, application-specific embedded system that works only for voice commands, we address the problem in a generic setting where a user can define a specific type of sound as primary (i.e., a relevant or essential sound type for the application), or secondary (i.e., a non-essential and potentially privacy concerning sound). For example, the voice of a user issuing a command is a primary source for home hubs, whereas any identifiable background noises such as the sounds from appliances, other conversations are examples of secondary sounds. Furthermore, instead of proposing modifications to existing home hubs, we build an independent embedded system that connects to a home hub via its audio input. Considering the aesthetics of home hubs, we envision the proposed system as a smart sleeve or a cover for these home hubs. The proposed system has necessary hardware and software to capture the audio, isolate signals from distinct sound sources, filter out signals that are from unwanted sources, and process the signals to enforce policies such as personalization before the signals enter into an untrusted system like Amazon Echo or Google Home. The device is programmable, i.e., an end user is able to configure it for different usage scenarios.

Developing such an embedded system poses several challenges. First, in order to isolate acoustic sources, we are required to use an array of microphones. Continuously sampling multiple microphones at high rates, at all times, and then processing them in real-time is extremely CPU, memory, and time demanding for resource-constrained systems. Second, to train the system to distinguish primary and secondary sources, we are required to collect audio samples from an end user to create person or context specific acoustic models. To the users, it would be an inconvenience if we require them to record a large number of audio samples for each type of sound in their home. Third, because no acoustic source separation is perfect, there will always be residuals of secondary sources after the source separation has been completed. These residuals contain enough information to infer personal or contextual information, and hence, they must be eliminated to ensure protection against information leakage.

In this paper, we address all these challenges and develop a complete system called the *SoundSifter*. The hardware of SoundSifter consists of a low-cost, open-source, embedded platform that drives an array of microphones at variable rates. Five software modules perform five major acoustic processing tasks: to orchestrate the sampling rates of the microphones, to align the signals, to isolate sound sources, to identify primary source, and to post process the stream to remove residuals and perform speaker identification. At the end of the processing, audio data is streamed into the home hub. We thoroughly evaluate the system components, algorithms, and the full system using empirical data as well as real deployment scenarios in multiple home environments.

The contributions of this paper are the following:

- We describe SoundSifter, the first system that addresses the overhearing problem of voice-enabled personal assistant devices like Amazon Echo, and provides an efficient, pragmatic solution to problems such as information leakage, and unauthorized or false commands due to the presence of unwanted sound sources in the environment.

- We devise an algorithm that predicts a spectral property of incoming audio to control the sampling rates of the microphone array to achieve an efficient acoustic source separation.

- We devise an algorithm that estimates noise directly from the secondary sources and nullifies residuals of secondary signals from the primary source.

- We conduct empirical and real-world experiments to demonstrate that SoundSifter runs in real-time, is noise resilient, and supports selective and personalized voice commands that commercial voice-enabled home hubs do not.

2. BACKGROUND

We provide background on source separation, a specific source separation algorithm, and terminology that is used later in the paper.

2.1 Source Separation

The term *'blind source separation'* [26] refers to the generic problem of retrieving N unobserved sources only from the knowledge of P observed mixtures of these sources. The problem was first formulated to model neural processing of human brains [34], and has later been extended and studied in many other contexts such as biomedical applications [42, 60], communication [29, 27], finance [23, 25], security [49, 48], and acoustics [61, 33, 65]. To the acoustic processing community, this problem is popularly known as the *'cocktail party problem,'* where sources represent human voices.

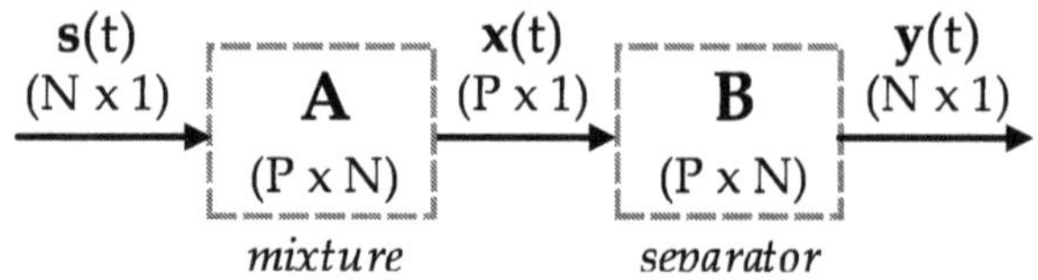

Figure 1: Generic model for source separation.

In this paper, all sources are acoustic, and each microphone observes a weighted combination of N sound sources. Assuming $\mathbf{s}(t) = (s_1(t), ..., s_N(t))^T \in \mathbb{R}^N$ denotes the sources, $\mathbf{x}(t) = (x_1(t), ..., x_P(t))^T \in \mathbb{R}^P$ denotes the observed mixtures, $(.)^T$ stands for matrix transpose operation, and $\mathbf{A}$ denotes an unknown mapping from $\mathbb{R}^N$ to $\mathbb{R}^P$, we can write: $\forall t \in \mathbb{Z} \quad \mathbf{x}(t) = \mathbf{A}\mathbf{s}(t)$.

The equation above is of a *linear instantaneous* model, which is the most commonly used model for source separation. This does not explicitly model noise, as it can be implicitly modeled as an additional source. In Figure 1, $\mathbf{A}$ is a *mixing* matrix that mixes N acoustic sources to produce P output streams. Retrieving the sources is equivalent to finding $\mathbf{B}$, the inverse or *separator* matrix. The separated outputs are expressed as: $\forall t \in \mathbb{Z} \quad \mathbf{y}(t) = \mathbf{B}\mathbf{x}(t)$. When $N \leq P$, $\mathbf{A}$ is invertible. But for $N > P$, additional assumptions (e.g., sparsity [21]) may be required.

2.2 Fast ICA

There are many solutions to the source separation problem that make different assumptions about sources and use different mixing systems [40, 25, 32]. *Independent Component Analysis* (ICA) is one of the most popular solutions. This approach assumes that the acoustic sources are statistically independent from each other – which is in general true for our application scenario. For example, voice commands to an Amazon Echo device and unwanted background sounds are unlikely to have any statistical correlations among themselves.

Fast ICA [38] is a popular, efficient independent component analysis-based source separation algorithm. It isolates the sources by iteratively maximizing a measure of mutual independence among the sources. In Fast ICA, *non-Gaussianity* [26] of the sources is taken as the measure.

Using matrix notation, $\mathbf{x}(t)$ is expressed as $X \in \mathbb{R}^{P \times T}$. FastICA iteratively updates a weight vector $W \in \mathbb{R}^P$ to maximize non-Gaussianity of the projection $W^T X$ using the following two steps in a loop:

$$W^+ \leftarrow E\{X\phi(W^T X)\} - E\{\phi'(W^T X)\}W$$
$$W \leftarrow W^+ / \,||W^+|| \tag{1}$$

Here, $\phi(x) = \tanh(x)$, $\phi'(x)$ is its derivative, and E{} is average over columns of a matrix. W is initialized to a random vector, and the loop stops when there is no significant change in it. Note that, for simplicity, we only show how to isolate one source in Equation 1; for multiple sources, this needs to be repeated for each source. We also omit the preprocessing steps that involves prewhitening [26] matrix X.

2.3 Measure of Residual Signals

Because no source separation is perfect, there are always residues of secondary sources within the isolated stream of audio that is supposed to carry signals from the primary source only. We use a metric to quantify this residual with the following equation:

$$\xi_i = ||x_i(t) - y_i(t)||_2 \tag{2}$$

Here, ξ_i denotes the amount of residuals in the ith source after source separation, which is expressed as the l^2-norm of the difference between primary signals before and after source separation. We use this metric in our evaluations to quantify the quality of source separation.

3. OVERVIEW OF SOUNDSIFTER

SoundSifter is motivated by the need of a smart acoustic filter that inspects audio signals and takes proper actions such as filtering sounds from unwanted secondary sources and checking the content of primary signals before letting them into a voice-enabled home hub or any such continuous listening devices.

SoundSifter connects to a home hub or a mobile device's audio jack, and can be thought of as an extension to their on-board audio I/O subsystem. It captures and processes all incoming audio streams, isolates audio signals from distinct sources, identifies and blocks out any sound that has not been labeled 'primary' by a user during its installation, and only lets processed audio enter into a hub for further application-specific processing.

3.1 Basic Workflow

Figure 2(a) shows how SoundSifter sits between audio sources and a home hub. Further details of its internal processing blocks are shown in Figure 2(b). The system has an *Audio I/O Controller* that controls an array of microphones (required for source separation), a speaker, Bluetooth and an audio jack to support external audio I/O. The *Source Separator* executes the acoustic source separation algorithm by controlling the microphones via the audio I/O controller and using precomputed acoustic models. The *Post Processing* module further filters and obfuscates the already separated primary stream to eliminate traces of residuals from other sources and to enforce policies (read from a configuration file) such as personalized commands. The policies are further described in 3.3 as usage scenarios. Finally, the processed audio output is let go into the home hub via the audio jack.

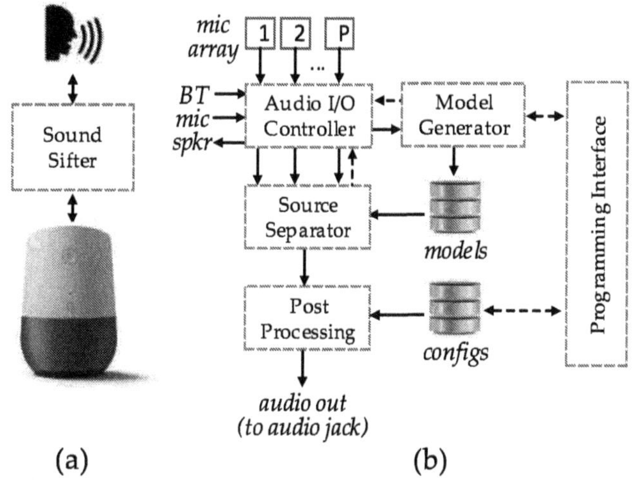

Figure 2: (a) System interface, and (b) block diagram of SoundSifter.

3.2 Initial Setup and Programming

SoundSifter needs to be programmed once for each use case (described in the next section). Programming the device essentially means creating acoustic models for each type of *primary* sound involved in a scenario. Because these sounds are often user- or home-specific, this process requires the active engagement of a user. To make the process simple, a user is provided with a mobile app that is as easy as using a media player. The mobile app connects to SoundSifter over Bluetooth, and interacts with it by sending programming commands and receiving responses. *No audio data are exchanged between the devices.*

In the app, the user is guided to send commands to SoundSifter to record $10s - 30s$ audio for each type of primary sound, label them, and specify in which scenario they will be used. The system also needs some examples of a few common types of secondary sounds for the application scenario. However, it does not require a user to record and label all possible secondary sounds. We empirically determined that as long as SoundSifter has 2-3 types of secondary sounds per use case, it is capable of detecting primary vs secondary sounds with a high accuracy and a negligible false positive rate.

Once the recording and labeling phase is over, SoundSifter uses an algorithm to create acoustic models, deletes all raw audio data, and only the labeled models are stored inside the device in a configuration file.

3.3 Usage Scenarios

We describe two motivating scenarios for SoundSifter that are specific to voice-controlled home hubs.

Voice-only mode: Continuous listening devices of today hear everything in their surrounding acoustic environment. The goal of *voice-only* mode is to ensure that only speech signals enter into these devices while all other sound sources in a home environment such as sounds from TV, appliances, non-voice human sounds such as laughter, crying, coughing, sounds of an activity such as cooking, cleaning, etc. are completely filtered out of the system. This is achieved in SoundSifter by using a combination of source separation, recognition, and suppression.

Personalization: Command personalization may be of multiple types: voice commands containing an exact sequence of words or an utterance, voice commands that contain a certain keyword or a set of keywords in it and voice commands of a certain person. These are achievable by first applying the voice-only mode, and then performing additional acoustic processing such as speech-to-text and speaker identification. Although we only mention home hub related usage scenarios of SoundSifter in this section, the generic notion of primary and secondary sound allows us to configure the system for other applications where it can filter in/out different primary/secondary sounds as well. Furthermore, we did not implement a speech-to-text converter in our system due to time constraints, which we leave as future work.

4. STUDYING THE PROBLEM

Prior to the development of SoundSifter, we performed studies and experiments to understand the nature of the challenge.

4.1 Need for Source Separation

As an alternative to source separation, we looked into simpler solutions such as filtering and noise cancellation. However, those attempts failed since the sounds that may be present in the environment overlap with one another in the frequency domain.

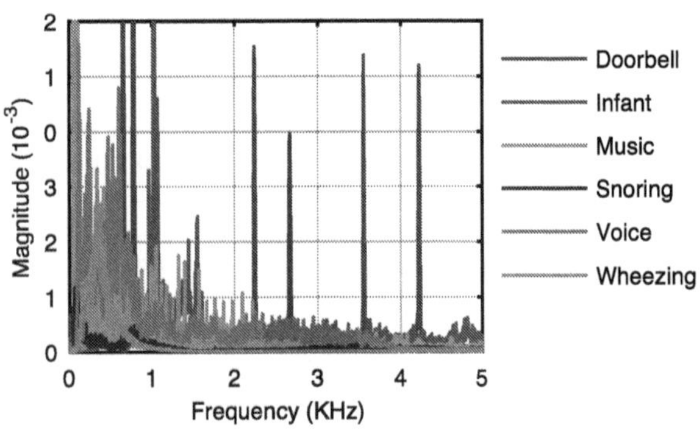

Figure 3: Frequency plots of variety of sounds.

In Figure 3 we plot frequency characteristics of a selected set of sounds. For example, speech (< 4 KHz) covers the full range of snoring (< 1.5 KHz) and asthmatic wheeze (< 1.3 KHz). Crying infants and doorbell sounds range from 500 Hz to 1.6 KHz and 4.2 KHz, respectively. Music overlaps with all sounds. Besides these, we also analyzed home appliances such as a blender, a washing machine, door slams, toilet flushes, speech signals of different sexes and age groups, and asthmatic crackling, and came to the conclusion that spatial information is the most effective method for identifying and isolating primary information containing signals from other types of unwanted sounds in a general purpose setting.

4.2 Number of Microphones

For effective source separation, we are required to use an array of microphones. In theory, the number of microphones should equal the number of simultaneously active sources. However, for sparse sources like audio (sources that do not produce a continuous stream) , source separation can be performed with fewer microphones.

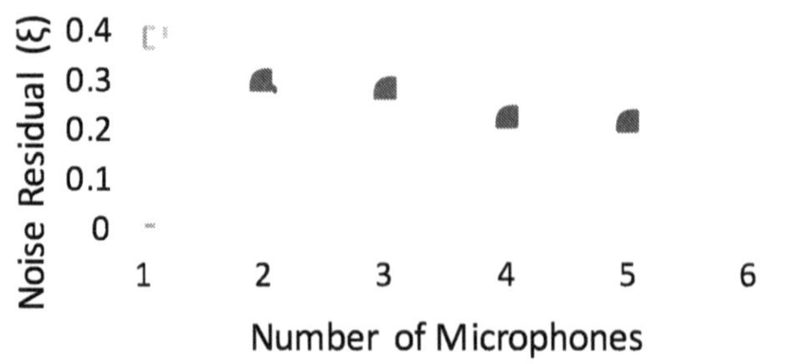

Figure 4: Source separation error for different number of microphones.

To determine an adequate number of microphones for source separation, we perform an experiment where we use an array of five microphones that captures audio signals from 2–5 simultaneously active sources: voice (primary sound), ringing phone, piano, songs, and television. Figure 4 shows the quality of source separation in terms of mean residuals (the lower the better) as we vary the number of microphones for different number of active sources. We observe that the residuals drop with more microphones. However, the reduction is not great for more than four microphones. Hence, we use four microphones in our system and use an additional noise removal step to nullify the remaining residuals.

4.3 Benefit of Rate Adaptation

According to the Nyquist theorem [55], the sampling rate of each microphone must be at least twice of the maximum frequency of any source. However, sampling an array of microphones at a very high rate costs significant CPU, memory, and power consumption. Note that our system is suitable for portable home hub devices, where a plug-in power is not always an option. In such cases, limited processing power is a challenge.

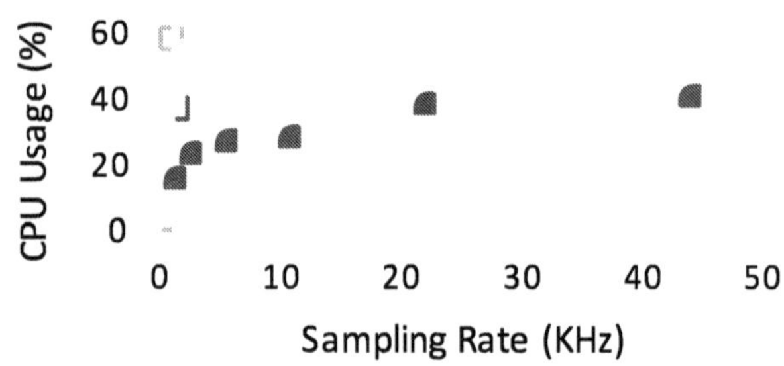

Figure 5: CPU usage increases with sampling rate.

To validate this, we conduct an experiment using an ARM Cortex A8-based microcontroller. In Figure 5, we observe that as the sampling rate is increased, CPU usage increases sharply. Memory consumption also increases from 22 KB to 704 KB as we vary the sampling rate. Based on this observation, we decide not to sample the microphones at the highest rate at all times; instead, we adopt a predictive scheme where we probabilistically choose a sufficient sampling rate for the microphone array based on previous knowledge on sound sources and signals that the system has just seen.

4.4 Modeling Sounds

After isolating the sources, for SoundSifter to determine which sounds to let in and which ones to block, it has to identify the source that represents the primary sound. Because primary sounds in different usage scenarios are highly subjective, SoundSifter must obtain a sufficiently large number of audio samples directly from the end user to create a robust and accurate sound classifier. On one hand, we need a large amount of training audio from the user for a robust classification. On the other hand, requiring a user to collect these data is likely to be error prone and also an inconvenience to them. Hence, it is customary to investigate techniques to create robust acoustic classifiers that generate accurate and robust models based on a limited amount of training data.

4.5 Need for Residue Removal

A crucial observation during our study has been that even after source separation, when we look into the stream of primary signals, we find traces of secondary sources. We realize that even though the residues are too weak to be heard, using machine learning, they can be identified and recognized.

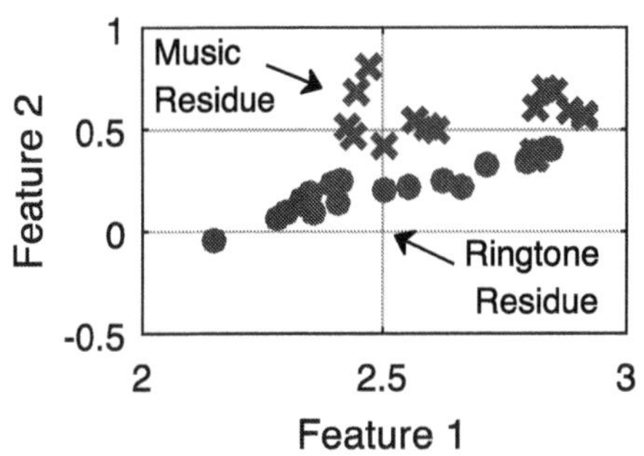

Figure 6: Effect of residue on primary source.

To illustrate the vulnerability of signal residue, we conducted a small scale study. We performed source separation for two cases – speech with: 1) music, and 2) a ringing phone in the background. In both cases, the same set of 20 utterances is synthetically mixed (to keep the primary sound identical) with the two background sounds. After source separation, we take the separated speech streams, compute Mel-frequency cepstral coefficient (MFCC) [57] features, and plot the utterances (total 40) in a 2D feature space as shown in Figure 6. In this figure, feature 1 and feature 2 denote the two highest ranked components of MFCC. It is interesting to observe that even though the residues of music and ring tone are not audible, their presence in the speech stream is statistically significant – which is enough to distinguish the two cases.

4.6 Analog Data Acquisition

A practical engineering challenge that we face with multi-channel audio data acquisition has been the inability of commodity embedded hardware platforms to sample analog signals at a very high rate. For example, considering the worst case where we are required to drive four analog microphones at 44.1 KHz, we need an aggregate sampling rate of 176.4 KHz. Achieving such a high rate of analog reading using off-the-shelf Linux-based embedded platforms such as Arduinos, Raspberry Pis, or Beaglebones is non-trivial. We address this implementation challenge and believe our solution will be helpful to anyone who wants to read analog audio at a high (e.g. MHz) rate.

5. ALGORITHM DESIGN

The audio processing pipeline inside SoundSifter has five major stages. Figure 7 shows the stages and their interconnections. The first two stages prepare the audio streams from the microphone array for the source separation stage. These two stages together implement the proposed sampling rate adaptation scheme in order to lower the CPU and memory consumption of SoundSifter. We use FastICA [38] to perform the actual source separation. The last two stages perform further processing to identify the primary source and to nullify the residuals of other sources in it.

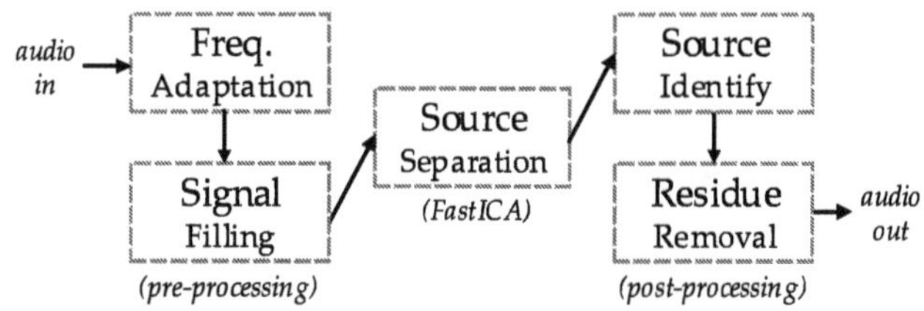

Figure 7: Components and interconnections inside SoundSifter's audio processing pipeline.

In this section, we describe the first and the last two stages of SoundSifter's audio processing pipeline, i.e. the pre-processing and post-processing stages to demonstrate how these stages work in concert to improve the efficiency and effectiveness in mitigating information leakage from unwanted acoustic sources with SoundSifter.

5.1 Frequency Adaptation

SoundSifter adopts a predictive scheme to determine an adequate sampling rate for the microphone array. Sampling rate adaptation in SoundSifter happens periodically, and the predicted rate is estimated based on the knowledge of the portion of the audio that the system has already seen. SoundSifter keeps an evolving Markov [53] model, whose transition probabilities help determine the expected maximum frequency of incoming audio, given the measured maximum frequencies of the audio samples received during the last few ms.

Predicting the absolute value of the maximum frequency of incoming audio signals is practically impossible in a generic setting. However, if we divide the full range of audible frequencies into discrete levels, the transitions from one level to another can be predicted with a higher confidence. For this, SoundSifter uses six ranges of frequencies by dividing the maximum sampling rate into six disjoint sets $44.1/2^h$ KHz, where $0 \leq h \leq 5$. We denote these by the set $\{f_i\}$, where $0 \leq i \leq 5$.

Furthermore, since we are aiming at applying the *past predicts the future* principle, a question that immediately comes up is how much past data to use for an accurate prediction of the desired sampling rate? To determine this, we conduct an experiment to quantify the look-back duration. We experiment with two different Markov models:

- **1-Step Look-back:** Uses a 6-state Markov model, where each state corresponds to a frequency in $\{f_i\}$, resulting in a 6×6 transition matrix having transitions of the form $f_i \rightarrow f_j$.

- **2-Step Look-back:** Uses a 36-state Markov model, where each state corresponds to a pair of frequencies (f_i, f_j), resulting in a 36×36 transition matrix having transitions of the form $(f_i, f_j) \rightarrow (f_j, f_k)$.

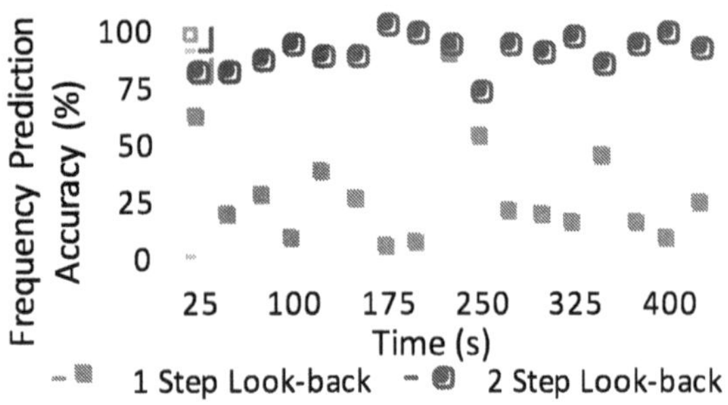

Figure 8: 2-Step Look-back performs better than 1-Step Look-back for loud music

Figure 8 shows a comparison of these two frequency prediction approaches for an 8-minute recording of loud music. Sampling frequency is adapted every 500 ms, compared with the ground truth, and the prediction accuracy is reported every 25 seconds. We observe that the 2-step look-back, i.e. the 36 state Markov model is a significant improvement over the 1-step look-back and has an average prediction accuracy of 88.23% for this very challenging case. Higher than 2-step look-back might show a slightly better accuracy, but such a model would result in an explosion of states. Hence, we use the 2-step look-back model in SoundSifter.

The proposed Markov model evolves over time. Initially, all transition probabilities in the model are set so that the microphones are sampled at the highest rate. As the model starts to make predictions, the probabilities are updated following a simple reward and punishment process where every correct/incorrect predict is rewarded/punished by increasing/decreasing the probability. Both the processes of making a prediction and updating the probability are $\mathcal{O}(1)$ operations.

Ideally one would expect SoundSifter to adapt all its microphones to the minimum required frequency of the moment, but there is a small caveat. Because frequency prediction is not 100% accurate, there is a chance that occasionally we will have mispredictions. Cases when the predicted frequency is lower than the desired one, we will not be able to correct it in the next step unless we have an oracle. To address this, we keep the sampling frequency of one microphone fixed at 44.1 KHz, while the sampling rates of all other microphones are adapted as described above. In case of mispredictions, this microphone serves as the oracle and helps determine the correct frequency.

5.2 Signal Prediction and Filling

Adapting sampling rates at runtime has its benefits, but it also introduces an *alignment* problem during source separation. By default, standard source separation algorithms such as the FastICA assume that all microphones are sampled at a known fixed rate. In SoundSifter, this assumption does not hold anymore, i.e. different microphones may be sampled at different rates. Therefore, we are required to re-align samples from all the microphones and fill the gaps (missing samples) in each of the low rate microphones. Because we work with a small amount of signals at a time, although we expand the low rate samples, the process does not increase the total memory consumption significantly.

We illustrate this using two microphones: $x_i(t)$ and $x_j(t)$, supposing they are sampled at 44.1 KHz and 11.025 KHz, respectively. Within a certain period of time (e.g., between two consecutive frequency adaptation events), the first microphone will have four times more samples than the second microphone. If we align them in time, there will be three missing values in the second stream for each sample. If we assume a matrix of samples where each row corresponds to one microphone, the resultant matrix after alignment would look like the following:

$$\begin{bmatrix} x_{i1} & x_{i2} & x_{i3} & x_{i4} & x_{i5} & x_{i6} & x_{i7} & x_{i8} & x_{i9} & \dots \\ x_{j1} & ? & ? & ? & x_{j5} & ? & ? & ? & x_{j9} & \dots \end{bmatrix}$$

To fill the missing values in the matrix, we formulate it as an interpolation problem and try to predict the missing values in two ways:

- **Linear Interpolation:** Uses line segments to join consecutive points and any intermediate missing value is predicted as a point on the line segment.

- **Cubic Spline Interpolation:** Uses piece-wise third order polynomials [20] to construct a smooth curve that is used to interpolate missing samples.

The benefit of linear interpolation is that it is faster (e.g., 58 times when compared to cubic spline for one second audio) than its higher order counterpart, but it performs very poorly in predicting audio samples if the gaps between given points are large. Cubic spline produces smoother curves and performs comparatively better for large gaps in missing values, but its running time is slower. We pick linear interpolation and a suitable length for interpolation, so that it runs fast and is also fairly accurate.

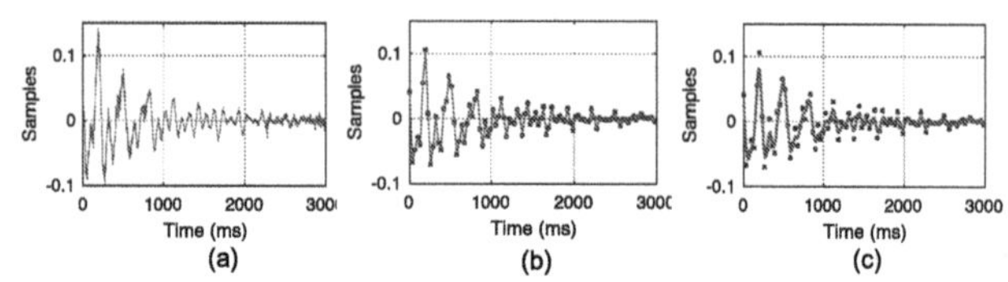

Figure 9: Predicting missing values of a signal(a) using linear(b) and spline(c) interpolation.

Figure 9 compares both linear and spline methods for signal interpolation to *raise up-sample* a signal from 1.378 KHz to 44.1 KHz. We observe that for 10 ms sample windows, linear interpolation produces faster and better results than cubic splines.

5.3 Modeling and Recognizing Sounds

After source separation, SoundSifter classifies each isolated source as primary or secondary. If we had sufficient training examples for each type of sound from an end user, the problem would be as simple as creating a standard machine learning classifier. However, to reduce the burden of data collection on a user and to improve the robustness of the created classifier in a principled way, we perform an additional *data augmentation* step prior to creating the classifier model. Recall that this is a one time step that happens during the installation and programming of SoundSifter for a particular usage scenario.

5.3.1 Data Augmentation

The basic principle behind data augmentation [28, 44] is to generate new training examples from existing ones by perturbing one or more acoustic characteristics. In SoundSifter, we use two specific types of augmentation techniques to increase the user contributed data size by about 13 times. These techniques are listed in Table 1.

Action	Description
f-warping	Remapping the frequency axis: $f_i \rightarrow \alpha f_i$, where $\alpha \in [0.8, 1.2]$.
Inject Noise	Superimposing simulated noise. Noise models are created offline.

Table 1: Data augmentation techniques applied to increase user-contributed samples.

To apply frequency warping [41], each sample goes through a mapping phase 10 times, each time using a different α that is chosen uniformly at random. Simulated random noise [56] is applied to about one-third of these examples to further augment the data set. Overall, we obtain a 13.33-fold boost in the number of training examples giving us original samples as well as their perturbed versions that are resilient to noise and changes in frequency due to environmental effect.

5.3.2 Feature Extraction and Classification

For each audio frame, a 13-element MFCC feature vector is computed. Following common practice, a number of consecutive feature vectors are used to calculate 13 deltas and 13 double deltas to obtain 39-element feature vectors for each frame. Finally, the mean, standard deviation, and range of these vectors are taken to obtain a single 39-element feature vector. A random forest [36] classifier is used to create the final classifier.

For speaker identification, we extend the feature vector of the previous step to include *pitch* as an extra feature. Following [51], we estimate pitch using the *zero crossing rate* (ZCR) of the audio in the time domain:

$$ZCR = 0.5 \times \sum_{i=2}^{n} |sign(s_i) - sign(s_{i-1})| \quad (3)$$

Here, s_i represents audio samples, n is the length of a frame and $sign(x)$ is either $+1$ or -1 depending on whether $(x > 0)$ or $(x < 0)$.

5.4 Eliminating Secondary Residues

After source separation and source identification, we obtain a primary and a number of secondary sources. As seen previously in Figure 4, the residuals were not zero even in the best case, and in Figure 6 we observed that such residuals are significant enough to recognize secondary sources embedded within the isolated primary stream.

In order to nullify these residuals we employ a customized *adaptive noise cancellation* technique [62]. Standard noise cancellation algorithms either assume simple Gaussian noises or use sophisticated hardware to capture noise sources to 'subtract' noise spectra from the main audio stream. In SoundSifter, we are lucky to have the separated secondary source streams readily available as a by product of source separation. These secondary streams are used as negative feedback to remove their respective residues from the primary stream.

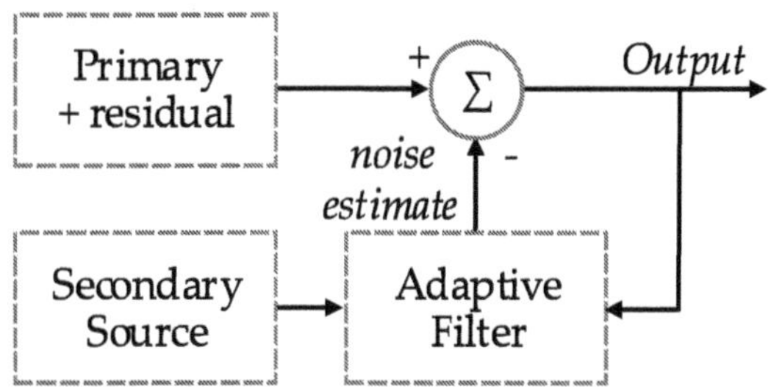

Figure 10: Leveraging isolated secondary sources to nullify their residue through a customized adaptive noise cancellation process.

Figure 10 shows the noise cancellation process where secondary sources are iteratively used to estimate residual noise signals contributed by each of them, which are then subtracted from the primary source to obtain residue-free signals. As an illustration, we consider p and n_i as the primary and secondary sources after the source separation step, respectively. An input to the noise canceller is $(p + n_i^r)$, where n_i^r denotes the residuals. The secondary source n_i is another input to the canceller that is passed through an adaptive filter to produce an output $\widehat{n}_i^r$ that is a close replica of n_i^r. The output of the adaptive filter is subtracted from the primary input to produce the system output $z = p + n_i^r - \widehat{n}_i^r$, which indicates the error signal for the adaptive process.

We adjust the filter using least mean squares (LMS) [63] algorithm that minimizes the output power. We use a stochastic gradient descent method where the filter weights are adapted based on the error at the current time step. The weight update function for the least mean squares algorithm is:

$$\mathrm{W}_{n+1} = \mathrm{W}_n - \mu \nabla \epsilon[n] \quad (4)$$

Here, ϵ represents the mean-square error, and μ is a constant that controls the speed of convergence.

6. IMPLEMENTATION NOTES

Due to space limitations we only describe some key implementation issues.

6.1 Amazon Alexa Voice Service

To demonstrate SoundSifter, we must connect it to a home hub such as Amazon Echo or Google Home. However, at present, none of these devices come with an audio input where we can pipe in the processed audio from SoundSifter. Hence, we use Amazon Voice Service (AVS) to turn a Raspberry Pi into an Alexa-enabled device which provides us with multiple options for audio inputs, i.e. audio jacks as well as Bluetooth. We followed the step-by-step procedure [1] that Amazon recommends to enable their voice service API in Raspberry Pi platform. Figure 11 shows our custom home hub in a 3D printed case, which is functionally identical to an Amazon Echo device.

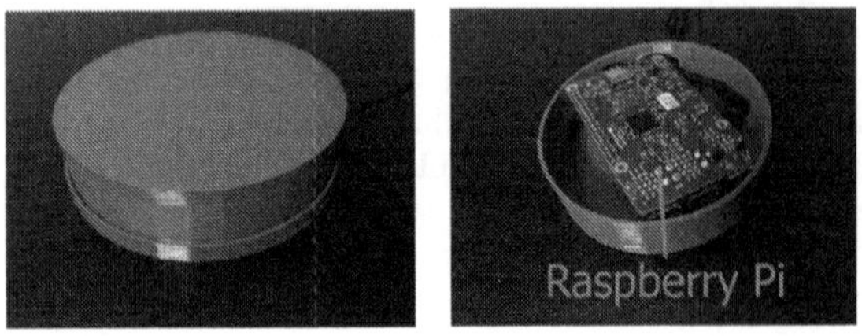

Figure 11: Alexa-enabled Raspberry Pi in a case.

6.2 SoundSifter in a BeagleBone Black

We have developed SoundSifter based on an open-source hardware platform called the Beaglebone Black [3]. An advantage of BeagleBone Black over other open platforms is that, besides the main ARM Cortex-A8 CPU, it has two additional cores known as the *programmable real-time units* (PRUs) [4]. Each PRU provides fast (200 MHz, 32-bit) real-time access to a number of I/O pins. This lets us sample multiple analog audio inputs at a very high rate.

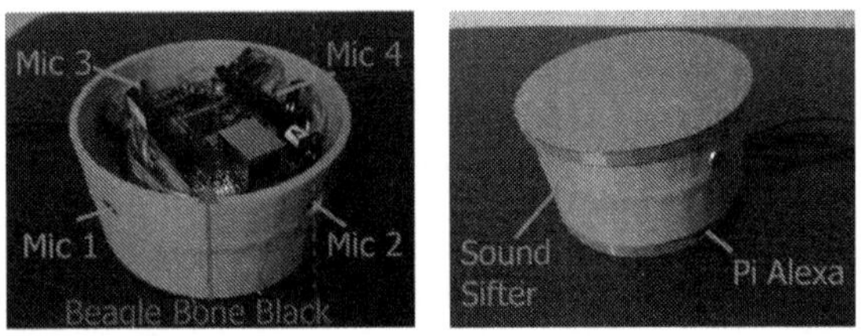

Figure 12: (Left) SoundSifter in its open case. (Right) the case sits on top of Alexa as a cover.

We use a PRU enabled BeagleBone Black as SoundSifter's processor. For the microphone array, we use four Electret microphones [17]. For aesthetics, we 3D-print a case that contains the complete SoundSifter system. In Figure 12 we show the SoundSifter inside a green open case (left). The lower half of this case is hollow, which allows us to put this on top of the Alexa device of Figure 11 as a cover (right).

6.3 Libraries

For Fast ICA we used the Modular toolkit for Data Processing (MDP) [12], which is a Python-based data processing framework. We use the Pandas [14] library for interpolation. We use libpruio [11] for PRUs, which is designed for easy configuration and data handling at high speed. To use this library, we load kernel driver uio_pruss and enable PRU subsystems by loading the universal device tree overlay [6].

7. EVALUATION

We perform three types of experiments. First, we evaluate the execution time, CPU, and memory usage of SoundSifter. Second, we evaluate the four key algorithms of SoundSifter using an empirical dataset. Third, we perform an end-to-end evaluation of different use cases of SoundSifter and compare the performance with an Amazon Echo device.

7.1 Microbenchmarks

Figure 13 shows execution times of five major components inside SoundSifter's audio processing pipeline for processing one second of audio. Frequency adaptation is a constant time operation that takes only 1 ms. It is essentially a matrix look-up operation in the transition matrix. Signal alignment and filling using linear interpolation takes 35 ms on average. As expected, the most time consuming operation in SoundSifter is the source separation step that takes about 179 ms. For source identification, SoundSifter takes 121 ms to calculate the features and 3 ms for classification. The last component of SoundSifter residue removal takes 54.68 ms. Overall, SoundSifter's execution time is 394 ms for processing 1 second audio, which means, the system runs in real-time.

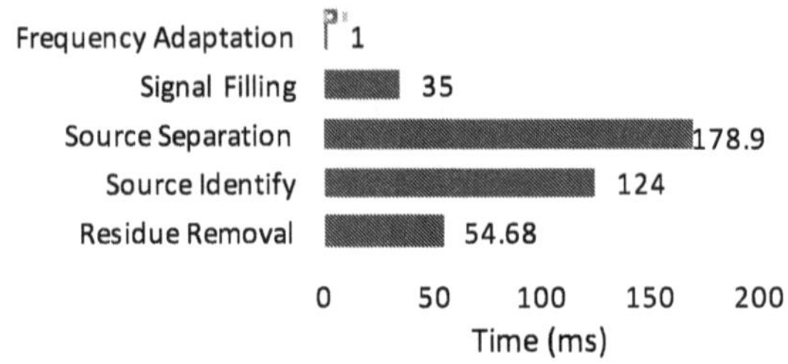

Figure 13: Run-time Analysis.

Table 2 lists the CPU and memory usage for the components of the audio processing pipeline. The most expensive operation is source separation. It requires 57.4% of the CPU and 5.2% memory. Other tasks such as source identification, signal filling, and residue removal use 50.8%, 33.6% and 11.5% of the CPU, respectively.

	CPU (%)	Memory (%)
Signal Filling	33.6	2.8
Source Separation	57.4	5.2
Source Identify	50.8	6.3
Residue Removal	11.5	2.5

Table 2: CPU and memory usage.

7.2 Algorithm Evaluation

To evaluate various components of SoundSifter, we use an empirical dataset which is segmented into three categories of sounds as described in Table 3. We collect this data in a 15 square feet room. For some of the analyses, such as (Figure 14, 16, 17, 19), where we want to evaluate the performance of the system at the maximum sampling rate (i.e. 44.1 KHz), we have used a multi-channel microphone setup [18]. This has allowed us to evaluate the proposed algorithms over a wider range of sampling rates. In the final prototype of SoundSifter, we, however, use Electret microphones [7] which have a frequency range of 20 Hz to 20 kHz. This is not an issue as long as the application, where SoundSifter is in use, deals with signals < 20 kHz. For example, in our chosen applications, the maximum frequency of any sound type in the environment is 10 KHz.

7.2.1 Frequency Adaptation

We compare SoundSifter's 2-step look-based frequency adaptation algorithm's accuracy with that of a 1-step look back Markov model in four test scenarios. These scenarios represent: 1) a person talking, 2) two-person conversation and

Dataset	Count	Examples	Length
Speech	150	conversations (1-10 persons)	200 *min*
Home	54	TV, phone, mouse, keyboard	75 *min*
Song	10	rock, country	55 *min*

Table 3: Description of the empirical dataset.

a TV in the background, 3) two-person conversation with a loud song in the background, and 4) two-person conversation while both TV and loud music are playing.

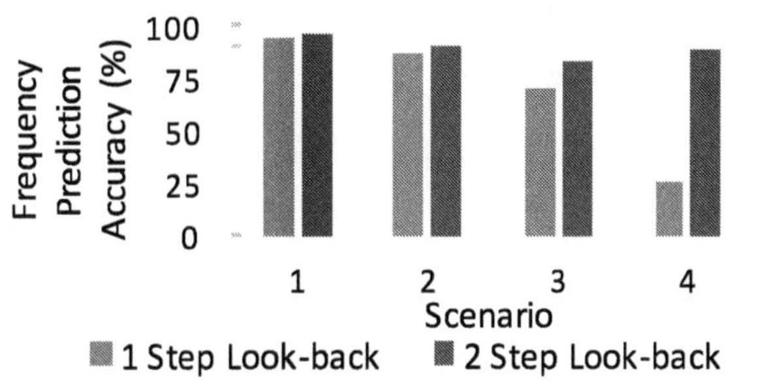

Figure 14: SoundSifter has higher accuracy than 1 Step Look-back for all scenarios.

In Figure 14, we observe that although the performance of both approaches drop as the scenarios become harder, the 2-step look-back model always performs better than the 1-step look-back method. The 2-step look-back model maintains an accuracy in the range of 88.24%-95.26%, whereas the 1-step look-back model's accuracy drops from 94.63% to 25.18%.

A reason behind SoundSifter's frequency adaptation was to reduce resource consumption of the embedded system. To evaluate this, we compare SoundSifter's CPU usage with that of a BeagleBone Black that is sampling four sensors at 44.1 KHz. We consider three scenarios demonstrating three different types of acoustic environments: 1) a noisy environment where a high-volume song is playing, 2) a living room where two persons are talking and a television is running, and 3) a relatively quiet environment where two persons are talking. The ranges of frequencies in these three scenarios are 11.03–5.51 KHz, 5.51–2.76 KHz, and ≤2.76 KHz, respectively.

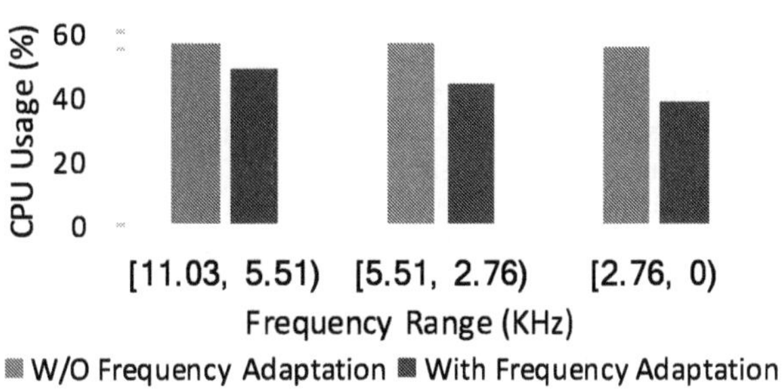

Figure 15: Frequency adaptation reduces CPU usage especially for lower frequency ranges.

Figure 15 shows that as the range of frequencies of the sound sources vary, because of the adaptive nature of SoundSifter, its CPU usage decreases from 48.3%-38.1%. The CPU usage of the BeagleBone remains fixed at 55.8% at all times.

7.2.2 Signal Prediction and Filling

We measure the performance of signal prediction and filling of SoundSifter by comparing its performance with a cubic spline-based interpolation scheme. We take a 44.1 KHz audio and down-sample it to produce five signal streams having the rates of 1.378 KHz, 2.756 KHz, 5.512 KHz, 11.025 KHz, 22.05 KHz, respectively. These are then up-sampled again to get back to 44.1 KHz, by using two interpolation methods: linear (as done in SoundSifter) and cubic spline. The quality of interpolation is measured in terms of their correlation with the original 44.1 KHz signals. We run this experiment on 150 speech clips of 200 minutes, 10 song clips of 50 minutes and four sound clips of 50 minutes.

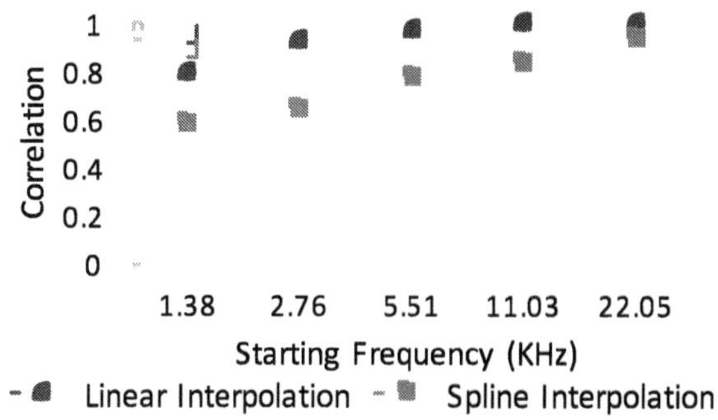

Figure 16: Linear Interpolation is more effective than Spline Interpolation for Signal Prediction and Filling.

Figure 16 shows that for 22.05 KHz, the predicted signals in SoundSifter show 98% correlation, whereas spline interpolation shows 93%. For lower frequencies, spline's performance drops significantly. SoundSifter's predicted signal shows more than 90% correlation even for 2.756 KHz. At 1.378 KHz, SoundSifter' correlation drops to 79%, which is still significantly higher than that of spline interpolation.

7.2.3 Sound Modeling and Recognition

We illustrate the performance of SoundSifter's sound modeling and recognition with the help of two scenarios: 1) voice-only mode, and 2) personalized mode.

For the voice only mode, we test the accuracy of primary and secondary source recognition after source separation, where speech is kept as the primary source.

In Figure 17, we observe that SoundSifter's data augmentation technique outperforms a classifier that is trained without data augmentation. For 2-3 sources, SoundSifter shows 89%-90.14% accuracy, whereas without data augmentation, a classifier achieves only 66%-70% accuracy. As the number of secondary sources increases, we see that without data augmentation the accuracy drops below 50% for 4-5 sources. SoundSifter's classification accuracy remains stable even when the number of sources is high. For 4-5 sources, SoundSifter achieves 89.13%-92.78% accuracy, and its false positive rate has always been 0%.

For the personalized mode, we want to recognize the particular user's commands and ignore anything else. For this, we collect 64 voice commands from three persons as primary sources and 53 voice commands from seven persons as

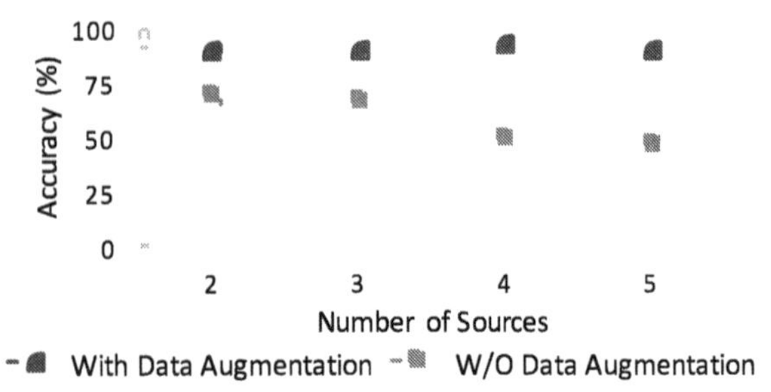

Figure 17: SoundSifter's data augmentation technique improves modeling accuracy

secondary sources. For primary speaker recognition, SoundSifter achieves 94.87% accuracy. From Figure 18, we see that SoundSifter is able to detect all the secondary users' commands, resulting in a 0% false positive rates. For primary speaker detection, SoundSifter was able to detect 58 out of 64 primary commands. Hence, this shows that SoundSifter is able to accept or reject commands based on personalization.

Actual \ Predicted	Primary	Secondary
Primary	58	6
Secondary	0	53

Figure 18: Confusion matrix for primary speaker recognition among up to 10 persons.

7.2.4 *Residue Removal*

We quantify the effectiveness of residue removal by showing that the residue in the separated signals is reduced after applying the process. For this experiment, we consider audio clips from a varying number of sound sources and apply Fast ICA with and without residual removal and compare the noise residual (ξ) we get from these two approaches.

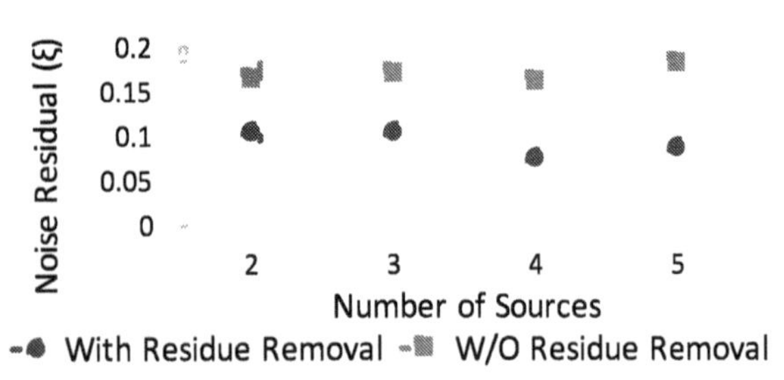

Figure 19: Residue Removal reduces noise residual from the primary signal.

From Figure 19, we see that for 2, 3, 4 and 5 sources Fast ICA without residual removal has 0.164, 0.169, 0.159 and 0.181 noise residual, whereas Fast ICA with residual removal has 0.102, 0.101, 0.073 and 0.084 noise residual, respectively. From this result, we deduce that using Fast ICA with residual removal has better performance for removing residue from the signal than using only Fast ICA.

7.3 Full System Evaluation

7.3.1 *Scenarios*

To demonstrate the effectiveness of SoundSifter, we compare its performance with an Amazon Echo device in three different scenarios. Table 4 lists the scenarios.

Scenario	Participants	Noise Level
Voice Mode (normal)	15	13 dB
Voice Mode (noisy)	10	51 dB
Personalized Mode	10	13 dB

Table 4: Description of the scenarios.

These scenarios are designed to illustrate SoundSifter's performance under different conditions and demands. In the first scenario, we consider a normal environment where only one person commands SoundSifter and Echo at the same time. In this experiment, we want to demonstrate that the source separation and residue removal steps do not damage the quality of the audio signals in SoundSifter. 50 commands from 15 different participants are used in this experiment.

For the second scenario, we consider a noisy environment. We ask our participants to issue commands while loud music is playing in the background. We want to show that due to source separation and residue removal, SoundSifter is more resilient to noise than Amazon Echo. We have collected 50 commands from 10 different participants for this scenario.

In the third scenario, we want to demonstrate that SoundSifter is personalized for a particular user and an intruder is not able to issue arbitrary commands to SoundSifter. Amazon Echo does not have this feature. For this experiment, we consider one of the ten participants as the primary user and the other nine users as intruders. 50 voice commands for both the primary user and the intruders are used in this experiment.

7.3.2 *Comparison with Amazon Echo*

From Figure 20, we see that in the first scenario, both SoundSifter and Echo are able to respond to all 50 commands. Hence, the source separation and residue removal steps of SoundSifter did not affect the quality of audio. In the second scenario, SoundSifter responds to 46 out of 50 commands, whereas Echo was only able to respond to 26 of them. This shows that SoundSifter is more resilient than Echo in a noisy environment.

In the third scenario, because Echo does not have any personalization support, it was unable to detect any intruders. On the other hand, from Figure 21, we find that SoundSifter is able to detect all 50 of the intruder's commands. This shows the strength of the special feature of SoundSifter that is not currently supported by any commercial home hub devices.

8. DISCUSSION

At present, home hub devices like Google Home and Amazon Echo do not have any audio input port where we can pipe in processed audio from SoundSifter. This is why we

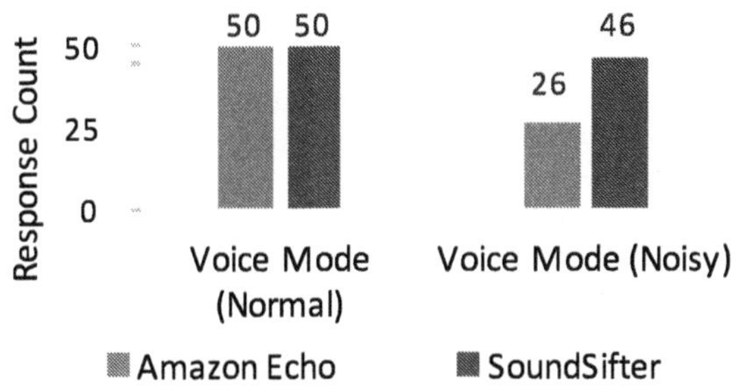

Figure 20: For noisy voice mode, SoundSifter was able to respond to 46 commands whereas, Echo responded to only 26 commands.

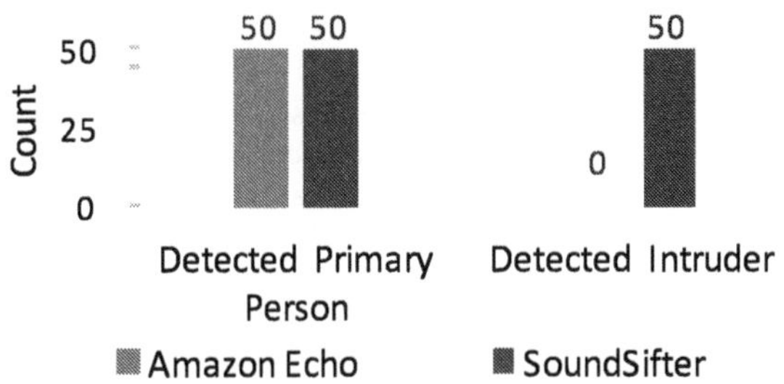

Figure 21: For personalized mode, SoundSifter was able to detect all 50 intruder commands, Amazon Echo fails to detect any of them.

had to develop a custom Amazon Echo clone using a Raspberry Pi. For our system to work seamlessly with a commercial home hub, either the device has to have an audio jack or it has to support open source software, so that our algorithms can be run on them.

In SoundSifter, the calculation of audio features takes a significant amount of computation time. Hence, the system is not fully ready for applications that require a very low latency. To address this issue, as future work, we aim to develop new acoustic features that are lightweight but similar to MFCC features in terms of performance.

The accuracy of the sound classifier depends on training, which is done by the end user who has to record audio samples of his voice commands and secondary sound types. This may be cumbersome to many users, and if the classifier is not trained sufficiently, the accuracy of primary source classification may drop. To address this issue, as a future extension, we plan to develop new classifiers that require a small number of training examples.

SoundSifter is not connected to the Internet, and audio processing happens inside the device. After processing, SoundSifter deletes the audio stream periodically. However, our system is secure as long as a hacker does not tamper with the device physically (e.g. by connecting extra wires to get raw data) or inject software Trojans (e.g., by altering the source code to dump the memory to files or by disabling/bypassing the algorithms during processing).

9. RELATED WORK

Solutions to the source separation problem under different assumptions on sources and mixing systems fall into three main categories. The first category is based on *Independent Component Analysis* (ICA) [40], where statistical independence of sources is exploited to estimate the sources. Although efficient implementations exist [38, 39], these algorithms have certain fundamental limitations, e.g., they support at most one Gaussian source, and do not exploit signal properties such as non-negativity or sparsity. The second category applies *Non-negative Matrix Factorization* (NMF) [25] to exploit non-negativity of real-world signals. However, their lack of statistical assumptions on data does not guarantee a correct decomposition of sources. The third type is based on *Sparse Component Analysis* (SCA) [32], which exploits sparsity in signals, e.g., acoustic signals. In this paper, we could have used any of the three methods, but we implement FastICA [39, 38] which is a proven and well-used algorithm.

In many digital systems, dynamic voltage and frequency scaling [47, 59, 24, 35, 31] are applied to scale up/down the clock frequency of the entire system to lower the power consumption. Our problem is significantly different and harder than that since we are required to dynamically adapt sampling frequencies of an array of microphones (each one is assigned a different rate) and make sure that the independent component analysis framework for source separation still works.

Standard practices toward dealing with limited training data fall broadly into two categories – *data augmentation* and *classifier fusion*, which are often used together. Data augmentation techniques [28, 44] generate new training examples by perturbing acoustic characteristics of existing examples, e.g., frequency warping [41], modifying tempo [43], and adding simulated reverberation [30], and noise [56]. In classifier fusion [58, 54], outputs of multiple classifiers are combined to improve the overall accuracy. These techniques vary from simple voting and averaging [45], to ranking [64, 37], to learning decision templates [46, 37]. In this paper, we only use data augmentation and avoided classifier fusion since that would require sharing and exchanging classifier models of different users – which may violate their privacy.

10. CONCLUSION

This paper describes a system that mitigates information leakage due to the presence of unwanted sound sources in an acoustic environment when using voice-enabled personal assistant devices like Amazon Echo. We developed new algorithms to make acoustic source separation CPU and memory efficient, and to remove residuals of unwanted signals from the main audio stream. The performance of the system has been compared with that of commercial continuous listening devices to show that it accurately filters out unwanted sounds and thus protects against personal and contextual information leakage where existing devices fail.

11. REFERENCES

[1] Alexa AVS. https://github.com/alexa/alexa-avs-sample-app/wiki/Raspberry-Pi.

[2] Amazon Echo: Always Ready, Connected, and Fast. www.amazon.com/echo.

[3] BeagleBone Black. http://beagleboard.org/black.

[4] Beaglebone black pru. http://beagleboard.org/pru.

[5] Belkin WeMo Switch. http://www.belkin.com/us/Products/home-automation.

[6] Device tree overlay. https://github.com/beagleboard/bb.org-overlays.

[7] Electret mic. https://www.adafruit.com/product/1713.

[8] Google Home. https://madeby.google.com/home/.

[9] Google Nest. https://nest.com/.

[10] iOS SiRi from Apple. http://www.apple.com/ios/siri/.

[11] libpruio. http://users.freebasic-portal.de/tjf/Projekte/libpruio/doc/html/index.html.

[12] Modular toolkit for data processing (mdp). http://mdp-toolkit.sourceforge.net/.

[13] OK Google Voice Search and Actions. https://support.google.com/websearch/answer/2940021?hl=en.

[14] Pandas library. http://pandas.pydata.org/pandas-docs/stable/generated/pandas.Series.interpolate.html.

[15] Phillips Hue. http://www2.meethue.com/en-us/.

[16] Say hello to Cortana. http://www.microsoft.com/en-us/mobile/experiences/cortana/.

[17] SparkFun Electret Microphone Breakout. http://www.ti.com/product/OPA344.

[18] Tascam. http://www.kraftmusic.com/tascam-trackpack-4x4-complete-recording-studio-bonus-pak.html.

[19] TP Link Smart Plug. http://www.tp-link.com/en/products/list-5258.html.

[20] B. A. Barsky, R. H. Bartels, and J. C. Beatty. *An Introduction to Splines for Use in Computer Graphics and Geometric Modeling.* Los Altos, Calif.: M. Kaufmann Publishers, 1987.

[21] P. Bofill and M. Zibulevsky. Underdetermined blind source separation using sparse representations. *Signal processing*, 81(11):2353–2362, 2001.

[22] S. Boll. Suppression of acoustic noise in speech using spectral subtraction. *IEEE Transactions on acoustics, speech, and signal processing*, 27(2):113–120, 1979.

[23] S.-M. Cha and L.-W. Chan. Applying independent component analysis to factor model in finance. In *International Conference on Intelligent Data Engineering and Automated Learning*, pages 538–544. Springer, 2000.

[24] K. Choi, R. Soma, and M. Pedram. Fine-grained dynamic voltage and frequency scaling for precise energy and performance tradeoff based on the ratio of off-chip access to on-chip computation times. *IEEE transactions on computer-aided design of integrated circuits and systems*, 24(1):18–28, 2005.

[25] A. Cichocki, R. Zdunek, A. H. Phan, and S.-i. Amari. *Nonnegative matrix and tensor factorizations: applications to exploratory multi-way data analysis and blind source separation.* John Wiley & Sons, 2009.

[26] P. Comon and C. Jutten. *Handbook of Blind Source Separation: Independent component analysis and applications.* Academic press, 2010.

[27] S. Cruces-Alvarez, A. Cichocki, and L. Castedo-Ribas. An iterative inversion approach to blind source separation. *IEEE Transactions on Neural Networks*, 11(6):1423–1437, 2000.

[28] X. Cui, V. Goel, and B. Kingsbury. Data augmentation for deep neural network acoustic modeling. *IEEE/ACM Transactions on Audio, Speech and Language Processing (TASLP)*, 23(9):1469–1477, 2015.

[29] K. I. Diamantaras and T. Papadimitriou. Mimo blind deconvolution using subspace-based filter deflation. In *Acoustics, Speech, and Signal Processing, 2004. Proceedings.(ICASSP'04). IEEE International Conference on*, volume 4, pages iv–433. IEEE, 2004.

[30] R. F. Dickerson, E. Hoque, P. Asare, S. Nirjon, and J. A. Stankovic. Resonate: reverberation environment simulation for improved classification of speech models. In *Proceedings of the 13th international symposium on Information processing in sensor networks*, pages 107–118. IEEE Press, 2014.

[31] W. R. Dieter, S. Datta, and W. K. Kai. Power reduction by varying sampling rate. In *Proceedings of the 2005 international symposium on Low power electronics and design*, pages 227–232. ACM, 2005.

[32] R. Gribonval and S. Lesage. A survey of sparse component analysis for blind source separation: principles, perspectives, and new challenges. In *ESANN'06 proceedings-14th European Symposium on Artificial Neural Networks*, pages 323–330. d-side publi., 2006.

[33] S. Haykin and Z. Chen. The cocktail party problem. *Neural computation*, 17(9):1875–1902, 2005.

[34] J. Herault and C. Jutten. Space or time adaptive signal processing by neural network models. In *Neural networks for computing*, volume 151, pages 206–211. AIP Publishing, 1986.

[35] S. Herbert and D. Marculescu. Analysis of dynamic voltage/frequency scaling in chip-multiprocessors. In *Low Power Electronics and Design (ISLPED), 2007 ACM/IEEE International Symposium on*, pages 38–43. IEEE, 2007.

[36] T. K. Ho. Random decision forests. In *Document Analysis and Recognition, 1995., Proceedings of the Third International Conference on*, volume 1, pages 278–282. IEEE, 1995.

[37] T. K. Ho, J. J. Hull, and S. N. Srihari. Decision combination in multiple classifier systems. *IEEE transactions on pattern analysis and machine intelligence*, 16(1):66–75, 1994.

[38] A. Hyvarinen. Fast and robust fixed-point algorithms for independent component analysis. *IEEE transactions on Neural Networks*, 10(3):626–634, 1999.

[39] A. Hyvärinen and E. Oja. A fast fixed-point algorithm for independent component analysis. *Neural computation*, 9(7):1483–1492, 1997.

[40] A. Hyvärinen and E. Oja. Independent component analysis: algorithms and applications. *Neural networks*, 13(4):411–430, 2000.

[41] N. Jaitly and G. E. Hinton. Vocal tract length perturbation (vtlp) improves speech recognition. In

Proc. ICML Workshop on Deep Learning for Audio, Speech and Language, 2013.

[42] T.-P. Jung, S. Makeig, C. Humphries, T.-W. Lee, M. J. Mckeown, V. Iragui, and T. J. Sejnowski. Removing electroencephalographic artifacts by blind source separation. *Psychophysiology*, 37(02):163–178, 2000.

[43] N. Kanda, R. Takeda, and Y. Obuchi. Elastic spectral distortion for low resource speech recognition with deep neural networks. In *Automatic Speech Recognition and Understanding (ASRU), 2013 IEEE Workshop on*, pages 309–314. IEEE, 2013.

[44] T. Ko, V. Peddinti, D. Povey, and S. Khudanpur. Audio augmentation for speech recognition. In *Proceedings of INTERSPEECH*, 2015.

[45] L. I. Kuncheva. A theoretical study on six classifier fusion strategies. *IEEE Transactions on pattern analysis and machine intelligence*, 24(2):281–286, 2002.

[46] L. I. Kuncheva, J. C. Bezdek, and R. P. Duin. Decision templates for multiple classifier fusion: an experimental comparison. *Pattern recognition*, 34(2):299–314, 2001.

[47] E. Le Sueur and G. Heiser. Dynamic voltage and frequency scaling: The laws of diminishing returns. In *Proceedings of the 2010 international conference on Power aware computing and systems*, pages 1–8, 2010.

[48] S. Li, C. Li, K.-T. Lo, and G. Chen. Cryptanalyzing an encryption scheme based on blind source separation. *IEEE Transactions on Circuits and Systems I: Regular Papers*, 55(4):1055–1063, 2008.

[49] Q.-H. Lin, F.-L. Yin, T.-M. Mei, and H. Liang. A blind source separation based method for speech encryption. *IEEE Transactions on Circuits and Systems I: Regular Papers*, 53(6):1320–1328, 2006.

[50] P. C. Loizou. *Speech enhancement: theory and practice.* CRC press, 2013.

[51] H. Lu, A. B. Brush, B. Priyantha, A. K. Karlson, and J. Liu. Speakersense: energy efficient unobtrusive speaker identification on mobile phones. In *International Conference on Pervasive Computing*, pages 188–205. Springer, 2011.

[52] R. Martin. Spectral subtraction based on minimum statistics. *power*, 6:8, 1994.

[53] S. P. Meyn and R. L. Tweedie. *Markov chains and stochastic stability.* Springer Science & Business Media, 2012.

[54] E. Miluzzo, C. T. Cornelius, A. Ramaswamy, T. Choudhury, Z. Liu, and A. T. Campbell. Darwin phones: the evolution of sensing and inference on mobile phones. In *Proceedings of the 8th international conference on Mobile systems, applications, and services*, pages 5–20. ACM, 2010.

[55] S. K. Mitra and J. F. Kaiser. *Handbook for digital signal processing.* John Wiley & Sons, Inc., 1993.

[56] N. Morales, L. Gu, and Y. Gao. Adding noise to improve noise robustness in speech recognition. In *INTERSPEECH*, pages 930–933, 2007.

[57] S. Nirjon, R. F. Dickerson, P. Asare, Q. Li, D. Hong, J. A. Stankovic, P. Hu, G. Shen, and X. Jiang. Auditeur: A mobile-cloud service platform for acoustic event detection on smartphones. In *Proceeding of the 11th annual international conference on Mobile systems, applications, and services*, pages 403–416. ACM, 2013.

[58] D. Ruta and B. Gabrys. An overview of classifier fusion methods. *Computing and Information systems*, 7(1):1–10, 2000.

[59] G. Semeraro, G. Magklis, R. Balasubramonian, D. H. Albonesi, S. Dwarkadas, and M. L. Scott. Energy-efficient processor design using multiple clock domains with dynamic voltage and frequency scaling. In *High-Performance Computer Architecture, 2002. Proceedings. Eighth International Symposium on*, pages 29–40. IEEE, 2002.

[60] G. Srivastava, S. Crottaz-Herbette, K. Lau, G. Glover, and V. Menon. Ica-based procedures for removing ballistocardiogram artifacts from eeg data acquired in the mri scanner. *Neuroimage*, 24(1):50–60, 2005.

[61] E. Vincent, R. Gribonval, and C. Févotte. Performance measurement in blind audio source separation. *IEEE transactions on audio, speech, and language processing*, 14(4):1462–1469, 2006.

[62] B. Widrow, J. R. Glover, J. M. McCool, J. Kaunitz, C. S. Williams, R. H. Hearn, J. R. Zeidler, J. E. Dong, and R. C. Goodlin. Adaptive noise cancelling: Principles and applications. *Proceedings of the IEEE*, 63(12):1692–1716, 1975.

[63] B. Widrow and S. D. Stearns. Adaptive signal processing. *Englewood Cliffs, NJ, Prentice-Hall, Inc., 1985, 491 p.*, 1, 1985.

[64] K. Woods, W. P. Kegelmeyer, and K. W. Bowyer. Combination of multiple classifiers using local accuracy estimates. *IEEE Transactions on Pattern Analysis and Machine Intelligence*, 19(4):405–410, 1997.

[65] M. Zibulevsky and B. A. Pearlmutter. Blind source separation by sparse decomposition in a signal dictionary. *Neural computation*, 13(4):863–882, 2001.

BatMapper: Acoustic Sensing Based Indoor Floor Plan Construction Using Smartphones

Bing Zhou[1], Mohammed Elbadry[2], Ruipeng Gao[3], Fan Ye[1]
[1]Department of Electrical and Computer Engineering, Stony Brook University
[2]Department of Computer Science, Stony Brook University
[3]School of Software Engineering, Beijing Jiaotong University
{bing.zhou, mohammed.salah, fan.ye}@stonybrook.edu
rpgao@bjtu.edu.cn

ABSTRACT

The lack of digital floor plans is a huge obstacle to pervasive indoor location based services (LBS). Recent floor plan construction work crowdsources mobile sensing data from smartphone users for scalability. However, they incur long time (e.g., weeks or months) and tremendous efforts in data collection, and many rely on images thus suffering technical and privacy limitations. In this paper, we propose *BatMapper*, which explores a previously untapped sensing modality – acoustics – for fast, fine grained and low cost floor plan construction. We design sound signals suitable for heterogeneous microphones on commodity smartphones, and acoustic signal processing techniques to produce accurate distance measurements to nearby objects. We further develop robust probabilistic echo-object association, recursive outlier removal and probabilistic resampling algorithms to identify the correspondence between distances and objects, thus the geometry of corridors and rooms. We compensate minute hand sway movements to identify small surface recessions, thus detecting doors automatically. Experiments in real buildings show BatMapper achieves $1-2cm$ distance accuracy in ranges up around $4m$; a $2 \sim 3$ minute walk generates fine grained corridor shapes, detects doors at 92% precision and $1 \sim 2m$ location error at 90-percentile; and tens of seconds of measurement gestures produce room geometry with errors $< 0.3m$ at 80-percentile, at $1-2$ orders of magnitude less data amounts and user efforts.

Keywords

Acoustic Sensing; Indoor Floor Plans

1. INTRODUCTION

Online digital maps (e.g., Google Maps) have provided great convenience for location based services (LBS) outdoors such as finding nearby point-of-interests (POIs) and navigation. However, for indoor environments where people spend over 80% of the time [17], such maps are extremely scarce and unavailable in most buildings. This has become a huge obstacle to pervasive indoor LBS.

Accurate, scalable indoor floor plan construction at low costs is urgently needed. Autonomous robots equipped with high precision special sensors (e.g., laser rangers [33], depth cameras [16], sonars [35]) can produce high quality maps. However, the high manufacturing costs, operational and logistic obstacles make it difficult to deploy robots in large quantities. Recently some work [2, 8, 15, 5, 4] have leveraged crowdsourced data (e.g., WiFi, inertial, images) from commodity mobile devices to achieve scalability. However, they require large amounts of data to combat inevitable errors and noises in crowdsourcing, hence expensive total efforts and long data collection times. Those using images also face common limitations in vision techniques: dark/changed lighting, blurry images, glass walls, and restrictions on phototaking due to privacy concerns.

In this paper, we propose BatMapper, a novel acoustic sensing based system for accurate floor plan construction using commodity smartphones. Unlike inertial [2] or WiFi data [19, 12] that are inherently noisy, acoustics is capable of producing very accurate (e.g., a few cm's) distance measurements. Unlike images [8], its performance is not affected by lighting conditions or transparent objects, nor does it cause privacy concerns. A single person can finish the measurements of a floor in a few minutes, eliminating the long time needed to crowdsource large amounts [11] of data from many users.

Despite its potentials, accurate and robust acoustic based floor plan construction is far from straightforward. Commodity smartphone speakers and microphones are designed with power, sensitivity intended mainly for low frequency human voice and music; their characteristics are not conducive for acoustic mapping. Due to the existence of numerous surrounding objects, many echoes, not just those bouncing off large surfaces like walls, but also those from smaller objects or over multiple surfaces, will be received. We must reliably determine which echoes, thus distances, correspond to interested objects/surfaces. Finally, the activities and efforts needed from the user must be convenient and minimal, so as to cover the whole floor in short time.

We make the following contributions in this work:

- We explore different acoustic signal designs and identify frequencies, pulse lengths, modulation and reshaping suitable for heterogeneous microphones in commodity smartphones, and echo detection techniques

Permission to make digital or hard copies of all or part of this work for personal or classroom use is granted without fee provided that copies are not made or distributed for profit or commercial advantage and that copies bear this notice and the full citation on the first page. Copyrights for components of this work owned by others than ACM must be honored. Abstracting with credit is permitted. To copy otherwise, or republish, to post on servers or to redistribute to lists, requires prior specific permission and/or a fee. Request permissions from permissions@acm.org.

MobiSys'17, June 19-23, 2017, Niagara Falls, NY, USA
© 2017 ACM. ISBN 978-1-4503-4928-4/17/06...$15.00
DOI: http://dx.doi.org/10.1145/3081333.3081363

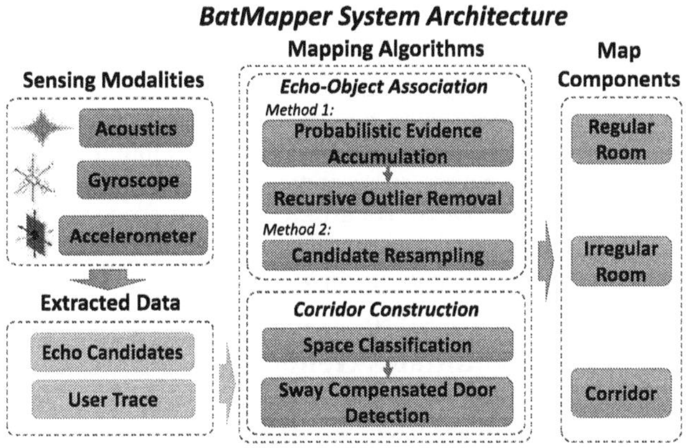

Figure 1: BatMapper takes acoustic and inertial data and uses a series of algorithms to produce the geometry of corridors and rooms, thus the full floor map.

that achieve ranging accuracy of $1-2cm$ in distances up to $\sim 4m$.

- We analyze the constraints and dependencies in distances among echoes from different surfaces, and develop probabilistic evidence accumulation and recursive outlier removal algorithms to reliably associate echo distances to reflection surfaces. We compensate the minute hand sway movement during walking, and automatically detect doors by their small recessions, thus increased distances.

- We propose measurement gestures and a probabilistic resampling algorithm for fast, robust room size/shape estimation in tens of seconds. We design classification algorithms to distinguish corridor segments, turning corners, open spaces, and cluttered areas for fine grained and more robust mapping.

- We build a prototype and extensive experiments in real buildings show that a $2\sim 3$ minute walk can produce fine-grained corridor shapes and detect recessed doors at precision of 92% and location error of $1\sim 2m$ at 90-percentile; the measurement gesture can estimate room geometry at errors $< 0.3m$ at 80-percentile. Compared to state of the art, the amounts of user efforts and data are both reduced by $1\sim 2$ orders of magnitude.

To the best of our knowledge, BatMapper is the first to explore acoustic sensing for floor plan construction using commodity smartphones, demonstrating robust, accurate results while cutting user efforts and data amounts by orders of magnitude.

2. OVERVIEW

BatMapper leverages three sensing modalities: acoustic, gyroscope and accelerometer for fast, accurate floor plan construction (Figure 1). The user walks along corridors and inside rooms while holding the phone. The phone keeps emitting and recording sound signals. It detects sound reflections (i.e., echoes) and measures their distances/amplitudes, from which relative positions of objects (e.g., walls) are inferred, and combined with user traces for floor plans.

By measuring the time between the sound emission and echo reception, the distances to objects are estimated. Although sonar systems have used such principles for exploring and mapping the ocean floor for decades, smartphone hardware is not designed for acoustic mapping purposes. Unlike sonar systems customarily equipped with arrays of tens of ultrasound transducers, the phone usually has one main speaker, two microphones with heterogeneous characteristics, the top for recording and background noise cancellation, the bottom for near field human voice. The speaker and microphones are intended for low frequency human voice and music (up to $\sim 1K/4KHz$), not high frequency ultrasound.

We design a series of algorithms to overcome these difficulties. We design sound signals suitable for heterogeneous microphones, and processing techniques to produce multiple echo candidates and their distances, amplitudes. The candidates are inherently noisy due to cluttered objects, multi-surface reflections, and lack direction information. *Echo-object association*, detecting which echo thus distance corresponds to which object (e.g., walls), is critical.

We propose robust algorithms for echo-object association to derive geometries of corridors and irregular rooms: a *probabilistic evidence accumulation* wall-distance association algorithm computes probabilities of echoes bouncing off different surfaces using relationships among various distances; a *recursive outlier removal* further eliminates residual incorrect associations caused by cluttered/moving objects. A *sway compensation* technique is designed to extract and compensate hand sway during walking and its disturbance to distance, thus small surface recessions ($\sim 10cm$) are reliably identified and door locations detected. Distinct patterns in inertial and distances are combined to classify corridors, corners, open spaces and cluttered areas. A probabilistic *candidate resampling* algorithm can measure regular room geometry in tens of seconds using left-right phone movement gestures.

3. ACOUSTIC SENSING

The acoustic ranging module in BatMapper consists of sound emitting, sound recording by two microphones, and a series of signal processing steps to produce distance/amplitude measurements for echo candidates in both microphones (Figure 2). Unlike some existing work [10] that only shows the received echoes and requires the user to guess and manually pick the one for a specific object, we leverage dual microphones and develop signal processing techniques for accurate and reliable peak detection, thus echo distance measurements.

3.1 Sound Signal Design

Due to the hardware limitations and heterogeneous properties of the two microphones, the sound signal design critically impacts the ranging accuracy and reliability. After extensive experiments and analysis of different frequency modulations, pulse lengths and wave shapes, we use a two-pulse signal, one at $3ms$ and frequency range $8\sim 16KHz$ and the other $1ms$ and $8\sim 10KHz$, both linear frequency increasing sine waves with Hanning window reshaping [13] and separated by $40ms$ delay (Figure 3).

Frequency Modulation and Pulse Length. We leverage a chirp signal with linear frequency increase over time,

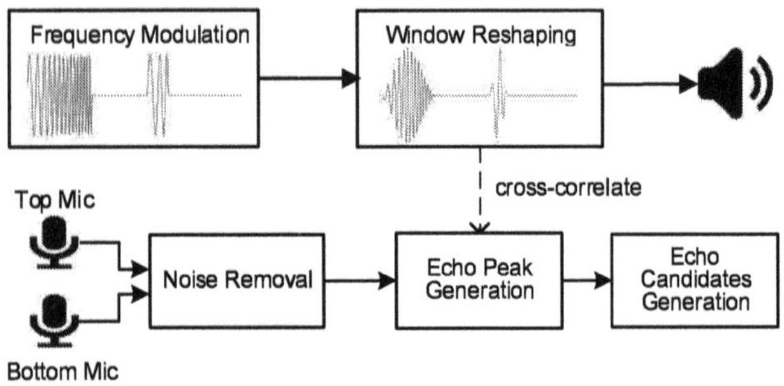

Figure 2: A particular sound signal and multiple signal processing steps produce echo candidates.

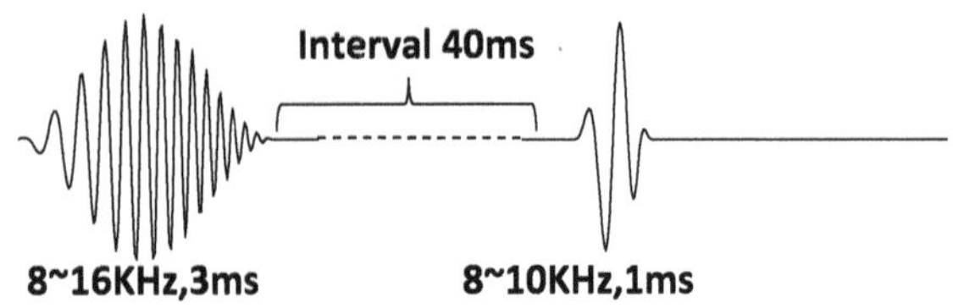

Figure 3: The signal contains two pulses: higher frequency with longer duration for top microphone, and lower frequency with shorter duration for the bottom one.

commonly used in sonar systems. It has an f_0 of the carrier frequency, f_1 the final frequency. The frequency keeps increasing linearly from f_0 to f_1. We choose two frequencies based on several factors of commodity smartphone hardware. First, the frequency range should not exceed the physical capability of a normal smartphone speaker, which is usually capped below $20KHz$. Second, the frequency range should be set apart from background noise, such as human voice usually under $1KHz$, and music instruments under $4KHz$. Hence we set the minimum carrier frequency as $8KHz$. Third, we need to consider heterogeneous frequency response properties of the two microphones. The bottom one is designed for close range human voice capturing, and the other (usually at the top) for background noise cancellation. We conduct extensive experiments with sound signals of different frequency ranges, intensities and lengths. We find that the top microphone is more sensitive but has higher noise levels. The bottom one has less noise, and sensitive to lower frequencies (e.g., human voice). We experiment with different frequency ranges and find that a wider range $[f_0, f_1]$ makes the echo peaks more distinct, thus easier to detect. Lastly, with the same emitting energy, low frequency sounds propagate farther than high frequency ones. Reflections could be too weak to be detected if the frequency is set too high. Increasing the chirp length can also increase the total energy, but it also increases overlaps between adjacent echoes from objects of similar distances, hence reducing the measurement resolution. The final signal design is a balance among all the above factors, with two signals of $1ms$ $8-10KHz$ for the bottom microphone, and $3ms$ $8-16KHz$ for the top one suitable for their properties.

Final Signal for Emitting. We apply a Hanning window [13] on the two pulses to reshape their envelops to increase their peak to side lobe ratio, thus higher signal to noise ratio (SNR). We join the two pulses and separate them by a delay in between, so one emitting signal includes two pulses for both microphones. To ensure echoes from two pulses do not overlap, the delay must be sufficient. From experiments, objects more than 6 meters away create very weak echoes, which can be ignored. Thus the minimum delay between two pulses corresponds to the farthest range, which is $\frac{6m \times 2}{343m/s} = 35ms$. We give a bit buffer space and set it at $40ms$. This would allow $1000/(3+40+1+40) \approx 12Hz$ emitting frequency, sufficient for a user to take fine grained measurements while walking.

3.2 Echo Candidates Generation

Noise Removal. The received signals will go through a Butterworth bandpass filter, $8 \sim 10KHz$ and $8 \sim 16KHz$ for the bottom/top microphone, to remove background noise. Without such filtering, weak reflections can be buried in the noise. This step is critical for collecting data in noisy environments.

Echo Peak Generation. Next we cross-correlate the signal with its respective pulse, a common technique [26] that produces a peak for each echo, and obtain the upper envelop for the signal. Then we chop the envelop into segments of small time windows of $35ms$, each containing echoes from one pulse only.

We need to determine the start of these windows. The first peak will always be the direct sound from the speaker to the microphone, and it has the highest amplitude. It will be used as the starting point. Before we find peak locations, we use a low pass filter moving average to eliminate small outlier peaks and smooth the envelop.

Echo Candidates Generation. For each emitted chirp, multiple peaks corresponding to different echoes are detected. E.g., a chirp in a small room will create echoes from all sidewalls, the ceiling and floor, even echoes reflected multiple times. How to *associate echoes to objects*, deciding which corresponds to which, is critical to derive the geometry of the environment.

Using a threshold, we can select only the top-K strongest peaks, which are hopefully from larger, closer objects. More candidates will cover those interested objects (e.g., wall surfaces), but too many candidates may also include echoes from other smaller, irrelevant objects (e.g., desks, chairs), making distance-wall association more difficult. After extensive experiments, we choose top 6 peaks for the top microphone, because it is more sensitive and has stronger echoes from faraway objects, and top 10 for the bottom one, because it is less sensitive and may miss echoes from faraway walls.

4. FLOOR PLAN CONSTRUCTION

A floor plan includes corridors and rooms. The shapes, sizes of corridors and the locations of doors along corridors form the map skeleton; the contours of rooms augment the skeleton and complete the map.

4.1 Corridor Construction

We combine user traces and acoustic distance measurements to both sides of walls for fast, light weight, and accurate corridor construction. The user holds the phone horizontally, and walks along corridors continuously. A few minutes' walking is enough to cover a floor of decent sizes (e.g., $40 \times 40m^2$). This incurs minimal user efforts, and minimal phone rotations which minimizes gyroscope drifts for robust

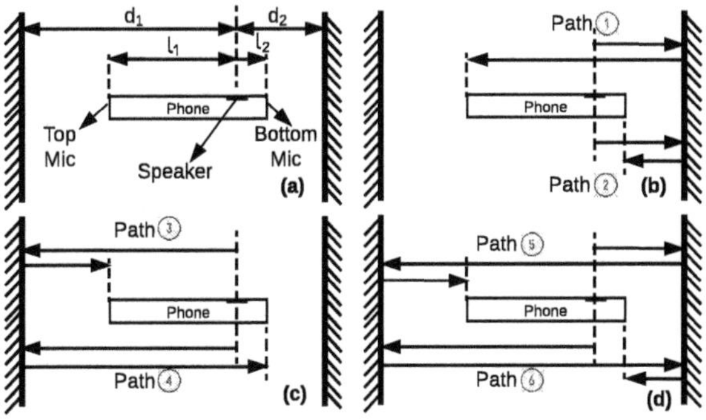

Figure 4: Position of speaker and microphones on the phone, and sound travelling paths of strong echoes in corridor.

user traces. Door locations are automatically determined by detecting small distance increases caused by doors usually slightly recessed ($\sim 10cm$) from walls. To handle many echoes and outliers from sound reverberation over multiple surfaces (e.g., floor, ceiling, and sidewalls) and moving objects/people, we design a *probabilistic evidence accumulation* algorithm, and *recursive outlier removal* to robustly associate distances to different sidewalls. Inevitable hand movements during walking cause distance variations comparable to the small recess depth of doors. Distance may be increased/decreased, causing false detection or missing of doors. We design a *sway compensation* technique that can correct such minute distance variations for reliable, automatic door detection.

Distance-Wall Association. To identify which distance corresponds to which objects, thus the geometry of corridors, we analyze the relationships among the distances and amplitudes of echo candidates from both microphones, and devise a probabilistic evidence accumulation (PEA) method for distance-wall association.

Figure 4 shows a phone held perpendicular to both sidewalls in a corridor, and reflection paths of strong echoes received by microphones [1]. In Figure 4(a), d_1, d_2 are distances from the speaker to the left/right wall (the width of corridor $d = d_1 + d_2$); l_1 and l_2 are the constant distances from speaker to the two microphones (the length of the phone $l = l_1 + l_2$).

In path 1,2 (Figure 4(b)), the sound bounces off the right wall once, and is received by top/bottom microphones. The echoes are likely very strong due to short travel distances, and similarly for echoes from left wall in path 3, 4 (Figure 4(c)). The echoes bouncing both sidewalls can still be detected, with less amplitude due to longer travel distances (Figure 4(d)). In reality, we find the top microphone can detect echoes from path 1,3,5 in most cases, and the bottom microphone can detect those from path 2 but miss some from path 4, 6 due to its low sensitivity to far field sounds.

Let $\{c_i^t\}$, $\{d_i^t\}$, $\{s_i^t\}$ ($i = \{1, \cdots, 6\}$) denote the sets of the 6 strongest echo candidates, their distance measurements and amplitudes from the top microphone; $\{c_i^b\}$, $\{d_i^b\}$, $\{s_i^b\}$ ($i = \{1, \cdots, 10\}$) those from the bottom microphone. Given these sets, our problem is to estimate the probability $P(c_i^u : path\ k)$ that a given candidate $c_i^u, u \in \{t, b\}$ travels along path k. The distances of candidates with greatest probabilities will be used to infer path lengths, thus corridor geometry such as width l.

1) $P(c_i^b : path\ 2)$: we combine two evidences. If c_i^b is a direct echo from the right wall, a) it is likely to have the highest amplitude in $\{s_i^b\}$. Thus

$$P_1 = f_1(1 - s_i^b / \max_i(s_i^b)) \tag{1}$$

where $f_1(\cdot) \sim \mathcal{N}(0, \sigma_1^2)$ is the PDF function of a Gaussian distribution, commonly used in Bayesian Networks to represent probabilities of such evidences. b) considering path 1 and 2, there must exist a candidate from top microphone c_j^t that travels path 1 where $d_j^t - d_i^b = l$. We model this probability as:

$$P_2 = f_2(\min_j(\mid d_j^t - d_i^b - l \mid)) \tag{2}$$

where $f_2(\cdot) \sim \mathcal{N}(0, \sigma_2^2)$. We combine the two evidences to compute $P(c_i^b : path\ 2) = P_1 \cdot P_2$.

2) $P(c_i^t : path\ 3)$: we combine three evidences. If c_i^t is a direct echo from the left wall, a) it is likely to have a high amplitude in $\{s_i^t\}$ [2]. We model this probability as:

$$P_3 = f_3(1 - s_i^t / \max_i(s_i^t)) \tag{3}$$

where $f_3(\cdot) \sim \mathcal{N}(0, \sigma_3^2)$. b) a c_i^t along path 1 can generate a high amplitude. We exclude it by the evidence of a corresponding c_j^b along path 2 computed in step 1. A large $P(c_j^b : path\ 2)$ indicates less likely c_i^t goes path 2.

$$P_4 = 1 - P(c_j^b : path\ 2) \tag{4}$$

where $j = \arg\min_j (\mid d_i^t - d_j^b - l \mid)$. c) two other echoes c_j^t, c_k^t must exist such that $d_i^t + d_j^t - d_k^t = l_1$. Hence

$$P_5 = f_5(\min_{j,k} \mid d_i^t + d_j^t - d_k^t - l_1 \mid); \tag{5}$$

where $j, k \in \{1, \dots, 6\}, j \neq i, k \neq i, j \neq k$, $f_5(\cdot) \sim \mathcal{N}(0, \sigma_5^2)$. We combine the three evidences for $P(c_i^t : path\ 3) = P_3 \cdot P_4 \cdot P_5$.

3) $P(c_i^t : path\ 5)$: if echo c_i^t bounces off right then left wall along path 5: a) considering distance relationship among path 1,3,5. There must exist two other echoes c_j^t, c_k^t such that $d_i^t - d_j^t - d_k^t = l_1$, hence

$$P_6 = f_5(\min_{j,k} \mid d_i^t - d_j^t - d_k^t + l_1 \mid); \tag{6}$$

where $j, k \in \{1, \dots, 6\}, j \neq i, k \neq i, j \neq k$ and $f_5(\cdot) \sim \mathcal{N}(0, \sigma_5^2)$. b) considering distance relationship among path 2,3,5. There must exist another c_j^t and c_k^b such that $d_i^t - d_j^t - d_k^b = l_2$, hence

$$P_7 = f_7(\min_{j,k} \mid d_i^t - d_j^t - d_k^b - l_2 \mid); \tag{7}$$

where $j \in \{1, \dots, 6\}, j \neq i, k \in \{1, \dots, 10\}$, $f_7(\cdot) \sim \mathcal{N}(0, \sigma_7^2)$. We combine them to get $P(c_i^t : path\ 5) = P_6 \cdot P_7$.

Parameter Learning. The variances $\{\sigma_1, \sigma_2, \sigma_3, \sigma_5, \sigma_7\}$ in the above are needed to compute probabilities. We conduct experiments in the corridor and collect training data

[1]Echoes coming from floor/ceiling have much less amplitudes because microphone openings are facing sidewalls. Their echo travel distance relationships also differ from those of sidewalls, thus will generate much smaller probabilities and be filtered out by PEA.

[2]Depending on where the phone is positioned left/right, it may or may not be the strongest.

samples where the traveled paths of echoes are labeled. Given a sample collection $\{x_i\}$ from a normal distribution, its mean and variance can be estimated [14] as $\mu = \sum_{j=1}^{n} \frac{x_j}{n}$ and $\hat{\sigma} = \frac{1}{n}\sum_{j=1}^{n}(x_i - \mu)^2$. We also find these parameters do not change much in different buildings, and learning them once produce accurate results in corridors with width $1.5 \sim 4m$.

Recursive Outlier Removal. After the above computation, we obtain the probabilities for each c_i^b traveling path 2, and each c_i^t traveling path 3 and 5. Initially, we select the candidate with the highest probability for each path. However, outliers can happen due to signal noises, moving objects/people during data collection. We propose a recursive outlier removal (ROR) algorithm to detect and replace outliers.

Assume a continuous sequence of n chirps emitted at time $\{t_i\}$. Without loss of generality, consider the top microphone's candidate set of the 6 strongest echoes at t_i. The one with the highest probability travelling path 3 has distance $d^{[i]}$. We define a similarity score $s = \sqrt{\alpha(d^{[i]} - d^{[j]})^2 + \beta(t_i - t_j)^2}$. For each $d^{[i]}$, count the number of $d^{[j]}$'s where $s < \epsilon$ (a threshold), $j \in \{i - n/2, i + n/2\}, j \neq i$. If the count is less than a threshold k, $d^{[i]}$ is considered an outlier. The candidate with the next highest probability traveling path 3 replaces the outlier. The above repeats for the new candidate, until it is not detected as an outlier, or all the 6 candidates at t_i are exhausted – the average of other non-outlier $d^{[j]}$ at neighboring times will be used. We find in reality the process quickly terminates as outlier count decreases exponentially.

4.2 Door Detection and Space Classification

The intuition for door detection is quite simple: doors are usually recessed from the frame and wall, thus creating slight increase in distance [3]. However, identifying such recessed doors is challenging. There is an inevitable left-right swaying of the hand during human walking, causing distance variations comparable to the recessed depth ($\sim 10cm$). This can increase/decrease the distance, thus generating false or missed detections.

Sway Compensation based Door Detection. Existing techniques [37, 28] can construct user traces by step counting, heading estimation and dead reckoning with accelerometer and gyroscope, but not slight movements of hand swaying. We use Figure 5 to illustrate the process. Figure 5(a) is the aggregated accelerometer amplitude after a low pass filter. Peaks occur when either foot hits the ground. Figure 5(b) is the distance to the right sidewall, which shows highly correlated patterns: a high peak or a low valley when the left/right foot hits the ground. Figure 5(c) is the distance to the left sidewall, which has larger noise due to longer distance and more distance variations caused by more doors. Figure 5(d) shows the measured corridor width where distance changes to left/right sidewalls cancel out each other. Using an empirical threshold of $\frac{2}{3}d$, where d is the recession depth, we detect sudden increase and decrease to identify corridor segments having doors.

Due to disturbances and noises in measurements, the above cannot reliably tell the boundaries of doors, or which side of the wall the door exists, or distinguish adjacent/overlap

[3]We survey 30 buildings around a university campus. Almost all doors are recessed except a few for special purposes.

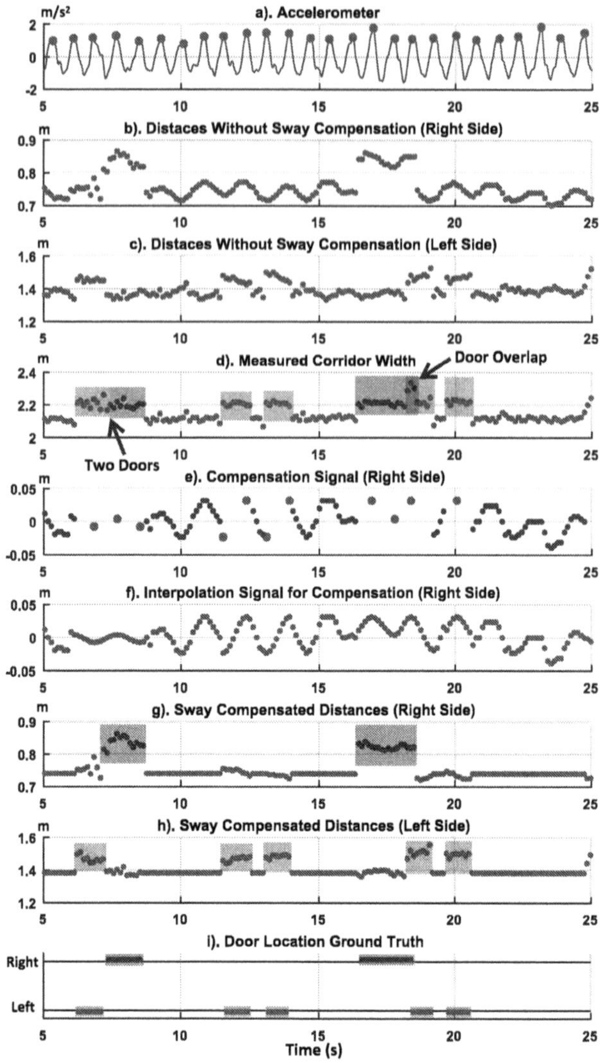

Figure 5: Phone sway while walking and compensation.

doors on opposite sides (Figure 5(d)). We compensate the sway to obtain accurate distance to each side. Segments without doors on either side are detected in Figure 5(d). The average of each segment is deducted from Figure 5(b) to obtain Figure 5(e), the compensation signal. The locations of missing peaks and valleys in Figure 5(e) are those of respective peaks in acceleration (Figure 5(a)), and their amplitudes are estimated using nearest neighboring peak or valley in Figure 5(e). The signal is fully interpolated using sinusoid (Figure 5(f)), and deducted from Figure 5(b) to obtain the compensated distance Figure 5(g). We repeat the same process for Figure 5(c) and obtain Figure 5(h). Finally we detect doors on each side in Figure 5(g,h) by detecting distance inreases/decreases using threshold $\frac{2}{3}d$. For each increasing point, a door is detected if a decreasing point exists within the following $(d_w - \varepsilon, d_w + \varepsilon)$ range, where d_w is the door width, ε a tolerance threshold. This further filters out false detections.

Space Classification. Besides straight corridors, large open space (e.g., lobby), stair entrances and corners also

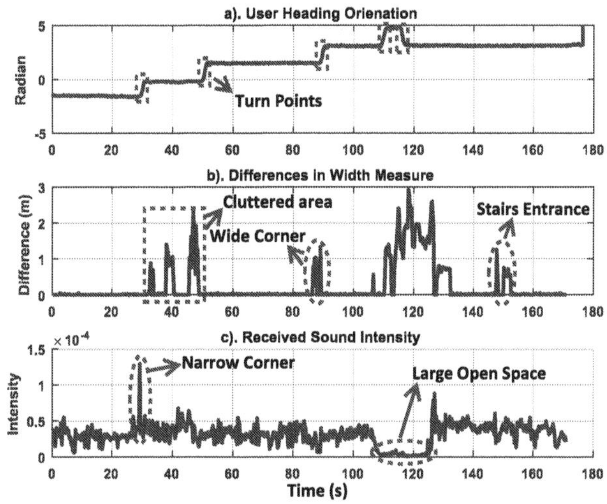

Figure 6: Different data patterns to illustrate rules of space classification.

exist. We leverage inertial and acoustic data to classify the space. By identifying large changes in heading direction, we can detect straight trajectory segments (Figure 6(a)). We further analyze the total width d and total energy of received echoes from the bottom microphone, because it is more sensitive to distance changes.

Intuitively, the total width equals the sum of distances to two sidewalls in corridors, and the echo energy is strong in narrow space while weak in large open space. We use Figure 6(b,c) to illustrate classification rules. The high peak around $30s$ in Figure 6(c) indicates a narrow corner because it has a high intensity and an orientation change. Width disturbances at $40 \sim 50s$ in Figure 6(b) have normal corresponding power, which indicates the size of the space is comparable to corridor, but it is more complex. This turns out to be a cluttered area of storage boxes. The width disturbance around $90s$ in Figure 6(b) indicates a wide corner, since we have a large orientation change and normal power. The drop in power $(110 - 125s)$ in Figure 6(c) shows the user is passing a large open space, and there are large width disturbances in Figure 6(b) as well. The last width disturbance in Figure 6(b) has no orientation change and normal power, corresponding to a stair entrance.

The above rules are largely distinct and exclusive to each other, with occasional exception (e.g., cluttered area vs. stair entrance) that may require further efforts. Their main purpose is not to provide 100% classification accuracy, but to detect and exclude non-corridor segments, so as to avoid false door detections caused by disturbances and false walls in large open spaces beyond measurement range.

5. ROOM CONSTRUCTION

Different methods are used for rooms of two types: 1) small, regular rooms and 2) irregular or large rooms. Rectangle or polygon rooms smaller than $8 \times 8m^2$ are type 1, including bathrooms, bedrooms, personal offices and laboratories [4]. Type 2 are either irregular shapes or over $8 \times 8m^2$, such as large classrooms, lobbies, auditoriums.

[4]Experiments show that the maximum distance that can be reliably measured is 4m to each side.

5.1 Regular Room Construction

We design a fast room construction method that obtains the width/depth of a regular room using a simple measurement gesture [5]. Without loss of generality, we explain using the top microphone. The user holds the phone in front of his body, clicks a button to trigger the phone to emit many chirps quickly (e.g., 50 in 5s), producing N distance measurements as the original set $D^O = \{d_1^O, d_2^O, ..., d_N^O\}$. Each distance has an equal probability of coming from the left wall.

The user stretches his arm and moves the phone to the right side; it emits multiple chirps (e.g., 10 in 1s) and produces an update set $D^U = \{d_1^U, d_2^U, ..., d_M^U\}$. We use the following candidate weight update and resampling to obtain distance from certain directions. Then the user moves the phone to left, repeat the process. The user may need to move the phone left/right a few times to produce reliable results.

Candidate Resampling. Candidate Resampling recalculates the probabilities of distance candidates over multiple measurements. The intuition is to "penalize" those that behave inconsistently given the phone's movement. For example, echoes coming from the front wall are assigned smaller weights because their distances do not change much in left/right movements. They will have much smaller weights and thus less likely to be chosen during resampling.

We compute the weight ω_j for each $d_j^O \in D^O$ as:

$$w_j = f(d_k^U - d_j^O - \mu), \quad k = \arg\min_k (| d_k^U - d_j^O - \mu |) \quad (8)$$

where $f(\cdot)$ is the likelihood function which has the form as PDF of Gaussian distribution $\mathcal{N}(0, \sigma^2)$ that describes the similarity between actual distance change $d_k^U - d_j^O$ and expected move distance μ, $d_k^U \in D^U$ is a distance measurement in the update set, σ is the variance tolerating estimation errors in moving distance. Assuming the phone is held by the right hand, we set $\mu = 0.3m$ and $\mu = 0.5m$ for left/right movement, σ at 0.2 empirically. A new set is formed by sampling N distances from the original set, each with probabilities proportional to their weights. The original set is then replaced by the new set.

The user may need to move the phone left/right multiple times. Each time the correct distance will be reinforced and incorrect ones penalized. Thus the results quickly converge (i.e., showing a distance with dominating probability) after a couple left/right movements, which can be done in tens of seconds. Although clutters along the movement directions may create echoes, such echoes are unstable compared to those from our targeted large surfaces (e.g., walls). Hence they are assigned lower probabilities and eventually removed. For better robustness and quick convergence, the user should avoid large objects, such as large furniture, along the moving directions. The user can turn 90° and repeat the above process to measure the other two walls. The total height between ceiling and floor can also be measured by holding and moving the phone vertically.

5.2 Irregular/Large Room Construction

For irregular/large rooms, we combine user traces and acoustic measurements for construction. Due to the limited sensing range, the fast construction method does not work

[5]Most rooms are cluttered and have larger size than corridor width, thus PEA cannot work reliably in this case.

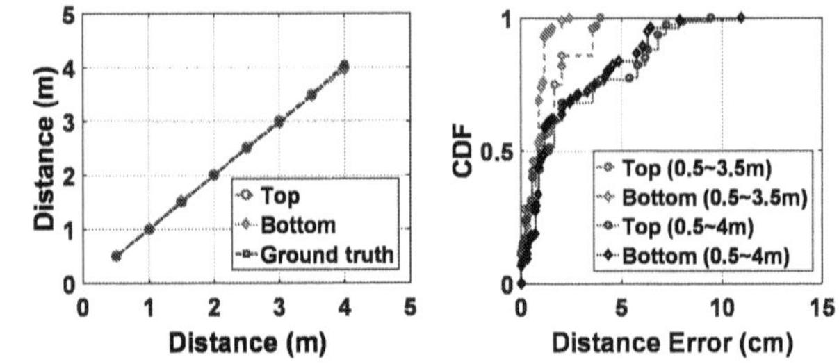

(a) Distance measurements. (b) Measurement errors.

Figure 7: Distance candidate accuracy and error for both top and bottom microphones.

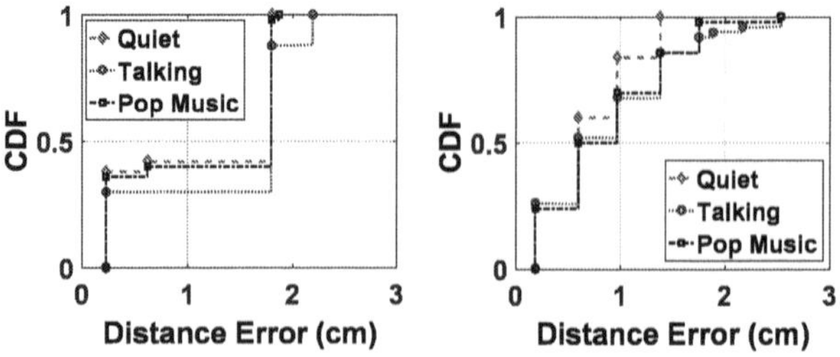

(a) Top microphone (b) Bottom microphone

Figure 8: CDF for measurement errors of both microphones in different scenarios: quiet room, human talking, and pop music at a fixed distance of 3.5 meters.

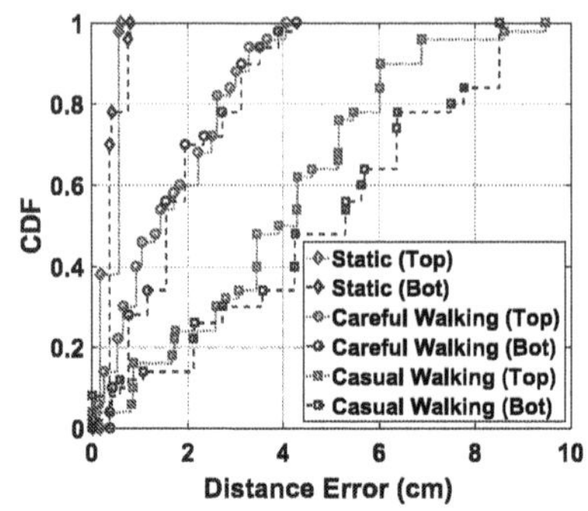

Figure 9: Distance measurement accuracy to a wall while the user is static or walking at a fixed distance of 1 meter.

for irregular or large rooms. The user must walk a full loop around the internal boundaries of the room, and measure the distance to the wall continuously. We combine the user trace and distance measurements to create the room boundaries. In this case, we walk close to the wall on right while holding the phone, and leverage PEA to identify the distance from the wall to bottom microphone. $P_1 \cdot P_2$ in PEA does not rely on left sidewall, thus we can get reliable distance measurements. As long as objects do not fully block line of sight to the wall, the acoustics can detect distance to walls reliably. Compared to approaches [2, 8, 15] using only user traces that can be distorted by objects, this method can generate much more accurate room shapes.

6. EVALUATION

We use Huawei Honor 6 smartphone for data collection and evaluate BatMapper from several aspects: acoustic measurements, algorithm performance, mapping performance, data amounts and user efforts. We conduct data collection in 3 large buildings, including a $40 \times 60m^2$ laboratory, a $50 \times 60m^2$ teaching building, and a $45 \times 45m^2$ office building. We use the composite sensor game rotation vector in Android that leverages accelerometer and gyroscope, which proves more reliable than integrating gyroscope data for orientation. The trajectory is further calibrated with a constant orientation drift rate and walking loop closure [6] when available.

6.1 Acoustic Measurements

Distance Accuracy. Accuracy of distance is the first step and basis for accurate floor plans. To evaluate the signal design and processing techniques, we select a plain wall in an empty space, and measure the distance to the wall at different locations. We vary the location thus the ground truth distance from $0.5 \sim 4m$ with steps of $0.5m$, and repeat 20 times at each location. Figure 7(a) shows that the distance measurements for both microphones have small errors up to $3.5m$ range, and grow larger at $4m$. Figure 7(b) shows the CDF for all measurement errors in ranges $0.5 \sim 3.5m$ and $0.5 \sim 4m$ for both microphones. For the range $0.5 \sim 3.5m$, the error is within $1 - 2cm$ at 80-percentile, and the maximum within $4cm$. For ranges up to $4m$, we still get reasonable high accuracy of $5cm$ at 80-percentile, and the maximum $\sim 10cm$. The effective range of $\sim 3.5m$ is sufficient to measure distances to both sidewalls simultaneously, at accuracy better than door recession depth ($\sim 10cm$).

Background Noise Tolerance. Background noises such as human speech and music are common, especially in public buildings. We evaluate their impact by comparing 3 scenarios: quiet room, human talking and pop music from another smartphone $1m$ away at maximum volume. We do 50 measurements at $3.5m$ from a wall. Figure 8(a), 8(b) show the CDF of measurement errors for the top and bottom microphones. The top microphone has most errors at $1.8cm$ and at most $2.2cm$ under all scenarios, which shows high noise tolerance. The bottom microphone has $\sim 1.4cm$ error at 90-percentile in quiet room, and $\sim 1.75cm$ under human talking or pop music, both with comparable performance. Because the higher frequency band $8 \sim 16KHz$ for the top microphone is far from human voice or music (up to $\sim 1K/4KHz$), it has better noise tolerance. The bottom microphone uses a lower frequency band $8 \sim 10KHz$, and it is designed to be more sensitive to human voice. Thus the slight less tolerance to noises. However, both are quite accurate, with $2.5cm$ error at most. We also tested other closer distances, there's only $< 2cm$ impact by noise.

Impact of User Movement. The user's walking causes inevitable movements to the phone, thus disturbances to distance measurements. We compare 3 scenarios with the user standing still, walking stably/carefully, and walking casually, along a straight line with $1m$ distance to the right sidewall. Figure 9 shows the CDF for measurement errors. The maximum error is $\sim 1cm$ for both microphones when the user stands still. For careful walking it increases to $4cm$, while casual walking further increases it to $\sim 9cm$. This becomes comparable to door recession depth ($\sim 10cm$), and shows the necessity of sway compensation for robust door

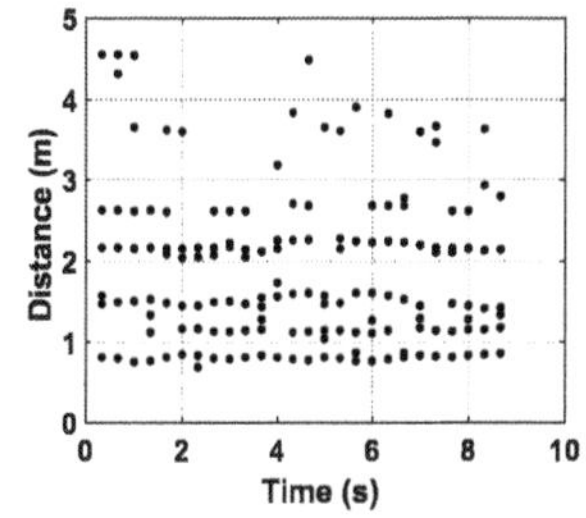

(a) 6 distance candidates per sample to left wall

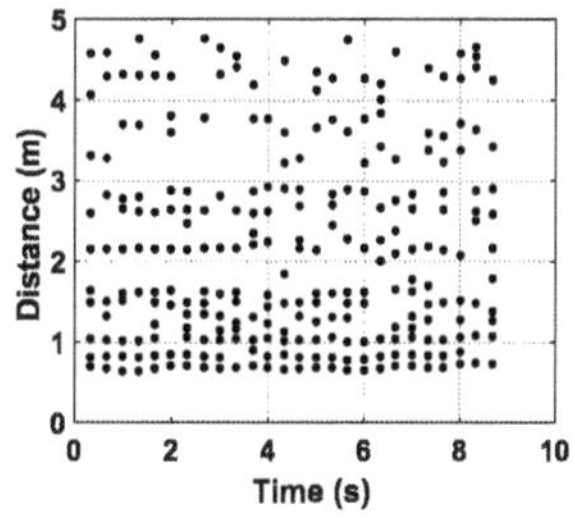

(b) 10 distance candidates per sample to right wall

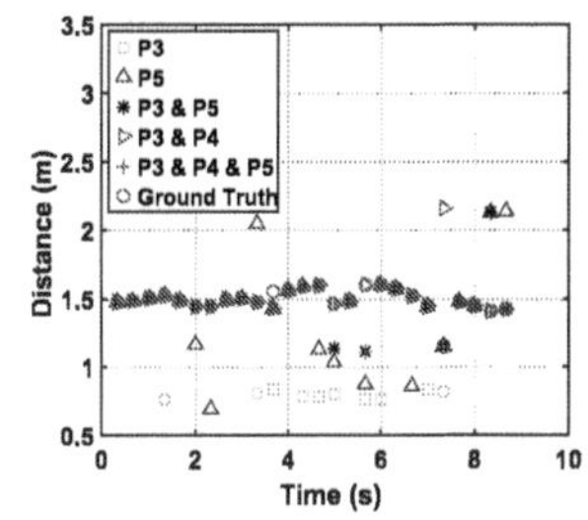

(c) PEA distance estimation for left wall

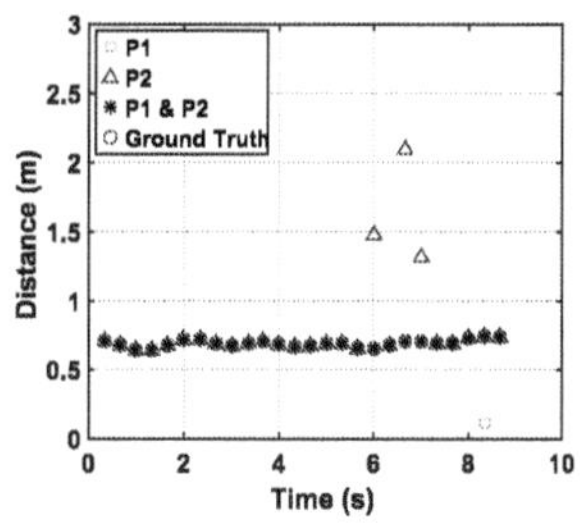

(d) PEA distance estimation for right wall

Figure 10: Measurement candidates in a corridor and PEA estimation results for candidates from left and right under different conditions.

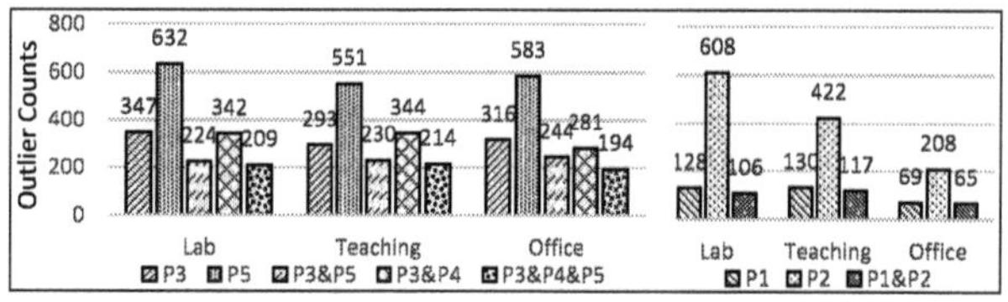

Figure 11: Outlier counts after different evidence combinations in PEA for three buildings.

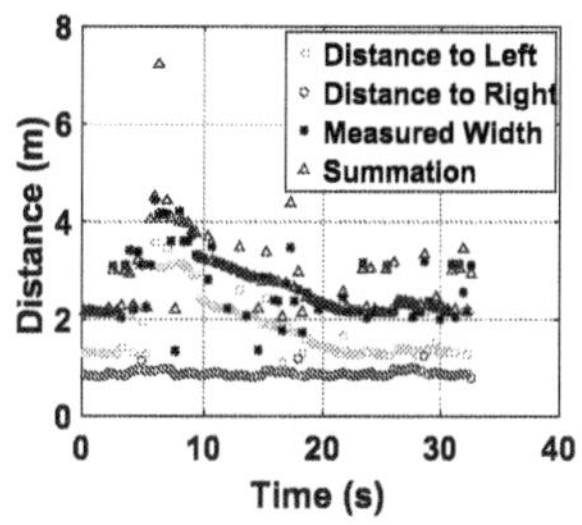

(a) Before ROR

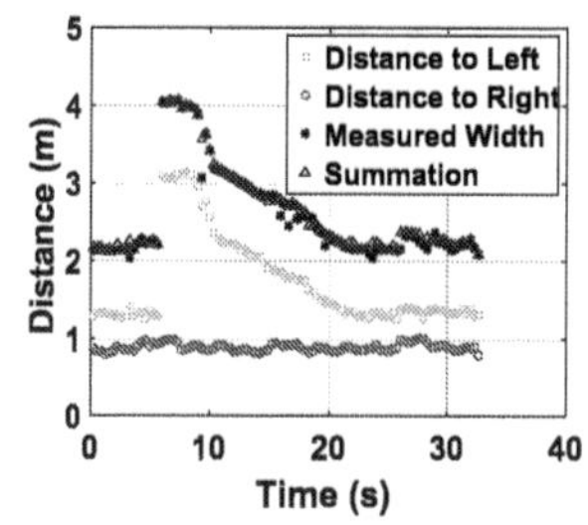

(b) After ROR

Figure 12: After ROR, outliers are removed, and all measured width and summation pairs match well.

detection.

6.2 Mapping Algorithm Evaluation

Probabilistic Evidence Accumulation. We collect data in a corridor segment and show the distance-wall association results with PEA. Figure 10(a), 10(b) show that each sound signal (emitted at $\sim 3Hz$) produces 6, 10 distance candidates to the left/right sidewalls, and all but one of them corresponds to respective $\sim 1.5m, \sim 0.7m$ ground truth. Figure 10(c) shows candidates with the maximum probability by different combinations of evidences in PEA. Using P_3 has 10 outliers in 26 samples, and all of them are distance to right wall ($\sim 0.7m$). This is because the top microphone is sensitive enough to produce high amplitudes for echoes from both sidewalls. Using $P_3 \cdot P_4$ filters most of them and leaves only 2 outliers. Using P_5 only also has 10 outliers and combining $P_3 \cdot P_5$ reduces to 5. In this example, $P_3 \cdot P_4 \cdot P_5$ has 2 outliers. Later systematic evaluation (Figure 11) shows it can further reduce outliers by $7-20\%$ compared to $P_3 \cdot P_4$. Figure 10(d) shows similar results. Using P_1 or P_2 only has 1, 3 outliers while combining $P_1 \cdot P_2$ completely eliminate all outliers. Note this experiment is for a "clean" environment without disturbances such as people passing by. In reality more outliers will happen.

We systematically evaluate PEA performance by analyzing data from corridor segments of three buildings, each has a total number of 1015, 830, and 885 samples. Results show that the number of outliers decreases as more evidences are accumulated (Figure 11). For left wall distance candidates, using P_3, P_5 only has on average $35\%, 64.7\%$ outliers. By accumulating two evidences, $P_3 \cdot P_5$ and $P_3 \cdot P_4$ reduce outliers to 25.57% and 35.42% respectively. Accumulating all evidences reduces this ratio to 22.6%. For right wall distance candidates, P_1 and P_2 has an average of 12% and 45.35% outliers respectively, combining both evidences reduces outliers to 10.5%.

Recursive Outlier Removal. The output of PEA is fed to ROR to further remove outliers. We select a walk along a corridor with a triangle area on one side, and illustrate results before and after ROR. Figure 12(a) shows the distances to the left/right walls, their summations, and the measured corridor width by identifying echoes bouncing both walls in PEA. Without outliers, the summation and measured width should be the same. Although most left/right distances are correct, there are quite some obvious outliers to the left, and a few to the right before ROR, which are caused by wrong data association. Thus they produce many unmatched summation and width measurements pairs.

Figure 12(b) shows the results after ROR. There are no outliers for either side, and all summation and width measurement pair match quite well. Besides, the $\sim 2m$ width jump around $6s$ and gradual decrease till $22s$ are preserved, showing clearly the triangle area. ROR can preserve such sharp changes while replacing outliers with correct candidates. Naive outlier removal methods such as moving average will lose such abrupt distance variations, blurring door frame boundaries critical for door detection. Methods such as Kalman filters [36] are not suitable: they assume the measurements follow a Gaussian distribution around the true value. While outliers by wrong data association are around distances to incorrect objects, thus not the true values needed (i.e., distances to walls). Figure 13 shows the number of remaining outliers after each iteration of ROR. About half of the outliers are removed at first iteration. For candidates to both sidewalls, the remaining outlier counts are less than 25 ($<\sim 2.5\%$) after all available candidates are exhausted. They are further removed and replaced by the average of respective non-outlier neighbors.

Candidate Resampling. We illustrate the distance distribution upon more updates with the user standing in a room, at $\sim 2m$ to the left wall. Initially, the phone emit-

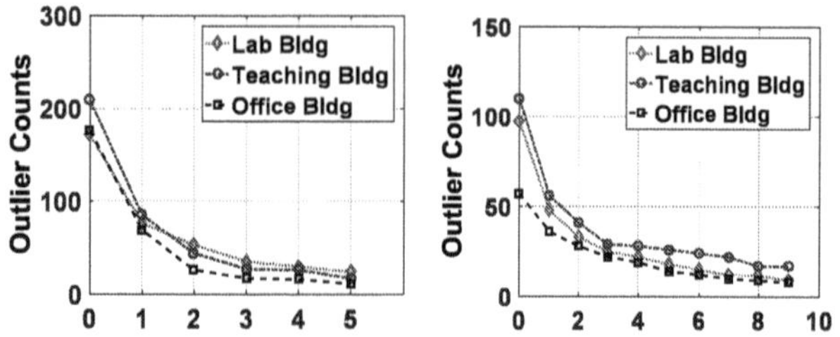

(a) Outlier in left distance (b) Outlier in right distance

Figure 13: Residual outlier counts of each iteration until ROR termination.

s 50 signals which produces 300 distance candidate (top microphone only, 6 per signal). Figure 14 shows the histogram of this original candidate set. Many candidates have large counts ($20-30$), thus difficult to tell which is the true distance. After the first update (moving the phone to the right), the correct candidate ($\sim 2m$) have the highest count (~ 85). After 4 updates, it becomes dominant (200 counts) while all others reduce to < 10 counts. This shows the robustness and effectiveness of candidate resampling to quickly converge to the correct result.

6.3 Mapping Performance

Corridor construction consists of door detection/location and corridor shape. Corridor shape is the skeleton of the whole map, and door locations indicate positions of each room. They are the most critical components in the floor plan.

Door Detection. We summarize door detection results for 3 buildings in Table 1. Except main entrances, there are 38, 47, and 30 doors in each building. True positive (TP) denotes the number of correctly detected doors, false positive (FP) the number of falsely detected (non-existent) doors, false negative (FN) denotes the number of missed doors. Precision is defined as $precision = TP/(TP + FP)$ and recall is $recall = TP/(TP + FN)$. Both precision and recall are $\sim 90\%$, and office has slightly lower precision because of the recessed poster windows along corridors.

Table 1: Door detection performance.

Bldg	Total	TP	FP	FN	Precision	Recall
Lab	38	34	2	4	94.44%	89.47%
Teaching	47	41	2	6	95.35%	87.23%
Office	30	26	5	4	83.87%	86.67%

Door Location. Figure 15 shows the CDF for door location errors in 3 buildings, and Figure 17 shows the constructed map and respective ground truth. For teaching and office building, the error is $< 2m$ at maximum, and $< 1m$ at 80-percentile. The error is slightly larger and a few large ones $3 \sim 4m$ for the lab building. This is due to longer user trajectory, and lack of loop closure for calibration. A slight orientation deviation in the long horizontal corridor segment can cause larger location errors for doors at the end.

Corridor Shape Accuracy. Figure 17 shows constructed corridor shapes are highly accurate. The corridor width error is within $1 \sim 3cm$ centimeters, almost negligible. The maps also show fine details. Recessed areas such as stairs, water fountains, or triangle areas are detected, which are difficult to identify using only trajectories.

Regular Rooms. We measure 18 regular rooms which we can access, with size from $2.32 \times 2.49m^2$ up to $7.86 \times 7.28m^2$. Figure 16 show the CDF of 36 length/depth measurements. The 80-percentile error is around $0.3m$, which shows that the CR algorithm can obtain reasonable accuracy for rooms. The error mainly comes from large objects (e.g., furniture) next to walls or recessions of windows. Large errors $0.5 \sim 1.5m$ are caused by false candidate association (e.g., large furniture in the middle).

Acoustic-aided Irregular/Large Rooms. Figure 18 show 4 examples of constructed irregular rooms using pure trace and acoustic-aided approach. Due to inaccessible areas (e.g., blocked by furniture), users cannot always walk close to the wall. Hence the trajectory cannot accurately recover the actual shape. Acoustic measurements can avoid many such issues and produce shapes much closer to ground truth. Figure 19 shows the recall of 15 large rooms with sizes from $\sim 5 \times 5m^2$ irregular shape rooms to $18 \times 22m^2$ large lobbies. The median recall is improved from 78% to 88%.

Final Map. Overlaying room shapes to respective door locations produces the final map. We are able to access only some of the rooms in these three buildings. Due to space limit, we omit such final maps.

6.4 Data Amount and User Effort

Table 2 shows the data amount and time for constructing corridor areas in the three buildings. BatMapper only takes $1 \sim 2.5min$ to gather $1.5 \sim 3.5MB$ data for corridor area construction, which incurs very little human effort and overhead in data collection.

Table 2: Data amount and data collection time for corridor construction by BatMapper.

Bldg	Audio	Inertial	Total	Time
Lab	2861 KB	657 KB	3518 KB	145s
Teaching (A)	2102 KB	470 KB	2572 KB	106s
Teaching (B)	1186 KB	276 KB	1462 KB	60s
Office	2427 KB	716 KB	3143 KB	122s

We also compare the data amount and time needed of corridor area construction to five previous designs: CrowdInside [2], Jigsaw [8], iMoon [5], CrowdMap [4] and Walkie-Markie [30]. CrowdInside collects a number of mobile traces (~ 100) covering all corridor areas, and uses unique anchor points (e.g., locations with GPS reception or special inertial data signature such as stairs) to enhance dead-reckoning accuracy. Jigsaw and iMoon combine vision and mobile techniques and generate complete floor plans or indoor 3D models. They both utilize Structure from Motion [31], which is a compute-intensive technique that requires many images. CrowdMap generates indoor panorama via video. For three buildings, more than $60K$ key frames are collected over six months. Walkie-Markie requires dense Wi-Fi AP deployment and many user walk rounds (e.g., 30), and it provides a rough corridor map but not rooms. For a typical indoor scenario with 30 landmarks/doors, assuming each photo at 816×612 resolution, the image storage of Jigsaw, iMoon and CrowdMap is around $360MB$, $180MB$ and $1.6GB$, respectively.

Table 3 shows the comparison in data amount, time needed and 80-percentile mapping accuracy. BatMapper cuts down the data amount and data collection time by orders

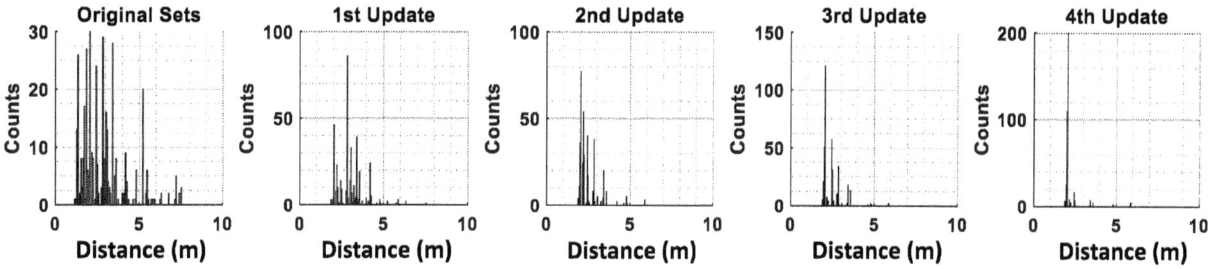

Figure 14: The real distance ($2m$) candidate becomes increasingly more dominant in the histogram.

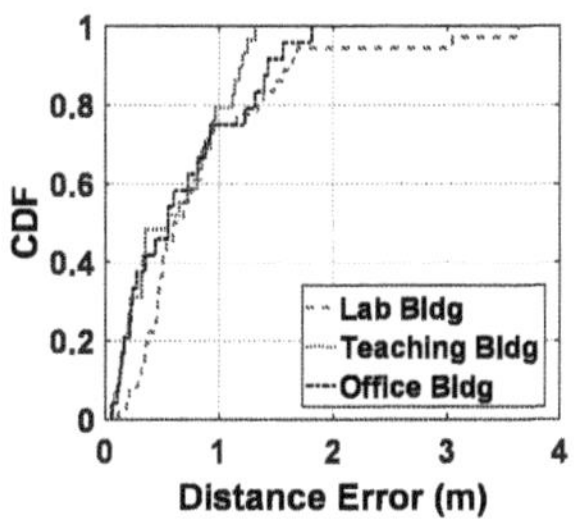

Figure 15: CDF of door location errors for three buildings.

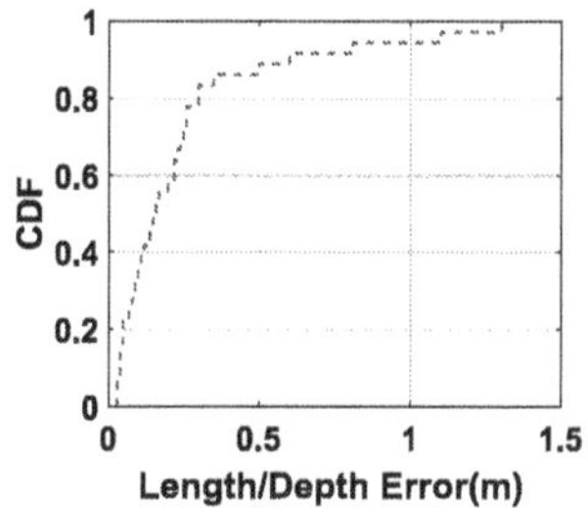

Figure 16: CDF for room length/depth measurements.

Table 3: Data amount, data collection time and door location accuracy comparison.

	Data	Time	Accuracy
CrowdInside [2]	$\sim 100\ MB$	$\sim 300\ mins$	$\sim 5m$
Jigsaw [8]	$\sim 360\ MB$	$\sim 20\ hours$	$\sim 2m$
iMoon [5]	$\sim 180\ MB$	$\sim 3\ weeks$	$\sim 2m$
CrowdMap [4]	$\sim 1.6\ GB$	$\sim 2\ months$	$\sim 1.5m$
Walkie-Markie [30]	$\sim 30\ MB$	$\sim 90\ mins$	$\sim 1.5m$
BatMapper	$\sim 4\ MB$	$\sim 3\ mins$	$\sim 1m$

of magnitude ($4MB$ vs. $30MB \sim 1.6GB$, $3min$ vs. hours, days), and provides accurate and complete floor plans comparable to the state-of-the-art.

6.5 Miscellaneous

Energy. We test the power consumption of data collection using a power monitor. The standby current consumption with screen on is $\sim 150mA$ with Wi-Fi, cellular off and no applications running in the background. Data collection for BatMapper requires accelerometer ($\sim 0.25mA$), gyroscope ($\sim 6.1mA$), and sound emitting/recording ($\sim 20mA$). Considering the battery capacity of $3100mAh$, data collection for one building (assuming 3 minutes for corridor, 30 minutes for 20 rooms) only consumes an additional $14.5mAh$, which is less than 0.47%. Considering the standby current, total energy cost is $\sim 97mAh$, which is 3.1%, negligible for daily use. DSP.Ear [9] can further reduce the power consumption for acoustic sensing.

Different Phones. Smartphones have different physical layouts, e.g., the speaker at the bottom instead of the back. Such a phone can be held perpendicular to sidewalls, with the speaker facing the right sidewall. A different set of distance relationships can be derived to reconfigure the PEA framework (mainly changes of phone length and covariance parameters.). We test our design on a more recent smart phone, Huawei P9, with the speaker at the bottom. Figure 20 shows the distance measurements of both microphones and the resulting distances after PEA and ROR. Raw measurements with such configuration turns to be much "cleaner" since the speaker faces side walls, hence echoes from floor/ceiling are suppressed. We also select Samsung Note 3 as another test phone, and obtain comparable results. A sample corridor segment with doors is shown in Figure 21.

7. DISCUSSION

Crowdsourcing. Crowdsourcing can collect large amounts of data from many users. To ensure scalability and data quality, effective incentive mechanisms are usually necessary. The cognitive, time overheads and operational complexity to users must be minimized. Compared to existing work, BatMapper does not need effort intensive image-taking; it cuts the data amount and collection time dramatically. It can be used by a dedicated user, or used in crowdsourcing for greatly reduced user efforts and incentive. Current design still requires a human to walk around the building and every room for data collection. A system that uses a drone to automatically survey the floor systematically and collect all data would avoid such human efforts.

Map Refinement. Accurate user trajectories are important to the overall shape and size of corridors. We plan to further leverage building internal layout rules (e.g., 90° turns, straight walls) to calibrate and refine the constructed map, especially where corridors all have a fixed width. Although BatMapper can detect fine granularity geometry, it does not yet reliably classify and label different functional areas (e.g., water fountains, stairs). Classification using additional data (e.g., TransitLabel[7], DeepEar [18]) would be needed.

Automatic Stitching. We adopt several simple rules (e.g., dividing long walks into a few short segments/loops, and loop closure) to help ensure accurate trajectories. A building with a typical size of $2000 \sim 3000m^2$ may be divided into 2-3 segments/loops, which need to be manually stitched together. One may leverage multiple sensing modalities, such as Wi-Fi signals and a few images at joining areas of loops to stitch them together automatically.

Complex Environments. For buildings with large open spaces (e.g., shopping malls) instead of narrow corridors, users need to walk extensively along the walls due to the limited acoustic ranging distance; this may add to the user effort. As long as the trajectories are accurate, the layout of walls will be precise and reliable. Some learning meth-

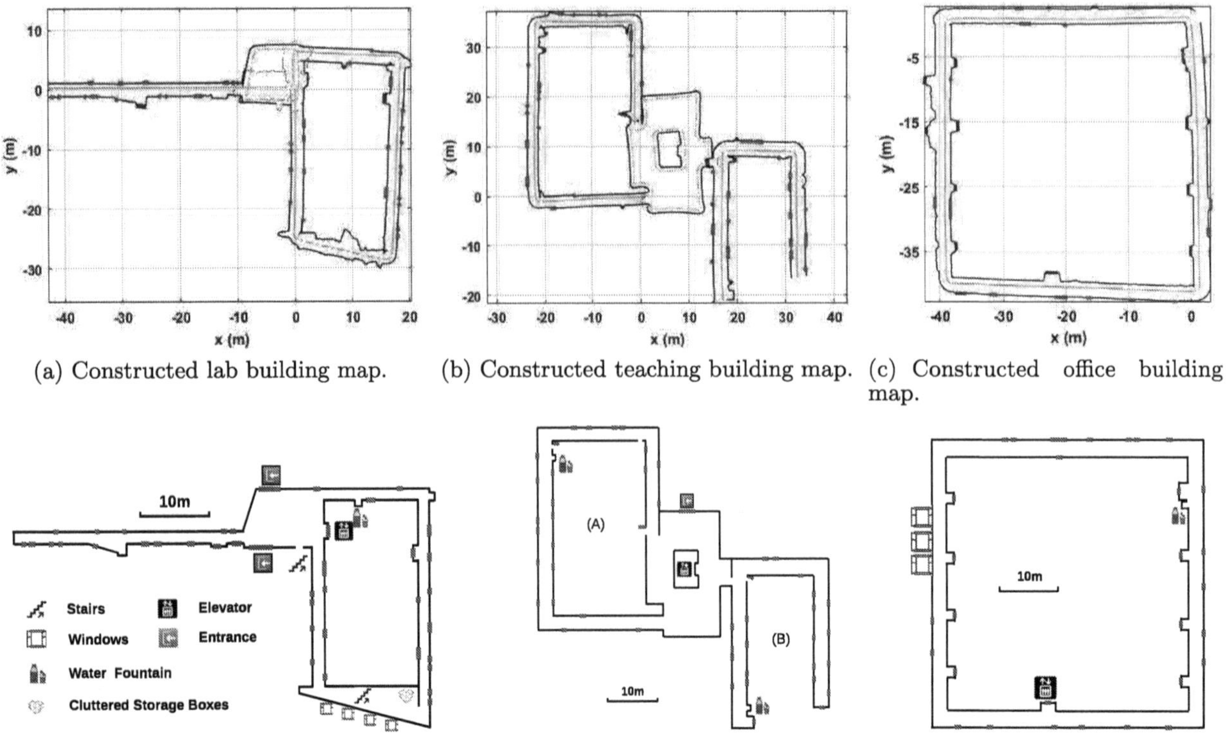

(a) Constructed lab building map. (b) Constructed teaching building map. (c) Constructed office building map.

(d) Ground truth of lab building. (e) Ground truth of teaching building. (f) Ground truth of office building.

Figure 17: (a),(b),(c) are constructed maps: green line is user trace, solid line indicates corridor while dotted in open space; black lines are constructed walls, doors are marked using red, thick line segments, and large recessions marked as blue. (d),(e),(f) are respective ground truth.

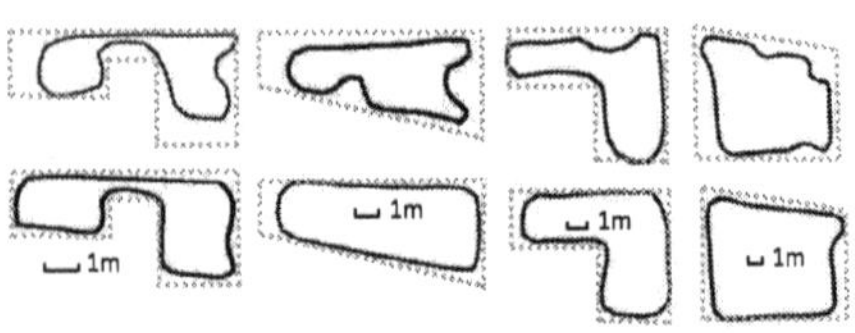

Figure 18: 4 pure trace based room shapes (top), and acoustic-aided ones (bottom). Ground truth are shown as dotted lines.

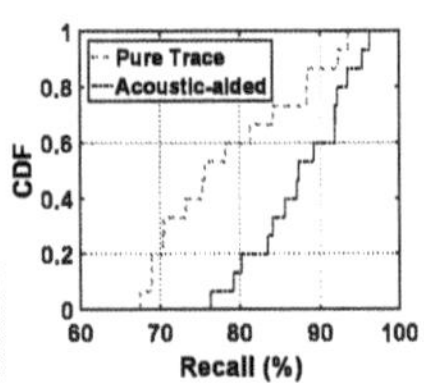

Figure 19: Recall of trace and acoustic based room shapes.

ods [34] may be applied to recognize different features (e.g., wide openings as entrances to stores). Additionally, vision based techniques (e.g., Jigsaw [8]) may be used to enhance the map construction wherever limiting factors (e.g., glass walls, dark lighting) do not exist.

Microphone/Speaker Layout. We plan to extend the current design to a broader category of mobile devices with different layouts of microphones and speakers. Customized configurations of constraints and parameters need to be derived according to the layout of microphones and speakers. This would allow various makes/models of mobile devices to be used for floor plan construction.

8. RELATED WORK

Acoustic Sensing. Acoustics has been used for ranging, localization, tracking, stress and encounter detection. BeepBeep [27], SwordFight [43] estimate the distance between two mobile devices instead of to objects. Graham *et al.* [10] use smartphones to show echo peaks and require the user to manually determine their association to objects, which can be cumbersome for practical use. Liu *et al.* [20] use cross-correlation to estimate arrival time difference for keystrokes snooping. Yang *et al.* [40] leverage mobile acoustic sensing to detect driver phone usage in a vehicle. Liu *et al.* [19] use acoustic ranging estimates among peer phones as constraints to improve their localization accuracy. GuoGuo [21] uses an anchor network that transmits spatial beacon signals to achieve centimeter-level localization accuracy. For tracking, UbiK [38], AAMouse [41], LLAP [39], FingerIO [25] leverage phase shift in received signals and achieve $\sim 1cm$ or higher accuracy for near field finger gesture tracking. CAT [23] leverages external speakers and uses FMCW [32] for phone movement tracking at mm-level accuracy. ApenaApp [24] monitors the minute chest and abdomen breathing movements using FMCW on smartphones. StressSense [22] detects stress of users unobtrusively in unconstrained acoustic environments using smartphones. DopEnc [42] uses an acoustic-based approach for identifying persons the user encounters during interaction.

Compared to them, BatMapper shares cross-correlation based echo detection similar to some work [10, 20, 19]. However its focus is on automatic echo-object association, which has not been addressed in previous work. We also propose techniques specifically designed for acoustic based floor plan construction, including sway compensation for automatic door detection, and candidate resampling for room construc-

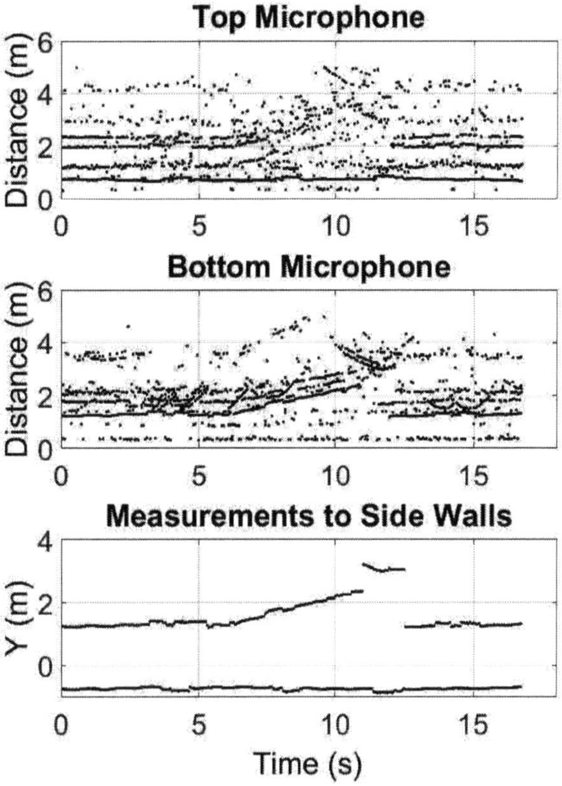

Figure 20: Distance measurements from Huawei P9, and distance to side walls after PEA and ROR.

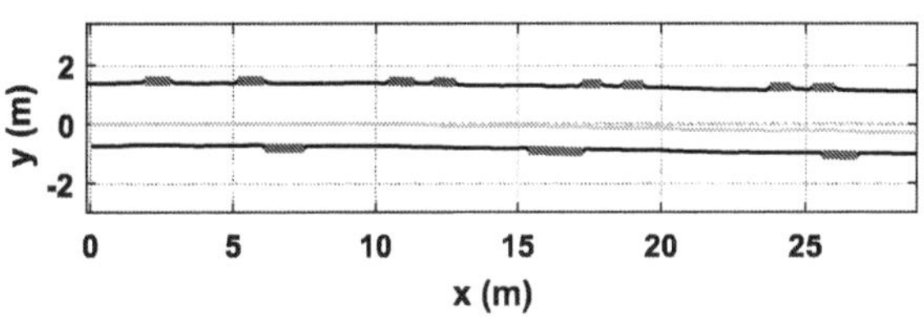

Figure 21: Sample corridor produced by Samsung Note3.

tion.

Indoor Floor Plans. Indoor floor plan construction has become an urgent problem for LBS. Robotic approaches can produce accurate maps, but they usually require expensive special hardware (e.g., laser rangers [33], depth cameras [16], sonars [35]) and deploying robots in massive numbers is logistically impractical. Vision based techniques [31, 29, 1] can generate 3D models of building interior, but they incur high computing overhead, and face privacy and technical limitations (e.g., glass walls, blurry images). Recent mobile device based approaches largely rely on crowdsourcing to achieve scalability. CrowdInside [2] uses inertial data with anchor points to approximate shapes of accessible areas. Jiang *et al.* [15] leverage Wi-Fi signatures to detect room and hallway adjacency, and combine with user trajectories to construct hallways. Walkie-Markie [30] recognizes points of reversing Wi-Fi signal strength to calibrate trajectories for corridors. Some recent work combines vision and mobile techniques to produce fine-grained floor plans. Jigsaw [8] leverages images to generate geometry attributes and spatial constraints of indoor landmarks. iMoon [5] builds 3D models of indoor environment from crowdsourced 2D photos, and compiles a navigation mesh from the generated 3D models. Indoor Crowd [3] produces panoramic maps of indoor environments by stitching images together. CrowdMap [4] detects line segments in such panoramic views and identifies room corners for room reconstruction. Such work usually requires significant amounts of data and crowdsourcing efforts; those using images/videos also face privacy restrictions.

Compared to them, BatMapper cuts down data amount and user efforts by orders of magnitude using acoustics, thus avoiding privacy constraints while achieving comparable accuracy to the state-of-the-art. TransitLabel[7] uses multi-modality data (e.g, acoustic, inertial, magnetic) to infer the types of functional areas and assign them human readable semantic labels. BatMapper focuses on floor plan geometry and does not address semantic labeling yet.

9. CONCLUSION

In this paper, we propose *BatMapper*, which leverages acoustics on commodity smartphones for fast, fine grained and low cost floor plan construction. A 2 $\sim$ 3 minute walk can produce fine grained corridor shapes, detect doors at 1 $\sim$ $2m$ 90-percentile location error and $\sim$ 90% precision. Accurate room geometries are derived using a measurement gesture in tens of seconds. Compared to latest work, BatMapper builds fine grained maps of comparable accuracy at 1-2 orders of magnitude less data amounts and user efforts.

10. ACKNOWLEDGEMENTS

This work is supported in part by a 2016 Google Faculty Research Award, and BJTU funding R16RC00030.

11. REFERENCES

[1] Project Tango, 2017. https://get.google.com/tango/.

[2] M. Alzantot and M. Youssef. Crowdinside: automatic construction of indoor floorplans. In *Proceedings of the 20th International Conference on Advances in Geographic Information Systems*, pages 99–108. ACM, 2012.

[3] S. Chen, M. Li, K. Ren, X. Fu, and C. Qiao. Rise of the indoor crowd: Reconstruction of building interior view via mobile crowdsourcing. In *ACM SenSys*, pages 59–71, 2015.

[4] S. Chen, M. Li, K. Ren, and C. Qiao. Crowd map: Accurate reconstruction of indoor floor plans from crowdsourced sensor-rich videos. In *Distributed Computing Systems (ICDCS), 2015 IEEE 35th International Conference on*, pages 1–10. IEEE, 2015.

[5] J. Dong, Y. Xiao, M. Noreikis, Z. Ou, and A. Ylä-Jääski. imoon: Using smartphones for image-based indoor navigation. In *Proceedings of the 13th ACM Conference on Embedded Networked Sensor Systems*, pages 85–97. ACM, 2015.

[6] G. Dubbelman, I. Esteban, and K. Schutte. Efficient trajectory bending with applications to loop closure. In *Intelligent Robots and Systems (IROS), 2010 IEEE/RSJ International Conference on*, pages 4836–4842. IEEE, 2010.

[7] M. Elhamshary, M. Youssef, A. Uchiyama, H. Yamaguchi, and T. Higashino. Transitlabel: A crowd-sensing system for automatic labeling of transit stations semantics. In *Proceedings of the 14th Annual International Conference on Mobile Systems, Applications, and Services*, pages 193–206. ACM, 2016.

[8] R. Gao, M. Zhao, T. Ye, F. Ye, Y. Wang, K. Bian, T. Wang, and X. Li. Jigsaw: Indoor floor plan reconstruction via mobile crowdsensing. In *Proceedings of the 20th annual international conference on Mobile computing and networking*, pages 249–260. ACM, 2014.

[9] P. Georgiev, N. D. Lane, K. K. Rachuri, and C. Mascolo. Dsp. ear: Leveraging co-processor support for continuous audio sensing on smartphones. In *Proceedings of the 12th ACM Conference on Embedded Network Sensor Systems*, pages 295–309. ACM, 2014.

[10] D. Graham, G. Simmons, D. T. Nguyen, and G. Zhou. A software-based sonar ranging sensor for smart phones. *IEEE Internet of Things Journal*, 2(6):479–489, 2015.

[11] M. H. Hennecke and G. A. Fink. Towards acoustic self-localization of ad hoc smartphone arrays. In *Hands-free Speech Communication and Microphone Arrays (HSCMA), 2011 Joint Workshop on*, pages 127–132. IEEE, 2011.

[12] D. Huang, R. Nandakumar, and S. Gollakota. Feasibility and limits of wi-fi imaging. In *Proceedings of the 12th ACM Conference on Embedded Network Sensor Systems*, pages 266–279. ACM, 2014.

[13] E. C. Ifeachor and B. W. Jervis. *Digital signal processing: a practical approach.* Pearson Education, 2002.

[14] E. T. Jaynes, J. E. T., and G. L. Bretthorst. *Probability Theory: The Logic of Science.* Cambridge University Press, 2003.

[15] Y. Jiang, Y. Xiang, X. Pan, K. Li, Q. Lv, R. P. Dick, L. Shang, and M. Hannigan. Hallway based automatic indoor floorplan construction using room fingerprints. In *Ubicomp*, 2013.

[16] K. Khoshelham and S. O. Elberink. Accuracy and resolution of kinect depth data for indoor mapping applications. *Sensors*, 12(2):1437–1454, 2012.

[17] N. E. Klepeis, W. C. Nelson, W. R. Ott, J. P. Robinson, A. M. Tsang, P. Switzer, J. V. Behar, S. C. Hern, W. H. Engelmann, et al. The national human activity pattern survey (nhaps): a resource for assessing exposure to environmental pollutants. *Journal of exposure analysis and environmental epidemiology*, 11(3):231–252, 2001.

[18] N. D. Lane, P. Georgiev, and L. Qendro. Deepear: robust smartphone audio sensing in unconstrained acoustic environments using deep learning. In *Proceedings of the 2015 ACM International Joint Conference on Pervasive and Ubiquitous Computing*, pages 283–294. ACM, 2015.

[19] H. Liu, Y. Gan, J. Yang, S. Sidhom, Y. Wang, Y. Chen, and F. Ye. Push the limit of wifi based localization for smartphones. In *ACM Mobicom 2012*.

[20] J. Liu, Y. Wang, G. Kar, Y. Chen, J. Yang, and M. Gruteser. Snooping keystrokes with mm-level audio ranging on a single phone. In *Proceedings of the 21st Annual International Conference on Mobile Computing and Networking*, pages 142–154. ACM, 2015.

[21] K. Liu, X. Liu, and X. Li. Guoguo: Enabling fine-grained indoor localization via smartphone. In *Proceeding of the 11th annual international conference on Mobile systems, applications, and services*, pages 235–248. ACM, 2013.

[22] H. Lu, D. Frauendorfer, M. Rabbi, M. S. Mast, G. T. Chittaranjan, A. T. Campbell, D. Gatica-Perez, and T. Choudhury. Stresssense: Detecting stress in unconstrained acoustic environments using smartphones. In *Proceedings of the 2012 ACM Conference on Ubiquitous Computing*, pages 351–360. ACM, 2012.

[23] W. Mao, J. He, and L. Qiu. Cat: high-precision acoustic motion tracking. In *Proceedings of the 22nd Annual International Conference on Mobile Computing and Networking*, pages 69–81. ACM, 2016.

[24] R. Nandakumar, S. Gollakota, and N. Watson. Contactless sleep apnea detection on smartphones. In *Proceedings of the 13th Annual International Conference on Mobile Systems, Applications, and Services*, pages 45–57. ACM, 2015.

[25] R. Nandakumar, V. Iyer, D. Tan, and S. Gollakota. Fingerio: Using active sonar for fine-grained finger tracking. In *Proceedings of the 2016 CHI Conference on Human Factors in Computing Systems*, pages 1515–1525. ACM, 2016.

[26] S. J. Orfanidis. *Optimum signal processing: An introduction.* 2nd Edition, Prentice-Hall, Englewood Cliffs, NJ, 1996.

[27] C. Peng, G. Shen, Y. Zhang, Y. Li, and K. Tan. Beepbeep: A high accuracy acoustic ranging system using cots mobile devices. In *ACM SenSys*, 2007.

[28] N. Roy, H. Wang, and R. R. Choudhury. I am a smartphone and i can tell my users walking direction. In *Mobisys*, 2014.

[29] A. Sankar and S. Seitz. Capturing indoor scenes with smartphones. In *Proceedings of the 25th annual ACM symposium on User interface software and technology*, pages 403–412. ACM, 2012.

[30] G. Shen, Z. Chen, P. Zhang, T. Moscibroda, and Y. Zhang. Walkie-markie: Indoor pathway mapping made easy. In *NSDI*, 2013.

[31] N. Snavely, I. Simon, M. Goesele, R. Szeliski, and M. Seitzs. Scene reconstruction and visualization from community photo collections. *Proceedings of the IEEE*, 1998.

[32] A. G. Stove. Linear fmcw radar techniques. In *IEE Proceedings F-Radar and Signal Processing*, volume 139, pages 343–350. IET, 1992.

[33] H. Surmann, A. Nüchter, and J. Hertzberg. An autonomous mobile robot with a 3d laser range finder for 3d exploration and digitalization of indoor environments. *Robotics and Autonomous Systems*, 45(3):181–198, 2003.

[34] J. A. Suykens and J. Vandewalle. Least squares support vector machine classifiers. *Neural processing letters*, 9(3):293–300, 1999.

[35] J. D. Tardós, J. Neira, P. M. Newman, and J. J. Leonard. Robust mapping and localization in indoor

environments using sonar data. *The International Journal of Robotics Research*, 21(4):311–330, 2002.

[36] J.-A. Ting, E. Theodorou, and S. Schaal. A kalman filter for robust outlier detection. In *Intelligent Robots and Systems, 2007. IROS 2007. IEEE/RSJ International Conference on*, pages 1514–1519. IEEE, 2007.

[37] H. Wang, S. Sen, A. Elgohary, M. Farid, M. Youssef, and R. R. Choudhury. No need to war-drive: Unsupervised indoor localization. In *MobiSys*, 2012.

[38] J. Wang, K. Zhao, X. Zhang, and C. Peng. Ubiquitous keyboard for small mobile devices: Harnessing multipath fading for fine-grained keystroke localization. In *Proceedings of ACM MobiSys*, pages 14–27, 2014.

[39] W. Wang, A. X. Liu, and K. Sun. Device-free gesture tracking using acoustic signals. In *Proceedings of the 22nd Annual International Conference on Mobile Computing and Networking*, pages 82–94. ACM, 2016.

[40] J. Yang, S. Sidhom, G. Chandrasekaran, T. Vu, H. Liu, N. Cecan, Y. Chen, M. Gruteser, and R. P. Martin. Detecting driver phone use leveraging car speakers. In *ACM MobiCom*, 2011.

[41] S. Yun, Y.-C. Chen, and L. Qiu. Turning a mobile device into a mouse in the air. In *Proceedings of ACM MobiSys*, pages 15–29, 2015.

[42] H. Zhang, W. Du, P. Zhou, M. Li, and P. Mohapatra. Dopenc: acoustic-based encounter profiling using smartphones. In *Proceedings of the 22nd Annual International Conference on Mobile Computing and Networking*, pages 294–307. ACM, 2016.

[43] Z. Zhang, D. Chu, X. Chen, and T. Moscibroda. Swordfight: enabling a new class of phone-to-phone action games on commodity phones. In *Proceedings of the 10th international conference on Mobile systems, applications, and services*, pages 1–14. ACM, 2012.

MobileDeepPill: A Small-Footprint Mobile Deep Learning System for Recognizing Unconstrained Pill Images

Xiao Zeng, Kai Cao, Mi Zhang
Michigan State University

ABSTRACT

Correct identification of prescription pills based on their visual appearance is a key step required to assure patient safety and facilitate more effective patient care. With the availability of high-quality cameras and computational power on smartphones, it is possible and helpful to identify unknown prescription pills using smartphones. Towards this goal, in 2016, the U.S. National Library of Medicine (NLM) of the National Institutes of Health (NIH) announced a nationwide competition, calling for the creation of a mobile vision system that can recognize pills automatically from a mobile phone picture under unconstrained real-world settings. In this paper, we present the design and evaluation of such mobile pill image recognition system called *MobileDeepPill*. The development of MobileDeepPill involves three key innovations: a triplet loss function which attains invariances to real-world noisiness that deteriorates the quality of pill images taken by mobile phones; a multi-CNNs model that collectively captures the shape, color and imprints characteristics of the pills; and a Knowledge Distillation-based deep model compression framework that significantly reduces the size of the multi-CNNs model without deteriorating its recognition performance. Our deep learning-based pill image recognition algorithm wins the First Prize (champion) of the NIH NLM Pill Image Recognition Challenge. Given its promising performance, we believe MobileDeepPill helps NIH tackle a critical problem with significant societal impact and will benefit millions of healthcare personnel and the general public.

CCS Concepts

•Human-centered computing → Ubiquitous and mobile computing; •Computing methodologies → Visual content-based indexing and retrieval;

Keywords

Mobile Deep Learning Systems; Unconstrained Pill Image Recognition; Deep Neural Network Model Compression; Mobile Health

Permission to make digital or hard copies of all or part of this work for personal or classroom use is granted without fee provided that copies are not made or distributed for profit or commercial advantage and that copies bear this notice and the full citation on the first page. Copyrights for components of this work owned by others than ACM must be honored. Abstracting with credit is permitted. To copy otherwise, or republish, to post on servers or to redistribute to lists, requires prior specific permission and/or a fee. Request permissions from permissions@acm.org.

MobiSys'17, June 19–23, 2017, Niagara Falls, NY, USA.
© 2017 ACM. ISBN 978-1-4503-4928-4/17/06. . . $15.00
DOI: http://dx.doi.org/10.1145/3081333.3081336

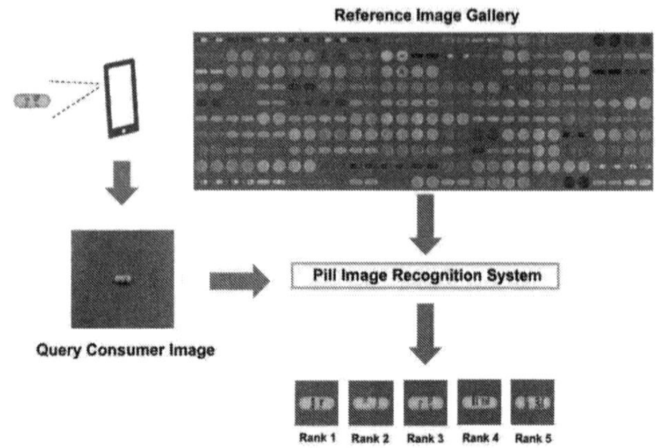

Figure 1: Illustration of the unconstrained pill image recognition problem.

1. INTRODUCTION

Smartphones with built-in high-quality cameras are ubiquitous today. These cameras coupled with advanced computer vision algorithms are turning smartphones into powerful tools for people to retrieve information from the physical world. In recent years, a number of such mobile vision systems have become applicable for daily-life tasks and have demonstrated impressive performance in unconstrained real-world settings. For example, Google Translate app can accurately translate texts on books, road signs, and menus from one language into another [2]. As another example, Amazon shopping app is capable of recognizing objects appeared in the scene and labeling them with associated product information [1].

In 2016, the U.S. National Library of Medicine (NLM) of the National Institutes of Health (NIH) announced a nationwide competition, calling for the creation of a mobile vision system that can recognize pills automatically from a mobile phone picture under unconstrained real-world settings [4]. This competition is motivated by the imperative need for a mobile pill recognition tool that can provide a simple way to recognize mystery pills, prevent unnecessary medication errors, and most importantly, save people's lives in urgent cases. Figure 1 illustrates this unconstrained pill image recognition problem. As shown, a user takes an image of a pill using his or her mobile phone. The pill image recognition system takes the image as input, compares it against thousands of high-quality pill images in the database, and returns a list of most similar pills to the user. The images taken by mobile phones in the unconstrained real-world settings are called *consumer images*. The images stored in the database are called *reference images*, which are taken by higher-resolution cameras in the controlled laboratory setting. However, developing such pill image recognition system is challenging. This is because in mobile unconstrained scenarios, the quality of photos taken by mobile phones can be easily deteriorated by a variety of factors such as illumination, shading, background, and phone orientation. Moreover, the number of types of prescription pills manufactured by pharmaceutical companies is large. Existing solutions are not capable of handling such large number of types and thus fail when the scale is increased considerably.

Over the past few years, deep learning has become the dominant approach in machine learning due to its impressive capability of handling large-scale learning problems [20]. Deep learning-based approaches have achieved state-of-the-art performance in solving a variety of computer vision problems such as object recognition [18], face recognition [27], video classification [17], and scene understanding [28]. However, deep learning-based approaches are very expensive in terms of computation, memory, and power consumption. As such, given the resource constraints of mobile devices, most of the existing deep learning-based mobile vision systems offload the workload to the cloud [9, 12]. Unfortunately, cloud offloading becomes impossible when the Internet connection is lost. It also suffers from unpredictable end-to-end network delay, which can be affected by many factors such as distance between mobile device and cloud, network bandwidth and data quantity. More importantly, the medication an individual takes contains very sensitive and private information about his or her medical record. Uploading pill images onto the cloud constitutes a great danger to an individual's privacy [6].

In this paper, we present the design, implementation, and evaluation of *MobileDeepPill*, a small-footprint mobile deep learning system that achieves state-of-the-art performance on recognizing unconstrained pill images without cloud offloading. The development of MobileDeepPill includes three key innovations. First, MobileDeepPill employs a triplet loss function [24] to attain invariances to real-world noisiness that deteriorates the quality of pill images taken by mobile phones. Second, MobileDeepPill involves a novel pill image recognition algorithm based on deep Convolutional Neural Network (CNN) [18]. Protected by patent laws, each manufactured prescribed pill is uniquely characterized by the combination of its shape, color and imprints. MobileDeepPill achieves state-of-the-art pill image recognition performance by utilizing a multi-CNNs architecture that collectively captures the shape, color and imprints characteristics of the pills. Third, MobileDeepPill incorporates a novel deep model compression technique based on Knowledge Distillation [15]. The model compression technique significantly reduces the size of the multi-CNNs model without deteriorating its recognition performance by designing a much smaller model and training it using the knowledge extracted from the multi-CNNs model. As a result, MobileDeepPill is able to perform accurate pill image recognition on commodity smartphones efficiently.

The innovations involved in MobileDeepPill are *generic* which can be applied to the development of a wide range of mobile sensing systems powered by on-device deep learning algorithms. First, data collected by mobile sensing systems is likely to be noisy. The triplet loss function can be leveraged to build mobile sensing systems that are resilient to noisiness in unconstrained mobile conditions. Second, the proposed multi-CNNs architecture can be used to build mobile sensing systems that perform inferences based on fusing knowledge extracted from multiple sensing modalities. Finally, the proposed Knowledge Distillation-based model compression framework allows practitioners who want to adopt large off-the-shelf deep convolutional models to generate small-footprint models for resource-limited mobile sensing systems without deteriorating its recognition performance.

Summary of Experimental Results: We have conducted a rich set of experiments to examine both the recognition and system performance of MobileDeepPill. To examine the recognition performance, we have evaluated MobileDeepPill on the official NIH NLM Pill Image Recognition Challenge dataset under two evaluation schemes [4]. To examine the system performance, we have implemented MobileDeepPill on three platforms with different computing power: 1) a desktop installed with an Intel i7-5930k CPU and a Nvidia GTX 1080 GPU (cloud CPU and GPU), 2) a Nvidia Jetson TX1 mobile development board equipped with a Nvidia Tegra X1 GPU (high-end mobile GPU), and 3) a Samsung Galaxy S7 edge smartphone (mobile CPU). Our results show that:

- MobileDeepPill achieves state-of-the-art unconstrained pill image recognition performance. Specifically, in the one-side pill recognition scheme, MobileDeepPill achieves an average 52.7% Top-1 accuracy and 81.7% Top-5 accuracy. In the two-side pill recognition scheme, MobileDeepPill achieves an average 73.7% Top-1 accuracy and 95.6% Top-5 accuracy.
- Our Knowledge Distillation-based deep model compression technique significantly reduces the number of parameters (by 86.8%) and floating-point operations per second (FLOPS) (by 62.8%) of the multi-CNNs model without deteriorating the recognition performance. As a result, MobileDeepPill only requires 34MB runtime memory to run the multi-CNNs model and is able to perform low-power (7665mJ), near real-time (1.58s) pill image recognition on commodity smartphones without cloud offloading. With the support of high-end mobile GPU, the runtime performance of MobileDeepPill is significantly improved (270ms) for real-time usage.

Summary of Contributions: In this work, we introduce the first mobile vision system that achieves real-world applicable performance for recognizing unconstrained pill images. *Our deep learning-based pill image recognition algorithm achieves the best recognition performance among all the contestants and wins the First Prize (champion) of the NIH NLM Pill Image Recognition Challenge.* Moreover, our Knowledge Distillation-based deep model compression technique is *complementary* to existing deep model compression techniques developed for mobile devices [19, 7], thus representing a unique contribution.

The need for a mobile pill recognition tool is more important today than ever before. Given its great performance, we believe MobileDeepPill helps NIH tackle a critical problem with significant societal impact and will benefit millions of healthcare personnel and the general public.

2. CHALLENGES AND OUR SOLUTIONS

Accurately recognizing unconstrained pill images on mobile devices without cloud offloading presents a number of challenges. In this section, we describe these challenges followed by explaining how MobileDeepPill addresses these challenges.

Differences between Reference and Consumer Images: The goal of unconstrained pill image recognition is to match the consumer image of a pill with its corresponding reference image. Figure 2 shows five pairs of consumer images and reference images of the same pills. As shown, depending on how people take the pictures using their phones, and due to the deterioration caused by a variety of real-world noisiness such as shading, blur, illumination and background, consumer image and reference image of the same pill look very different. As a consequence, the recognition accuracy will suffer if we use the model trained on reference images to recognize pills appeared in consumer images. To address this challenge,

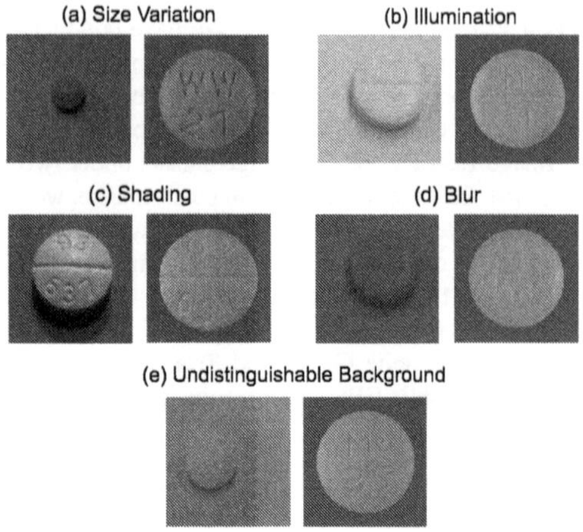

Figure 2: Illustration of differences between reference and consumer images of the same pills under five different scenarios. For each scenario, the image on the left is the consumer image; and the image on the right is the reference image of the same pill.

we employ a *triplet loss function* [24] to learn features that attain invariances to the noisiness illustrated in Figure 2 using CNNs. As such, MobileDeepPill can accurately match consumer images and reference images of the same pills even if they look different.

Unreliable Pill Characteristics: Although each prescribed pill can be identified by its unique combination of color, shape and imprints, the characteristics of a pill may appear differently in consumer images caused by real-world noisiness. For example, as shown in Figure 2 (b), a white pill turns into a yellow pill when the illumination in the environment is yellow. To address this challenge, we propose a *multi-CNNs architecture*. Specifically, we generate the gray and gradient images of the original color pill images to train three independent CNNs. CNNs trained on gray and gradient images not only alleviate the dependency on color information which can be deteriorated in unconstrained conditions, but also attain enhanced shape and imprint information which is helpful in distinguishing different pills. By combining the outputs of these three CNNs, MobileDeepPill becomes more resilient to the unreliability of pill characteristics.

Lack of Training Samples: A large volume of training images that contain significant variations is needed to ensure the robustness of our pill image recognition system in mobile settings. Unfortunately, collecting a large volume of diverse consumer images for all types of pills is very challenging. To address this challenge, we perform a number of *data augmentation* techniques to generate new augmented images. The data augmentation techniques generate variations that mimic the variations occurred in mobile settings. With the large amount of newly generated augmented images, CNNs are effectively trained. As a result, MobileDeepPill becomes more robust to the diverse variations in mobile settings.

Resource Constraints of Mobile Devices: To best protect the privacy of the user, pill images need to be completely processed inside mobile devices without cloud offloading. However, CNNs that achieve state-of-the-art accuracy in computer vision tasks usually consume hundreds of MB of memory and billions of FLOPS [18, 27, 25, 14]. Although mobile devices today are equipped with powerful computing resources, they are not designed for efficiently running such computation and memory intensive models. To address this challenge, we propose a novel deep neural network model compression technique based on *Knowledge Distillation* [15], which significantly reduces the memory footprint and FLOPS of CNNs without deteriorating the recognition accuracy. As such, MobileDeepPill can be efficiently running on today's commodity mobile phones while still achieving state-of-the-art recognition accuracy.

To the best of our knowledge, MobileDeepPill is the first mobile system that addresses these challenges and achieves real-world applicable performance.

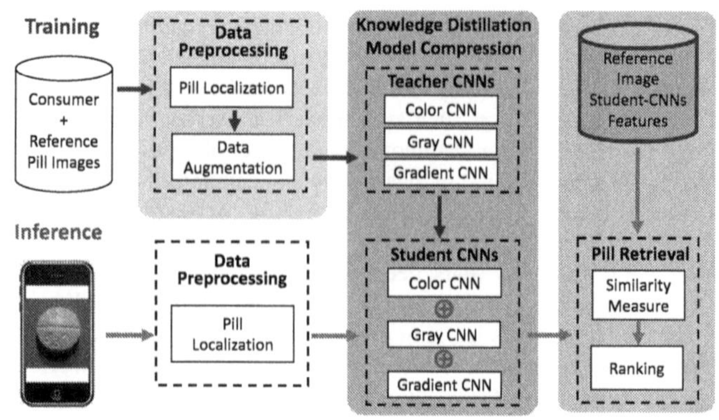

Figure 3: The system architecture of MobileDeepPill. Blue arrows represent flow in training stage. Green arrows represent flow in inference stage.

3. SYSTEM OVERVIEW

The system architecture of MobileDeepPill is illustrated in Figure 3. As shown, the training stage and the inference stage contain different system components.

In the training stage, MobileDeepPill first localizes and segments the pill in every consumer and reference image. It then performs data augmentation on the segmented consumer and reference images to generate new augmented images to increase the number of training samples. For every original and augmented image in the training set, MobileDeepPill generates the gray and gradient images of the original color pill images to train three independent CNNs: *Color CNN*, *Gray CNN*, and *Gradient CNN*. Finally, these three CNNs are imported as *Teacher CNNs* into the *Knowledge Distillation Model Compression* framework to derive three small-footprint *Student CNNs*.

In the inference stage, given a consumer image taken by the smartphone, MobileDeepPill first localizes and segments the pill in the consumer image. The segmented consumer image is then fed into the *Student CNNs* to extract CNN features. These features will be compared with the CNN features of all the reference images. Finally, the ranking based on the similarity between the consumer image and all the reference images in the CNN feature space is generated in descending order. Based on the ranking, the reference images of the top N pill candidates are returned to the user.

In the next two sections, we describe the design of MobileDeepPill in details.

4. MULTI-CNNS BASED PILL IMAGE PROCESSING

4.1 Data Preprocessing

4.1.1 Pill Localization

The backgrounds of pill images do not contain useful information to help identify pills, and in real-world settings, can become a source of noises that will affect recognition accuracy. Therefore,

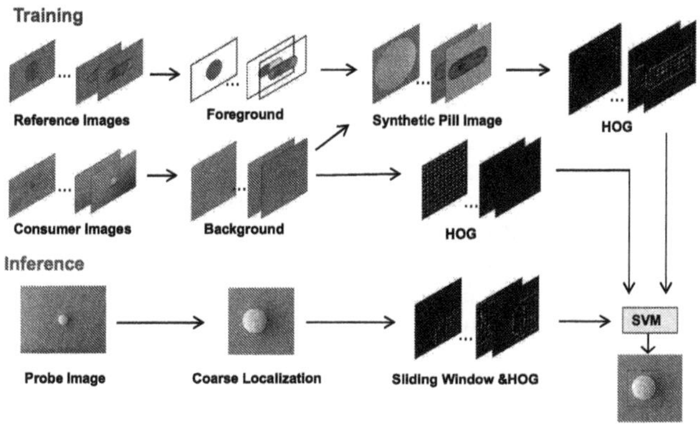

Figure 4: Illustration of pill localization approach for consumer images.

it is necessary to localize and segment the pills in the images in the first place. Considering the differences between reference images and consumer images, we propose two different localization schemes for reference images and consumer images, respectively.

Pill Localization for Reference Images: Since reference images were taken by high-resolution professional cameras in controlled settings, the backgrounds of reference images are uniform and only contain plain texture. As such, we use a simple gradient detection method to localize and segment pills in reference images. Specifically, the gradient detection method finds the image gradients that exceed a given threshold. These gradients strongly imply the location of the pill in a reference image. Using morphologically image operations, the largest connected region, which is also the region of the pill in the reference image is obtained.

Pill Localization for Consumer Images: Directly applying the gradient detection method to consumer images does not achieve good performance because consumer images contain diverse backgrounds. To address this problem, we adopt a learning-based approach to train a pill detector using Support Vector Machine (SVM). Figure 4 provides a graphical overview of our pill localization approach for consumer images. Specifically, we leverage the localization results of reference images and use them as positive localization samples. We manually extract backgrounds of consumer images and use them as negative localization samples. We then use these positive and negative samples as training data and compute the histogram of oriented gradients (HOG) of each sample as features to train the SVM-based pill detector. We localize and segment the pill in a consumer image by first using the gradient detection method to obtain the coarse location of the pill in the image. A sliding window is then used to crop image patches inside the coarse region. These patches are then fed into the trained SVM. The patch with the highest probability is considered as the pill location.

4.1.2 *Data Augmentation*

We have applied three data augmentation techniques on the segmented pill images. Specifically, we have applied Gaussian filtering to simulate blur images; we have zoomed the images by a random factor in the range of (0.8, 1.2) to ensure our system is robust to pill size variation; and finally, we have applied random translation (in the range of (-5, 5) pixels) and rotation (in the range of (-6, 6) degrees) to the segmented pill images to ensure our system is less sensitive to localization errors.

4.2 Feature Learning Using Triplet Loss and Deep Convolutional Neural Networks

4.2.1 *Triplet Loss*

The goal of unconstrained pill image recognition is to match the consumer image of a pill with its corresponding reference image. However, as illustrated in Figure 2, due to the deterioration caused in unconstrained conditions, consumer images and reference images of the same pills may look very different. To this end, we employ a triplet loss function (i.e., triplet loss) to address this problem. Triplet loss has been successfully used for addressing variations in expression, pose, and illumination in the problem of unconstrained face recognition [24]. In the context of unconstrained pill recognition, we use triplet loss to guide the training of CNNs to create a new feature space such that in this feature space, the distances between consumer and reference images of the same pills are small, whereas the distances between consumer and reference images of different pills are large.

Specifically, triplet loss takes a set of three images (i.e., triplet) as its input: an *anchor image* I^a, a *positive image* I^p, and a *negative image* I^n. Among them, the *anchor image* and the *positive image* are from the same pill, while the *negative image* is from a different pill. The objective of triplet loss is to find an embedding $f(I)$, from an image I into a d-dimensional feature space $\mathbb{R}^d$, such that in the feature space, the anchor image is closer to all positive images, *independent of the deterioration caused by real-world noisiness*, than to any negative image. This objective can be translated into the following mathematical formulation:

$$\|f(I^a) - f(I^p)\|_2^2 + \alpha < \|f(I^a) - f(I^n)\|_2^2 \quad (1)$$

and the corresponding triplet loss function is formulated as:

$$\mathcal{L} = \max(\|f(I^a) - f(I^p)\|_2^2 - \|f(I^a) - f(I^n)\|_2^2 + \alpha, 0) \quad (2)$$

where α is a margin that controls the distance between the positive pair (I^a, I^p) and negative pair (I^a, I^n).

Figure 5 illustrates the effect of triplet loss. As shown, in the original image space, due to real-world noisiness, the *anchor image* I^a is closer to the *negative image* I^n compared to the *positive image* I^p. This leads to the consequence where the *anchor image* I^a is misclassified to the same pill as the *negative image* I^n. By

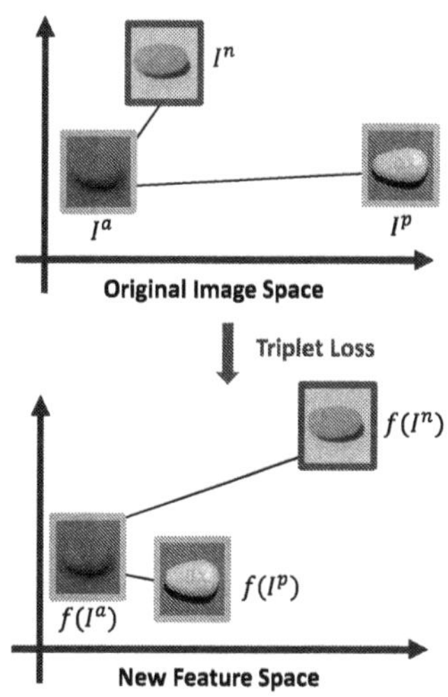

Figure 5: Illustration of the effect of triplet loss. The colors of bounding boxes indicate the classes of the pills.

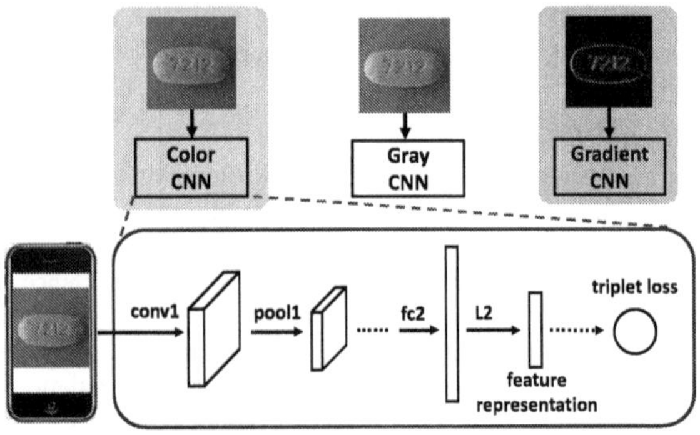

Figure 6: Illustration of the multi-CNNs architecture of MobileDeepPill.

employing triplet loss, the three pill images I^a, I^p, and I^n are projected into a new feature space where the *anchor image* I^a is closer to the *positive image* I^p compared to the *negative image* I^n. As a result, the *anchor image* I^a is correctly classified to the same pill as the *positive image* I^p.

4.2.2 Triplet Generation

One critical issue of employing triplet loss is how to generate the correct triplets. This is because triplets that are generated using random combination method do not contain much useful information. As a result, these randomly selected triplets do not contribute to the CNN training and thus lead to slow convergence [24].

To address this problem, we have designed an online scheme that generates informative triplets from intermediate results during the training process. The key idea is to generate triplets based on current pill ranking. Specifically, for an image in the training dataset, we treat it as I^a and randomly select I^p from the same pill class. We leverage the current ranking of I^a and choose its neighboring pill class in the ranking as I^n. The rationale behind this strategy is that we want the CNN to learn features that are distinctive among different pill classes, especially among very similar pills. As an example, assume we have I^a and its corresponding reference image ranks $10th$. We randomly select one pill that ranks close to $10th$ as the negative image I^n. As we have observed in our experiments, our online triplet generation scheme successfully generates informative triplets that contribute to improving the CNN model as well as fast convergence during the training process.

4.2.3 Multi-CNNs Architecture

Figure 6 shows the multi-CNNs architecture of our MobileDeepPill system. As illustrated, the multi-CNNs architecture consists of three independent CNNs: *Color CNN*, *Gray CNN*, and *Gradient CNN*. These three CNNs play different roles and extract complementary features that collectively capture the shape, color and imprints characteristics of the pills. Specifically, *Color CNN* is responsible for extracting color information of the pills; and *Gray CNN* and *Gradient CNN* are responsible for extracting shape and imprints information of the pills.

We design the network architecture of the three CNNs based on AlexNet [18]. All the three CNNs have the same network architecture except the first convolutional layer. This is because for *Color CNN*, the input is the RGB color images and thus the number of input channels is three; whereas for *Gray CNN* and *Gradient CNN*, the input is the gray and gradient images respectively and thus the number of input channels is one. Table 1 provides the details of the network architecture of *Color CNN*. As shown, the network consists of five convolutional layers (*conv1* to *conv5*), three pooling layers (*pool1*, *pool2*, and *pool5*), and two fully connected layers (*fc1* and *fc2*). Finally, on top of the *fc2* layer, a L2 normalization layer is added to output the feature representation $f(I)$.

Layer	Size In	Size Out	Kernel
conv1	$227 \times 227 \times 3$	$55 \times 55 \times 96$	$11 \times 11, 4$
pool1	$55 \times 55 \times 96$	$27 \times 27 \times 96$	$3 \times 3, 2$
conv2	$27 \times 27 \times 96$	$27 \times 27 \times 256$	$5 \times 5, 1$
pool2	$27 \times 27 \times 256$	$13 \times 13 \times 256$	$3 \times 3, 2$
conv3	$13 \times 13 \times 256$	$13 \times 13 \times 384$	$3 \times 3, 1$
conv4	$13 \times 13 \times 384$	$13 \times 13 \times 384$	$3 \times 3, 1$
conv5	$13 \times 13 \times 384$	$13 \times 13 \times 256$	$3 \times 3, 1$
pool5	$13 \times 13 \times 256$	$6 \times 6 \times 256$	$3 \times 3, 2$
fc1	$6 \times 6 \times 256$	1024	
fc2	1024	128	
L2	128	128	

Table 1: The network architecture of *Color CNN*. The parameters in the Size In and Size Out columns follow the format of $height \times width \times \#kernels$. The parameters in the Kernel column follow the format of $height \times width, stride$. The network architecture of *Gray CNN* and *Gradient CNN* are the same except the Size In of *conv1* is $227 \times 227 \times 1$.

4.3 Pill Retrieval

Given a query consumer image taken by a smartphone, the objective of pill retrieval is to compare the query consumer image to the reference images of all pill classes and then output a similarity ranking in a descending order. MobileDeepPill achieves this by measuring the similarity between consumer and reference images in the learned CNN feature space. Specifically, we use the cosine distance as the metric to calculate a similarity score:

$$S = f(I_q)^T f(I_{ref}) \tag{3}$$

where I_q is the query consumer image and I_{ref} is the reference image that I_q is compared to. Since we have three independent CNNs, three similarity scores S_{color}, S_{gray} and $S_{gradient}$ are calculated respectively. Finally, since color, shape and imprints information is complementary for identifying pills, a final similarity score is calculated as the unweighted sum of S_{color}, S_{gray} and $S_{gradient}$.

$$S_{final} = S_{color} + S_{gray} + S_{gradient} \tag{4}$$

5. KNOWLEDGE DISTILLATION-BASED MODEL COMPRESSION

Although our multi-CNNs model is able to extract complementary features that collectively capture the color, shape, and imprints characteristics of pills, it contains about 40 million parameters and consumes over 3.2 billion FLOPS (see Table 3 for breakdown details). The large number of parameters makes the model memory intensive; and the high FLOPS makes the model computation intensive. Although mobile devices today are equipped with powerful computing resources, they are not designed for efficiently running such memory and computation intensive model.

To address this problem, MobileDeepPill adopts a novel deep neural network model compression technique based on Knowledge Distillation [15]. It compresses the large multi-CNNs model into a small network with much smaller numbers of parameters and FLOPS, and can be efficiently running on mobile devices without deteriorating the recognition accuracy. The Knowledge Distillation model compression framework involves two networks: a *student network* which is the original large network to be compressed; and a *student network* which is the desired small network to be designed. By training the student network to imitate the outputs of the teacher network, the knowledge of the teacher network is transferred to the student network. Although there are a few existing model compression techniques developed for mobile devices, they focus on compressing pretrained large networks [19, 7]. In contrast, by following a number of optimization strategies, our compression technique focuses on designing and training a new network architecture with a much smaller footprint.

In this section, we first provide the background knowledge of Knowledge Distillation. We then describe the strategies that guide the design of the student network. By following these strategies, we describe the architecture of the newly designed student network, and compare it with the original network (i.e., teacher network). Finally, we describe how to use the teacher network to train the student network.

5.1 A Primer on Knowledge Distillation

Knowledge Distillation was first introduced by Hinton *et al.* as a framework for model compression [15]. It aims to train a small network (i.e., *student network*) using the outputs of the original large network (i.e., *teacher network*). By doing it, the teacher network transfers its knowledge learned from data to the student network.

In [15], this framework is applied to the object recognition problem where the outputs of both teacher and student networks are softmax outputs $P_t = softmax(\mathbf{a}_t^L)$ and $P_s = softmax(\mathbf{a}_s^L)$:

$$P_t^\tau = softmax(\frac{\mathbf{a}_t^L}{\tau}) \quad (5)$$

$$P_s^\tau = softmax(\frac{\mathbf{a}_s^L}{\tau}) \quad (6)$$

where $\mathbf{a}^L$ is the activation of the last layer L and $\tau > 1$ is the relaxation to soften the outputs of both teacher and student networks. Based on the softmax outputs, the student network is trained to optimize the following loss function:

$$\mathcal{L} = \mathcal{H}(\mathbf{y}, P_s) + \lambda\mathcal{H}(P_t^\tau, P_s^\tau) \quad (7)$$

where $\mathcal{H}$ is the cross-entropy, $\mathbf{y}$ are true labels, and λ controls how much knowledge should be transferred from the teacher network.

In our work, since our goal is to compress the large multi-CNNs model without deteriorating its recognition performance, we use the following simplified loss function instead to only enforce the student network to imitate the outputs of the teacher network.

$$\mathcal{L} = \left\|(\mathbf{a}_t^L - \mathbf{a}_s^L)\right\|_2^2 \quad (8)$$

5.2 Student Network Design Strategies

The overarching goal of the student network design is to minimize the computational cost (i.e., the number of FLOPS) and memory footprint (i.e., the numbers of model parameters) while maintaining the recognition performance. As such, the design of the student network involves the examination of the trade-offs between recognition performance and a number of factors of the deep neural network architecture including depth, width, filter numbers, and filter sizes. However, this is a very complicated problem due to the complexity of the deep neural network architecture. To simplify the problem, we adopt the *layer replacement* scheme proposed in [13]. The core of the *layer replacement* scheme is that, at each time, one or a few layers are replaced by some other layers that preserve the recognition performance, without changing the other layers. Based on this scheme, we use the teacher network as the starting point, and progressively modify the teacher network architecture by examining the trade-offs between the recognition performance and the network architecture factors through a series of controlled experiments. This process not only leads to a small-footprint student network that maintains the recognition performance as its teacher network, but also helps formulate a number of strategies that can guide model compression.

In the following, we describe these strategies one by one. It is worthwhile to note that many similar strategies have been validated by other researchers in building compressed models for other tasks such as object recognition [13, 16]. Therefore, we expect our student network design strategies are helpful to building small-footprint deep neural network models on resource limited platforms like mobile phones and wearables for many other applications.

Strategy 1: Late downsampling. Late downsampling refers to maintaining large activation maps (i.e., the outputs of convolutional layers) at early layers and downsampling activation maps at later layers. It has been shown that late downsampling not only helps reduce the number of model parameters but also leads to higher recognition performance by keeping activation maps at early layers large to preserve information contained in images [16]. As such, when designing the student network, we propose to perform late downsampling to enhance recognition performance while reducing the number of model parameters.

Strategy 2: Use 1×1 filters for channel reduction. The concept of 1×1 filter was first introduced in [22]. It has been shown in GoogLeNet [26] that the 1×1 filter can significantly reduce the channel dimensions without sacrificing recognition accuracy. As such, when designing the student network, we propose to insert a new convolutional layer that uses 1×1 filter before the first fully-connected layer. By doing so, the number of parameters of the first fully-connected layer can be significantly reduced.

Strategy 3: Split one convolutional layer into multiple convolutional layers with filter number trade-off. Increasing network depth by adding extra layers has been demonstrated to be the key to improving accuracy [25, 26, 13]. However, adding extra layers also increases the number of model parameters. As such, when designing the student network, we propose to split one convolutional layer into two sub convolutional layers to increase depth. We also propose to adjust the filter number of the two sub convolutional layers such that the number of parameters is reduced or remains roughly the same. By doing this, the student network becomes deeper without increasing the number of model parameters.

Strategy 4: Split one convolutional layer into multiple convolutional layers with filter size trade-off. The receptive field of a convolutional layer determines how much information is preserved in that layer and thus plays a key role on recognition performance. It has been shown that the receptive field of one convolutional layer with large filter size (e.g., 5×5, 7×7) is equivalent to stacking multiple 3×3 convolutional layers [26]. This finding shows a way to increase the network depth by trading off filter size. As such, when designing the student network, we propose to split one convolutional layer that uses larger filter size into multiple 3×3 convolutional layers. By doing this, the student network becomes deeper without loosing the receptive field.

Strategy 5: Reduce filter number without splitting. Keeping increasing the network depth does not necessarily lead to accuracy improvement. This is because deeper networks are more difficult to train due to the degradation problem [14]. As such, when designing the student network, we propose to reduce the number of filters when increasing the depth does not help to improve the recognition accuracy. By doing this, it reduces the numbers of model parameters and FLOPS.

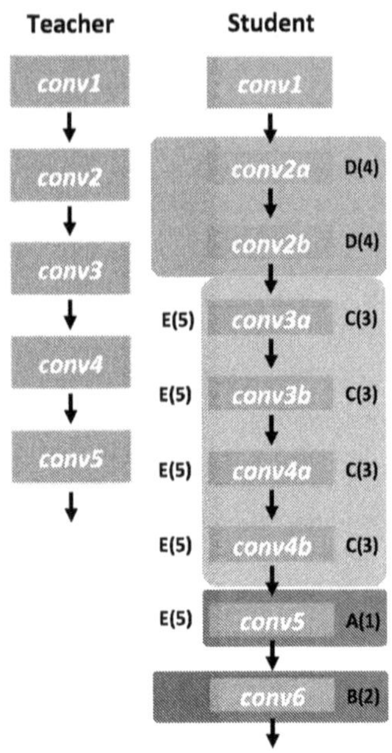

Figure 7: Illustration of the student network design process with the annotated strategy numbers and model symbols. Syntax: model symbol (strategy number).

5.3 Student Network Architecture

By following the above design strategies step by step, we gradually transform the teacher network into the student network. In this section, we go through the models generated at each step. The model to be generated at the next step is built on top of the current model. To help illustrate the whole process, Figure 7 is plotted with the annotated strategy numbers and model symbols. In addition, to illustrate the progress we have made at each step towards building a small-footprint student network, Table 2 lists the numbers of model parameters and FLOPS for each model.

Model A: We have followed **Strategy 1** to derive this model. Specifically, we perform late downsampling at *conv5* by changing its stride from 1 to 2. As a result, the number of parameters in *fc1* is reduced by 75%, dropping from $1024 \times 6 \times 6 \times 256$ to $1024 \times 3 \times 3 \times 256$.

Model B: We have followed **Strategy 2** to derive this model. Specifically, we add a new layer *conv6* comprised of 64 1×1 filters after *conv5*. As a result, the network depth increases one; the channels of activation maps after *conv6* are reduced to 64; and the number of parameters in *fc1* is reduced by 75%, dropping from $1024 \times 3 \times 3 \times 256$ to $1024 \times 3 \times 3 \times 64$.

Model C: We have followed **Strategy 3** to derive this model. Specifically, we split *conv3* and *conv4* into two sub convolutional layers *conv3a*, *conv3b* and *conv4a*, *conv4b*, respectively. As a result, the network depth increases two; and the filter number is reduced to 256.

Model D: We have followed **Strategy 4** to derive this model. Specifically, we split *conv2* into two sub convolutional layers *conv2a* and *conv2b*. As a result, the network depth increases one; and the filter size is reduced to 3×3.

Model E (Student Network): We have followed **Strategy 5** to derive this model. As a result, the numbers of filters in *conv3a*, *conv3b*, *conv4a*, *conv4b*, and *conv5* are further reduced to 128.

Model	T	A	B	C	D	E
# params (m)	13.32	6.24	4.49	4.34	3.69	1.76
FLOPS (m)	1093	984	973	985	676	407

Table 2: The numbers of parameters and FLOPS for each model during the student network design process (T = teacher network, m = million).

Table 3 and Table 4 show the details of the architecture of the teacher network and the student network of *Color CNN*, respectively. For *Gray CNN* and *Gradient CNN*, the architecture is the same as *Color CNN* except for the first layer where the number of parameters is 12k and the number of FLOPS is 37.4m. As shown in the tables, the generated student network only has 1.76m parameters and 407m FLOPS. Compared to the original teacher network, the corresponding compression ratio is 7.6 (13.32m / 1.76m) for the number of parameters, and 2.7 (1093m / 407m) for FLOPS.

Layer	Size Out	Kernel	# params	FLOPS
conv1	$55 \times 55 \times 96$	$11 \times 11, 4$	35k	112.2m
pool1	$27 \times 27 \times 96$	$3 \times 3, 2$		
conv2	$27 \times 27 \times 256$	$5 \times 5, 1$	615k	447.9m
pool2	$13 \times 13 \times 256$	$3 \times 3, 2$		
conv3	$13 \times 13 \times 384$	$3 \times 3, 1$	885k	149.5m
conv4	$13 \times 13 \times 384$	$3 \times 3, 1$	1330k	224.3m
conv5	$13 \times 13 \times 256$	$3 \times 3, 1$	885k	149.5m
pool5	$6 \times 6 \times 256$	$3 \times 3, 2$		
fc1	1024		9440k	9.4m
fc2	128		131k	0.1m
Total			13.32m	1093m

Table 3: The architecture of the *Color CNN* teacher network (Model T).

Layer	Size Out	Kernel	# params	FLOPS
conv1	$55 \times 55 \times 96$	$11 \times 11, 4$	35k	112.2m
pool1	$27 \times 27 \times 96$	$3 \times 3, 2$		
conv2a	$27 \times 27 \times 128$	$3 \times 3, 1$	111k	80.6m
conv2b	$27 \times 27 \times 128$	$3 \times 3, 1$	147k	107.5m
pool2	$13 \times 13 \times 128$	$3 \times 3, 2$		
conv3a	$13 \times 13 \times 128$	$3 \times 3, 1$	148k	24.9m
conv3b	$13 \times 13 \times 128$	$3 \times 3, 1$	148k	24.9m
conv4a	$13 \times 13 \times 128$	$3 \times 3, 1$	148k	24.9m
conv4b	$13 \times 13 \times 128$	$3 \times 3, 1$	148k	24.9m
conv5	$7 \times 7 \times 128$	$3 \times 3, 2$	148k	6.2m
conv6	$7 \times 7 \times 64$	$1 \times 1, 1$	8k	0.4m
pool6	$3 \times 3 \times 64$	$3 \times 3, 2$		
fc1	1024		591k	0.6m
fc2	128		131k	0.1m
Total			1.76m	407m

Table 4: The architecture of the *Color CNN* student network (Model E).

5.4 Student Network Training

In our proposed system, the teacher networks are our original color, gray and gradient CNNs described in section 4.2.3. Given the newly designed student network architecture in section 5.3, we apply the Knowledge Distillation framework described in section 5.1 to train the student network.

The training process consists of two stages. In the first stage, we let the student network learn by itself by training the student network using triplet loss. In the second stage, we let the pretrained teacher network train and transfer knowledge to the student network using Knowledge Distillation. By doing this, the student network learns the low-level features better and achieves much better generalization performance.

6. EVALUATION

6.1 Experimental Setup

6.1.1 Dataset

We conduct our experiments using the official NIH NLM Pill Image Recognition Challenge dataset [4]. The dataset contains 1000 distinct pills and has two categories of pill images:

Reference Images: This category contains 2000 reference images of the 1000 pills, with one image for the front side of the pill and one image for the back side of the pill. These images were taken under the same controlled laboratory settings using a high-resolution camera directly above the front and back sides of the pills.

Consumer Images: This category contains 5000 consumer images of the 1000 pills. These images were taken by digital cameras in mobile phones in real-world settings. For each of the 1000 pills, there are five consumer images taken under different conditions with variations in camera angle, illumination, and background.

6.1.2 Evaluation Metrics

To evaluate the pill recognition performance of MobileDeepPill, we use the Mean Average Precision (MAP) and Top-K accuracy as the evaluation metrics.

Mean Average Precision (MAP): MAP is the evaluation metric used in the official NIH NLM Pill Image Recognition Challenge. It is defined as:

$$MAP = \frac{1}{N}\sum_{i=1}^{N}\left(\frac{1}{N_i}\sum_{j=1}^{N_i}\frac{j}{MT(i,j)}\right) \tag{9}$$

where N denotes the number of query images used for evaluation, N_i is the number of genuine images which is always 2 because there are two sides for each pill, and $MT(i,j)$ are the rankings of two genuine images.

Top-K Accuracy: In practice, users are usually only interested in the top K pill candidates (e.g., K equal to 1, 5) retrieved by the system. Thus we employ Top-K accuracy as another metric to assess the recognition performance, which is defined as the ratio of the number of query images whose true mates are within the top K candidates retrieved by the system to the number of query images.

Besides the pill recognition performance, we also evaluate the system performance of MobileDeepPill including runtime, runtime memory, and energy consumption.

6.1.3 Evaluation Schemes and Protocol

Evaluation Schemes: We evaluate the recognition performance under the following two schemes:

- **One-Side Pill Recognition:** In this scheme, the system takes one consumer image, either front side or back side of a pill, as the input. The goal is to retrieve the reference image of either side of the same pill.
- **Two-Side Pill Recognition:** In this scheme, the system takes two consumer images, both front and back side of the same pill, as the input. The goal is to retrieve the reference images of both sides of the same pill.

Evaluation Protocol: For each evaluation scheme, we use 5-fold cross validation as the evaluation protocol. Specifically, we evenly split the 1000 pills into 5 folds of mutually exclusive pill sets, with the front side and back side of the same pill in the same fold. As such, each fold contains 200 distinct pills with 400 reference images (two reference images for each pill) and their corresponding 1000 consumer images. During training, we use all the images in four folds. During testing, we use the consumer images in the remaining fold as query images and all the reference images in 5 folds as gallery images.

6.2 Pill Image Recognition Performance

6.2.1 Superiority of Multi-CNNs over Single-CNN

Table 5 lists the recognition performance of the Single-CNN model (i.e., *Color CNN*) and the Multi-CNNs model in terms of MAP and Top-K accuracy (K = 1, 5) under both one-side and two-side pill recognition schemes. As shown, in both schemes, the Multi-CNNs model outperforms the Single-CNN model by a large margin across all three metrics. Specifically, in the one-side pill recognition scheme, MAP score increases 0.14 (from 0.242 to 0.382); Top-1 accuracy increases 27.1% (from 26.0% to 53.1%); and Top-5 accuracy increases 29.9% (from 53.2% to 83.1%). In the two-side pill recognition scheme, MAP score increases 0.27 (from 0.567 to 0.837); Top-1 accuracy increases 31% (from 43.1% to 74.1%); and Top-5 accuracy increases 22.9% (from 73.5% to 96.4%). This result demonstrates the significant superiority of the Multi-CNNs model over the Single-CNN model. This is because for the Single-CNN model (i.e., *Color CNN*), its recognition performance suffers when the color of the pill is changed in unconstrained conditions. In contrast, even if the color of the pill is changed, the Multi-CNNs model can still count on the shape and imprints information extracted from the *Gray CNN* and *Gradient CNN* to retrieve the correct pill. It is also worthwhile to note that both Single-CNN and Multi-CNNs achieve much better recognition performance in the two-side scheme than in the one-side scheme. This result indicates that providing both front and end side images of the query pill can significantly enhance the recognition performance.

6.2.2 Capability of the Student Network

Table 5 also compares the recognition performance between the teacher network and the student network. Two types of student network are considered: 1) *student network with KD*, which is the compressed Multi-CNNs model trained with Knowledge Distillation; and 2) *student network without KD*, which is the compressed Multi-CNNs model trained without Knowledge Distillation. As shown, for *student network with KD*, even if the student network has much fewer parameters, with the knowledge passed from the teacher network, it achieves almost equivalent recognition performance as the teacher network. For example, in the two-side pill recognition scheme, *student network with KD* achieves 95.6% Top-5 accuracy, which is only 0.8% less than the teacher network. This result indicates that the student network, though small in size, is able to absorb the knowledge passed from the teacher network, which demonstrates the effectiveness of our Knowledge Distillation-based model compression technique. In contrast, for *student network without KD*, by learning from the training dataset by itself with no knowledge passed from the teacher network, it has a significant performance drop across all three metrics in both schemes compared to the teacher network.

Finally, Figure 8 plots the Cumulative Match Characteristic (CMC) curves for both one-side and two-side pill recognition schemes to illustrate the trend of the Top-K accuracy across different models. As shown, in both one-side and two-side schemes, *student network with KD* is closely aligned with the teacher network from Top-1 to Top-20 accuracy. It also consistently outperforms *student network without KD* and the Single-CNN model from Top-1 to Top-20 accuracy. These results demonstrate once again the effectiveness of our Knowledge Distillation-based model compression technique.

Model	One-Side Pill Recognition			Two-Side Pill Recognition		
	MAP	Top-1	Top-5	MAP	Top-1	Top-5
Single-CNN	0.242 ± 0.008	$26.0 \pm 1.2\%$	53.2 ± 1.9	0.567 ± 0.007	$43.1 \pm 1.2\%$	$73.5 \pm 1.0\%$
Multi-CNNs (Teacher Network)	$\mathbf{0.382 \pm 0.008}$	$\mathbf{53.1 \pm 1.0\%}$	$\mathbf{83.1 \pm 0.9\%}$	$\mathbf{0.837 \pm 0.007}$	$\mathbf{74.1 \pm 0.8\%}$	$\mathbf{96.4 \pm 0.8\%}$
Student Network with KD	0.375 ± 0.009	$52.7 \pm 1.1\%$	$81.7 \pm 1.1\%$	0.829 ± 0.007	$73.7 \pm 1.0\%$	$95.6 \pm 0.5\%$
Student Network without KD	0.353 ± 0.008	$47.1 \pm 1.0\%$	$76.6 \pm 1.1\%$	0.779 ± 0.007	$67.5 \pm 0.9\%$	$90.6 \pm 0.7\%$

Table 5: Summary of unconstrained pill image recognition results (KD = Knowledge Distillation).

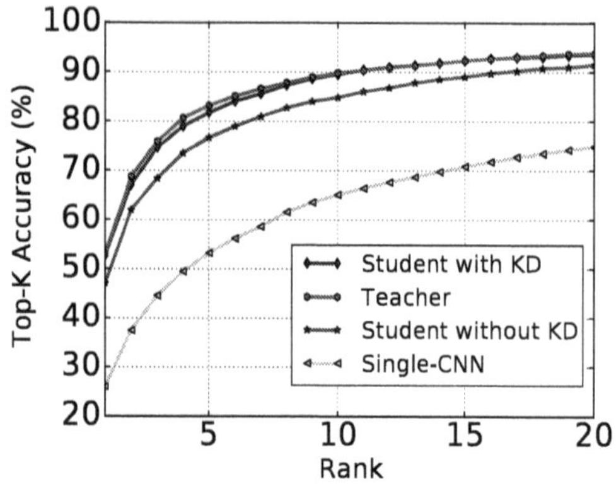

(a) The CMC curve of the One-Side Pill Recognition scheme.

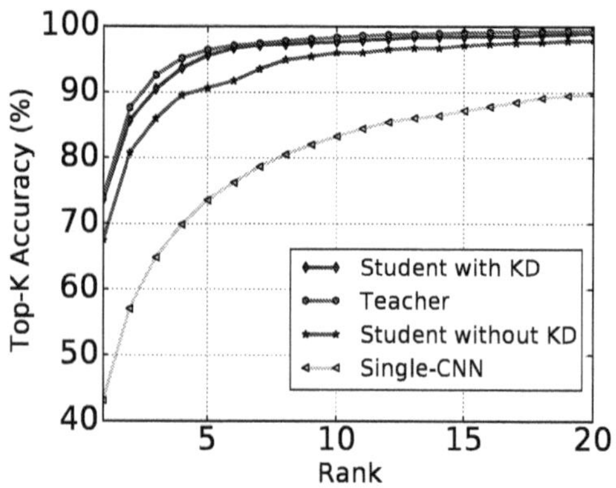

(b) The CMC curve of the Two-Side Pill Recognition scheme.

Figure 8: The Cumulative Match Characteristic (CMC) curves of two evaluation schemes. The horizontal axis is the rank K; and the vertical axis is the corresponding Top-K accuracy.

6.3 System Performance

To evaluate the system performance of MobileDeepPill, we have implemented MobileDeepPill end-to-end on three hardware platforms. Our goal is to profile the system performance of MobileDeepPill across platforms with different computing power. Specifically, we use a desktop installed with an Intel i7-5930k CPU and a Nvidia GTX 1080 GPU to simulate a cloud server; we use a Nvidia Jetson TX1 mobile development board that contains a Nvidia Tegra X1 GPU to simulate the next-generation smartphone with built-in high-end mobile GPU; and we use the Samsung Galaxy S7 edge as the commodity smartphone platform and run MobileDeepPill on its CPU. Figure 9 shows the three hardware platforms. The specs of those three hardware platforms are summarized in Table 6.

To provide a comprehensive evaluation, we have evaluated the system performance of all the six models listed in Table 2 (i.e., Model T, A, B, C, D, and E) in terms of runtime performance, runtime memory performance, and energy consumption. In the following, we report their system performance respectively.

(a) Desktop with Intel i7-5930k CPU and Nvidia GTX 1080 GPU (b) Nvidia Jetson TX1 (c) Samsung Galaxy S7 edge

Figure 9: Hardware platforms.

Platform	CPU		RAM	GPU		
	Cores	Speed		Cores	GFLOPS	Speed
Desktop	6	3.7 GHz	32 GB	2560	8228	1.67 GHz
Jetson TX1	4	1.9GHz	4GB	256	512	1 GHz
Galaxy S7 edge	8	2.3 GHz	4 GB	-	-	-

Table 6: The specs of the three hardware platforms.

6.3.1 *Runtime Performance*

To evaluate the runtime performance of MobileDeepPill, we measure the average processing time consumed at each computing stage during inference. An inference carried out by MobileDeepPill consists of four computing stages: 1) coarse-grained localization, 2) fine-grained localization, 3) CNN feature extraction, and 4) pill retrieval. We run 2000 inferences and report the average runtime at each stage. Specifically, since the computations at stages 1), 2) and 4) only involve CPU, we first examine the runtime performance of these three stages. Table 7 lists the CPU runtime of these three stages on the three hardware platforms. As shown, among the three hardware platforms, the Galaxy S7 edge has the worst runtime performance. Among the three computing stages, fine-grained localization has the worst runtime performance. This is because it involves extracting HOG features which is computation intensive.

Platform	Coarse-Grained Localization	Fine-Grained Localization	Pill Retrieval
Desktop	0.2	6.1	1.2
Jetson TX1	0.5	39.8	2.7
Galaxy S7 edge	47.2	165.1	39.4

Table 7: CPU runtime of coarse-grained localization, fine-grained localization, and pill retrieval computing stages during inference (unit: ms).

Next we evaluate the runtime performance of stage 3) of all the six CNN models listed in Table 2 on the three platforms. Figure 10 illustrates the results and we have three observations. First, the CNN runtime on GPU is significantly lower than the CNN runtime on CPU across all six CNN models, demonstrating the significant superiority of GPU over CPU for running CNN models. For each CNN model, GPU achieves at least 30X speedup over CPU on the desktop platform; and at least 58X speedup on the mobile platforms (i.e., TX1 and S7 edge). Second, our model compression technique effectively reduces CNN runtime on both desktop and mobile platforms. Specifically, on the desktop platform, the student network (i.e., Model E) achieves 1.43X (163ms / 114ms) speedup on CPU

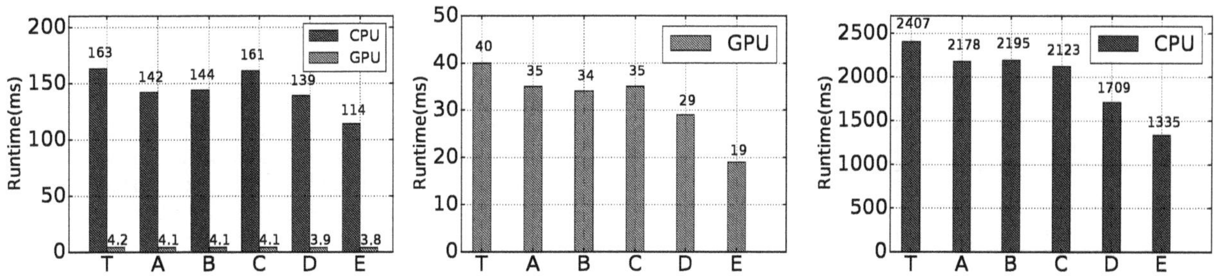

(a) CNN runtime performance on Desktop (b) CNN runtime performance on TX1 (c) CNN runtime performance on S7 edge

Figure 10: CNN runtime performance on three platforms (T = teacher network, E = student network).

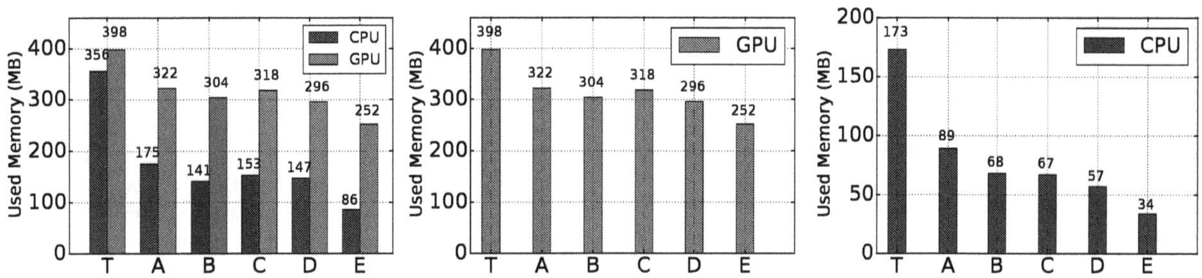

(a) CNN runtime memory usage on Desktop (b) CNN runtime memory usage on TX1 (c) CNN runtime memory usage on S7 edge

Figure 11: CNN runtime memory usage on three platforms (T = teacher network, E = student network).

and 1.1X (4.2ms / 3.8ms) speedup on GPU over the teacher network (i.e., Model T); on the mobile platforms, the student network achieves 1.8X (2407ms / 1335ms) speedup on CPU and 2.1X (40ms / 19ms) speedup on GPU over the teacher network. Finally, the reduction in runtime is not as significant as the reduction in FLOPS listed in Table 2. This is due to the parallel operations in the CNN inference implementations. As an example, on the desktop platform, the GPU runtime barely changes as the CNN model size decreases. This is because the operations on the GTX 1080 GPU are highly parallel.

6.3.2 Runtime Memory Usage

We evaluate the runtime memory usage of all six CNN models on the three platforms. To accurately measure the CNN runtime memory usage, for Galaxy S7 edge, garbage collection operation is invoked each time before we measure the runtime memory usage. For the desktop and Jetson TX1, we subtract the memory usage before the CNN model is loaded and only report the memory usage that is allocated to the CNN model only. Figure 11 illustrates the results. As shown, our model compression technique effectively reduces the CNN runtime memory usage on both desktop and mobile platforms. In particular, the student network only requires 34MB runtime memory to run on the commodity Samsung Galaxy S7 edge smartphone, achieving a reduction of 139MB runtime memory compared to its teacher network (173MB).

6.3.3 Energy Consumption

To evaluate the energy consumption of MobileDeepPill, we measure the average energy consumption at each computing stage during inference on two mobile platforms: Galaxy S7 edge and Jetson TX1. We use the Monsoon power monitor [3] to measure the power consumption of Galaxy S7 edge and the PWRcheck power analyzer [5] to measure the power consumption of Jetson TX1. We run 2000 inferences and report the average energy consumption at each stage. Table 8 and Table 9 show the energy consumption of Galaxy S7 edge and Jetson TX1 at each computing stage, respectively. As shown, the most power hungry stage is the CNN feature extraction. This is expected because CNN contains much more computing operations than any other stage. More interestingly, although the difference in power consumption between the teacher network and the student network is not large, due to the significant runtime reduction, the student network consumes much less energy than the teacher network, reducing energy consumption by 47.6% (from 13350mJ to 7000mJ) on Galaxy S7 edge and by 62.2% (from 471mJ to 178mJ) on Jetson TX1.

Stage	Power (mW)	Time (ms)	Energy (mJ)
Sleep	39.7	-	-
Screen-On	567.6	-	-
App-On	1180.9	-	-
Coarse-Grained Localization	2895.1	47.2	137
Fine-Grained Localization	2473.5	165.1	408
Teacher Network (CPU)	5546.2	2407	13350
Student Network (CPU)	5243.8	1335	7000
Pill Retrieval	3042.7	39.4	120
Total (Teacher)	-	-	14015
Total (Student)	-	-	7665

Table 8: Energy consumption on Samsung Galaxy S7 edge smartphone.

Stage	Power (mW)	Time (ms)	Energy (mJ)
Idle	3564.9	-	-
Coarse-Grained Localization	5711.3	0.5	3
Fine-Grained Localization	5849.5	39.8	233
Teacher Network (GPU)	11763.4	40	471
Student Network (GPU)	9378.7	19	178
Pill Retrieval	6533.1	2.7	18
Total (Teacher)	-	-	725
Total (Student)	-	-	432

Table 9: Energy consumption on Nvidia Jetson TX1.

Platform	Model	CPU	GPU
Galaxy S7 edge	Teacher Network	3560	-
	Student Network	6509	-
Jetson TX1	Teacher Network	-	68822
	Student Network	-	115500

Table 10: Estimated numbers of inferences with a 3600mAh battery.

Finally, we report the estimated number of inferences that can be performed with a fully charged 3600mAh battery, assuming an ideal discharge curve. As listed in Table 10, when the teacher network is used, S7 edge can process a total number of 3560 inferences. In comparison, when the student network is used, the total number of inferences can be processed is increased to 6509.

7. DISCUSSION AND FUTURE WORK

Impact on Pill Image Recognition Technology: MobileDeepPill represents the state-of-the-art mobile vision system for pill image recognition in unconstrained real-world settings. It demonstrates the superiority of deep learning-based approaches which learn features automatically over traditional approaches which use hand-crafted features designed based on domain knowledge. Given its promising performance and the prevalence of mobile phones, we envision that MobileDeepPill can become a widely used tool that provides people with a simple and convenient way to identify mystery pills and fetch pill information when needed.

Generality of MobileDeepPill: Although MobileDeepPill is designed for solving unconstrained pill image recognition problem using mobile phones, many techniques involved in MobileDeepPill can be generalized to the development of other mobile sensing systems with on-device deep learning algorithms. First, the quality of the sensor data collected by mobile sensing systems can be easily deteriorated by a variety of noises in unconstrained mobile conditions. The employment of triplet loss can enhance the resilience of mobile sensing systems to those noises. Second, modern mobile sensing systems normally utilize more than one sensing modalities to capture information from users and their surrounding environment. The multi-CNNs architecture can be applied to building mobile sensing systems that need to combine information from multiple sensor data sources. Finally, the general trend on developing new deep neural networks has been to make the networks larger and more complicated to maximize the recognition performance without considering model size and computational complexity. The Knowledge Distillation-based model compression technique can be applied to any large deep convolutional models to reduce their numbers of parameters and FLOPS so that the compressed models can efficiently run on the resource-limited mobile sensing systems.

Opportunities for Improvement: There are opportunities to make MobileDeepPill better. As an example, MobileDeepPill currently does not support recognizing multiple pills appeared in one image. To solve this issue, as the first step, algorithms that can accurately detect and localize multiple pills need to be developed. After the pills are localized and segmented, the orientation of each individual pill must be determined, and each pill must be oriented correctly before sending to the pill recognition system for identification. We leave it as our future work.

8. RELATED WORK

Our work is related to two research areas: 1) pill image recognition; and 2) deep neural network model compression. In this section, we provide a brief review of the most relevant work within each area.

Pill Image Recognition: Due to the lack of large openly available datasets, there are only a few works on pill image recognition, and most of them focus on pill images taken in well-controlled conditions. Lee *et al.* [21] developed a system called Pill-ID to recognize illicit pills using Hu moment and Grid intensity, where the illicit pills are of high quality and manually cropped. Caban *et al.* [8] proposed a pill recognition scheme using shape, imprint and color features. However, they used augmented images which were generated by random perturbation of the reference images to evaluate the system. All of these methods used hand-crafted features designed based on domain knowledge for recognition. In contrast, MobileDeepPill is the first work on developing deep learning-based approach to automatically learn the features for recognizing unconstrained pill images.

Deep Neural Network Model Compression: Model compression for deep neural networks has attracted significant attention in recent years due to the imperative demand on running deep learning models on resource limited platforms. In general, deep neural network model compression techniques can be grouped into two categories. The first category is focused on compressing pretrained large networks. For example, Han *et al.* [11] proposed a network pruning method that identifies important connections in the deep neural network and removes all the unimportant connections whose weights are lower than a threshold. Rastegari *et al.* [23] developed Binary-Weight-Networks and XNOR-Networks that compress networks by approximating standard convolutional operations using binary operations. Denton *et al.* [10] exploited the redundancy present within the convolutional filters to derive approximations using Singular Vector Decomposition (SVD) that significantly reduce the computation and memory footprint. The second category is focused on designing and training small networks directly. For example, Iandola *et al.* [16] proposed a squeeze layer that only has 1×1 filters to re-design the network architecture. The generated smart network achieves AlexNet-level accuracy with 50x fewer parameters. MobileDeepPill follows the idea of the second category. It uses a number of strategies to design a new network architecture with a much smaller footprint and learns the parameters of the smart network via the knowledge distillation framework [15].

9. CONCLUSION

In this paper, we presented the design, implementation and evaluation of MobileDeepPill, a small-footprint mobile vision system for recognizing unconstrained pill images. Based on a novel multi-CNNs architecture, MobileDeepPill achieves state-of-the-art pill image recognition performance with 52.7% Top-1 accuracy and 81.7% Top-5 accuracy in one-side pill recognition scheme as well as 73.7% Top-1 accuracy and 95.6% Top-5 accuracy in two-side pill recognition scheme. By leveraging a novel Knowledge Distillation-based deep model compression framework, MobileDeepPill only requires 34MB runtime memory to run the multi-CNNs model and is able to perform low-power, near real-time pill image recognition on commodity smartphones without cloud offloading. With the support of high-end mobile GPU, the runtime performance is significantly improved from 1.58s to 270ms.

10. ACKNOWLEDGEMENT

We would like to thank the National Library of Medicine (NLM) of the National Institutes of Health (NIH) for organizing the Pill Image Recognition Challenge and providing the pill image dataset. We are also grateful to the anonymous MobiSys reviewers for their valuable reviews and insightful comments. This research was partially funded by NSF awards #1565604 and #1617627.

11. REFERENCES

[1] Amazon Shopping Mobile App. https://itunes.apple.com/us/app/amazon-app-shop-scan-compare/id297606951?mt=8.

[2] Google Translate. https://play.google.com/store/apps/details?id=com.google.android.apps.translate&hl=en.

[3] Monsoon Power Monitor. https://www.msoon.com/LabEquipment/PowerMonitor/.

[4] NIH NLM Pill Image Recognition Challenge. https://pir.nlm.nih.gov/challenge/.

[5] PWRcheck DC power analyzer. http://www.westmountainradio.com/product_info.php?products_id=pwrcheck.

[6] Your Prescriptions and Your Privacy. https://www.privacyrights.org/consumer-guides/your-prescriptions-and-your-privacy-california-medical-privacy-series.

[7] S. Bhattacharya and N. D. Lane. Sparsification and separation of deep learning layers for constrained resource inference on wearables. In *Proceedings of the 14th ACM Conference on Embedded Network Sensor Systems CD-ROM*, pages 176–189. ACM, 2016.

[8] J. J. Caban, A. Rosebrock, and T. S. Yoo. Automatic identification of prescription drugs using shape distribution models. In *2012 19th IEEE International Conference on Image Processing*, pages 1005–1008. IEEE, 2012.

[9] T. Y.-H. Chen, L. Ravindranath, S. Deng, P. Bahl, and H. Balakrishnan. Glimpse: Continuous, real-time object recognition on mobile devices. In *Proceedings of the 13th ACM Conference on Embedded Networked Sensor Systems*, pages 155–168. ACM, 2015.

[10] E. L. Denton, W. Zaremba, J. Bruna, Y. LeCun, and R. Fergus. Exploiting linear structure within convolutional networks for efficient evaluation. In *Advances in Neural Information Processing Systems*, pages 1269–1277, 2014.

[11] S. Han, J. Pool, J. Tran, and W. Dally. Learning both weights and connections for efficient neural network. In *Advances in Neural Information Processing Systems*, pages 1135–1143, 2015.

[12] S. Han, H. Shen, M. Philipose, S. Agarwal, A. Wolman, and A. Krishnamurthy. Mcdnn: An approximation-based execution framework for deep stream processing under resource constraints. In *Proceedings of the 14th Annual International Conference on Mobile Systems, Applications, and Services*, MobiSys '16, pages 123–136, New York, NY, USA, 2016. ACM.

[13] K. He and J. Sun. Convolutional neural networks at constrained time cost. In *Proceedings of the IEEE Conference on Computer Vision and Pattern Recognition*, pages 5353–5360, 2015.

[14] K. He, X. Zhang, S. Ren, and J. Sun. Deep residual learning for image recognition. In *Proceedings of the IEEE Conference on Computer Vision and Pattern Recognition*, pages 770–778, 2016.

[15] G. Hinton, O. Vinyals, and J. Dean. Distilling the knowledge in a neural network. *arXiv preprint arXiv:1503.02531*, 2015.

[16] F. N. Iandola, M. W. Moskewicz, K. Ashraf, S. Han, W. J. Dally, and K. Keutzer. Squeezenet: Alexnet-level accuracy with 50x fewer parameters and< 1mb model size. *arXiv preprint arXiv:1602.07360*, 2016.

[17] A. Karpathy, G. Toderici, S. Shetty, T. Leung, R. Sukthankar, and L. Fei-Fei. Large-scale video classification with convolutional neural networks. In *Proceedings of the IEEE conference on Computer Vision and Pattern Recognition*, pages 1725–1732, 2014.

[18] A. Krizhevsky, I. Sutskever, and G. E. Hinton. Imagenet classification with deep convolutional neural networks. In *Advances in neural information processing systems*, pages 1097–1105, 2012.

[19] N. D. Lane, S. Bhattacharya, P. Georgiev, C. Forlivesi, L. Jiao, L. Qendro, and F. Kawsar. Deepx: A software accelerator for low-power deep learning inference on mobile devices. In *2016 15th ACM/IEEE International Conference on Information Processing in Sensor Networks (IPSN)*, pages 1–12. IEEE, 2016.

[20] Y. LeCun, Y. Bengio, and G. Hinton. Deep learning. *Nature*, 521(7553):436–444, 2015.

[21] Y.-B. Lee, U. Park, A. K. Jain, and S.-W. Lee. Pill-id: Matching and retrieval of drug pill images. *Pattern Recognition Letters*, 33(7):904–910, 2012.

[22] M. Lin, Q. Chen, and S. Yan. Network in network. *arXiv preprint arXiv:1312.4400*, 2013.

[23] M. Rastegari, V. Ordonez, J. Redmon, and A. Farhadi. Xnor-net: Imagenet classification using binary convolutional neural networks. *arXiv preprint arXiv:1603.05279*, 2016.

[24] F. Schroff, D. Kalenichenko, and J. Philbin. Facenet: A unified embedding for face recognition and clustering. In *Proceedings of the IEEE Conference on Computer Vision and Pattern Recognition*, pages 815–823, 2015.

[25] K. Simonyan and A. Zisserman. Very deep convolutional networks for large-scale image recognition. *arXiv preprint arXiv:1409.1556*, 2014.

[26] C. Szegedy, W. Liu, Y. Jia, P. Sermanet, S. Reed, D. Anguelov, D. Erhan, V. Vanhoucke, and A. Rabinovich. Going deeper with convolutions. In *Proceedings of the IEEE Conference on Computer Vision and Pattern Recognition*, pages 1–9, 2015.

[27] Y. Taigman, M. Yang, M. Ranzato, and L. Wolf. Deepface: Closing the gap to human-level performance in face verification. In *Proceedings of the IEEE Conference on Computer Vision and Pattern Recognition*, pages 1701–1708, 2014.

[28] B. Zhou, A. Lapedriza, J. Xiao, A. Torralba, and A. Oliva. Learning deep features for scene recognition using places database. In *Advances in neural information processing systems*, pages 487–495, 2014.

DeepEye: Resource Efficient Local Execution of Multiple Deep Vision Models using Wearable Commodity Hardware

Akhil Mathur[‡], Nicholas D. Lane[‡†], Sourav Bhattacharya[‡]
Aidan Boran[‡], Claudio Forlivesi[‡], Fahim Kawsar[‡]
[‡]Nokia Bell Labs, [†]University College London

ABSTRACT

Wearable devices with in-built cameras present interesting opportunities for users to capture various aspects of their daily life and are potentially also useful in supporting users with low vision in their everyday tasks. However, state-of-the-art image wearables available in the market are limited to capturing images periodically and do not provide any real-time analysis of the data that might be useful for the wearers.

In this paper, we present DeepEye - a match-box sized wearable camera that is capable of running multiple cloud-scale deep learning models locally on the device, thereby enabling rich analysis of the captured images in near real-time without offloading them to the cloud. DeepEye is powered by a commodity wearable processor (Snapdragon 410) which ensures its wearable form factor. The software architecture for DeepEye addresses a key limitation with executing multiple deep learning models on constrained hardware, that is their limited runtime memory. We propose a novel inference software pipeline that targets the local execution of multiple deep vision models (specifically, CNNs) by interleaving the execution of computation-heavy convolutional layers with the loading of memory-heavy fully-connected layers.

Beyond this core idea, the execution framework incorporates: a memory caching scheme and a selective use of model compression techniques that further minimizes memory bottlenecks. Through a series of experiments, we show that our execution framework outperforms the baseline approaches significantly in terms of inference latency, memory requirements and energy consumption.

Keywords

Wearables; deep learning; embedded devices; computer vision; local execution

1. INTRODUCTION

Mobile vision systems have been built for decades, with recent example systems from research including SenseCam [1], Gabriel [2] and ThirdEye [3]. All of these systems capture images from devices worn by the user which are then processed by vision algorithms for extracting high-level information in service of a range of applications; for example, cognitive assistance, physical analytics, mobile health, memory augmentation and lifelogging. Now even commercial systems of this type are for sale with the most popular examples being Google Glass [4] and the Narrative Clip [5]. Fortuitously, as wearable cameras start to become mainstream the ability of computational models to understand the images they collect has also undergone a revolution in its abilities. Powered by rapid innovation in the area of deep learning for some image tasks (recognizing a face [6], locating an image geographically [7], or deciding if an image is memorable or not [8]) these models are even equalling human performance.

However, currently there exists a huge gap between this growing computational ability to understand images and the ability of wearable resource constrained devices to execute them. While this is an active area of research [9, 10, 11, 12, 13, 14], still today virtually no *wearable* devices in either research or sold commercial locally process the images they collect with deep learning models; and are limited, at best to processing them in the cloud (e.g., systems like [15]) which exposes users to privacy risks as highly sensitive personal images are handled by a third party. In fact, many devices like the Narrative Clip simply capture the image, transfer them to the cloud for later analysis – and perform no local computation on the image at all. Alternatively, research prototypes like Gabriel [2] that is based on Google Glass do perform some mixture of local and cloud-based processing of images using shallow image modeling algorithms (that are not as accurate as deep learning models); but, this processing comes at a cost with Gabriel having only 1 or 2 hours of battery life (reported in [2]).

The aim of this paper is to explore the future of wearable vision systems, where devices can locally process images with bleeding edge deep learning algorithms towards realizing a wide range of mobile vision based applications. In this work, we aim to not investigate what will it take for a *single* deep vision model to run efficiently – instead we attempt to run *multiple* concurrent deep learning algorithms using a wearable form-factor prototype. *We believe this is a critical system design issue that will enable important ubiquitous computing and mobile computing applications, many of which are already developed and studied [1, 16, 17, 18, 19, 20, 21], but remain impractical for large-scale deployment because suitable wearable devices are not yet available.*

In this work we present the design, implementation and evaluation of *DeepEye*; a one-of-a-kind wearable that is capable of executing 5 state-of-the-art deep vision models entirely on the device on images that are periodically captured (with a default sampling rate of 30 seconds). DeepEye is unlike any current wearable vision device in its capability to process images without cloud support, an ability that affords critical privacy assurances to users who

Permission to make digital or hard copies of all or part of this work for personal or classroom use is granted without fee provided that copies are not made or distributed for profit or commercial advantage and that copies bear this notice and the full citation on the first page. Copyrights for components of this work owned by others than the author(s) must be honored. Abstracting with credit is permitted. To copy otherwise, or republish, to post on servers or to redistribute to lists, requires prior specific permission and/or a fee. Request permissions from permissions@acm.org.

MobiSys'17, June 19-23, 2017, Niagara Falls, NY, USA

© 2017 Copyright held by the owner/author(s). Publication rights licensed to ACM.

ISBN 978-1-4503-4928-4/17/06. . . $15.00

DOI: http://dx.doi.org/10.1145/3081333.3081359

can trust their images never have to leave the device. In its current form the prototype device weighs 60gm and it has dimensions of 44 X 68 X 12 mm (illustrations are available in Figures 1 and 8). Although it has general support for all forms of Convolutional (CNNs) and Deep Neural Network models (DNNs) [22] (the most popular two forms of deep learning) – we evaluate it within this paper while supporting deep models that perform the following image tasks: face recognition, counting salient images in a scence, visual scene recognition, object detection, age and gender assessment of faces and more unusually the prediction of the memorability of an image [8]. Using these models it would be possible to use DeepEye to realize a wide range of vision applications; for example, a life-logging application that smartly filters images based on their expected memorability. Importantly, under this workload DeepEye still manages to maintain a battery life of nearly 17 hours with it taking only 10.10 seconds (depending on the model set used) to compute all deep models.

Two core enablers allow DeepEye to provide these levels of efficient mobile image processing. The first is the hardware design that combines a Qualcomm Snapdragon 410 processor (the same found in many smartwatches) with a custom integrated carrier board of our own design consisting of a 5 megapixel camera sensor and a 2400 mAh LiPo battery. The second enabler is an inference pipeline optimized specifically to cope with the needs of multiple models. Multiple deep model inference execution presents specific bottlenecks separate to those of single models; for instance, it becomes impossible to always keep all layers for each model in memory. Our inference pipeline optimizes *at the level of individual deep learning layers* and builds on a fundamental inter-model optimization insight: namely, that CNNs are comprised of a combination of computation-heavy convolutional layers and memory-heavy fully-connected layers. While convolutional layers tax the memory resources lightly, they are computationally demanding; in contrast, fully-connected layers have the exact opposite resource demands. Due to these orthogonal resource demands of memory and compute, it is possible to schedule and batch layers together from multiple models that better maximizes the resource of constrained devices and avoids bottlenecks that prevents multiple deep models from being executed. This core idea is complemented with a layer caching scheme and a selective use of SVD-based layer compression that further minimizes memory bottlenecks.

Finally – to complement our system and resource efficiency focus – we investigate the accuracy of the deep models used within DeepEye by testing them against images collected by actual wearable cameras (specifically Narrative Clips [5]). This is important because these models were not trained with data captured by wearable cameras and this will negatively impact their performance. Typically their accuracy numbers are assessed with data that is not representative of wearable devices. To address this, more than 18,000 images are provided from the authors of [23] which we have further labeled with image entities (≈4000) using Amazon Mechanical Turk (detailed in § 5.6). Overall, our findings indicate that deep models' accuracy does (as expected) decline than typical reported values primarily due to the nature of egocentric images (e.g., low lighting conditions, object occlusion). As such, there is a clear need to fine-tune these deep models for objects and scenarios commonly found in egocentric images.

The scientific contributions of this work include:

- We design the proof-of-concept DeepEye wearable. This is a first-of-its-kind device that is capable of executing multiple deep learning based vision algorithms purely locally. Comparable wearables from research, and those available commercially, at best may be able to run just a single example deep model – but none are designed to, or capable of, executing multiple models.
- We develop an inference pipeline for wearables designed to meet the challenges faced when multiple models are being executed (large memory footprint, shear computational overhead). This pipeline primarily relies on increasing processor utilization by scheduling layers with orthogonal bottlenecks.
- We build prototype hardware to demonstrate the feasibility of our design. This prototype relies on a commodity SoC (containing both CPU and GPU) and is capable of capturing/processing images with 5 deep models within reasonable resource bounds.
- We perform an extensive evaluation of the performance of DeepEye including its: inference pipeline, hardware, and even the accuracy of these models using images typical of wearable devices. We show that relative to alternatives, like serially performing inference using all models, the DeepEye offer more than 1.7x gains in execution latency.

Device	Weight (gm)	Lifetime (hours)	Cloud?	Inference?
DeepEye	60	16	No	Yes
Gabriel [2]	42	1	Yes	Yes
SenseCam [1]	93.5	24	No	No
Autographer [24]	59	24	No	No
Narrative Clip [5]	19	30	No	No

Table 1: Comparison of DeepEye with recent and/or popular wearables from the literature and available commercially

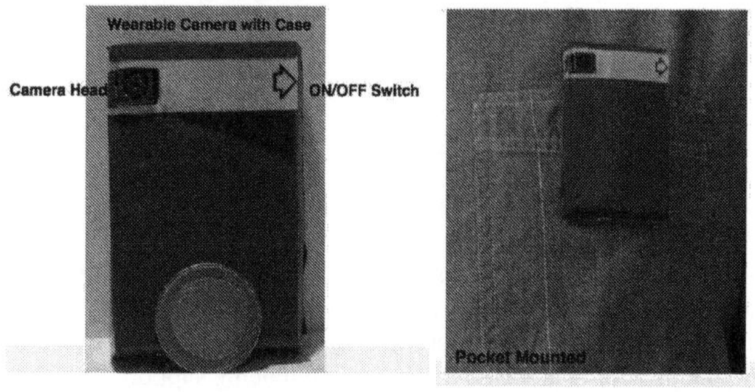

Figure 1: DeepEye Prototype. Device is comfortable being placed in the front pocket of the user's shirt.

2. DeepEye OVERVIEW

In this section we begin by systematically describing DeepEye and summarizing the capabilities of this wearable. DeepEye extends current capabilities of wearables by allowing simultaneous execution of multiple large-scale deep vision models locally in an efficient manner. The main use-cases of running multiple vision models include: (i) *logging of everyday* life, while capturing various aspects of the environment, (ii) providing navigation and social support for partially blind people in real-world situations, and (iii) enabling privacy-aware inferencing on personal devices by running all inferences on locally, completely avoiding cloud-based services. Moreover, as new sensors are becoming increasingly available on mobile platforms, application developers are adding new features that require a number of different inference tasks to be executed simultaneously.

2.1 Existing Camera Wearables

In Table 1, we summarize various camera-based wearable devices proposed in the literature as well as those commercially available

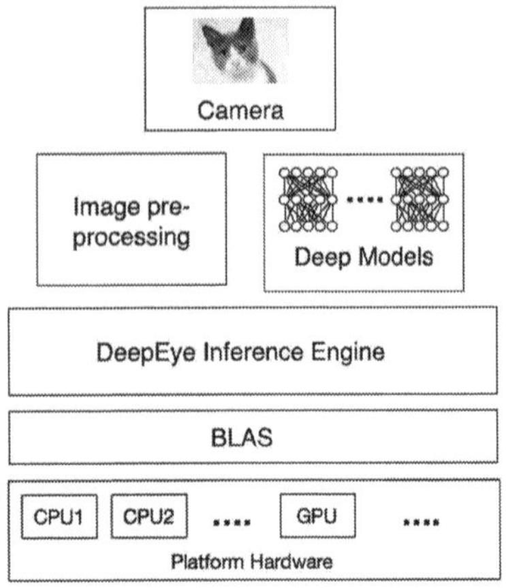

Figure 2: Software architecture of DeepEye

in the market, along with their form factors and capabilities. A common observation is that most camera-capture wearables such as Narrative Clip or Autographer only capture and stores images without providing any kind of context inferencing support. Further, devices such as the Gabriel [2] which provide inference on the collected images do so by offloading computations to a cloud backend. Contrary to existing wearables, DeepEye makes a significant leap forward by addressing technical challenges in simultaneously executing a number of very large vision models locally, which has not been attempted previously. Figure 1 illustrates a fully functional prototype of DeepEye.

2.2 Design Considerations

The primary design goal for DeepEye is to support the execution of multiple deep vision models locally on the device, which can enable a new class of applications for camera-based wearables. In this vein, the following three key design considerations have shaped the design of DeepEye:

- **Multiple Model Execution:** Study of how a system will behave, and what needs to be optimized when a number of models need to be locally executed periodically on the device. This means no single model can completely reside in memory constantly. This is also similar to the situation where a single large deep model is too big to reside completely at memory, this can become an increasingly critical issue due to the direction of deep models to be 100s and even 1000s layers deep – which is much larger than the 10 to 20 layers more often seen today.
- **Wearable Continous Vision Device:** The device should have a battery life able to last the typical waking hours of a day, within a form-factor that is comfortable for the user. Ideally a form-factor not significantly larger than existing devices today (such as the Narrative Clip) but still enabling a transformative increase in the amount of vision based deep models applicable to collected images.
- **Minimal Accuracy Loss Optimizations:** The device should minimize the accuracy losses associated with common optimization techniques which trade-off accuracy for resource reduction. As such, the core techniques we target in our design seek to increase the utilization of the device SoC and the efficiencies available in multiple model situations.

2.3 Architecture and Dataflow

We briefly describe the operation of DeepEye to provide context for how data is processed, and thus how the optimizations discussed in the following section are applied. Figure 2 depicts the overall architecture of our system, and its main components are as follows:

- **Layer Store Initialization:** Before DeepEye ever runs it must be initialized based on the collection of deep models to be executed. Each layer of the model is separated, and dependencies from the model architecture noted. DeepEye treats layers as the unit that are processed and once all layers of a model are processed then the output of the entire model is determined. At this phase logical dependencies between models can also be configured. For example, some models may only operate on face, therefore they should only be activated when a face is detected (by a face recognition model). Note: For the purposes of experiments all models execute regardless of such dependencies.
- **Sampling and Pre-processing:** At a configurable sampling rate images are taken and held temporarily for each deep model to be applied. At this phase the various types of pre-processing required by each model are applied so that their input layer can be initialized when it runs.
- **Inference Engine:** As described in the next section, this engine manages when different CNN layers are processed and how layers are cached to reduce overhead such as the paging in and out of layers. Individual layers are executed by DeepEye with the aim to reduce the resources consumed by all models collectively. The execution time of a total collection of models defines an upper bound on the camera sampling frequency; it is prohibited for the camera to sample photos at a rate faster than the system can process them locally. DeepEye can offer image inferences in the form of local API calls that applications can then be built.
- **BLAS:** In order to optimize the numeric operations on the hardware, DeepEye uses the optimized BLAS library for numeric computations. The inference engine passes the layers to be executed on the hardware to BLAS, which in turn distributes their computations across the multiple processors available on the device.

3. MULTIPLE MODEL DEEP INFERENCE PIPELINE

In this section we describe the inference pipeline of DeepEye. We begin by providing a primer on a Convolutional Neural Network (CNN) which is a popular deep learning model architecture for computer vision models. Next, we describe the major bottlenecks in running one or multiple CNN models on resource-constrained devices. To address these bottlenecks, we propose a new execution pipeline which includes a number of optimization strategies and a novel scheduling technique.

3.1 CNNs on Embedded Devices

Here we focus on the challenges associated with running CNN models on resource-constrained embedded devices. We begin by providing a brief overview of how a CNN model generates inference from the raw data, and then explain the challenges in executing the various layers of a CNN on embedded devices such as DeepEye.

Convolutional Neural Network Primer. CNNs are an alternative to DNNs (Deep Neural Networks) that still share many architectural similarities. As shown in Figure 3, a CNN is composed of one or more: convolutional layers, pooling or sub-sampling layers, and fully connected layers (with this final type being equivalent to those used in DNNs). The aim of these layers is to extract simple representations at high resolution from the input data, and then

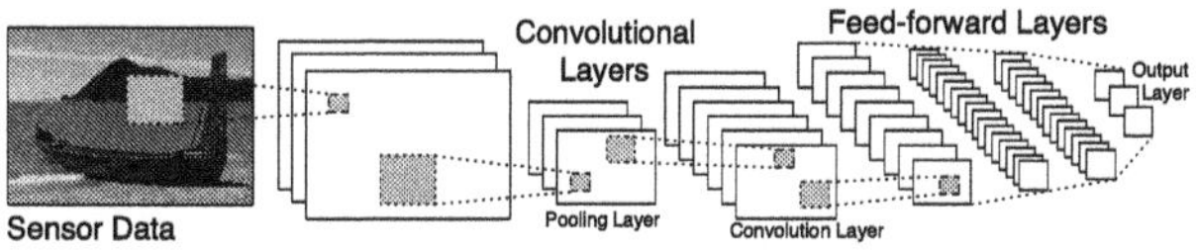

Figure 3: A CNN mixes convolutional and feed-forward layers.

converting these into more complex representations, but at much coarser resolutions within subsequent layers. This is achieved by first applying convolutional filters (with small kernel width) to capture local data properties. Next follow max or min pooling layers causing representations to be invariant to translations, this also acts as a form of dimensionality reduction. Finally, fully connected layers (i.e., a DNN) are applied to complete classification. Inference under a CNN operates only on a single segment of data (i.e., an image) at a time. Data is provided to convolutional layers at the head of the architecture. This can be considered a form of feature extraction before the fully connected layers are engaged. Inference then proceeds exactly as previously described for DNNs until ultimately a classification is reached.

CNN bottlenecks on resource-constrained devices. As has been reported in prior literature [9], the memory overhead in executing a deep model is dominated by the loading of weight parameters of fully-connected (fc) layers. In comparison, the convolutional kernels are small is size and take significantly less time to load. On the other hand, the computational overhead in deep model execution is dominated by the convolution operations, which are an order of magnitude higher than the matrix multiplication operations in the fc layers. In the context of wearable and embedded devices, the slow disc read and memory bus speed could be a major bottleneck is loading FC layers into the memory, and increase the latency of model execution. We study this bottleneck through a experiment on eight popular vision-based CNN models, where we run the models on an embedded platform (Qualcomm Snapdragon 410c) and measure the load and execution times of all the individual layers. In Figure 4 we summarize the results from this experiment and show the breakdown of average[1] time taken to load the fully-connected layers and execute the convolutional layers. The experiment reveals that on this embedded platform, the loading of fully-connected layers is the most expensive operation, even more than the loading and execution of convolutional layers by a factor of 1.3 (ObjectNet) to 2.15 (MemNet). As such, if we can explore opportunities to reduce the loading time of FC-layers, it will speed up the entire inference pipeline. In §3.2, we propose employing layer caching and layer compression techniques on the FC-layers to achieve latency gains in execution of deep models on constrained devices.

Bottlenecks in running multiple CNNs on embedded devices. As the demand for simultaneously running a number of deep models increases, we quickly run into a situation when the available memory on an embedded platform becomes insufficient to hold all the deep models. Under this situation, a common strategy is to run the deep models sequentially, i.e., loading one model at a time, run inferencing and clearing model memory before moving on to the next model. However this repeated paging-in and paging-out of large models adds significant overhead to the inference process, especially in the case of continuous inference systems such as DeepEye. Moreover, there can be cases where a deep model is so large that it cannot fit into the available memory on an embedded platform – in these scenarios, a common approach is to break the deep

[1] All models have been executed 100 times and we report the average here.

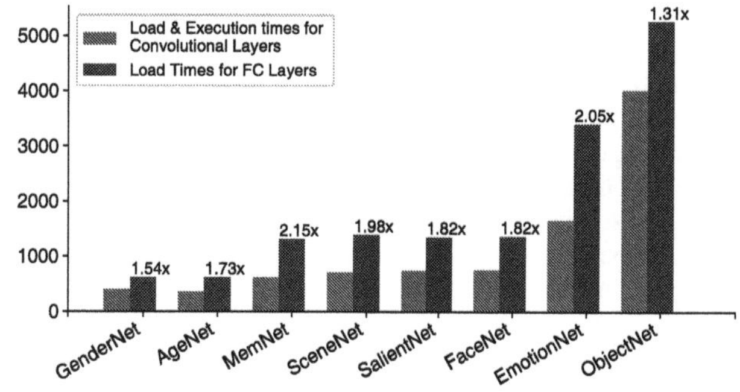

Figure 4: Understanding the bottleneck in deep vision model execution on embedded platforms. Loading model parameters is the single most time consuming task, which was seen across eight different models popular within the computer vision community.

model into its constituent layers, which are then paged-in to memory and executed in series. Even then, the bottleneck associated with loading of model parameters into memory still exists, and in fact it is amplified due to the presence of multiple deep models. In §3.2, we present a new technique of scheduling the execution of deep model layers which provides latency gains over the series execution – our approach exploits a key property of CNN models which is that the execution of layers follow a strict order (i.e. fc layers are executed on the output of the convolution layers), and aims to interleave the execution of convolution layers with loading of FC layers.

3.2 DeepEye Inference Engine

In this section, we present an overview of the inference pipeline used by DeepEye for executing multiple CNN models on resource-constrained devices. The key innovation in the pipeline is a novel approach of interleaving the loading of fully-connected layers with the execution of convolutional layers. We also discuss how our inference pipeline incorporates layer caching, model compression, and image hashing (detailed in § 3.3) to provide additional latency gains over the baseline approaches. Note that the pipeline is independent of the underlying processor, and can be applied to any available processor (e.g., CPU, DSP) on the system.

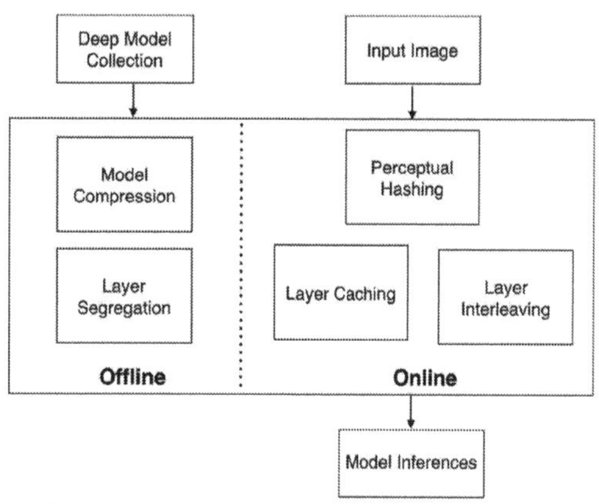

Figure 5: Overview of the DeepEye Inference Engine

Figure 5 illustrates the various components of the deep inference engine. The inference engine is initialized offline by segregating all model layers into computation- and memory-heavy layers, i.e. convolutional and fully-connected layers respectively. Next, the engine allows various kinds of model compression techniques to be applied on the pool of layers. Currently, DeepEye supports the SVD-based layer compression technique proposed in the DeepX toolkit [25] for model compression, however more techniques could be added in future. In the online phase while computing the inference, the engine reads an input image from the camera, calculates a perceptual hash vector [26] (detailed in the subsequent sections) for the image, and compares it with the hash values of the last five images. If the hash similarity is above a certain threshold (i.e., the images are similar), the inference pipeline is terminated and the inference output corresponding to the nearest hash vector is returned. If the image hash does not match the previous five images, the inference pipelines continues by applying various pre-processing steps on the image to generate the necessary input expected by the individual models in the pipeline. Once the preprocessing of the image is completed, the results are immediately fed to the input layer (convolutional layers) of all the models. Thereafter, the caching and interleaved execution of convolution and FC layers take place (detailed in § 3.3), which finally results in an inference output for each model. The inference results are then written to the disc or can be passed onto any user-facing apps through API calls.

3.3 Optimization Techniques

In the following subsections, we discuss each of the optimization techniques employed by the DeepEye engine.

Runtime Interleaving: The core runtime optimization in DeepEye's execution pipeline is based on the idea of processing different layers from a pool of deep vision models in parallel to reduce the execution latency. As discussed above, the loading of FC layers and the execution of convolution layers are the two most expensive operations in running a deep model on embedded devices. Interestingly, due to the feed-forward inferencing followed in deep models, the memory-heavy FC layers are only executed after the input is fully processed by the convolution layers – as such, the loading of FC layers can potentially be interleaved with the execution of convolution layers. Naturally, the case of multiple model inferences allows for greater opportunities to parallelize the aforementioned execution and loading processes across multiple models.

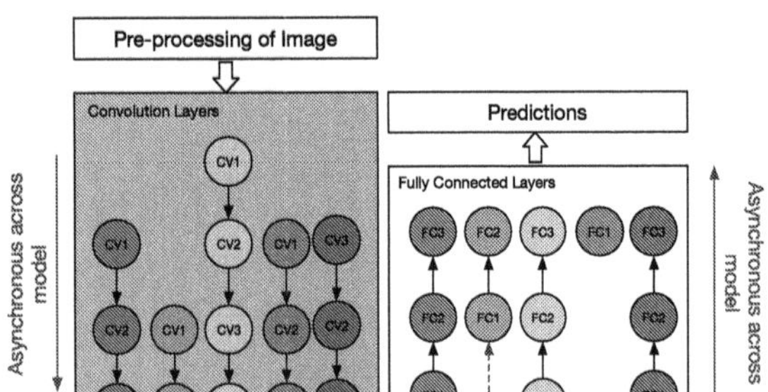

Figure 6: Runtime interleaving of convolutional and FC layers

Figure 6 depicts the overview of the runtime interleaving for an example case of five deep models. As indicated before, we first segregate all model layers into two pools, namely convolution layers and fully-connected layers. We next spawn two threads, namely *convolution-execution* thread and *data-loading* thread. In the convolution-execution thread, the convolution filter parameters of all models are loaded into the memory and the convolution operations begin on the pre-processed input data for each model. We take advantage of the underlying BLAS numeric library used in our implementation (detailed in § 4.2) to perform efficient multi-threaded numerical operations (e.g., convolutions) – as such we do not spawn separate convolution-execution threads for each model. Instead we adopt a FIFO queue based execution strategy for the convolutional layers across models. For example, as shown in Figure 6, three layers of convolution operations for red model are carried out by this thread, which are followed by two layers of yellow and three layers of the grey model. The *data-loading* thread which is spawned in parallel with the convolution thread is responsible for loading the FC layer parameters for all models into the memory, again in a pipelined manner (i.e., one model after the other).

The objective of the *convolution-execution* thread is to perform all convolutions on the input image, and pass the results of the final convolution layer of each model to the *data-loading* thread. When the *data-loading* thread finishes loading the FC layer parameters for a model, it can use the pre-computed convolution outputs from the *convolution-execution* and proceed to obtain the final classification results.

The latency gain G from runtime interleaving can be computed as:

$$G = \frac{t_{conv} + t_{fc\_load}}{max\{t_{conv}, t_{fc\_load}\}} \quad (1)$$

where, t_{conv} represents the time taken to load the convolution filters and execute the convolution operations for all models, and t_{fc_load} represents the time taken to load all FC layer parameters into the memory. As such, the numerator in Equation 1 corresponds to the baseline case where convolution execution and loading of FC layers is done in series, while the denominator corresponds to the interleaved execution where the total time is the maximum of both threads' execution times. Note that the eventual execution of FC layers on the output generated from the convolutional layers in common in both series and interleaved approaches – as such, it is not accounted for while calculating the latency gain (G) due to interleaving.

The denominator of equation 1 can be simplified using the following equation which expresses the maximum of two numbers in terms of their sum and difference:

$$max\{a, b\} = \frac{1}{2}(a + b + |a - b|) \quad (2)$$

By substituting (2) in (1), we get:

$$\begin{aligned} G &= \frac{2}{1 + \frac{|t_{fc\_load} - t_{conv}|}{t_{fc\_load} + t_{conv}}} \\ &= \frac{2}{1 + \lambda} \end{aligned} \quad (3)$$

where $\lambda = \frac{|t_{fc\_load} - t_{conv}|}{t_{fc\_load} + t_{conv}}$ stands for the *interleaving factor* and captures the difference between t_{conv} and t_{fc_load}. As λ increases, the interleaving gain G decreases – and when $\lambda = 0$ (i.e., time taken to load the FC layers is the same as time taken to run the convolutions), the gain G is maximized to 2x. In § 5, we experiment with different values of λ to showcase interleaving gains in multiple scenarios.

Caching of Memory-Heavy Layers: For continuous-sensing applications and devices such as DeepEye, caching of layer parameters into the memory could be potentially useful, as it saves significant time required to load thousands of parameters into memory for each inference. As loading the parameters for fully connected layers is one of the main time-consuming operations in the inference process, the idea strategy would be the keep all parameters of these FC layers into memory. However, the limited runtime memory on the embedded devices becomes a bottleneck to load all the layer parameters, more so in the case of executing multiple deep models.

DeepEye adopts a greedy approach for caching the layers parameters of the FC layers to maximize memory utilization. It monitors the available runtime memory and caches the k largest FC layers from the model pool that can fit into the memory. In case the available memory cannot fit all k layers, it caches $k-1$ largest layers, and again greedily repeat the process to cache the second-largest layers into the remaining memory. As layer caching effectively reduces the total load time for the FC layers (t_{fc_load}), it is likely to reduce the value of λ and increase the latency gains by interleaving.

Model Compression: In addition to layer caching, another potential approach to reduce the load times of the memory-heavy FC layers is to employ model compression techniques. The goal of model compression techniques is to reduce the size and execution latency for a single deep model, at the expense of some accuracy loss. In our work, we use the SVD-based layer factorization approach proposed in the DeepX toolkit [25, 27] to compress the FC layers of all deep models. The SVD-factorization technique takes the weight matrix containing the matrix multiplication parameters for two adjacent FC layers, and factorizes it into two matrices which together contain lesser parameters than the original matrix. As a result of this factorization, the total number of parameters in the FC layers are reduced, which in turn lowers the load time of the FC layers (t_{fc_load}). This also reduces the value of λ (as the difference between t_{fc_load} and t_{conv} reduces), and hence increases the latency gains (G) from interleaving. However, it is interesting to note that if too much compression (C) is applied to the FC layers such that $t_{conv} > C * t_{fc\_load}$ i.e., if the convolution execution time starts dominating the FC loading operation, then the gains due to compression will no longer be observable.

Pre-empt using Hashing: In continuous image capture systems such as DeepEye, it is likely that consecutively captured images are similar in their content – this situation often arises in everyday life logging, for e.g., when the wearer is stationary or the capture device is kept on a table. If the system can identify such similar images, it need not run the entire inference pipeline on the image, and a significant amount of computations and energy could be saved over time. Although, stationary conditions can be adequately detected by inertial sensors like accelerometer, in this work we rely on an image-based hashing technique to detect image similarity. More specifically, we apply a *perceptual hashing* algorithm [26] on the input images and store hash values of the last five images along with their predictions. Perceptual hashing functions are widely used to establish the *perceptual similarity* of multimedia content – this is done by extracting a series of features from the content (i.e., the raw image) and applying a hash function on those features. DeepEye uses the Radial Variance Based Hash function as implemented in [26]. When a new image is captured, we first compute the hash of the image and then calculate its *hamming* distance to all five previously stored hashes. If the hamming distance is found to be smaller than a predefined threshold, we then pre-empt execution of all deep models and return the classes stored for the image with smallest hamming distance. In our implementation we use a distance threshold of 26, which is suggested by the developers of the hashing algorithm.

4. EMBEDDED IMPLEMENTATION

In this section we describe the hardware implementation of DeepEye with a quad-core Qualcomm Snapdragon 410 processor. We

Figure 7: DeepEye Hardware Prototype

also describe our current software implementation designed to run multiple deep models on DeepEye using the Torch framework.

4.1 Hardware Prototype

DeepEye is powered by a quad-core Qualcomm Snapdragon 410 processor on a custom integrated carrier board, and includes a 2400 mAh LiPo battery. We intend to open-source the design of DeepEye hardware soon to help other researchers build similar wearable devices.

Snapdragon 410 Series APQ8016. The DeepEye wearable camera consists of a System On Chip (SOC) mounted on a carrier board as shown in Figure 8. The SOC has a quad core ARM processor (Snapdragon 410 Series APQ8016 from Qualcomm), a Qualcomm Adreno 306 GPU, 8GB of flash storage and 700MB of usable RAM. The carrier board allows the SOC to be plugged in and provides ports for a Camera Serial Interface (CSI) camera, a UART for programming and debug, i2C and SPI GPIOs for connecting sensors.

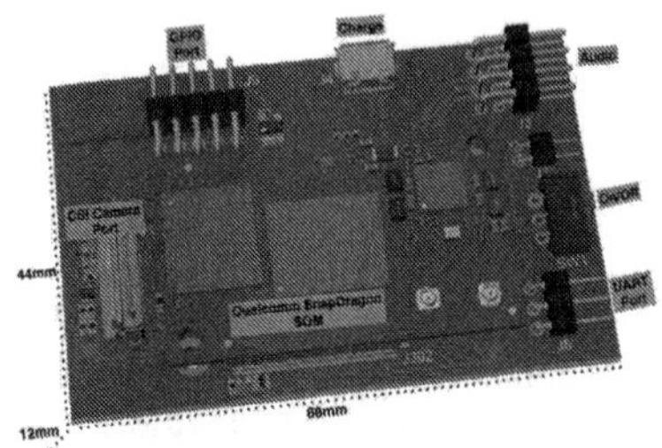

Figure 8: DeepEye Qualcomm SoC and Custom Integrated Carrier Board

Custom Integrated Carrier Board. The carrier board is powered by a 3.7v LiPo battery. The SoC provides power management and recharging circuitry while the carrier board provides a micro usb connector for charging. The DeepEye wearable runs a custom build of Linaro Debian linux based on the 4.3 Linux kernel. The custom build adds driver support of high-speed CSI camera and removes unused devices (HDMI bridge, DSI panel, USB hub) by using a custom Linux kernel and device tree. The camera module uses a 5 Megapixels Omnivision OV5640 camera sensor.

The DeepEye wearable has a small form factor (44 X 68 X 12 mm), and includes a 2400mAh LiPo battery. The device weights 24gm without the battery, and 60 gm with the battery attached to it, thus making it practical for everyday use.

4.2 Software Implementation

Our current software implementation for DeepEye uses an optimized version of the Torch deep learning framework for doing inference on the embedded device. The motivations for using Torch were the availability of state-of-the-art vision models for this framework, and its excellent portability to embedded platforms. By removing non-essential components from the Torch framework, we were able to keep these benefits while also reducing the overhead of the framework relative to a custom C++ runtime. We now discuss the major components of our implementation:

BLAS Runtime. While executing deep model inferencing, the main computational load remains in performing matrix multiplications [28, 25, 27]. In our current implementation of DeepEye we use the highly optimized BLAS library [29] for running the convolutions and the matrix multiplications needed in the fully-connected layers. In the current implementation we use Torch as our deep learning inferencing engine, which supports multi-threading for deep model execution. The Torch framework loads the model layers into the memory and send them to the BLAS library for computation. Thereafter, BLAS distributes the actual computational tasks across the CPU or GPU cores as specified by the model. Note that DeepEye is agnostic to the underlying deep learning framework and can be easily integrated with other engines supporting multi-threaded execution, e.g., TensorFlow and Theano.

Control Subsystem. We implement the data-flow runtime as described in §2 in the following manner. DeepEye camera captures an image every 30 seconds, and saves it to the disk. This image is then loaded in the Torch framework and a number of pre-processing operations are done on it. Although these operations are specific to each deep model, they broadly include cropping, resizing and mean normalization of the input image.

Next, the deep vision models are read from the storage and loaded into the shared memory in a layer-wise manner by Torch, that is each layer is paged-in the memory, where it operates on its input data and generates the input for the next layer. Thereafter, the layer is paged-out of memory and the next layer is paged-in. As described in §3, these load/execute are done in series in the baseline case and by applying interleaving (and other optimizations) in our proposed approach.

DeepEye is capable of using both the CPU and GPU on Snapdragon 410c for running convolution operations. The Snapdragon on-board GPU however lacks OpenCL support, therefore we implemented an Open-GL based Convolution Engine (described in next subsection) which can run convolution operations using OpenGL shaders. When the system has to compute a convolution (which is the dominant operation in the initial layers of a CNN), it can execute the operation on the quad-core CPU (using Torch) or on the GPU (using the Open-GL engine).

Open-GL Convolution Acceleration. OpenGL is a 3-D drawing specification which allows applications to accelerate graphics using an accelerated rendering pipeline implemented in the GPU. Recently a subset of OpenGL, named OpenGL ES, has made it possible for other computational algorithms to execute on the GPU, if they could map their data into graphical objects, such as bitmaps, textures and vertex buffers. In the case of deep learning models, our key idea is to represent the input to a convolution layer as a bitmap object, then apply an OpenGL Shader to it to convert it to another bitmap, which is then fed to the subsequent layers.

5. EVALUATION

In this section, we first benchmark the performance of various optimization techniques described in §3 viz. layer interleaving, layer caching, and model compression against the baseline approach of executing deep models in a layer-wise fashion. Next, we present two case studies inspired by real-world applications of DeepEye and highlight latency and energy gains achieved by our proposed inference pipeline. Note that we take a CPU-centric approach in our experiments – i.e., all experiments were conducted on the on-board quad-core CPU of DeepEye. Later, we also discuss using the on-board GPU for running the inference pipeline and highlight why it does not add to any latency gains. Our main findings can be summarized as follows:

- DeepEye can last for more than 33 hours on a single battery charge, assuming an image is captured and analyzed by the deep learning models every minute.
- Our proposed execution approach of layer interleaving and layer caching results in nearly 2x gains in runtime over the baseline method of series execution.
- The interleaved execution technique could work in tandem with model compression, and serve as a way to offset the accuracy losses due to compression while providing comparable latency gains.

5.1 Methodology

We used the Qualcomm Dragonboard 410c, which is the development board for the Snapdragon 410 processor to perform the experiments for evaluating the performance of DeepEye and its optimization techniques. For energy measurements, we instrumented the power lead of the Dragonboard 410c to connect an Ammeter to it. We also disabled those peripherals (e.g. HDMI port, SD Card, WiFi chip) on the Dragonboard which are not present on DeepEye to get accurate energy measurements. As representative workload for our experiments, we used eight state-of-the-art pre-trained deep learning models trained for a variety of computer vision tasks. In the next section, we present more details about the deep models used for evaluation.

Deep Models: In total, we used eight CNN models of varying sizes and computational complexities that are representative of common vision tasks. All these models are pre-trained and available as open-source models from Torch or Caffe framework websites. A summary of these models is also presented in Table 2.

FaceNet [30]: Face detection is a popular task for any image capturing system, and is a necessary step for algorithms which aim to detect smile or emotions in an image. Here, we use a face detection CNN model that can detect faces in a wide range of orientations.

AgeNet and GenderNet [31]: AgeNet and GenderNet models aim to predict the age (8 categories) and gender (2 categories) of a person from an input image. The models have been trained using around 20K images.

EmotionNet [32]: This model aims to recognize the emotion on a person's face by analyzing the input image. The input to this model is a cropped RGB image of the face, and it outputs confidence scores for 8 different emotions: angry, disgust, happy, sad, surprise, fear and neutral. The authors of this model also offer additional emotion recognition models, all of which when used together offer state-of-the-art performance – however, for the sake of experimentation - we only use the model that operates on RGB values.

SalientNet [33]: This model aims to compute the saliency of an input image, by predicting the existence and the number of salient objects in a given scene. Models such as SalientNet could be particularly useful to filter out non-salient images from the lifelog outputs.

ObjectNet [34]: Detecting various objects present in an image is of utmost importance to both our representative use-cases. For this, we consider a popular CNN model named VGG which supports more than 1000 object classes (e.g., dog, car).

MemNet [35]: The aim of this model is to determine how memorable an image is (with actual output being a "memorability score"). Experiments indicate MemNet has the ability to select images that

Scenario	Model	Size	Architecture
Lifelogging	SceneNet	240MB	c:8[†]; p:3[‡]; fc:3[*]
Lifelogging	MemNet	233MB	c:8[†]; p:3[‡]; fc:3[*]
Lifelogging	SalientNet	233MB	c:8[†]; p:3[‡]; fc:3[*]
Vision Support	AgeNet	46MB	c:3[†]; p:3[‡]; fc:3[*]
Vision Support	GenderNet	46MB	c:3[†]; p:3[‡]; fc:3[*]
Vision Support	EmotionNet	419MB	c:5[†]; p:3[‡]; fc:3[*]
Both	FaceNet	230MB	c:8[†]; p:3[‡]; fc:3[*]
Both	ObjectNet	553MB	c:13[†]; p:5[‡]; fc:3[*]

[†]*convolution layers*; [‡]*pooling layers*; [*]*fully connected layers*

Table 2: Representative deep models and scenarios used for evaluating DeepEye

are memorable with similar success to those of human labelers. This model could also be potentially useful to assist lifeloggers in browsing through the thousands of images captured by DeepEye.

SceneNet [36]: A total of 476 scene types are recognized by this model. Example scenes include: bedrooms, kitchens, forests.

Scenarios. We logically group the deep models into two scenarios to illustrate practical use-cases of DeepEye, namely *i) lifelogging*, and *ii) vision support*. Lifelogging, i.e. capturing and archiving our everyday lives, has been a primary use-case for camera-based wearable devices such as the Microsoft SenseCam and Narrative Clip. For demonstrating a lifelogging scenario with DeepEye, we use models which can detect objects, places, faces in an image, along with inferring the saliency and memorability of the image. Another important application for camera wearables could be to support users with visual impairment, in that the wearable can analyze the captured images and provide non-visual (e.g. audio or haptic) feedback to the user. For demonstrating this scenario, we chose models that could detect the faces or object in an image, along with inferring the age, gender and emotion of people in the image. Both scenarios along with the models associated with them are summarized in Table 2.

5.2 Interleaving Analysis

Here we evaluate the impact of layer interleaving on the overall inference time of deep models. We first show the gains achieved in inference time by using layer interleaving in both application scenarios mentioned earlier. Then we empirically validate the sensitivity of interleaving gains as shown in Equation 3, by varying the value of the *interleaving factor* λ.

Setup. To evaluate the benefits of interleaving, we run the five deep models in each scenario in both series (baseline) and interleaved manner. No other optimization (e.g., caching, compression) is applied to the models. Next, in order to explore the sensitivity of interleaving as per Equation 3, we constructed model pipelines of various sizes in both scenarios. For example, in a scenario with 5 models, there are $^5C_2$ possible pipelines of 2 models in it, $^5C_3$ pipelines of 3 models and so on. In total, we generated 52 different pipelines for both scenarios, with each pipeline having a different length and combination of models. We executed each pipeline in the baseline Series condition and calculated the value of *interleaving factor* λ for it. Then we ran each pipeline in an interleaved way and calculate the inference time gain over the baseline condition. Below we present our findings for both the experiments.

Results. Figure 9 illustrates the reduction in inference time in the interleaved case for both scenarios. We clearly observe a reduction in inference time in both scenarios (1.29x in Lifelogging scenario and 1.4x in the Vision Support scenario), although the magnitude of reduction is different. To explore it further, in Figure 10, we plot

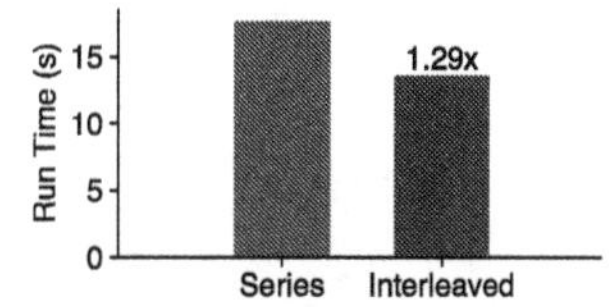

(a) Scenario: Lifelogging

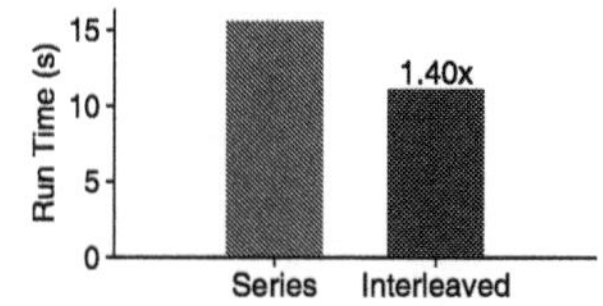

(b) Scenario: Vision Support

Figure 9: Latency comparison between series and interleaved execution. The values on the bars show the latency gains due to interleaved execution.

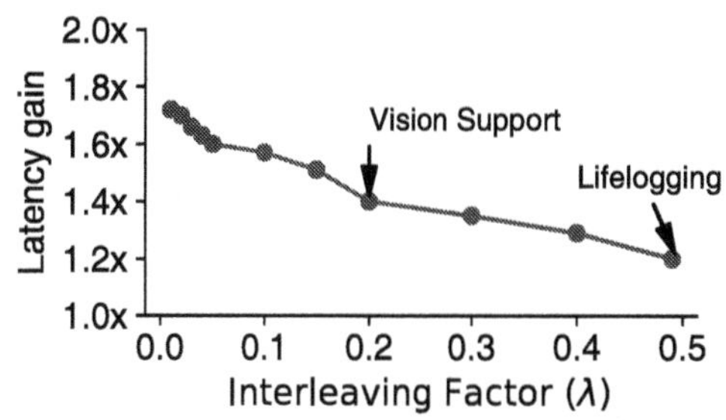

Figure 10: Latency gain under different values of λ

the latency gain (due to interleaving) against 10 different values of λ obtained from executing various combination of model pipelines. We can observe that as the value of λ increases, the latency gains due to interleaving decrease. As λ is proportional to the difference between execution time of convolution layers and load time of FC layers, this implies that if both these times are of the same order, the interleaving gains are maximized. For example, the Lifelogging scenario has a higher value of λ than the Vision Support scenario (due to the choice of models in them), and therefore exhibits lower latency gains.

To sum up, we found the interleaved execution provides a way to maximize the resource usage on the device, and provides latency gains without any loss in inference accuracy.

5.3 Interleaving Meets Model Compression

Our findings from interleaving analysis shows that although interleaving outperforms the baseline series execution, its latency gain has an upper bound of 2x when t_{fc_load} equals t_{conv} (Equation 3). However, this is difficult to achieve in practice as the loading times of FC layers are higher than the execution times of the convolution layers as shown in the model profiles in Figure 4. In this section, we investigate if model compression techniques proposed in the literature can reduce the load times of the FC layers, thereby increasing the latency gains in the interleaved execution.

Setup. For studying model compression, we choose four deep models from our model pool, namely SceneNet, MemNet, SalientNet, and FaceNet. On each model, we apply four levels of compression using the SVD-based weight factorization scheme proposed in prior literature such as the DeepX toolkit [25, 27, 37]. The SVD-based compression approach reduces the total parameters (and operations) in a fully-connected layer by factorizing it into two smaller layers, with some loss in overall inference accuracy. Our experiments apply four levels of compression (10%, 20%, 70%, 80%) to all FC-layers of the deep models, and we report the latency gains in each compression setting. The motivation to apply high compressions (70%, 80%) is to empirically show that the compression gains peak at a certain point, after which compression does not provide any additive gains to the interleaved execution.

Results. In Figure 11, we compare the performance of interleaved execution approach against series baseline and model compression

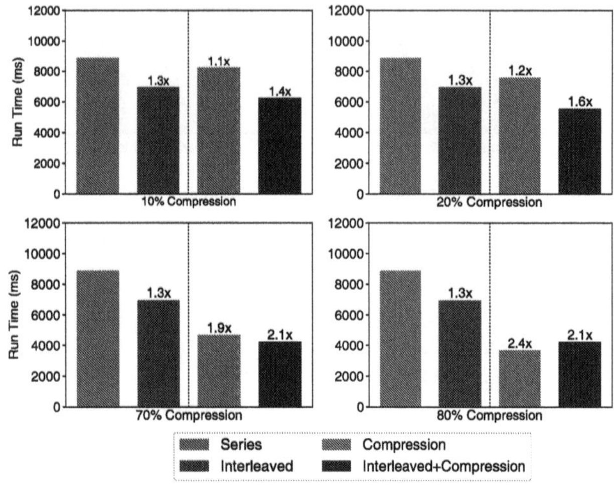

Figure 11: Performance of layer interleaving in combination with model compression approaches. The values on the bars show the latency gain in each case over the baseline Series execution approach.

for our selected 4-model pipeline. There are three key insights that emerge from Figure 11: firstly, as the compression ratio increases, the latency gain also increases for both compression-only approach and compression+interleaving, with the latter outperforming the other techniques. For example, in the 20% compression scenario, applying interleaving with compression provides a latency gain of 1.6x, as opposed to 1.2x provided by compression alone. Secondly, we observe that when the amount of compression applied to the model is too high (e.g., 80%), the interleaved execution no longer benefits from it, because the convolution execution starts dominating the overall runtime in the interleaved case. Finally, it is evident that interleaving can be used as a tool to offset against the accuracy loss caused by model compression. For example, we found that with 30% compression applied to the models, the pipeline can run 1.4x faster in the baseline case (not represented in the figure). However, the same 1.4x speedup can be achieved by applying 10% compression and interleaving the execution of layers as shown in Figure 11. As such, interleaving provides a way to get same latency gains with lesser compression and lesser accuracy losses.

5.4 Caching Analysis

In this section, we explore the benefits of caching memory-heavy layers on the overall runtime of the deep model pipeline. For continuous sensing wearables, caching of memory-heavy layer parameters into the memory could be potentially useful, as it saves significant time required to load thousands of parameters into memory for each inference.

Setup. For this experiment, four deep models from the Table 2 namely SceneNet, MemNet, SalientNet, and FaceNet are chosen as the workload. Although DeepEye has roughly (5̃70 MB) of available runtime memory, other low-end wearable devices often have much less runtime memory. As such, for a detailed evaluation of the caching approach, we simulate three more cases with runtime memory of 150MB, 300MB, and 400MB. In each case, we adopt a greedy approach to cache the n largest FC layers from the model pool into the memory. In case the available memory cannot fit all n layers, then we cache $n-1$ largest layers, and again greedily repeat the process to cache the second-largest layers into the remaining memory. In the following, we compare the latency gains by layer caching in series and interleaved execution approaches.

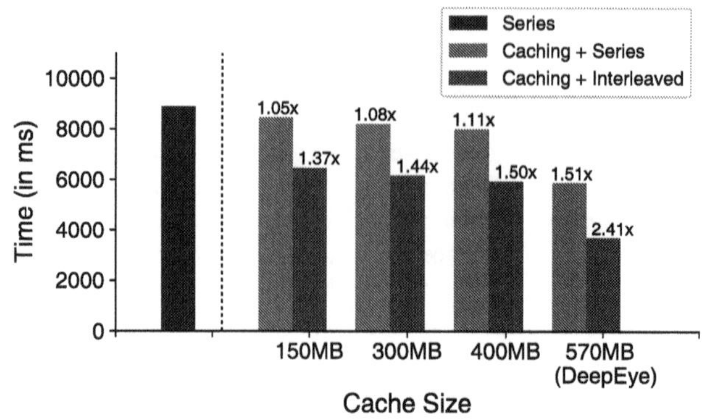

Figure 12: Performance of layer interleaving in combination with layer caching. The values on the bars show the latency gain in each case over the baseline Series execution approach.

Scenario	Latency per inference	Estimated Battery Life
Lifelogging	10.10s (1.74x gain)	33 hours
Vision Support	8.23x (1.88x gain)	43 hours

Table 3: Performance of DeepEye in the two application scenarios

Results. Figure 12 shows that as the runtime memory available on the device increases, we are able to cache more FC-layer parameters into the memory and hence achieve higher latency gains for both series and interleaved caching scenarios. For example, with 570MB available memory (as is the case on DeepEye), the caching-series execution approach gives a 1.51x latency gain whereas the caching-interleaved execution provides a 2.41x speedup over the baseline. Interestingly, it is worth noting that the interleaved-caching approach is able to provide a similar speedup (1.5x) with 400MB of runtime memory, whereas the caching-series approach would need an additional 170MB runtime memory to achieve the same speedup. As such, constrained devices with limited runtime memory can benefit by implementing the interleaved-caching mechanism for deep model execution.

The findings from the above experiments highlight the gains in inference latency on applying the various optimization techniques used by DeepEye. In the next section, we will present two case studies where we apply these optimizations on two real-world applications of continuous camera capture devices.

5.5 Case Studies

In this section, we evaluate the performance of DeepEye on the two scenarios described in previous section, namely *i) lifelogging*, and *ii) vision support*. Each scenario consist of five deep learning vision models as summarized in Table 2. We begin by presenting the overall performance when these scenarios are run on DeepEye, and then present detailed latency and energy results.

DeepEye Performance: We applied layer caching, compression, and interleaving to the pool of deep model layers and calculated the latency and energy consumed for performing one inference. Battery life is estimated from the per-inference energy consumption, assuming that an inference will be made every 1 minute. In Table 3, we show the per-inference latency and battery life of DeepEye when it executes each of the application scenarios. We observe the DeepEye provides at least 1.74x latency gain for both application scenarios, and the estimated battery life for the device is more than 33 hours.

Execution time: Here we provide a detailed breakdown of the inference execution time for both the scenarios. For each scenario, we compare the baseline Series execution approach against the interleaved execution approach, with various optimizations (caching, compression) added to it. For scenario #1 (Lifelogging), we cached the largest fully connected layers of FaceNet, MemnNet and SalientNet into the memory, while for use-case #2 (Visual Impairment Support), we stored in memory the first fully-connected layers of VGG, GenderNet and AgeNet. As for model compression, we applied a 20% compression to each FC layer by using the SVD-based factorization approach discussed earlier.

In Figures 13a and 13b, we plot the total time taken to run the two model pipelines on the DeepEye CPU in four different execution conditions. The results are averaged over 10 iterations. We observe that the baseline approach of loading and running the layers in series without caching has the worst runtime performance – the time taken to run the entire inference pipeline being 17.57 seconds (in Scenario 1) and 15.51 seconds (in Scenario 2). On the contrary, layer interleaving in combination with caching and compression outperforms all other approaches – the runtime for the model pipeline in Scenario 1 and Scenario 2 are 10.10 seconds (~1.74x faster than baseline) and 8.23 seconds (~1.88x faster than baseline) respectively.

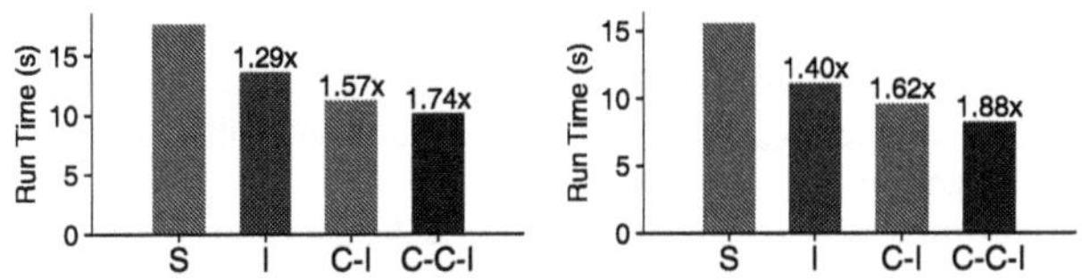

(a) Scenario: Lifelogging (b) Scenario: Vision Support

Figure 13: Latency comparison when executing the scenario pipelines on DeepEye. S = Series, I = Interleaved, C-I = Caching+Interleaved, C-C-I = Compression+Caching+Interleaved

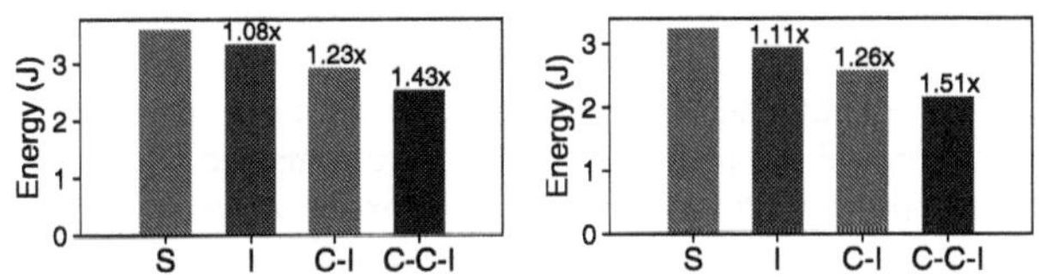

(a) Scenario: Lifelogging (b) Scenario: Vision Support

Figure 14: Energy comparison when executing the scenario pipelines on DeepEye. S = Series, I = Interleaved, C-I = Caching+Interleaved, C-C-I = Compression+Caching+Interleaved

Energy Performance. We measured the average current flow during each execution of a model pipeline, and used it to calculate the total energy consumption. In Figures 14a and 14b, we plot the energy consumed to run the two scenarios on DeepEye in various experiment conditions. Our findings show that by applying caching and compression in the interleaved execution case, DeepEye requires nearly 1.43x less energy than the baseline approach. Although the observed energy saving for one single execution may not be considered significant, these savings get compounded over time and can result in few additional hours of battery life as we will discuss next.

In Figure 15, we show the effect of image capture frequency on the expected battery life of DeepEye. These calculations were done by adding the energy consumption during idle time, energy cost of taking a picture, and the cost of one execution of the model pipeline. We observe that in the case of an image being captured and analyzed every 30 seconds, DeepEye's battery will last 16.85 hours for the Lifelogging scenario and 21.6 hours for the Vision Support scenario using our proposed optimization techniques. In a more reasonable case of an image being captured and analyzed every 1 minute, the battery lasts for 33 hours (9 hours more than the baseline) for Lifelogging and 43 hours (12 hours more than baseline) for the Vision Support scenario.

Hashing Performance. Now we present the findings of applying the *perceptual hashing* technique (discussed in §3) on a dataset of 18,735 egocentric images as described in §5.6. We chose a window-size of 5, that is we compute and store hash values of five recent images in the workload. For each new image, we compute its hash and calculate its hamming distance to all previously stored hashes. With a distance threshold of 26 (as suggested by the developers of the hashing algorithm), we found that for roughly 18% of all images in the dataset, we could pre-empt the execution of all deep models and return the classes stored for the image with smallest hamming distance. This approach eventually results in significant energy savings, and increases the battery life of the device.

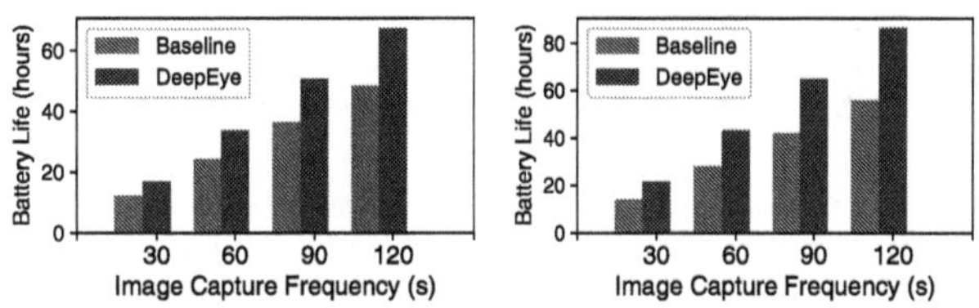

(a) Scenario: Lifelogging (b) Scenario: Vision Support

Figure 15: Comparison of estimated battery life of DeepEye assuming different image capture frequencies. This does not include energy gains from perceptual hashing, which will increase the battery life of DeepEye.

GPU execution. Finally, we evaluated the runtime of our model pipelines by running them on both CPU and GPU. While executing the models on a GPU, we observed a 1.6x gain in execution of the convolution layers over CPU-only approach. However, as the CPU and GPU have a shared memory on the Snapdragon 410c, the loading time of fully connected layers into the memory remains the primary bottleneck. As such, even with faster convolution operations on the GPU, we do not gain much in terms of the overall inference time due to the bottleneck of loading fc layer parameters into the memory – moreover, using the GPU consumes additional energy which reduces the battery life of the wearable. Therefore, in the current version of DeepEye, we only employ the CPU for doing model computations.

5.6 Inference Accuracy

In this subsection we discuss the accuracy of the deep learning models used in our experiments on egocentric images. Note that the deep models used in our experiments were pre-trained on a wide variety of images, not specifically on egocentric images captured from a wearable. As such, we would like to understand how well these models perform on egocentric images, and whether they need extensive re-training in the future.

Dataset. For our evaluation, we used the egocentric image dataset from the authors of [23], which consists of a total of 18,735 images captured by 7 users wearing a Narrative Clip for 20 days. The Narrative Clip has the same camera resolution as DeepEye, therefore its images are representative of what will be captured by DeepEye. The dataset is rich in diversity, as the users were wearing the Narrative Clip in different contexts: while attending a conference, on

Figure 16: Examples of egocentric images captured from a Narrative Clip

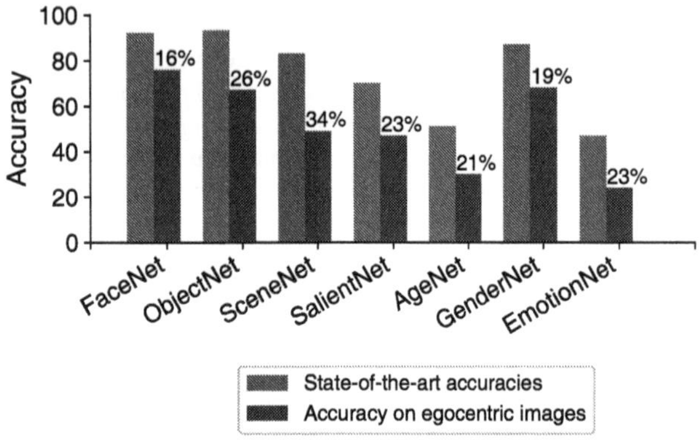

Figure 17: Accuracy of the pre-trained deep models on egocentric images. Numbers on the bars represent accuracy loss compared to the state-of-the-art accuracies, which happes because the models are not fine-tuned for egocentric images.

holiday, during the weekend, and during the week. A sample of the images in the dataset is shown in Figure 16.

Ground Truth Collection. The dataset from [23] is largely unlabeled for evaluating the models used in our experiment, with the exception of face labeling. For a subset of 4912 images in the dataset, the authors have labeled whether the image consists of a 'face' or not. As such, these images could be used to evaluate the accuracy of FaceNet in our experiments. To collect the ground truth for evaluation of other models, we ran two crowdsourcing tasks on Amazon Mechanical Turk.

In the first task, we asked workers to choose labels for the face images (extracted from the original dataset) viz. their age (8 age categories), gender (male/female) and emotion (7 categories). The label choices were the same as the output classes in AgeNet, GenderNet and EmotionNet. In the second task, we asked workers to label 4000 different images from the dataset viz. the number of salient objects in them (for evaluating SalientNet), objects seen in the image (for evaluating ObjectNet) and the places seen in the image (for evaluating SceneNet). While the original ObjectNet and SceneNet models consist of 1000 and 205 classes respectively, we only asked the workers to choose from object and scene classes that are expected to be captured in routine life (e.g. laptop, office, home, building, cup, fruit). We did not evaluate the accuracy for MemNet as it was difficult for crowd workers to label the memorability of an image captured by somebody else.

Results. Before presenting the results, it is worth pointing that none of the models used in our experiments were fine-tuned for egocentric images. Egocentric images typically have poor lighting conditions, multiple objects in them and they may even have the object or person of interest occluded by other objects – thereby making it challenging to get an accurate inference.

In Figure 17, we plot the accuracy of the models as observed on the egocentric image database. For ObjectNet and SceneNet, we present the top-5 accuracies, that is the ground-truth category is within the top-5 predicted categories. For other models, we present the top-1 accuracy. We observe that the face-based models, such as FaceNet, AgeNet, GenderNet, and EmotionNet have lower accuracies drops (numbers shown on top of the bars) as compared to the state-of-the-art accuracies. On the other hand, models which aim to analyze the scene (e.g., SceneNet or ObjectNet) reported much higher accuracies drops. Specifically for SceneNet, images captured indoors (e.g. at home in the evening) had a high number of misclassifications – we believe that the poor indoor lighting conditions made it challenging for the classifier to infer the location. Overall, these results suggest that fine-tuning the pre-trained models on egocentric images is required to achieve their reported accuracies.

6. DISCUSSION

We now discuss a key set of issues related to the design and evaluation of DeepEye.

Beyond Just Vision-based Deep Models. We believe the optimization techniques described will operate successfully even in models that are not image based. Our design of DeepEye and the optimizations we discover exploits characteristics of layers (such as fully-connected feed-forward layers in relation to other layer types) that should be suitable for other mobile platforms that target other uses of deep learning. For example, audio understanding and emotion recognition.

Relevance of Deep Learning Specific Accelerators. Existing accelerators such as [38, 39] are not able to execute multiple deep models as DeepEye is able to. While their performance for individual models we use (such as AlexNet and VGG based models) may execute more efficiently on this purpose-built hardware, how they will support multiple model situations remains unstudied.

Complementary to Many Existing Optimizations. Because model-centric techniques that use sparse-coding [27], SVD [40], node pruning [41] alter the layers of deep models themselves they are compatible with scheduling and caching approaches we develop here. As we show in the evaluation when the proposed methods and such model compression techniques are combined, the performance impact with respect to the accuracy trade-off can be impressive and better than the trade-offs possible with the original technique itself.

User Trials of DeepEye. Currently DeepEye has not yet been deployed. The focus of this work has been the development of hardware and software techniques that at this stage are evaluated through a trace-dataset. However, we will begin deployments of these devices for limited periods of time moving forward.

Improving Deep Model Accuracy. In this work we report some of the first observations of deep models running against egocentric first-person images as are captured by wearable cameras like DeepEye. To our knowledge, our work along with [15] has evaluated the accuracy of these techniques on such image workloads. We reported that the inference accuracies for all models drop when they are applied on egocentric images. These reported accuracy numbers are expected to improve when techniques such as fine-tuning are applied to these models using the training images captured by DeepEye.

Privacy Concerns. Like any wearable camera, with DeepEye there are significant potential privacy concerns that must be respected. For this reason DeepEye never retains any images at any stage. Only inference results are kept. This is quite unlike most wearables that perform heavy image processing that will most often rely on the cloud. Users also benefit from a very simple mental model of where their data is and is not. They can assure themselves that data never leaves DeepEye unless they install an application that does so.

7. RELATED WORK

DeepEye follows in a line of wearable and mobile vision systems that have been prototyped for decades. Relatively recent examples include SenseCam [1], Gabriel [2] and ThirdEye [3]. A central difference to these systems is that DeepEye performs image processing using deep learning models; this is significant because this brings state-of-the-art models for various image task to a wearable platform, rather either simplified alternative learning algorithms executing locally or complex models running remotely. While few mobile systems (such as smartphones [42, 43]) and virtually no wearable systems (i.e., those with a smaller form factor) use a single deep learning for local processing, in contrast DeepEye integrates multiple concurrently executing models. DeepEye explores an area that is only just emerging (cloud-free deep learning for mobile vision), and more than that leaps beyond existing systems with single models to study what we believe will be a important upcoming step; specifically, how these systems can cope with (and benefit from) multiple executing deep learning models.

More importantly, DeepEye contributes significantly as a enabler of experiments to study these issues because all hardware and software will be open-sourced. In the area of mobile vision, perhaps the central systems question has been how these systems can be made to be energy (and more broadly resource) efficient [12, 14]. The DeepEye wearable and its cloud-free focus allows us to further understand when and if the cloud should be incorporated especially in relation to multiple deep model scenarios. Few studies of this type currently exist into the performance of deep models on mobile hardware; those that do exist (such as [28]) have not yet examined the multi-model problem, and more importantly have not made the type of observations for future optimizations in this area that we have done in this paper (see earlier section). SDKs for using mobile GPUs and deep models are starting to arrive (such as [11]). In contrast, other directions being take start at a more algorithmic level and consider how the models themselves can be different towards being more efficient [13, 44]. But interestingly most of the understanding of mobile and optimized deep learning currently exists in commercial settings (such as [42]) although software approaches to cloud offloading [9] and device-side acceleration [45] are arriving. The experiments we report here are some of the first to focus specifically on large deep models designed for image processing on a wearable. Examples of deep learning on wearables form-factors are very rare up to this point and have not considered the CNN architecture needed for images; in comparison work like [46] and [47] consider LSTM and RBMs respectively.

Finally, a key part of the future of deep learning on mobiles and wearables undoubtedly will include consideration of custom hardware. Such hardware options are evolving in research [48][39] and in industry [38]; DeepEye contributes to this examination by exploring the limit of conventional hardware through the combination of a conventional processor and custom supporting daughter board. Interesting ideas in co-design involving low-level ML components and sennsor array are also emerging towards more efficicent vision processing systems [10]. But because DeepEye leverages a general-purpose hardware its observations will more easily translate into other more popular SoCs, than deep learning specific hardware options. Furthermore, the observations for rethinking and optimizing the software-based inference pipeline is just as needed as any hardware innovations because, as we highlighted here, many optimization opportunities exist within the inference algorithms available.

8. CONCLUSION

In this paper, we empirically study two key areas pertaining to mobile vision systems moving forward. First, the raw feasibility, and overall system performance, of wearable form-factor devices to meet the needs of cloud-free deep learning-based vision processing of periodically captured images. We study this within the context of a powerful conventional small form-factor processor, and purpose-built daughter board, under a real-world image workload of ≈4000 images collected from a user trial with actual commercial wearable device. Second, we focus on a key aspect of execution support for these models – namely, the challenges presented by simultaneous inference of multiple models on the same image. This will be a building block behavior of vision systems as most applications require multiple types of analysis (i.e., multiple models) to be performed on a single image. We highlighted the core bottlenecks with executing multiple deep models on constrained devices, and proposed methods to manage these issues in the inference process when concurrent images are processed. We believe our techniques will be of broad interest for mobile systems and vision researchers at large, and will lead to more research in this space.

9. REFERENCES

[1] S. Hodges, L. Williams, E. Berry, S. Izadi, J. Srinivasan, A. Butler, G. Smyth, N. Kapur, and K. Wood, "Sensecam: A retrospective memory aid," in *UbiComp 2006: Ubiquitous Computing*. Springer, 2006, pp. 177–193.

[2] K. Ha, Z. Chen, W. Hu, W. Richter, P. Pillai, and M. Satyanarayanan, "Towards wearable cognitive assistance," in *Proceedings of the 12th Annual International Conference on Mobile Systems, Applications, and Services*, ser. MobiSys '14. New York, NY, USA: ACM, 2014, pp. 68–81. [Online]. Available: http://doi.acm.org/10.1145/2594368.2594383

[3] S. Rallapalli, A. Ganesan, K. Chintalapudi, V. N. Padmanabhan, and L. Qiu, "Enabling physical analytics in retail stores using smart glasses," in *Proceedings of the 20th Annual International Conference on Mobile Computing and Networking*, ser. MobiCom '14. New York, NY, USA: ACM, 2014, pp. 115–126. [Online]. Available: http://doi.acm.org/10.1145/2639108.2639126

[4] "Google Glass," https://developers.google.com/glass/distribute/glass-at-work.

[5] "Narrative Clip 1," http://getnarrative.com/narrative-clip-1.

[6] Y. Taigman, M. Yang, M. Ranzato, and L. Wolf, "Deepface: Closing the gap to human-level performance in face verification," in *Conference on Computer Vision and Pattern Recognition (CVPR)*, 2014.

[7] T. Weyand, I. Kostrikov, and J. Philbin, "Planet - photo geolocation with convolutional neural networks," *CoRR*, vol. abs/1602.05314, 2016. [Online]. Available: http://arxiv.org/abs/1602.05314

[8] A. Khosla, A. S. Raju, A. Torralba, and A. Oliva, "Understanding and predicting image memorability at a large scale," in *International Conference on Computer Vision (ICCV)*, 2015.

[9] S. Han, H. Shen, M. Philipose, S. Agarwal, A. Wolman, and A. Krishnamurthy, "Mcdnn: An execution framework for deep neural networks on resource-constrained devicesg," in

Proceedings of the 14th Annual International Conference on Mobile Systems, Applications, and Services, 2016.

[10] M. Philipose, "Efficient object detection via adaptive online selection of sensor-array elements," in *Proceedings of the Twenty-Eighth AAAI Conference on Artificial Intelligence*, ser. AAAI'14. AAAI Press, 2014, pp. 2817–2823. [Online]. Available: http://dl.acm.org/citation.cfm?id=2892753.2892942

[11] L. N. Huynh, R. K. Balan, and Y. Lee, "Deepsense: A gpu-based deep convolutional neural network framework on commodity mobile devices," in *Proceedings of the 2016 Workshop on Wearable Systems and Applications*, ser. WearSys '16. New York, NY, USA: ACM, 2016, pp. 25–30. [Online]. Available: http://doi.acm.org/10.1145/2935643.2935650

[12] R. LiKamWa, B. Priyantha, M. Philipose, L. Zhong, and P. Bahl, "Energy characterization and optimization of image sensing toward continuous mobile vision," in *Proceeding of the 11th Annual International Conference on Mobile Systems, Applications, and Services*, ser. MobiSys '13. New York, NY, USA: ACM, 2013, pp. 69–82. [Online]. Available: http://doi.acm.org/10.1145/2462456.2464448

[13] H. Shen, S. Han, M. Philipose, and A. Krishnamurthy, "Fast video classification via adaptive cascading of deep models," *arXiv preprint arXiv:1611.06453*, 2016.

[14] P. Bahl, M. Philipose, and L. Zhong, "Vision: cloud-powered sight for all: showing the cloud what you see," in *Proceedings of the third ACM workshop on Mobile cloud computing and services*. ACM, 2012, pp. 53–60.

[15] D. Castro, S. Hickson, V. Bettadapura, E. Thomaz, G. Abowd, H. Christensen, and I. Essa, "Predicting daily activities from egocentric images using deep learning," in *Proceedings of the 2015 ACM International Symposium on Wearable Computers*, ser. ISWC '15. New York, NY, USA: ACM, 2015, pp. 75–82. [Online]. Available: http://doi.acm.org/10.1145/2802083.2808398

[16] P. Kelly, A. Doherty, E. Berry, S. Hodges, A. M. Batterham, and C. Foster, "Can we use digital life-log images to investigate active and sedentary travel behaviour? results from a pilot study," *Int J Behav Nutr Phys Act*, vol. 8, no. 44, p. 44, 2011.

[17] A. Grimes, M. Bednar, J. D. Bolter, and R. E. Grinter, "Eatwell: sharing nutrition-related memories in a low-income community," in *Proceedings of the 2008 ACM conference on Computer supported cooperative work*. ACM, 2008, pp. 87–96.

[18] R. Sarvas and D. M. Frohlich, *From snapshots to social media-the changing picture of domestic photography*. Springer Science & Business Media, 2011.

[19] I. Li, A. K. Dey, and J. Forlizzi, "Understanding my data, myself: supporting self-reflection with ubicomp technologies," in *Proceedings of the 13th international conference on Ubiquitous computing*. ACM, 2011, pp. 405–414.

[20] H. Pirsiavash and D. Ramanan, "Detecting activities of daily living in first-person camera views," in *Computer Vision and Pattern Recognition (CVPR), 2012 IEEE Conference on*. IEEE, 2012, pp. 2847–2854.

[21] A. J. Sellen, A. Fogg, M. Aitken, S. Hodges, C. Rother, and K. Wood, "Do life-logging technologies support memory for the past?: an experimental study using sensecam," in *Proceedings of the SIGCHI conference on Human factors in computing systems*. ACM, 2007, pp. 81–90.

[22] L. Deng and D. Yu, "Deep learning: Methods and applications," Tech. Rep. MSR-TR-2014-21, January 2014. [Online]. Available: http://research.microsoft.com/apps/pubs/default.aspx?id=209355

[23] M. Dimiccoli, M. Bolaños, E. Talavera, M. Aghaei, S. G. Nikolov, and P. Radeva, "Sr-clustering: Semantic regularized clustering for egocentric photo streams segmentation," *arXiv preprint arXiv:1512.07143*, 2015.

[24] "Autographer," http://getnarrative.com/narrative-clip-1.

[25] N. D. Lane, S. Bhattacharya, C. Forlivesi, P. Georgiev, L. Jiao, L. Qendro, , and F. Kawsar, "Deepx: A software accelerator for low-power deep learning inference on mobile devices," in *IPSN 2016*.

[26] "Perceptual Hashing," http://www.phash.org/.

[27] S. Bhattacharya and N. D. Lane, "Sparsification and separation of deep learning layers for constrained resource inference on wearables," in *ACM Conference on Embedded Networked Sensor Systems (SenSys)*, 2016.

[28] N. D. Lane, S. Bhattacharya, P. Georgiev, C. Forlivesi, and F. Kawsar, "An early resource characterization of deep learning on wearables, smartphones and internet-of-things devices," in *Proceedings of the 2015 International Workshop on Internet of Things Towards Applications*, ser. IoT-App '15. New York, NY, USA: ACM, 2015, pp. 7–12. [Online]. Available: http://doi.acm.org/10.1145/2820975.2820980

[29] "BLAS library," http://www.netlib.org/blas/.

[30] S. S. Farfade, M. J. Saberian, and L.-J. Li, "Multi-view face detection using deep convolutional neural networks," in *Proceedings of the 5th ACM on International Conference on Multimedia Retrieval*. ACM, 2015, pp. 643–650.

[31] G. Levi and T. Hassner, "Age and gender classification using convolutional neural networks," in *Proceedings of the IEEE Conference on Computer Vision and Pattern Recognition Workshops*, 2015, pp. 34–42.

[32] G. Levi and T. Hasner, "Emotion recognition in the wild via convolutional neural networks and mapped binary patterns," in *Proceedings of the 2015 ACM on International Conference on Multimodal Interaction*, 2015, pp. 503–510.

[33] J. Zhang, S. Ma, M. Sameki, S. Sclaroff, M. Betke, Z. Lin, X. Shen, B. Price, and R. Mech, "Salient object subitizing," in *Proceedings of the IEEE Conference on Computer Vision and Pattern Recognition*, 2015, pp. 4045–4054.

[34] K. Simonyan and A. Zisserman, "Very deep convolutional networks for large-scale image recognition," *arXiv preprint arXiv:1409.1556*, 2014.

[35] A. Khosla, A. S. Raju, A. Torralba, and A. Oliva, "Understanding and predicting image memorability at a large scale," in *Proceedings of the IEEE International Conference on Computer Vision*, 2015, pp. 2390–2398.

[36] B. Zhou, A. Lapedriza, J. Xiao, A. Torralba, and A. Oliva, "Learning deep features for scene recognition using places database," in *Advances in neural information processing systems*, 2014, pp. 487–495.

[37] N. Lane, S. Bhattacharya, A. Mathur, C. Forlivesi, and F. Kawsar, "Dxtk: Enabling resource-efficient deep learning on mobile and embedded devices with the deepx toolkit," in *Proceedings of the 8th EAI International Conference on Mobile Computing, Applications and Services*, ser. MobiCASE'16. ICST, Brussels, Belgium, Belgium: ICST (Institute for Computer Sciences, Social-Informatics and Telecommunications Engineering), 2016, pp. 98–107.

[Online]. Available: https://doi.org/10.4108/eai.30-11-2016.2267463
[38] "Movidius," http://www.movidius.com/.
[39] T. Chen, Z. Du, N. Sun, J. Wang, C. Wu, Y. Chen, and O. Temam, "Diannao: A small-footprint high-throughput accelerator for ubiquitous machine-learning," in *Proceedings of the 19th International Conference on Architectural Support for Programming Languages and Operating Systems*, ser. ASPLOS '14. New York, NY, USA: ACM, 2014, pp. 269–284. [Online]. Available: http://doi.acm.org/10.1145/2541940.2541967
[40] J. Xue, J. Li, and Y. Gong, "Restructuring of deep neural network acoustic models with singular value decomposition," in *INTERSPEECH*, 2013, pp. 2365–2369.
[41] S. Han, J. Pool, J. Tran, and W. Dally, "Learning both weights and connections for efficient neural network," in *Advances in Neural Information Processing Systems (NIPS)*, 2015, pp. 1135–1143.
[42] "How Google Translate squeezes deep learning onto a phone," http://googleresearch.blogspot.co.uk/2015/07/how-google-translate-squeezes-deep.html.
[43] "Happy Halloween! Baidu Research Introduces FaceYou," http://uk.reuters.com/article/idUKnMKWYbQbJa+1ea+MKW20151029.
[44] S. Venkataramani, V. Bahl, X.-S. Hua, J. Liu, J. Li, M. Phillipose, B. Priyantha, and M. Shoaib, "Sapphire: an always-on context-aware computer vision system for portable devices," in *2015 Design, Automation & Test in Europe Conference & Exhibition (DATE)*. IEEE, 2015, pp. 1491–1496.
[45] N. D. Lane, S. Bhattacharya, P. Georgiev, C. Forlivesi, L. Jiao, L. Qendro, and F. Kawsar, "Deepx: A software accelerator for low-power deep learning inference on mobile devices," in *Proceedings of the 15th International Conference on Information Processing in Sensor Networks*, 2016.
[46] T. Beltramelli and S. Risi, "Deep-spying: Spying using smartwatch and deep learning," *CoRR*, vol. abs/1512.05616, 2015. [Online]. Available: http://arxiv.org/abs/1512.05616
[47] S. Bhattacharya and N. D. Lane, "From smart to deep: Robust activity recognition on smartwatches using deep learning," in *Proceedings of the Second Workshop on Sensing Systems and Applications Using Wrist Worn Smart Devices*, 2016.
[48] R. LiKamWa, Y. Hou, J. Gao, M. Polansky, and L. Zhong, "Redeye: Analog convnet image sensor architecture for continuous mobile vision," in *International Symposium on Computer Architecture (ISCA)*, 2016.

DeepMon: Mobile GPU-based Deep Learning Framework for Continuous Vision Applications

Loc N. Huynh, Youngki Lee, Rajesh Krishna Balan
Singapore Management University
{nlhuynh.2014, youngkilee, rajesh}@smu.edu.sg

ABSTRACT

The rapid emergence of head-mounted devices such as the Microsoft Holo-lens enables a wide variety of continuous vision applications. Such applications often adopt deep-learning algorithms such as CNN and RNN to extract rich contextual information from the first-person-view video streams. Despite the high accuracy, use of deep learning algorithms in mobile devices raises critical challenges, i.e., high processing latency and power consumption. In this paper, we propose DeepMon, a mobile deep learning inference system to run a variety of deep learning inferences purely on a mobile device in a fast and energy-efficient manner. For this, we designed a suite of optimization techniques to efficiently offload convolutional layers to mobile GPUs and accelerate the processing; note that the convolutional layers are the common performance bottleneck of many deep learning models. Our experimental results show that DeepMon can classify an image over the VGG-VeryDeep-16 deep learning model in 644ms on Samsung Galaxy S7, taking an important step towards continuous vision without imposing any privacy concerns nor networking cost.

Keywords

Mobile GPU; Mobile Sensing; Deep Learning; Continuous Vision

1. INTRODUCTION

The popularity of head-mounted augmented reality (AR) devices such as the Microsoft Hololens [4] and the Google Glass [3] has given rise to a new class of continuous mobile vision applications. These range from identifying road signs in real time to provide directions [15], to identifying people in the environment to give guidance to individuals suffering from dementia [12]. In all these use cases, the commonality is the need to perform computer vision algorithms in real time on a continuous video stream provided by the AR devices.

The current state-of-the-art approach to continuous video processing is to use a deep neural network (DNN) approach where the video streams are processed by a large and well-trained convolutional neural network (CNN) or recurrent neural network (RNN). However, these networks require large amounts of CPU and memory resources to run efficiently. It has thus proved challenging to achieve adequate performance when executing large deep learning networks on commodity mobile devices. For example, a commonly used object recognition model, VGG-Verydeep-16 [46], has 13 convolutional layers and three fully connected layers and takes ≈100 seconds to process a single image using CPU on a Samsung Galaxy S7 smartphone.

One way to overcome this limitation is to use cloud resources to run the required DNNs [25]. However, this introduces significant privacy concerns (as the video feed is now available on the cloud server) in addition to possible latency, and energy concerns depending on where the cloud is located and what network interface (LTE etc.) is used.

In this paper, we present a system, called *DeepMon*[1], that uses the graphics processing unit (GPU) on mobile devices to execute the large DNNs required for continuous video processing. *DeepMon* can achieve continuous video processing (at about 1-2 frames per second) of full HD (1080p) video frames using just the memory, CPU, and GPU resources of a commodity smartphone. This speedup allows *DeepMon* to be used, with a larger processing pipeline where *DeepMon* can extract features from video frames that can then be processed by cloud resources to produce a complete knowledge. This greatly reduces the privacy impact of using a cloud (as only features and not actual video frames are sent to the cloud) as well as the latency and energy concerns (the feature set is much smaller than the full video image). However, in this paper, we focus solely on the optimisations and techniques to reduce the local processing time from multiple seconds to ≈600ms per frame and leave the integration with a complete cloud-enabled solution to future work.

Before building *DeepMon*, we analysed various deep learning models (e.g., VGG-Verydeep-16 [46] and YOLO [43]) to identify their performance bottlenecks. We noticed that they commonly adopt a large number of convolutional layers (to extract and refine features) along with a small number of fully connected layers (to make inferences). Our measurement showed that the convolutional layer processing takes a significant portion of the entire processing – e.g. 88.7% for VGG-Verydeep-16 and 85% for YOLO (see Section 4).

We thus focused on techniques to reduce the processing latency of convolutional layers. One clear solution was to offload the DNN convolutional layer computation to the mobile GPU as these layers have highly parallel and repetitive processing structures. However, prior offloading techniques were developed for server-class GPUs and required re-design/optimization for mobile GPUs with much

[1]The git repo of *DeepMon* is available at https://github.com/JC1DA/DeepMon and the videos are at http://is.gd/DeepMon

Permission to make digital or hard copies of all or part of this work for personal or classroom use is granted without fee provided that copies are not made or distributed for profit or commercial advantage and that copies bear this notice and the full citation on the first page. Copyrights for components of this work owned by others than ACM must be honored. Abstracting with credit is permitted. To copy otherwise, or republish, to post on servers or to redistribute to lists, requires prior specific permission and/or a fee. Request permissions from permissions@acm.org.

MobiSys '17, June 19–23, 2017, Niagara Falls, NY, USA.
© 2017 ACM. ISBN 978-1-4503-4928-4/17/06...$15.00
DOI: http://dx.doi.org/10.1145/3081333.3081360

smaller number of processing cores and memory bandwidth; for instance, NVidia GTX 980 GPU for desktops have 2,048 GPU cores and 224GB/s memory read/write bandwidth while Mali T880 GPU on Samsung Galaxy S7 has 12 GPU cores and 25.6GB/s memory bandwidth.

We developed a suite of optimizations for processing convolutional layers on mobile GPUs. First, we designed a smart caching mechanism specially designed for convolutional layers. The key idea is to exploit the similarity between consecutive frames in first-person-view videos. Our mechanism is unique in that it utilizes the internal processing structure of convolutional layers to reuse the intermediate results of the previous frame to calculate the current frame, instead of just simply reusing its final output. Second, we decompose the matrices used in the convolutional layers to accelerate the multiplications between high-dimensional matrices, which are the bottleneck when running convolutional layers on GPUs. Also, we applied a number of system-level optimizations (described in Section 6 to accelerate the matrix calculation in mobile GPUs).

We implemented *DeepMon* using OpenCL [7] and Vulkan [9] and tested it on various mobile GPUs (Adreno 420, Adreno 430, and Mali T 880) with multiple large DNN models. For developers to adopt various DNN models in *DeepMon*, we also developed a tool that automatically converts pre-trained legacy models and loads them to *DeepMon* with its various optimization strategies applied.

Our results show that *DeepMon* significantly accelerates the processing of large DNNs. For example, the latency of VGG-VeryDeep-16 model-based inference reduces ≈5 times compared to the naive GPU-based implementation with just a marginal reduction in inference accuracy (≈5%). This enables low-latency image classifications (i.e., 3 frames per 2 seconds). Note: VGG-Verydeep-16 is the model many applications such as face recognition (Deep Face from Oxford [42]) and object detection (YOLO [43] and Fast R-CNN [22]) rely on. In addition, we conducted experiments on other models for object detection (such as YOLO) on commodity smartphones (Samsung Galaxy S7, Note 4, etc.). Our results showed that our proposed techniques could achieve a latency of 644ms for VGG-Verydeep-16 and 1,006ms for YOLO on Samsung Galaxy S7.

The contributions of our paper can be summarized as follows:

- To the best of our knowledge, *DeepMon* is the first system to allow large DNNs to run on commodity mobile devices at a low latency. Prior work, such as DeepX [35] and MCDNN [25], has focused on smaller DNNs, cloud computation, and non-commodity more powerful mobile devices such as the Tegra K1.
- We devised a suite of optimization techniques to reduce the processing latency of the convolutional layers of DNNs. Our smart caching mechanism leverages similarities of consecutive images to cache internally processed data within the deep convolutional neural network. Also, we adopted and improved state-of-the-art matrix multiplication techniques such as model decomposition [31] and unfolding [14] to accelerate multiplication operations (the bottleneck operation in convolutional layers) on mobile GPUs.
- We shared lessons about implementing *DeepMon* on OpenCL and Vulkan and scaling it to support various mobile GPUs. Prior work has focused primarily on CUDA [6] which, to the best of our knowledge, is not supported by commodity smartphones. *DeepMon's* OpenCL implementation can be deployed on a variety of Android-based devices with Snapdragon and Exynos chipsets while its Vulkan implementation (the first such implementation we could find) can be deployed on recent iPhone models such as the iPhone 7. Finally, developers can easily load pre-trained legacy models on various mobile GPUs by using *DeepMon's* model converting tool.
- We conducted extensive experiments showing that *DeepMon* can execute very deep models such as VGG-Verydeep-16 on video streams in near real-time, reducing the processing latency to execute one frame from 3 seconds down to 644 ms.

2. RELATED WORK

Deep Learning on Mobile Devices. Lane et al. took important first steps towards the real-time execution of DNN and CNN on mobile devices [35, 36]. DeepEar [36] showed the feasibility of running entire DNNs for audio sensing applications on low-power mobile DSPs. DeepX [35] then enabled the execution of DNN and CNN on mobile devices by splitting computations across multiple co-processors. We believe that *DeepMon* can complement DeepX in the following ways. First, DeepX is effective in reducing the latency of fully-connected layers while our framework focuses on reducing the latency of convolutional layers. Also, *DeepMon* supports OpenCL, Vulkan and GPUs on commercially available mobile devices in the market whereas DeepX was prototyped on more powerful hardware such as Tegra K1 and Snapdragon 801 on external development kits.

DeepSense [28] presented early evidence that using a GPU could help improve the latency of DNN computations – *DeepMon* extends that work by providing many more optimisations, a full implementation, and extensive evaluation. Recently, Glimpse [15] leveraged the cloud to enable real-time object detection and tracking while MCDNN [25] executed deep learning algorithms across mobile devices and clouds. MCDNN [25] proposed efficient optimization techniques such as building multiple smaller DNN models to recognize frequently appearing objects, sharing visual features between applications and optimizing task offloading to the clouds. However, we tackled the problem of executing the full deep learning pipelines solely within a mobile device using its GPU. In addition, while *DeepMon* shares a high-level concept with MCDNN (about re-using the DNN computation), *DeepMon's* caching technique re-uses the intermediate partial results while processing convolutional layers, enabling much more fine-granule sharing of computation across consecutive images.

Mobile Continuous Vision. Gabriel [24] uses cloudlets to support cognitive assistance applications while LiKamWa et al. presented optimization techniques for image sensors to enable continuous mobile vision [38] and Starfish [39] to support concurrent execution of multiple vision applications. *DeepMon* also aims at enabling continuous vision applications by focusing on efficiently executing deep DNNs locally on mobile devices.

Deep Learning Optimization. In the machine learning communities, there has been work to reduce the training time of CNNs and DNNs [40]. There has been some work to optimize inference time; for example, Vanhoucke et al. [50] and Jaderberg et al. [29] presented optimization techniques to reduce the inference latency (e.g., using fixed point arithmetic and SSSE3/SSE4 instructions on x86 machines). *DeepMon* uses these techniques and develops additional optimization techniques to further reduce the latency of mobile-driven continuous vision applications.

Restructuring DNN models has been widely studied to reduce the size of the model and accelerate the inference speed [18, 23, 29, 32, 34, 45]. Recently, Bhattacharya and Lane proposed a frame-

	App	Size (M)	Top-1 Acc. (%)	Top-5 Acc. (%)	Arch.
Deep Models					
VGG-VeryDeep-16	IR	138.4	71.7	90.5	13c,5p,3fc
VGG-Face	FR	145	98.95	-	13c,5p,3fc
YOLO	IR	275	63.4	-	24c,4p,2fc
Shallow Models					
AlexNet	IR	60.8	58.2	80.8	5c,3p,3fc
VGG-F	IR	60.8	58.6	80.9	5c,3p,3fc
VGG-M	IR	102.9	63.1	84.5	5c,3p,3fc
LRCN (CNN+LSTM)	AR	62.5	68.2	-	5c,3p,2lrn, 3fc

Application (IR: image recognition, FR: face recognition, AR: activity recognition),
Size: number of parameters,
Architecture (c: convolutional layers, p: pooling layers, fc: fully connected layers, lrn: local response normalization)

Table 1: Comparison of DNN Models

work to sparsify fully-connected layers and separate convolutional kernels, reducing the memory and computational costs of DNN/CNN significantly for wearables [34]. Kim et al. proposed a *Tucker-2 decomposition* technique [32]. It decomposes a tensor into three smaller ones, accelerating convolutional layer execution for mobile devices. *DeepMon* adopts the Tucker-2 decomposition and tailor it to work with our caching technique to further reduce the execution latency of convolutional layers.

3. MOTIVATING SCENARIOS

The following usage scenarios drove the development of *DeepMon*.

Speaker Identification: In this scenario, a user is wearing a pair of AR glasses and moving through a conference venue. The video stream captured by the glass is continuously processed to identify the faces of the people in view. As people are identified, information about them, such as their name, their last interaction with the user, etc., is overlayed in the glass's display.

Safety For The Elderly: In this scenario, the AR glasses are worn by an elderly person going about their regular daily chores. The glass's video feed is constantly processed to detect objects, such as oncoming traffic if a road is being crossed, or obstacles on the pavement when walking, that need to be brought to the attention of the user. In this way, the user can react early and appropriately to various situations.

Both of these scenarios, face and object detection, share similarities; (a) they both need to be performed in near real-time – identifying people after they have left or hazards after they have been hit are both undesirable outcomes, (b) the image screen may contain images (children, relatives, etc.) that should not be sent to a cloud service, (c) they can still be useful even at low frame rates, for example, face and object recognition that operates at 1 to 2 frames per second can still provide near real-time feedback to a user who is walking, and finally, (d) the state-of-the-art solutions for both problems use deep DNNs – deep DNNs are DNNs that have many computational layers (usually more than 10) that substantially increase the accuracy at the expense of higher latencies and computational requirements. In the rest of this paper, we describe how *DeepMon* enables both face and objection detection deep DNN models to run at 1 to 2 frames per second on commodity smartphones.

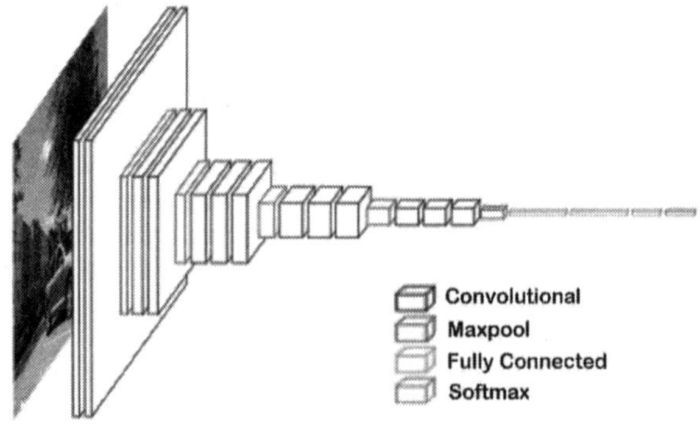

Figure 1: Macroarchitecture of VGG-VeryDeep-16 [1]

4. DEEP LEARNING PIPELINES

Vision applications use many deep learning pipelines. We explored the most popularly used models, such as AlexNet, VGG-F, VGG-VeryDeep-16, YOLO, Fast R-CNN (Region-based CNN), to characterize their computational requirements and performance – summary provided in Table 1. In this paper, we primarily focus on models (VGG-VeryDeep-16 and YOLO in particular) that adopt more than 15 processing layers to achieve higher accuracy.

4.1 Background on Various Models

VGG-VeryDeep-16 and VGG-Face. Figure 1 shows the detailed processing structure of VGG-VeryDeep-16. The architecture is composed of 13 convolutional layers, 5 pooling layers, and 3 fully-connected layers. Convolutional layers are in charge of extracting various features from an image and refining them while fully connected layers make inferences from extracted features. Pooling layers convert the data from the previous layer to feed to the next input layer. The softmax layer is the final layer to aggregate and normalize the scores generated by the last fully connected layer and outputs the final classification result.

VGG-VeryDeep-16 [46] is used to classify images into one of 1,000 different image types with a confidence probability; it outputs top-N image types with the probability per type. VGG-Face [42], is based on VGG-VeryDeep-16, and performs face recognition. We only use VGG-VeryDeep-16 in our evaluation as VGG-Face has the same structural and algorithmic properties.

YOLO [43] recognizes and locates objects in an image. YOLO can be trained with different datasets. For example, YOLO trained with the VOC dataset [2] identifies 20 objects and tracks their locations while YOLO trained with the Pascal VOC dataset [8] can identify and localize 80 different objects. The architecture of YOLO is composed of 24 convolutional layers and two fully connected layers, resulting in higher computational requirements compared to VGG-VeryDeep-16 or VGG-Face.

Other Models. There are other smaller-sized but popular models used for image classification, such as VGG-F [13], AlexNet [33], and VGG-M [13]. Their architecture incorporates a much smaller number of layers; for example, they use just 5 convolutional layers to extract features and 4 fully connected layers for inference. These models are much smaller than VGG-VeryDeep-16 or YOLO with correspondingly lower accuracies given the same train and test data. We omit these shallow models from the rest of the paper as (i) they have already been studied by prior work [35, 36], and (ii) higher accuracy object and face recognition would be more usable for end user applications.

	Conv. (ms)	FC. (ms)	Pooling (ms)	Total (ms)
VGG-VeryDeep-16	2,647	294	40	2,984
YOLO	3,345	536.1	44.9	3,935
(CNN+LSTM)	5,488.8	161.7	2,158.8	8,301

Table 2: Latency Breakdown

At the other end, some extremely deep models achieve even higher accuracies. For instance, ResNet-152 [26] has 152 layers and achieves 3.62% higher accuracy compared to VGG-VeryDeep-16. However, we noticed that the accuracy improvements of such models are marginal compared to the models that have 15 to 25 layers while incurring much higher computational costs. We do not expect those extremely deep models can be run on mobile devices in near real-time and thus exclude them from this work.

There are other models such as Faster-RCNN [22] for object detection and *Long-term Recurrent Convolutional Networks* (LRCN [19]) for activity recognition – LRCN is the combination of CNN and *Long Short Term Memory* (LSTM [27]). These models have some common characteristics with VGG-VeryDeep-16 or AlexNet and also modify the structures to achieve better performance and accuracy. Even though they are applied in different scenarios, we noticed that they have lots of commonality with VGG-based models and our workload characterization and optimization techniques apply well to these models.

Effect of the model depth on accuracy and latency. In general, the deeper the model becomes, the higher accuracy it achieves for the same classification task. This increase in accuracy has been validated by recent results [49] (although there are a few special cases where a shallow network is equally accurate). For instance, AlexNet with 5 convolutional layers achieves 80.8% top-5 accuracy to recognize an image while VGG-Verydeep-16 with 13 convolutional layers achieves 90.5% top-5 accuracy. Also, ResNet-152 with 152 layers shows 94.3% top-5 accuracy. On the other hand, deeper models impose much higher computational or memory requirements; For example, the number of operations required to execute VGG-VeryDeep-16 is 21 times more than that of AlexNet while ResNet-152 requires 4 times more memory space than VGG-VeryDeep-16.

4.2 Workload Characterization

We noticed important common characteristics in the workloads of deep deep-learning models that drove the optimisations in *DeepMon*. First, each deep model has a large number of computational layers – with the accuracy of the model increasing as more layers (convolutional layers in particular) were added. Second, the majority of the layers are convolutional layers. Convolutional layers play a critical role to extract useful features from images and then refine them; in particular, they apply various types of *filters* over the small blocks of an image to abstract out visual features such as edges and shapes. Table 1 confirms that, in deep models, the most processing layers are convolutional layers, with a small number of fully connected layers and pooling layers.

Hence, it is likely that most of the processing time is spent in convolutional layers. To check if this was the case, we measured the running time of different deep learning models on a Samsung Galaxy S7 and broke down the processing latency per layer type. To do this, we implemented a GPU-based deep learning execution framework (without any optimization techniques applied).

Table 2 shows the execution time broken down per layer type (i.e., convolutional, fully-connected, and pooling). It indicates that the convolutional layers dominate the processing time. For VGG-VeryDeep-16, over 88.7 % of the processing time is occupied by the convolutional layers followed by 9.8% and 1.3% for fully-connected layers and pooling layers, respectively. For the YOLO model, over 85% of computation time is spent in convolutional layers. The reasons for these time breakdowns are (i) there are many more convolutional layers than other layers in deep models, and (ii) the total number of addition and multiplication operations within convolutional layers is much higher compared to fully connected layers and pooling layers (e.g. VGG-VeryDeep-16 requires 15,346M addition and multiplication operations for convolutional layers while only 123M operations are necessary for fully connected layers). These results suggest that optimizing the processing time of convolutional layers would lead to huge improvements in overall model processing latencies.

5. DESIGN CONSIDERATIONS

We developed *DeepMon* with the following design goals:

No cloud offloading: Our primary design goal, for this paper, was to use local phone resources only without any cloud offloading to process deep DNNs as this area has compelling use cases without any viable solutions. There are also scenarios, such as processing of sensitive video feeds or video processing in places with poor or expensive networking connectivity, where offloading is either unwanted (due to privacy concerns) or impossible (due to networking issues). We do plan to extend our solution to support cyber foraging (e.g. MAUI [16] and Chroma [10, 11]), where local and cloud resources are used in a dynamic fashion.

Near real-time latency: Our intended application scenarios, described in Section 3, both require near-real time processing of image streams to give on-the-fly feedback to the users. However, we do not aim to provide strict real-time support (e.g., < 50ms with strict inter-frame timings) as we do not believe this is possible with current commodity smartphones and deep DNNs. Instead, we aim to push the research boundary to provide 1-2 frames per second processing capability (the current state-of-the-art is 1 frame every 3-4 seconds).

Minimal accuracy loss: While achieving near-real-time processing latencies is good, it cannot be done at the cost of accuracy – otherwise improving latency becomes trivially easy. We thus require *DeepMon* to be only about 5% less accurate than running the same model on a desktop PC.

Efficient power use. Minimizing the energy use of *DeepMon* is essential as we aim at running complex deep learning pipelines on mobile devices. In this paper, we focused on reducing the power consumption of executing deep learning pipeline on a mobile device and rely optimising the power consumption of the video camera (to capture and store continuous video feeds) to prior work [38].

Support a wide range of mobile GPUs and programming APIs: There has been prior work [25, 35] that used external mobile development boards, such as the Tegra K1, to test their solutions. We designed *DeepMon* to work well on commodity smartphones and tested it across a range of mobile phones and programming APIs (the full list of test devices is shown in Table 3). In particular, *DeepMon* supports both the OpenCL [7] and Vulkan [9] programming APIs.

6. IMPLEMENTATION

In this section, we first show the overall architecture of *DeepMon*, and then describe, in detail, the various techniques we adopted to optimize the execution of deep learning pipelines.

Phone	GPU	APIs	# GPU Cores (#ALUs)	Memory Size (GB)	Memory Bandwid. (GB/s)
Samsung S7	Mali T880	OpenCL/ Vulkan	12	4	25.6
Samsung Note 4	Adreno 420	OpenCL	4 (128)	3	12.8
Sony Z5	Adreno 430	OpenCL	4 (192)	3	12.8

Table 3: Specs for Commodity Mobile GPUs

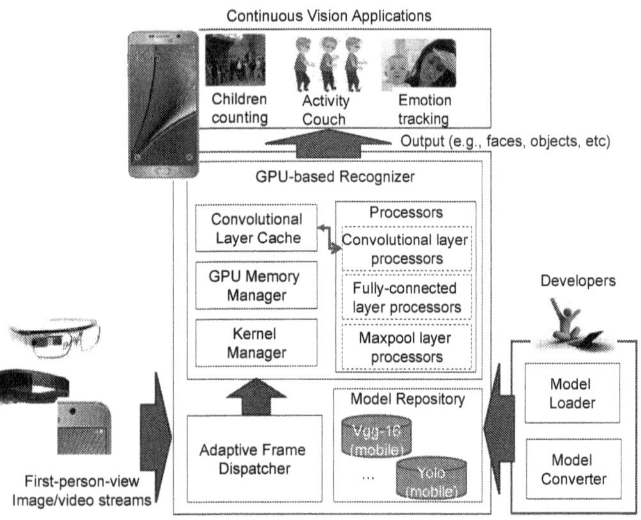

Figure 2: *DeepMon* System Architecture

6.1 Architecture Overview

Figure 2 shows the overall architecture of *DeepMon*, and Table 4 summarizes our techniques. *DeepMon* works through two different phases: (1) the model conversion phase to convert existing models to run on mobile GPUs, and (2) the inference phase to process image streams using the converted model to recognize useful information.

Model conversion and loading. To use *DeepMon*, developers first need to convert existing deep learning models (built for desktop GPUs) to fit on mobile GPUs. For this, we provide *model converter* and *model loader* tools – the current *DeepMon* prototype can convert a variety of existing models including the ones described in Table 1. The model converter adapts the configurations and parameters of an existing model and generates a new model that can run efficiently on mobile GPUs (See Section 6.4). The model loader then loads the generated model on *DeepMon*– it allocates adequate memory spaces to lay out input data for efficient convolution computation and structures the processors for all the layers composing the model (See Section 6.2)

DeepMon currently supports the models from three different deep learning frameworks, namely *Caffe* [30], *Matconvnet* [51] and *YOLO* [43].

Real-time Inference. During the inference phase, *DeepMon* takes a stream of first-person-view images as its input. The *frame dispatcher* selects important frames to recognize and feeds them to the GPU-based recognizer. Then, the *GPU-based recognizer* executes the deep learning pipeline and outputs its inference results to the applications of interest. During the execution, it applies a suite of optimization techniques, such as convolutional layer caching and matrix multiplication optimizations, to boost the recognition speed (explained in detail in Sections 6.3 and 6.5).

DeepMon supports both OpenCL and Vulkan and was tested on phones with Adreno and Mali GPUs. We present our evaluation results for various GPUs and Vulcan in Section 7.6 and 7.7.

Techniques	Description	Evaluation
Model Conversion/Loading	Section 6.2	-
Convolutional Layer Caching	Section 6.3	Section 7.2–7.5& Section 7.8–7.9
Layer Decomposition	Section 6.4	Section 7.2–7.5
Convolution Optimizations	Section 6.5	Section 7.2–7.5
Scaling to various GPUs/APIs	Section 6.6&6.2	Section 7.6&7.7

Table 4: Summary of *DeepMon's* techniques

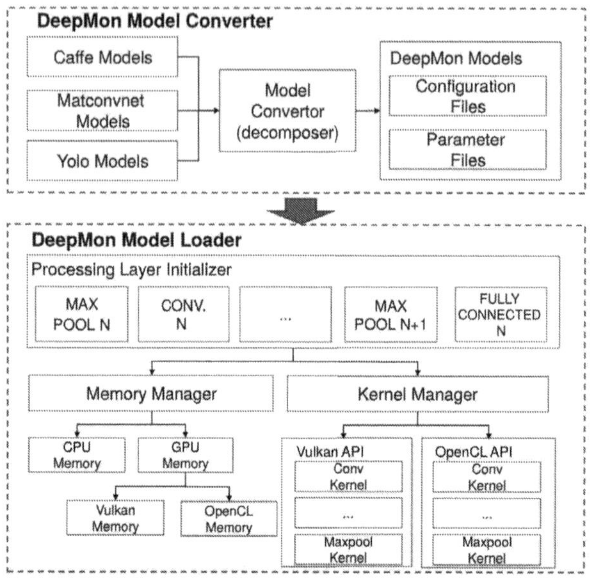

Figure 3: The Flow of Model Conversation and Loading

6.2 Loading Models into Mobile GPUs

Figure 3 shows the detailed flow of the model conversion and loading process. First, the model convertor decides how to layout the input data into the memory space. The challenge here occurs mainly because the memory space is linear while the input data are multi-dimensional matrices. The wrong unfolding of the multi-dimensional data into a linear space would result in huge fragmentation of the data, which will slow down the convolution processing significantly. Intuitively, the model converter lays out the data such that matrix multiplications can be done by reading consecutive memory blocks and reusing them as much as possible once they are in memory. This is particularly important for devices with low memory bandwidth (e.g. Samsung Galaxy Note 4 and Sony Xperia Z5).

Once the data layout is decided, the *model loader* initializes all the necessary additional layers (e.g. convolutional, pooling, fully-connected, etc.) within the *DeepMon's* recognizer. During initialization, *DeepMon* performs two important tasks: (a) memory allocation and (b) kernel code compilation.

First, upon layer initialization, *DeepMon* needs to allocate memory spaces to store the metadata (e.g. size of filters, input size,

(a) An image at time t_0 (Left)
(b) An image at time $t_0 + 500ms$ (Middle)
(c) The same image blocks marked as black (Right)

Figure 4: Example First-Person-View Images

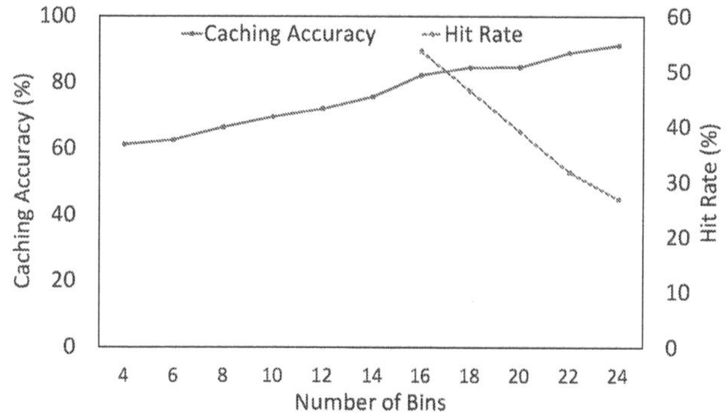

Figure 5: Effect of the Number of Bins on Caching

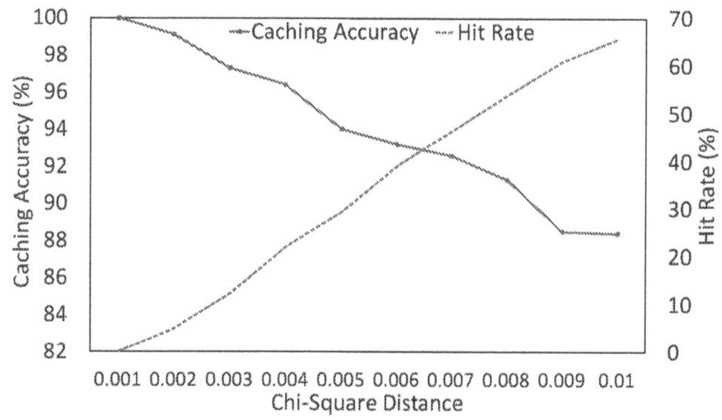

Figure 6: Effect of the Distance Values on Caching

output size, etc.) or parameter values. *DeepMon* stores all the metadata in the host memory (or CPU memory) for easy data access and stores all the parameters in the device memory (or GPU memory). The GPU memory space is allocated based on the API used (OpenCL or Vulkan). The memory space for the actual input and output data is also allocated in the GPU memory for efficient computation. This space can be mapped to the host memory when necessary (e.g. to return final output to application).

Second, a specific *kernel code*, containing the code block to be parallelized by the layer, needs to be built and loaded. Building these kernel code is handled differently for OpenCL and Vulkan. For OpenCL, a kernel is written in the OpenCL C-like language. It does not require pre-built binary code for any specific device – Instead, it supports compilation capabilities on the target device itself, making it easy to be ported to other OpenCL-enabled devices. Vulkan, on the other hand, uses SPIR-V (Standard Portable Intermediate Representation), an intermediate language for graphics and parallel computation. In Vulkan, SPIR-V code can be loaded onto various Vulkan-enabled devices without building binary code. *DeepMon* prepares two separate convolutional implementations in advance and compiles the kernel code on demand, based on the chosen API, when a layer is initialized and loads the kernel into memory.

6.3 Convolutional Layer Caching

As shown earlier (Section 4), the convolutional layers are the main performance bottlenecks. To accelerate the computation of these layers, we designed a caching mechanism optimised for convolutional layers. Our key observation is that first-person-view images tend not to change much over a short time duration. For example, Figure 4 shows three first-person-view images; the left and middle images were taken at time t_0 and $t_0 + 500ms$ while the rightmost image, taken at time $t_0 + 500ms$ shows the same image blocks (marked as black).

In particular, the background of images across multiple continuous image frames often remains still while foreground objects tend to move. Such commonality in images incurs heavy repetition in the execution of convolutional layers as applying the full pipeline on one image at a time applies the same convolution computations on many different "repeated" frames and sub-frames.

Our caching mechanism reduces this repetitive computation significantly. A plausible caching approach would be to reuse the final result from the previous frame when the difference between frames is under a certain threshold (Chen et al. [15] proposed a similar idea). However, this approach would not work in many cases as foreground objects (that take a small portion of the entire image but are important to recognize) tend to change noticeably while the background images do not. This makes the previously cached results either stale (on a cache hit) or incurs lots of cache misses. To overcome this, we *cache the partial results of convolutional layers* – i.e., we reuse the convolution outputs for the unchanged blocks of an image while recalculating convolutions for the changed blocks.

6.3.1 Caching Mechanism

The overall flow of our caching mechanism is as follows. First, we divide the image into a grid (e.g. an 8x8 grid) where each grid block contains a fixed number of pixels. During the execution, we compare corresponding blocks, $b_{(t-1)}$ and b_t of two consecutive images to determine if the outputs of the previous convolutional layer, $b_{(t-1)}$, are reusable (i.e., it is a cache hit). Upon a cache hit, *DeepMon* skips the convolution computation on the pixels within the entire block. *DeepMon* caches the convolution outputs for the first N convolutional layers only (where N is determined empirically for every model) since the computation for the later convolutional layers are often quite small, and the caching overhead is higher than the benefit. Cached values expire after a certain duration – for example, we set the default expiration times, determined empirically, to 650ms for VGG-VeryDeep-16 and 1000ms for YOLO.

However, the key challenge with this caching scheme is that it is a non-trivial task to determine if the two image blocks are similar or not. Indeed, if the image comparison is too heavyweight, the caching overhead will quickly exceed its benefit. There are a few image comparison algorithms with high comparison accuracy, for example SIFT-based [41] and Hog-based [17] algorithms. However, their computational cost is high and not suitable for our cache design (See Section 7.9 for the relevant results.).

To solve this problem, we adopted a light-weight algorithm based on colour histograms. For the two image blocks to compare, we compute the histogram of the colour distribution and compute a *chi-square distance metric*. If the distance is less than a pre-defined threshold, the cell is marked as "reusable".

For efficient caching, it is important to choose the right number of bins (to calculate the histogram) and the distance threshold. We carefully chose the right parameters through empirical studies using AlexNet. First, we investigated the effect of the number of bins by fixing the distance parameter to 0.005. Figure 5 shows that as the number of bins increases, the accuracy increases while the number of "cacheable" blocks decreases; in the figure, the caching accuracy indicates how closely *DeepMon* outputs the final classification results with respect comparing to the original model. We also explored the effect of distance threshold – the number of bins was set to 16. Figure 6 shows the trade-off between accuracy and cache hit rates for various distance threshold values. We use the cross-over points of the accuracy and hit rate to decide a plausible number of bins and distance threshold value.

To make caching work efficiently along with our GPU-based recognizer, we carefully re-implemented our GPU-specific kernels. Intuitively, we first initialize all the memory spaces (that need to contain the output of a convolutional layer) with the cached results. Only for those blocks with cache misses, *DeepMon* maps the new outputs into the corresponding memory spaces. This makes updating uncached results easy.

When reusing cached results, we had to be careful about the edges of an image block. Figure 7 shows two examples of caching applied on a block size of 4x4 in a convolutional layer with a filter size of 3x3. Figure 7(a) shows an example where a convolutional filter is applied to the edge of the cached block. In this case, the output value becomes non-cachable as the 3x3 block being calculated may refer to non-cachable data (data outside of cached block). For that reason, *DeepMon* will not reuse the results for the edges of the block. However, when two or more consecutive blocks can be cached, as shown in Figure 7(b), *DeepMon* reuses the cached results for the edges that are shared by the cacheable consecutive blocks. Importantly, for the models we are considering, the block size is quite large for the first few convolutional layers (e.g. 28x28 pixels for the first layer for VGG-VeryDeep-16), making this caching technique effective for all those layers.

6.4 Convolutional Layer Decomposition

We further optimize convolutional layers by decomposing the convolutional parameters. Convolutional layers are well-known to have redundant parameters [29], making them computationally inefficient on resource-constrained devices. Prior research have provided a few different methods (such as the tucker decomposition [32] and CP decomposition [37]) to decompose a convolutional layer into three smaller convolutional layers so that the total computation of the decomposed layers is less than that of the original layer.

DeepMon adopts a variance of the Tucker decomposition named *Tucker-2* [32] over other alternatives since it is a better match to *DeepMon's* caching algorithm. The weights of a convolutional layer are often represented as a tensor *T* of size *[N x C x D x D]* in which *N* and *C* are the numbers of input and output channels, respectively, while *D* is the size of the filters. Tucker-2 decomposes *T* into three smaller tensors *T1, T2, T2* with the sizes of *[C' x C x 1 x 1], [N' x C' x D x D], [N x N' x 1 x 1]* respectively, where the number of new input and output channels (i.e. N' and C') are reduced compared to those in the original tensor (i.e. *N* and *C*). Intuitively, the decomposition reduces the number of dot product operations from *(N x C x D x D)* to *(C' x C) + (N' x C' x D x D) + (N x N')*, enabling *DeepMon* to further reduce the latency.

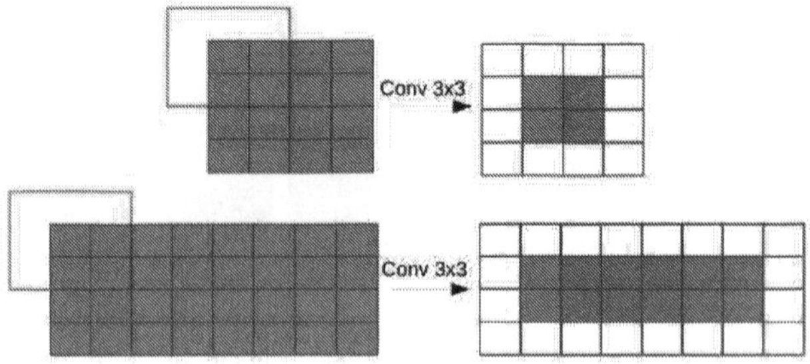

(a) Example with a 4x4 Block and a 3x3 Filter (Top)
(b) Example with two 4x4 Consecutive Blocks and a 3x3 Filter (Bottom)

Figure 7: Caching on the Edge of an Image Block

Tucker-2 decomposition is more appropriate to be used with our caching technique due to its unique characteristic – two of the decomposed layers have the filters with the size of *[1 x 1]*. *[1 x 1]* filters do not reduce the input size to the subsequent layers, keeping the cacheable block size across layers; note that if the block sizes get reduced, the overhead to compute cache hit/miss will increase, compromising the benefit of caching. On the other hand, other decomposition methods use filters larger than *[1 x 1]*, reducing the size of *cachable* blocks and making the caching less effective. Moreover, the *[1 x 1]* filter does not require separate handling of the edges of cacheable blocks (as shown in the Figure 7). This enables us to develop a more efficient GPU-kernel to reduce the latency further.

The non-trivial problem, here, is to choose the right *N' and C'*. In practice, manual trial and error is still a common yet inefficient approach that requires a lot of effort. Instead, we devised a *double binary search algorithm* to reduce the amount of effort needed. The key idea behind the algorithm is to find *N' and C'* that maximizes the variance when we reconstruct the original tensor (e.g. similar to principle component analysis). We define the desired variance that we need to sufficiently reconstruct the tensor and then use binary search to find the parameters that best produce the required variance. Finally, we fine-tune the model to recover from the possible loss in its accuracy.

6.5 Optimizing Convolutional Operation

The execution of a deep learning pipeline heavily relies on matrix multiplication. However, linear algebra libraries for OpenCL (such as ClBlast and ViennaCL used in Caffe) are tuned for desktop GPUs and do not perform efficiently on smartphones.

To accelerate convolutional operation, existing frameworks use a technique called *unfolding* that converts inputs into a large matrix and then uses matrix multiplication on the unfolded input and filters to compute the result [14]. The unfolding technique requires a large amount of memory and bandwidth when executing convolutional layers. Unfortunately, the memory bandwidth on mobile GPU is quite small compared to server GPU. This makes the unfolding technique unsuitable for *DeepMon*.

Deeper observations showed that convolutional operations performed without unfolding tend to consume less bandwidth for memory access. However, it also stores the data, in memory, in a non-contiguous fashion, making it inefficient when running on memory-constrained mobile GPUs. Our second observation is that carefully laying out the convolutional weights in the format of *[N x D x D x*

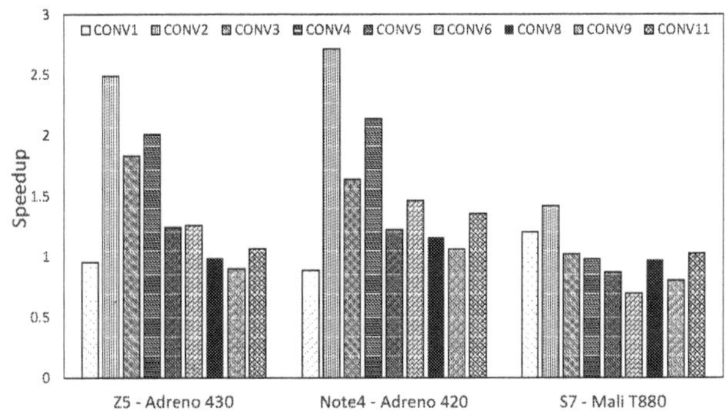

Figure 8: Speedup Comparison with ClBlast

C] and its input in *[H x W x C]* makes it more GPU friendly as we can read multiple items at the same time using OpenCL functionality. We also note that Caffe and YOLO use the format of *[N x C x D x D]* for the weights of convolutional layers.

Figure 8 shows the speedup between our implementation and conventional unfolding approach. We benchmark two approaches using convolutional layers extracted from VGG-VeryDeep-16. We drop convolutional layer 7, 10, 11 and 12 from our benchmark since they have similar parameters to the other layers. We extract unfolding kernel from Caffe and use ClBlast library (one of three linear algebra used in Caffe) to do convolutional operations. Results show that on lower bandwidth devices (Note 4 and Z5), our approach almost provides the better latency (speedup > 1). However, on S7, since the device has integrated LPDDR4 which has doubled bandwidth comparing to two other devices, conventional approach starts to benefit at some layers. We additionally validated the latency of convolutional layers with another commonly-used library, ViennaCL (on Caffe). We found out that ViennaCL performs slower than ClBlast on Samsung Galaxy S7 – mainly due to its lack of support to optimize various parameters.

We further reduce the processing latency of the convolutional operations by using half floating point precision in OpenCL. Since the memory bandwidth is limited on the mobile devices (compared to desktop machines), it is highly useful to reduce the size of memory reads and writes by half by dropping the last half digits of the data. Our results, shown in Section 7, indicate that this optimisation is effective at reducing latency without any significant impact on the accuracy.

6.6 Scaling to Various Mobile GPUs

We implemented a number of techniques to allow *DeepMon* to support various types of mobile GPUs. The most important consideration was to adapt to the different memory architectures of different mobile GPUs and the ways in which they read/write data from the main memory.

Mobile GPUs support unified memory access that allows GPUs to directly access the main memory and use it as its own memory. However, the main memory is shared among the many components of a mobile device and its data read/write bandwidth is limited. This limited bandwidth could slow down the processing of *DeepMon* as DNN execution usually requires the GPU to read a large amount of data from the main memory.

One possible solution is to use *local memory* on the GPU chipset itself. The local memory is a small memory (for instance 8KB on Adreno 330 and 32KB on Adreno 430) which is used as a cache to accelerate memory access during computation (data is first loaded

	conv_1 (ms)	conv_2 (ms)	conv_3 (ms)	conv_4 (ms)
Host memory	78.66	667.10	340.59	757.12
GPU local memory	63.98	526.9	262.57	584.80

Table 5: Benefit of using GPU Local Memory

into local memory and is reused during computation). However, the size and architecture of the local memory vary across different GPUs. For example, different Adreno boards have different sizes of local memory while Mali GPUs have no local memory. Such differences are the key challenge in making *DeepMon* support different mobile GPUs.

We address this issue by building kernel codes that can exploit different amounts of local memory (including a kernel code for no memory) and dynamically uses the appropriate code at runtime. In particular, when executing convolution layers, if the memory requirement for a single filter fits into the small local memory, we adaptively use kernel code that supports that amount of local memory. Otherwise, we use the non-local-memory version.

We also build the kernel code in a way that the filters within a convolutional layer are shared to evaluate all input values. Accordingly, for the first layer of VGG-VeryDeep-16, we can fit all 64 filters with the size of *[3 x 3 x 3]* into the 8KB local memory of the Xperia Z5. For the deeper layers that require more than available local memory, *DeepMon* loads a subset of filters into the local memory and compute partial outputs at a time. We also find out that the half floating point approximation reduces the size of filters by half, allowing *DeepMon* to load more filters into the local memory. Table 5 shows the processing time for the four first convolutional layers while executing VGG-VeryDeep-16 on the Sony Xperia Z5 phone. It indicates that the use of local memory accelerates the processing time by 23-30%.

7. EXPERIMENTS

7.1 Experimental Setup

We extensively measured the performance of *DeepMon* with a variety of deep learning models and mobile GPUs.

Workloads. We used a variety of deep learning models as shown in Table 1. We mainly report the results for two deep models, VGG-VeryDeep-16 and YOLO, and report the results for other models only when they are significant. We used the VGG-VeryDeep-16 model trained with the ILSVRC2012 train dataset [44] and YOLO trained with the Pascal VOC 2007 train dataset [8].

Metrics and datasets. We used processing latency, accuracy, and powerer consumption as our key evaluation metrics. For the latency, we measured the duration to process an image, i.e., $t_1 - t_2$ where t_1 is the time that *DeepMon* outputs the inference result and t_2 is the time that *DeepMon* receives the input image. For the latency evaluation, we used two test datasets: (i) the *UCF101* dataset [48] comprising 13,421 short videos (less than a minute long) created for activity recognition and (ii) LENA dataset [47] consists of 200 first-person-view videos captured from Google Glasses, and report the average latency across all processed frames along with the 95% confidence interval. We used the UCF101 dataset by default while we report the performance for LENA dataset in Section 7.8 and Section 7.9.

For accuracy, we measured the percentage of accuracy drop compared to the original models. We focused on the drop as our goal is not to improve the accuracy but to keep it close to that of the original models while accelerating inference speed. Note: unlike prior

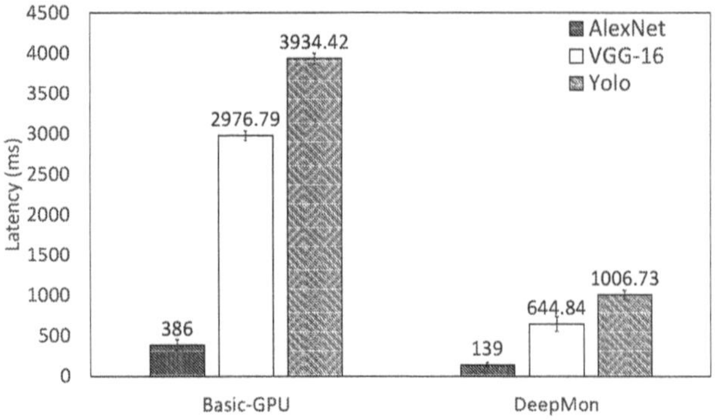

Figure 9: Overall Processing Latency

work [25], we did not reduce the total number of possible output categories (e.g., the number of objects that can be recognized by the model). For the accuracy evaluation, we used the ILSVRC2012 [44] validation dataset for VGG-VeryDeep-16 and the Pascal VOC 2007 test dataset [20] for YOLO, and calculated the average accuracy over each test dataset. For YOLO, we used the mean average precision (mAP), which is a standard metric to evaluate the YOLO's accuracy regarding both object recognition and localization [21].

Finally, we measured the power consumption using the Monsoon power monitor [5]. We reported the average energy consumption of the smartphone while processing an image in uAh by measuring the baseline energy consumption before running the processing logic and deducting the baseline from the measured value. For energy evaluation, we used the UCF101 dataset (the same dataset used in the latency evaluation), and report the average energy consumption across all processed frames along with the 95% confidence interval.

Alternatives. We compared the performance of *DeepMon* with other plausible smartphone-based alternatives such as *basic-CPU* and *basic-GPU*, and a few cloud-based alternatives. *basic-CPU* only uses the mobile CPUs to compute the full deep learning pipelines while *basic-GPU* utilizes the mobile GPUs for all processing layers without optimization. For the cloud-based approaches, the mobile device sends images to a cloud server, the server processes the images and return the results back to the mobile device (details of the cloud-based alternatives are explained in Section 7.4). Also, to look into the benefit of *DeepMon*, we applied different combinations of the optimization techniques presented in Section 6 such as convolutional layer caching (denoted as CA in the figures), layer decomposition (DC), and half floating-point calculation (HF).

Devices and APIs. We used a Samsung Galaxy S7 (with Mali T880 GPU), a Samsung Galaxy Note 4 (with Adreno 420), and a Sony Xperia Z5 (with Adreno 430) as our experiment devices. Unless mentioned, we used the S7 as the default device. Also, we used the OpenCL implementation of *DeepMon* by default while we measured the performance of the Vulkan implementation in Section 7.7.

7.2 Processing Latency

We first study the overall processing latency of *DeepMon* in comparison with naive approaches. Figure 9 shows the results, on an S7, for the three models: AlexNet (trained with the ILSVRC2012 train dataset), VGG-VeryDeep-16 and YOLO.

The figure shows that *DeepMon* accelerates the processing of deep learning models by 3-5 times compared to *basic-GPU*. *DeepMon* processes VGG-VeryDeep-16, a model with 13 convolutional layers and 3 fully-connected layers, at the latency of 644ms, enabling near real-time processing of continuous image streams. YOLO

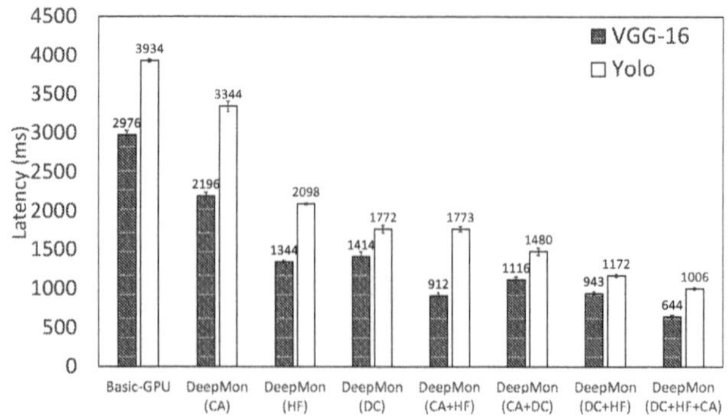

CA: Convolutional Layer Caching
DC: Layer Decomposition
HF: Half Floating-Point Optimization

Figure 10: *DeepMon* Latency Breakdown

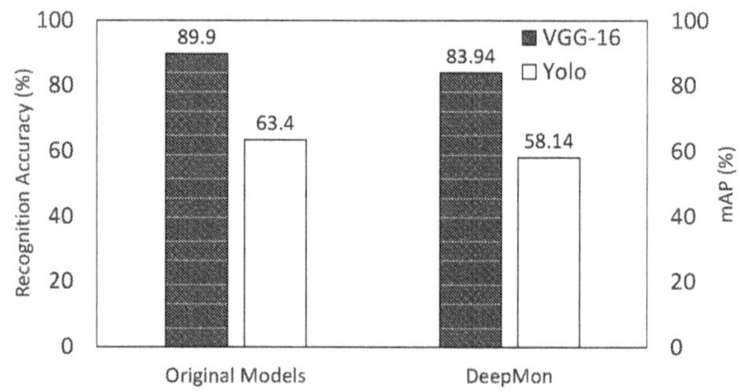

We reported the classification accuracy for VGG-VeryDeep-16 and the mean average precision (mAP) for YOLO.

Figure 11: Recognition Accuracy

takes about 1 second as it includes more number of convolutional layers to track their locations of the objects.

For smaller models such as AlexNet (or equivalents such as VGG-F or VGG-M with 5 convolutional layers and 3 fully-connected layers), *DeepMon* can process an image with just 139 ms of latency. Note: The processing time of *basic-CPU* is slower by one or two orders of magnitude depending on the model. It takes 6345ms for *basic-CPU* to process an image using AlexNet, which is 45.6 times slower than *DeepMon*.

Digging deeper, we analysed which *DeepMon* techniques contribute to the processing benefits. Figure 10 shows the latency breakdown for VGG-VeryDeep-16 and YOLO while cumulatively applying the various optimization techniques. The results show that all techniques significantly contribute to the latency reduction for VGG-VeryDeep-16. For YOLO, the benefit of the caching was smaller than VGG-VeryDeep-16 as the layer decomposition technique highly optimizes the first few convolutional layers, making the reuse of the cached results less beneficial.

7.3 Recognition Accuracy

Next, we investigate how much accuracy *DeepMon* compromises in return for the latency benefits. Figure 11 shows the classification accuracy of the original VGG-VeryDeep-16 and the mAP of YOLO as well as the converted models optimized to run on *DeepMon*. The figure shows that *DeepMon* drops about 5-6% of ac-

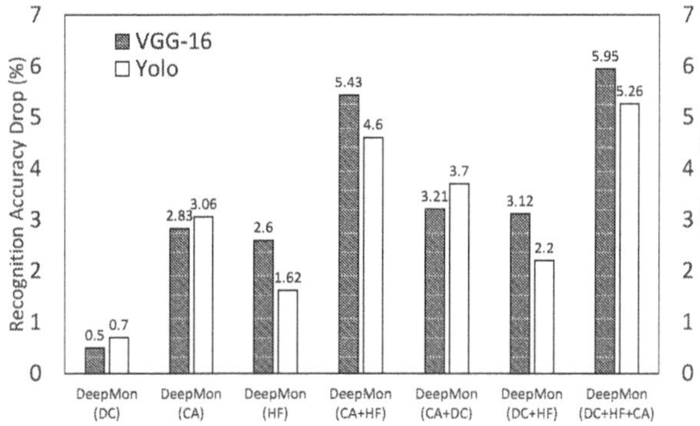

CA: Convolutional Layer Caching
DC: Layer Decomposition
HF: Half Floating-Point Optimization

Figure 12: Breakdown of *DeepMon* Accuracy Drop

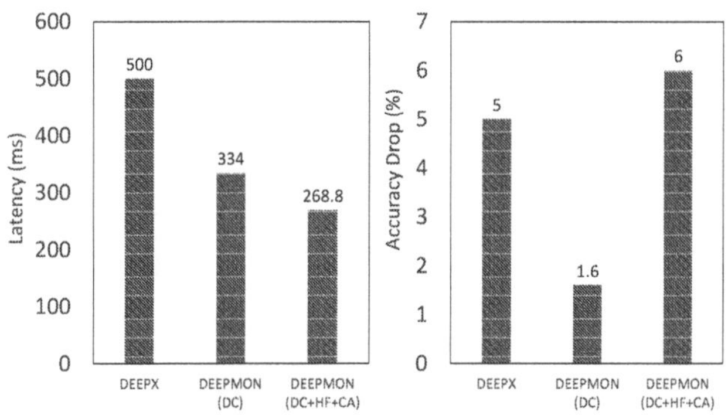

(a) Inference Latency (Left)
(b) Accuracy Drop (Right)

Figure 13: Comparison to DeepX on Samsung Galaxy S5

curacy while accelerating the latency 4-5 times. We designed our techniques to keep the properties of the original architecture, thus minimizing the impact on the recognition output. Note that Fast-YOLO [43], a lightweight version of YOLO shows the lower mAP of 52.7%, which is 5.44% lower than that of *DeepMon*, while the latency benefit of Fast-YOLO was similar to *DeepMon* (i.e., ≈4.5 times when experimented on Samsung S7).

We further analysed which of *DeepMon's* components contributed to the accuracy drop. Figure 12 shows the results by applying the three different techniques that affect the accuracy. The accuracy drop by layer decomposition is marginal, indicating that our binary-search-based decomposition selects suitable decomposition parameters. Also, the convolutional layer caching reduces accuracy by about ≈3%, showing that the use of cached results marginally affects the accuracy for video streams.

7.4 Comparison with Other Approaches

We now compare the processing latency of *DeepMon* with DeepX, the state-of-the-art mobile deep learning inference engine. Figure 13 shows the latency and accuracy drop of DeepX and *DeepMon*; we ran AlexNet using the SnapDragon 801 processor. DeepX consumes 500ms to process an image with an accuracy drop of 5%. *DeepMon's* latency was 269ms, twice as fast as DeepX, when all techniques are applied while its accuracy drop was 1% higher at 6%. *DeepMon* can be adjusted to only use the layer decomposition

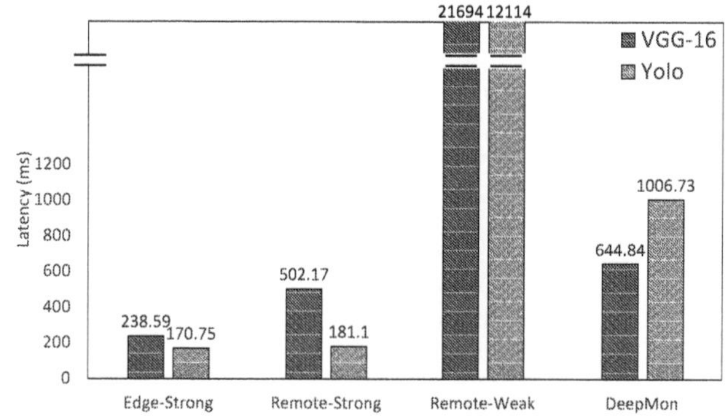

Figure 14: Comparison with the Cloud-based Approach

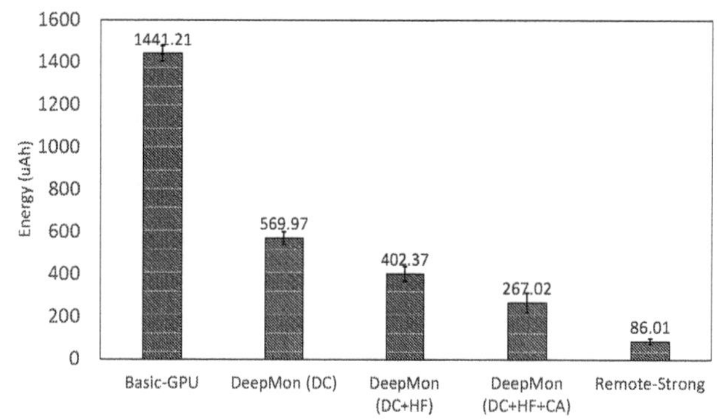

Figure 15: Overall Power Consumption

method which achieves 333ms latency (≈33% faster than DeepX), but with only a 1.6% accuracy drop.

We also compared the latency of *DeepMon* with the cloud-based alternatives. Figure 14 shows the results. We used three different cloud variants: *edge-strong*, *remote-strong*, and *remote-weak*. For, *edge-strong*, the mobile phone and the server was connected through the local Wi-Fi network while the server is equipped with a NVidia GTX 980 GPU (2,048 GPU cores, 8GB memory size and 224GB/s memory bandwidth). For *remote-strong* and *remote-weak*, we used Amazon EC2 servers (in particular g2.2xlarge and t2.medium instances respectively) located in the EC2 Asia Pacific (Singapore) datacenter. *remote-strong* was equipped with a K520 GPU (with 8 cores and 15 GB of memory) with while *remote-weak* had no GPU. We used the Caffe [30] and YOLO [43] frameworks to run the models on the cloud.

edge-strong is 2.7 times faster than *DeepMon* while *remote-strong* is only 28% faster than *DeepMon*for VGG-VeryDeep-16. The latencies of *remote-weak* were 33.6 and 12 times slower than *DeepMon* , respectively, due to its CPU-based execution of deep learning models. This suggests that we can leverage cloud services for home- or office-based applications where the user can offload the data safely to the edge servers with low networking latency and fewer privacy concerns. On the other hand, we need to be careful about using the remote clouds even when the users are willing to send the data. The cost for *remote-strong* (using g2.2xlarge server instance) is 1 USD per hour, imposing huge service cost for continuous vision applications. We can use less powerful instances, although doing so might not improve the latency as indicated by the numbers for *remote-weak*.

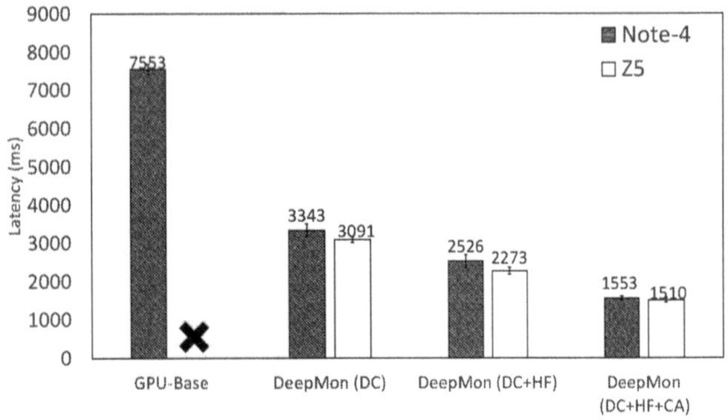

Figure 16: Processing Latency for Different GPUs

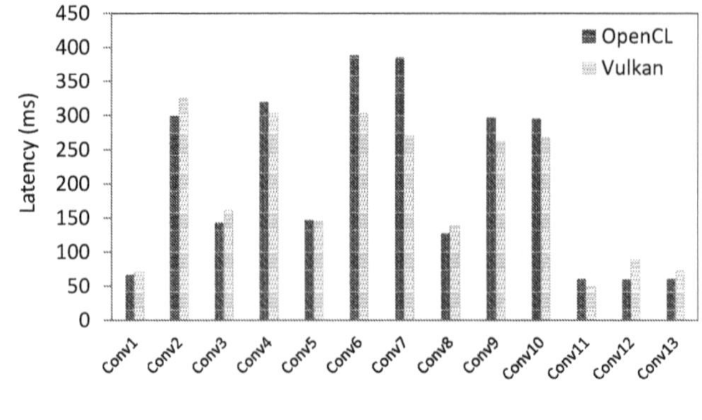

Figure 17: Performance of Vulkan

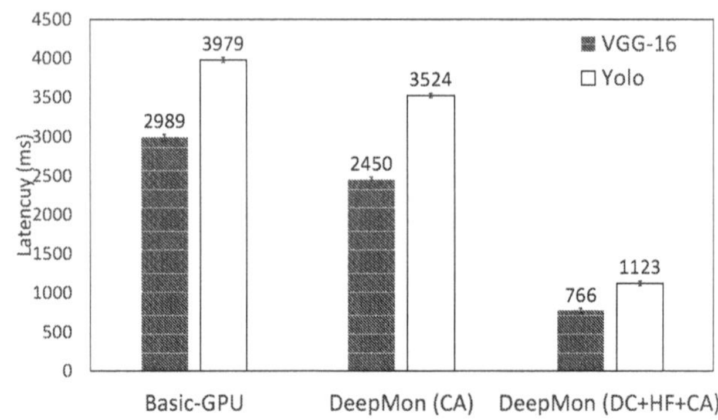

Figure 18: Latency on the LENA Dataset

7.5 Power Consumption

We now investigate the power consumption of *DeepMon* in comparison with *basic-GPU*, *remote-strong*, and *remote-weak*. Figure 15 shows the overall power consumption for each approach along with the breakdown. All *DeepMon* measurements were done on Samsung Note 4 as it has a detachable battery that could be tapped with the Monsoon power meter.

The figure shows that *DeepMon* is lower than the power consumption of basic-GPU by more than 5 times for both VGG-VeryDeep-16 and YOLO. This savings is mostly from the reduced processing time. *remote-strong* consumes 3 times lesser power as the mobile device consumes power only to send the image to the cloud and then goes into power saving mode until it receives the result. However, as stated earlier, you need a large expensive server instance to see small latency benefits compared to *DeepMon*.

7.6 Latency on Other Mobile GPUs

We next studied the processing latency of *DeepMon* across different GPUs. We used a Samsung Galaxy Note 4 (with Adreno 420) and a Sony Xperia Z5 (Adreno 430). Figure 16 shows the results. While the latency reduction pattern by all our optimization strategies remains similar, the absolute processing latency increases by 2.4 times for the Note 4 and 2.34 times for the Z5, compared to the Samsung Galaxy S7 (with Mali T 880). Even though the direct comparison between Mali and Adreno is non-trivial, Mali's faster performance is likely to result from having more GPU cores and higher memory bandwidth compared to Adreno 420 and 430. We also noticed that the original VGG-VeryDeep-16 model cannot be run on Z5 due to the limitations of the heap memory size – although it can run after the decomposition technique reduces the model size by half.

7.7 Latency of Vulkan

We also explored the performance of the Vulkan implementation of *DeepMon*. We used the Samsung Galaxy S7 that supports both Vulkan and OpenCL. Figure 17 shows the processing time per convolutional layer for VGG-VeryDeep-16. Even though there are small differences in processing time per layer (compared to OpenCL), all our techniques are equally effective on Vulkan as well, resulting in similar overall processing times.

7.8 Performance on First-Person-View Videos

We further evaluated the latency and accuracy of *DeepMon* over the first-person-view dataset, LENA, which could be the typical workload for *DeepMon*. For accuracy, we reported the percentage of frames that the base model and *DeepMon* outputs the different classification result – we define this as the output difference ratio. For VGG-VeryDeep-16, we consider that the output is different when the top-1 classification results of the base model and *DeepMon* are different. For YOLO, we consider that the output is different when the positions of the detected object (indicated as rectangles on the image) overlap less than 50% (i.e., *Intersection-Over-Union (IoU)* < 50%).

Figure 18 shows the latency of *DeepMon* on the entire LENA dataset. *DeepMon* shows ≈4 times of overall latency reduction, which is comparable to the benefit over the UCF101 dataset. In particular, our caching technique reduced ≈22% and ≈13% of the total execution times of VGG-Verydeep-16 and YOLO, respectively. The reduction rate was slightly decreased compared to that of the UCF101 dataset since the first-person-view videos tend to have more frequent changes in the recorded scenes due to continuous head movement. However, the results show that our caching technique is still effective for the first-person-view videos.

Figure 19 shows the output difference ratio. *DeepMon* produces different outputs for 25.89% and 12.28% of the total frames compared to the base VGG-VeryDeep-16 and YOLO models, respectively. We empirically looked into such differently-classified frames and found out that most of those frames are not correctly classified or do not have a matching class in the base model, margin-ally affecting the actual accuracy.

Interestingly, the output difference ratio of VGG-Verydeep-16 is much higher than that of YOLO. This is because VGG-Verydeep-16 always outputs one of the 1,000 pre-trained classes even though the target frame is unlikely to be one of the 1,000 classes; for the consecutive frames with low classification confidences, their top-1 classified objects vary sensitively from one frame to another (al-

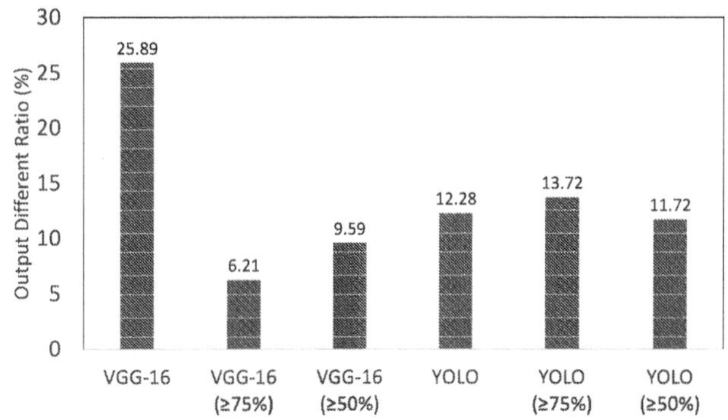

VGG-16(≥75%) indicates the accuracy evaluated only on the videos with the average confident score above 75%. Similar explanation applies to VGG-16(≥50%), YOLO(≥75%), and YOLO(≥50%).

Figure 19: Accuracy on the LENA Dataset

	SIFT-based	Histogram-based
Overhead (ms)	2,580	4.77
Overall latency change (ms)	2,064 (increased)	-534 (decreased)
Output difference ratio (%)	3.875	6.21
Cache hit rate (%)	31.4	35.52

Table 6: Caching Performance Analysis

though the frames include the same object), making our caching results different from the newly calculated ones. We further calculated the output difference ratio only over the videos that have the average classification confidence higher than 75% and 50%, and the output difference ratio was reduced to 6.21 and 9.59, respectively. For YOLO, the output difference ratio did not vary much since the model eliminated "others" when its classification confidence was below a certain threshold.

7.9 Convolutional Layer Caching Performance

We further studied how our caching technique performed over the LENA dataset. We used Vgg-VeryDeep-16 for this study. Table 6 shows the results on the videos with the average confidence score over 75%. *DeepMon* (with its histogram-based caching) shows the average latency reduction of 538 ms. The benefit comes from 35.52% of cache hits, significantly reducing unnecessary recalculation of convolution operations. We noticed that the latency reduction was ≈20% less than that of the UCF101 dataset. As expected, the cache hit rate over LENA, the first-person-view dataset, was lower compared the cache hit rate over the UCF101 dataset. This is mainly because head-mounted cameras tend to move more than third-person-view cameras, resulting in bigger differences between the two consecutive images.

We also compared our proposed histogram-based caching algorithm against an alternative using SIFT features [41]. Although SIFT-based algorithm provides the lower output difference ratio (3.875%) than the ratio of the histogram-based algorithm (6.21%), extracting SIFT features from multiple blocks of an image is highly time-consuming; it took over 2.5 seconds to calculate SIFT features for an image (across all convolutional layers). Due to high overhead to calculate the SIFT features, it cannot be used to compare image blocks for caching. On the other hand, our histogram-based approach can compare blocks of an image within 5 ms, making it much more suitable to be adopted for our caching algorithm.

	Base	Base+HF	DC	DC+HF
VGG-Verydeep-16(MB)	578	289	517	258.5
YOLO(MB)	1,116	558	1,002	501

"Base" indicates the original model.

Table 7: Memory Footprint

7.10 Memory Footprint

Table 7 shows the memory footprint for VGG-Verydeep-16 and YOLO. The memory usage is well within the available memory spaces of commodity mobile devices, showing that *DeepMon* manages its memory usage efficiently. Also, the decomposition and half-floating point approximation reduce the memory usage of *DeepMon*; they reduce the memory usage from 578MB and 1116MB down to 258.5MB and 501MB for VGG-Verydeep-16 and YOLO, respectively. For the models that require large memory spaces, other optimization techniques such as *Singular Value Decomposition* (SVD) [35] can be applied to further reduce the memory usage.

DeepMon mainly uses the memory to load the model and stores input and output of a layer. *DeepMon* stores the entire model within system memory for efficient inference since it is time-consuming to load the model on-demand from the external memory. On the other hand, *DeepMon* only stores input and output of the currently executing layer – it discards all output data from previous layers once they become of no use to keep memory usage as low as possible. Accordingly, memory usage of *DeepMon* is capped at the size of the model and the largest input and output size of a single layer.

8. CONCLUSION

In this paper, we present *DeepMon*, a system for enabling the low-latency execution of deep DNNs on a mobile GPU. *DeepMon* uses various optimisation techniques including the convolutional layer caching, decomposition, and matrix multiplication optimizations to achieve significant speedups (over 3-4x) compared to state-of-the-art current solutions. In particular, *DeepMon* allows DNN-based face/object detection models, such as VGG-VeryDeep-16 and YOLO, to process video frames at 1 to 2 frames per second. We implemented *DeepMon* in both OpenCL and Vulkan and tested it's effectiveness using three different mobile GPUs (Adreno 420, Adreno 430, and Mali T 880) and against alternative solutions such as state-of-the-art research systems (DeepX) and plausible cloud-based solutions. Our results show that *DeepMon* significantly outperforms all local-computation-only based solutions with a marginal drop in accuracy and that *DeepMon's* latency and accuracy combination can only be bettered by using very large (and expensive) cloud server instances with very good networking connectivity. Videos of *DeepMon* in action are available at http://is.gd/DeepMon. Also, *DeepMon*'s source code can be found at https://github.com/JC1DA/DeepMon.

9. ACKNOWLEDGEMENTS

We sincerely thank our shepherd, Matthai Philipose, for providing excellent iterative feedback that greatly improved our paper. We also thank the anonymous reviewers for their valuable comments. This research is supported by the National Research Foundation, Prime Minister's Office, Singapore under its IDM Futures Funding Initiative.

10. REFERENCES

[1] A brief report of the heuritech deep learning meetup 5. https://blog.heuritech.com/2016/02/29/a-brief-report-of-the-heuritech-deep-learning-meetup-5/. Accessed: 2016-12-8.

[2] Common objects in context. http://mscoco.org/. Accessed: 2016-12-8.

[3] Google glass. https://developers.google.com/glass/. Accessed: 2016-12-8.

[4] Hololens. https://www.microsoft.com/microsoft-hololens/en-us. Accessed: 2016-12-8.

[5] Monsoon power monitor. https://www.msoon.com/LabEquipment/PowerMonitor/. Accessed: 2016-12-8.

[6] Nvidia cuda toolkit. https://developer.nvidia.com/cuda-toolkit. Accessed: 2016-12-8.

[7] Opencl. https://www.khronos.org/opencl/. Accessed: 2016-12-8.

[8] Pascal visual object classes. http://host.robots.ox.ac.uk/pascal/VOC/. Accessed: 2016-12-8.

[9] Vulkan. https://www.khronos.org/vulkan/. Accessed: 2016-12-8.

[10] Balan, R. K., Gergle, D., Satyanarayanan, M., and Herbsleb, J. Simplifying cyber foraging for mobile devices. *Proceedings of the 5th International Conference on Mobile Systems, Applications and Services*, MobiSys '07, pages 272–285, New York, NY, USA, 2007. ACM.

[11] Balan, R. K., Satyanarayanan, M., Park, S. Y., and Okoshi, T. Tactics-based remote execution for mobile computing. *Proceedings of the 1st International Conference on Mobile Systems, Applications and Services*, MobiSys '03, pages 273–286, New York, NY, USA, 2003. ACM.

[12] Boger, J., Hoey, J., Poupart, P., Boutilier, C., Fernie, G., and Mihailidis, A. A planning system based on markov decision processes to guide people with dementia through activities of daily living. *IEEE Transactions on Information Technology in Biomedicine*, 10(2):323–333, 2006.

[13] Chatfield, K., Simonyan, K., Vedaldi, A., and Zisserman, A. Return of the devil in the details: Delving deep into convolutional nets. *arXiv preprint arXiv:1405.3531*, 2014.

[14] Chellapilla, K., Puri, S., and Simard, P. High Performance Convolutional Neural Networks for Document Processing. In Lorette, G., editor, *Tenth International Workshop on Frontiers in Handwriting Recognition*, La Baule (France), Oct. 2006. Université de Rennes 1, Suvisoft. http://www.suvisoft.com.

[15] Chen, T. Y.-H., Ravindranath, L., Deng, S., Bahl, P., and Balakrishnan, H. Glimpse: Continuous, real-time object recognition on mobile devices. *Proceedings of the 13th ACM Conference on Embedded Networked Sensor Systems*, SenSys '15, pages 155–168, New York, NY, USA, 2015. ACM.

[16] Cuervo, E., Balasubramanian, A., Cho, D.-k., Wolman, A., Saroiu, S., Chandra, R., and Bahl, P. Maui: Making smartphones last longer with code offload. *Proceedings of the 8th International Conference on Mobile Systems, Applications, and Services*, MobiSys '10, pages 49–62, New York, NY, USA, 2010. ACM.

[17] Dalal, N. and Triggs, B. Histograms of oriented gradients for human detection. *Proceedings of 2005 IEEE Computer Society Conference on Computer Vision and Pattern Recognition*, volume 1 of *CVPR '05*, pages 886–893. IEEE, 2005.

[18] Denton, E. L., Zaremba, W., Bruna, J., LeCun, Y., and Fergus, R. Exploiting linear structure within convolutional networks for efficient evaluation. *Advances in Neural Information Processing Systems*, pages 1269–1277, 2014.

[19] Donahue, J., Anne Hendricks, L., Guadarrama, S., Rohrbach, M., Venugopalan, S., Saenko, K., and Darrell, T. Long-term recurrent convolutional networks for visual recognition and description. *Proceedings of the IEEE Conference on Computer Vision and Pattern Recognition*, CVPR '15, pages 2625–2634, 2015.

[20] Everingham, M., Eslami, S. A., Van Gool, L., Williams, C. K., Winn, J., and Zisserman, A. The pascal visual object classes challenge: A retrospective. *International Journal of Computer Vision*, 111(1):98–136, 2015.

[21] Everingham, M., Van Gool, L., Williams, C. K., Winn, J., and Zisserman, A. The pascal visual object classes (voc) challenge. *International Journal of Computer Vision*, 88(2):303–338, 2010.

[22] Girshick, R. Fast r-cnn. *Proceedings of the IEEE International Conference on Computer Vision*, pages 1440–1448, 2015.

[23] Grasedyck, L., Kressner, D., and Tobler, C. A literature survey of low-rank tensor approximation techniques. *GAMM-Mitteilungen*, 36(1):53–78, 2013.

[24] Ha, K., Chen, Z., Hu, W., Richter, W., Pillai, P., and Satyanarayanan, M. Towards wearable cognitive assistance. *Proceedings of the 12th Annual International Conference on Mobile Systems, Applications, and Services*, MobiSys '14, pages 68–81, New York, NY, USA, 2014. ACM.

[25] Han, S., Shen, H., Philipose, M., Agarwal, S., Wolman, A., and Krishnamurthy, A. Mcdnn: An approximation-based execution framework for deep stream processing under resource constraints. *Proceedings of the 14th Annual International Conference on Mobile Systems, Applications, and Services*, MobiSys '16, pages 123–136, New York, NY, USA, 2016. ACM.

[26] He, K., Zhang, X., Ren, S., and Sun, J. Deep residual learning for image recognition. *Proceedings of the IEEE Conference on Computer Vision and Pattern Recognition*, pages 770–778, 2016.

[27] Hochreiter, S. and Schmidhuber, J. Long short-term memory. *Neural computation*, 9(8):1735–1780, 1997.

[28] Huynh, L. N., Balan, R. K., and Lee, Y. Deepsense: A gpu-based deep convolutional neural network framework on commodity mobile devices. *Proceedings of the 2016 Workshop on Wearable Systems and Applications*, WearSys '16, pages 25–30, New York, NY, USA, 2016. ACM.

[29] Jaderberg, M., Vedaldi, A., and Zisserman, A. Speeding up convolutional neural networks with low rank expansions. *CoRR*, abs/1405.3866, 2014.

[30] Jia, Y., Shelhamer, E., Donahue, J., Karayev, S., Long, J., Girshick, R., Guadarrama, S., and Darrell, T. Caffe: Convolutional architecture for fast feature embedding. *Proceedings of the 22nd ACM international conference on Multimedia*, pages 675–678. ACM, 2014.

[31] Kim, Y., Park, E., Yoo, S., Choi, T., Yang, L., and Shin, D. Compression of deep convolutional neural networks for fast and low power mobile applications. *CoRR*, abs/1511.06530, 2015.

[32] Kim, Y.-D., Park, E., Yoo, S., Choi, T., Yang, L., and Shin, D. Compression of deep convolutional neural networks for fast and low power mobile applications. *arXiv preprint arXiv:1511.06530*, 2015.

[33] Krizhevsky, A., Sutskever, I., and Hinton, G. E. Imagenet classification with deep convolutional neural networks. *Advances in Neural Information Processing Systems*, pages 1097–1105, 2012.

[34] Lane, N. and Bhattacharya, S. Sparsifying deep learning layers for constrained resource inference on wearables. *Proceedings of the 14th ACM Conference on Embedded Network Sensor Systems*, pages 176–189. ACM, 2016.

[35] Lane, N. D., Bhattacharya, S., Georgiev, P., Forlivesi, C., Jiao, L., Qendro, L., and Kawsar, F. Deepx: A software accelerator for low-power deep learning inference on mobile devices. *2016 15th ACM/IEEE International Conference on Information Processing in Sensor Networks*, IPSN '16, pages 1–12. IEEE, 2016.

[36] Lane, N. D., Georgiev, P., and Qendro, L. Deepear: Robust smartphone audio sensing in unconstrained acoustic environments using deep learning. *Proceedings of the 2015 ACM International Joint Conference on Pervasive and Ubiquitous Computing*, UbiComp '15, pages 283–294, New York, NY, USA, 2015. ACM.

[37] Lebedev, V., Ganin, Y., Rakhuba, M., Oseledets, I., and Lempitsky, V. Speeding-up convolutional neural networks using fine-tuned cp-decomposition. *arXiv preprint arXiv:1412.6553*, 2014.

[38] LiKamWa, R., Priyantha, B., Philipose, M., Zhong, L., and Bahl, P. Energy characterization and optimization of image sensing toward continuous mobile vision. *Proceeding of the 11th Annual International Conference on Mobile Systems, Applications, and Services*, MobiSys '13, pages 69–82, New York, NY, USA, 2013. ACM.

[39] LiKamWa, R. and Zhong, L. Starfish: Efficient concurrency support for computer vision applications. *Proceedings of the 13th Annual International Conference on Mobile Systems, Applications, and Services*, MobiSys '15, pages 213–226, New York, NY, USA, 2015. ACM.

[40] Mathieu, M., Henaff, M., and LeCun, Y. Fast training of convolutional networks through ffts. *CoRR*, abs/1312.5851, 2013.

[41] Morel, J.-M. and Yu, G. Asift: A new framework for fully affine invariant image comparison. *SIAM Journal on Imaging Sciences*, 2(2):438–469, 2009.

[42] Parkhi, O. M., Vedaldi, A., and Zisserman, A. Deep face recognition. *Proceedings of 2015 British Machine Vision Conference*, volume 1, page 6, 2015.

[43] Redmon, J., Divvala, S., Girshick, R., and Farhadi, A. You only look once: Unified, real-time object detection. *arXiv preprint arXiv:1506.02640*, 2015.

[44] Russakovsky, O., Deng, J., Su, H., Krause, J., Satheesh, S., Ma, S., Huang, Z., Karpathy, A., Khosla, A., Bernstein, M., et al. Imagenet large scale visual recognition challenge. *International Journal of Computer Vision*, 115(3):211–252, 2015.

[45] Sainath, T. N., Kingsbury, B., Sindhwani, V., Arisoy, E., and Ramabhadran, B. Low-rank matrix factorization for deep neural network training with high-dimensional output targets. *Proceedings of 2013 IEEE International Conference on Acoustics, Speech and Signal Processing*, ICASSP '13, pages 6655–6659. IEEE, 2013.

[46] Simonyan, K. and Zisserman, A. Very deep convolutional networks for large-scale image recognition. *arXiv preprint arXiv:1409.1556*, 2014.

[47] Song, S., Chandrasekhar, V., Cheung, N.-M., Narayan, S., Li, L., and Lim, J.-H. Activity recognition in egocentric life-logging videos. *Asian Conference on Computer Vision*, pages 445–458. Springer, 2014.

[48] Soomro, K., Zamir, A. R., and Shah, M. Ucf101: A dataset of 101 human actions classes from videos in the wild. *arXiv preprint arXiv:1212.0402*, 2012.

[49] Urban, G., Geras, K. J., Kahou, S. E., Aslan, Ö., Wang, S., Caruana, R., Mohamed, A., Philipose, M., and Richardson, M. Do deep convolutional nets really need to be deep (or even convolutional)? *CoRR*, abs/1603.05691, 2016.

[50] Vanhoucke, V., Senior, A., and Mao, M. Z. Improving the speed of neural networks on cpus. *Deep Learning and Unsupervised Feature Learning Workshop, NIPS 2011*, 2011.

[51] Vedaldi, A. and Lenc, K. Matconvnet: Convolutional neural networks for matlab. *Proceedings of the 23rd ACM International Conference on Multimedia*, pages 689–692. ACM, 2015.

Enabling High-Precision Visible Light Localization in Today's Buildings

Shilin Zhu and Xinyu Zhang
University of Wisconsin-Madison
{szhu,xyzhang}@ece.wisc.edu

ABSTRACT

For over one decade, research in visible light positioning has focused on using modulated LEDs as location landmarks. But the need for specialized LED fixtures, and the associated retrofitting cost, has been hindering the adoption of VLP. In this paper, we forgo this approach and design iLAMP to enable reliable, high-precision VLP using conventional LEDs and fluorescent lamps inside today's buildings. Our key observation is that these lamps intrinsically possess hidden visual features, which are imperceptible to human eyes, but can be extracted by capturing and processing the lamps' images using a computational imaging framework. Simply using commodity smartphones' front cameras, our approach can identify lamps within a building with close to 100% accuracy. Furthermore, we develop a geometrical model which combines the camera image with gyroscope/accelerometer output, to estimate a smartphone's 3D location and heading direction relative to each lamp landmark. Our field tests demonstrate a mean localization (heading) precision of 3 cm (2.6°) and 90-percentile 3.5 cm (2.8°), even if a single lamp falls in the camera's field of view.

1. INTRODUCTION

Over the past decade, there has been a concerted research effort in developing an accurate, reliable, and ready-to-use indoor localization system for smartphones. Such a system can enable a multitude of location-based services. Some of the use cases include: precise navigation to rooms/items of interest in office buildings, museums, airports, and shopping centers; targeted advertisement, product recommendation and coupon delivery in retail stores; consumer analytics through aggregated foot-traffic patterns and dwell time; multi-players augmented-reality games, *etc.* To unleash these services and trigger wide adoption, the localization technology must provide the business operators or customers a compelling quality of experience, specifically in terms of: high precision, high robustness, low cost (in terms of location sensor hardware and infrastructure maintenance), and mobile friendliness (low latency and low power consumption).

Despite a wide spectrum of indoor localization technologies, there has been very limited adoption into real-world scenarios, mainly because of the challenges in simultaneously satisfying the above key metrics. Mainstream approaches, especially those based on RF signals, focused intensively on improving the location precision. In particular, recent multi-antenna based solutions have achieved a median precision of decimeters [1–3]. But they fall short of robustness in real building environment—the 90% location error often reaches 3 to 10 meters [1–3], which may jeopardize user experience. The root cause lies in the elusive nature of the wireless channel. High precision RF localization relies on phase or received signal strength (RSS), metrics that can be easily affected by ambient multipath reflections. In effect, human body blockage, reflection and even hand gestures can significantly disturb such wireless channel profiles [4, 5].

As an alternative modality, visible light positioning (VLP) holds potential to overcome the instability owing to the almost multipath-free propagation. VLP can achieve decimeter to centimeter precision, using specialized "beaconing LEDs" as location landmarks, and photodiodes [6–8] or smartphone cameras [9–11] as location sensors. However, deploying such VLP systems at building scale entails changing the fixtures/bulbs at substantial retrofitting cost. To date, fluorescent lights (FLs) occupy 85% of the commercial buildings in the US [12]. Even the *basic LEDs* only account for 12%, and will take another 10 to 15 years to dominate the market [12], not to mention the smart beaconing LEDs. A recent solution, LiTell [13], enabled low-cost VLP by sensing FLs' inherent flickering frequencies. However, these frequency features are extremely weak. They are detectable only on FLs, under low ceilings (< 2.5 m) and with high-resolution back cameras. Moreover, such features can discriminate individual lights with only 60% accuracy, which hampers reliability.

In this paper, we propose a novel VLP system, called iLAMP, to fill the missing spot that meets the multi-faceted challenges. iLAMP uses a smartphone camera to discriminate existing FLs and LEDs, based on visual features extracted from a computational imaging framework. Furthermore, it can reliably derive the smartphone's heading direction and 3D location at centimeter precision, even when a single light landmark is visible. Leveraging the ubiquitous lighting infrastructure, iLAMP can bring highly reliable and accurate indoor localization to today's buildings, at no extra hardware cost.

The key challenge for iLAMP lies in discriminating the incumbent lights, which have no beacon-generation hardware and often come from the same model when deployed in a building. Nonetheless, iLAMP's computational imaging solution can extrapolate hidden features from images of the lights. It stores these features as unique signatures in a server database during the setup phase, and uses simple feature matching mechanism to derive a light's identity during the run-time localization phase. The *main feature* that iLAMP harnesses is the *spatial radiance pattern* (SRP), defined as the radiance intensity distribution across a light's

Permission to make digital or hard copies of all or part of this work for personal or classroom use is granted without fee provided that copies are not made or distributed for profit or commercial advantage and that copies bear this notice and the full citation on the first page. Copyrights for components of this work owned by others than ACM must be honored. Abstracting with credit is permitted. To copy otherwise, or republish, to post on servers or to redistribute to lists, requires prior specific permission and/or a fee. Request permissions from permissions@acm.org.

MobiSys '17, June 19–23, 2017, Niagara Falls, NY, USA.
© 2017 ACM. ISBN 978-1-4503-4928-4/17/06...$15.00
DOI: http://dx.doi.org/10.1145/3081333.3081335

body. This SRP feature is resilient to the camera's viewing angle/distance, and highly diverse among lights due to inevitable manufacturing variations. In addition, iLAMP employs two sets of *assistant features*, derived from the smartphone's ambient light sensor (ALS) and camera RGB output, respectively, as coarse-grained pre-filters to curtail the computational cost in matching the main feature. Low computational load in turn translates into low response latency.

Once a light landmark is identified, a camera-based VLP system can employ the photogrammetry technique in computer vision [14] to derive a smartphone's physical location relative to the landmarks. State-of-the-art VLP solutions [6, 10] often require 3+ lights for triangulation, but smartphone cameras typically have a narrow FoV of only around 60° and can hardly capture more than one lights simultaneously in practical buildings. In contrast, iLAMP employs a *sensor-assisted photogrammetry* mechanism, which harnesses the inherent spatial heterogeneity of the radiance pattern, to estimate the phone's azimuth orientation, and subsequently its 3D location, even if a single light is visible.

Existing camera-based VLP [9,10,13] focused on full-operation mode, with camera always on, consuming substantial power (2 to 3 W [10,13]). Observing that ceiling luminaries tend to be scattered, iLAMP turns on a camera only when it gauges that a light falls in its FoV. The key idea is to use the smartphone's ALS as a gating device, and derive the intensity correlation between the ALS and camera through simple offline calibration. With this smart camera scheduler, we can duty cycle the operation and substantially reduce the power consumption.

We have implemented iLAMP as an Android application connected to a backend database server, and evaluated its performance against the aforementioned challenging requirements. Our experiments in real-world buildings show that iLAMP achieves around 95% accuracy in identifying different ceiling lights even when using radiance pattern alone, and close to 100% when combining the two assistant features. iLAMP achieves a mean location precision of 3.2 cm and 90-percentile of 3.5 cm under a single light, and even higher when multiple lights are visible. iLAMP also estimates the phone's azimuth (heading direction) with a small error of 2.6° and 90-percentile of 2.8°. More importantly, the performance remains highly stable under practical disturbing factors, such as random variation of phone orientation and phone-to-ceiling distance. Even under extremely sparse light deployment, iLAMP can still be combined with motion-sensor based dead-reckoning mechanisms, and maintain a few decimeters of location precision. In addition, iLAMP is efficient: it has a low end-to-end latency of 400-700 ms, and total power consumption of 927 mW on a smartphone (less than 1/2 compared with LiTell [13] or Luxapose [10]).

Despite more than one decade of research [15], VLP has not been widely adopted. The main contribution of iLAMP is to fill the sweet spot between accuracy, cost and reliability, and enable a VLP system that is immediately usable in today's buildings. More specifically,

(i) We design novel computational imaging mechanisms to extrapolate intrinsic visual features from incumbent FLs and LEDs, allowing them to be distinguishable at no extra hardware cost. We further introduce simple feature compression and matching schemes to make the light identification computationally efficient and robust to image distortion.

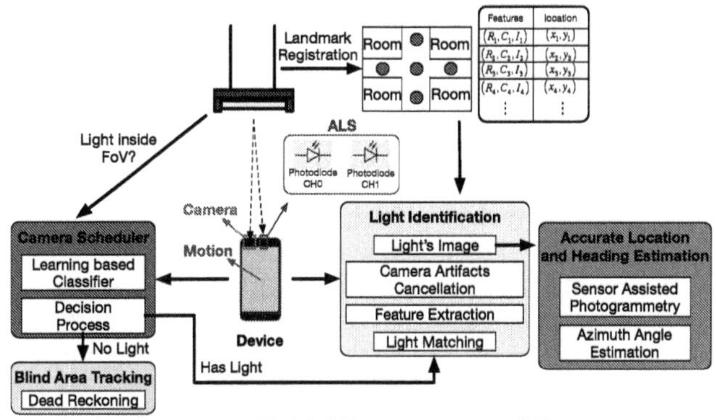

Figure 1: iLAMP system workflow.

(ii) We introduce a sensor assisted photogrammetry technique which can precisely locate a smartphone's 3D position and heading direction, even when a single light landmark is available.

(iii) We design a camera scheduling mechanism that duty cycles the power hungry camera based on its correlation with the low-power ALS. The mechanism can be generalized to all camera-based VLP systems.

2. iLAMP OVERVIEW

Main challenges and design goals. iLAMP builds its components around four major design goals: *(i)* Reliably discriminating existing ceiling lights with close to 0 confusion probability under a wide range of usage scenarios (various light models, ceiling heights, phone orientation, sunlight interference, *etc.*). *(ii)* Accurately estimating heading direction and 3D location with centimeter precision even under a single light. *(iii)* High computational efficiency, and real-time response to localization requests with sub-second end-to-end latency. *(iv)* High energy efficiency for continuous location tracking. Finally, iLAMP aims for an immediately usable localization system that is compatible with typical smartphone hardware.

System workflow. *iLAMP* comprises three main modules: light identification, phone location/heading estimation, and camera scheduling. Fig. 1 illustrates their work flow.

To bootstrap the system, we need to take a *benchmark image* for each light, extract its visual features, and register the ⟨*feature vector, location*⟩ pair in a server database. This *landmark registration* procedure only needs to be done once for each light. The light fixtures' locations are usually known at installation time; even manual survey of the locations is simple as the lights tend to be deployed regularly over space. Registering the lights' locations is also the minimal bootstrapping effort needed for all other VLP systems.

At run-time, the smartphone takes an image, preprocesses it to eliminate camera artifacts and remove background pixels (Sec. 3.1). It then extracts the *main feature* (*i.e.*, spatial radiance pattern) from pixels representing the light's body, and *compresses* the feature into a small-sized array (Sec. 3.1). Meanwhile, iLAMP computes two *assistant features*: the color pattern based on the image's RGB values, and the infrared to visible light intensity ratio (I2V ratio) based on the smartphone's ambient light sensor (ALS) (Sec. 4.1). These three features form a vector and are sent to the server. The server runs a hierarchical *light identification* algorithm: It uses the assistant features to narrow down the search space, and then looks up the database to identify the landmark whose main feature best matches the current light (Sec. 3.2).

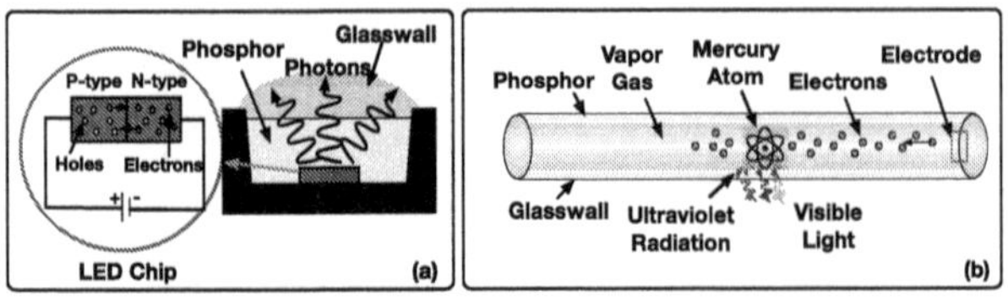

Figure 2: Physical principle of visible light emission of LED and fluorescent.

Once the light landmark is identified, iLAMP uses its *sensor assisted photogrammetry* to compute the phone's 3D location relative to the landmark, based on the camera image and the phone's gravity sensor output (Sec. 5.1). This approach also estimates the azimuth (heading direction) of the phone to substitute the notoriously inaccurate smartphone compass [16] (Sec. 5.2).

Both the light identification and location/heading estimation modules need the camera image as input. To curtail the camera's power consumption, iLAMP executes its *camera scheduler* to adaptively turn on the camera (Sec. 4.2). To ensure reliability of light identification, iLAMP only proceeds with those images containing at least one full light. When no light is visible, iLAMP uses the conventional motion-sensor based dead-reckoning method [17] to keep track of the phone's movement.

3. DISCRIMINATING LIGHTS USING HIDDEN VISUAL FEATURES

3.1 The Hidden Fingerprints of Incumbent Lights

3.1.1 Understanding the Optical Properties of LEDs and Fluorescent Lights

To understand the origin of the visual features in conventional FLs and LEDs, we first explain their working principles (Fig. 2). *Light-Emitting Diodes (LEDs)* generate light through a semiconductor chip (a *p-n* junction diode). Under a suitable voltage, the electrons within the chip will fall into a lower energy level when meeting a hole, emitting energy in the form of photons. An LED lamp typically comprises multiple LED chips, and integrates with optical lenses/glass-walls to reshape its radiation pattern. The wavelength of the light emitted, and thus its color, depends on the materials forming the LED chip. Most commercial white LEDs are formed by coating blue-color (or ultraviolet/RGB) LED chips with multiple phosphor layers of different colors [18,19]. Due to inevitable manufacturing variations, *e.g.*, phosphor thickness/composition and non-uniformity of the glass-wall, different areas of an LED lamp may manifest different optical properties (radiant flux, color temperature, *etc.*).

Fluorescent lights (FLs) use an electronic ballast to excite mercury vapor inside a lamp tube, which produces short-wave ultraviolet light that then causes a phosphor coating to radiate visible light. In FLs, characteristics of electrons and Mercury atoms traveled inside vapor gas can bring different radiance power and spatial pattern across the light tube's body. Non-uniformity of the phosphor coating and the glass wall further varies the emission characteristics, even among FLs of the same model.

Although the variations of optical properties are invisible to human eyes, they can be revealed by the computational imaging mechanisms in iLAMP, which we detail below.

3.1.2 Extracting a Lamp's Spatial Radiance Pattern

We now introduce how iLAMP extracts the hidden visual features from a light (lamp), based on the principle of camera image formation (Fig. 3).

Figure 3: Principle of image formation.

Radiance characterizes the radiation property of a surface patch (either on a light source or a reflecting surface). It corresponds roughly to the brightness, and is defined as the amount of light radiated from the surface patch per solid angle per unit area (expressed in Watts per m^2 per steradian) [20]. Radiance is an intrinsic property of the light emitter. By definition, it is independent of viewing angle. It is also independent of distance, because the sampled surface area increases quadratically with the viewing distance, canceling the inverse-square path loss of optical signals [20].

On the other hand, a camera quantizes the *irradiance* E, defined as the light power per unit area (W/m^2) captured on its image sensor, and bears the following relation with radiance R_s:

$$E = \frac{\pi}{4} R_s \frac{l_0^2}{f^2} \cos\alpha^4 \tag{1}$$

where l_0 and f denote the camera lens' diameter and focal length, respectively. α is the incidental angle from the emitter to the camera. If emitter tilts away from light, the same amount of light strikes bigger sensor area which decreases E. But in practice, most cameras have a small FoV of around $60°$, corresponding to $\alpha = 30°$ and $\cos\alpha^4 = 0.997 \approx 1$.

Therefore, *the irradiance of a camera image only depends on the intrinsic radiance property of the scene, and is independent of the scene-to-camera distance/angle.* This should not be confused with the *light intensity*, which is known to be affected by the distance/angle factors.

Ultimately, the camera electronics post-process the image and convert the matrix of irradiance values (representing the whole scene) into a matrix of *pixel values.* This conversion follows a *camera response function* which should ideally be linear. Different camera models often use different gamma correction into their image processing pipeline which may make the response function non-linear. Nonetheless, the linearity can be restored by a standard one-time camera response calibration procedure [21], which only requires using the camera to capture the same scene under multiple exposure settings.

In iLAMP, we use the *spatial radiance pattern* (SRP) to characterize a lamp, which is defined as the distribution of radiance values across the lamp's body. Owing to the aforementioned linear relation, we can use the 2D matrix of pixel values as feature, which is independent of orientation/distance just like radiance itself. Although SRP is invisible to human eyes, it can be revealed by looking into values of all pixels of two-dimensional image. Fig. 4 plots the SRP of a set of ceiling-mounted LEDs (FLs) of the same model, which clearly shows distinguishable spatial patterns.

Since an image can contain millions of pixels, directly using the pixel-by-pixel SRP is computationally intensive. We thus employ a simple *feature compression* mechanism that abstracts the 2D SRP matrix into a small array. Consider the most commonly adopted linear light fixtures in commercial buildings. iLAMP first fits the image of such a light fixture in the Cartesian coordination. It then computes each row's and column's average radiance and standard deviation (*std.*), which compactly represents the spatial distribution

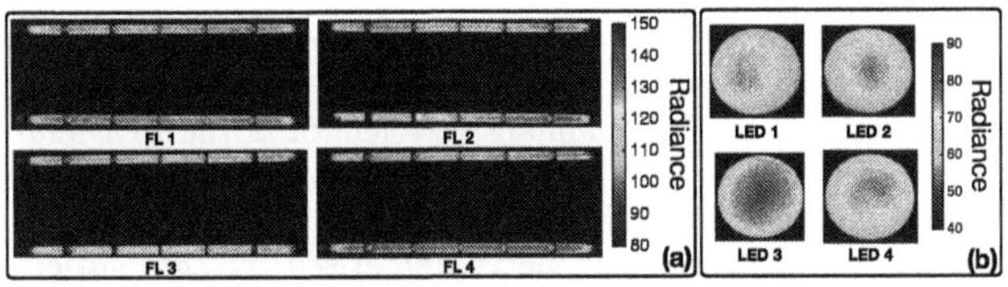

Figure 4: Example spatial radiance pattern of (a) 4 FLs and (b) 4 LEDs of the same model. The notches on the FLs are due to the cover structure.

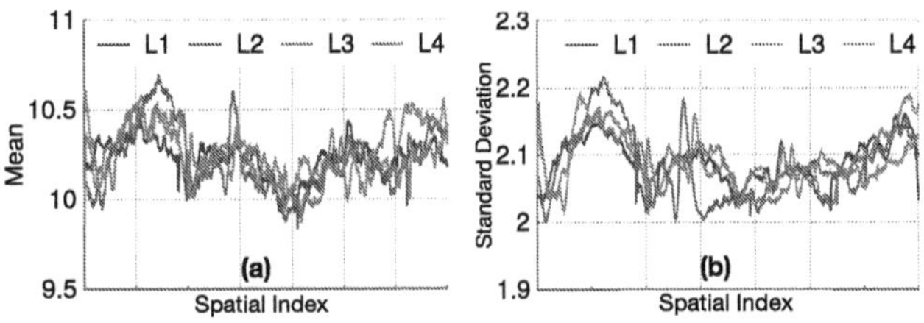

Figure 5: SRP (mean and *std*) of 4 FLs after compression.

of radiance. Therefore, we can reduce a radiance pattern of $M \times N$ pixels to a vector of size $M+N$, where M and N represents the number of rows and columns, respectively. For round shaped lamps, we use the polar coordinates, *i.e.*, radiation distribution along radial and angular directions *w.r.t.* the center of the lamp. Fig. 5 plots the compressed SRP of 4 FLs of the same model, which clearly demonstrate distinguishable patterns. Note that the small-scale fluctuation and variation are quite different.

3.1.3 Overcoming Camera Artifacts

We now describe the preprocessing needed before feeding a camera image into the aforementioned SRP extraction. Fig. 6 illustrates these operations.

Contour extraction. By default, iLAMP sets the camera's exposure time to its minimum to maximize the contrast, which renders the background pixels almost dark. Given an image, iLAMP runs a contour extraction to obtain the pixels belonging to the lamp's body, and remove the background. Direct contour extraction needs to involve millions of pixels. To reduce the computational cost, we first subsample the image, and then run the classical edge-detection based contour extraction algorithm [22] on this sub-sampled image. To reduce the dark noises within the image, we configure the ISO to the minimum value. Sub-sampling does not corrupt the contour extraction since most of the lights inside modern buildings have regular shapes. We eventually scale up the extracted contour to fit the original image and use this contour as a mask to filter out background pixels. Given the contour, we then run a shape similarity check against a benchmark image in the database to determine if a full lamp is captured.

Compensating the Color Filter Array (CFA). Cameras commonly use a two-dimensional CFA to collect photons. Each array element corresponds to a particular R, G, or B pixel sensor, interleaved across rows and columns. The heterogeneous distribution of RGB sensors may distort the SRP, because different color pixels may scale the radiance differently, depending on the color spectrum of the light emission. We thus normalize the RAW value of each pixel output, by the average value of all pixels with the same color, so as to compensate for the CFA distortion caused by existence of different colors.

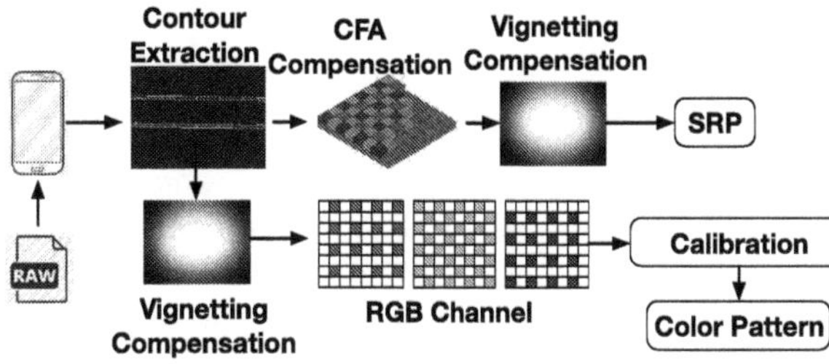

Figure 6: Image preprocessing to compensate for undesired effect of camera.

Compenstating the vignetting effect. Vignetting is a natural artifact of the imperfect camera lens, which causes lower brightness at peripheral pixels than at the center of the image. To prevent vignetting from distorting the SRP, we run a one-time camera calibration following [23], which fits each row/column of an image with a 6-th order polynomial curve. At run-time, we normalize the pixels along each row/column by its corresponding fitting curve.

Compensating the heterogeneity among camera models. Different smartphones may have different camera models with different color and intensity responses. We thus normalize the camera's average RGB and luminance values by a fixed proportion (corresponding to this specific camera) to match the standard ones stored in the database, for all the images taken by this camera. Note that different camera models may have different proportions for normalization and this one-time calibration has low overhead for each camera model. This ensures the light identification works even if the features in the server database are captured using a different camera model.

3.2 Robust SRP Matching Under Distance/ Orientation Distortion

After extracting the SRP from the current light's image, iLAMP needs to find the best matching light inside the server database. Using the Euclidean distance as a matching metric is feasible but highly vulnerable to image distortions. Depending on the phone's holding position, the run-time phone-to-ceiling distance may differ from that when the ground-truth SRPs are created for the database. Longer distances lead to fewer pixels that portrait the light, hence fewer elements in the SRP array. The phone's orientation change may also cause phase shift and deformation effect on the SRP.

DTW formulation. In iLAMP, we use the dynamic time warping (DTW) to deal with such distance/orientation distortions. DTW has been widely adopted in measuring similarity between two time series (*e.g.*, sequences of speech), owing to its robustness against signal compressing, stretching, and phase shift. Given an SRP array of length C obtained by camera and a candidate array of length D in our database, DTW first constructs an $C \times D$ matrix, with each element (c, d) being the distance between corresponding elements c and d in the two arrays. To find the best way to align these two arrays, DTW needs to retrieve a path through the matrix with the minimum cumulative distance, referred to as the warping cost or *DTW distance*. When the two arrays are exactly the same, the path simply traverses the diagonal of the matrix. In more general cases, DTW can be solved using a known dynamic programming formulation [24].

iLAMP uses the DTW distance to measure the similarity between each pair of SRP arrays. Recall that an SRP array

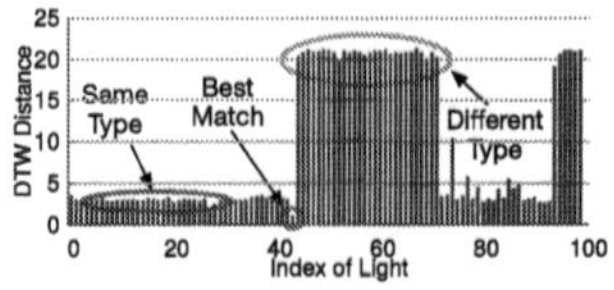

Figure 7: Uniqueness of main feature.

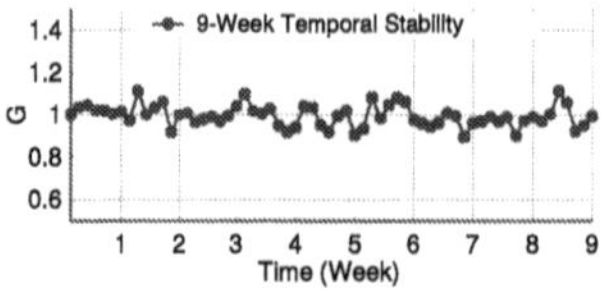

Figure 8: Stability of main feature with time.

concatenates two sequences: the mean values ($\boldsymbol{S_1}$) and *std.* values ($\boldsymbol{S_1}$), respectively, which may have different ranges. We thus compute the total DTW distance as: $DTW(\boldsymbol{S_1}) + DTW(\boldsymbol{S_2}) \cdot mean(\boldsymbol{S_1})/mean(\boldsymbol{S_2})$, where the scaling is used to make the two distances addable. Finally, the candidate with the minimum total DTW distance will be used as the best match.

Microbenchmark verification of light identification. We now use the DTW metric to benchmark the *uniqueness* and *temporal stability* of the SRP feature. Fig. 7 plots an example of DTW distances among 100 lights in our office building using one light. All DTW distances have been normalized by the minimum one (*i.e.*, DTW_{min}). We observe that the DTW distance between images of the same light is obviously the smallest, implying the SRP feature is highly unique. The DTW distance with others is much larger, due to manufacturing variations among the same light model, and physical appearances (cover, shape, *etc.*) among different models.

To simplify the evaluation of uniqueness, we introduce a metric called ***normalized tolerance gap***, defined as

$$G = \frac{DTW^c_{smin} - DTW^c_{min}}{DTW^n_{smin} - DTW^n_{min}} \tag{2}$$

where DTW^c_{min} denotes DTW distance between an image and the benchmark image of the same light (in the database). DTW^c_{smin} denotes the minimum DTW distance with all other lights in the database. Here the superscript c represents variable conditions such as time, distance, orientation *etc.* DTW^n_{smin} and DTW^n_{min} represent counterpart definitions for an image taken under similar condition as when the database benchmark (normal condition) was created.

This G factor essentially represents a microscopic metric to study the DTW matching alone. Note that a series always matches best with itself, *i.e.*, $DTW^n_{min} < DTW^n_{smin}$. Therefore, $G > 0$ *iff* $DTW^c_{smin} - DTW^c_{min} > 0$. In other words, *a light's image can be correctly matched to its database image iff the **G metric** is a positive number.* Normally, G should be close to 1. A close-to-zero G implies that the light identification may fail under minor disturbances. Occasional wrong light identification may confuse the location with a light that is far away. Such errors can be easily corrected using spatial smoothing as in [13].

Figure 8 plots the G metric of a randomly selected light across 9 weeks. Since we cannot exactly reproduce the condition when the database image was create, G varies across measurements, but it always stays around 1 and well above 0, implying that the light identification is stable over time.

4. EFFICIENT FEATURE MATCHING

4.1 Improving Computational Efficiency

In this section, we introduce how the two assistant features help reducing the computational cost in light identification.

Color pattern. An FL or LED lamp's color temperature rating reflects the power spectrum distribution of the optical frequencies that it emits, which manifests through the "softness" of its white color. The exact color temperature pattern is determined by the dominant wavelength of the LED chip (or FL vapor), as well as the composition/thickness of the phosphor layers with different colors.

Color temperature can be characterized by *chromaticity* and *luminance* [18], representing color quality and brightness. Both metrics are almost unaffected by distance/orientation, but manufacturing variations inevitably deviate them from their nominal ratings. To capture such variations, we first compute $\overline{P}_R, \overline{P}_G, \overline{P}_B$, *i.e.*, the average value of the R, G, and B channel, respectively, across all pixels inside the image of the lamp. We then use the value ratio $\overline{P}_R/\overline{P}_G$ and $\overline{P}_G/\overline{P}_B$ to represent the lamp's chromaticity. On the other hand, the luminance Y follows a linear relation with the RGB values [25] and it is directly related to radiance:

$$Y = \mathcal{A}[\overline{P}_R, \overline{P}_G, \overline{P}_B]^T \tag{3}$$

where $\mathcal{A}$ is a vector of Color Space Transform (CST) Matrix [26]. CST is camera-specific (which maps from camera color space to CIE XYZ) and this is why we need to compensate the heterogeneity among camera models after RGB and luminance extraction as mentioned in Sec. 3.1.3.

We note that the RGB values are interleaved in a RAW image due to the use of CFA (Sec. 3.1.3). Thus, assume CFA outputs a matrix of $m \times n$ pixel values, JPEG's interpolation effect will fill each pixel with all 3 RGB values, expanding the matrix to $m \times n \times 3$. Different models of smartphone cameras may have different color configurations, and hence different RGB readings even when capturing the same scene. We thus need a one-time calibration of a camera, so that its RGB readings become consistent with the camera that was used to create the feature database. Since the main feature (SRP) alone has high confidence in identifying a light (albeit at high computational cost), iLAMP runs the SRP matching once, to identify one light that the user's camera captured. Suppose the mean power of the captured R channel is $\overline{P}_R$, and that of the database is $\overline{P}_{R0}$. Then, iLAMP scales the user camera's subsequent R channel measurements by $\overline{P}_R/\overline{P}_{R0}$, when computing the chromaticity and brightness. The same scaling process is used on the other two channels. To prevent unnecessary twisting of the colors, we set the camera's white balancing to a fixed mode (*e.g.*, daylight).

Infrared to visible intensity ratio (I2V ratio). The visible light wavelength ranges from 400 nm to 700 nm, but an FL and LED's emission spectrum can go up to 1000 nm [27] and 800 nm [19]. Optical signal leakage beyond 700 nm falls in the infrared spectrum, and the signal intensity depends on the heat generated inside the light, subject to manufacturing variation. Smartphone cameras have built-in infrared filters and cannot directly estimate the infrared intensity. Fortunately, we can repurpose the smartphone ALS as an infrared intensity sensor. Mainstream smartphones' ALS comprises two photodiodes: CH0, used primarily for sensing ambient light intensity (for adjusting screen brightness); and CH1, an infrared sensor originally used to detect proximity between the phone screen and user's cheek. One can directly measure infrared intensity using CH1, yet the measurement will vary wildly as the phone-to-light distance/orientation changes. To make the infrared intensity a stable feature, iLAMP normalize the CH1 reading by the CH0. Since the two photodiodes' frequencies are close and their FoVs are designed to cover similar range, the impact of

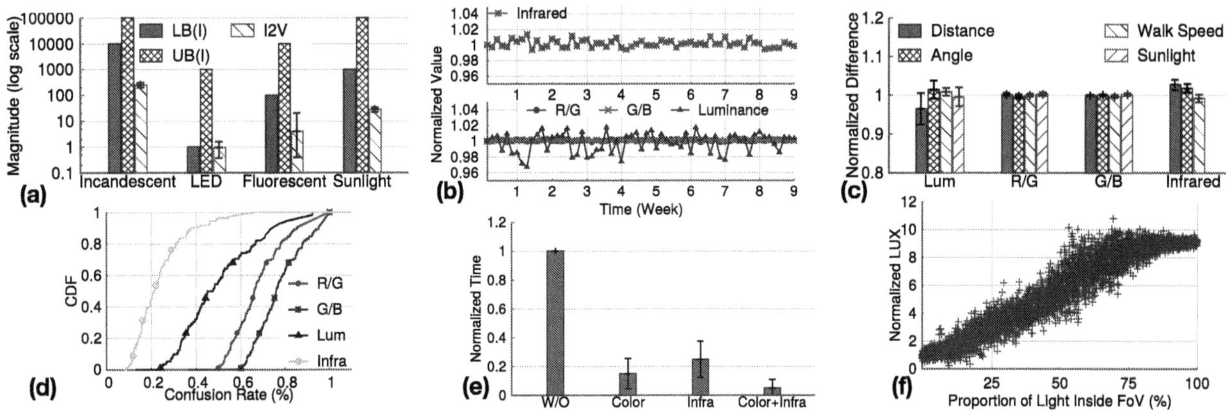

Figure 9: (a) Infrared emission of different source of lights; (b) Stability of assistant features over time; (c) The robustness of color features to overcome different distortions; (d) Confusion rate of assistant features among different lights; (e) Improving computational efficiency via hierarchical feature matching; (f) Correlation between ALS and fraction of lamp inside camera FoV.

distance/orientation on them is similar and can be canceled out after normalization.

It is also worth noting that sunlight has a wide optical spectrum and may interfere the I2V ratio. But such interference can be easily detected because sunlight has a much stronger Infrared emission. Fig. 9(a) shows the infrared intensity ("LB/UB" means lower/upper bound) and I2V on incandescent, LED, fluorescent and sunlight that we measured under a variety of conditions. For artificial lights, LB and UB are determined by distance (from 2 meters to close to 0 meter) and for natural sunlight, they are determined throughout an entire sunny day from early morning to late night. We see that the absolute values of infrared intensity is at least an order of magnitude higher than that of FLs and LEDs, even in a partially shaded region with indirect sunlight (the "LB" case), and sunlight's I2V is an order of magnitude lower than that of incandescent. Therefore, whenever iLAMP detects an ultra-strong infrared value and small I2V, it degrades to a fail-safe mode, disabling I2V ratio computation and instead uses the color pattern alone as assistant feature.

Hierarchical feature matching using assistant features. Computing the DTW distance between two main feature arrays involves quadratic complexity *w.r.t.* the array size which equals $(M + N)$. This translates into tens of ms computation time for a million-pixel image, but the computation cost increases linearly with the number of lights. To curtail the cost, iLAMP uses the assistant features to prefilter the candidate lights before running the DTW over the main feature. Note that the assistant features may be affected slightly by random factors, *e.g.*, distance/orientation and ambient interference. We thus empirically set an upperbound drift for each of the assistant features to guarantee we do not filter out the correct light. For the pre-filtering, we rule out the lights whose feature values deviate beyond the bound, which only requires a linear comparison across all lights in the database.

To get an intuitive understanding of the feature stability, Fig. 9(b) plots the color pattern and I2V ratio across 9 weeks, measured on a randomly selected FL in our office building, and normalized *w.r.t.* the first-day measurement. We can see that *the assistant features are highly stable over time*, with a maximum deviation of ±0.26% for the chromaticity (RGB ratio), ±3.2% for the luminance, ±1.3% for the I2V ratio, and the error is unbiased. We further evaluate the stability over usage behaviors/scenarios, by varying the distance (±1m from holding position), angle (±45°), sunlight intensity (direct sunlight from glass window on a side wall) and walking speed (0 to 2 m/s). From the results (Fig. 9)(c), we observe that the features are almost unaffected, with maximum deviation of ±7%, ±0.5% and ±4% (shown in error bars), for luminance, RGB ratio and I2V, respectively.

We thus set a conservative threshold of ±14%, ±1% and ±8% as the upper-bound drift for these three sets of features, respectively. For different light models, these thresholds can be calibrated *a priori*; but even without calibration, a conservative threshold can be used at the expense of lower discrimination (and less saving in computation).

Note that the RGB ratio is much more stable compared with luminance, as it only depends on the physical properties of the lights, such as phosphor thickness/composition.

Microbenchmark verification of computational cost. To verify the effectiveness of hierarchical feature matching, we first examine how distinguishable the assistant features are among different lights, under the same experimental setup as in Sec. 3.2. We use *confusion rate* as a metric, defined for each light $\mathcal{L}$, as the fraction of candidate lights whose feature are indistinguishable from $\mathcal{L}$, *i.e.*, the feature difference is smaller than the aforementioned upperbound threshold.

The results in Fig. 9(d) show that, although these assistant features are not as unique as the SRP, they can filter out majority of the lights. In particular, the $\overline{P}_R/\overline{P}_G$, $\overline{P}_G/\overline{P}_B$, luminance Y and I2V features have a mean confusion rate of 65%, 78% , 48%, 23%, respectively. This means on average, these assistant features can narrow down the search space to a small fraction $(0.65 \times 0.78 \times 0.48 \times 0.23 = 6\%)$ of the light candidates, assuming the features are independent across lights.

The effectiveness of discrimination in turn translates into a smaller search space for the SRP, and lower computational cost. To verify this, we use a server machine (i7-4770, 3.9 GHz) to run the light matching over 550 lights in our office building. We found that, to identify one light, a brute-force DTW matching over the million-pixel images of all light candidates takes almost 2.5 hours. Our SRP compression reduces the computation time to about 5 seconds. Fig. 9(e) shows how the hierarchical feature matching further reduces this value. We see that the color pattern or I2V ratio alone reduces the latency to below 30%, and together cut it down to around 10.6% (0.53 second), which enables real-time localization response.

4.2 Camera Scheduling

To save power, iLAMP duty-cycles the camera and turns it on only if it is likely to capture a full lamp. Note that the smartphone's camera and light sensor have comparable FoVs and the same orientation, *i.e.*, the same norm vector with respect to phone's screen surface. Therefore, the ALS ambient light intensity should be proportional to the fraction of lamp body captured by the camera. To test this hypothesis, we walk below a light many times and intentionally vary the phone's holding position/orientation to its extremes. The scatter plot in Fig. 9(f) shows the normalized ALS ambient light intensity (*w.r.t.* the case with no light) vs. lamp fraction across 300 samples, which clearly shows a quasi-linear relation. We thus use a least square method to approximate the statistical relation, so that we can predict the availability of a full lamp by just reading the low power ALS.

More specifically, let $C_p \in [0, 1]$ be the fraction of the lamp captured by camera at a random position/orientation p. Let I_p be the corresponding ALS reading. Then,

$$C_p = I_p \cdot \phi_p + \epsilon_p \tag{4}$$

where the unknown parameter ϕ_p is a linear coefficient and ϵ_p represents errors which are assumed to be zero-mean Gaussian. To materialize this linear relation, we need to train the camera scheduler by randomly changing the phone orientation/distance, just as in real use cases. This will generate a random set of samples, corresponding to measured values $I = [I_p, I_{p-1}, \cdots, I_0]'$ and $C = [C_p, C_{p-1}, \cdots, C_0]'$. This dataset is created within the regarded light area. We then use the least square method [28] to solve for the parameter ϕ_p:

$$\phi_p = (I'I)^{-1} I'C \tag{5}$$

At run-time, given an ALS measurement I_p, we estimate $C_p = \phi_p I_p$ and turn on the camera if $C_p > 0.5$. Here we set a conservative threshold of below 1, because the camera has a setup latency of around 0.2 s, and needs to be triggered slightly ahead of time. Note that strong sunlight may mislead the camera scheduling. Thus, we switch to a fail-safe mode and keep the camera on when sunlight is detected based on ALS's infrared reading (Sec. 4.1).

The parameter training procedure can be done by each user at run-time, as iLAMP collects more and more ground-truth samples. Inside one building, different types of lamps may be deployed, corresponding to different ϕ_p. Yet iLAMP can choose the parameter that is likely to fit the nearby lights. In the worst case, iLAMP can choose the parameter so as to turn on the camera aggressively — this may reduce the power saving from camera scheduler but does not compromise the localization accuracy of iLAMP.

5. SENSOR ASSISTED PHOTOGRAMMETRY

Once a light landmark is identified and its location obtained from the database, iLAMP pinpoints the phone's location relative to that light landmark, which also provides the phone's global location within the building map. iLAMP further computes the phone's horizontal orientation, *i.e.*, heading direction, based on a geometrical model.

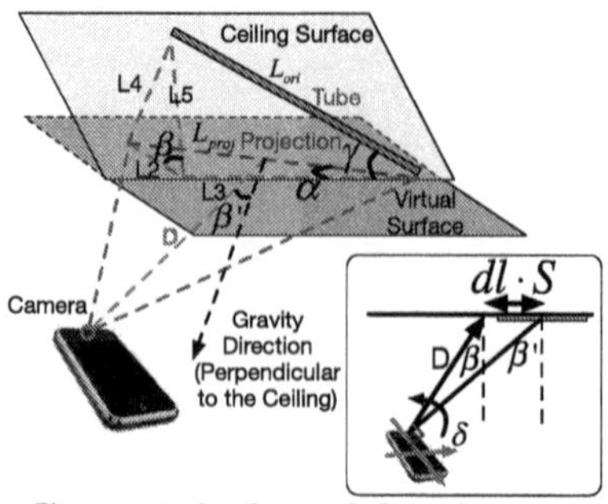

Figure 10: Geometrical model to locate a phone under a single light.

5.1 Estimating 3D Location

Our geometrical model analyzes the phone-to-light distance/orientation based on how the light's body is projected into the phone camera. The model also takes as input the standard gravity sensor output [29] from the phone's accelerometer/gyroscope. The gravity reading, unlike compass, is known to be accurate and unaffected by ferromagnetic interferences [16]. Our model abstracts a tube light as a line segment with known physical length L_{ori}. Later we will generalize it to arbitrary light shapes (Sec. 5.2).

Fig. 5.1 illustrates the geometrical model. Here L_3 is the intersection line between the ceiling plane, and the phone's *virtual surface plane* (a plane parallel to the phone surface but intersects with the lowest points on the lamp). Without loss of generality, we assume the ceiling to be perpendicular to the gravity. L_4 is perpendicular to the virtual surface plane. L_5 is a line segment within the ceiling plane and $L_5 \perp L_3$. L_{proj} is the projection of the light tube onto the virtual surface plane. α, β, β' and γ are various angles between the line segments.

Following these definitions, the following geometrical relations are straightforward: $L_{ori} = \sqrt{L_3^2 + L_5^2}$, $L_{proj} = \sqrt{L_2^2 + L_3^2}$, $L_3 = L_{proj} \cos\alpha$, $L_2 = L_5 \cos\beta = L_{proj} \sin\alpha$. Here β represents the angle between the ceiling surface and virtual plane, which can be obtained from gravity sensor ($\cos\beta = \frac{G_z}{\sqrt{G_x^2+G_y^2+G_z^2}}$ where G_* represents the earth gravity projected to the *-axis of phone). α is the phone's azimuth angle relative to the light which will be computed following Sec. 5.2. We can then obtain a *shrink factor* F between the original length of light tube L_{ori} and the length of its projection L_{proj}:

$$F = \frac{L_{ori}}{L_{proj}} = \sqrt{\cos^2\alpha + \left(\frac{\sin\alpha}{\cos\beta}\right)^2} \tag{6}$$

Further, we can compute the angle γ as:

$$\gamma = \cos^{-1}\frac{L_3}{L_{ori}} = \cos^{-1}\left(\frac{cos\alpha}{F}\right) \tag{7}$$

Suppose the camera has a focal length f and size of a single pixel L_{pix}, and the light's long side has N_{pix} pixels on the image. Following the camera imaging principle (*i.e.*, the pinhole model) [20], we have:

$$\frac{L_{proj}}{D} = \frac{N_{pix} \cdot L_{pix}}{f} \tag{8}$$

From which we obtain the phone-to-light distance D, *i.e.*, distance between the camera and the light tube's projection on the virtual surface plane. We further obtain the distance projection on each of the 3D axes as:

$$D_x = D \cdot \sin\beta' \cdot \cos\gamma, D_y = D \cdot \sin\beta' \cdot \sin\gamma, D_z = D \cdot \cos\beta' \tag{9}$$

Here the angle $\beta' = \beta$ if the center of the light aligns with the center of the image (because the gravity and D are perpendicular to L_5 and L_2, respectively). But this no longer holds when the user does not perfectly point the camera to the light. In such general cases, the deviation angle can be approximated as $\delta \approx (dl \cdot S)/D$ (Fig. 5.1), where S is the scaling factor between the physical length of the lamp with that measured on the image. dl is the horizontal or vertical (on image's coordination) pixel distance from the light's center to image center, which is scaled to a physical distance by S. The angular approximation holds since typically $D \gg dl \cdot S$ given the narrow FoV of camera. We then compensate the deviation angle as: $\beta' = \beta - \delta$ if δ is clockwise and $\beta' = \beta + \delta$ if δ is counterclockwise (Fig. 5.1). This approximation and compensation of δ is done twice, for pitch and roll angle, separately.

5.2 Estimating Heading Direction

In iLAMP, the server database stores not only the location, but also azimuth direction of each light landmark relative to the north. We then compute the phone's azimuth angle relative to the landmark's direction.

We observe that the SRP is typically distributed non-uniformly across a lamp's body (see, *e.g.*, Fig. 4). Therefore, we can define the azimuth direction even for symmetrically shaped lamps. When a smartphone changes its azimuth orientation, the SRP it measures should be rotated accordingly. So the run-time SRP of a light is a rotated version of the database version (*w.r.t.* the x-axis in the Cartesian coordinates or the 0-degree vector in the polar coordinates). The rotation angle is a direct output of the DTW matching procedure.

The above heuristic works straightforwardly when the phone is held flat, *i.e.*, the phone's azimuth plane is parallel to the ceiling and hence the pitch/roll angle equals 0 (this is also the way when the database image was taken). Under arbitrary roll/pitch/yaw angles, the light's contour may be distorted slightly, and the ratio between its width/length may deviate from the database version. But we can still fit the contour to the most similar shape in the database. Without loss of generality, consider the most commonly used rectangular lamp. Suppose P and Q are midpoints on the edges of the best-fit rectangle (Fig. 11). Then the relative azimuth between the phone and the light is:

$$\theta = \arctan \frac{y_P - y_Q}{x_P - x_Q} \tag{10}$$

where the coordinates of P and Q on the image are available after contour extraction (Sec. 3.1.3). Note that fitting the original contour to a rectangle may inject some errors but we will show the resulting heading estimation error is still quite small. For non-rectangular shaped lights, we can define a virtual rectangle (Fig. 11) corresponding to the north, and execute the same model. After obtaining heading estimation θ, we first subtract the yaw angle (*i.e.*, rotation angle with z-axis) and then obtain α in Sec. 5.1 to realize 3D localization as we mentioned previously.

5.3 Blind Area Tracking

In the "blind" area with no light coverage, alternative location tracking strategies can be employed to complement iLAMP and fill in the gap. We choose the classical motion-sensor based dead-reckoning as it is ready to use on most mobile devices. Specifically, we implement dead-reckoning following FootPath [17], which counts steps based on sharp

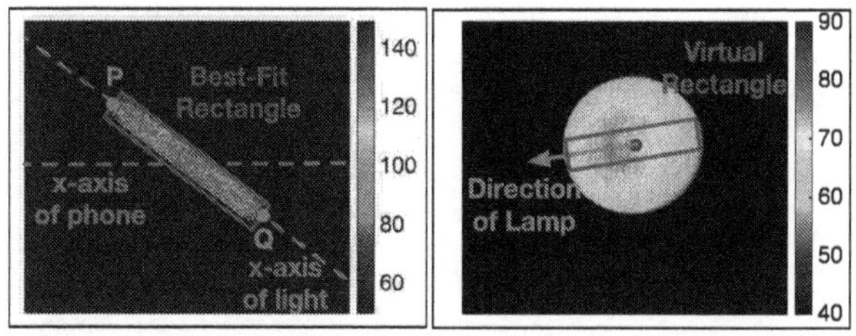

Figure 11: Heading estimation of rectangle light tube and circular bulb.

drops of phone acceleration, and uses the compass azimuth reading as heading direction. FootPath assumes a fixed stride length. In iLAMP, we estimate a user's average stride length based on the ground-truth distance between two lamps. This estimation is run between consecutive lamps, and used subsequently to translate step counts into walking distance.

Dead-reckoning is known to suffer from drift, due to the inaccurate compass and noise accumulation of the accelerometer over time [30]. Fortunately, whenever the user moves to a new light from blind area, iLAMP automatically runs the light matching and localization to correct the drift. Most indoor environment has densely deployed luminaries with a few meters of separation. Hence the blind area tends to be small and the dead-reckoning error can be well confined.

6. IMPLEMENTATION

We implement iLAMP based on a simple client-server architecture. The client side is an Android application that captures and preprocesses the images. More computationally intensive tasks are offloaded to the server which also hosts the light landmark's location database. Given an image input, the client executes the contour extraction (Sec. 3.1.3), extracts and compresses the SRP (Sec. 3.1.2). Meanwhile, it also computes the assistant features, *i.e.* RGB color pattern and I2V ratio, from the image and light sensors, respectively. The light intensity is measured by the smartphone's ALS based on an open-source driver [31], which streams the sensor readings to the user-space through SYSFS interfaces. Both the SRP and assistant features are subsequently sent to the server for matching.

The server executes the light matching mechanisms (Sec. 3.2 and Sec. 4.1) and returns the matching light landmark's global location on the floor map. Meanwhile, the client computes its 3D location and azimuth relative to the light landmark (Sec. 5), and converts the result into its own global location once it gets the server feedback. To prompt the landmark database, we have implemented a graphical user interface, which takes the building floor plan as input, and allows a user to mark a landmark's position within and associate it with a sample image of the light. We use a mobile laser ranger to measure the landmark location *w.r.t.* the floor map. We emphasize that such landmark registration procedure is needed for all infrastructure based localization schemes. For VLP systems, registering each light only takes tens of seconds, given that most of the lights in a building have similar shapes and have regular geometrical separations.

7. EXPERIMENTAL EVALUATION

7.1 Effectiveness of Light Identification

We first evaluate the accuracy and robustness of iLAMP in identifying light landmarks.

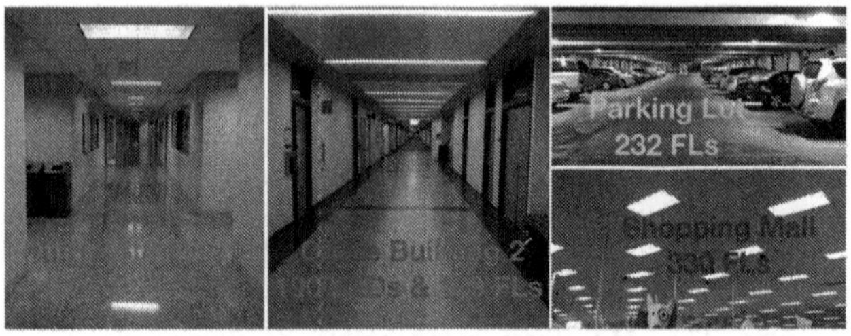

Figure 12: Field test in large buildings.

Accuracy. To represent typical use cases of indoor localization/navigation, we choose 4 different environments (Fig. 12): office 1 (588 FLs, 2.5 m ceiling), office 2 (a mix of 190 LEDs and 129 FLs, 3 m ceiling), semi-open parking ramp (232 FLs, 2.5 m ceiling) and retail store (330 FLs, 6 m ceiling). Except in the parking ramp, all the ceiling lights have plastic covers/decorators and multiple lights may be co-located inside the same house. By default, we use a Nexus 5X phone, held comfortably at around 1.2 m above the floor, capturing RAW image from its front camera. Robustness of iLAMP across different configurations will be tested subsequently.

Fig. 13(a) plots the fraction of lights that are correctly identified without any confusion with any other one inside the same building. We observe that the *main feature alone* can achieve more than 96% identification accuracy for typical buildings with up to 3 m ceilings, and more than 82% accuracy even for a 6 m ceiling. When combining the main and assistant features together through hierarchical feature matching (Sec. 4.1), the accuracy is boosted to above 95% for all the buildings. Therefore, the assistant features not only reduce computational cost, but also bring the light matching accuracy close to 100%.

The results also show that JPEG images have relatively lower discrimination accuracy when JPEG images are captured by user as well as stored in database. This is because JPEG compression processes the RAW pixels through non-linear operations, which may distort the SRP. However, the assistant features are unaffected and can still bring the accuracy above 90%. The minor residual error can be easily eliminated by combining two consecutive lights' features as the user moves as in [13]. Therefore, even for those phone models that do not support RAW output, iLAMP can still achieve much higher accuracy in light identification than the most advanced VLP system LiTell [13].

Robustness. Multiple factors in practical usage scenarios may disturb the light identification. In the following micro-benchmarks, we test the sensitivity of the SRP features to such factors, using the G metric defined in Sec. 3.2. We randomly pick one light and find its best DTW match in the database, under various disturbing factors[1]. Here we vary each following variable while keeping others fixed to their typical values.

(i) Phone orientation and height variation. The images in iLAMP's database are captured when holding the phone flat at a certain height. But the run-time images may differ as users' height and holding position varies. We first test the impact of height deviation inside Office 1, by deviating the phone from 0 m to 1.2 m relative to the height when creating the database image. We adjust the height using a tripod.

As shown in Fig. 13(b), the DTW tolerance gap G decreases with height deviation, since distance affects the number of pixels of a light's image. Fortunately, the main features are diverse enough, and DTW can tolerate the missing/addition pixels (*i.e.*, contraction and stretching) due to image distortion. Consequently, G is still well above 0 even if the height deviates from the database benchmark by 1.2 m (typically from the holding position to the ground). We further rotate the phone around the axial direction of the tube, so that the relative orientation (radiation angle from the lamp and incidental angle into the phone) changes by up to 45° (maximum deviation to ensure the entire light can still be captured). Fig. 13(c) shows that the G metric deviates slightly, but remains well above 0 even with 45° angular deviation. These two experiments verify that *iLAMP can maintain high light identification accuracy even if the run-time capturing height/orientation deviates from the database benchmark by a practical offset.* Note that severe distortion may happen under certain cases, *e.g.*, when the phone rotates its pitch angle which results in perspective changes. Such effects can be compensated through classical computer vision techniques, but are beyond the scope of the present work.

(ii) Image resolution and ceiling height. To further test iLAMP's robustness against JPEG compression, we adjust the JPEG's resolution of Nexus 5X from its default 5MP to lower than 1.3MP, while using the same 5 MP images in the database for light matching. From Fig. 13(d), we can see that a more aggressive JPEG compression reduces the diversity of visual features among lights. But even at a low resolution of 1.56 MP, the G metric remains above 0. When the image resolution degrades to below 1.3MP, G becomes close to 0, implying that confusion among lights occurs. Nonetheless, today's mainstream front-cameras mostly have higher than 2 MP resolution, which ensures iLAMP's robustness. Note that the RAW image quality is unaffected by the JPEG resolution. It only depends on the size of the image sensor within the camera. On the other hand, increasing the ceiling height has the same effect as reducing the image resolution. Fig. 13(e) quantifies the effects by proportionally sub-sampling the image, which shows that the accuracy remains above 70% even under the extreme case with 10 m height ceiling. In contrast, alternative solutions that leverage frequency features [13] can only correctly discriminate individual lights with 40% accuracy even at a low ceiling height of 2.5 m.

(iii) Partial light distortion. Although iLAMP invokes light matching only if a full light is captured, it can also run in an aggressive mode and responds even if a partial light is visible. Fig. 13(f) plots the light matching accuracy, where we intentionally vary the fraction of a light inside the camera FoV (an entire light fixture includes 2 to 3 tubes, occupying 1.2 m × 0.6 m in Office Building 1). The resulting G *degrades only slightly even when only* $1/2$ *of the light is visible in common office buildings.* Besides the SRP itself, the resilience is also attributed to the assistant features, which capture the average color pattern or I2V ratio and remain stable even with a partial light image.

(iv) Ambient sunlight interference. Certain buildings may install sidewall windows through which sunlight can peek in and interfere the camera imaging. We verify the impact by placing the smartphone 1.5 m under an FL immediate to a window in Office 1. Fig. 13(g) plots the measured G metric

[1]We use office building 1 and Nexus 5X as the representative testbed and device for the rest of the experiments, unless otherwise stated.

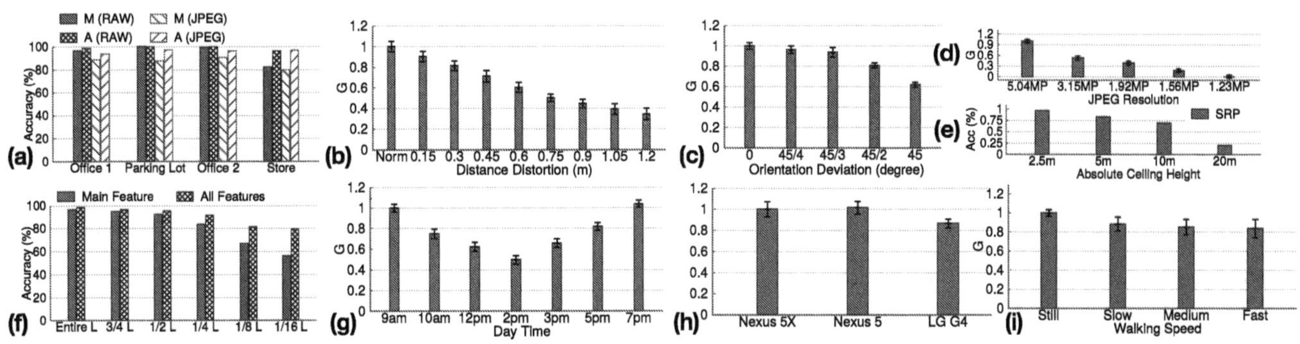

Figure 13: (a) Accuracy of light identification with Main (M) feature or All (A) features; Impact of (b) distance variations (relative to normal holding position); (c) specific orientation variations; (d) different camera resolutions and (e) ceiling heights; (f) partial light; (g) ambient sunlight interferences; (h) device heterogeneity; (i) walking speed on main SRP feature.

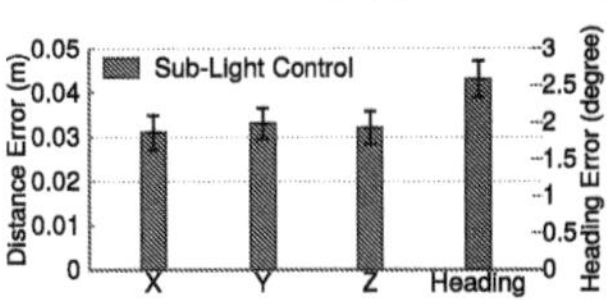

Figure 14: 3D location and heading estimation even under a single light landmark.

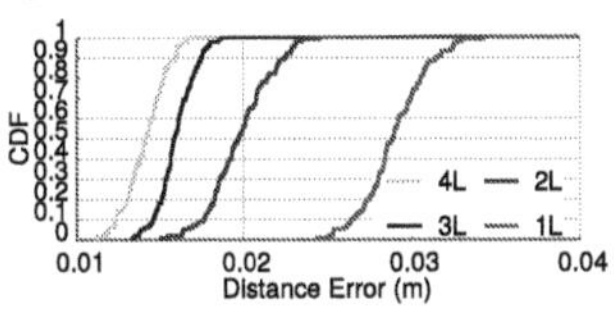

Figure 15: Localization precision improves as more light landmarks fall in the camera's FoV.

across a sunny day. At 2pm, the sunlight has the smallest incidental angle of approximately 30°, which results in the lowest G, but still well above 0. Therefore, *iLAMP's light discrimination mechanism is robust against normal indoor sunlight interference.* Although the sunlight may slightly reduce the image contrast, the scaling effect can be easily counteracted by the DTW matching. In case when there is strong direct sunlight with incidental angle close to 0 (*i.e.*, coming from the same angle as the lamp), the camera tends to be saturated and the lamp's image is no longer viable for feature extraction. But such cases rarely occur in practice.

(v) Device heterogeneity. To test how iLAMP works across different camera hardware, we create the database using Nexus 5X (5 MP, 1.4μm sensor), and then test the light discrimination accuracy using *calibrated* LG G4 (8 MP, 1.2 μm), Nexus 5 (8 MP, 1.4μm). The Nexus 5 front-camera cannot output RAW image, so we use its rear camera instead. We use these phones to capture the same light, and then compute the corresponding G metric. Fig. 13(h) shows that the G metric varies negligibly and well above 0 across phone models, implying that *iLAMP's light identification accuracy is almost unaffected even if the run-time images are captured using different phones than the database images.*

(vi) Walking speed. The user's walking speed may affect the image quality because most front-cameras do not have an optical image stabilizer. To measure the impact, we walk and hold the phone in stable at slow (≈0.5 m/s), medium (≈1 m/s) and fast (≈ 2 m/s) speed across one light. Fig. 13(i) shows that the G metric remains around 1, implying *iLAMP's light discrimination mechanism is robust against the walking patterns.*

7.2 Precision of Location and Heading Estimation

To verify the sensor-assisted photogrammetry, we place the phone under a tube FL at 25 random spots, with horizontal displacement up to 1.6 m, and vertical up to 2 m. At each spot, we randomly rotate the phone at 3 different roll/yaw/pitch angles. Fig. 14 plots the mean and 90-percentile (error bars) accuracy. We observe that *iLAMP achieves a mean localization precision of around 3.2 cm and 90-percentile of 3.5 cm across all axis, and mean heading estimation error of* 2.6° *and 90-percentile of* 2.8°. Further, we repeat the experiment by mounting multiple lamps closely on the ceiling, and take a simple average of the location estimation *w.r.t.* each lamp. Fig. 15 further shows that, as the number of lights increases to 4, the 3D localization error (90-percentile) drops to 1.7 cm, implying that *iLAMP's accuracy further improves under densely deployed light fixtures.*

We further conduct *field tests* and use iLAMP to navigate across two environments (Fig. 16): *(i)* a $9 \times 9m^2$ research lab with *densely deployed* ceiling FLs which ensures 1 or 2 lights are always visible to the phone and thus no blind area tracking is needed); *(ii)* a $90 \times 70m^2$ office building corridor with *sparse* light deployment (3 m separation). Thus both room and corridor are included. In both scenarios, ground-truth is created by placing markers with different colors along a predefined track. We use Google Tango [32], which is known to have centimeter precision. We stick it with the smartphone so that it runs spatially in sync with iLAMP. Here we follow the best-practice guideline of Google Tango to ensure a highly accurate ground truth trace assisted by these unique markers on the floor [32]. A user walks across the track while naturally holding the phone with Tango and sends a localization request through iLAMP when passing each marker position.

Fig. 16(a) shows that the location trace measured by iLAMP is highly consistent with the ground truth. For clarity, Fig. 17 further plots the error vector on the horizontal plane across all the sampled spots. iLAMP demonstrates a 90-percentile precision of around 2.7 cm, which is consistent with the previous controlled test.

Fig. 16(b) and Fig. 18 plot the localization traces and error vectors inside the large office environment. Since lights are visible intermittently, iLAMP invokes the blind area tracking (Sec. 5.3) occasionally. When the dead-reckoning (DR) is used alone, the mean error is around 3 m, consistent with state-of-the-art evaluation [17]. iLAMP can intermittently correct the DR drift, reducing the mean error to 0.18 m and 90-percentile to 0.44 m. Therefore, *iLAMP not only provides absolute position fixes to DR, but also enhances its precision by an order of magnitude in environment with sparse light installation.*

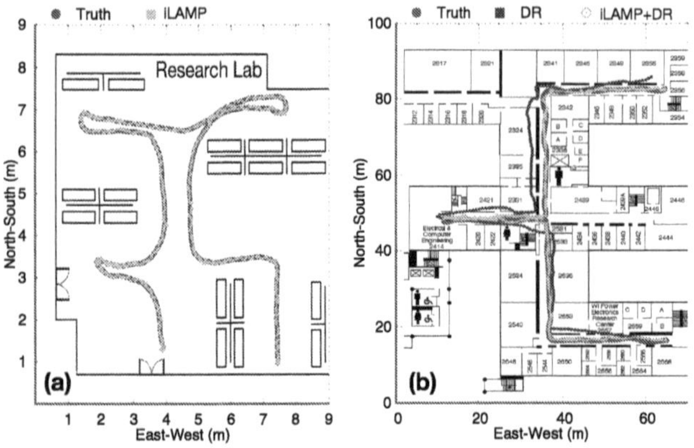

Figure 16: Field tests of real-time navigation.

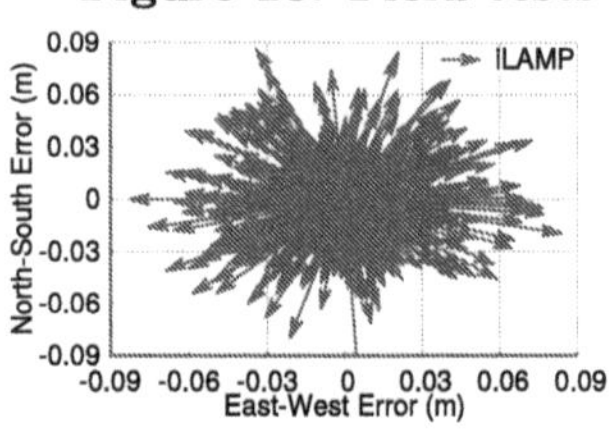

Figure 17: Error vector in environment with densely deployed lights.

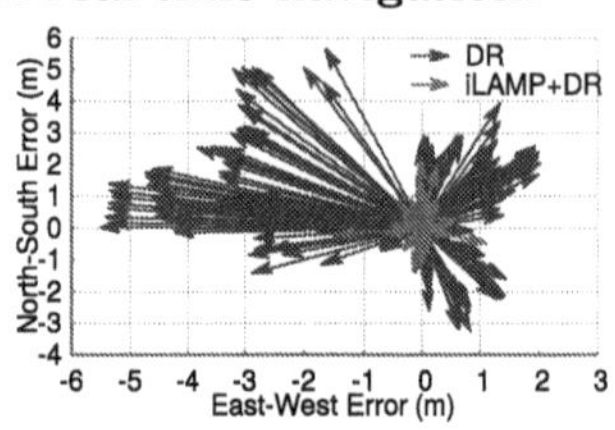

Figure 18: Error vectors under sparse light deployment (with blind area tracking).

7.3 System Efficiency

Latency. iLAMP's end-to-end operations can break down into 3 steps: local processing (feature extraction) on the phone, phone-to-server data transmission, and light matching on the server. We time-stamp these operations and plot the latency in Fig. 19. The measurement is done on a Nexus 5X client and an Intel i7-4770 3.9 GHz server. We observe the end-to-end latency takes 0.37 to 0.7 s per localization operation, and is roughly proportional to the number of lights inside a building. The local processing and transmission takes only around 160 ms on the smartphone, and is invariant across environment. Remarkably, the light matching procedure on the server dominates the computational cost, taking almost 0.6 s inside the large Office 1 with 588 light fixtures. This latency can be reduced substantially through several measures: (i) An optimized C-based DTW implementation which replaces our current Matlab implementation on the server. (ii) A multi-thread implementation that harnesses the server's multiple CPU cores. In addition, iLAMP can easily scale to a large number of clients, because the clients' DTW computation and database lookups are independent and can be easily distributed across many servers.

Energy efficiency. We use the Monsoon power monitor [33] to measure the smartphone's power consumption when running iLAMP on Nexus 5X inside the Office 1 (Fig. 12). Fig. 20 plots the real-time power consumption as the user walks across 7 lights, which demonstrates that the camera scheduler can judiciously turn off the camera in the blind region. We further run the test across 100 lights and examine the average power consumption. Fig. 21 further plots the fraction of camera-on time, verifying that setting the C_p threshold to an intermediate value makes a balanced tradeoff: it is more responsive compared with an aggressive strategy (*i.e.*, camera on if $C_p \approx 1$), yet saves more power compared with a conservative strategy (*i.e.*, camera on if $C_p > 0$).

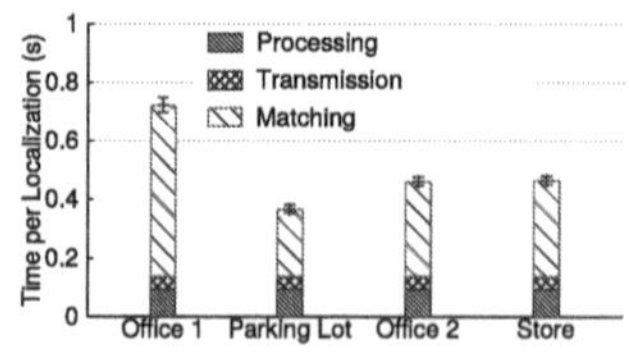

Figure 19: Breakdown of localization latency (using a single CPU core).

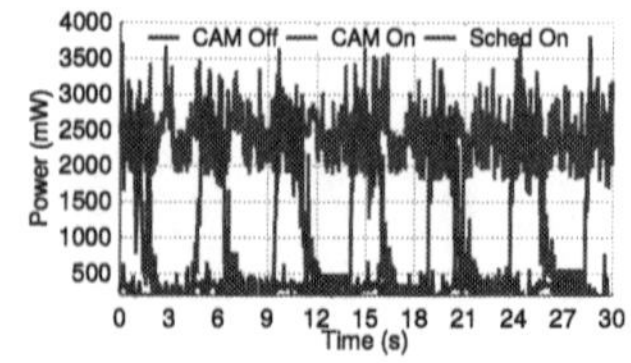

Figure 20: A snapshot of power consumption.

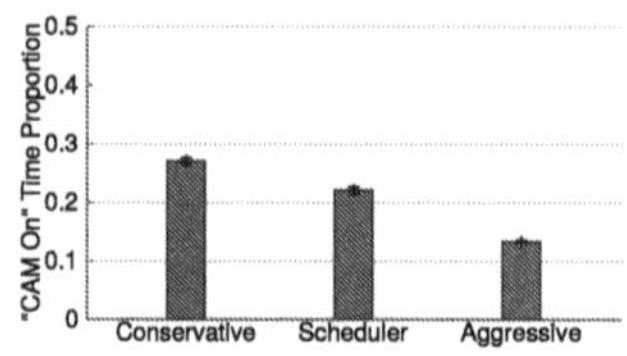

Figure 21: Robustness of camera scheduler.

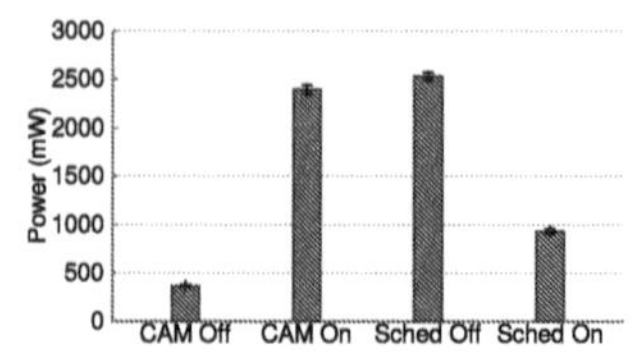

Figure 22: Breakdown of average power consumption.

Fig. 22 provides a breakdown analysis of the power consumption. Even without running iLAMP, the camera alone escalates the system power consumption to 2.5 W ("CAM on"). Turning on iLAMP's processing only adds less than 100 mW ("Sched off"). With the camera scheduler activated ("Sched on"), *iLAMP can effectively reduce the power consumption to 0.93 W — a 62% reduction.* For buildings with dense light deployment, the power saving will be smaller, but iLAMP can still duty cycle the camera based on how frequently the localization is needed.

8. DISCUSSION

Bootstrapping overhead. The landmark survey is a critical bootstrapping step in all infrastructure based localization systems. Specific to iLAMP, it requires capturing the features of each lamp and marks the lamp on a floor plan. This procedure only needs to be done once. It involves much less overhead compared with traditional WiFi fingerprinting, which requires surveying each location spot instead of landmark. iLAMP's sensor-assisted photogrammetry technique needs to know the physical size (edge width and length) of each light fixture, but the measurement needs to be done mostly only for a few representative lights because most of the lights in a building come from the same hardware model. As a contrast, the WiFi APs' locations can be much harder to identify because many of the APs are hidden from users and are accessible only to building managers.

Robustness under various lamp shapes and image distortions. Most of the large commercial buildings we observed and experimented with embed their light fixtures inside the ceiling. Or they house the light bulbs/tubes with a cover that reshapes majority of the light beam towards the floor. Therefore, a 2D camera image mainly captures the azimuth cross-section of the light fixtures. Changing the imaging perspective, or cutting/distorting part of the image (or equivalently adding certain non-cross-section parts) does not affect the light identification in a noticeable way (Sec. 7.1). However, certain pendant lamps or chandeliers may largely expose the side fractions of their bodies. To deal with such cases, iLAMP can fall back to a conservative mode, and trigger light identification only if the image shape matches cross-section of the light taken in the database.

Our current implementation of iLAMP captures the ceiling light fixtures' tubes as well as covers to extrapolate unique features. Whereas ambient physical accessories may enrich a light's feature, they may also make the light identification sensitive to phone orientation or perspective changes. For example, the partition structures in certain FL fixtures may occupy different fraction of the image depending on the phone's horizontal position relative to the light. As mentioned in Sec. 7.1, such artifacts can be reduced by using proper structural analysis and computer vision techniques, but the solution is beyond the scope of this work.

Integration with alternative localization modalities. RF localization can be an alternative to dead-reckoning in iLAMP's blind area tracking. But to achieve high accuracy, RF localization schemes often require dense AP deployment, known AP locations, and CSI readings [1–3], which are not readily available for most of today's buildings and smartphones. Yet simple AP identities can inform iLAMP of the building or section it is in, which can become assistant features to help iLAMP narrow down its search space. iLAMP works best when the phone is held with camera facing up. RF localization may complement the cases when the phone is not exposed to LoS lights (*e.g.*, in user's pocket). Existing system's light features such as flickering frequency [13] can also be introduced as one assistant feature of iLAMP.

Privacy issues. iLAMP sets the camera exposure time to a very small value to make the ceiling light stand out of the background. In fact, the background is rendered black in all the indoor environment we have tested. Moreover, iLAMP compresses the image features into a single row and column, so no visible information will be leaked to the server. Overall, iLAMP easily preserves user privacy, unlike other visual localization approaches such as SLAM [34] which needs to capture physical scenes.

9. RELATED WORKS

Over the past two decades of research in indoor localization, RF based approaches garnered the most attention due to the wide adoption of WiFi. RF localization falls in two general categories: *fingerprinting* and *model-driven*. The fingerprinting method associates each location with the RSS [35] or channel state information (CSI) [36, 37] measured *w.r.t.* multiple access points (APs). Such RF metrics are known to be unreliable due to the small-scale fading effects, caused by multipath reflections, device movement, and human activities. Also, the fingerprinting procedure is labor intensive, requiring a blanket survey of all location spots [36, 37] This should not be confused with the much simpler landmark registration procedure which marks landmark (*e.g.*, WiFi APs or ceiling lights) positions within a floor map.

Model-driven RF localization can directly compute the line-of-sight distance/angle between APs and the mobile device, based on propagation time [2, 38] or angle-of-arrival (AoA) [1, 3]. However, due to the intrinsic instability of the wireless channel, the reliability of such approaches remains an issue: despite the decimeter-level median precision, the 90-percentile error remains at 2 to 10 meters when tested in real buildings [1–3]. Hence, they may suffice for long-term navigation, but will impair user experience in other applications that require instant and precise location fix, such as item localization and targeted advertisement in retail stores.

Since the early conceptual development in 2004 [15], existing VLP research focused intensively on two issues: light identification and device localization. Almost all the VLP solutions in the past decade used modulated smart LEDs that send digital identification beacons [7–11]. Although LiTell [13] obviates the need for such specialized LEDs, it only works for FLs with natural flickering frequencies. LiTell's frequency-based features have high confusion rate (60% even when discriminating a small population of 100 lights). So it has to combine multiple lights sequentially to enrich the feature, resulting in longer latency. Its limitation to low ceilings and back-cameras also hampers its real-world usage. In contrast, iLAMP reduces the confusion rate close to 0, and works readily with low-resolution front-cameras and high ceilings. As for device localization, PD based VLP systems follow the Lambertian radiation model to compute distance using RSS, and location using trilateration. But the RSS-distance model no longer holds for tube lights [7], and when collimating or diffusing covers/lenses are used for uniform illumination [39]. Camera based VLP [10,11] overcomes the limitation using AoA-based photogrammetry. LiTell [13] builds on this approach and transforms the distortion of lamp shape into camera position. Yet its model is applicable only for tube lights, and when the camera is held flat (Sec. 5). Besides, LiTell cannot identify the phone's azimuth orientation.

Motion sensors can track a user's relative movement via dead-reckoning [17, 40, 41], but need to be calibrated by other approaches that provide absolute location fixes [30]. State-of-the-art vision-based robotic systems integrate motion sensors with a camera to realize visual-inertial odometry (VIO) or SLAM [34], which tracks user movement continuously via image differential [42]. But the performance suffers in environment with uniform visual features (*e.g.*, office hallways) or dynamic scenes (*e.g.*, retail stores) while requiring both specific camera and continuous power consumption by video recording [34]. iLAMP hints to a new principle that can benefit the vast research in VIO and SLAM: using a computational imaging approach, many of the seemingly homogeneous scenes can become distinguishable, and hence contribute to higher precision in VIO and SLAM with commodity smartphones. Using lights instead of the ambient scenes also brings several key advantages. In particular, the lights have high contrast from the background, and are deployed regularly at discrete points. These properties simplify landmark registration and lower the image processing overhead, thus enabling accurate, real-time, and energy efficient localization.

10. CONCLUSION

Despite decades of research, accurate, robust, and low-cost indoor localization is still recognized as a grand challenge in mobile computing [43]. In this paper, we proposed iLAMP as a novel visible light localization system to confront this challenge. iLAMP uses a smartphone to efficiently extract the intrinsic visual features in unmodified LED/FL lamps, and identify each lamp as landmark with close to 100% confidence. iLAMP further introduces a sensor assisted photogrammetry technique to estimate the smartphone's 3D location (heading direction) with a small 90-percentile error of 3.5 cm (2.8°). Our Android implementation also demonstrated iLAMP as a low-latency and energy efficient localization system readily usable in today's buildings. Future research is also required to improve the robustness and extendability of our prototype and combine with other VLP or RF localization schemes.

11. REFERENCES

[1] J. Xiong and K. Jamieson, "ArrayTrack: A Fine-grained Indoor Location System," in *Proc. of USENIX NSDI*, 2013.

[2] D. Vasisht, S. Kumar, and D. Katabi, "Decimeter-level Localization with a Single WiFi Access Point," in *USENIX NSDI*, 2016.

[3] M. Kotaru, K. Joshi, D. Bharadia, and S. Katti, "SpotFi: Decimeter Level Localization Using WiFi," in *Proc. of ACM SIGCOMM*, 2015.

[4] H. Liu, Y. Gan, J. Yang, S. Sidhom, Y. Wang, Y. Chen, and F. Ye, "Push the Limit of WiFi Based Localization for Smartphones," in *Proc. of ACM MobiCom*, 2012.

[5] Q. Pu, S. Gupta, S. Gollakota, and S. Patel, "Whole-home Gesture Recognition Using Wireless Signals," in *ACM MobiCom*, 2013.

[6] L. Li, P. Hu, C. Peng, G. Shen, and F. Zhao, "Epsilon: A Visible Light Based Positioning System," in *Proc. of USENIX NSDI*, 2014.

[7] B. Xie, K. Chen, G. Tan, M. Lu, Y. Liu, J. Wu, and T. He, "LIPS: A Light Intensity–Based Positioning System for Indoor Environments," *ACM Transactions on Sensor Networks*, vol. 12, no. 4, 2016.

[8] B. Xie, G. Tan, and T. He, "SpinLight: A High Accuracy and Robust Light Positioning System for Indoor Applications," in *Prof. of ACM SenSys*, 2015.

[9] N. Rajagopal, P. Lazik, and A. Rowe, "Visual Light Landmarks for Mobile Devices," in *Proc. of ACM/IEEE IPSN*, 2014.

[10] Y.-S. Kuo, P. Pannuto, K.-J. Hsiao, and P. Dutta, "Luxapose: Indoor Positioning with Mobile Phones and Visible Light," in *Proc. of ACM MobiCom*, 2014.

[11] Z. Yang, Z. Wang, J. Zhang, C. Huang, and Q. Zhang, "Wearables Can Afford: Light-weight Indoor Positioning with Visible Light," in *Proc. of ACM MobiSys*, 2015.

[12] U.S. Department of Energy, "Energy Savings Forecast of Solid-State Lighting in General Illumination Applications," Aug. 2014.

[13] C. Zhang and X. Zhang, "LiTell: Robust Indoor Localization Using Unmodified Light Fixtures," in *Proc. of ACM MobiCom*, 2016.

[14] R. Lukac, *Computational Photography: Methods and Applications*. CRC Press, 2016.

[15] S. Horikawa, T. Komine, S. Haruyama, and M. Nakagawa, "Pervasive Visible Light Positioning System using White LED Lighting," *Technical report of IEICE DSP*, vol. 103, no. 719, 2004.

[16] P. Zhou, M. Li, and G. Shen, "Use it free: Instantly knowing your phone attitude," in *Proc. of ACM MobiCom*, 2014.

[17] J. Ã. B. Link, P. Smith, N. Viol, and K. Wehrle, "FootPath: Accurate Map-Based Indoor Navigation Using Smartphones," in *International Conference on Indoor Positioning and Indoor Navigation (IPIN)*, 2011.

[18] T. Q. Khanh, P. Bodrogi, Q. T. Vinh, and H. Winkler, *LED Lighting : Technology and Perception*. Willey, 2014.

[19] S. Pimputkar, J. S. Speck, S. P. DenBaars, and S. Nakamura, "Prospects for led lighting," *Nature Photonics*, vol. 3, no. 4, pp. 180–182, 2009.

[20] M. W. Burke, *Image Acquisition: Handbook of machine vision engineering: Volume 1*. Springer, 1996.

[21] G. B. Garcia, O. D. Suarez, J. L. E. Aranda, J. S. Tercero, and I. S. Gracia, *Learning Image Processing with OpenCV*. Packt Publishing, 2015.

[22] B. Gary and K. Adrian, "Learning opencv: Computer vision with the opencv library," *O'Reilly USA*, 2008.

[23] D. B. Goldman and J.-H. Chen, "Vignette and Exposure Calibration and Compensation," in *IEEE International Conference on Computer Vision (ICCV)*, vol. 1, 2005.

[24] E. Keogh and A. Ratanamahatana, "Everything You Know About Dynamic Time Warping is Wrong," *SIG-KDD Workshop on Mining Temporal and Sequential Data*, 2004.

[25] H. S. Fairman, M. H. Brill, H. Hemmendinger *et al.*, "How the cie 1931 color-matching functions were derived from wright-guild data," *Color Research & Application*, vol. 22, no. 1, pp. 11–23, 1997.

[26] C. CIE, "Commission internationale de l'eclairage proceedings, 1931," 1932.

[27] R. Narasimhan, M. D. Audeh, and J. M. Kahn, "Effect of Electronic-Ballast Fluorescent Lighting on Wireless Infrared Links," http://wireless.stanford.edu/papers/Ravi/iee1996ir.pdf, 1996.

[28] C. M. Bishop, "Pattern recognition," *Machine Learning*, vol. 128, 2006.

[29] Android Developers, "Gravity Sensor," https://source.android.com/devices/sensors/sensor-types.html#gravity, 2016.

[30] H. Wang, S. Sen, A. Elgohary, M. Farid, M. Youssef, and R. R. Choudhury, "No Need to War-drive: Unsupervised Indoor Localization," in *Proc. of ACM MobiSys*, 2012.

[31] Avago, "Avago 9930 linux driver," 2016. [Online]. Available: http://github.com/CyanogenMod/android_kernel_lge_hammerhead/blob/cm-13.0/drivers/misc/apds993x.c

[32] Google Tango Developer Guide, "https://developers.google.com/tango/overview/motion-tracking."

[33] Monsoon Solutions, Inc., "Monsoon Power Monitor," https://www.msoon.com/LabEquipment/PowerMonitor/.

[34] C. Cadena, L. Carlone, H. Carrillo, Y. Latif, D. Scaramuzza, J. Neira, I. D. Reid, and J. J. Leonard, "Simultaneous Localization And Mapping: Present, Future, and the Robust-Perception Age," *CoRR*, vol. abs/1606.05830, 2016.

[35] P. Bahl and V. Padmanabhan, "RADAR: an In-Building RF-Based User Location and Tracking System," in *Proc. of IEEE INFOCOM*, 2000.

[36] Y. Chen, D. Lymberopoulos, J. Liu, and B. Priyantha, "FM-based Indoor Localization," in *Proc. of ACM MobiSys*, 2012.

[37] S. Sen, B. Radunovic, R. R. Choudhury, and T. Minka, "You Are Facing the Mona Lisa: Spot Localization Using PHY Layer Information," in *Proc. of ACM MobiSys*, 2012.

[38] S. Sen, D. Kim, S. Laroche, K.-H. Kim, and J. Lee, "Bringing CUPID Indoor Positioning System to Practice," in *International Conference on World Wide Web (WWW)*, 2015.

[39] A. J. W. Whang, Y. Y. Chen, and Y. T. Teng, "Designing Uniform Illumination Systems by Surface-Tailored Lens and Configurations of LED Arrays," *Journal of Display Technology*, vol. 5, no. 3, 2009.

[40] F. Li, C. Zhao, G. Ding, J. Gong, C. Liu, and F. Zhao, "A Reliable and Accurate Indoor Localization Method Using Phone Inertial Sensors," in *Proc. of ACM Conference on Ubiquitous Computing (UbiComp)*, 2012.

[41] Q. Xu, R. Zheng, and S. Hranilovic, "Idyll: indoor localization using inertial and light sensors on smartphones," in *Proceedings of the 2015 ACM International Joint Conference on Pervasive and Ubiquitous Computing*. ACM, 2015, pp. 307–318.

[42] C. Forster, L. Carlone, F. Dellaert, and D. Scaramuzza, "On-Manifold Preintegration for Real-Time Visual-Inertial Odometry," *IEEE Transactions on Robotics*, 2016.

[43] D. Lymberopoulos, J. Liu, X. Yang, R. R. Choudhury, V. Handziski, and S. Sen, "A Realistic Evaluation and Comparison of Indoor Location Technologies: Experiences and Lessons Learned," in *Proc. of ACM/IEEE IPSN*, 2015.

POLI: Long-Range Visible Light Communications Using Polarized Light Intensity Modulation

Chun-Ling Chan†, Hsin-Mu Tsai†, Kate Ching-Ju Lin‡
†Department of Computer Science and Information Engineering, National Taiwan University, Taiwan
‡Department of Computer Science, National Chiao Tung University, Taiwan
r03922036@ntu.edu.tw, hsinmu@csie.ntu.edu.tw, katelin@cs.nctu.edu.tw

ABSTRACT

Recent studies have demonstrated the potential of light-to-camera communications for realizing applications such as localization, augmented reality and vehicle-to-vehicle communications. However, the fundamental requirement of visible light communications, *flicker-free illumination*, becomes a key limitation hindering existing technologies from serving a camera at larger distances. To break this limitation, this paper presents POLI, a light-to-camera communication system that exploits a novel *POlarized Light Intensity modulation* scheme to provide reliable communications for a wide range of distances. The key idea of POLI is to hide the information with the polarization direction of the light, to which human eyes are insensitive. Taking advantage of this, POLI can change the intensity of the polarized light as slowly as possible, at a rate determined by the range the system would support, but does not generate flickers. By using an optical component to "transform polarization directions to colors", POLI allows a camera to leverage its received RGB values as the three spatial dimensions to recover the information carried in different data streams. POLI further incorporates a number of designs to tackle the non-linearity effect of a camera, which is especially critical for an intensity-based modulation scheme. We implemented a prototype using the USRP N200 combined with off-the-shelf optical components. The experimental results show that POLI delivers to its camera receiver a throughput proportional to the dynamic channel conditions. The achievable throughput can be up to 71 bytes per second at short distances, while the service range can be up to 40 meters.

1. INTRODUCTION

Light-to-camera communications has recently become an emerging network paradigm. The potential applications that greatly benefit from such a system include advanced driving assistance system (ADAS) and augmented reality. For example, real-time status information about a particular vehicle, such as its speed, bearing, and brake status, can be emitted by its LED tail lights, or users can capture the information required for augmented reality based navigation in a large museum from ceiling lights. The key to the success of the above applications is: communication range! However, most existing designs [9, 23, 17, 18] only support a room-level communication range, limiting their applicability.

The main challenge of enabling long-range light-to-camera communications is to combat with severe path losses. Essentially, the intensity of a pixel in an image is the amount of optical energy accumulated by the sensing area of that pixel within the exposure duration, i.e., when the shutter is open. Hence, a camera at longer distances experiences a larger path loss and no longer accumulates sufficient energy for reliable decoding. To extend the service range, a simple solution is to extend the exposure time and, thereby, increase the signal strength. Unfortunately, there exists a limit of the longest exposure time a camera can use. In particular, any exposure time longer than a symbol duration could cause *inter-symbol interference*, meaning that a camera would receive mixtures of consecutive symbols in an image, making all of the mixed symbols undecodable. One might think that, to avoid symbol mixtures, we may further enlarge the symbol duration accordingly, which, however, could lead to observable flickers. This, hence, sets a hard limit for a non-flickering light to enable long-range and reliable communications.

In this paper, we introduce POLI, a light-to-camera communication system that uses *POlarized Light Intensity modulation* to overcome the above fundamental limitation, allowing a distant camera of a few tens of meters to still receive reliably. The key idea of POLI is to circumvent the limitation set by the flicker-free requirement using a novel optical design that leverages an extra dimension – polarization. To do so, instead of directly modulating a light source, we modulate the polarized lights along different directions, while still maintaining the emitted light intensity stable all the time. Since human eyes are insensitive to polarization, there no longer exist any limitation on the symbol duration and, thereby, the exposure time a camera can use. To realize such a system, however, a few key questions need to be answered.

First, how do we hide observable flickers, even when the signal has significant energy at lower frequency? POLI tackles this challenge by a novel polarization intensity modulation scheme. The scheme creates a signal such that the total intensity of light in different polarization directions is kept constant over time, while the intensity of each polarized light can be changed independently even at a very low frequency. On the other hand, polarization of light also serves as a tool to multiplex different data streams and boost the data rate.

Then, how exactly should a camera recover the information embedded in different polarizations of light? A camera typically accumulates the intensity of all the polarizations of light, but now needs to detect intensity changes along some particular polarizations of light. To do so, inspired by [35], POLI makes use of an optical rotatory dispersor to *transform polarization direction into colors*. Since

Permission to make digital or hard copies of all or part of this work for personal or classroom use is granted without fee provided that copies are not made or distributed for profit or commercial advantage and that copies bear this notice and the full citation on the first page. Copyrights for components of this work owned by others than the author(s) must be honored. Abstracting with credit is permitted. To copy otherwise, or republish, to post on servers or to redistribute to lists, requires prior specific permission and/or a fee. Request permissions from permissions@acm.org.

MobiSys'17, June 19-23, 2017, Niagara Falls, NY, USA

© 2017 Copyright held by the owner/author(s). Publication rights licensed to ACM.

ISBN 978-1-4503-4928-4/17/06...$15.00

DOI: http://dx.doi.org/10.1145/3081333.3081352

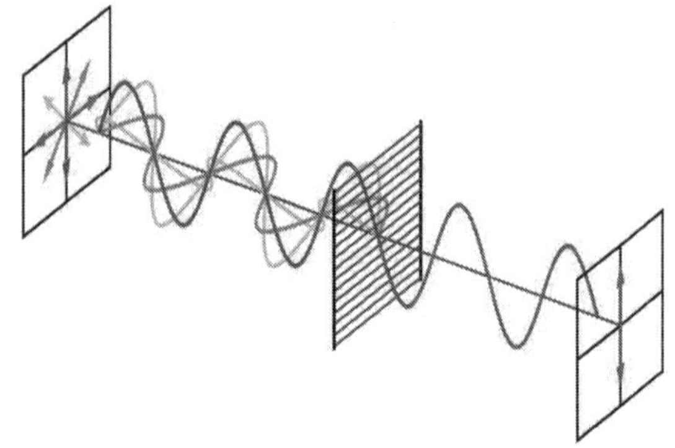

Figure 1: **Optical polarization.** Unpolarized light can be converted to polarized light after passing the first polarizer, which is then partially blocked by the second polarizer.

a commodity camera captures the red, green, and blue (RGB) values at each pixel of an image, these three color components can be thought of the spatial dimensions of a camera, which behaves like a three-antenna device that has three degrees of freedom and can separate three simultaneous data streams. Therefore, by attaching a polarizer, a camera receiver should be able to observe colors and recover information modulated in different polarized color beams.

Finally, how does the system deal with non-linearity of a camera? This non-linearity effect would introduce two practical problems. First, most existing MIMO decoders are linear equalizers, which would produce large decoding errors if the channels are non-linear. Second, each camera has a limited dynamic range: incoming light waves saturate the output at short distances and generate low pixel values with little changes at long distances. We solve the first problem by a new channel estimation scheme that improves decoding reliability even for non-linear channels. To further alleviate the impact of non-linearity, we propose an automatic gain control scheme that adapts the exposure time to dynamic channels such that the received intensity can be mostly within the linearity range of a camera, thereby enabling reliable communications in a wide range of distance.

We have built a prototype of POLI using the USRP N200 radio platforms to control the three LEDs and generated intensity varying polarized lights, which are then converted to color beams by a dispersor. A Point Grey Grasshopper camera is used as the receiver to measure the RGB values of the combined color beam and perform MIMO decoding. The performance of POLI is evaluated via testbed experiments, and our key findings are as follows:

- The intensity of the combined white light of the transmitted polarized color beams is nearly constant, thereby indistinguishable to human eyes. However, by installing a polarizer, a camera can clearly detect the variation in its received RGB values and use MIMO decoding to separate the concurrent streams modulated in different color beams.
- Each exposure time has its own optimal operational range. Without proper configuration, the linearity of the received RGB intensity might be too poor to ensure reliable decoding. By enabling POLI's gain control, a receiver can quickly identify its suitable exposure time and achieve a symbol delivery ratio very close to the one produced by the optimal configuration.
- POLI provides a camera a throughput proportional to its channel condition. As the baud rate is set to 30 symbols per second, the effective throughput at distances 5 m and 10 m are, on average, 34 and 9 bytes per second, respectively. The service range can even be extended to 40 meters with an error rate of only 10%.
- The service range is determined by the baud rate (i.e., inverse of the symbol interval) used by a transmitter. With POLI, a transmitter can flexibly reduce its baud rate in order to extend its service range. The smallest baud rate is now no longer limited by a lowest frequency required by existing light-to-camera communication systems to prevent observable flickering, and can be reduced to 5 Hz or less.

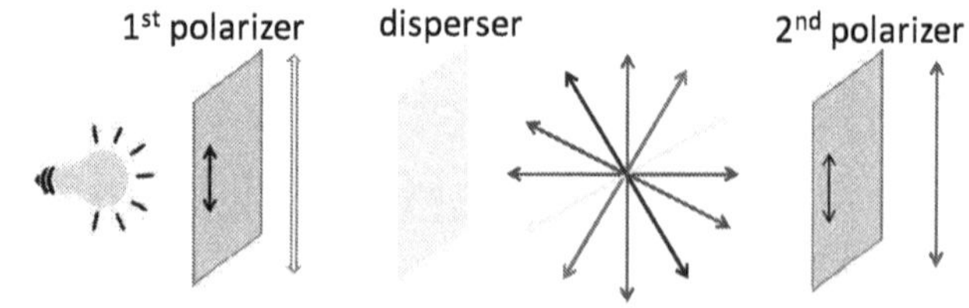

Figure 2: **Transmitting a color beam via dispersion.** The dispersor diverts polarized light from the first polarizer into several color beams in different polarizations; then, the second polarizer only allows a polarized color beam to traverse.

2. PRIMER

2.1 Polarization

Most common sources of visible light, such as LED, typically emit unpolarized light, which consists of a mixture of waves with different polarizations. To generate polarized light, one can pass unpolarized light through an optical polarizing filter or simply "polarizer", as shown in Fig. 1. A polarizer[1]. This polarization effect will not be perceived by users since human eyes cannot detect polarization directions. To measure the oscillating direction of polarized light, we can pass the light source through another polarizing filter, as shown in Fig. 1. Then, the intensity of the beam traversing through the second filter will be determined by the angle θ between the directions of the two polarizers. According to the Malus's law [8], the intensity of the beam passing through two polarizers can be given by

$$I = I_0 \cos^2 \theta, \quad (1)$$

where I_0 indicates the original light intensity. From the equation, we get that, ideally, the light can completely pass through the filters if the directions of the two polarizers are in parallel. However, the light is fully blocked if one filter is perpendicular to the other.

2.2 Dispersion

Dispersor is an optical material that can separate a white light into components of different wavelengths (i.e., different colors) and rotate them to different polarization directions. If we simply place a dispersor in front of a light source, human eye or image sensors still see the white light since all those dispersed polarized color beams are combined together. A possible way to emit a color beam is to place a dispersor in between two linear polarizers, as shown in Fig. 2. The first polarizer makes unpolarized light become linearly

[1]Polarizers can further be classified into *absorptive polarizers* and *beam splitting polarizers* allows only a particular polarization to pass through, while blocking the waves oscillating in all the other directions. The former absorbs the unwanted polarizations, while the later reflects the unwanted polarizations. We use absorptive polarizers in our work and simply refer to the term "polarizer" as the absorptive polarizer.

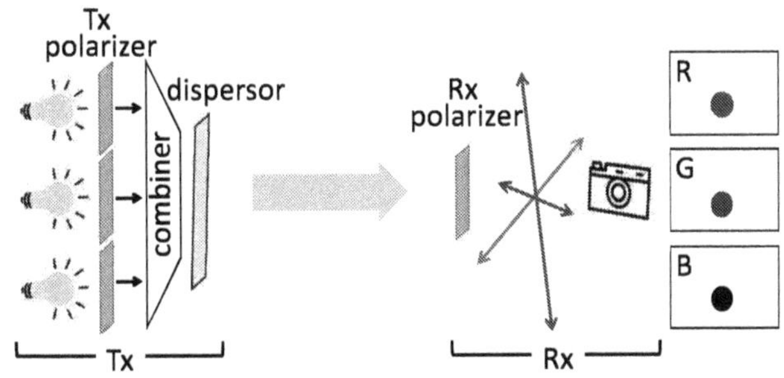

Figure 3: **POLI's design.** Light from the three LEDs is diverted into color beams along different polarization directions. By filtering them through another polarizer, the receiver only senses three color beams aligned in different polarizations, which can be recovered using MIMO decoding technologies.

polarized light. The dispersor then diverts the polarized light into several color beams (each with a distinct wavelength) in different polarization directions [35]. Since human eyes cannot detect polarizations, without the second polarizer, people still see the white light, though the light intensity might be slightly lowered after dispersion. However, by attaching the second polarizer to a receiving image sensor (or camera), the receiver only receives one particular color beam that aligns along the direction of its polarizer and can, hence, traverse through. By combining a dispersor with two polarizers, we can tune the direction of either polarizer to change the color of the light beam and explicitly control the RGB intensity of the image pixels occupied by a transmitting light. This gives us an opportunity to realize intensity-based modulation, which is more suitable for long-range VLC, without causing flickers, and the information can easily be recovered by measuring the received RGB intensity. We will explain in Sec. 3 why such polarization intensity modulation provides reliability even at a long distance.

2.3 Intensity Modulation

Intensity modulation represents digital data as variations in the intensity of a light source. The basic operation is intrinsically the same with traditional *amplitude modulation* used in RF-based systems. The only difference is that a light source can only emit non-negative amplitude and, hence, should represent data using light intensity, i.e., the amount of energy. For example, for M-ary intensity modulation (M-IM), each symbol is assigned one of M different intensity values, which are usually uniformly distributed between the maximum intensity $I_{\max}$ and minimum intensity $I_{\min}$ as follow:

$$I_m = \frac{I_{\max} - I_{\min}}{M-1}(m-1) + I_{\min}, \forall m = 1, \cdots, M. \quad (2)$$

Each intensity is then used to represent a unique sequence of $\log_2 M$ digital bits. Hence, the ideal data rate of intensity modulation equals to $\frac{\log_2 M}{T}$, where T is the symbol duration. Such intensity modulation is more resilient to small occupied areas of a light in an image or can even work for single-pixel light sensors. However, varying intensity is intrusive as human eyes will perceive flickers. Therefore, our goal is to develop a system that can alternatively vary the intensity of each color component, while stabilizing the aggregated intensity of color beams.

3. DESIGN

3.1 Overview

The key of POLI is to develop a novel modulation technique, called *polarization intensity modulation* (PIM). To avoid flickering while maintaining the nice properties of intensity modulation, POLI's PIM represents digital bits using the intensity of RGB values received by a camera or light sensor, instead of the intensity of the transmitting light. To do so, we combine three LED light bulbs and a dispersor as a transmitter, as shown in Fig. 3. Each LED is attached a linear polarizer that converts unpolarized light to polarized light and operates like an *antenna* in a traditional MIMO wireless device. To ensure that each light source can be converted to a different color beam, we equip the three polarizers along three different directions. The three light beams are then aggregated via a beam combiner, which passes the combined light through the dispersor for diverting the color beams along different directions.

POLI's receiver can be either a rolling shutter camera, a global shutter camera or a color sensor. To detect color intensity modulated by the transmitted light, the receiver attaches another polarizer in front of its lens. If only a single LED is transmitting, the camera will only receive a single color beam, as shown in Fig. 2.[2] However, since POLI combines three LEDs, each with a polarizer along a different direction, the camera thus receives the combination of the three different color beams, each of which is from a transmitting LED light, as shown in Fig. 3. By changing the intensity of each LED, and thereby the intensity of each color beam, the camera will receive varying RGB values in those pixels occupied by the combined color beam (see Sec. 3.2). Note that a camera now receives in three dimensions, i.e., three RGB intensity values. Hence, POLI's design is analogous to a 3×3 MIMO system and can further leverage the multiplexing gain to boost the data rate. Specifically, a 3-antenna MIMO system can typically deliver three data streams simultaneously. In POLI, the intensity variation of the three LEDs can be thought of three data streams, which can be recovered from the three received RGB values (see Sec. 3.3) using MIMO decoding algorithms.

However, since the color intensity received by a camera not only depends on the transmitted light intensity, but also its configured exposure time. If the exposure time is not properly selected, the received RGB intensity might saturate due to over exposure or become too low due to under exposure, as a result leading to non-linear channel response. This non-linearity effect makes standard linear MIMO equalizers ineffective. To resolve this non-linearity problem, we propose a table lookup decoding method in Sec. 3.3 to recover the combined signals, and further develop an automatic gain control scheme in Sec. 3.4 to adapt the exposure time of a receiver to dynamic channel conditions so as to enlarge the linearity range.

3.2 Polarization Intensity Modulation

The proposed *Polarization Intensity Modulation* (PIM) is a technique that varies the intensity of a polarized light beam, instead of the aggregated light intensity. In particular, each LED changes its light intensity over time, while the intensities of the three lights are well-controlled such that the total intensity output by the beam combiner can still be a constant. Consider a simple case where only a single LED light bulb i is transmitting using a unit of intensity. The dispersor diverts the light into multiple color beams, but only one of the beams passing through the receiver's polarizer is captured in the image. Let $\mathbf{c}_i = (R_i, G_i, B_i)$ denote the RGB inten-

[2]For ease of description, we mainly consider the scenario with a single transmitting light. However, the design can be easily extended to a scenario with multiple transmitters if the receiver is a camera, which can leverage its high spatial resolution of image sensors to separate multiple transmitters at different locations.

sity of the received color beam captured in the image when LED i transmits signals with a unit of intensity. This color intensity vector $\mathbf{c}_i$ can be thought of a unique channel between the i-th transmitting light and the receiving camera, similar to the channels of a 1×3 MIMO link. To simplify the description, for now we temporarily assume that the received intensity of each RGB component is linearly proportional to the intensity of the transmitted light. In other words, if the transmitting LED changes its light intensity to x, the received color vector becomes $(R_i, G_i, B_i)x$. In POLI, each LED i, $i = 1, 2, 3$, sets its intensity to $x_i(t)$ at time t. The camera then receives the combination of the three color beams, and the RGB values of each pixel occupied by the light beam can be expressed by

$$\begin{pmatrix} y_R \\ y_G \\ y_B \end{pmatrix} = \begin{pmatrix} R_1 \\ G_1 \\ B_1 \end{pmatrix} x_1 + \begin{pmatrix} R_2 \\ G_2 \\ B_2 \end{pmatrix} x_2 + \begin{pmatrix} R_3 \\ G_3 \\ B_3 \end{pmatrix} x_3. \quad (3)$$

To ensure that the above three equations are linearly independent, the polarizers in front of three lights should be attached along three different directions. We place them in 10°, 60° and 100° in our implementation, but any configuration of three independent directions works. Note that the intensity of the combined light beam should keep constant. Hence, the following total intensity constraint should always hold:

$$x_1 + x_2 + x_3 = I_{\text{total}}, \quad (4)$$

where I_{total} is the constant light intensity of POLI's transmitter. Subject to this constraint, we use x_1 and x_2 as data symbols, but use x_3 as a *complement* to satisfy Eq. 4. That is, similar to power control in most of RF-based systems, POLI should also perform *intensity control* by setting x_3 to $I_{\text{total}} - x_1 - x_2$. Hence, Eq. 3 can be rewritten as the following vector form:

$$\mathbf{y} = \mathbf{c}_1 x_1 + \mathbf{c}_2 x_2 + \mathbf{c}_3 (I_{\text{total}} - x_1 - x_2), \quad (5)$$

where $\mathbf{c}_i$ is the unique channel vector between the i-th transmitting LED and a receiving camera.

Due to this intensity constraint, though POLI consists of three LED light bulbs, there are, however, only two lights available for carrying data signals x_1 and x_2. In particular, we call the first two LEDs the *data light sources* and call the last LED the *complementary light source*. Then, for each of the data light sources, we use an M-ary PIM (M-PIM) symbol to represent any $\log_2 M$ bits of information. The intensity of each M-PIM symbol I_m for $m = 1, \cdots, M$ is given by

$$I_m = \frac{I_{\text{total}}/2 - I_{\min}}{M-1} * (m-1) + I_{\min}, \text{for } m = 1, \cdots, M, \quad (6)$$

where $I_{\text{total}}/2$ is the maximum intensity allocated to a data light source and $I_{\min}$ is the minimum intensity. Then, the combination of the intensity of two light bulbs, i.e., $\mathbf{x} = (x_1, x_2)$ at time t represents a unique pattern of $2\log_2 M$ bits, and we collect all the combinations as the symbol set $\mathbb{S}$. For example, if POLI adopts 16-PIM, each light bulb encodes four bits into 16 intensity levels. Then, the symbol set $\mathbb{S}$ includes 256 symbol vectors, and any transmitted symbol vector can be expressed by

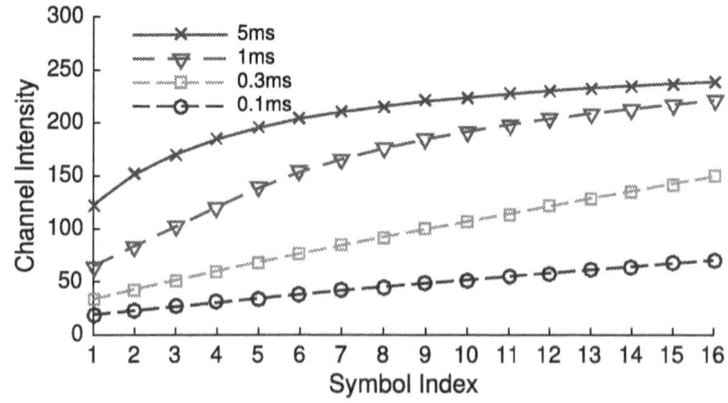

Figure 4: **Non-linearity of intensity-modulated signals.** A camera usually has a poor linearity, especially when the exposure time is not set properly. This non-linearity effect hinders us from using the conventional linear MIMO equalizer, e.g., zero-forcing, to recover the signals.

$$\mathbf{x}(t) = (x_1(t), x_2(t)) = \begin{cases} (I_1, I_1) & \text{for bit pattern 1} \\ (I_1, I_2) & \text{for bit pattern 2} \\ \vdots & \\ (I_1, I_{16}) & \text{for bit pattern 16} \\ (I_2, I_1) & \text{for bit pattern 17} \\ \vdots & \\ (I_{16}, I_{16}) & \text{for bit pattern 256.} \end{cases} \quad (7)$$

Then, the camera receives one of the 256 possible RGB intensity vectors and maps it back to the digital bits.

3.3 Channel Estimation and Demodulation

Due to the analogy between our POLI and a 3×3 MIMO system, in theory, we can recover the three unknowns, x_1, x_2 and x_3, in Eq. 3 using the standard linear MIMO decoders, such as the *zero forcing equalizer* [29]. However, the feasibility of linear equalizers relies on an assumption of *signal linearity*, which refers to as the property that the received signal should be linearly proportional to the transmitted signal. However, in a visible light communication system, the image intensity is determined by not only the intensity of the transmitting light but also camera sensitivity or configurations, such as exposure time. For example, if the exposure time is set to too long, the RGB intensity is very likely to saturate, i.e., close to 255. Similarly, if the exposure time is too short, the received RGB intensity would be very close to 0 most of the time. Hence, a VLC system usually is not a perfect linear system. To verify this point, we measure the RGB intensity received by a camera deployed at distance 1 m when only the first LED modulates its signals using 16-Ary PIM (i.e., 16 different intensity values). The maximum and minimum transmitted intensity, $I_{\max}$ and $I_{\min}$, are set to 35 and 150, respectively. Fig. 4 only plots the intensity of the blue color when the exposure time is set to four different values. The results show that, for some configurations of the exposure time, e.g., 5 ms, the received intensity quickly saturates when the transmitter increases its amplitude. That is, an improper exposure time could lead to poor linearity. If this is the case, decoding the received symbols using traditional linear equalizers could produce a high error rate.

Table 1: **Intensity-to-symbol lookup table.**

Rx RGB Intensity $f(\mathbf{x})$	Tx symbol $\mathbf{x} = (x_1, x_2)$
$(R_{1,1}, G_{1,1}, B_{1,1})$	(I_1, I_1)
$\vdots$	$\vdots$
$(R_{1,M}, G_{1,M}, B_{1,M})$	(I_1, I_M)
$(R_{2,1}, G_{2,1}, B_{2,1})$	(I_2, I_1)
$\vdots$	$\vdots$
$(R_{2,M}, G_{2,M}, B_{2,M})$	(I_2, I_M)
$\vdots$	$\vdots$
$(R_{M,M}, G_{M,M}, B_{M,M})$	(I_M, I_M)

To resolve this non-linearity issue, we exploit a table lookup decoding scheme to recover the multiplexing streams. In particular, instead of learning the channels (i.e., the intensity vectors $\mathbf{c}_i$ from LED i) and decoding via linear MIMO equalizers, we alternatively allow each receiver to measure the intensity-to-symbol table that directly maps the received RGB intensity values to the most likely transmitted symbol. Such table lookup decoding is simple but effective mainly because, in POLI, though the received RGB intensity is non-linear, it, however, does not change is quite stable since the optical fading is much more static as compared to the fading of RF signals. Hence, the lookup table does not need to be updated frequently if the light-to-camera link distance does not change much.

To realize table lookup decoding, POLI's transmitter sends some known training symbols in the beginning of a packet for each receiving camera to update its intensity-to-symbol lookup table. To reduce the training overhead, the transmitter only samples a small subset of symbol vectors (I_i, I_j) from $\mathbb{S}$ as the training symbol vectors. A camera measures the received RGB intensity of the training symbol vectors, as the blue entries shown in Table 1, and leverage *piecewise bilinear interpolation* to estimate the RGB intensity of the remaining symbol vectors, as the black entries shown in Table 1. By *piecewise bilinear interpolation*, we mean that the estimated RGB intensity of a non-training symbol vector is learned from taking bilinear interpolation of a few closest training symbol vectors. By collecting the intensity of a sufficient number of training symbol vectors, such piecewise linear interpolation should approximately fit the actual non-linear channels, e.g., the channels shown in Fig. 4. In particular, we adopt grid sampling to select the training symbol vectors. In particular, the set of the selected training symbol vectors can be expressed as

$$\mathbb{S}_{\text{train}} = \{(I_i, I_j) : 1 \leq i, j \leq M, i \bmod d{=}1, j \bmod d{=}1\}, \quad (8)$$

where d denotes the sampling interval, meaning that each data LED samples one out of every d possible intensity values as a training known symbol. Then, we can adjust the interval d to determine the density of training symbols. Given the measured RGB intensity of the training symbol vectors, the receiver performs *bilinear interpolation* for the non-training symbol vectors within a rectilinear 2D grid formed the four closet training symbol vectors, as illustrated in Fig. 5. For example, for the symbol vectors (I_i, I_j), $1 \leq i \leq d, 1 \leq j \leq d$, their RGB intensity intensity is estimated by bilinear interpolation of the measured RGB intensity of the four training symbol vectors, $(I_1, I_1), (I_1, I_d), (I_d, I_1)$ and (I_d, I_d). Since each grid performs its interpolation independently, this piecewise interpolation can alleviate the non-linearity problem when the training symbol vectors are sampled dense enough. We will show in §5.1 that 16 training symbols are sufficient to produce a fairly good decoding reliability. As compared to traditional linear equalizers, which also need to send a few training symbols from each antenna, POLI only needs slightly higher channel estimation overhead, but can effectively resolve the non-linearity problem.

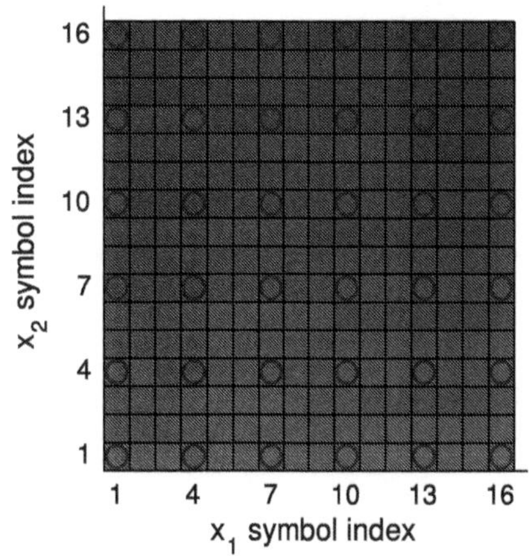

Figure 5: **Channel estimation via piecewise bilinear interpolation.** We select the symbol vectors (the blue circles) at the corners of a grid as training symbol vectors, and estimate the received RGB intensity of the other symbol vectors (the color of each block) within a grid using bilinear interpolation.

Given the intensity-to-symbol lookup table, a receiver can recover its symbols using ML (Maximum Likelihood) decoding. In particular, let $\mathbf{x} = (x_1, x_2) \in \mathbb{S}$ denote any possible symbol vector sent by the transmitter's two data LEDs and let $f(\mathbf{x})$ be the measured or interpolated RGB intensity corresponding to $\mathbf{x}$. Then, ML detection of a symbol vector can be written as

$$\hat{\mathbf{x}} = \arg\min_{\mathbf{x} \in \mathbb{S}} \|\mathbf{y} - f(\mathbf{x})\|^2, \quad (9)$$

where $\mathbf{y}$ is the received RGB intensity vector. Though enabling ML requires a receiver to search the whole space, this complexity is, however, acceptable for a VLC system, in which the bandwidth (i.e., the frame rate) of a receiving camera is usually much smaller than RF devices, giving a camera receiver a long enough time to decode every symbol.

Detailed protocols of POLI. To realize the above ML detection in practice, we collect several data symbols as a packet, and broadcast a delimiter and the training symbols in the beginning of each packet, as shown in Fig. 6. The delimiter consists of 20 known symbols that are used for a receiver to detect the beginning of a packet. The delimiter is followed by the training symbols for a receiver to update its intensity-to-symbol table. Since different receiving cameras usually have different frame rates, a receiver's sampling interval is usually different from the symbol duration of the transmitted light signals. Therefore, the transmitter should configure its symbol duration such that any receiver can at least receive each symbol in at least one image frame. To improve reliability, we let the symbol baud rate be four times of the frame rate of a receiving camera in our implementation. With this configuration, a receiver can receive a symbol across four image frames and take the average intensity to perform table lookup decoding. One might doubt that a receiver would receive the mixture of two consecutive symbols in an image frame if a receiver is not tightly synchronized with its transmitter. This is however rarely happens since a camera does not receive the light signals all the time, but only during the exposure time, which

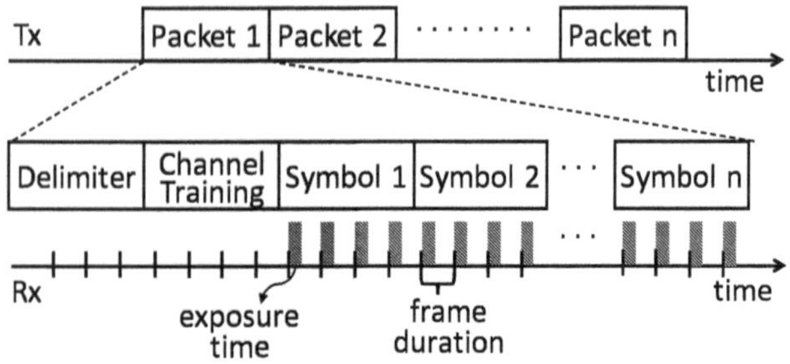

Figure 6: **Protocol and packet format.** Each packet preceded with a delimiter and a few channel training symbols for a receiver to detect the packet and train its lookup table.

is actually much shorter than a frame interval, as shown in Fig. 6. Therefore, the probability that a symbol boundary happens to locate within an exposure time is fairly small.[3]

3.4 Automatic Gain Control

Though POLI leverages table lookup decoding to alleviate the impact of non-linearity, the symbol error rate might still be high if the channel is extremely non-linear since the distance between the intensity RGB intensity $f(\mathbf{x})$ of any two neighboring symbol vectors might become too small. To improve the decoding success probability, a receiver should adapt its exposure time to dynamic environmental conditions, such as the distance to the transmitter and the strength of the ambient light. More specifically, to minimize the symbol error rate, a receiver should search the best exposure time such that the received intensity of POLI's PIM signals can be mostly within the linearity range of the receiver. This task is fundamentally the same with *automatic gain control* (AGC) required in most of RF-based communication systems.

To achieve this goal, we adopt a simple adaptation scheme to search the best configuration during data reception. The high-level idea is to decrease the exposure time if the maximum received RGB intensity is too large, while increasing it if the minimum intensity is too small. In particular, a receiver maintains a window of K frames and keeps tracking its maximum and minimum received intensity among the pixels occupied by the light in those K frames. For each pixel, we use $\max(R, G, B)$ to represent its intensity as searching for the maximum intensity, while using $\min(R, G, B)$ to represent its intensity as looking for the minimum intensity. The receiver switches to the next longer exposure time if the minimum intensity is lower than a threshold $P_{\min}$, while switching to the next shorter exposure time if the maximum intensity is higher than a threshold $P_{\max}$. We set $P_{\max} = 255 * (1 - \alpha)$ and $P_{\min} = 255 * \beta$, where α and β are small margins used to prevent saturation and low intensity, respectively. In our experiments, the two values are heuristically chosen without much efforts, but can usually ensure quick convergence for static scenarios.

The last thing worth noting is that the longest feasible exposure time is bounded by the symbol duration used by the transmitter. Otherwise, if the exposure time is longer than a symbol duration, the receiver will expose two or more consecutive symbols in an image frame, leading to inter-symbol interference. In other words, since a farther receiver usually receives a lower intensity and needs to use a longer exposure time, to extend POLI's service range, we should enlarge the symbol duration. This, however, reduces the achievable data rate. We will experimentally evaluate this tradeoff in Sec. 5.

[3]If, unfortunately, the exposure time really overlaps with the symbol boundary, we leverage the delimiter to detect the symbol boundary and remove those mixture frames.

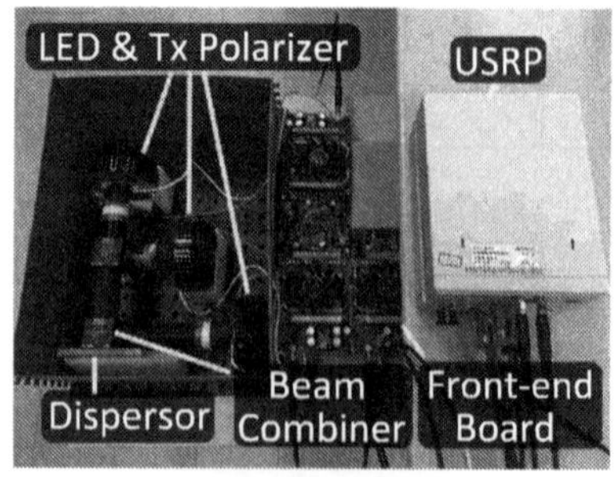

(a) Transmitter

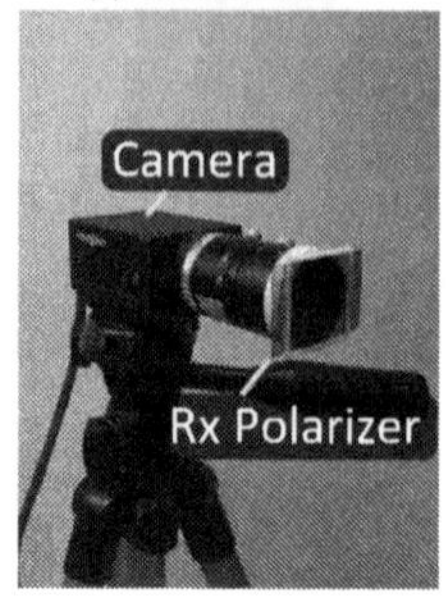

(b) Receiver

Figure 7: **POLI prototype.**

4. IMPLEMENTATION

We combine three Bridgelux BXRA-W0802 12.5 watt LED light bulbs as POLI's transmitter. Each LED light is controlled by an Ettus USRP (Universal Software Radio Peripheral) N200 board [1] through a VLC front-end board, as shown in Fig. 7(a). In particular, the USRP board is equipped with a LFTX daughterboard that can generates voltage varying signals with a sampling rate between 0 and 30 MHz. The voltage signals are then converted to the current varying signals by the front-end board to drives an LED light. The intensity of a transmitting LED can be tuned by adjusting the voltage of the signals sent by the USRP controller. Each LED is controlled by one USRP board, and the three USRPs are synchronized through an external clock [2] so that they can update their intensity at exactly the same time. A polarizer is attached to each of the three LEDs, and the directions of the three polarizers are aligned to 10, 60 and 100 degrees, respectively. The three light beams are then aggregated by a Thorlabs CM1-BS013 beam combiner [3], which passes the combined light beam through an EDC7723 LCD dispersor.

At the receiver side, we use a Point Grey Grasshopper camera with a global shutter that outputs the received optical signals as image frames with a resolution of 1920×1200, as shown in Fig. 7(b). The Grasshopper camera provides flexibility to tune the parameters, including the frame rate, the exposure time and the gain. Without otherwise stated, we let the camera receive a few random symbols and adapt its gain accordingly before data reception. The captured images are saved as the JPG or RAW formats for offline processing and decoding in a Linux system. Though the evaluation is done offline, we collect the traces over real channels to evaluate the performance with consideration of channel variation and the impact of imperfect channel estimation.

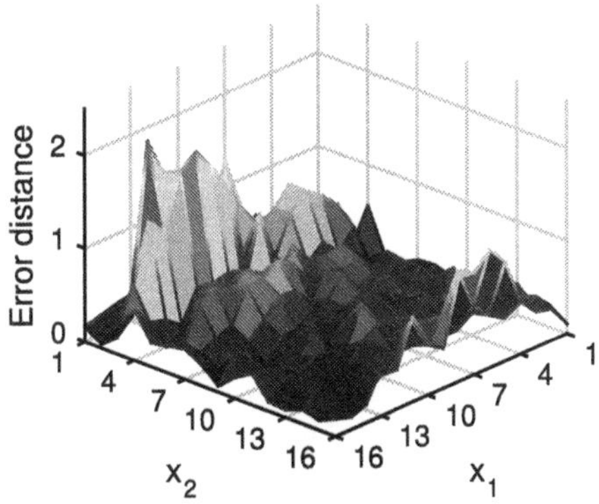

(a) Linear sampling (JPG image)

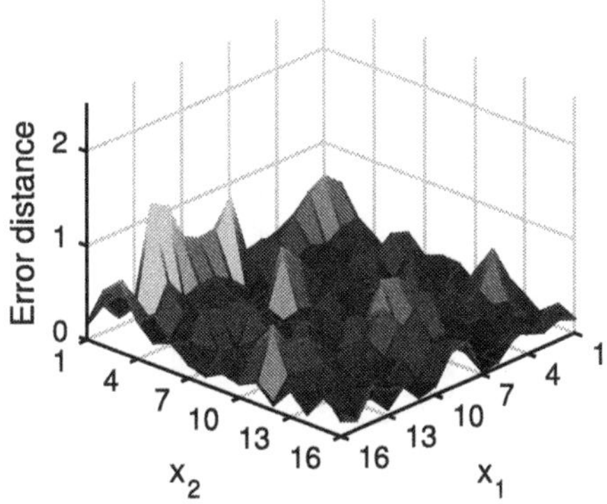

(b) Grid sampling (JPG image)

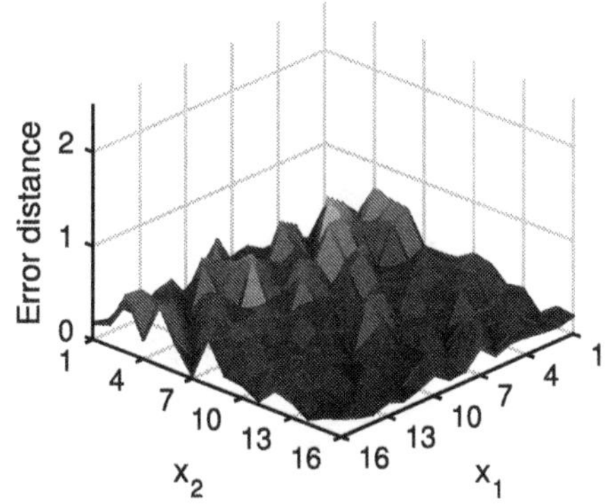

(c) Grid sampling (RAW image)

Figure 8: **Error distance per symbol.** The distribution of error distances is non-uniform because of the non-linearity effect inherently in a VLC system. The error could be large for some intensity regions, as shown in (a), if the symbols are decoded using a linear equalizer. Our ML-based decoding alleviates the impact of non-linearity and reduces the decoding error, as shown in (b). The errors can further be reduced if a camera outputs RAW images, which do not distort the received information, as shown in (c).

Parameter	Options	Default
Transmission baud rate	5,15,30,60 (Hz)	30 (Hz)
Camera frame rate	20,60,120,240 (fps)	120 (fps)
Exposure time	0.08,1,7,16,30 (ms)	7 (ms)
Modulation order	8,16,32	16
Min/Max intensity in PIM, $I_{\min}, I_{\max}$	-	35,150
Training symbol sampling distance d	3,5,15	3
Threshold for AGC, $P_{\min}$, $P_{\max}$	-	80,150
Image format	JPG, RAW	RAW

Table 2: **Parameters and default values.**

5. RESULTS

We conduct testbed experiments to characterize the benchmark performance of POLI, including the channel estimation error, the required channel training cost, the impact of channel correlation and exposure time configuration. For testing a more challenging case in indoor environments, we experiment when all interfering lights, three light fixtures, each with 4 14W T5 fluorescent tubes, are turned on during normal daylight. They would generate ambient light which adds noises to the received signal. We also conduct some experiments in an outdoor environment during the daytime to test how POLI works in this more challenging scenario. The performance of POLI is evaluated in terms of the *i) symbol delivery ratio*, which is defined as the number of correctly delivered symbols divided by the total number of transmitted symbols, and the *ii) effective throughput*, which is defined as the symbol rate multiplied by the symbol delivery ratio. Other default parameter settings are listed in Table 2.

5.1 Micro benchmark

5.1.1 Demodulation Errors

We first check the effectiveness of our table lookup decoding with grid-based training and compare it with traditional linear equalization.

Experiment setup: A receiving camera is deployed at a distance 1 m away from the transmitter, which modulates the signals using 16-Ary PIM. We compare our table lookup ML decoding with the traditional ZF decoding. For our ML decoding, the transmitter adopts grid sampling and set the sampling interval d (in Eq. 8) to 5. For ZF decoding, we randomly select 12 known training symbol vectors for a receiver to train its channel vectors $\mathbf{c}_i, i = 1, 2, 3$. The transmitter first broadcasts the training symbols and then transmits all the 256 possible symbols iteratively. For each experiment, the training symbols are only sent once, while we repeat symbol transmissions for four iterations. To check the impact of channel non-linearity on decoding errors, we calculate the error distance between the true received intensity and the estimated intensity (i.e., $f(\mathbf{x})$ in the table for ML and $\sum_i \mathbf{c}_i x_i$ for ZF). Since the intensity information might be distorted after image compression, we further check whether such compression would affect the error distance by saving the frames as the JPG and RAW formates, respectively.

Results: Fig. 8 illustrates the error distance, i.e., the distance between the expected color intensity estimated by the learned channels and the actual measured color intensity, for ZF (JPG), ML (JPG) and ML (RAW), respectively. The results show that the error distances of ZF are much larger than that of our table lookup decoding. For ZF, the errors for symbols with a larger index, i.e., those corresponding to a higher transmitted intensity, are much larger. This is because, as shown in Fig. 4, the non-linear effect usually occurs in the high intensity region when the receiving camera uses an exposure time that causes overexposure. By enabling our table lookup ML decoding with grid-based sampling, the impact of non-linearity can be minimized as the bilinear interpolation is performed only within a grid, instead of the whole symbol vector space. We can also observe that the RAW image format, as shown in Fig. 8(c), produces a much smaller error than the JPG image format, as shown in Fig. 8(b). This explains that image compression introduces additional noise and further worsens the non-linearity problem.

5.1.2 Channel Training Cost

Since the training symbols sent per-packet are an overhead of the system, we next check how many training symbols are sufficient for a receiver to achieve reliable decoding.

Experiment setup: We use the same sampling strategy as the previous experiment to select the training symbols for 16-ary PIM, but

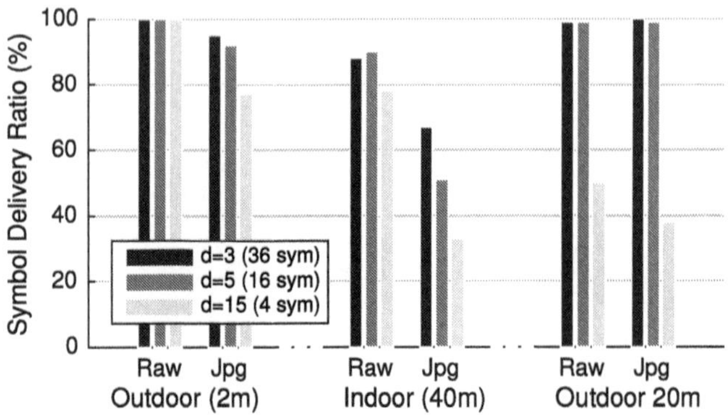

Figure 9: **The impact of the training cost on the symbol delivery ratio.** When the channels are less linear, e.g., as the link distance becomes longer, more training symbols, i.e., a smaller sampling interval, are required to perform piecewise bilinear interpolation and approximate the real channels. From our measurements, training symbols are dense enough to achieve accurate channel estimation as $d = 5$.

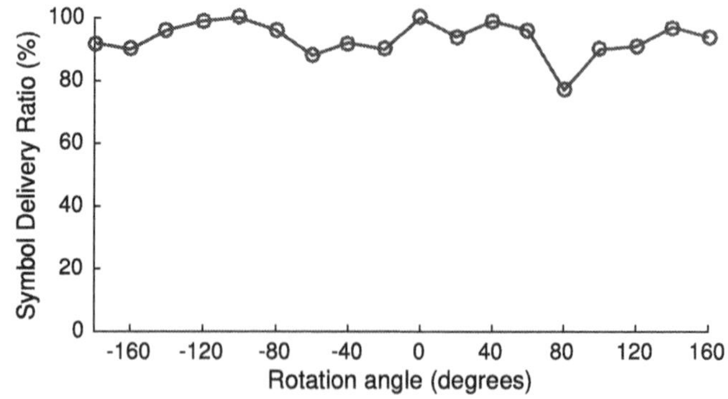

Figure 10: **Impact of rotation on channel correlation.** Similar to most of MIMO systems, the practical achievable multiplexing gain is determined by the correlation between the channel vectors. POLI achieves a high symbol delivery ratio, except for some worse spots with a polarization direction lead to a higher channel correlation.

now try different sampling densities. In particular, each LED selects one training symbol out of every $d = 3$, 5 and 15 symbols, respectively. Then, the RGB intensity of non-training symbols within a grid is trained via bilinear interpolation according to the measured intensity of the four corner symbol vectors. The transmitter sends 100 randomly-generated data symbols after broadcasting the training symbols, while the receiver decodes the data symbols and calculates the symbol delivery ratio, which is defined as the number of the correctly recovered symbols to the total number of the received symbols. To further examine the impact of environmental dynamics on the performance of channel estimation, we repeat this experiment in three different scenarios, namely outdoor with the link distance of 2 m, indoor with the link distance of 40 m and outdoor with the link distance of 20 m.

Results: We plot the average symbol delivery ratio of the three scenarios in Fig. 9 when the frames are recorded as the JPG and RAW formats, respectively. The results show that four training symbols ($d = 15$) are not dense enough to eliminate the non-linearity effect, while performing piecewise interpolation with 16 training symbols ($d = 5$) can almost avoid symbol errors in the short-range scenarios, i.e., outdoor 2 m and indoor 40 m. We hence use 16 training symbols ($d = 5$) as our default setting for channel training and bilinear interpolation.

The case of indoor 40 m is more challenging and suffers from a higher error rate because the received intensity is already too low even when the longest exposure time is configured. However, our POLI can still ensure that the camera still receives more than half of the symbols correctly even in such a critical condition. The results show that, in general, RAW images produce a higher decoding success probability than JPG images, especially in the challenging long distance scenario. This explains why compression becomes a key factor that determines the final decoding performance when the received signal strength is not sufficiently high. Therefore, to support a very long range service, such as in a vehicular network, we might need to use a camera that is capable of outputting RAW images.

5.1.3 Impact of Rotation on Channel Correlation

The achievable spatial multiplexing gain of a multi-antenna system is typically determined by channel correlation among different received signals. For example, though a 3×3 MIMO system can theoretically support three simultaneous transmissions, the real throughput gain, however, cannot be triple if the channel vectors, i.e., $\mathbf{c}_1, \mathbf{c}_2$ and $\mathbf{c}_3$ in POLI, are not fully orthogonal with each other. In POLI, the channel vectors are determined by polarization rotation after the dispersion as well as the polarization direction at the receiver. Since a receiver might rotate to an arbitrary orientation, thereby changing its polarization direction, we hence check how varying channel correlation due to the receiver's rotation affects the symbol delivery rate.

Experiment setup: We place a receiving camera at 1 m away from the transmitter, which is sending random symbols of 32-Ary PIM signals. The exposure time of the receiver is set to 0.08 ms. We rotate the receiver to any orientation between 0 and 360 degrees. For each setting, the receiver recovers 100 symbols and measures its symbol delivery ratio for various rotations.

Result: We plot the symbol delivery ratios for various rotations in Fig. 10. The results confirm that POLI often achieves a symbol delivery ratio larger than 90%, showing that the color channels are mostly uncorrelated in most of the cases. The receiver might sometimes get bad luck to rotate to a polarization direction, e.g., rotating 80 degrees as shown in Fig. 10, that results in two color channel vectors $\mathbf{c}_1$ and $\mathbf{c}_2$ with a higher correlation, making it much harder to separate two simultaneous symbols. This problem is, however, unavoidable in most of the MIMO systems, including the RF communication protocols such as 802.11ac. In POLI, a possible way to remedy this situation is to replace the receiver's polarizer with a *liquid crystal cell* (LCC), i.e., a 1 pixel LCD, which can *electronically* adjust its polarization direction by charging it with different amounts of voltage. With the support of LCC, the receiver now should be able to search for a polarization direction maximizing channel orthogonality, and thereby the SNR of the received signals. We leave this as a flexible deployment choice.

5.1.4 Impact of Exposure Time on Service Range

The receiver's linearity range is closely related to its exposure time. We now check what is the optimal exposure time with respective to different distances of a light-camera link.

Experiment setup: In this experiment, we change the distance of the light-camera link, ranging from 1 m to 10 m. Both the transmitting light and the receiving camera are static. For each tested distance, we let the transmitter continuously send random 32-Ary

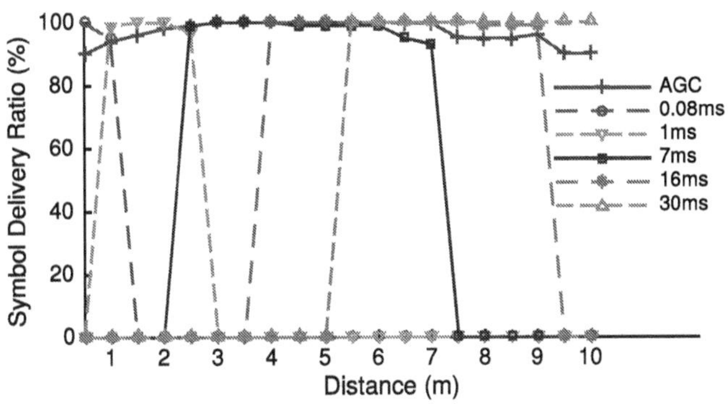

Figure 11: **Impact of exposure time on the service range.** Different exposure times have different operational ranges. A long distance link suffers from more severe fading and, hence, should configure a larger exposure time. With POLI's exposure time adaptation, we are able to quickly converge to a proper configuration and achieve a high delivery ratio at any distance.

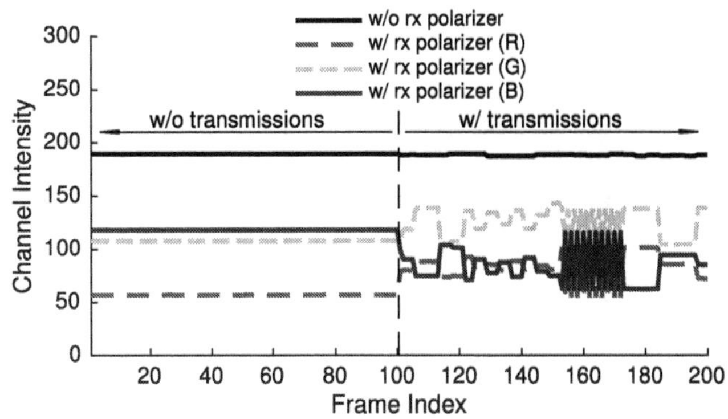

Figure 12: **Intensity variation.** POLI's PIM ensures that only a receiver attached with a polarizer can see intensity variation in its captured images, while the intensity variation of the aggregated light sent by the transmitter is very small and, thereby, indistinguishable by human eyes.

PIM symbols, while the receiver iteratively switches between all the five available exposure times. By this setup, the receiver could test different exposure times under a similar channel condition. The receiver then records 100 received symbols for every setting of the exposure times, and calculates the symbol delivery ratio of each exposure time, which is used to represent the performance when our AGC is disabled. For each tested distance, we then use the symbol traces of the five exposure time to offline emulate our automatic gain control (AGC), with the initial exposure time set to 7 ms and the thresholds $P_{\max}$ and $P_{\min}$ set to 80 and 150, respectively. The receiver then counts the number of correctly recovered symbols, during adaptation and after convergence, and calculates the achievable symbol delivery ratio when AGC is enabled.

Result: We plot in Fig. 11 the symbol delivery ratio of different exposure times (i.e., AGC disabled) and the symbol delivery ratio of our AGC, respectively, at different distances. The results verify that each exposure time has its own optimal operational range. Without proper configuration, the received intensity might be too dark or too bright, implying that the linearity range is too small to reliably detect all the possible symbol vectors. A camera usually receives a lower intensity at a long distance due to optical channel fading. Therefore, if a far receiver still configures a short exposure time, the received intensity will be too dark to be decodable. Similarly, a near receiver should configure a short exposure time to avoid overexposure. POLI adapts the exposure time to the receiver's channel condition, and can achieve a symbol delivery ratio close to the one achieved by the optimal exposure time. Since we only collect 100 symbols to evaluate the performance of AGC, the high delivery ratio also implies that our AGC can quickly converge to the optimal setting. Otherwise, if the convergence time is long, the symbol losses during adaptation would greatly degrade the overall delivery ratio.

5.1.5 User Perception

We finally evaluate whether POLI's polarization intensity modulation would cause flickers and become perceptible by human eyes.

Experiment setup: To numerically analyze how much illumination of POLI is perceived by human eyes, we remove the receiver's polarizer and measure the received aggregated light intensity sent by the three LEDs. We use the default settings listed in Table 2. The experiment is divided into two phases: *no-transmission phase* and *transmission phase*. In the *no-transmission* phase, each of the three LEDs continuously illuminate with a fixed randomly-selected intensity, but still ensures that the aggregated intensity equals to I_{total}, i.e., the constant total intensity used in POLI. In the *transmission* phase, the first two LEDs send random symbols, while the third LED illuminates the complementary intensity, following POLI's PIM design. Since human eyes (or a camera without a polarizer) still see the white light emitted by the transmitter, we use the average of the measured RGB values to represent the perceived light intensity. For comparison, we also allow the receiver to measure the received RGB values of the same signals with its polarizer installed.

Result: Fig. 12 illustrates that, after data transmissions, the change in the aggregated light intensity is negligible because POLI' PIM ensures that the total intensity keeps unchanged even when data are represented by intensity-based modulation. This figure further confirms that the variation of the RGB values is indeed large enough as expected, showing that our PIM can indeed modulate the *polarized color beams* with different intensity levels to increase the data rate. The figure demonstrates that our POLI successfully realizes an intensity-based modulation scheme, but introduces nearly no backlight intensity variation.

5.2 Throughput Performance

We now measure the overall network performance of POLI when the receiver is static but placed at different distances.

Experiment setup: In this experiment, we setup a light-to-camera link with a distance ranging from 1 m to 20 m. In each experiment, the transmitter sends 10 packets, each consists of a delimiter, the training symbols and 10 data symbols modulated by 32-PIM. The receiver updates its lookup table every packet and decodes the data symbols using the up-to-date table. The receiver applies POLI's automatic gain control and initializes its exposure time to 7 ms. Since some cameras on the market allow the user to manually configure the gain, we further check whether increasing the gain of a camera can extend the operational distance of POLI. Specifically, we further experiment when the camera locates at distance 20 m but increases its gain to 15 or 24. We test four different baud rates (the inverse of a symbol duration) to check how it affects the achievable service range. For each setting, we fix the location of the transmitter, but deploy the receiver at 5 randomly-selected locations at the specified distance and output the average result.

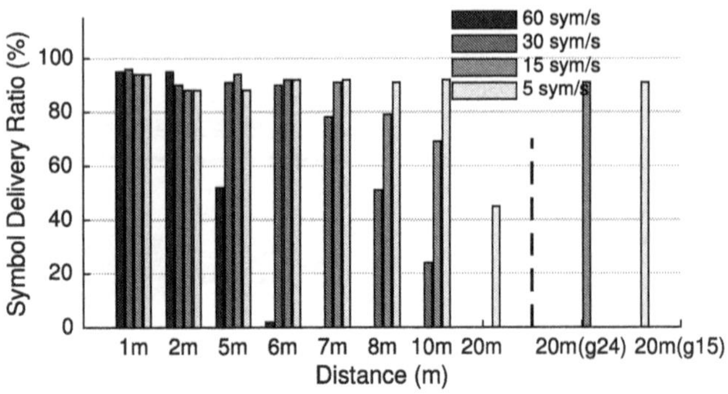

Figure 13: **Symbol delivery ratio at different distances.** The service range of different baud rates will be different. The maximum service range of a baud rate is bounded by the maximal feasible exposure time a receiver can use without suffering from the mixture frame problem.

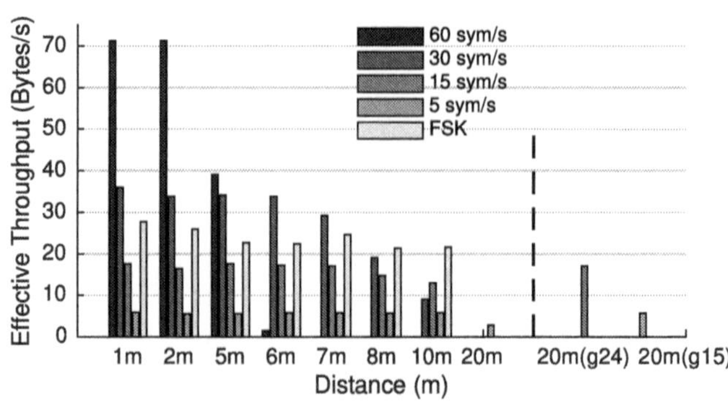

Figure 14: **Throughput at different distances.** A higher baud rate supports a shorter range but produce a higher throughput for a receiver within the service range. A transmitter can pick a baud rate to balance the tradeoff between the achievable throughput and the service range.

We further compare our POLI with conventional frequency modulation, i.e., frequency-shift keying (FSK) [18, 17]. The number of frequencies available for modulation is closely related to the link distance. We manually test the largest detectable frequency and smallest detectable frequency for each different link distance, and configure the frequency spacing as suggested in [18]. Intuitively, the more detectable frequencies we can use, the higher rate a receiver can get. For fair comparison, we similarly search the best exposure time setting, i.e., the one minimizing the symbol error rate, for FSK. Since FSK can only be applied in rolling-shutter cameras, we use a Pointgrey Flea3 camera with the same lens of POLI for FSK experiments. The output power of the transmitter, using only one LED, is configured to be the same as the total output power of the 3 LED lights of POLI.

Results: We plot the symbol delivery ratios and the effective throughput at various distances in Fig. 13 and Fig. 14, respectively. The figures show:

- The conventional FSK-based VLC scheme achieves a throughput comparable to our POLI at short distances. Its throughput, however, drops to zero when the distance is longer than 20m. The main reason is that the FSK-based scheme relies on a receiver being able to detect and estimate the width of dark and bright strips of a transmitting light from the captured images. However, at longer distances, light intensity decades significantly, and longer shutter time is required for the image sensor to collect sufficient light. However, in such cases the contrast of the strips becomes very small and hard to detect. Thus, the throughput of FSK eventually reduces to zero.
- Reducing the baud rate, i.e., increasing the symbol duration, extends POLI's service distance to 20 m since a receiver can avoid the symbol mixture problem even if it switches to a long exposure time. As a result, receivers can adaptively increase its exposure time to achieve a high enough signal strength for reliable decoding.
- As shown in Fig. 14, though a smaller symbol duration can only support a limited transmission range, its higher baud rate, however, corresponds to a higher effective throughput if a receiver is at shorter distance and has a high enough signal strength even when a small exposure time is used. The service range of this experiment is shorter than that shown in Fig. 9 since this experiment uses a higher-order modulation, i.e., 32-PIM, which needs a higher SNR to reliably decode the symbols. However, by increasing the camera gain, we can again achieve a fairly low error rate.
- We can observe from the two figures that the selection of a proper baud rate is actually very similar to the bit-rate adaptation problem [6, 33, 12, 22, 7, 20, 30], i.e., how to adapt the transmission bit-rate according to the SNR of a receiver, considered in 802.11 or a cellular system. By enabling a feedback channel to learn the channel condition of the worst receiver we want to serve, the transmitter can adaptively adjust its baud rate and make the best tradeoff between the achievable effective throughput and the service range. As this work mainly focuses on extending the communication distance, we leave the above baud rate adaptation problem as our future studies.

6. RELATED WORK

We can categorize recent related works into the following categories.

Light-to-camera communications: A number of literatures have focused on enabling light-to-camera communications. The systems [9, 23, 17, 18] leverages a high sampling rate of the rolling shutter effect of CMOS cameras to increase the data rate. However, these works all require the light sources to occupy a sufficient large number of rows in the captured image so as to capture the rolling shutter effect, which is, however, infeasible in along range scenario. Moreover, those systems need a receiving camera to operate at a low exposure time, which prevents the receiver at longer distances from getting sufficient intensity for reliable decoding. ColorBars [14] utilizes Color Shift Keying (CSK) to modulate data using different LED colors. However, the transmission range is very limited due to the high requirement on the received intensity. In [24], Luo *et al.* enable long range, low SNR communications through undersampled frequency shift OOK (UFSOOK). However, this approach does not utilize the dimensions spanned by the RGB space of a camera, as a result supporting a very low data rate, i.e., 0.5 bits per image. PIXEL [35] uses an LCD to modulate bits into the polarization directions of a light, and spans the polarized lights using a dispersor to ensure uniform intensity contrast among all the receiving directions. However, the transmission rate is limited by the low response time of an LCD.

Screen-to-camera communications: Recent works [5, 21, 13, 15, 34, 4, 16, 19, 31] modulate a huge number of pixels on a screen to boost the throughput of camera communication links. Strata [16] implements the adaptive coding, supporting different transmission distances by adding layered coding to QR codes. COBRA [13] enhances the SNR of a screen-to-camera link by carrying additional color information in traditional barcodes. Further improvements include LightSync [15], which solves the inter-frame symbol problem caused by un-synchronization between a transmitter and a receiver, VRCodes (NewsFlash) [34], Inframe++ [31], Implicit-Code [27] and HiLight [19], which embeds extra information that could be extracted by a camera but not human eyes into the images. The work [4] proposes a rate adaptation scheme for camera-based communications. Benefiting from the high resolution of a screen, the above works all provide a high throughput. Nevertheless, this high resolution could hardly be captured by a distant camera. Also, the screen flickers as performing transmission may be obtrusive to human eyes.

Light-to-photodiode communications: Photodiodes features a high sampling rate and a high intensity resolution as compared to cameras. Many proposals [25, 32, 10, 28, 11] explore various application scenarios for the light-to-photodiode technology. LED-to-LED and OpenVLC [25, 32] use LED as the transceiver of a system, simplifying the hardware design of a communication system and enabling half-duplex communications. OWC [11] characterizes the optical channels of different optical modulations, and Li-Fi [10] provides numerous empirical data and boost the throughput so as to be comparable with an RF link. DarkLight [28] focuses on enabling communications with a low-duty cycle transmitter. The high intensity resolution of a photodiode provides a capability of of capturing signals far away; however, a photodiode sums all the incoming lights from different incidence angles, it usually takes a larger overhead to eliminate cross interference from multiple transmitters.

Bit-rate adaptation in WiFi: A number of literatures [6, 33, 12, 22, 7, 20, 30] have investigated the algorithms for bit-rate adaptation in 802.11. They either allow bit-rate selection at the transmitter side or receiver side, according to the dynamic channel condition of a transmission link. POLI's baud rate selection problem is similar to the conventional WiFi rate adaptation problem. However, unlike most of RF protocols supporting duplex communications, VLC usually supports an one-way light-to-camera communication. Fortunately, some recent research [25, 26] is dedicated to enable two-way visible light communications. We could expect that baud rate selection would be less a problem in the future with the support of duplex capability.

7. CONCLUSION AND FUTURE WORK

In this paper, we presented POLI, the first light-to-camera communication system that can serve camera receivers at long distance while the transmitter generates no flickers observable to human eyes. POLI uses a novel polarized light intensity modulation to allow the use of low frequency band in the signal, so that the data symbols can be transmitted at slower speed. As a result, without introducing inter-symbol interference, a camera receiver can use longer exposure time to accumulate sufficient energy, even at long distances, for reliable communications. POLI uses an optical rotatory dispersor to transform polarizations into color beams, and hence color cameras can take advantage of the three outputs of R, G, and B values to separate and demodulate the three transmitted data streams in different polarization directions, boosting the achievable data rate. POLI also incorporates a low-overhead channel estimation scheme and automatic gain control to deal with the channel non-linearity issue. We implemented POLI with off-the-shelf components and software defined radios (USRP). The evaluation results obtained from the prototype show that POLI produces throughput proportional to the channel condition, 34 bytes/s at 5 meters and 9 bytes/s at 10 meters, respectively, and can serve receivers at an extended range of 40 meters with an error rate of only 10%.

POLI makes an important step toward enabling long-range VLC. Some future works are worth investigated to further improve the reliability and applicability of POLI. First, in our experiments, we only report the raw loss rate and throughput. Therefore, though the loss rate at longer distances gets higher, we can combine POLI with proper error correction codes, such as FEC, to ensure low-rate reliable transmissions, thereby extending the service range of VLC. Second, while our trace-driven offline decoding evaluates the performance of POLI with real channels, we, however, do not deal with the synchronization issue between a transmitting light and a receiving camera, which could be a practical issue as implementing real-time decoding. Such a synchronization issue can be resolved by proper initial calibration, similar to the solution used in [18]. Finally, while the current proof-of-concept prototype uses off-the-shelf optical components, which has much larger dimensions than necessary, we believe that eventually with mass production the design can be shrank down to the size of a single LED chip, similar to the RGB LED chip available on today's market.

8. ACKNOWLEDGEMENT

This research was supported in part by the Ministry of Science and Technology of Taiwan (MOST 106-2633-E-002-001, MOST 104-2628-E-009-014-MY2), National Taiwan University (NTU 106R104045), Intel Corporation, and Delta Electronics.

9. REFERENCES

[1] Ettus Inc., universal software radio peripheral. http://ettus.com.

[2] Jackson Labs Technologies Inc., Fury GPSDO. http://www.jackson-labs.com/index.php/products/fury.

[3] Thorlabs Inc., non-polarizing beamsplitter cubes in 30 mm cage cubes. https://www.thorlabs.com.

[4] A. Ashok, M. Gruteser, N. Mandayam, T. Kwon, W. Yuan, M. Varga, and K. Dana. Rate adaptation in visual MIMO. In *IEEE SECON*, 2011.

[5] A. Ashok, M. Gruteser, N. Mandayam, J. Silva, M. Varga, and K. Dana. Challenge: Mobile optical networks through visual MIMO. In *ACM MobiCom*, 2010.

[6] J. Bicket. *Bit-rate Selection in Wireless Networks*. PhD thesis, Massachusetts Institute of Technology, 2005.

[7] J. Camp and E. Knightly. Modulation Rate Adaptation in Urban and Vehicular Environments: Cross-layer Implementation and Experimental Evaluation. In *MobiCom*, 2008.

[8] E. Collett. *Field Guide to Polarization*. SPIE Press, 2005.

[9] C. Danakis, M. Afgani, G. Povey, I. Underwood, and H. Haas. Using a CMOS camera sensor for visible light communication. In *IEEE Globecom*, 2012.

[10] S. Dimitrov and H. Haas. *Principles of LED Light Communications*. Principles of LED Light Communications: Towards Networked Li-Fi. Cambridge University Press, 2015.

[11] Z. Ghassemlooy, W. Popoola, and S. Rajbhandari. Optical wireless communications: System and channel modelling with MATLAB. Boca Raton, FL, USA, 2012. CRC Press, Inc.

[12] D. Halperin, W. Hu, A. Sheth, and D. Wetherall. Predictable 802.11 Packet Delivery from Wireless Channel Measurements. In *ACM SIGCOMM*, 2010.

[13] T. Hao, R. Zhou, and G. Xing. COBRA: Color barcode streaming for smartphone systems. In *ACM MobiSys*, 2012.

[14] P. Hu, P. H. Pathak, X. Feng, H. Fu, and P. Mohapatra. ColorBars: Increasing data rate of LED-to-camera communication using color shift keying. In *ACM CoNEXT*, 2015.

[15] W. Hu, H. Gu, and Q. Pu. LightSync: Unsynchronized visual communication over screen-camera links. In *ACM MobiCom*, 2013.

[16] W. Hu, J. Mao, Z. Huang, Y. Xue, J. She, K. Bian, and G. Shen. Strata: Layered coding for scalable visual communication. In *ACM MobiCom*, 2014.

[17] Y.-S. Kuo, P. Pannuto, K.-J. Hsiao, and P. Dutta. Luxapose: Indoor positioning with mobile phones and visible light. In *ACM MobiCom*, 2014.

[18] H.-Y. Lee, H.-M. Lin, Y.-L. Wei, H.-I. Wu, H.-M. Tsai, and K. C.-J. Lin. Rollinglight: Enabling line-of-sight light-to-camera communications. In *ACM MobiSys*, 2015.

[19] T. Li, C. An, X. Xiao, A. T. Campbell, and X. Zhou. Real-time screen-camera communication behind any scene. In *ACM MobiSys*, 2015.

[20] K. C.-J. Lin, N. Kushman, and D. Katabi. ZipTx: Harnessing Partial Packets in 802.11 Networks. In *ACM MobiCom*, 2008.

[21] S. D. Perli, N. Ahmed, and D. Katabi. Pixnet: Interference-free wireless links using LCD-camera pairs. In *ACM MobiCom*, 2010.

[22] H. Rahul, F. Edalat, D. Katabi, and C. Sodini. Frequency-Aware Rate Adaptation and MAC Protocols. In *ACM MOBICOM*, 2009.

[23] N. Rajagopal, P. Lazik, and A. Rowe. Visual light landmarks for mobile devices. In *IEEE IPSN*, 2014.

[24] R. D. Roberts. Undersampled frequency shift ON-OFF keying (UFSOOK) for camera communications (CamCom). In *IEEE Wireless and Optical Communication Conference*, 2013.

[25] S. Schmid, G. Corbellini, S. Mangold, and T. R. Gross. LED-to-LED visible light communication networks. In *ACM MobiHoc*, 2013.

[26] S. Schmid, T. Richner, S. Mangold, and T. R. Gross. EnLighting: An indoor visible light communication system based on networked light bulbs. In *IEEE SECON*, 2016.

[27] S. Shi, L. Chen, W. Hu, and M. Gruteser. Reading between lines: High-rate, non-intrusive visual codes within regular videos via ImplicitCode. In *ACM UbiComp*, 2015.

[28] Z. Tian, K. Wright, and X. Zhou. The DarkLight Rises: Visible light communication in the dark. In *ACM MobiCom*, 2016.

[29] D. Tse and P. Vishwanath. *Fundamentals of Wireless Communications*. Cambridge University Press, 2005.

[30] M. Vutukuru, H. Balakrishnan, and K. Jamieson. Cross-Layer Wireless Bit Rate Adaptation. In *ACM SIGCOMM*, 2009.

[31] A. Wang, Z. Li, C. Peng, G. Shen, G. Fang, and B. Zeng. Inframe++: Achieve simultaneous screen-human viewing and hidden screen-camera communication. In *ACM MobiSys*, 2015.

[32] Q. Wang, D. Giustiniano, and D. Puccinelli. OpenVLC: Software-defined visible light embedded networks. In *ACM MobiCom Workshop on Visible Light Communication Systems*, 2014.

[33] S. H. Y. Wong, H. Yang, S. Lu, and V. Bharghavan. Robust rate adaptation for 802.11 wireless networks. In *ACM MobiCom*, 2006.

[34] G. Woo, A. Lippman, and R. Raskar. Vrcodes: Unobtrusive and active visual codes for interaction by exploiting rolling shutter. In *IEEE International Symposium on Mixed and Augmented Reality (ISMAR)*, 2012.

[35] Z. Yang, Z. Wang, J. Zhang, C. Huang, and Q. Zhang. Wearables can afford: Light-weight indoor positioning with visible light. In ACM MobiSys,2015.

Card-stunt as a Service: Empowering a Massively Packed Crowd for Instant Collective Expressiveness

Chungkuk Yoo[1*], Inseok Hwang[2†], Seungwoo Kang[3], Myung-Chul Kim[4], Seonghoon Kim[1], Daeyoung Won[1], Yu Gu[4], Junehwa Song[1]
[1]KAIST, [2]IBM Research, [3]KOREATECH, [4]IBM
[1]{ckyoo, shkim, daeyoung, junesong}@nclab.kaist.ac.kr,
[2,4]{ihwang, mckima, yugu}@us.ibm.com, [3]swkang@koreatech.ac.kr

ABSTRACT

Imagine a densely packed crowd that gathers to convey a common message, such as people in a candlelight vigil or a protest. We envision an innovation through mobile computing technologies to empower such a crowd by enabling them simply to hold their phones up and create a massive collective visualization on top of them. We propose Card-stunt as a Service (CaaS). CaaS is a service enabling a densely packed crowd to instantly visualize symbols using their mobile devices and a server-side service. The key challenge toward realizing an instant collective visualization is how to achieve instant, infrastructure-free, decimeter-level localization of individuals in a massively packed crowd, while maintaining low latency. CaaS addresses the challenges by mobile visible-light angle-of-arrival (AoA) sensing and scalable constrained optimization. It reconstructs relative locations of all individuals and dispatches individualized timed pixels to each one so that they can do their part in the overall visualization. We evaluate CaaS with extensive experiments under diverse reality settings as well as under synthetic workloads scaling up to tens of thousands of people. We deploy CaaS to 49 participants so that they successfully perform a collective visualization cheering up MobiSys.

CCS Concepts

•Human-centered computing → Ubiquitous and mobile computing systems and tools; Collaborative content creation; Computer supported cooperative work; •Information systems → Spatial-temporal systems; Mobile information processing systems;

Keywords

collective visualization; relative localization; visible light communication; optimization; card stunt; mobile-crowd service

*This work was done in part when the first author was on an internship at IBM Research - Austin.
†The corresponding author.

Permission to make digital or hard copies of all or part of this work for personal or classroom use is granted without fee provided that copies are not made or distributed for profit or commercial advantage and that copies bear this notice and the full citation on the first page. Copyrights for components of this work owned by others than the author(s) must be honored. Abstracting with credit is permitted. To copy otherwise, or republish, to post on servers or to redistribute to lists, requires prior specific permission and/or a fee. Request permissions from permissions@acm.org.

MobiSys'17, June 19-23, 2017, Niagara Falls, NY, USA

© 2017 Copyright held by the owner/author(s). Publication rights licensed to ACM.

ISBN 978-1-4503-4928-4/17/06. . . $15.00

DOI: http://dx.doi.org/10.1145/3081333.3081357

(a) Candlelight vigil. (b) Card stunt at a stadium.

Figure 1: Massive collective visualization examples.

1. INTRODUCTION

Consider a densely packed crowd gathered in a public space to express a common voice to the community. Such a scene may resemble that seen in Figure 1a, in which over 4000 people participate in a candlelight vigil for memorial and social awareness purposes [7]. Imagine they hold not candles but their phones; each phone automatically glows on and off in a coordinated way such that the entire set of phones collectively visualize a massive symbol or image on top of the crowd.

Why would we want it? It will provide a new prominent medium empowering the crowd's message and attracting the community to listen; people will be able to express their message in a more impactful and visually compelling way by synthesizing their scattered voices, banners, and flags into a single massive one. Fundamentally, it would be an innovation in the way that mobile computing technologies facilitate a new form of instant collaborative crowd activities in the real world, through which people can stimulate their community. In application-wide, such a mobile technology would serve not only public activism but also diverse collective visualization events, such as commercial promotions, flash mobs, sport fans, and collective artistic works, etc.

In this paper, we propose Card-stunt as a Service (CaaS), metaphorically named after the traditional massive sport-supporting activities that could be seen in a stadium (see Figure 1b). CaaS is a new genre of mobile-crowd service to help densely packed crowds express their messages with impact. It enables a crowd to instantly and collectively visualize textual or graphical symbols using their mobile devices. For instance, Figure 2 demonstrates a small group of people using CaaS to perform small-scale, collective visualizations. Imagine a visualization of this kind created by a much larger number of people and at a higher people-per-symbol density.

How would we realize a dynamic, high-quality collective visualization today without CaaS? We refer to the process of planning a traditional card stunt; it requires month-long planning for each venue, rehearsals for specific participants, and often significant budget to hire a professional production [5]. Such a huge cost

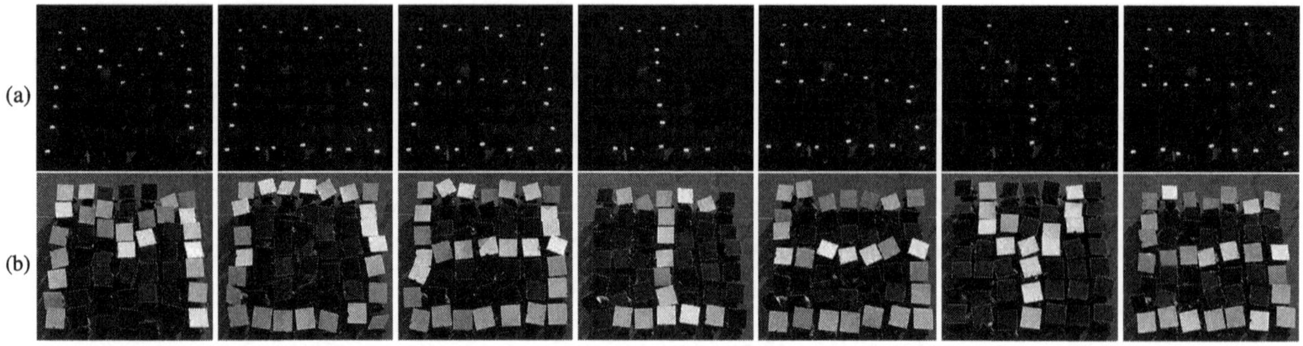

Figure 2: Small-scale demonstrations of CaaS with $7 \times 7 = 49$ participants. (a) Night mode with glowing phone screens. (b) Daylight mode with pieces of cardboard raised or flipped upon individual cues given to each user's phone.

of time, money, and labor would be impractical to most people in our collective visualization scenarios.

CaaS requires none; as soon as a crowd packs into a place like a public square, CaaS lets them instantly create collective visualizations. CaaS automatically determines each user's relative location within the crowd, divides a symbol into a 2-D matrix of pixels, and assigns each pixel to the mobile device at the right location. Each device locally displays the assigned pixel in full-screen. To visualize time-varying symbols, each mobile device may be assigned a timed sequence of pixels. On occasions when sunlight is so strong that a phone's display is indiscernible at full-brightness, CaaS may glow a phone's flashlight instead at the visualization phase. Alternatively, users may improvise physical cardboard with each side colored differently. CaaS can send cues to users' phones, directing them to flip the cardboard and ensure a visual signal even in bright sunlight as shown in Figure 2b.

Our unique challenge to realize an instant collective visualization is how to achieve (1) infrastructure-free, (2) decimeter-level localization of individuals, (3) in a densely packed crowd, while (4) maintaining a low latency for people possibly scaling up to tens of thousands. We do not assume any localization infrastructure like beacons [45] or WiFi access points [41, 49], as those are unlikely in typical gathering places like public squares or wide boulevards. Likewise, existing peer-to-peer localization schemes [21, 58, 68, 72] are not an option, as the one-by-one pair-wise sensing is impractical to handle the high density of people in a crowd.

CaaS tackles those challenges through elaborate mobile-side visible-light angle-of-arrival (AoA) sensing and server-side constrained optimization. To ensure CaaS is suitable for real-world deployment, we carefully devise and implement: (1) fast and robust multi-target visual AoA observations under diverse lighting conditions, partial occlusions, and varying phone orientations when handheld, and (2) scalable and accurate computation strategies to reconstruct the optimal device locations given all the AoA observations. We built a working prototype and conducted extensive experiments to evaluate the step-by-step performances of CaaS under diverse conditions discussed above. We deployed CaaS to 49 co-located participants, where CaaS demonstrated successful reconstruction of individual locations at a typical error radius of 15 cm.

Our contributions are three-fold. First, we set forth the agenda that mobile computing technologies empower people of a common voice and convey a massive real-world impact. Second, we propose CaaS, a mobile service enabling a densely packed crowd to create collective visualizations in an instant, impromptu, and infrastructure-free way. Third, we present our CaaS architecture, novel sensing and computing strategies, and real-world implementation issues to realize accurate reconstruction of densely packed individuals' locations within a reasonably short time.

2. CROWD CHARACTERISTICS

As for the target applications of CaaS to enable large collective visualization, we mainly consider real-world events with densely packed crowds that are relatively stationary and strongly motivated to participate. Examples may be seen in the form of organized fan activities in stadiums [18], commercial promotions [14], or public campaigns [4]. Aside from these existing examples, we also envision that public activism could be a new promising area where CaaS would make an impact. Although large-scale events for public activism are sometimes stereotyped as involving high mobility and unorganized dynamic actions, we note that there exist real protests with peaceful, stationary, and well-organized crowds. Recent examples include the series of candlelight vigils in South Korea in 2016 [15, 20] and the Romanian protests in 2017 [13]. CaaS targets such relatively stationary crowds so that one-time localization results would remain valid for the visualization session.

We analyzed the characteristics of such crowds based on news articles, video footage, journalism literature [9, 13, 15, 20, 36]. We found a few common elements. Notably, their inter-person distances are very small; a participant is most likely surrounded by others within arm's length. Our finding is supported by the studies of political gatherings, (e.g. [36]) which report an average inter-person distance of 0.75 meters. Our analysis also indicates that crowd participants are well-organized and highly motivated. To achieve their goal, they cooperate with a few coordinators in front of them giving actionable cues or chants [9]. Crowd participants will often tolerate significant physical discomfort, as well as financial and temporal cost in order to achieve their goals. For example, the 2016 South Korean candlelight vigils [15, 20] recurred every weekend for five months, during which hundreds of thousands of people gathered, despite freezing temperatures. Similarly, sport fans performing card stunts in a stadium often practice for weeks and pay nontrivial costs (e.g. even a simplest card stunt may cost USD 1 – 3 per person, a higher quality card stunt may cost USD 6 – 29 per person; The rates may further vary depending on the number of symbols and the complexity of the stunts [5]). We believe that CaaS would be highly attractive to such crowds not only in quickly creating massive visualizations but also resulting in very small cost and minimal effort, e.g., holding up their phones overhead for a while, which would be negligible compared to conventional efforts.

2.1 Requirements of CaaS

Imagine a target crowd like those described above. To support an instant collective visualization above such a crowd, CaaS has to: (1) obtain each participant's relative location in the crowd, (2) map each participant to a pixel of the symbol to visualize, (3) let each participant's device know the assigned pixel (or a timed sequence of pixels), and (4) complete (1)–(3) in a short, interactive time.

Figure 3: People raising their phones overhead

In this paper, we address the key technical challenges mainly stemming from (1) and (4). Note that (2) and (3) are straightforward once (1) is complete. For (1) and (4), we derive the following specific localization requirements from our crowd characteristics.

- Infrastructure-free and off-the-shelf phones only. A crowd may gather in a public square or a wide street, which do not generally have fine-grained localization infrastructure like beacons. Crowd members require no special device but their phones.
- High-density crowd support. A collective visualization event deals with densely packed people of hundreds or more, with often an average spacing of only 0.75 meters between each other [36]. Relative localization should support such a density and scale.
- Decimeter-level location accuracy. In such a high-density crowd we should keep individual location errors within one's tiny personal space. Higher errors may cause swapped pixels in the visualization, degrading the readability.
- Fast and scalable reconstruction. Once a crowd forms, the relative localization should be completed in a reasonably short time so that the visualization can start momentarily. Members of both small and large crowds (tens to tens of thousands) should not be required to wait too long to negatively impact interactivity (e.g. 10 seconds unless they are given another task to focus on [53]).

2.2 Limitations of Existing Approaches

Infrastructure-based localization: GPS is commonly available in smartphones. However, its typical location error ranges from 5 to 10 meters [71], which is insufficient to distinguish adjacent people in the crowds. Coin-GPS addresses the indoor unavailability of GPS [54], but the issues of low accuracy and high-gain antenna requirement remain. Higher accuracies are achieved by other techniques relying on pre-installed infrastructure such as WiFi access points [49], beacons [45], and modified LEDs [40, 43, 44]. However, such infrastructure is neither generally available in public spaces, nor is it likely to be installed by crowds on the spot. For example, a state-of-the-art system of visible light sensing [44] achieves 2D localization error of 4 cm, but requires an indoor space with extensive instrumentation, i.e., hundreds of LED lights on the ceiling and hundreds of photodiodes on the floor.

Peer-to-peer relative localization: Peer-to-peer ranging and triangulation among devices is an alternative. Existing techniques have a pair of devices exchange sound chirps or wireless packets and measure TDoA (time difference of arrival) or ToF (time of flight), then convert them into distances [58, 68, 72]. Although those state-of-the-art systems achieve centi- or decimeter level accuracy that is sufficiently accurate for CaaS, the challenges come from a large number of people and limited channel capacity making simultaneous multi-pair sensing difficult. For example, BeepBeep [58] requires all the devices to generate and listen to sound signals one after another. It needs an interval of one second to separate each adjacent sound signal. Chronos [68] takes much less time, i.e., 84 ms, to range a single pair of devices. However, nearby devices around the ranging pair should wait so as not to interfere with this pair's ranging process, as Chronos actively probes all WiFi channels between the pair. In both techniques, the total ranging time for all N devices would be proportional to N; they quickly become intractable in massively packed scenarios like we have assumed.

In short, CaaS deals with high people density where one-by-one pair-wise sensing is infeasible for timely all-pair relative localization, not to mention other issues aggravated in high-density crowds such as elevated channel noise levels and multipath effects.

3. CaaS DESIGN

3.1 Vision-based Collective Localization with Crowd Cooperation

For timely relative localization of all individuals in a dense crowd with no infrastructure and no known reference locations, CaaS adopts visible-light AoA (angle of arrival) observations between cameras and displays of the participants' phones, followed by server-side optimization. This offers key advantages to the CaaS context: multiple pairs can sense simultaneously while hardly interfering with each other. Most smartphone cameras have sufficiently good image resolutions and optical systems capable of high-precision AoA observation from a light source within their FoV (field of view); the multi-path issue is hardly a concern compared to wireless- or sound-based sensing. Collectively processing mobile-side AoA observations, server-side optimization enables all devices' relative locations to be reconstructed in an accurate and timely manner.

3.2 Use Case

Applying the approach of vision-based collective localization, we design CaaS for target crowds described in Section 2 to realize collective visualization under the following use case.

1. Once a crowd packs together in a public square for a collective visualization event, each participant runs the CaaS Mobile Application. Each phone contacts the server and joins the event.
2. The event coordinator's device provides a user interface through which she can choose a symbol to visualize, see how many people have joined, and broadcast a cue to them. The symbols could be pre-determined through the participants' consensus in online communities prior to the event. Once a sufficient number of people have joined, the coordinator triggers a request to each users' phone, instructing them to raise their phones overhead.
3. People raise their phones overhead to maximize the line-of-sight chances among the devices, as shown in Figure 3. The application gives audio-tactile feedback to help a user hold the phone at a preferred orientation.
4. Each phone begins visual observation through its camera, while displaying an encoded identifier on the screen. The application notifies a user to lower the phone when either a certain number of distinct devices have been detected or a timer expires.
5. The observations are sent to the server; the participants wait until the server computes their relative locations. They may keep their arms lowered during server computations.
6. Soon enough (e.g., a few seconds), each phone is assigned a pixel specific to its relative location ensuring that each user provides the correct part of the symbol to be visualized.
7. The phone glows the assigned pixel color on full screen. In bright daylight, users might choose to raise a piece of cardboard upon a cue from the phone. The pixels or cues change synchronously if they are given a timed sequence.
8. The coordinator may choose the next symbols without reperforming the localization as long as the crowd remains stationary.

3.3 Main Technical Challenges

To realize the high-level approach above, we have faced multiple technical challenges in reality. In particular, Section 3.4 through Section 6 discuss our system architecture, key techniques, and experiments to address the following main technical problems:

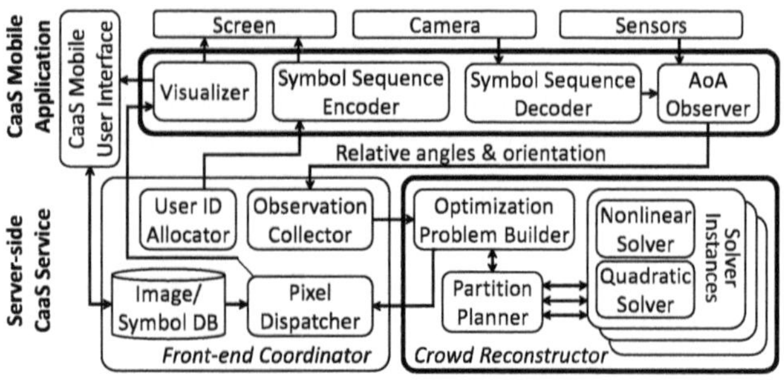

Figure 4: CaaS architecture.

- On the mobile-side, CaaS requires fast and robust multi-target visual observations under diverse lighting conditions, partial occlusions, and handheld phone conditions. Target device screens are seen as too small to observers' cameras, e.g., a 5-inch screen at 6 meters away makes only a few pixels on an observer's FoV. Even worse, we found that extremely diverse lighting conditions in reality make it very hard to identify any content on target screens — too dark under daylight and white-saturated at night. We address these challenges to visual observation in Section 4.
- On the server-side, given all the mobile-side AoA observations, CaaS requires accurate reconstruction of all individual devices' locations quickly enough not to negatively impact interactivity. The computing time for optimal reconstruction should remain short even for tens of thousands of people. Despite accurate mobile-side observations, residual sensor drifts and camera displacements still cause erroneous reconstruction. We also encounter that the reconstruction time rapidly grows for increasing numbers of participants, e.g., more than an hour for a thousand people. We address the server-side challenges in Section 5.

In addition to the above technical issues, there are a number of human and environmental factors that have the potential to strongly impact the success of CaaS. These include (*i*) physical discomfort associated with holding a phone for extended time periods, (*ii*) the dynamicity of crowds, (*iii*) individual height differences, (*iv*) cellular connectivity, and (*v*) time synchronization. In Section 7, we explore the issues in detail and discuss how most of them would be non-critical or transient, based on our real-world observations, our conjecture therefrom, and feasible solutions.

3.4 CaaS Architecture

The CaaS architecture consists of mobile applications and server-side services (Figure 4). Each instance of the CaaS Mobile Application observes local AoAs and displays the assigned pixels. The server-side CaaS service collects the observations, computes all devices' relative locations, and determines the pixel for each device.

CaaS Mobile Application. The *CaaS Mobile User Interface* provides a user with user interfaces to join a collective visualization event, view original images or symbols to be displayed in an event, and give individual cues to raise a phone overhead. It also provides a feature for the coordinators to choose one of the images or symbols that the participants agreed upon beforehand, and to broadcast notifications to the participants such as "Raise your phone." Upon joining an event, the *Symbol Sequence Encoder* retrieves a device-specific identifier (ID) from the server, encodes it into a visual symbol sequence, and displays the code on its screen. At the same time, the *Symbol Sequence Decoder* detects and decodes symbol sequences from the main camera. For each code decoded, the *AoA Observer* measures its AoA from its on-image location and applies sensor compensations. The decoded ID and its AoA values are sent to the server. The *Visualizer* displays the pixels in sequence, which

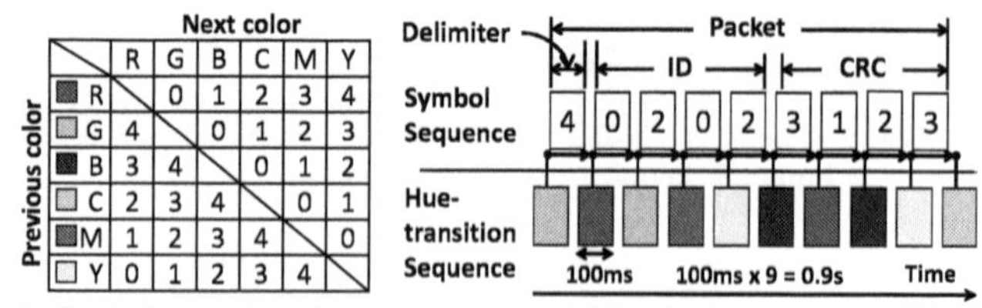

(a) Symbol encoding scheme. (b) Packet format.

Figure 5: Hue transition-based symbol encoding and packet format.

are assigned to the device by the server. The key challenges are to detect multiple symbol sequences and measure AoAs under diverse lighting conditions, partial occlusions, and varying phone orientations. Section 4 discusses these steps in more detail.

Server-side CaaS Service. The *Observation Collector* collects the mobile-side observations. Once collection is done, the *Crowd Reconstructor* computes individual devices' relative locations using the observations. To achieve this, our *Optimization Problem Builder* builds a constrained optimization problem describing the optimal locations of the devices for the given observation results. The *Partition Planner* intelligently divides the problem into smaller pieces with low inter-dependencies, and invokes one or more *Solver Instances*. Once the optimization is complete, the *Crowd Reconstructor* returns the reconstructed locations to the *Pixel Dispatcher*, which determines a pixel for each device and dispatches it to the corresponding *CaaS Mobile Application*. The key server-side challenges lie within the *Crowd Reconstructor*, which performs sub-meter localizations of densely packed devices within a short and scalable response time. Section 5 presents our basic strategy and advanced issues faced in reality.

4. OBSERVING RELATIVE ANGLES

The key steps in mobile observation are (1) detecting visual symbol sequences seen on an observer's camera, (2) decoding each symbol sequence to identify an observed device, and (3) measuring the AoA from a device. This section presents our symbol coding, real-world issues, AoA measurements, and observing performance.

4.1 Designing Visual Symbol Sequences

Our collective visualization scenarios pose a number of challenges to mobile visual observations. First, the target devices are seen as too small, e.g., a 5-inch screen as far as 9 meters away. Furthermore, this represents a best case, since in reality the target phone is handheld overhead, making its observed representation slanted or partially occluded. Second, the external lighting conditions are highly diverse, ranging from a sunny street to a midnight candlelight vigil. Third, multi-target observations should be completed quickly so that people do not hold their phones overhead for long. These challenges make spatial codes inviable [29, 32, 70]. In our experiments, even a state-of-the-art technique [32] fails to support code detection on a small screen at the envisaged distances, even if occlusions are completely avoided.

Our alternative is to adopt temporally coded full-screen symbols inspired by [52, 61]. We favor a lightweight design in order to enable real-time multi-target detection, and find optimal parameters to ensure a high throughput and thereby quickly complete the observations. We encode data (e.g., device ID) into a sequence of k-level quantized hue values. Hue is a component in HSB (Hue Saturation Brightness) color spaces, representing a chromatic element of a color orthogonal to brightness and saturation.

Figure 5b illustrates our packet structure, beginning with a leading delimiter symbol followed by data symbols and CRC (Cyclic Redundancy Check) symbols. Note that we apply differential coding; a symbol is not defined one-on-one for each hue level but for a

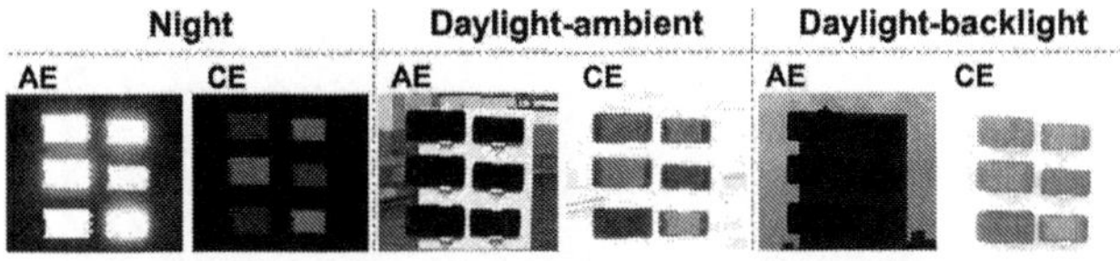

Figure 6: Phone screens under different lighting conditions with (AE: auto, CE: custom-found) exposure settings.

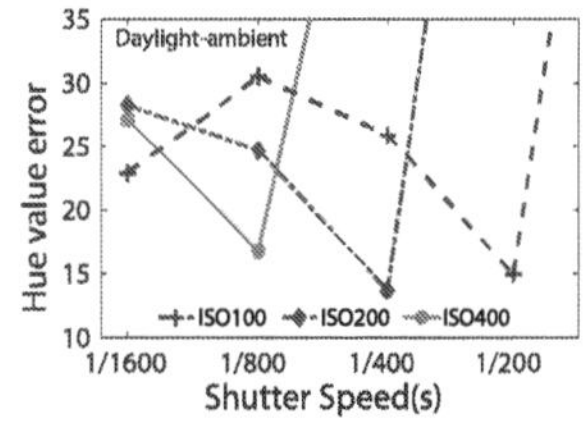

Figure 7: Tuning exposure.

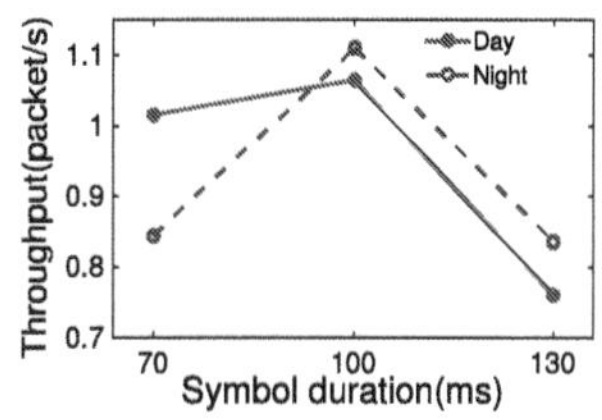

Figure 8: symbol durations.

temporal hue transition. This use of differential coding has the effect of improving throughput. Our early implementations used one-on-one coding, but testing revealed that observing devices can often encounter randomly occurring non-symbol hue sequences that have a valid packet structure, i.e. the sequence begins with the delimiter hue and then contains a sequence of non-delimiter cues; the decoder rejected such false-positive sequence at the CRC checker, but the high frequency of such false-positives requires an extended CRC to ensure that all occurrences are reliably rejected.

By contrast, our revised design with differential coding greatly reduces the occurrences of such false-positive sequences. Since each legitimate packet is expected to change its hue level between every consecutive pair of frames (a scenario that is unlikely to naturally occur), any pixel areas whose hue levels do not change between frames can be rejected early even before reaching the CRC checker. Overall, our differential coding approach has a reduced reliance on CRC when compared to the one-on-one coding approach, achieving an equivalent false-positive rejection rate with much fewer CRC symbols per packet. Thus we can make each packet shorter, resulting in higher throughput. Replacing the single-symbol delimiter with a multi-symbol preamble might be an alternative to early rejection of non-packet sequences, but it makes a packet longer than using differential coding.

Figure 5a illustrates our mapping table for a case of $k = 6$, which maps a hue transition pair onto a base-5 digit, i.e., a symbol. Note that we determined $k = 6$ through extensive experiments, which are discussed in Section 4.2. For the leading delimiter, we assigned the digit "4" among the available five digits. We used the remaining available digits (0, 1, 2, 3) for the device identifier and the CRC. Therefore, the 9-symbol packet with 6-level hue quantization can represent $4^4 = 256$ different device identifiers. The sender repeatedly transmits this packet in full-screen.

4.2 Code Parameters

Exposure settings. In theory, the hue component is defined orthogonally to the brightness component. Still, we found that external lighting conditions often cause the observer to see a distorted hue value that is large enough to result in a wrong quantization level, i.e., a symbol error. Figure 6 shows pictures of phone screens; the one taken under daylight is too dark to recognize the hue, whereas the other taken at night is white-saturated. This is mainly caused by the auto-exposure feature of cameras. When taking a picture, this feature automatically optimizes the ISO value and exposure time based on the ambient brightness. We overcome this issue by enforcing custom exposure settings for three major outdoor lighting conditions—night, daylight-ambient, and daylight-backlight (i.e., camera faces the sun). Figure 7 shows the mean errors of the observed hue values from those originally transmitted. Our experiments show the smallest hue value errors at ISO 200 and 1/400 s exposure time both in night and daylight-ambient conditions, whereas in a daylight-backlight condition, the smallest hue value errors are found at at ISO 100 and 1/400 s exposure time. The errors soar once the exposure is too long to saturate the image sensor. Figure 6 shows the effectiveness of these custom settings.

The CaaS Mobile Application automatically determines the current lighting conditions using the time of day and built-in sensors and manipulates the exposure settings accordingly using Camera2 APIs available in Android 5.0+. Given the phone is outdoors, it is obvious to determine either daylight or night condition from the time of day. To further determine either daylight-ambient or daylight-backlight conditions, CaaS first computes the sun's celestial orientation based on the date, time, and geographic location of a device. Then it sets the daylight-backlight condition if the sun would be seen within the camera's FoV at a current device's orientation. CaaS would be able to adopt an advanced image processing technique to determine whether an image is back-lit [23].

Hue quantization levels. A higher throughput is desirable to help users lower their phones earlier. A finer-grained quantization level (i.e., a higher k) in our coding gives higher bits per symbol. However, a higher k may increase SER (symbol error rate) which degrades the throughput. Thus we need to find a good value of k at which the effective throughput is maximized. Interestingly, we found good k values differ across the display types: OLEDs and LCDs. Experiments in daylight ambient conditions, using a three-meter distance between devices and optimal exposure settings, show the best throughput of 1.11 packets at both $k = 6$ and 7 for OLEDs; $k = 6$ achieves zero SER, whereas $k = 7$ increases the bits-per-symbol but the throughput remains the same, since the increment is nullified by the degraded SER. For LCDs, the optimal k value is 14. Further experiments indicate an optimal k value of 7 (OLED) and 20 (LCD) in both daylight-backlight and night conditions. Since CaaS has no way to know the display type of an arbitrary target display a priori, use of the lower k value for each lighting condition is most appropriate. For our prototype, we select a conservative k value of 6 for use across all lighting conditions

Symbol duration. For given k quantized hue levels, another parameter impacting the throughput is the symbol duration; a shorter symbol duration gives higher bits per symbol but increases SER. Most smartphone displays refresh at 60 Hz [17]. However, most smartphone cameras capture frames at a maximum of 30 fps, where Nyquist-Shannon sampling theorem gives the theoretical minimum symbol duration of 67 ms (= 15 Hz symbol rate). Figure 8 reports the throughput for varying symbol durations. For 70 ms daylight, the higher bits per symbol and SER break even, resulting in comparable throughput with 100 ms. Our final choice is 100 ms due to the real issue of occasional frame drops from cameras, which having 3 frames per symbol is more robust against.

At this symbol duration, a single 9-symbol packet transmission takes 1 second because a the packet is encoded into a sequence of $9+1 = 10$ hue levels. However, as discussed earlier, CaaS Mobile Application repetitively transmits the same packets. If 9-symbol packets are concatenated N times, this data stream will be encoded into a sequence of $N \times 9 + 1$ hue levels. Thus, the average time duration per packet will converge to 900 ms as N increases.

4.3 Real-world Issues

Rolling shutter effect. We experienced that observer devices often detect incorrect hue transitions that include a phantom hue level that was not shown either before or after the transition at the target

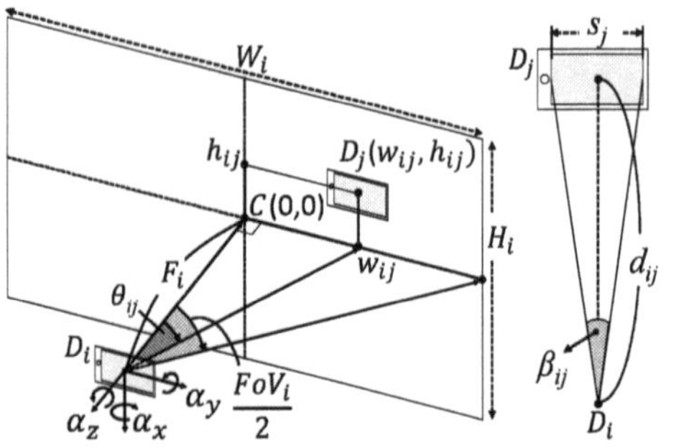

Figure 9: An observer D_i's camera sees a target D_j's display.

(a) (b) (c)

Figure 10: (a) Rolling shutter effect during a (R to G) transition. (b)-(c) Visual observation experiment setup.

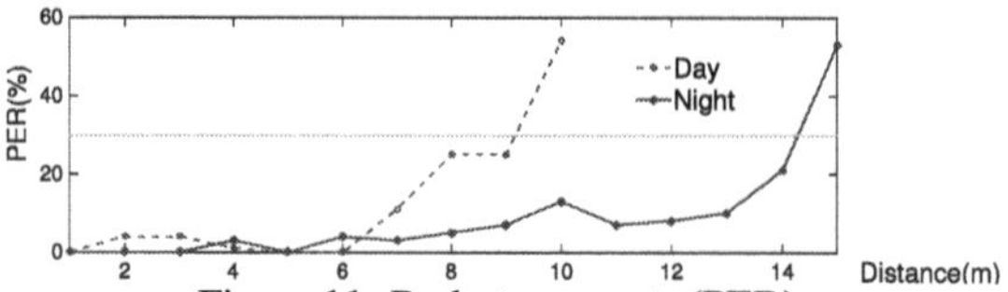

Figure 11: Packet error rate (PER).

screens. This is a result of rolling shutter effects, an anomaly in digital photography whereby a single frame consists of pixels each of which is captured at slightly different times. The reason is that an image sensor usually captures a frame by rapidly scanning the sensing pixels vertically or horizontally, not taking a snapshot of the entire scene at once. Figure 10a shows an example frame affected by rolling shutter. This frame is captured while the shown target device was making an R-to-G transition. Apparently, the reddish pixels around the bottom-left corner are captured slightly before the transition, whereas the greenish pixels around the top-right corner are captured slightly after the transition. The yellowish pixels in the middle are exposed to both colors at the very moment of transition, resulting in averaged colors. Due to the yellowish pixels, an observer device may mis-decode this frame into either R-to-Y or Y-to-G transitions. We filter out this anomaly by exploiting the characteristics of the effect: 1) a wrongly quantized hue level is a mixture of two valid hue levels detected consecutively, and 2) this hue level is seen only from a single frame. Note that we also check the symbol duration to ensure the valid duration of 100 ms (3 frames). But this duration alone is not a reliable measure due to frame drops and inconsistent frame intervals in reality.

Real-time image processing. To ensure the real-time constraint of 33 ms per frame, we implemented the Symbol Sequence Decoder in Android RenderScript for flexible parallelism on multi-core CPUs and GPUs. Our RenderScript implementation processes a single frame in 15.2 ms, whereas our alternative implementation in Android NDK (Native Development Kit) takes 56.5 ms. Note that it could be possible to utilize parallelism by using OpenCL [12] in our NDK implementation, but an OpenCL is unavailable to some phone models, e.g., Google Nexus family, unless rooted.

Our decoder divides a 1280×960 frame into 25600 subframes of 8×6 pixels each. In parallel, each subframe is downsampled by 4 to 1. Taking a raw frame at 640×480 narrowed FoV in some phone models. By contrast, downsampling had a negligible impact on the accuracy. For each subframe, the decoder finds a single quantized hue level dominating this subframe. At each subframe location, a packet is detected upon the transitions of the dominant hue levels that conforms to our symbol definitions in Figure 5, as well as passes CRC. The decoded ID is associated with the subframe location to compute its AoA.

4.4 AoA Measurement

Figure 9 shows the geometry of two devices, the main camera of an observer device D_i and the display of a target device D_j. Our goal for AoA measurement is that D_i measures the horizontal angle θ_{ij} between C (center of D_i's image plane) and w_{ij} (horizontal pixel coordinate of D_j as seen on D_i's image plane). We can derive θ_{ij} as a function of w_{ij} and F_i (focal length of D_i in pixels):

$$\theta_{ij} = \arctan 2\left(w_{ij}, F_i\right), \qquad (1)$$

where $F_i = \frac{W_i}{2}\left(\tan\frac{FoV_i}{2}\right)^{-1}$, W_i is the pixel width of the image plane, FoV_i is the horizontal FoV in radian available runtime through Android APIs, $\arctan 2(y,x)$ is a two-variable extension of $\arctan\frac{y}{x}$ defined over $(-\pi,\pi]$ range [2].

This is an ideal case when D_i is at a perfect landscape orientation and standing upright, i.e., $\alpha_x = 0, \alpha_y = 0, \alpha_z = 0$. In reality, a device held in a user's hand would have nonzero orientation angles, resulting in wrong w_{ij} and θ_{ij}. To reorient w_{ij} and evaluate the true θ_{ij}, we first define an X-Y-Z intrinsic rotation, where the element rotation angles α_x, α_y, and α_z are obtained by the built-in Android API, the magnetometer, and the gravity sensor. Figure 10c defines the axes of rotation. Each observing device applies Z- and Y- rotation matrices R_z and R_y to the pre-rotation (h_{ij}, w_{ij}, z_{ij}), where z_{ij} is the point where a virtual sphere of the radius F_i intersects with a line originating from (h_{ij}, w_{ij}) orthogonal to D_i's image plane. The post-rotation coordinates are given by:

$$\begin{bmatrix} h'_{ij} & w'_{ij} & z'_{ij} \end{bmatrix}^T = R_x(\alpha_x)R_y(\alpha_y)R_z(\alpha_z)\begin{bmatrix} h_{ij} & w_{ij} & z_{ij} \end{bmatrix},$$

where R_x, R_y, R_z denote the 3-D rotation matrices with respect to x-, y- and z-axis, respectively. Then, we compute the re-oriented θ'_{ij} by (1) and w'_{ij}. The CaaS Mobile Application sends θ'_{ij} to the server-side *Observation Collector*. Note that to make θ'_{ij} compatible with a server-side reference orientation, each device also reports its own α_x along with the observation so that the server normalizes θ'_{ij} with respect to the mean of all devices' α_x.

Vision-based AoA sensing also gives a rough estimate of the physical distance to the observed device. In Figure 9, the distance d_{ij} is given by $d_{ij} = s_j/2\tan\frac{\angle\beta_{ij}}{2}$, where s_j is the screen's physical length and $\angle\beta_{ij}$ is its horizontal angular width seen by D_i. We can obtain s_j from D_j's specification. In reality, D_j may be slanted or partially occluded, resulting in a smaller $\angle\beta_{ij}$ to D_i's view. Thus, d_{ij} is not a definite distance but only an upper-bound that the real distance could be at most. We include d_{ij} as an upper-bound distance constraint for our optimization in Section 5.1.

4.5 Mobile-side Observation Performance

We evaluate the mobile-side observation performance using two Nexus 5s, one for an observer and the other for a target. The display size is 4.95 inches and the camera's FoV is 59.6°×46.7°.

PER in handheld observations. Figure 11 shows the PER (packet error rate) when two devices are hand-held by participants. The observed device transmits 9-symbol packets 100 times for each lighting and distance condition. The PER remains low within a certain

Lighting, orientation	Night Ideal	Day Ideal	Day Random	Day Hand-held
(Avg, σ)	(0.64, 0.44)	(0.53, 0.31)	(1.29, 0.69)	(1.23, 1.03)

Table 1: Observation angle error (degree).

distance, i.e., under 10% until 9 meters at night, under 5% until 6 meters under daylight. As discussed in Section 4.2, the average packet duration is less than 1 second for a 9-symbol packet; even for extended identifier digits supporting 10000+ people, 1.5 seconds will suffice. Thus repeated observations for a few seconds will boost the chances of successful decoding at further distances. Without considering the rolling shutter effect, the PER increases to 33% for observation even at 1 meter away at night.

Accuracy of AoA measurement. We evaluate the accuracy of the observation angle θ_{ij} in controlled settings. We conduct a set of measurements under varying conditions of ground truth angles, distances, ambient lighting, and observer orientations. We measure the error of θ_{ij}, i.e., the absolute difference between an estimated angle and a ground truth angle varying within the camera's FoV.

First, we evaluate the angle errors under the ideal orientation, i.e., two devices heading in the same direction and mounted on landscape tripods (Figure 10b). The ground truth observation angle is set by a protractor at ±25°, ±20°, ±10°, and 0° at distances from 1 to 10 meters at every 1 meter increment. This means that we measured the accuracy at 70 different locations under each lighting condition. The average AoA error on 70 different locations is reported in Table 1. We test two lighting conditions: daylight (55000 lux) and night (0 lux). Results indicate that errors in observation angles are typically small, i.e., less than 0.7° on average regardless of ground truth angles and lighting conditions, as shown in Table 1.

Next, we evaluate the accuracy at realistic phone orientations under the daylight conditions: (1) an observer device randomly oriented but firmly held on a tripod (Figure 10c), and (2) both devices hand-held by human participants. For (1), we measured the rotation angles after an arbitrary rotation that happened to be: $\alpha_x = -20°$, $\alpha_y = 7.4°$, and $\alpha_z = 7.4°$. For (2), two persons raised their phones overhead and stood at the corresponding observation angle and distance. For each of the two conditions, we measured AoA errors at 70 different locations as mentioned above and obtained the average. Table 1 shows slightly increased errors compared to the ideal cases. These errors may be due to possible compass offset [75]. Section 5.2 addresses server-side compensation for this error.

5. RECONSTRUCTING CROWD LOCATIONS

The CaaS server first collects the mobile-side observations – tuples of (D_i, D_j, θ_{ij}). Each tuple indicates that an observer D_i has visually identified a target D_j at an angle of θ_{ij}. Based on the observations, it then reconstructs the locations of all devices by solving a constrained optimization problem. We present how we formulate the optimization problem and discuss our approaches to improving reconstruction accuracy and scalability for large crowds.

5.1 Formulating an Optimization Problem

We build an optimization problem subject to a set of geometric constraints. The goal is to compute device locations that produce inter-device angles closest to the real observed angles.

Constraints. We begin with a geometric illustration of an observation (D_i, D_j, θ_{ij}), as shown in Figure 12. Device D_i's camera observed another device D_j's ID at a relative angle of θ_{ij}. The coordinates of the two devices (x_i, y_i) and (x_j, y_j) as well as the distance between them are all unknown. In theory, this observation enforces one constraint, which is that D_j should exist at an arbitrary point only on the line originating from (x_i, y_i) towards the direction

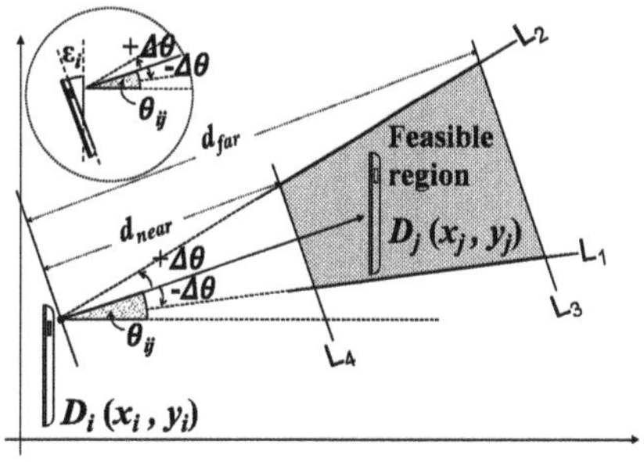

Figure 12: Cartesian plane for constrained optimization.

of D_i's camera at a slope of θ_{ij}. In reality, however, we consider a possible imprecise observation of θ_{ij} and physical limitations. Thus we define a so-called *feasible region* where D_j would exist, which is the trapezoidal area enclosed by four lines (L_1, L_2, L_3, and L_4) highlighted in Figure 12. The rationale for these lines is as follows: (1) L_1 and L_2 are employed to incorporate possible error bounds of θ_{ij}; we set the slopes of L_1 and L_2 to be apart from θ_{ij} by $-\Delta\theta$ and $+\Delta\theta$, respectively. (2) We incorporate the upper-bound distance that comes with each observation by which D_j could be apart from D_i at most as discussed in Section 4.4. Also, D_i and D_j should be apart by at least a single person's torso width. These two distance constraints define L_3 and L_4 as orthogonal lines to $\overline{D_iD_j}$ and distant from D_i by d_{far} and d_{near}, respectively.

Putting them together, we derive the constraints associated with the observation (D_i, D_j, θ_{ij}): four linear inequalities (2) through (5) defining the region enclosed by $L_1 - L_4$:

$$L_1: \ y_j \geq \tan(\theta_{ij} - \Delta\theta)(x - x_i) + y_i, \tag{2}$$

$$L_2: \ y_j \leq \tan(\theta_{ij} + \Delta\theta)(x - x_i) + y_i, \tag{3}$$

$$L_3: \ x_j \leq \frac{1}{\tan\left(\theta_{ij} + \frac{\pi}{2}\right)} \{y_j - (y_i + d_{fy})\} + (x_i + d_{fx}), \tag{4}$$

$$L_4: \ x_j \geq \frac{1}{\tan\left(\theta_{ij} + \frac{\pi}{2}\right)} \{y_j - (y_i + d_{ny})\} + (x_i + d_{nx}), \tag{5}$$

$$\text{where } d_{fx} = d_{far}\cos\theta_{ij}, \ d_{fy} = d_{far}\sin\theta_{ij},$$
$$d_{nx} = d_{near}\cos\theta_{ij}, \ d_{ny} = d_{near}\sin\theta_{ij}.$$

Constraints (4) and (5) place x_j on the left-hand side to deal with a zero slope instead of an infinite slope when $\theta_{ij} = 0$. Having the constraints in linear forms is favorable to lowering the computational complexity. Back to the original problem with N devices, we build the whole constraints set by concatenating all the inequalities for each (D_i, D_j) pair where an observation exists in between.

Cost function. We define a cost function as the gross unsigned difference between the reproduced angles and the observed angles. Consider N devices and the observations among some of them. Let O denote a set of device pairs (i, j) where an observation from D_i to D_j exists. The goal is to find $(x_1, y_1, ..., x_N, y_N)$, minimizing the error between θ_{ij} and the computed slope of $\overline{D_iD_j}$ after reconstruction. The cost function f and its gradient are given by:

$$f(x_1, y_1, ..., x_N, y_N)$$
$$= \sum_{(i,j)\in O} \{\arctan 2(y_j - y_i, \ x_j - x_i) - \theta_{ij}\}^2, \tag{6}$$

$$\nabla f = \sum_{i=1}^{N} \left(\frac{\partial f}{\partial x_i}\hat{\mathbf{x}}_i + \frac{\partial f}{\partial y_i}\hat{\mathbf{y}}_i \right). \tag{7}$$

Note that f must be differentiable to warrant a gradient. Thus we use a square term for the unsigned angular difference in (6). $\arctan 2(y, x)$ is differentiable by x and y except where $\sqrt{x^2 + y^2} + x = 0$. This singularity is not in our domain because D_i and D_j

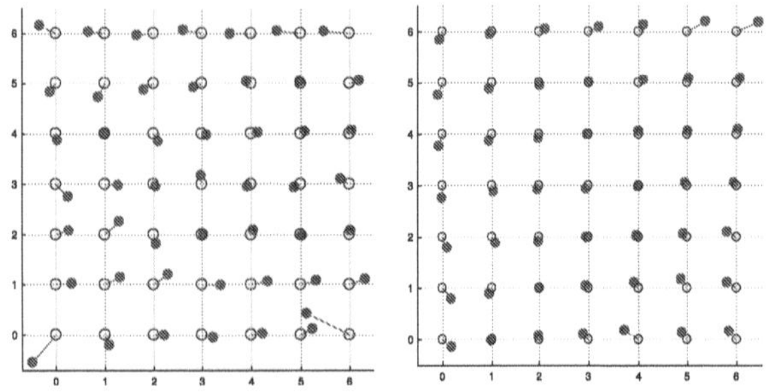

(a) Baseline reconstruction results. Mean LE: 0.26 mpd (b) Camera displacements overlooked. Mean LE: 0.14 mpd

Figure 13: Reconstructed locations of 49 phones placed on 7×7 grids. 1 mpd=75 cm. Blue hollow circles (○) denote ground truth locations. Red solid circles (●) denote the computed locations.

do not overlap, observations are unidirectional, and we define the Cartesian plane to always place D_i to the left side of D_j.

Although we focus on only the "relative" locations, we need one fixed reference point on the Cartesian plane to keep our problem domain bounded. Without loss of generality, we anchor a single arbitrary device at the origin: $x_1 = 0, y_1 = 0$.

Now the reconstruction problem is translated into a nonlinear programming problem to find $(x_1, y_1, ..., x_N, y_N)$, minimizing f in (6) subject to linear inequality constraints (2) – (5) and two linear equality constraints of $x_1 = 0, y_1 = 0$. Several algorithms are available to solve this family of problems [22, 69]. CaaS uses `fmincon`, an off-the-shelf implementation of these algorithms in MATLAB.

5.2 Tackling Error Factors

To represent location accuracy in our collective visualization context, we define a unit *Mean Person Distance* (mpd) — the mean distance between adjacent people on their ground truth locations. We report the individual location error (LE) and the average location error (Mean LE) in units of mpd. Although the physical distance of 1 mpd may vary in different crowds, we refer to an average inter-person distance of 0.75 meters from [36]. We set 1 mpd to be 0.75 m in controlled experiments unless specified otherwise.

Through experiments with real phones, we found that the technique proposed in Section 5.1 results in noticeable localization errors. Figure 13a shows an example reconstruction for 49 phones placed on 7×7 grids. The location errors are shown in units of mpd. Every phone is localized within LE < 1 mpd.

5.2.1 Incorporating Compass Offset

In spite of the mobile-side reorientation of local coordinates, we still observed some errors in the device's horizontal heading α_x due to the gyroscope drift and magnetometer interferences [75]. We found that the local measurements of α_y and α_z are more reliable which the gravity sensor mostly determines.

To compensate possible errors in the devices' α_x readings, we define a variable ε_i that is an observer-specific error between its true horizontal heading and the measured one. For an observer D_i, we presume ε_i is a constant for a short period of time, representing a static offset in its α_x readings. Formally, we revise our cost function f to make it possible to manipulate ε_i within a moderate interval:

$$f(x_1, y_1, ..., x_N, y_N, \varepsilon_1, ..., \varepsilon_N) = \sum_{(i,j) \in O} \left\{ \arctan 2\{y_j - y_i,\, x_j - x_i\} - (\theta_{ij} + \varepsilon_i) \right\}^2 \quad (8)$$

$$\text{where } -\Delta\varepsilon \leq \varepsilon_i \leq +\Delta\varepsilon, \text{ for } 1 \leq i \leq N \quad (9)$$

The gradient in Equation (7) incorporates ε_i terms, and our linear inequality constraints incorporate the constraint (9). We found $\Delta\varepsilon = 20°$ works for most cases. Figure 13b shows an improved reconstruction by applying ε_i terms.

5.2.2 Incorporating Off-centered Camera

Figure 13b exhibits small but consistent angular shifts by 3–10° in the reconstructed locations. The shifts are slightly counterclockwise from the ground truth. The reason is that the camera lenses are not centered on the phones' body, but displaced by 4.3 cm to 6.5 cm. In landscape view, this creates an effect as if the observer device were slightly aside from the true location.

We resolved this issue by replacing the observer's Y-axis coordinates y_i with $y_i + \delta_i$ in (2) – (5) and (8); δ_i is a per-device constant indicating the displacement of the camera from the phone's center. We approximate δ_i as the half of the phone's screen height given by Android API. Figure 20a shows improved reconstruction (Mean LE: 0.07 mpd) after including camera displacements. Note that the target's coordinates (x_j, y_j) remain the same in the equations because the observer mostly sees the center of the target's display.

5.3 Keeping Computing Time Scalable

Our mobile-side experiments have dealt with a relatively small number of people (or devices) ($N < 50$) due to the practical challenges associated with recruiting a larger number. Still, we can test the Crowd Reconstructor with synthetic workloads of a larger N. We built a mobile-side simulator that (1) generates ground-truth locations for given N simulated people and (2) synthesizes realistic observations among the devices. The ground-truth locations are generated to roughly form a given spatial formation, and have the inter-person distances follow a given statistic distribution, i.e., a normal distribution of $\mu = 0.75$ and $\sigma = 0.2$. The observation syntheses incorporate the real camera's FoV, distance bounds, and imperfect orientations that we learned previously. Using the synthetic observations, we measured the reconstruction time on a server running on moderate hardware – Intel i7 2.8 GHz CPU, 16 GB RAM.

Figure 14a shows that our implementation of Crowd Reconstructor takes significant computing time as N increases, becoming impractical at $N = 200$. This means that, even after mobile-side observations are completed, the people must still wait for many minutes until the reconstruction completes and card stunts are fully ready.

5.3.1 Accelerating with Initial Location Estimates

So far we have bootstrapped the nonlinear optimization algorithm with random initial locations. We observed that initial values more similar to the ground truth locations make the algorithm converge faster. To obtain approximate initial values at much less complexity, we build a linearly constrained quadratic programming problem. Figure 14c illustrates our quadratic cost function, which is the vertical distance between (x_j, y_j) and the line from (x_i, y_i) at a slope $\tan\theta_{ij}$. Our quadratic-formed cost function is given by:

$$f_a(x_1, y_1, ...) = \sum_{(i,j) \in O} \left[\{(x_j - x_i)\tan\theta_{ij} + (y_i + \delta_i)\} - y_j \right]^2$$

We used `quadprog`, an off-the-shelf quadratic programming implementation in MATLAB, to find (x_i, y_i)s which minimize f_a, subject to the same constraints as in Section 5.1. Figure 14b shows the computing times of this quadratic programming for $N \leq 10000$ as well as Mean LE of the estimated initial locations. These initial locations exhibit much larger Mean LEs by an order of magnitude compared to those achieved by nonlinear optimization (plotted together in Figure 14a). Still, we observe that providing these initial locations to the nonlinear optimization saves an average of 43.5% computing time compared to random bootstrapping.

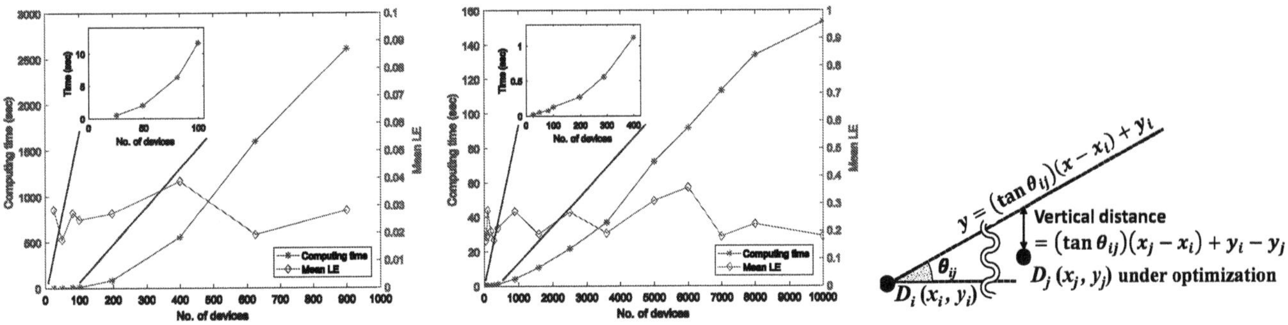

(a) Nonlinear optimization for $N < 1000$ (b) Quadratic optimization for $N \leq 10000$ (c) Quadratic cost function geometry.

Figure 14: (a), (b): Computing time and Mean LE for varying N. (c): Quadratic cost function.

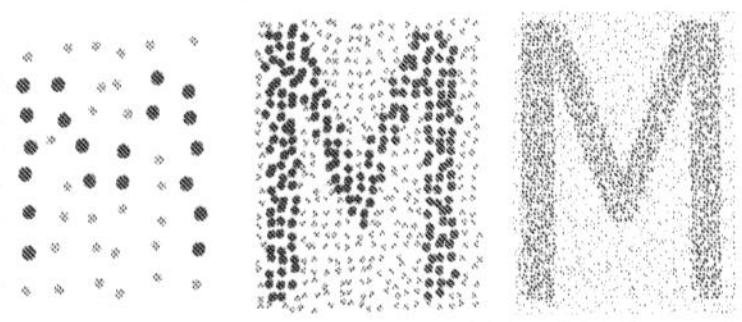

Figure 15: Visualizations for N=48, 500, 5000 at similar localization errors (0.18<Mean LE<0.21). Red dots and gray dots denote ground truth locations whose pixels are on and off, respectively.

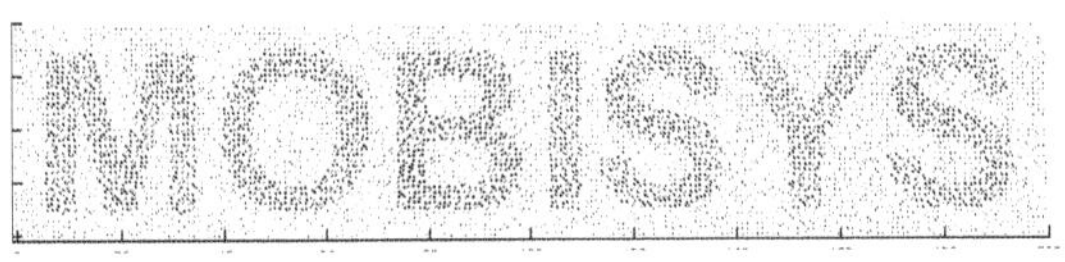

Figure 16: Visualization only with initial locations.

5.3.2 *Diminishing Relative Impacts in Larger Crowds*

So far the reduced computing time is still too long to be practical for N in an order of hundreds or more. We need a different level of breakthrough. Our insight is that, for a larger N, a relaxed reconstruction accuracy may not impact much on the visualization quality. Figure 15 shows the varying visualization quality for different N even at a similar Mean LE. These visualizations are created by CaaS using simulator-generated observations and determining on or off for each device. The resulting pixels are visualized on their ground truth locations. The main factor of varying quality is the pixels-per-symbol. For $N = 48$ only 1 pixel stroke width is allowed per symbol, compared to many pixels in the stroke for $N = 5000$.

In this light, we address that even the initial location estimates would achieve practical accuracies for large Ns. To demonstrate this strategy, we generated the ground truth locations and observations of 8000 people in formation at an aspect ratio of 1:5. Their locations are estimated only by quadratic programming. Then each device is set on or off based on its estimated location. Figure 16 shows the resulting visualization that would appear on top of their ground truth locations. A future question would be: how large N is good enough for this strategy? It may depend on the visualization complexity and the ratio of 1 mpd to the whole crowd area.

5.3.3 *Partitioning into Subproblems for Parallelism*

Section 5.3.2 showed huge time saving by orders of magnitude, e.g., 1000-device reconstruction in less than 5 seconds. Still, the ever-growing computing time is no longer practical for N in the next order of magnitude. For $N = 10000$ it exceeds 2 minutes. It is time to seek parallelism. We exploit our problem's locality from the nature that the mobile-side observations are spatially bounded.

Figure 17 shows such locality for $N = 10000$. The sparsity pattern is a symmetric matrix where (i, j)-th and (j, i)-th elements are set if D_i and D_j has an observation in between. While the original

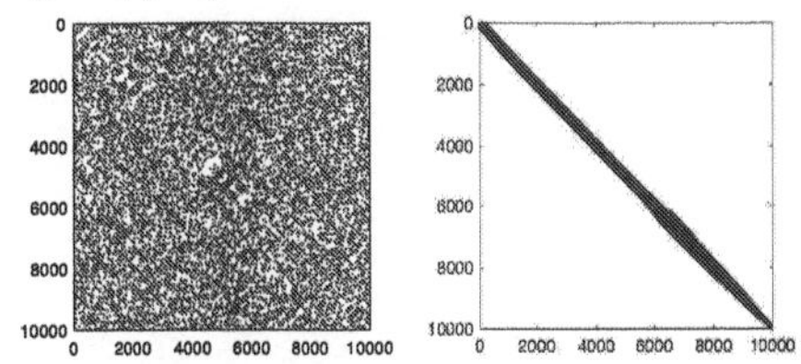

Figure 17: Sparsity pattern of observations for 10000 devices (left) and its RCM reordered matrix (right)

	No. of partitions		1	4	8	16	32
$N = 10000$	Mean LE		0.27	0.26	0.31	0.44	0.46
	Max subprob. time (s)		153	31.7	7.31	1.13	0.45
	% of devices that	$1 \leq LE < 2$	0.10	0.13	1.98	1.69	2.50
		$2 \leq LE < 3$	0	0	0.03	0.03	0
		$LE \geq 3$	0	0	0	0.16	0.10
	No. of partitions		1	16	32	64	128
$N = 40000$	Mean LE		0.26	0.29	0.32	0.50	10.62
	Max subprob. time (s)		1061	21.2	7.52	2.40	0.72
	% of devices that	$1 \leq LE < 2$	0.16	0.23	0.43	8.86	20.6
		$2 \leq LE < 3$	0	0	0.02	0.03	4.04
		$LE \geq 3$	0	0	0	0.03	20.3

Table 2: Trade-offs along with the number of partitions

matrix (left) looks chaotic, applying RCM reordering [26] on the device indices reveals a matrix of strong diagonal locality (right).

We use this reordered diagonal to partition the devices into subgroups, keeping most dependencies therein. This way, only a few observations at the partition borders are discarded. Figure 18a shows how we partition a problem of $N = 10000$ into 4 subproblems of $N = 2500$ each and where the observation losses occur. Figure 18b–18e shows the reconstruction of each subproblem computed independently. While computing the original problem as is took 153 seconds, a subproblem took 31.7 seconds at most. This subproblem computing time further decreases for a greater degree of parallelism, e.g. 7.31 seconds for 8-way. The RCM reordering and putting together the subproblem results take a trivial runtime, e.g., less than 300 ms for 8-way, $N = 10000$.

Finer parallelism creates more partition borders and discards more observations. Table 2 shows a trade-off among the number of partitions, Mean LE, and subproblem computing times. Still most devices are localized at LE < 1 mpd even in small-sized partitions computable in a few seconds, except for 128-way, $N = 40000$.

6. DEPLOYMENT AND EVALUATION

6.1 Reconstruction under Controlled Settings

We evaluate the reconstruction performance under controlled settings using 49 phones of the models: Nexus (5, 6, 5X, 6P) and Galaxy S6, with display sizes of 4.95 to 5.96 inches and horizontal FoVs of 59.6° to 68.1°. To study under different practical condi-

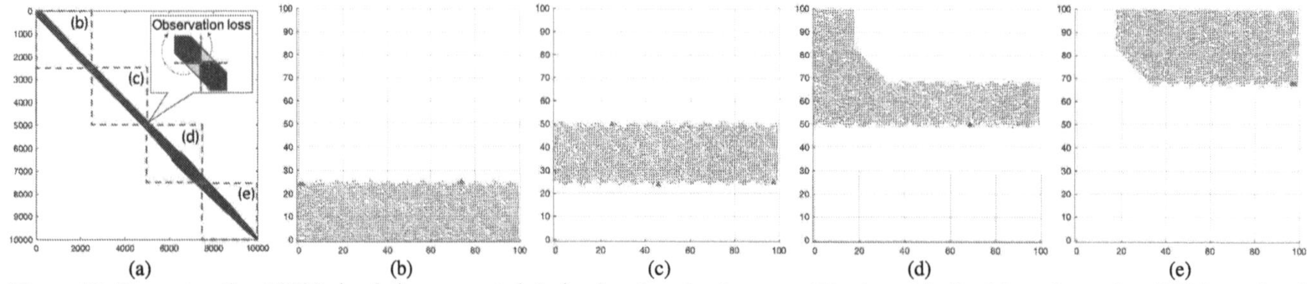

Figure 18: Reconstructing 10000 simulation-generated device locations by 4-way partitioning. (a): Partitions denoted on RCM-reordered sparsity matrix. (b)–(d): Reconstruction results for each partitioned subproblem. Red solid circles (•) denote reconstructed device locations within LE<1 mpd. Green triangles (▲) denote reconstructed device locations where 1 mpd $\leq$ LE $<$ 2 mpd.

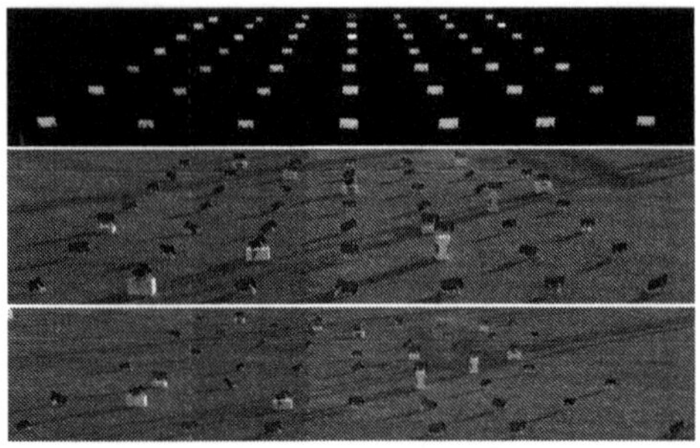

Figure 19: Reconstruction test in varying (orientation, placement, lighting) conditions. Top to bottom: (ideal, uniform, night), (realistic, uniform, day), (realistic, variable, day)

Condition	Mean LE	σ
(I, U, N)	0.068	0.049
(I, U, D)	0.125	0.087
(R, U, D)	0.107	0.067
(R, V, D)	0.105	0.081

(a) Controlled test with 49 phones.

Condition	Mean LE	σ
(R, U, N)	0.186	0.113
(R, U, D)	0.178	0.123
(R, V, N)	0.196	0.133
(R, V, D)	0.168	0.114

(b) Deployment with 49 people

Table 3: Reconstruction errors: Mean LE and σ in mpd. Condition notations: (Orientation {**I**deal | **R**ealistic}, Spacing {**U**niform | **V**ariable}, Lighting {**D**ay | **N**ight})

tions, we conduct experimental trials under different conditions of (*i*) ambient lighting (day (69000 lux) vs. night), (*ii*) orientation (ideal vs. realistic), and (*iii*) device placement (uniformly spaced vs. variably spaced). For the realistic orientations, we applied random rotations around the X or Z axis and height variation, i.e., placing randomly selected devices on boxes 8 – 20 cm high. For device placements, we placed each device on 7×7 grid points with 75-cm spacing in between. For the condition of variable-spaced placements, each device was placed on a randomly selected grid point among 9×9 grid points each spaced by 75 cm. All devices were fixed on the same type of holders. Figure 19 shows the setup. For brevity we use an ordered triple notation (orientation, placement, lighting) to denote an experiment condition. For example (ideal, uniform, night) indicates the conditions of ideal orientation, uniformly spaced placements, and dark lighting at night.

For evaluation, we measure Mean LE in units of mpd as defined in Section 5.2. Figure 20a and 20b show the reconstruction of the 49 phone locations in varying conditions. The reconstruction is close to the ground truth locations; no single device's LE exceeds 0.3 mpd (23 cm). Table 3a shows Mean LEs $\leq$ 0.13 mpd (10 cm) in every condition. The errors are small enough that the the pixel assignments do not deviate from the optimal ones. The lowest error was observed at night because of the large number of observed devices. The average number of observed devices at night is 4.9, while 4.0 and 4.3 devices were observed in (realistic, uniform, day) and (realistic, variable, day), respectively. Counter-intuitively, in (ideal, uniform, day) conditions we observed the fewest, 2.6, because a device would likely occlude those immediately behind it.

6.2 Small Deployment on 49 Participants

We conducted small-scale deployments using CaaS to reconstruct a crowd of 49 participants and demonstrate CaaS-guided collective visualization. We deployed twice — once under daylight (73200 lux) and another time at night. We recruited the participants from a campus bulletin board. To rule out learning effects, each deployment was conducted with different groups of 49 participants (age: 18 – 35). Everyone voluntarily participated and was compensated with a gift card worth either USD 10 or 15. Those in the daylight group were given the higher valued cards because their visualizations were expected to take more time to flip the cardboard upon the cues given from their CaaS Mobile Application (see Figure 2b). The night deployment took less time because the visualization was automatically done by the glowing phones (see Figure 2a). Our deployment plan was reviewed by the IRB and classified as exempt, meeting the minimal risk research criteria.

The daylight group included 38 males and 11 females (height: 155 – 181 cm). The night group included 32 males and 17 females (height: 155 – 187 cm). For those using iPhones or Android phones below 5.0, we provided our own. The phone models included: Nexus (5, 6, 5X, 6P) and Galaxy (S6, Note5) with display sizes of 4.95 to 5.96 inches and horizontal FoVs of 59.6° to 68.1°.

We demonstrate scenarios in which those 49 participants collectively visualize one letter at a time with their phones (at night) or cardboard (under daylight). Each person was responsible for one of the 49 pixels. We asked the participants to stand on 7×7 grids with 75 cm spacing (see Figure 21a). We also conducted variably spaced cases; each participant stood on a random grid point of their choice out of 81 points of a 9×9 grid (see Figure 21b). Importantly, the ground truth locations of the phones are not aligned on the grids in either case. Each phone is handheld, so that there is a random displacement from the center of the human body. We manually labeled the ground truth locations as seen in the snapshots.

In our deployment, visual observation sessions of each device took from 4.6 up to 30 seconds until 4 to 6 distinct devices were observed. This time included 1) visualizing hue transition sequences and observing AoAs, 2) network delay of sending a cue for "Raise your phone" from the CaaS server to each participant, and 3) human factors from a few sluggish users raising their phones late. We set the observation timeout as 30 seconds to address occasional human factor delays. We believe that the timeout would not be too long for highly motivated people with a specific purpose.

Table 3b lists Mean LEs$\leq$ 0.2 mpd (15 cm) in every condition. No single device's LE exceeded 0.5 mpd (33 cm). Mean LEs slightly grew compared to the controlled cases because (1) the overhead handheld phones underwent minor motions and (2) the ground

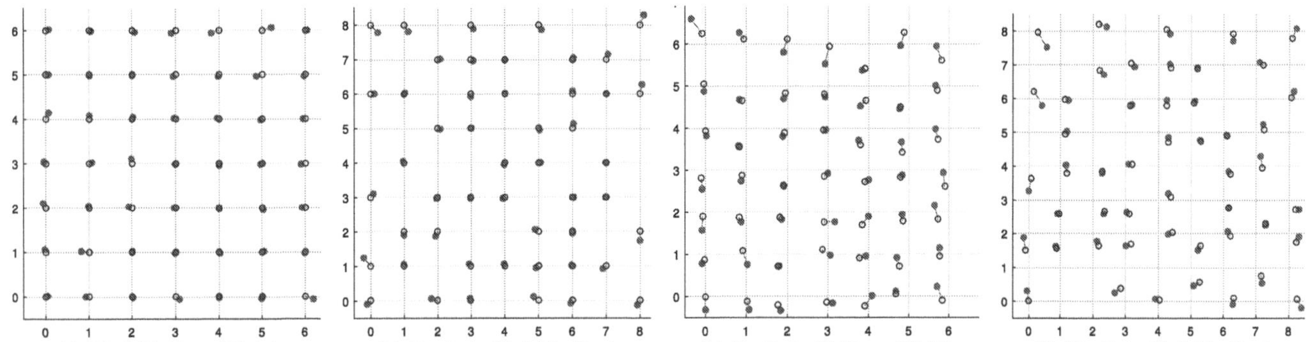

(a) (Ideal, Uniform, Night) (b) (Realistic, Variable, Day) (c) (Realistic, Uniform, Night) (d) (Realistic, Variable, Day)

Figure 20: Reconstruction performance. (a)–(b): controlled setting, (c)–(d): real deployments with human participants. Blue hollow circles (∘) denote ground truth locations. Red solid circles (•) denote computed locations. Every phone is localized within LE<1 mpd.

(a) Uniform spacing (night) (b) Variable spacing (day)

Figure 21: Two cases of small-scale deployment setting.

truth locations seen from the snapshot picture may have differed from the true locations when each device captured the AoAs. Figures 20c and 20d show the reconstruction of the 49 people's devices and the labeled ground truth locations. Figure 2 show their CaaS-guided card stunts showing "MOBISYS" one letter after another.

7. DISCUSSION

Participants' cooperation: Our use case expects the participants to hold their phones overhead during the initial localization. While this might sound burdensome, we target highly motivated participants as discussed in Section 2. They would feel it insignificant compared to their other efforts. Our experiments showed that the initial localization during which a CaaS user needs to hold the phone overhead takes as low as 4.6 seconds. As for following the coordinator's cues, such motivated participants would be as cooperative as they have been in conventional public gatherings.

Dynamicity of crowd. CaaS is mainly designed for stationary, cooperative, densely packed crowds [9, 13, 15, 18, 20]. As discussed in Section 2, CaaS participants are highly motivated and cooperative to convey their common voices, so they may be willing to remain stationary while using CaaS. Still, some might inevitably move, join or leave while CaaS is in action. An efficient way to handle a newly joined or relocated user is to initiate a localized reconstruction for a subgroup of devices in the vicinity of the new user. Users that have left the visualization could be detected through events triggered when the CaaS Mobile Application is closed on the devices. To enable a newly joined device to detect nearby devices, the CaaS Mobile Applications could sporadically toggle Bluetooth discoverability [46, 57]. Only a tiny fraction of the devices should be discoverable at a time to avoid channel flooding. Detecting a few nearby device identifiers would suffice for the CaaS server to define a spatial subgroup to be reconstructed.

Potential cellular bottleneck. CaaS needs Internet access for each device to send AoA measurements to the CaaS server. Concurrent cellular traffic from tens of thousands of densely packed users would render the nearby base stations irresponsive [39]. Despite the tiny payload (< 1kB) to/from a CaaS Mobile Application, they may produce a short, concurrent burst of messages at the initial localization. We believe that this issue is transient due to the upcoming 5th Generation (5G) Mobile Networks. We discuss the feasibility of Internet access via 5G networks and other alternatives.

- A major goal of 5G networks is to support simultaneous connectivity for a large number of devices. The 5G White Paper from the Next Generation Mobile Networks (NGMN) Alliance [11] specifies the capability of providing simultaneous Internet connectivity to 150000 devices per square km. It also specifies a stadium example with an equivalent density — 30000 simultaneously connected devices in a stadium with 25.6 Mbps average rate per device. Moreover, high-density connectivity load will be further distributed as such an area will most likely be covered by multiple cell towers, each likely owned by different mobile carriers. Even one carrier may operate multiple cell towers in an overlapped manner. We envision that, in the near future with 5G networks operational, packed participants of CaaS in a stadium or in a public square will be able to connect to the CaaS server.
- Adopting ad-hoc network techniques would be an alternative to reduce simultaneous connections to a cell tower. Shafiq et al. proposed a connection-sharing technique to reduce network overload [62]. Notably, they showed its efficiency in a scenario very similar to CaaS (e.g., a stadium). Adopting the connection sharing into CaaS will greatly reduce the simultaneous connections to a nearby cell tower. While a device (namely D_A) is connected to the CaaS server via a cellular network, dozens of nearby devices around D_A send their AoA measurement data to D_A via Bluetooth or WiFi Direct. D_A then sends the collected data as well as its own measurement to the CaaS server via a cellular connection. This way, only a small portion of the devices connect to cellular networks, but all devices still communicate with the server. The individual CaaS messages are very small (<1kB), which are favorable to keep the aggregated message size not burdensome for D_A to send via the cellular connection.
- While CaaS aims at public spaces where rich WiFi infrastructure is unlikely, stadium-specific scenarios may benefit from WiFi infrastructure available at some advanced stadiums. There were 700 WiFi access points in operation at New Orleans Superdome during the Super Bowl in 2013 [27]. IBM Smarter Stadiums [8] and Cisco Connected Stadiums [6] offer dense WiFi connectivity for tens of thousands of fans in a stadium, which will soon be deployed in Atlanta Stadium [3] and Texas A&M Stadium [19].

Time synchronization. To visualize animated symbols, CaaS requires a method to synchronize the local clocks of the participants' devices. The desired time-sync resolution depends on the dynamicity of card stunt contents. For example, a 30-fps animated image would require a fine-grained time-sync resolution smaller than 33 milliseconds. On the other hand, intermittently changing images such as those in conventional manual card stunts may tolerate even a few seconds of time-sync resolution. Our deployment shown in Figure 2 is the latter case, i.e., showing one character at a time for several seconds and than changing to the next one. In the deployment, we did not observe a noticeable out-of-sync problem even without any time-sync method. Nonetheless, CaaS needs time-sync functionality to support faster animations. Below we discuss a few time-sync options available to off-the-shelf smartphones:

- GPS achieves a typical error in the order of sub-microseconds [48]. This is favorable for CaaS since most scenarios are expected to be outdoor events. An Android device can compute its local clock relative to a global reference clock from the satellites [1].
- Network Time Protocol (NTP) is an alternative for sub-second time-sync resolution, achieving a typical error in the order of tens of milliseconds (WiFi) or hundreds of milliseconds (4G) [47].
- Cellular networks provide a built-in time-sync feature, Network Identity and Time Zone (NITZ) [10], but it is not an option for CaaS because its typical error is in the order of minutes.

Facing similar directions: The initial localization works best when the participants face similar directions. The visible light observation is not omnidirectional but constrained within moderate angular ranges; e.g., Nexus 5's camera has an FoV of 59°, and the display exhibits dimmer brightness at peripheral viewing angles. Having the phones see similar directions creates a much higher probability that one phone's camera and another one's display are in the line of sight. This would not be an issue because CaaS will likely target crowds whose participants are naturally facing similar directions, e.g., the stage, the coordinator, or the arena [9, 18, 20]. For further assistance, the CaaS Mobile Application provides sensor-assisted audio-tactile feedback to hold the phone at a certain 3-D orientation, i.e., the display faces forward and the main camera faces backward. Our experiments showed that each phone sees not only the one immediately behind it but many phones within its FoV and a certain range, achieving simultaneous multi-target observations.

Different heights of participants: Even after the phones are aligned, one may argue that not many screens may be seen in a device's FoV due to the different heights of people. We find this hardly a problem. Given a smartphone camera's typical vertical FoV of 46°, an observer device is able to see other devices behind it as long as the height difference is within ± 32 cm for a horizontal distance of 0.75 meters; the tolerable height difference grows for people more than 0.75 meter away. For the height distribution of U.S. adults, a 32-cm interval centered at the median covers 98% of the same-gender adults, and 92% of whole adults [16]. In our deployment, we found no problem from height differences. Stepped floors in a stadium may amplify the height differences, but the audio-tactile feedback may consider the floor slope to tilt properly. The coordinator UI may include a simple pointing feature to estimate the floor slope.

Participant feedback: The CaaS Mobile Application shows the symbol to be visualized, so that a participant can opt out anytime. It may be unusual though, as we assume motivated crowds that agreed to the symbols in online communities prior to the event.

8. RELATED WORK

Stitching small displays. Technologies for stitching multiple displays have been proposed in the HCI and mobile computing literature. However, such techniques are poorly suited to the scenarios addressed by CaaS. Phone as a pixel [61] and Where's my pixel [42] use a global camera with an omniscient view to see all participants' phone screens within its FoV. In CaaS scenarios, such a camera would need to be high enough to have a holistic view of the crowd. Requiring such a mid-air camera would greatly increase the barrier to entry, in direct opposition to our objective to offer a commodity service that does not require the installation of additional hardware into public spaces. MagMobile [33] uses specialized hardware attached to all devices to detect the spatial arrangement between two collocated devices in very close proximity up to a few centimeters. Again, CaaS should support unmodified off-the-shelf smartphones. Other approaches require structured light [56], fiducial markers [60], short-range infrared [51], programmable tiles [59] and so on. MovieTile [55] stitches displays by having users repeat pinching gestures for every adjacent device to determine their relative directions. Such a pair-wise gesture would not be user-friendly, fast, nor precise.

Relative localization of distributed devices. We discussed closely related works for peer-to-peer ranging in Section 2.2. In addition to these previously described works, APIT [31] is an influential early work in wireless sensors using radio connectivity among sensor nodes. A large volume of works are based on the radio connectivity principle [74], dual-mode radio [21], or acoustic signals [30]. However, within large-scale densely packed devices, existing connectivity-based approaches would suffer from excessive noise, multipath interferences, and signal attenuation. Event-driven approaches inject events to the system and utilize the detection patterns to infer the individual locations [63, 64, 73], but they require dedicated event generators/detectors such as a moving aerial vehicle emitting focused light beams. While CaaS scenarios address mostly stationary people, moving object tracking or interpersonal ranging techniques [25, 38, 65, 35, 37, 34] may complement CaaS to promptly address individuals joining and leaving.

Facilitating public activism. In the last decade, online social media and mobile connectivity have influenced public activism [24, 28, 66, 67]. Still it remains unclear if social media really facilitates public activism and supports users in the changing of wider societal perceptions [50]. CaaS may complement such online influences to facilitate public activism by attracting real-world attention.

9. CONCLUSION

This paper presented Card-stunt as a Service (CaaS), a service enabling a densely packed crowd to instantly visualize symbols collectively using their mobile devices and server-side services. CaaS features novel robust mobile visual observation and scalable optimization techniques to achieve high-density, infrastructure-free, and fast crowd reconstruction in real environments. Our implementation is robust and effective, demonstrating decimeter-level accuracies in real 49-person deployments, regardless of devices orientation and placement, and of lighting conditions. Our scalable computing strategy exhibits steadily low computing time even for simulated groups of tens of thousands of devices. Beyond the scenarios mainly discussed, CaaS would open up creative opportunities for people to express their ideas in a massive and prominent way.

10. ACKNOWLEDGEMENTS

We thank our shepherd, Dr. Sarah Clinch and the anonymous reviewers for their valuable comments. The corresponding author is Inseok Hwang. This work was partly supported by the National Research Foundation of Korea(NRF) grants funded by the Korea government(MSIP: Ministry of Science, ICT & Future Planning) (No. 2017R1C1B1010619 and 2017R1A2B3010504).

11. REFERENCES

[1] Android API, getFullBiasNanos. https://developer.android.com/reference/android/location/GnssClock.html#getFullBiasNanos(). Accessed: April 2, 2017.

[2] atan2. http://linux.die.net/man/3/atan2. Accessed: December 8, 2016.

[3] Atlanta stadium with IBM smarter stadiums. https://www-03.ibm.com/press/us/en/pressrelease/46116.wss. Accessed: April 14, 2017.

[4] Autism speaks card stunt. http://www.cardstunts.com/autism-speaks-card-stunt/. Accessed: April 8, 2017.

[5] Card Stunts by Kivett Productions. http://www.cardstunts.com/. Accessed: December 8, 2016.

[6] Cisco connected stadium Wi-Fi solution. http://www.cisco.com/c/dam/en_us/solutions/industries/docs/sports/c78-675063_dSheet.pdf. Accessed: April 14, 2017.

[7] Guinness record-setting candlelight vigil. http://english.hani.co.kr/arti/english_edition/e_national/687413.html. Accessed: December 8, 2016.

[8] IBM smarter stadiums. https://www.ibm.com/sports. Accessed: April 14, 2017.

[9] Iceland fans together with national team performs "Viking war chant". https://www.youtube.com/watch?v=BM6U1tmDjUA. Accessed: April 8, 2017.

[10] Network identity and timezone (nitz); service description. https://portal.3gpp.org/desktopmodules/Specifications/SpecificationDetails.aspx?specificationId=576. Accessed: April 8, 2017.

[11] NGMN Alliance. 5g white paper. https://www.ngmn.org/uploads/media/NGMN_5G_White_Paper_V1_0.pdf. Accessed: December 8, 2016.

[12] OpenCL framework. https://www.khronos.org/opencl/. Accessed: April 6, 2017.

[13] Protesters create giant Romanian flag. http://www.wsj.com/video/protesters-create-giant-romanian-flag/6EA2237F-2C08-4422-AD55-4BE0D09B637A.html. Accessed: April 8, 2017.

[14] Schneider's 80th anniversary. http://www.cardstunts.com/schneiders-80th-anniversary/. Accessed: April 8, 2017.

[15] South Korean protesters march against president again. http://edition.cnn.com/2016/11/12/asia/south-korean-protest-president-park/. Accessed: April 8, 2017.

[16] Statistical abstract of the united states: 2011. U.S. Census Bureau.

[17] SurfaceFlinger and Hardware Composer. https://source.android.com/devices/graphics/arch-sf-hwc.html. Accessed: December 5, 2016.

[18] Texas A&M completes world's largest card stunt. http://tamu.247sports.com/Bolt/AM-completes-worlds-largest-card-stunt-40896549. Accessed: April 8, 2017.

[19] Texas A&M's Kyle Field fiber for the future, stadium tech report. http://www.corning.com/media/worldwide/coc/documents/TA&M_SINGLEPAGE_LOW.pdf. Accessed: April 14, 2017.

[20] Thousands call on South Korea's Park to step down. http://edition.cnn.com/2016/11/05/asia/south-korea-president-protests/. Accessed: April 8, 2017.

[21] N. Banerjee, S. Agarwal, P. Bahl, R. Chandra, A. Wolman, and M. Corner. Virtual compass: relative positioning to sense mobile social interactions. In *Proceedings of the 8th International Conference on Pervasive Computing (Pervasive '10)*, pages 1–21. Springer, 2010.

[22] R. H. Byrd, M. E. Hribar, and J. Nocedal. An interior point algorithm for large-scale nonlinear programming. *SIAM Journal on Optimization*, 9(4):877–900, 1999.

[23] C.-L. Chin and C.-T. Lin. Detection and compensation algorithm for backlight images with fuzzy logic and adaptive compensation curve. *International Journal of Pattern Recognition and Artificial Intelligence*, 19(08):1041–1057, 2005.

[24] A. Choudhary, W. Hendrix, K. Lee, D. Palsetia, and W.-K. Liao. Social media evolution of the egyptian revolution. *Communications of the ACM*, 55(5):74–80, 2012.

[25] I. Constandache, X. Bao, M. Azizyan, and R. R. Choudhury. Did you see bob?: human localization using mobile phones. In *Proceedings of the Sixteenth Annual International Conference on Mobile Computing and Networking (MobiCom'10)*, pages 149–160. ACM, 2010.

[26] E. Cuthill and J. McKee. Reducing the bandwidth of sparse symmetric matrices. In *Proceedings of the 1969 24th national conference*, pages 157–172. ACM, 1969.

[27] J. Erman and K. K. Ramakrishnan. Understanding the super-sized traffic of the super bowl. In *Proceedings of the 2013 Internet Measurement Conference*, pages 353–360. ACM, 2013.

[28] S. González-Bailón, J. Borge-Holthoefer, A. Rivero, and Y. Moreno. The dynamics of protest recruitment through an online network. *Scientific reports*, 1, 2011.

[29] T. Hao, R. Zhou, and G. Xing. Cobra: color barcode streaming for smartphone systems. In *Proceedings of the 10th International Conference on Mobile Systems, Applications, and Services (MobiSys'12)*, pages 85–98. ACM, 2012.

[30] M. Hazas, C. Kray, H. Gellersen, H. Agbota, G. Kortuem, and A. Krohn. A relative positioning system for co-located mobile devices. In *Proceedings of the 3rd International Conference on Mobile Systems, Applications, and Services (MobiSys'05)*, pages 177–190. ACM, 2005.

[31] T. He, C. Huang, B. M. Blum, J. A. Stankovic, and T. Abdelzaher. Range-free localization schemes for large scale sensor networks. In *Proceedings of the 9th Annual International Conference on Mobile Computing and Networking (MobiCom'03)*, pages 81–95. ACM, 2003.

[32] F. Hermans, L. McNamara, G. Sörös, C. Rohner, T. Voigt, and E. Ngai. Focus: Robust visual codes for everyone. In *Proceedings of the 14th ACM International Conference on Mobile Systems, Applications, and Services (MobiSys'16)*, pages 319–332. ACM, 2016.

[33] D.-Y. Huang, C.-P. Lin, Y.-P. Hung, T.-W. Chang, N.-H. Yu, M.-L. Tsai, and M. Y. Chen. Magmobile: enhancing social interactions with rapid view-stitching games of mobile devices. In *Proceedings of the 11th International Conference on Mobile and Ubiquitous Multimedia (MUM'12)*, number 61. ACM, 2012.

[34] I. Hwang, H. Jang, T. Park, A. Choi, C. Hwang, Y. Choi, L. Nachman, and J. Song. Toward delegated observation of kindergarten children's exploratory behaviors in field trips. In *Proceedings of the 13th International Conference on*

Ubiquitous Computing (UbiComp'11), pages 555–556. ACM, 2011.

[35] I. Hwang, H. Jang, T. Park, A. Choi, Y. Lee, C. Hwang, Y. Choi, L. Nachman, and J. Song. Leveraging children's behavioral distribution and singularities in new interactive environments: Study in kindergarten field trips. In *Proceedings of the 10th International Conference on Pervasive Computing (Pervasive'12)*, pages 39–56. Springer, 2012.

[36] H. Jacobs. To count a crowd. *Columbia Journalism Review*, 6(1):37, 1967.

[37] H. Jang, S. P. Choe, I. Hwang, C. Hwang, L. Nachman, and J. Song. Rubberband: augmenting teacher's awareness of spatially isolated children on kindergarten field trips. In *Proceedings of the 2012 ACM Conference on Ubiquitous Computing (UbiComp'12)*, pages 236–239. ACM, 2012.

[38] J. Jun, Y. Gu, L. Cheng, B. Lu, J. Sun, T. Zhu, and J. Niu. Social-loc: Improving indoor localization with social sensing. In *Proceedings of the 11th ACM Conference on Embedded Networked Sensor Systems (SenSys'13)*, number 14. ACM, 2013.

[39] J. Jurgensen. Concert crowds flounder in digital dead zones. *The Wall Street Journal*, 2014. Accessed: December 8, 2016.

[40] Y.-S. Kuo, P. Pannuto, K.-J. Hsiao, and P. Dutta. Luxapose: Indoor positioning with mobile phones and visible light. In *Proceedings of the 20th Annual International Conference on Mobile Computing and Networking (MobiCom'14)*, pages 447–458. ACM, 2014.

[41] A. LaMarca, Y. Chawathe, S. Consolvo, J. Hightower, I. Smith, J. Scott, T. Sohn, J. Howard, J. Hughes, F. Potter, J. Tabert, P. Powledge, G. Borriello, and B. SchilitShow. Place lab: Device positioning using radio beacons in the wild. In *Proceedings of the Third International Conference on Pervasive Computing (Pervasive'05)*, pages 116–133. Springer, 2005.

[42] C. Lewis, A. Chandler, and J. Finney. Where's my pixel? multi-view reconstruction of smart led displays. In *The Fifth International Conference on Mobile Ubiquitous Computing, Systems, Services and Technologies (UBICOMM'11)*, pages 83–89. IARIA, 2011.

[43] L. Li, P. Hu, C. Peng, G. Shen, and F. Zhao. Epsilon: A visible light based positioning system. In *Proceedings of the 11th USENIX Symposium on Networked Systems Design and Implementation (NSDI'14)*, pages 331–343, 2014.

[44] T. Li, Q. Liu, and X. Zhou. Practical human sensing in the light. In *Proceedings of the 14th ACM International Conference on Mobile Systems, Applications, and Services (MobiSys'16)*, pages 71–84. ACM, 2016.

[45] K. Liu, X. Liu, and X. Li. Guoguo: Enabling fine-grained indoor localization via smartphone. In *Proceeding of the 11th International Conference on Mobile Systems, Applications, and Services (MobiSys'13)*, pages 235–248. ACM, 2013.

[46] C. Luo and M. C. Chan. Socialweaver: collaborative inference of human conversation networks using smartphones. In *Proceedings of the 11th ACM Conference on Embedded Networked Sensor Systems (SenSys'13)*, number 20. ACM, 2013.

[47] S. K. Mani, R. Durairajan, P. Barford, and J. Sommers. Mntp: Enhancing time synchronization for mobile devices. In *Proceedings of the 2016 Internet Measurement Conference*, pages 335–348. ACM, 2016.

[48] J. Mannermaa, K. Kalliomaki, T. Manstén, and S. Turunen. Timing performance of various GPS receivers. In *Frequency and Time Forum, 1999 and the IEEE International Frequency Control Symposium, 1999., Proceedings of the 1999 Joint Meeting of the European*, volume 1, pages 287–290. IEEE, 1999.

[49] A. T. Mariakakis, S. Sen, J. Lee, and K.-H. Kim. Sail: single access point-based indoor localization. In *Proceedings of the 12th International Conference on Mobile Systems, Applications, and Services (MobiSys'14)*, pages 315–328. ACM, 2014.

[50] D. McCafferty. Activism vs. slacktivism. *Communications of the ACM*, 54(12):17–19, 2011.

[51] D. Merrill, J. Kalanithi, and P. Maes. Siftables: towards sensor network user interfaces. In *Proceedings of the 1st international conference on Tangible and Embedded Interaction (TEI'07)*, pages 75–78. ACM, 2007.

[52] K. Miyaoku, S. Higashino, and Y. Tonomura. C-blink: a hue-difference-based light signal marker for large screen interaction via any mobile terminal. In *Proceedings of the 17th Annual ACM Symposium on User Interface Software and Technology (UIST'04)*, pages 147–156. ACM, 2004.

[53] J. Nielsen. *Usability engineering*. Elsevier, 1994.

[54] S. Nirjon, J. Liu, G. DeJean, B. Priyantha, Y. Jin, and T. Hart. Coin-GPS: indoor localization from direct GPS receiving. In *Proceedings of the 12th International Conference on Mobile Systems, Applications, and Services (MobiSys'14)*, pages 301–314. ACM, 2014.

[55] T. Ohta and J. Tanaka. Movietile: interactively adjustable free shape multi-display of mobile devices. In *SIGGRAPH Asia 2015 Mobile Graphics and Interactive Applications*, number 18. ACM, 2015.

[56] T. Okatani and K. Deguchi. Easy calibration of a multi-projector display system. *International journal of computer vision*, 85(1):1–18, 2009.

[57] D. O. Olguín, B. N. Waber, T. Kim, A. Mohan, K. Ara, and A. Pentland. Sensible organizations: Technology and methodology for automatically measuring organizational behavior. *Systems, Man, and Cybernetics, Part B: Cybernetics, IEEE Transactions on*, 39(1):43–55, 2009.

[58] C. Peng, G. Shen, Y. Zhang, Y. Li, and K. Tan. Beepbeep: a high accuracy acoustic ranging system using cots mobile devices. In *Proceedings of the 5th International Conference on Embedded Networked Sensor Systems (SenSys'07)*, pages 1–14. ACM, 2007.

[59] J. Rekimoto. Squama: a programmable window and wall for future physical architectures. In *Proceedings of the 2012 ACM Conference on Ubiquitous Computing (UbiComp'12)*, pages 667–668. ACM, 2012.

[60] A. Schmitz, M. Li, V. Schönefeld, and L. Kobbelt. Ad-hoc multi-displays for mobile interactive applications. In *Eurographics (Areas Papers)*, pages 45–52, 2010.

[61] J. Schwarz, D. Klionsky, C. Harrison, P. Dietz, and A. Wilson. Phone as a pixel: enabling ad-hoc, large-scale displays using mobile devices. In *Proceedings of the SIGCHI Conference on Human Factors in Computing Systems (CHI'12)*, pages 2235–2238. ACM, 2012.

[62] M. Z. Shafiq, L. Ji, A. X. Liu, J. Pang, S. Venkataraman, and J. Wang. A first look at cellular network performance during crowded events. In *ACM SIGMETRICS Performance Evaluation Review*, volume 41, pages 17–28. ACM, 2013.

[63] R. Stoleru, T. He, J. A. Stankovic, and D. Luebke. A high-accuracy, low-cost localization system for wireless

sensor networks. In *Proceedings of the 3rd International Conference on Embedded Networked Sensor Systems (SenSys'05)*, pages 13–26. ACM, 2005.

[64] R. Stoleru, P. Vicaire, T. He, and J. A. Stankovic. Stardust: a flexible architecture for passive localization in wireless sensor networks. In *Proceedings of the 4th International Conference on Embedded Networked Sensor Systems (SenSys'06)*, pages 57–70. ACM, 2006.

[65] A. Symington and N. Trigoni. Encounter based sensor tracking. In *Proceedings of the thirteenth ACM International Symposium on Mobile Ad Hoc Networking and Computing (MobiHoc'12)*, pages 15–24. ACM, 2012.

[66] S. Valenzuela. Unpacking the use of social media for protest behavior the roles of information, opinion expression, and activism. *American Behavioral Scientist*, 57(7):920–942, 2013.

[67] O. Varol, E. Ferrara, C. L. Ogan, F. Menczer, and A. Flammini. Evolution of online user behavior during a social upheaval. In *Proceedings of the 2014 ACM Conference on Web Science (WebSci'14)*, pages 81–90. ACM, 2014.

[68] D. Vasisht, S. Kumar, and D. Katabi. Decimeter-level localization with a single WiFi access point. In *Proceedings of 13th USENIX Symposium on Networked Systems Design and Implementation (NSDI'16)*, pages 165–178, 2016.

[69] R. A. Waltz, J. L. Morales, J. Nocedal, and D. Orban. An interior algorithm for nonlinear optimization that combines line search and trust region steps. *Mathematical programming*, 107(3):391–408, 2006.

[70] A. Wang, Z. Li, C. Peng, G. Shen, G. Fang, and B. Zeng. Inframe++: Achieve simultaneous screen-human viewing and hidden screen-camera communication. In *Proceedings of the 13th International Conference on Mobile Systems, Applications, and Services (MobiSys'15)*, pages 181–195. ACM, 2015.

[71] P. A. Zandbergen. Accuracy of iphone locations: A comparison of assisted GPS, WiFi and cellular positioning. *Transactions in GIS*, 13(s1):5–25, 2009.

[72] Z. Zhang, D. Chu, X. Chen, and T. Moscibroda. Swordfight: Enabling a new class of phone-to-phone action games on commodity phones. In *Proceedings of the 10th International Conference on Mobile Systems, Applications, and Services (MobiSys'12)*, pages 1–14. ACM, 2012.

[73] Z. Zhong and T. He. Msp: multi-sequence positioning of wireless sensor nodes. In *Proceedings of the 5th international Conference on Embedded Networked Sensor Systems (SenSys'07)*, pages 15–28. ACM, 2007.

[74] Z. Zhong and T. He. Achieving range-free localization beyond connectivity. In *Proceedings of the 7th ACM Conference on Embedded Networked Sensor Systems (SenSys'09)*, pages 281–294. ACM, 2009.

[75] P. Zhou, M. Li, and G. Shen. Use it free: Instantly knowing your phone attitude. In *Proceedings of the 20th Annual International Conference on Mobile Computing and Networking (MobiCom'14)*, pages 605–616. ACM, 2014.

CELLI: Indoor Positioning Using Polarized Sweeping Light Beams

Yu-Lin Wei†, Chang-Jung Huang†, Hsin-Mu Tsai†, Kate Ching-Ju Lin‡

†Department of Computer Science and Information Engineering, National Taiwan University, Taiwan

‡Department of Computer Science, National Chiao Tung University, Taiwan

{r03922027,r02922061,hsinmu}@csie.ntu.edu.tw, katelin@cs.nctu.edu.tw

ABSTRACT

Existing visible light positioning (VLP) systems leverage the high image resolution of a receiving camera to support high positioning accuracy. However, power-hungry cameras might not always be applicable for many scenarios, such as smart factories, in which small objects require to be accurately localized and tracked. In this paper, we introduce CELLI, an indoor VLP system that only uses a single luminary as the transmitter and requires only a simple light sensor to achieve an extremely high accuracy with centimeter-level error. The key idea is to provide the spatial resolution capability from the transmitter instead of the receiver, so that the complexity of the receiver can be minimized. In particular, a small LCD is installed at the transmitter to project a large number of narrow and interference-free polarized light beams to different spatial *cells*. A receiving light sensor identifies its located cell by detecting the unique polarization-modulated signals projected to that cell. CELLI further incorporates a number of novel designs to overcome the technical challenges such as reducing the positioning latency, which is typically limited by the long optical response time of an LCD, and transforming a cell coordinate to the global 3D position using only a single light. We have prototyped our design using off-the-shelf optical and electrical components, and experimentally shown that CELLI achieves a median 3D positioning error less than 11.8 cm and a median 2D positioning error to less than 2.7 cm.

1. INTRODUCTION

Indoor positioning enables location-based services for a wide range of commercial applications [8]. Seeking to maximize their efficiency, smart factories in the next decade requires assets and personnel to be constantly tracked, automated vehicles navigating themselves to transport goods, and robots in the assembly lines manipulating objects with precision. To turn these into reality, it is essential to have a positioning technology with centimeter-level accuracy, while being applicable even for small objects or able to be directly attached to existing equipment. The use cases set stringent energy consumption, computation, and cost constraints that need to be overcome by the positioning technology.

Permission to make digital or hard copies of all or part of this work for personal or classroom use is granted without fee provided that copies are not made or distributed for profit or commercial advantage and that copies bear this notice and the full citation on the first page. Copyrights for components of this work owned by others than the author(s) must be honored. Abstracting with credit is permitted. To copy otherwise, or republish, to post on servers or to redistribute to lists, requires prior specific permission and/or a fee. Request permissions from permissions@acm.org.

MobiSys'17, June 19-23, 2017, Niagara Falls, NY, USA

© 2017 Copyright held by the owner/author(s). Publication rights licensed to ACM.

ISBN 978-1-4503-4928-4/17/06...$15.00

DOI: http://dx.doi.org/10.1145/3081333.3081352

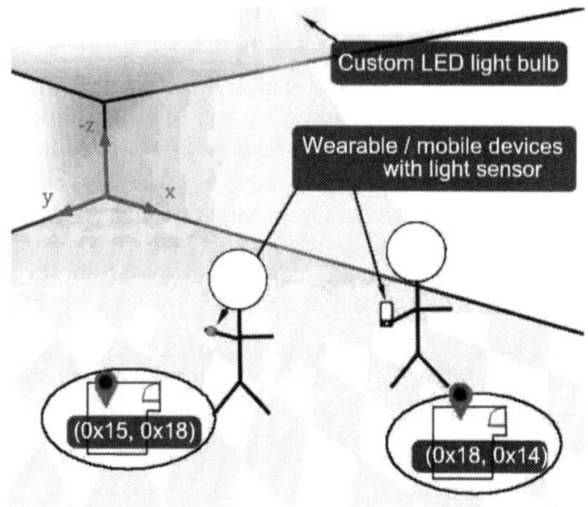

Figure 1: Positioning with CELLI. CELLI provides accurate positioning using one light bulb and a simple light sensor.

While RFID-based positioning technologies [18–22, 26] are especially suitable for object localization or tracking, their accuracy, however, could degrade significantly in a multipath-rich environment, such as a factory with metallic objects everywhere. Recent works [12, 14–16, 24] have demonstrated that visible light signals can be utilized to get rid of the critical multipath problem and deliver accurate positioning estimation with sub-meter accuracy. In these systems, taking advantage of the high image resolution, a commodity camera is able to capture at least three transmitting luminaries in the same image and leverages some geometric properties to estimate its location. However, the need for multiple captured luminaries prevents those designs from being applied on small objects, which might only be able to be equipped with a simple light sensor (i.e., single-pixel photodiode). Also, supporting positioning services with dense modified lighting equipments creates additional difficulty for widely deployment.

In this paper, we propose CELLI, a novel visible light positioning system that can perform centimeter-level 3D positioning with only a single transmitting luminary and a simple receiving light sensor. The key innovative idea of CELLI is to transfer the spatial resolution capability from the receiver to the transmitter. Making use of a small liquid crystal display (LCD) panel, CELLI's transmitter projects a large number of fine-grained, parallel, and yet interference-free light beams toward the service area. As a result, CELLI only needs a small light sensor, instead of a commodity camera, as the receiver, which can be easily integrated with small objects or devices. At a certain location, the light sensor receives the light beam from a particular pixel of the LCD, which carries the information about *the coordinate of a fine-grained cell.* The positioning signals are modulated using the polarization direction of a light source. Hence, human eyes perceive non-flickering white light from the transmitting luminary, preserving its main function – illumination.

Realizing the idea, however, is not trivial, due to the following challenges: First, CELLI's transmitter changes the states of LCD pixels to modulate the light beams with positioning information. However, the long optical response time of an LCD, i.e., the time for a pixel to completely change between states, could take hundreds of milliseconds. If we naïvely transmit the bits of the location identifier, it would take several seconds to complete positioning once, due to the large number of state changes (i.e., bit flipping). To address this issue, we modulate the positioning signals using a modified *pulse position modulation* (PPM) scheme, which incorporates only 4 state changes in a complete positioning cycle. In particular, taking advantage of PPM's single pulse property, we propose a *pre-switching* mechanism to reduce the positioning cycle from 1.8 seconds to 0.6 seconds, but still keep each LCD pixel staying at a state for a sufficient time to settle, maintaining a high signal strength for accurate positioning.

In addition, in CELLI, the light sensor only receives the 2D coordinate from a transmitting light. This renders conventional triangulation and trilateration techniques inapplicable and makes 3D positioning a challenging task. To further convert the received 2D coordinate to the actual 3D position, the system should be able to estimate the receiver height (the projected distance along the Z axis in Fig. 1) as well as the corresponding size of the projected cell. To achieve this goal, CELLI employs a novel *dual-lens optical design* to project two independent sets of light beams to the service area. A receiver would capture two light beams respectively from both sets of projection, enabling it to accurately estimate the Z-axis distance and, thereby, its 3D position, using an angle-of-arrival based technique.

Finally, since CELLI uses the polarization direction of a light beam to represent the positioning information, the received signal strength of an angle-of-polarization-modulated signal could drop significantly [24] when the receiver rotates to certain orientations with respect to the transmitter. To ensure that a receiver gets a signal strength high enough for accurate positioning, CELLI incorporates an electronic polarizer in front of the receiving light sensor. Combined with a simple search algorithm, the electronic polarizer adaptively rotates its polarization direction that best matches the incoming light polarization and maintains sufficient received signal strength. CELLI's receiver can, hence, perform accurate positioning in any of the 360 degree orientations.

We have implemented a prototype of CELLI using commodity optical compoments and development boards, and tested the impact of different types of LCDs. The key findings from our testbed experiments are as follows:

- CELLI combines PPM with a simple but effective pre-switching scheme to shorten the positioning cycle from 1.8 seconds (required by the traditional bit-pattern approach) to 0.6 seconds, while keeping mostly the same positioning accuracy.
- CELLI resolves the problem of intensity contrast drop due to arbitrary rotation by applying an additional electronic polarizer at the receiver. By dynamically adapting the polarization direction, the receiver can always observe a similar intensity contrast, independent of its orientation.
- The interference from a neighboring cell 2 cm further away is negligible. Taking advantage of the dense narrow yet interference-free light beams generated by a high-resolution LCD, CELLI produces a 2D positioning error no larger than 3.3cm.

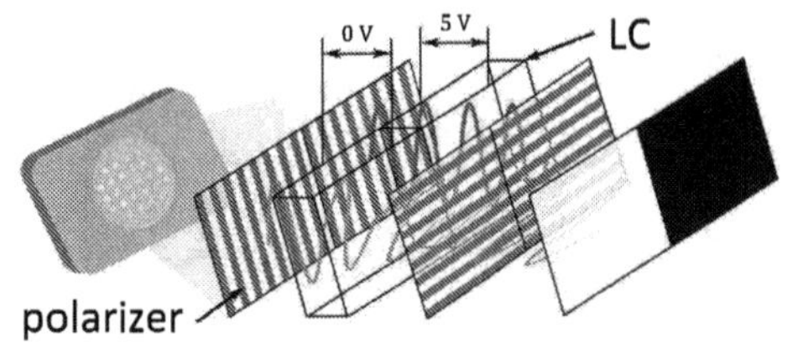

Figure 2: LCD operation principle. Each LC pixel twists the polarization direction of the light according to the applied voltage.

- With the novel dual-lens design, CELLI can further support 3D positioning with a median error of only 11.8 cm.

2. LCD PRIMER

2.1 Principle of Operation

LCD is a widely-used display technology on all types of screens, e.g., computers, mobile devices, TV, projectors, etc. An LCD is composed of a liquid crystal (LC) array between two polarization filters that are *perpendicular to each other*, as shown in Fig. 2. A polarizing filter (or polarizer) is an optical filter that allows only one particular polarization of the incoming light to pass through while filtering out all the remaining polarizations. Therefore, the first polarizer of an LCD can convert an unpolarized light source to a polarized light beam. Each LC cell (or pixel) in the array then twists the polarization direction of the incoming light according to the voltage applied. The intensity of the polarized light passing through the second polarizer, I_θ, varies with the angle between the polarization direction and the second filter, θ, which can be expressed as

$$I_\theta = I_0 \cos^2 \theta, \tag{1}$$

where I_0 is the initial intensity of the polarized light before passing the second filter [10]. Hence, by controlling the voltage applied to each LC pixel, we can tune the angle θ and change the intensity a narrow light beam accordingly. For example, when no voltage is applied, the pixel twists the polarized light by 90 degrees, making the polarization direction of the light become parallel to the second polarizer. The polarized light can, hence, completely pass through the LCD. On the contrary, when full voltage is applied, the LC pixel does not twist the polarization direction of light, and, hence, the polarized light stays perpendicular to the second polarizer. In this case, the polarized light will be fully blocked and a black pixel is displayed. CELLI leverages the spatial resolution of an LCD to simultaneously emit a large number of well-modulated narrow light beams and achieve find-grained positioning.

2.2 Types and Characteristics

Most LCDs on the market can be categorized into *passive matrix* and *active matrix* according to the control circuit design [17]. Passive matrix LCDs, such as STN LCDs, cannot adjust the voltage of each pixel independently, but can only control a column of pixels or a row of pixels at a time. As a result, a passive LCD suffers from a lower contrast ratio and long response time, but features low price, high optical transparency and energy efficiency. For example, a common low-cost STN LCD (~$10 each) can support a resolution up to 128 by 64 pixels.

On the contrary, active matrix LCDs are able to control each pixel of the LC array independently using a thin transistor film (TFT) array over the LC layer. Active LCDs usually support a greater contrast ratio with the cost of lower optical transparency and

LCD Type	Passive Matrix	Active Matrix
Addressing	row/column control circuit	thin film transistor
Energy Consuming	Low	High
Cost	Low	High
Transparency	High	Low
Contrast Ratio	Low	High
Response Time	Long	Short

Table 1: Comparison between passive and active matrix LCDs.

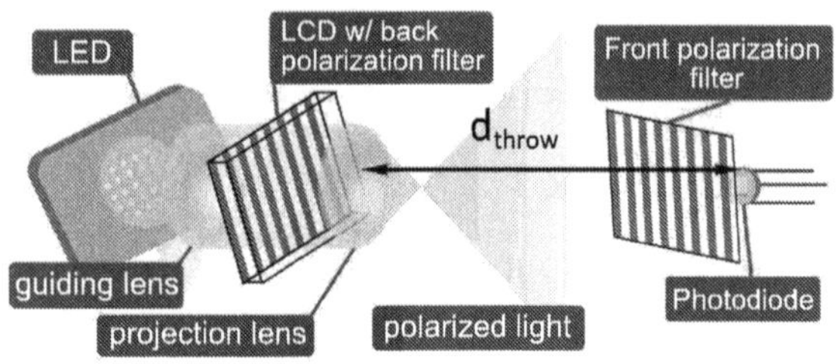

Figure 3: CELLI system design. CELLI utilizes a LCD to generate polarized light beams, each of which is then projected to a small cell in the service area.

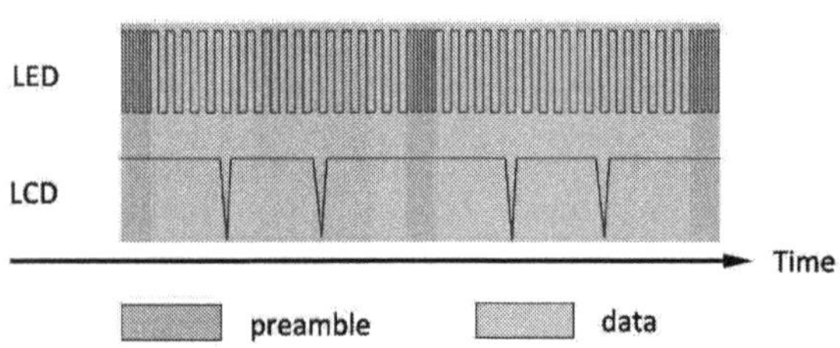

Figure 4: Positioning cycles. CELLI modulates the LED back-light using the preamble frequency to indicate the beginning of a positioning cycle.

higher energy consumption required by the additional TFT layer. Also, the response time of active LCDs is much shorter than passive LCDs since the delay of changing the state of one LCD pixel is smaller than that of updating a group of pixels or the entire LCD frame. The detailed comparison between passive and active LCDs is summarized in Table 1, and we will check in Sec. 5.1 CELLI's positioning performance when different types of LCDs are applied.

3. SYSTEM DESIGN

3.1 Overview

CELLI aims to provide accurate indoor positioning using only a single luminary. On the transmitter side, we place an LCD between two lenses to modulate the light from an LED light source, which emits unpolarized light, as shown in Fig. 3. The *guiding lens*, which sits in front of the LED light source, refracts the light to enter the LCD in parallel. Then, each pixel of the LCD modulates the angle of polarization of the incoming light to generate a narrow and polarized light beam. The *projection lens* refracts the parallel light beams out of the LCD, and projects them toward non-overlapping locations, denoted as *cells* hereafter, in a positioning service area. By carefully selecting this lens, CELLI can flexibly control the tradeoff between accuracy and the dimensions of the service area. We detach the second filter from the LCD, but attach it in front of the receiving light sensor, such that, between the transmitter and the receiver, only the angle of polarization varies. As human eyes are insensitive to this variation, flickers are not observed. The second polarizer makes sure that the light sensor can observe the intensity changes induced by the change of each pixel's polarization angle. In particular, we explicitly adjust the states of the LCD's pixels to generate positioning signals such that the receiving light sensor at different cells observes different and unique bright-dark sequences over time (see Sec. 3.2 for the details). Taking advantage of the high spatial resolution of the LCD, CELLI is able to achieve fine-grained positioning.

Realizing such cell positioning, however, requires us to overcome two practical challenges. First, with CELLI, the receiver can only identify its coordinate, instead of the absolute position. To convert coordinate to position, the receiver further needs the information about its *height*, which is defined as the *throw distance* between the transmitter and the cell plane of the receiver, as shown in Fig. 3. To allow a receiver to estimate its own height, we introduce a dual-lens design at the transmitter such that each receiver can capture two different positioning signals from two projection lenses (see Sec. 3.3). Once detecting two different bright-dark sequences, the receiver can leverage some fundamental geometric properties to estimate its height and thereby its absolute location. Second, the receiver may be rotated to an arbitrary orientation during positioning. Since rotation changes the angle between the LCD at the transmitter and the polarizer installed at the receiver, the bright-dark pattern might become indistinguishable at the receiver at certain angles [24], resulting in received signal strength insufficient for positioning. We resolve this issue by replacing the receiver's polarizer with a liquid crystal cell (LCC), i.e., a "single pixel LCD", which acts as an electronic polarizer whose orientation can be dynamically adjusted. With the LCC, the receiver can search for the polarizer direction of its LC that best matches the polarization of the incoming signal, maximizing the contrast of the bright-dark signals, and thereby improving detection accuracy (see Sec. 3.4).

3.2 Coordinate Detection

CELLI partitions time into disjoint positioning cycles, as shown in Fig. 4. Each positioning cycle can be further divided into T time slots. CELLI modulates the LED back-light using two frequencies: the preamble frequency and data frequency. The preamble frequency is transmitted for a small period of time, e.g., 10 ms, at the beginning of each positioning cycle, as the reference starting time before every round of positioning data signals, which are then sent with the back-light modulating at the data frequency. A receiver starts the positioning procedure by correlating the received signal with the preamble carrier in order to detect the preamble and tag the reference starting point.

Modulating positioning signals. To transmit a unique bright-dark sequence toward each cell, CELLI utilizes the characteristics of the LCD mentioned in Sec. 2.2 to realize *Pulse Position Modulation* (PPM) [9], which transmits only one or a few signal pulses in the T possible time slots. In particular, each pixel in the x-th column and the y-th row is assigned a coordinate (x, y) and broadcasts the positioning messages to the corresponding cell. To represent (x, y) using PPM, CELLI partitions the duration of a position cycle into the *column scanning* phase and the *row scanning* phase. Let T_x and T_y denote the durations of the column and row scanning phases, respectively, and, hence, $T = T_x + T_y$. Each pixel then switches

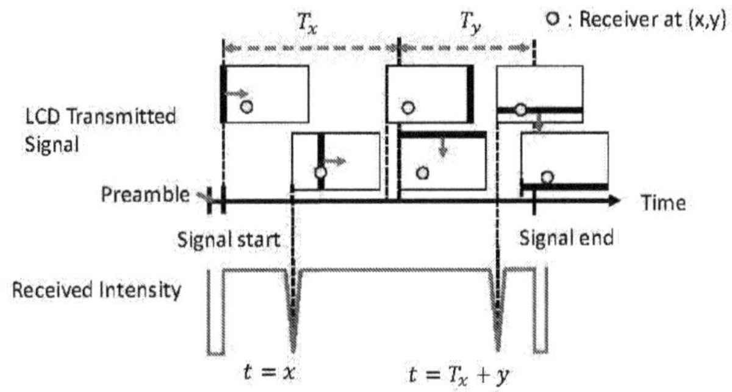

Figure 5: CELLI's PPM modulation. The transmitter delivers PPM signals by sweeping a strip horizontally and then vertically.

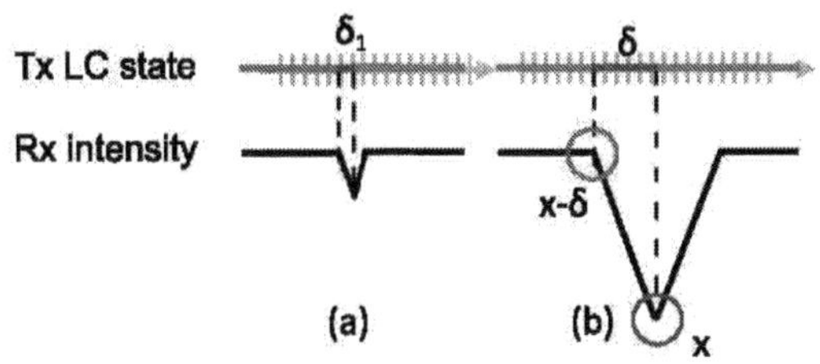

Figure 6: Pre-switching for increasing the intensity contrast. CELLI lets each pixel pre-switch its state so as to ensure complete state transition.

its polarization angle $\theta_{x,y}(t)$ at time slot t as follows:

$$\theta_{x,y}(t) = \begin{cases} 90^\circ & \text{, if } t = x \text{ or } t = T_x + y \\ 0^\circ & \text{, otherwise.} \end{cases} \quad (2)$$

A nice property of this PPM scanning scheme is that each pixel rarely changes its state. Specifically, the traditional bit-pattern scheme uses black and white states as bit 0 and bit 1 to represent the binary identifier of each cell, and, hence, needs to frequently switch the state of each pixel between "0" (dark) and "1" (bright). However, CELLI's PPM allows each pixel (x, y) to switch its state only *four times*, i.e., at time slots x and $T_x + y$ (from 0° to 90°) and at time slots $x + 1$ and $T_x + y + 1$ (from 90° to 0°).

Assume that the receiver's polarizer is placed with an angle of 0°. Then, it receives the dark intensity at only time slots x and $T_x + y$, but receives the bright intensity at all the remaining time slots, as shown in Fig. 5. Hence, with PPM, the positioning signals sent by the transmitter is visually similar to the effect of sweeping a vertical strip column by column, within the column scanning phase T_x, and then sweeping a horizontal strip row by row, within the row scanning phase T_y, as shown in Fig. 5. However, for a receiver to be able to detect the dark signal, the duration of each time slot, denoted by T_{switch}, should at least be larger than the optical response time. The main reason is that each transmitting LCD pixel cannot *immediately* change it polarization state from one angle to another. Hence, if a time slot is too short, the contrast between the bright and dark intensities could be insufficient to distinguish, as shown in Fig. 6(a), since the transmitter might not completely change its angle from 0° to 90°.

To further shorten the positioning cycle without sacrificing the positioning resolution, we need to design an approach to reduce the duration of each time slot, while maintaining the contrast of the bright-dark signals. To achieve this goal, our solution is to shorten the duration of a state transition time-slot T_{switch} but, alternatively,

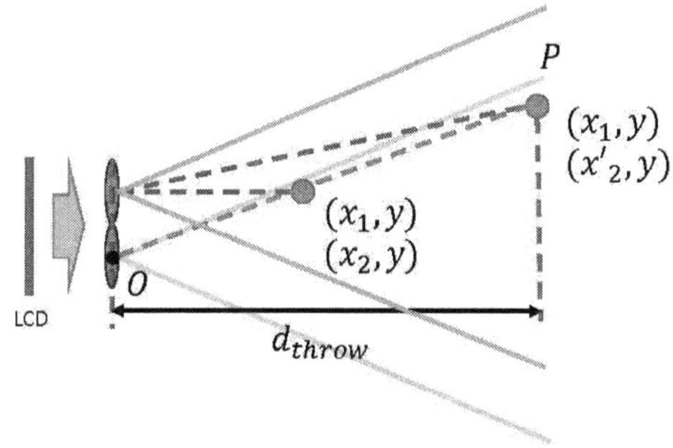

Figure 7: Height estimation by dual-lens. A receiver could detect the same 2D coordinate at different heights. Our dual-lens design allows a receiver to estimate its height even if it is served by only a single transmitting light.

modulate the positioning signals as follows:

$$\theta_{x,y}(t) = \begin{cases} 90^\circ & \text{, if } x - \delta < t \leq x \text{ or} \\ & \quad (T_x + y - \delta) < t \leq T_x + y \\ 0^\circ & \text{, otherwise.} \end{cases} \quad (3)$$

We can see from the above equation that each pixel (x, y) *pre-switches* to the 90° state at time slot $x - \delta + 1$ and $T_x + y - \delta + 1$, respectively, and stays in this state for δ time slots. To maximize the contrast of the bright-dark signals, we should carefully pick the value of δ such that the total time a pixel stays in the 90° state is larger than its response time. Fig. 6(b) illustrates that this pre-switching scheme allows each transmitting pixel (x, y) to gradually switch to the *actual* 90° state, i.e., reaching the darkest intensity, at time slots x and $T_x + y$, respectively. Therefore, the receiver can still detect the deep of the received signals and estimate its location accurately. With this pre-switching, CELLI now reduces the duration of each time slot, thereby shortening the whole positioning cycle. Therefore, CELLI can achieve fine-grained positioning resolution even with some cheap and low-end LCDs with larger response time (i.e., longer latency for a state transition).

Combining PPM with bit-pattern. While TFT LCDs are capable of updating the state of each pixel independently, some STN LCDs can only update *a group of pixels* at a time. Hence, if we incorporate an STN LCD in the transmitter, CELLI's PPM should treat a group of pixels as a coordinate. Each pixel, again, sends the PPM signals according to its assigned coordinate. However, such group-based scanning can only provide block-level positioning accuracy. To overcome this limitation, we further adopt a hybrid approach that combines CELLI's PPM with the traditional bit-pattern scheme. That is, to achieve pixel-level accuracy, after sending our PPM signals, each pixel within a group further delivers a unique assigned bit-pattern to the corresponding cell. It is worth noting that, since the bit-pattern scheme cannot take advantage of the previously mentioned pre-switching scheme due to its frequency state changes, the duration of a time slot needs to be increased to allow sufficient time for pixels to change their states.

3.3 From 2D Coordinate to 3D Positioning

CELLI's PPM signals only allow receivers to identify their coordinates, instead of absolute locations. Consider the example shown in Fig. 7. If a receiver identifies its coordinate (x_1, y), it still does not know what its exact location is since any points along the line

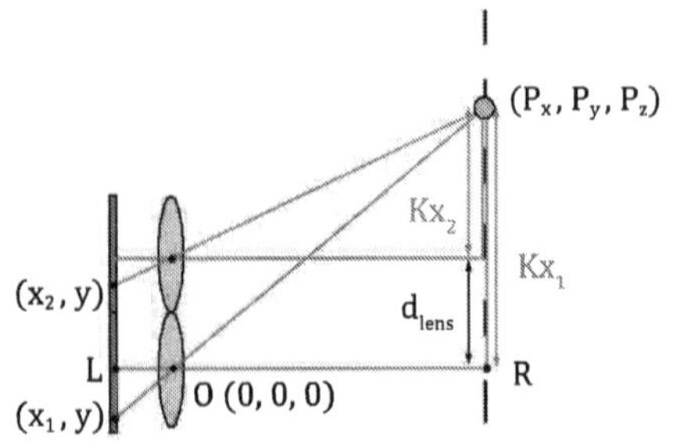

Figure 8: Converting the coordinate to the actual position. The receiver leverages some geometric properties to estimate its height, and thereby 3D position.

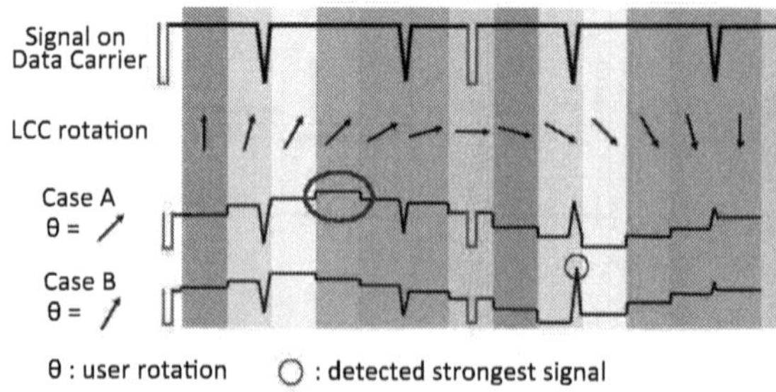

Figure 9: Polarization adaptation using LCC. CELLI uses a LCC to search for a proper polarization angle that gives a high intensity contrast.

segment $\overline{OP}$ receive the same signals from the LCD pixel (x_1, y). To enable a receiver to convert its coordinate to the location, we introduce a dual-lens design at the transmitter. In particular, we replace the original single projection lens with two side-by-side lenses, each of which is covered by half of the pixels of the LCD. With dual lenses, the transmitting light projects to two areas, mostly overlapped with each other, on a surface, as shown in Fig. 7. The LCD pixels, thus, are also partitioned into two sets. Each set has its own coordinate system, with the origin located at the center of each lens. Then, each pixel still broadcasts the positioning signal according to its assigned coordinate using Eq. 3. With these two coordinate systems, the receiver now captures two dark signals in the *column scanning* phase, each of which is from one of the two projection lenses[1]. We can observe from Fig. 8 that, though any point along $\overline{OP}$ receives the same coordinate from the bottom lens, it, however, receives a different coordinate from the top lens.

With such a dual-lens design, a receiver can use the two detected coordinates, (x_1, y) and (x_2, y), from the two lenses, to calculate its global 3D location (P_x, P_y, P_z). Here, we assume the origin of the global coordinate system locates at the center of the bottom lens. To find P_x and P_y, we define K as an unknown scaling factor representing the conversion ratio of the actual physical size of a cell to the unit of our coordinate system, which is determined by the receiver height, P_z. That is, the scaler K is a function of the height, i.e., $K = f(P_z)$. Then, the actual position can be represented by

$$P_x = Kx_1 = Kx_2 + d_{\text{lens}} \text{ and } P_y = Ky, \tag{4}$$

which can be rewritten as

$$K = d_{\text{lens}} \frac{1}{x_1 - x_2}, \tag{5}$$

where d_{lens} is the distance between the origins of the two lenses. Thus, K can be calculated from the detected values of x_1 and x_2, if d_{lens} is known.

The next question is how do we know the value of the constant d_{lens}? Directly measuring the distance between the two lenses might generate measuring error that introduces additional inaccuracy. However, we can see from Eq. 5 that the unknown scaling factor K is a linear function of $\frac{1}{x_1 - x_2}$. This also implies that, since all the cells on a service plane at distance P_z have the same scaling factor K, they must observe the same value of $x_1 - x_2$. Therefore, to more precisely determine the coefficient d_{lens}, we instead measure the true values of K and $\frac{1}{x_1 - x_2}$ at a few known receiver positions, and adopt linear regression to estimate d_{lens}.

[1]Note that, with our dual-lens design, a receiver still receives only one y-axis coordinate since the two lenses are placed side-by-side horizontally.

Given that the value of K is now known, the receiver can calculate its global position along the first two dimensions, P_x and P_y, based on Eq. 4. The receiver can further make use of some geometric properties to learn P_z, which is equal to the throw distance between the LCD origin and the plane where the receiver is located, denoted by $\overline{OR}$ as shown in Fig. 8. Using the property of similar triangles, we can estimate the distance $\overline{OR}$, i.e., the position along the z-axis P_z, by

$$P_z = \overline{OR} = \left(\frac{\overline{OL}}{d_x}\right) K, \tag{6}$$

where $\overline{OL}$ is the distance between the LCD plane and the lens center and d_x is the size of a pixel of the LCD along the x-axis. Again, the distance $\overline{OR}$ is a linear function of K, and we adopt linear regression to learn the constant coefficient $\frac{\overline{OL}}{d_x}$, which is independent of the receiver height, in a similar way[2]. In summary, by estimating the scaling factor K, the receiver can easily learn its three-dimensional global position (P_x, P_y, P_z) based on Eq. 4 and Eq. 6.

3.4 Dealing with Rotation

So far, we assume that the orientation of the polarizer in front of the receiving light sensor perfectly matches the orientation of the LCD in the transmitter (i.e., the relative angle $= 0°$). Thus, when the transmitter alternates the polarization angle of the emitted light beam between $0°$ and $90°$, the receiver can observe the maximum difference between received intensities (i.e., contrast) of these two states, according to Eq. 1. However, in reality, a receiver might have an arbitrary rotation with respect to the transmitter. Since the received intensity is determined by the inter-polarization angle between the polarization angle of the emitted light beam and the receiver's polarizer, with this additional rotation, the angle no longer alternates between $0°$ and $90°$. In the most critical case when the receiver is rotated to a relative angle of $45°$, the inter-polarization angle stays the same at $45°$ when a pixel is set to either a polarization angle of $0°$ or $90°$. As a result, the receiver observes the same intensity in both the bright and dark states and, therefore, can hardly recover the positioning signal.

To address this problem, we replace the receiver's polarizer with a *liquid crystal cell* (LCC) [2], i.e., a one-pixel LCD, which serves as an electronic polarizer. By applying different voltages to the LCC, we can rotate the polarizer orientation to any desirable angle

[2]This linear relationship will be destroyed if the conjunction point of the two lenses is not exactly aligned with the center of the LCD. This offset can be easily calibrated by geometric transformations. We skip the details due to space limitation.

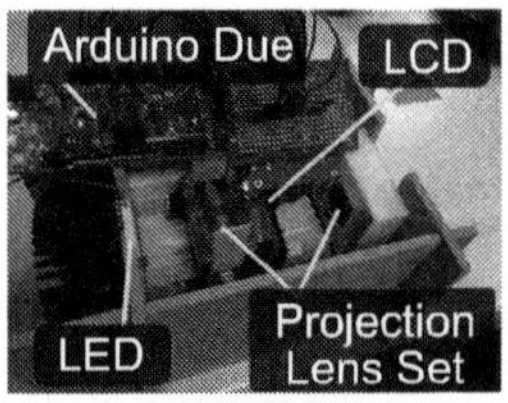

(a) Transmitter

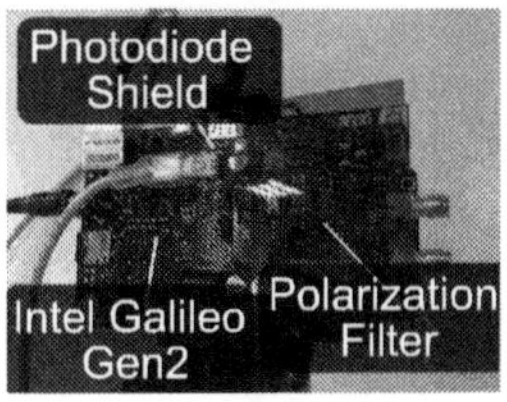

(c) Receiver

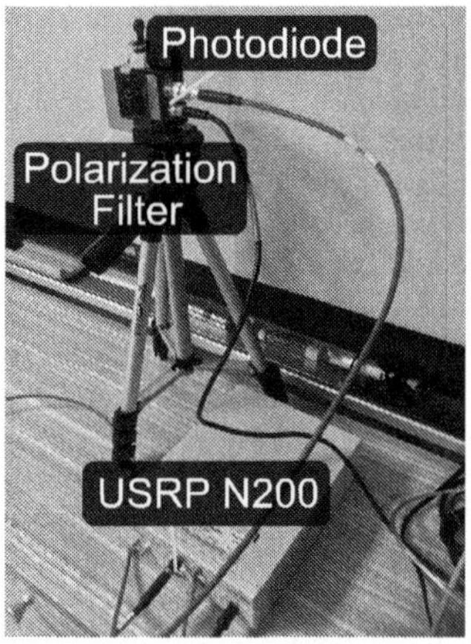

(b) Channel measurement receiver

Figure 10: STN prototype

between 0° and 180°.[3] Hence, by tuning the voltage of the LCC, we can search for a proper polarization angle that maximizes the contrast of the received intensities. To reduce the search complexity, in our implementation, we use only 11 LCC rotation angles. In addition, since it is time-consuming to receive the signal of a complete positioning cycle for every tested LCC rotation angle, to further reduce the search time, we apply the following optimization. For each tested rotation angle, the receiver only measures the maximum received intensity during a small fixed period of time, e.g., 50ms, which is much shorter than a positioning cycle. Then, after testing all candidate angles, the receiver rotates the LCC by the tested angle that reaches the maximum intensity during the whole testing interval, as shown in Fig. 9. The rationale behind this design is that the identified angle should be the one that switches the receiver's polarization such that the relative angle between its polarization direction and the LCD's polarization is closest to either 0° or 90°, thereby producing the maximum contrast.

Note that, due to our PPM signal design, for most of the time, CELLI's transmitter emits light beams with a polarization angle of 0°. Hence, the identified angle producing the maximum intensity is usually the one that best aligns the LCD's orientation and the direction of the receiver's electronic polarizer (i.e., relative angle = 0°), e.g., case A in Fig. 9. Then, the receiver can apply our decoding algorithm to detect the dark signals and estimate its location without any change. However, for a very special case where the receiver happens to observe the maximum intensity when the transmitting light beam is set to the 90° state, i.e., case B in Fig. 9, the relative angle between the LCD and the orientation of the receiver's electronic polarizer is approximately 90°. In this case, the receiver now observes the dark signals for most of time, while seeing the bright signals only when the transmitting light beam is switched to the 90° state. This, however, can be easily solved by taking the inverse of the bright-dark pattern, i.e., $y' = y_{\max} - y$, where y denotes the original received signals and $y_{\max}$ is the maximum intensity of the received signals. After such inversion, the receiver can again apply the normal decoding algorithm to find its location.

[3]A commodity LCC usually only supports rotation up to 90°. To further extend the supported range, we place two LCCs back-to-back to rotate the polarizer to any angle between 0° and 180°.

(a) Transmitter

(b) Receiver

Figure 11: CELLI prototype

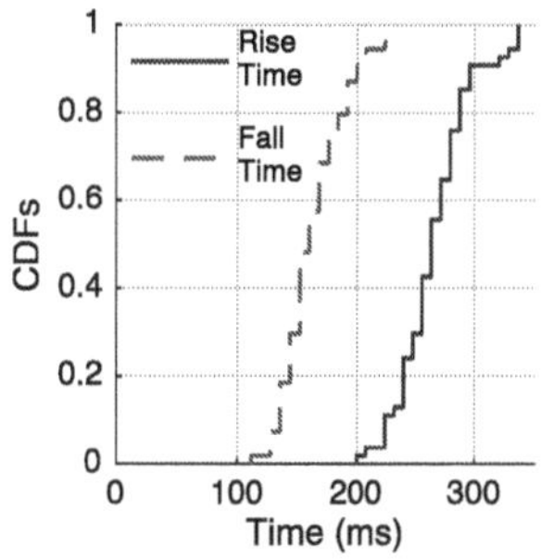

(a) STN

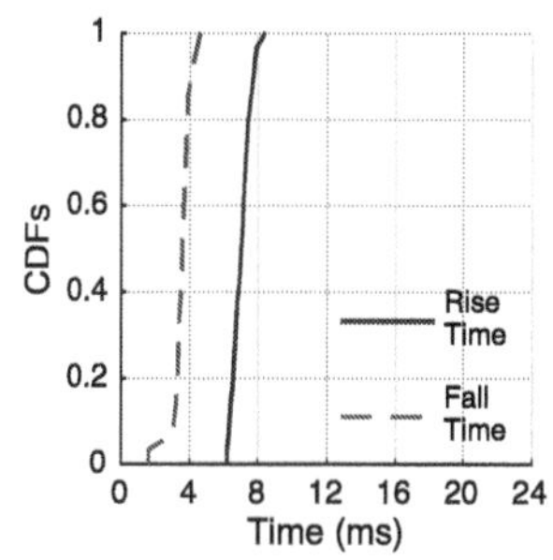

(b) TFT

Figure 12: Response time comparison. The response time of some LCDs is quite large, meaning that reducing the positioning latency is a critical challenge.

4. IMPLEMENTATION

We implement two prototypes of CELLI's transmitter (Tx), one using a passive LCD and the other using an active LCD to check how their characteristics (discussed in Sec. 2) affect CELLI's positioning accuracy. For the passive LCD, we use the STN (super-twisted nematic) LCD with a resolution of 128×64 pixels from NewHeaven Display [3], and control it by an Arduino development board, as shown in Fig. 10(a). For the active LCD, we use the TN (twisted nematic) TFT LCD with a resolution of 320×240 pixels and a controller built in from 4D Systems [1]. Both prototypes use XLamp® CXA2540 as the backlight LED, as shown in Fig. 11(a).

At the receiver side, we implement three different prototypes according to the characteristics of the optical channel. All the three receiver prototypes consist of a photodiode with human eye sensitivity, a polarization filter and a microprocessor. The first prototype is designed for benchmark channel measurement, where we use an experimental photodiode [7] as the receiver to increase the precision of channel characterizations, as shown in Fig. 10(b). For the STN Tx, we use SFH206K [4] as the receiving photodiode. Since the positioning cycle is longer, we choose Intel Galileo Gen2, which provides a larger memory size and computational power, as the motherboard, as shown in Fig. 10(c). Finally, since the TFT Tx features a shorter positioning cycle, we use a microprocessor [6] combined with a photodiode [5] to implement real-time positioning, as shown in Fig. 11(b).

5. RESULTS

In this section, we first conduct benchmark measurements to characterize two common types of LCDs, and check the feasibility of CELLI's dual lens design. Experiments are carried out in a typical conference room with normal daylight and all 12 light fixtures turned on. Each light fixture has four 14W T5 fluorescent tubes.

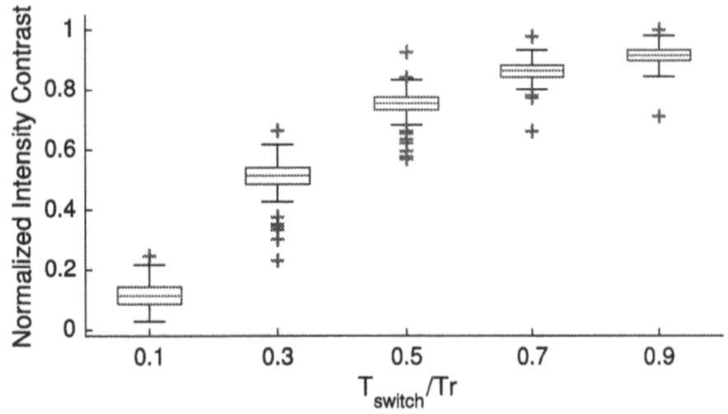

Figure 13: Impact of the state transition duration on the received intensity contrast. The intensity contrast drops significantly if an LCD pixel is not given sufficient time to change its state.

This represents a worst-case indoor scenario where both daylight and light fixtures add noises to the received signal. For ease of experiments, we place the transmitter horizontally, similar to how a projector is usually placed, and setup the receiver on the projected surface, set at distances 175 cm and 225 cm, respectively, away from the transmitting light. The two tested distances correspond to the typical distances between the ceiling and human shoulder or chest, respectively. The performance metrics used in our evaluation are defined as follows:

- *Normalized intensity:* It equals the ratio of the received intensity of a light signal to the maximum light intensity.
- *Signal strength:* The received raw signals are converted to the frequency domain signals via FFT. The signal strength is defined as the amplitude of the peak frequency.
- *Intensity contrast:* It is defined as the difference between the maximum and minimum received intensities.

5.1 Benchmark

As mentioned in Sec. 2.2, different types of LCDs could have very different characteristics. We first empirically compare both the passive STN LCD and the active TFT LCD in terms of the response time, cross-cell interference and the transmittance. We then check the performance of different sampling strategies as finding the regression models used in our dual-lens height estimation.

5.1.1 LCD Response Time

We first measure the duration required by each LCD pixel to complete a state transition.

Experiment setup: In this experiment, a region of 10 by 10 pixels at the center of the LCD flash at a frequency of 0.5 Hz (i.e., switching once every two seconds) for a backlight operating on the frequency of 1000 Hz. This flashing rate (0.5 Hz) is configured to guarantee that each LCD pixel can completely change its state so that the photodiode can measure the maximum intensity contrast between the dark and bright states of the received signals. To find the latency required to ensure a high enough intensity contrast, the transmitter performs 30 rounds of state transitions, and the receiver measures the time gap that the *normalized intensity contrast* raises from 10% to 90% or falls from 90% to 10%. Here, the normalized contrast is the expected contrast divided by the maximum contrast.

Results: Fig. 12 plots the CDFs of the response time for both types of LCDs. The results show that the response time of the STN LCD ranges from 100 ms to 250 ms, while the response time of the TFT LCD is no more than 8 ms. Due to this, the positioning cycle may be very long if we use an STN LCD. If we force the STN LCD to change the state faster than its response time, the achievable intensity contrast of the received signals would be greatly reduced, leading to a weak signal strength. To verify this point, we further measure the intensity contrast when the duration of state switching T_{switch} is smaller than the LCD's response time, denoted by T_r, and compare it to the maximum intensity contrast. Fig. 13 plots the *normalized* intensity contrasts, i.e., the measured contrasts divided by the maximum contrast, for various settings of T_{switch}. The results show that the intensity contrast decreases significantly even if the switching duration is only reduced to half of the response time. CELLI's PPM addresses this practical challenge by reducing the time interval of each switching time-slot but leveraging pre-switching to ensure that each state can still last for a long enough duration by setting $T_{\text{switch}}\delta$ equal to the response time. Hence, our design significantly shortens the positioning cycle, while still keeping the signal strength high.

5.1.2 Interference from Neighboring Cells

We next check whether the light signal from one LCD pixel to a cell will leak to the neighboring cells and degrade the signal recovery probability in those cells.

Experiment setup: In this experiment, a receiver is placed in the origin at distance 175 cm and 225 cm, respectively, apart from the transmitter. That is, the global location of the receiver is set to $(0, 0, 175)$ and $(0, 0, 225)$, respectively. We then let each of the 10 by 10 pixels at the center of the LCD *sequentially* transmit the modulated light signals, which switch between the states 0° and 90° at 0.5 Hz. Namely, at any point of time, only a single LCD pixel is transmitting. The receiver, locating in the origin $(0, 0)$, measures the strength of an interfering signal that steers its beam to a neighboring cell (x, y) rather than $(0, 0)$. Then, the measured signal strength is refereed to as the interference from cell (x, y) at the same height, i.e., on the same projected plane.

Results: As shown in Fig. 14, the leakage interference from an STN LCD is slightly less than that from a TFT LCD. Fig. 14(b) shows that, in the case of the TFT LCD at distance 175 cm, the interfering signal strength from the cells in the left-bottom corner is stronger. This is because the resolution of the TFT LCD is higher, making it more difficult to precisely deploy the receiver in a specific cell, i.e., the origin in our setting. As a result, the measured interference map is shifted a little bit due to this small deployment error. However, both types of LCDs generate nearly no interference, i.e., -10dB or less, to a neighboring cell 2 cm away. This confirms that the directionality of light beams from multiple pixels of an LCD is the key to make the success of CELLI's fine-grained positioning.

5.1.3 Transmittance

We now check how the intensity of the illuminating light source degrades as passing through the transmitter's LCD.

Experiment setup: We configure the backlight LED to transmit a 1000 Hz carrier wave. A receiver is placed in different cells at distance 225 cm. All the pixels of the LCD set their states to 0° such that the receiver would receive the maximum intensity from the light passing through the LCD. It then compares the intensity of the received signals when the LCD is installed and is removed, respectively. The received intensity is then normalized by the maximum intensity among all the measurements, which is then converted to decibel (dB).

Results: Fig. 15(a) and Fig. 15(b) illustrate the normalized intensity for the STN LCD and TFT LCD, respectively. The x-axis of the figure is the x-axis position of the receiver with respect to the origin of the coordinate system. The results show that the trans-

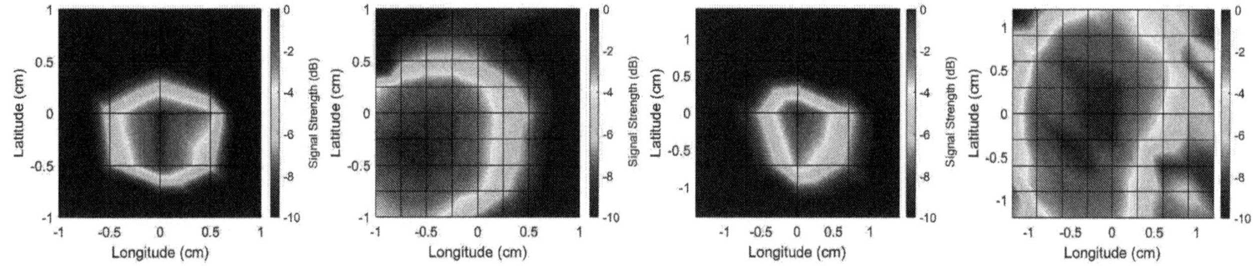

(a) STN LCD at 175cm (b) TFT LCD at 175cm (c) STN LCD at 225 cm (d) TFT LCD at 225 cm

Figure 14: Cross-cell leakage interference. Both types of LCDs generate nearly no interference, i.e., -10 dB or less, to a cell 2 cm away.

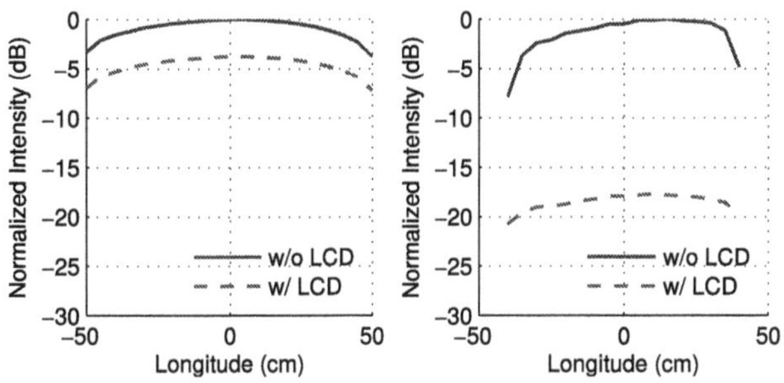

(a) STN (b) TFT

Figure 15: Transparency comparison. An TFT LCD locks a large amount of light. While the TFT LCD provides a better positioning accuracy, some additional light sources for illumination purpose might be required.

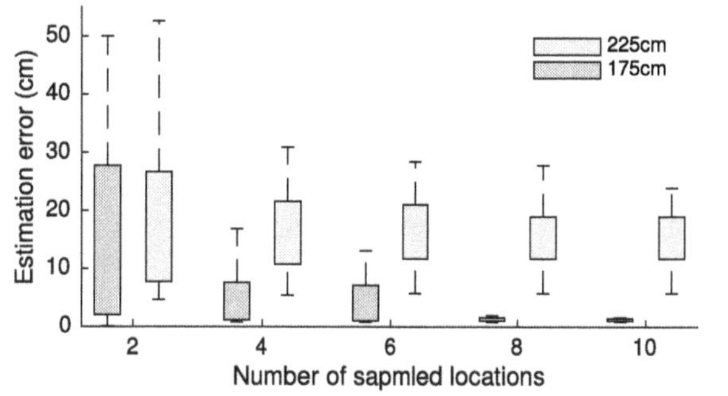

Figure 16: Fingerprinting cost. A small fingerprinting overhead allows us to train a very accurate regression model for height estimation.

mittance of the STN LCD is higher than that of the TFT LCD. By supporting CELLI's positioning service with the STN LCD, the intensity reduction is -3.7 dB, implying that the light intensity for illumination is reduced to around 43%. On the other hand, the TFT LCD introduces a much larger intensity reduction. Due to this intensity blockage effect, when the TFT LCD is used, it is likely that the transmitting light cannot be simultaneously used as illumination sources, and the environment would need some additional light sources for illumination purposes.

5.1.4 Fingerprinting cost

When CELLI is used only for 2D positioning, no prior training is required. For 3D positioning, as mentioned in Sec. 3.3, CELLI uses regression to learn the coefficients of the linear function converting a coordinate to the absolute position. This task needs to be performed for the transmitter only if the manufacturing error of lens configuration is not negligible, and can be done as part of the manufacturing process. To reduce the training cost, we now test how many location samples are sufficient for learning an accurate regression model.

Experiment setup: We adopt the TFT LCD in this experiment. A few positioning cells at heights 175cm and 225 cm, respectively, are sampled to train the regression model. An intuitive training method is to directly use the measured values (x_1-x_2) of randomly-selected fingerprint locations to train the regression model. However, noisy training data might degrade the accuracy of regression. Note that, as explained in Sec. 3.3, a receiver, in theory, observes the same coordinate difference $(x_1 - x_2)$ in all the cells at a given height. With this property, for each height, we instead find the median value of $(x_1 - x_2)$ of the sampled fingerprint locations to filter out the noisy data. Then, only the median values of $(x_1 - x_2)$ at the two heights are used to train the regression model. We compare the prediction accuracy as various numbers of fingerprint locations are sampled. For each setting, we repeat 50 rounds of random sampling and learn a regression model for each round of sampling. We then place the receiver in other cells to test the accuracy of the regression model.

Result: Fig. 16 shows the box plots of the height estimation errors when the number of training samples per height varies from 2 to 10. The results demonstrate that our regression-based estimation can achieve a very high accuracy as we only sample eight out of 320×240 cells to train the linear coefficient. It confirms that the fingerprint cost of learning the linear function is quite small. The results further show that the estimation error at height 225 cm is slightly larger than 175 cm. The main reason is that the dimension of each cell on the projected plane at 225 cm is larger than that at 175 cm. As a result, an error on coordinate detection translates to a larger height estimation error.

5.1.5 Impact of PPM Cycle Duration

We finally check how the duration of state switching T_{switch}, and thereby the positioning cycle, affects the positioning accuracy.

Experiment setup: We use the TFT LCD at the transmitter side and place the receiver in a randomly-selected cell at 225 cm. The switching duration T_{switch} is varied from 0.5 to 4 milliseconds, corresponding to a positioning cycle from 0.3 to 2.4 seconds. The pre-switching parameter δ should be updated according to T_{switch} such that the duration of the 90° state, δT_{switch}, can still be roughly the same with the LCD response time. For each setting, we repeat the experiment with different randomly-selected cells for 40 times.

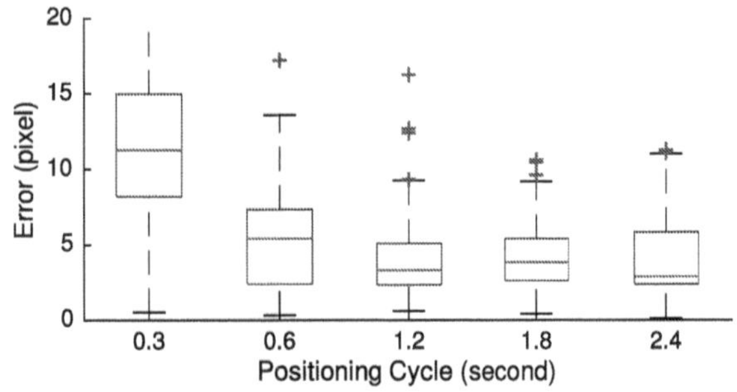

Figure 17: Impact of positioning cycle. With CELLI's pre-switching design, we reduce the positioning cycle to 0.6 s, but maintaining a comparable positioning accuracy.

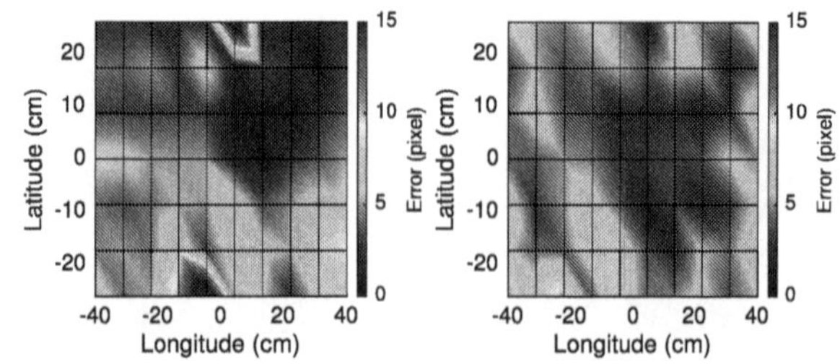

(a) Bit-pattern (b) PPM

Figure 18: Comparison between bit-pattern and PPM. The estimation error of bit-pattern and PPM are 4.18 pixels and 4.27 pixels, respectively, at height 225 cm.

Result: Fig. 17 shows the box plot of the coordinate estimation errors of all the measures for each tested positioning cycle. The results demonstrate that, though the transmitter ensures that the duration of the 90° state keeps constant, the positioning error still increases slightly when the positioning cycle is shorten. The main reason is that, while we are able to change the sampling rate of the transmitter, i.e.,$1/T_{\text{switch}}$, the sampling rate at the receiver, called r_{Rx}, is, however, a constant. As a result, the same error of identifying the sample index of the deep received signal will correspond to different coordinate estimation errors when T_{switch} varies. Consider an example that the true deep is the k-th received sample, but the receiver incorrectly detects the $(k-\epsilon)$-th received sample as the deep. Then, since CELLI's PPM uses the time-slot of the deep signal to represent the coordinate, the constant error time gap ϵ/r_{Rx} corresponds to more time-slots of the transmitter's state switching and, thereby a larger coordinate estimation error, when T_{switch} is smaller. However, we can see that the increase in coordinate detection errors is fairly small when we reduce the positioning cycle from 2.4 seconds to 0.6 seconds. Therefore, in our later evaluation, we set the positioning cycle to 0.6 seconds so as to achieve a balance between the positioning latency and accuracy.

5.2 Positioning Accuracy

We now conduct several experiments to evaluate the overall positioning performance of CELLI under different scenarios. The experiments are designed to answer the following questions:

- What is the positioning error in various cells at different heights, i.e., on different projected planes?
- How the types of LCDs (STN and TFT) affect the position accuracy?
- Does a receiver suffer from arbitrary rotation?

5.2.1 Comparison between Bit-pattern and PPM

We first compare the accuracy of the bit-pattern positioning signals and our PPM positioning signals.

Experiment Setup: We place a receiver in all the different cells at height 225 cm. Since the response time of the STN LCD is too long, a positioning cycle of the bit-pattern scheme would be more than 3 seconds, which is too long to realize practical positioning applications. We hence only evaluate the performance of the TFT LCD in this experiment. Since the bit-pattern scheme does not allow pre-switching, we cannot reduce the duration of state switching, T_{switch}, which is hence set to the inverse of the refresh rate of the TFT LCD, i.e., 100 ms. For our PPM scheme, we then reduce T_{switch} to 1 ms, but set the pre-switching parameter to $\delta = 12$. For each possible positioning cell, we collect ten measurements and output the average error.

Result: Fig. 18(a) and (b) plot the average 2D positioning errors of all the cells for bit-pattern and PPM, respectively. The median errors of the bit-pattern and PPM approaches are 1.22 cm (4.18 pixel) and 1.25 cm (4.27 pixel), respectively. Though the two schemes offer similar positioning accuracy, they, however, introduce a very different positioning latency. In particular, the positioning cycle of PPM is only 0.6 second, while the bit-pattern approach requires every pixel to take 1.8 seconds to deliver its coordinate.

5.2.2 Impact of the LCD types

We next check the positioning accuracy when different types of LCDs are applied in CELLI.

Experiment Setup: We place a receiver in all the different cells at height 175 cm and 225 cm, respectively, to receive the PPM signals from the transmitting light. Based on Fig. 12, the average response time of the STN LCD and the TFT LCD are 5.3 ms and 212 ms, respectively. Hence, for the STN LCD, we set T_{switch} to 5 ms and set the pre-switching parameter δ to 15. We choose these parameters to limit the entire positioning cycle within 2 seconds, which is the timing requirement of most practical positioning applications, while keeping δT_{switch} large enough to achieve an acceptable intensity contrast. As for the TFT LCD, we set $(T_{\text{switch}}, \delta) = (1\text{ ms}, 12)$, as mentioned in Sec. 5.1.5, to keep the positioning period short. Each pixel of the LCD is assigned a distinct coordinate. Therefore, the dimensions of each coordinate for the STN LCD and the TFT LCD are different, depending on their resolutions. The receiver repeats the positioning procedure 10 times in each cell and calculates the average positioning error.

Result: Fig. 19 plots the average 2D positioning errors of all the cells for the both LCDs in height 175 cm and 225 cm, respectively. The results show that both LCDs achieve a fairly accurate positioning with an median error lower than 3 cm, regardless of the positioning height. The TFT LCD achieves a higher accuracy since the TFT LCD offers a much higher resolution than the STN LCD. For the STN LCD, the errors in the top area are slightly larger due to the imperfection of the optical components. In particular, since the intensity of the light passing through the projection lens is usually not uniform, this non-uniform transmittance leads to non-uniform errors in both height configurations. The problem can be alleviated by using better optical components.

5.2.3 Impact of Receiver Rotation

We next check whether a receiver with rotation can still find its location.

Experiment setup: In this experiment, the transmitter uses the TFT LCD. We place a receiver in 10 different cells at height 225 cm. In each cell, the receiver rotates to different orientations, and ap-

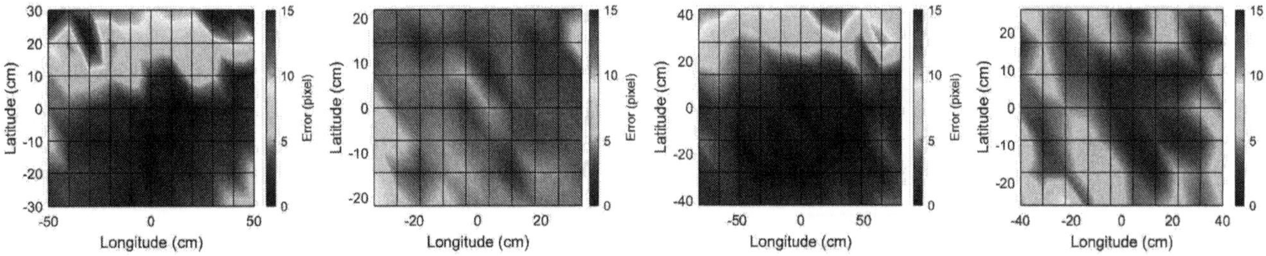

(a) STN LCD at 175cm (b) TFT LCD at 175cm (c) STN LCD at 225 cm (d) TFT LCD at 225 cm

Figure 19: Performance of both LCD types. Both LCDs achieve a fairly high positioning accuracy with a median error lower than 3 cm.

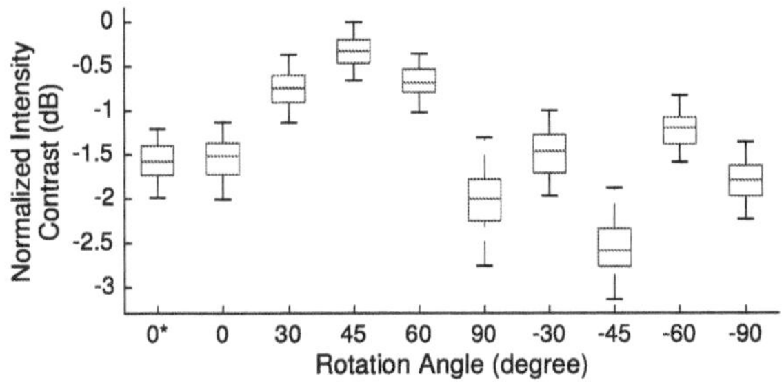

Figure 20: Impact of rotation. By dynamically adapting the receiver's polarizer direction, the achievable intensity contrast becomes similar for any receiver orientation. (The index 0* means the case where both the orientation and the polarizer direction of a receiver is 0° and the LC adaptation is disabled.)

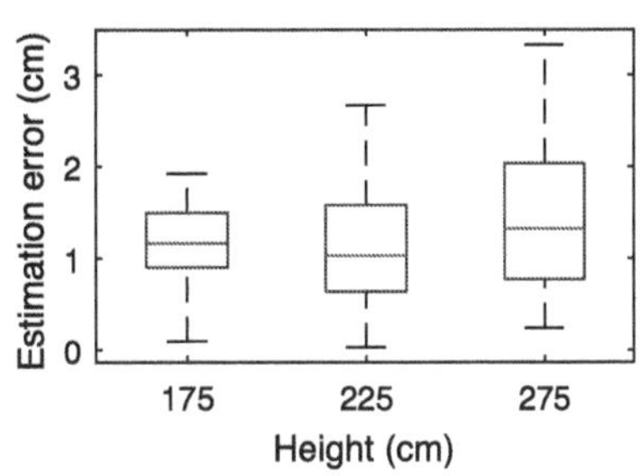

Figure 21: Impact of positioning height. The estimation errors of all heights in common indoor environment are all very small, with median error less than 1.5 cm.

plies the algorithm mentioned in Sec. 3.4 to adjust the polarization direction of its LC. We also measure the received intensity when the receiver has no rotation and does not apply the LC as baseline for comparison. The effectiveness of LC adjustment is evaluated in terms of the intensity contrast.

Result: The results in Fig. 20 show that, by testing a few sampled LC angles, the receiver can automatically configure its polarization direction to achieve a intensity contrast comparable to that of the baseline no-rotation scenario. The median reduction of the intensity contrast is no more than 2dB. A receiver can, hence, reliably recover the PPM signals and estimate its coordinate even if it rotates to an arbitrary orientation.

5.2.4 *Impact of Positioning Height*

We next check whether the positioning height affects the positioning accuracy.

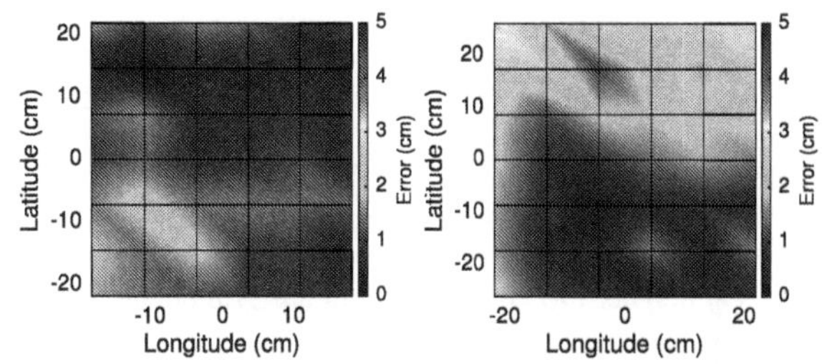

(a) height=175 cm (b) height=225 cm

Figure 22: 2D positioning error. CELLI achieves a median error 1.07 cm and 1.59 cm at height 175 cm and 225 cm, respectively.

Experiment setup: In this experiment, the transmitter uses the TFT LCD. Other than the heights of 175 and 225 cm, we further test a more challenging case of height 275cm, which is almost the longest distance in typical indoor environments. We place the receiver in 12 randomly selected cells at these three heights.

Result: The results in Fig. 21 show that CELLI can provide extremely accurate positioning at all common positioning distances in indoor enviroments. The median positioning errors at height 175, 225, and 275 cm are 1.17, 1.03, and 1.32 cm respectively. This is because CELLI utilizes PPM to modulate the positioning information, which could tolerate low SNR and hence can perform reliably even when the height increases and the intensity gets smaller in the 275cm case.

5.2.5 *Accuracy of 2D and 3D Positioning*

We finally check CELLI's positioning accuracy.

Experiment setup: In this experiment, the transmitter uses the TFT LCD with the pre-switching parameter $\delta = 12$ and the switching duration $T_{\text{switch}} = 1$ ms, while the receiver is deployed at heights 175 cm and 225 cm, respectively. The receiver applies the proposed LC-based polarization adaptation and the dual-lens coordinate-to-position conversion schemes to find its global location.

Result: We first demonstrate the 2D positioning accuracy in Fig. 22. The results show that the 2D positioning error is 1.6 cm on average and 3.3 cm at worst. This implies that, assuming the height of a position area is given (which is a reasonable assumption for some IoT applications, such as smart factories), CELLI can provide extremely fine-grained positioning. Fig. 23 illustrates the 3D positioning errors when the height of a receiver is unknown and is estimated based on Eq. 6. The results show that the positioning errors is higher as compared to 2D positioning. The root cause is that the x-axis and y-axis positions are estimated based on only Eq. 5. However, the z-axis coordinate P_z is estimated from both Eq. 5 and

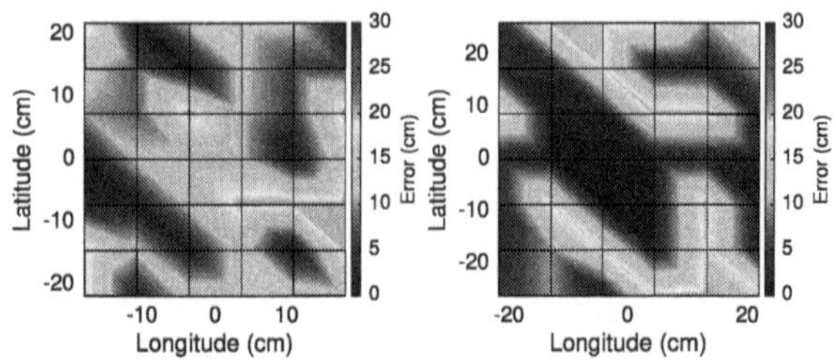

(a) height=175 cm (b) height=225 cm

Figure 23: 3D positioning error. Though the error along the z-dimension is slightly larger, CELLI can still provide sub-meter accuracy. The median errors at height 175 cm and 225 cm, respectively, are 11.81 and 2.65 cm respectively.

Eq. 6. Hence, the aggregated errors of the coefficients in the both equations caused by regression increase the positioning errors in the z-dimension, which have been confirmed in Fig. 16. Even with a slightly higher height estimation error, the accuracy of CELLI's overall 3D positioning is still fairly high. The median 3D positioning errors at heights 175 cm and 225 cm are 11.8 cm and 2.7 cm, respectively.

6. RELATED WORK

We categorize the existing works on indoor visible light positioning to camera-based and photodiode-based approaches.

Light-to-Camera Positioning: PIXEL [24] uses a single-pixel LCD and a disperser in front of a light source to disperse the polarized lights of different wavelength, i.e., different colors, along different light oscillation directions. By attaching the second polarizer to a receiving camera, the camera can observe different colors form different light sources and estimate the Angle-of-Arrival (AoA) of each light according to the received color. By collecting the AoA of more than three light sources, CELLI leverages conventional AoA-based positioning algorithms to identify its own location. However, the positioning error of AoA-based positioning algorithms is typically up to tens of centimeters. Some other works [12, 14, 15, 25] utilize computer vision and triangulation techniques to estimate the location of a camera based on the location of multiple lights captured in an image. The above approaches all require multiple light sources, increasing the deployment overhead and cost. Moreover, those solutions usually introduce a significant overhead on image processing, and the estimation may fail in complex environments where the light sources in the image cannot be reliably located. More importantly, the positioning resolution of the above camera-based solutions heavily rely on the resolution of a captured image. They may perform worse for low-resolution cameras or even cannot be applied on single-pixel photodiodes. Also, camera-based technologies may be suitable for human positioning, but not object positioning, in which energy consumption and computational overhead are major concerns.

Light-to-Photodiode Positioning: Some works [11, 27] migrate the idea of RF-based triangulation to optical channels. In [11], a receiver estimates its location based on the signal strength received from at least three transmitting lights operating in different frequencies. Benefiting from the independent, clear and low multipath channel characteristics of visible light, the positioning error can be much smaller than RF-based triangulation, e.g., 2 centimeters. It, however, requires a 3-LED transmitting array in each 60 cm by 60 cm cell to perform positioning. In addition, the work does not evaluate how the interference from neighboring cells affects the positioning performance. SpinLight [23] covers the infrared light source by a 3D-printed spinning lampshade with holes. By explicitly designing the patterns of printed holes, the light source can only pass through those holes and projects bright-dark patterns onto a positioning service area such that a receiving photodiode can estimate its location based on the received light intensity. However, this design can only use infrared, which is imperceptible to human eyes, but not common LED lights. Otherwise, human eyes will visually see the patterns shaded by the lampshade. In addition, this system can only allow a receiver to estimate its coordinate, instead of the global 3D location. By contrast, CELLI is a pioneer work that needs only a single light source and a single-pixel photodiode to enable 3D positioning.

7. DISCUSSION

This section briefly discusses the limitations of this work and potential directions for future research.

Range (throw-distance). Our experimental results report the positioning accuracy within typical throw distances of 175, 225, and 275 cm, respectively corresponding to ceiling to user's shoulder, chest, and floor distances in the common case of 3 meter ceiling height. Although not evaluated in this paper, in less common settings with larger ceiling height, despite lower received signal strength, we expect similar positioning accuracy due to the energy efficient PPM scheme. The output power of the backlight can also be increased to compensate for the larger range, which could also be required for illumination purposes.

Service area. Our implementation has a service area of 160 cm by 84 cm (with 225 cm throw distance). If a larger service area is desired, a projection lens with smaller focal length can be used, allowing CELLI to produce a larger projection, at the cost of decreased signal strength. An alternative approach is to use multiple CELLI transmitters such that positioning can be performed at any of their service areas. Different transmitters use different preambles and data frequencies such that a receiver can demodulate the signal at possible frequencies and locate itself correctly even if some service areas overlap.

RX and TX instrumentation. As mentioned in Sec. 4, we built our prototypes with off-the-shelf components. In other words, many components were not customized for the system and far from optimized in both size and efficiency. In real application scenarios, a transmitter could be further compressed into a light bulb size by carefully choosing the guiding lens of proper focal length, while a receiver could be implemented by only a chip composed of low-cost photodiode, a MCU, and a small battery.

Comparison to RFID. Past works have shown that RFID can be used for fairly accurate indoor positioning in both line-of-sight and non-line-of-sight cases, and its tags do not require an energy source. CELLI, on the other hand, also has a few advantages over RFID. First, multipath propagation is less prominent for optical signals, and therefore CELLI can have good accuracy in a wider range of environments. Second, CELLI utilizes the lighting infrastructure, and potentially can reduce the cost to deploy transmitters compared to deploying RFID readers.

Some future works could overcome CELLI's limitations. CELLI receiver can be modified to use a small solar panel [13] to provide its power, eliminating the need for an energy source. In addition, although the optical signal processing scheme in CELLI receiver currently runs on an off-the-shelf microprocessor, its low complexity provides opportunities for easy generation of an application-specific integrated circuit (ASIC), enabling a low-cost, energy-efficient receiver solution comparable to passive RFID tags.

8. CONCLUSION

In this paper, we present CELLI, an accurate indoor positioning system using only a single custom light as the transmitter and a simple light sensor as the receiver, making our designs applicable even for energy-constrained small objects. By utilizing the high spatial resolution of an LCD, CELLI can emit a large number of narrow but interference-free light beams that project distinct positioning information to different cells in a service area. CELLI combines a novel pre-switching mechanism with PPM to significantly shorten the positioning cycle, and furthers leverage a dual-lens design to support 3D positioning even using only a single transmitting light. We demonstrate via testbed experiments that CELLI achieves a centimeter-level 3D positioning accuracy, and the error of 2D positioning can be 3.3 cm at worst.

9. ACKNOWLEDGEMENT

This research was supported in part by the Ministry of Science and Technology of Taiwan (MOST 106-2633-E-002-001, MOST 104-2628-E-009-014-MY2), National Taiwan University (NTU-10 6R104045), Intel Corporation, and Delta Electronics.

10. REFERENCES

[1] 4D Systems | uLCD-28PTU. http://www.4dsystems.com.au.

[2] Good Display | GDC8811. http://www.good-display.com.

[3] NHD-C12864GG-RN-GBW. http://www.newhavendisplay.com.

[4] OSRAM Opto Semiconductors | SFH 206 K | PIN Photodiodes in Through hole. http://www.osram-os.com/os.

[5] OSRAM Opto Semiconductors | SFH 2430 | SMT PIN Photodiodes . http://www.osram-os.com/os.

[6] STM32F405RG - High-performance foundation line. http://www.st.com/content/st_com/en.html.

[7] Thorlabs | PDA100A Si Switchable Gain Detector. https://www.thorlabs.com.

[8] J. Armstrong, Y. A. Sekercioglu, and A. Neild. Visible light positioning: a roadmap for international standardization. *IEEE Communications Magazine*, 51(12):68–73, December 2013.

[9] J. Hamkins. Pulse position modulation. *Handbook of Computer Networks: Key Concepts, Data Transmission, and Digital and Optical Networks, Volume 1*, pages 492–508, 2007.

[10] A. Jha. *A Textbook of Applied Physics*, volume 1. IK International Pvt Ltd, 2009.

[11] H.-S. Kim, D.-R. Kim, S.-H. Yang, Y.-H. Son, and S.-K. Han. An indoor visible light communication positioning system using a RF carrier allocation technique. *Journal of Lightwave Technology*, 31(1):134–144, 2013.

[12] Y.-S. Kuo, P. Pannuto, K.-J. Hsiao, and P. Dutta. Luxapose: Indoor positioning with mobile phones and visible light. In *ACM MobiCom*, 2014.

[13] J. Li, A. Liu, G. Shen, L. Li, C. Sun, and F. Zhao. Retro-VLC: Enabling Battery-free Duplex Visible Light Communication for Mobile and IoT Applications. In *Proceedings of the 16th International Workshop on Mobile Computing Systems and Applications*, HotMobile '15, pages 21–26, New York, NY, USA, 2015.

[14] L. Li, P. Hu, C. Peng, G. Shen, and F. Zhao. Epsilon: A visible light based positioning system. In *USENIX NSDI*, 2014.

[15] M. S. Rahman, M. M. Haque, and K.-D. Kim. Indoor positioning by led visible light communication and image sensors. *International Journal of Electrical and Computer Engineering*, 1(2):161, 2011.

[16] N. Rajagopal, P. Lazik, and A. Rowe. Visual light landmarks for mobile devices. In *Proceedings of the 13th international symposium on Information processing in sensor networks*. IEEE Press, 2014.

[17] T. Scheffer and J. Nehring. Supertwisted nematic (stn) liquid crystal displays. *Annual Review of Materials Science*, 27(1):555–583, 1997.

[18] L. Shangguan and K. Jamieson. The design and implementation of a mobile rfid tag sorting robot. In *ACM MobiSys*, 2016.

[19] L. Shangguan, Z. Li, Z. Yang, M. Li, and Y. Liu. Otrack: Order tracking for luggage in mobile rfid systems. In *2013 Proceedings IEEE INFOCOM*, 2013.

[20] J. Wang, F. Adib, R. Knepper, D. Katabi, and D. Rus. Rf-compass: Robot object manipulation using rfids. In *ACM MobiCom*, 2013.

[21] J. Wang and D. Katabi. Dude, where's my card?: Rfid positioning that works with multipath and non-line of sight. In *ACM SIGCOMM*, 2013.

[22] J. Wang, D. Vasisht, and D. Katabi. Rf-idraw: Virtual touch screen in the air using rf signals. In *ACM SIGCOMM*, 2014.

[23] B. Xie, G. Tan, and T. He. Spinlight: A high accuracy and robust light positioning system for indoor applications. In *ACM SenSys*, 2015.

[24] Z. Yang, Z. Wang, J. Zhang, C. Huang, and Q. Zhang. Wearables can afford: Light-weight indoor positioning with visible light. In *ACM MobiSys*, 2015.

[25] M. Yoshino, S. Haruyama, and M. Nakagawa. High-accuracy positioning system using visible LED lights and image sensor. In *IEEE Radio and Wireless Symposium*, pages 439–442, 2008.

[26] Y. Zhao, Y. Liu, and L. M. Ni. Vire: Active rfid-based localization using virtual reference elimination. In *2007 International Conference on Parallel Processing (ICPP 2007)*, 2007.

[27] Z. Zhou, M. Kavehrad, and P. Deng. Indoor positioning algorithm using light-emitting diode visible light communications. *Optical Engineering*, 51(8):085009–1–085009–6, 2012.

Poster: Multicamera Synchronization for Smartphones using Optimally Modulated Illuminations

Koki Kudo Masanori Sugimoto
Hokkaido University
Sapporo, Japan
{kudou@main, sugi@}ist.hokudai.ac.jp

Takayuki Akiyama Hiromichi Hashizume
SOKENDAI/ NII
Hayama/Tokyo, Japan
{tak, has}@nii.ac.jp

ABSTRACT

The paper describes a rapid and accurate time-synchronization technique for smartphones using their built-in cameras and its preliminary evaluations for application development.

Keywords

Smartphone, camera synchronization, LED illumination

1. INTRODUCTION

The proposed technique is applicable to a motion-capture, 3D video or a pseudo high-speed camera system using multiple smartphone built-in cameras by controlling their shutter timings. Existing time-synchronization techniques (e.g.[1]) are assumed to be run on a realtime OS, or need long time because of frequent message exchanges between devices. Achieving rapid and accurate time-synchronization is hence difficult. We reported a time-difference estimation technique between a LED light and a 60 fps camera, and achieved 0.0174 ms estimation errors at the 90th percentile using 4 frames (0.067 sec)[2]. We extended this technique and conducted preliminary evaluations using smartphones.

2. PROPOSED TECHNIQUE

An optimally modulated signal emitted from a LED and its time difference t_D ($0 \leq t_D < 1/f_S$) from a camera is derived theoretically, if given the camera frame rate f_S, exposure time ratio η and intensity values of four consecutive frames (see [2] for details). The synchronization of a LED and a smartphone is conducted by first obtaining t_D, setting the camera frame rate to $f_S^{'} = 1/(2/f_S - t_D)$ ($f_S^{'} < f_S$) and then returning to f_S. Synchronizing multiple smartphones is conducted individually in the same manner.

3. EXPERIMENTS AND FUTURE PLAN

Apple iPhone 6s and iPhone 7 Plus were used. A LED (OptoSupply OSB56A5111A) connected to a function generator (NF Corporation, WF1948) emitted an optimally modulated signal for a camera with parameters $\eta = 0.50$ and $f_S = 60$ (Hz). The time synchronization software was programmed with Swift3.0. Cumulative distribution functions (CDFs) of time synchronization errors in a no ambient light setting is shown in Figure 1 (a). The proposed technique using iPhone 6s and iPhone 7 Plus achieved 0.176 ms and 0.160 ms errors at the 90th percentile, respectively. From Figure 1 (b), errors and standard deviations did not change remarkably by repeating time synchronization calculations. Figure 1 (c) shows the time drifts of the smartphones after the completion of their synchronization were stable and different from each other, which must be considered in developing applications.

The following issues are to be investigated: (1) efficient methods for synchronizing heterogeneous smartphones (different models, vendors and camera parameters) and (2) useful applications. For example, a 120 fps pseudo high-speed camera was configured by using the two smartphones whose shutter release timing difference was adjusted to 1/120 sec (Figure 2).

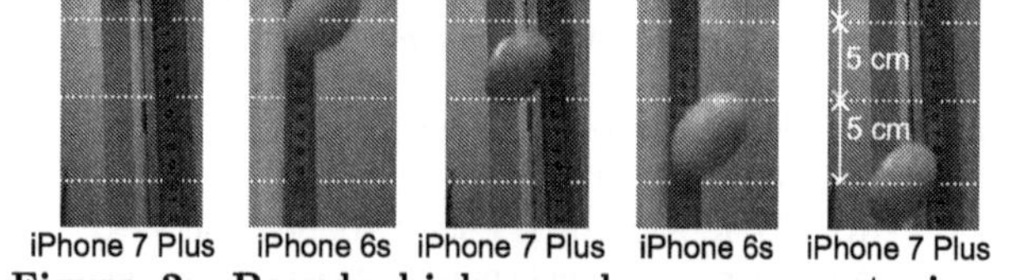

Figure 1: (a)CDFs (b) Errors and standard deviations ($n = 100$) and (c) Time drifts

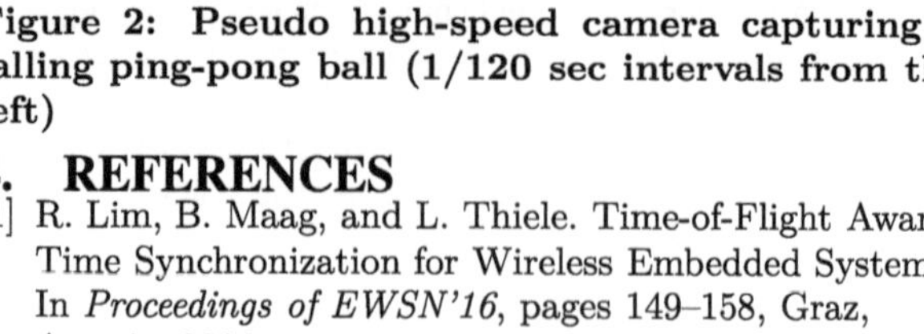

Figure 2: Pseudo high-speed camera capturing a falling ping-pong ball (1/120 sec intervals from the left)

4. REFERENCES

[1] R. Lim, B. Maag, and L. Thiele. Time-of-Flight Aware Time Synchronization for Wireless Embedded Systems. In *Proceedings of EWSN'16*, pages 149–158, Graz, Austria, 2016.

[2] M. Sugimoto, H. Kumaki, T. Akiyama, and H. Hashizume. Optimally Modulated Illumination for Rapid and Accurate Time Synchronization. *IEEE Transactions on Signal Processing*, 65(2):505–516, 2017.

Permission to make digital or hard copies of part or all of this work for personal or classroom use is granted without fee provided that copies are not made or distributed for profit or commercial advantage and that copies bear this notice and the full citation on the first page. Copyrights for third-party components of this work must be honored. For all other uses, contact the owner/author(s).

MobiSys'17 June 19-23, 2017, Niagara Falls, NY, USA

© 2017 Copyright held by the owner/author(s).

ACM ISBN 978-1-4503-4928-4/17/06.

DOI: http://dx.doi.org/10.1145/3081333.3089292

Poster: Sdguard — An Android Application Implementing Privacy Protection and Ransomware Detection

Shuangxi Hong Chuanchang Liu Bingfei Ren Junliang Chen
hongshuangxi_2008@126.com{lcc3265, rbf, chjl}@bupt.edu.cn
State Key Laboratory of Networking and Switching Technology of
Beijing University of Posts and Telecommunications
Beijing, 100876, China

Keywords
Android System; FUSE Filesystem; Permission Control; Ransomware

Currently, the smartphone has become an essential communication and amusement tool, which has strong computing power and a variety of functions. Especially, the market share of smartphone with android system account for 84% in 2016[1]. Under android system, a large of privacy data (e.g. photos or videos) are stored in external storage (emulated Sdcard storage), which can be accessed by installed apps. This not only results in privacy leakage but also incurs ransomware attack[2] (e.g. simplocker). Therefore, we present Sdguard, an app, can implement fine-grain permission control based on Linux DAC mechanism, and detect ransomware which encrypts content of file stored in external storage or lock user screen.

To install Sdguard app, we need to ensure that the smartphone has been rooted and use FUSE filesystem on external storage. During installing, sdcard daemon of android (i.e. FUSE daemon) is replaced by our customized sdcard daemon. After rebooting system, the customized daemon is loaded, and each component of Sdguard is running.

Figure 1 shows the architecture of the Sdguard app, which consists of two service components (activity stack monitor and I/O log analyzer) and an access control list. When an app creates a file, the customized FUSE daemon modifies owner and group of the file according to UID and GID of the app. Meanwhile, when an app read or write a file, the module of permission checker verifies its UID and permission to determine access action (allowing or refusing). I/O recorder can record all I/O operations to external storage, and then write log to a file. I/O log analyzer parses log file to try finding malicious action. We also create some decoy files which can be accessed by installed apps. We can find one type of ransomware which encrypts file. User can set some specific access rules to installed apps through access control list. This can meet some personal demand of user. The activity stack monitor service is in charge of monitoring activity stack of android system. The monitor only observes an activity which locates top stack. When finding an activity of certain app except lock-screen app (android system app) locates top stack for long time, we may think the app is ransomware which can lock user screen and kill its process to eliminate threat.

Permission to make digital or hard copies of part or all of this work for personal or classroom use is granted without fee provided that copies are not made or distributed for profit or commercial advantage and that copies bear this notice and the full citation on the first page. Copyrights for third-party components of this work must be honored. For all other uses, contact the Owner/Author.
MobiSys'17, June 19-23, 2017, Niagara Falls, NY, USA
© 2017 Copyright is held by the owner/author(s)
ACM ISBN 978-1-4503-4928-4/17/06.
http://dx.doi.org/10.1145/3081333.3089293

To enable monitoring activity stack, and starting automatically, the Sdguard application must delear related permissions, such as GET_TASK and RECEIVE_BOOT_COMPLETED. In short, the Sdguard app may be easily installed by manual way or OTA on the most of android version, and prevent privacy leakage from external storage. A user can grant/revoke certain permissions to an installed application through modifying Access control list. In addition, the Sdguard also effectively eliminate influence of ransomware.

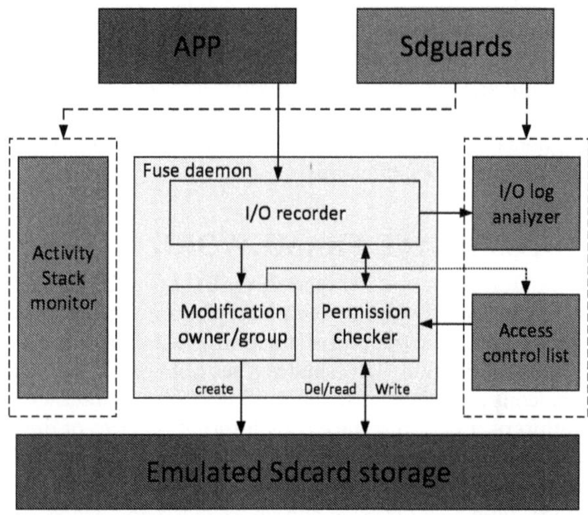

Figure 1: Sdguard app architecture and its component

This work has been sponsored by National Natural Science Foundation of China under (Grant No. U1536112), National Grand Fundamental Research 973 Program of China under (Grant No. 2013CB329102). The authors would also like to thank reviewers for their constructive comments.

REFERENCES

[1] 2016. android OS of global smartphone shipments.[Online]. Available: https://www.statista.com/statistics/236027/globalsmartphone-os-market-share-of-android/

[2] ANDRONIO, N., ZANERO, S., and MAGGI, F., 2015. HelDroid: Dissecting and Detecting Mobile Ransomware. In *Research in Attacks, Intrusions, and Defenses: 18th International Symposium, RAID 2015, Kyoto, Japan,November 2-4, 2015. Proceedings*, H. BOS, F. MONROSE and G. BLANC Eds. Springer International Publishing, Cham, 382-404. DOI= http://dx.doi.org/10.1007/978-3-319-26362-5_18.

Poster: MobiTemplate: A Template-based Rapid Cross-Platform Mobile Application Development Environment

Yimeng Feng, Bo Cheng, Shuai Zhao, Zhongyi Zhai, Zhaoning Wang, Meng Niu, Junliang Chen
State Key Laboratory of Networking and Switching Technology
Beijing University of Posts and Telecommunications, Beijing, China
fyimeng@bupt.edu.cn, chengbo@bupt.edu.cn

1. INTRODUCTION

Customizable mobile services are usually expressed with complex services composed of different atomic services. Fine-grained atomic mobile services are not so convenient for end users to reuse. Considering that in identical or similar service domains, a great deal of the business logics and functions are reusable within the scope. So we present a template-based framework to allow reuse of services and to achieve rapid mobile application development. The reusable fine-grained service logics and functions are encapsulated into comparatively coarse-grained templates, from which the designers can create the personalized composite services and edit the templates efficiently.

2. TEMPLATE FRAMEWORK

MobiTemplate = <TemplateInfo, UI, Local Interface, Remote Interface, Logic>. TemplateInfo is a set of the basic information of the templates, including its name, description and related domain. UI includes a set of bars, including buttons, icons and diagrams, which allows users to interact with computers. Local Interface calls internal services of devices, including camera, wifi and location. Remote Interface connects to services of the third party, such as video analyzing service, phone call service and short message service. Logic expresses the order of atomic services, such as sequential logic and combinational logic.

At (a) part of the Figure, it describes the process from extracting identical or similar services into templates. Templates are divided by different domain and the templates can be reused in identical or similar domain. The (b) part of the Figure shows the process of creating a template. The five red circle are the components of MobiTemplate. Also this environment can generate cross-platform mobile applications, which refers to our previous work: EasyApp.[1] Buttons in the blue circle can create mobile device installation packages. EasyApp allows end-users to develop mobile applications by native APIs. While, MobiTemplate separates similar and identical domains of services into templates. Using templates instead of using native APIs can reduce time of mobile application development.

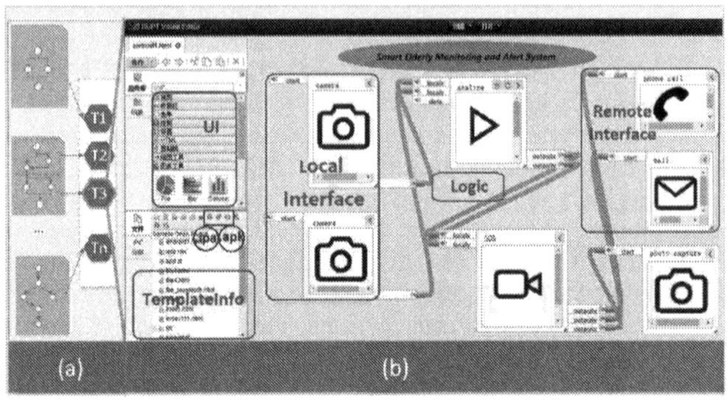

Figure 1: A template framework

Smart devices at home can help us live comfortably and it consists of many scenarios. As shown in the (b) part of the figure, we implement a template named Smart Elderly Monitoring and Alert System (SEMAS) as an example. Firstly, two cameras at home monitor the safety of the elderly. Secondly, the video analyzing service is called. Thirdly, an emergency program is invoked if the analyzing service reports anomaly. Fourthly, three services (a call, a short message, and a screenshot service from cameras) are used to inform caregivers. Cameras are invoked through local Interface, phone call service and short message service are invoked from the third party (Remote Interface). The combination of each service names the logic in MobiTemplate.

Permission to make digital or hard copies of part or all of this work for personal or classroom use is granted without fee provided that copies are not made or distributed for profit or commercial advantage and that copies bear this notice and the full citation on the first page. Copyrights for third-party components of this work must be honored. For all other uses, contact the owner/author(s).

MobiSys'17 June 19-23, 2017, Niagara Falls, NY, USA

© 2017 Copyright held by the owner/author(s).

ACM ISBN 978-1-4503-4928-4/17/06.
DOI: http://dx.doi.org/10.1145/3081333.3089294

3. ACKNOWLEDGEMENTS

The research reported in this paper is supported by National High-tech R&D Program of China (863 Program) under Grant No. 2013AA102301; National Grand Fundamental Research 973 Program of China under Grant No. 2013CB329102 (Corresponding author: Bo Cheng)

4. REFERENCES

[1] Z. Wang, B. Cheng, Z. Zhai, Y. Jin, Y. Feng, and J. Chen. Easyapp: A cross-platform mobile applications development environment based on osgi. In *Proceedings of the 2016 conference on ACM SIGCOMM 2016 Conference*, 2016.

Poster: Mobile Power Management Using FreeRTOS-based Uninterruptable Generator Supply

Chulju Lee
Dept. Computer Science & Engineering
Hanyang University, Ansan 15588, Korea
chlee0709@hanyang.ac.kr

Kyungtae Kang
Dept. Computer Science & Engineering
Hanyang University, Ansan 15588, Korea
ktkang@hanyang.ac.kr

ABSTRACT

Current designs of battery-powered uninterruptible power supplies only provide power for a short time, and offer few control options. We combined a compact synchronous generator with a battery with 10% of the capacity of a UPS of the same rating to produce an uninterruptible generator supply (UGS). The controller of this UGS runs FreeRTOS, which enables it to respond quickly to a power outage. A wifi module provides connectivity to a web server for real-time monitoring and management on a remote PC or cellphone.

CCS Concepts

•Computer systems organization → Real-time operating systems; Real-time operating systems; •Software and its engineering → Power management;

Keywords

Mobile power management; FreeRTOS; UGS

1. MOBIL POWER MANAGEMENT

Fig. 1 is a block diagram of our UGS and its management module. The controller, which has an ARM Cortex-M4 core running FreeRTOS^{TM} [1], monitors the supply and the battery state. When an outage occurs, energy from the battery is used to support the load while a compact synchronous generator is started.

The controller also transmits the status of the UGS to a web server, which can start and stop the generator. We used Python and Tornado to develop this server, and the data from the UGS are stored in a PostgreSQL database. Fig. 2a shows a chart of the status over time produced by an implementation of this server on a laptop. Finally, a user can monitor and control the UGS using a smartphone which accesses the server over the web, as shown in Fig. 2b.

Fig. 2c shows a prototype of our FreeRTOS-based UGS for mobile power management. In experiments with this prototype, it was demonstrated that it provided convenience for users and reduced the maintenance costs when managing power. Furthermore, the output voltage exhibited a stable waveform, as shown in Fig. 2d, which means that good quality power was supplied to load from our UGS in real time, in the case of a power outage.

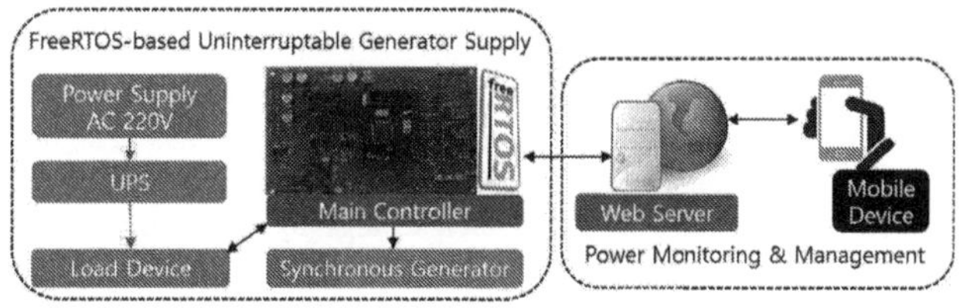

Figure 1: Block diagram of proposed mobile power management system.

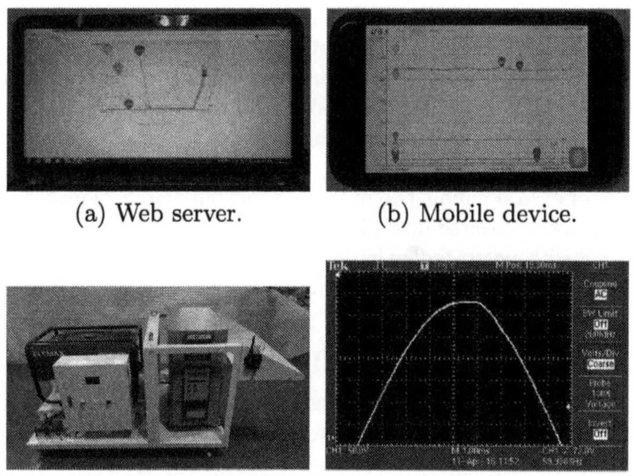

(a) Web server. (b) Mobile device.

(c) Prototype UGS. (d) Output Voltage

Figure 2: Mobile power management using the proposed FreeRTOS-based uninterruptible generator supply.

2. ACKNOWLEDGMENTS

This work was supported by IITP grant funded by the Ministry of Science, ICT and Future Planning (2014-0-00065 (Resilient CPS Research), IITP-2017-2014-0-00636). (Corresponding author: K. Kang)

3. REFERENCES

[1] Introduction to FreeRTOS. [Online]. Available at http://www.freertos.org/RTOS.html

Permission to make digital or hard copies of part or all of this work for personal or classroom use is granted without fee provided that copies are not made or distributed for profit or commercial advantage and that copies bear this notice and the full citation on the first page. Copyrights for third-party components of this work must be honored. For all other uses, contact the owner/author(s).

MobiSys'17 June 19-23, 2017, Niagara Falls, NY, USA

© 2017 Copyright held by the owner/author(s).

ACM ISBN 978-1-4503-4928-4/17/06.

DOI: http://dx.doi.org/10.1145/3081333.3089295

Poster: Charge My Phone As I Instruct

Liang He
University of Michigan
2260 Hayward St.
Ann Arbor, MI, 48109
lianghe@umich.edu

Yu-Chih Tung
University of Michigan
2260 Hayward St.
Ann Arbor, MI, 48109
yctung@umich.edu

Kang G. Shin
University of Michigan
2260 Hayward St.
Ann Arbor, MI, 48109
kgshin@umich.edu

1. INTRODUCTION

Charging mobile devices fast alleviates users' impatience in waiting for their devices to be charged. So, fast charging has been the focus of both industry and academia, developing and deploying various technologies, such as Quick Charge by Qualcomm, TurboPower by Motorola, Flash Charge by OPPO, etc.

Fast charging, unfortunately, accelerates the capacity fading of device battery because it follows the *Constant Current, Constant Voltage* (CCCV) charge principle without considering the behavior of how users charge their devices. CCCV charging principle is a two-phase charging process consisting of (i) Constant-Current Charge (CC-Chg) and (ii) Constant-Voltage Charge (CV-Chg) [2] where CV-Chg is usually triggered at the end of charging (e.g., 80–100%) to stabilize the battery condition. However, fast charging technologies are agnostic of users' available charging time, resulting in premature termination of the planned charging if users only have limited time. This, in turn, leads to an incomplete CV-Chg phase or even skipping it completely. From our empirical measurements, we discovered that *CV-Chg relaxes the batteries and slows down their capacity fading by up to* 80% [1] — incomplete CV-Chg shortens the battery life significantly over time!

2. USER-INTERACTIVE CHARGING

The negative effects of fast charging motivated us the design of `iCharge`, a novel user-interactive charging paradigm that tailors the device charging to the users' real-time needs [1], as illustrated in Fig. 1. `iCharge` allows users to specify their available charging time, displays the charged capacity if Relaxation-aware (`R-Aware`) or fast charging is used, and adopts their selection of a charging method in the charging plan. Unlike fast charging, `R-Aware` maximizes the charged capacity while ensuring the use of CV-Chg to relax the battery, thus improving battery health and device operation time in the long run. We have evaluated `R-Aware` via laboratory experiments over 15 months with advanced battery testing systems, as shown in Fig. 2 — `R-Aware` slows down battery capacity fading by 36% on average. We have also implemented `R-Aware` as a system component on various Android devices, corroborating its compatibility with commodity devices.

Permission to make digital or hard copies of part or all of this work for personal or classroom use is granted without fee provided that copies are not made or distributed for profit or commercial advantage and that copies bear this notice and the full citation on the first page. Copyrights for third-party components of this work must be honored. For all other uses, contact the owner/author(s).

MobiSys'17 June 19-23, 2017, Niagara Falls, NY, USA

© 2017 Copyright held by the owner/author(s).

ACM ISBN 978-1-4503-4928-4/17/06.

DOI: http://dx.doi.org/10.1145/3081333.3089296

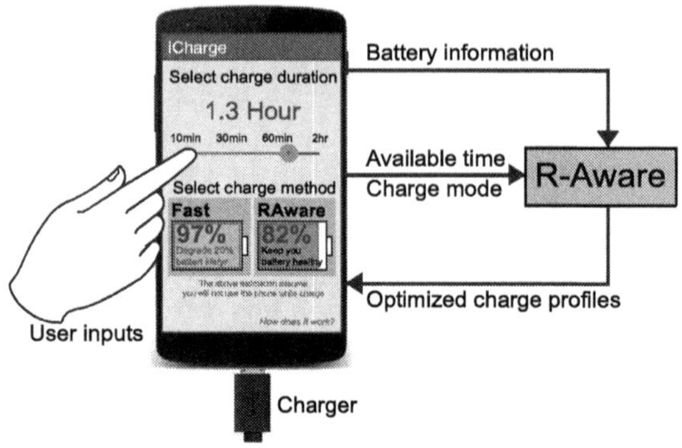

Figure 1: `iCharge` overview: tailoring the device charging to the user's available time and selection of charging method.

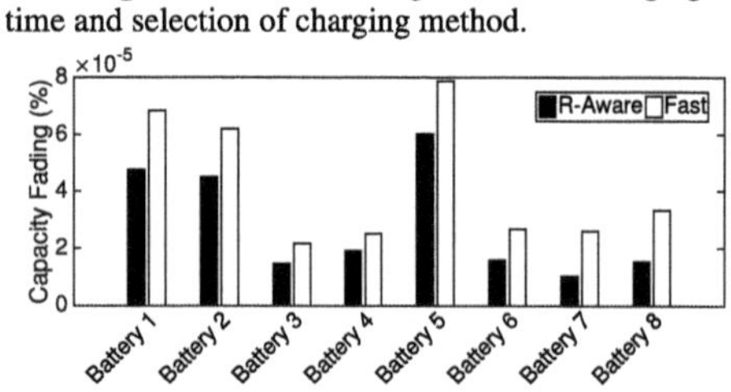

Figure 2: `R-Aware` slows down batteries' capacity by 36% on average.

Note that `R-Aware` is not designed to replace fast charging algorithms but offers an attractive alternative to keep the device battery healthier at the expense of a slower charging rate. For example, when no charging options are provided by users, `iCharge` charges the device by using the default fast charging algorithms to preserve user experience when a high charging rate is required. We have performed user studies to collect feedback on `iCharge`. First, we conducted a questionnaire-based survey of 146 participants, in which 89% of them noticed the capacity fading of their device batteries. Although some participants normally purchase new phones every year, 77% of them still want to use `iCharge` in order to keep their device battery healthy. Second, we had 13 users used a conceptual app of `iCharge` over 3 weeks, showing their preference of `R-Aware` to fast charging for 36% of all charging cases.

3. ACKNOWLEDGMENTS

The work reported in this paper was supported by NSF under Grant CNS-1446117.

4. REFERENCES

[1] L. He, Y.-C. Tung, and K. G. Shin. User-interactive charging of mobile devices. In *MobiSys'17*, 2017.

[2] A. Sanpei. Charging Method for Secondary Battery. US Patent, 5,237,259, 1993.

Poster: Docker-Based Self-Organizing IoT Services Architecture for Smarthome

Meng Niu, Bo Cheng, Zhongyi Zhai, Yimeng Feng, Junliang Chen
State Key Laboratory of Networking and Switching Technology
Beijing University of Posts and Telecommunications, Beijing, China
buptniumeng@163.com, chengbo@bupt.edu.cn

1. INTRODUCTION

Internet of Things(IoT) was first coined in 1999 by Kevin Ashton.[1] However with the technologies advancement, it seems that intelligent devices will invisibly be embedded in our life in few years. Enormous amounts of data need be exchanged every seconds.[2] It calls for a seamless effect and easily interpretable communicating architecture. The research proposal will try to address some challenges and possible path in IoT enabled smarthome. It focuses primarily on two categories. Firstly, devices in IoT field is always distributed. So, there is a distributed IoT services architecture instead of traditional control-center solution. However, those devices are also limited in a certain area (such as a home local network). In order to reduce delay and burden, those distributed devices collect context information though a self-organizing broadcast network, and determine their next action based on that context data. Secondly, using *Docker* (a lightweight hardware-agnostic and platform-agnostic container) to package services. In our smarthome network, IoT services are distributed across different home electronics. *Docker* shields all the differences, so that we can quickly deploy and update module in the smarthome network after purchasing new electronics.

2. IOT SERVICES ARCHITECTURE

In the traditional IoT-enabled smarthome solution, all users' orders from mobile and devices information are measured by the central server. It is a heavy burden for the central server. We release some compute tasks to home electronics (such as television). Over these devices, we deploy related IoT services. And these services are wrapped by *Docker*. *Docker container* shields all differences. So services can be heterogeneous and accessible migration between devices. It is friendly while adding new node and updating the home network. As shown in Figure 1, these services communicate with other services though broadcast, and constitute a self-organizing network, just like *Ad-Hoc* (a wireless self-organizing communication network). And for sensors web,

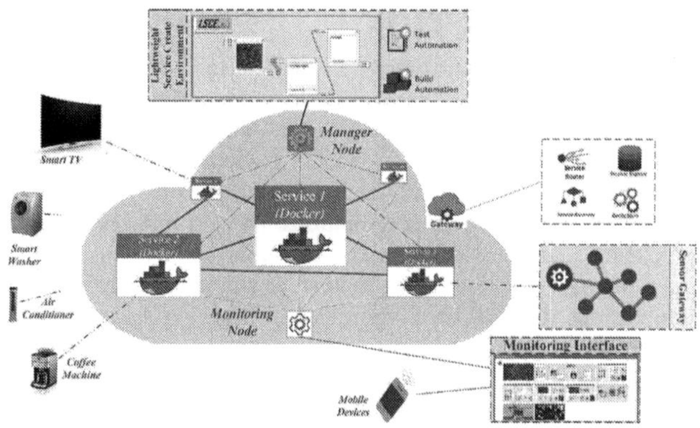

Figure 1: the IoT Services Architecture

they access the network though sensor gateway which is also wrapped by *Docker*. Services collect and process context information though the *Docker* web and then decide the devices' next action.

Over more, we have a drag-drop-way orchestrator called *LSCE4IoT* for service creation. A manager node will analyze created business information and then distribute the choreographer information. Based on the choreographer information and context data, device nodes determine which next node to send data to. Besides manager node, we also insert a monitoring node to catches network's statues though broadcast data and return monitoring information to users' screen.

Though this Docker-based self-organizing IoT services network, the smart home devices sense and measure the context information efficiently, and support users' daily lifestyle.

3. ACKNOWLEDGMENTS

The research reported in this paper is supported by National High-tech R&D Program of China (863 Program) under Grant No. 2013AA102301; National Grand Fundamental Research 973 Program of China under Grant No. 2013CB329102. (Corresponding author: Bo Cheng).

4. REFERENCES

[1] K. Ashton. That "internet of things" thing. *RFID Journal*, 22(7):97–114, 2009.

[2] J. Gubbi, R. Buyya, S. Marusic, and M. Palaniswami. Internet of things (iot): A vision, architectural elements, and future directions. *Future generation computer systems*, 29(7):1645–1660, 2013.

Permission to make digital or hard copies of part or all of this work for personal or classroom use is granted without fee provided that copies are not made or distributed for profit or commercial advantage and that copies bear this notice and the full citation on the first page. Copyrights for third-party components of this work must be honored. For all other uses, contact the owner/author(s).

MobiSys '17, June 19–23, 2017, Niagara Falls, NY, USA.

© 2017 Copyright held by the owner/author(s).

ACM ISBN 978-1-4503-4928-4/17/06..

DOI: http://dx.doi.org/10.1145/3081333.3089297

Poster: Improve Push Notification on Smartwatches

Xing Liu
Indiana University
Bloomington, IN
xl45@indiana.edu

Yunsheng Yao
Indiana University
Bloomington, IN
yy29@indiana.edu

Feng Qian
Indiana University
Bloomington, IN
fengqian@indiana.edu

1. INTRODUCTION

Receiving push notifications is one of the key features of smartwatches. In our recent measurement study involving 27 smartwatch users [1], we found that push notifications are used by more than 200 applications, dominated by instant messaging, emails, social media, *etc.* In this work, we propose a suite of methods to optimize the performance, energy efficiency, and usability of smartwatch push notifications, which have several salient features distinguishing them from regular notifications received on a smartphone: requiring heavy phone-watch cooperation, being delivered over short-range Bluetooth link, and incurring non-trivial energy consumption on watches with very limited battery capacity. Considering these factors, our proposed work focuses on four aspects as elaborated below.

• **To Push or not to Push.** We found that when a notification is available on the phone side, apps/OS employ naïve policies to determine whether to push or not to the watch. For example, many Android apps push a notification when and only when the phone-side app is not running in the foreground. Such a policy may cause unnecessary pushes when the user is interacting with the phone (so she can already see the message in the notification bar on the phone), or cause useful pushes to be skipped when the user puts the phone aside (with the app running in the foreground) and walks away. Ideally, in most use cases, an app should perform pushes only when the user is *not* interacting with the phone. We thus plan to design and implement an API that intelligently determines whether to push or not to push by leveraging diverse types of information sources such as the user interaction level, the application type, and the physical distance between the watch and the phone. The API needs to be reliable and lightweight.

• **When to Push.** Today's smartphones perform pushes immediately when notifications are available. Doing so minimizes the latency while oftentimes incurring energy overhead on watches, which need to fully wake up and keep the display on for several seconds when a notification arrives. Despite such short wake-up sessions that account for only 2% of the overall usage period based on our crowd-sourced measurement, their energy footprint is as high as 27% of the overall watch energy consumption. To reduce the energy consumption incurred by push, we leverage the fact that different types of notifications have different delay tolerance levels. For many delay-tolerant notifications, they can be pushed to the watch in a single bundle, or be pushed when the watch wakes up. Batching or piggybacking message delivery is not a new concept. However we face several unique challenges here such as determining the delay tolerance level for notifications, devising an energy-efficient push strategy, and designing an interface allowing users to conveniently read multiple notifications on the watch.

• **How to Push.** On most smartwatches, notifications are pushed over the Bluetooth (BT/BLE) channel established between the phone and the wearable. However, the range of a BT link is short, and some vendors intentionally reduce the BT antenna power for energy saving purpose. As a result, handovers between BT and WiFi (many smartwatches have built-in WiFi) may frequently happen. We found that on commodity Android watches, a handover may take a long time to finish, leading to long delays for time-sensitive notifications such as chat. The problem we try to address is thus to ensure good push performance during frequent handovers. We observed from our user study that the arrival of notifications exhibits a strong bursty pattern. Within a burst of notifications, the watch can predict the loss of the BT connectivity and preemptively establish the WiFi channel. Notifications with high priority will then be pushed over both channels to ensure their prompt and reliable delivery.

• **What to Push.** When a notification arrives at the watch, watch-side apps may allow users to take further actions such as launching a phone-side activity, opening a URL, or taking voice input. We found that these actions only involve a small set of homogeneous operations across a wide range of apps. Here our idea is to allow the phone not only to push regular contents such as text and image, but also to push an "applet" defining the operations that the user can take. The applet is expected to be small, simple, and cacheable. It can be easily crafted using OS-provided APIs. This approach can help reduce watch apps' development overhead or even eliminate most watch-side apps whose sole job is to handle simple interactions upon receiving notifications. The challenges include making the applets lightweight, secure, and cover common interaction options that a user may take.

On-going Work and Future Plan. We are working on designing and implementing the above four optimizations. We plan to integrate them into a holistic software framework. Evaluations will be conducted using both in-lab controlled experiments and our on-going smartwatch user study [1].

Permission to make digital or hard copies of part or all of this work for personal or classroom use is granted without fee provided that copies are not made or distributed for profit or commercial advantage and that copies bear this notice and the full citation on the first page. Copyrights for third-party components of this work must be honored. For all other uses, contact the owner/author(s).

MobiSys'17 June 19-23, 2017, Niagara Falls, NY, USA

© 2017 Copyright held by the owner/author(s).

ACM ISBN 978-1-4503-4928-4/17/06.
DOI: http://dx.doi.org/10.1145/3081333.3089298

2. REFERENCES

[1] LIU, X., CHEN, T., QIAN, F., GUO, Z., LIN, F. X., WANG, X., AND CHEN, K. Characterizing Smartwatch Usage in the Wild. In *MobiSys* (2017).

Poster: Mobile Photo Data Management as a Platform Service

Kyungho Jeon, Sharath Chandrashekhara, Karthik Dantu, Steven Y. Ko
Department of Computer Science and Engineering
University at Buffalo, The State University of New York
Buffalo, New York
{kyunghoj, sc296, kdantu, stevko}@buffalo.edu

ABSTRACT

This poster presents Pixelsior, a new mobile platform service for photo data management in mobile apps.

1. INTRODUCTION

Many popular apps for mobile platforms interact with photo data. In those apps, interacting with photo data means not only to capture and to store them but also to classify, annotate, and enhance images either automatically or manually.

Implementing photo data interaction features is not a trivial task. However, such features are not well supported by mobile platforms. For example, Android provides only the basic functionality around managing photo data: i) encoding and decoding an image, ii) storing the encoded image in a file, and iii) indexing its metadata. Therefore, individual apps have to implement all the advanced features on their own or include libraries that provide such features, even though the same features may have been available in other apps in the device. Considering the rapid advances in image processing technologies, this siloed development effort is wasted and hampers the apps' adoption of new technologies. Even worse, individual implementations may result in fragmented data management problems as follows: i) An app may not be able to understand the relationship between two images, even though one is a mere resize of another. ii) Textual information extracted from an image by an app cannot be shared with other apps.

2. DESIGN

To overcome the challenges in mobile photo data, we design a platform, Pixelsior, that provides a new abstraction for photo data and a programming interface around the abstraction. The new abstraction encapsulate photo data within a logical object which has: a set of attributes and custom metadata tags and multiple images and relationship among them—for example, an image and a resize of the image. Also, the platform enables an image processing functionality developed by a third party to be installed on the platform and be used by every app in the device. Figure 1 illustrates the architecture of Pixelsior.

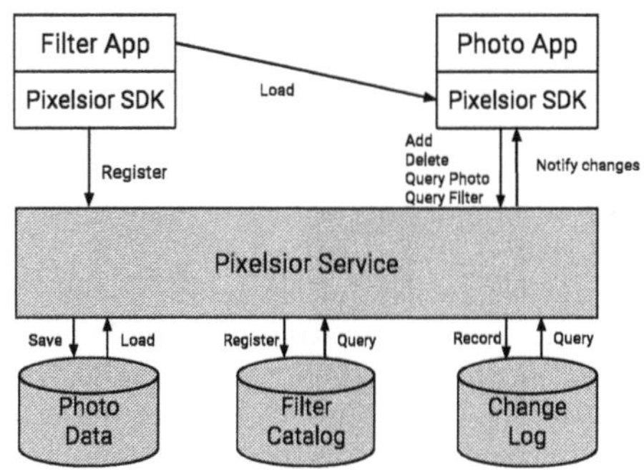

Figure 1: System Architecture of Pixelsior

3. RESULT AND DISCUSSION

Our initial prototype shows that our approach introduces low overhead (e.g., less than 10% in loading an image of 816 $\times$ 612 pixels) while allowing a clean programming interface and a set of context-aware policies for efficient mobile apps.

This new abstraction not only gives a principled interface for apps, but also enables interesting tradeoffs in how to store and retrieve photo data. For example, a photo-editing app may choose to store filters applied on a photo, instead of resulting images to reduce its storage space usage.

Pixelsior is a new approach in managing photo data in mobile apps. Even though past work has explored i) how to upload photo data with more privacy [1] or ii) how to control sharing of photo data in a finger granularity [2], they did not explore a new abstraction and interface to manage photo data as Pixelsior does.

4. REFERENCES

[1] M.-R. Ra, R. Govindan, and A. Ortega. P3: Toward privacy-preserving photo sharing. In *NSDI 13*.

[2] Y. Xu, T. Hunt, Y. Kwon, M. Georgiev, V. Shmatikov, and E. Witchel. Earp: Principled storage, sharing, and protection for mobile apps. In *NSDI 16*.

Permission to make digital or hard copies of part or all of this work for personal or classroom use is granted without fee provided that copies are not made or distributed for profit or commercial advantage and that copies bear this notice and the full citation on the first page. Copyrights for third-party components of this work must be honored. For all other uses, contact the owner/author(s).

MobiSys'17 June 19-23, 2017, Niagara Falls, NY, USA

© 2017 Copyright held by the owner/author(s).

ACM ISBN 978-1-4503-4928-4/17/06.
DOI: http://dx.doi.org/10.1145/3081333.3089299

Poster: Towards Quick Angular Check to Rebuff Forged Position Attacks in Vehicular Communication

Yongtae Park and Seungho Kuk
Intelligent Machines Laboratory, Korea University, Republic of Korea
{ytpark, shkuk}@korea.ac.kr

1. MOTIVATION

Although Wireless Access in Vehicular Environment (WAVE) will be legally enforced from 2020 after the recent move by the U.S. Government [1], there is still an unresolved security issue. It is data plausibility, which is not addressed in any standard that comprises the WAVE framework. In particular, an attacker may forge false position values in safety beacons in order to cause unsafe response from startled receiving vehicles. The data plausibility is a longstanding issue for which various approaches based on sensor fusion, behavior analysis and communication constraints have been proposed. However, none of these completely solve the problem.

In this work, we propose an approach in the third category, based on physical constraints of radio communication, to defend against position forgers including stationary roadside attackers. Our approach has certain advantages over the previous approaches. First, it can work even when the sensor-based position check does not work, e.g. in non-line-of-sight (NLoS) condition. This is because most vehicle sensors such as camera, radar, and LiDAR are LoS devices. Second, it can work when the behavioral analysis may fail. For one, the behavioral analysis cannot be applied to a stopped vehicle, since it does not exhibit any movement behavior. Our proposal also departs from existing communication constraints based schemes relying on maximum distance check. This is because the maximum communication distance is a poorly defined variable since it depends on many constantly changing environmental factors and varying transmission power used by the congestion control algorithm. The angle of arrival checking approach is immune to these problems.

2. QUICK ANGULAR CHECK SYSTEM USING ANGLE OF ARRIVAL

In this work, we propose an angle of arrival (AoA) based method to invalidate position forging adversaries such as roadside attackers. Our method is based on the fact that the attacker can falsify the location information of the safety message but cannot lie about the physical location from where the message is transmitted. For example, the relative angle between vehicles can be detected by the AoA of the beacon signal. Therefore, when an attacker tries to induce unsafe reaction from the drivers of the vehicles in its vicinity through the position forgery, it is possible to detect whether the attacker forged its position information by comparing with the measured AoA. Based on the above description, we design a quick angular check system for forgery detection as shown in Fig.1.

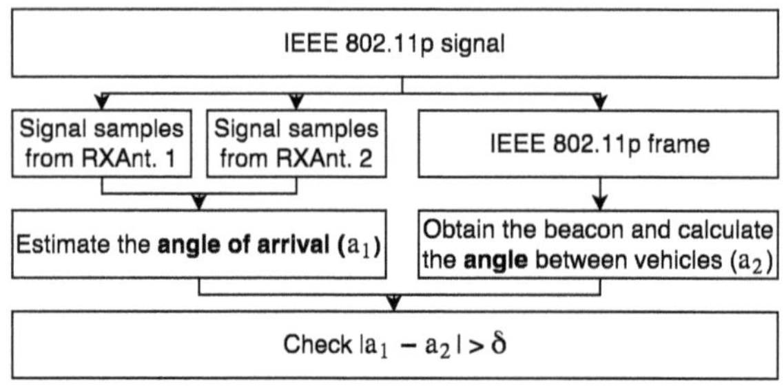

Figure 1: Quick angular check system design

3. PRELIMINARY EVALUATION

We implement a testbed using Chemtronics' On-Board Unit (OBU) and Ettus's Universal Software Radio Peripheral (USRP) B210 with two 5.9 GHz dipole antennas. The USRP B210 allows the use of a synchronized digital signal sample by receiving the safety beacon from the OBU with two antennas. In order to process the digital signal sample, we listen to the WAVE channel using GNU Radio's IEEE 802.11p software on the Linux laptop to detect the short preamble of the beacon and collect signal samples of the following long preamble. The signal samples are analyzed using the MUSIC algorithm that is one of the best AoA estimation methods.

Varying the angle between the OBU and B210, we perform an experiment to measure AoA and compare it with the actual angle. The experimental result shows that more than 96.5% of the measured AoAs have an error within 5 degrees. Based on this, we could confirm that our proposed system can estimate the direction of the actual signal through the AoA, and it is possible to detect messages and attack vehicles that falsify the position except in the same direction.

4. ACKNOWLEDGEMENT

This work was supported by a Korea University Grant.

5. REFERENCES

[1] National Highway Traffic Safety Administration (NHTSA). U.S. DOT advances deployment of Connected Vehicle Technology to prevent hundreds of thousands of crashes. URL: https://www.nhtsa.gov/press-releases/us-dot-advances-deployment-connected-vehicle-technology-prevent-hundreds-thousands, Dec 2016.

Permission to make digital or hard copies of part or all of this work for personal or classroom use is granted without fee provided that copies are not made or distributed for profit or commercial advantage and that copies bear this notice and the full citation on the first page. Copyrights for third-party components of this work must be honored. For all other uses, contact the owner/author(s).

MobiSys'17 June 19-23, 2017, Niagara Falls, NY, USA

© 2017 Copyright held by the owner/author(s).

ACM ISBN 978-1-4503-4928-4/17/06.
DOI: http://dx.doi.org/10.1145/3081333.3089300

Poster: Visual Cue-Based VRU Protection on Smartphones

Taeho Kim, Wongoo Han, Yongtae Park
Intelligent Machines Laboratory, Korea University, Republic of Korea
{taehokim, wongoohan, ytpark}@korea.ac.kr

1. MOTIVATION

As autonomous vehicles loom as reality, and the vehicle communication starts to be enforced by law from 2020, protecting vulnerable road users (VRUs) using vehicle communication is receiving attention. The current vehicle-to-pedestrian (V2P) communication as stipulated by the standards such as SAE J2735 implies that it is the vehicles that take the responsibility for VRU protection. User devices are essentially beacons that transmit Personal Safety Messages (PSMs), and upon receiving PSMs, the drivers (or autonomous vehicles) take necessary measures to protect them. We, however, believe that the road users also need information about nearby vehicles to protect themselves from dangerous situations.

Using other technologies than the standard Dedicated Short Range Communication (DSRC), there have been existing works for VRU protection. They use Wi-Fi or Wi-Fi Direct as replacements of DSRC [1]. An automaker tested DSRC for VRU protection [2], but no technical detail has been presented. An important issue with the existing VRU protection proposals is that they are fraught with *false alarms*, which lowers the utility of the whole idea. Although one can come up with a highly precise collision prediction model, any such model will generate a huge number of false alarms, especially in urban environments. For example, if a pedestrian walks along a sidewalk well protected from the driveway, all passing vehicles will generate an alert to the pedestrian and *vice versa*. So our approach instead provides intuitive visual cues to the smartphone user looking at the screen, so that they can use their discretion to determine the level of danger for themselves.

2. VRU PROTECTION PLATFORM

In this work, we propose visual cue-based VRU protection method, particularly targeting the road users whose head is buried in a smartphone. First, we develop the working DSRC module that can be connected to a smartphone (Fig.1) and the software module including Wireless Access in Vehicular Environments (WAVE) and SAE J2735 protocols, so that the smartphone can communicate with other vehicles. The DSRC module not only transmits PSMs, but receives the other vehicle's Basic Safety Messages (BSMs) using IEEE 802.11p/ 1609.4 protocols through a wireless channel. After receiving the BSMs, the module provides the messages to the smartphone via the USB port.

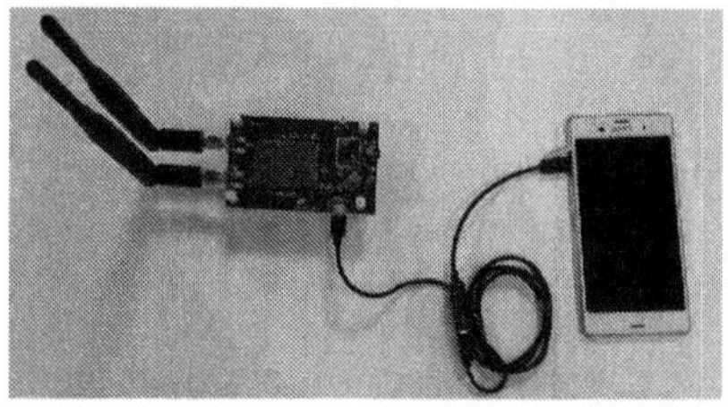

Figure 1: DSRC V2P prototype module attached to smartphone via USB port

3. VISUAL CUE-BASED VRU PROTECTION

Second, we propose a method to inform smartphone users of the risk by using visual cues on the edges of the smartphone. In a sense, it is similar to the LED-lighted crosswalks in the Netherlands that gives visual cues in the peripheral vision of the smartphone user [3]. We implement an application that highlights the screen edge on the incoming vehicle side, and the highlighted part moves along the edge and changes color and intensity according to the relative speed and location of the passing vehicle (Fig.2). It is computed using the GPS coordinate, heading and speed information of the vehicle in the BSM and those of the smartphone, along with the attitude of the phone that is detected by sensors.

Figure 2: Smartphone screen with the edge on the incoming vehicle side hightlighted

4. ACKNOWLEDGEMENT

This work was supported by a Korea University Grant.

5. REFERENCES

[1] K. Dhondge et al. WiFiHonk: Smartphone-Based Beacon Stuffed WiFi Car2X-Communication System for Vulnerable Road User Safety. In *IEEE VTC Spring*, 2014.

[2] Honda. Honda Demonstrates Advanced Vehicle-to-Pedestrian and Vehicle-to-Motorcycle Safety Technologies, 2013.

[3] J. Titcomb. Pavement lights installed near Dutch schools to guide smartphone-obsessed pedestrians. Telegraph, February 2017.

Permission to make digital or hard copies of part or all of this work for personal or classroom use is granted without fee provided that copies are not made or distributed for profit or commercial advantage and that copies bear this notice and the full citation on the first page. Copyrights for third-party components of this work must be honored. For all other uses, contact the owner/author(s).

MobiSys'17 June 19-23, 2017, Niagara Falls, NY, USA

© 2017 Copyright held by the owner/author(s).

ACM ISBN 978-1-4503-4928-4/17/06.

DOI: http://dx.doi.org/10.1145/3081333.3089301

Poster: A Lightweight Live Migration Platform with Container-based Virtualization for System Resilience

Jaemyoun Lee
Hanyang University, Ansan 15588, Korea
jaemyoun@hanyang.ac.kr

Kyungtae Kang
Hanyang University, Ansan 15588, Korea
ktkang@hanyang.ac.kr

ABSTRACT

When integrated with push notifications, a live migration function can be used to ensure that systems have a high reliability in cases of hardware failures. However, the dependencies for a large range of hardware devices need to be addressed before realizing emergency live migration. Our platform introduces container-based light virtualization and an automated build function to isolate an application so that it can be deployed on different devices such as Edison, Raspberry Pi model B, BeagleBone Black, and Odroid XU3, as shown in Fig. 1.

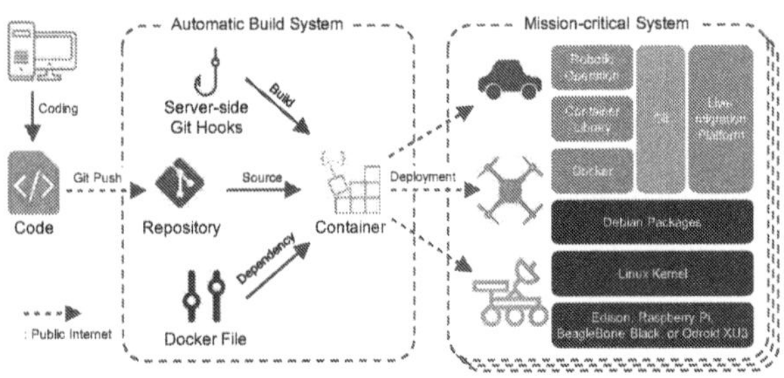

Figure 1: Our automatic deployment platform.

1. LIVE MIGRATION PLATFORM

Emergency live migration, in conjunction with a primary backup scheme, can improve the reliability of applications by coping with unexpected errors in devices. Fig. 2 shows how our platform can consolidate emergency live migration to ensure a high system resilience.

A device installed with an application container [1] conducts sensing and actuating procedures, and transmits data generated during a mission to object-based storage for a cloud application. When it discovers a faulty device, it searches for a surplus device that is available, and migrates all mission-related applications and data from the faulty device to the surplus device to continue the mission.

Permission to make digital or hard copies of part or all of this work for personal or classroom use is granted without fee provided that copies are not made or distributed for profit or commercial advantage and that copies bear this notice and the full citation on the first page. Copyrights for third-party components of this work must be honored. For all other uses, contact the owner/author(s).

MobiSys'17 June 19-23, 2017, Niagara Falls, NY, USA

© 2017 Copyright held by the owner/author(s).

ACM ISBN 978-1-4503-4928-4/17/06.
DOI: http://dx.doi.org/10.1145/3081333.3089302

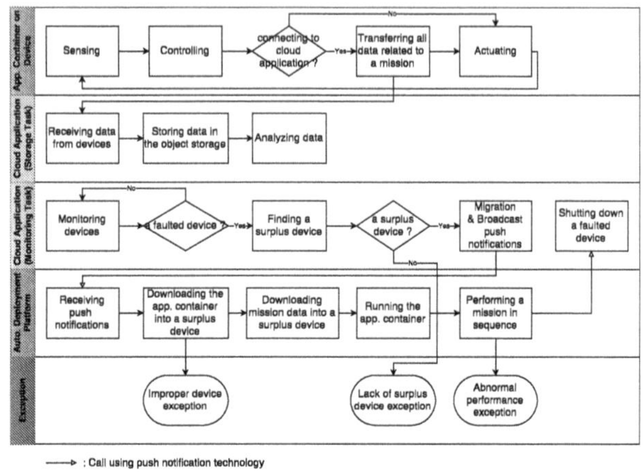

Figure 2: Proposed platform for emergency live migration.

The migration procedures are initiated by a push notification. First, the application container for the mission is downloaded onto the surplus device, and subsequently, the data needed to perform the mission are downloaded. Then the downloaded container is initialized and executed, and finally, the migration platform sends a push notification to the cloud application to shut down the faulty device.

In an experiment using a model electronic vehicle, it was observed that the right device seamlessly controlled the vehicle, despite the sudden stoppage of the left device. This demonstrates that our platform can improve the reliability of systems by facilitating emergency migration.

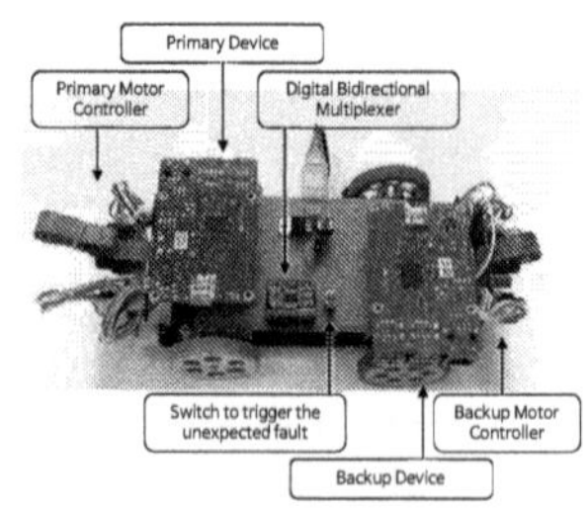

Figure 3: Testing vehicle.

2. ACKNOWLEDGMENTS

This work was supported by IITP grant funded by the Korean government (2014-0-00065, Resilient CPS Research).

3. REFERENCES

[1] S. Soltesz, H. Pötzl, M. E. Fiuczynski, A. Bavier, and L. Peterson. Container-based operating system virtualization: A scalable, high-performance alternative to hypervisors. In *EuroSys*, pages 275–287, March 2007.

Poster: Application-Layer Optimization of Performance vs Energy in Mobile Network I/O

Kemal Guner and Tevfik Kosar
Department of Computer Science and Engineering
University at Buffalo (SUNY)
Buffalo, NY 14260-2500
{kemalgne, tkosar}@buffalo.edu

Extended Abstract

The number of smartphone users globally has already exceeded 2 Billion, and this number is expected to reach 3 Billion by 2020 [2]. It is also estimated that smartphone mobile data traffic (cellular + WiFi) will reach 370 Exabytes per year by that time, exceeding PC Internet traffic the first time in the history [4]. An average smartphone consumes between 300 – 1200 milliwatts power [1] depending on the type of applications it is running, and most of the energy in smartphone applications is spent for networked I/O. During an active data transfer, the cellular (i.e., GSM) and WiFi components of a smartphone consume more power than its CPU, RAM, and even LCD+graphics card at the highest brightness level [3, 1]. Although the mobile data traffic and the amount of energy spent for it increase at a very fast pace, the battery capacities of smartphones do not increase at the same rate. In this work, we analyze the effects of different application layer data transfer protocol parameters (such as the number of parallel data streams per file, the level of concurrent file transfers, and the I/O request size) on mobile data transfer throughput and energy consumption.

Figure 1 shows the achieved end-to-end throughput, total energy consumption, and the change in instantaneous power consumption during a wide-area data transfer with increased concurrency level. This figure presents the break point for the throughput versus energy consumption trade-off very well. As long as the energy gain due to the decreased transfer time is more than the loss due to the increased instantaneous power consumption, then we save energy at this device while increasing the throughput. But this is not always the case. We observe that although the throughput continues to increase up to a certain concurrency level, the total energy consumption does not continue to decrease, instead comes to a balance and starts increasing again. The main reason for this is the server and network components are typically not energy proportional. When used wisely, these parameters have a potential to improve the end-to-end data transfer performance and decrease total energy consumption at a great extent, but improper use of these parameters can also hurt the performance of the data transfers due to increased load at the end-systems and congested links in the network. For this reason, it is crucial to find the best combination for these parameters with the least intrusion and overhead to the system resource utilization and power consumption.

Our contributions within this work are the following: (1) To the best of our knowledge, we are first to provide an in depth analysis of the effects of application layer data transfer protocol parameters on the energy consumption of mobile phones. (2) We show that significant energy savings can be achieved with application-layer solutions at the mobile systems during data transfer with no or minimal performance penalty. (3) We also show that, in many cases, performance increase and energy savings can be achieved simultaneously.

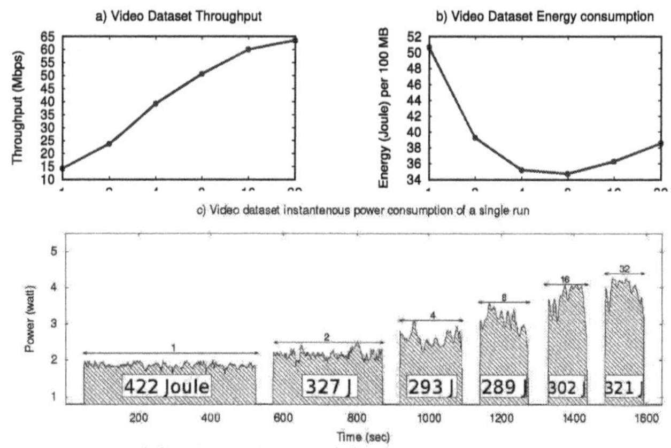

Figure 1: (a) Throughput; (b) Energy Consumption; and (c) Instantaneous Power Consumption of a data transfer with increased level of concurrency.

Permission to make digital or hard copies of part or all of this work for personal or classroom use is granted without fee provided that copies are not made or distributed for profit or commercial advantage and that copies bear this notice and the full citation on the first page. Copyrights for third-party components of this work must be honored. For all other uses, contact the owner/author(s).

MobiSys'17 June 19-23, 2017, Niagara Falls, NY, USA

© 2017 Copyright held by the owner/author(s).

ACM ISBN 978-1-4503-4928-4/17/06.
DOI: http://dx.doi.org/10.1145/3081333.3089303

1. REFERENCES

[1] A. Carroll and G. Heiser. An analysis of power consumption in a smartphone. In *USENIX annual technical conference*, volume 14. Boston, MA, 2010.

[2] E. A. Edwards, J. Lumsden, C. Rivas, L. Steed, L. Edwards, A. Thiyagarajan, R. Sohanpal, H. Caton, C. Griffiths, M. Munafò, et al. Gamification for health promotion: systematic review of behaviour change techniques in smartphone apps. *BMJ open*, 6(10):e012447, 2016.

[3] A. Pathak, Y. C. Hu, and M. Zhang. Where is the energy spent inside my app?: fine grained energy accounting on smartphones with eprof. In *Proceedings of the 7th ACM european conference on Computer Systems*, pages 29–42. ACM, 2012.

[4] C. Systems. Visual networking index: Forecast and methodology, 2015–2020, June 2016.

Poster: Vocal Resonance as a Passive Biometric

Rui Liu, Cory Cornelius[†], Reza Rawassizadeh, Ron Peterson, and David Kotz
Dept. of Computer Science, Dartmouth College and [†]Intel Labs

1. INTRODUCTION

With continuing advances in the development of low-power electronics, including sensors and actuators, we anticipate a rapid expansion of pervasive computing. Wearable devices, in particular, require new modes for interaction – many have no keyboard or touchscreen.

In this work, we focus on *user authentication* on wearable devices. For an entertainment device, such as a VR headset, it can recognize the user and load the right game profile or music playlist. For a house climate-control system, it can adjust the environment to the wearer's preference. Most compellingly, for a health-monitoring device, it can label the sensor data with the correct identity so that the data can be stored in the correct health record. (A mix-up of sensor data could lead to incorrect decisions, with harm to the patient.)

Because not all devices are personal devices – *my* phone, *your* fitness sensor – many devices will need to automatically recognize their wearer. They may have no interface for user identification (or PIN or password for authentication). Thus, we need a simple, wearable biometric technique to identify the user – which could be embedded in one authentication device that shares the identity with a body-area network of other devices (earlier confirmed to be on the same body [1]). This device should be trained once, for each user that might wear it, but thenceforth be completely automatic. Although a wristband could use a physiological biometric to recognize its wearer [2]; we seek an alternative biometric, notably, one that might work for devices mounted on the head, neck, or chest.

2. VOCAL RESONANCE

We present a novel, unobtrusive biometric measurement that can support user identification in wearable body-mounted devices: *vocal resonance*, that is, the sound of the person's voice as it travels through the person's body. In our method, a microphone is placed into contact with the body. It records audio samples and compares them with a model, built earlier during a training phase. If the samples fit the model, then we conclude that (a) the speaker is indeed the person for whom we trained the model, and (b) the microphone device is physically *on* the speaker's body. If we train the device for a set of known users, the device should be able to identify which of those people is wearing the device, or that none of them are wearing the device.

We explore two machine-learning approaches; our first approach runs *stand-alone*, processing all data on the microphone-enabled wearable device. Our second approach off-loads data to a *remote host* to run a more expensive deep-learning algorithm. In the latter, we aim to achieve higher accuracy in anticipation of the day when these complex algorithms can be migrated into wearable or portable devices.

3. RESULTS

This poster shows that our system achieves reliable speaker identification through a wearable, body-contact microphone, can reliably distinguish among multiple individuals, and can distinguish between the situation where the microphone is on the body of the identified speaker and where the microphone is simply nearby, even on another body. We evaluated the feasibility of this biometric through two distinct machine-learning algorithms, and evaluated their performance on data from 25 volunteer subjects. We found that a Recurrent Neural Network (RNN) with Long Short Term Memory (LSTM), in combination with a fully-connected layer architecture, achieved the best accuracy (95.6%). Furthermore, we implemented two wearable prototypes and verified that the algorithms have acceptable latency and energy consumption when used for occasional or periodic verification or identification.

4. ACKNOWLEDGMENTS

This work is a research program supported by ISTS at Dartmouth College funded by NSF under award numbers CNS-0910842 and CNS-1329686, and by the Department of Health and Human Services (SHARP program) under award number 90TR0003-01.

5. REFERENCES

[1] C. Cornelius and D. Kotz. Recognizing whether sensors are on the same body. *Journal of Pervasive and Mobile Computing*, 8(6):822–836, Dec. 2012.

[2] C. Cornelius, R. Peterson, J. Skinner, R. Halter, and D. Kotz. A wearable system that knows who wears it. In *Proceedings of the International Conference on Mobile Systems, Applications, and Services (MobiSys)*, pages 55–67, June 2014.

Permission to make digital or hard copies of part or all of this work for personal or classroom use is granted without fee provided that copies are not made or distributed for profit or commercial advantage and that copies bear this notice and the full citation on the first page. Copyrights for third-party components of this work must be honored. For all other uses, contact the owner/author(s).

MobiSys'17 June 19-23, 2017, Niagara Falls, NY, USA

© 2017 Copyright held by the owner/author(s).

ACM ISBN 978-1-4503-4928-4/17/06.

DOI: http://dx.doi.org/10.1145/3081333.3089304

Poster: Occupancy State Detection using WiFi Signals

Elahe Soltanaghaei
University of Virginia
Charlottesville, VA, USA
es3ce@virginia.edu

Avinash Kalyanaraman
University of Virginia
Charlottesville, VA, USA
ak3ka@virginia.edu

Kamin Whitehouse
University of Virginia
Charlottesville, VA, USA
whitehouse@virginia.edu

ABSTRACT

A large amount of energy could be saved by detecting home occupancy and automatically controlling the lights, HVAC, water heating, and other mechanical systems. Existing systems rely on motion information, which usually fail to detect occupied rooms with stationary people. In this project, we study the possibility of converting commodity WiFi access points to occupancy sensors by exploiting multipath reflections as individual spatial sensors. The proposed method measures fine-grained distortions caused by human body on phase and amplitude of WiFi signals. Our initial results suggest that formulating WiFi parameters into angle of arrival provides a more sensitive metric to measure occupancy.

1. WIFI-BASED DETECTION

Homes, the spaces we spend more than 60% of our time in, are becoming increasingly automated, with automatic control of lights, heating and cooling systems. However these smart applications require knowledge of the occupancy state of the spaces in a home. Such knowledge can benefit both monetarily and environmentally, as homes consume nearly 40% of the total US energy budget, and 70% of all electricity, with heating and cooling responsible for nearly 45% of it [1].

Recent advances in wireless techniques such as MIMO-OFDM have extended its use to a device-free human sensing tool. The previous WiFi-base detection works [2] require the mobility of the target to detect signal interference with human body. To overcome this limitation, we leverage on the ubiquity of commodity WiFi devices to detect both the stationary and moving targets. The presence of several WiFi-enabled devices in a building such as laptops or smart TVs creates a wireless mesh, which can serve as a sensor network and provides rich information about the environment. However, in indoor places such as homes, WiFi signals suffer from rich multipath propagation, which distorts the received signal and masks the weak signal variations produced by the stationary body. Hence, monitoring disturbance on wireless signal strength is ineffective for occupancy detection.

Permission to make digital or hard copies of part or all of this work for personal or classroom use is granted without fee provided that copies are not made or distributed for profit or commercial advantage and that copies bear this notice and the full citation on the first page. Copyrights for third-party components of this work must be honored. For all other uses, contact the owner/author(s).

MobiSys'17 June 19-23, 2017, Niagara Falls, NY, USA

© 2017 Copyright held by the owner/author(s).

ACM ISBN 978-1-4503-4928-4/17/06.
DOI: http://dx.doi.org/10.1145/3081333.3089305

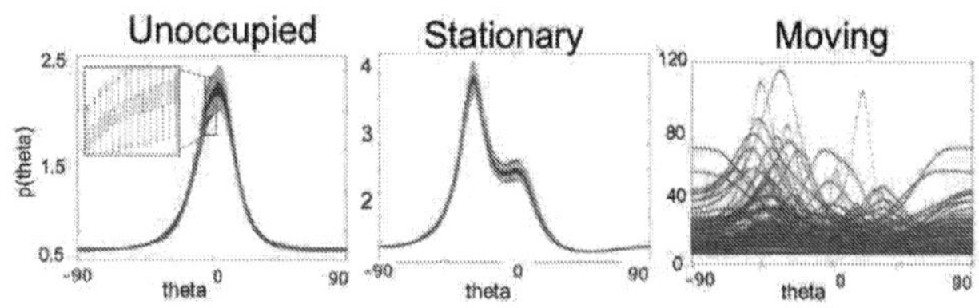

Figure 1: Changes in multipath characteristics of empty room in the presence of people.

In this project, we take advantage of the multipath distortions by converting them into a stable metric to detect occupancy. For that, we resolve and analyze multipath reflections of an empty room and characterize superimposed signals with their angle of arrivals. Then, we detect a person's presence by looking for changes in the multipath environment. We hypothesize that analyzing multipath reflections is a more sensitive approach because people affect the multipath reflections even when they are perfectly still, while other approaches require the person to be moving at least a little bit.

Figure 1 illustrates the presence effect of a person on the resolved AoA pseudo-spectrum for a sample experiment. The figure contains the variations in the power values for each angle across 1000 packets shown in a boxplot. Changes in the resolved angles of the scenario with a stationary target, and temporal changes caused by movements of the moving target reveal that the multipath resolution and resolved angle of arrivals play a key role in determining the occupancy. To implement this idea, we leverage the PHY layer Channel State Information (CSI) provided by commercial WiFi NICs, which provides fine-grained channel responses at the granularity of OFDM subcarriers. To evaluate this hypothesis, we do an in-depth analysis with different occupancy states of unoccupied, stationary target, and moving target. Our initial results show that we can detect the occupancy states with 96.7% accuracy, compared to the conventional signal strength-based solution with 56.1% and 76% accuracies.

2. REFERENCES

[1] E. Soltanaghaei and K. Whitehouse. Walksense: Classifying home occupancy states using walkway sensing. In *BuildSys*. ACM, 2016.

[2] Z. Zhou, Z. Yang, C. Wu, L. Shangguan, and Y. Liu. Towards omnidirectional passive human detection. In *INFOCOM*. IEEE, 2013.

Poster: Smartwatch Knows How Much You Drink

Takashi Hamatani, Moustafa Elhamshary, Akira Uchiyama, and Teruo Higashino
Graduate School of Information Science and Technology, Osaka University
{h-takasi, m.elhamshary, uchiyama, higashino}@ist.osaka-u.ac.jp

1. INTRODUCTION

Water accounts for about 60% of the human body, and when the body loses it (e.g., through urine, sweat, etc.) in higher rate than its intake rate (through drinking), dehydration symptoms occur. The dehydration causes many severe health problems like organ and cognitive impairment. Therefore, it is critical for the human to drink water in a sustained manner to avoid dehydration. To prevent humans from dehydration, continuous day-scale tracking of the water intake is needed. Nonetheless, it is challenging as we need to gauge the volume of water the user drink or use smart bottles like [1] to automatically keep track of the water intake.

In the previous studies [2, 3], wrist-worn devices are used to record food and medicine intake. They detected fine-grained human activities such as biting, using utensils during food intake; and opening medicine bottle, pouring medicine capsules during medication ingestion. Also, Amft Oliver and et al. [4] employ highly accurate wrist-worn inertial sensors to recognize fine-grained micro actions during the drinking activity. However, their method employs Xsens sensor which is very expensive and too bulky to be used during daily activities over large time. In addition, it does not target the estimation of water intake amount which is the enabler for potential health assistance Apps.

In this paper, we propose an unobtrusive method to recognize the drinking activity as well as estimate the water intake amount in milliliter scale by leveraging smartwatches. Our basic idea is to track the arm motion and discriminate the drinking activities from the similar hand-based motions like food intake, phone calls, etc. Thereafter, we estimate the water intake amount from the drinking duration. To achieve this, we adopt a two-layer classification architecture (Figure 1). The first classification layer (Macro-activity classifier) separates the drinking activity from other activities (walking, sitting, etc.) by using a large observation window. The second layer (Micro-activity classifier) detects the sequential micro-actions (hold the bottle, drink, and release it) taking place during the drinking activity using a smaller window.

Permission to make digital or hard copies of part or all of this work for personal or classroom use is granted without fee provided that copies are not made or distributed for profit or commercial advantage and that copies bear this notice and the full citation on the first page. Copyrights for third-party components of this work must be honored. For all other uses, contact the owner/author(s).

MobiSys'17 June 19-23, 2017, Niagara Falls, NY, USA

© 2017 Copyright held by the owner/author(s).

ACM ISBN 978-1-4503-4928-4/17/06.
DOI: http://dx.doi.org/10.1145/3081333.3089306

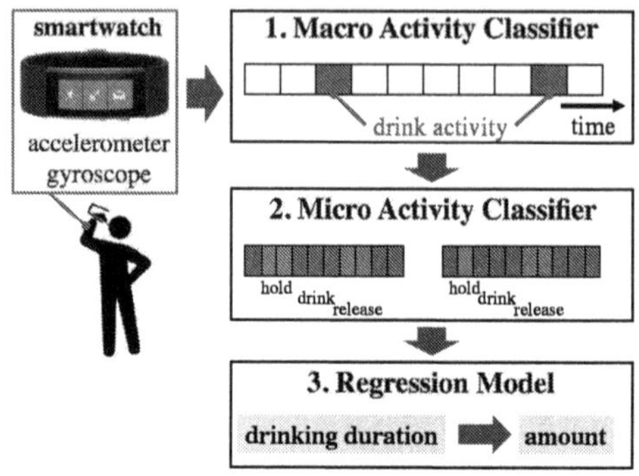

Figure 1: System Architecture

Both classifiers are conditional random fields which are built upon different statistical features from the gyroscope and accelerometer values. Finally, the amount of water intake is derived from the drinking-gesture duration through a regression model.

We validated our work by collecting 450 minutes dataset of seven different activities from six subjects using Microsoft band smartwatches. The results show that precision and recall of macro-activity recognition are 0.879 and 0.907 and for micro-activity inference are 0.890 and 0.906. Also, the system has the relative error of 15.2% in the estimation of water intake amount. These results indicate that our method is promising for recognizing drinking activity and tracking daily water intake. Currently, we are expanding our method in different directions including collecting larger dataset in the wild, using heterogeneous smartwatches, among others.

2. REFERENCES

[1] Hidrate Spark. https://hidratespark.com/

[2] H. Kalantarian et al. A smartwatch-based medication adherence system. In *Proc. of BSN 2015*, pages 1–6. IEEE, 2015.

[3] R. I. Ramos-Garcia et al. Improving the recognition of eating gestures using intergesture sequential dependencies. *IEEE J Biomed Health Inform*, 19(3):825–831, 2015.

[4] O. Amft et al. Towards wearable sensing-based assessment of fluid intake. In *Proc. of PerCom 2010 Workshops*, pages 298–303. IEEE, 2010.

Poster: EPS – Edge-hosted Personal Services for Mobile Users

Pengzhan Hao, Yongshu Bai, Xin Zhang, and Yifan Zhang
Department of Computer Science
SUNY Binghamton
Binghamton, NY
{phao3, ybai4, xzhang99, zhangy}@binghamton.edu

Introduction. Being powered by battery and the reliance on expensive cellular data while users are on the move are holding *smart mobile devices* from being widely used in those long-lasted, computation-intensive, or highly network-reliant usage scenarios. In the meantime, more and more mobile workloads and optimizations now rely on the cloud, such as mobile cloud offloading, cloud-based mobile web optimization, and cloud-based network traffic redundancy reduction. However, it is hard to perform *large-scale* and *personalized* support or optimization for mobile workloads without significant computation resource increase on the cloud, as well as higher bandwidth requirement on the networks.

We target solving the above two problems by enabling *edge-hosed personalized services* (EPS for short). The idea of EPS is twofold. One is enabling developer-customizable and power-and-traffic-efficient network communication on the "last-hop" communication between mobile devices and the network edge. The other is distributing cloud services for mobile workloads to network edge, so that they can be done on a personalized basis, while enjoying much lower communication latency to/from mobile devices. Our approach is to deploy on the network edge certain computation endpoints (named as "service carriers"), each of which performs some specific service for individual users. The goal is to build a practical, secure, efficient and scalable framework that supports *customized communication protocols* between network edge and mobile devices, as well as *customizable collaborative workloads/optimizations* on mobile devices and the edge.

Motivation usage scenarios. Many mobile workloads can be significantly benefited from customized communication protocols for reduced network traffic and prolonged battery life. One such scenario is *cloud-storage-backed mobile document editing*: a user edits office suite documents on his smartphones/tablets. The content changes made by the user are sent to cloud storage, and can be further synchronized in real-time to other devices owned by the user or his collaborators. We find that all current cloud storage services transmit almost the entire file even for one character change, despite the fact that deduplication and delta-encoding are

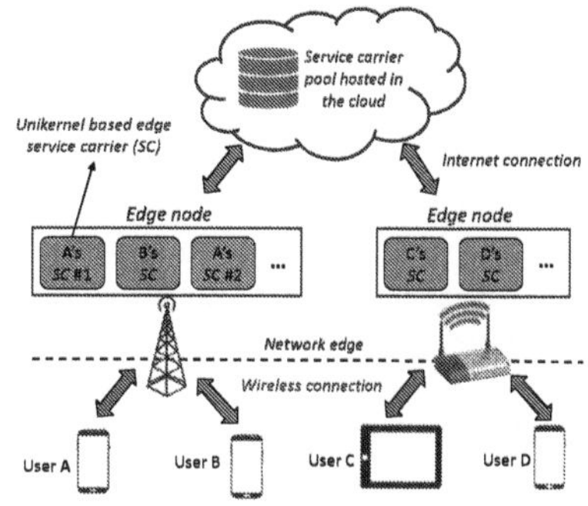

Figure 1: EPS Architecture

being applied. An effective solution would require changes on the cloud storage providers side, which can take a long time to be deployed. With an EPS that enables customized communication protocol for such scenario, we can significantly reduce network traffic generated by mobile devices. There are many other usage scenarios that can be benefited from EPS. For example, EPS can enable personalized web data reduction (e.g., through compression, image transcoding), personalized web caching on the edge, and personalized preconnecting and prefetching for mobile web.

EPS architecture. Figure 1 shows the architecture of EPS. When users move to a new location, their service carriers can be migrated from the previous edge node to the current one through the cloud-based service carrier pool. The service carrier is designed to be a Unikernel [1]. We choose Unikernel because of two main reasons. First, Unikernels are extremely small and lightweight, so that they can be migrated to and booted on resource-constrained edge nodes quickly. Second, Unikernels provide perfect resource isolation. This ideal to ensure user data security and privacy on an edge node, which also runs other users' services.

Ongoing work. We have implemented an EPS for the cloud-storage-backed mobile document editing usage scenario mentioned previously. Our current implementation of the EPS's service carrier is a Unikernel running on Xen hypervisor on an x86 desktop server. We are working on porting our implementation onto ARM boards. In the meantime, we have also started the process of designing and building a programming and system framework that allows mobile application developers to take advantage of EPS to improve mobile user experiences.

Acknowledgments. This work is being supported in part by NSF Award #1566375.

References

[1] A. Madhavapeddy and D. J. Scott. Unikernels: Rise of the virtual library operating system. *Queue*, 11(11):30, 2013.

Permission to make digital or hard copies of part or all of this work for personal or classroom use is granted without fee provided that copies are not made or distributed for profit or commercial advantage and that copies bear this notice and the full citation on the first page. Copyrights for third-party components of this work must be honored. For all other uses, contact the owner/author(s).

MobiSys'17 June 19-23, 2017, Niagara Falls, NY, USA

© 2017 Copyright held by the owner/author(s).

ACM ISBN 978-1-4503-4928-4/17/06.
DOI: http://dx.doi.org/10.1145/3081333.3089307

Poster: HeartFit – An Intuitive Smartphone Application for Well-being of Hypertensive Patients

Syeda Farzia Afroze[1],Faysal Hossain Shezan[2],Sadia Sharmin [3]
Department of Computer Science and Engineering
Bangladesh University of Engineering and Technology
[1]farziaa@gmail.com,[2]faysalhossain2007@gmail.com,[3] sadiasharmin@cse.buet.ac.bd

ABSTRACT

Hypertension is the single most significant risk factor for heart disease, stroke and kidney disease. The key causes of hypertension can be directly linked to the lifestyle of the patient, including age, family history, smoking, obesity etc. Our work consists of an interactive mobile application that acquires these lifestyle information and use several recommendation techniques to warn and guide the user towards well-being. So far, this is one of the earliest approaches in this domain for a developing country like Bangladesh.

Keywords

m-Health; Human Computer Interaction; Hypertension; Recommendation System

1 Introduction

Hypertension is a chronic condition where blood pressure persistently remains high. Smart phones present us with ample scope to monitor a person's lifestyle and diminish the risks associated with hypertension. This paper aims at detecting the risk level of hypertension of a person and based on the analysis it will make the person aware of the drawback of such disease.

2 Motivation

As of 2012, in Bangladesh, approximately 20% of adult and 40 to 65% of elderly people suffered from hypertension. Although significant works on this topic have been carried out in developed countries [1,2], they are not fitted for the people of Bangladesh owing to the socioeconomic reasons, lack of technological awareness etc. Due to insufficient medical care facilities and lack of health-care awareness among people of Bangladesh, patients only visit doctors when they start showing symptoms of diseases caused by hypertension, and by then it might be already too late.

3 Methodology

The target of our work is to analyze user data, determine the risk level of hypertension and related diseases, and provide relevant recommendations. For this, we have modeled a system with three major fragments: **input, processing** and **output**.The whole system architecture is shown in Figure 1. A user will provide his basic information to our system through the mobile application. We have categorized the input mainly into two divisions: static information and dynamic information. The static information will be obtained only once, when the user uses our app for the first time. It includes age, height and heredity information of a user.

Dynamic information is acquired after a certain interval taking into consideration of some important factors, such as risk level and other constraints. These include social, physical, psychological and lifestyle information.

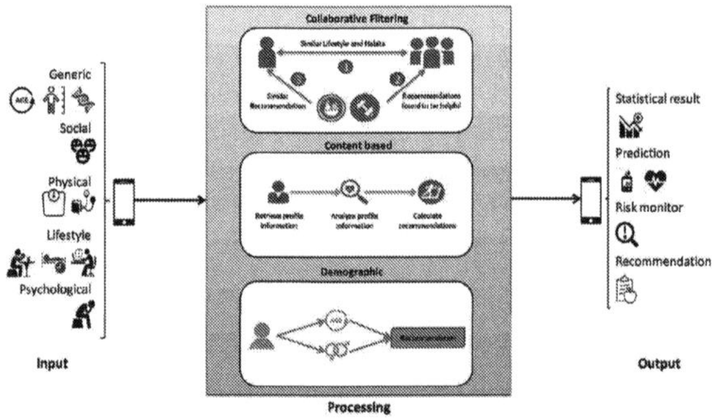

Figure 1: System Architecture

We have introduced three different approaches for constructing our recommendation system: **Collaborative Filtering, Content Based Analysis** and **Demographic Analysis**

4 Conclusion

Hypertension may cause several life-threatening diseases without any prior indication. Thus, having an app installed in a user's mobile that regularly monitors his activities and guides him accordingly is extremely beneficial.

5 References

[1] Valérie Gay and Peter Leijdekkers. A health monitoring system using smart phones and wearable sensors. *International Journal of ARM*, 8(2):29–35, 2007.

[2] A Mertens, S Becker, S Theis, P Rasche, M Wille, C Bröhl, L Finken, and C Schlick. Mobile technology improves therapy-adherence rates in elderly patients undergoing rehabilitationâĂŤa crossover design study. In *Advances in Human Factors and Ergonomics in Healthcare*, pages 295–308. Springer, 2017.

Permission to make digital or hard copies of part or all of this work for personal or classroom use is granted without fee provided that copies are not made or distributed for profit or commercial advantage and that copies bear this notice and the full citation on the first page. Copyrights for third-party components of this work must be honored. For all other uses, contact the owner/author(s).

MobiSys'17 June 19-23, 2017, Niagara Falls, NY, USA

© 2017 Copyright held by the owner/author(s).

ACM ISBN 978-1-4503-4928-4/17/06.
DOI: http://dx.doi.org/10.1145/3081333.3089308

Poster: Flood Monitoring using Computer Vision

Bhavana B Nair
Amrita Center for Wireless Networks & Applications (AmritaWNA)
Amrita School of Engineering, Amritapuri
Amrita Vishwa Vidyapeetham
Amrita University, India
bhavanabnair@am.amrita.edu

Sethuraman N Rao
Amrita Center for Wireless Networks & Applications (AmritaWNA)
Amrita School of Engineering, Amritapuri
Amrita Vishwa Vidyapeetham
Amrita University, India
sethuramanrao@am.amrita.edu

1. INTRODUCTION

Urban floods have become a constant threat to human life and property. Also, high resolution cameras in smart phones have become ubiquitous. This work involves using Computer Vision [1] [2] algorithms to estimate the depth of flooding based on images taken by the general public which are geo-tagged and time-stamped. This approach will help in the implementation of effective and timely urban flood relief and management. This data can also be used to assess the effectiveness of preventive measures taken in the past and to plan remedial measures in the future.

2. OBJECTIVE

Estimate the water level in a flooded region using the human height as reference. Steps [Figure 1] :

- Detection of human face and segmenting the human part in the image using deep learning algorithm. Human segmentation [3] helps to find the pixel position of the water line.
- Classify each detected human face as male or female and use average male/female height as the reference.
- Assume the human height to be 8 times that of the bounding box around the face (Golden Ratio).
- Once the pixel positions of the human feet (where the extrapolated bounding box ends) and the water line are known, they can be used to estimate the water depth.

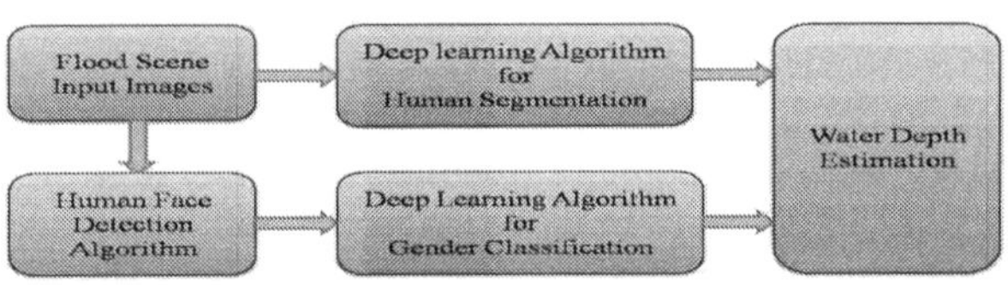

Figure 1: System Architecture

Permission to make digital or hard copies of part or all of this work for personal or classroom use is granted without fee provided that copies are not made or distributed for profit or commercial advantage and that copies bear this notice and the full citation on the first page. Copyrights for third-party components of this work must be honored. For all other uses, contact the owner/author(s).

MobiSys'17 June 19-23, 2017, Niagara Falls, NY, USA

© 2017 Copyright held by the owner/author(s).

ACM ISBN 978-1-4503-4928-4/17/06.
DOI: http://dx.doi.org/10.1145/3081333.3089309

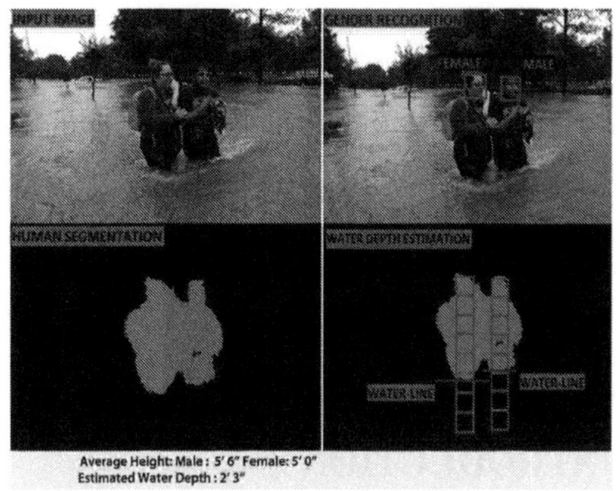

Figure 2: Water Depth Estimation

3. EXPERIMENTAL RESULTS

The steps involved in flood depth estimation and the results obtained are shown in Figure 2.

4. CONCLUSION & FUTURE WORK

In this work, Computer Vision is used to estimate the flood water depth based on images of humans wading through water. One challenge in this approach is that human face detection algorithm may fail with low resolution images. Possible future work includes:

1. Water segmentation to find the water line.
2. Further refinement of the reference human height based on detection of age, ethnicity, etc.
3. Water depth estimation based on reference height of other objects such as vehicles, buildings, electric posts, etc., in the image.

5. REFERENCES

[1] R. Narayanan, V. M. Lekshmy, S. Rao, and K. Sasidhar. A novel approach to urban flood monitoring using computer vision. In *ICCCNT*, pages 1–7, July 2014.

[2] G Uma, R. Narayanan, P. Venkat Rangan, and Balaji Hariharan. Re-orchestration of remote teaching environment in elearning. In *ICEIS 2016*, pages 223–229, 2016.

[3] R. Narayanan, Balaji Hariharan, G Uma, and P. Venkat Rangan. Instructor contour extraction and overlay for near-real presence in e-learning systems. In *CSEDU 2016*, pages 353–358, 2016.

Poster: Impact of Ground Truth Errors on Wi-Fi Localization Accuracy*

Andrei Popleteev
SnT, University of Luxembourg
contact@popleteev.com

ABSTRACT

This study investigates the impact of small ground truth (GT) errors on indoor positioning systems based on Wi-Fi fingerprinting. The results demonstrate that even centimeter-scale GT deviations cause severe degradation of measured localization accuracy.

Keywords

Indoor localization; performance evaluation; small-scale fading; ground truth; fingerprinting; RSS; WLAN.

1. INTRODUCTION

Fingerprinting-based indoor positioning systems are often trained and tested in the same reference points [1]. In reality, however, these "same" points can be decimeters apart, depending on the chosen ground truth (GT) methodology [2].

On one hand, minor GT errors seem negligible in comparison to meter-scale Wi-Fi localization errors. On the other hand, small-scale fading of Wi-Fi signals — the result of radio wave interference with its own reflections from surrounding obstacles — causes significant spatial variations of received signal strength (RSS) at sub-wavelength distances ($\lambda = 12.5$ cm for Wi-Fi). While location tracking systems can detect and mitigate such variations when the user moves [3], this is not possible for non-tracking (single-shot) systems.

In this study we demonstrate that minor GT errors are amplified by small-scale fading and can introduce multi-meter positioning errors, thus affecting benchmarking results of an indoor localization system.

*This work was supported by the National Research Fund of Luxembourg (C14/IS/8311593).

Permission to make digital or hard copies of part or all of this work for personal or classroom use is granted without fee provided that copies are not made or distributed for profit or commercial advantage and that copies bear this notice and the full citation on the first page. Copyrights for third-party components of this work must be honored. For all other uses, contact the owner/author(s).

MobiSys'17 June 19-23, 2017, Niagara Falls, NY, USA

© 2017 Copyright held by the owner/author(s).

ACM ISBN 978-1-4503-4928-4/17/06.
DOI: http://dx.doi.org/10.1145/3081333.3089310

2. PERFORMANCE EVALUATION

To evaluate the impact of imprecise GT, we collected a training Wi-Fi RSS dataset (using a 3×4 grid with 2 m step) and several testing datasets, with increasing deviation from the original GT positions. To minimize the impact of non GT related factors, the experiment was conducted in otherwise idealized conditions: same device, same orientation, same hour, minimal human presence. The results show that even centimeter-scale dislocations between the calibration and testing points significantly reduce the localization accuracy (Figure 1).

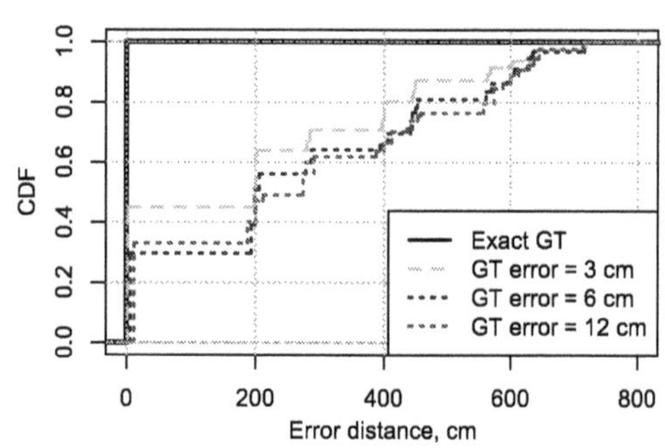

Figure 1: Localization accuracy and GT error.

We thus propose GT quality as a new methodological factor that affects Wi-Fi fingerprinting performance. Curiously, this makes localization accuracy directly dependent on the experimenter's diligence. Moreover, this partially explains some of the already known accuracy-limiting factors (such as device diversity, different-person evaluation, accuracy degradation with time) as they are also associated with GT errors.

3. REFERENCES

[1] S. Adler, S. Schmitt, K. Wolter, and M. Kyas. A survey of experimental evaluation in indoor localization research. In *Proc. IPIN-2015*, 2015.

[2] A. Popleteev. HIPS: Human-based indoor positioning system. In *Proc. IPIN-2016*, 2016.

[3] M. Youssef and A. Agrawala. Small-scale compensation for WLAN location determination systems. In *Proc. WCNC-2003*, 2003.

Poster: *Observe. Patternize. Mimic.* Leveraging Patterns in Mobile-User Behavior for Enterprise Applications

Uma Parthavi Moravapalle[a], Shruti Sanadhya[b], Cheng-Lin Tsao[c] and Raghupathy Sivakumar[a]
[a]Georgia Tech.; [b]Hewlett Packard Labs; [c]Anthem Innovation Studio

1. OVERVIEW

Application Mobilization, or the ability of an enterprise employee to rely on mobile devices such as smartphones and tablets, to continue to perform business workflows even when mobile, is seen as a game changer to improve productivity[1]. However, the practical adoption of enterprise mobility is very much in its infancy, and seemingly has barriers. We posit that these barriers include *heavy user-burden in accomplishing tasks* (e.g. number of actions required to execute a workflow), *high cost of mobile access* (e.g. latency for content fetching), and *irrelevance of available mobile functions* (e.g. mobile app defeaturization done inappropriately).The novelty of our research is in a **unified observe-patternize-mimic paradigm** we explore to address these barriers, based on a simple question: *could patterns in user-behavior be learned, and leveraged for reducing user-burden?* If patterns are discovered, then we show that intelligent mimicking of these patterns at appropriate junctures can considerably relieve the mobile-user burden. We motivate this paradigm through three application scenarios representing *read*, *write*, and *act* usage modalities.

2. OBSERVE. PATTERNIZE. MIMIC.

Precog (read): An enterprise worker might consume web content from different locations (e.g. work, home, customer office etc.), sometimes over high cost/latency networks (e.g. 3G/4G cellular). By observing the user's browsing behavior to extract content access patterns, and using these patterns to intelligently prefetch web content that the user is likely to need in the future over cheaper networks (e.g. WiFi), we can achieve cost/latency benefits. Existing solutions are either name-based (prefetch most used URLs and hence irrelevant for dynamic web) or are network-unaware (do not consider differing network costs i.e. WiFi is cheaper than cellular). Thus, we propose *Precog*, a solution that leverages consistency in page layouts to identify repeating user actions (e.g. clicking top stories) on cellular networks and preplays them on WiFi before the cellular access. We find that *Precog* can achieve up to 37% latency reduction through mobile browser action traces collected from 8 users (see fig. 1a).

This work was funded in part by the National Science Foundation under grants CNS-1513884 and CNS-1319455, and the Wayne J. Holman Endowed Chair.

[1]http://www.techrepublic.com/article/infographic-byod-is-popular-but-not-widely-supported-by-it/

Permission to make digital or hard copies of part or all of this work for personal or classroom use is granted without fee provided that copies are not made or distributed for profit or commercial advantage and that copies bear this notice and the full citation on the first page. Copyrights for third-party components of this work must be honored. For all other uses, contact the owner/author(s).

MobiSys'17 June 19-23, 2017, Niagara Falls, NY, USA

© 2017 Copyright held by the owner/author(s).

ACM ISBN 978-1-4503-4928-4/17/06.
DOI: http://dx.doi.org/10.1145/3081333.3089311

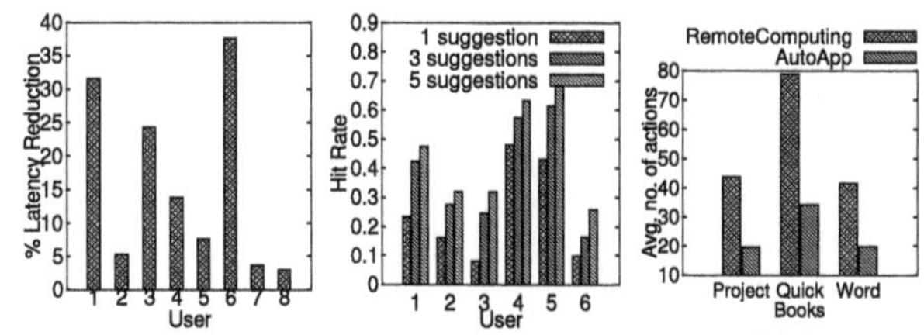

(a) Read (b) Write (c) Act

Figure 1: Benefits of intelligent pattern mimic

Precog observes and extracts patterns in user's actions on a webpage while on cellular and preplays these actions over WiFi for latency and cost benefits.

Dejavu (write): An enterprise worker spends an inordinate amount of time on responding to email queries from co-workers, many of which can be similar or identical in nature. Our proposed research *Dejavu* observes the user's mailbox and automatically suggests email responses for emails using the content already present on the mailbox. *Dejavu* extracts important keywords from an inbox email, matches these keywords to emails already in the mailbox, and suggests emails that are closest to the current email (min. 60% similarity) as responses. Using the mailbox data from 6 users (see fig. 1b), we found that this simple matching approach in *Dejavu* can find suggestions that have >60% match with actual response (hitrate) for 33% of all emails (1 suggestion) on average.

Dejavu observes emails in a user's mailbox to suggest responses that closely match keywords in an inbox email and reduces user burden of typing the response.

AutoApp (act): One promising strategy for application mobilization is defeaturization - where-in the number of features exposed on the mobile app is a tiny fraction of what the desktop version supports. This is accomplished today through manual and static design and remains the same for all users. Our proposed solution, *AutoApp*, is based on application refactoring on remote computing, with a server running the application and a client with a remote view. Unlike remote computing, *AutoApp* observes desktop usage patterns, defeaturizes the application to contain only commonly used features, condenses some patterns into macros, and transforms the UI elements of the original application view to smartphone native UI elements. A preliminary prototype for *AutoApp* for Windows applications (Quickbooks, Project and Word) with a manual transformation of application views, showed up to 66% reduction in the number of actions to perform a task compared to remote computing (fig. 1c).

AutoApp observes desktop application usage to customize defeaturization for each individual user, thereby reducing the task burden of performing workflows.

Poster: RTDroid: A Real-Time Solution with Android

Yin Yan, Karthik Dantu, Steven Y. Ko, Lukasz Ziarek
Department of Computer Science and Engineering
The State University of New York at Buffalo
{yinyan, kdantu, stevko, lziarek}@buffalo.edu

ABSTRACT

Since the introduction of the smartphone, mobile computing has become pervasive in our society. Meanwhile, Mobile devices have evolved far beyond the stereotypical personal devices and been employed in various traditional real-time embedded domains. Of the currently available mobile systems, Android has seen the most widespread deployment outside of the consumer electronics market. Its open source nature has prompted its ubiquitous adoption in sensing, medical, robotics, and autopilot applications. However, it is not surprising that Android does not provide any real-time guarantee since it is designed as a mobile system and optimised for mobility, user experience, and energy efficiency.

Although there has been much interest [1, 2, 3] in adopting Android in real-time contexts, surprisingly little work has been done to examine the suitability of Android for real-time systems. Existing work only provides solutions to traditional problems, including real-time garbage collection at the virtual machine layer, real-time OS scheduling and resource management. While it is critical to address these issues, it is by no means sufficient. After all, Android is a vast system that is more than a Java virtual machine and a kernel.

Our work [4, 6, 7] examines the internals of Android, the Android programming model, libraries and core systems services. We discuss the implications and challenges of adapting Android constructs and core system services for real-time and present a solution for each, name RTDroid, *as a whole system*. It is unique in that it redesigns Android's internal components, replaces Android's Dalvik/ART with a real-time Java virtual machine, FijiVM, and leverages off-the-shelf real-time OSes.

RTDroid also provides an event-driven programming model [5] for the development of real-time applications. To retain a familiar style of Android application, we make a number of changes to the Android abstractions and how they interact with the underlying system as well as each other. We aim to leave legacy Android code unaffected and expose real-time features to components which have timeliness requirements. More specifically, Our programming model consist of four parts: 1) real-time constructs for real-time expressiveness, 2) a real-time extension to Android's application manifest for the real-time configuration, 3) real-time communication channels that enable construct interactions with real-time semantics, 4) pause-less memory management with scoped memory.

To validate the predictability of RTDroid's implementation, we firstly report a number of micro benchmark results with RTDroid basic constructs. Then, we demonstrate three real-world applications implemented in RTDroid and provide statistic results. Our results illustrate that, at least in these use-cases, the modified platform delivers significantly better time predictability than stock Android and reduces the code complexity as compared to the traditional real-time programming paradigm, RTSJ.

Permission to make digital or hard copies of part or all of this work for personal or classroom use is granted without fee provided that copies are not made or distributed for profit or commercial advantage and that copies bear this notice and the full citation on the first page. Copyrights for third-party components of this work must be honored. For all other uses, contact the owner/author(s).

MobiSys'17 June 19-23, 2017, Niagara Falls, NY, USA

© 2017 Copyright held by the owner/author(s).

ACM ISBN 978-1-4503-4928-4/17/06...$15.00

DOI: http://dx.doi.org/10.1145/3081333.3089312

References

[1] Thomas Gerlitz, Igor Kalkov, John Schommer, Dominik Franke, and Stefan Kowalewski. Non-blocking garbage collection for real-time android. In *Proceedings of the 11th International Workshop on Java Technologies for Real-time and Embedded Systems*, JTRES '13, 2013.

[2] Igor Kalkov, Dominik Franke, John F. Schommer, and Stefan Kowalewski. A Real-Time Extension to The Android Platform. In *Proceedings of the 10th International Workshop on Java Technologies for Real-time and Embedded Systems*, JTRES '12, pages 105–114, New York, NY, USA, 2012. ACM.

[3] Cláudio Maia, Luís Nogueira, and Luis Miguel Pinho. Evaluating Android OS for Embedded Real-Time Systems. In *Proceedings of the 6th International Workshop on Operating Systems Platforms for Embedded Real-Time Applications, Brussels, Belgium*, OSPERT '10, pages 63–70, 2010.

[4] Yin Yan, Shaun Cosgrove, Varun Anand, Amit Kulkarni, Sree Harsha Konduri, Steven Y Ko, and Lukasz Ziarek. Rtdroid: A design for real-time android. *IEEE Transactions on Mobile Computing*, 15(10):2564–2584, 2016.

[5] Yin Yan, Karthik Dantu, Steve Ko, Jan Vitek, and Lukasz Ziarek. Making Android Run on Time. In *Real-Time and Embedded Technology and Application Symposium*, RTAS '17, Washington, DC, USA, April 2017. IEEE Computer Society.

[6] Yin Yan, Sree Harsha Konduri, Amit Kulkarni, Varun Anand, Steve Ko, and Lukasz Ziarek. RTDroid: A Design for Real-Time Android. In *Proceedings of the 11th International Workshop on Java Technologies for Real-time and Embedded Systems*, JTRES '13, New York, NY, USA, 2013. ACM.

[7] Yin Yan, Sree Harsha Konduri, Amit Kulkarni, Varun Anand, Steve Ko, and Lukasz Ziarek. Real-Time Android with RT-Droid. In *The 12th International Conference on Mobile Systems, Applications, and Services*, MOBISYS '14, New York, NY, USA, 2014. ACM.

Poster: Securing Device Inputs for Smartphones Using Hypervisor Based Approach

Xin Zhang, Yongshu Bai, Pengzhan Hao, and Yifan Zhang
Department of Computer Science
SUNY Binghamton
Binghamton, NY
{xzhang99, ybai4, phao3, zhangy}@binghamton.edu

Introduction. Smartphone device inputs, such as inputs from touchscreen, sensors, and GPS, carry sensitive user information, but are vulnerable to passive and active attacks. In one category of the attacks, attackers can passively infer or actively steal sensitive user info from smartphone device inputs. In another category, attackers can tamper with or forge smartphone device inputs to disrupt services relying on those input data or even gain control of the smartphone. We present our ongoing design and implementation of SDIF, a Secure Device Input Framework for smartphones.

System architecture. Figure 1 shows the architecture of SDIF on an Android smartphone. The core components of SDIF are *a small and dedicated bare-metal hypervisor built using ARM hardware virtualization support* and *a user-space sandbox framework*, which collectively ensure SDIF's support for unmodified OSes and apps. SDIF secures smartphone device inputs with two novel designs:

• First, SDIF enables *a secure path between smartphone input devices and the protected applications*, allowing device input streams to be securely transferred between the two endpoints. On the device endpoint, SDIF relies on the dedicated bare-metal hypervisor to achieve secure device I/O management. By trapping and inspecting sensitive activities, the SDIF hypervisor can monitor the I/O operations in the system without modifying any code of the OS. On the application endpoint, SDIF relies on the user-space sandbox framework to provide necessary utilities for the applications to communicate with the input devices via the secure path. To connect the two endpoints, a communication protocol specifying how device inputs are transmitted between the endpoints via the secure path is needed. We are currently exploring three different communication protocol designs on two different secure paths, aiming to ensure that no attacker can infer or steal user information from device inputs when the user is interacting with the protected applications.

• Second, to ensure that the input devices are properly configured when device drivers read data from the devices, and that device drivers themselves will not tampered with the data before handing them over to the OS, SDIF ports the device driver functionalities to the hypervisor, which provides a trusted execution environment. However, this brings a notable challenge, which is the need of minimizing the hypervisor's code size (and hence minimizing its TCB). SDIF addresses this challenge by porting only the driver functionalities that are critical for trusted device data reading, which is a small part in driver's code, into the hypervisor, such that the original unmodified device driver and the hypervisor can collectively achieve trusted device data reading. The above two designs collectively guarantee that the device inputs that a protected application receives have not been tampered with.

Permission to make digital or hard copies of part or all of this work for personal or classroom use is granted without fee provided that copies are not made or distributed for profit or commercial advantage and that copies bear this notice and the full citation on the first page. Copyrights for third-party components of this work must be honored. For all other uses, contact the owner/author(s).

MobiSys'17 June 19-23, 2017, Niagara Falls, NY, USA

© 2017 Copyright held by the owner/author(s).

ACM ISBN 978-1-4503-4928-4/17/06.
DOI: http://dx.doi.org/10.1145/3081333.3089313

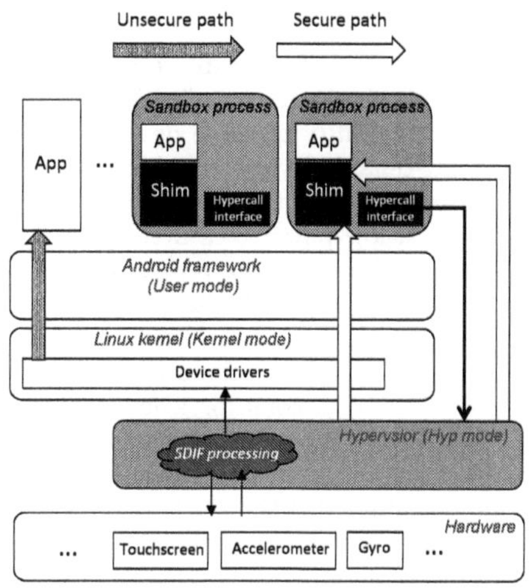

Figure 1: SDIF overview (shaded parts are the components of SDIF).

Ongoing implementation. We are in the active process of implementing SDIF system on real hardware, and plan to validate the our designs by performing real-world experiments on the prototype system. Due to the easiness of flashing and running customized bootloaders, we use ARM development boards featuring commercial smartphone SoCs as our prototype and experiment platforms. Our initial platform consists of an ODROID XU3 development board, a 9 inch 10-points capacitive multi touchscreen, and a WiFi module. The ODROID XU3 features Samsung Exynos 5422 SoC, which is currently used on many popular smartphones such as the Samsung Galaxy S5. We also have a plan to port the implementation to and validate it on ARMv8 architecture.

Acknowledgments. This work is being supported in part by NSF Award #1566375.

Poster: Memory Protection in Ultra-Low-Power Multi-Application Wearables

Taylor Hardin†, Josiah Hester*, Patrick Proctor†, Jacob Sorber*, David Kotz†
†Dartmouth College and *Clemson University

1. INTRODUCTION

An increasing number of wearable devices support the execution of multiple third-party applications, increasing the functionality and flexibility of these devices. These multi-application, multi-tenant devices provide users with more options, and application developers with a standard platform. Typical ultra-low-power wearable devices, however, lack the type of hardware memory protection mechanisms – such as Memory Management Units (MMU) – needed to safely separate applications. At best, they provide a Memory Protection Unit (MPU), which allows the user to configure read/write/execute permissions for a few distinct regions of memory. At worst, no hardware memory protection is provided. MPU capabilities vary across hardware platforms, with many shortcomings: (1) the MPU may only support a few distinct memory regions (fewer than one per application), (2) the MPU may not protect all regions of memory, like hardware registers, and (3) MPU protection boundary rules can be arcane, because they depend on opaque hardware implementations. Our key observation is that by supplementing a limited segment MPU with runtime checks, and using compile-time static analysis to explicitly layout applications in memory, we can guarantee application isolation (sandboxing) even on these limited MPUs, with lower overhead than software-only solutions.

2. APPROACH

Ultra-low-power microcontrollers have historically not offered MPUs; only recently have MPUs become more prevalent, but many lack the functionality for sufficient memory management and protection. Thus, those who develop multi-application, multi-tenant platforms isolate applications using compile-time or run-time software sandboxing (e.g., AmuletOS [1]), imposing limits on application developers and adding time/space overhead to running applications. We have developed methods, however, to leverage the limited MPUs and thereby reduce overhead cost by narrowing the use of software-based approaches.

Permission to make digital or hard copies of part or all of this work for personal or classroom use is granted without fee provided that copies are not made or distributed for profit or commercial advantage and that copies bear this notice and the full citation on the first page. Copyrights for third-party components of this work must be honored. For all other uses, contact the owner/author(s).

MobiSys'17 June 19-23, 2017, Niagara Falls, NY, USA

© 2017 Copyright held by the owner/author(s).

ACM ISBN 978-1-4503-4928-4/17/06.
DOI: http://dx.doi.org/10.1145/3081333.3089314

Our prototype solution runs on the MSP430 microcontroller (specifically, MSP430FR5989); its MPU supports four memory regions (with some restrictions). At compile time, our solution splits memory into three coarse-grained sections: 1) OS stack, 2) OS code, and 3) applications. Each application in Section 3 is then further divided into code and stack segments. By providing each application with its own stack we can ensure that applications are not able to glean or modify sensitive stack information from the system or other applications. This layout allows us to use the MPU to prevent all illegal accesses above the currently executing application's stack. Since we need only check memory references below the current application's stack, our method eliminates half of the number of compiler-inserted runtime checks. The compiler inserts code for MPU management, enabling cross-domain "system calls" from the application to the OS, and arranging the MPU boundaries when the OS or another application needs to run next.

3. CONTRIBUTION

The poster summarizes the current state of MPU hardware used in ultra-low-power wearables, and evaluates our prototype solution. For applications with a high frequency of memory accesses, our approach induces less overhead than software-only solutions, and gives more freedom to application developers (by avoiding the need for language or compile-time restrictions imposed by many software solutions). With minimal changes, our solution can be applied to other MPUs with varying degrees of functionality. Given these observations, we propose changes to existing MPU hardware that would decrease runtime overhead and/or eliminate the need for software checks. Please follow us at amulet-project.org.

Acknowledgements. This research results from a research program at the Institute for Security, Technology, and Society, supported by the National Science Foundation under award numbers CNS-1314281, CNS-1314342, CNS-1619970, and CNS-1619950. The Amulet logo was designed by the DALI Lab at Dartmouth College. The views and conclusions contained in this document are those of the authors and should not be interpreted as necessarily representing the official policies, either expressed or implied, of the sponsors.

4. REFERENCES

[1] J. Hester et al. Amulet: An Energy-Efficient, Multi-Application Wearable Platform. In *Proceedings of the ACM Conferences on Embedded Networked Sensor Systems (SenSys)*, pages 216-229. ACM, Nov. 2016.

Poster: Android Malware Detection using Multi-Flows and API Patterns

Feng Shen, Justin Del Vecchio, Aziz Mohaisen, Steven Y. Ko, Lukasz Ziarek
University at Buffalo, The State University of New York
{fengshen, jmdv, mohaisen, stevko, lziarek}@buffalo.edu

ABSTRACT

This paper proposes a new technique for detecting mobile malware based on information flow analysis. Our approach focuses on the *structure* of information flows we gather in our analysis, and the *patterns* of behavior present in information flows. Our analysis not only gathers *simple* flows that have a single source and a single sink, but also *Multi-Flows* that either start from a single source and flow to multiple sinks, or start from multiple sources and flow to a single sink. This analysis captures more complex behavior that both recent malware and recent benign applications exhibit. We leverage *N-gram analysis* to understand both unique and common behavioral patterns present in Multi-Flows. Our tool leverages N-gram analysis over sequences of API calls that occur along control flow paths in Multi-Flows to precisely analyze Multi-Flows with respect to app behavior.

Using our approach, we show that there is a need to look beyond simple flows in order to effectively leverage information flow analysis for malware detection. By analyzing recently-collected malware, we show there has been an evolution in malware beyond simply collecting sensitive information and immediately exposing it. Many previous systems focus on identifying the existence of *simple* information flows—i.e. considering an information flow as just a (source, sink) pair. However, modern malware performs complex computations before, during, and after collecting sensitive information and tends to aggregate data before exposing it. A simple (source, sink) view of information flow does not adequately capture such behavior.

The uniqueness of our approach comes from the following two features. First, our information flow analysis represent an information flow not as a simple (source, sink) pair, but as *a sequence of API calls*. This gives us the ability to distinguish different flows with same sources and sinks based on the *computation* performed along the information flow. Second, our information flow analysis detects Multi-Flows, flows that either start with a single source and flow to multiple sinks, or start with multiple sources and flow to a single sink. We treat such flows as a single flow, instead of multiple distinct flows. Fig. 1 shows a comparison of a Multi-Flow and its corresponding simple flows. This allows us to examine the *structure* of the flows themselves. We leverage machine learning techniques to extract features from Multi-Flows and their API sequences (N-gram analysis) and use these features to perform SVM-based classification.

Based on this approach, we build an open source implementation of Multi-Flow analysis and API sequencing in the BlueSeal framework [2] [3] [1], along with N-gram analysis and a SVM-based classifier. We also conduct a detailed evaluation study, highlighting the differences in old and new apps. We leverage the app behavior extracted as features from both Multi-Flows and their API usage patterns and apply machine learning techniques to automatically identify malware based on the structure of its computation over sensitive data. We test our tool on a set of 1,576 benign apps downloaded from Google Play and 2,422 known malicious apps. Our results show that app behavior difference on sensitive data can be a significant factor in malware detection.

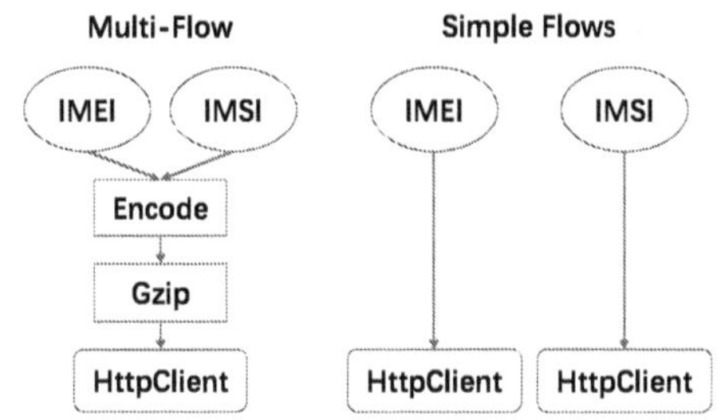

Figure 1: Multi-Flow vs Simple Flows

Permission to make digital or hard copies of part or all of this work for personal or classroom use is granted without fee provided that copies are not made or distributed for profit or commercial advantage and that copies bear this notice and the full citation on the first page. Copyrights for third-party components of this work must be honored. For all other uses, contact the owner/author(s).
MobiSys'17 June 19-23, 2017, Niagara Falls, NY, USA
© 2017 Copyright held by the owner/author(s).
ACM ISBN 978-1-4503-4928-4/17/06.
DOI: http://dx.doi.org/10.1145/3081333.3089315

References

[1] S. Holavanalli, D. Manuel, V. Nanjundaswamy, B. Rosenberg, F. Shen, S. Y. Ko, and L. Ziarek. Flow permissions for android. In *Proceedings of the 28th IEEE/ACM International Conference on Automated Software Engineering (ASE 2013)*, 2013.

[2] F. Shen, J. Del Vecchio, A. Mohaisen, S. Y. Ko, and L. Ziarek. Android malware detection using complex-flows. In *Proceedings of The 37th IEEE International Conference on Distributed Computing Systems*, ICDCS '17.

[3] F. Shen, N. Vishnubhotla, C. Todarka, M. Arora, B. Dhandapani, E. J. Lehner, S. Y. Ko, and L. Ziarek. Information flows as a permission mechanism. In *Proceedings of the 29th ACM/IEEE International Conference on Automated Software Engineering*, ASE '14.

Poster: Camera Images Offloading in Low-resource Wireless Networks

Wei Xiong, Mariya Zheleva
University at Albany, SUNY
{wxiong, mzheleva}@albany.edu

1. MOTIVATION AND METHODOLOGY

Camera snapshot images are widely used in IoT applications such as smart farming and weather monitoring, which generate large volumes of image data. However, when these settings are in rural areas or poorly-performing networks, the images offloading usually exhausts the limited network resources. While we can certainly revamp the network links, we can also optimize the payload at the same time[1]. From our site survey we see that for consecutive camera snapshots, there is a notable similarity among the contents, especially from fixed-positioned cameras used in IoT environments.

Methodology. We design a system that computes and transfers only the "difference" between consecutive images, thus drastically reducing the network offered load. Original images are then restored at the server side. Our system uses a middlebox to intercept camera images, compute the "difference" across image series before uploading them to the server. The middlebox is plug-and-play and can be deployed on a cheap single board computer near the cameras; for example, on an OpenWRT-based access point serving the cameras. Also, we use another counterpart module on the server to "decode" the payload and restore the original image. In this early implementation, we use *Pillow* as the imaging tool and *Scapy* to manipulate packets passed through. Because of lossy compression operations used in both "encode" and "decode" stages, the restored image may introduce some small error compared to the original image, but the approach significantly reduces the payload transferred which is a good choice to alleviate poorly performing networks.

2. PRELIMINARY EVALUATION

We choose 330 traffic cameras in New York[2]. For each camera, we download 100 consecutive images at a 10-second interval. Our selected cameras provide a wide diversity of images, ranging from streets and highways to bridges and tunnels. From any two consecutive images of the same camera, we subtract latter image B from previous image A to get the difference (aka, the payload in our proposed system). We calculate the size of reduced image δ comparing to B as shown in Fig.2. We then add δ and A to get the restored image B'. We calculate the `structural similarity` between B and B', denoted as accuracy in Fig.1.

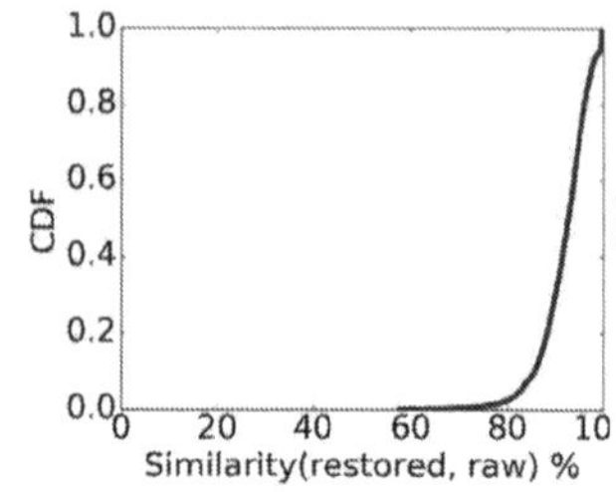

Figure 1: Accuracy

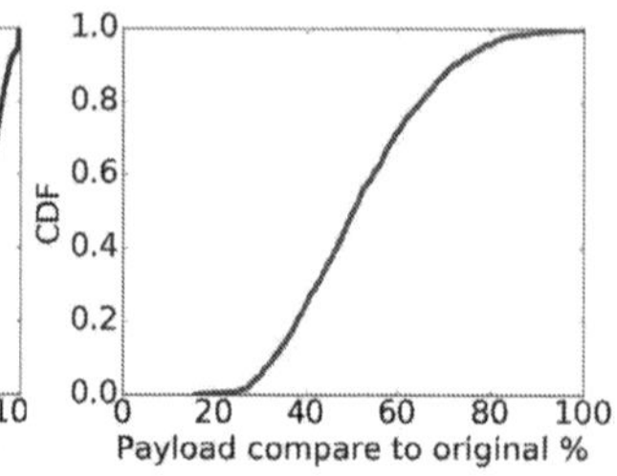

Figure 2: Reduced payload

Note that there is a difference due to what we called one-step optimization and multi-step optimization. Denote A, B and C as consecutive images, f_1, f_2 as decoding and encoding respectively. The above result shows

$$Sim(C,\ f_2(B + f_1(C - B))) \tag{1}$$

But instead of using raw image B, we do

$$\begin{aligned} &Sim(C,\ f_2(B' + f_1(C - B'))) \\ &\text{where} \quad B' = f_2(A + f_1(B - A)) \end{aligned} \tag{2}$$

Apparently (2) does not necessarily yield same accuracy as (1) does. However (2) leads to a higher sum of reduced payload. Therefore in order to achieve the result shown, we assume using one-step optimization, meaning the middlebox should offload the raw image in every other cycle. While it can certainly perform multi-steps optimization, the trade-off between the compound error on similarity and the sum of reduced payload could be one aspect of our further study. Also, we notice the worst accuracy comes from camera images with random striping noise, which should be further studied in order to deal with noise and other external factors.

3. REFERENCES

[1] W. Hu et al. The case for offload shaping. In *Proceedings of the 16th International Workshop on Mobile Computing Systems and Applications*, pages 51–56. ACM, 2015.

[2] NYC Traffic Cameras. http://dotsignals.org.

Permission to make digital or hard copies of part or all of this work for personal or classroom use is granted without fee provided that copies are not made or distributed for profit or commercial advantage and that copies bear this notice and the full citation on the first page. Copyrights for third-party components of this work must be honored. For all other uses, contact the owner/author(s).

MobiSys'17 June 19-23, 2017, Niagara Falls, NY, USA

© 2017 Copyright held by the owner/author(s).

ACM ISBN 978-1-4503-4928-4/17/06.

DOI: http://dx.doi.org/10.1145/3081333.3089316

Poster: Redundancy-Aided Vehicular Networking

HyunJong Lee

Jason Flinn

University of Michigan

Vehicular applications are increasingly connected to cloud services. For example, route planning, gas price applications, and Siri-like personal assistants all respond to user queries based in part on cloud processing. Network communication thus is often a substantial component of user-perceived latency in vehicular applications.

Current vehicular computing platforms typically connect to the cloud using a single cellular network provider. Network conditions can change rapidly as a vehicle moves due to geographical variation in coverage, radio shadows, and differing traffic density. Such variation is often exacerbated by connection re-establishment after an interface has entered a sleep state.

Thus, vehicular applications can often appear unresponsive due to high wireless network latency. Even worse, the responsiveness is unpredictable; high tail latency makes some user interactions take longer, even when most interactions complete in an acceptable amount of time. This unpredictability is especially worrisome in a vehicular environment, in which occasional unexpected performance anomalies distract the driver of the vehicle.

Smartphones mitigate poor network performance by switching among multiple networks (e.g., WiFi and cellular). Such a strategy makes sense when performance is predictable. However, it provides little help for the unexpected tail latencies common in vehicular environments.

In our work, we are mitigating tail latency for vehicular applications by redundantly sending data over multiple wireless networks for user-facing applications. Rather than estimate network latency and bandwidth as scalar values, we calculate the expected distribution of these values for each wireless networks. If the error bounds for the expected time to transmit small amounts of data over at least two different wireless networks overlap with each other, our vehicular platform transmits the data over both networks. At the cost of redundant transmission of data, this strategy improves the average user-perceived delay in vehicle-cloud applications. More importantly, it substantially reduces tail latency.

The opportunities for employing redundant transmission are considerable in vehicular computing. Not only can the vehicular platform employ built-in cellular and WiFi interfaces, but the platform can also communicate with multiple cellular providers by tethering with smartphones carried by passengers within the vehicle.

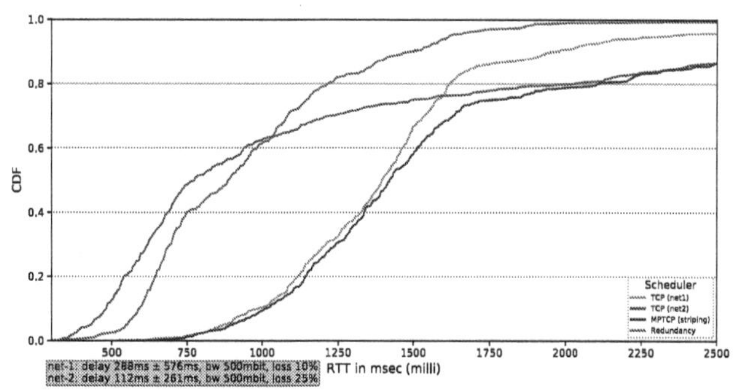

Figure 1: 10K data transfer by different schedulers

We argue that the downsides of employing redundancy are surprisingly small. The user-facing applications for which we are employing redundancy transmit small amounts of data. Indeed, an application transmitting bulk data would benefit little from redundancy, and our vehicular platform would not employ redundancy for such a purpose. Thus, the total amount of bytes sent redundantly is small. Energy considerations are also minimal since vehicular platforms are typically powered by the automobile engine.

Our prototype system for *Redundancy-Aided Vehicular Networking* (RAVEN) reduces tail latency for vehicular applications via redundant network transmission. RAVEN is implemented on top of MPTCP, a recent extension of TCP to support multipath networks. MPTCP binds a single application TCP connection to multiple TCP subflows to stripe data over multiple physical networks. RAVEN implements a new MPTCP scheduler that selectively transmits small data redundantly over these subflows. We have developed a statistical model that provides latency estimates for each physical network within a configurable confidence level. When redundancy has a substantial confidence to reduce tail latency, RAVEN transmits the data redundantly over multiple subflows to improve responsiveness of user-facing applications.

We are currently evaluating RAVEN in many wireless network scenarios. For instance, consider the common situation where two wireless networks are experiencing unexpected packet loss. As shown in Fig. 1, RAVEN outperforms both MPTCP and a strategy that selects either wireless network for exclusive transmission. The improvement in performance is most noticeable at the 99% percentile in the CDF, where redundancy substantially reduces tail network latency compared to generic MPTCP and TCP over either network.

Permission to make digital or hard copies of part or all of this work for personal or classroom use is granted without fee provided that copies are not made or distributed for profit or commercial advantage and that copies bear this notice and the full citation on the first page. Copyrights for third-party components of this work must be honored. For all other uses, contact the Owner/Author(s). Copyright is held by the owner/author(s).
MobiSys '17, June 19–23, 2017, Niagara Falls, NY, USA.
ACM ISBN 978-1-4503-4928-4/17/06.
DOI: http://dx.doi.org/10.1145/3081333.3089317

Poster: *Twirl*: On the Benefits of Adapting Orientation of a WiFi Access-Point

Yubing Jian, Shruti Lall, and Raghupathy Sivakumar
Georgia Institute of Technology
{yubing, slall, siva}@ece.gatech.edu

1. OVERVIEW

The position of a wireless access point (AP) in wireless networks has been found to have a considerable impact on the overall network performance in indoor scenarios. Recent work has investigated the impact of the AP's location on the received signal strength of clients [1], and has shown that a 1.7x throughput improvement can be achieved by simply moving the AP in a 2ft. x 2ft. region. The benefits of small scale AP mobility is chiefly caused by mitigating multipath effects. In fact, the multipath effect has a significant impact on network performance, and can be dramatically altered even with mere centimeter level movement of a Tx or a Rx. In this work, we investigate how network throughput performance can be improved if the AP *is able to adapt its orientation.* We consider two types of orientation changes - that of the AP's base platform (base orientation), and that of its antennas (antenna orientation). We show using experimental analysis that network throughput performance can be improved 1.8x by simply adapting AP's orientation.

2. EXPERIMENTAL SETUP

To validate the impact of AP orientation on network performance, *three* different environments are studied; namely, a research lab, a home, and a classroom. In each environment, we measure the throughput performance for a single AP and a single client (on weekends or at nights to reduce the impact of interference). The specifications are as follows: AP - *Netgear AC 2350*; Client - *Lenovo Y700*; Traffic Direction - *Downlink*; Channel between AP and its client - *NLOS*; WiFi type - *802.11ac*; Duration - *20s * 3*; Throughput Measurement tool - *Iperf3*. The metric used is the *Average Gain*, which is the ratio of the maximum throughput to the average throughput.

3. ANALYSIS AND INSIGHTS

Impact of Base Orientation: We evaluate the network performance with 12 different base orientations that are obtained by rotating the AP with a 30° step size belonging to the set: {0°,30°,...,330°}. From Fig. 1, changing only the base orientation can improve the network performance up to 1.5x. Also, it is clear that the performance improvement varies across the different scenarios. This can be attributed to the fact that multipath is very site-specific.

Permission to make digital or hard copies of part or all of this work for personal or classroom use is granted without fee provided that copies are not made or distributed for profit or commercial advantage and that copies bear this notice and the full citation on the first page. Copyrights for third-party components of this work must be honored. For all other uses, contact the owner/author(s).
MobiSys'17 June 19-23, 2017, Niagara Falls, NY, USA
© 2017 Copyright held by the owner/author(s).
ACM ISBN 978-1-4503-4928-4/17/06.
DOI: http://dx.doi.org/10.1145/3081333.3089318

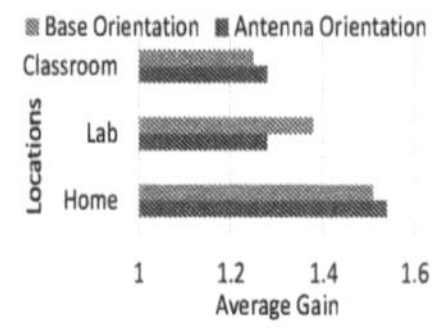

Figure 1: Base vs. Antenna Orientation

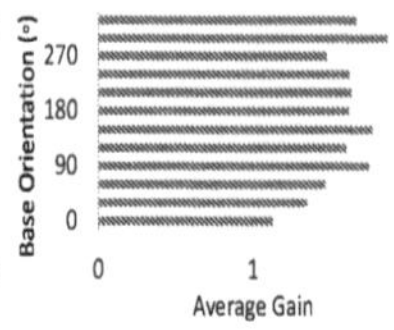

Figure 2: Joint Orientation

Figure 3: Robotic Platform

Impact of Antenna Orientation: There are 4 antennas, and each antenna has a 45° or a 90° antenna orientation configuration; there are therefore 16 different antenna orientation configurations for which the network performance is investigated. Similar to the results of changing base orientation, changing the antenna orientation is capable of improving the network performance up to 1.5x as shown in Fig. 1.

Impact of Joint Orientation (Twirl): The impact of changing both the antenna and base orientation, defined as *Twirl* orientation, is also evaluated. We evaluate the network performance in the lab environment with 12 different base orientations, and at each base orientation, we evaluate 16 different antenna orientations; for a total of 192 different configurations. The average gain is calculated as the ratios of the maximum throughput of all 192 configurations over the average throughput for each base orientation. Fig. 2 shows that Twirl can deliver network performance improvement of up to 1.8x.

Summary: The results show that the network throughput performance can be improved by as much as 1.8x through simply adapting the orientation of the AP. This is comparable to the improvement achieved by AP relocation [1]. This indicates that multipath effects can be mitigated without physically relocating the AP using large-scale movement. The results also indicate the promising potential of orientation adaptation of AP.

4. ROBOTIC PLATFORM

We show a possible platform for Twirl in Fig. 3. Base orientation can be achieved using *iRobot Create 2*, which can be programmed to rotate and move in a specific trajectory in a 2D space. Antenna orientation can be achieved using *Global Specialties R700 Robotic Arm*, which is a 6 degree-of-freedom programmable robotic arm.

5. ACKNOWLEDGEMENTS

This work was funded in part by the National Science Foundation under grants CNS-1513884 and CNS-1319455, and the Wayne J. Holman Endowed Chair.

6. REFERENCES

[1] M. Gowda, A. Dhekne, and R. Roy Choudhury, "The case for robotic wireless networks," in *Proceedings of International Conference on World Wide Web*, 2016, pp. 1317–1327.

Poster: Online Map Matching for Passive Indoor Positioning Systems

Huy Tran
Portland State University
hptran@pdx.edu

Santosh Pandey
Cisco Systems
sanpande@cisco.com

Nirupama Bulusu
Portland State University
nbulusu@pdx.edu

ABSTRACT

Passive indoor positioning systems (PIPS) enable non-invasive tracking of mobile devices (e.g., smartphones, Wi-Fi tags) using enterprise network infrastructure. This empowers operators of large airports and retail facilities to optimize cost-intensive resource allocation as well as to provide location-based services to their customers such as geo-fencing and proximity marketing. However, existing PIPS often generate noisy location estimates due to unpredictable interference and attenuation of wireless signals in indoor environments. To address this problem, we propose a novel map matching approach that uses a floor map to constrain location estimates to possible paths a mobile user can take.

1. INTRODUCTION

Figure 1 describes the online map matching problem. PIPS such as Cisco's Hyperlocation [1] use signal strength and angle of arrival of Wi-Fi signals to track these devices. Map matching for such PIPS is challenging because of four reasons. First, location estimates are noisy. The mean error can range from 3 to 7 m. Second, a floor map can contain many possible paths. Third, location estimates are temporally sparse due to the latency incurred in sampling Wi-Fi signal strengths from a user device and in the location estimation process. The time difference between two consecutive location estimates can vary by as much as four seconds. Fourth, the location estimates often lag the corresponding actual locations of the user device.

We propose a novel map matching approach that applies proximity and topological constraints to select path segments by modeling these constraints with a Hidden Markov Model. *Our main contribution is a new topological constraint based on our observation that a mobile user often takes a small number of turns between two consecutive locations that correspond to the location estimates generated by the system.*

To evaluate our work, we perform thirty experiments on two different building floors, with two participants, to collect location estimates and corresponding ground truth data. In each experiment, a participant walks on a floor for five minutes while holding a phone (iPhone 6S). Our results demonstrate improved map matching accuracy with our proposed constraint compared to travel time and travel distance constraints [2] on a floor having dense path segments. Our map matching approach aligns 50% of location estimates on correct path segments taken by mobile users and lagging the corresponding actual locations up to 7 m.

We acknowledge that this result is not comparable with the accuracy of active indoor positioning systems in which a mobile device uses additional information such as fingerprint data and inertial sensor data to estimate the device locations. However, improving PIPS with a map matching technique brings two important benefits: low energy consumption at the user's mobile device and not encumbering every user with application installation on his/her device.

Acknowledgement — This research was supported by Cisco University grant CG594206.

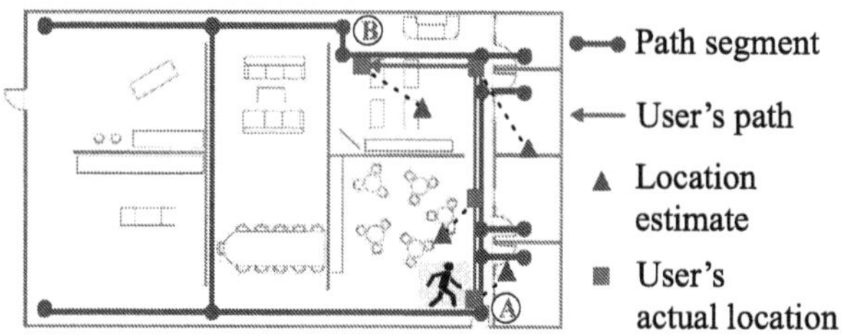

Figure 1: A user walks from location A to location B on the floor map and is currently at B. Given the floor map composed of the path segments and the sequence of time-stamped location estimates, the map matching problem is to determine to which path segment the current location estimate must be aligned.

2. REFERENCES

[1] Cisco Hyperlocation module with advanced security. http://www.cisco.com/c/en/us/products/interfaces-modules/aironet-hyperlocation-module-advanced-security/index.html.

[2] P. Newson and J. Krumm. Hidden Markov map matching through noise and sparseness. In *Proc. of the 17th ACM SIGSPATIAL*, pages 336–343, 2009.

Permission to make digital or hard copies of part or all of this work for personal or classroom use is granted without fee provided that copies are not made or distributed for profit or commercial advantage and that copies bear this notice and the full citation on the first page. Copyrights for third-party components of this work must be honored. For all other uses, contact the owner/author(s).

MobiSys'17 June 19-23, 2017, Niagara Falls, NY, USA

© 2017 Copyright held by the owner/author(s).

ACM ISBN 978-1-4503-4928-4/17/06.
DOI: http://dx.doi.org/10.1145/3081333.3089319

Poster: Auracle – A Wearable Device for Detecting and Monitoring Eating Behavior

Shengjie Bi†, Ellen Davenport†, Jun Gong†, Ronald Peterson†,
Joseph Skinner†, Kevin Storer*, Tao Wang†, Kelly Caine*, Ryan Halter†,
David Kotz†, Kofi Odame†, Jacob Sorber*, Xing-Dong Yang†
†Dartmouth College and *Clemson University

1. INTRODUCTION

Chronic disease is one of the most pressing health challenges facing the United States (and an increasing set of other countries). The onset or progression of diseases like obesity, diabetes, and metabolic disorder are strongly related to eating behavior, and scientists are still trying to fully understand the complex mixture of diet, exercise, genetics, sociocultural context, and physical environment that lead to these diseases. Health science, however, has no effective means for automatically measuring eating behavior in free-living conditions.

The **Auracle** aims to be a wearable earpiece that detects eating behavior, to be fielded by health-science researchers in their efforts to study eating behavior and ultimately to develop interventions useful to individuals striving to address chronic disease related to eating.

2. APPROACH

In the Auracle project we are developing an electronic earpiece (worn unobtrusively behind the ear) that senses sound (microphone) and muscle activity (EMG) to detect eating activities. While other work has used similar sensors (e.g., [2, 3]), the Auracle aims to monitor eating throughout a waking day, unobtrusively, in free-living conditions. We anticipate the earpiece will have the capability to communicate privately to its wearer through sound; the wearer can respond through intuitive input mechanisms. Finally, the earpiece will offload eating records to the wearer's smartphone for longer-term storage and for richer interactions.

Computational jewelry is beginning to appear in several form factors: bracelets, pendants, rings, and eyewear. Indeed, each location provides distinct opportunities and challenges. We see great promise in an earpiece form factor. First, the ear has long served as a culturally acceptable location for wearable objects, both ornamental (jewelry) and practical (glasses, headphones, hearing aids). Second, the ear is an ideal location for detecting and measuring behaviors relevant to health and wellness, such as eating, drinking, smoking, and speaking. Third, it could offer strong security (biometrically identifying its wearer with vocal resonance [1]). Finally, it provides rich opportunities for unobtrusive communication with the wearer via sound, speech, and touch.

Permission to make digital or hard copies of part or all of this work for personal or classroom use is granted without fee provided that copies are not made or distributed for profit or commercial advantage and that copies bear this notice and the full citation on the first page. Copyrights for third-party components of this work must be honored. For all other uses, contact the owner/author(s).

MobiSys'17 June 19-23, 2017, Niagara Falls, NY, USA

© 2017 Copyright held by the owner/author(s).

ACM ISBN 978-1-4503-4928-4/17/06.
DOI: http://dx.doi.org/10.1145/3081333.3089320

3. RESULTS

Our initial experiments evaluated several sensors and algorithms to determine their suitability for recognizing eating activities, with a focus on two popular sensors for eating recognition (based on acoustic and electromyography (EMG) sensors, individually and combined). We built a data-acquisition system using two off-the-shelf sensors and conducted a study with 20 participants. In controlled laboratory experiments, our preliminary results show that this system can detect eating with an accuracy exceeding 90.9% while the crunchiness level of food varies.

Our initial wearable prototype embeds an Arduino platform in a comfortable elastic headband (Figure 1); this prototype will allow us to conduct experiments in a broader variety of settings and with a broader variety of food types. The poster includes preliminary results of these experiments.

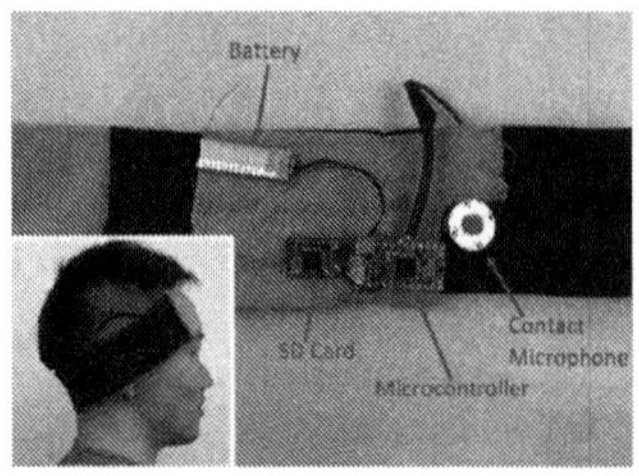

Figure 1: Wearable prototype

With the Auracle device unobtrusively mounted behind the participant's ear, we can enable extended experimentation in free-living conditions in support of health science. Please follow us at auracle-project.org.

4. REFERENCES

[1] C. Cornelius et al. Vocal resonance as a biometric for pervasive wearable devices. Technical Report TR2014-747, Dartmouth, Feb. 2014.
[2] T. Rahman et al. Bodybeat: A mobile system for sensing non-speech body sounds. In *MobiSys*, 2014.
[3] R. Zhang and O. Amft. Bite glasses: Measuring chewing using EMG and bone vibration in smart eyeglasses. In *ACM Int'l Symp. on Wearable Computers*, 2016.

Poster: *Characters vs. Words* - Observations on Command Design for Brain-Computer Interfaces

Mohit Agarwal
Georgia Institute of Technology
magarwal37@gatech.edu

Raghupathy Sivakumar
Georgia Institute of Technology
siva@gatech.edu

1. OVERVIEW

Brain-computer interfaces (BCIs) allow users to communicate to a nearby computing device (computer, smartphone, etc.) using thoughts or other covert actions that result in a detectable change in brain-waves. Consider a BCI command to be a *word* consisting of a sequence of *characters*. Each character is a thought or action that can be reliably detected through brain waves. For this work, we specifically consider *eye-blinks* as the user action of interest. Eye-blinks are an interesting modality for BCI commands because of their easy detectability and naturalness (and hence covertness). It turns out that there is an interesting trade-off between the complexity of characters and the length of words. In this work, we perform a user-study to answer a simple, but important, question pertaining to eye-blinks based BCI command design: *do users prefer shorter characters (and hence longer words) or shorter words (and hence longer characters) when performing commands?* (Fig.1 and 2, where **B** denotes an eye-blink) We present a simple eye-blink language consisting of words and characters and use real user-experiments to study the aforementioned trade-off.

{BB BB BB BB}

Figure 1: Shorter Characters

{BBBB BBBB}

Figure 2: Shorter Words

2. EYE-BLINK COMMANDS

We use the multiplicity of eye-blinks to construct eye-blink words, and represent them with numerals (for e.g. "2" represents a double blink). A command thus consists of a sequence of words separated by "non eye-blinks", and is represented with numerals enclosed in square brackets separated by ","s (for e.g. [2,3] denotes a double eye-blink followed by a non eye-blink, and then a triple eye-blink). Generically, this can be represented as,

$$\{\ [A_1, A_2, \ldots A_n] \mid i, A_i \in \mathcal{N} \text{ and } A_i \leq M\ , i \leq N\}$$

where M and N represent the lengths of the character and the word respectively. A character cannot be "1" (or single-blink) because of the high natural frequency of its occurence (leading to false positives). We also restrict the scope of our study to a maximum value of 4 for both M and N. This results in 117 different permutations and 31 unique combinations of commands. Since the sum of the total number of double-blinks (#2), triple-blinks (#3) and 4-blinks (#4) is equal to the command length (i.e., #2 + #3 + #4 = N), the 31 command combinations can be mapped in a 3D space with three axes as #2, #3 and #4. These commands lie on 3 parallel planes, which are shown in Fig. 3. To reduce the experimental complexity, we select a set of *representative commands* such that all commands in Fig.3 are within a 1-hop distance from the representative commands while minimizing the cardinality of the representative set. This results in 13 different commands (marked in Fig.3 with green circles). We add two additional commands ([4,2,3] and [4,2,2,4]) in order to study the effect of permutation in command usability, making it a total of 15 commands for experimental analysis.

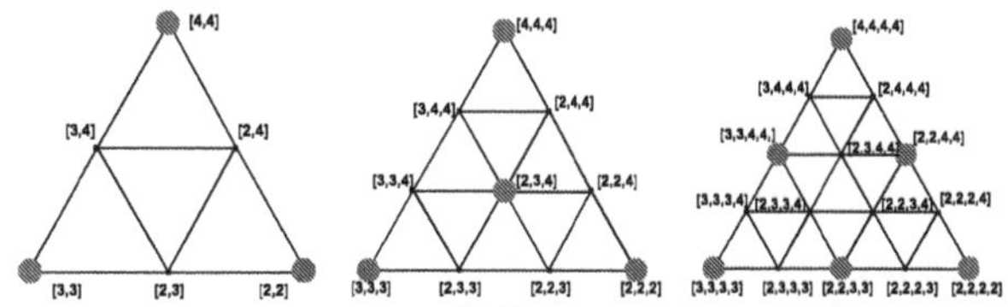

(a) N=2 (b) N=3 (c) N=4

Figure 3: Eye-Blink Commands

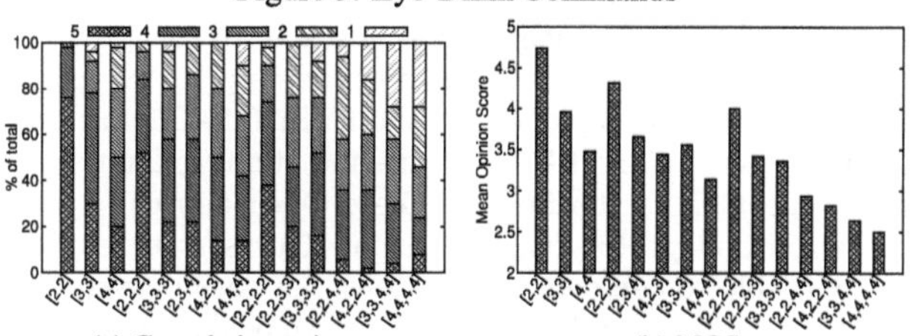

(a) Cumulative ratings (b) MOS

Figure 4: Experimental Results

3. EXPERIMENTAL INSIGHTS

For the user study, we ask 50 users to perform the 15 blink commands, and rate them on an mean opinion score (MOS) scale of 1 to 5 (1 being most difficult, 5 being very easy). Fig.4a, and 4b show percentage distribution of MOS scores for each command, and the average MOS score aggregated over 50 users, respectively. The following interesting and non-intuitive insights can be observed:

- Longer commands with shorter word lengths are preferred over shorter commands with longer word lengths. For e.g. [2,2,2,2] is more comfortable (MOS: 4.0, % of 5s: 38%) as compared to [4,4] (MOS: 3.48, % of 5s: 20%).
- Thus, for a given BCI application with a required vocabulary size, N should be increased before M to ensure user comfort.
- For a particular character combination, different character permutations impacts usability (e.g. [2,3,4] and [4,2,3] has % of 5s as 22% and 14%, and MOS of 3.66 and 3.44 respectively).

Exploring the command usability with different permutations and extending the analysis to other BCI modalities is a part of ongoing work.

Acknowledgements: This work was funded in part by the National Science Foundation under grants CNS-1513884 and CNS-1319455, and the Wayne J. Holman Endowed Chair.

Permission to make digital or hard copies of part or all of this work for personal or classroom use is granted without fee provided that copies are not made or distributed for profit or commercial advantage and that copies bear this notice and the full citation on the first page. Copyrights for third-party components of this work must be honored. For all other uses, contact the owner/author(s).

MobiSys'17 June 19-23, 2017, Niagara Falls, NY, USA

© 2017 Copyright held by the owner/author(s).

ACM ISBN 978-1-4503-4928-4/17/06.

DOI: http://dx.doi.org/10.1145/3081333.3089321

Poster: Field Testing Vehicular Networks using OpenC2X

Florian Klingler, Gurjashan Singh Pannu, Christoph Sommer,
Bastian Bloessl and Falko Dressler
Heinz Nixdorf Institute and Dept. of Computer Science, Paderborn University, Germany
{klingler,gurjashan.pannu,sommer,bloessl,dressler}@ccs-labs.org

ABSTRACT

We present OpenC2X, an Open Source approach to field testing of vehicular networking solutions. Field Operational Test (FOT) and real-world experimentation are becoming more relevant to our research community as well as to industry and regulation. Unfortunately, available commercial solutions make experimental modifications to the protocol stack time consuming or prohibit it completely. To overcome this limitation, we implemented the ETSI ITS-G5 stack on a standard embedded PC hardware and running Linux system. OpenC2X is the first complete Open Source experimentation and prototyping platform. Our system is fully interoperable to commercial solutions, yet easily extensible with new protocols and applications for vehicular networks.

1. INTRODUCTION

In the last decade, we have seen many striking advances in the field of vehicular networks. The work led to the standardization of access layers (DSRC, IEEE 802.11p) as well as complete network stacks (IEEE WAVE, ETSI ITS-G5, ARIB T109) [3]. As protocols matured, the focus shifted towards Field Operational Tests (FOTs) in order to identify possible limitations and to ensure seamless integration in real-world applications. As of today, Japan already started to deploy DSRC using its local ARIB standard and car makers in both Europe and the US announced first units to become standard in selected cars.

FOTs are usually conducted with proprietary commercial equipment, which limits the ability to modify or even fine-tune protocol layers. To overcome this limitation, we developed OpenC2X [2], the first Open Source experimentation and prototyping platform that can easily be extended and parameterized for R&D on vehicular networking protocols. We continued and extended previous work to present version 2.0 of our framework, which is fully compatible to commercial tools like the Cohda Wireless MK5, a popular choice for FOTs. It is now possible to use OpenC2X to investigate and validate details of (almost) all protocol layers. We plan extending the platform with a Software Defined Radio (SDR) to even allow fine-tuning the physical layer [1].

Permission to make digital or hard copies of part or all of this work for personal or classroom use is granted without fee provided that copies are not made or distributed for profit or commercial advantage and that copies bear this notice and the full citation on the first page. Copyrights for third-party components of this work must be honored. For all other uses, contact the owner/author(s).

MobiSys'17 June 19-23, 2017, Niagara Falls, NY, USA

© 2017 Copyright held by the owner/author(s).

ACM ISBN 978-1-4503-4928-4/17/06.
DOI: http://dx.doi.org/10.1145/3081333.3089322

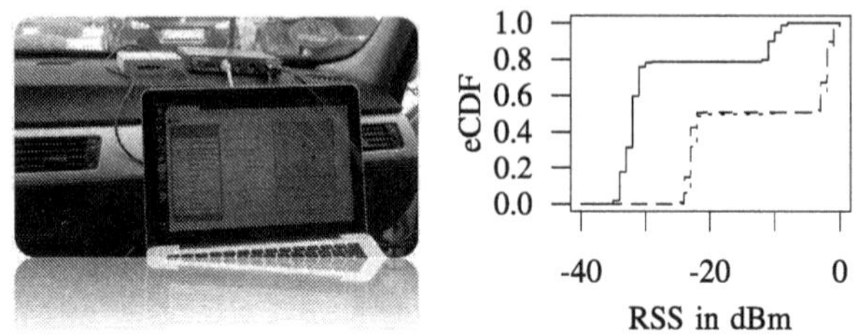

Figure 1: Setup and results of OpenC2X running on an embedded Linux system in the car.

2. FIELD TESTING WITH OPENC2X

Field testing using OpenC2X is simple as our software runs on a standard Linux system. It uses Atheros 9k WLAN cards, which can operate on the 5.9 GHz band, using 10 MHz channels and all parameters according to the IEEE 802.11p standard. We support almost all aspects of the ETSI ITS-G5 standard, particularly, congestion control mechanisms according to Decentralized Congestion Control (DCC), a mechanism that is considered for the US IEEE WAVE standard as well. In a set of experiments, we explored the capabilities of OpenC2X. The hardware setup and sample results are depicted in Figure 1. We confirmed interoperability with the Cohda Wireless MK5 by sending and receiving Cooperative Awareness Messages (CAMs) and Decentralized Environmental Notification Messages (DENMs). Our OpenC2X system also connects to typical GPS receivers as well as to the car's CAN bus via an ELM 327 based OBD-II adapter. The system also features a graphical web interface that shows and logs detailed information about the ego vehicle, neighboring vehicles, and the latest CAMs and DENMs.

3. REFERENCES

[1] B. Bloessl, M. Segata, C. Sommer, and F. Dressler. Towards an Open Source IEEE 802.11p Stack: A Full SDR-based Transceiver in GNURadio. In *IEEE VNC 2013*, pages 143–149, Boston, MA, Dec. 2013.

[2] S. Laux, G. S. Pannu, S. Schneider, J. Tiemann, F. Klingler, C. Sommer, and F. Dressler. OpenC2X - An Open Source Experimental and Prototyping Platform Supporting ETSI ITS-G5. In *IEEE VNC 2016, Demo Session*, pages 152–153, Columbus, OH, Dec. 2016.

[3] C. Sommer and F. Dressler. *Vehicular Networking*. Cambridge University Press, Nov. 2014.

Poster: ARM Errata and their Software Workarounds

Nisal Menuka and Lin Zhong
Rice University, Houston, TX
{nisal.menuka, lzhong}@rice.edu

Like software, hardware also has bugs. These bugs, or *errata*, can cause unexpected behaviors, reducing performance and causing malfunctions in the entire system. As there is no way to fix an erratum after hardware is deployed, its harmful effects are often mitigated by software workarounds, usually in low-level software such as operating system. The goal of our work is to ensure system correctness and security against the harmful effects of errata and their workarounds. The first step is to systematically understand them in the wild.

In this poster, we present our early results from analyzing errata in the ARM Cortex-A family of microarchitecture, introduced by ARM itself, and their workarounds. We studied publicly available ARM errata documentations and examined source code of low-level software, namely Linux kernel, U-Boot and ARM Trusted firmware. ARM classifies errata in to three categories: A - critical error with no acceptable workaround available, B - significant error with acceptable workaround available and C - minor error. Figure 1 (Left) shows distribution of the errata we analyzed according to these categories.

Unfixed Errata and Spurious Workarounds

We found most errata do not have workarounds in the low-level software we examined. We found workarounds for only about 50 errata, less than 20% of those documented by ARM. Figure 1 (Right) shows the workarounds we identified according to applicable ARM cores. Out of the 115 Category B errata, less than half have workarounds. Recall these errata can cause significant errors and their workarounds are available according to ARM.

On the other hand, we found that workarounds intended for one architecture are sometimes enabled for another. For example, the official kernel repository for Cortex-A8 based BeagleBone Black [1] had three errata workarounds intended for Cortex-A9 in its default configuration. The same problem also was found in [2] and the maintainer disabled four spurious errata workarounds after we reported them.

How and Where Errata were Fixed

We found workarounds fix errata in two different ways. The more common way is to configure the processor during initialization so that the erratum would never occur. Such workarounds usually

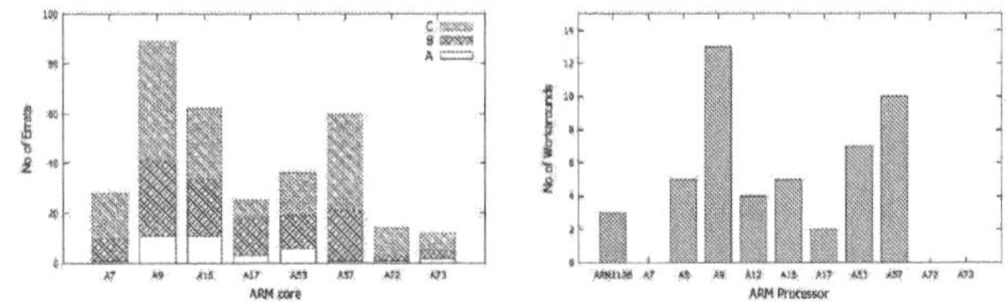

Figure 1: (Left) Errata distribution according to categories; (Right) Workarounds found in Linux kernel, U-Boot and ARM Trusted Firmware categorized according to applicable ARM core.

modify processor control registers. 22 out of 32 workarounds we identified in the Linux kernel falls in to this category and require the kernel to run in the secure state. For example, cause of ARM errata 742230 which affects Cortex-A9 is faulty execution of the Data Memory Barrier (`DMB`) instruction. The workaround for this erratum is to configure a secure state register to decode `DMB` as the Data Synchronization Barrier (`DSB`) instruction. `DSB` functionally subsumes `DMB`. This workaround can reduce system performance slightly.

The rest of the 32 workarounds modify necessary code, e.g., by adding new instructions and replacing instructions. For example, the workaround for ARM errata 754322 for Cortex-A9 adds a `DSB` instruction in the code for context switching, which increases the latter's overhead. Note that this workaround was enabled spuriously for Beaglebone Black in [2], where we measured the overhead to be 1.3% on average for each context switch.

Errata workarounds that modify code must be applied in the kernel, e.g., that for ARM errata 753422, for obvious reasons. However, errata workarounds that configure the secure state registers appear to be better applied before the Linux kernel boots, in the bootloader. This is because the bootloader itself may trigger an erratum and must work around it. Additionally, if the kernel boots in a non-secure state, it cannot write into secure state registers. The bootloader is more likely to run in the secure state. However, with the ARM TrustZone technology, a normal world bootloader does not run in the secure state. As a result, workarounds that require access to secure state registers must be applied even early, e.g., in the firmware.

We observe that some workarounds for the same errata exist in both the Linux Kernel and the bootloader. The Linux kernel community has already reached the consensus not to accept any more errata workarounds if they can be applied in the bootloaders.

Permission to make digital or hard copies of part or all of this work for personal or classroom use is granted without fee provided that copies are not made or distributed for profit or commercial advantage and that copies bear this notice and the full citation on the first page. Copyrights for third-party components of this work must be honored. For all other uses, contact the owner/author(s).

MobiSys'17 June 19-23, 2017, Niagara Falls, NY, USA

© 2017 Copyright held by the owner/author(s).

ACM ISBN 978-1-4503-4928-4/17/06.
DOI: http://dx.doi.org/10.1145/3081333.3089323

References

[1] The official beagleboard and beaglebone kernel repository. https://github.com/beagleboard/linux. Accessed 03/01/2017.

[2] Robertcnelson/bb-kernel. https://github.com/RobertCNelson/bb-kernel. Accessed 03/01/2017.

Poster: Extensive Evaluation of Emotional Contagion on Smiling Selfies over Social Network

Wataru Sasaki, Mikio Obuchi, Kazuki Egashira, Naohiro Isokawa, Yuki Furukawa, Yuuki Nishiyama, Tadashi Okoshi, Jin Nakazawa
Graduate School of Media and Governance, Keio University
wataru@ht.sfc.keio.ac.jp

ABSTRACT

We propose "SmileWave", the first selfie social networking service to reveal the existence of emotional cognation through smiling selfies on the social network. We conducted multiple rounds of in-the-wild user studies with 86 cumulative total users for total duration of 5 weeks. Throughout the entire study, we confirmed the occurrence of smile-based emotional contagion over social network, not only in the momentary duration but in longer term period.

Keywords: Emotional Contagion; Social Network; Mobile Sensing.

1. BACKGROUND

In our daily lives, we have experiences such that we become happier when we see people smiling happily. A specific mechanism occurring in such emotional propagation is called "emotional contagion", where people experience the same emotion expressed by someone when communicating with them [1]. Emotional contagion on the online communication has not been well investigated yet. In this research, we aim to reveal how emotional contagion occurs and propagates on the social network and particularly spotlight smile selfie photos as communication media. To address the problem above, we propose "SmileWave", a photo-based social networking service that analyzes the changes in user's smile degree on looking at posted smiling selfies posted by other users. The features of SmileWave are (1) real-time feedback to users, (2) ease of use anytime and anywhere and (3) simple user interface and high usability. Figure 1 shows the overview of SmileWave.

2. EVALUTAION AND RESULTS

Firstly, we conducted an in-the-wild user study with 48 participants for 30 days [2]. Next, we further conducted the second extensive in-the-wild user study with 38 participants for 2 weeks, preparing the second generation of SmileWave with brush-ups/fixes. We found that there is a change in the effect on smile-based emotional contagion, by showing smile selfies with higher smile degree, not only in the momentary duration but also in longer term duration. We also found that there is a stronger effect on smile-based emotional contagion after she/he viewed the posted selfie photos ordered from the one with the lower smile degree to the one with the higher degree. Those differences were found with statistical significance in our ANOVA analysis.

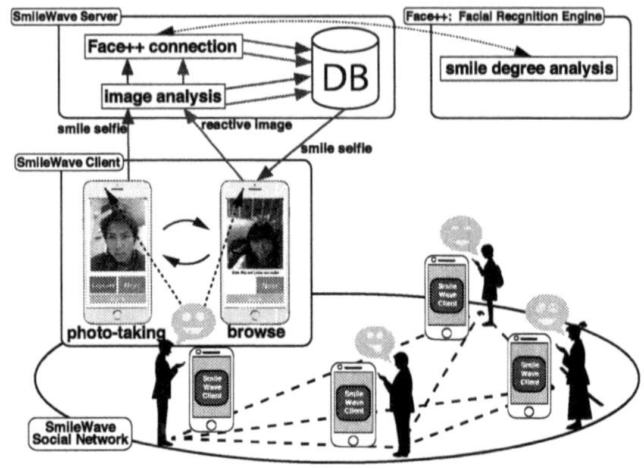

Figure 1: Overview of the SmileWave System

3. CONCLUSION AND FUTURE WORK

We conclude that smile-based emotional contagion over the social network is occurring. Our future work includes longer-term and larger-scale user study to validate SmileWave's performance on the degree of happiness directly.

4. ACKNOWLEDGMENTS

This work was supported (in part) by National Institute of Information and Communications Technology, (in part) by RIKEN, Japan and (in part) by Ministry of Education, Culture, Sports, Science and Technology (MEXT) Grant-in-Aid for the "Program for Leading Graduate Schools".

5. REFERENCES

[1] E. Hatfield, J. T. Cacioppo, and R. L. Rapson. Emotional Contagion. *Current Directions in Psychological Science*, 2:96–100, 1993.

[2] W. Sasaki, Y. Furukawa, Y. Nishiyama, T. Okoshi, J. Nakazawa, and H. Tokuda. *Poster Abstract: SmileWave - Sensing and Analysis of Smile-Based Emotional Contagion over Social Network.* Institute of Electrical and Electronics Engineers Inc., United States, 4 2016.

Permission to make digital or hard copies of part or all of this work for personal or classroom use is granted without fee provided that copies are not made or distributed for profit or commercial advantage and that copies bear this notice and the full citation on the first page. Copyrights for third-party components of this work must be honored. For all other uses, contact the owner/author(s).

MobiSys '17, June 19–23, 2017, Niagara Falls, NY, USA.

© 2017 Copyright held by the owner/author(s).

ACM ISBN 978-1-4503-4928-4/17/06
DOI: http://dx.doi.org/10.1145/3081333.3089324

Demo: Mobile Contextual Advertising Platform based on Tiny Text Intelligence

Jung-Hyun Lee, So-Young Jun, So-Jung Park, Kang-Min Kim, SangKeun Lee
Department of Computer Science and Engineering
Korea University, Seoul, Republic of Korea
{jhbslpd, syzzang, sojungpark, kangmin89, yalphy}@korea.ac.kr

ABSTRACT

In-app advertising has become a significant source of revenue for mobile app. In order to improve the effectiveness of in-app ads, most ad networks focus on targeting a user based on the user's personal information collected from their ad library inside mobile apps and the global knowledge built from big data on ad servers. However, sharing user's sensitive information with the ad servers may raise privacy concerns. As opposed to targeting users, mobile contextual advertising seeks to target the app page a user is viewing.

In this demo, we present a novel mobile contextual advertising platform, called *MoCA*, which is designed to improve the semantic relevance of in-app ads in a stand-alone, privacy-protecting manner on mobile devices. MoCA understands the semantics of app page and ads, and then matches semantically relevant ads to the page inside mobile devices. To the best of our knowledge, this is the first work to implement the mobile contextual advertising platform based on the semantic approach without resort to ad servers.

The technical challenge is to perform the classification and searching task of the semantic approach, which needs high computational resources, inside mobile devices with limited hardware resources. To this end, MoCA utilizes the *tiny text intelligence* [1] that is suitable for the mobile environment. It consists of the light-weight classifier and the similarity model on the compressed knowledge base which requires only 34.3MB storage. The tiny text intelligence has been utilized and its effectiveness has already been proven for several intelligent services [2].

Figure 1 illustrates the system architecture of MoCA. In the background process, MoCA first pre-collects ad candidates from ad servers. In the real-time process, it scrapes the dynamic content of the app page viewed by the user through its ad library, and then captures the semantics of the content and matches semantically relevant ads from ad candidates by utilizing the tiny text intelligence.

We evaluate the relevance of the ads shown by MoCA using a real-world dataset consisting of app pages crawled from popular apps in the Google Play Store. We observe that MoCA achieves the relevance performance of as much as 93.1% compared to the semantic approach in the server environment. We also observe that the average runtime and energy consumption of the real-time process on 1,000 ad candidates is 0.965 seconds and 0.352 mAh per ad request, which is equivalent to 2.73 seconds of music play. These results show that the overhead of MoCA is not considerable.

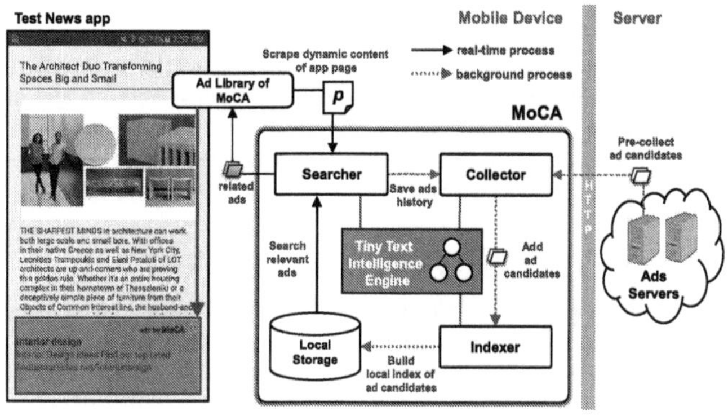

Figure 1: System architecture of MoCA

We implement a MoCA prototype and a test app using its ad library as independent applications on Android OS. The test app is a simple news aggregation app that shows a list of recent news articles dynamically crawled from the RSS feed of Wall Street Journal. During the demo session, users will be able to read the recent news articles along with relevant ads dynamically provided by MoCA. The demo video is also available here: https://youtu.be/G2O0j7ucYCk.

Acknowledgment

This research was supported by Basic Science Research Program through the National Research Foundation of Korea (NRF) funded by the Ministry of Science, ICT and Future Planning (number 2015R1A2A1A15052701).

1. REFERENCES

[1] J. Ha, J.-H. Lee, and S. Lee. EPE: An embedded personalization engine for mobile users. *IEEE Internet Computing*, 18(1):30–37, January 2014.

[2] W.-J. Ryu, J.-H. Lee, K.-M. Kim, and S. Lee. meCurate: Personalized curation service using a tiny text intelligence. In *Proc. WWW '17 Companion*, pages 269–272, 2017.

Permission to make digital or hard copies of part or all of this work for personal or classroom use is granted without fee provided that copies are not made or distributed for profit or commercial advantage and that copies bear this notice and the full citation on the first page. Copyrights for third-party components of this work must be honored. For all other uses, contact the owner/author(s).

MobiSys'17, June 19-23, 2017, Niagara Falls, NY, USA.

© 2017 Copyright held by the owner/author(s).

ACM ISBN 978-1-4503-4928-4/17/06.
DOI: http://dx.doi.org/10.1145/3081333.3089326

Demo: BlueMountain: An Architecture to Customize Data Management on Mobile Systems

Sharath Chandrashekhara, Taeyeon Ki, Kyungho Jeon, Karthik Dantu, Steven Y. Ko
Department of Computer Science and Engineering
University at Buffalo, The State University of New York
{sc296, tki, kyunghoj, kdantu, stevko}@buffalo.edu

ABSTRACT

BlueMountain is a system that enables building pluggable data management solutions which can be linked with any Android app at runtime, without requiring any modifications to the Android platform. BlueMountain simplifies the app development, provides flexibility to end users, and works with existing apps.

1. MOTIVATION AND OVERVIEW

Modern apps on mobile systems employ sophisticated data management solutions, including local file and database storage as well as cloud services for user/app data. However, data management in mobile apps does not provide enough flexibility to either developers or users.

To address this problem, we have designed a pluggable data management solution for modern mobile platforms like Android. Our goal is to allow data management mechanisms and policies to be implemented independently of core app logic and provide users a higher control over their data. To achieve this, we envision two kinds of apps. The first category is regular apps that one can currently find in app stores such as Google Play. The second category is what we call *data management apps*. These apps are meant to be *pluggable* and always used in conjunction with regular apps for the purpose of managing their data. A regular app delegates all its data management decisions to a data management app. Depending on their needs, the users will choose a data management app to use for each regular app. For example, a user in this ecosystem could install a regular note-taking app with a data management app designed to extend battery life while syncing notes to cloud. At the same time, another user could install the same note-taking app, but with a data management app that syncs all notes with the user's personal devices.

To realize the aforementioned separation, we propose BlueMountain, which has three distinct features: (i) It defines a clean interface for data management apps, which mimics the interface for Android's files, database, and key-value storage. (ii) It enables dynamic binding between a data management app and a regular app, so that a user can choose which data management app to use for each regular app. (iii) It automatically transforms existing apps

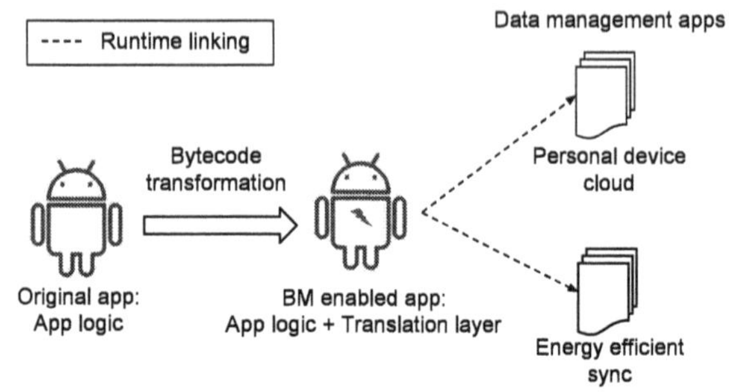

Figure 1: BlueMountain Workflow Example

to leverage BlueMountain's functionality via Java bytecode instrumentation [5]. Figure 1 shows a visualization of this workflow.

We have built BlueMountain system for Android and implemented a layer that translates the Android Storage APIs—files, databases and key-value storage to our interface. We have also built five data management apps. Two of these apps (inspired by PS-Cloud [3] and QuickSync [4]) are designed to manage files while the other three are designed to manage databases using various cloud syncing strategies. We evaluate our system by measuring the overhead using micro-benchmarks as well as end-to-end performance with five data management apps described above. We show that our system is practical and the overhead remains less than 10% in most of the cases and goes up to 30% in the worst case. Lastly, we show that our approach *supports existing apps* by automatically transforming 400 apps downloaded from Google Play to leverage our framework and verifying the correctness of their functionality. We have measured the increase in code size, energy, and heap usage due to instrumentation and show that the overhead is minimal.

2. DEMO

Our demo [1] shows an app downloaded from Google Play, Ex., 'Photo talks' [2], instrumented with BlueMountain framework and working with one of the data management app that we have built (Ex. automatic syncing of photos generated by 'Photo talks' with all of user's devices and Dropbox).

3. REFERENCES

[1] Demo. https://goo.gl/QthkKa.
[2] Photo talks: speech bubbles. https://goo.gl/8CRheK.
[3] S. Bazarbayev et al. Pscloud: a durable context-aware personal storage cloud. In *HotDep 2013*.
[4] Y. Cui et al. Quicksync: Improving synchronization efficiency for mobile cloud storage services. In *MobiCom 2015*.
[5] T. Ki et al. Reptor: Enabling api virtualization on android for platform openness. In *MobiSys 2017*.

Permission to make digital or hard copies of part or all of this work for personal or classroom use is granted without fee provided that copies are not made or distributed for profit or commercial advantage and that copies bear this notice and the full citation on the first page. Copyrights for third-party components of this work must be honored. For all other uses, contact the owner/author(s).
MobiSys'17 June 19-23, 2017, Niagara Falls, NY, USA
© 2017 Copyright held by the owner/author(s).
ACM ISBN 978-1-4503-4928-4/17/06.
DOI: http://dx.doi.org/10.1145/3081333.3089327

Demo: Fusing Mobile Sensors for Paper Keyboard On-the-Go

Anh Nguyen[†*], Duy Nguyen[††*], Nhan Nguyen[††], Ashwin Ashok[‡]
Binh Nguyen[††], Bao Pham[††], and Tam Vu[†]
[†]University of Colorado Boulder, [‡]Georgia State University, [††]University of Science, Vietnam
{Anh.TL.Nguyen, Tam.Vu}@Colorado.EDU[†], aashok@gsu.edu[‡]
{ngtbinh, ptbao}@hcmus.edu.vn, {nmduy881994, nttmailg}@gmail.com[††]

ABSTRACT

Using touchscreens has largely limited user inputs to small form-factor devices. To address this constraint, we explore a novel input mechanism, dubbed PaperKey, that enables users to interact with mobile devices by performing multi-finger typing gestures on a surface where the device is placed. Using acceleration signals on the device, PaperKey infers the user's type events and then leverages a vision-based technique for detecting the exact typing locations on a paper keyboard layout. Compared to single audio, image, or vibration sensing, this work accurately localizes keystrokes with faster processing speed. Additionally, this mechanism keeps the mobility of devices by working without external sensors.

Keywords

Multi-finger Typing; Touching Vibration; Vision-based Localization; Paper Keyboard

1. INTRODUCTION

Technology has led to the development of modern mobile and wearable devices. In contradiction with their ceaseless increases in efficiency and power, their shape and size are miniaturized so that their dominant form of inputting text today remains as small virtual on-screen keyboards. Although such keyboards are easily integrable and relatively easier to use, they have to adapt to different finger sizes and such adaptability is impractical in reality.

Together with a suite of sensors built in mobile devices, recent contributions have seen the growth of different user input techniques through sensing. However, some text-entry methods require carried piece of a bulky external hardware [1, 2], which is not convenient for mobile users. On the other hand, most of them leverage only the single sensor to detect keystrokes [3, 4]. Consequently, achieving high accuracy requires hacking device hardware to enable special ways of signal sensing and data collection.

In this work, we demonstrate a novel touch-free mechanism, dubbed *PaperKey* [1], that fuses an accelerometer and a smartphone forward camera to accurately detect keys pressed at natural typing speed. Specifically, when a user taps one key on the keyboard layout placed on the same surface as the phone is standing, it creates vibrations on the surface recorded by the accelerometer. Due to no constraint on the number of involved fingers in camera images, after determining a touch event of a finger on the surface, the actual typing finger is identified and the coordinate location of the pressed key is then determined, with respect to the keyboard, using image processing algorithms.

'*' marks co-primary authors.

[1]Demo video is available at https://youtu.be/dZ1OEtj-laY

Permission to make digital or hard copies of part or all of this work for personal or classroom use is granted without fee provided that copies are not made or distributed for profit or commercial advantage and that copies bear this notice and the full citation on the first page. Copyrights for third-party components of this work must be honored. For all other uses, contact the owner/author(s).

MobiSys'17 June 19-23, 2017, Niagara Falls, NY, USA

© 2017 Copyright held by the owner/author(s).

ACM ISBN 978-1-4503-4928-4/17/06.

DOI: http://dx.doi.org/10.1145/3081333.3089328

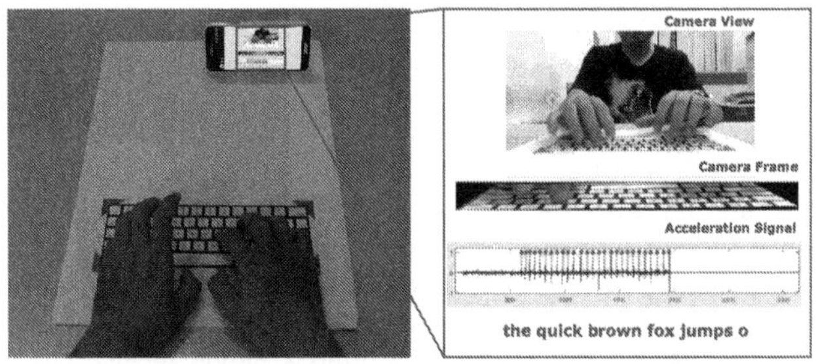

(a) Demo Setup (b) Smartphone Screenshot

Figure 1: A typical demonstration of PaperKey

2. DEMO

We will demonstrate our PaperKey system using various Android smartphone models with a self-designed keyboard layout. Specifically, the self-designed layout will be printed in color on a paper and be placed on a flat-surface table. The smartphone will then be stood horizontally on the layout at a location where its front camera can capture the whole keyboard in the closest distance. Figure 1 visualizes a setup of our demonstration along with the phone and the keyboard.

We will also demonstrate the capability of PaperKey to accurately detect actual keystrokes using the fusion of data from multiple sensors. Users will freely type their own sentences using the paper keyboard with natural typing speed. Moreover, there will be no limit of choosing their input ways in terms of different number of typing fingers and hands.

3. REFERENCES

[1] J. Liu et al. VibKeyboard: Virtual keyboard leveraging physical vibration: Demo. In *ACM MobiCom '16*, pages 507–508, 2016.

[2] Tap. http://www.tapwithus.com/. Accessed: March 28, 2017.

[3] J. Wang et al. Ubiquitous keyboard for small mobile devices: Harnessing multipath fading for fine-grained keystroke localization. In *ACM MobiSys '14*, pages 14–27, 2014.

[4] Y. Yin et al. CamK: A camera-based keyboard for small mobile devices. In *IEEE INFOCOM '16*, pages 1–9, 2016.

Demo: sigSocial: A Novel Social Media Aggregation Service using a Tiny Text Intelligence

Hyunwoong Bang, Hyunsub Kim, and SangKeun Lee
Department of Computer Science and Engineering, Korea University
{sijongyeoil, embrapers263, yalphy}@korea.ac.kr

1. INTRODUCTION

We present an entirely novel concept of retrieving social media data, called *sigSocial*. It integrates social media data of various sources, using a semantic classifier. Nowadays, people use multiple social media simultaneously, acquiring information with ease. However, accessing numerous services to reach different channels is bothersome. Also, the volume of information one can process is limited. Our aim is to reduce this burden, providing easiness and efficiency. In other words, we attempt to build a single service that integrates information from various platforms.

The application has three main features. First, it enables users to explore multiple social media without accessing them separately. Second, it organizes information retrieved from social medias into well-defined classes. Finally, it works as a stand-alone application, the mechanism of which is internal to the device, not relying on any external servers or networks. This method respects user privacy, which has recently gained much attention.

2. TECHNIQUES

The biggest obstacle is to combine information obtained from multiple sources. In addition, protecting personal information is also crucial. We use open APIs and collection tools for social media, and direct live information to a single database. The subsequent challenge is the classification, which typically requires extensive computational resources, within limited resources of a mobile device. The solution we use is the *tiny text intelligence* [1], optimized for mobile environment. It consists of the light-weight classifier and the similarity model on the compressed knowledge base which requires only 34.3MB storage. The tiny text intelligence has been utilized and its effectiveness has already been proven for several intelligent services [2][3]. In this demo, we utilize the classifier to organize social media data according to their classified classes. Using the classifier, *sigSocial* works in a privacy-protecting manner without sending out any personal information. Users read the semantically well-organized social media data. The entire process is illustrated in Figure 1. *sigSocial* demonstrates the concept of collecting and organizing social media data on a user's device.

Permission to make digital or hard copies of part or all of this work for personal or classroom use is granted without fee provided that copies are not made or distributed for profit or commercial advantage and that copies bear this notice and the full citation on the first page. Copyrights for third-party components of this work must be honored. For all other uses, contact the owner/author(s).

MobiSys'17, June 19-23, 2017, Niagara Falls, NY, USA.

© 2017 Copyright held by the owner/author(s).

ACM ISBN 978-1-4503-4928-4/17/06.
DOI: http://dx.doi.org/10.1145/3081333.3089329

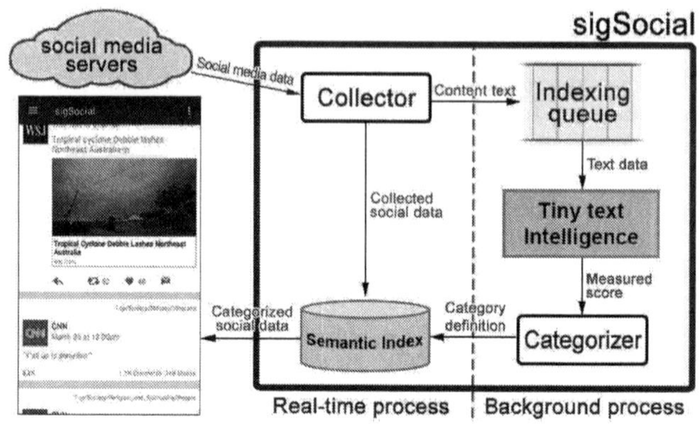

Figure 1: System Architecture

3. DEMONSTRATION

In this demo, we present *sigSocial* in the form of an Android application. *sigSocial* gathers and processes social media data from different sources, including Facebook, Twitter, RSS feeds, and YouTube subscription feeds. Three main features are provided within the program: gathering social media data, classifying social media data semantically, and presenting the classified data.

Acknowledgment

This research was supported by Basic Science Research Program through the National Research Foundation of Korea (NRF) funded by the Ministry of Science, ICT and Future Planning (number 2015R1A2A1A10052665).

4. REFERENCES

[1] J. Ha, J.-H. Lee, and S. Lee. EPE: An embedded personalization engine for mobile users. *IEEE Internet Computing*, 18(1):30-37, January/February 2014.

[2] H. Shin, H. Oh, W.-J. Ryu, and S. Lee. sigAlbum: An embedded photo service using a tiny text intelligence. In *Proc. UbiComp'16*, pp.373-376, 2016.

[3] W.-J. Ryu, J.-H. Lee, K.-M. Kim, and S. Lee. meCurate: Personalized curation service using a tiny text intelligence. In *Proc. WWW'17 Companion*, pp.269-272, 2017.

Demo: Fully Automated UI Testing System for Large-scale Android Apps Using Multiple Devices

Taeyeon Ki, Alexander Simeonov, Chang Min Park, Karthik Dantu, Steven Y. Ko, Lukasz Ziarek
Department of Computer Science and Engineering
University at Buffalo, The State University of New York
{tki, agsimeon, cpark22, kdantu, stevko, lziarek}@buffalo.edu

Abstract

We demonstrate AutoClicker, a fully automated UI testing system for *large-scale* Android apps using *multiple devices*. It provides a way to quickly and easily verify that a large number of Android apps behave correctly at runtime in a repeatable manner.

1. INTRODUCTION

Recently, many researchers leverage app instrumentation techniques to achieve different goals, such as improving energy efficiency for always-on sensing [4], or providing mobile deep links [3]. With compiler validation, One can easily check that instrumented apps are correctly transformed at compilation time. However, verifying if a large number of instrumented apps behave correctly at runtime is still challenging and time-consuming. This is because researchers have to schedule many apps for testing and use multiple devices in parallel in order to facilitate testing. Moreover, researchers need to understand app testing APIs and libraries, and build a system using them. To address this issue, we have developed AutoClicker, which is a fully automated UI testing system that does not require any testing scripts or manual efforts. Only a set of apps to test and a set of real devices or emulators are required.

2. ARCHITECTURE OVERVIEW

AutoClicker takes a set of apps and a set of devices as input and generates logs and result plots. AutoClicker provides command-line options such as testing time, the number of runs, runtime type (Dalvik, ART), cleanup mode, etc. It uses adb (Android Debugging Bridge) to control devices connected to AutoClicker. AutoClicker has six core components as shown in the Figure 1. Device Controller detects all devices including real devices or emulators connected to it, and checks device conditions such as battery level, occupied status, and so on. From this information, APK distributor selects a device and an app that is not tested yet. It installs and launches the app on a device to start testing. UI Inspector leverages Android UI Automator [1], which can inspect all UI elements and their hierarchy for an app running on a device. Using this information, Random Event Generator generates random UI events such as button clicks and text input. In the background, Log Collector captures all logs that the app under test generates. To reduce the log size, it filters out unnecessary logs. The processes mentioned above are repeated until all apps are completely tested. Then, Graph Generator draws a result plot by analyzing the logs. For each run, AutoClicker restores a predefined image to clean up for testing consistency if the cleanup mode is enabled.

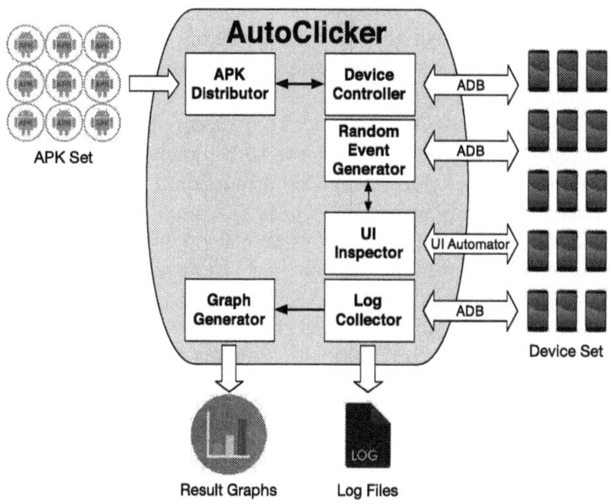

Figure 1: AutoClicker Architecture

Permission to make digital or hard copies of part or all of this work for personal or classroom use is granted without fee provided that copies are not made or distributed for profit or commercial advantage and that copies bear this notice and the full citation on the first page. Copyrights for third-party components of this work must be honored. For all other uses, contact the owner/author(s).
MobiSys'17 June 19-23, 2017, Niagara Falls, NY, USA
© 2017 Copyright held by the owner/author(s).
ACM ISBN 978-1-4503-4928-4/17/06.
DOI: http://dx.doi.org/10.1145/3081333.3089330

3. DEMONSTRATION

In this demo, we will show the capabilities of AutoClicker on a normal desktop connected to fourteen Nexus 5 devices running Android 4.4 for Dalvik and Android 6.0.1 for ART. We will test 2,207 apps downloaded from Google Play 10 times for one minute. During testing, AutoClicker will verify if the runtime behavior of each app in the test set is correct. A demo video of AutoClicker can be found from [2].

4. REFERENCES

[1] Android UI Automator. https://goo.gl/xSxzoj.

[2] AutoClicker Demo. https://goo.gl/O4yweO.

[3] T. Azim, O. Riva, and S. Nath. ulink: Enabling user-defined deep linking to app content. In *Proceedings of the 14th Annual International Conference on Mobile Systems, Applications, and Services*, MobiSys '16, 2016.

[4] H. Shen, A. Balasubramanian, A. LaMarca, and D. Wetherall. Enhancing Mobile Apps to Use Sensor Hubs Without Programmer Effort. In *Proceedings of the 2015 ACM International Joint Conference on Pervasive and Ubiquitous Computing*, UbiComp '15, 2015.

DEMO: DeepMon - Building Mobile GPU Deep Learning Models for Continuous Vision Applications

Loc N. Huynh, Rajesh Krishna Balan, Youngki Lee
Singapore Management University
{nlhuynh.2014, rajesh, youngkilee}@smu.edu.sg

Keywords

Mobile GPU; Mobile Sensing; Deep Learning; Continuous Vision

1. INTRODUCTION

Deep learning has revolutionized vision sensing applications in terms of accuracy comparing to other techniques. Its breakthrough comes from the ability to extract complex high level features directly from sensor data. However, deep learning models are still yet to be natively supported on mobile devices due to high computational requirements. In this paper, we present *DeepMon*, a next generation of *DeepSense* [1] framework, to enable deep learning models on conventional mobile devices (e.g. Samsung Galaxy S7) for continuous vision sensing applications. Firstly, *DeepMon* exploits similarity between consecutive video frames for intermediate data caching within models to enhance inference latency. Secondly, *DeepMon* leverages approximation technique (e.g. Tucker decomposition) to build up approximated models with negligible impact on accuracy. Thirdly, *DeepMon* offloads heavy computation onto integrated mobile GPU to significantly reduce execution time of the model.

2. SYSTEM OVERVIEW

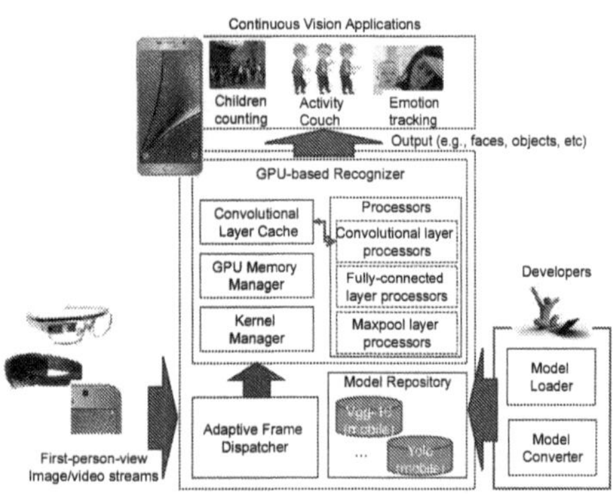

Figure 1: *DeepMon* System Architecture

DeepMon consists of 3 main components (Figure 1).

1) Adaptive frame dispatcher: takes responsibility for choosing important frames and submits them to recognizer.

Permission to make digital or hard copies of part or all of this work for personal or classroom use is granted without fee provided that copies are not made or distributed for profit or commercial advantage and that copies bear this notice and the full citation on the first page. Copyrights for third-party components of this work must be honored. For all other uses, contact the owner/author(s).

MobiSys'17 June 19-23, 2017, Niagara Falls, NY, USA

© 2017 Copyright held by the owner/author(s).

ACM ISBN 978-1-4503-4928-4/17/06.
DOI: http://dx.doi.org/10.1145/3081333.3089331

Phone	GPU	APIs	# GPU Cores (#ALUs)	Memory Size (GB)	Memory Bandwid. (GB/s)
Samsung S7	Mali T880	OpenCL/ Vulkan	12	4	25.6
Sony Z5	Adreno 430	OpenCL	4 (192)	3	12.8

Table 1: Specs for Commodity Mobile GPUs

2) Model repository: stores pre-trained models for various tasks such as image recognition, object detection. *DeepMon's* models are not limited to those we provided but can be converted from other framework such as Caffe [2] via our external *model converter*.

3) GPU-based recognizer: processes interesting frames and sends the output back to applications of interests. At first, *DeepMon* compares the current frame with the previous one to see if any regions within a frame should be recomputed to reduce the total computation. After that, caching kernels will be launched to compute only specific regions of the frame, followed by precision reduction if configured by applications.

3. DEMONSTRATION

We demonstrate our *DeepMon* framework on two latest devices, Samsung Galaxy S7 and Z5. Both are commodity smartphone devices running on two different GPU architectures. Galaxy S7 integrates Mali GPU while Z5 uses Adreno GPU as shown in table 1.

In our demonstration, we will trigger Yolo object detection [3] continuously on video streams to localize 20 objects (e.g. persopn, dog, cat, etc.) and show detected bounding boxes on the screen.

4. REFERENCES

[1] L. N. Huynh, R. K. Balan, and Y. Lee. Deepsense: A gpu-based deep convolutional neural network framework on commodity mobile devices. In *Proceedings of the 2016 Workshop on Wearable Systems and Applications*, pages 25–30. ACM, 2016.

[2] Y. Jia, E. Shelhamer, J. Donahue, S. Karayev, J. Long, R. Girshick, S. Guadarrama, and T. Darrell. Caffe: Convolutional architecture for fast feature embedding. In *Proceedings of the 22nd ACM international conference on Multimedia*, pages 675–678. ACM, 2014.

[3] J. Redmon, S. Divvala, R. Girshick, and A. Farhadi. You only look once: Unified, real-time object detection. *arXiv preprint arXiv:1506.02640*, 2015.

Demo: Card-stunt as a Service: Empowering a Massively Packed Crowd for Instant Collective Expressiveness

Chungkuk Yoo[1], Inseok Hwang[2], Seungwoo Kang[3] Myung-Chul Kim[4],
Seonghoon Kim[1], Daeyoung Won[1], Yu Gu[4], Junehwa Song[1]
[1]KAIST, [2]IBM Research, [3]KOREATECH, [4]IBM
[1]{ckyoo, shkim, daeyoung, junesong}@nclab.kaist.ac.kr,
[2,4]{ihwang, mckima, yugu}@us.ibm.com, [3]swkang@koreatech.ac.kr

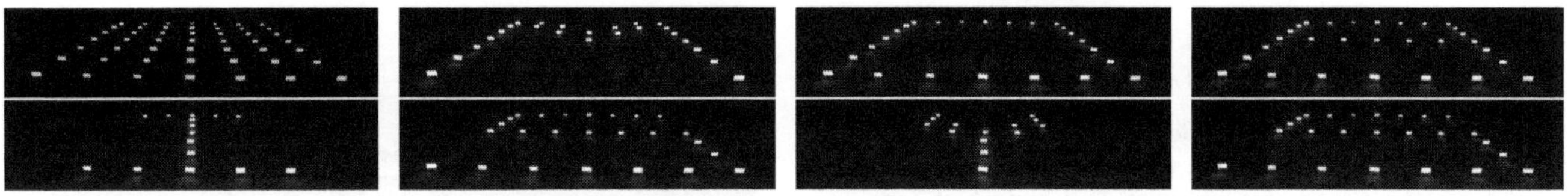

Figure 1: CaaS displays "MOBISYS" one letter after another on 49 smartphones.

1. INTRODUCTION

Consider a massive crowd who gathered together to convey their common voice to public, e.g., supporters of a team sitting together in a stadium, people doing a candlelight vigil in a public square, and so on. Imagine that they hold up their smartphone displays which collectively compose a huge public screen; the crowd's messages are now shown big on the top of them. We present CaaS [3], a mobile service to realize such an instant, massive, collective visualization with commodity smartphones and cloud services. In this demo, we demonstrate the collective localization feature of CaaS so that the audience can watch a given pattern or symbol collectively displayed on top of arbitrarily positioned phones (See the video demo, https://goo.gl/GfsORc).

2. CHALLENGES AND APPROACH

The key challenge to enable CaaS is instantly localizing a large number of devices, even up to tens of thousands, within accuracy and latency tolerances, without any custom infrastructure other than commodity smartphones and Internet connectivity. Existing approaches for stitching small displays require a custom infrastructure to localize each device such as an omniscient camera [2]. GPS is not accurate enough to clearly distinguish individual devices of a packed crowd, which are often less than one meter apart from each other. While existing device-to-device localization techniques [1] even provide centimeter-level accuracies, they are hardly applicable to the problem of localizing a large number of densely packed co-located devices with tight time constraints.

To address the challenge, CaaS utilizes simultaneous AoA (angle of arrival) sensing through VLC (visual-light communication) among all participating devices. As shown in Figure 2, when a screen of 'A' transmits its identifier signals encoded in hue transition sequences, the rear camera of 'B' captures the signals seen within its FoV (field of view). B computes the AoA between its camera and the center of A's screen. To maximize line-of-sight paths between devices, all participants are asked to hold up their smartphones overhead for a few seconds at the same time. After sensing AoAs, each device sends observed AoA data to a CaaS cloud server which reconstructs the device locations to be optimal for the given observed AoAs and some error margins. The details of whole process for localization are presented in [3].

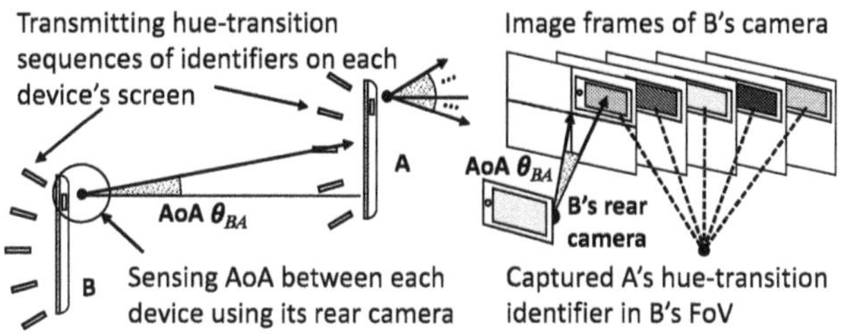

Figure 2: VLC for AoA sensing between smartphones.

3. DEMONSTRATION

We will demonstrate CaaS with arbitrarily located multiple devices on a table. Due to a limited number of devices under our ownership, the devices to be shipped to the demo venue may be fewer than those recruited in our full deployments [3]. Once AoA sensings are complete, CaaS server interface shows the relative localization result within a few seconds. As soon as the CaaS coordinator chooses an image to show, the image is pixelated to fit the spatial placements of the devices. Each device displays the right pixel with respect to its relative location. Animated images also can be displayed (See Figure 1). We believe CaaS will create new user experience for co-located crowds. CaaS would help them express their messages through a huge collective display consisting of small lights from individual smartphone.

4. REFERENCES

[1] C. Peng et al. Beepbeep: a high accuracy acoustic ranging system using cots mobile devices. In *Proc. SenSys'07*. ACM, 2007.

[2] J. Schwarz et al. Phone as a pixel: enabling ad-hoc, large-scale displays using mobile devices. In *Proc. CHI'12*. ACM, 2012.

[3] C. Yoo et al. Card-stunt as a service: Empowering a massively packed crowd for instant collective expressiveness. In *Proc. MobiSys'17*. ACM, 2017.

Permission to make digital or hard copies of part or all of this work for personal or classroom use is granted without fee provided that copies are not made or distributed for profit or commercial advantage and that copies bear this notice and the full citation on the first page. Copyrights for third-party components of this work must be honored. For all other uses, contact the owner/author(s).

MobiSys'17 June 19-23, 2017, Niagara Falls, NY, USA

© 2017 Copyright held by the owner/author(s).

ACM ISBN 978-1-4503-4928-4/17/06.
DOI: http://dx.doi.org/10.1145/3081333.3089332

Demo: AWSense – A Framework for Collecting Sensing Data from the Apple Watch

Katrin Hänsel, Hamed Haddadi, Akram Alomainy
Queen Mary University of London
London, UK
{k.hansel, hamed.haddadi, a.alomainy}@qmul.ac.uk

ABSTRACT

We present a framework - AWSense - for eased sensing data collection from an Apple Watch wearable device. The framework eases the access, transmission and export of sensing data from the device. This data comprises: heart rate, raw acceleration, and computed device motion. In our demo, we present sample applications built on top of this framework to show its capabilities, of real-time presentation and recording of the sensing data.

1. INTRODUCTION

Mobile phones have been equipped with a variety of sensors, e.g. accelerometers, gyroscopes, which have been used in mobile sensing research [1]. With the introduction of wearable devices, this trend has transferred over to wearables like smartwatches and fitness trackers. Those sensors can be utilised to enhance mobile and wearable sensing research. We made our framework and two demo applications available on Github[1].

2. FRAMEWORK ARCHITECTURE

The *AWSense* framework consists of two parts: the core and connect framework.

The *AWSense Core* is designed to be run on the Apple Watch alone and it contains the main sensing functionality. It can be incorporated into watch apps to make data access easier. It allows the subscription to real-time sensing events, configuration of sensors and the start of a sensing session. The sensors currently available are:

- Raw acceleration (including gravity), configurable up to 100 Hz
- Device Motion (computed linear acceleration, rotation rate, gravity and attitude), configurable up to 100 Hz
- Heart rate

[1]https://github.com/MiezelKat/AWSense

Permission to make digital or hard copies of part or all of this work for personal or classroom use is granted without fee provided that copies are not made or distributed for profit or commercial advantage and that copies bear this notice and the full citation on the first page. Copyrights for third-party components of this work must be honored. For all other uses, contact the owner/author(s).

MobiSys'17 June 19–23, 2017, Niagara Falls, NY, USA

© 2017 Copyright held by the owner/author(s).

ACM ISBN 978-1-4503-4928-4/17/06.
DOI: http://dx.doi.org/10.1145/3081333.3089333

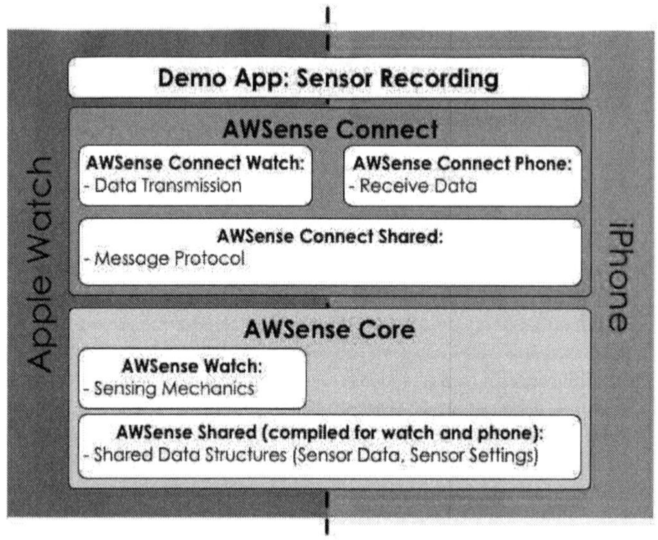

The *AWSense Connect* part builds on top of the *Core* and manages the communication between the phone and watch. The phone-side API allows the the configuration of sensors, subscription to events and start of a remote sensing session on the Apple Watch. The configuration, sensor data, and events are all transferred through an own message protocol. This message protocol offers several message types to configure and control a sensing session. The wearable sensing data is buffered on the watch and sent in batches to decrease battery consumption and communication load. The buffer size and time between transmissions are hereby flexibly configurable to match the purpose of the application. There is the option to store the sensing data in a CSV format on the iPhone. It can then be downloaded for further use.

3. DEMONSTRATION

We will demonstrate a test applications built on top of the *AWSense* framework to show, real-time data presentation and data export. We will also present previous data recordings made with our framework.

4. REFERENCES

[1] N. Lane, E. Miluzzo, H. Lu, D. Peebles, T. Choudhury, and A. Campbell. A survey of mobile phone sensing. *IEEE Communications Magazine*, 48(9):140–150, 2010.

Demo: Riding the Non-linearities to Record Ultrasound with Smartphones

Nirupam Roy, Haitham Hassanieh, Romit Roy Choudhury
University of Illinois at Urbana-Champaign

ABSTRACT

We demonstrate that high frequency ultrasonic sounds can be designed to become recordable by unmodified smartphone microphones, while remaining inaudible to humans. The core idea lies in exploiting non-linearities in microphone hardware with a combination of ultrasound frequencies. These frequencies can be regulated to carry data bits, thereby enabling an acoustic (but inaudible) communication channel to today's microphones. Other applications include jamming spy microphones in the environment, live watermarking of music in a concert, and even acoustic Denial-of-Service (DoS) attacks.

System Overview

Microphones, like human ears, operate at audible frequencies, hence cannot record ultrasonic sounds (>24kHz). *BackDoor* [1] shows the possibility of designing ultrasonic signals that humans cannot hear but microphones can record. The core intuition is to exploit the inherent non-linearities in the diaphragm and the amplifiers of the microphones. *BackDoor* generates a set of carefully modulated frequencies, which, due to these non-linearities, produces predictable "*shadow*" frequencies within the recordable range of the microphone. In the simplest case, *BackDoor* plays two tones at say 40kHz and 50kHz. When these tones arrive together at the microphone's power amplifier, they are amplified as expected, but also multiplied due to fundamental non-linearities in the system. Multiplication of frequencies f_1 and f_2 result in frequency components at $(f_1 - f_2)$ and $(f_1 + f_2)$. Given that $(f_1 - f_2)$ is 10kHz in this case, well within the microphone's range, the signal passes unaltered through the low pass filter (LPF). Human ears, on the other hand, do not exhibit such non-linearities and the 40kHz and 50kHz sounds remain inaudible. Figure 1 illustrates the effect. Importantly, the microphone does not require any modification, enabling billions of phones, laptops, and IoT devices to leverage the capability. This opens new applications in security and communications.

Permission to make digital or hard copies of part or all of this work for personal or classroom use is granted without fee provided that copies are not made or distributed for profit or commercial advantage and that copies bear this notice and the full citation on the first page. Copyrights for third-party components of this work must be honored. For all other uses, contact the owner/author(s).

MobiSys'17 June 19-23, 2017, Niagara Falls, NY, USA

© 2017 Copyright held by the owner/author(s).

ACM ISBN 978-1-4503-4928-4/17/06.
DOI: http://dx.doi.org/10.1145/3081333.3089334

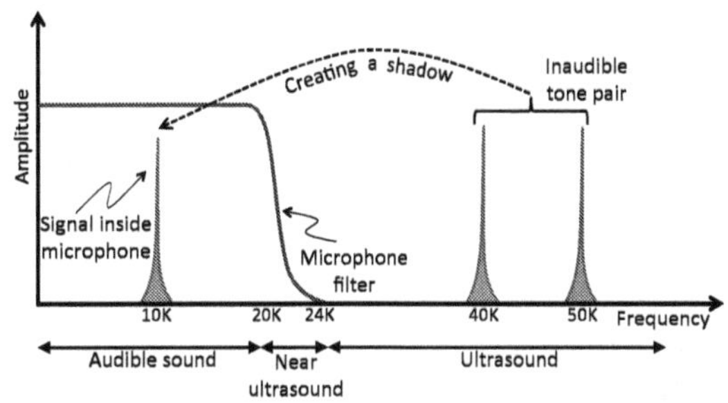

Figure 1: The main idea underlying *BackDoor*.

Given microphones record these inaudible sounds, it should be possible to silently jam spy microphones from recording. Military and government officials can secure private and confidential meetings from electronic eavesdropping; cinemas and concerts can prevent unauthorized recording of movies and live performances. On the other hand, *BackDoor* can utilize the entire microphone spectrum for inaudible acoustic communication that enables an alternative channel for the IoT devices. In this demonstration we explain the core intuitions behind *BackDoor* and show its initial prototypes.

Demonstration

We develop three different transmitter prototypes – (1) a pair of fixed frequency tone generators to demonstrate the nonlinearity in microphones, (2) a frequency modulated (FM) transmitter setup for communication, and (3) a speaker array for jamming. A programmable waveform generator drives the speakers with frequency modulated signals. The audience can receive BackDoor signals on their smartphones to experience the inaudible jamming effect. We have also developed an android application to demonstrate the communication prototype.

Acknowledgement

We are grateful to the Joan and Lalit Bahl Fellowship, Qualcomm, IBM, and NSF (award number: 1619313) for partially funding this research.

1. REFERENCES

[1] Roy, N., Hassanieh, H., and Roy Choudhury, R. Backdoor: Making microphones hear inaudible sounds. In *Proceeding of the 15th annual international conference on Mobile systems, applications, and services* (2017), ACM.

Demo: Detecting Group Formations using iBeacon Technology

Kleomenis Katevas†, Laurissa Tokarchuk†, Hamed Haddadi†, Richard G. Clegg†, Muhammad Irfan†◇
†Queen Mary University of London, UK. ◇University of Genova, Italy.
k.katevas@qmul.ac.uk

1. INTRODUCTION

Researchers from different disciplines have examined crowd behavior in the past by employing a variety of methods including ethnographic studies, computer vision techniques and manual annotation based data analysis. However, because of the inherent difficulties in collecting, processing and analyzing the data, it is difficult to obtain large data sets for study. In this work we present a system for detecting stationary interactions inside crowds, depending entirely on the sensors available in a modern smartphone device such as Bluetooth Smart (BLE) and Accelerometer. By utilizing Apple's iBeacon^{TM} implementation of Bluetooth Smart using SensingKit[1], our open-source multi-platform mobile sensing framework [1], we are able to detect the proximity of users carrying a smartphone in their pocket. We then use an algorithm based on graph theory to predict group interactions inside the crowd. Previous work in this area has been limited to the detection of interactions between only two people and therefore our approach goes beyond current state of the art in its ability to detect group formations with more than two people involved. Our approach is particularly beneficial to the design and implementation of crowd behavior analytics, design of influence strategies, and algorithms for crowd reconfiguration.

2. DEMONSTRATION

As shown in Figure 1, our system consists of: an iOS mobile application titled CrowdSense[3], and a cloud-based server back-end. Each user needs to have CrowdSense installed, enabling his/her device to both broadcast as an iBeacon^{TM}, but at the same time scan for other beacons around the space. The app is also collecting the Linear Acceleration of the device, classifying the user's motion activity between 'stationary' and 'in motion'. Our back-end receives the data in real-time and visualizes the detected group formations though a web interface. Additionally, it produces analytics about the detected crowd such as: types of interactions over time, clustering and degree distributions. For more information about how our technology works, please refer to [2].

Our setup includes some iPhone devices with the CrowdSense app installed, that will be given to people interested in our demo. Since CrowdSense is available in the AppStore, users could also use their personal devices to participate. The back-end will analyze the streamed data, detect the users' social interactions in real-time and visualize them on a screen through a web-interface. A video recording of an actual social event (e.g. a conference coffee break) will also be displayed on another screen, while our system will analyze more complex scenarios of interactions happening in that event.

The purpose of this demo is to present a technology that is capable of providing in-depth analytics about how the crowd behaves during social events. A video showcase of the demo can be found at: https://www.sensingkit.org/MobiSys17-Demo.m4v.

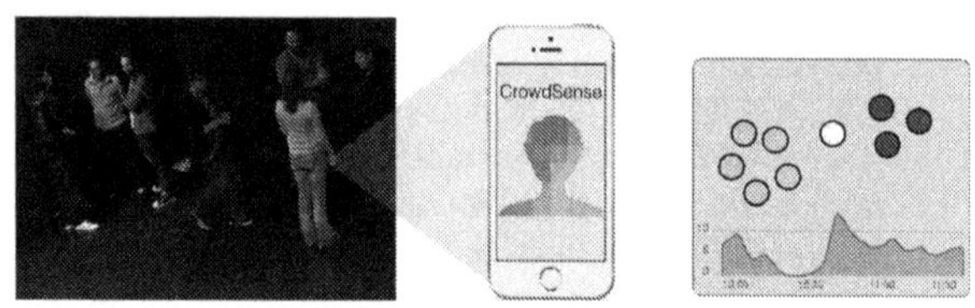

Figure 1: System Design

Acknowledgments

This work is supported by funding from the UK Defense Science and Technology Laboratory.

3. REFERENCES

[1] K. Katevas, H. Haddadi, and L. Tokarchuk. Sensingkit: Evaluating the sensor power consumption in ios devices. In *2016 12th International Conference on Intelligent Environments (IE)*, pages 222–225, Sept 2016.

[2] K. Katevas, H. Haddadi, L. Tokarchuk, and R. G. Clegg. Detecting group formations using iBeacon technology. In *Proceedings of the 2016 ACM International Joint Conference on Pervasive and Ubiquitous Computing: Adjunct*, UbiComp '16, pages 742–752, New York, NY, USA, 2016. ACM.

[3] Kleomenis Katevas. CrowdSense for iOS. https://itunes.apple.com/app/crowdsense/id930853606.

[1] https://www.sensingkit.org

Permission to make digital or hard copies of part or all of this work for personal or classroom use is granted without fee provided that copies are not made or distributed for profit or commercial advantage and that copies bear this notice and the full citation on the first page. Copyrights for third-party components of this work must be honored. For all other uses, contact the owner/author(s).

MobiSys'17 June 19-23, 2017, Niagara Falls, NY, USA

© 2017 Copyright held by the owner/author(s).

ACM ISBN 978-1-4503-4928-4/17/06.

DOI: http://dx.doi.org/10.1145/3081333.3089335

Demo: Enabling Dynamic Gesture Mapping with UI Events

Chang Min Park, Taeyeon Ki, Karthik Dantu, Steven Y. Ko, Lukasz Ziarek
Department of Computer Science and Engineering
University at Buffalo, The State University of New York
{cpark22, tki, kdantu, stevko, lziarek}@buffalo.edu

Abstract

We demonstrate Gesto, a dynamic gesture mapping tool. It provides users to map any gesture to a certain UI event that the users need. Also, the mapping can be easily changed by users.

1. INTRODUCTION

On mobile devices, a user can interact with an app using UI events such as button clicks or text input. However, it is often hard for a user to perform UI actions directly on a device. For example, a user may need to perform UI events while exercising or when wearing thick gloves. To address this issue, many researchers proposed to use gestures such as shaking to enable a new mode of interaction between a user and an app [1, 3, 4]. However, previous approaches all have a limitation that gestures are mapped statically to certain UI elements, and users cannot easily configure the mappings.

Gesto is a new system that allows dynamic mappings between gestures and UI events. Users can easily change the mappings whenever they need.

2. ARCHITECTURE OVERVIEW

Gesto allows various gesture APIs that users can map with UI events. Gesto consists of two parts which are recording and performing. When a single wave gesture is detected, Gesto waits for a gesture to map with UI events. After a certain gesture was detected, Gesto goes to the launcher activity and records the sequnce of user input. Gesto can detect all UI elements and save which UI element is used by users. It also saves activity hierarchy, which shows all activities opened during recording, starting with main activity. This approach is similar to uLink [2], but we use it for correct recording of UI events to map with gestures later, not a deep link. The recording is turned off by double wave. All the UI events that users do are saved during recording. Once the gesture is succesfully mapped with some UI events, the saved UI events can be performed by triggering gesture as shown in Figure 1. Gesto firstly checks if the gesture is mapped with some UI events. If not, it informs that no UI event is mapped for that particular gesture. If yes, it goes to main activity and loads a saved activity hierarchy. Then, it sees which UI events were recorded by users. After perfoming all UI events for a certain activity, it moves to another activity and does the same task. After performing all saved UI events, Gesto ends. By triggering a previously-used followed by a single wave, it overrides the previous mapping and records a new mapping.

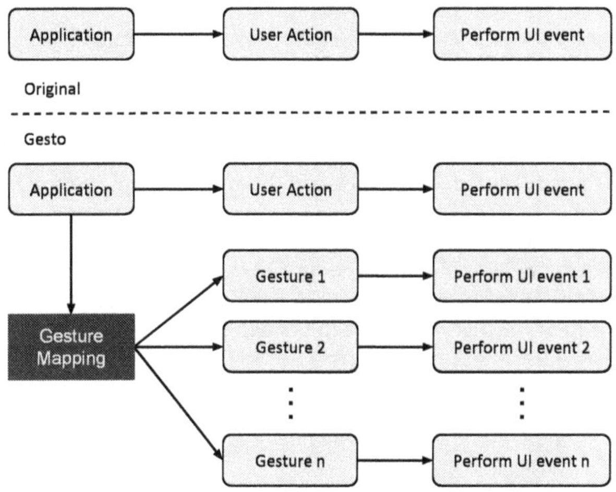

Figure 1: Gesto Architecture

3. DEMONSTRATION

In this demo, we will show how easily users can map various gestures with UI events. We will test several apps to show that Gesto can detect all UI elements and succcessfully map those with gestures. Also, we will show the UI events are actully performed when mapped gestures are triggerd.

4. REFERENCES

[1] Daniel Ashbrook and Thad Starner. Magic: A motion gesture design tool. In CHI, New York, NY, USA, 2010. ACM.

[2] Tanzirul Azim, Oriana Riva, and Suman Nath. ulink: Enabling user-defined deep linking to app content. In MobiSys, New York, NY, USA, 2016. ACM.

[3] Rainhard Findling and Muhammad Muaaz. Shakeunlock: Securely unlock mobile devices by shaking them together. In MoMM, New York, NY, USA, 2014. ACM.

[4] Ryo Izuta, Kazuya Murao, Tsutomu Terada, and Masahiko Tsukamoto. Early gesture recognition method with an accelerometer. In MoMM, New York, NY, USA, 2014. ACM.

Permission to make digital or hard copies of part or all of this work for personal or classroom use is granted without fee provided that copies are not made or distributed for profit or commercial advantage and that copies bear this notice and the full citation on the first page. Copyrights for third-party components of this work must be honored. For all other uses, contact the owner/author(s).

MobiSys'17 June 19-23, 2017, Niagara Falls, NY, USA

© 2017 Copyright held by the owner/author(s).

ACM ISBN 978-1-4503-4928-4/17/06.
DOI: http://dx.doi.org/10.1145/3081333.3089336

Demo: iBlink: Smart Glasses for Facial Paralysis Patients

Sijie Xiong†, Sujie Zhu†, Yisheng Ji†, Binyao Jiang†, Xiaohua Tian†,
Xuesheng Zheng‡, Xinbing Wang†
†School of Electronic, Info. & Electrical Engineering, Shanghai Jiao Tong University, China
‡Xin Hua Hospital Affiliated to Shanghai Jiao Tong University School of Medicine, China
†{qq420778733, zhusujie, acetanil, emberspirit, xtian, xwang8}@sjtu.edu.cn,
‡pheiphei@126.com

Extended Abstract

Facial paralysis is a disease caused by nerve damage, which can make patients lose facial movements. Facial paralysis patients usually have muscles on one side of the face noticeably droop, which seriously impacts the person's quality of life as shown in Fig. 1. Worse still, the eye on the affected side is unable to blink and will become dry and infected by debries, which can incur eye damage even blindness. To the best of scientists' knowledge, the paralysis is due to the pressure incurred by infection in the tunnel containing main trunk of facial nerves, where the tunnel is inside of the people's head termed as the Facial canal.

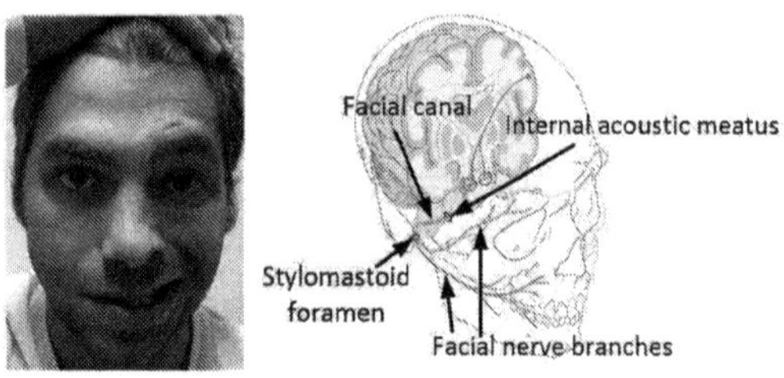

Figure 1: Anatomy of facial nerves.

In this demo, we present *iBlink* [1], a novel system to help paralysis patients to blink. Paralysis usually occurs in just one side of the face, and clinical trials show that electrical stimulation could trigger blink. Based on such observations, the basic idea of *iBlink* is to monitor the normal side of the face with a camera and stimulate the paralysed side, so that eye-movements of the both sides become symmetric.

Several challenges need to be overcome in the design of *iBlink*. First, since different patients require different configurations of the stimulation impulse to enable blinking according to our precedent Medtronic Keypoint electromyography(EMG) clinical trials, the system has to accommodate individual diversity. Second, because the accuracy of blink detection is significantly influenced by illumination conditions, the system has to adapt to varied environment. Third, the system has to be power efficient, which is common challenge for all mobile devices.

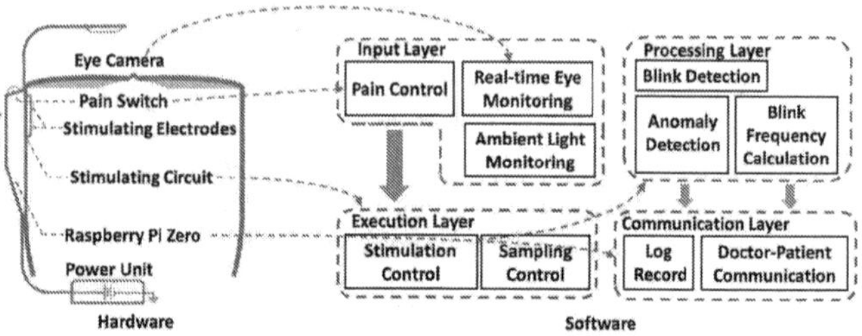

Figure 2: Design of the iBlink system

The architecture design of *iBlink* is shown in Fig. 2. The camera installed in front of the eyes monitors eye-movements in real time. The Raspberry Pi Zero platform processes the images captured by the eye camera, which also monitors the ambient lighting condition. The Raspberry PI Zero and stimulation circuits are located on the patient's paralyzed side of the face, where Raspberry PI Zero and stimulation circuits are in the outer side of the glass frame, and two stimulating electrodes are in the inner side of the frame pressing on the patient's face skin. The Wi-Fi and Bluetooth interfaces in Raspberry PI Zero can be utilized for communication with smartphones.

The software consists of four layers: input layer, processing layer, execution layer and communication layer. The input layer captures the input images and ambient illumination data from the camera and pain control action from the pain switch. The processing layer deals with the data captured by input layer to select day-and-night model, detect anomalous blink, and calculate blink frequency. The execution layer includes stimulation control and sampling control. The stimulation control adjusts the electric stimulation parameters for the patients automatically based on detection results from the processing layer. The sampling control adjusts the sampling frequency of the camera based on the blink frequency calculated in the processing layer. The communication layer collects patients' pathology data and transmits the data to doctors.

Permission to make digital or hard copies of part or all of this work for personal or classroom use is granted without fee provided that copies are not made or distributed for profit or commercial advantage and that copies bear this notice and the full citation on the first page. Copyrights for third-party components of this work must be honored. For all other uses, contact the owner/author(s).
MobiSys'17 June 19-23, 2017, Niagara Falls, NY, USA
© 2017 Copyright held by the owner/author(s).
ACM ISBN 978-1-4503-4928-4/17/06.
DOI: http://dx.doi.org/10.1145/3081333.3089337

1. REFERENCES

[1] S. Xiong, S. Zhu, Y. Ji, B. Jiang, X. Tian, X. Zheng, X. Wang, to appear "iBlink: Smart Glasses for Facial Paralysis Patients," in *Proc of ACM Mobisys'17.*

Demo: Reptor: Enabling API Virtualization on Android for Platform Openness

Taeyeon Ki, Alexander Simeonov, Chang Min Park, Karthik Dantu, Steven Y. Ko, Lukasz Ziarek
Department of Computer Science and Engineering
University at Buffalo, The State University of New York
{tki, agsimeon, cpark22, kdantu, stevko, lziarek}@buffalo.edu

Abstract

We demonstrate Reptor, a bytecode instrumentation tool enabling *API virtualization* on Android. It provides a general way to alter functionality of platform APIs on Android. With Reptor, third-party developers can modify the behavior of platform APIs according to their needs. All modifications are completely at the app layer without modifying the underlying platform. This allows practical openness—third-party developers can easily distribute their modifications for a platform without the need to update the entire platform.

1. INTRODUCTION

Oftentimes, mobile platform source code is closed. For example, the source code for iOS and Windows Mobile is closed. Third parties cannot really examine and modify the source code. One exception is Android that is open to the public. Third-party developers can access and modify the source code. However, there is no easy way to deploy the platform modifications to large-scale users. This is because Google or major mobile vendors such as Samsung and LG, control the platform distribution channels. In other words, there are only a select few players who can control the innovation on Android. Thus, there is a stiff barrier to realize novel ideas to make advances. To mitigate this lack of mobile platform openness, we propose a new technique called *API virtualization* to enable open innovation in Android. API virtualization allows third-party developers to modify, reimplement, or customize the behavior of platform APIs and deploy them seamlessly.

2. API VIRTUALIZATION

API virtualization is a shim layer between the platform layer and the app layer as shown in Figure 1. We create replacement classes for all platform API classes used by an app, and modify the existing code in the app to use the replacement classes instead of the original platform API classes. This shim layer contains all replacement classes and is injected into the app. In other words, API virtualization is self-contained in the app layer allowing for seamless modifications. Third-party developers can easily modify the behavior of platform APIs by modifying the implementation of replacement

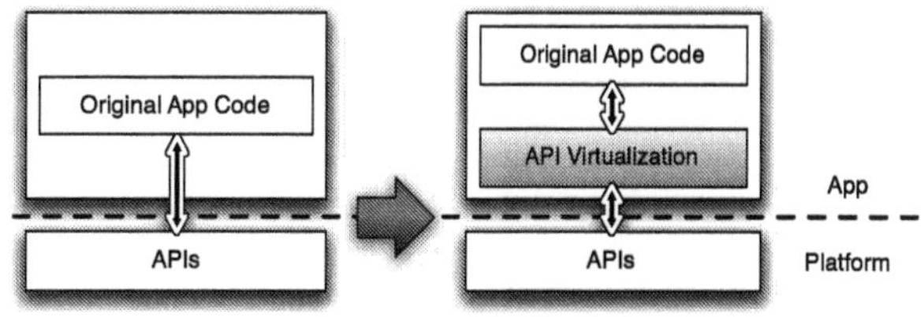

Figure 1: API Virtualization

classes. Moreover, third-party developers seamlessly deploy their instrumented version of app through regular app distribution channels such as Google Play. This approach has an extra benefit that per-app customizations are possible. One example is when each app is tailored to sync with public cloud or secure cloud depending on its purpose as envisioned by BlueMountain [2].

We have implemented a prototype of API virtualization called Reptor on Android. To correctly realize API virtualization, we have carefully addressed many practical challenges. These challenges mainly come from Android's event-driven programming model and its development language, Java. Java has a variety of features such as polymorphism, which means that a child class object can be cast to a parent class anywhere in an app. Also, the child class can define its own functionality or use some of the parent class's functionality. Therefore, known techniques such as search-and-replace approach and call site instrumentation are not suitable for API virtualization due to the features.

3. DEMONSTRATION

To concretely demonstrate the power of Reptor, we will show three use cases. The first use case of Reptor is a vendor-tied library switching. In this use case, we automatically transform Airbnb app developed with Googles library to use Amazons library by using Reptor, specifically Google Maps APIs to Amazon Maps APIs. The second use case is a runtime permission mechanism that asks a user to grant permission to an app at run time, mirroring the iOS permission model. In this use case, we use Twitter as a target app. The third use case is an HTTP-to-HTTPS translator, which makes an app use HTTPS instead of HTTP if HTTPS is available on a requested URL. We have posted demo videos of the use cases on our YouTube channel [1].

4. REFERENCES

[1] Reptor Use Case Demos. https://goo.gl/hGTjpL.
[2] S. Chandrashekhara, K. Marcus, R. G. M. Subramanya, H. S. Karve, K. Dantu, and S. Y. Ko. Enabling Automated, Rich, and Versatile Data Management for Android Apps with BlueMountain. In HotStorage, 2015.

Permission to make digital or hard copies of part or all of this work for personal or classroom use is granted without fee provided that copies are not made or distributed for profit or commercial advantage and that copies bear this notice and the full citation on the first page. Copyrights for third-party components of this work must be honored. For all other uses, contact the owner/author(s).
MobiSys'17 June 19-23, 2017, Niagara Falls, NY, USA
© 2017 Copyright held by the owner/author(s).
ACM ISBN 978-1-4503-4928-4/17/06.
DOI: http://dx.doi.org/10.1145/3081333.3089338

Demo: CELLI - Indoor Positioning using Polarized Sweeping Light Beams

Yu-Lin Wei†, Chang-Jung Huang†, Hsin-Mu Tsai†, Kate Ching-Ju Lin‡
†Department of Computer Science and Information Engineering, National Taiwan University, Taiwan
‡Department of Computer Science, National Chiao Tung University, Taiwan
{r03922027,r02922061,hsinmu}@csie.ntu.edu.tw, katelin@cs.nctu.edu.tw

1. INTRODUCTION

Indoor positioning enables location-based services for a wide range of commercial applications [4]. Existing visible light positioning (VLP) systems [5, 7] leverage the high image resolution of a receiving camera to support high positioning accuracy. However, power-hungry cameras are not desirable in many scenarios, e.g., smart factories, where small objects need to be accurately located and tracked.

In this demo, we introduce CELLI, an indoor VLP system that only uses a single luminary as the transmitter and requires only a simple light sensor to achieve high accuracy with centimeter-level error. The key idea is to provide the spatial resolution capability from the transmitter instead of the receiver, so that the complexity of the receiver can be minimized. In particular, a small Liquid Crystal Display (LCD) is installed at the transmitter to project a large number of narrow and interference-free polarized light beams to different spatial *cells*. A receiving light sensor identifies its located cell by detecting the unique polarization-modulated signals projected to that cell, as shown in Fig. 1.

CELLI further incorporates several novel designs to overcome the technical challenges such as reducing the positioning latency, which is typically limited by the long optical response time of an LCD, and transforming a cell coordinate to the global 3D position using only a single light. We have prototyped our design using off-the-shelf optical and electronic components, and experimentally shown that CELLI achieves a median 3D positioning error less than 12 cm and a median 2D error less than 2.7 cm.

2. IMPLEMENTATION

We implement CELLI's transmitter using the Twisted Nematic (TN) Thin Film Transistor (TFT) LCD with a resolution of 320×240 pixels, featuring a short 4 ms response time, affordable price (less than $30 U.S. Dollar), and built-in controller [1]. The backlight LED used is a XLamp® CXA2540. The compact Tx prototype is shown in Fig. 2(a).

We built the receiver prototype with a microprocessor (MCU) [3] combined with a photodiode component [2] and a Liquid Crystal Cell (LCC) in front. The receiver provides a sampling rate up to 10 kHz and can perform real-time positioning, as shown in Fig. 2(b).

Permission to make digital or hard copies of part or all of this work for personal or classroom use is granted without fee provided that copies are not made or distributed for profit or commercial advantage and that copies bear this notice and the full citation on the first page. Copyrights for third-party components of this work must be honored. For all other uses, contact the owner/author(s).

MobiSys'17 June 19-23, 2017, Niagara Falls, NY, USA

© 2017 Copyright held by the owner/author(s).

ACM ISBN 978-1-4503-4928-4/17/06.
DOI: http://dx.doi.org/10.1145/3081333.3089339

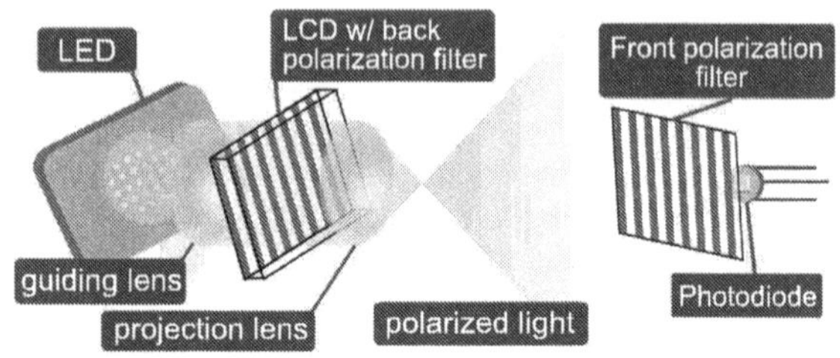

Figure 1: CELLI system design.

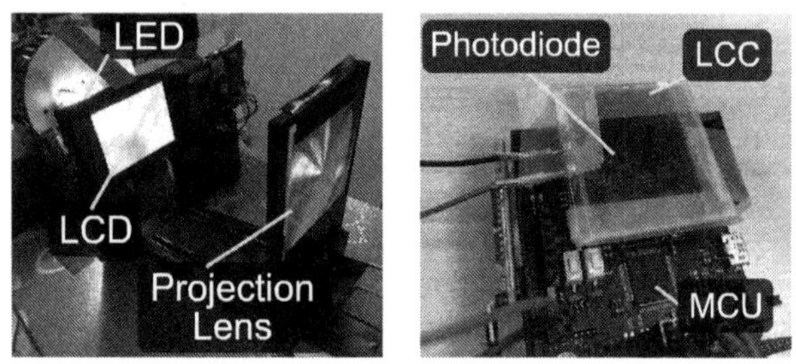

(a) Transmitter **(b)** Receiver

Figure 2: TFT prototype

More detailed information can be found in [6].

3. DEMO VIDEO

The demo video can be viewed at https://goo.gl/qTTo4i.

4. REFERENCES

[1] 4D Systems | uLCD-28PTU. http://www.4dsystems.com.au.
[2] OSRAM Opto Semiconductors | SFH 2430 | SMT PIN Photodiodes . http://www.osram-os.com/os.
[3] STM32F405RG - High-performance foundation line. http://www.st.com/content/st_com/en.html.
[4] J. Armstrong, Y. A. Sekercioglu, and A. Neild. Visible light positioning: a roadmap for international standardization. *IEEE Communications Magazine*, 51(12):68–73, December 2013.
[5] Y.-S. Kuo, P. Pannuto, K.-J. Hsiao, and P. Dutta. Luxapose: Indoor positioning with mobile phones and visible light. In *ACM MobiCom*, 2014.
[6] Y.-L. Wei, C.-J. Huang, H.-M. Tsai, and K. C.-J. Lin. CELLI: Indoor positioning using polarized sweeping light beams. In *ACM MobiSys*, 2017.
[7] Z. Yang, Z. Wang, J. Zhang, C. Huang, and Q. Zhang. Wearables can afford: Light-weight indoor positioning with visible light. In *ACM MobiSys*, 2015.

Demo: Live Video Stream Triggers

Lenin Ravindranath, Matthai Philipose, Peter Bodik, Paramvir Bahl
Microsoft Research
Redmond, WA, USA
lenin@microsoft.com, matthaip@microsoft.com, peterb@microsoft.com, bahl@microsoft.com

Live streaming is an increasingly popular way to broadcast videos ranging from formal news channels to kitten cams to home security camera feeds. Live streaming marries the rich detail of video with the timeliness of live transmission and the ease of use of consumer cameras, thus promising to vastly increase the amount of detailed, up-to-the minute information available about the real world. The volume of potentially interesting footage brings up the question of how end-users can avoid being glued to one (or worse, many) streams of videos waiting for events of interest. In this demo, we present Lookout, a system that allows users to register standing queries, called *triggers* over live video streams. Lookout then notifies the user when events of interest to them occur in their streams of interest. For example, a user could point to a cat cam and write a trigger that sends a notification when the cat wakes up and starts moving. Users can also write triggers to look for certain news being covered in a live new channel, a gamer moving to a certain level in a Twitch stream, a stranger showing up in a outdoor surveillance camera, etc.

Research: Lookout allows users to specify streams of interest and write standing queries on a webpage or mobile app, processes these queries on a continuous basis on a cloud backend and notifies the user when the queries are satisfied. In doing so, Lookout addresses several research challenges. It proposes an expressive but efficient query language that allows users to specify useful spatial and temporal queries over video. It provides a cloud-based architecture to index and serve these queries. It includes several techniques to make cloud-based processing efficient, including feedback-based frame selection, decoupled visual processing and text-based search, cost-effective division of labor between CPU and GPU, and techniques for efficient execution of visual processing algorithms, especially Deep Neural Networks (DNNs).

Permission to make digital or hard copies of part or all of this work for personal or classroom use is granted without fee provided that copies are not made or distributed for profit or commercial advantage and that copies bear this notice and the full citation on the first page. Copyrights for third-party components of this work must be honored. For all other uses, contact the owner/author(s).
MobiSys'17 June 19-23, 2017, Niagara Falls, NY, USA
© 2017 Copyright held by the owner/author(s).
ACM ISBN 978-1-4503-4928-4/17/06.
DOI: http://dx.doi.org/10.1145/3081333.3089340

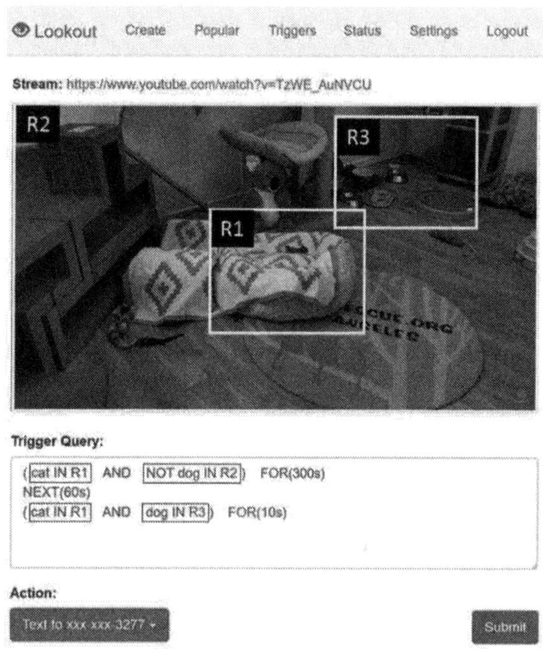

Figure 1: Trigger on a live foster cam with a cat and a dog. The trigger looks for "dog stealing cat's food when the cat is asleep".

Demo: The demo will provide a web page that allows users to add new live streams of interest to them, including, e.g., those from YouTube Live. We will also have one or more on-site cameras from which we will stream live. For each stream, the user can specify a trigger consisting of *atomic queries*, which are regions of interest with entities (object names, text and faces) of interest, and compositions of these atoms using AND, OR, NOT, FOR (indicating temporal extent of the atom), NEXT (indicating temporal sequencing of atoms), WITHIN (indicating temporal neighborhood next to an atom). The user can associate actions such as text/email-based notification or recording the video snippet. Figure 1 shows the current interface for Lookout with a complex trigger.

ALOHA to the Web
Keynote

Norman Abramson
Professor Emeritus
University of Hawaii
norm@hawaii.edu

ABSTRACT
Wireless access to the Internet today is provided predominantly by random access ALOHA channels connecting a wide variety of user devices. ALOHA channels were first analyzed, implemented and demonstrated in the ALOHA network at the University of Hawaii in June, 1971. In this talk we provide a history of the ALOHA Network from a technological point of view illustrated with photos of the original ALOHA equipment designed and built at UH in the early 1970's.

The architectural design choices made in the original ALOHA Network were influenced by the perceived traffic demands of ALOHA users. As ALOHA based random access channels were adopted by other types of networks (satellite, Ethernet, WiFi, mobile phone, cable) and other types of users, some of these design choices were reevaluated so that the architecture of networks utilizing ALOHA assumed several different forms. We use the history of the ALOHA Network to categorize these forms and to speculate on future choices of network architecture.

Permission to make digital or hard copies of part or all of this work for personal or classroom use is granted without fee provided that copies are not made or distributed for profit or commercial advantage and that copies bear this notice and the full citation on the first page. Copyrights for third-party components of this work must be honored. For all other uses, contact the Owner/Author(s). Copyright is held by the owner/author(s).
MobiSys '17, June 19–23, 2017, Niagara Falls, NY, USA.
ACM ISBN 978-1-4503-4928-4/17/06.
DOI: http://dx.doi.org/10.1145/3081333.3081475

BIO
Norman Abramson is Professor Emeritus at the University of Hawaii. He has served as Professor of Electrical Engineering, Professor and Chair of Information Science and Director of the ALOHA Network at UH. He has also been a member of the faculty at Stanford, and a visiting member of the faculty at Berkeley, Harvard and MIT.

Abramson is the recipient of various awards for his work on random access channels and the ALOHA Network, the first wireless data network. Among these awards are the Eduard Rhein Foundation Technology Award (Munich, 2000), the IEEE Alexander Graham Bell Medal (Philadelphia, 2007) and the NEC C&C Foundation Award (Tokyo, 2011). Abramson received an A.B. in physics from Harvard College in 1953, an M.A. in physics from UCLA in 1955, and a Ph.D. in Electrical Engineering from Stanford in 1958.

SchrodinText: Strong Protection of Sensitive Textual Content of Mobile Applications

Ardalan Amiri Sani
Computer Science Department
University of California, Irvine
ardalan@uci.edu

Abstract

Many mobile applications deliver and show *sensitive and private textual content* to users including messages, social network posts, account information, and verification codes. All such textual content must only be displayed to the user but must be strongly protected from unauthorized access in the device. Unfortunately, this is not the case in mobile devices today: malware that can compromise the operating system, e.g., gain root or kernel privileges, can easily access textual content of other applications.

In this paper, we present SchrodinText, a system solution for strongly protecting the confidentiality of application's selected UI textual content from a fully compromised operating system. SchrodinText leverages a novel security monitor based on two hardware features on modern ARM processors: virtualization hardware and TrustZone. Our key contribution is a set of novel techniques that allow the operating system to perform the text rendering without needing access to the text itself, hence minimizing the Trusted Computing Base (TCB). These techniques, collectively called *oblivious rendering*, enable the operating system to rasterize and lay out all the characters without access to the text; the monitor only *resolves* the right character glyphs onto the framebuffer *observed* by the user and protects them from the operating system, e.g., against DMA attacks. We present our prototype using an ARM Juno development board and Android operating system. We show that SchrodinText incurs noticeable overhead but that its performance is usable.

> *"If one has left this entire system to itself for an hour, one would say that the cat still lives if meanwhile no atom has decayed. The first atomic decay would have poisoned it. The psi-function of the entire system would express this by having in it the* ***living and dead cat*** *(pardon the expression) mixed or smeared out in equal parts. It is typical of these cases that an indeterminacy originally restricted to the atomic domain becomes transformed into macroscopic indeterminacy, which can then be* ***resolved*** *by direct* ***observation****."*
>
> \- *Erwin Schrödinger*[1]

[1] https://en.wikipedia.org/wiki/Schrodingers_cat

Permission to make digital or hard copies of all or part of this work for personal or classroom use is granted without fee provided that copies are not made or distributed for profit or commercial advantage and that copies bear this notice and the full citation on the first page. Copyrights for components of this work owned by others than the author(s) must be honored. Abstracting with credit is permitted. To copy otherwise, or republish, to post on servers or to redistribute to lists, requires prior specific permission and/or a fee. Request permissions from permissions@acm.org.

MobiSys'17, June 19-23, 2017, Niagara Falls, NY, USA

© 2017 Copyright held by the owner/author(s). Publication rights licensed to ACM.

ISBN 978-1-4503-4928-4/17/06...$15.00

DOI: http://dx.doi.org/10.1145/3081333.3081346

Keywords

Text protection; Mobile devices; UI safety; TrustZone; Virtualization

1. INTRODUCTION

There are millions of mobile applications today. The textual content that many of these applications show to the user in their UI can contain extremely sensitive and private information, such as social security number, bank account information, private messages, passwords (in a password vault), and verification codes used for two-factor authentication. *Such content must only be displayed to the user but must be otherwise protected against unauthorized access by malware.* Indeed, Zhou et al. found 644 malware samples (in 27 families) that harvest "user's information, including user accounts and short messages stored on the phones" [54]. Application developers attempt to defeat this by encrypting the raw text in their backend server and send the ciphertext to the mobile application. However, the application needs to decrypt the ciphertext before passing it to the operating system for rendering and showing to the user. Therefore, malware that compromises the operating system (or even just its graphics stack) can access the content.

This is a growing concern as mobile operating systems are increasingly large and unreliable. Malware hiding inside ordinary unprivileged applications can easily compromise the operating system and gain root or kernel privileges [50, 53]. Such malware can then attempt to extract sensitive content from other applications using various methods. For example on Android, these methods include but are not limited to the following. Malware with root privilege can (*i*) take a screenshot of the device UI, which might contain the aforementioned sensitive text or (*ii*) replace Android's UI rendering libraries; the compromised library can then leak the textual content of victim applications. Or malware with kernel privileges can (*i*) access the application's memory in order to read the plaintext after decryption or (*ii*) read the texture buffers allocated by the graphics stack to hold the character glyphs used in the text.

Unfortunately, as noted by Checkoway et al. [23], it is extremely difficult to fully protect an application from a compromised operating system. Yet, we ask ourselves: *can we at least protect the confidentiality of selected sensitive textual content of the application's UI in such an environment?* We care about protecting selected textual content since most, if not all, sensitive information delivered to the user via apps is in textual format.

In this paper, we present a system solution, called *Schrod-*

inText, designed to meet this goal. Our solution leverages novel hardware features in ARM processors to create a security monitor for showing and protecting the text. The monitor leverages both virtualization and TrustZone hardware available on modern ARM processor. The monitor is more privileged than the operating system and is used to protect the selected textual content shown on the display.

In SchrodinText, the application's backend server encrypts the text with a key only available to the monitor, hence protecting it from the operating system. However, this raises an important challenge: the text needs to be rendered by the graphics stack in the operating system. The final pixels displayed to the user depend on the font type, size, and color chosen by the app developer, all of which are available and understandable by the operating system, and not the monitor. The graphics stack includes several libraries and frameworks as well as kernel device drivers and is one of the largest and most complicated components of the operating system. Therefore, how can the monitor display the textual content to the user given that the graphics stack is implemented by the operating system?

At first glance, it seems like a feasible solution to this problem is to move the graphics stack to the monitor. However, such an approach would significantly bloat the Trusted Computing Base (TCB) of the monitor. A large TCB would make the monitor vulnerable to attacks itself hence defeating the original purpose. An alternative approach might then be to support a minimal and simplified version of the graphics stack in the monitor, in order to keep the TCB small. Unfortunately, with this approach, the content rendered by the monitor would not be visually well-integrated with the rest of the content, which are rendered by the complete graphics stack in the operating system. Moreover, such a solution would not be able to easily benefit from updates to the operating system graphics stack, which, for example, might introduce new fonts and effects from untrusted sources.

In SchrodinText, we introduce an alternative solution that addresses all of these shortcomings: *oblivious rendering*. With this solution, SchrodinText implements the text rendering fully in the operating system without access to the text itself, hence resulting in visually well-integrated content while minimizing the TCB of the monitor. The key idea is to have the operating system rasterize all the possible character glyphs given the attributes of the text selected by the developer, e.g., font type, size, and color. The resultant glyphs are then shared with the monitor using a simple and low-level memory API (referred to as glyph-book API hereafter). The monitor then decrypts the ciphertext and uses that to *resolve* the right glyphs onto the framebuffer *observed* by the user[2]. With SchrodinText, *the protected text will be visible to the user on the display but not available to the operating system, e.g., in a screenshot.*

We address two important challenges in SchrodinText. First, the operating system needs to perform the layout of text (i.e., determining the location on the UI to place each character), which not only depends on the relative size of the font to the size of text UI widget, it also depends on the text itself as different characters have varying widths. To address this challenge, we choose to limit SchrodinText to *monospaced fonts*, in which all characters have a fixed width. In addition, we introduce a technique for determining the line-breaks without access to the text, called *oblivious line-breaking*. These two techniques allow the operating system to perform the layout in full, only needing access to the *number of characters* in the text, and not the text itself.

Second, once character glyphs are rasterized and their locations are determined, they must be composited on top of other layers in the framebuffer and displayed to the user. Android on modern mobile devices uses the GPU for compositing. Exposing the resolved glyphs to the GPU makes them vulnerable to attacks by the operating system since the GPU is programmed by the operating system. We use two techniques, namely *multi-view pages* and *two-stage compositing*, to securely perform the compositing while protecting the resolved glyphs. Collectively, these two techniques allow us to use the operating system and GPU for compositing of non-protected textures and use the monitor (but not the GPU) for compositing the protected text glyphs, all the while protecting them from the operating system and other DMA-capable devices.

It is important to note that SchrodinText protects the *output text* of the applications but not the *input text*. That is, it protects the textual content that is shown to the user, such as received messages, bank account information, health records, and verification codes in two-factor authentication. It, however, does not protect the text input by the user, including outgoing messages and typed passwords. Protecting the input text also requires protecting the input stack in the operating system, which is out of the scope of this work.

We have designed SchrodinText with ease of use for developers in mind. More specifically, we provide a simple UI widget, called `SchrodinTextView`, which is a modified version of `TextView` used in Android to embed text in application's UI. The developer can simply embed this widget in the UI, very similar to existing widgets. The cloud backend sends the ciphertext to the application, which then binds it to the widget by a call to a `setCiphertext()` function, also passing a handle to the key needed to decrypt the text (the key is known to the monitor but not the operating system). SchrodinText takes care of rendering the text, showing it to the user, and protecting it from the operating system. To demonstrate the practicality of this API, we incorporate it in a messaging application to show and strongly protect the received messages.

SchrodinText does not require any changes to the mobile device hardware; it however requires its monitor to be deployed in the hypervisor and TrustZone secure world, and requires modifications to the operating system kernel and user space rendering libraries. Hence, we envision SchrodinText to be deployed by mobile device vendors, e.g., Google, Samsung, HTC, and Apple.

We implement SchrodinText for Android running on an ARM Juno development board, the only board that allows non-vendors to program the hypervisor and TrustZone secure world, to the best of our knowledge. We show that SchrodinText incurs modest memory and performance overheads. More specifically, depending on the font size, it can use an additional 150 kB to 4.8 MB for storing the glyph-books. Also, depending on the size of the framebuffer and the number and size of the glyphs, it can use an additional 104 kB to a maximum of 15.8 MB for creating protected

[2]This also explains our choice of the system name. Similar to Schrödinger's cat (which, put in simple words, can be dead or alive until it is observed), the actual characters in a text protected by SchrodinText are not determined until they are resolved (by the monitor) and displayed to the user

views of the framebuffer. Moreover, it increases the text rendering latency by about 30 ms to 270 ms for UI pages having 20 to 1000 characters (of font size 14 sp) protected by SchrodinText. Only 4 ms to 170 ms of this added latency is for the monitor-based compositing, which allows for acceptable scrolling performance especially for UI surfaces with smaller number of characters in them. Finally, SchrodinText increases the overall CPU usage in this rendering period by about 1 to 3 times, but does not use more than 19% of overall CPU resources in the system. While SchrodinText's overhead is noticeably higher than that of normal text, we believe that its performance is usable and the overhead is justified given the strong protection guarantees that it provides, especially for small number of protected characters.

2. BACKGROUND & ATTACKS

2.1 Android's Text Rendering

Here, we provide a basic overview of text rendering in Android. For more details, we refer the interested reader to [2].

There are three main operations in text rendering: glyph rasterization, layout, and compositing. Rasterization generates the glyphs of characters given the selected font type and size. The glyphs contain the pixel information of the characters at the target size on the screen. They, however, do not contain the RGB color information; they only contain the alpha channel information (hence one byte per pixel). The rasterized glyphs are stored in a texture buffer. This buffer is later used in compositing.

Layout determines the location of each character on the UI surface, and hence on the framebuffer. The location depends on the size and location of the widget enclosing the text, the surface size (which itself depends on the display size), and glyph sizes, which depend on the text itself as different character glyphs can have varying widths.

The last step is compositing. Once the character glyphs are ready in the texture buffer and their locations on the framebuffer are known, GPU is used (through the OpenGL framework) to read the glyphs and composite them on the right location in the framebuffer. The color of the text is applied at this stage. Compositing is achieved with alpha-blending, where the text glyphs are blended onto the surface below them, e.g., a background image. The framebuffer is then shared with the display controller for showing to the user.

2.2 Attacks

In this work, we are concerned with malware that attempts to steal textual content of other applications' UIs. Here, we explain *why* and *how* malware might perform such an attack.

Why? There are several categories of mobile applications with important text that malware might attempt to extract. One category is apps with user's private and sensitive information, e.g., messages in a messaging app, posts in a social networking app, bank account information in a banking app, or the social security number (SSN) in a finance app. Indeed, an important category of mobile malware is *spyware*, which attempts to monitor user's sensitive information, e.g., SMS messages. Some examples of such spyware are TheTruthSpy [15] and LetMeSpy [10]. Moreover, Zhou et al. found 644 malware samples (in 27 families) that harvest "user's information, including user accounts and short messages stored on the phones" [54].

Another category is apps that reveal passwords or one-time tokens to the user. For example, a password vault app might show user's passwords to her on the display. As another example, a two-factor authentication application, such as Microsoft and Google Authenticators [9, 12], or a messaging application might show a verification code to the user.

How? Here, we mention a few possible methods that malware can use to extract textual content of victim applications. For most of the attacks, malware, originally packaged as a normal app, should exploit a vulnerability in the operating system in order to escalate its privileges for root access or to execute code with kernel privileges. Malware can use various methods to gain root privilege [53], e.g., rowhammer attack [50]. To gain kernel privileges, it can try code injection [38] or Return-Oriented Programming [22, 48].

With root privileges, malware will be able to use two methods to access other applications' textual content. First, malware can simply capture a screenshot of the screen, which, if taken at the right time, will contain sensitive information displayed to the user. Second, it can replace text rendering libraries in Android with a malicious one. The replacement library can then be used to extract the text of other applications, which will load this library for text rendering. Whenever a victim application calls *setText()* on a text widget and passes a string, this string will be available to the library, which can then communicate it with malware, e.g., by writing it to a file.

With kernel privileges, in addition to the aforementioned attacks, malware can either access the application's memory in order to read the plaintext after decryption or read the texture buffers allocated by the graphics stack to hold the character glyphs used in the text.

3. OVERVIEW

3.1 Key Idea and Design

Our goal is to provide strong protection for sensitive and private textual content in mobile applications' UIs, even in the presence of a compromised operating system. Our key insight is that such content must be displayed to the user only; operating system should not have access to it. Towards this goal, we leverage novel hardware features on modern ARM processors, including virtualization and TrustZone hardware, to create a security monitor. Our key contribution is *oblivious rendering*, a set of techniques that allows the operating system to perform all the stages of text rendering without having access to the text itself. The monitor then resolves the right text on the framebuffer.

3.2 SchrodinText UI Widget

In SchrodinText, we do not protect all the textual content of an app. Only selected text, as determined by the application developer, will be protected. We achieve this by providing a new UI widget for protected text, called `SchrodinTextView`, which is mostly similar to the existing `TextView` widget in Android's application programming framework. The developer can position the widget on any desired location in one of application's UI surfaces, i.e., Android activities. The main difference is that, instead of setting a string

```
void drawText(byte[] ciphertext,
              int keyHandle)
{
    String text =
        decrypt(ciphertext, keyHandle);
    TextView view = (TextView)
        findViewById(R.id.textWidget);
    view.setText(text);
}
```

```
void drawText(byte[] ciphertext,
              int textLen,
              int keyHandle)
{
    SchrodinTextView view = (SchrodinTextView)
        findViewById(R.id.textWidget);
    view.setCiphertext(ciphertext, textLen,
                       keyHandle);
}
```

Figure 1: Rendering protected text using Android's `TextView` (Left) vs. `SchrodinTextView` (Right).

as the content of the widget (using **`setText(String text)`**), the encrypted version of the text, i.e., ciphertext, will be set as the content (using **`setCiphertext(byte[] ciphertext, ...)`**).

Figure 1 shows a sample code snippet for both **`SchrodinTextView`** and Android's **`TextView`**. In both cases, we assume that the developer attempts to use encryption for protection of the text. As can be seen, in the existing approach, the application first decrypts the ciphertext (e.g., using Android's Keystore system [1]), and passes it to the operating system for rendering by calling the **`setText()`** method with the plaintext. While encryption of the text can protect the text from eavesdropping in the network, it cannot protect it from the operating system since the plaintext is available in the application's memory and even passed to the operating system for rendering.

However, with **`SchrodinTextView`**, the ciphertext never gets decrypted by the application; it is simply passed to the operating system and eventually decrypted in the monitor. However, with **`SchrodinTextView`**, the rendering API (**`setCiphertext()`** needs two additional argument: **`textLen`**, which is the number of characters in the text, needed for layout by the operating system (see §4), and **`keyHandle`**, which informs the monitor of the key to use to decrypt the ciphertext. As these examples show, the amount of effort needed for using **`SchrodinTextView`** is comparable with that for using Android's **`TextView`**.

3.3 Workflow

The typical usage of SchrodinText is to allow the application to show a text to the user where the text is sent to the application from its backend server in the cloud. Figure 2 shows a basic overview of SchrodinText including the sequence of events taking place in it. The sequence is as follows. (1) The application's backend server exchanges a key with the monitor (§3.5). (2) The backend then uses the key to encrypt the text and send the ciphertext to the application. The server also sends the length (i.e., number of characters) of the encrypted text and the key handle. (3) The application on the mobile device uses **`SchrodinTextView`** to show this text. As arguments of this widget, it passes the ciphertext, the length of the text, and the key handle. Moreover, the application configures the widget with the desired font properties (e.g., type, size, and color). (4) Based on this metadata, the operating system rasterizes all the character glyphs and shares them with the monitor through a novel *glyph-book* memory API (§4.1.1) along with the ciphertext and the location of text characters on the framebuffer. (5) The monitor decrypts the ciphertext and uses that to resolve the right glyphs onto the right location on framebuffer shown

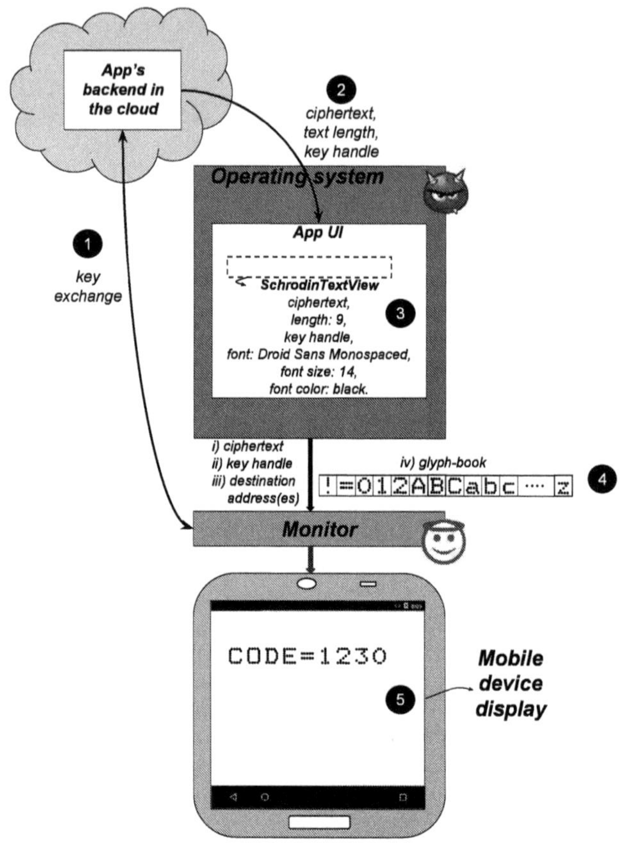

Figure 2: Overview of SchrodinText's workflow.

on the display. When resolving the glyph, the monitor also protects the corresponding framebuffer pages from the operating system (to avoid read-back) by leveraging nested page tables and IOMMUs provided by the virtualization hardware. To do this, the monitor uses the *multi-view* pages technique, in which the operating system and DMA-capable devices see one view of a corresponding framebuffer page without the text on it, whereas the display sees a different version with the text on it.

To better understand these steps, consider a messaging application. At install/login time, the application's cloud backend performs a handshake with the monitor to establish a shared secret key. From then on, the backend will encrypt all the messages with this key before delivering them to the application. The application then uses a **`SchrodinTextView`** to pass the ciphertext for display. The ciphertext is eventually passed to the monitor, which decrypts it and show it on the display (using the glyph-book and layout information provided by the operating system).

Note that while in most use cases of SchrodinText, the ciphertext is sent from the application's cloud backend, in some use cases, the ciphertext might be retrieved from the local storage of the mobile device. For example, a messaging application might be used to show previously communicated messages. Or a password vault might store the ciphertext of a password in storage and show it to the user when needed.

The operating system performs the layout without access to the text itself. To make this possible, in addition to other techniques (§4.2), we limit the available fonts for `SchrodinTextView` to monospaced fonts, in which all character glyphs have similar widths. This allows the operating system to compute the relative location of each character without knowing the actual text. While monospaced fonts are not as common as normal fonts, they are well supported in mobile devices. For example, Roboto, the new typeface used in Android, provides 10 different styles of monospaced fonts [14], while it provides 12 different styles of normal fonts [13]. Similarly, the older typeface in Android, i.e., Droid Sans, supported one monospaced style [8] and two normal styles [7].

3.4 SchrodinText's Security Monitor

The monitor is built on top of two novel hardware security features in modern ARM processors. The first one is the ARM TrustZone [5, 19, 51] that divides the execution into two worlds: normal world and secure world. The normal world hosts the main operating system, such as Android. The secure world hosts security critical components. Moreover, the secure world has access to a device-unique key [18], which is not accessible to the normal world. This makes the secure world ideal for cryptographic operations. Indeed, on Android-based smartphones, Keystore can be implemented in the secure world [1].

The second hardware feature, recently added to ARM processors, is virtualization hardware [27]. It adds a new privilege mode in the normal world (in addition to the user and kernel modes). This new mode, i.e., the *hyp* mode, can be used to host a hypervisor. Among others, virtualization hardware comprises of (*i*) nested page tables, which map the operating system's physical pages to different machine pages (hence virtualizing the memory for the operating system), and (*ii*) I/O Memory Management Unit (IOMMU) components (referred to as System MMU or SMMU in ARM's terminology [4]), which map the physical pages seen in Direct Memory Access (DMA) operations by I/O devices, such as the GPU and display, to different machine pages (hence virtualizing the memory for these I/O devices).

Our monitor uses these hardware components for different purposes. It uses the virtualization hardware to host a hypervisor. The hypervisor is more privileged than the operating system and hence can display the protected text on the framebuffer, while preventing the operating system from accessing it. It does so by creating different views of the framebuffer pages using the nested page tables and IOMMU (§5.1). The monitor uses the secure world for cryptographic key management and operations.

3.5 Key Management

As mentioned earlier, the ciphertext is shipped from application's cloud backend to the mobile device. The backend encrypts the text with a key shared with the monitor. Therefore, before the server can use the key, it must establish and share it with the monitor. Different methods can be used for sharing a secret key. For example, the monitor can first generate a public and private key pair and share the public key with the cloud so that it can generate and share a secret key with the monitor. Alternatively, other key sharing mechanisms, such as Diffie-Hellman key exchange [29], might be used to safely share a secret key. In the rest of the paper, we simply assume that the application's cloud backend has already shared a key with the TrustZone's secure world on the device.

Note that it is possible to use public-key encryption for the protected text. That is, the cloud backend can encrypt the text with a public key, for which the private key is only known to the monitor. In SchrodinText, we use symmetric-key encryption since it incurs less computational overhead.

3.6 Threat Model

We assume a powerful adversary. Specifically, we assume that malware, originally disguised in an application, can compromise the operating system and gain root or kernel privileges (§2.2).

We assume that our monitor is protected from malware. First, the monitor is protected by the secure boot. Used on many modern commodity devices, secure boot performs integrity measurements of software loaded in memory at boot time, and compares it with the expected value (available as a signed measurement provided by the vendor). If the measurements do not match, a notice is shown to the user informing her that the loaded image is tampered with. We assume that the secure boot protects the TrustZone secure world runtime and the hypervisor. Therefore, no other entity, other than the device manufacturer, can deploy or modify the hypervisor and secure world runtime. Second, we assume that the hypervisor and the secure world are safe against runtime attacks due to their small sizes and narrow attack surfaces. While runtime attacks on these components have been demonstrated in the past [21, 28], they are much less frequent than runtime attacks on the operating system.

As mentioned in §3.5, we assume that the application's cloud backend can safely share a secret key with the monitor and protect the key from unauthorized access (note that the monitor protects the key on the device). If the key is compromised, SchrodinText will be ineffective as the adversary can simply decrypt the ciphertext.

In SchrodinText, we protect the text from some known side-channel attacks. More specifically, the monitor flushes the cache after writing to the protected view of framebuffer pages to defeat cache side-channel attacks. Moreover, the monitor is not easily vulnerable to timing channels as alpha-blending in the monitor uses the same number of loop iterations for all glyphs.

In SchrodinText, we protect the text in `SchrodinTextView` from access by the adversary, i.e., *confidentiality* guarantee. We do not, however, provide any *integrity* or *availability* guarantees.

Integrity. There are two ways to mount integrity attacks on the sensitive text. First, although an attacker does not possess the encryption keys, he could still modify the ciphertext arbitrarily. SchrodinText would still decrypt the modified ciphertext, but the plaintext now will be "garbage". Second, the attacker could replace one ciphertext with another (perhaps provided to another secure application). The monitor cannot prevent such an attacks because it cannot verify if the ciphertext comes from the foreground application or not.

One might wonder how SchrodinText can provide additional defenses against these attacks. For the first attack, SchrodinText could use a cryptographically secure hash function to detect arbitrary ciphertext modifications. For the second attack, however, the monitor would need to be able to detect the foreground application. This would unfortunately come with significant additional bloat in the TCB.

Availability. An attacker with root or kernel privileges can prevent the text in a `SchrodinTextView` to be shown at all. It can achieve so by modifying the graphics stack so that the rendering of text in `SchrodinTextView` is not fully performed, e.g., by blocking hypercalls to the monitor.

3.7 Trusted Computing Base

We assume that the monitor is trusted. This means that both the TrustZone secure world runtime and the hypervisor are trusted. If malware can compromise the secure world, it can extract the protected keys and decrypt the content. If it can compromise the hypervisor, it can revert the protection of memory pages and access the final rendered pixels on the framebuffer or it can simply extract the decrypted text. We also assume that the security hardware is trusted including the virtualization and TrustZone hardware. We do not, however, trust the I/O devices, such as GPU and display; we protect against DMA attacks by them using IOMMUs. The SchrodinText's monitor uses different IOMMUs for different I/O devices. It uses one to give the display controller read-only access to all memory pages so that the display can show the framebuffer (but not leak its content). It also uses other IOMMUs to prevent any access by the GPU and other DMA-capable devices to these protected pages. Therefore, the operating system cannot abuse these devices to access the framebuffer pages containing protected text. §5 will elaborate on these issues.

4. OBLIVIOUS RENDERING

In SchrodinText, we enable the operating system, which controls the full graphics stack, to perform the text rendering without access to the text itself. We refer to the set of techniques that make this possible as *oblivious rendering*. As mentioned in §2.1, rendering comprises of three stages: rasterization, layout, and compositing. All of these stages face important challenges in oblivious rendering. For rasterization, our solution is to have the operating system rasterize all printing ASCII characters. For layout, the operating system determines the location of the n-th character on the display. Finally, for compositing, the operating system composites all the content excluding the text protected by SchrodinText. The monitor then composites the text on top of the rest of the content. Next, we will elaborate on these three techniques. More specifically, in this section, we mainly discuss rasterization and layout. In the next section, we address compositing.

Straw-man solution 1: One option is to implement the rasterization and layout in the cloud. For this, the application can inform the cloud backend of the font type, size, and color, as well as the size of the UI. The cloud backend can then rasterize the glyphs and lay them out on a buffer and send the encrypted pixels to the application, which can then use the monitor to composite that on the screen. Such a solution has important drawbacks. First, it complicates the cloud backend implementation as it must now be able to lay out and rasterize the text exactly as it would be done by the mobile device. This would, for example, require access to the right fonts on the target platform. The diversity of mobile devices in practice will make this challenging for the cloud backend. Second, this approach increases the network bandwidth consumption. In this case, texts will consume network bandwidth as much as images do.

Straw-man solution 2: The second option is to move the graphics stack to the monitor, e.g., to the TrustZone secure world, so that rasterization and layout (as well as compositing) are fully performed in a trusted environment. This approach has important shortcomings as well. First, it significantly increases the size of the TCB. Second, if only a minimal portion of the graphics stack were to be used in the monitor (to keep the TCB small), the content rendered by the monitor would not be visually well-integrated with the rest of the content, which are rendered by the complete graphics stack in the operating system. Third, this solution makes updates to the graphics stack more difficult. For example, new fonts from untrusted sources cannot be used.

4.1 Glyph Rasterization

One of the key components of our oblivious rendering technique is its rasterization. Given that the operating system does not have access to the text, the key idea behind our solution is to have the operating system rasterize all the character glyphs given the font type and other metadata, e.g., size and color. The operating system can then pass all of these glyphs to the monitor using a novel memory abstraction, called glyph-book. Depending on the plaintext, the monitor can then resolve the right glyphs on the desired location on the framebuffer (the address of which is determined by the operating system in layout and provided to the monitor).

It is important to note that the glyphs resulting from rasterization in SchrodinText are different from those resulting from normal Android's rasterization (§2.1). In the latter, the glyphs simply contain the alpha channel information (one byte per pixel). The colors are then applied by the GPU at compositing time. In SchrodinText, however, compositing is performed by the monitor (see §5), which merely implements simple alpha-blending. Therefore, we apply the color in the rasterization phase resulting in fully colored glyphs (4 bytes (RGBA) per pixel).

4.1.1 Glyph-Book

The glyph-book API is at the core of oblivious rendering in SchrodinText. It is implemented by the monitor and exposed to the operating system through three hypercalls. We have abstracted this low-level API in a C++ class for the convenience of integrating them with the graphics libraries. The methods supported by this class are as follows:

1) *Constructor*:
```
GlyphBook::GlyphBook(
unsigned int glyphSize, unsigned int numGlyphs,
void *ciphertext, unsigned int ciphertextSize,
int keyHandle);
```

The constructor allocates `numGlyphs` buffers of size `glyphSize` each. Each buffer will hold one of the character glyphs rasterized by the operating system. The number of buffers is the number of printing ASCII characters (ASCII characters

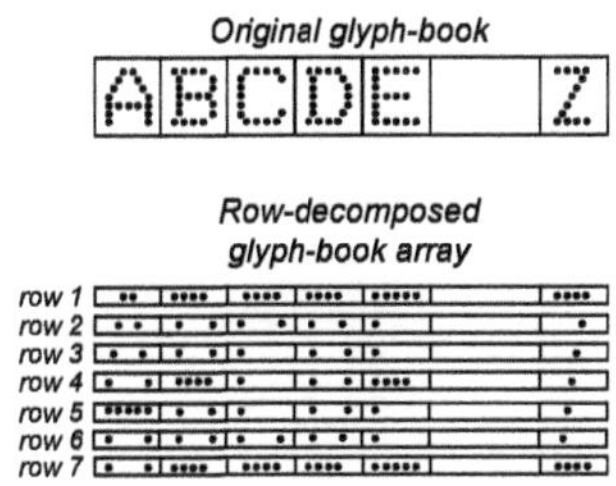

Figure 3: Row-decomposed glyph-book array.

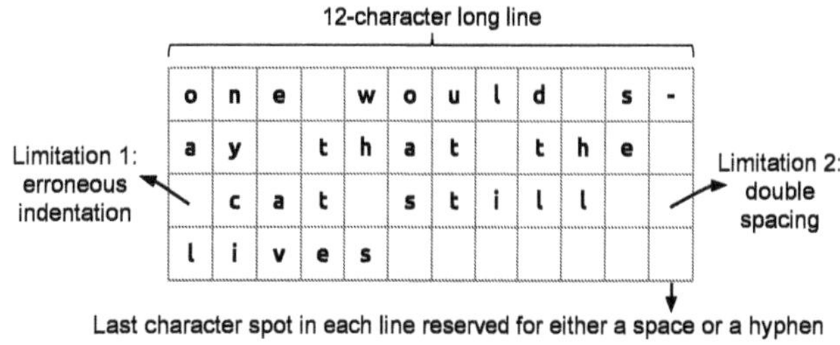

Figure 4: Oblivious line-breaking demonstration.

32 to 126, a total of 95 characters). The constructor also receives the ciphertext (`ciphertext`), the size of the buffer holding the ciphertext (`ciphertextSize`), and a handle to a pre-established key to be used for decrypting the ciphertext in the monitor (`keyHandle`).

2) *Getter*: `uint8_t *GlyphBook::getBuffer( unsigned int i);`

The getter simply returns a pointer to the i-th buffer in a glyph-book. Note that the getter is handled fully in the operating system and does not need to interact with the monitor. The rendering library uses the getter method to populate the glyph-book.

3) *Resolver*: `int GlyphBook::resolve( uint8_t *dstAddr, unsigned int textPos, bool conditional);`

The resolver blends the right glyph for the `textPos`-th character of the text into the destination (`dstAddr`) address. The right glyph depends on the text, which is known to the monitor. The monitor uses the ASCII value of the `textPos`-th character to compute the index into the array of buffers containing the glyphs and alpha-blends that to the destination. The last argument of this API (`conditional`) is used to ask the monitor for conditional resolve, which will be discussed in §4.2.

For example, assume that the ciphertext encrypts the string "CODE=1230". Once the glyph-book is shared with the monitor, the operating system calls the `resolver` API 9 times, once per character. At first, it calls the API for the first character; the monitor then uses the plaintext, retrieves the ASCII value of the first character (67 for C), and uses that as an index in the array[3] to retrieve the glyph, and blends it onto the framebuffer address provided by the operating system.

Note that the resolver first protects the destination framebuffer pages before blending the content onto them. The protection is done using the multi-view pages technique (§5.1). It also adds this destination address to a list, needed by the destructor.

4) *Destructor*: `GlyphBook::~GlyphBook();`

The destructor iterates through the aforementioned list of protected pages, zeros out the content copied by the resolver, and unprotects them.

4.1.2 Row-Decomposition of the Glyph-Book

It is critical to keep the implementation of the glyph-book API minimal in the monitor. Therefore, we implement the `resolve` API to perform alpha-blending on a contiguous memory buffer (determined by a start address (`dstAddr`) and size (`glyphSize`)). However, blending a character glyph into the framebuffer cannot simply be performed using a contiguous memory buffer as the glyph comprises of multiple rows, and these rows are not contiguous on the framebuffer.

The first solution that we considered was to update the implementation of the `resolve` API so that it could take a glyph, iterate over its rows, and blend them onto the right addresses in the framebuffer (derived from a single address pointing to the location of the first row of the glyph in the framebuffer and the widths of the framebuffer). However, we rejected this solution since it would complicate the monitor's implementation.

To address this challenge, we decompose the glyphs into their rows and store them in separate glyph-books. In this case, the operating system creates one glyph-book consisting of the first rows of all glyphs, another including the second rows, and so on. The operating system then issues multiple resolve API calls on all of these glyph-books passing the destination address of corresponding rows in these calls. Since the pixels in a row are contiguous in memory, the monitor's resolve API blends them on a contiguous destination address in the framebuffer. Figure 3 illustrates this technique.

4.2 Layout

In SchrodinText, we also perform the layout in the operating system without access to the text. Note that the operating system knows the number of the characters in the string to be shown in the widget as this is one of the arguments of `setCiphertext()` in `SchrodinTextView`. Moreover, we limit the `SchrodinTextView` to monospaced fonts. With monospaced fonts, the operating system can compute the location of each character relative to the previous one without knowing the exact characters since all character glyphs have equal widths.

However, even with monospaced fonts, we face an important challenge: determining the *line-breaks* and *consequent hyphenation*. The first straw-man approach that we considered was to inform the operating system of the lengths of the words in the text, e.g., a 4 character word followed by a 5 character word for a total of 10 characters (including the space). This way, the operating system could determine appropriate line breaks and hyphenation. However, this approach would enable the operating system to gain side-channel information about the text using word-length frequency analysis.

Our solution to solve this challenge is called *oblivious line-breaking* that determines the line breaks without word-length information. In this solution, the operating system reserves the last character spot in the line for either a space or a hyphen. For that spot, it issues a *conditional resolve* to the monitor (§4.1.1). More specifically, it asks the monitor

[3]More specifically, (67-32) is the index since the first glyph in the glyph-book corresponds to space with ASCII value of 32. The previous 32 ASCII values are non-printing.

to leave that spot empty if either the preceding or proceeding characters in the plaintext is a space (ASCII #32) and to fill it with a hyphen (ASCII #45), otherwise.

Figure 4 illustrates a sample text laid out over 4 lines using this technique. As can be seen, this technique has two limitations: *erroneous indentation* and *double spacing*. The former happens when the first character in the line is a space. The latter happens when the character before the last in the line is a space. While less elegant compared to more advanced layout algorithms, SchrodinText performs adequately well, resulting in fully readable text (the errors are at most two character glyphs wide).

Finally, note that SchrodinText's layout does not support tab spaces or newlines. For the former, multiple spaces must be used. For the latter, separate `SchrodinTextViews` need to be utilized.

5. SECURE COMPOSITING

In this section, we focus on compositing in SchrodinText and its challenges. Once rasterized glyphs are ready and their locations are determined, the next stage is to composite the right glyphs on top of other graphics layers, e.g., background image in the app, and generate the framebuffer to be displayed to the user. Compositing the protected text in SchrodinText must meet the following requirements: the text on the framebuffer must be visible to the display controller so that it can be shown to the user. It, however, must not be available to the operating system for read-back (either with direct access or through DMA). Also, the operating system must be able to composite all the unprotected content with the GPU as it normally does for performance.

We use two techniques to meet these goals: *multi-view pages* and *two-stage compositing*. The former technique uses the CPU MMU and various IOMMUs in the ARM SoC to provide different views of the framebuffer pages containing protected text pixels. The latter technique allows the operating system to perform its own compositing using the GPU and enables the monitor to composite the protected text in CPU. Below, we describe these two techniques in more details.

5.1 Multi-View Pages

Normally, a memory page (determined by its physical address from the operating system's perspective) is available to the operating system and all I/O devices for access. That is, reading a page either directly from the operating system (using CPU's load instructions) or reading it using I/O devices (with DMA) will return the same values. A *multi-view page* changes this paradigm. With this technique, access to the same page by the operating system and I/O devices can return different values.

We implement this technique using the nested page tables and IOMMUs in the ARM SoC. Using the nested page tables and IOMMUs, the monitor can map a physical address seen by the operating system and DMA-capable devices, respectively, to different pages in memory. Figure 5 shows an overview of this technique. For a given page of interest, the monitor maintains two underlying pages (i.e., *views*), a *protected view* and an *unprotected view*. The two have similar content except that the protected text pixels are blended on the protected view only. The monitor then maps the protected view in the IOMMU in front of the display controller; it maps the unprotected view for the operating system (using the MMU) and the rest of DMA-capable devices (using the IOMMUs in front of them). When calling the `resolve` API of the glyph-book abstraction on a given page for the first time, the monitor creates the protected view, copies the content of the unprotected view into it, blends the right glyph buffers to the protected view, and then maps it to the display's IOMMU at the same physical address. For the following `resolve` API calls on the page, the monitor simply performs alpha-blending on the protected view, but not the unprotected one.

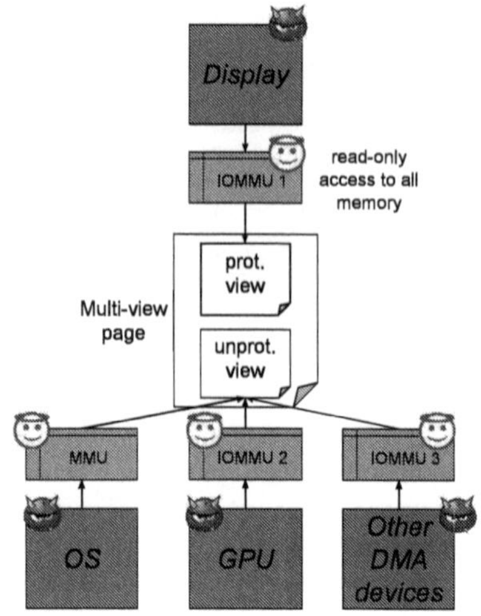

Figure 5: Multi-view pages.

5.2 Two-Stage Compositing

In Android and on all modern smartphones equipped with GPUs, the compositing is performed by the GPU for best performance. GPU compositing creates an important challenge for SchrodinText as it requires the GPU to have read-access to the resolved text glyphs. Given that the GPU is programmed by the operating system, GPU compositing would create a channel for the operating system to access the resolved glyphs.

We considered different solutions for this problem. The first option was to perform all compositing by the GPU and perform sanity checks in the monitor on the GPU instructions issued by the operating system to guarantee that the resolved glyphs are only copied to the framebuffer (which is protected from the operating system). However, this solution would significantly bloat the monitor's TCB as it would require it to parse and understand the GPU instructions. Moreover, this solution would make the monitor highly specific to the GPU model, which would make it challenging to port to other devices with different GPUs. The second solution that we considered was to execute the compositing fully by the CPU. This solution would however significantly degrade the graphics performance even for contents that are not protected.

We thus adopted a third solution, called *two-stage compositing*, which is a middle ground between these two solutions. In this solution, in the first stage, the operating system composites the unprotected layers using the GPU. In the second stage, the monitor composites the protected text using the CPU. Figure 6 illustrates this approach.

Once the application's UI surface is moved out of the visible region, e.g., pushed to the background or obscured by the dragged notification bar, the operating system must replace the content of the framebuffer including the protected pages in it. To do this, the operating system can simply call the destructor of the glyph-books. The destructor will wipe the rendered text and unprotect the protected page (visually resulting in the text disappearing from the display). In order to improve the performance, if the surface will be used in the future, the operating system can keep the current framebuffer in memory, replace it with another framebuffer, and replace it back when the previous surface needs to be shown. We have not implemented this optimization.

Compositing requires the monitor to implement alpha-blending. We currently implement this in software in the monitor with less than 20 lines of code. Note that while simple, our current alpha-blending implementation incurs noticeable computational overhead as it loops over all the pixels in the character glyphs and blends them on top of the background pixels. In §8.5, we evaluate the CPU overhead of SchrodinText, which includes the computational overhead of alpha-blending. In the future, we plan to investigate using alpha-blending hardware support in the display controller to accelerate this operation in the monitor [49].

5.3 Security Analysis

Display controller and its driver. The display has access to the protected view of the page. This raises an important concern: since the display controller is programmable by the operating system (through the display controller driver), it can be compromised by the operating system and then used to access the protected view. To address this concern, we map all the memory pages as read-only in the IOMMU of the display. Therefore, the display hardware is not able to leak out the protected content to any other locations in the memory. Moreover, a compromised display controller driver cannot access the content using CPU instructions since it is limited by the nested page tables. It cannot trigger a DMA request on its own either; it needs to program the display controller to do so, which is then limited by the IOMMU.

GPU. One might wonder whether the GPU can be abused by the operating system to access the protected views. To protect against this, the monitor maps the unprotected view of the pages into the IOMMU in front of the GPU. That is, SchrodinText programs this IOMMU to prevent the GPU to have any access (whether read or write) to the memory pages holding the protected text. This IOMMU is set in this restricted mode before the protected text is composited on the framebuffer by the monitor and is disabled after zeroing out the pages holding the text.

6. APPLICATION INTEGRATION

To demonstrate practicality and ease-of-use of SchrodinText, we have used it in a messaging application. More specifically, we have modified the open source `Xabber` application (an XMPP client) [17] so that all the received messages are displayed to the user using the `SchrodinTextView` widget. This only required us to modify a few lines of code, in order to use `SchrodinTextView` instead of `TextView`.

7. IMPLEMENTATION

We have implemented SchrodinText on an ARM Juno r0 development board [20]. To the best of our knowledge, ARM

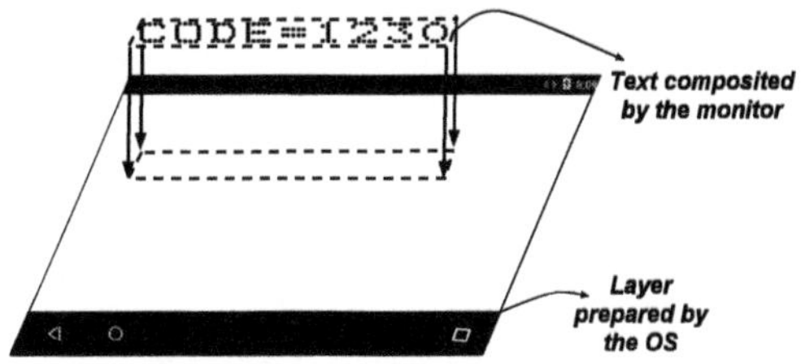

Figure 6: Secure two-stage compositing.

Juno boards are the only devices that allow us to program both the hypervisor and the TrustZone secure world runtime, both of which are needed for our prototype. The Juno r0 development board incorporates 6 CPUs (2 Cortex-A57 and 4 Cortex-A53 in the big.LITTLE architecture).

In our prototype, we use Android Marshmallow (version 6.0-16.04) for the normal world operating system, which uses the Linux kernel version 3.18. The operating system is configured with 1 GB of memory. We use Xen version 4.6 for the hypervisor and Open-TEE version 16.04 for the secure world runtime. We use AES encryption for the ciphertext and use the mbed TLS library [11] in the secure world to decrypt it.

Our multi-view page approach requires controlling the IOMMUs (i.e., SMMUs in ARM) for various DMA-capable devices. On the Juno board, we leverage four SMMUs: one MMU-400 in front of the GPU, one MMU-401 in front of the display, one MMU-401 in front of the DMA engine, and one MMU-401 in front of the USB devices. Note that the board incorporates SMMUs for other components such as the PCI interface. However, we disable these components in our prototype.

We implement our oblivious rendering in two parts. First is the implementation of the glyph-book abstraction in the hypervisor. We also implement a proxy layer in the operating system kernel to enable the user space rendering libraries to invoke the hypercalls provided by the glyph-book in the hypervisor. Second is the implementation of the `SchrodinTextView` in Android. This requires modifications to the text rendering libraries in Android including the Java-based implementation of the text widget and its corresponding native layer, the Minikin layout library, and the hardware-accelerated UI rendering library.

8. EVALUATION

In this section, we evaluate the protection and TCB reduction provided by SchrodinText as well its rendering overhead. More specifically, for the latter, we measure the added memory usage and latency compared to using existing `TextView` widgets supported by Android. Note that we conduct our experiments in a freshly installed Android operating system with no applications installed other than the default ones. Moreover, we reboot the operating system before every experiment. In practice, however, the overhead of SchrodinText can affect other apps running concurrently in the system as well. To capture such an effect, we also measure and report the CPU usage incurred by SchrodinText.

8.1 Protection

As mentioned in §2.2, there are various ways for an attacker to extract other applications' textual content. In this section, we experimentally demonstrate how SchrodinText

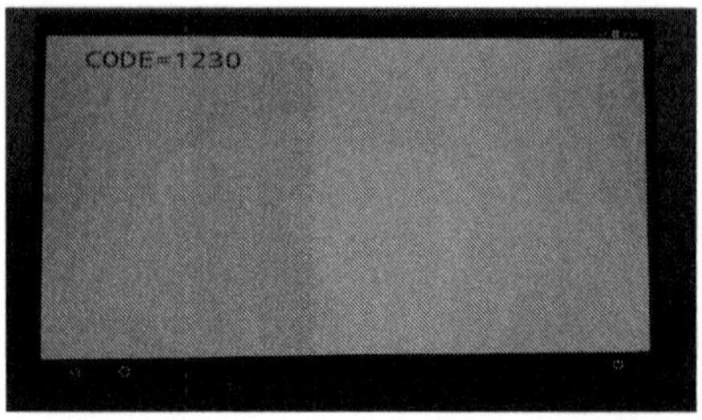

(a) What the user sees on the display

(b) What the operating system sees in the framebuffer

Figure 7: SchrodinText protects the text against framebuffer read-back attacks.

will protect against framebuffer read-back attack (e.g., taking a screenshot). SchrodinText's protection against the rest of the attacks is simple to explain as it never decrypts the ciphertext in the operating system. As a result, extraction through a compromised graphics stack (including text rendering libraries) and memory dumping is ineffective.

SchrodinText protects against framebuffer read-back attack due to its protection of the framebuffer pages (using the multi-view page technique). To evaluate this, we use `SchrodinTextView` to show a text on the application's UI, and then attempt to extract the text by taking a snapshot of the framebuffer content (we have root privilege, mimicking an attacker with such a privilege). Figure 7 illustrates the outcome of this experiment. Figure 7 (a) is a photo of what is seen on the display, taken by an external camera. Figure 7 (b) is a screenshot resulting from reading the framebuffer in the operating system. As can be seen, the text shows up on the screen but not on the screenshot. Everything else is the same including the white background, Android's notification bar on the top, and Android's virtual buttons on the bottom of the screen. The size of the screen is large since our Juno development board uses an external display.

8.2 TCB Reduction

SchrodinText eliminates large swaths of code that would otherwise have to be trusted. Without SchrodinText, we would have to trust a large portion of the operating system including its kernel (which itself contains various device drivers such as the GPU driver) and the user space graphics stack (including UI related frameworks and libraries). We tried to measure the size of the latter. The components that we identified contain about half a million lines of code (not including closed source libraries such as OpenGL).

SchrodinText does add additional code, but this codebase is small. Notably, it requires a hypervisor, which is much smaller than the operating system kernel. Moreover, the hypervisor is not only specific to SchrodinText and can be used for other security purposes in the system as well [26,41]. The part of the hypervisor that we developed for SchrodinText is only approximately a thousand lines of code. Finally, SchrodinText does not add any new functionality to the TrustZone secure world other than what is already available in it in commodity devices, i.e., key management and decryption of a ciphertext (§3.4).

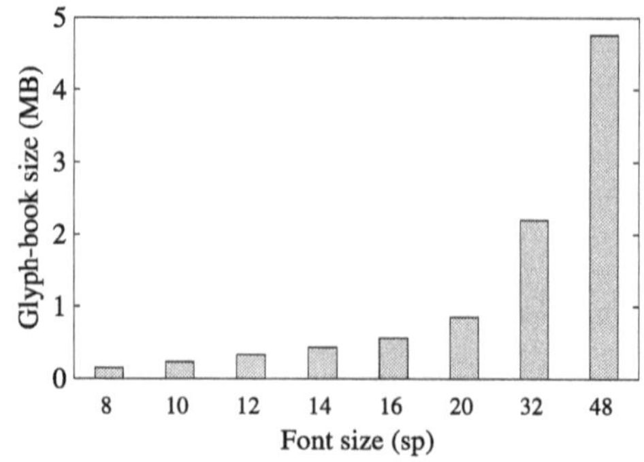

Figure 8: Size of glyph book for varying font sizes. The font size unit is in sp (scale-independent pixel).

8.3 Memory Usage

There are two sources of memory overhead in SchrodinText: memory used for the glyph-book (§4) and for multi-view pages (§5.1).

Glyph-book. The operating system needs to render the colored glyphs for all the characters given the font type, size, and color. We measure the size of the glyph-book for the default monospaced font in Android installed on our board (Droid Sans Monospaced) for varying font sizes. Figure 8 shows the results. It shows that the size of the glyph-book is small for normal font sizes (a few hundreds of kB, e.g., 150 kB for font size 8 sp). The glyph-book size does however become exponentially large for larger fonts, e.g., about 4.8 MB for font size 48 sp. The exponential growth is due to glyphs being two dimensional.

Multi-view pages. The monitor needs to create a protected view of every framebuffer page that contains protected text pixels. The amount of memory used for this depends on the number of characters and their size. A single character glyph affects several memory pages. For example, a single glyph in Droid Sans Monospaced font at sizes 8 sp and 48 sp affect 26 and 146 pages, respectively, resulting in 104 kB and 584 kB of memory needed for the protected views. However, two consecutive glyphs will not use twice as much as they mostly affect the same memory pages on the framebuffer.

At most, multi-view pages can result in as much memory as the size of the framebuffer, which depends on the screen size and its resolution. For example, the size of the framebuffer in the Juno board (which is connected to a 27" display) is about 15.8 MB. The size of the framebuffer is however often smaller on commodity devices. For example on a Nexus 5 smartphone, the framebuffer size is about 8 MB.

8.4 Rendering Latency

SchrodinText increases the rendering latency. We measure this latency from the time that the text widget (either

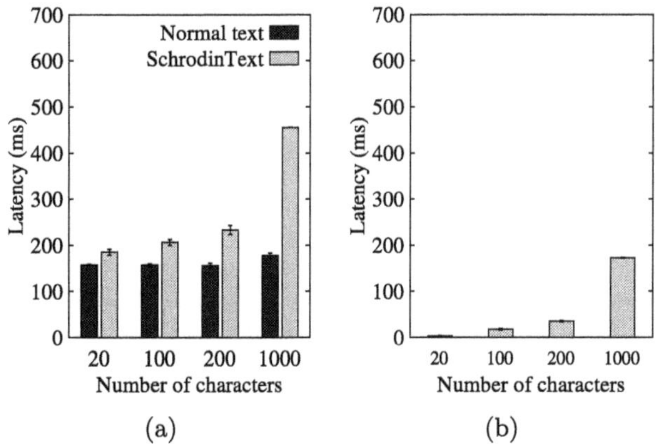

Figure 9: (a) Overall text rendering latency. (b) Monitor compositing latency in SchrodinText.

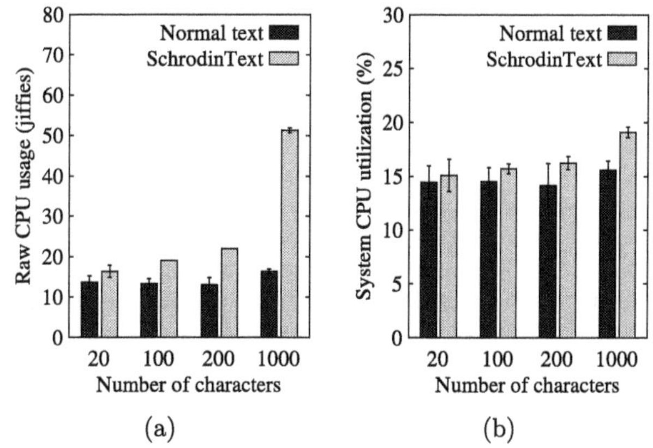

Figure 10: (a) Raw CPU usage. (b) System CPU utilization during rendering.

`SchrodinTextView` or `TextView`) is created until when the renderer is finished rendering the text. We perform experiments with application's UI pages with a varying number of characters in them. We use four different numbers: 20 characters representing a small text such as SSN, account information, and password; 100 and 200 characters representing messages; and 1000 characters representing a UI full of text. We use font size 14 sp in the experiments and divide the text into maximum 35 character lines, each line in a separate widget. A major contributor to the latency is the time needed for monitor-based compositing, which results in one hypercall per row of each glyph used in the text. We measure this latency as well.

8.5 CPU Usage

Figure 9 shows the results. We have repeated each experiments three times and shown the average and standard deviation. There are three observations. First, SchrodinText adds modest latency to the overall text rendering (about 30 ms to 270 ms for 20 to 1000 protected characters). This impacts the latency incurred when a UI surface is first created, e.g., at application's launch time. We believe that this latency is usable given that mobile application's launch latency has an average of 2 seconds [42] and can be as high as 20 seconds [52]. Moreover, predictive app preloading can be used with SchrodinText to further hide this latency [42,52]. Second, for small number of characters on the screen, the latency is small. Only when the screen is full of text, e.g., with 1000 characters, the latency becomes noticeable. Finally, SchrodinText can support scrolling text pages with adequate framerate. More specifically, the scrolling performance is determined by the compositing latency. As the figure shows, SchrodinText's compositing incurs small latency (4 ms to 170 ms for 20 to 1000 protected characters). At 200 characters, compositing takes about 35 ms, which can support scrolling at near 29 (= 1000/35) Frames Per Second (FPS). At 1000 characters, however, compositing takes about 170 ms, which would cap the scrolling framerate to about 5 (= 1000/170) FPS. As can be seen in Figure 9, the latency in the monitor increases exponentially with the number of characters. This is due to the alpha-blending in the monitor, which operates on each pixel, resulting in exponential latency increase for two dimensional character glyphs.

We also measured the time needed to construct the glyph-book for various font sizes. Regardless of the font size, constructing the glyph-book does not take more than 30 ms, often much less. Although small, this time can be removed from the rendering latency by proactively creating the glyph-book or caching it for future use.

We measure the CPU usage overhead of rendering in SchrodinText. We measure the CPU usage overhead by measuring the amount of CPU used in the system from the beginning to the end of the text rendering period. Some of the CPU usage in this period might be due to other processes running in the background. We make sure to minimize this effect by not installing any other apps than the one under experiment and a few default ones available in the system. Also, the application itself is simple and does nothing but showing the text.

Figure 10 shows the results. Figure 10 (a) shows the raw CPU usage in jiffies (a unit of time used in Linux). It shows that the total amount of CPU usage has increased by 1-3×. This is because SchrodinText incurs computational overhead when creating the glyph-book as well as blending all the pixels in software (§5.2). In contrast, normal text in Android is blended fully in GPU, reducing the CPU usage.

Despite the overall increase in CPU usage, SchrodinText does not saturate the CPUs available in the system. Figure 10 (b) shows the CPU utilization in the system (the ratio of time when CPU is used to when it is idle). The SchrodinText's rendering components run mostly in a single thread incurring no more than 19% CPU utilization during the rendering period, slightly more than that of the normal text rendering.

9. RELATED WORK

9.1 Untrusted Operating System

Research on untrusted operating systems shares our motivation: modern commodity operating systems are too large and complex to be safe. Hence, many systems have attempted to protect the applications from the operating system assuming that the operating system can easily gets compromised by other malicious applications. Overshadow [25] and Inktag [35] were some of the early such systems. They use the hypervisor to protect the application. Recently, Intel added the Software Guard Extensions (SGX) [40] allowing the application to to create an isolated execution environment, i.e., an enclave, and protect itself, e.g., its memory, from the operating system. Unfortunately, the job of full protection of an application from its operating system is a daunting task. Checkoway et al. showed that the operating system has many ways to attack an application, e.g., by controlling the random number generator [23].

Dealing with untrusted operating systems in mobile devices has been an active line of work as well. Mobile solutions often use the TrustZone hardware for this purpose. They allow sensitive frameworks to be offloaded to the secure world and hence isolated from the operating system. For example, AdAttester [36] pushes the display and touchscreen drivers to the secure world allowing it to provide guarantees for ad providers, e.g., that the ad is shown correctly and that the click on the ad is not fake. TLR [46] provides a managed runtime (based on .NET) to run the security sensitive parts of application in the secure world. Trusted sensors [33,34,39,47] use a trusted hardware component (either TrustZone or Mobile Trusted Module (MTM) [16]) to provide authenticity guarantees for sensor readings. More specifically, the trusted sensor framework in [39] moves the sensor driver to the secure world and use the cryptographic operation support in it to sign the sensor readings. And YouProve [34] uses the trusted hardware to provide signed statements about transformed sensor readings generated in the device. Finally, SIMlet [43] uses the TrustZone to provide a trustworthy framework to monitor a mobile device's network traffic in order to enable content providers and mobile users to co-pay for the cost of network traffic.

In pocket hypervisors [26], Cox et al. envisioned the hypervisor to be used for providing security services in mobile devices. SchrodinText is one realization of this decade-old mobile computing vision.

There exists solutions for building a trusted path between an application (or an Internet service) and the user, assuming that the operating system is untrusted [37,55]. Zhou et al. [55] use a hypervisor to give an application direct, exclusive, and protected access to I/O devices, e.g., keyboard and display. In contrast, SchrodinText does not give any applications exclusive access to the display. It allows the operating system to manage the display as it normally does. It, however, protects selected textual content that the application shows to the user. Li et al. [37] use the secure world to protect the framebuffer and enforce background/foreground colors for it (to match the LED colors also enforced by the secure world) in order to protect against a framebuffer overlay attack. Their work, however, does not protect selected textual content on the UI.

Virtual Machine Introspection (VMI) uses the hypervisor for intrusion detection [30–32] and for detection of malicious activities in the operating system. SchrodinText is related to VMI as it uses the hypervisor to protect the textual content on the UI against a malicious operating system.

Finally, unlike these systems, SchrodinText leverages both the hypervisor and the TrustZone secure world.

9.2 Digital Rights Management

Digital Rights Management (DRM) is a framework that allows mobile devices to protect the digital media (such as video and audio) from unauthorized access. This framework allows the application's cloud backend, e.g., Netflix cloud service, to encrypt the content and share them with the application. Current implementation of DRM in Android decrypt the content in user space system services and hence are also vulnerable to the attacks by a compromised operating system. Future devices, however, are starting to embrace full hardware implementation for DRM, such as ARM Mali-V500 video processor [3]. In such a device, the encrypted content is delivered to a video processor hardware (integrated with the TrustZone secure world), which decodes the content and passes it to the display, all hidden from the operating system. It is however important to note that protecting digital video in this manner is relatively simpler than textual content for two reasons: First, the video does not need to be rendered; it already comes with all the pixel information available. All the video decoder hardware has to do is to decrypt the content and show it on the display. Hence, the operating system role is minimal. Second, the video is often full-screen and not fully integrated with the app UI. In contrast for text, the exact pixels to be rendered depend on the selected font type, size, and color as well as the size of the UI, text widget, and the display, most of them are not known to the cloud backend. Moreover, textual content is embedded in the app UI and highly integrated with it. However, we note that once such video processors are available in commodity devices, SchrodinText can use them for accelerating its software-based compositing.

9.3 Others

Unfortunately, protecting the UI integrity in Android has been challenging allowing an attacker to hijack the UI, which has triggered research into finding mitigations [24,44,45]. As mentioned in §3.6, SchrodinText does not provide integrity guarantees. Instead, it provides strong confidentiality guarantee for selected textual content on the UI.

CAPTCHA [6] attempts to identify human users (vs. computers) by showing a distorted text on the display and asking the user to type the text (a task difficult for a computer to do). Unlike SchrodinText, CAPTCHA does not protect the confidentiality of content shown on the display.

10. CONCLUSIONS

We presented SchrodinText, a system solution for strongly protecting application's sensitive textual content from malware that has compromised the operating system. SchrodinText leverages modern security hardware features on ARM platforms to protect and display the text. Our key contribution was oblivious rendering, a set of novel techniques to allow the operating system to perform the rendering without having access to the text, allowing us to keep the monitor, and hence the TCB, small. Our evaluation on the ARM Juno development board shows that SchrodinText incurs noticeable overhead but that its performance is usable. We believe that SchrodinText can be used to safely display various sensitive textual information to mobile users.

Acknowledgments

The author would like to thank the anonymous MobiSys reviewers and the paper shepherd, Rajesh Krishna Balan, for their insightful feedback. He would also like to thank Stefan Saroiu for the helpful and constructive discussions regarding this paper.

11. REFERENCES

[1] Android Keystore System. https://developer.android.com/training/articles/keystore.html.

[2] Android's Font Renderer. https://medium.com/@romainguy/androids-font-renderer-c368bbde87d9#.rvl02m0u0.

[3] Arm mali-v500.

[4] ARM SMMU. http://www.arm.com/files/pdf/System-MMU-Whitepaper-v8.0.pdf.

[5] ARM TrustZone. http://www.arm.com/products/processors/technologies/trustzone/index.php.

[6] CAPTCHA. http://www.captcha.net/.

[7] Droid sans fonts.

[8] Droid sans monospaced font.

[9] Google Authenticator. https://play.google.com/store/apps/details?id=com.google.android.apps.authenticator2.

[10] LetMeSpy. http://www.letmespy.com/.

[11] mbed TLS. https://tls.mbed.org/.

[12] Microsoft Authenticator. https://play.google.com/store/apps/details?id=com.azure.authenticator.

[13] Roboto fonts.

[14] Roboto monospaced fonts.

[15] TheTruthSpy. http://thetruthspy.com/.

[16] Trusted computing group mobile specifications.

[17] Xabber: open source xmpp client for android.

[18] ARM Security Technology, Building a Secure System using TrustZone Technology. http://infocenter.arm.com/help/topic/com.arm.doc.prd29-genc-009492c/PRD29-GENC-009492C_trustzone_security_whitepaper.pdf, 2004.

[19] TrustZone: Integrated Hardware and Software Security: Enabling Trusted Computing in Embedded Systems. In *ARM White Paper*, 2004.

[20] ARM. Juno ARM Development Platform SoC, Revision r0p0, Technical Overview. *ARM DTO*, 0038A (ID040516), 2014.

[21] A. M. Azab, K. Swidowski, J. M. Bhutkar, W. Shen, R. Wang, and P. Ning. SKEE: A Lightweight Secure Kernel-level Execution Environment for ARM. In *Proc. ACM MobiSys*, 2016.

[22] S. Checkoway, L. Davi, A. Dmitrienko, A. Sadeghi, H. Shacham, and M. Winandy. Return-Oriented Programming without Returns. In *Proc. ACM CCS*, 2010.

[23] S. Checkoway and H. Shacham. Iago Attacks: Why the System Call API is a Bad Untrusted RPC Interface. In *Proc. ACM ASPLOS*, 2013.

[24] Q. A. Chen, Z. Qian, and Z. M. Mao. Peeking into Your App without Actually Seeing It: UI State Inference and Novel Android Attacks. In *Proc. USENIX Security*, 2014.

[25] X. Chen, T. Garfinkel, E. C. Lewis, P. Subrahmanyam, C. A. Waldspurger, D. Boneh, J. Dwoskin, and D. R. K. Ports. Overshadow: a Virtualization-Based Approach to Retrofitting Protection in Commodity Operating Systems. In *Proc. ACM ASPLOS*, 2008.

[26] L. P. Cox and P. M. Chen. Pocket Hypervisors: Opportunities and Challenges. In *Proc. IEEE/ACM HotMobile*, 2007.

[27] C. Dall and J. Nieh. KVM/ARM: The Design and Implementation of the Linux ARM Hypervisor. In *Proc. ACM ASPLOS*, 2014.

[28] N. V. Database. Vulnerability summary for cve-2015-6639.

[29] W. Diffie and M. Hellman. New Directions in Cryptography. *IEEE transactions on Information Theory*, 22(6):644–654, 1976.

[30] B. Dolan-Gavitt, T. Leek, M. Zhivich, J. Giffin, and W. Lee. Virtuoso: Narrowing the Semantic Gap in Virtual Machine Introspection. In *Proc. IEEE Security and Privacy (S&P)*, 2011.

[31] Y. Fu and Z. Lin. Space Traveling across VM: Automatically Bridging the Semantic Gap in Virtual Machine Introspection via Online Kernel Data Redirection. In *Proc. IEEE Security and Privacy (S&P)*, 2012.

[32] T. Garfinkel and M. Rosenblum. A Virtual Machine Introspection Based Architecture for Intrusion Detection. In *Proc. Internet Society NDSS*, 2003.

[33] P. Gilbert, L. P. Cox, J. Jung, and D. Wetherall. Toward Trustworthy Mobile Sensing. In *Proc. ACM Workshop on Mobile Computing Systems & Applications (HotMobile)*, 2010.

[34] P. Gilbert, J. Jung, K. Lee, H. Qin, D. Sharkey, A. Sheth, and L. P. Cox. YouProve: Authenticity and Fidelity in Mobile Sensing. In *Proc. ACM SenSys*, 2011.

[35] O. S. Hofmann, S. Kim, A. M. Dunn, M. Z. Lee, and E. Witchel. InkTag: Secure Applications on an Untrusted Operating System. In *Proc. ACM ASPLOS*, 2013.

[36] W. Li, H. Li, H. Chen, and Y. Xia. AdAttester: Secure Online Mobile Advertisement Attestation Using TrustZone. In *Proc. ACM MobiSys*, 2015.

[37] W. Li, M. Ma, J. Han, Y. Xia, B. Zang, C. Chu, and T. Li. Building Trusted Path on Untrusted Device Drivers for Mobile Devices. In *Proc. ACM Asia-Pacific Workshop on Systems (APSys)*, 2014.

[38] A. Lineberry. Malicious Code Injection via /dev/mem. *Black Hat Europe*, page 11, 2009.

[39] H. Liu, S. Saroiu, A. Wolman, and H. Raj. Software Abstractions for Trusted Sensors. In *Proc. ACM MobiSys*, 2012.

[40] F. McKeen, I. Alexandrovich, A. Berenzon, C. V. Rozas, H. Shafi, V. Shanbhogue, and U. R. Savagaonkar. Innovative Instructions and Software Model for Isolated Execution. In *Proc. Inter. Workshop on Hardware and Architectural Support for Security and Privacy (HASP)*, page 10, 2013.

[41] S. Mirzamohammadi and A. Amiri Sani. Viola: Trustworthy Sensor Notifications for Enhanced Privacy on Mobile Systems. In *Proc. ACM MobiSys*, 2016.

[42] A. Rahmati, C. Shepard, C. Tossell, L. Zhong, and P. Kortum. Practical Context Awareness: Measuring and Utilizing the Context Dependency of Mobile Usage. *IEEE Transactions on Mobile Computing*, 14(9):1932–1946, 2015.

[43] H. Raj, S. Saroiu, A. Wolman, and J. Padhye. Splitting the Bill for Mobile Data with SIMlets. In *Proc. ACM HotMobile*, 2013.

[44] C. Ren, P. Liu, and S. Zhu. WindowGuard:

Systematic Protection of GUI Security in Android. In *Proc. Internet Society NDSS*, 2017.

[45] C. Ren, Y. Zhang, H. Xue, T. Wei, and P. Liu. Towards Discovering and Understanding Task Hijacking in Android. In *Proc. USENIX Security*, 2015.

[46] N. Santos, H. Raj, S. Saroiu, and A. Wolman. Using ARM TrustZone to Build a Trusted Language Runtime for Mobile Applications. In *Proc. ACM ASPLOS*, 2014.

[47] S. Saroiu and A. Wolman. I Am a Sensor, and I Approve This Message. In *Proc. ACM Workshop on Mobile Computing Systems & Applications (HotMobile)*, 2010.

[48] H. Shacham. The Geometry of Innocent Flesh on the Bone: Return-into-libc without Function Calls (on the x86). In *Proc. ACM CCS*, 2007.

[49] Texas Instruments. Architecture Reference Manual, OMAP4430 Multimedia Device Silicon Revision 2.x. SWPU231N, 2010.

[50] V. van der Veen, Y. Fratantonio, M. Lindorfer, D. Gruss, C. Maurice, G. Vigna, H. Bos, K. Razavi, and C. Giuffrida. Drammer: Deterministic Rowhammer Attacks on Mobile Platforms. In *Proc. ACM CCS*, 2016.

[51] J. Winter. Trusted Computing Building Blocks for Embedded Linux-based ARM TrustZone Platforms. In *Proc. ACM Workshop on Scalable Trusted Computing (STC)*, 2008.

[52] T. Yan, D. Chu, D. Ganesan, A. Kansal, and J. Liu. Fast App Launching for Mobile Devices Using Predictive User Context. In *Proc. ACM MobiSys*, 2012.

[53] H. Zhang, D. She, and Z. Qian. Android Root and its Providers: A double-Edged Sword. In *Proc. ACM CCS*, 2015.

[54] Y. Zhou and X. Jiang. Dissecting Android Malware: Characterization and Evolution. In *IEEE Symposium on Security and Privacy*, 2012.

[55] Z. Zhou, V. D. Gligor, J. Newsome, and J. M. McCune. Building Verifiable Trusted Path on Commodity x86 Computers. In *Proc. IEEE Symposium on Security and Privacy (S&P)*, 2012.

Matthan: Drone Presence Detection by Identifying Physical Signatures in the Drone's RF Communication

Phuc Nguyen[†‡], Hoang Truong[†‡], Mahesh Ravindranathan[‡], Anh Nguyen[†‡], Richard Han[‡] and Tam Vu[†‡]
[†]University of Colorado, Denver, [‡]University of Colorado, Boulder
{phuc.v.nguyen, hoang.truong,anh.t4.nguyen, tam.vu}@ucdenver.edu,
{mahesh.ravindranathan, richard.han}@colorado.edu

ABSTRACT

Drones are increasingly flying in sensitive airspace where their presence may cause harm, such as near airports, forest fires, large crowded events, secure buildings, and even jails. This problem is likely to expand given the rapid proliferation of drones for commerce, monitoring, recreation, and other applications. A cost-effective detection system is needed to warn of the presence of drones in such cases. In this paper, we explore the feasibility of inexpensive RF-based detection of the presence of drones. We examine whether physical characteristics of the drone, such as body vibration and body shifting, can be detected in the wireless signal transmitted by drones during communication. We consider whether the received drone signals are uniquely differentiated from other mobile wireless phenomena such as cars equipped with Wi-Fi or humans carrying a mobile phone. The sensitivity of detection at distances of hundreds of meters as well as the accuracy of the overall detection system are evaluated using software defined radio (SDR) implementation.

1. INTRODUCTION

With the advent of inexpensive commercially available unmanned aerial vehicles (UAV), drones are rapidly rising in popularity as a host of a wide class of applications ranging from commercial delivery [27], environment monitoring [2], photography [26], policing [81], fire fighting [73], just to name a few. However, with the rise in drone usage, there has also been a rise in incidents involving drones, such as mid-air collisions, damage to property, and violations of privacy.

In particular, drones are increasingly flying in sensitive airspace where their presence may cause harm, such as near airports, forest fires, large crowded events, and even jails. For example, Dubai airport, the third busiest airport in the world, reported that in 2016 it had to shut down three times to avoid unauthorized drone activity [16]. In 2015, drones were used to smuggle drugs and contraband into a Maryland prison [59]. A quadcopter crashed on the White House lawn [36], raising concerns about the safety of buildings and political leaders. The presence of drones has interfered with and grounded aircraft fighting forest fires [46]. Drone crashes have also disrupted sporting events such as the US Open tennis tournament as well as a World Cup skiing race [79, 15]. In fact, based on FAA data, more than 300 drone incidents were reported in California alone between April 2014 and Jan 2016 [74], which is equivalent of 15 incidents per month on average or 1 incident every two days.

A variety of approaches have been explored to interdict drones. These include shooting nets at the drones to tamper with their propeller to bring them down [66], using lasers to shoot down drones [78], spoofing GPS to confuse a drone's localization system [33], hijacking the software of drones by hacking into them [58], using other drones to hunt down unauthorized drones [16], and even training eagles to attack and disable drones [4].

However, these interdiction strategies typically presume that the presence of the drone has already been detected. Recent work has sought to develop drone detection systems that leverage either microphone, camera, or radar to sense the presence of drones [23, 20, 1]. Each approach has its own limitations. Audio-based approaches can be confused by other sounds in noisy environments, has limited range, and cannot detect drones that employ noise canceling techniques [49]. Camera-based approaches require good lighting conditions, high quality lens, and camera with ultra-high resolution for detecting drones at long distance. Thermal and IR imaging cameras for long distance are prohibitively expensive and have limited coverage. Radio-frequency techniques based on active radar introduce RF interference. Geofencing is useful to prevent drones from flying into fixed areas known a priori as sensitive [74], but requires manufacturers to install such software and is less useful to prohibit drones from flying around temporary event venues (we refer readers to the related work Section 6 for thorough discussions of advantages and drawbacks of each approach).

In this paper, we consider an approach to detect the presence drone by passively eavesdropping on the RF communication between a drone and its controller (Wi-Fi standard). Such communication mode often happens over standard unlicensed spectrum for which a low-cost COTS hardware can be utilized for observation. Prior work utilizing passive RF to identify drones has sought, for example, to detect the frequency of transmission, the MAC address of the drone, and the frequency of packet communication [19, 57, 53]. All these techniques suffer from various limitations, as described in the related work section, and none seek to discern whether

Permission to make digital or hard copies of all or part of this work for personal or classroom use is granted without fee provided that copies are not made or distributed for profit or commercial advantage and that copies bear this notice and the full citation on the first page. Copyrights for components of this work owned by others than ACM must be honored. Abstracting with credit is permitted. To copy otherwise, or republish, to post on servers or to redistribute to lists, requires prior specific permission and/or a fee. Request permissions from permissions@acm.org.

MobiSys'17, June 19-23, 2017, Niagara Falls, NY, USA

© 2017 ACM. ISBN 978-1-4503-4928-4/17/06...$15.00

DOI: http://dx.doi.org/10.1145/3081333.3081354

physical signatures of the drone's motion are manifested in the drone's RF signal.

In this work, we investigate the fundamental aerodynamic and motion control mechanisms of drones to identify two key inherent types of movement of the drone's body, namely *body shifting* caused by the spinning propellers and *body vibration* due to navigation and environmental impact corrections. We validate our hypothesis on the existence of such movements through empirical studies and then conduct a theoretical analysis on the characteristics of such movements. We also explore the feasibility of reconstructing such movement by using passive RF sensing. We then propose Matthan, a system that incorporates a number of algorithms to detect the presence of drone from both body vibration and shifting. It employs low cost software-defined radios (SDRs) to eavesdrop on Wi-Fi channels used in drone-to-controller communication. We demonstrate that this system can detect the physical signatures to uniquely identify an individual drone and effectively differentiate it from other mobile wireless devices at distances of hundreds of meters. Matthan is currently able to detect Wi-Fi embedded individual drones independently at any point in time. We are investigating detection of drones that communicate at other RF frequencies to identify multiple drones at the same time.

Our paper makes the following contributions. We

- identify the relationship between the drone controller's compensation reaction and its body shifting
- identify a second frequency component in the RF signal that we attribute to the drone's propellers
- show that both of these on-board physical phenomena are manifested in the received RF signal
- devise an algorithm to detect drones from their RF-based signature based on both body vibration and body shifting physical characteristics marked on the continuous data stream between drones and their controllers
- verify that this algorithm can detect drone signatures at Wi-Fi frequencies that are uniquely differentiated from other mobile Wi-Fi devices, such as cars and walking cellphone users
- confirm that this algorithm can operate at distances of hundreds of meters using a directional antenna with a 21 degree beamwidth
- discover that this algorithm could be used to begin differentiating the seven different drones tested

In the following, we first describe in Section 2 the basics of drone flight and validate, using sensors attached to the drone, that the drone vibrates at the propeller frequency and that body shifting causes correlated disturbances in the RF signal. In Section 3, we develop a model to explain the influence of both types of body motion on the RF signal, and present our drone detection algorithm, which utilizes both frequency analysis to detect body vibration in the RF signal and wavelet analysis to detect shifts in the drone during flight. We provide a performance evaluation in Section 4 considering different types of evidence, then conduct an analysis over a variety of drones, environments, and distances. We conclude the paper with a discussion of the current drawbacks of Matthan, related work, and a summary.

2. FUNDAMENTAL AERODYNAMICS AND PHYSICAL SIGNATURES OF DRONES

Matthan relies on the unique physical signatures that persist across drones to detect and differentiate them from other moving objects. In this section, we start by providing the background on aerodynamic principles that allows drones to move towards a desired direction or remain balanced while flying. We then derive two unique physical signatures, namely *body shifting* and *body vibration*, that are present on all drones that have propellers. We empirically prove the existence of such signatures and then perform a formal analysis to show how such signature can be captured from the radio signals that are emitted from the drones for communicating with their remote controller.

2.1 Drone Movement and Control Background

Drones or micro air vehicles (MAVs) can be made from a form of helicopter, an airplane, a multirotors or even a balloon. In that, helicopter and multirotors are the most common drones due to simplicity of manufactoring. As its name indicated, a multirotor [43] has multiple rotors with a much simpler flying control mechanism compared to that of a helicopter [31]. Instead of changing its wing's pitch and speed using a complex rotor as found in helicopters to maintain balance and maneuver, a multirotor operates by simply changing its motors' speed. Therefore, no complex mechanical parts is required. Partly due to this simplicity, multirotor-based drones are much more popular than their counterpart helicopters [45]. Since it has multiple similar rotors arranged symmetrically, a multirotor can keep its balance more easily even when it carries additional load (e.g. cameras, packages). The change in the center of mass can be tolerated by simply adjusting the rotors' speed. These advantages of multirotor become even more significant when it comes to small-sized drones since integrating sophisticated controlling mechanics as in a helicopter requires a large form factor, increasing cost and size of the drone's footprint. Therefore, most of today's commercial drones are of the multirotor type and the same trend is predicted for the near future [63]. As a result, we focus on this type of drone in this paper.

Drone equilibrium conditions. The popular designs of multirotors include 4-, 6-,and 8-rotors which are naturally termed quadcopter, hexacopter and octocopter respectively. The most popular one is the quadrotor, which has four similar propellers arranged in either "×" configuration or "+" configuration with equal distance from its the center of mass. The rotation direction of each propellers depends on its relative position. Let the indexes of the propellers be numbered sequentially from #1 to #4. If the propeller #1 rotates clockwise, for example, the ones #2 and #4 will rotate counter-clockwise while #3 will rotate clockwise as illustrated in Figure 1. To facilitate our analysis in the remaining sections of this paper, let ω_i with $i = 1..n$ be the rotation speed of each propeller. Without losing the generality, we only focus on analyzing quadrotors ($n = 4$).

Let F_i with $i = 1..4$ be the forces generated by the propellers i and m be the mass of the quadrotors. Since the quadrotor is symmetric, if L is the distance between the center of the quadrotor and each propeller, the moment generated by each propeller is calculated by $M_i = L * F_i$. In an ideal environment, in order to keep balance and remain

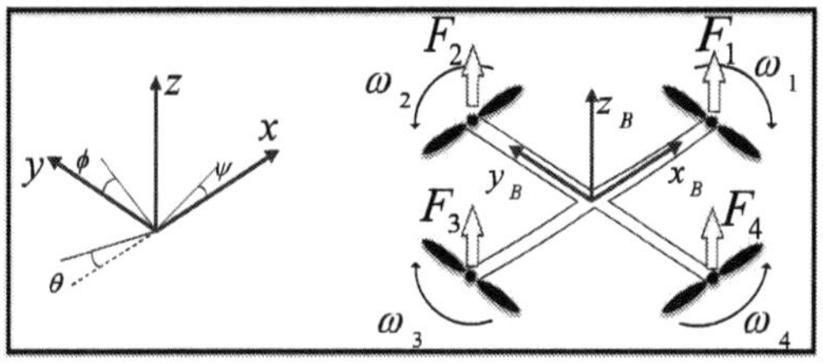

Figure 1: Earth and quadrotor reference systems.

in equilibrium state, the quadrotor must obey these four physical conditions:

(1) $\sum_{i=1}^{4} F_i = -mg$ (Equilibrium of forces),
(2) $\sum_{i=1}^{4} F_i || g$ (Equilibrium of directions),
(3) $\sum_{i=1}^{4} M_i = 0$ (Equilibrium of moments), and
(4) $(\omega_1 + \omega_2) - (\omega_3 + \omega_4) = 0$ (Equilibrium of rotation speeds).

If one or more of those conditions are violated, the quadrotor will leave equilibrium state and start making movement as depicted in Figure 1. Two reference systems are used to represent the position and orientation of the quadrotor. The inertial reference system, i.e. the Earth frame (denoted x, y, z-axes) provides the absolute linear position of the quadrotor; and the quadrotor reference system, i.e. the Body frame (denoted x_B, y_B, z_B-axes) gives the angular position with three Euler angles. Roll angle (ϕ), Pitch angle (θ) and Yaw angle (ψ) determine the rotation of the quadrotor around the x, y, z-axes respectively.

Drone maneuvering conditions. Any movement of a quadrotor can be created by a combination of four basic movements: roll rotation, pitch rotation, yaw rotation and altitude change. Each of these movements is created by briefly violating the above equilibrium conditions by applying proper angular speeds to each propeller, $\omega_{1..4}$. For example, to create a roll rotation, $\omega_{1..4}$ must be applied such that $(\omega_1+\omega_4)-(\omega_2+\omega_3) \neq 0$. Similarly, to generate a pitch rotation, the drone needs to change the angular speeds of different rotors such that $(\omega_1+\omega_2)-(\omega_3+\omega_4) \neq 0$. To move the drone up and down, the rotation speeds should be changed to adjust the thrust force F so that $\sum_{n=1}^{4} F_i \neq -mg$.

2.2 Body Shifting and Body Vibration as Drone's Physical Signatures

Many different controllers have been introduced in the literature following aforementioned principles, including PID [72, 21, 83, 8], back-stepping [41, 82], nonlinear H∞ [62], LQR [8], and nonlinear controllers with nested saturation[12, 24], to stabilize and maneuver drones. Beside taking the desired direction as inputs, these controllers also need to take into account the impacts of the unpredictable environments, such as wind, and the inaccuracy of its sensors and actuators. Since these factors are nondeterministic and occur often, the controller needs to frequently react to and compensate for them, causing undesirable physical movement of the drone. In particular, the undesirable movements can be the result of the controller's reaction to (a) an environmental change, e.g., a gust of wind, a magnetic storm; (b) numerical errors inside control loop of the drone itself, e.g. the imperfection of converting from speed of rotation to the exact targeted pitch, roll, yaw angles [31, 32, 9]; and (c) by the vibration caused by propeller's movement [31]. We leverage these undesirable yet persistent movements as unique signa-

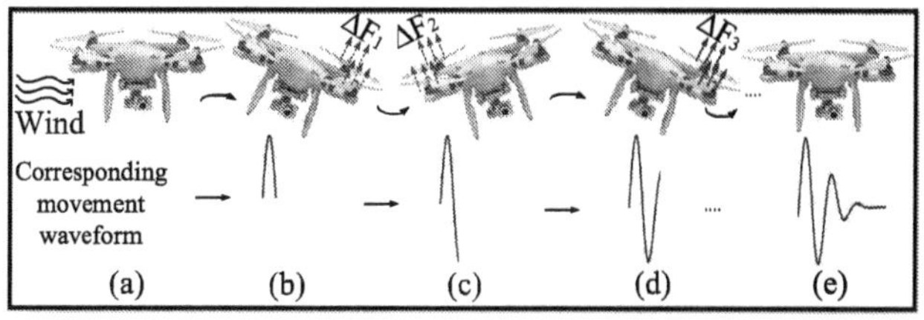

Figure 2: An example illustrated the drone shifts its body due to the effect from an unexpected wind. The additional force ΔF are created by speeding up corresponding propellers to balance the drone.

tures of drones, which can be used to differentiate a drone from other moving objects. The movements of interest fall into two main categories: *the drone's body shifting* and *the drone's body vibration.*

Drone body shifting. Body shifting occurs as a sequence of discrete events. Figure 2 illustrates the drone's body movement caused by wind (a, b) as the result of a rebalancing effort from the drone's controlling mechanism (c, d). Beside the drifting its body does due to the effect of environmental conditions, the drone body also usually changes its body orientation and direction when it flies. The angular velocity of the rotor i, denoted ω_i, creates force F_i in the direction of the rotor's axis. The angular velocity and acceleration of the rotor also need to create torque τ_{M_i} around the rotor axis: $F_i = k\omega_i^2, \tau_{M_i} = b\omega_i^2 + I_M\omega_i^*$ in which ω_i is the rotation speed of rotor i, k is the lift constant, b is the drag constant, the inertial movement of the rotor is I_M. The impact from ω_i^* is usually small and thus it is omitted. When the wind creates an additional force that changes the balance of the drone, the drag force now becomes $\tau_{M_i} + \Delta F_1$. To make the drone return to a stable state, the propeller on the right side will speed up to create an additional force $\Delta F_2, (\Delta F_1 \approx \Delta F_2)$ against the force generated by the wind. When the drone is balanced, if the additional forceΔ F_2 stays longer than expected, it creates a side effect to the drone body that makes the drone unbalanced again. Next, the controlling algorithm will changes the propeller speed expecting the drone to go to the balanced state. This process will be repeated and take several iterations until the drone gets to its equilibrium. We consider this behavior to be one signature of a flying drone that can be used to distinguish it from other flying objects, e.g. birds. Because of the waveform's resemblance to a wavelet, this stimulated our interest in developing a wavelet-based detector for drone body shifting, as explained later.

Drone body vibrations. The drone body is vibrated within a certain frequency range and such vibrations are usually caused by the rotation of its propellers [31, 32]. In the literature, several works have been conducted to analyze the vibration of helicopters caused by their propeller's rotation [38, 30, 40]. The resulting vibration is the vector sum of vertical, longitudinal, and lateral vibrations. More specifically, in forced vibration, the frequency of the vibration is close to the frequency of the force or motion applied, and the magnitude of the vibration depends on the actual mechanical system [5]. The steady-state solution of the forced vibration system with damping subjected to a sinusoidal force $F(t) = Fsin(2\pi ft)$ can be expressed as $x(t) = Xsin(2\pi ft + \phi)$, where $x(t)$ is the vibration function, X is the amplitude of the vibration, f is the vibration frequency, which is the same as the engine operating speed, and ϕ is the phase.

Thus far, we have discussed two types of drone's inherent body movements that happen when the drone is flying. However, these types of movement are unexplored in the literature. To validate our hypothesis, we conduct a set of experiment to validate the drone body shifting and body vibration signatures. We also conduct a feasibility check to confirm whether an RF-based technique can be used to detect the drone by observing its signatures.

2.3 Preliminary Validation of Drone Body Movements

This section presents a set of experiments to validate the signatures of the drone as mentioned earlier. We conduct two main experiments to explore the body movement characteristics of the drone using (1) inertial measurement units (IMUs) and (2) a wireless sensing hardware. In the first experiment, we attach external IMUs, to the drone's frame underneath each propeller to capture the drone's body movements. Secondly, we also attach firmly a 2.4 GHz wireless transmitting antenna to the drone. The RF signal from the transmitter is captured by a wireless receiver placed 2 meters apart. The goal here is to validate whether the drone body movements are observable by analyzing the received wireless samples. We present results here from experiments conducted for the Parrot Bebop [56] in an indoor environment. Similar confirmation was obtained using the DJI Phantom [22].

2.3.1 *Validating Drone Body Movements using IMUs*

We inspected behaviors of the drone including taking off, hovering, and flying. The drone is augmented with 4 IMUs (MPU 9150 [69]) each of which is mounted beneath propeller. The data from these IMUs are gathered by an Arduino Pro Mini board [3] and then are sent to a computer via Bluetooth Module HC-05 [7]. A camera was also used to record the start, the end, and the movement of the drone during testing sessions. The objectives of the experiments are to answer the following questions: *(a) Does the drone vibrate and move its body when flying as predicted in the previous analysis?, (b) What are the frequencies of such vibrations and movement patterns?, (c) When there is no wind, will the drone body shifting still persist?*

The spectrogram of the collected signal is shown in Figure 3. There are two dominant frequencies that are observable from the data. The low frequency (less than 10Hz) components happen at 10^{th}(s), 20^{th}(s), 32^{th}(s), 40^{th}(s), and 53^{th}(s), which correspond to the drone's body shifting (confirmed from recorded videos). In addition, the second dominant frequency at 50th to 70th Hz represents the vibration frequency of the drone body caused by propellers. These results answer the first two questions we mentioned earlier, that the drone constantly vibrates and create iterative body shiftings when it flies. The observed data also shown that the body vibration and body shifting can happen at the same time at some moments.

To answer the third question, we setup a closed indoor experiment where wind is blocked to a minimal level and the drone circles within a small room. Analyzing the captured IMU data in both time and frequency domain gives us two conclusions: the drone body vibration is still present from

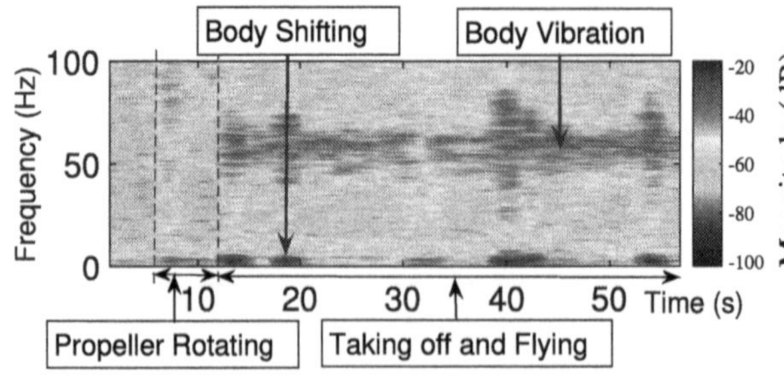

Figure 3: An example illustrates the movement captured by IMUs attached to the Bebop drone.

the IMU data even without wind; and the body shifting still happens during the time the drone tries to adjust its pitch and yaw angles to fly in a circular shape. Such drone body movements happen when the drone tries to change its pitch, roll, and yaw angles. In summary, we empirically confirmed that the drone body is shifted even in a windless environment, and the drone body continuously vibrates when it flies. In the next subsection, we will conduct another experiment to validate whether those movements can be captured using RF signals.

2.3.2 *Feasibility Check: Capturing Drone Body Movements using RF Signals*

We conduct the second set of experiments to check the feasibility of capturing the drone movements using RF signals. A wireless transmission antenna is attached to the drone. A wireless receiving antenna is placed at a fixed location to capture the signal sent from the transmitter (which is attached to the drone as illustrated in Figure 4). We used USRP B200 mini software-defined radios (SDR) [77] to control the transmitter and receiver antennas. The antennas are connected to USRP SDRs through cables of 6m length. The transmitter antenna emits a single tone wireless signal at 2.4 GHz when the drone is flying. The key idea is to capture the change in RSSI and phase of the transmitted single tone signal to infer the drone body movements. In addition, we also attached the IMUs to the drone and collect the data as the ground truth. The objectives of this experiment are to answer the following questions: *Do received wireless samples correspond to the movements of the drone (a) for body shifting? and (b) for body vibration?*

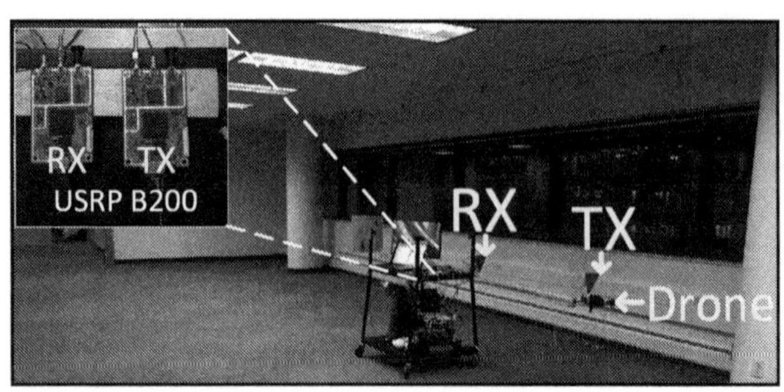

Figure 4: The setup for the indoor environment.

The results showed that it is possible to capture body shifting and body vibration in the RF domain. First, in Figure 5, we plot the raw data obtained from accelerometer

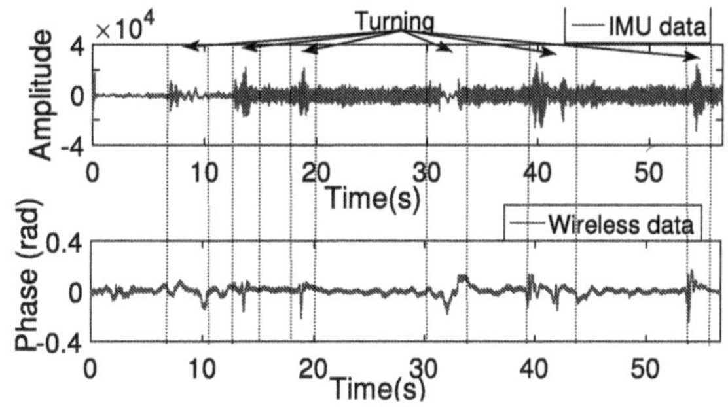

Figure 5: Signals captured by the IMU and from RF.

data and the phase of the received RF signal. Note that the SDR listens to a WiFi band and demodulates the signal to baseband, after which we compute the FFT. As shown in the figure, the body shifting peaks corresponding to turning are clearly identifiable and correlated on both accelerometer and RF data.

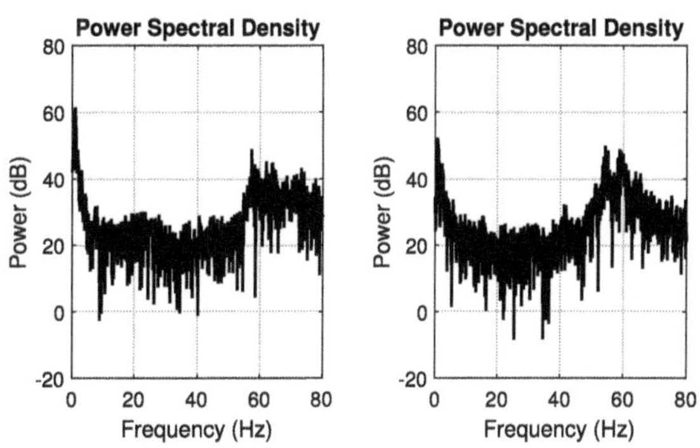

Figure 6: The frequency distribution of the signal from IMU (left) and RF (right).

We conducted experiments to see whether the measured vibration frequency of the IMU matches what we see in the frequency domain of the RF signal. We confirmed that the peak frequency detected in the frequency domain repeatedly matches what we observed via the IMUs. Figure 6 illustrates the frequency distribution of RF signal captured with peaks around the 60 Hz mark, which is similar to the peak on the IMU measurements.

3. MATTHAN DRONE PRESENCE DETECTION

We design Matthan, a system that detects the above-mentioned body movements, namely body shifting and body vibration, by passively listening on the radio channels that the drone is using to communicate with its remote controller. A number of algorithms are introduced to capture such miniature physical signatures and to identify if it is coming from a drone. In the following subsection, we first formally define our problem and identify challenges in realizing such a system. We then present the body vibration detection method and body shifting detection method before describing a fusion algorithm that combines the two types of movements into a single classifier.

3.1 Problem Formulation

To detect the presence of drones, Matthan listens to the channel that is used by the drones to communicate with its remote controller. Let the signal broadcast by the drone to its remote control be $\tilde{t}(t)$ at time t. The signal Matthan received by listening is $\tilde{r}(t)$. Since the movements of interest are at frequencies that are a few orders of magnitude lower than the carrier frequency or the data rate, $\tilde{r}(t)$ can be filtered to obtain only the low frequency components. Let $\tilde{r_f}(t)$ be the filtered signal. We then have:

$$\tilde{r_f}(t) = q(t) + \eta(t) \tag{1}$$

where $q(t)$ is the signal that contains the drone body shifting and body vibration, and $\eta(t)$, which is the environment noise. After removing the DC components, $\eta(t)$ becomes a signal with zero-mean and some variance. Previous experiments show that the drone body vibration happens continuously over a specific range of frequencies when the drone is flying. In addition, we also found that the drone body shifting has a form that is close to a wavelet $\psi(t)$ due to the characteristic of its rebalancing and control loop mechanisms. Hence, the drone signal $q(t)$ can be written as:

$$q(t) = \psi(t) + Xsin(2\pi ft + \phi) \tag{2}$$

where $\psi(t)$ is the function represents the drone body shifting. $\psi(t)$ is the function containing different dominant single tone cosine signals that have amplitude $\hat{A}(\psi)$, frequency $\hat{f}(\psi)$, and phase $\hat{\phi}(\psi)$. And X,ϕ, and f are the amplitude, phase, and frequency of the drone body vibration. In summary, the key objectives of Matthan are to identify the drone body shifting ($\hat{A}(\psi)$, $\hat{f}(\psi)$, $\hat{\phi}(\psi)$) and the drone body vibration (X,ϕ, f).

■ **Challenges.** However, accurate and robust drone detection based on RF signals is hard due to the following challenges:

1) Movements-RF translation. The drone body shifting and movement information are buried in the wireless signal. This limits the maximum detection range that can be obtained from the system at different environment.

2) The body shifting can happen at different scales. Different drones creates different types of body shifting according to their controlling mechanism and accuracy as well as their physical characteristics (weight, structures, and etc.). The signal can be detected at different magnitudes as well as frequencies. However, the shape of the body shifting signal stays relatively constant. We propose a wavelet based technique that is resilient to the scale and magnitude of the physical body shift.

3) Interference from static APs. The drone may communicate at the same frequency channel with the wireless APs in the environment. The detection algorithm should be able to distinguish between the signals from the static APs and the signal from the drone. The solution for the next challenge is used to solve this problem.

4) Interference from mobile APs. A mobile AP carried by a human walking or an embedded AP on a moving vehicle, e.g. bus, could create similar wireless signals as the drone, which could affect the detection results (assuming the AP operates at the same frequency with the drone's communication channel). We propose a technique that differentiates the drone from other static or mobile APs based on identifying the body vibration of the drone using RF.

5) Environment noise. The noisy and heterogeneous environment makes the problem much more challenging. We introduce an evidence-based classifier to make the detection more robust. The drone presence is detected based on the availability of multiple lines of evidence that uniquely identify the physical characteristics of the drone (i.e., body shifting and body vibration).
6) Variety of drones. Drones vary in terms of having different numbers of propellors, weights, sizes, speeds, and communication mechanisms. We present a confusion matrix showing that Matthan's detection approach is promising in terms of discriminating among the specific set of drones that we tested.

3.2 Drone Detection Algorithm

In this section, we present Matthan's detection algorithms. Since the drone body shifting happens at different scales and environments, it can be detected at different magnitudes as well as frequencies. However, the shape of the signal stays relatively constant. We propose a wavelet-based technique that is resilient to the scale and magnitude of the physical body shift. In addition, we design a Fourier analysis to detect the drone body vibration. We then design an evidence-based algorithm taking the input from wavelet and Fourier analysis to make the final decision.

3.2.1 Drone Body Shifting Detection

We use wavelet analysis to detect the drone body shifting. A wavelet is a wave-like oscillation with an amplitude that begins at zero, increases, and then decreases back to zero. Wavelets are especially good at capturing brief oscillations. From the results of our experiment (Sec. 2.2), the behavior of the drone body shifting is similar to the form of a wavelet. This characteristic will result in high coefficients when multiplying the wireless signal $\tilde{r}(t)$ with scaled versions of the mother wavelet.

The wavelet, denoted by $w(t)$, maintains local information in both the time and frequency domains. It is defined as a waveform that satisfies the following condition: $\int_{-\infty}^{+\infty} w(t)dt = 0$. The Wavelet Transform [71] uses as the wavelet that satisfies the condition of dynamic scaling and shifting function, $w_{s,p}$,

$$w_{s,p}(t) = \frac{1}{\sqrt{s}} w\left(\frac{t-p}{s}\right) \tag{3}$$

where $w_{s,p}(t)$ are the integrated and integral transformation signal, s is the scale and p is the shift parameter, which can also be the central location of the wavelet in the time domain. The wavelet can be stretched and translated with flexible windows by adjusting s and p, respectively. The wavelet transform of the wireless received samples $\tilde{r}(t)$ using transform coefficient $W(s,p)$ is calculated as following:

$$\begin{aligned} W(s,p) &= \int_{-\infty}^{+\infty} \tilde{r_f}(t)\overline{w_{s,p}}(t)dt \\ &= \frac{1}{\sqrt{s}} \int_{-\infty}^{+\infty} \tilde{r_f}(t)\overline{w_{s,p}}\left(\frac{t-p}{s}\right)dt \end{aligned} \tag{4}$$

where $\overline{w_{s,p}}(t)$ represents the complex conjugate of $w_{s,p}(t)$. The result of the wavelet transform gives us a correlation function of the template signal at different scales (frequency bands) in both the time and frequency domains. As in Equation 4, the correlation function $W(s,p)(t)$ has two main fea-

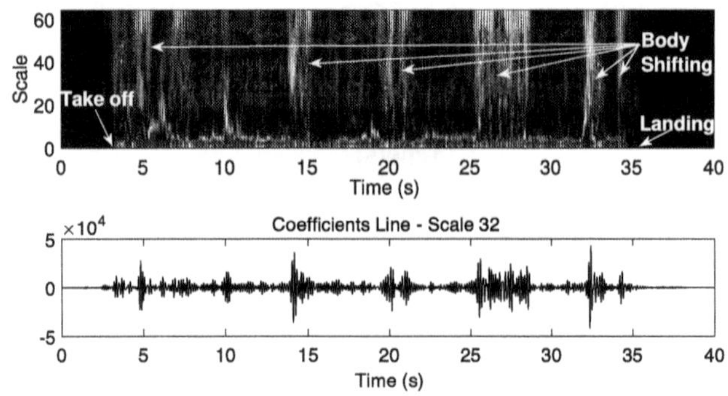

Figure 7: An example wavelet analysis of body shifting detection

tures as follows. (1) The time resolution is high with high frequencies while the frequency resolution is high with low frequency signals. When multiplying the high frequency component of the signal with the high frequency of the wavelet, the correlation result will indicate the exact location where it happens. This can be used to identify the very first body shifting event created by the drone. (2) As the wavelet has local existence in both time and frequency domain, the point of discontinuity in the signal can be detected with high sensitivity. As the discontinuity (generated by body shifting) is considered as an event and happens quickly in time, the result of correlation with high frequency wavelet will be readily captured.

Let $W_m(s,p)$, $W_{vi}(s,p)$, and $W_\eta(s,p)$ be the wavelet transform coefficients of the signal caused by the drone body shifting, drone body vibration, and the noise, respectively. The wavelet transform coefficient of the sum of the signals is calculated as follows:

$$W_{m+vi+\eta}(s,p) = W_m(s,p) + W_{vi}(s,p) + W_\eta(s,p) \tag{5}$$

Because of the linearity property, the coefficients of the wavelet transform enable us to precisely identify the body shifting event in the time domain when there is a signal discontinuity. As the drone body vibration and the noise are quite constant over time, these behaviors decay quickly after different levels of scaling, leaving the body shifting component. The wavelet transform coefficients then give us two valuable pieces of information for event detection: the location and the duration of each body shifting event. Figure 7 (top) depicts the results of the wavelet transform at 64 scales of the received wireless samples where the drone body shifting events are correctly identified.

To identify exact time and frequency of the drone body shifting, Matthan decomposes the signal into a sequence of sub-frequency bands and approximates the energy of each frequency band. Energy of each sub-frequency is calculated as following:

$$\xi_i = \int |f_i(t)|^2 dt = \sum_{k=1}^{n} |f_i(k)|^2 \tag{6}$$

where $f_i(t)$ is the signal of i frequency band, $f_i(k)$ is its discrete value. The system compares the energy of each frequency band, then reconstructs the coefficient of special sub frequencies that have enough energy and contain the frequency of drone body shifting.

The center of the signal can be calculated according to the definition of the gravitational center in mechanics, namely the center of the body shifting event in time is given as:

$$t_{center} = \frac{\int t|f(t)|^2 dt}{\int |f(t)|^2 dt} \tag{7}$$

Then, the width of the window function of the STFT can be calculated from the central point to the point where the coefficient value $W_{s,p}$ drops down to the noise band. Hence, the above results gives us the time center and the width of the function. We then can perform STFT to analyze the frequency of the drone body movement. The peak of the frequency distribution resulting from STFT identifies the frequency of drone body shifting $\psi(t)$.

3.2.2 *Drone Body Vibration Detection*

As seen earlier in Figure 3, the drone's vibration creates a periodic signal that is well-reflected in the FFT-based spectrogram. Conversely, a wavelet transform that is better-suited for capturing transitory phenomena such as a body shifting event is not well-suited for drone vibration detection. Consequently, we employ a frequency domain approach to identifying the presence of the drone's vibration signal. Recall that the wireless signal component that is affected by the drone body vibration has the form of $Xsin(2\pi ft + \phi)$. From the received wireless sample $\tilde{r}(t)$, an efficient approximation of the drone's vibration frequency is to identify the dominant frequency component that has maximum power spectrum density (PSD) through the STFT. Then, the approximation of the drone's vibration frequency f_v is as follows:

$$f_v = \max_{[f_{min} \to f_{max}]} \left(|\sum_{k=1}^{N} \tilde{r_f}(t) e^{-j2\pi ftk}|^2 \right) \tag{8}$$

where N is the number samples. After f is estimated, it can be used to estimate the amplitudes and phases of different frequency channels using the following: $X = \frac{2}{N} \, |\sum_{k=1}^{N} \tilde{r_f}(t)e^{-j2\pi ftk}|$, and $\phi = actan\frac{-\sum_{k=1}^{N} \tilde{r_f}(t)sin(2\pi ftk)}{\sum_{k=1}^{N} \tilde{r_f}(t)cos(2\pi ftk)}$. In this way, the system obtains the desired quantities $[X, \phi, f]$.

3.2.3 *Evidence-Based Drone Detection Algorithm*

We design an algorithm to determine if a drone is present by first gathering evidence from multiple sources that relate to drone body shifting and vibration, then combine these sources of evidence to form a binary classifier. The overview structure of Matthan is illustrated in Figure 8.

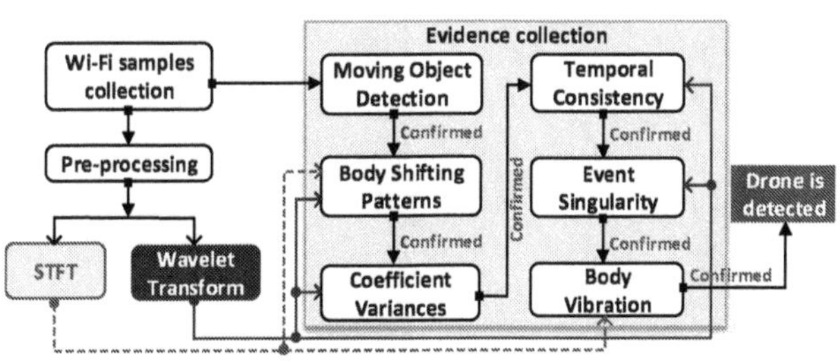

Figure 8: Overview architecture of Matthan.

■ **Evidence #1: Moving Object**. The first evidence to collect is the presence of a moving object using RF signals. This of course is not a unique indication of a drone but of any moving object such as a human walking while carrying a phone or a phone inside a car. Matthan calculates the standard deviation of the received wireless signal and compares it with the standard deviation of the environment at the time of initialization. The standar deviation of the signal without moving objects, denoted by δ_0 is an environment independent quantity [76] and it represents the received signal changes caused by electronic noise. Received signals are dominated by *quantization errors* and *electronic noise*. Therefore, the signal follows a Gaussian distribution with zero-mean after DC removal [76]. On the other hand, when the drone or other moving object is in the environment, the received signals are expected to follow the distribution of multipath fading because it dominates the other noise sources. A log-normal, Ricean, or Rayleigh distribution is expected to represent the distribution of the collected data with such multipath affects. As a result, the comparison between the standard deviation of the signal at test and δ_0 can be done to confirm this evidence.

■ **Evidence #2: Drone Body Shifting**. As mentioned in Section 3.2.1, the drone body shifting event serves as one of the main indications of drone presence detection. Since the shifting follows a certain pattern in space, it can be amplified and detected using wavelet transformation. We use Mexican hat wavelet [67] as the template of comparison because this wavelet has a similar waveform to the drone's body shifting event shown before. It is important to note that the speed (i.e how fast it shifts) and amplitude (i.e. how much it moves) of the shifting might vary from one movement to another. Therefore, our evidence confirmation method must be designed to detect a specific range of speeds (i.e. frequency) and amplitudes (i.e. wavelet scale). We propose a two-step process for confirming the body shifting by looking at the signal from both frequency and wavelet domains. In particular, we (1) acquire the frequency of the body shifting as shown in Section 3.2.1. We then (2) compare the waveform of the shifting with the template by calculating the coefficient between the two using the Dynamic Time Wrapping technique [28, 75]. The evidence is confirmed when the frequency is less than 5Hz and the coefficient is under a preset threshold. This threshold is determined by the practical possible range of body shifting amplitude.

■ **Evidence #3: Coefficient Invariance**: This evidence is to confirm that the body shifting is a discrete event that is similar to the template. The intuition for this evidence stems from the fact that body shifting movements are unexpected and non-uniform events triggered by various environmental and electronic artifacts. As a result, two or more consecutive body shifting motions are not expected to be similar. As one of the wavelet transformation properties, coefficient invariance can be used to confirm if a template is present on a trunk of signal once and only once. In particular, the coefficients are retained and even enhanced as the transformation scale increases [13] for each body shifting event. Hence, if the signal is of the template form and non-repetitive for 4 consecutive body shifting cycles, the body shifting event is confirmed. In short, the coefficient invariance evidence is confirmed if the coefficient magnitude monotonically increases across multiple body shifting events detected by evidence #2 as the transformation scale increases.

- **Evidence #4: Temporal Consistency**: While the previous evidence (#3) can capture the discontinuity and repetitive of an event, it could also introduce false positive by counting *short* and *discrete surges* of signals caused by noises in the environment. This evidence is introduced to address this very issue. The key idea is to observe the spread of the signal at different sampling rates. As the sampling rate reduces, the coefficient of the noise (discrete surges) decays because the wireless samples that represent the surges are reduced or disappear. Let t_1 be the spread of the signal at sampling rate f_{s1}, t_2 be the spread of the signal at sampling rate f_{s2}, $f_1 > f_2$. t_1 and t_2 can be approximated from the spread of the wavelet coefficient that is over the threshold. Wavelet decomposition [44] is used to collect this evidence. If t_1 and t_2 at two consecutive levels of decomposition are close to each other, the evidence is confirmed.

- **Evidence #5: Event Singularity**: As the fluctuation of the drone is in the wavelet pattern, the direction of fluctuation is very unique. The direction of the body shifting can be obtained by the sign of extremum of the *wavelet coefficients*. The direction must be changed between two consecutive extrema at the same frequency with that of the body shifting at different levels of decomposition. To confirm the fluctuation is from the drone body, the sign of the extremum coefficient needs to alternate while the magnitudes of coefficients remain similar. While evidence #2 shows the similarity of the signal representing body shifting and the template, evidences #3 and #4 make sure there is no false positive due to the noises in the RF domain, evidence #5 confirms that the change of body shifting behavior should cross-interleave the balance state.

- **Evidence #6: Drone Body Vibration**: As shown in subsection 3.2.2, the drone body vibration is observable through a short-time Fourier analysis. The evidence is obtained when maximum power distribution of the peak frequency belongs to the range of drone's body vibration. This evidence is used to identify the drone versus other interference sources such as mobile AP carrying by a walking user or the embedded AP on a moving vehicle.

The different forms of evidence are collected at each time window. The decision is made based on the number of forms of evidence that are confirmed on each window. We sort the evidence based on their uniqueness as the signature for drones. All the evidence is combined linearly for the final decision of detection. That is, Matthan concludes a drone is present only when all the forms of evidence are confirmed. In Section 4, we show the contribution of each form of evidence to the accuracy of Matthan.

4. PERFORMANCE EVALUATION

4.1 Experimental Setup

We implement Matthan using the SDR USRP B200 mini [77]. The USRP board is sampled at 100kHz to collect wireless samples from the drone's communication channel. The USRP board is configured as a receiver connecting to a 2.4GHz 20dBi gain directional antenna [37]. The wireless samples collected from USRP are sent to a laptop for data processing and filtering. The Wi-Fi channel of the drone's communication is identified by Wi-Fi Analyzer [25]. This application provides the channel ID and frequency for listening to the drone's communication. The collected data are stored in binary files and further processed using MATLAB.

We conducted experiments in three different environments including a parking lot in the downtown of a city (*urban*), a soccer field inside our university (*campus*), and an open field (*sub-urban*) as depicted in Figure 9. In each environment, the data are collected when the drone is flying at different distances with respect to our receiver. We collect data at the maximum distance of 100m, 200m, and 600m in urban, campus, and sub-urban environments, respectively. The drone is controlled to *take off* and *hover* within the coverage area of the antenna receiver's beam during all experiments.

Figure 9: Testing locations: (a) Urban (Parking area), (b) University campus, and (c) Sub-urban

The experiment was conducted on 7 different drones of different models and manufacturers as shown in Figure 10, including the Parrot Bebop [56], Protocol Dronium One Special Edition [60], Sky Viper [68], Swift Stream [70], Parrot AR DRone [55], Protocol Galileo Stealth [61], and DJI Phantom [22]. The Bebop, Dronium, Skype Viper, ARDrone, and DJI Phantom send Wi-Fi signals from the Wi-Fi card mounted on their body for either controlling the channel or streaming video. Protocol Galileo Stealth and Swift Stream emit Wi-Fi signals from the plug-n-play cameras came with the drones.

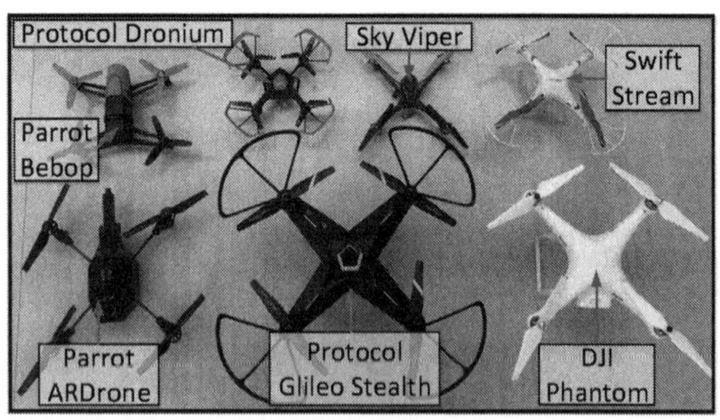

Figure 10: Drones used during experiments

To test whether the drone's RF signal could be differentiated from those of other mobile wireless devices, we also

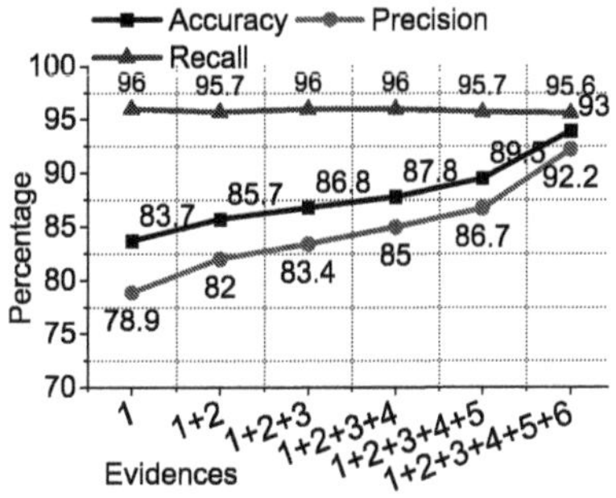

Figure 11: Detection accuracy with increasing forms of evidence.

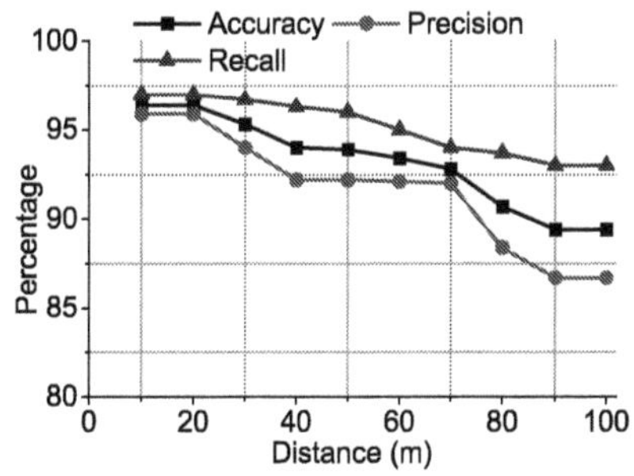

Figure 12: Detection accuracy at different distances.

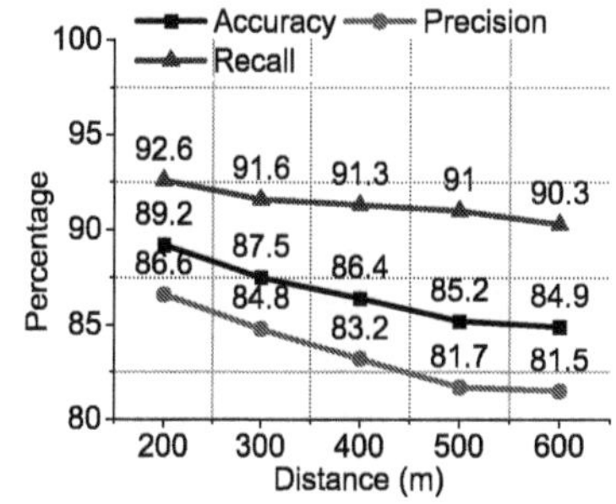

Figure 13: Detection accuracy at long distances.

evaluated two other scenarios when a mobile AP was carried inside a moving vehicle or by a walking person. First, the user configures a mobile device to create a Hotspot (mobile AP) to emit Wi-Fi signals. We use another mobile phone (client phone) to connect to the mobile AP. The client phone streams Youtube video continuously. We asked the user to carry both client and the mobile AP to walk around at a distance of 50m away from the wireless system. Secondly, the client and mobile AP are placed inside a car which moves around in the coverage area of the wireless system at a distance of 50m to 100m away. The vehicle is moving at 20 mph (32 km/h) speed. In both scenarios, the mobile AP and client are always within the coverage area of the system.

We then segmented the collected data into two main types: *drone* and *no drone*. Each segment has a length of 10 seconds. The "drone" data contains the wireless segments that correspond to the moment where the drone is flying in the environment. Similarly, the "no drone" data contains the wireless segments that correspond to the moment at which there is no drone in the environment (the drone is completely turned off). More specifically, the "no drone" data contains types of data including "environment noises", "human carrying mobile AP", and "mobile AP augmented inside a car".

4.2 Evaluation Results

In this section, we evaluate the performance of Matthan at different distances (from 10m to 600m), with 7 different types of drones, and at different environmental setups (urban, campus, sub-urban). We use *accuracy*, *precision* and *recall* as the performance metrics for evaluation. The *accuracy*, *precision*, and *recall* are calculated from True Positive (TP), True Negative (TN), False Positive (FP), and False Negative (FN). The calculations are given as follows: $accuracy = \frac{TP+TN}{TP+FP+FN+TN}$, $precision = \frac{TP}{TP+FP}$, and $recall = \frac{TP}{TP+FN}$.

4.2.1 Detection Performance vs. Number of Evidences

As stated in Section 3, Matthan makes detection decision by collecting evidences that are resulted from its analysis of the collected wireless samples.

We run the evaluation on the segmented data set of 600 segments of 10 seconds data (300 segments of drone's presence and 300 other segments from the environment, human walker carrying mobile AP, and mobile AP inside a moving car). This data is collected when the Bebop is at 50m distance from the Matthan system. The performance of detection is shown in Figure 11 in which the evidence IDs are corresponding to the IDs presented in Section 3. As can be seen, the accuracy of the system is as low as 83.7% when the system uses only the first form of evidence to detect the drone. More importantly, the system obtained a precision of detection around 78.9%. Such performance is not really usable for reliable detection. So, the first evidence only helps to detect the drone in an environment where the system receives minimal interference from other Wi-Fi sources. However, based on this evidence, Matthan cannot detect the drone within environments that contain a large amount of interference. When more evidences are combined, the performance increases significantly. More specifically, we can observe how the false positive rate diminishes and precision correspondingly rises as more evidences are integrated. Initially, the precision of the system is as low as 78.9% with only one part of evidence and increases successively to 86.7% once the first five forms of evidence are considered. Matthan does not recognize all of the wireless samples representing a human carrying an AP or a mobile AP inside a car as drone data because the standard deviations of the wireless samples in these cases are sometime smaller than the detection threshold. From our observations, the standard deviations of the signal in these scenarios are only incorrectly identified as the signal from the drone only when the user goes toward or backward Matthan (with distance less than 5m). Finally, when the vibration detection is considered (evidence #6), the overall *precision* rises to 92.2% (corresponding with 93.9% of *accuracy* and 95.6% for *recall*). This result is obtained due to the fact that the last evidence is well-represented for the uniqueness of drone's body vibration in the environment.

4.2.2 Impact of distance

We also analyze the impact of the distance between the detection system and the drone on Matthan's performance. The evaluation is conducted for both short and long distances. At short distances, we analyze the performance of the system when the drone is from 10m to 100m away. Bebop data from the urban environment experiment is presented for this analysis. At each location, 600 segments of data are analyzed (300 segments of drone's presence). All 6 forms of evidence are used to calculate the results of detection. The results are shown in Figure 12. The system obtained up to 96.5% of *accuracy*, 95.9% of *precision* and 97% of *recall* when the drone is 10m away from the detection system. When the distance increases, the performance of the detection falls to 89.4% of *accuracy*, 86.7% of *precision* and 93% of *recall* at 100m. Note that with audio-based detection techniques, the most recent report shows that the

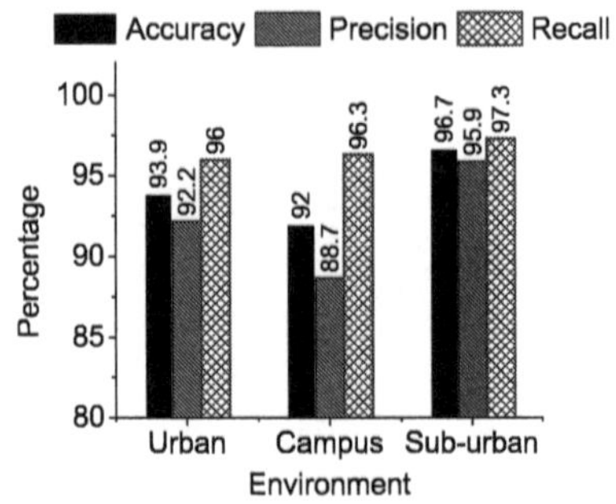

Figure 14: Detection accuracy in different environments.

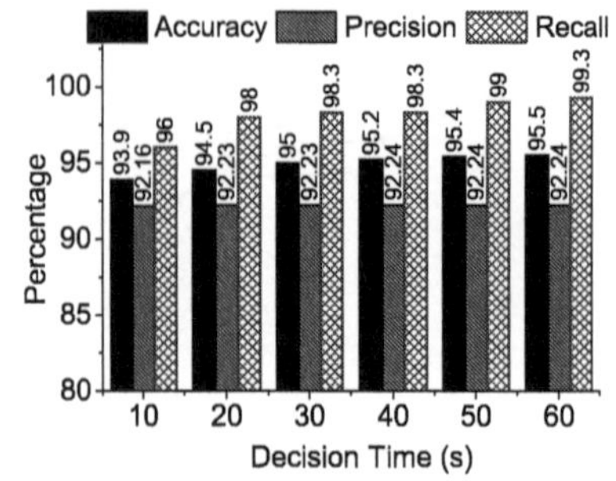

Figure 15: Detection accuracy with different decision times.

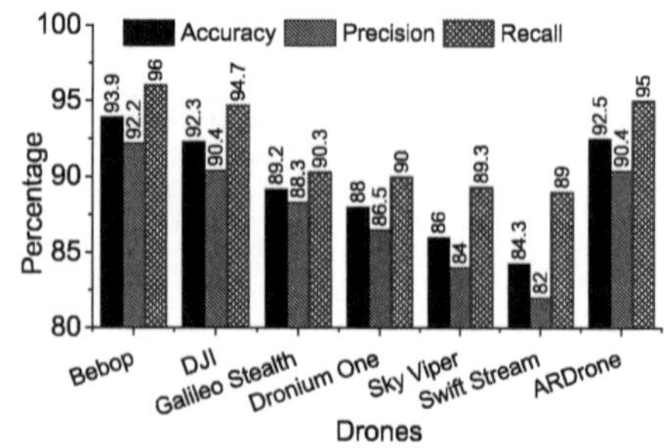

Figure 16: Performance across different drones.

drones are correctly detected with distance less than 30m, and this technique completely fails with distance more than 50m [29]. Similarly, video techniques can be performed for detection at distances less than 50m with large drones [65, 64].

The Matthan's performance is further evaluated when the distance between the drone and Matthan is from 200m to 600m. We used a sub-urban data set for this evaluation. We used 200 segments (100 segments with drones' presence) at each distance to evaluate the system. Figure 13 shows the performance of Matthan at these longer distances. The system obtained 84.9% of *accuracy*, 81.5% of *precision*, and 90.3% of *recall* at 600m distance. We were limited to 600m due to the space constraints of the testing location, but hope to find another venue with greater range.

4.2.3 Impact of environmental setup

We also evaluate the impact of the environment noise to Matthan's performance. We use the 50m data set from the Bebop drone at three locations (urban, campus, and sub-urban) for this evaluation. The impact of mobile APs is also taken into account. One half of the data set are from the drone, another half includes the data from the environmental noises and human carrying a mobile AP. The data from mobile APs inside the campus environment is not available because we cannot drive a car inside the campus. The results of drone detection are shown in Figure 14. We use 600 segments of data and 300 segments from the drone's presence. The system obtained the best performance in the sub-urban environment as this area has little effect from environmental noise as well as multi-path reflection. The system can achieve up to 96.7% of *accuracy*, 95.9% and 97.3% of *precision* and *recall*, respectively. The campus environment has a number of wireless access points operating over different Wi-Fi channels, and hence it is found that the drone communication channel usually interferes with other static APs in the campus environment. At the time of the experiment, there were 16 Wi-Fi APs in the same vicinity using Wi-Fi Analyzer app [25]. Therefore, the system creates more false alarms (false positive) in the campus environment compared with urban and sub-urban environments. However, Matthan still performs 92% of *accuracy*, 88.7% of *precision* and 96.3% of *recall* in the most interfering environment (campus).

4.2.4 Impact of time budget

Detecting the drone is also challenging due to the limited time budget within which the drone flies across the detection system. We are interested in analyzing the detection accuracy of Matthan with different time budgets for detection. The key motivation is to understand the performance when the drone stays longer inside the coverage area. We use the data set from the Bebop drone at 50m distance in an urban environment for this evaluation. We use 600 segments of data with 300 segments from the drone's presence. We increase the duration of each measurement (segment) from 10s to 60s, and a decision is made for each segment. Figure 15 shows the performance obtained for different time budgets. Matthan obtains up to 95.5% of accuracy with 60s budget of detection. The *accuracy* and *recall* increase as we give more time for Matthan to make a decision, unlike the *precision*.

4.2.5 Performance across different drones

We evaluate the performance of Matthan for different types of drones including Parrot Bebop [56], Protocol Dronium One Special Edition [60], Sky Viper [68], Swift Stream [70], Parrot AR DRone [55], Protocol Galileo Stealth [61], and DJI Phantom [22]. Galileo Stealth and Swift Stream and some small drones in the market are usually configured at a specific frequency that does not belong to any Wi-Fi's channel. These drones are very light-weight and cannot carry much weight. They usually utilize a Wi-Fi camera for video streaming and navigation. As the camera is attached to the drone, the wireless signal emitted by the Wi-Fi camera would be very similar to the controlling signal from the drones if there is no shock absorbing mechanism is in-place for the camera. We found that it is the case in the drone of our procession in this experiment. Figure 16 shows the accuracy of detecting different drones using Matthan. Matthan performs with the highest detection results for heavy drones such as Bebop, DJI, Galileo Stealth, and ARDrone. We found that those four drones generate similar signatures in body shifting as well as vibration frequency range. The Dronium and Swift Stream drones are more light-weight. We observed that there was less vibration generated in the light-weight drones than the heavier ones, which explains the improved results for the heavier drones.

4.2.6 Drone classification

It is also important to identify which drone is flying in the coverage area after detecting its presence. Though it is not the focus of this work, we want to explore if it is even possible with Matthan. We conducted a classifier based on the physical characteristics of the drones to detect them. The key idea is to identify the frequency of vibration of each drone to detect/classify it. Drones are often uniquely designed in weight, structure, materials, propellers' size and so on. .

Drone	Bebop	DJI	Galieo	Dronium
f_v (Hz)	60	100	140	35
Drone	**Sky Viper**	**Swift Stream**	**AR Drone**	
f_v (Hz)	50	20	70	

Table 1: A table summary of the vibration frequency of different drones f_v.

Those characteristics affect the forces generated by the propellers and therefore also affect the vibration frequency of the drones. We employed a similar experimental setup as in section 2.3.1. We attached the IMUs to different drones to collect the motion data. The motion data is then analyzed to determine the central and the dominant frequencies of vibration. According to this central frequency, we approximate the vibration frequency windows as in Table 1.

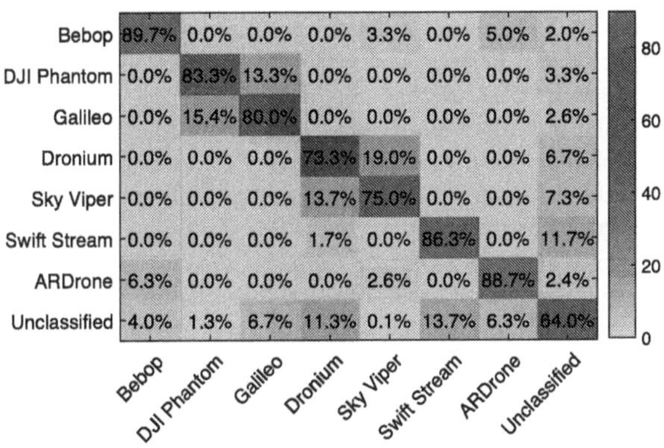

Figure 17: Confusion matrix from drone classification based on FFT analysis.

5. DISCUSSION

Our system has focused on detecting the presence of drones through their unique inherent physical movement signatures on WiFi domain. We wish to expand our experiments to consider a wider variety of drones and greater distances. Our system should be expanded to incorporate automated channel sensing [47, 48, 14, 35], as the current experiments fix the eavesdropping to a specific communication channel. Such an approach should improve our ability to detect diverse drones that operate with different protocols over the same unlicensed Wi-Fi frequency bands, or that communicate on non-Wi-Fi frequency bands. Our system should also be enhanced to integrate automated antenna steering/ beamforming, as our current experiments fix the direction of the antenna. Note that the directional antenna is only used for improving the gain of detection at a certain direction, omi-directional antenna can also be used to detect the presence of the drone. Localizing the position of the drones is the next logical step, but this consideration is outside the scope of this paper.

We would like to conduct experiments that test non-line-of-sight RF detection in the presence of occlusions such as buildings. We intend to pursue further the extent to which Matthan can distinguish between individual drones as well as different types of drones. We also desire to conduct a more detailed examination of fusion algorithms such as boosting and bagging for combining multiple weak detectors into a stronger fused detector. In addition, we wish to detect other aspects of the drone beyond merely its presence, such as its location, speed and direction. Also in the future we hope to address the fact that our system is not currently capable of detecting multiple drones in the same vicinity at the same time. Moreover, we would like to evaluate the impact of the environment, e.g. windy condition, to the accuracy of detection. Finally, while reactive control [9] is considered as one solutions to reduce a number of body-shifting events, Matthan's algorithm can be slightly modified to update the weight of each evidence to focus more on the impact of the drone's body vibration in detection.

6. RELATED WORK

Multiple sensing modalities have been employed for drone detection, including audio, video and RF. First, an acoustic approach collects a database of acoustic signatures from different drones and uses this database to compare with observed sound signals to make a decision [23]. Challenges to this approach include detection accuracy in noisy urban environments and at distance, keeping this database updated, and new quieter drone models [50].

Second, a video-based solution employs a camera to detect drones [20]. Challenges to this approach include operation at night, compute-intensive image processing that must distinguish between a drone and say a bird at distance, and occlusion by buildings that limit distance in an urban environment. Thermal cameras have been proposed to detect drones at night [34] but are a relatively expensive technique.

A variety of RF-based solutions have been proposed for drone detection. One approach is to monitor the 1MHz - 6.8GHz band, and any unknown transmitter is assumed to be a drone [19]. This would suffer from false positives. Another approach is MAC address collection and analysis [57], but this can be bypassed easily by spoofing the MAC address. The frequency of packet communication on the uplink and downlink between the drone and its controller has also been used for detection[53]. However, other periodic packet sources at similar rates such as VOIP traffic could be mistaken as drone communication.

Radar-based techniques actively transmit RF waves and look for the reflection to determine the presence of the drone. WiDop [1] is a non-coherent radar system which exploits the modulation produced by a target in a clutter with a non-coherent X-band radar. WiDop is claimed to have advantages over a coherent radar in terms of low cost radar and high range, but there exist disadvantages due to the radar angle and lack of high precision. Another radar technique is passive bistatic radar [80, 10, 52, 51, 54], which consists of a passive receiver to process a received signal from a known source of transmission and reflected signals from the moving target. These systems have advantages of low cost, fast update of the target position and variable frequency allocation. In conjunction with the usage of abundant WiFi sources as reference transmitters, multiple algorithms [17, 6] have been proposed for signal processing in passive bistatic radar systems such as MTI and LS adaptive filters [11] or compressive sensing [42]. Moreover, multistatic radar [18, 39], which includes more than two receivers, is also used to detect flying objects by calculating the radar cross section. The use of multiple receivers increase the accuracy of the system. Radar generally introduces interference due to active transmissions, which is especially problematic when there is a large amount of legitimate packet traffic over RF bands such as Wi-Fi, especially in crowded environments.

7. CONCLUSION

This paper introduced Matthan, a system for detecting the presence of drones by identifying unique signatures of a drone's body vibration and body shifting in the Wi-Fi signal transmitted by a drone. The joint detector integrates evidence from both a frequency-based detector that looks for the maximum frequency peak to be in the range of 50-220 Hz to indicate drone body vibration as well as a wavelet-based detector that captures the sudden shifts of the drone's body by computing wavelets at different scales from the temporal RF signal. Matthan was prototyped and evaluated using SDR radios in three different real-world environments. When given a mix of data containing both drone and non-drone cases (Wi-Fi-equipped car, walking user with a smartphone on, and no drone scenarios), we showed that Matthan is capable of differentiating drone signals from other mobile wireless devices by achieving high accuracy, precision and recall, all above 90 percent at 50 meters. We also showed how Matthan's accuracy, precision and recall varies with distance, dropping to 90 percent accuracy and 80-85 percent precision and recall at a distance of 600 meters. Matthan's performance was studied across seven different drones, where the performance varied only moderately, and was tested across three different environments, again varying only moderately in performance. We also present how Matthan's performance improves as it is allowed more time to accumulate data. Finally, a confusion matrix illustrates Matthan's potential to identify specific drones from among seven different drones.

Acknowledgements

We thank the shepherd Heather Zheng, the anonymous reviewers, and Shane Transue for their insightful comments. This research was partially funded by NSF grant 1602428.

8. REFERENCES

[1] R. Abileah, P. A. Fox, and J. W. Maresca Jr. Detection of low observable objects in clutter using non-coherent radars, Feb. 23 2016. US Patent 9,268,008.

[2] Amazon. Amazon prime air. https://goo.gl/Ags0YJ, 2016. [Online; accessed Nov 01, 2016].

[3] Arduino. Pro mini. https://goo.gl/AGFeCN, 2016. [Online; accessed Nov 01, 2016].

[4] BBC. Dutch police fight drones with eagles. https://goo.gl/PnJCcd, September 12, 2016.

[5] L. L. Beranek. *Noise and vibration control engineering: principles and applications.* Wiley, 1992.

[6] Berger et al. Signal processing for passive radar using ofdm waveforms. *IEEE Journal of Selected Topics in Signal Processing*, pages 226–238, 2010.

[7] Bluetooth. Bluetooth hc-05. https://goo.gl/0PKs6r, 2016. [Online; accessed Nov 01, 2016].

[8] S. Bouabdallah, A. Noth, and R. Siegwart. PID vs LQ control techniques applied to an indoor micro quadrotor. pages 2451–2456, 2004.

[9] E. Bregu, N. Casamassima, D. Cantoni, L. Mottola, and K. Whitehouse. Reactive control of autonomous drones. In *ACM MobiSys*, pages 207–219, 2016.

[10] J. Brown, K. Woodbridge, A. Stove, and S. Watts. Air target detection using airborne passive bistatic radar. *Electronics letters*, pages 1396–1397, 2010.

[11] Buonanno et al. Wifi-based passive bistatic radar by using moving target indicator and least square adaptive filtering. In *IEEE International Symposium on Phased Array Systems & Technology*, pages 174–179, 2013.

[12] Castillo et al. Real-time stabilization and tracking of a four-rotor mini rotorcraft. *IEEE Transactions on Control Systems Technology*, pages 510–516, 2004.

[13] P. Chaovalit et al. Discrete Wavelet Transform-based Time Series Analysis and Mining. *ACM Comput. Surv.*, pages 6:1–6:37, 2011.

[14] R. I. C. Chiang et al. A Quantitative Analysis of Spectral Occupancy Measurements for Cognitive Radio. In *IEEE VTC*, pages 3016–3020, 2007.

[15] CNN. Drone crashes onto piste, misses champion skier by inches. https://goo.gl/jtPdLh, 2015. [Online; accessed Nov 01, 2016].

[16] CNN. Dubai deploys a 'drone hunter' to keep its airport open. https://goo.gl/iXJMu3, 2016. [Online; accessed Nov 01, 2016].

[17] F. Colone et al. A multistage processing algorithm for disturbance removal and target detection in passive bistatic radar. *IEEE Transactions on Aerospace and Electronic Systems*, pages 698–722, 2009.

[18] E. Conte et al. Multistatic radar detection: synthesis and comparison of optimum and suboptimum receivers. *Communications, Radar and Signal Processing, IEE Proceedings F*, pages 484–494, 1983.

[19] DDC-LLC. Domestic drone countermeasures. https://goo.gl/ZAju6O.

[20] DeDrone. Drone tracker. http://www.dedrone.com/en/, 2016. [Online; accessed Nov 01, 2016].

[21] I. C. Dikmen, A. Arisoy, and H. Temeltas. Attitude control of a quadrotor. In *RAST*, pages 722–727, 2009.

[22] DJI. DJI Phantom. http://www.dji.com/, 2016. [Online; accessed Nov 01, 2016].

[23] DroneShield. Drone detection. https://goo.gl/y5ZuMm, 2016. [Online; accessed Nov 01, 2016].

[24] J. Escareno, S. Salazar-Cruz, and R. Lozano. Embedded control of a four-rotor UAV. In *American Control Conference*, page 6, 2006.

[25] Farproc. Wifi analyzer. http://tinyurl.com/8yqxge9.

[26] J. Fleureau et al. Generic Drone Control Platform for Autonomous Capture of Cinema Scenes. In *ACM MobiSys Dronet*, pages 35–40, 2016.

[27] FlexReport. The economics of drone delivery. https://goo.gl/RN4irU, 2016. [Online; accessed Nov 01, 2016].

[28] T. Giorgino. Computing and visualizing dynamic time warping alignments in R: The dtw package. *Journal of Statistical Software*, pages 1–24, 2009.

[29] L. Hauzenberger and E. H. Ohlsson. Drone detection using audio analysis. Master's thesis, Department of Electrical and Information Technology, Lund University, Lund, Scania, Sweden, 2015. https://goo.gl/58BGoN.

[30] R. Heffernan et al. Vibration analysis of the SA349/2 helicopter. *NASA Technical Memorandum 102794*, 1991.

[31] G. Hoffmann et al. Quadrotor Helicopter Flight Dynamics and Control: Theory and Experiment. In *AIAA Guidance, Navigation and Control Conference and Exhibit*. 2007.

[32] H. Huang et al. Aerodynamics and control of autonomous quadrotor helicopters in aggressive maneuvering. In *IEEE ICRA*, pages 3277–3282, 2009.

[33] T. HUMPHREYS. Statement on the security threat posed by unmanned aerial systems and possible countermeasures, 2015.

[34] IEC. IEC infrared systems: Banshee. https://goo.gl/TLDjFb, 2016. [Online; accessed Nov 01, 2016].

[35] M. H. Islam et al. Spectrum Survey in Singapore: Occupancy Measurements and Analyses. In *EAI CROWNCOM*, pages 1–7, 2008.

[36] B. Jansen. Drone crash at white house reveals security risks. USA Today, January 26, 2015.

[37] L-Com. 2.4 / 5.1-5.8 GHz 20dBi Flat Panel Antenna. https://goo.gl/77WdQD, 2016. [Online; accessed Nov 01, 2016].

[38] Y.-C. Lai and S.-S. Jan. Attitude estimation based on fusion of gyroscopes and single antenna GPS for small UAVs under the influence of vibration. *GPS Solutions*, pages 67–77, 2011.

[39] S. K. Laleh et al. Detection, identification and tracking of flying objects in three dimensions using multistatic radars. *Int'l J. of Communications, Network and System Sciences*, 2009.

[40] X. Liu and R. Randall. Blind source separation of internal combustion engine piston slap from other measured vibration signals. *Mechanical Systems and Signal Processing*, pages 1196–1208, 2005.

[41] T. Madani and A. Benallegue. Backstepping Control for a Quadrotor Helicopter. In *IEEE/RSJ IROS*, pages 3255–3260, 2006.

[42] P. Maechler et al. Compressive sensing for wifi-based passive bistatic radar. In *EUSIPCO*, pages 1444–1448, 2012.

[43] R. Mahony, V. Kumar, and P. Corke. Multirotor aerial vehicles: Modeling, estimation, and control of quadrotor. *IEEE robotics & automation magazine*, pages 20–32, 2012.

[44] S. G. Mallat. A Theory for Multiresolution Signal Decomposition: The Wavelet Representation. *IEEE Trans. Pattern Anal. Mach. Intell.*, pages 674–693, July 1989.

[45] Marketsandmarkets. Multirotor uav market worth $2.28 billion by 2020. https://goo.gl/1M43OD, 2016. [Online; accessed Nov 01, 2016].

[46] P. McGreevy. Private drones are putting firefighters in 'immediate danger,' california fire official says. LA Times, August 18, 2015.

[47] M. A. McHenry and S. Chunduri. Nsf spectrum occupancy measurement project summary. *Shared Spectrum Company Report*, 2005.

[48] M. A. McHenry et al. C. s. chicago spectrum occupancy measurements and analysis and a long-term studies proposal. *TAPAS*, 2005.

[49] Z. Naboulsi. Drone detection: What works and what doesn't. https://goo.gl/MkfHoF, 2016. [Online; accessed Nov 01, 2016].

[50] Newshub. Big noise for kiwis' quiet drone. https://goo.gl/ioa6hj, April 25, 2016.

[51] Nguyen et al. WiKiSpiro: Non-contact Respiration Volume Monitoring During Sleep. pages 27–29, New York, NY, USA, 2016.

[52] P. Nguyen et al. Continuous and fine-grained breathing volume monitoring from afar using wireless signals. In *IEEE INFOCOM 2016*, pages 1–9, 2016.

[53] P. Nguyen, M. Ravindranatha, A. Nguyen, R. Han, and T. Vu. Investigating cost-effective rf-based detection of drones. In *ACM MobiSys Dronet*, pages 17–22, 2016.

[54] N. P. et al. Continuous and Fine-grained Respiration Volume Monitoring Using Continuous Wave Radar. In *ACM MobiCom*, pages 266–268. ACM, 2015.

[55] Parrot. ARDrone. https://goo.gl/deJFd6, 2016. [Online; accessed Nov 01, 2016].

[56] Parrot. Parrot Bebop Drone. https://goo.gl/xZ36IF, 2016. [Online; accessed Nov 01, 2016].

[57] M. Peacock and M. N. Johnstone. Towards detection and control of civilian unmanned aerial vehicles. 2013.

[58] J.-S. Pleban et al. Hacking and securing the ar. drone 2.0 quadcopter: investigations for improving the security of a toy. In *SPIE Electronic Imaging*, 2014.

[59] W. Post. Prisons try to stop drones from delivering drugs, porn and cellphones to inmates. https://goo.gl/6DapQM, October 13, 2016.

[60] Protocol New York. Dronium ONE - Special Edition WiFi. https://goo.gl/u4NjuS, 2016. [Online; accessed Nov 01, 2016].

[61] Protocol New York. Protocol Galileo Stealth. https://goo.gl/TVGPkx, 2016. [Online; accessed Nov 01, 2016].

[62] G. V. Raffo and dothers. An Integral Predictive/Nonlinear H∞ Control Structure for a Quadrotor Helicopter. *Automatica*, pages 29–39, 2010.

[63] Reportbuyer. Global multi-rotor drone market - analysis and forecast 2016-2022 (focus on major applications payloads and, pricing). https://goo.gl/Z6Z2gF, 2017. [Online; accessed Apr 17, 2017].

[64] A. Rozantsev, V. Lepetit, and P. Fua. Flying Objects Detection from a Single Moving Camera. In *Conference on Computer Vision and Pattern Recognition (CVPR)*, 2015.

[65] A. Rozantsev, V. Lepetit, and P. Fua. Detecting Flying Objects using a Single Moving Camera. *IEEE Transactions on Pattern Analysis and Machine Intelligence*, pages 879 – 892, 2017.

[66] D. Sathyamoorthy. A review of security threats of unmanned aerial vehicles and mitigation steps.

[67] L.-K. Shark and C. Yu. Design of Matched Wavelets Based on Generalized Mexican-hat Function. *Signal Process.*, pages 1451–1469, 2006.

[68] Skyrocket. Sky Viper. http://sky-viper.com/, 2016. [Online; accessed Nov 01, 2016].

[69] Sparkfun-InvenSense. Mpu 9150. https://goo.gl/Hh3viK, 2016. [Online; accessed Nov 01, 2016].

[70] S. Stream. Swiftstreamrc. https://goo.gl/sB0Kro, 2016. [Online; accessed Nov 01, 2016].

[71] C. Taswell and K. C. McGill. Algorithm 735: Wavelet transform algorithms for finite-duration discrete-time signals. *ACM Trans. Math. Softw.*, pages 398–412, 1994.

[72] A. Tayebi and S. McGilvray. Attitude stabilization of a four-rotor aerial robot. In *IEEE CDC*, pages 1216–1221, 2004.

[73] Techcrunch. Firefighting drone serves as a reminder to be careful with crowdfunding campaigns. https://goo.gl/WwFgWk, 2016. [Online; accessed Nov 01, 2016].

[74] L. Times. To keep drones out of high-risk areas, companies try hijacking them and shooting them down. https://goo.gl/MqDag5, 2016. [Online; accessed Nov 01, 2016].

[75] P. Tormene et al. Matching incomplete time series with dynamic time warping: An algorithm and an application to post-stroke rehabilitation. *Artificial Intelligence in Medicine*, pages 11–34, 2008.

[76] D. Tse and P. Viswanath. *Fundamentals of Wireless Communication*. 2005.

[77] USRP. B200 Mini. https://goo.gl/7ssQDP, 2016. [Online; accessed Nov 01, 2016].

[78] R. Vander Schaaf. *What technologies or integrating concepts are needed for the US military to counter future missile threats looking out to 2040?* PhD thesis, US Army, 2014.

[79] D. Waldstein. Drone crash interrupts match. New York Times, September 3, 2015.

[80] N. J. Willis and H. D. Griffiths. *Advances in bistatic radar*. SciTech Publishing, 2007.

[81] Wired. Surrey now has the uk's 'largest' police drone project. https://goo.gl/VzrdQf, 2016. [Online; accessed Nov 01, 2016].

[82] K. M. Zemalache, L. Beji, and H. Marref. Control of an under-actuated system: application a four rotors rotorcraft. In *IEEEROBIO*, pages 404–409, 2005.

[83] Z. Zuo. Trajectory tracking control design with command-filtered compensation for a quadrotor. *IET Control Theory Applications*, pages 2343–2355, 2010.

System Service Call-oriented Symbolic Execution of Android Framework with Applications to Vulnerability Discovery and Exploit Generation

Lannan Luo[†]*, Qiang Zeng[‡]*, Chen Cao[§], Kai Chen[§♭], Jian Liu[§♭], Limin Liu[§♭], Neng Gao[§♭], Min Yang[≀], Xinyu Xing[†], and Peng Liu[†]
[†]The Pennsylvania State University, USA
[‡]Temple University, USA
[§]SKLOIS, Institute of Information Engineering, Chinese Academy of Sciences
[♭]School of Cyber Security, University of Chinese Academy of Sciences
[≀]Fudan University, China
{lzl144, xxing, pliu}@ist.psu.edu, {qzeng}@temple.edu,
{caochen, chenkai, liujian6, liulimin, gaoneng}@iie.ac.cn, {m_yang}@fudan.edu.cn

ABSTRACT

Android Application Framework is an integral and foundational part of the Android system. Each of the 1.4 billion Android devices relies on the system services of Android Framework to manage applications and system resources. Given its critical role, a vulnerability in the framework can be exploited to launch large-scale cyber attacks and cause severe harms to user security and privacy. Recently, many vulnerabilities in Android Framework were exposed, showing that it is vulnerable and exploitable. However, most of the existing research has been limited to analyzing Android applications, while there are very few techniques and tools developed for analyzing Android Framework. In particular, to our knowledge, there is no previous work that analyzes the framework through symbolic execution, an approach that has proven to be very powerful for vulnerability discovery and exploit generation. We design and build the first system, CENTAUR, that enables symbolic execution of Android Framework. Due to some unique characteristics of the framework, such as its middleware nature and extraordinary complexity, many new challenges arise and are tackled in CENTAUR. In addition, we demonstrate how the system can be applied to discovering new vulnerability instances, which can be exploited by several recently uncovered attacks against the framework, and to generating PoC exploits.

Keywords

Symbolic execution; concolic execution; vulnerability discovery; exploit generation; Android Framework

*These two authors have contributed equally.

Permission to make digital or hard copies of all or part of this work for personal or classroom use is granted without fee provided that copies are not made or distributed for profit or commercial advantage and that copies bear this notice and the full citation on the first page. Copyrights for components of this work owned by others than ACM must be honored. Abstracting with credit is permitted. To copy otherwise, or republish, to post on servers or to redistribute to lists, requires prior specific permission and/or a fee. Request permissions from permissions@acm.org.

MobiSys'17, June 19-23, 2017, Niagara Falls, NY, USA
© 2017 ACM. ISBN 978-1-4503-4928-4/17/06...$15.00
DOI: http://dx.doi.org/10.1145/3081333.3081361

1. INTRODUCTION

The global smartphone market is booming and Android dominates the market with a share of 87.6% [30]. As of 2016, there were 1.4 billion active Android devices [52] and over 65 billion Android apps that had been downloaded and installed [49]. An Android app relies on the Android Application Framework (*Android Framework*, for short) to make it useful. For example, all the user interface designs and multi-tasking features would not work without WMS (Window Manager Service) and AMS (Activity Manager Service) provided by Android Framework; as another example, apps cannot obtain the GPS location without LMS (Location Manager Service) of the framework. Therefore, Android Framework is an integral and foundational part of the Android system; it runs on each Android device for managing all applications and providing a generic abstraction for hardware access [26]. Recently, many vulnerabilities in Android Framework were identified [16, 17, 19, 18]. A vulnerability in the framework can lead to large-scale cyber attacks and cause serious harms to user security and privacy. For example, malicious apps can exploit such vulnerabilities to steal user passwords, take pictures in the background, launch UI spoofing attacks, and tamper with user data [45, 47, 48].

Despite the critical role of Android Framework and the security concerns due to the vulnerabilities hidden in its several million lines of code, most of the existing work has been focused on analyzing Android applications [20, 3, 13, 35, 39, 34, 44, 21, 56, 10, 11, 36, 12, 55, 53]. Very few systems and tools are available for analyzing Android Framework [4, 23, 6]; as a result, the insecurity analysis of the framework has been imprecise and/or requires significant manual effort [47, 45]. For example, Shao et al. [47] uncovered a very interesting type of Android Framework vulnerabilities that are due to inconsistent permission checking (detailed in Section 7.2); however, due to the overwhelming amount of manual effort needed to validate their findings, the process of vulnerability discovery was tedious and error-prone; moreover, the reported vulnerabilities were hard to verify since no PoC exploits were provided. Thus, there is an urgent need for techniques and tools for *precise* and *automated* insecurity analysis of Android Framework. In particular, to our knowledge, there is no

Figure 1: The getProviders service interface method.

```
1 // Defined in the LocationManagerService class
2 List<String> getProviders(Criteria criteria,
      boolean enabledOnly) {
3   int uid = Binder.getCallingUid();
4   int level = getAllowedResolutionLevel(uid);
5   ArrayList<String> out = new ArrayList<String>();
6   for (LocationProviderInterface p : mProviders) {
7     if(level >= p.requriedLevel) {
8       ...
9       out.add(p.name);
10    }
11  }
12  return out;
13 }
14 int getAllowedResolutionLevel(int uid) {
15   // Inside checkPermission(), the function
       getUserIdLPr() is invoked
16   HashSet ps = mContext.checkPermission(uid);
17   if(ps.contains(ACCESS_FINE_LOCATION))
18     return 2;
19   else if (ps.contains(ACCESS_COARSE_LOCATION))
20     return 1;
21   else
22     return 0;
23 }
24
25 // Defined in the Settings class
26 static final int FIRST_APPLICATION_UID = 10000;
27 static final int PER_USER_RANGE = 100000;
28 ArrayList<Object> mUserIds;
29 Object getUserIdLPr(int uid) {
30   if (uid >= FIRST_APPLICATION_UID) {
31     uid %= PER_USER_RANGE;
32     int index = uid - FIRST_APPLICATION_UID;
33     return mUserIds.get(index);
34   }
35 }
```

tool that is able to analyze the framework through *symbolic execution*, a precise and automated analysis approach that has proven to be very powerful for automatic vulnerability discovery and exploit generation [5, 9, 25].

This work is to fill the critical gap, aiming to (1) design and build a system that enables symbolic execution of the Android Framework code, and (2) given the description of a new type of attacks exploiting Android Framework, apply the system to precisely and automatically finding zero-day vulnerability instances and generating PoC exploits to validate the findings; such exploits can also be fed into defense systems for automated malware signature generation [5, 15].

While many symbolic execution systems have been proposed for analyzing *Windows programs* [24, 25, 7], *Unix programs* [5, 9, 8], and *Android apps* [38, 1, 31, 37, 54], none has explored how to effectively analyze such complex middleware as Android Framework. Due to unique characteristics of Android Framework, many new challenges arise when building its symbolic execution system.

First, most of the existing systems target stand-alone executables and start analysis of the code from the `main` function, while Android Framework is a large piece of middleware with a very complex initialization phase, which parses system and app settings and then prepares all the system services. Symbolic execution that starts from the main entry of Android Framework, `SystemServer.main`, would quickly cause state explosion and hence cannot reach deep code paths. On the other hand, Android Framework exports system services to apps in the form of a large number of *service interface methods* (also called *entrypoint methods*); e.g., in Android Framework 5.0, there are 3,079 entrypoint methods exported. Our insight is that, instead of analyzing Android Framework as a whole, the capability of analyzing each entrypoint method separately is the key to the *scalability* of the analysis.

However, if the analyzer skips the initialization phase and directly analyzes a service interface method, the context information, such as the type and value of variables, is missing and thus many problems may be caused, as is the case in Under-Constrained Symbolic Execution (UCSE) [42, 22, 43].

For example, Figure 1 shows the code for the service interface method `getProviders`,[1] which returns the names of the GPS providers that the calling app is allowed to access. Line 16 contains a virtual function call to `checkPermission` through `mContext`, a reference variable of the `Context` type; `Context` is an abstract class extended by four classes, including `ContextWrapper`, `ContextImpl`, `BridgeContext`, and `MockContext`, each of which implements the function `checkPermission`. Without the concrete *type* information of the object pointed to by `mContext`, it is hard to precisely determine the dispatch target of the call. Such virtual function calls prevail in the framework code.

Similarly, without the value information of variables, the state explosion problem can be exacerbated. For example, consider `mProviders` in Line 6 as an example, which is an ArrayList that stores the currently installed GPS providers; if the elements in the list are unknown, it is difficult to carry out a loop that iterates through the list. One workaround is to regard the list as a symbolic input and then handle it using lazy initialization [32]; this way, however, the loop becomes unbounded and elements of the list become symbolic, which unnecessarily exacerbates the state explosion problem.

Therefore, while it increases the scalability of analysis by symbolically executing each service interface method separately, *how to deal with the situation of the missing context information is a challenging problem (C1)*. To resolve it, we employ an analysis scheme that combines concrete execution and symbolic execution, allowing analysis to start from an arbitrary middleware API method (Section 3).

Second, Android Framework contains a large number of data structures maintained for both system services and apps. From the perspective of finding vulnerabilities exploitable by a malicious app, variables that are derived from the malicious app are under control of attackers, and thus should be specified as symbolic inputs, such that branches depending on them are all explored during the analysis. However, given a malicious app, the variables derived from it *scatter* in the form of object fields and array elements in numerous data structures.

In Figure 1, for example, `mUserIds` at Line 28 is an ArrayList that stores the information of all the installed apps with one element for each app. The object pointed to by `ps` at Line 16 is an element of `mUserIds` (Line 33); the object is derived from the calling app and thus should be handled as a symbolic input, such that all the branches in the function `getAllowedResolutionLevel` will be explored by considering different values of the object. While it is not difficult to identify variables derived from the calling app once one

[1]The code snippet has been modified slightly from the original to ease the understanding.

understands the program logic, how to automate the process, given the large number of complex data structures in the framework, is an intriguing new problem as well as a challenge (**C2**).

Our hypothesis is that, as the framework stores information for multiple clients (i.e., apps), there must exist fixed *patterns* used to access the client-specific information when the framework services a client call, and this hypothesis is validated through our investigation. Based on the patterns how client-specific variables are accessed upon a system service call, a customized taint analysis approach, called *slim tainting*, is designed to precisely and automatically pinpoint client-specific variables (Section 4).

Third, a straightforward design is to place the symbolic execution engine inside the Android system, such that the analyzer can make use of the host execution environment including the native libraries and other supporting processes (e.g., the Service Manager process used to register and query system services). But this way the symbolic executor is tightly coupled with Android, and the implementation has to handle compatibility with the Android Runtime (ART) in terms of thread management, instruction execution, binary representation of objects, and garbage collection. This significantly complicates the implementation of the symbolic executor and makes the system brittle and hard to debug due to various incompatibility issues. Moreover, since it is unlikely to modularize the code for symbolic execution based on this design, whenever a new version of the Android system is released the symbolic execution code has to be re-inserted. To avoid the complicated and brittle implementation and the endless maintenance, a decoupled architecture is desired. However, *how to design an architecture that can make use of the Android execution environment without leading to a complicated and coupled implementation is a challenge (**C3**).*

We propose a decoupled design which builds the symbolic executor outside the Android system but is still able to make use of the Android execution environment. An innovative and critical component of the system is to migrate information generated in Android, such as the classes and objects, to the symbolic execution environment (Section 5).

We have overcome the challenges above and implemented the symbolic execution system named CENTAUR for symbolic execution of the Java code in Android Framework. The source code for CENTAUR is publicly available.[2] CENTAUR is a path exploration system that can effectively assist automatic and precise vulnerability discovery. We concretely demonstrate how CENTAUR can be applied to vulnerability discovery by considering several recently uncovered attacks that exploit the framework vulnerabilities. We show that the process minimizes the manual effort and guarantees zero-false positives, in contrast with recent researches on finding Android Framework vulnerabilities that rely on laborious and error-prone manual work [47, 45]. Finally, we make use of CENTAUR to generate PoC exploits to validate the findings. We make the following contributions.

- To our knowledge, CENTAUR is the first system that supports symbolic execution of Android Framework. It provides an approach to exploring paths in Android Framework automatically and precisely. The proposed techniques can potentially be applied to symbolic execution of other complex middleware.
- Unlike previous symbolic execution schemes that either start analysis from the main function or analyze a non-main function without the context information, we employ a scheme that allows service interface methods of middleware to be analyzed separately for much improved scalability and meanwhile provides a complete execution context.
- A novel tainting analysis technique is proposed to precisely identify the framework variables derived from a given app. It is particularly suitable for vulnerability discovery as it considers all possible values under the control of a malicious app.
- An innovative architecture that builds the symbolic executor out of the Android system is proposed. A powerful algorithm that migrates the execution context information from Android to the symbolic executor is designed.
- We have implemented CENTAUR and evaluated it in terms of the effectiveness and precision in finding vulnerabilities and generating PoC exploits.

[2]https://github.com/Android-Framewrok-Symbolic-Executor/Centaur

The remainder of the paper is organized as follows. Section 2 covers some background about Android Framework and symbolic execution. Section 3 gives an overview of the system. Section 4 describes how to identify variables as symbolic inputs. Section 5 presents how to migrate the execution context. Section 6 describes the implementation details, and Section 7 describes the evaluation. The related work is discussed in Section 8, and the paper is concluded in Section 9.

2. BACKGROUND

Android Framework. Android Framework provides a collection of system services, which implements many fundamental functionalities, such as managing the life cycle of all apps, organizing activities into tasks, and managing app packages. Most of the system services, except for the media services, run as threads in the System Server process [26]. Thus, the System Server process plays a central role in Android Framework. This work uses the services in this process as examples to illustrate the ideas and techniques, which should be applicable to other services.

A system service exposes its service interface methods invokable by apps, and a *system service call* is handled in the form of a remote procedural call through the IPC mechanism Binder, which dispatches the call to one of the threads of the target system service. Android Framework is mainly implemented in Java. E.g., in Android Framework 5.0, there are 2.4 million lines of Java code and 880 thousand lines of C/C++ code. Currently, CENTAUR can only perform symbolic execution of Java code.

Symbolic execution. Symbolic execution provides a means of efficiently exploring execution paths [33]. For example, consider the function `getAllowedResolutionLevel` in Figure 1, by assigning a symbolic value (as opposed to assigning concrete values as in fuzzing) to `ps`, symbolic execution analysis can iterate every of the three paths and precisely provide the condition that the symbolic value should satisfy for executing a given path; e.g., the symbolic execution analysis can produce the path condition for reaching Line 18: `ps.contains(ACCESS_FINE_LOCATION)`.

Symbolic execution is particularly suitable for vulnerability discovery for several reasons. First, it performs an efficient and automatic path exploration and ideally explores all possible paths. So that it is able to discover as many vulnerability instances as possible. Second, for each path explored, it records a path condition, which is a symbolic expression describing the condition that should be satisfied by the input values in order that the path is taken. Consequently, by resolving the path condition, one can obtain the concrete input values that force the execution to follow the corresponding path; the concrete input values can be used to construct exploits, and can be fed into real program execution for verifying the suspected vulnerability. This way, it guarantees zero false-positives in vulnerability discovery.

One of the main challenges in applying symbolic execution to large-sized programs is to cope with the path explosion problem, as the number of distinct execution paths is exponential in the number of branches that depend on symbolic values. We mitigate the problem using multiple ways, such as analyzing service interface methods separately and precisely identifying variables as symbolic inputs.

3. SYSTEM OVERVIEW

Our observation of Android Framework is that its execution consists of the initialization phase and the ready-for-use phase, and the initialization phase is fairly stable when the system restarts, since the system boots mainly according to the system configuration, which itself is stable. Thus, to resolve the problem of the missing context information (**C1**), we propose a *phased concrete-to-symbolic execution* (PC2SE) for analyzing middleware software like Android Framework; it runs the initialization phase as whole-system concrete execution and then performs symbolic execution starting at one of the entrypoint methods under the execution context provided by the concrete execution. It avoids the state space explosion due to the complex initialization phase and meanwhile provides the context for symbolic execution, such that the type and value information of the *input variables* (i.e., non-locally defined variables read during symbolic execution) is available.

When starting the symbolic execution from an entrypoint method, if only the parameters of the entrypoint method are set as symbolic inputs [40], the path exploration will be severely limited, leading to *over-constrained* symbolic execution. In the framework, variables derived from the malicious app (mainly its manifest file) are also under control of attackers and can affect the execution of system service calls; thus, those variables should also be set as symbolic inputs. To resolve **C2** (i.e., identifying variables derived from the malicious app as symbolic inputs), instead of tracking how information is flowed from an app to the framework, we investigate how the app-specific variables in the framework are accessed and propose *slim tainting* to identify those variables as symbolic inputs on the fly during path exploration by capturing the characteristic access patterns (Section 4). This way, the path exploration considers all possible values of these variables.

To address **C3** (i.e., to avoid complicated implementation and endless maintenance due to the coupled design), we propose a novel architecture that is suitable for PC2SE, as shown

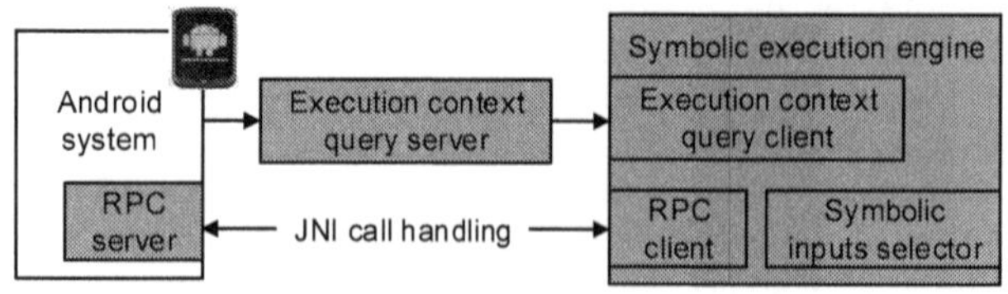

Figure 2: Architecture of Centaur.

in Figure 2, where the symbolic execution engine is built outside of Android. As the symbolic execution engine does not need to take care of the comparability issues but is specialized for path exploration, its design and implementation are largely simplified. Plus, since the code for the symbolic executor is separated from Android code, it does not need to be maintained when the Android system is updated.

The whole-system concrete execution is performed in the Android system. Between the Android system and the symbolic execution engine is the execution context query server, which migrates the context information from Android to the symbolic execution engine. How to correctly interpret the *semantics* of the bytes and bits in the heap captured at Android and to mitigate the information properly will be discussed in Section 5. Finally, an RPC server placed inside the Android system, and JNI calls during path exploration are delegated to the RPC server, which will be discussed in Section 6.

4. IDENTIFYING SYMBOLIC INPUTS

4.1 App-specific Variables

To deal with over-constrained symbolic execution, it is vital to set Android Framework variables that are derived from the malicious app as symbolic inputs, such that execution paths due to all possible values of these variables are explored by symbolic execution.

A closer look at Android Framework reveals that there are two distinct types of variables. The first type, called *non-app-specific* variables, are allocated regardless of apps in the system. For example, the aforementioned `LocationManagerService.mProviders` ArrayList (Line 6 in Figure 1) exists no matter what apps are running. This type of variables should not be specified as symbolic inputs, since they are not derived from the malicious app.

The second type, called *app-specific* variables, stores app-specific information. Some variables store information for all installed apps; for instance, `Settings.mUserIds` is an ArrayList that stores the installation data of each installed app (the code path, signature, granted permissions, etc.). Others store the information of running apps, such as task affinities, intents, and back stacks. Unlike the Linux kernel, which stores most information of a process in a centralized structure `task_struct`, the app-specific information in Android is stored in the many data structures for the system services: Android Framework code is structured as a set of system service classes, each of which points to some objects and arrays for storing app-specific information. Therefore, given an app, the framework variables derived from it scatter and exist as objects fields and array elements among the many data structures.

Note that the task of selecting variables as symbolic inputs is not only to find the app-specific variables but also to

Figure 3: Example of retrieving information from a hash-table-based variable mPackages.

```
// Defined in the PackageManagerService class
HashMap<String, PackageParser.Package> mPackages;
int checkPermission(String perm, String pkgNm){
  PackageParser.Package p = mPackages.get(pkgNm);
   ...
}
```

locate fields or elements within the variables that are derived from a given malicious app. For instance, in addition to determining **Settings.mUserIds** is an app-specific variable, we need to locate which element in the array is derived from the malicious app. Thus, the task is like looking for a needle in a large pile of hay considering the large number of complex data structures.

4.2 Access Patterns

In order to determine which variables are derived from a given app, a natural method is to track how the information flows from the app to Android Framework via tainting. However, such information flow is very complex involving multiple intricate steps, including app installation, system boot, and starting the app. Given the complexity of these steps and the huge amount of code involved, it is very difficult, if not impossible, to precisely track the information flow using taint analysis. Note that existing taint analysis, such as TaintDroid [20], Chex [35], and TaintART [50], is able to track whether the information of the return values (e.g., GPS locations) of specific system service calls flow to specific sinks (e.g., sending to network), but none is able to track how the whole app-level information propagates to Android Framework variables. Moreover, conventional tainting techniques suffer from the well-know overtainting and undertainting issues, which lead to imprecise tainting results.

Instead of proposing a even more complex taint analysis technique to track the information flow, we resolve the challenge from a novel angle by looking at how the app-specific variables are retrieved and marking them as symbolic inputs in the process of path exploration. Our hypothesis is that, as the framework stores information for multiple apps, there must exist specific ways to retrieve the information for a given app (i.e., the calling app), rather than any other app, when servicing a system service call. Our further investigation has validated the hypothesis and revealed that app-specific variables are stored in two categories of data structures, array-based ones (built-in arrays, ArrayList, SparseArray, etc.) and hash-table-based ones (HashMap, HashSet, etc.), and the two categories are accessed in two characteristic ways, respectively.

First, given an array-based variable, the framework retrieves an app's information in the array using an index that is a function of the app's unique UID (an app's UID is assigned upon installation and not changed). Our investigation further shows that there are two such formulas used to calculate the index. One is ($uid\%100,000 - 10,000$), converting the user app's UID into an index to retrieve the element for the app from a built-in array or ArrayList; the other one is ($uid\%100,000$), which is used to calculate the index into a SparseArray. Two magic numbers appear in

Table 1: Taint Propagation Logic. Register variables are referenced by v_X. $\tau(y) \leftarrow \tau(x)$ means setting the taint tag of y to the taint tag of x.

Inst. / Function	Operation Semantics	Taint Propagation
isub	$v_B \leftarrow v_A - C$	if C == 10,000, $\tau(v_B) \leftarrow \tau(v_A)$
irem	$v_B \leftarrow v_A \% C$	if C == 100, 000, $\tau(v_B) \leftarrow \tau(v_A)$
concat	$v_C \leftarrow v_A$.concat(v_B)	$\tau(v_C) \leftarrow \tau(v_A)$

the formulas and are worth interpretation. 10,000 means **FIRST_APPLICATION_UID** (Line 26 in Figure 1), indicating the smallest UID an user app can have, while 100,000 means **PER_USER_RANGE** (Line 27 in Figure 1), indicating the largest UID plus one. For example, as shown in Figure 1, the function **getUserIdLpr** (Line 29) utilizes the first formula to calculate the index into the ArrayList **Settings.mUserIds** (Lines 31 and 32).

Second, for hash-table-based variables, no matter it is hash table or a set, the package name (or the package name concatenated with a component name) is used as the key to access elements. Figure 3 shows an example of retrieving information from a hash-table-based variable.

While there are a large variety of data structures in the framework, our investigation shows that they commonly follow the two fixed access patterns to retrieve the app-specific information when servicing a system service call.

4.3 Slim Tainting

We thus propose *slim taint analysis* that tracks and recognizes the characteristic access patterns above on the fly during path exploration and sets variables as symbolic inputs when app-specific information is accessed.

Next, we elaborate slim tainting. Similar to other tainting techniques, it consists of taint sources, taint propagation logic, and taint sinks. (1) The return values of **getCallingUID** and **getPackageName** are set as taint sources; they are unique identifications of an app. (2) The taint propagation logic as shown in Table 1 is very simple, involving only two instructions and one string concatenation function. They are all derived from the access patterns described in Section 4.2. (3) Finally, the taint sinks include the **get** functions of the collection data structures as well as bytecode instructions for loading elements from built-in arrays, such as **iaload** (loads from an array of integers) and **aaload** (loads from an array of references); they check whether the index or key is tainted, and if so, the target element is flagged as a symbolic input.

Example: Let us take the code in Figure 1 as an example to illustrate how the slim taint analysis works. First, due to the call to **getCallingUID** (Line 3), its return value **uid** obtains the taint. Second, the taint propagates along Lines 31 and 32 according to the taint propagation logic. Finally, at Line 33, the **get** function works as a sink to set the element (and *only* this element) accessed through the tainted index as a symbolic input.

Slim tainting comprises very specific taint sources and a simple but precise taint propagation logic; it thus avoids the overtainting and undertainting issues. Section 6 includes its implementation details. It is worth mentioning that the implementation intercepts some specific function calls and changes the interpretation of several bytecode instructions; it does not need to change a single line of the source code of

Android Framework and does not need any code annotation. Therefore, it is precise and automatic. When the Android system evolves, new access patterns may be used. In that case, we need to update some details of slim tainting in terms of, e.g., taint sources and propagation logic. But the idea of capturing access patterns should still be applicable.

5. EXECUTION CONTEXT MIGRATION

The decoupled architectural design requires that the execution context due to the concrete execution be mitigated from the Android system to the analyzer. Note that, in the execution context, the program counter, the register file, and the stack all obtain their fresh content when symbolic execution starts at the analyzer; only the heap in the execution context, which is a collection of classes and objects, needs to be migrated. The heap memory image in the execution context is called a *snapshot* for short. Three problems have to be resolved for migrating the heap information captured in a snapshot: (1) how to obtain the semantics of the bits and bytes in a snapshot? (2) how to conduct the migration during symbolic execution? and (3) how to bootstrap the migration?

5.1 Snapshot Parsing and Information Query

A heap snapshot is nothing but an array of bits. However, it would not work if we simply copy the array of bits to the JVM instance for symbolic execution, because the ART process in Android and the JVM instance for symbolic execution differ significantly in terms of the low-level representation of classes and objects. E.g., in our implementation, each object in our symbolic executor needs extra space for recording the taint and the symbolic expression; plus, its heap memory management is different from the one used in Android. On the other hand, given an object, both ART and our JVM should agree on the number of the contained fields, according to the class definition file, and their values. Therefore, given an object, our migration is not to copy its bits but to copy the values of all its fields.

Thus, the parser analyzes the snapshot to obtain all the active objects (and classes) and, for each object (and class), records the values of its fields. The information is organized in a two-tier data structure: the first tier maps an object (or class) address to a second-tier data structure instance, which maps field names of an object (or class) or element indexes of an array to their values.

After the snapshot is parsed and its information is stored, the *execution context query server* (in Figure 2) is used to service requests from the symbolic exectuor by returning the information about objects, classes and arrays. Multiple query interfaces are provided: given a reference value, the type of the corresponding object can be queried; given a reference value of an object and the name of one of its fields, the field value can be queried. Snapshot parsing and information query provide the foundation for heap information migration.

5.2 Migration Algorithm

Given an object in the concrete execution world, for fields of primitive types we can simply copy the field values after allocating the space from the symbolic executor for the object. But what about fields of the reference type? A deep copy is too inefficient while a simple shallow copy of the reference value will not work as the reference value only indicates the object location in the concrete execution world (where the snapshot has been captured). We choose to enforce *a variant of the simple shallow copy*: when an object is migrated, we simply copy all the field values, but for each reference-typed field, we mark that it indicates a reference value in the concrete execution world (a boolean attribute `snapshotRef` is associated with each reference-typed field to indicate whether the filed value is a location in the concrete or symbolic execution world); later, when one of such reference-typed fields is used to access its target object, the target object is either migrated or, if it has been migrated, the field value is updated with the reference value in the symbolic exectuion world.

Therefore, a hash table, `conc2Sym`, is maintained to map reference values in the concrete execution world to ones in the symbolic execution world. Every time an object o is migrated, a new pair $\langle r_c, r_s \rangle$ is added to the hash table, where r_c is the reference value of o in the concrete execution world and r_s symbolic. The hash table is maintained for two purposes. First, it prevents duplicate migration of an

Algorithm 1 Migration of heap information.

```
function GETFIELD(index)
    objRef = peekStackTop()
    fdInfo = getFdInfo(index)            ▷ Class-specific info.
    fd = getFd(objRef, fdInfo)           ▷ objRef-specific info.
    if !fd.getSnapshotRefAttribute() then
        return super.getfield(index)
    end if
    concRef = fd.getValue()
    symRef = conc2Sym.get(concRef)
    if symRef == NULL then
        fdType = fdInfo.getFdType()
        if fdType == strRef then
            str = snapshot.getStr(concRef)
            symRef = searchConstantPool(str);
            if symRef == NULL then
                symRef = newString(str);
            end if
        else if fdType == arrayRef then
            entryType = fdType.getEntryType()
            len = snapshot.getArrayLen(concRef)
            symRef = newArray(entryType, len)
            snapshot.copyEntries(symRef, concRef)
        else                             ▷ Other reference types
            symRef = newObj(fdType)
            snapshot.copyFields(symRef, concRef)
        end if
        conc2Sym.addPair(concRef, symRef)
    end if
    fd.setValue(symRef)
    fd.setSnapshotRefAttribute(false)
    return super.getfield(index)
end function

function INITCLASS(classInfo)
    if snapshot.isInitialized(classInfo) then
        snapshot.copyStaticFields(classInfo)
    else
        super.initClass(classInfo)
        handleBootstrapField(classInfo)
    end if
end function
```

Table 2: Bytecode instructions (and function) used for migrating heap information.

Instruction	Stack [before]→[after]	Description
`getfield`	objRef → value	get a field value of an object
`getstatic`	→value	get a static field value of a class
`aaload`	arrayRef, index → value	load onto the stack a reference from an array
`initClass`	N/A	invoked for class initialization

object; that is, an object pointed to by r_c is migrated only if r_c is not found in the hash table. Second, the hash table is used to translate reference values in the concrete execution world, if they exist in the hash table, to ones in the symbolic execution world.

The hash table **conc2Sym** *is handled as part of the process state, and gets stored and restored as the path exploration advances and backtracks*, respectively; this way, the migration status keeps consistent during path exploration.

The heap execution context migration algorithm, which is built into the symbolic execution engine, is implemented by overriding a couple of bytecode instructions, shown in Table 1, which includes, for each instruction, the effect that the instruction has on the operand stack and the instruction description. Algorithm 1 shows the main migration procedures.

5.2.1 Migrating Objects

The instruction **getfield** is used to access non-static fields in an object. Given a reference to an object (this object must have been migrated; Section 5.3 covers the reason) on the stack (Line 2), the instruction **getfield** pushes a field value of the object onto the stack. Below we describe how an object pointed to by a field when this field is accessed through **getfield**.

If the field's **snapshotRef** attribute is **false** (Line 5), which means that either it is a primitive-typed field or it has a reference value in the symbolic execution world, the instruction's interpretation is not changed (Line 6); i.e., the filed value is simply pushed onto the stack. If **snapshotRef** is **true** and the field value **concRef** is not found in **conc2Sym** (Line 10), the object should be migrated (Lines 11–26); after migration, the pair ⟨*concRef*, *symRef*⟩ is added to **conc2Sym** (Line 27).

How to migrate an object is determined by its type (Line 11). (Recall that, given the reference value, which is the value of the field being accessed, the the execution context query server can locate and return the target object information, i.e., its type and contained field values, from the concrete execution world.) (1) If the object is a string, the algorithm first searches for a string that has the same value within the runtime constant pool in the VM for symbolic execution. If not found, a new string with the same value is created in the symbolic world (Lines 12–17). (2) If the object is an array, an array is allocated and all the elements are copied to the new array (Lines 18–22). This algorithm performs a shallow copy. Thus, for a multi-dimensional array, e.g., $A[5][10]$, only the five elements in the top-level array are copied at this moment. Later, when any of the five elements is accessed, the instruction **aaload** has to be invoked, which is the reason the interpretation of **aaload** (not shown in Algorithm 1) is also overridden, i.e., to migrate second-level arrays. Due to the shallow copy, an array object is not copied until a

Figure 4: Example of a test driver.

```
public TestDriver() {
  @fromSnapshot
  private static com.android.server.
    LocationManagerService mService;
  public static void main() {
    // The parameters are configured as symbolic
    inputs, so their values do not matter
    mService.getProviders(null, false);
  }
}
```

reference to the object is accessed. (3) A reference to an ordinary object is handled by allocating a new object and copying all its fields (Lines 23–25).

While non-static fields are accessed through **getfield**, access to static fields is through **getstatic**. Thus, to migrate objects pointed to by static fields, the interpretation of **getstatic** has to be overridden, and the interpretation is similar to that of **getfield** and is thus omitted.

5.2.2 Migrating Classes

When an operation (e.g., an object of a class is created or a class's static fields are accessed for the first time) triggers initialization of a class during symbolic execution, **initClass** is invoked by the underlying VM for symbolic execution automatically. For classes that have been initialized during concrete execution, the symbolic executor has to make sure that they are migrated instead of being initialized, considering that the static fields have obtained their values during concrete execution. Thus, when **initClass** is invoked, the symbolic executor first checks whether the class has been initialized in the concrete execution world; if so, the enclosed static fields in the class are copied from the snapshot to the symbolic execution world (Line 36). In particular, when an object of some class is created in the symbolic world for the first time due to migration (Line 24), it triggers the invocation of **initClass** first, which migrates the class.

5.3 Bootstrapping

An important invariant kept during migration is that, when a field of an object o (resp. an element of an array A) is accessed, o (resp. A) must have been migrated in the symbolic execution world. Assume f is the field whose access triggers the migration of the first object; a natural question is "*where does f reside?*" The answer is that f, called the *bootstrap* field, resides in the test driver class, and it is a reference to the system service class that contains the entrypoint method. Listing 4 shows an example of a test driver. A custom annotation **fromSnapshot** is used to specify the bootstrap field, which is recognized and handled by the migration algorithm; specifically, when the **TestDriver** class is initialized, it sets the bootstrap field value to the reference value of the system service object in the concrete execution world (note that all the system service classes adopt the *singleton* design pattern, so there is no ambiguity when specifying the reference value).

Example. In Listing 4, when the **TestDriver** class is initialized, the migration algorithm sets the value of the bootstrap field to the reference to the Location Manager service object in the snapshot; as a result, when the bootstrap field is accessed, the service object is migrated correctly. The migration of classes and objects form a *migration tree*, which grows as classes and objects get migrated, rooted at the class

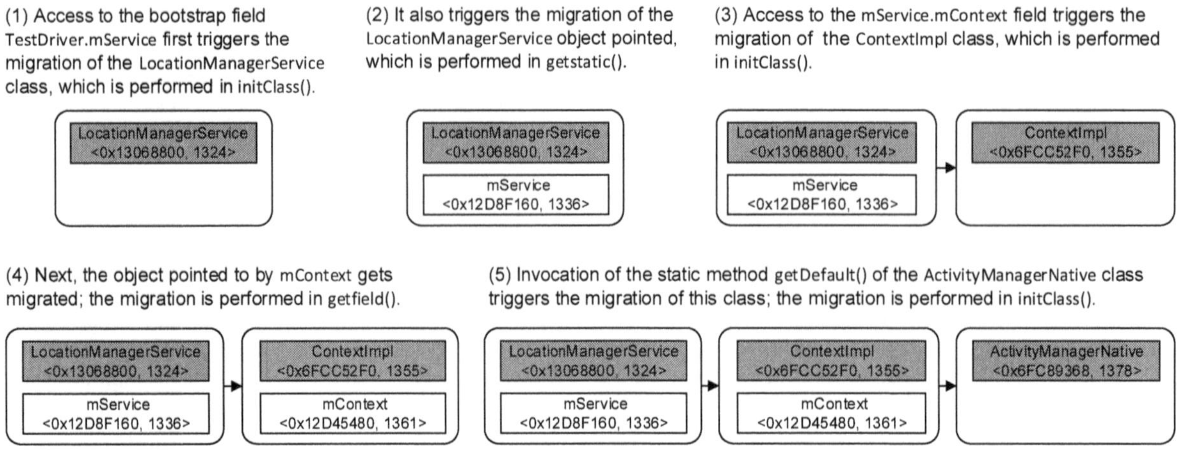

Figure 5: An example of migrating the heap. Grey rectangles and white ones denote classes and objects, respectively. For each class and object, `<conRef, symRef>` denotes the mapping between the reference value in the concrete execution world and that in the symbolic world. The migration of a class also triggers the migration of all its super classes, which are not shown for simplicity.

and object corresponding to the bootstrap field type. We use the code in Listing 4 as an example to partially illustrate how a migration tree grows, as shown in Figure 5, where the root node is the class and object for `LocationManagerService`. Note that the step (5), `getDefault` is invoked due to the call to `getProviders`.

6. IMPLEMENTATION DETAILS

Background on SPF. We built the symbolic executor based on Symbolic PathFinder (SPF) [41], a symbolic execution framework on top of Java PathFinder (JPF) [51]. SPF can be understood as a non-standard Java bytecode interpreter, which enforces path exploration when interpreting the code; e.g., when interpreting an `if` statement, it creates two program states so that both branches will be explored. It provides a set of path selection policies that can be chosen from and various constraint solvers for resolving path conditions.

SPF can be extended by overriding methods that are used to interpret bytecode instructions. It also supports the interception of arbitrary function calls for customized handling during the analysis. Specifically, JPF provides a mechanism called *Model Java Interface* (MJI) that intercepts method invocations for custom handling. CENTAUR makes use of MJI to intercept certain method calls (e.g., `getCallingUid`, `getPackageName`, and the `get` functions of various collection data structures), and redirects them to our custom implementation of these functions. Finally, attributes can be added to associate with each of the class/object fields on the heap and variables on the stack to record and track states of interest, such as taints and symbolic expressions.

We added 6,285 lines of code for implementing CENTAUR through extending SPF. Significant effort has been saved by building upon SPF, which is made possible thanks to the decoupled design.

Classpath. The Java source code in Android is compiled into `.jar` files, which comprise standard `.class` files, and the symbolic executor is built to analyze Java bytecode in such `.class` files. The classpath below shows the classes analyzed by the symbolic executor.

```
classpath=test_driver_dir;\
services_intermediates/classes-full-debug.jar;\
framework_intermeidates/classes-full-debug.jar;\
core-libart_intermediates/classes-full-debug.jar
```

The first line specifies the directory containing the test driver, the next two lines spercify the Android Framework code, and the last line the core libraries of ART, such as utility, io, and math libraries. Several classes (e.g., `java.lang.class`, `.Thread`, `.StackTraceElement`) are modeled by the symbolic executor, but `core-libart` contains the Android version of these classes; hences, these specific classes have to be excluded from `core-libart` to avoid failures due to duplication.

Slim tainting. Slim tainting is built into the symbolic executor by modifying the interpretation of instructions, such as `isub` (subtraction), `irem` (modular), and `*aload`, and intercepting functions, such as `getPackageName`, `getCallingUID`, `String.concat` (string concatenation), and various `get` functions of collection data structures. CENTAUR adds one attribute indicating the taint and another indicating the symbolic input property for each field, array element, and call-stack variable; Thanks to JPF's supports for interception of function calls and adding field attributes without modifying the framework source code, there is no maintenance effort needed when there are new versions of Android released, as long as the app-specific variable access patterns (Section 4.2) are not changed.

Capturing and Parsing Snapshots. After a heap memory snapshot of an Android Framework process is captured (using the `dumpheap` utility), it is first converted to a standard `.hprof` file using the `hprof-conv` utility in the Android SDK. The standard `.hprof` file format opens up the possibility of parsing the snapshot using many existing tools. In our case, the file is then parsed to extract the list of classes and objects stored in the `.hprof` file using a hprof file parser [29]. The extracted information is then organized into the memory space of the execution context query server.

Dealing with Messaging. Two messaging mechanisms that are frequently used by system services are Message Handler and State Machine calls. A message handler is associated with a thread's message queue, and is used to send messages to the message queue and handle them as messages come out of the queue [28]. To deal with messages sent to a queue, we propose to replace the call to `sendMessage(message)` with a call to the destination handler's `handleMessage(message)`. We connect the senders and receivers for messages sent through State Machine in a similar way.

Handling JNI calls. Part of Android Framework is implemented in native code, which is invoked through the Java Native Interface (JNI) mechanism. Multiple ways are adopted to handle JNI calls during symbolic execution. (1) Methods that return the calling UID (`getCallingUid()`) and the package name (`getPackage-Name()`) of the client app are modeled to return the corresponding information for the malicious app. (2) The return values of other native methods that return app-specific information of the malicious app are specified as symbolic inputs. For example, many native methods declared in the package `android.content.res` access application resources. (3) For native methods that do not have return values are ignored. (4) Other calls to native methods are delegated back to Android through remote procedure calls (RPCs). The RPC client in the symbolic executor is built similar to jpf-nhandler [46]. While jpf-nhandler delegates native calls to a host JVM, our client delegates them to an app running as the RPC server in a remote Android system (Figure 2) and handels native calls using reflection on demand. The *GSON* library [27] is used for marshalling and unmarshalling method parameters and return values, which are transmitted between the RPC server and client via socket.

7. EVALUATION

We compare CENTAUR against under-constrained symbolic execution (UCSE) in Section 7.1. Both can start symbolic execution from system interface methods to reach the code deep in the program, but CENTAUR makes use of the execution context provided by concrete execution. Ideally, we should also compare the PC2SE scheme used in CENTAUR against symbolic execution that starts from the main entry of Android Framework, that is, `SystemServer.main`, but note that our symbolic executor runs outside Android, while at the initialization phase the System Server heavily relies on the Android environment, such as the file systems and other supporting processes, to finish its initialization, meaning that it is unlikely to initialize the System Server process outside the Android environment. We thus compare PC2SE with UCSE only.

CENTAUR provides strong support for vulnerability discovery and exploit generation. To demonstrate how CENTAUR can be applied to assisting vulnerability discovery, we investigate two distinct types of recently uncovered attacks that exploit Android Framework vulnerabilities. The investigation in Sections 7.2 and 7.3 shows how zero-day vulnerability instances can be discovered through the application of CENTAUR.

Finally, the reliability of the approach is investigated. We present exploit generation experiments based on snapshots captured at different times, and analyze the consistency of the results in Section 7.4.

The experiments were performed on a machine with an Intel Core i7 4.0Ghz Quad Core processor and 32GB RAM running Linux kernel 3.13. Exploits were generated on Android Framework 5.0 and verified using different versions of Android systems.

We use a *skeleton app* to act as the malicious app; it contains all the aspects of a regular app, including the manifest file, activities, and services, but does not implement any essential functionality; in particular, the skeleton app used in our experiments borrows the manifest file from the Android developer website, which has "every element that it can contain" [2]. In practice, the analyst can choose any app as the malicious app.

7.1 Comparison with Under-constrained Symbolic Execution (UCSE)

The first issue of applying UCSE to symbolic execution of Android Framework is that virtual function calls are frequently used in the framework code, but the runtime types of the receiver objects are unknown. UCSE constructs the receiver objects based on the type hierarchy or relying on manual specifications, which either explores spurious paths or requires much manual effort.

The second issues is that input variables which are treated as concrete inputs in CENTAUR are treated as symbolic inputs in UCSE. UCSE handles such symbolic inputs using lazy initialization, which causes the following problems: (1) loops that iterate through collection data structures are unbounded, and (2) the generated concrete values may be unrealistic.

We tried to perform UCSE of Android Framework using Java PathFinder, which kept crashing when it was applied directly. We spent a lot of time and tedious effort modifying the framework code (e.g., adding the type information about objects pointed to by references to assist dynamic dispatching) to make the symbolic execution possible. We thus only modified the code with respect to the `getProviders` API and the `startActivity`. UCSE spent 138m when analyzing `getProviders` and ran out of memory in the case of `startActivity`, while CENTAUR finished them within 26s and 42m 37s, respectively.

Therefore, path exploration without precise information of the execution context causes many problems, such as requiring tedious manual annotation effort and exploring spurious paths. CENTAUR resolves the problems by migrating the execution context from the concrete execution world to symbolic execution.

7.2 Investigating Inconsistent Security Policy Enforcement (ISPE)

Background. Android Framework utilizes a permission-based security model, which provides controlled access to various system resources. However, a sensitive operation may be reached from different paths, which may enforce security checks inconsistently. As a result, an attacker with insufficient privilege may perform sensitive operations by taking paths that lack security checks. Recently, static analysis combined with manual code inspection has been applied to finding such inconsistent security enforcement cases in Android Framework [47]. The system, called *Kratos*, first builds a call graph based on the Android Framework code. With the call graph, it finds all the execution paths that can reach sensitive operations. Kratos then compares the paths pairwise to identify paths that reach the same sensitive operation with inconsistent security checks enforced, and reports them as suspected ISPE vulnerabilities, in that they violate the security property that *all paths should have consistent permissions for reaching a given sensitive operation.*

Combined approach for bug finding. Static analysis based on the reachability analysis for finding ISPE bugs may report false positives, as some paths are infeasible in real executions. Currently, manual effort is used to scrutinize the code along each reported path, which is laborious and tedious; moreover, it is difficult to verify the correctness of the manual inspection results.

We propose to combine static analysis and symbolic execution to find ISPE bugs. For each suspected vulnerability reported by static analysis, CENTAUR (1) finds all feasible paths that reach the sensitive operation, (2) gives permissions needed for each feasible path (the needed permissions are included in each path condition), (3) verifies permission consistency among the feasible paths, and (4) generates inputs that exercise the feasible paths to verify suspected vulnerabilities. It thus demonstrates the uses of CENTAUR comprehensively. All the steps have been performed automatically, in contrast with previous work that relies on tedious and error-prone manual inspection. Plus, zero false positives are guaranteed as all suspected vulnerabilities are validated by the runtime log.

Result summary. Table 3 summarizes the experiment results (the vulnerability shown in the last row is discussed in Section 7.3). For each vulnerability, the table lists the vulnerability description, entrypoint(s), the min/max number of migrated classes among different paths, the min/max number of migrated objects among different paths, the number of sets of concrete values generated ("—" means it can be exploited unconditionally; note that we generate one set of concrete values for each unique path explored), the number of sets that can be used to generate exploits, the symbolic execution time, and the code coverage.

Given an entrypoint method, there may be multiple paths that reach the sensitive operation, and the classes and objects involved in the paths may vary, as illustrated by the min/max number of migrated classes and objects. Note that when migrating a class, all its super classes are also migrated, which is the reason the number of migrated classes is greater than that of objects. In the majority of the cases, the symbolic execution of an entrypoint method is finished within less one minute. Note that in some cases we have a relatively low code coverage, e.g., in `WSI.addOrUpdateNetwork`; it is mainly because branches that rely on non-app-specific variables are not iterated, as we consider those variables as concrete inputs. We are only interested in branches that can be affected by the variables derived from the malicious app.

New findings. It is notable that some of our results are inconsistent with those of Kratos. First, for the fifth vulnerability in Table 3, Kratos reports that it does not exist in Android Framework 5.0, while CENTAUR shows that it still exist (i.e., different permissions are required by the two system interface methods for reaching the sensitive resource) and the result is verified by the log. Second, for the sixth vulnerability in Table 3, Kratos reports only one permission `CONNECTIVITY_INTERNAL` for invoking `NsdService.setEnabled`, while CENTAUR reports two permissions, `CONNECTIVITY_INTERNAL` and `WRITE_SETTINGS`. The more thorough and accurate results demonstrate the advantages of the hybrid approach.

A detailed example. As an example, we describe in detail how the combined approach was applied to finding the

Figure 6: `startActivityUncheckedLocked()`.

```
final int startActivityUncheckedLocked(
    ActivityRecord r, ActivityRecord sourceRecord,
     IVoiceInteractionSession voiceSession,
    IVoiceInteractor voiceInteractor, int
    startFlags, boolean doResume, Bundle options,
     TaskRecord inTask) {...}
```

first vulnerability in Table 3. (1) First, the static analysis based on path reachability and pairwise path comparison finds that both `getProviders(Criteria, boolean)` and `getAllProviders()` (in the `LocationManagerService` class) have paths reaching the same sensitive operation that returns the names of the installed GPS providers, and the two paths can be executed with inconsistent permissions; thus, it is a suspected vulnerability. (2) Next, CENTAUR is applied to check automatically whether there exist paths that can reach the sensitive operation from the two service interface methods. Specifically, after the Android system is initialized and the skeleton app is launched, a heap memory snapshot of the System Server process is captured, and provides execution context for symbolic execution, and symbolic execution starts from the two service interface methods respectively.

Compared to previous work that relies on enormous and error-prone manual inspection, the combined approach of call graph reachability analysis and symbolic execution eliminates the need for manual work and guarantees zero false positives. It is potential to apply this approach to finding other types of vulnerabilities in Android Framework.

7.3 Investigating Task Hijacking Attacks

Background. The Activity Manager Service allows activities of different apps to reside in the same *task*, which is a collection of activities that users interact with when performing a certain job. The activities in a given task are arranged in a *back stack*, pushed in the order they were opened; users can navigate back using the "Back" button. This feature can be exploited by a malicious app if its activities are manipulated to reside side by side with the victim apps in the same task and hijack the user sessions of the victim apps. This is a design flaw rather than a program bug, but can be exploited to implement UI spoofing, denial-of-service, and user monitoring attacks [45]. For example, a malicious app may start a malicious activity that impersonates the victim activity, and the UI spoofing attack succeeds if the fake activity resides in the same back stack as the victim activity, and the user may mistake the fake malicious activity for the victim one. This case illustrates unique characteristics of exploits that take advantage of Android Framework vulnerabilities: the malicious "input" is not some single input (a command parameter, a network packet, etc.) but a separate app.

Vulnerability discovery. We use the `EditEventActivity` activity of the `calendar` app as an example victim activity. In the skeleton app, the main activity of the skeleton app starts the malicious activity, denoted by M. The goal of the attack is that M, when it is started, will reside in the same task as the victim activity. A bug is identified if such attacks against the victim activity is feasible. We capture the heap memory snapshot when the victim app and the skeleton app are started and the main activity of the skeleton app is to start the malicious activity.

Table 3: List of vulnerabilities and analysis statistics. (*LMS*, *TSI*, *PIM*, *WMS*, *AMS*, *WSI*, *NS*, and *ASS* represent LocationManagerService, TelecomServiceImpl, PhoneInterfaceManager, WindowManagerService, ActivityManagerService, WifiServiceImpl, NsdService, and ActivityStackSupervisor, respectively.)

No.	Vulnerability description	Entrypoint(s)	# of migrated classes		# of migrated objects		# of all sets	# of legal sets	Analysis time	Code coverage (%)
			min	max	min	max				
1	Access installed providers with insuf. privilege	LMS.getAllProviders()	55	55	4	4	—	—	19s	92.3
		LMS.getProviders(Criteria,boolean)	77	93	14	42	66	66	26s	45.8
2	Read phone state with insuf. privilege	TSI.getCallState()	48	48	3	3	—	—	14s	72.4
		TSI.isInCall()	62	69	17	20	1	1	32s	83.5
		TSI.isRinging()	60	65	16	18	1	1	35s	
3	End phone calls with insuf. privilege	TSI.endCall()	81	83	21	24	1	1	29s	91.3
		PIM.endCall()	80	85	23	26	1	1	38s	89.4
4	Close system dialogs with insuf. privilege	WMS.closeSystemDialogs(String)	57	57	6	6	—	—	17s	69.1
		AMS.closeSystemDialogs(String)	63	67	11	15	2	2	29s	56.0
5	Set up HTTP proxy working in PAC mode with insuf. privilege	WSI.addOrUpdateNetwork()	67	122	23	52	16	16	26s	30.4
		WSI.getWifiServiceMessenger()	65	84	21	24	1	1	18s	57.3
6	Enable/Disable mDNS daemon with insuf. privilege	NS.setEnabled(boolean)	75	114	28	53	1	1	44s	47.2
		NS.getMessenger()	80	81	11	14	1	1	18s	62.4
7	Task hijacking	ASS.startActivityUncheckedLocked()	324	387	136	182	2,020	810	42m 37s	58.3

Figure 7: An example set of concrete input values.

```
(r.intent.mFlags == 0x10080000) &&
(r.launchMode == LAUNCH_SINGLE_TASK) &&
(r.mLaunchTaskBehind == true) &&
(options == null) &&
(r.resultTo == null) &&
(r.info.documentLaunchMode == 0) &&
(r.info.targetActivity == null) &&
(r.taskAffinity == "android.task.calendar")
```

While the method for starting an activity is **startActivity**, the task selection is done in **startActivityUncheckedLocked**, which is invoked by **startActivity**. We thus performed the symbolic execution of **startActivityUncheckedLocked** to simplify the path exploration; it has eight parameters as shown in Figure 6. The first parameter **r** is an **ActivityRecord** instance storing the information of M, while the second storing that of the caller activity. The description of other parameters is omitted. They are set to symbolic inputs. The constraint indicating that *the task selected for M is exactly the one hosting the victim activity* is added to each of the path conditions when it is to be resolved; that is, $\langle m.task.taskId == v.task.taskId\rangle$, where m and v represent the **activityRecords** of the malicious activity and the victim activity, respectively. A feasible path is found if the path condition is resolvable.

Exploit generation. The symbolic execution generated 2,020 sets of concrete input values (each set corresponds to a unique path), among which some contain illegal concrete values, e.g., due to requiring the malicious activity's package and activity names to be equal to those of the victim activity. Simple scripts were written to filter out illegal concrete values (1,210 sets totally). Figure 7 shows an example of the rest 810 sets of legal concrete values. In this example, *r.intent.mFlags* and *options* (whose type is **Bundle**) guide how to set the two parameters of **startActivity(Intent, Bundle)**, respectively, and others instruct how to configure the malicious activity; for example, **r.launchMode** is mapped to the **android:launchMode** in the manifest file. Figure 8 shows the exploit generated according to the set of concrete values, and it has verified that the exploit can be used to launch task hijacking successfully.

Figure 8: Exploit example.

```
// Snippet of AndroidManifest.xml
<activity android:name=".maliciousActivity"
     android:launchMode="singleTask"
     android:taskAffinity="android.task.calendar"
     android:documentLaunchMode="none" />
// The main activity starts the malicious
   activity
public void onCreate(Bundle savedInstanceState) {
  Intent i = new Intent(this, maliciousActivity.
     class);
  intent.setFlags(0x10080000);
  // null is due to "options == null"
  startActivity(i, null);
}
```

Table 4: Effectiveness of the generated exploits.

Android version	4.0	4.1	4.2	4.3	4.4	5.0
# of effective exploits	434	674	674	674	702	810

We then examined whether the exploits generated on Android 5.0 were effective on other versions of Android systems. Table 4 lists the results, which show that the effectiveness of the exploits are affected by the versions of Android systems. Further investigation has revealed that the difference is mainly caused by code changes. For example, the new exploiting condition **FLAG_ACTIVITY_NEW_DOCUMENT** is not introduced until Android 5.0 (discussed below); the API **startActivity(Intent, Bundle)** is not included in version 4.0, and thus only exploits with **options == null** can be used for invoking **startActivity(Intent)**.

Newly discovered exploiting condition. The path conditions generated from symbolic execution reveal an extra exploiting condition (requiring a specific bit in the bitflags *r.intent.mFlags* be 0) that was not reported in previous work [45]. Compared to previous work that relies on *ad hoc* manual effort for discovering the exploiting conditions, CENTAUR finds them in a systematic and automatic way.

7.4 Consistency of Exploits Generated with Different Snapshots

We then investigated whether snapshots captured at different times affected exploit generation. After the system was initialized, 20 snapshots were captured at intervals of 5 minutes on Android 5.0 with random user interactions during the intervals. For each vulnerability listed in Table 3, symbolic execution was performed with each of the 20 snapshots providing the execution context. The results show that, for each vulnerability, the same sets of path conditions were generated with different snapshots, which means that the resulting exploits with the different snapshots are consistent.

There are several reasons that explain the consistency of exploits. First, if a malicious app does not rely on other apps to exploit a vulnerability (e.g., inconsistent security policy enforcement), access control is enforced in Android Framework to make sure the information of other apps is not accessed. Thus, the configurations and statuses of other apps do not affect the path exploration. On the other hand, for exploits that rely on the statuses of other apps (e.g., the victim app in task hijacking attacks), the path exploration may depend on the statuses of one or more apps; hence, during symbolic execution, reasonable setting up is established consistently; for example, the victim activity should already be started in the task hijacking case prior to capturing snapshots. The results show that an attack succeeds as long as the same statuses recur.

Finally, the values of non-app-specific variables do not affect path exploration, at least, in our cases. For example, in the case of inconsistent security policy enforcement vulnerabilities due to accessing the names of installed providers, the path exploration does not depend on the concrete values of the related non-app-specific variable (i.e., `LocationManagerService.mProviders`), although different provider names may be returned by the service calls when different providers are installed.

8. RELATED WORK

DART is the first concolic testing tool that uses symbolic analysis in concert with concrete execution to improve code coverage [24]. It runs the tested unit code on random inputs and symbolically gathers constraints at decision points that use input values; then, it negates one of these symbolic constraints to generate the next test case. DART [24], EXE [9], KLEE [8], and S^2E [14] all make use of concrete execution to execute external code or uninterpreted functions, similar to our handling of JNI calls. In CENTAUR, concrete execution is not only used for handling uninterpreted functions (i.e., JNI calls), but also for the initialization of Android Framework in order to set up the execution context for the symbolic execution phase.

Symbolic PathFinder (SPF) can switch to symbolic execution at any point of concrete execution [40]. SPF aims at generating unit test cases, so it simply specifies function parameters as symbolic inputs, which leads to over-constrained symbolic execution. We make use of concrete execution in the initialization phase, which makes the analysis results *sensible* and *easy to interpret*. Plus, PC2SE aims at generating exploits that can be embedded into malicious apps, so it finds variables derived from the malicious app, in addition to the function parameters, and uses them as symbolic inputs. Finally, we have proposed a novel architectural design that decouples symbolic executor from the concrete execution environment to obtain a modularized implementation.

Symbolic execution has been applied to vulnerability discovery and exploit generation in previous work. For example, SAGE has successfully found many vulnerabilities of Windows programs [25], leveraging the technique described in DART [24]. SAGE has demonstrated symbolic execution can be very useful for finding vulnerabilities. AEG has shown vulnerability discovery and exploit generation given vulnerable Unix programs [5]. Automatic patch-based exploit generation (APEG) generates exploits based on information in patches [7]. SAGE, APEG, and AEG all consider stand-alone native Windows or Unix executables, while our work analyzes Android Framework, a piece of middleware that manages all executables running upon it. Many unique challenges arise and are addressed in this work.

There has been a lot of work that applies symbolic execution to Android apps for test input generation or security enhancement [38, 1, 31, 37, 54]. For example, Jensen et al. proposed to use concolic execution to build summaries of individual event handlers and then generate event sequences backward, in order to find event sequences that reach a given target line of code in the Android app [31]. To our knowledge, our system is the first that supports symbolic execution of Android Framework.

9. CONCLUSIONS

We have introduced the first system, called CENTAUR, for symbolic execution of Android Framework. To avoid state space explosion due to the complex initialization, the Phased Concrete-to-Symbolic Execution is proposed that runs concrete execution for the initialization phase, providing execution context to symbolic execution. Among the large number of variables in the execution context, slim tainting tracks characteristic access patterns to identify variables derived from the malicious apps as symbolic inputs. In order to decouple the implementation of CENTAUR from Android, the execution context provided by concrete execution is migrated from an Android ART process to a Java VM. We have implemented the system and evaluated it. The evaluation shows that CENTAUR is very effective in both vulnerability discovery and exploit generation. Given that symbolic execution has proven to be a very useful technique, we plan to apply CENTAUR to other purposes in future work, such as automatic API specification generation, fine-grained malware analysis, and testing.

10. ACKNOWLEDGMENTS

We thank anonymous reviewers and our shepherd Dr. Luca Mottola for their constructive comments. Dr. Peng Liu and Lannan Luo were supported by ARO W911NF-13-1-0421 (MURI), NSF CCF-1320605, NSF SBE-1422215, NSF CNS-1422594, and NSF CNS-1505664. Dr. Kai Chen was supported by NSFC U1536106, 61100226, Youth Innovation Promotion Association CAS, and strategic priority research program of CAS (XDA06010701). Dr. Min Yang was funded by the National Program on Key Basic Research (NO.2015CB358800) and NSFC U1636204.

11. REFERENCES

[1] S. Anand, M. Naik, H. Yang, and M. J. Harrold. Automated concolic testing of smartphone apps. In *FSE*, 2012.

[2] App Manifest. https://developer.android.com/guide/topics/manifest/manifest-intro.html.

[3] S. Arzt, S. Rasthofer, C. Fritz, E. Bodden, A. Bartel, J. Klein, Y. L. Traon, D. Octeau, and P. McDaniel. FlowDroid: Precise context, flow, field, object-sensitive and lifecycle-aware taint analysis for Android apps. In *PLDI*, 2014.

[4] K. W. Y. Au, Y. F. Zhou, Z. Huang, and D. Lie. PScout: analyzing the android permission specification. In *CCS*, 2012.

[5] T. Avgerinos, S. K. Cha, B. L. T. Hao, and D. Brumley. AEG: automatic exploit generation. In *Communications of the ACM*, 2014.

[6] M. Backes, S. Bugiel, E. Derr, P. McDaniel, D. Octeau, and S. Weisgerber. On demystifying the android application framework: Re-visiting android permission specification analysis. In *USENIX Security*, 2016.

[7] D. Brumley, P. Poosankam, D. Song, and J. Zheng. Automatic patch-based exploit generation is possible: Techniques and implications. In *USENIX Security*, 2008.

[8] C. Cadar, D. Dunbar, and D. R. Engler. KLEE: unassisted and automatic generation of high-coverage tests for complex systems programs. In *OSDI*, 2008.

[9] C. Cadar, V. Ganesh, P. M. Pawlowski, D. L. Dill, and D. R. Engler. EXE: automatically generating inputs of death. In *CCS*, 2006.

[10] Y. Cao, Y. Fratantonio, A. Bianchi, M. Egele, C. Kruegel, G. Vigna, and Y. Chen. EdgeMiner: automatically detecting implicit control flow transitions through the android framework. In *NDSS*, 2015.

[11] K. Chen, P. Liu, and Y. Zhang. Achieving accuracy and scalability simultaneously in detecting application clones on Android markets. In *ICSE*, 2014.

[12] K. Chen, P. Wang, Y. Lee, X. Wang, N. Zhang, H. Huang, WeiZou, and P. Liu. Finding unknown malice in 10 seconds: Mass vetting for new threats at the Google-Play scale. In *USENIX Security*, 2015.

[13] E. Chin, A. P. Felt, K. Greenwood, and D. Wagner. Analyzing inter-application communication in android. In *Proceedings of the 9th international conference on Mobile systems, applications, and services*, pages 239–252, 2011.

[14] V. Chipounov, V. Kuznetsov, and G. Candea. S2E: a platform for in-vivo multi-path analysis of software systems. In *ASPLOS*, 2011.

[15] M. Costa, M. Castro, L. Zhou, L. Zhang, and M. Peinado. Bouncer: securing software by blocking bad input. In *SOSP*, 2007.

[16] CVE-2015-6628. https://www.cvedetails.com/cve/CVE-2015-6628/.

[17] CVE-2016-2496. https://www.cvedetails.com/cve/CVE-2016-2496/.

[18] CVE-2016-3750. https://www.cvedetails.com/cve/CVE-2016-3750/.

[19] CVE-2016-3759. https://www.cvedetails.com/cve/CVE-2016-3759/.

[20] W. Enck, P. Gilbert, B.-G. Chun, L. P. Cox, J. Jung, P. McDaniel, and A. N. Sheth. TaintDroid: An information-flow tracking system for realtime privacy monitoring on smartphones. In *OSDI*, 2010.

[21] W. Enck, M. Ongtang, and P. McDaniel. On lightweight mobile phone application certification. In *Proceedings of the 16th ACM conference on Computer and communications security*, pages 235–245. ACM, 2009.

[22] D. Engler and D. Dunbar. Under-constrained execution: marking automatic code destruction easy and scalable. In *ISSTA*, 2007.

[23] A. P. Felt, E. Chin, S. Hanna, D. Song, and D. Wagner. Android permissions demystified. In *CCS*, 2011.

[24] P. Godefroid, N. Klarlund, and K. Sen. DART: directed automated random testing. In *PLDI*, 2005.

[25] P. Godefroid, M. Y. Levin, and D. Molnar. Automated whitebox fuzz testing. In *NDSS*, 2008.

[26] Google. Android Interfaces and Architecture. https://source.android.com/devices/.

[27] GSON. https://sites.google.com/site/gson/Home.

[28] Handler. https://developer.android.com/reference/android/os/Handler.html.

[29] HPROF Parser. https://github.com/eaftan/hprof-parser.

[30] IDC. Smartphone OS Market Share, 2016. https://www.idc.com/prodserv/smartphone-os-market-share.jsp.

[31] C. S. Jensen, M. R. Prasad, and A. Moller. Automated testing with targeted event sequence generation. In *ISSTA*, 2013.

[32] S. Khurshid, C. S. Păsăreanu, and W. Visser. Generalized symbolic execution for model checking and testing. In *TACAS*, 2003.

[33] J. C. King. Symbolic execution and program testing. *Communications of the ACM*, 19(7):385–394, 1976.

[34] L. Li, A. Bartel, T. F. Bissyandé, J. Klein, Y. Le Traon, S. Arzt, S. Rasthofer, E. Bodden, D. Octeau, and P. McDaniel. Iccta: Detecting inter-component privacy leaks in android apps. In *Proceedings of the 37th International Conference on Software Engineering*, pages 280–291, 2015.

[35] L. Lu, Z. Li, Z. Wu, W. Lee, and G. Jiang. Chex: statically vetting android apps for component hijacking vulnerabilities. In *Proceedings of the 2012 ACM conference on Computer and communications security*, pages 229–240, 2012.

[36] L. Luo, J. Ming, D. Wu, P. Liu, and S. Zhu. Semantics-based obfuscation-resilient binary code similarity comparison with applications to software plagiarism detection. In *FSE*, 2014.

[37] N. Mirzaei, H. Bagheri, R. Mahmood, and S. Malek. SIG-Droid: automated system input generation for android applications. In *ISSRE*, 2015.

[38] N. Mirzaei, S. Malek, C. S. Păsăreanu, N. Esfahani, and R. Mahmood. Testing android apps through symbolic execution. In *Software Engineering Notes*, 2012.

[39] D. Octeau, P. McDaniel, S. Jha, A. Bartel, E. Bodden, J. Klein, and Y. Le Traon. Effective inter-component communication mapping in android: An essential step towards holistic security analysis. In *Presented as part*

of the 22nd USENIX Security Symposium (USENIX Security 13), pages 543–558, 2013.

[40] C. S. Păsăreanu, P. C. Mehlitz, D. H. Bushnell, K. Gundy-Burlet, M. Lowry, S. Person, and M. Pape. Combining unit-level symbolic execution and system-level concrete execution for testing nasa software. In *ISSTA*, 2008.

[41] C. S. Păsăreanu, W. Visser, D. Bushnell, J. Geldenhuys, P. Mehlitz, and N. Rungta. Symbolic PathFinder: integrating symbolic execution with model checking for java bytecode analysis. In *ASE*, 2013.

[42] D. A. Ramos and D. Engler. Under-Constrained Symbolic Execution: correctness checking for real code. In *USENIX Security*, 2015.

[43] D. A. Ramos and D. R. Engler. Practical, low-effort equivalence verification of real code. In *CAV*, 2011.

[44] V. Rastogi, Y. Chen, and W. Enck. Appsplayground: automatic security analysis of smartphone applications. In *Proceedings of the third ACM conference on Data and application security and privacy*, pages 209–220, 2013.

[45] C. Ren, Y. Zhang, H. Xue, T. Wei, and P. Liu. Towards discovering and understanding task hijacking in android. In *USENIX Security*, 2015.

[46] N. Shafiei and F. van Breugel. Automatic handling of native methods in Java PathFinder. In *SPIN Symposium on Model Checking of Software*, 2014.

[47] Y. Shao, J. Ott, Q. A. Chen, Z. Qian, and Z. M. Mao. Kratos: discovering inconsistent security policy enforcement in the android framework. In *NDSS*, 2016.

[48] Stagefright. https://en.wikipedia.org/wiki/Stagefright_(bug).

[49] Statista. Cumulative number of apps downloaded from the Google Play, 2016. https://www.statista.com/statistics/281106/number-of-android-app-downloads-from-google-play/.

[50] M. Sun, T. Wei, and J. Lui. Taintart: A practical multi-level information-flow tracking system for android runtime. In *Proceedings of the 2016 ACM SIGSAC Conference on Computer and Communications Security*, pages 331–342. ACM, 2016.

[51] W. Visser, K. Havelund, G. Brat, S. Park, and F. Lerda. Model checking programs. In *ASE*, 2003.

[52] WSJ. Google says android has 1.4 billion active users. www.wsj.com/articles/google-says-android-has-1-4-billion-active-users-1443546856.

[53] L.-K. Yan and H. Yin. DroidScope: Seamlessly reconstructing os and dalvik semantic views for dynamic android malware analysis. In *USENIX Security*, 2012.

[54] Z. Yang, M. Yang, Y. Zhang, G. Gu, P. Ning, and X. S. Wang. Appintent: Analyzing sensitive data transmission in android for privacy leakage detection. In *Proceedings of the 2013 ACM SIGSAC conference on Computer & communications security*, pages 1043–1054. ACM, 2013.

[55] Y. Zhou and X. Jiang. Dissecting Android malware: Characterization and evolution. In *S&P*, 2012.

[56] Y. Zhou, Z. Wang, W. Zhou, and X. Jiang. Hey, you, get off of my market: Detecting malicious apps in official and alternative android markets. In *NDSS*, volume 25, pages 50–52, 2012.

Enabling Gesture-based Interactions with Objects

Longfei Shangguan
Dept. of Computer Science
Princeton University
longfeis@cs.princeton.edu

Zimu Zhou
Dept. of Electrical Engineering
ETH Zurich
zzhou@tik.ee.ethz.ch

Kyle Jamieson
Dept. of Computer Science
Princeton University
kylej@cs.princeton.edu

ABSTRACT

Increasing numbers of everyday objects in libraries, stores and warehouses are instrumented with passive RFID tags, resulting in a ripe opportunity for gesture-based interactions with people. By a simple act of picking up and gesturing with an RFID-tagged object, users can send their opinions and sentiments about that object to the cloud. Prior work in RFID-based gesture tracking relies on multiple bulky and expensive antennas and readers to function, which incurs unacceptable infrastructure costs for large-scale ubiquitous deployment (over an entire warehouse or mall, for example) thus hindering practical adoption. In this paper, we propose Pantomime, the first RFID-based gesture recognition system that uses just a single antenna per geographical area of coverage. Our key insight is to replace the conventional multiple antenna single tag tracking framework with an equivalent multiple tag single antenna system. Through a novel tag coordination protocol and a lightweight tracking algorithm, Pantomime enables accurate gesture tracking that works for objects tagged with just two RFID tags. We implement a real-time prototype of Pantomime with commercial off-the-shelf (COTS) RFID readers and antennas. Extensive evaluations and real-world case studies in a classroom and a retail store demonstrate that Pantomime achieves comparable gesture tracking accuracy (87%) to state-of-the-art multi-antenna schemes (88%) at a minimal deployment cost.

Keywords

RFID; Tracking; Human-object interaction

1. INTRODUCTION

A promising vision for the future Internet of Things (IoT) is to enable input [3, 33, 35, 40], control [1, 13, 28, 38], and interaction [19, 20, 34] via natural gestures: writing and drawing anywhere with any smart objects. Radio Frequency IDentification (RFID) technology holds promise for such capabilities due to the massive existing deployment of small, low-cost RFID tags attached to almost every product and commodity in stores and warehouses. Through tracking the detailed shape of motions of any tagged object held in a user's hand by an RFID reader, the user can perform gestures or write in the air to input his/her comments of the object as an augmented interaction mechanism in stores and warehouses.

Table 1— Comparison of infrastructure deployment in representative RFID-based localization and gesture tracking systems.

System	Antennas	Hardware
RF-IDraw [40]	8	COTS RFID
Tagoram [46]	4	COTS RFID
Backpos [22]	4	COTS RFID
Yunfei *et al.* [23]	4	dedicated tag & reader
PolarDraw [33]	2	linearly-polarized antenna
Pantomime	**1**	**COTS RFID**

Despite active research on RFID-based localization and gesture tracking [22, 23, 33, 40, 46], we argue that existing schemes do not scale up to very large real world scenarios such as coverage over an entire mall or warehouse. State-of-the-art systems use techniques such as motion-based synthetic aperture radar [32, 46], multi-frequency continuous wave radar [23], and electromagnetic polarization discrimination [33], which achieve centimeter- or even millimeter-accurate localization or tracking accuracy. Yet all of them require multiple bulky and expensive antennas to function (Table 1). Due to the extremely asymmetric cost of RFID reader antennas (over \$100) and passive RFID tags (lower than 15 cents) [37], real-world RFID systems are usually deployed to cover a large number of tagged objects with a minimal number of antennas. As a result, a tagged object is often covered by one antenna only, impeding the adoption of the above multi-antenna approaches. We quantify the infrastructure costs for covering a typical indoor space with multi-antenna based systems in §3.1.

In this paper, we present the design and implementation of Pantomime, the first RFID-based human-object interaction system that can track the object motion with a single antenna per geographical area of coverage. The basic idea is to attach multiple RFID tags to an object to compose a tag array. Owning to the reciprocity of the wireless channel, a multi-tag single antenna system is in a sense equivalent to a multi-antenna single tag system. Thus Pantomime can track the motion of a tag-array attached object using a single antenna by tracking the relative movements of the antenna in the frame of the reference of this tag array. The $650\times$[1] gap in cost between an RFID antenna and a passive tag guarantees that it is far more cost-effective to attach multiple tags to every object within a reading range than deploying additional antennas. With one antenna, Pantomime sets a new standard for RFID-based gesture tracking with a minimal supporting infrastructure, and opening new possibilities for pervasive in-air writing, non-intrusive shop-

[1] For a 15-cent tag and \$100 antenna.

Permission to make digital or hard copies of all or part of this work for personal or classroom use is granted without fee provided that copies are not made or distributed for profit or commercial advantage and that copies bear this notice and the full citation on the first page. Copyrights for components of this work owned by others than the author(s) must be honored. Abstracting with credit is permitted. To copy otherwise, or republish, to post on servers or to redistribute to lists, requires prior specific permission and/or a fee. Request permissions from permissions@acm.org.

MobiSys'17, June 19-23, 2017, Niagara Falls, NY, USA

© 2017 Copyright held by the owner/author(s). Publication rights licensed to ACM.

ISBN 978-1-4503-4928-4/17/06...\$15.00

DOI: http://dx.doi.org/10.1145/3081333.3081364

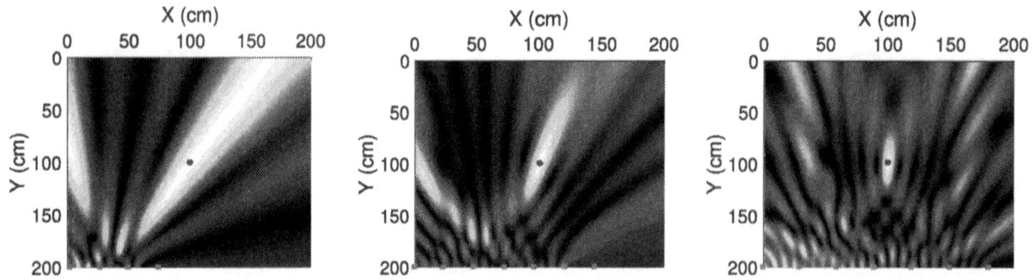

(a)— $n = 4$, $s = 20$cm; (b)— $n = 7$, $s = 20$cm; (c)— $n = 7$, $s = 30$cm;

Figure 1— Hologram generated by an antenna array with different number of antennas and antenna spacing. The green square represents the antenna, the purple dot indicates the ground truth location of the tag. n and s is the number of antennas and antenna spacing, respectively.

Table 2— Impact of coupling effect on phase readings.

Tag spacing (cm)	4.00	3.00	2.00	1.00	0.50
Phase error (degree)	4.6	10.3	26.3	53.9	81.4

ping behavior identification, and instant commodity reviewing services.

A natural question arises over whether it is feasible to directly apply the algorithms designed for multi-antenna single tag systems such as Angle-of-Arrival (AoA) [40, 45] and hologram based methods [32, 46] to multi-tag single antenna systems by swapping the roles of antennas and tags. We argue that such a naive swapping will lead to severe degradation in gesture tracking performance. Multi-antenna based approaches often make certain requirements on antenna quantity and spacing. However, it is often difficult to attach tag arrays to small object to fulfill these requirements. Specifically, AoA based schemes [40, 45] achieve a high angular resolution by processing phase measurements collected from a large antenna array. Attaching large numbers of tags on small objects, *e.g.*, a book spine, will result in closely spaced tags. A small tag spacing then leads to significant coupling effects between adjacent tags [32, 44], which can cause sizable errors in phase readings (Table 2), and consequently, unacceptable errors for object motion tracking. On the other hand, hologram-based methods [32, 46] demand both sufficient antenna spacing and number of antennas to yield satisfactory beam resolution (Figure 1). Yet it is unrealistic to simultaneously achieve large tag spacing and tag quantity on the surfaces of small objects.

In addition to the difficulty to meet the requirements on tag spacing and tag population to yield a desirable resolution for gesture tracking, the adoption of tag arrays to each inventory object or retail item also brings a new challenge: *low per-tag reading rate*. By attaching two tags to each object within the reading range of a reader antenna, the tag population also doubles. Since standard UHF RFID readers exploit the slotted ALOHA protocol [29] to interrogate RFID tags, a boosted tag population will cause significant tag reply collisions. Hence the reading rate (the number of successful tag interrogations per second) of each tag will drop by almost half, leading to sparsely-collected measurements that may even fail to accurately track gestures performed at a normal speed. We quantify the impact of tag population on per-tag reading rate in §3.2.

Pantomime addresses the above challenges by incorporating (i) a MAC layer tag filtering algorithm to boost the reading rate of those tags attached to the target object, and (ii) a novel Extended Kalman Filter (EKF) based tracking algorithm that tracks fine-grained object motions in a 2D plane with a limited number of tags attached to an object. Specifically, Pantomime works as follows. It detects tag movement by examining the statistical distribution of their phase readings. These moving tags are target tags for tracking. Pantomime then stops those stationary tags from responding to the reader, thereby reducing the RF traffic load and response collisions to improve the reading rate of the target tags. As the object moves (so does the tag array attached to it), Pantomime tracks the relative location and the heading of the antenna in the frame of the reference of the tag array. Finally, the relative locations of the antenna, together with a kinetic model based tracking result are fed into an EKF fusion model to further enhance the tracking accuracy.

Contributions and Roadmap. We design and implement the first RFID-based human-object interaction system that enables users to input their opinions and sentiments of an object through instant gestures. We demonstrate the potential widespread applicability of Pantomime for augmented interactions with two real-world case studies: whiteboard handwriting tracking and retail-store item querying (§2). Although attaching multiple tags on an object to infer the object orientation has been studied [44], Pantomime is the first system we are aware of that uses a tag array for gesture-based human-object interaction. We present quantitative experimental measurements to demonstrate the antenna coverage problem and the low tag reading rate issue in real-world scenarios (§3). Novel techniques introduced in §4 (Design) address these challenges, and thus have the potential to be applied to existing RFID infrastructure deployments without deploying additional hardware. We implement Pantomime using COTS RFID devices (§5), evaluate both end-to-end performance and microbenchmarks in laboratory environments (§6), and compare it with two state-of-the-arts tracking systems: four-antenna Tagoram [46] and two-antenna PolarDraw [33]. The result shows that Pantomime achieves competitive tracking performance using a single antenna. We review related work in §7, discuss limitations in §8 and conclude in §9.

2. CASE STUDY

In this section, we demonstrate the potential applicability of Pantomime for gesture-based object interaction with two real-world case studies: whiteboard handwriting tracking and retail-store item querying.

2.1 Whiteboard handwriting tracking

Although previous work [33, 40] has shown the feasibility of handwriting tracking using multi-antenna RFID systems, this case study aims to demonstrate that handwriting tracking is viable with a single antenna. Enabling handwriting tracking with minimal RFID infrastructure is essential to promote RFID-based sensing technologies to smart homes, classrooms, and offices, where RFID systems haven't been pervasively deployed.

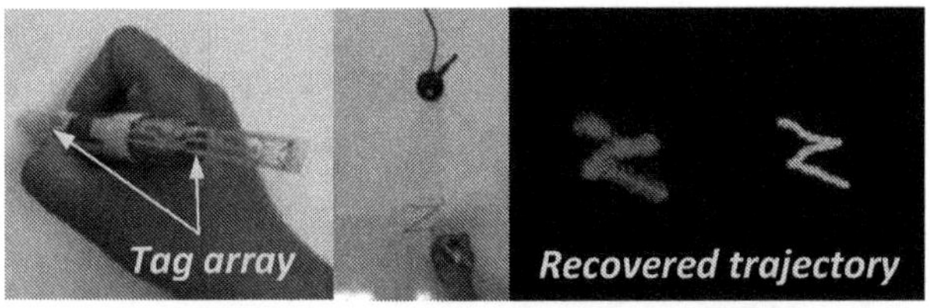

Figure 2— Handwriting tracking: the antenna is placed near the pen for a better illustration. Tag spacing = 2.7cm.

Figure 3— Retail store case study. Tag spacing = 5.4cm.

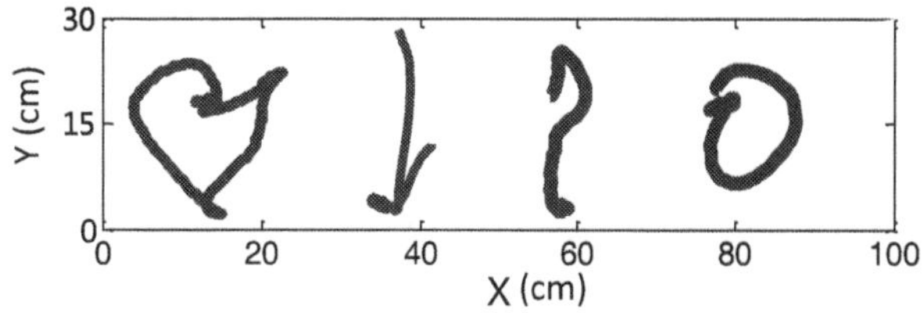

Figure 4— Recovered trajectory: ♡, ↓, ? and O.

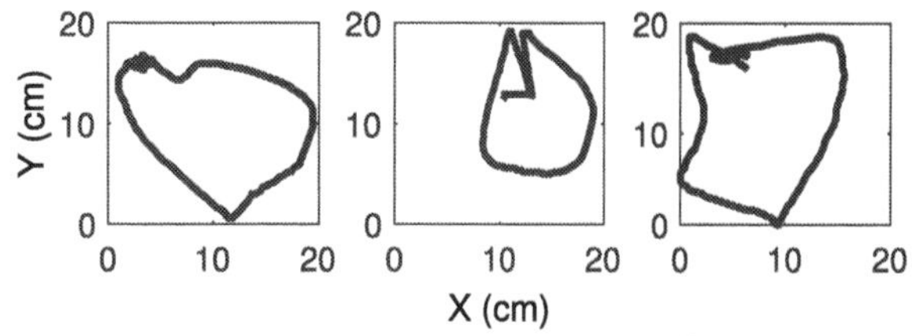

Figure 5— Recovered gesture when a user writes ♡ in the air using retail items with different weights: the weight of the retail item decreases from the left to the right.

As an illustration, we deploy Pantomime in a classroom. We install an antenna on top of a whiteboard and attach two passive RFID tags to a marker pen as in Figure 2. A volunteer is then asked to write letters at random on the whiteboard using the tagged marker pen. We plot the ground-truth trajectory of the marker pen and the trajectory captured by Pantomime. In Figure 2, the red arrows show the motion headings inferred by Pantomime, which are input into our fusion algorithm to derive the final trajectory denoted by the green line. Compared with the ground-truth, the recovered letter is stretched and rotated due to tracking errors. However, the trajectory shape of this letter Z is well preserved and can be easily recognized. This result clearly demonstrates the viability of Pantomime to track the handwriting with high fidelity. In §6.3, we quantitatively evaluate the quality of the trajectories recovered by Pantomime and compare it with the state-of-the-art multi-antenna RFID tracking systems.

2.2 Retail-store item querying

Acquiring customers' opinions on groceries is desired for shopkeepers to optimize the trading strategy and profit. While large online retailers *e.g.* Amazon can directly collect opinions of items via online feedback systems, most small to medium sized offline retailers still lack effective methods to acquire customers' opinion on groceries. With proper incentive mechanisms such as coupons and discounts, customers might be motivated to provide instant and offline opinions on the goods if there is an interactive way to express their opinions. This case study aims to demonstrate the viability of enabling RFID-based customer interactions, including offering feedback on the price and quality of daily goods, and reporting out-of-date items by performing the following in-air gestures with the item held in hand:

♡: I like this item;	↓: Too expensive;
?: Price unclear;	O: Item (*e.g.*, milk, bread) Out-of-date;

This gesture set is designed to include gestures consisting of both *straight lines* and *curves*. Figure 3 shows the deployment of Pantomime in a retail store, where passive RFID tags are attached to 40 items, with two tags on each item. A volunteer is asked to randomly pick up the items and perform the four gestures above. Figure 4 shows the recovered trajectories of the gestures. Apparently, the strokes in each gesture are warped or stretched due to the fact that the volunteer may change the item orientation unintentionally during gesturing. An interesting finding is that the recovered trajectories are more easily recognized when performing gestures holding a heavier item, as shown in Figure 5. A partial explanation might be that the volunteer will hold the item more steadily if it is heavy, which helps to keep the orientation of the tag array unchanged. Note that we do not quantitatively evaluate the recognition accuracy of these four gestures. Our aim is to demonstrate that the trajectories of such free-hand drawing-like gestures tracked by Pantomime are recognizable by humans. Selecting a specific machine learning algorithm for gesture recognition is out of the scope of this work.

3. CHALLENGES

The previous section demonstrates potential applications of Pantomime for emerging augmented interactions. In this section, we conduct two quantitative measurements on (i) antenna coverage and (ii) per-tag reading rate with different antenna and tag population settings to show (i) the difficulty of adopting multi-antenna based tag tracking schemes with a cost-effective system deployment and (ii) the new challenge introduced by tag arrays.

3.1 Antenna crisis

To quantitatively measure the number of antennas needed to deploy existing RFID-based localization and tracking systems in medium-sized stores and warehouses, we conduct simulations in a 100m x 100m rectangular region. The region is divided into 1m x 1m *blocks*. We deploy different numbers of antennas in this region and calculate the *four-coverage ratio* (Backpos [22] and Tagoram [46]) and *eight-coverage ratio* (RF-IDraw [40]) of these blocks. Here an *n-coverage ratio* is defined as the percentage of blocks that can be covered by at least *n* reader antennas among all blocks. To make a conservative estimation of the number of antennas required for *n-coverage*, we set a wider beam-width (120°) and a higher antenna gain (20 dBm) of each antenna in our simulation. Figure 6 illustrates the coverage ratio under different numbers of antennas. We can see that over 85% of the region is covered by at least one antenna when deploying 220 antennas. In contrast, 900 antennas are

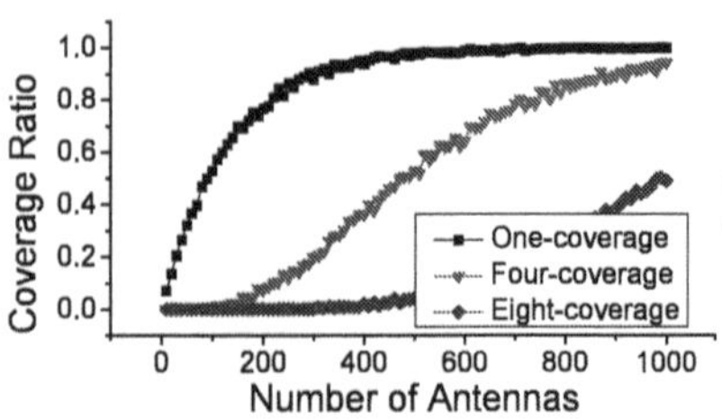

Figure 6— Coverage ratio vs. Number of antennas (simulation).

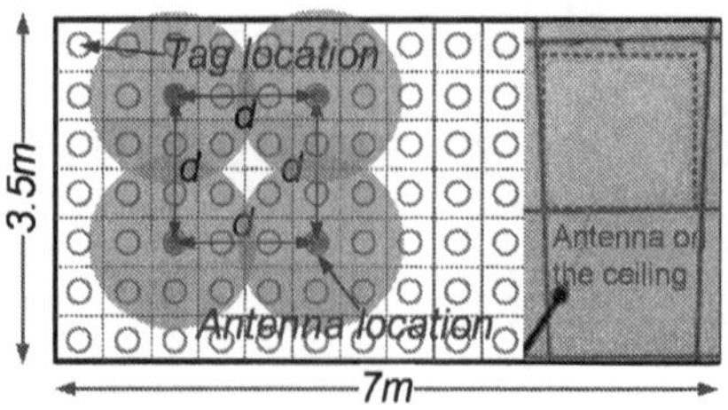

Figure 7— Coverage testing setup.

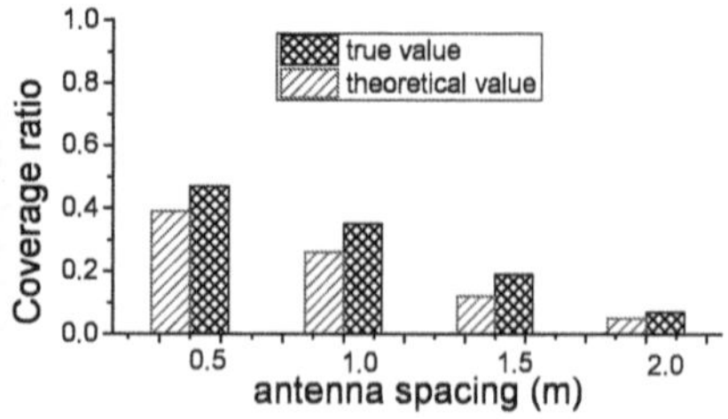

Figure 8— Four coverage ratio vs. antenna spacing d (experimental).

Table 3— The average readings (times/sec) of tag (**T**) and reader (**R**) under different tag population (n) settings.

	$n = 1$	2	5	20	50	100
T	51.23	46.32	21.92	15.34	7.78	4.14
R	51.23	92.64	109.6	306.79	388.84	413.52

required in order to provide a 85% four-coverage ratio. For eight-coverage, 1,000 antennas can only achieve around 54% coverage ratio. The result clearly shows that the multiple antenna coverage requirement will cause an "antenna crisis" – the number of antennas required grows dramatically with the expansion of the area to be covered.

To better understand the antenna coverage problem in real-world deployment, we deploy multiple antennas in a laboratory to examine the antenna coverage ratio. In this experiment, we mount four circularly polarized antennas [16] on the ceiling 3 m above the floor in a 3.5 m x 7 m laboratory, place an RFID tag in different locations in the room (white circles in Figure 7), and measure the number of antennas that can interrogate the tag. We estimate the coverage ratio as the number of locations that are covered by four antennas over different antenna spacing, and plot the results in Figure 8. As shown, four antennas with a spacing d of 0.5 m yields a 47% four-coverage ratio, which is moderately higher than the theoretical value due to multi-path reflections. Given a spacing d of 2 m, which resembles the antenna deployment in a real-world RFID system [41], the four-coverage ratio drops dramatically to only 7%. In summary, Deploying a multi-antenna RFID tracking system in malls, supermarkets, and warehouses will incur significant infrastructure costs.

3.2 Low tag reading rate

A high tag reading rate is essential to accurately track tag movement. Insufficient reading rates are especially harmful to phase-based rfid tracking schemes because phase readings repeat from 0 to 2π every wavelength, and a low reading rate will fail to capture the consecutive phase changes when the tag moves fast, resulting in an ambiguity in the tag's displacement. In gesture or handwriting tracking applications, a tagged object can move at a speed ranging from 0.5 m/s to 3.0 m/s [9]. Thus the tag should be read at a minimal rate of 8 Hz to 46 Hz to avoid this phase ambiguity, given a wavelength of 32 cm (UHF frequency 920.625 MHz).

Commercial RFID readers adopt Slotted ALOHA protocol [29] to interrogate tags within the reading range. Each tag randomly picks a time slot to reply. A collision occurs when multiple tags reply in the same slot and the reader will fail to decode any of them. Although the allocated slots can scale to the tag population [46], collisions occur much more frequently for a large tag population due to the limited frame length [31], which decreases the per-tag reading rate. In this experiment, we examine the average tag reading rate with different numbers of tags in an indoor laboratory environment. Specifically, we place an RFID antenna 2 m away from a bookshelf to interrogate tags attached to the spine of books. As shown in Table 3, the reader's reading rate (**R**) increases significantly as tag population grows. However, the average per-tag reading rate ((**T**)) drops significantly from 46 Hz to around 4 Hz with 100 tags. Such a low tag reading rate fails to meet the theoretical minimum requirement for gesture tracking. As we further attach multiple tags on each object, there will be more MAC contention and more collisions, resulting in a much lower per-tag reading rate.

4. DESIGN

This section first introduces our proposed technique for boosting the tag reading rate, followed by the virtual antenna tracking algorithm, and finally movement translation, the processing step that outputs the trajectory of the tagged object.

4.1 Boosting the tag reading rate

The basic idea to boost the reading rate of the tag array is to make the reader interrogate these target tags only, instead of all tags within the reading range of the reader. Here *target tags* refer to the tags on an object that a user holds in hand and performs gestures with. *Non-target tags* are the tags on other stationary objects nearby. Thus the reading rate boosting scheme contains two steps: (i) identifying the target tags and (ii) blocking non-target tags from responding to the reader.

Inferring the target tags. To differentiate target and non-target tags, we leverage the intuition that the pick-up action will make target tag moving, hence leading to continuous phase changes of these target tags. In contrast, the non-target tags keeps stationary and their phase reading remains. To validate the above intuition, we attach 40 tags to 20 books (two tags per book), and place an RFID antenna 4 m away to interrogate the tags. The per-tag reading rate in this experiment is around 10 Hz. We collect phase measurements under four settings: a clear Line-Of-Sight (LOS) path between the tags and the antenna, people stands by to create reflection paths, people stands in between to block the LOS path, and people pick up a book to review. Figure 9 illustrates these testing setups.

For each testing case, we randomly pick up a tag and plot their phase readings in Figure 10. As shown, the phase readings remain stable in clear LOS path condition. When the people walks to the bookshelf and generate a reflection path, we can see the phase readings of the stationary tag jumps from a stable level to another stable level. Similar trend happens when the human walks to block the LOS path between the tag and the antenna. However, when the tag is picked up by the volunteer, we can see the phase readings of this tag change constantly across the whole cycle of $[0, 2\pi]$. Hence it is possible to distinguish the target tags by observing its phase changing trend.

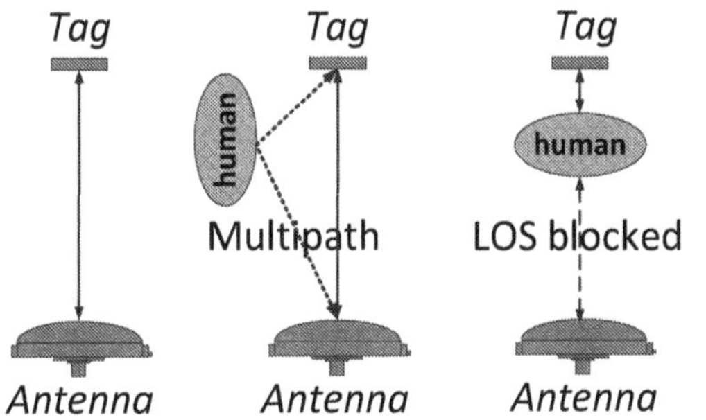

Figure 9— Examining the motion-induced phase changes.

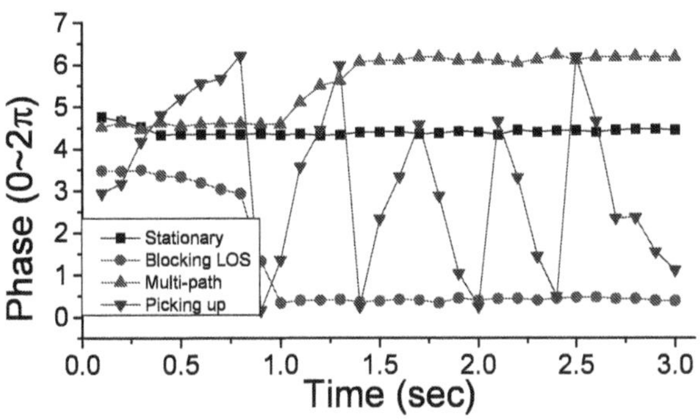

Figure 10— Phase pattern of tags under different motion states.

In Pantomime, we quantify the phase changing trend using an entropy metric. Low entropy correlates with narrow phase distribution likely from a stationary, non-target tag, while high entropy indicates a wider phase distribution possibly from a moving, target tag. Specifically, we split the range of phase readings $[0, 2\pi]$ into N bins with equal bin size. The bin size is empirically set to 0.5 radians (see §6.2). Given a set of phase readings of tag i, let n_j be the number of phase readings within j^{th} bin. We write the entropy of tag i as:

$$e_i = -\frac{1}{\lg(N-1)} \sum_{j=1}^{N} p_i^j \lg p_i^j \quad (1)$$

where $p_i^j = \frac{n_j}{\sum_{k=1}^{N} n_k}$.[2] Pantomime then formulates the following hypothesis test with H_0 representing the hypothesis of a moving, target tag and H_1 of a stationary, non-target tag:

$$\begin{cases} H_0 : e_i \geq \gamma \\ H_1 : e_i < \gamma, \end{cases} \quad (2)$$

where γ denotes a predefined threshold. We conduct micro-benchmarks to test various γ settings and empirically set it to 0.7 (§6.2), which yields a satisfactory detection performance. As false positives may still exist, Pantomime further filters out those target tags whose siblings are detected as non-target tags. Here the siblings of a tag represent the remaining tags in the same tag array.

Blocking the reply of non-target tags. After finding out the target tags, our next step is to stop non-target tags from replying to the reader, thereby reducing the amount of RF traffic and response collisions to improve the reading rate of the target tags. To achieve this goal, we manipulate the EPC-standard C1G2 low-level tag interrogation process [7]. As Figure 11 shows, at the beginning of

[2] we set $\lg p_i^j$ to 0 when $p_i^j = 0$.

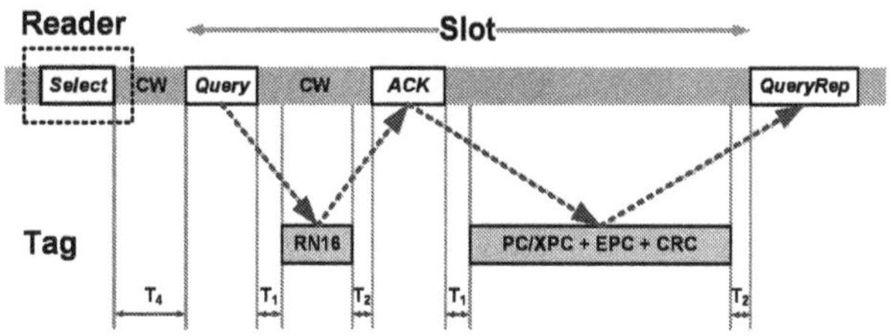

Figure 11— Low-level reader to tag communication.

each inventory round (frame), the reader executes a *SELECT* command to choose tags for inventory and access. After receiving this command, the tags satisfying this selection criteria will enter the *READY* state, indicating that they are ready to reply. Other tags will keep silent (and not reply) until the end of this inventory round. By setting the *SELECT* criteria, we can thus stop the stationary tags from replying. The default setting of *SELECT* is to let all tags reply. In Pantomime, after detecting the target tags, we set the *SELECT* command to read the target tags alone by specifying the 96-bit EPC code of these tags. This is achieved by calling the function setC1G2TagInventoryMask of the C1G2Filter class provided by the Low-level Reader Protocol (LLRP) API.

After performing a gesture, the user may place the object back to the rack, resulting in a significant phase fluctuations due to the object motions, and then relatively stable phase readings when the object becomes stationary. Pantomime detects this state transition by examining the variance of phase readings within every five seconds. A small variance indicates the object has been placed back on the rack, hence Pantomime will reconfigure the tag mask to let all tags reply. We test different variance threshold and set it to 0.3, which yields an empirically minimum false positive rate.

4.2 Virtual antenna trajectory tracking

To track the object motion using a single antenna, we track the location changes of the antenna in the frame of the reference of the tag array and transform into a gesture trajectory in physical coordinates via motion translation. In Pantomime, we keep tracking the relative location of the antenna by estimating the change in tag-to-antenna distances. However, the accuracy of such ranging-based tracking algorithm is undesirable due to multi-path reflection and thermal noises [46]. In Pantomime, we further improve the accuracy of ranging-based tracking by incorporating a kinetic model and an Extended Kalman Filter (EKF) fusion framework. In the following parts, we first introduce our ranging-based tracking algorithm, and then describe how to improve its tracking accuracy with EKF model.

4.2.1 Pseudo-ranging tracking algorithm

Let $P_t = (x_t, y_t)$ be the virtual position of the antenna at time t; $R_j = (x_{R_j}, y_{R_j})$ be the location of tag j in the frame of reference of the tag array, which is known a prior. The distance from the antenna to tag j can be represented as:

$$d_t^j = \|P_t, R_j\| = \sqrt{(x_t - x_{R_j})^2 + (y_t - y_{R_j})^2} = \lambda \left(\frac{\theta_t^j}{4\pi} \right) + s_j \quad (3)$$

where θ_t^j is the phase reading of tag j at time t; s_j is an unknown distance offset. We assume the object moves within half a wavelength (≈16 cm) during consecutive tag readings.[3] Accordingly,

[3] That is, no faster than 3 m/s given the reading rate of 46 Hz, which can be achieved after boosting the tag reading rate.

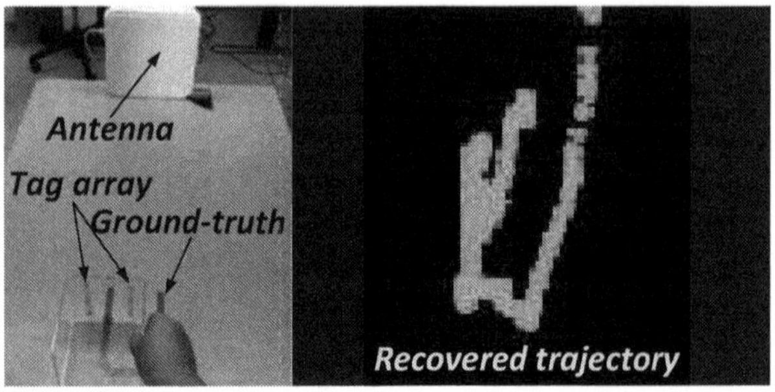

Figure 12— Recovering the trajectory of the moving cube based on pseudo-ranging.

the virtual moving distance of the antenna during time t and $t+1$ can be computed as follows:

$$\Delta d_{t+1}^{j} = \begin{cases} (\theta_{t+1}^{j} - \theta_{t}^{j}) \cdot \lambda/(4\pi), & \text{if } |\theta_{t+1}^{j} - \theta_{t}^{j}| < \pi \\ (\theta_{t+1}^{j} - \theta_{t}^{j} - 2\pi) \cdot \lambda/(4\pi), & \text{if } \theta_{t+1}^{j} - \theta_{t}^{j} \geq \pi \\ (\theta_{t+1}^{j} - \theta_{t}^{j} + 2\pi) \cdot \lambda/(4\pi), & \text{if } \theta_{t+1}^{j} - \theta_{t}^{j} \leq -\pi \end{cases} \tag{4}$$

Now the distance between the reader antenna and each tag can be updated as follows:

$$d_{t+1}^{j} = \|P_{t+1}, R_j\| = d_t^j + \Delta d_{t+1}^{j} = d_1^j + s_j + \sum_{k=1}^{t+1} \Delta d_k^j \tag{5}$$

In the above equation, we cannot compute d_{t+1}^{j} due to the unknown distance offset s_j. However, s_j is a constant value and will not change throughout the object's movement. Hence we omit s_j and define the *pseudo-distance* between the antenna and tag j as follows:

$$\hat{d}_{t+1}^{j} = d_1^j + \sum_{k=1}^{t+1} \Delta d_k^j \tag{6}$$

In the above equation, d_1^j and $\sum_{k=1}^{t+1} \Delta d_k^j$ can be computed using Equation 3 and Equation 4, respectively. Thus we can estimate the antenna's position (P_t) at each time point and determine its virtual moving trajectory in the frame of the reference of the tag array with at least two tags.

The pseudo-ranging tracking algorithm works in two steps: computing the pseudo initial distance d_1^j between the antenna and each tag j, and then consecutively estimating the new location of the antenna as the object (antenna array) moves. Specifically, in each time frame, the algorithm computes the virtual moving distance Δd_{t+1}^{j} of the antenna and updates the pseudo-distance $\hat{d}_{t+1}^{j}$ between each tag and the antenna. With $\hat{d}_{t+1}^{j}$, the algorithm estimates the antenna's virtual location via trilateration.

Figure 12 shows the trajectory of a letter U recovered by the pseudo-ranging tracking algorithm. As shown, the recovered trajectory preserves the rough shape of the letter. However, there are sharp and abrupt discontinuities in the trajectory, especially at the corners of the shape. This is because the location of the antenna is estimated independently each time. Therefore, large location deviation occurs during consecutive location estimates due to phase noises and multi-path effect. To avoid unexpected discontinuities in the recovered trajectory, we further leverage heading information to bound the deviation of successive location estimates.

Antenna heading inference. In Figure 13(b), suppose the antenna moves from position A to B within two tag readings. Since the sampling rate of the tag is high, hence we know $|AB| \ll |AT_2|$. Thus it is reasonable to approximate the antenna's displacement along the radial direction $|AB_2|$ with Δd. On the other hand, since the antenna's position A is estimated through the position-velocity model (described later), it is thus feasible to determine the heading of $\angle\overrightarrow{AB_2}$ as well. Taking one step further, we can infer the displacement and the heading of $\angle\overrightarrow{AB_1}$ and $\angle\overrightarrow{AB_3}$ in a similar way (as shown in Figure 13(c)), and finally determine the antenna heading by summing up these vectors.

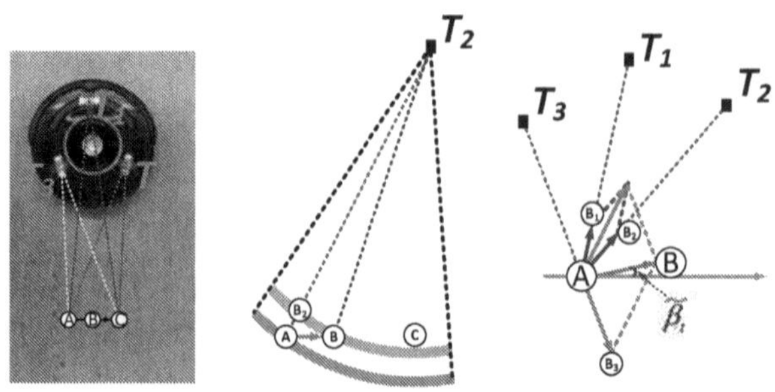

(a) (b) (c)

Figure 13— An illustration of the antenna heading inference. The antenna virtually moves from point A to point B and our algorithm continuously tracks the antenna heading during its virtual movement.

4.2.2 *Kinetic model based tracking algorithm*

Position-velocity model. We employ constant acceleration model-[21] to characterize the hand motion. So the antenna movement suits this model as well. In the frame of reference of the tag array, consider the discrete time model: let T be the window size in *ms*. Within each window, the state of the antenna can be characterized by its location $P = [x_t, y_t]$, velocity $V = [\dot{x}_t, \dot{y}_t]$ and acceleration $A = [\ddot{x}_t, \ddot{y}_t]$:

$$X_t = [P, V, A] = [x_t, \dot{x}_t, \ddot{x}_t, y_t, \dot{y}_t, \ddot{y}_t] \tag{7}$$

The state transition model can be written as:

$$X_{t+1} = f(X_t) + W_t = AX_t{}^T + W_t$$

$$= \begin{bmatrix} 1 & T & T^2/2 & 0 & 0 & 0 \\ 0 & 1 & T & 0 & 0 & 0 \\ 0 & 0 & 1 & 0 & 0 & 0 \\ 0 & 0 & 0 & 1 & T & T^2/2 \\ 0 & 0 & 0 & 0 & 1 & T \\ 0 & 0 & 0 & 0 & 0 & 1 \end{bmatrix} \cdot \begin{bmatrix} x_t \\ \dot{x}_t \\ \ddot{x}_t \\ y_t \\ \dot{y}_t \\ \ddot{y}_t \end{bmatrix} + \begin{bmatrix} T^2/2 & 0 \\ T & 0 \\ 1 & 0 \\ 0 & T^2/2 \\ 0 & t \\ 0 & 1 \end{bmatrix} \cdot \begin{bmatrix} n_t^x \\ n_t^y \end{bmatrix}$$

where A models the state transition of the antenna from window t to $t+1$. Vector W_t takes thermal noise into account, which follows normal distribution with zero mean and covariance matrix Q_t: $W_t \sim \mathcal{N}(0, Q_t)$. With the antenna heading and the position-velocity model, it is viable to track the virtual movement of the antenna in the frame of reference of the tag array, and accordingly the movements of the tagged object. However, since the acceleration of the hand gesture may change abruptly, the constant acceleration model fails to accurately characterize the shape of the virtual antenna motion.

4.3 Fusion Algorithm

As pointed out previously, the ranging-based method can recover the rough shape of the virtual antenna movement yet fail to characterize the trajectory smoothly. Conversely, the kinetic model based method could track the trajectory smoothly, yet fail to accurately characterize its shape with natural hand movements. We thus leverage the Extended Karman Filter (EKF) model to fuse the tracking results of these two tracking algorithms for a better result.

Observation. Let N be the number of tags attached to the object. The observation function is defined as:

$$Y_{t+1} = h(X_{t+1}) + V_{t+1} = \begin{bmatrix} \|P_{t+1}, R_1\| \\ \|P_{t+1}, R_2\| \\ \vdots \\ \|P_{t+1}, R_N\| \end{bmatrix} + V_{t+1} = \begin{bmatrix} d_t^1 + \Delta d_{t+1}^1 \\ d_t^2 + \Delta d_{t+1}^2 \\ \vdots \\ d_t^N + \Delta d_{t+1}^N \end{bmatrix} + V_{t+1} \tag{8}$$

where V_{t+1} is the ranging errors due to phase noises. We empirically set V_{t+1} to $\frac{1}{10} \cdot mean(\Delta d_t^j)$, where $mean(\Delta d_t^j)$ is the average value of the change of the distance between the antenna and each tag. $h(.)$ is a non-linear function that relates observations and states.

EKF-based Motion Tracking. The EKF-based fusion algorithm consists of three steps: linearization, prediction and updating. We detail them in turn in the following parts.

Linearization. In Equation 8, the nonlinear function $h(.)$ can be linearized about X_0 as follows:

$$Y_t - Y_{t-1} = H_t \Delta X_t + V_t \tag{9}$$

where H_t is the Jacobian matrix of $h(.)$ with respect to X_n.

Predicting phase. Given the estimate $\hat{X}_{t|t}$ of X_t, the predicted state $\hat{X}_{t+1|t}$ is calculated as:

$$\hat{X}_{t+1|t} = F_t \hat{X}_{t|t} \tag{10}$$

where $F_t = \frac{\partial f}{\partial X}|_{\hat{X}_{t|t}}$ is the Jacobian matrix of $f(.)$. The prediction error covariance matrix $\hat{P}_{t+1|t}$ associated to the predicted state estimation $\hat{X}_{t+1|t}$ is evaluated from the previous estimate $\hat{P}_{t|t}$:

$$\hat{P}_{t+1|t} = F_t \hat{P}_{t|t} F_t^T + Q_t \tag{11}$$

The predicted measurement is then computed as follows:

$$\hat{Y}_{t+1|t} = h(\hat{X}_{t+1|t}) + V_{t+1} \tag{12}$$

Updating phase. Once the system acquires new phase readings at time $t+1$, it computes the difference between the measurement and the predicted measurement as follows:

$$\gamma_{t+1} = Y_{t+1} - \hat{Y}_{t+1|t} \tag{13}$$

with the covariance:

$$S_{t+1} = H_{t+1} \hat{P}_{t+1|t} H_{t+1}^T + R_{t+1} \tag{14}$$

where $H_{t+1} = \frac{\partial h}{\partial X}|_{\hat{X}_{t+1|t}}$ is the Jacobian matrix of the state transition function $f(.)$ with respect to the predicted state $\hat{X}_{t+1|t}$. After that, it computes the EKF gain as follows:

$$K_{t+1} = P_{t+1|t} H_{t+1} (\hat{S}_{t+1})^{-1} \tag{15}$$

Finally, the algorithm computes a posterior state estimate $X_{t+1|t+1}$ and the corresponding covariance matrix $\hat{P}_{t+1|t+1}$ by correcting the priori state estimate $\hat{X}_{t+1|t}$ and $\hat{P}_{t+1|t}$:

$$\hat{X}_{t+1|t+1} = \hat{X}_{t+1|t} + K_{t+1} \gamma_{t+1} \tag{16}$$

$$\hat{P}_{t+1|t+1} = (I_N - K_{t+1} H_{t+1}) \hat{P}_{t+1|t} \tag{17}$$

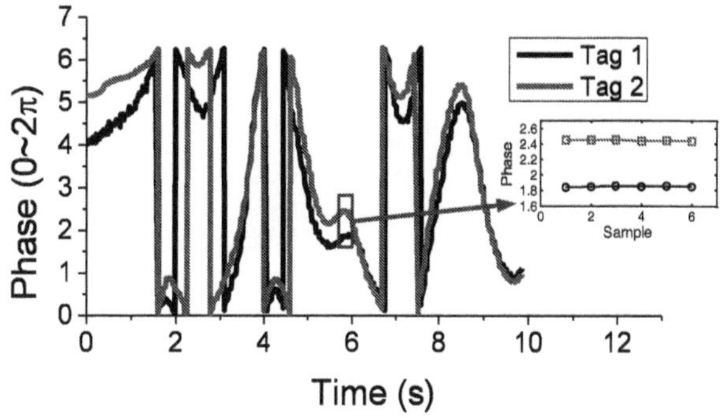

Figure 14— Phase readings of two tags attached to an object that has been picked up for gesturing.

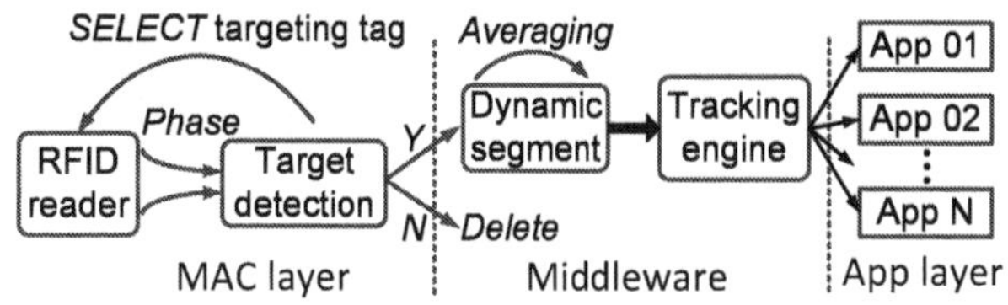

Figure 15— System workflow of Pantomime.

4.4 Motion Translation

Let $S = \{P_1, P_2, ..., P_t\}$ be the recovered trajectory of the antenna in the frame of reference of the tag array and S' be the real trajectory of the object in the frame of the reference of the physical world. We can recover S' by rotating S by π:

$$S' = S \cdot \begin{bmatrix} \cos\pi & -\sin\pi \\ \sin\pi & \cos\pi \end{bmatrix} \tag{18}$$

5. IMPLEMENTATION

So far we have provided the algorithmic basis of how Pantomime works. This section describes its implementation.

RF-sensing module. The hardware of the RF-sensing module consists of three parts: an ImpinJ Speedway R420 RFID reader [11], an RFMAX indoor RFID antenna [16], and multiple Avery Dennison AD-227m5 UHF passive RFID tags [5]. The reader interrogates RFID tags and sends phase readings to a Lenovo ThinkCentre PC for processing.

Frontend software. Figure 15 shows the workflow of Pantomime. The reader interrogates tags using the Low Level RFID Protocol (LLRP) API. We implement the reading rate control function in the MAC layer. Once the target tags are detected, the reader stops other stationary tags from replying in the following frames. The phase readings of target tags are then delivered to the middleware layer for segmentation and tracking. The output of the middleware layer is the trajectory of the antenna in the frame of the reference of the tag array, which can be integrated to various applications (after trajectory translation) such as virtual touch screen and in-air book reviewing. The software is implemented in C# and it tracks the object in real-time.

Dynamic segmentation. To minimize the noises and interference, Pantomime segments phase streams into windows and uses the average phase in each window as the input of the tracking engine. The window size is critical to our system. If it is too small, Pantomime needs to frequently feed the phase readings to the tracking engine, leading to significant computational overhead. If the window size

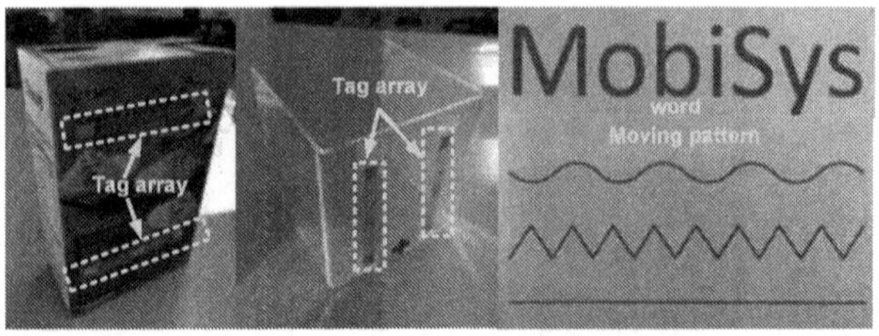

Figure 16— Experimental setup: We construct tag arrays by attaching multiple tags to a food package and a plastic cube, and move them along trajectories printed on paper.

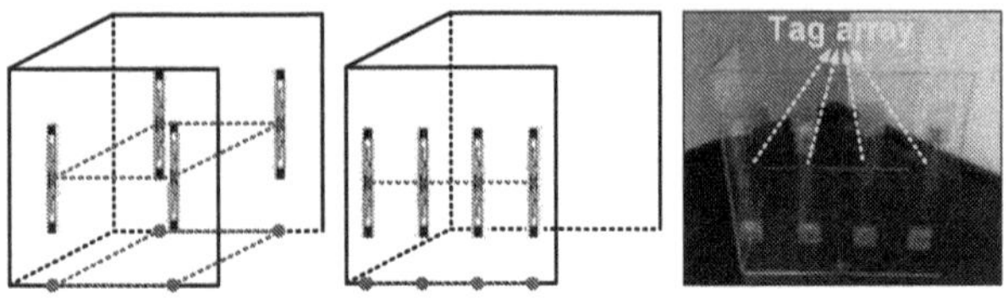

(a) (b) (c)

Figure 17— Different layout of tag arrays.

is too large, the phase changes induced by motions are likely to average out, resulting in tracking errors. Either case will degrade the system performance.

In Pantomime, we design a dynamic segmentation mechanism. It is based on the following finding: if the object moves slowly, the phase will change slowly and smoothly, and we can safely expand the window size. If the object moves fast, the phase will change rapidly, we need to reduce the window size to preserve the detail of the phase profile. Specifically, Pantomime updates the window size as follows:

if v_t - v_{t-1} < -v_{TH} & $W_t + W_a < W_{max}$ **then**
  $W_{t+1} \leftarrow W_t + W_a$;
else if v_t - v_{t-1} > v_{TH} & $W_t - W_a > W_{min}$ **then**
  $W_{t+1} \leftarrow W_t - W_a$;
else
  $W_{t+1} \leftarrow W_t$;
end if

where W_α is a constant to control the window length; v_t is the moving speed of the tag in the time window t; v_{TH} is the moving speed threshold. Within each window, the window size updates until it surpasses or falls below the maximum and minimum window size W_{max} and W_{min}, respectively. We test a wide range of parameter settings, and empirically set v_{TH}, initial window size W, W_α, W_{max} and W_{min} to 0.1 m/s, 40 ms, 20 ms, 200 ms and 20 ms, respectively.

6. EVALUATION

In this section, we present the experimental evaluation results of Pantomime, starting with the experimental methodology, microbenchmarks and ending with field studies.

6.1 Experimental methodology

We attach RFID tags to both a food package and a plastic cube to form a tag array and move the array along printed trajectories. The trajectories cover different English letters, words (with different lengths) and paths (see Figure 16).

We use *recognition accuracy* to quantify the performance of Pantomime. The *recognition accuracy* is defined as the fraction of correctly recognized hand-written letters/words over total number of hand-written letters/words. For letter recognition, we use LipiTk [10], an open-source handwriting recognition toolkit.

Table 4— FP/FN rate under different γ and bin size settings.

		Bin size			
		0.5 (rad)	**1**	**1.5**	**2**
γ	**0.1**	0.72/0.01	0.72/0.01	0.72/0.01	0.81/0.03
	0.3	0.51/0.01	0.51/0.01	0.53/0.02	0.74/0.05
	0.5	0.21/0.03	0.21/0.03	0.21/0.04	0.43/0.06
	0.7	**0.03/0.03**	0.06/0.03	0.06/0.07	0.14/0.09
	0.9	0.02/0.06	0.02/0.06	0.02/0.10	0.06/0.12

6.2 Microbenchmarks

In these microbenchmark experiments, we answer the following questions:

1. *How do bin size and γ affect tag detection?*
2. *How does tag reading rate affect tracking performance?*
3. *How does array size affect tracking performance?*
4. *How does array layout affect tracking performance?*
5. *Does the EKF fusion algorithm improve tracking accuracy?*

Configuring bin size and γ. We first perform a sensitivity analysis, examining how the bin size and the threshold γ affect the targeting tag detection accuracy. In this experiment, two volunteers randomly pick up a book from 20 tagged books. Each experiment is repeated 50 times, and we get 100 phase series in total. We also collect 100 phase series of those stationary tags, whose wireless links are blocked or reflected by nearby humans. We then vary the bin size and γ to find an appropriate setting. Table 4 summarizes the False Positive (FP) rate and False Negative (FN) rate with different the bin size and γ. The desired parameter setting should minimize both the FP and FN rates. Suggested by the experimental result, we set the bin size and γ to 0.5 rad and 0.7, which optimize the overall detection performance.

Impact of tag reading rate. We then examine the impact of the tag reading rate. In this experiment, we randomly pick 10 letters from 26 English letters and let a volunteer write these letters using the two-tag array cube (see Figure 16). We change the tag population in the antenna's reading range to control the tag reading rate. Figure 18 shows the recognition accuracy. As expected, the recognition accuracy is sensitive to the average tag reading rate. It achieves an accuracy below 20% when the reading rate is around 8 Hz, and then jumps to around 80% when the average per-tag reading rate is 31 Hz. In contrast, Pantomime achieves constantly high recognition accuracy after boosting the tag reading rate, with the accuracies all above 87%, which verifies the efficacy of our tag reading rate boosting protocol.

Impact of array layout. We then examine the impact of the array layout. As shown in Figure 17, we attach four tags to a plastic cube, forming a rectangle array and a linear array. We randomly choose 10 letters from the English alphabet, and invite a volunteer to write each letter 10 times using these two different tag-array. The letter recognition accuracy is shown in Table 5. As the result shows, Pantomime achieves 92% letter recognition accuracy with the rectangle array. The recognition accuracy drops slightly to 86% with the linear array. The performance gap here indicates that the nature of sparse tag distribution in the rectangle array helps to improve the tracking accuracy.

Impact of array size. We next examine the impact of the array size. Similar to previous experiments, we invite a volunteer to write

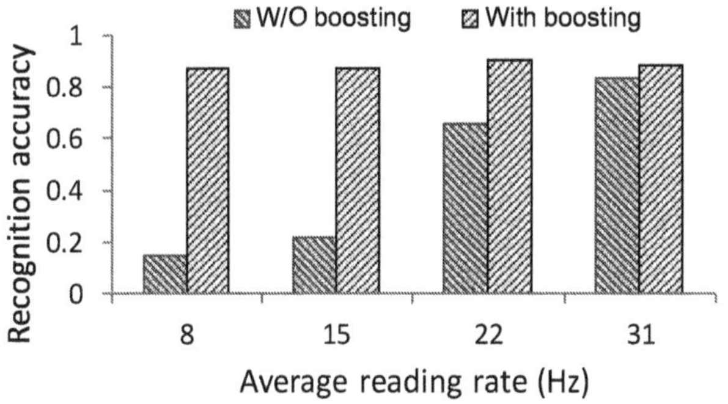

Figure 18— Impact of reading rate.

Table 5— Impact of Array layout.

	Rectangle array	Linear array
Recognition accuracy	92%	86%

10 letters using a linear tag array of size 2 to 5. Figure 19 shows the recognition accuracy. As we see, the recognition accuracy increases as we attach more tags to the cube. This is because compared with a small tag array, the large tag array can help average out ranging noise. However, the performance gap between the small array (*e.g.*, two-tag array) and the larger one (*e.g.*, five-tag array) is confined to a small range (below 5% in the experiment), indicating that the large array marginally improves tracking accuracy.

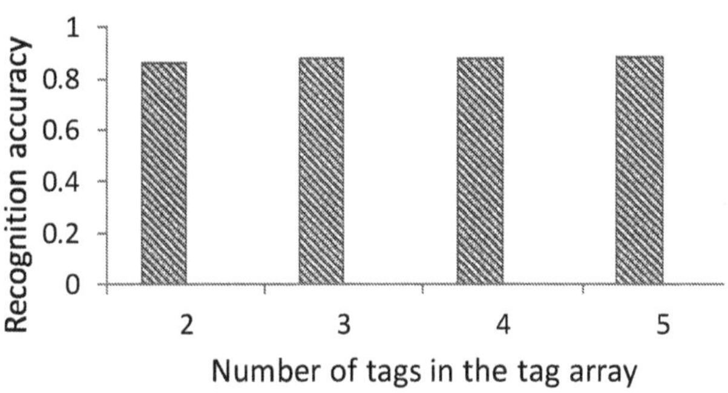

Figure 19— Impact of array size.

Gain of fusion algorithm. This experiment validates the gain of the EKF fusion algorithm for gesture tracking. Four volunteers are asked to use the two-tag array to write 10 letters randomly chosen from the 26 English letters. These written letters are then put into the LipiTk for letter recognition. The result is shown in Figure 20. Pantomime achieves a relatively stable performance over all four volunteers, with a maximum and minimum recognition accuracy of 87% and 83%, respectively. In contrast, when solely running the pseudo ranging-based tracking algorithm, Pantomime achieves undesirable performance over the four volunteers, with a maximum recognition accuracy of around 56%. This result demonstrates that the EKF fusion algorithm significantly improves the tracking accuracy.

6.3 Field study

We conduct field studies in a laboratory environment. In the field study, we attach two tags to a food package to form a stylus (see Figure 16). A volunteer is asked to use this light-weighted stylus

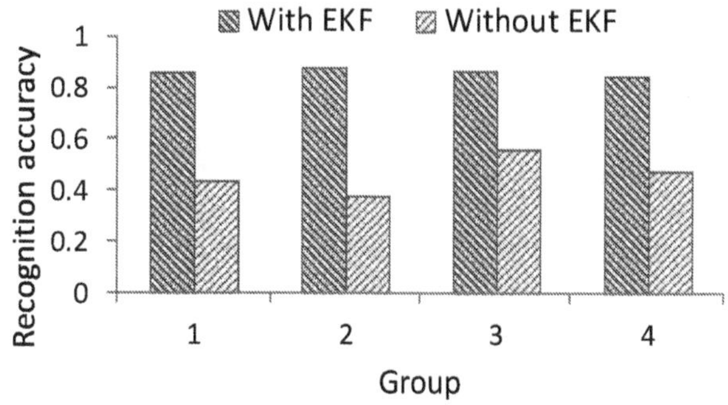

Figure 20— Examine the EKF gain.

to write given characters. We are of particular interest in answering the following questions:

1. *Is* Pantomime *robust to different moving patterns?*
2. *Is* Pantomime *resilient to multi-path effect?*
3. Does tag-to-reader distance affect the tracking accuracy?
4. *Does backing material affect the tracking accuracy?*
5. *How does* Pantomime *perform compared with other state-of-the-art systems?*
6. Can we adapt Pantomime to multi-antenna settings?

Robustness to moving patterns. We first examine whether Pantomime can successfully track different kinds of trajectories for future drawing applications. These trajectories include three kinds of fundamental line drawings [36]: straight lines, wave lines, and jagged lines, as shown in Figure 16. Figure 21 shows the recovered trajectories. As shown, the recovered wave line and jagged line are not self-symmetric due to tracking errors. However, each of them still preserves its unique line pattern, making them distinguishable to human beings. Also, we can see the recovered straight line is still smooth despite deviating from its ground truth at small scale.

Figure 21— Wave line, jagged line, and straight line, as outputs of Pantomime.

We further show a sample of the recovered trajectory of letters M o b i S y s in Figure 22. The recovered trajectories of letters o and s are quite smooth, manifesting that Pantomime is capable of capturing the continuously moving heading changes. The detailed shapes of these seven letters are well preserved.

Resilience to multi-path reflections. We then examine the impact of both static and dynamic multi-path on the tracking performance.

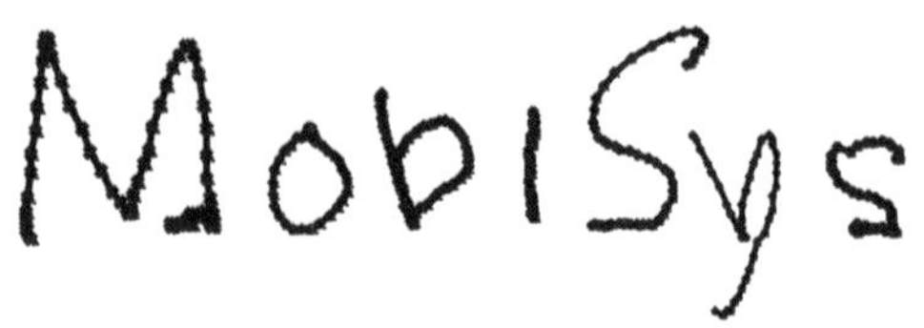

Figure 22— Recovered trajectories for M, o, b, i, S, y, s.

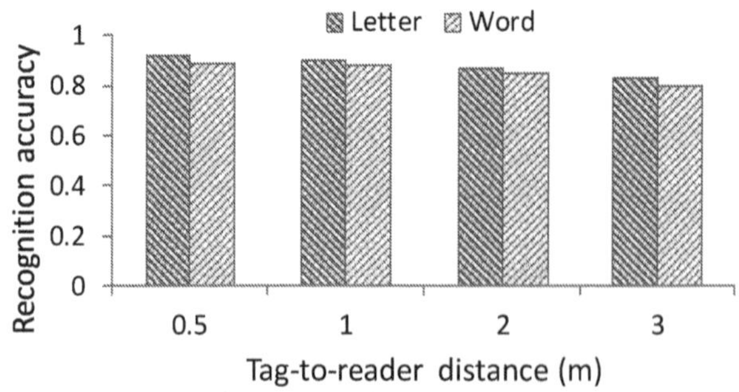

Figure 24— Impact of tag-to-reader distance.

Figure 25— Making a stylus using everyday object.

For static multi-path, we put two metal lockers around the experiment field to reflect the backscatter signals. For dynamic multi-path, a volunteer walks around near the experiment field at normal walking speed to generate dynamic reflections. Another volunteer then writes 10 letters and 10 words using the stylus, with each letter written for 10 times. Figure 23 shows the recognition result of these letters and words under different multi-path reflections. The recognition accuracy for both the letter and the word slightly decreases as we introduce the multi-path effect. However, with static multi-path, Pantomime still achieves around 85% and 80% accuracy for letter and word recognition, respectively. With dynamic multi-path, Pantomime achieves around 80% and 71% accuracy for letter and word recognition, respectively. The small performance gap between the no multi-path case and the multi-path cases shows that Pantomime is not very sensitive to both the static and dynamic multi-path.

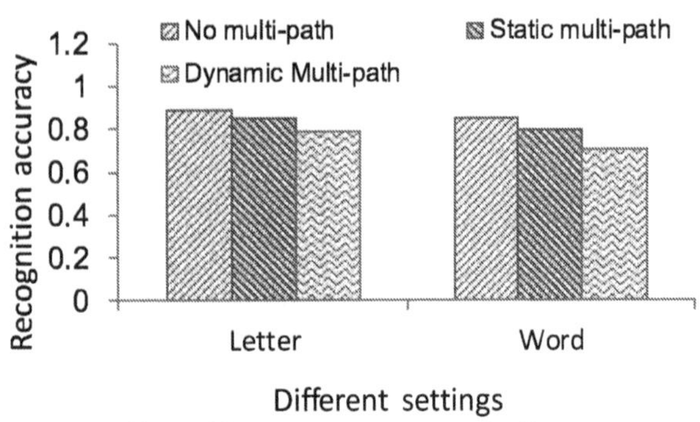

Figure 23— Impact the multi-path effect.

Impact of tag-to-reader distance. We further examine the system performance under different tag-to-reader distance settings. In this trail of experiments, we place an RFID antenna 3m, 2m, 1m, and 0.5m away from a stage. In each tag-to-reader distance setting, we invite a volunteer to stand on this stage and write ten letters and ten words using the plastic stylus. Each letter and word is repeated ten times. Figure 24 shows the result. As shown, when the stage is 0.5m away from the reader antenna, Pantomime achieves 92% letter recognition accuracy and 89% word recognition accuracy, respectively. As we expand the distance between the stage and the reader antenna, the signal will experience relatively intense multi-path propagation. Hence both the letter and the word recognition accuracy drops slightly. Nevertheless, both the letter and the word recognition accuracy still maintain above 80% when the reader is 3m away from the stage.

Impact of backing material. We next examine the impact of backing material on the system performance. In this trail of experiments, we attach a two-tag array on four kinds of items (as shown in Figure 25): a woolen puppet (W), an empty ceramic mug (C), a plastic bubble cushion (P), and a leather wallet (L). We then ask a volunteer to use these four kinds of items as a stylus to write 10 letters in the air, with each letter been written for 10 times. The letter is randomly chosen from 26 English alphabet letters. The letter recognition accuracy of these four kinds of stylus is shown in Table 6. As shown, we can category the recognition accuracy of these five kinds of stylus into two groups. The first groups include the woolen puppet, the bubble cushion and the leather bag, they all achieve a letter recognition accuracy over 84%, and there is no significant difference in their recognition accuracy. Another group only contains the empty ceramic mug, which achieves 2% recognition accuracy. To understand the reason behind this poor performance, we further check the phase readings of this stylus and find that the tag reading rate maintains in a very low level (below 5 Hz), probably due to the strong signal reflection property of this kind of material. Such a low tag reading rate renders the phase readings discontinuous during the stylus movement. Accordingly, Pantomime is unable to recover the profile of the stylus's movement, resulting in a low letter recognition accuracy.

Table 6— Letter recognition accuracy using different stylus.

	W	**C**	**P**	**L**
Letter recognition accuracy	85%	2%	84%	88%

Comparison with state-of-the-art. We further compare Pantomime against two state-of-the-art RFID-based tracking systems[4]: Tagoram [46] and PolarDraw [33]. Tagoram adopts four circularly polarized antennas to track one moving tag using a hologram method. PolarDraw adopts two linearly polarized antennas and simultaneously estimates the moving direction (based on RSS change) and distance (based on phase change) of a moving tag.

For a fair comparison, we conduct two sets of experiments. In the first experiment, we deploy multiple antennas (four for Tago-

[4]We do not compare with Wi-Fi based solutions because most of Wi-Fi based works cannot track the gesture trajectory and associate the gesture with the object that the user is interacting with.

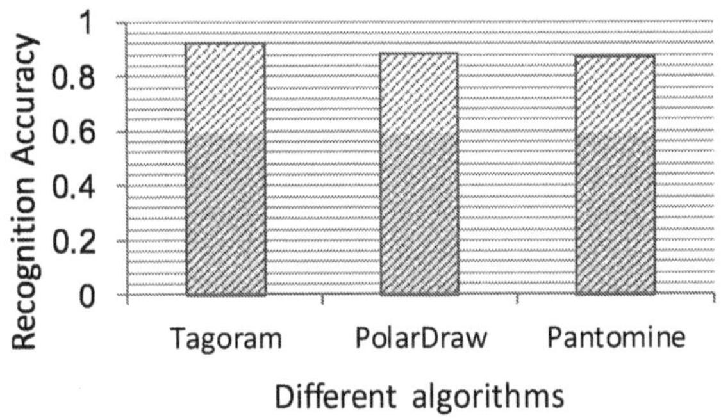

Figure 26— Recognition accuracy achieved by different system in Multi-antenna settings.

ram and two for PolarDraw) to track handwriting and compare the recognition accuray with Pantomime. Figure 26 shows the result. With four antennas, Tagoram achieves an average recognition accuracy of 92%. While for the two-antenna PolarDraw, the average recognition accuracy is 88%. Our single antenna based Pantomime achieves an average recognition accuracy 87%, which is slightly lower than Tagoram but similar to PolarDraw. With natural language processing techniques like [25], we believe recognition accuracy can be improved even further.

In the second experiment, we use one antenna and attach multiple tags (four for Tagoram and Two for PolarDraw) to the food package to compose a multi-tag single antenna tracking system. We then implement Tagoram and Polardraw to track the virtual movement of the antenna in the frame of the reference of the tag array. The recovered trajectories are rotated and fed into the letter recognition software. Figure 27 shows the recognition result. As expected, Tagoram achieves inferior performance due to the low beam resolution. PolarDraw's performance also degrades because of the limited array spacing and the stiff writing style (*i.e.*, writing without rotation). In contrast, Pantomime achieves consistently high recognition accuracy (88%), which is superior to both Tagoram and PolarDraw.

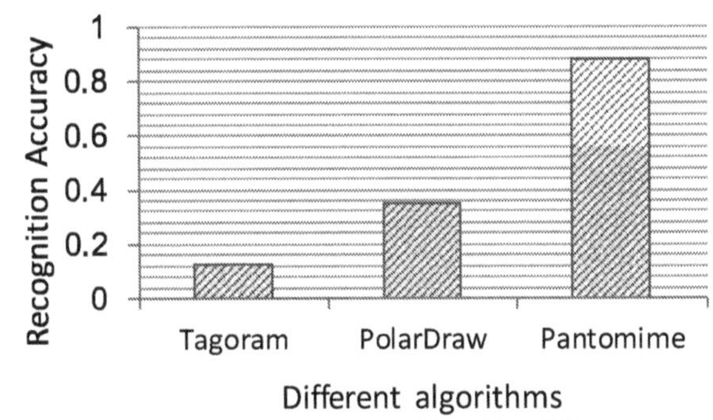

Figure 27— Recognition accuracy achieved by different system in Multi-tag settings.

Multi-antenna Pantomime **vs. multi-tag** Pantomime.We further build a multi-antenna version of Pantomime and compare it with the multi-tag Pantomime. The multi--antenna version of Pantomime is composed of three RFID antennas. The antenna spacing is 0.3m. A volunteer stands 1.5m away from the antenna array, writing 10 letters and 10 words using a mark pen (attached with one RFID tag), as shown in Figure 28. For comparison, we let the volunteer write the same letters and words using a plastic cube, where we attach

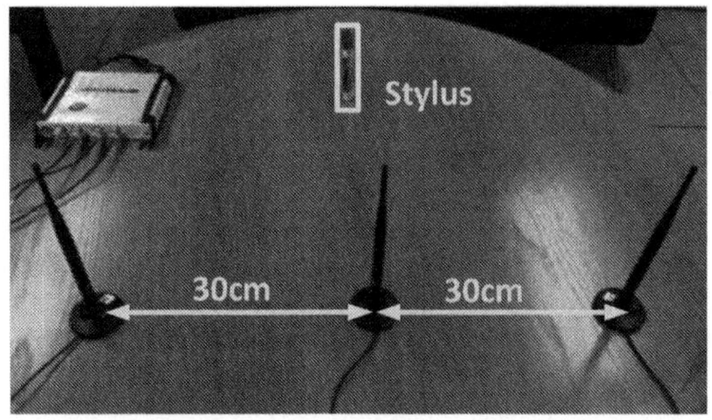

Figure 28— Setups of the multi-antenna version of Pantomime.

three tags to compose a linear tag array. The tag spacing is 4cm. Both the letters and the words are chosen randomly. We summarize the letter and word recognition accuracy in Table 7. As shown, the multi-antenna version of Pantomime (termed as A-Pantomime) achieves a better performance than the tag-array based Pantomime in both letter and word recognition. Specifically, A-Pantomime achieves an overall accuracy of 92% and 89% in letter and word recognition, respectively. In contrast, Pantomime achieves 85% and 82% word and letter recognition accuracy, respectively. The performance gap between A-Pantomime and Pantomime may be due to the asymmetric layout: the spacing between antennas is 0.3m while the spacing between tags is 4cm due to the limited surface space of the item held in hand. However, the performance gap is marginal, which verifies our assumption that a multi-antenna-single-tag system is equivalent to a multi-tag-single-antenna system in performance, yet at much lower cost due to the huge price gap between an antenna and a tag.

Table 7— Recognition accuracy of A-Pantomime and Pantomime.

	Antenna-array	**Tag-array**
Letter recognition accuracy	92%	85%
Word recognition accuracy	89%	82%

7. RELATED WORK

Despite commercial gesture recognition systems such as Kinect-[14] and Leap Motion [18], these vision or infrared based solutions are infeasible for deployment in stores and warehouses, where they are expected to cover a wide range and operate even in non-line-of-sight conditions. Alternatively, researchers have explored context sensing via wireless signals, especially Wi-Fi, with the vision to enable pervasive context-awareness with minimal costs [1, 2, 4, 28, 35, 42, 43, 47]. Although these systems enable device-free sensing in smart homes and offices, they do not associate a gesture with a specific object, which motivates our work. Pantomime is inspired by this trend of wireless sensing, and is particularly related to the following categories of efforts.

Wireless gesture and activity sensing. There has been active research on leveraging wireless signals to track gestures and activities [1, 2, 4, 28, 35, 42, 43], especially using Wi-Fi signals from commodity infrastructure. E-eyes [43] exploits CSI from COTS Wi-Fi network interface cards (NICs) for household activity recognitions. CARM [42] models the relationship between motion speeds and the CSI amplitude, and builds an SVM classifier to recognize location-independent human activities. WiKey [4] decodes keystrokes based on CSI patterns while WiGest [1] leverages RSSI patterns for gesture based device control. WiSee [28] extracts

Doppler frequency shifts from Wi-Fi signals for arm gesture recognition. WiDraw [35] tracks hand motions by measuring angle-of-arrival (AoA) extracted from CSI. Although these systems enable device-free sensing for context-awareness in smart homes and offices, they do not associate a gesture with a specific RFID-tagged object, as Pantomime does.

RFID-based gesture and activity sensing. The ubiquitous deployment of RFID tags makes them promising for interactions and activity recognition with everyday objects. TagFall [30] leverages RFID for fall detection. FEMO [8] extracts Doppler signatures to classify and assess the quality of free-weight activities by attaching RFID tags to dumbbells. ShopMiner [34] harnesses the phase patterns of RFID tags attached to garments to infer shopping behaviors in physical clothing stores. IDSense [20] combines RSSI and phase patterns of RFID tags to identify touching and moving events of the tagged objects. PaperID [19] extract features from RSSI, phase and reading rate for gesture recognition on traces printed or drawn on paper with conductive ink. AllSee [13] powers an RFID-like gesture recognition interface by backscattering ambient wireless signals. While some of them [13, 19] have enabled gesture recognition with a single antenna, they rely on machine learning to recognize a predefined set of gestures. Pantomime is complementary in that Pantomime outputs the trajectory shapes of object motions, which can be further fed into different machine learning algorithms for scalable gesture recognition and other applications such as handwriting tracking and drawing. Pantomime is most close to works on RFID-based gesture tracking [33, 40]. RF-IDraw [40] exploits carefully designed antenna arrays to track the AoA of finger motions. PolarDraw [33] leverages the polarization mismatch of two linearly polarized antennas to track handwriting. Pantomime advances the area by achieving comparable gesture tracking performance using one single antenna, thus yielding the minimal costs for RFID-based gesture tracking.

RFID-based localization and tracking. LANDMARC [26] is the first active RFID based localization scheme by deploying anchor tags. PinIt [39] exploits the multi-path profile of RFID tags attached to books to locate these tagged books in NLOS environments. The adoption of anchor tags for profile matching incurs high cost and the decimeter localization accuracy is unfit for fine-grained gesture tracking. Other works leverage Synthetic Aperatures Radar (SAR) or Inverse SAR (ISAR) to track RFID tags at centimeter-scale accuracies. In [24], the authors introduce a hologram-based scheme to track a moving tag on a transponder. In [27], the authors leverage the tag mobility and adopt ISAR to localize an RFID tag. Tagoram [46] introduces a multi-antenna based hologram method to localize and track tag motion trajectories with error centimeter accuracies. However, all these SAR-based schemes require multiple bulky and expensive RFID antennas to function, impeding their deployment in stores and warehouses. In addition, both SAR and ISAR based schemes track the RFID tag by calculating its position for each time point. Conversely, Pantomime tracks the tag array via the changes of the tag-to-reader distances without pinpointing its absolute position. Tagyro [44] attaches multiple tags on an object to track its 3D *orientation* using differential phase-based hologram. However, it does not consider the limited tag reading and insufficient antenna coverage issues. Pantomime is designed for the fine-grained gesture tracking and we show that hologram-based methods fail to achieve this goal due to the space limitation of the object and the antenna crisis.

8. DISCUSSION

We discuss limitations and opportunities for improvement.

Identifying the beginning of the gesture. Pantomime needs to detect the beginning of the gesture in the phase stream for gesture tracking. The technique we propose is based on instructing users to hold the tagged object for a short period before performing a gesture, which results in relatively stable phase readings that naturally separate the pick-up action and the gestures (see Figure 14). Similar to the activity detection algorithm used in [8], Pantomime uses K-L divergence [15] to identify these short resting periods, and tracks the gesture hereafter.

Support for multiple users. Our current prototype supports single user gesture tracking per antenna, because when a user performs gestures in front of an antenna, Pantomime blocks all the remaining tags within its reading range from replying. Pantomime can support multiple users by letting the reader interrogate both target and non-target tags at different sampling rates, *e.g.*, sampling all target tags at a high frequency, yet sampling only one tag attached to each of the remaining objects at a lower rate for multiple user detection. However, this requires modifications of the MAC protocol and we leave it for future work.

Trade-off between multi-tag and multi-antenna systems. Recent research on MIMO RFID readers [17] has lowered down the cost of a multi-antenna system, yet an RFID antenna can still cost 100 USD, more than 600 times the cost of an RFID tag (15 cent). Thus the additional cost to deploy 3 more antennas to support four-coverage ratio can support attaching a 2-tag array to around 2000 objects. Since the typical effective reading area of a ceiling-mounted RFID antenna is about $10m^2$, it is reasonable that there will be fewer than 1500 objects placed on shelves in stores and warehouses within this effective reading area. Therefore, a multi-tag system like Pantomime is a more cost-effective alternative to current multi-antenna solutions. Multi-tag solutions also have the advantages of improving the item detection probability [6], which is desirable in store and warehouse management to reduce potential financial losses.

Practicality of hardware solutions. Note that Pantomime serves as a proof-of-concept to show the benefits of attaching multiple tags on each object. Our aim is to provide a new object interaction mechanism for stores and warehouses, where the adoption of low-cost, widely accessible infrastructure is essential. In principle, recent research on multi-antenna RFID tags [12] is also applicable in our scenarios with customized MAC protocols, and will avoid the challenge of reading rate. We envision the future commercialization of multi-antenna RFID tags will further decrease the cost of multi-tag systems like Pantomime.

9. CONCLUSION

In this paper, we present the design, implementation and evaluation of Pantomime, a gesture tracking system with a single RFID antenna. Through both comprehensive experiments and real-world case studies, we demonstrate that Pantomime achieves comparable gesture tracking accuracy to the state-of-the-art multi-antenna methods, showing the potential to support various gesture-based object interactions with a minimal deployment cost. In the future we plan to extend Pantomime to multi-user cases and deploy it in an entire warehouse/mall for large-scale and long-term studies.

Acknowledgements

We thank our shepherd Shyam Gollakota and the anonymous reviewers for their helpful feedback. This material is based upon work supported by the National Science Foundation under Grant No. 1617161.

References

[1] H. Abdelnasser, M. Youssef, K. A. Harras. Wigest: A ubiquitous wifi-based gesture recognition system. *INFOCOM*, 2015.

[2] F. Adib, Z. Kabelac, D. Katabi, R. Miller. 3D Tracking via body radio reflections. *NSDI*, 2014.

[3] S. Agrawal, I. Constandache, S. Gaonkar, R. Roy Choudhury, K. Caves, F. DeRuyter. Using mobile phones to write in air. *MobiSys*, 2011.

[4] K. Ali, A. X. Liu, W. Wang, M. Shahzad. Keystroke recognition using WiFi signals. *MobiCom*, 2015.

[5] Avery-Dennison UHF RFID inlay *AD-227m5*. Web page.

[6] L. Bolotnyy, S. Krize, G. Robins. The practicality of multi-tag rfid systems. *IWRT*, 2007.

[7] EPC radio-frequency identity protocols class-1 generation-2 uhf rfid protocols for communications at 860 MHz - 960 MHz. .

[8] H. Ding, L. Shangguan, Z. Yang, J. Han, Z. Zhou, P. Yang, W. Xi, J. Zhao. Femo: A platform for free-weight exercise monitoring with RFIDs. *SenSys*, 2015.

[9] S. Gupta, D. Morris, S. Patel, D. Tan. Soundwave: using the doppler effect to sense gestures. *CHI*, 2012.

[10] LipiTk: online hand writing recognition toolkit. Web page.

[11] ImpinJ Speedway R420 reader. Web page.

[12] N. C. Karmakar, M. Zomorrodi, C. Divarathne. *Advanced Chipless RFID: MIMO-Based Imaging at 60 GHz-ML Detection*. John Wiley & Sons, 2016.

[13] B. Kellogg, V. Talla, S. Gollakota. Bringing gesture recognition to all devices. *NSDI*, 2015.

[14] Microsoft Kinect. Web page.

[15] Kullback-Leibler Divergence. Web page.

[16] RFMAX S9028PCR (LP) outdoor RFID antenna. Web page.

[17] R. Langwieser, C. Angerer, A. L. Scholtz. A uhf frontend for mimo applications in rfid. *RWS*, 124–127, 2010.

[18] Leap Motion. Web page.

[19] H. Li, E. Brockmeyer, E. J. Carter, J. Fromm, S. E. Hudson, S. N. Patel, A. Sample. Paperid: A technique for drawing functional battery-free wireless interfaces on paper. *CHI*, 2016.

[20] H. Li, C. Ye, A. P. Sample. Idsense: A human object interaction detection system based on passive uhf rfid. *CHI*, 2015.

[21] X. R. Li, V. P. Jilkov. Survey of maneuvering target tracking: dynamic models. *AeroSense 2000*, 2000.

[22] T. Liu, Y. Liu, L. Yang, Y. Guo, C. Wang. Backpos: High accuracy backscatter positioning system. *IEEE TMC*, **15**(3), 586–598, 2016.

[23] Y. Ma, X. Hui, E. C. Kan. 3d real-time indoor localization via broadband nonlinear backscatter in passive devices with centimeter precision. *MobiCom*, 2016.

[24] R. Miesen, F. Kirsch, M. Vossiek. Holographic localization of passive uhf rfid transponders. *RFID*, 2011.

[25] A. Nasr, F. Béchet, J.-F. Rey, B. Favre, J. Le Roux. Macaon: An nlp tool suite for processing word lattices. *ACL*, 2011.

[26] L. M. Ni, Y. Liu, Y. C. Lau, A. P. Patil. LANDMARC: indoor location sensing using active RFID. *Wireless networks*, 2004.

[27] A. Parr, R. Miesen, M. Vossiek. Inverse sar approach for localization of moving rfid tags. *RFID*, 2013.

[28] Q. Pu, S. Gupta, S. Gollakota, S. Patel. Whole-home gesture recognition using wireless signals. *MobiCom*, 2013.

[29] L. G. Roberts. Aloha packet system with and without slots and capture. *ACM SIGCOMM Computer Communication Review*, 1975.

[30] W. Ruan, L. Yao, Q. Z. Sheng, N. Falkner, X. Li, T. Gu. Tagfall: Towards unobstructive fine-grained fall detection based on uhf passive rfid tags. *MOBIQUITOUS*, 2015.

[31] M. Shahzad, A. X. Liu. Every bit counts: fast and scalable rfid estimation. *MobiCom*, 2012.

[32] L. Shangguan, K. Jamieson. The design and implementation of a mobile rfid tag sorting robot. *MobiSys*, 2016.

[33] L. Shangguan, K. Jamieson. Leveraging electromagnetic polarization in a two-antenna whiteboard in the air. *CoNEXT*, 2016.

[34] L. Shangguan, Z. Zhou, X. Zheng, L. Yang, Y. Liu, J. Han. Shopminer: Mining customer shopping behavior in physical clothing stores with cots RFID devices. *SenSys*, 2015.

[35] L. Sun, S. Sen, D. Koutsonikolas, K.-H. Kim. WiDraw: Enabling hands-free drawing in the air on commodity WiFi devices. *MobiCom*, 2015.

[36] Line Drawing: A Guide for Art Students. Web page.

[37] Tag price. Web page.

[38] J. Wang, F. Adib, R. Knepper, D. Katabi, D. Rus. RF-compass: Robot object manipulation using RFIDs. *MobiCom*, 2013.

[39] J. Wang, D. Katabi. Dude, where's my card? RFID positioning that works with multipath and non-line of sight. *SIGCOMM*, 2013.

[40] J. Wang, D. Vasisht, D. Katabi. RF-IDraw: Virtual touch screen in the air using RF signals. *SIGCOMM*, 2014.

[41] L. Wang, B. A. Norman, J. Rajgopal. Placement of multiple rfid reader antennas to maximise portal read accuracy. *International Journal of Radio Frequency Identification Technology and Applications*, 2007.

[42] W. Wang, A. Liu, M. Shahzad, K. Ling, S. Lu. Understanding and modeling of WiFi signal based human activity recognition. *MobiCom*, 2015.

[43] Y. Wang, J. Liu, Y. Chen, M. Gruteser, J. Yang, H. Liu. E-eyes: device-free location-oriented activity identification using fine-grained WiFi signatures. *MobiCom*, 2014.

[44] T. Wei, X. Zhang. Gyro in the air: tracking 3d orientation of batteryless internet-of-things. *MobiCom*, 2016.

[45] J. Xiong, K. Jamieson. ArrayTrack: A fine-grained indoor location system. *NSDI*, 2013.

[46] L. Yang, Y. Chen, X.-Y. Li, C. Xiao, M. Li, Y. Liu. Tagoram: Real-time tracking of mobile RFID tags to high precision using COTS devices. *MobiCom*, 2014.

[47] X. Zheng, J. Wang, L. Shangguan, Z. Zhou, Y. Liu. Smokey: Ubiquitous smoking detection with commercial wifi infrastructures. *INFOCOM*, 2016.

Position and Orientation Agnostic Gesture Recognition Using WiFi

Aditya Virmani and Muhammad Shahzad
Department of Computer Science
North Carolina State University
Raleigh, North Carolina, USA
{avirman2, mshahza}@ncsu.edu

ABSTRACT

WiFi based gesture recognition systems have recently proliferated due to the ubiquitous availability of WiFi in almost every modern building. The key limitation of existing WiFi based gesture recognition systems is that they require the user to be in the same configuration (*i.e.*, at the same position and in same orientation) when performing gestures at runtime as when providing training samples, which significantly restricts their practical usability. In this paper, we propose a WiFi based gesture recognition system, namely WiAG, which recognizes the gestures of the user irrespective of his/her configuration. The key idea behind WiAG is that it first requests the user to provide training samples for all gestures in only one configuration and then automatically generates virtual samples for all gestures in all possible configurations by applying our novel translation function on the training samples. Next, for each configuration, it generates a classification model using virtual samples corresponding to that configuration. To recognize gestures of a user at runtime, as soon as the user performs a gesture, WiAG first automatically estimates the configuration of the user and then evaluates the gesture against the classification model corresponding to that estimated configuration. Our evaluation results show that when user's configuration is not the same at runtime as at the time of providing training samples, WiAG significantly improves the gesture recognition accuracy from just 51.4% to 91.4%.

1. INTRODUCTION

1.1 Motivation and Problem Statement

Background: As computing devices are becoming smaller, smarter, and more ubiquitous, computing has started to embed in our environments in various forms such as intelligent thermostats [1–3, 6], smart appliances [5, 10], and remotely controllable household equipment [4, 7, 8, 11]. Consequently, we need new ways to seamlessly communicate and interact with such pervasive and always-available computing. A natural choice for such communication and interaction is human gestures because gestures are an integral part of the way humans communicate and interact with each other in their daily lives. Indeed, researchers have been developing various types of gesture recognition systems, which usually rely on cameras [18, 21, 25, 31, 33, 38], wearable sensors [22, 29, 34, 39, 49], or wireless signals [12, 27, 35]. Among these systems, WiFi based gesture recognition systems are receiving widespread interest because the cost and complexity of deploying a WiFi based gesture recognition system is potentially negligible. It needs as few as only two commodity WiFi devices, such as a laptop and an access point, which already exist in almost every modern building. The intuition behind WiFi based gesture recognition systems is that the wireless channel metrics, such as channel state information (CSI) and received signal strength (RSS), change when a user moves in a wireless environment. The patterns of change in these metrics are different for different gestures. WiFi based gesture recognition systems first learn these patterns of change using machine learning techniques for each predefined gesture and then recognize them as the user performs them at runtime.

Permission to make digital or hard copies of all or part of this work for personal or classroom use is granted without fee provided that copies are not made or distributed for profit or commercial advantage and that copies bear this notice and the full citation on the first page. Copyrights for components of this work owned by others than ACM must be honored. Abstracting with credit is permitted. To copy otherwise, or republish, to post on servers or to redistribute to lists, requires prior specific permission and/or a fee. Request permissions from permissions@acm.org.

MobiSys'17, June 19-23, 2017, Niagara Falls, NY, USA
© 2017 ACM. ISBN 978-1-4503-4928-4/17/06... $15.00
DOI: http://dx.doi.org/10.1145/3081333.3081340

Limitations of Prior Art: While several WiFi based gesture recognition systems have been proposed within the last few years, one of the limitations of the systems that work on commodity devices is that they recognize gestures with the reported accuracy only when either the *position* or the *orientation* of a user in the given environment does not change significantly compared to the position and orientation of the user at the time of providing training samples. Here, *position* is defined as the absolute location of the user in the given environment and *orientation* is defined as the direction in which the user is facing. Onward, we will use the term *configuration* to refer to position and orientation collectively. Two configurations are equal only if their corresponding positions and corresponding orientations are same.

The reason behind this limitation is that the patterns of change in wireless channel metrics due to a given gesture are different for different configurations of the user, and prior schemes do not take this into account. To illustrate this, consider a simple push gesture where a user moves her hand outward while facing towards the WiFi receiver. The amplitude of the signal reflected from the hand arriving at the WiFi receiver increases, as shown in Figure 1(a). Now consider the same push gesture by the user while facing away from the WiFi receiver. The amplitude of the signal decreases, as shown in Figure 1(b). This very simple illustration shows how same gesture results in different patterns of change in wireless channel metrics when performed in different configurations. Note that these two figures are obtained from real instances of the push gesture. We will provide our implementation details later in the paper.

Unfortunately, this limitation significantly restricts the practical usability of existing WiFi based gesture recognition systems due to the inconvenience of requiring the user to always be in the same configuration when performing gestures at runtime as at the time of providing training samples. It is absolutely imperative to address and overcome this limitation in order to take WiFi based gesture recognition to its next level of evolution and to bring it a step closer to real world deployment.

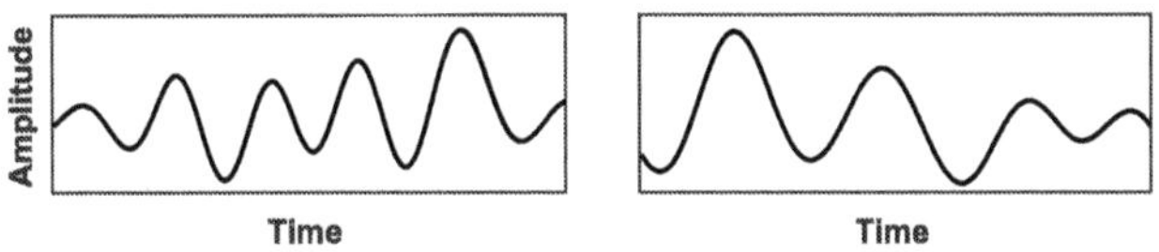

(a) Facing towards receiver (b) Facing away from receiver

Figure 1: Push gesture amplitude in two orientations

Problem Statement: In this paper, our goal is to design a WiFi based gesture recognition system that is agnostic to user's configuration, *i.e.*, it should recognize gestures of user irrespective of his/her configuration.

1.2 Proposed Approach

A seemingly obvious solution to making WiFi based gesture recognition agnostic to user's configuration is to first request the user to provide training samples for all gestures in all possible configurations in the given environment and then use these samples to learn patterns of change in wireless channel metrics for each gesture in all possible configurations. While this solution is theoretically plausible, it is impractical because the number of training samples to collect is prohibitively large and, therefore, almost impossible for a user to provide.

In this paper, we present a WiFi based configuration agnostic gesture recognition system (WiAG), which recognizes gestures irrespective of user's configuration and at the same time, requires user to provide training samples in only one configuration. We have designed WiAG to work on commodity WiFi devices, such as laptops. To measure changes in the wireless channel due to gestures, WiAG uses channel state information (CSI), which is a well known wireless channel metric and has been used in several existing WiFi based gesture and activity recognition systems [12,24,45,46].

The key component of WiAG is our novel theoretically grounded *translation function* that can generate *virtual samples* of a given gesture in any desired configuration using a real sample of that gesture collected from the user in a known configuration. The key property of this translation function is that the virtual sample of a gesture that it generates for the desired configuration is identical to the real sample that would result from a real user performing that gesture in that configuration. The key idea behind WiAG is that instead of requesting the user to provide training samples in all possible configurations, it first requests the user to provide training samples for all gestures in only one configuration and then automatically generates virtual samples for all gestures in all possible configurations by applying our translation function on each training sample. Next, for each configuration, it generates a k-nearest neighbor (k-NN) based classification model using the virtual samples of the gestures in that configuration. To recognize gestures of a user at runtime, as soon as the user performs a gesture, WiAG first automatically estimates the configuration of the user and then evaluates the gesture against the classification model corresponding to that estimated configuration.

1.3 Technical Challenges

In designing WiAG, we faced several technical challenges, out of which, we describe three here. The first challenge is to develop a theoretical model to estimate changes in CSI measurements due to human gestures. This model is required in order to develop our translation function. We develop this model by first quantifying the changes in CSI measurements caused by a point object in linear motion. Next, we extend the model for the point object to a human arm (or any limb used during gesture) in linear motion. As human gestures often comprise of non-linear motions of arm (*e.g.*, circle or wave gesture), we extend the model for arm in linear motion to arm in non-linear motion, and use this final model to develop our translation function.

The second challenge is to automatically estimate user's configuration when he/she performs a gesture. This estimate of user's configuration is required to select an appropriate classification model to evaluate the unknown gesture. To address this challenge, we made the formulation of our model for non-linear arm motion parametric in nature, where two of the parameters are the position and the orientation of user. To estimate user's configuration, we first ask the user to perform a preamble gesture and then solve our model to estimate the position and orientation using the CSI measurements observed during the preamble gesture.

The third challenge is to make WiAG resilient to static changes in the environment, such as adding an extra chair. Such static changes result in new multi-paths or change the lengths of existing multi-paths. Although they do not contribute dynamically changing variations to CSI measurements during the gestures, they still modify the net patterns of change observed in the CSI measurements. To address this challenge, we have developed our model for non-linear arm motion such that it characterizes the *change* in CSI measurements instead of the absolute CSI measurements. Consequently, the effects of the addition of new multi-paths or changes to the lengths of existing multi-paths as a result of static environmental changes get cancelled out in the model and the model only captures information about the multi-paths that are affected by moving objects, which in our case is user's arm.

1.4 Key Contributions

In this paper, we make following three key contributions. First, we present a novel translation function that enables position and orientation agnostic gesture recognition without requiring the user to provide training samples in all possible configurations. Second, we present a novel configuration estimation scheme that automatically identifies the position and orientation of the user. To the best of our knowledge, there is no prior work that can estimate the orientation of user without requiring the user to hold a device in hand, such as an RFID tag [36]. Third, we have implemented and extensively evaluated WiAG using commodity WiFi devices, which include a Thinkpad X200 laptop equipped with an Intel 5300 WiFi NIC and a TP-Link N750 access point. Our results from an extensive set of experiments show that when user's configuration is not the same at runtime as at the time of providing training samples, our translation function significantly improves the accuracy of gesture recognition from just 51.4% to 91.4%.

2. RELATED WORK

In this section, we describe prior WiFi based gesture recognition systems and explain why each of them requires the user to always be in the same configuration at the time of performing gestures as at the time of providing training samples. In addition to gesture recognition systems, researchers have also proposed WiFi based activity recognition systems and WiFi based micro-movement sensing systems. Due to space limitation and rather less relevance to gesture recognition, we do not individually describe each activity and micro-movement recognition system. Instead, we only mention them and point the interested readers to appropriate references.

Prior WiFi based systems can be divided into two broad categories: specialized-hardware (SH) based and commodity-devices (CD) based. The SH-based systems use software defined radios (SDRs), often along with specialized antennas or custom analog circuits, to capture changes in the wireless channel metrics due to human movements. The CD-based systems are implemented using commercially available devices, such as commodity laptops, and use the WiFi NICs in those devices to capture changes in the wireless channel metrics. The SH-based systems are usually slightly more accurate because SDRs can measure the wireless channel metrics more accurately compared to the WiFi NICs in commodity devices. Nonetheless, the CD-based systems have received a wider acceptance compared to the SH-based systems due to their potentially negligible deployment cost and complexity. Consequently, we have designed WiAG such that it can be implemented on commodity devices and does not require any specialized hardware. Next, we describe the existing work on CD-based systems followed by the SH-based systems.

2.1 CD-based Human Sensing using WiFi

To the best of our knowledge, Abdelnasser *et al.* proposed the only existing CD-based gesture recognition system, WiGest [12]. WiGest uses RSS as the wireless channel metric. WiGest recognizes gestures based on the patterns of change in primitives such as rising edge, falling edge and pause. As long as the user faces the same direction with respect to the receiver, WiGest can recognize gestures irrespective of where the user is with respect to the receiver. However, if the direction the user is facing changes, the patterns of change in the primitives also change, resulting in loss in accuracy. In comparison, WiAG does not require the direction of user to always be the same with respect to the receiver.

Researchers have also proposed other WiFi based human sensing systems that can be implemented on commodity devices, such as WiFall that detects a single human activity of falling [24], E-eyes [46] and CARM [45] that recognize daily human activities, such as brushing teeth, taking shower, and doing dishes in fixed user configurations, WiDraw that enables in-air drawing [40], WiHear that recognizes a predefined set of spoken words [43], WiKey that recognizes characters typed on keyboard [19], WifiU that identifies people based on their gait [44], FrogEye that counts the number of people in a crowd [47], and indoor localization schemes [37,48].

2.2 SH-based Human Sensing using WiFi

Pu *et al.* proposed WiSee that uses an SDR to monitor micro-level doppler shifts in a carrier wave to recognize gestures [35]. To make it relatively independent of user configuration, WiSee leverages a preamble gesture to first calibrate the sign of the subsequent Doppler shifts and then recognizes the gestures. Kellogg *et al.* proposed AllSee that uses an analog envelope-detection circuit to extract the amplitude of the received signal and learns the pattern of change in it to recognize gestures [27]. As the magnitude of shift in amplitude at the receiver depends on the direction of movement of hand and the distance between the receiver and the hand, AllSee works only if the user is at a predefined distance and in a predefined orientation with respect to the receiver. Furthermore, AllSee works only when the user is within a short distance of less than 2.5 feet from the receiver. Due to these limitations, the authors of AllSee proposed to keep the receiver in user's backpack or pocket to keep the configuration of user with respect to the receiver fixed. In comparison to both WiSee and AllSee, WiAG neither requires the user to be in a fixed configuration nor requires any specialized hardware.

Researchers have also proposed other WiFi based human sensing systems that utilize specialized hardware with objectives such as tracking humans [13,15,16], measuring movement speeds of different parts of human body [42], recognizing human gait [30], building images of nearby objects [26], measuring breathing and heart rates [17], and localizing multiple users [14].

3. TRANSLATION FUNCTION

In this section, we develop our translation function that can generate virtual samples of any given gesture in any desired configuration using a real sample of that gesture collected from the user in a known configuration. Note that any sample (either virtual or real) is essentially a time-series of the measurement values of one or more wireless channel metrics. Our translation function works on samples comprised of CSI measurements, which the commodity WiFi devices provide. Next, we first briefly describe what CSI measurements represent and then derive our translation function.

3.1 Channel State Information

Modern IEEE 802.11n/ac WiFi devices typically consist of multiple transmit and receive antennas and thus support MIMO. A MIMO channel between each transmit-receive (Tx-Rx) antenna pair comprises of 64 subcarriers (52 for data, 4 for pilot tones, and 8 for protective padding). WiFi devices continuously monitor the state of the wireless channel to effectively perform transmit power allocation and rate adaptation [23]. For this monitoring, they utilize CSI measurements, which they calculate internally using preambles in the received signals. Let $X(f,t)$ and $Y(f,t)$ be the frequency domain representations of transmitted and received signals, respectively, on a subcarrier with carrier frequency f at time t between a given Tx-Rx pair. The two signals are related by the expression $Y(f,t) = H(f,t) \times X(f,t)$, where $H(f,t)$ represents the channel frequency response (CFR) of the wireless channel for the subcarrier of $X(f,t)$ at time t between the given Tx-Rx pair. A CSI measurement essentially consists of these CFR values, one for each subcarrier between each Tx-Rx pair. Let N_{Tx} and N_{Rx} represent the number of transmitting and receiving antennas, respectively, and let S represent the number of subcarriers between each Tx-Rx pair. Each CSI measurement contains S matrices (*i.e.*, one matrix per subcarrier) of dimensions $N_{Tx} \times N_{Rx}$ each. Each matrix contains CFR values for its associated subcarrier between all Tx-Rx pairs. As WiFi NICs generate CSI measurements repeatedly (*e.g.*, Intel 5300 WiFi NIC generates up to 2500 measurements/sec [23]), we essentially obtain $S \times N_{Tx} \times N_{Rx}$ time-series of CFR values. Onward, we will call each time-series of CFR values a *CSI-stream*. As each CSI-stream is comprised of CFR values, next, we derive expressions that model the CFR in the absence and presence of gestures. These expressions will be used in deriving the translation function.

3.2 CFR Modeling without Gestures

CFR of a wireless channel for a subcarrier quantifies the change in magnitude and phase, which that subcarrier experiences when passing through that wireless channel. Consider a wireless signal propagating on a subcarrier with frequency f. At time t, we can represent this propagating signal by a sinusoid $S(f,t) = A(t) \times e^{j2\pi ft}$, where $A(t)$ is the amplitude of the sinusoid and f is the subcarrier frequency. Assume that this signal is travelling through a time-invariant free-space, *i.e.*, the space contains no objects, obstacles, or humans. Let $X(f)$ represent this signal when it was initially transmitted at time $t = 0$. Thus, $X(f) = S(f,0) = A(0) \times e^{j\times 0}$. Let $Y(f)$ represent this signal when it arrives at the receiver at time T after traveling a distance D. Thus, $Y(f) = S(f,T) = A(T) \times e^{j2\pi fT}$. It is a well known fact that the amplitude of a wireless signal travelling through free-space is inversely proportional to the square of the distance it travels; thus $A(T) \propto \frac{A(0)}{(cT)^2} \Rightarrow A(T) = k\frac{A(0)}{D^2}$, where c is the propagation speed of the wireless signal and k is the proportionality constant, which caters for the effects of the relatively stationary characteristics of environment (such as its thermal properties) on wireless signal. If the wavelength of the sinusoid is λ, the phase of the sinusoid at the receiver will be $2\pi fT = 2\pi\frac{c}{\lambda}T = 2\pi\frac{D}{\lambda}$. Thus, $Y(f) = k\frac{A(0)}{D^2} \times e^{j2\pi\frac{D}{\lambda}} = (\frac{k}{D^2} \times e^{j2\pi\frac{D}{\lambda}}) \times X(f)$. As $Y(f)$=$H(f)$×$X(f)$ for a time-invariant channel, we get

$$H(f) = k/D^2 \times e^{j2\pi\frac{D}{\lambda}} \tag{1}$$

The equation above quantifies the CFR of a time-invariant wireless channel in free-space for a subcarrier with wavelength λ (or frequency f, where $\lambda = \frac{c}{f}$).

Note that Eq. (1) models CFR for the ideal setting where there are no surfaces in the space that reflect the signal and the signal travels from the transmitter to the receiver on a single line-of-sight path. In practice, however, the signal that arrives at the receiver is a linear combination of several signals traveling through different paths due to reflections from objects in the space. Let N represent the number of such paths and let D_i represent the total length of the ith path. Assuming that the space is still time-invariant despite the presence of multiple objects (*i.e.*, all objects stay stationary), the CFR of the wireless channel in this space is quantified by the generalized version of Eq. (1) as below.

$$H(f) = \sum_{i=1}^{N} \frac{k}{D_i^2} \times e^{j2\pi\frac{D_i}{\lambda}} \tag{2}$$

3.3 CFR Modeling with Gestures

When a user is present in the environment, different paths that the signal traverses can be divided into two categories: non-user reflected paths and user reflected paths. Non-user reflected paths include both line-of-sight paths as well as the paths reflected from static objects. Such paths do not change due to human movements. We represent the aggregate CFR of all non-user reflected paths with a constant $H_s(f)$. The user reflected paths can be further divided into two subcategories. The first subcategory consists of the paths that go directly to the receiver after reflecting from the user, and the second subcategory consists of the paths that experience further reflections after reflecting from the user. Compared to the signals traveling on the paths belonging to the first subcategory, we assume that the signals traveling on the paths belonging to the second subcategory have relatively lower amplitudes when they arrive at the receiver, and are thus approximated with 0. Lets assume for now that there is only a single path of length D that is reflected from the arm of the user as he/she performs the gesture. We will soon incorporate the more complex scenario where multiple paths reflect from the arm. Let $H_D(f)$ represent the aggregate CFR of the wireless channel containing a stationary human. Based on Eq. (2), $H_D(f)$ is calculated as below.

$$H_D(f) = H_s(f) + k/D^2 \times e^{j2\pi\frac{D}{\lambda}} \tag{3}$$

This equation still assumes that the channel is time-invariant despite user's presence and is valid only if the user stays stationary. Next, we first derive an expression to calculate CFR when the user is not stationary anymore, rather moves the arm in a linear motion, such as doing a push gesture. After that, we extend this expression to calculate CFR when the user moves the arm in arbitrary directions to perform any desired gestures.

3.3.1 *Linear Gestures*

Consider a point object, initially situated at a distance D_1 from the receiver. Suppose the object moves at an angle θ with speed v for time t and arrives at the point situated at a distance D_2, as shown in Figure 2(a). Let $d = vt$ represent the distance that the object moves in time t. Using basic trigonometric identities, we get

$$D_2 \sin(\phi) = D_1 \sin(\theta) \tag{4}$$

$$D_2 \cos(\phi) = D_1 \cos(\theta) - d \tag{5}$$

Dividing Eq. (5) by Eq. (4), squaring the resultant, and adding 1 yields the following on simplification.

$$(D_2)^2 = (D_1)^2\Big\{1 + \Big(\frac{d}{D_1}\Big)^2 - 2\frac{d}{D_1}\cos(\theta)\Big\} \tag{6}$$

Replacing D in Eq. (3) with D_2 and substituting the value of $(D_2)^2$ from Eq. (6) into the denominator of the second term in Eq. (3), we get

$$H_{D_2}(f,t) = H_s(f) + \frac{k \times e^{j2\pi\frac{D_2}{\lambda}}}{(D_1)^2\Big\{1+\Big(\frac{d}{D_1}\Big)^2 - 2\frac{d}{D_1}\cos(\theta)\Big\}} \tag{7}$$

The equation above calculates CFR at time t when the point object has travelled a distance d and there is only one reflected path (*i.e.*, from the point object). Note that we have introduced t in the term $H_{D_2}(f,t)$ because $d = vt$, *i.e.*, the channel is no longer time-invariant due to change in the position of the point object with time.

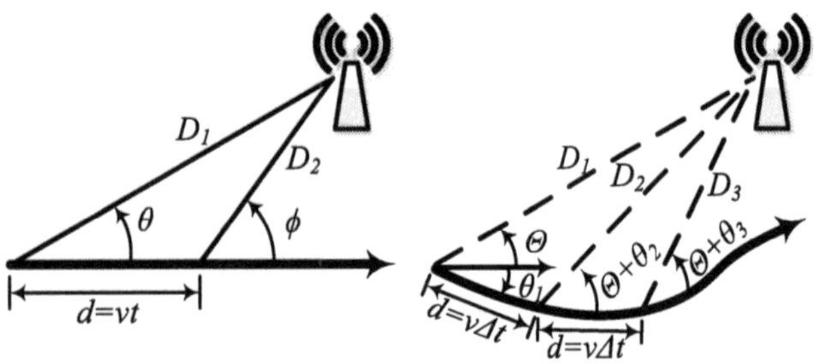

(a) Linear Gestures (b) Non-linear Gestures

Figure 2: CFR modeling for gestures

When a human performs a linear gesture, such as a push or pull, the entire arm moves, and not just a point object. The arm acts as a reflector and its area of cross-section changes in proportion to the distance moved by the arm. Consequently, the strength of the signal reflected off the arm changes proportionately too. To calculate total CFR at time t, represented by $H_T(f,t)$, that incorporates reflection from the entire arm, we adopt the following *simplified* model. We first divide the length of the portion of arm extended by time t into infinitesimal segments of size dd such that each segment offers a single reflected path (*i.e.*, acts like a point object). After that, we add the CFRs of paths reflected from each of these tiny segments by integrating the second term in Eq. (7) over d, which gives the following *approximation* for the total CFR (after substituting $d = vt$).

$$H_T(f,t) = H_s(f) + \int_0^t \frac{kv \times e^{j2\pi\frac{D_2}{\lambda}}}{(D_1)^2\left\{1+\left(\frac{vt}{D_1}\right)^2 - 2\frac{vt}{D_1}\cos(\theta)\right\}} \mathrm{d}t$$

Unfortunately, it is not straightforward to obtain the value of the constant $H_s(f)$. To eliminate it, we differentiate the equation above with respect to t. This differentiation also eliminates the contribution of any static object in the environment to the CFR, and thus, makes WiAG resilient to static changes in the environment, such as adding an extra chair. which results in the following equation.

$$\mathrm{d}H_T(f,t) = \frac{kv \times e^{j2\pi\frac{D_2}{\lambda}}}{(D_1)^2\left\{1+\left(\frac{vt}{D_1}\right)^2 - 2\frac{vt}{D_1}\cos(\theta)\right\}} \tag{8}$$

The physical interpretation of this equation is that it calculates the change introduced in the total CFR for subcarrier with frequency f at time t as a result of the reflection introduced/removed by a small surface area as the arm extends/retracts by a small distance. Thus, if we know the initial distance D_1 and the orientation θ of the user, we can estimate the change in CFR values due to linear gestures using the parametric formulation in Eq. (8). In practice, we obtain the values of $\mathrm{d}H_T(f,t)$ for any desired subcarrier by taking the first order difference of the CSI-stream of that subcarrier.

While Eq. (8) describes both amplitude and phase of the first order derivative of the total CFR, moving forward, we only utilize the amplitude information of the CFR because the noise contained in the amplitude values of CFR is additive in nature and relatively easy to filter out. Thus, it does not significantly affect the change in CFR amplitude due to user's gestures. Taking only the amplitude into consideration, Eq. (8) reduces into the following.

$$\|\mathrm{d}H_T(f,t)\| = \frac{kv}{(D_1)^2\left\{1+\left(\frac{vt}{D_1}\right)^2 - 2\frac{vt}{D_1}\cos(\theta)\right\}} \tag{9}$$

This equation calculates the amplitude of the first order derivative of total CFR for linear gestures, such as push and pull. Next, we extend this model to gestures with arbitrary directions of motion. We will use the resulting extended model to derive our translation function.

3.3.2 Non-linear Gestures

Consider a point object initially situated at a distance D_1 from the receiver. Suppose the object moves along an arbitrary non-linear path at a constant speed v, starting at an angle θ_1 with respect to the user orientation, *i.e.*, the direction the user is facing, as shown in Figure 2(b). Let Θ represent the absolute user orientation. After a short duration Δt, the object reaches a position where its distance from the receiver is D_2. The duration Δt is small enough such that the path followed by the object during this time can be approximated by a straight line. Until this point, the situation is exactly the same as discussed for linear-gestures in Section 3.3.1. At this point, the object continues to move, without stopping, at the same speed v but at an angle θ_2 with respect to the user orientation. After another short Δt, it reaches a position where its distance from the receiver is D_3 as shown in the Figure 2(b) The object continues to move like this without stopping.

As the object moves at a constant speed v, the distance d it covers in each Δt interval is constant, *i.e.*, $d = v \times \Delta t$. Following the same steps as we took to derive Eq. (6), we obtain the following equation.

$$(D_i)^2 = (D_{i-1})^2\left\{1+\left(\frac{d}{D_{i-1}}\right)^2 - 2\frac{d}{D_{i-1}}\cos(\theta_i+\Theta)\right\} \tag{10}$$

Let t_i represent the time when the object has moved through i segments along its path, *i.e.*, $t_i = i \times \Delta t$. If we can automatically calculate the values of D_1, all θ_i, Θ, k, and v (we will describe in Section 3.4.1 how we automatically calculate these values), we can calculate values of D_i for all i. Following the same steps as for linear gestures in Section 3.3.1, we arrive at an equation similar to Eq. (9) that calculates the change in the amplitude of total CFR during the ith short time interval Δt as a result of a very small change in reflection due to a small change in the position of the arm as it moves by a small distance. This equation is given below.

$$\|\mathrm{d}H_T(f,t_i)\| = \frac{kv}{(D_i)^2\left\{1+\left(\frac{d}{D_i}\right)^2 - 2\frac{d}{D_i}\cos(\theta_i+\Theta)\right\}} \tag{11}$$

Eqs. (10) and (11) are the generalized versions of Eqs. (6) and (9), respectively, and are thus valid for both non-linear as well as linear gestures. As mentioned earlier, we obtain the values of $\mathrm{d}H_T(f,t_i)$ for any desired subcarrier by taking the first order difference of the CSI-stream of that subcarrier. Through simple polar maths, it is easy to see that during consecutive CSI measurements (10ms apart), the fastest moving point on a human arm moves by less than 2cm, which is small enough for our context. Thus, our assumption that the path followed by any point on the arm during Δt interval can be approximated by a straight line holds in practice.

3.4 Gesture Translation

Next, we use Eq. (11) to derive our translation function. Recall that $\| \mathrm{d}H_T(f,t_i) \|$ represents the difference between consecutive CFR values in the CSI-stream of subcarrier with frequency f at times t_i and t_{i-1}. Let $V(f,t_i,X)$ represent the value of $\|\mathrm{d}H_T(f,t_i)\|$ when user is in configuration X. Eq. (11) can be written as.

$$V(f,t_i,X)\times\frac{(D_i^{\mathrm{X}})^2}{k^X v}\Big\{1+\Big(\frac{d}{D_i^{\mathrm{X}}}\Big)^2-2\frac{d}{D_i^{\mathrm{X}}}\cos(\theta_i^{\mathrm{X}}+\Theta^X)\Big\}=1$$

If a user provides a training sample in configuration A and we desire to translate it to configuration B, as the right hand side of the equation above is a constant, translated values of CFR, represented by $V(f,t_i,B)$, are given by the following equation.

$$V(f,t_i,B) = V(f,t_i,A)\times \frac{k^B(D_i^{\mathrm{A}})^2\Big\{1+\Big(\frac{d}{D_i^{\mathrm{A}}}\Big)^2-2\frac{d}{D_i^{\mathrm{A}}}\cos(\theta_i^{\mathrm{A}}+\Theta^A)\Big\}}{k^A(D_i^{\mathrm{B}})^2\Big\{1+\Big(\frac{d}{D_i^{\mathrm{B}}}\Big)^2-2\frac{d}{D_i^{\mathrm{B}}}\cos(\theta_i^{\mathrm{B}}+\Theta^B)\Big\}} \quad (12)$$

Eq. (12) is our gesture translation function. To apply this translation function, WiAG needs the values of the configuration parameters (D_1 and Θ), proportionality constant (k), shape parameters (all θ_i), and speed (v) at both configurations A (where the user provided training samples) and B (the desired configuration). Next, we describe how WiAG obtains the values of these parameters at both configurations.

3.4.1 *Parameter Estimation for Configuration A*

Config. Params. and Prop. Constant: We use our configuration estimation scheme to automatically calculate the values of D_1^{A}, Θ^{A}, and k^{A}. We will describe our configuration estimation scheme in Section 6.

Shape Parameters: To estimate the values of shape parameters θ_i^{A}, we request the user to hold a smart phone in hand for at least one sample per gesture when providing training data. The smart phone runs our custom application that applies standard algorithms on the measurements from the onboard inertial measurement unit (IMU) to calculate the direction and magnitude of displacement of hand along all three axes and obtains the values of all θ_i^{A}. *We emphasize here that we ask the user to hold a smart phone in hand* **only** *at the time of collecting training samples and* **never** *at the time of using the trained gesture recognition system at runtime.* In every sample during which the user holds the phone, the user is requested to hold it in same orientation.

Speed: We again use our smart phone app to calculate the speed of the gesture. Our app divides the length of the path the hand follows during the gesture by the duration of the gesture to calculate speed. We again emphasize that the user holds a smart phone in hand only during training samples.

3.4.2 *Parameter Estimation for Configuration B*

Config. Params. and Prop. Constant: When generating classification models, the values of configuration parameters at configuration B are already known (we will see this shortly). When recognizing an unknown gesture from user at runtime, we use our configuration estimation scheme (Section 6) to calculate these values.

Shape Parameters: We use the same values for shape parameters at configuration B as at configuration A, *i.e.*, $\forall i$, $\theta_i^{\mathrm{B}} = \theta_i^{\mathrm{A}}$, because we want the shape of the gesture to stay the same in the virtual samples.

Speed: We use the same value for speed at configuration B as at configuration A because the speed of gesture should not change in the virtual sample.

3.4.3 *Applying the Translation Function*

To generate a virtual sample of a given gesture at a desired configuration B using a sample of that gesture collected at configuration A, WiAG first estimates the values of all parameters for both configurations as described above, and then $\forall i$, uses Eq. (12) to calculate $V(f,t_i,B)$ corresponding to each value $V(f,t_i,A)$ in the first-order difference of the filtered CSI-streams of that gesture. Filtering will be discussed shortly.

4. WIAG - OVERVIEW

In this section, we provide an overview of WiAG and how it utilizes the translation function to perform position and orientation agnostic gesture recognition. To recognize gestures in any given environment, WiAG needs classification models for those gestures in all possible configurations in that environment. Theoretically, the number of possible configurations is infinite. However, practically, we observed that a change in position of up to 12 inches and a change in orientation of up to 45° does not have a significant impact on gesture recognition accuracy. Therefore, we recommend to generate classification models at all positions corresponding to the intersection points of an imaginary grid, where the side of each square in the grid is at most 12 inches in length. At each position, we recommend to generate classification models for at least $360°/45° = 8$ orientations. Given the training samples collected in a single known configuration, WiAG builds classification models for each configuration in the following four steps.

1) CSI-Stream Conditioning: In this step, WiAG performs two tasks: noise removal and gesture extraction. CSI-streams contain a large amount of noise that occludes the variations caused by gestures in the channel frequency response. To remove this noise, WiAG first applies a principal component analysis (PCA) based de-noising technique followed by Butterworth filtering. It then calculates the first order difference of the filtered streams. We call the resulting streams "differentiated principal component" (dPC) streams. To extract a gesture from the dPC-streams, *i.e.*, to identify the start and end times of the gesture, WiAG uses a supervised thresholding scheme. It then uses the values in dPC-streams contained between the start and end times for further processing.

2) Configuration Estimation: Before collecting any training samples, WiAG requests the user to first perform a preamble gesture in the configuration where the user will provide the training samples. Using the *d*PC-streams from the preamble gesture, WiAG estimates the configuration parameters and the proportionality constant by solving the CFR model derived in Section 3.

3) Gesture Translation: In this step, using the parameter values obtained from the second step along with the values of the shape parameters and speed obtained from the IMU, WiAG applies the translation function on each sample of each gesture extracted from the *d*PC-streams during the first step to generate virtual samples of the gestures in all configurations.

4) Classifier Training: In this step, for each configuration, WiAG takes the virtual samples of all gestures in that configuration from the third step and extracts appropriate features from them. It uses these features to perform *k*-NN based classification. Note that WiAG applies only the third and the fourth steps for each configuration in the given environment. The first and the second steps are applied only once on the training data.

Gesture Recognition: To recognize a gesture at runtime, WiAG requests the user to first perform a preamble gesture. The preamble gesture is not required if the time elapsed since the user performed the previous gesture is less than 10s. WiAG assumes that the user does not change configurations between consecutive gestures if they are separated in time by less than 10s. WiAG continuously applies CSI-stream Conditioning step on the incoming CSI-streams. As soon as it detects and extracts an unknown gesture, it checks whether more than 10s have elapsed since the previous gesture. If yes, WiAG applies the Configuration Estimation step, otherwise, it uses the values from previous most recently executed configuration estimation step. WiAG then takes the features (which it extracted during the fourth step) of the virtual samples corresponding to the estimated configuration and applies *k*-NN based classification to recognize the incoming gesture. Next, we describe CSI-Stream Conditioning, Configuration Estimation, and Classifier Training steps in detail. We do not discuss Gesture Translation step further because we have already described it in detail in Section 3.

5. CSI-STREAM CONDITIONING

In this section, we first explain how WiAG removes noise from CSI-streams and then describe how it detects the start and end of a gesture.

5.1 Noise Removal

The CSI-streams provided by WiFi NICs are extremely noisy. This noise occludes the variations caused by gestures, which makes it difficult to recognize them. The major source of noise in CSI-streams is the internal state transitions in sender and receiver WiFi NICs, such as transmission power changes and transmission rate adaptations. These state transitions manifest as high amplitude impulse and burst noises in CSI-streams. Before we describe how WiAG removes this noise, recall from Section 3.1 that there are 64 subcarriers between each Tx-Rx antenna pair. However, the driver of our Intel 5300 WiFi NIC reports CSI measurements for only 30 out of the 64 subcarriers. Therefore, we get only 30 CSI-streams for each Tx-Rx antenna pair.

To remove the noise, WiAG uses the de-noising scheme of CARM, proposed in [45]. We briefly summarize this scheme here and refer interested readers to [45] for details. CARM's de-noising scheme leverages the observation that human movements cause correlated changes in all CSI-streams. Principal component analysis (PCA) is a natural choice to capture these correlated changes. For each Tx-Rx pair, we first apply PCA on the 30 CSI-streams to capture all correlated human movements and then pass each of the resulting streams through a butterworth filter to remove any noise in the captured human movements. Consequently, we get 30 new streams per Tx-Rx pair, ordered based on the amount of information each stream contains. We call these new streams principle component (PC) streams. CARM recommends to use the second and third PC-streams for further processing because they contain little to no noise while at the same time clearly capture human movements. CARM does not use the first PC-stream because it captures the leftover correlated noise that the butterworth filter could not remove. We, however, chose to proceed only with the third component because we observed that the second component also captured some noise. Consequently, we get $N_{Tx} \times N_{Rx}$ PC-streams, one per Tx-Rx pair. Figure 3(a) shows three randomly chosen raw CSI-streams out of 30 CSI-streams between a Tx-Rx pair. We observe from this figure that these streams are indeed very noisy. Figure 3(b) shows the third PC-stream corresponding to the same duration as the CSI-streams in Figure 3(a). We observe that this PC-stream contains no visible noise while at the same time captures human gestures clearly.

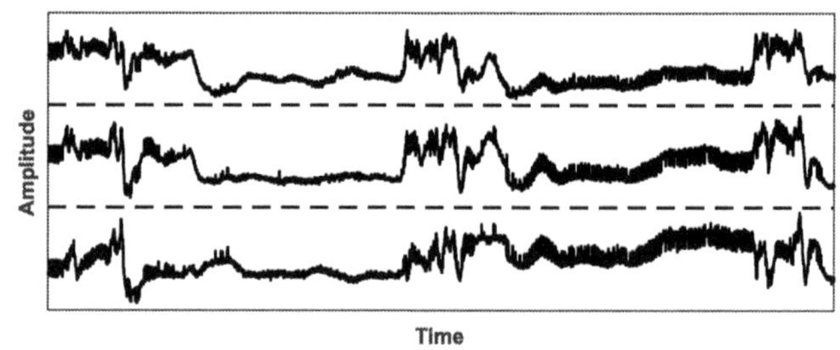

(a) Raw CSI-Streams

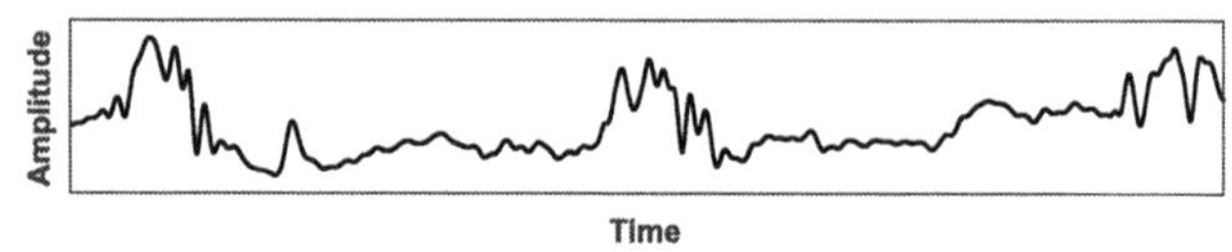

(b) Third PC-stream

Figure 3: CSI- and PC-streams

5.2 Gesture Detection

To detect the start and end of a gesture, like most gesture recognition systems (including non-WiFi based), we request the user to take brief pauses before and after the gesture. Figure 4(a) plots a PC-stream when the user performs a push gesture three times, with brief pauses before and after each gesture. We observe from this figure that there is an absolute increase or decrease in the stream values at the start or end of gestures. This happens due to change in the position of arm at the start and end of a gesture. This observation makes it challenging to develop a threshold based gesture detection scheme because one never knows where the arm will be at the start and when it will be at the end of an arbitrary gesture.

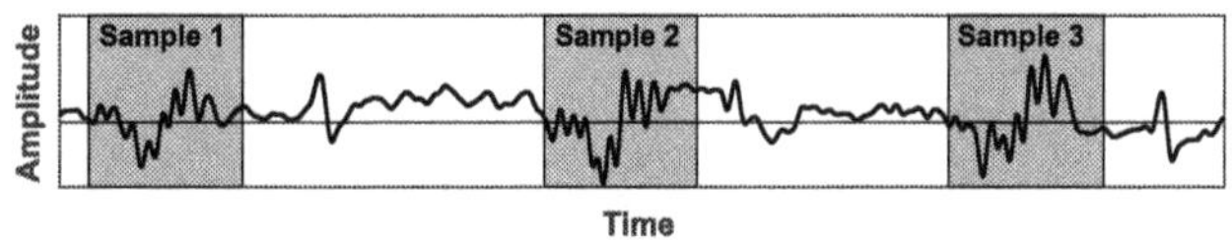

(a) Third PC-Stream

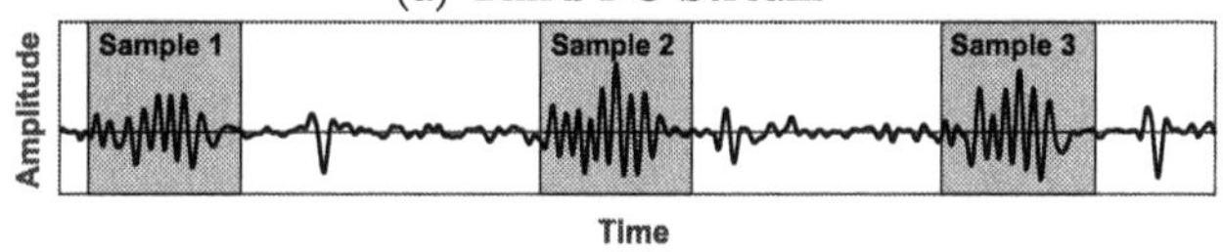

(b) Third dPC-stream

Figure 4: Effect of differentiation on PC-stream

We also observe from Figure 4(a) that during the pauses, the values in the PC-stream experience only small changes, whereas, during the gestures, they experience larger changes. WiAG leverages this observation to detect the start and end of gestures. More specifically, it takes the first order difference of the PC-stream by subtracting each value in the PC-stream from the next value. We represent this differentiated PC-stream with dPC-stream. Figure 4(b) plots the dPC-stream corresponding to the PC-stream in Figure 4(a). From this figure, we make two key observations. First, during the gestures, the amplitudes of variations in the dPC-stream are very high, whereas during the pauses, the amplitudes are very low. Second, the dPC-stream is centered around 0, especially during the pauses, regardless of what the position of the arm is at the start and end of gestures. These two observations enable us to set a threshold to identify the start and end of any gesture.

To identify the start and end of a gesture, WiAG monitors the time-separation between peaks in the dPC-stream of any one Tx-Rx pair. But first, it has to distinguish between peaks generated during gestures from the peaks generated during pauses. WiAG identifies peaks in the dPC-stream by comparing each value in the stream with the value before and the value after it. If any value is less than both values before and after it, that value is a local minima. Similarly, if any value is greater than the values before and after it, it is a local maxima. From the empirical study of our data set, we observed that the absolute amplitudes of almost 100% of the peaks during pauses is less than a threshold $T = 0.8$, whereas the absolute amplitudes of 98% of the peaks during gestures is greater than T. WiAG uses this threshold T to distinguish between peaks belonging to gestures from the peaks belonging to pauses.

While $T = 0.8$ in our data set, WiAG actually automatically calculates this threshold for any given environment by asking a user to first stay stationary and then move the arm randomly. WiAG takes the time when the user started moving the arm as input. Using one of the resulting dPC-streams, it calculates average μ_S of absolute amplitudes of peaks when the user was stationary and average μ_G of absolute amplitudes of peaks when the user was moving the arm, and sets the threshold as $T = (\mu_S + \mu_G)/2$.

After identifying all peaks with absolute amplitudes $>T$, WiAG makes groups of peaks that are close in time, *i.e.*, it groups together all peaks for which the largest time separation between any pair of consecutive peaks is no more than 300ms. Each group represents a gesture, where the start and end times of the gesture are the times of the first and last peaks in the group, respectively. With this method, WiAG successfully identified the start and end times of 96% of gestures in our data set while experiencing no false positives.

6. CONFIGURATION ESTIMATION

In this section, we explain how WiAG estimates the configuration parameters (D_1 and Θ) and the proportionality constant (k). For this purpose, WiAG requests the user to perform a preamble gesture, which in our implementation is a push gesture. We will later show that push is also one of the six gestures on which we evaluated WiAG. If a user wants to perform a push gesture, but is required to perform the preamble gesture first because the user has not performed any gesture in last 10 seconds, the user simply performs the push gesture twice, with a brief pause in between. WiAG treats the first gesture as the preamble gesture and the second as the regular gesture. As push is a linear gesture, our configuration estimation scheme is based on Eq. (9).

The terms $(\frac{vt}{D_1})^2 - 2\frac{vt}{D_1}\cos(\theta)$ in the denominator of Eq. (9) almost always evaluate to less than 1 because vt is the distance the hand travels, whose maximum value for a push gesture is approximately equal to the length of the arm. Furthermore, as D_1 is the distance of the user from the receiver, it is almost always greater than the length of the arm. Consequently, we can do binomial expansion of $\parallel \mathrm{d}H_T(f,t) \parallel$ in Eq. (9), which gives us

$$\parallel \mathrm{d}H_T(f,t) \parallel \approx \frac{kv}{(D_1)^2}\Big\{1 + \Big(2\frac{v}{D_1}\cos(\Theta)\Big) \times t - \Big(\frac{v^2}{D_1^2}(1 - 4\cos^2(\Theta))\Big) \times t^2\Big\}$$

Note the that we have replaced θ with Θ in the equation above because in our formulation for linear gestures, the orientation Θ of the user was represented by θ (see Figure 2(a)). The binomial expansion above expresses $\parallel \mathrm{d}H_T(f,t) \parallel$ as a polynomial in t. To estimate the values of D_1, Θ, and k, we fit a polynomial of degree n in least squares sense on an observed dPC-stream of the preamble gesture, which gives us $n+1$ polynomial coefficients. In our implementation, we used $n = 8$ as it provided the best fit. Let a_i represent the ith coefficient from the polynomial fit. By comparing the estimated values of the coefficients a_0, a_1, and a_2 from the polynomial fit with the coefficients of t^0, t^1, and t^2, we get

$$a_0 = \frac{kv}{(D_1)^2}, \qquad a_1 = \frac{kv}{(D_1)^2}\Big(2\frac{v}{D_1}cos(\Theta)\Big)$$
$$a_2 = -\frac{kv}{(D_1)^2}\Big(\frac{v^2}{D_1^2}(1 - 4\cos^2(\Theta))\Big)$$

Recall that we already know the value of v from our IMU based technique. Thus, we have three unknowns D_1, Θ, and k and three equations, which we solve simultaneously to obtain the values of these unknowns. Also recall that WiAG obtains $N_{Tx} \times N_{Rx}$ dPC-streams per gesture. Thus, it actually first estimates the coefficients a_0, a_1, and a_2 from each of the $N_{Tx} \times N_{Rx}$ dPC-streams and then uses their average values in the three equations above to estimate the values of D_1, Θ, and k.

7. CLASSIFIER TRAINING

WiAG builds a classification model for gestures in each configuration. As WiAG uses k-NN based classifier, the process of building the classification model in any given configuration essentially involves only extracting features form the virtual samples in that configuration. Recall from Section 4 that WiAG obtains virtual samples in any desired configuration by applying the three steps of CSI-Stream Conditioning, Configuration Estimation, and Gesture Translation. Next, we first describe how WiAG extracts features from virtual samples and then explain how it evaluates an unknown gesture.

7.1 Feature Extraction

WiAG uses discrete wavelet transform (DWT) to extract features from virtual samples. We chose DWT due to its inherent ability to extract features with high classification potential when time-series for different samples belonging to the same class have similar shapes while the time-series of different samples belonging to different classes have different shapes. DWT is a popular tool to extract features and has extensively been used in both WiFi based [12, 19, 45] as well as non-WiFi based human sensing systems [32, 41]. One of the reasons behind its popularity is that it provides a good resolution in both time and frequency and enables measurements of both fast and slow gestures. WiAG extracts features using DWT in the following four steps.

1) Aggregation: Recall that each virtual sample consists of $N_{Tx} \times N_{Rx}$ *d*PC-streams and that the CFR values across all *Tx*-*Rx* pairs are correlated. Consequently, all $N_{Tx} \times N_{Rx}$ *d*PC-streams are also correlated. We leverage this observation to combine these $N_{Tx} \times N_{Rx}$ *d*PC-streams into a single stream by first applying PCA on these streams and then picking the resulting PCA component with the largest Eigen value. We name this component *d*PC-component. The motivation behind combining these streams into a single stream is to reduce the computational cost of the k-NN based classifier when recognizing gestures at runtime.

2) Extrapolation: Due to human imprecisions, users almost always take different amounts of time to perform two samples of even the same gesture. Consequently, the number of points in the *d*PC-component of each virtual sample is also almost always different. To apply DWT, we need the number of points in *d*PC-component of every sample to be the same. From the exploratory study of our data set, we observed that our volunteers always took less than 10s to perform any gesture. As we will describe later, we measure CFR values from our WiFi NIC at a rate of 100 samples/sec. Consequently, each *d*PC-component always has less than 1000 points. Thus, we chose a number 1024 (>1000 and an exact power of 2, which makes it easy to apply DWT), and used smoothing splines [9] to extrapolate each *d*PC-component to 1024 points.

3) DWT: DWT is a hierarchical transform that gives *detail coefficients* at multiple *levels*, where the frequency span at any given level is half of the span at the level before it. When we apply DWT to a *d*PC-component, the resulting detail coefficients at any given DWT level represent the correlation between the *d*PC-component and the wavelet function at the frequency corresponding to that DWT level. The detail coefficients are also ordered according to their occurrence in time. In our implementation, we used Daubechies D4 wavelet because it is the most commonly used wavelet and also gave the highest accuracy in our experiments. Similarly, we used the detail coefficients corresponding to DWT level 3 due to its high accuracy. At level 3, we get $1024/2^3 = 128$ detail coefficients for each virtual sample. Due to space limitation, we do not give the theory and other details of DWT here, and refer interested readers to [20, 28].

4) Energy Calculation: While the detail coefficients contain distinct patterns for virtual samples of different gestures, we observed that these patterns also had slight shifts across the virtual samples of the same gesture due to human imprecisions. Thus, using these coefficients directly for classification results in relatively low accuracy. To mitigate this, WiAG distributes these 128 detail coefficients almost equally into 10 bins. More specifically, it puts the first 8 sets of 13 consecutive coefficients in first 8 bins and the remaining 2 sets of 12 consecutive coefficients in the remaining two bins. It then calculates the energy of each bin and uses it as a feature. The energy of a bin is equal to the sum of square of all values in it. Thus, WiAG extracts 10 features per virtual sample, which it uses for classification.

7.2 Recognizing Gestures at Runtime

To recognize a gesture at runtime, WiAG follows the steps described under "Gesture Recognition" in Section 4. Here we only describe how it applies the k-NN based classification step at the estimated user configuration. To classify an unknown gesture, WiAG first extracts the 10 features from its $N_{Tx} \times N_{Rx}$ *d*PC-streams. After that, it applies the k-NN classifier, which essentially looks at the k nearest neighbors of this unknown gesture in the 10 dimensional space containing all virtual samples of all gesture at the estimated configuration, and declares the unknown gesture to be the one whose virtual samples are most frequent among its k nearest neighbors. In our implementation, $k = 20$.

8. IMPLEMENTATION & EVALUATION

We implemented WiAG on a Thinkpad X200 laptop equipped with an Intel 5300 WiFi NIC attached to two omni-directional antennas. We installed the tool developed by Halperin *et al.* [24] on the laptop to obtain CSI measurements in the 2.4GHz WiFi frequency band with 20MHz bandwidth subcarriers. The laptop communicates with a TP-Link N750 access point (AP). In our implementation, the laptop and AP contain two and three antennas, respectively, *i.e.*, $N_{Tx} = 2$ and $N_{Rx} = 3$. To collect CSI measurements, we probed the AP using ping command every 10ms and achieved a sampling rate of 100 samples/sec. In comparison, existing schemes, such as CARM, ping the AP at very high rates of up to 2500 pings per second, which consumes a significant portion of the bandwidth, leaving little bandwidth for transferring actual data. Next, we first describe our evaluation setup along with information about the data we collected. After that, we evaluate the configuration estimation and gesture recognition accuracies of WiAG. Last, we evaluate the performance of WiAG under changing environmental conditions. All evaluations are done using using real world data.

8.1 Evaluation Setup

We collected 1427 samples from 10 volunteers for 6 gestures at 5 different positions on 8 different days. The names of the six gestures and the number of samples per gesture are listed in Table 1. Note that WiAG does not require the training samples to come from the same user whose gestures it has to recognize. Consequently, the number of volunteers in the data set is irrelevant. Nonetheless, we still collected samples from 10 volunteers. We collected these samples in a 25ft×16ft room that contains usual furniture including 7 chairs and 3 tables. Figure 5 shows the layout of the room along with the locations of access point (Tx), laptop (Rx), and the 5 positions (represented by triangles) where we collected samples. The ordered-pair under each triangle gives volunteers' absolute position in inches (with Tx being at origin) and the value above gives volunteers' orientation with respect to the receiver at that position. We collected these samples after obtaining IRB approval. To incorporate the effects of environmental changes, we randomly moved furniture in the room each day before collecting samples on that day.

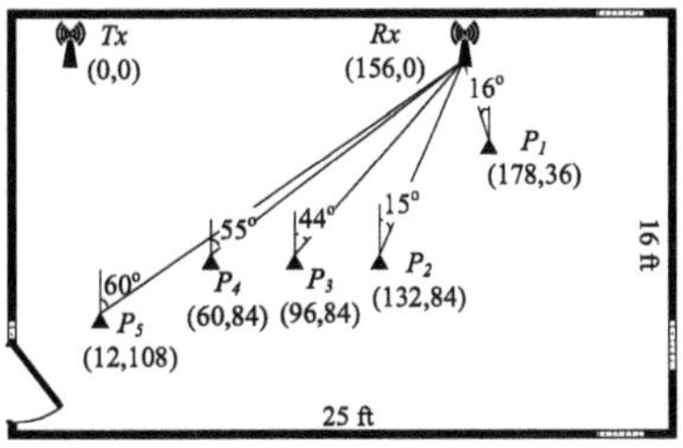

Figure 5: Layout of data collection environment

Gesture	Samples
Push	207
Pull	235
Flick	204
Circle	324
Throw	152
Dodge	305

Table 1: Summary of gesture data set

8.2 Orientation Estimation Accuracy

To evaluate WiAG's configuration estimation scheme, we show the performance of WiAG in estimating orientations of users. For this, we took all samples of the push gesture (recall that WiAG uses push gesture as preamble) from our data set and estimated user orientation from each sample. We report the performance of WiAG's orientation estimation in terms of *absolute error*, which is the absolute value of the difference between the estimated orientation and the actual orientation, measured in degrees. We observe from our experiments that WiAG achieves average absolute error of less than 23° in estimating user orientation. Figure 6 plots the CDF of absolute errors across all samples of push gesture collected at all positions. Recall that we recommended to generate classification models for 8 orientations per position, which corresponds to 45° per orientation. As WiAG achieves an average error of almost half of 45°, it can correctly identify the classification model that it should use when evaluating an unknown gesture. We also observed from our experiments that the smallest absolute error that WiAG achieved is just 1.3°.

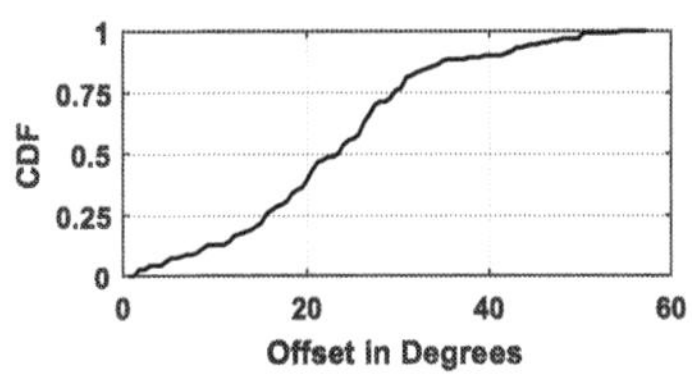

Figure 6: CDF of absolute error in WiAG's orientation estimation

8.3 Gesture Recognition Accuracy

Next, we first show WiAG's performance in recognizing gestures when only the orientation of user changes compared to the orientation of user at the time of providing training samples. For this set of experiments, the position of user stays the same. After that, we show the performance of WiAG when both orientation and position of user change. We report the gesture recognition performance of WiAG in terms of *accuracy*, which is defined as the percentage of samples correctly recognized.

Accuracy with Change in Orientation: For this set of experiments, in addition to collecting samples in the 44° orientation at position P_3 (see Figure 5), we also collected samples from our volunteers for all 6 gestures in two randomly chosen orientations of 134° and 314° at P_3. Next, we first obtained virtual samples corresponding to the 134° and 314° orientations using real samples collected in the 44° orientation, and then evaluated the real samples collected in the 134° and 314° orientations using the corresponding virtual samples. Figure 7(a) plots WiAG's aggregate accuracy across all gestures for each test orientation using a black bar and accuracy for individual gestures using patterned and grey-scale bars. We observe from this figure that WiAG achieves an aggregate accuracy of at least 89.9% across six gestures when trained and tested in different orientations. Figure 7(b) plots the accuracies when we repeat the same set of experiments, except that we use the samples in the 44° orientation directly without applying our translation function. We observe from this figure that the accuracy drops significantly to 47.62% and 53.26% for the two test orientations. This result has two implications: 1) change in orientation indeed severely deteriorates the accuracy of WiFi based gesture recognition, and 2) our translation function is very effective in making WiFi based gesture recognition agnostic to orientation.

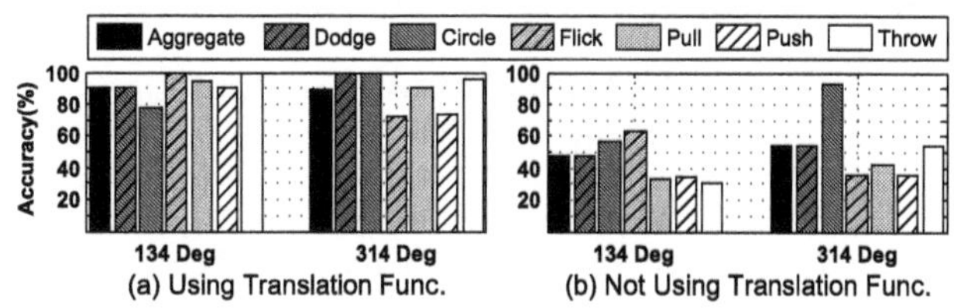

Figure 7: Accuracy with change in orientation

Accuracy with Change in Orientation and Position: For this set of experiments, we used the samples collected at position P_3 in 44° orientation and generated virtual samples corresponding to configurations at positions P_1, P_2, P_4 and P_5. We then evaluated the real samples collected at each of these four positions using the virtual samples generated for the corresponding configurations and applying the k-NN classifier. Our experimental results show that WiAG achieves an average accuracy of 91.4% in recognizing the six gestures in all 4 different configurations. Note that this accuracy is comparable to that reported by prior WiFi based gesture and activity recognition systems [12–16, 24, 27, 35, 42, 45, 46], which train and test in same configurations. Figure 8(a) plots WiAG's aggregate accuracy across all gestures in each configuration using a black bar and accuracy for individual gestures using patterned and grey-scale bars. We see in this figure that WiAG achieves an aggregate accuracy of no less than 90.6% across the six gestures. Figure 9(a) shows the confusion matrix for the six gestures across all four configurations. We see that WiAG achieves the highest average accuracy for the Push gesture.

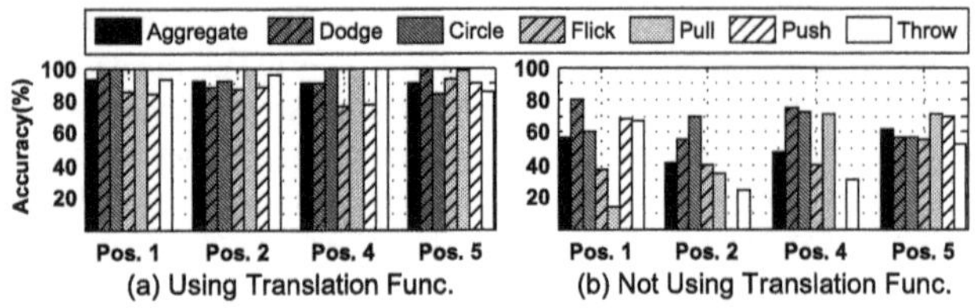

Figure 8: Accuracy with change in orientation & position

	Dodge	Circle	Flick	Pull	Push	Throw
Dodge	0.86	0.00	0.00	0.01	0.13	0.00
Circle	0.00	0.96	0.02	0.00	0.00	0.02
Flick	0.00	0.04	0.86	0.00	0.00	0.11
Pull	0.04	0.00	0.00	0.96	0.00	0.00
Push	0.03	0.00	0.00	0.01	0.96	0.00
Throw	0.00	0.07	0.04	0.00	0.00	0.88

(a) Using translation func.

	Dodge	Circle	Flick	Pull	Push	Throw
Dodge	0.43	0.02	0.00	0.29	0.23	0.03
Circle	0.01	0.50	0.23	0.00	0.00	0.26
Flick	0.03	0.03	0.51	0.00	0.00	0.43
Pull	0.11	0.02	0.00	0.78	0.09	0.00
Push	0.11	0.02	0.04	0.43	0.40	0.00
Throw	0.04	0.21	0.21	0.00	0.03	0.50

(b) Not using translation func.

Figure 9: Confusion matrix across all configurations

Figures 8(b) and 9(b) show results from the same set of experiments as conducted to generate Figures 8(a) and 9(a), respectively, except that we used the samples at P_3 in 44° orientation directly without applying our translation function. From Figure 8(b), we observe that even the highest aggregate accuracy among the 4 configurations is just 61.24%, which is significantly less than the minimum aggregate accuracy of 90.6% when using the translation function. We observe similar trends on comparing Figures 9(a) and 9(b). From Figure 9(b), we also observe that 43% of push gestures are recognized as pull because without taking orientation into account, push gesture in one orientation and pull gesture in another can appear very similar to the receiver. These observations show that our translation function indeed makes WiAG agnostic to position and orientation.

8.4 Effect of Environmental Changes

In this section, we evaluate the performance of WiAG when the number and position of stationary objects in an environment change across samples, such as moving or adding a chair. Recall from Section 8.1 that when collecting samples, we randomly moved furniture each day before collecting samples on that day. For this set of experiments, for each day in our data set, we evaluated the samples collected on that day using the samples collected on all other days and applying the k-NN classifier. Figure 10 shows the resulting average accuracy of WiAG across all gestures for each day in our data set. We observe from this figure that the accuracy of WiAG does not change significantly across days, which shows that the static environmental changes do not affect WiAG. WiAG achieves this property due to the differentiation step of Eq. (8).

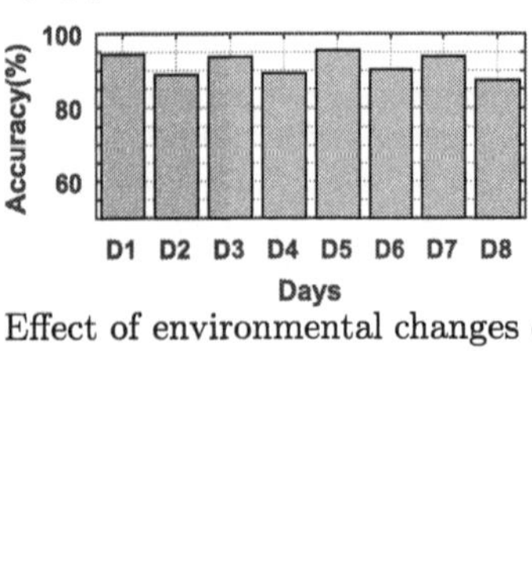

Figure 10: Effect of environmental changes on accuracy

9. CONCLUSION

In this paper, we proposed WiAG, a theoretically grounded position and orientation agnostic gesture recognition system. The key novelty of WiAG lies in its *translation function* that can generate virtual samples of any gesture in any desired configuration, and in its *configuration estimation scheme* that can estimate the position and orientation of user with respect to the receiver. The key technical depth of WiAG lies in its parametric formulation of the model for calculating changes in CFR due to linear and non-linear human gestures. This parametric formulation lies at the the heart of WiAG's translation function and configuration estimation scheme. We implemented WiAG using cheap, commercially available, commodity WiFi devices and demonstrated that when user's configuration is not the same as at the time of collecting training samples, using our translation function, WiAG significantly improves the gesture recognition accuracy from just 51.4% to 91.4%. We envision that WiAG will help the research on WiFi based gesture recognition to step into its next phase of evolution where it will become more ubiquitous, pervasive, and practical.

10. REFERENCES

[1] Allure Smart Thermostat. https://www.allure-energy.com/.

[2] Honeywell Lyric Thermostat. http://wifithermostat.com/Products/Lyric/.

[3] Honeywell Smart Thermostat. http://wifithermostat.com/Products/WiFiSmartThermostat/.

[4] Insteon LED Bulbs. http://www.insteon.com/led-bulbs/.

[5] LG Smart Appliances. http://www.lg.com/us/discover/smartthinq/thinq.

[6] Nest Thermostat. https://nest.com/thermostat/meet-nest-thermostat/.

[7] Philips Hue. http://www2.meethue.com/en-us/.

[8] Smart Home. http://www.smarthome.com/.

[9] Smoothing Spline Matlab. https://www.mathworks.com/help/curvefit/smoothing-splines.html.

[10] Whirlpool Smart Appliances. http://www.whirlpool.com/smart-appliances/.

[11] WiFi Plug. http://www.wifiplug.co.uk/.

[12] Abdelnasser, H., Youssef, M., and Harras, K. A. WiGest: A Ubiquitous WiFi-based Gesture Recognition System, May 2015.

[13] Adib, F., Hsu, C. Y., Mao, H., Katabi, D., and Durand, F. Capturing the Human Figure Through a Wall. *ACM Trans. Graph. 34*, 6 (Oct. 2015).

[14] Adib, F., Kabelac, Z., and Katabi, D. Multi-person Localization via RF Body Reflections. In *Proceedings of the 12th USENIX Conference on Networked Systems Design and Implementation* (Berkeley, CA, USA, 2015), NSDI'15, USENIX Association, pp. 279–292.

[15] Adib, F., Kabelac, Z., Katabi, D., and Miller, R. C. 3D Tracking via Body Radio Reflections. In *Proceedings of the 11th USENIX Conference on Networked Systems Design and Implementation* (Berkeley, CA, USA, 2014), NSDI'14, USENIX Association, pp. 317–329.

[16] Adib, F., and Katabi, D. See Through Walls with WiFi! *SIGCOMM Comput. Commun. Rev. 43*, 4 (Aug. 2013), 75–86.

[17] Adib, F., Mao, H., Kabelac, Z., Katabi, D., and Miller, R. C. Smart Homes That Monitor Breathing and Heart Rate. In *Proceedings of the 33rd Annual ACM Conference on Human Factors in Computing Systems* (New York, NY, USA, 2015), CHI '15, ACM, pp. 837–846.

[18] Aggarwal, J. K., and Michael, S. R. Human activity analysis: A review. *ACM Computing Surveys 43*, 3 (2011).

[19] Ali, K., Liu, A. X., Wang, W., and Shahzad, M. Keystroke Recognition Using WiFi Signals. In *Proceedings of the 21st Annual International Conference on Mobile Computing and Networking* (New York, NY, USA, 2015), MobiCom '15, ACM, pp. 90–102.

[20] Burrus, C. S., Gopinath, R. A., and Guo, H. Introduction to wavelets and wavelet transforms: a primer.

[21] Cheung, G. K., Kanade, T., Bouguet, J.-Y., and Holler, M. A real time system for robust 3d voxel reconstruction of human motions. In *Computer Vision and Pattern Recognition, 2000. Proceedings. IEEE Conference on* (2000), vol. 2, IEEE, pp. 714–720.

[22] Ertin, E., Stohs, N., Kumar, S., Raij, A., al'Absi, M., and Shah, S. AutoSense: unobtrusively wearable sensor suite for inferring the onset, causality, and consequences of stress in the field. In *Proceedings of ACM Sensys* (2011).

[23] Halperin, D., Hu, W., Sheth, A., and Wetherall, D. Tool release: Gathering 802.11n traces with channel state information. *ACM SIGCOMM CCR 41*, 1 (Jan. 2011), 53.

[24] Han, C., Wu, K., Wang, Y., and Ni, L. M. Wifall: Device-free fall detection by wireless networks. In *Proceedings of IEEE INFOCOM* (2014), pp. 271–279.

[25] Herda, L., Fua, P., Plänkers, R., Boulic, R., and Thalmann, D. Skeleton-based motion capture for robust reconstruction of human motion. In *Computer Animation 2000. Proceedings* (2000), IEEE, pp. 77–83.

[26] Huang, D., Nandakumar, R., and Gollakota, S. Feasibility and limits of wi-fi imaging. In *Proceedings of the 12th ACM Conference on Embedded Network Sensor Systems* (2014), ACM, pp. 266–279.

[27] Kellogg, B., Talla, V., and Gollakota, S. Bringing gesture recognition to all devices. In *Proceedings of the 11th USENIX Conference on Networked Systems Design and Implementation* (Berkeley, CA, USA, 2014), NSDI'14, USENIX Association, pp. 303–316.

[28] Lang, M., Guo, H., Odegard, J. E., Burrus, C. S., and Wells, R. O. Noise reduction using an undecimated discrete wavelet transform. *IEEE Signal Processing Letters 3*, 1 (1996), 10–12.

[29] Lemmey, T., Vonog, S., and Surin, N. System architecture and methods for distributed multi-sensor gesture processing, Aug. 15 2011. US Patent App. 13/210,370.

[30] Lyonnet, B., Ioana, C., and Amin, M. G. Human gait classification using microdoppler time-frequency signal representations. In *2010 IEEE Radar Conference* (2010), IEEE, pp. 915–919.

[31] Moeslund, T. B., Hilton, A., and Krüger, V. A survey of advances in vision-based human motion capture and analysis. *Computer vision and image understanding 104*, 2 (2006), 90–126.

[32] Ocak, H. Automatic detection of epileptic seizures in eeg using discrete wavelet transform and approximate entropy. *Expert Systems with Applications 36*, 2 (2009), 2027–2036.

[33] Oprisescu, S., Rasche, C., and Su, B. Automatic static hand gesture recognition using tof cameras. In *Signal Processing Conference (EUSIPCO), 2012 Proceedings of the 20th European* (2012), IEEE, pp. 2748–2751.

[34] Park, T., Lee, J., Hwang, I., Yoo, C., Nachman, L., and Song, J. E-gesture: a collaborative architecture for energy-efficient gesture recognition with hand-worn sensor and mobile devices. In *Proceedings of the 9th ACM Conference on Embedded Networked Sensor Systems* (2011), ACM, pp. 260–273.

[35] Pu, Q., Gupta, S., Gollakota, S., and Patel, S. Whole-home gesture recognition using wireless signals. In *Proceedings of the 19th Annual International Conference on Mobile Computing & Networking* (New York, NY, USA, 2013), MobiCom '13, ACM, pp. 27–38.

[36] Seco, F., Jiménez, A. R., and Zampella, F. Joint estimation of indoor position and orientation from rf signal strength measurements. In *Indoor Positioning and Indoor Navigation (IPIN), 2013 International Conference on* (2013), IEEE, pp. 1–8.

[37] Sen, S., Lee, J., Kim, K.-H., and Congdon, P. Avoiding multipath to revive inbuilding wifi localization. In *Proceeding of the 11th annual international conference on Mobile systems, applications, and services* (2013), ACM, pp. 249–262.

[38] Shotton, J., Sharp, T., Kipman, A., Fitzgibbon, A., Finocchio, M., Blake, A., Cook, M., and Moore, R. Real-time human pose recognition in parts from single depth images. *Communications of the ACM 56*, 1 (2013), 116–124.

[39] Singh, G., Nelson, A., Robucci, R., Patel, C., and Banerjee, N. Inviz: Low-power personalized gesture recognition using wearable textile capacitive sensor arrays. In *Pervasive Computing and Communications (PerCom), 2015 IEEE International Conference on* (2015), IEEE, pp. 198–206.

[40] Sun, L., Sen, S., Koutsonikolas, D., and Kim, K. H. WiDraw: Enabling Hands-free Drawing in the Air on Commodity WiFi Devices. In *Proceedings of the 21st Annual International Conference on Mobile Computing and Networking* (New York, NY, USA, 2015), MobiCom '15, ACM, pp. 77–89.

[41] Tzanetakis, G., Essl, G., and Cook, P. Audio analysis using the discrete wavelet transform. In *Proc. Conf. in Acoustics and Music Theory Applications* (2001).

[42] Van Dorp, P., and Groen, F. Feature-based human motion parameter estimation with radar. *IET Radar, Sonar & Navigation 2*, 2 (2008), 135–145.

[43] Wang, G., Zou, Y., Zhou, Z., Wu, K., and Ni, L. M. We can hear you with wi-fi! In *Proceedings of the 20th Annual International Conference on Mobile Computing and Networking* (New York, NY, USA, 2014), MobiCom '14, ACM, pp. 593–604.

[44] Wang, W., Liu, A. X., and Shahzad, M. Gait recognition using wifi signals. In *Proceedings of the 2016 ACM International Joint Conference on Pervasive and Ubiquitous Computing* (2016), ACM, pp. 363–373.

[45] Wang, W., Liu, A. X., Shahzad, M., Ling, K., and Lu, S. Understanding and modeling of wifi signal based human activity recognition. In *Proceedings of the 21st Annual International Conference on Mobile Computing and Networking* (2015), ACM, pp. 65–76.

[46] Wang, Y., Liu, J., Chen, Y., Gruteser, M., Yang, J., and Liu, H. E-eyes: Device-free Location-oriented Activity Identification Using Fine-grained WiFi Signatures. In *Proceedings of the 20th Annual International Conference on Mobile Computing and Networking* (New York, NY, USA, 2014), MobiCom '14, ACM, pp. 617–628.

[47] Xi, W., Zhao, J., Li, X.-Y., Zhao, K., Tang, S., Liu, X., and Jiang, Z. Electronic frog eye: Counting crowd using WiFi. In *Proceedings of IEEE INFOCOM* (2014).

[48] Yang, Z., Zhou, Z., and Liu, Y. From rssi to csi: Indoor localization via channel response. *ACM Computing Surveys (CSUR) 46*, 2 (2013), 25.

[49] Yatani, K., and Truong, K. N. Bodyscope: a wearable acoustic sensor for activity recognition. In *Proceedings of ACM UbiComp* (2012), pp. 341–350.

Object Recognition and Navigation using a Single Networking Device

Yanzi Zhu, Yuanshun Yao, Ben Y. Zhao and Haitao Zheng
Department of Computer Science, UC Santa Barbara
{yanzi, yao, ravenben, htzheng}@cs.ucsb.edu

ABSTRACT

Tomorrow's autonomous mobile devices need accurate, robust and real-time sensing of their operating environment. Today's solutions fall short. Vision or acoustic-based techniques are vulnerable against challenging lighting conditions or background noise, while more robust laser or RF solutions require either bulky expensive hardware or tight coordination between multiple devices.

This paper describes the design, implementation and evaluation of Ulysses, a practical environmental imaging system using colocated 60GHz radios on a *single* mobile device. Unlike alternatives that require specialized hardware, Ulysses reuses low-cost commodity networking chipsets available today. Ulysses' new imaging approach leverages RF beamforming, operates on specular (direct) reflection, and integrates the device's movement trajectory with sensing. Ulysses also includes a navigation component that uses the same 60GHz radios to compute "safety regions" where devices can move freely without collision, and to compute optimal paths for imaging within safety regions. Using our implementation of a small robotic car prototype, our experimental results show that Ulysses images objects meters away with cm-level precision, and provides accurate estimates of objects' surface materials.

1. INTRODUCTION

Autonomous devices are the future of mobile computing. Today, Amazon's drone-based home delivery system (Prime Air) has already received regulatory approval in the UK [20], and retailers like 7-up have performed drone deliveries on a smaller scale [33]. Meanwhile, Uber has already deployed a pilot program for self-driving passenger pickup vehicles in Pittsburgh [17]. With improved hardware and advances in robotics, autonomous robots can do much more than their capabilities today. One might imagine more powerful versions of the Roomba robot cleaning tables and countertops at home, personal robot companions that walk alongside the elderly or visually impaired, and first responder robots that identify and rescue survivors from natural or man-made disasters [18, 23].

One of the significant roadblocks on the path towards this vision is object imaging and recognition. Autonomous devices require knowledge about objects in their surroundings, including distance to the object, size, surface curvature and other properties. Such information allows devices to recognize and distinguish between nearby obstacles and potential target objects for interaction. Additionally, a practical imaging system must be portable enough to mount on mobile devices, and provide robust results in a wide range of environmental conditions.

Permission to make digital or hard copies of all or part of this work for personal or classroom use is granted without fee provided that copies are not made or distributed for profit or commercial advantage and that copies bear this notice and the full citation on the first page. Copyrights for components of this work owned by others than ACM must be honored. Abstracting with credit is permitted. To copy otherwise, or republish, to post on servers or to redistribute to lists, requires prior specific permission and/or a fee. Request permissions from permissions@acm.org.

MobiSys '17, June 19–23, 2017, Niagara Falls, NY, USA.
© 2017 ACM. ISBN 978-1-4503-4928-4/17/06...$15.00
DOI: http://dx.doi.org/10.1145/3081333.3081339

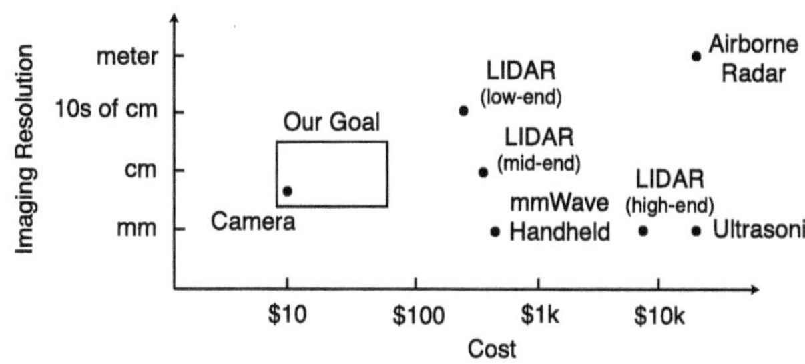

Figure 1: Comparing existing commercial single-device imaging products.

Of the numerous imaging products available today, few if any are appropriate for autonomous mobile devices. In Figure 1, we classify potential imaging solutions based on their precision and cost, including products based on sonar [40], computer vision [1], radar [9, 34] and LIDAR [2, 8, 45]. Nearly all of these approaches require specialized hardware that make them too costly (*e.g.*, > $250) and unwieldly for mobile devices[1]. The only exception is camera-based systems. Yet they are sensitive to lighting conditions and can fail badly when objects and their backgrounds have similar colors, (*e.g.*, the likely cause of the recent fatal accident in a driver-assisted Tesla [35, 30]).

Fortunately, researchers have made significant recent advances in radar systems, dramatically reducing their cost, size and weight. The first group of efforts developed specialized hardware operating in the WiFi bands (Frequency-Modulated Continuous Wave or FMCW radars). Leveraging the precise ranging capabilities of FMCW radars, researchers developed novel systems that detect and measure subtle human dynamics, *e.g.*, heartbeats and body movements [11, 12, 13]. The second group of efforts (re)uses commodity networking devices (non-FMCW hardware) to recognize static objects. Existing works use either two well-separated static WiFi radios [26] or two independently moving WiFi or 60GHz radios [22, 57].

[1]The cheapest mmWave handheld imager costs $500, weighs 5lb [9], and the cheapest low-end LIDAR costs $250 and offers 1D imaging at a resolution of tens of cms [8].

Imaging via a Single Networking Device. Our goal is to further advance the state of imaging systems based on commodity networking devices. Like [57, 22, 26], we focus on imaging static objects, but address the key limitation of requiring dual separate devices. We also integrate navigation with imaging, using the same networking radio to avoid obstacles. The result is a simple, single-device imaging system that recognizes details of objects meters away, using only the device's onboard networking radios. This supports a low-cost solution deployable in crowded spaces, robust to a variety of lighting and acoustic conditions, while avoiding the overhead and complexity of coordinating multiple devices.

Specifically, our approach is to use a pair of 60GHz networking chipsets, one transmitter (TX) and one receiver (RX), mounted on a single commodity mobile robot, separated by a (small) fixed distance (25–40cm). As the device moves by an object, the RX picks up reflections of signals sent by the TX, and uses changing angles of reflection along the path to reconstruct the surface shape, size, curvature, and material of the object. While the TX and RX beamform and analyze reflected beams to enable imaging, the device moves to emulate a large aperture antenna array. Finally, the mobile device can scan an area with multiple objects and map the area and the objects by navigating over a carefully computed path.

Our Contributions. This paper describes the design, implementation and evaluation of *Ulysses*, an object imaging system using a single compact mobile device and on-board 60GHz networking radios. Since phase noise from device tracking errors and colocating of the TX/RX pair introduce changes that invalidate existing radar and RF imaging algorithms, we must design a new imaging algorithm. Our work makes three key contributions:

- **A new imaging algorithm driven by specular reflection and beamforming.** Center to Ulysses is a new imaging algorithm that operates on *beamforming RSS*. As the device moves nearby an object, Ulysses captures the *specular* reflection off the object surface, uses the observed angular and amplitude values of the reflection to recognize tiny segments on the object surface, and then leverages device trajectory to assemble them and reconstruct the object surface details. In a nutshell, Ulysses emulates monostatic synthetic aperture radar (M-SAR) without using phase (for robustness), but using angular and signal strength information offered by the commodity 60GHz radios. Ulysses differs fundamentally from existing 60GHz imaging design [57], which explicitly avoids segment assembly.
- **Navigation based on 60GHz beamforming.** Ulysses also integrates robot navigation with imaging, focusing on defining "safety zones" where devices can move freely without collision, again using just the onboard 60GHz radios.
- **Prototype and evaluation using 802.11ad phased arrays and robot.** We prototype Ulysses using commodity 60GHz 802.11ad radios with phased arrays, which are cost effective ($5) and small enough (4.8cm × 2.4cm) for mobile devices. We then integrate Ulysses on a compact robotic car and evaluate it in multiple indoor and outdoor settings on objects of various sizes, shapes and materials. Our results show that Ulysses images objects meters away with cm-level precision, provides accurate estimates of the surface material, while safely and efficiently navigating in unknown, crowded environments. It is also robust against robot trajectory errors (up to 10cm). We also compare Ulysses to camera based imaging [1] and dual-device 60GHz imaging radar [57]. Ulysses achieves similar accuracy but eliminates the sensitivity to lighting and the need of two mobile devices.

Our prototype is primitive and limited by both hardware and device constraints. However, we believe these results demonstrate significant promise for this approach towards the development of an accurate, low-cost, and portable imaging system for single mobile devices. We discuss the limitations of our current design in §7, and potential solutions to be explored in upcoming work.

2. SINGLE DEVICE MOBILE IMAGING

As background, we describe in this section our target scenarios and constraints, the trade-offs for using 60GHz networking radios, the reason why existing imaging solutions cannot be applied, and the key challenges facing our single-device imaging design.

2.1 Scenarios and Requirements

Our basic operating scenario includes a compact mobile device, *e.g.,* a robot car or a drone, exploring an unknown environment by imaging nearby objects. Figure 2 shows two illustrative examples. The first is a robotic car tries to pick up specific objects inside an unknown room. Target objects are defined by size, shape and material, *e.g.,* a metal box of a specific size. To locate the objects, the robot navigates through the room while imaging each object or obstacle (without bumping into them). The second scenario is a vehicle (or a robot) tries to image the back of parked cars in an outdoor parking lot. For both scenarios, "imaging" an object means recognizing its size, shape and material.

The key requirements for our imaging system include:

- To be suitable for mobile devices, our imaging solution needs to be lightweight and low-cost, and compact enough to be mounted on a single compact mobile device like robot cars or drones (30–40cm in width).
- Our system must accurately image static objects, including recognition of object size, shape (curvature) and materials. These detailed information will greatly help with object recognition, especially in unknown environments.
- To satisfy today's application scenarios, our solution must attain accuracy (of location or size/shape) to a small number of centimeters, and image objects meters away.

2.2 A Case for 60GHz

Our goal is to achieve imaging using commodity networking radios on a single device. Both WiFi and 60GHz networking radios are attractive candidates because they are in unlicensed bands, and have commodity networking chipsets on the market today that are energy efficient and low-cost ($5–$30). We choose 60GHz radios because they offer high directionality (via real-time beamforming) in a small form-factor, so we can place both TX and RX radios on a single, compact mobile device. Furthermore, under high directionality, 60GHz propagation and reflection face minimum multipath effect, and are stable and predictable for both indoor and outdoor scenarios, as shown by prior studies [48, 55].

Figure 3 compares the sizes of a drone, a robot car, and our 60GHz array prototype. The 60GHz array uses a standard 8×16 rectangular array and is 2.4cm × 4.8cm in size. The compact and light-weight design makes it feasible to deploy both transmitter and receiver on a single autonomous device. To achieve the same directionality using WiFi requires antenna size at least 12 times larger. Furthermore, our initial prototype already offers real-time fine-grained beamforming, *i.e.* switching beam every 0.4ms. Commercial 60GHz chips offer beam switching at a higher speed of 50ns [51].

Compared to WiFi, the key limitations of 60GHz radios are reduced range and sensitivity to blockage and rain. But since our goal is to image objects a few meters away (rather than maintaining high-speed communications), these limitations are tolerable under

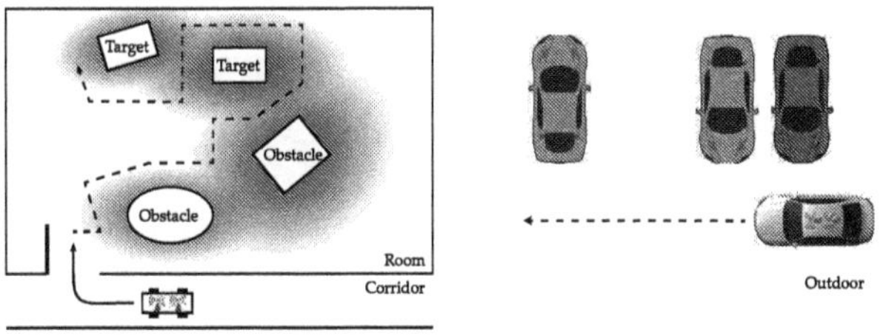

Figure 2: Illustration of two target scenarios where a robot explores an unknown room to image target objects, and a car drives by a set of parked cars to image them.

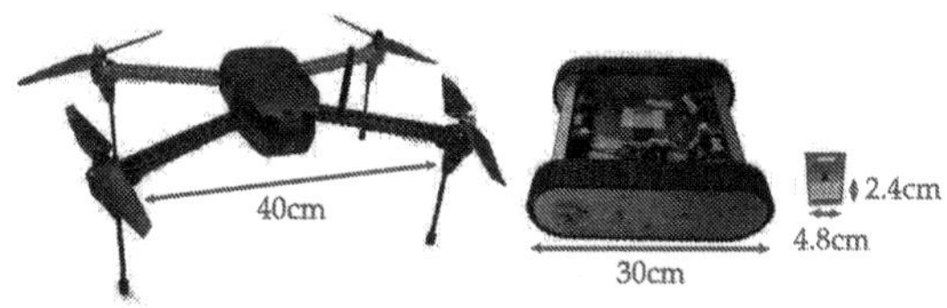

Figure 3: The actual size comparison of a drone, a robot car and our 60GHz array prototype. The array (16×8) is compact and both TX and RX can be mounted on a single mobile device.

our scenarios. Heavy rain only adds 0.2dB signal loss for a 10m imaging range.

2.3 The Need for a New Imaging Algorithm

A key design question is "can we apply existing radar or RF imaging algorithms to our system?" Unfortunately, our analysis shows that existing solutions fail to apply. As starter, FMCW based solutions (*e.g.*, mmWave handheld imagers [9, 10]) do not apply because they require specialized frequency-modulated hardware components that do not exist on commodity networking radios, and it will be difficult and costly to port them into networking radios. Next, prior design for WiFi mobile imaging [22] leverages the shadowing effect of WiFi propagation between two well-separated devices. This approach is not applicable to our scenario since it requires two independently moving mobile devices, and also 60GHz can hardly penetrate objects (thus there is no shadowing effect). Finally, the most relevant solutions are the monostatic synthetic aperture radar (M-SAR) algorithm [46] and variations, and the RSA algorithm for 60GHz mobile imaging [57], which we discuss next.

M-SAR and phase-based solutions. Using colocated transmitter and receiver, M-SAR [46] emulates a large antenna array by moving the device and aggregating both signal strength and phase measurements across locations. Unfortunately, M-SAR requires accurate phase construction along the device path to assemble the measurements. For 60GHz radios, this is only feasible when the device can track its trajectory to sub-millimeter-level accuracy. Prior work [57] have shown that even millimeter-level tracking errors translate into random, large phase noises and significant imaging errors. Similarly, prior works on WiFi object imaging [26], near-field mmWave object imaging [36] and tracking [53] all rely on accurate phase construction, and fail to apply here.

RSA. Developed for dual-device 60GHz mobile imaging [57], RSA tolerates trajectory noises by operating only on RSS. Yet it fails to apply to our system because our *new* requirement of colocating TX and RX breaks the fundamental assumption of its design. Specifically, RSA images an object surface by capturing and modeling the *scattering* reflection contributed by the entire surface as one unit. This methodology works when TX and RX are widely separated and moving independently, but breaks down when TX and RX are colocated and move in unison (discussed next).

2.4 Key Challenges

Challenge 1: Large phase noises. Like existing works on 60GHz mobile imaging [57], our system faces the challenge that (random) errors in trajectory tracking translate into large phase noises across signal measurements. When phase measurements are used in imaging, we observe large imaging errors (similar to [57]). Thus like [57]), we chose not to use phase measurements in our imaging design.

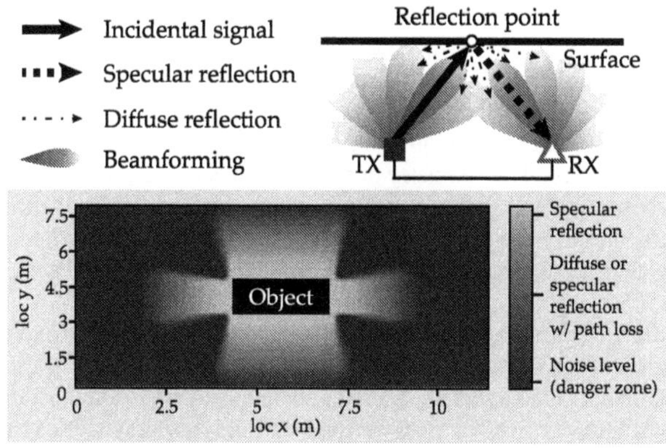

Figure 4: Colocated TX/RX leads to limited visibility of specular reflection, for both indoor and outdoor settings.

In addition to not using phase, we face several new challenges by colocating TX and RX on a single mobile device, separated by a small, fixed distance.

Challenge 2: Moving TX. Colocation means that TX moves with RX as the device travels. This breaks the foundation of RSA [57], which assumed a static TX with fixed beam direction (during imaging) that helped generate an "anchor point" for the entire surface. RSA fails when TX moves in unison with RX.

More importantly, while RSA assumed scattering (specular+diffuse) reflection due to static TX and mobile RX, our system operates on specular (or direct) reflection thanks to colocation. As shown by Figure 4, signal reflected from a surface generally includes both *specular* and *diffuse* components — specular reflection is focused on a single direction and diffuse reflections are scattered over a range of directions. Since object surfaces are much larger than 60GHz's 5mm wavelength, specular reflection, when captured, is much stronger than diffuse reflection. This and the fact that TX/RX are in close proximity, co-moving and beamforming, indicate that our system will operate on specular reflection along the device trajectory, both indoor and outdoor.

Challenge 3: Limited visibility. With colocation, the proximity between TX and RX means (specular) reflections from the object can only be detected in a small angular window, and thus at a limited set of locations. Using a rectangular object as an example, Figure 4 also shows the measured reflection signal strength around the object. Clearly the object is only "visible" at a small set of locations, especially near the four object corners.

Challenge 4: Navigation via 60GHz beamforming. Since each object is only "visible" at certain locations due to specular reflections, the mobile device must travel to find these visible locations to perform imaging. That is, the mobile device must integrate its navigation with its imaging process.

Rather than reinventing our own navigation algorithms, we seek to leverage existing navigation algorithms from the robotics community [15, 16, 39]. These algorithms typically assume cameras, sonar or LIDAR as sensors. Instead, we develop methods to compute "safety zones" for navigation based on 60GHz beamforming results, and to plan movement trajectories that facilitate the imaging process. To the best of our knowledge, we are the first to quantify safety zones using 60GHz beamforming.

3. ULYSSES

To address the above challenges, we introduce *Ulysses*, a single-device imaging system that uses 60GHz directional beams to detect and image unknown objects in far-field scenarios. Our key insight is that as TX and RX move in unison on certain trajectories and perform fine-grained beamforming, RX can *continuously* capture specular reflection contributed by each *small* segment of object surface. The geometry of specular reflection creates a strong tie between its angular properties and the surface shape of these segments. Ulysses then integrates these angular properties with the device trajectory to assemble the estimated "segments" and image the object.

Since Ulysses operates on the signal strength and angular information of 60GHz beamforming signals, it is robust against trajectory errors (up to a few cms). We confirm this by performing signal measurements on different trajectories. While these trajectories can deviate from each other by as much as 10cm, their RSS and angular values vary little. This observation aligns with that of [57].

Core Concepts. Ulysses includes three core components:

- a *sensing* module that uses 60GHz beamforming to detect and extract specular reflection off objects;
- an *imaging* module that leverages the geometry of specular reflection and converts device trajectory into a reliable estimate of the surface shape; in essence, our design emulates M-SAR's point aggregation process [46] without using phase;
- a *navigation* module that uses 60GHz beamforming to safely and efficiently explore the unknown environment and to identify paths for capturing specular reflection off objects and imaging them.

In the following, we present the core idea of each component and leave their design details to §4.

1. Sensing specular reflection via beamforming. As shown by Figure 5, at each location, Ulysses scans for objects using *real-time, fine-grained* RF beamforming. This beamforming function is defined by the 802.11ad standard for 60GHz networking [27], and supported by all commodity 802.11ad chipsets. Using beamforming, Ulysses leverages the high directionality of 60GHz antenna array to capture reflection signals in each fine-grained TX/RX beam directions. That is, without physically rotating the hardware device, Ulysses can sense surrounding objects in real-time.

Once the reflection signal is identified as specular (details in §4), Ulysses extracts the angular and signal strength information of the reflection signal, producing a sensing map per location. Figure 5 shows an example sensing map, which records the signal strength as a function of the TX and RX beam directions. The peak on the map is used to extract the Angle of Arrival (AoA) and the Angle of Transmission (AoT), representing the RX and TX beam directions that lead to the strongest reflection signal, respectively. Since the strongest reflection comes from the center line direction of both the TX beam and the RX beam, each tuple of AoA, AoT and the corresponding received signal strength (RSS) captures the specular reflection off *a very small segment of the surface*.

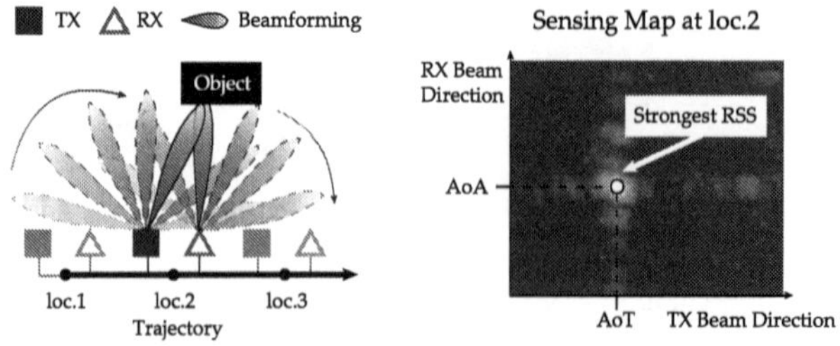

Figure 5: At each location, Ulysses scans objects by fine-grained beamforming. The result is a per-location sensing map that records the received signal strength as a function of TX and RX beam directions. The peak defines the $\{AoA, AoT, RSS\}$ tuple for imaging.

2. Imaging surface by projecting trajectory. The basic concept is shown by Figure 6. As the device moves around an object and "lights" up each small segment of the surface, the measured $\{AoA, AoT, RSS\}$ sequence allows us to compute the *normal line* of each small surface segment, *i.e.* a line that is perpendicular to the segment and represents its orientation.

Building an image of the object surface, however, requires both the normal line (orientation) and the location of each small segment. Since each segment location is the incident point of the reflection, ideally it can be estimated by intersecting AoA and AoT. Yet in practice the result is quite noisy due to both the quantization noise in beam steering (an inherent artifact of analog beamforming hardware design) and the trajectory noise in device movement. One might consider conventional RF ranging/positioning solutions, such as the time-of-flight method [32]. But under our far-field scenarios, these solutions only pinpoint the center of a surface rather than each tiny segment on a continuous surface.

Ulysses takes a different approach to image the surface without pinpointing each segment. Specifically, Ulysses first estimates the surface shape (size, curvature, orientation) without performing any ranging. It then estimates the center location of the object surface using *all* the beamforming measurements on the trajectory (thus achieving much higher accuracy), and "shifts" the estimated shape to the estimated surface center.

To estimate the surface shape, Ulysses leverages the fact that object surfaces are locally continuous, and thus the orientations of two neighboring surface segments are similar. Ulysses recovers the surface shape by projecting the device trajectory along the normal lines of every two segments. As shown by Figure 6, such projection can successfully reveal not only flat surfaces but also curved surfaces (details in §4).

3. Navigation by 60GHz beamforming. With colocation, a mobile device can only capture specular reflections at selected regions near an object. To navigate to these (unknown) locations while avoiding obstacles, Ulysses integrates 60GHz beamforming with prior work in robotic navigation [50]. Specifically, Ulysses leverages 60GHz reflection models to compute safety zones when reflection signal is present or absent, and uses them to guide device navigation. It also leverages beamforming sensing results to plan efficient trajectory around the object(s) to perform imaging.

4. ULYSSES DESIGN DETAILS

We present Ulysses' three modules in detail, starting from the sensing and imaging modules assuming a single object is present.

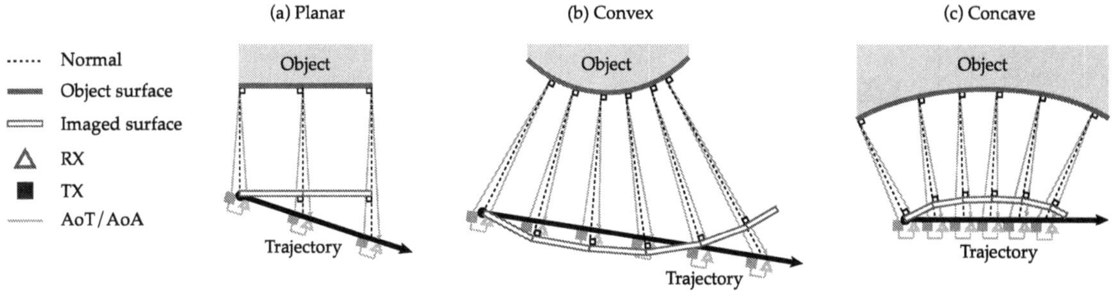

Figure 6: Estimate surface shape by projecting trajectory. At each measurement location on the trajectory, the captured $\{AoA, AoT, RSS\}$ is contributed by a small segment of the object surface. By projecting the trajectory segment guided by the two normal lines, we can estimate the shape of this surface segment. We then stitch these estimates up to build a continuous surface shape estimate.

We then discuss how Ulysses images multiple objects simultaneously, followed by the navigation module.

4.1 Sensing via Beamforming

The colocated TX/RX perform sensing using the fine-grained beamforming module in 802.11ad [27]. TX steers its beam towards each direction for a small period of time, *e.g.,* 25ms in our prototype, and sends out beacon packets repeatedly. RX steers its beam at a faster speed, *e.g.,* 0.5ms, and records the RSS value at each scanned direction. Upon capturing reflection signals, Ulysses identifies whether specular reflection is present, and extracts the $\{AoA, AoT, RSS\}$ tuple.

Detecting specular reflection. Being much stronger than diffuse reflection, specular reflection can be detected by examining the measured signal strength across locations. When moving from a region where specular reflection is invisible to a region where it becomes visible, the device will observe a sharp jump in the measured signal strength (at the strongest direction per location). Such variation is significantly stronger than those within each region. Thus Ulysses detects the presence of specular reflection if the signal strength variation (over space) exceeds some threshold.

Handling array sidelobes. Unlike laser, the beams of 60GHz arrays are not perfectly "clean" – it contains a strong main lobe and many weaker side lobes. The side lobes can be reflected towards RX by the target object, other objects or backgrounds, leading to noises in the sensing results. In Ulysses, we apply the method in [25] to distinguish the contribution of the main lobe from those of the side lobes. Thus these side lobes have minimal impact on our system.

4.2 Imaging by Projecting Trajectory

After detecting the presence of specular reflection, the Ulysses device will move following a scheduled trajectory $\mathbb{T}$ (see §4.4 for trajectory planning) to image the corresponding object. When moving, the device performs the aforementioned beamforming sensing. The sensing granularity depends on the beamforming sensing time and the moving speed, but should be at least once every 1cm to ensure cm-level imaging accuracy.

Recovering surface shape from trajectory. The imaging module takes as input the trajectory $\mathbb{T}$ and a sequence of measurement tuples $\{AoT_i, AoA_i, RSS_i\}_{i\in\mathbb{T}}$, where i is a measurement location on $\mathbb{T}$. Each tuple i corresponds to a segment of the object surface, whose normal line is $\theta_i = (AoT_i + AoA_i)/2$. Similarly, the trajectory $\mathbb{T}$ is also segmented, where each segment $\mathbb{T}_i$ starts from measurement location i and ends at $i+1$. Next, at each location i, $\mathbb{T}_i$ is projected onto a line that is perpendicular to both θ_i and θ_{i+1}, creating a surface estimate $\hat{\mathbb{S}}_i$. Finally, all the estimated segments are assembled in space by aligning the starting point of $\hat{\mathbb{S}}_{i+1}$ with the end point of $\hat{\mathbb{S}}_i$, creating a continuous surface shape $\hat{\mathbb{S}}$.

As discussed earlier, Ulysses does not locate each individual surface segment. As each segment is small (<1cm), even sub-cm error in ranging will create unnecessary ambiguity in shape estimation. Instead, Ulysses assembles the estimated segments given that object surface is locally continuous. Doing so means the imaging result might miss subtle surface details, *e.g.,* keys on a keyboard. This is not a requirement for our target scenarios, and we leave it to future work.

Computing surface boundaries and curvature. The surface curvature can be easily determined by intersecting all the normal lines $\{\theta_i\}_{i\in\mathbb{T}}$. For flat surfaces, these lines should not intersect; for convex surfaces, they intersect at a location in the TX beam direction; and for concave surfaces, they intersect at a location in the reverse TX beam direction.

The estimate on surface boundaries, *i.e.* width, depends on the curvature. For flat surfaces, the shape estimate $\hat{\mathbb{S}}$ has the same length of the true surface. For curved surfaces, $\hat{\mathbb{S}}$ is either an enlarged (convex) or compressed (concave) version of the true surface (see Figure 6). But since the true and estimated surface shapes share the same curvature center, *i.e.* the intersection of $\{\theta_i\}_{i\in\mathbb{T}}$, we can resize $\hat{\mathbb{S}}$ properly by estimating the radii of the true and estimated shapes.

To compute the curvature center, we intersect every pair of $\{\theta_i\}_{i\in\mathbb{T}}$, and take a majority vote to mitigate noise. We calculate the radius of the estimated surface by applying majority vote on the distance between each measurement location and the curvature center, again to mitigate noise. Finally, we compute the radius of the true surface as the distance between the curvature center and an estimate on the object center (discussed below).

One exception is when the device is further away from a concave object than its curvature center, *i.e.* the curvature center is in between the trajectory and the object center. Now the reflection will appear as coming from a convex surface. This can be easily detected and corrected by flipping the estimated (convex) shape $\hat{\mathbb{S}}$.

Estimating object surface center and material. We now estimate the center location of the object surface, which allows us to not only determine the surface curvature and width, but also place the estimated shape $\hat{\mathbb{S}}$ at the proper location. For robustness and accuracy, we estimate the surface center using all the sensing results along the trajectory. Specifically, we compute the intersection of each AoA and AoT pair and use the average over the trajectory as the estimate of surface center. After estimating the surface curva-

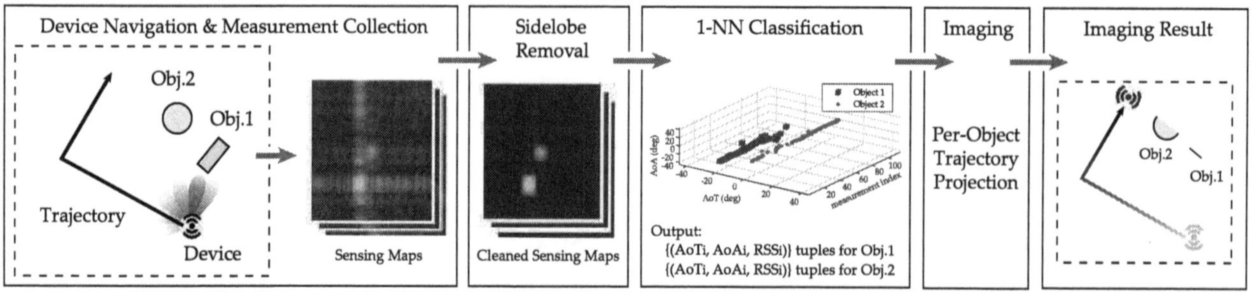

Figure 7: Ulysses can image *multiple* surfaces from a single trajectory. From a sequence of sensing maps, we extract per-object $\{AoA, AoT, RSS\}$ tuples via classification, and then image each object separately.

ture and radius, we the refine the center estimate accordingly. Note that when the radio hardware offers access to high-precision timing information, we can also leverage the time-of-flight method [32], which can achieve $< 10cm$ accuracy that is independent of object-to-device distance.

Finally, given estimates of surface curvature, width and center location, we can determine the materials by computing the signal reflection loss [57]. That is, we first predict RSS (at the trajectory center) assuming signal reflection leads to zero loss, and compare it to the measured RSS value. The difference between the two is the reflection loss and the corresponding material can be found from the widely used material-loss table [31].

4.3 Imaging Multiple Objects

The above discussion assumes there is only one object in the search space. When multiple objects (including background walls, etc) are present, the device may capture reflections from multiple surfaces along its trajectory. In this case, Ulysses follows the same algorithm to image each object, but first applies the following method to detect and extract reflection signals for each surface.

Extracting per-object reflection signals. Here we leverage two insights. *First*, thanks to 60GHz high directionality, the (specular) reflection seen by each individual RX beam generally only comes from a single surface. *Second*, along a continuous trajectory, the reflection from each object maintains a strong correlation over space. That is, the corresponding $\{AoT, AoA, RSS\}$ tuple per object varies smoothly along the trajectory.

With these in mind, we apply a classification-based method to separate contributions from different objects. Figure 7 illustrates the process. Given a sequence of sensing maps collected along the trajectory, we first remove the contributions of side lobes using [25]. If the cleaned sensing maps still contain multiple peaks, then multiple objects are observed. Next, from each of these peaks, we extract the $\{AoA, AoT, RSS\}$ tuples and apply 1-nn (1 nearest neighbor) [19] based classification to group the tuples along the trajectory to individual surfaces. Currently our classification uses equally weighted AoT and AoA, but not RSS. This is because the captured reflection signal per object can change from specular to diffuse reflection along the trajectory, creating large RSS variations that disrupt the classification. We leave further optimization of the classification to future work.

4.4 Navigation for Imaging

As mentioned earlier, a Ulysses device needs to navigate in an (unknown) environment safely to capture specular reflections off objects. The navigation design leverages rich literatures on robotic navigation/mapping to move within the unknown environment (*e.g.*, [15, 16, 39, 50]), and instead focuses on enabling navigation using the on-board 60GHz beamforming radios rather than sensors like sonar, Lidar/laser and camera that were used in conventional navigation systems. Ulysses' key contributions include methods to define safety zones for navigation and to schedule trajectory for imaging once an object becomes "visible".

Defining safety zones. A key input to robotic navigation is the *safety zone*. Defined with respect to the device's current location, it allows the device to move freely without bumping into objects [50]. While prior works compute safety zones using sensors like sonar and camera, we are the first to define them using just 60GHz beamforming radios.

1) Safety zone when no reflection is seen. While a Ulysses device has limited view on specular reflection, it will still capture (weak) diffuse reflections when in close proximity of an objection. Thus at locations where no reflection (above the noise floor) is seen, we build the safety zone as a circle whose radius γ is the *minimum* range that the device can capture any reflection in any beam direction from any object of reasonable size. That is, we determine γ based on the object that leads to the heaviest reflection loss.

We take an empirical approach to determine γ based on the following condition:

$$\frac{P_{TX} G_{TX} G_{RX}}{L_{path}(\gamma) L_{shape} L_{material}} = \text{noise floor} \quad (1)$$

where L_{path}, L_{shape} and $L_{material}$ are the path loss, the reflection loss due to shape and material, respectively. We compute γ by finding the heaviest L_{shape} and $L_{material}$ from any object. For L_{shape}, prior works have shown that for any given object, the sharp edge of the object leads to the weakest reflection, referred to as the wedge diffraction effect [14, 24]. Using testbed measurements on many household objects of different shapes and materials, we empirically validated this claim and found that L_{shape} is bounded by 24dB. For $L_{material}$ we use the widely known table of material vs. 60GHz reflection loss [31] and set it to $19.3dB$. This is the reflection loss of wooden objects which peaks among common household objects. We also manually measured other materials like leather and a deck of paper sheets, and found that they are no more than 19.3dB. Given the L_{shape} and $L_{material}$, we use (1) to derive $\gamma \approx 1m$.

2) Safety zone when observing reflection. In this case, RX will observe reflection signals (above the noise floor) at some beam directions. At the beam directions where reflection is absent, the safety zone is a round segment with $1m$ radius. At the beam directions where reflection is seen, the safety zone is a region between the current device and the object(s) since 60GHz waves cannot penetrate objects. Thus we approximate the safety zone as a round segment whose radius is the smallest separation between the device and the

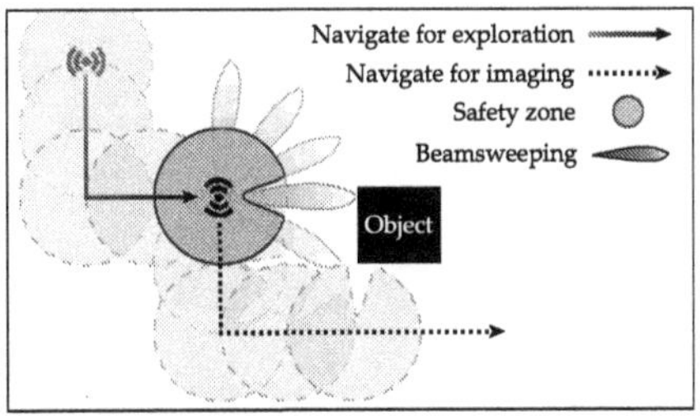

Figure 8: An illustration of Ulysses's navigation path to image an object and the corresponding safety zones.

object(s) that leads to the observed RSS value. For this we reuse (1) but replace the noise floor with the observed RSS.

One special case is that when an object is less than 1m away, the diffuse reflection signal becomes sufficiently strong and can be reliably captured at many RX beam directions. They can be utilized along with the specular reflection to pinpoint the object surface, *e.g.,* intersecting the AoAs and AoTs at many TX/RX beam directions. This is particularly useful when a robot rotates itself and suddenly faces an obstacle in close proximity and needs to avoid them.

Planning trajectory for imaging. When detecting reflection signals, a Ulysses device will move within its safety zone in a direction that is perpendicular to the normal line $\frac{AoA+AoT}{2}$. This not only allows Ulysses to identify the type of reflection (specular vs. diffuse) but also puts the device on an efficient trajectory for imaging (under specular reflection). Upon detecting diffuse reflection, the device will explore in other directions.

While traveling, a Ulysses device will periodically recalibrate the safety zone computation and adjust trajectory if necessary. In particular, when the trajectory coverage passes the edge of the object, it will observe a significant continuous drop of signal strength due to the aforementioned wedge diffraction effect. In this case, the device will re-compute the safety zone and rotate by 90° (or the closest value defined by the safety zone) to go around the object. Figure 8 illustrates how a device navigates to discover and image an object and the corresponding safety zones along the entire path. During the exploration segment of the trajectory, the safety zone is a full circle of 1m radius, which reduces into a partial circle when the device starts to image the object.

Finally, when multiple objects are present, Ulysses will choose a direction in the safety zone that is the average of the "optimal" trajectories across the objects, or even weighted by their RSS values. In some cases, it will image objects sequentially, sorted by their RSS values.

Avoiding walls. During navigation, the device will likely capture the reflection of a wall and attempt to image it by moving along it. This can be minimized based on the intuition that the wall is much larger than our target objects. Thus Ulysses includes a wall-avoidance feature that if enabled, will stop imaging an object if the detected shape is flat and more than $1m$ in width.

5. IMPLEMENTATION

Proof-of-concept hardware. We build a Ulysses prototype by placing two 60GHz radios on a robot car as the colocated TX and RX (see Figure 9(a)). Currently the two small 60GHz antennas are hard-attached to two wooden boxes so the prototype appears bulky. Yet it emulates a compact, mobile imaging robot where the arrays are placed on the robot front or top. We also do not use any software/hardware to synchronize the two radios.

Our robot car is from Nexus Robot [3]. We control its movement using the on-board Arduino chip (with a maximum speed of $1m/s$). The robot rotates at deg-level accuracy, thus we configure the robot to move in straight lines and avoid sub-deg-level rotation. Most of our rotations are 90° and we check the need for rotation every 0.5m. The trajectory error is random but bounded by $10cm$.

The 60GHz radios were donated by Facebook's Terragraph project [6] and follow the 802.11ad standard[2]. The Effective Isotropic Radiated Power (EIRP) is 32dBm, well-below the FCC regulation limit of 82dBm [5]. Each radio has an 8×16 rectangular phased array (6° horizontal and 12° vertical beamwidth), and is electronically steerable in the horizontal direction at a granularity of 1.5°. Each round of beamforming sweeps a 90° range (left and right 45°), and takes 1.6s due to the $0.4ms$ beam switching delay. To meet the real-time requirement (0.4s per measurement round for our robot car), we reduce the sweeping coverage from 90° to 45°. Note that the beam switching delay will be much smaller for production hardware, *e.g.,* 50ns in [51].

The imaging range depends on the surface material. For rough wood (>12dB loss), the horizontal imaging range is more than 10m. The vertical range depends on the vertical beam coverage (since our radios are mounted at a fixed height). Figure 10 plots the vertical coverage of our array: 1m when the object is 10m away and 0.5m when 5m away.

Navigation. We configure the robot to move at a speed of 2.5cm/s and performs beamforming sweep (which finishes within 0.4s) every 1cm. While moving, the robot keeps track of its location, scans the surroundings via beamforming, and updates the planned path and its safety area. During bootstrapping, we use an exploration algorithm known to the robotic community [39]. Within the safety zone, it searches for the local RSS maxima and terminates when the device detects RSS above the noise floor.

Identifying specular reflection. As discussed in §4, Ulysses examines the measured RSS over space to identify the type of reflection (specular vs. diffuse). Our measurements have shown that when the reflection transitions between specular and diffuse dominated scenarios, one in general observes a gradual, consistent RSS change by 20dB over ~10cm moving distance. Thus we empirically choose a 2dB threshold between any two consecutive to detect such continuous RSS change. This works well across all our experiments on many objects and environments.

Complexity. We implement all the computation in Matlab, running on a 2013 MacBook Pro laptop (2.4 GHz Intel Core i7 CPU and 8GB RAM). After collecting reflection measurements along a path segment, the imaging computation takes 0.5s–1s per meter for the given path. This can be further optimized by using a more efficient implementation, which we leave to future work. The navigation computation is nearly instantaneous.

6. EVALUATION

In this section, we use real-life experiments to evaluate our Ulysses prototype, focusing on imaging accuracy, navigation efficiency and safety. We also compare Ulysses to camera based imaging [1] and dual-device 60GHz mobile imaging [57].

[2] Facebook recently showcased similar devices at the Embedded Linux Conference [4] and deployed them in Downtown San Jose [7]. We hope that these devices will become commercially available soon.

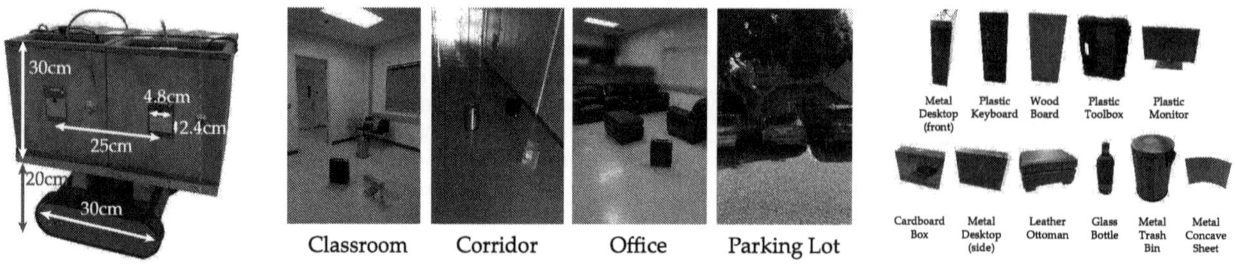

(a) Testbed (b) 3 Indoor and 1 Outdoor Environments (c) Objects

Figure 9: Our testbed prototype, evaluation environments, and experimental objects.

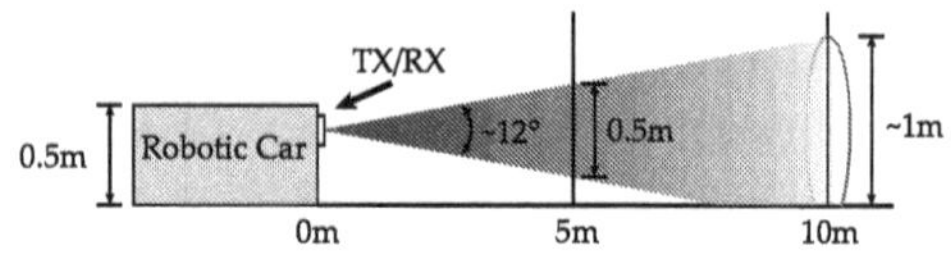

Figure 10: Since the TX/RX has a fixed height, the vertical imaging range depends on the vertical beam coverage. At 10m distance, any object placed within the 1m beam coverage can still be observed.

Experiment Configuration. We first perform experiments in three indoor environments (Figure 9(b)): a building corridor (of size $2.5m \times 50m$), a classroom (of size $8m \times 12m$) with randomly placed chairs as obstacles, and a standard office reception area ($5m \times 5m$) with leather seatings. We place one or multiple objects in these environments, some as target objects, some as obstacles. In total, we experiment with 11 household objects of various sizes (8–82cm in width), surface shapes (flat, convex, concave, complex), and materials (metallic, plastic, wood, glass, cardboard, leather). Figure 9 shows their physical pictures.

By default, we place our robot car based prototype either near the entry door of the classroom and the office or at the center of the corridor. Since our prototype cannot vary the height of the TX/RX, we instrument the system to focus on imaging objects in the ground level. When placing the objects, we vary their locations and orientations to the starting location of the robot car. We change the initial orientation of the robot to create different first-views of the environment, such as a door, walls, obstacles, target objects or nothing. This allows us to test our design under different startup conditions. We also vary the separation between the colocated TX and RX from 25cm to 50cm (we are unable to go below 25cm due to the hardware case constraint). We verify via experiments that in this range, the amount of separation has minimum impact since they all allow the system to identify the normal line efficiently. Thus we only show the results for 40cm separation for brevity.

We next experiment with Ulysses in an outdoor parking lot to image the back of parked cars (Figure 9(b)). We set the prototype on top of a mobile cart to emulate a vehicle, and move the car at a slow speed to compensate the beam switching delay.

All of our results are produced under (uncontrolled) device movement errors. While programmed to move in a straight line, the trajectory deviation is random and can reach 10cm. The orientation deviation is bounded by 1° per run.

6.1 Imaging Accuracy

Our imaging system outputs the shape, orientation, and material of the target object surface. We quantify the accuracy by the absolute error in each metric.

Imaging a surface via a straight line. Consider a simple scenario where Ulysses images a specific object surface by traveling on a straight line. In each experiment, we place an object in the center of the room and program the robot to move in a straight line. Due to random trajectory errors and measurement noises, the imaging outcome varies slightly across multiple runs. We report the median value over 6 runs per configuration. For sensitivity analysis, we vary the object to robot distance between 1m and 5m, and the object surface to trajectory angle between 0 and 10° (so that the robot can capture specular reflection).

For flat (or planar) surfaces, the estimates of surface width and orientation are not affected by the object-to-device distance and orientation. Thus Figure 11 (a) shows the results for the 9 planar surfaces that are 5m away from the robot. The median width error ranges between 2–5cm except for the large ottoman (it is of 82cm in width and the error is 7cm). The surface orientation error is bounded by 1°.

Our system can always identify the curvature type, *i.e.* planar, convex and concave. For curved surfaces, the orientation error is always bounded by 1° across all the configurations. Yet the accuracy of width estimation depends on the object-to-device distance. As discussed earlier, we need to estimate the location of surface center in order to resize the shape estimate. Since the accuracy of our current ranging method decreases with the object distance, the error in the ranging result propagates into the width estimation. Figure 11 (b) shows the width and orientation errors for the three curved objects that are 3m away from the robot. With our simple ranging method, the median width error of the metal trash can (convex) is 7cm, which increases to 8.8cm when the object-to-device distance is 5m. But by improving the ranging accuracy to $< 10cm$, the width error at both 3m and 5m will reduce to 6cm and 6.7cm, respectively.

Finally, our material estimation is accurate. Across our experiments, the ground-truth material always falls in the top-3 candidates provided by our imaging algorithm. This level of accuracy aligns with prior works that must place TX/RX on multiple devices [56, 57].

Imaging objects via navigation. Next we consider practical scenarios where the robot navigates around the object(s) to image them. For this we consider both single object and multiple object scenarios. Figure 12 shows three examples of our real-time navigation for imaging and the corresponding imaging results. Figure 12(a) shows that to image a metal desktop (of 40cm in width), the Ulysses device takes a rectangular trajectory following the shape of the object. This is because when reaching the edge of the object, detected by observing a significant and consistent drop of signals, the device will rotate 90° to circle around the corner. Figure 12(d) shows that the estimated object is almost a duplicate of the ground

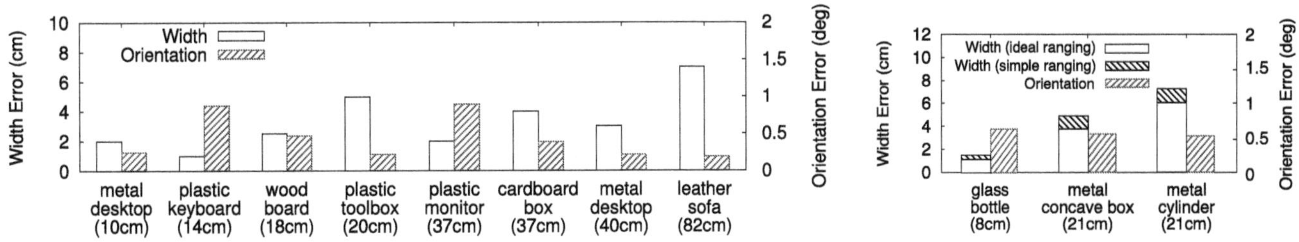

(a) Planar Surfaces (b) Curved Surfaces

Figure 11: Object imaging benchmarks for (a) planar surfaces (5m away) and (b) curved surfaces (3m away). Overall, we achieve $< 8cm$ error in width and $< 1^{\circ}$ error in orientation. We later show that when imaging the entire object, the per-surface error will reduce after we assemble different surfaces.

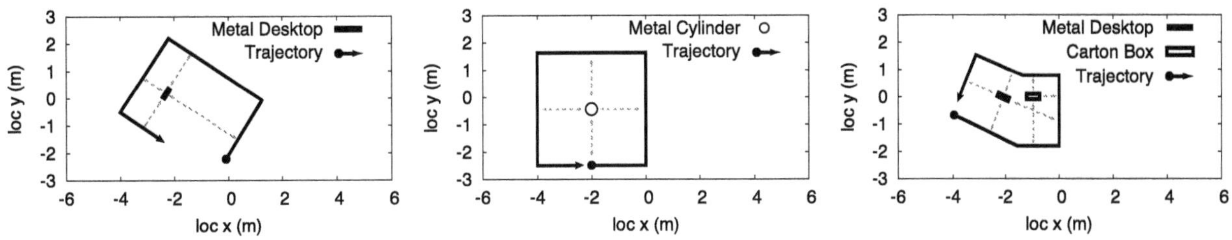

(a) Device path for a metal desktop, following the object shape (b) Device path for a metal cylinder, following a rectangular shape (c) Device path for multiple objects, following a complex shape

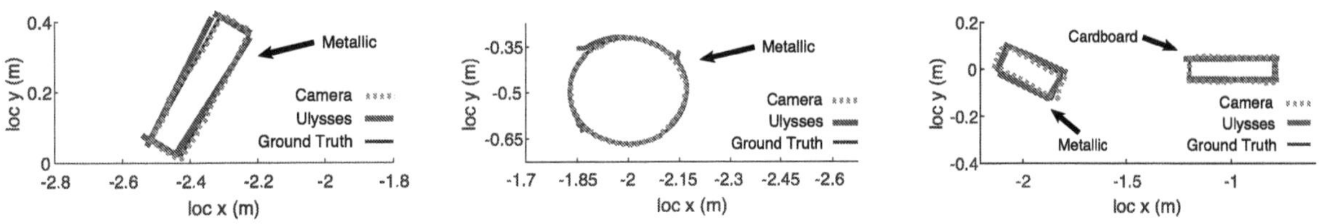

(d) Imaging result of a metal desktop (e) Imaging result of a metal cylinder (f) Imaging result of multiple objects

Figure 12: Ulysses navigates around the object and images the target(s) accurately.

error type	single-object		multi-object	
	median	max	median	max
surface boundary	2cm	5cm	2.5cm	4cm
curvature radius	3.5cm	5cm	-	-
orientation	0.47°	0.86°	0.58°	0.98°
object center	2cm	7cm	1.5cm	4cm

Table 1: Overall imaging errors under single- and multi-object scenarios, when the device navigates around the object to image the entire object.

truth ($< 3cm$ error in width). Another example in Figure 12(b) shows the navigation path around a circular object (the trash can) assuming the robot car can only rotate by 90°. In this case, the trajectory is rectangular, and does not follow the object surface shape. Yet the estimated object still closely aligns with the ground truth.

Figure 12(c) shows the scenario where our Ulysses device images two objects simultaneously. The corresponding trajectory planned by our system has a more complex shape, as the device rotates its moving direction slightly after identifying a different surface. The imaging result is accurate except it misses one side of carton box. This is because the corresponding reflection from this surface is blocked by the metal desktop.

Finally, Table 1 summarizes the distribution of the object imaging errors (surface boundaries, orientation, and object center location, and curvature radius for circular objects) across all of our experiments (using our simple ranging method). The maximum errors are bounded by 5cm for surface boundaries, 1° for orientation, and 7cm for object center location, while the median errors are bounded by 2.5cm, 0.58°, and 2cm, respectively. One interesting observation is that when we assemble the estimated surface segments to construct the entire object, the inherent geometry dependence across them also helps to correct the imaging error on individual surfaces. For example, the estimated surface segments for the trash can that is 5m away can have width errors up to 12cm, which reduce to below 5cm after assembly.

Impact of measurement granularity. Since each beamforming sweep takes 400ms, the measurement granularity (on the trajectory) varies with the robot speed. So far we configure the robot to move at 2.5cm/s, mapping to one measurement per 1cm. We then increase the speed to 5cm/s, mapping to one measurement per 2cm or half the granularity. In this case, the imaging results do degrade slightly, *i.e.* $< 2cm$ error in size estimation. However, this is only a limitation to our current hardware. Since commercial 60GHz chipsets will support a significantly faster beamforming sweep ($50ns/beam$ [51]), this will no longer be an issue.

Ulysses vs. RSA and Camera-based imaging. We also compare Ulysses to RSA, the dual-device 60GHz imaging system [57], and the camera-based imaging system. First, we implement the RSA algorithm on our platform, following the same scenarios of Figure 11, except that we place TX on a separated device 4m away from the object and well-separated from RX. Ulysses and RSA provide similar imaging results ($< 5cm$ error in width, and $< 1°$ error in surface orientation) thanks to 60GHz's directionality. But Ulysses outperforms RSA by using a single device, thus greatly simplifying navigation and eliminating device coordination overhead.

Second, we use a smartphone app called 123D Catch [1], a popular camera-based imaging solution from Autodesk. It captures a series of photos, analyzes them on the cloud, and reconstructs the captured environment. Like Ulysses, this is a single-device imaging solution. Since 123D Catch does not offer navigation, we set the smartphone to follow the same navigation paths of Ulysses. Figure 12 compares the imaging results of both systems, which are very close to each other. But when we turn off the light, or use it in a foggy day, 123D Catch fails completely and Ulysses is not affected. We also noticed that the camera app takes minutes and even hours to produce imaging results. Instead, Ulysses is of low computational cost and runs in real-time (<1s).

Outdoor Results. We also evaluate Ulysses in an outdoor parking lot, with the goal of imaging the back of parked cars to identify shape, size and material. Our results are promising, indicating cm-level accuracy in this scenario. Figure 13 shows an example imaging result of a parked car, where Ulysses correctly identifies the shape, size (to the cm-level accuracy) as well as the surface material.

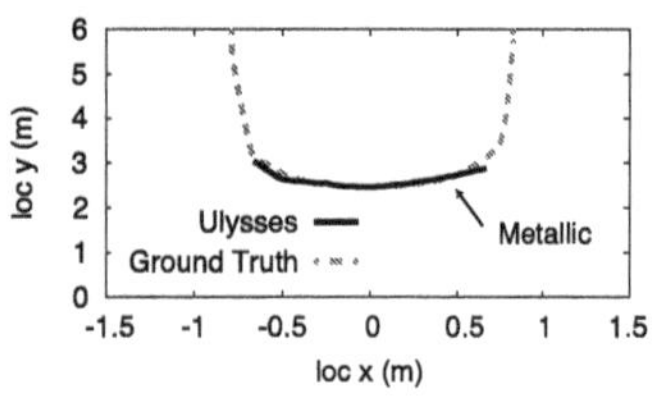

Figure 13: Imaging result of the back of a parked car.

6.2 Safe and Effective Navigation

Next we evaluate the safety and efficiency of our navigation design using 60GHz beamforming. We run experiments in three indoor environments with obstacles and objects on the floor. The device has zero start-up knowledge of the environment and cannot "see" the target object initially. In each experiment, we place three objects with 1m to 5m distance from each other, and perform 10 experiments per indoor environments. Across all 30 experiments, our prototype successfully navigates around all the obstacles and objects without any collision.

Figure 14(a) illustrates an example of the overall navigation path. The robot car starts in the center of the classroom facing away from all three objects, and seeks to "find the carton box". It first explores local areas in four directions within the 1m safety circle, and detects reflection in one direction and then adjusts its trajectory to go around the object to image it. The device then identifies the imaged object as a plastic monitor. This is not its target, thus the robot moves to discover and image the other two objects together.

Figure 14(b) shows another example in the corridor, a smaller environment due to the walls on the side. The robot's mission is to find the "metal desktop". At first the robot sees the wall reflection and attempts to image it. After moving 1m and finding the object is at least 1m in width, the robot gives up on that. It then finds two reflections and decides to image the one with stronger RSS. When approaching the wall, it turns left to avoid collision. After identifying the carton box, it senses new reflection signals and moves to image the other two object and locates the target.

Accuracy of safety zones. We also measure the safety zone at individual locations and confirm that they all do not overlap with any object or obstacle. Figure 14(c) shows a specific example in the narrow corridor of 2.5m in width where the device is in the middle of three objects. Although being conservative, the safety zone accurately captures the impact of the walls, the objects, and even the small pillars on the wall (5cm in width). As future work, we plan to compare our 60GHz based safety zone estimations to those using sonar and/or camera [15, 16, 42, 43].

7. LIMITATIONS AND FUTURE WORK

Handling large trajectory errors. Operating on angular and RSS measurements of reflections, Ulysses is robust against moderate trajectory tracking errors (our robot achieves $< 10cm$ deviations over straight lines). In this paper we limited our experiments to 2D movements where the trajectory tracking error is moderate. Under 3D movements, *e.g.,* drone flying, the tracking error might be (much) larger, leading to noisy angular and RSS measurements, thus affecting imaging and navigation performance.

A potential solution is to integrate SLAM into Ulysses [21, 44], which iteratively estimates the robot's current movement and the corresponding imaging outcome, using prior trajectory data and imaging results.

Handling device rotation errors. Moving in straight lines, our robot makes small rotation error ($< 1°$). Thus in our experiments, we did not observe any impact on Ulysses imaging and navigation. But under larger rotation errors, the accuracy of AoT and AoA computation may be affected. We plan to empirically examine this potential artifact, and improve our design if necessary.

Handling multipath reflection. 60GHz's high directionality and colocation of RX/TX effectively limit the chance that RX captures multiple reflections in a single beam. Yet, this can happen if two objects are placed in close proximity and have the same orientation with respect to the Ulysses device. Separating these signals requires very high channel sampling rate which is costly and hard to achieve.

Multipath reflection will have much less impact on imaging than navigation, because multipath is location-dependent and will appear on very few locations along a trajectory. One can potentially identify these "noisy" locations and compensate accordingly. Navigation requires computing safety zone for each location, thus the impact of multipath will be more visible. As multipath is location-specific (within a few cms), one potential solution is to derive per-location safety zones by integrating measurements at nearby locations.

Duty cycling 60GHz radios. Currently Ulysses assumes 60GHz radios are always available for imaging. In practice, we need to dutycycle/schedule imaging tasks on 60GHz radios to reduce energy consumption and/or allow radios to perform necessary communication tasks. We plan to study the tradeoff between imaging accuracy and the amount of 60GHz radio usage, with and without communication tasks.

Improving image resolution. Our current prototype achieves an image resolution of a few cms. We think this is partially due to the beam width, the beam steering accuracy and granularity of

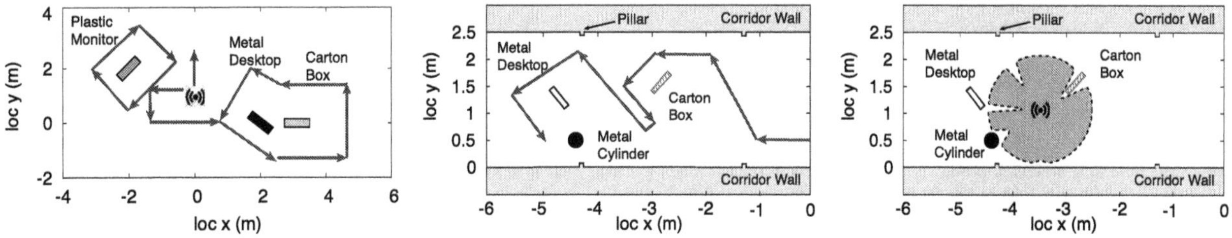

(a) Path in the classroom (b) Path in the corridor (c) Estimated safety zone example

Figure 14: Ulysses navigates in (a) the classroom and (b) the corridor without colliding into objects/walls. In (c) we plot an example of the estimated safety zone (the shaded region) at a specific location.

our 60GHz prototype, and the lack of precise timing information from the radios. Moving forward, we expect imaging accuracy to improve with better hardware availability and better software access to radio data. Finally, Ulysses does not assume TX and RX are tightly synchronized. We plan to study whether adding TX/RX synchronization can help improve imaging performance.

8. RELATED WORK

Reflection-based RF imaging and tracking. Recent works have leveraged signal reflection to perform imaging and target tracking in both WiFi and 60GHz bands. In the WiFi bands, researchers have used commodity WiFi chips [22, 26, 29, 47] or specialized FMCW hardware [11, 12, 13] to localize/image static objects, or measure human body dynamics as well as hand/finger motions. Others use commodity WiFi radios to recognize predefined hand gestures [41, 49], often leverage machine learning methods to distinguish different gestures and motions.

Existing efforts in 60GHz applied radar design to achieve precise object imaging and motion tracking of small targets. [36] uses FMCW hardware and applies SAR with sparse measurements in absence of device movement noises, while [53] uses three separate, static 60GHz radios to track subtle pen movements on a tablet. Both designs assume short object-device distance (30–50cm), rely on phase and do not face any device movement noise. Another direction is to use two mobile 60GHz radios to image static objects meters away at cm-level accuracy [57, 56], focusing on being robust to device path noises. Finally, the most relevant mmWave handheld imager is *Walleye* [9], which uses specialized hardware, costs $500, and weighs 5lb.

Acoustic-based tracking and imaging. Recent works use smartphone's speaker-mic pair to localize targets with cm- and mm-level accuracy [38, 52], while another develops new measuring methods to image objects using an audible frequency [37]. These acoustic systems are very appealing in short distance scenarios, but are sensitive to environmental noises. On the other hand, today's acoustic imaging products use ultrasound and are costly, *e.g.*, $45K [40].

LIDAR and vision-based solutions. Today, the state of the art in mobile imaging products is LIDAR, used by Google self-driving cars [45], with costs up to $75,000. Low-cost LIDAR prototypes are in the works, but must sacrifice range, precision and coverage (from 2D imaging to 1D). To our best knowledge, the cheapest version [8] still costs $250 per device, providing 1D imaging with 10s of centimeter precision; another recent version [2] improves precision to a few cms but costs $400.

Another widely studied area is vision-based solutions that use commodity cameras, *e.g.*, the commercial app 123D Catch [1], which we compare with in this work. As discussed earlier, these solutions face the challenge of being sensitive to lighting conditions and not being able to distinguish objects of similar colors.

In terms of imaging techniques, existing vision-based systems assume a stationary lighting source (TX) like [54, 28]. Using TX's location as a reference, these systems construct images of objects by exploiting either special illumination patterns or the image correlation of multiple reflection points observed at various locations. Our system uses a similar spatial correlation based approach, but differs by leveraging the directional 60GHz signals on a moving TX. One of our key contributions is the geometric method that integrates a sequence of observations (and spatial patterns) collected under a moving TX source.

Robotic navigation. Ulysses leverages the rich literature on robotic navigation in unknown environments (*e.g.*, [15, 16, 39, 50]). Our (new) contribution here is to define safety zones using the onboard 60GHz beamforming radios rather than sonar and camera [15, 16, 42, 43].

9. CONCLUSION

This paper describes our experiences in designing, implementing and evaluating an object imaging system for mobile devices using commodity 60GHz radios. Experiments on our prototype validate the feasibility of our colocated radio design, and confirm that our imaging and navigation algorithms can leverage onboard 60GHz radios for robust and accurate results. While the current prototype is limited by hardware constraints, we believe our results show significant promise for a low-cost, compact, single-device imaging system. We hope this work and followups will play a role in autonomous devices in the near future.

Acknowledgment

We would like to thank our shepherd Fadel Adib and the anonymous reviewers for their useful feedback, and the Facebook Terragraph team for providing the 60GHz testbed on which our experiments were carried out. This work is supported by NSF grants CNS-1518812 and CNS-1317153. Any opinions, findings, and conclusions or recommendations expressed in this material do not necessarily reflect the views of any funding agencies.

10. REFERENCES

[1] http://www.123dapp.com/catch.
[2] http://www.slamtec.com/.
[3] http://www.nexusrobot.com/.
[4] http://events.linuxfoundation.org/events/embedded-linux-conference/.
[5] https://apps.fcc.gov/edocs_public/attachmatch/FCC-13-112A1_Rcd.pdf.

[6] Introducing facebook's new terrestrial connectivity systems: Terragraph and project aries. https://code.facebook.com/posts/1072680049445290/introducing-facebook-s-new-terrestrial-connectivity-systems-terragraph-and-project-aries/.

[7] San josé partners with facebook for high-speed outdoor wi-fi. https://gcn.com/articles/2016/04/18/san-jose-facebook.aspx.

[8] ACKERMAN, E. Sweep is a $250 LIDAR with range of 40 meters that works outdoors. IEEE Spectrum, April 2016.

[9] ADAMS, C., HOLBROOK, D., AND SENGSTEN, R. A handheld active millimeter wave camera. In *Proc. of HST* (2010).

[10] ADAMS, C., HOLBROOK, D., AND SENGSTEN, R. A handheld active millimeter wave camera. In *HST* (2010).

[11] ADIB, F., HSU, C.-Y., MAO, H., KATABI, D., AND DURAND, F. Capturing the human figure through a wall. *ACM Transactions on Graphics 34*, 6 (2015), 219:1–219:13.

[12] ADIB, F., KABELAC, Z., AND KATABI, D. Multi-person localization via rf body reflections. In *Proc. of NSDI* (2015).

[13] ADIB, F., KABELAC, Z., KATABI, D., AND MILLER, R. C. 3d tracking via body radio reflections. In *Proc. of NSDI* (2014).

[14] ANDERSON, H. R. A ray-tracing propagation model for digital broadcast systems in urban areas. *IEEE Transactions on Broadcasting 39*, 3 (1993), 309–317.

[15] BORENSTEIN, J., AND KOREN, Y. Real-time obstacle avoidance for fast mobile robots in cluttered environments. In *Proc. of ICRA* (1990).

[16] BORENSTEIN, J., AND KOREN, Y. The vector field histogram-fast obstacle avoidance for mobile robots. *IEEE Transactions on Robotics and Automation 7*, 3 (1991), 278–288.

[17] BREWSTER, S. Uber starts self-driving car pickups in Pittsburgh. TechCrunch, September 2016.

[18] CAMERON, D., AND CUADRA, A. Meet the future first responders. Washington Post, June 2015.

[19] COVER, T., AND HART, P. Nearest neighbor pattern classification. *IEEE Transactions on Information Theory 13*, 1 (1967), 21–27.

[20] CUTHBERTSON, A. Amazon drone deliveries receive U.K. approval. NewsWeek, July 2016.

[21] DAVISON, A. J., REID, I. D., MOLTON, N. D., AND STASSE, O. MonoSLAM: Real-time single camera SLAM. *IEEE Transactions on Pattern Analysis and Machine Intelligence* (2007).

[22] DEPATLA, S., BUCKLAND, L., AND MOSTOFI, Y. X-ray vision with only wifi power measurements using rytov wave models. *IEEE Transactions on Vehicular Technology 64* (2015), 1376–1387.

[23] GERSHGORN, D. Google's robots are learning how to pick things up. Popular Science, March 2016.

[24] HACIVELIOĞLU, F., USLU, M. A., AND SEVGI, L. A matlab-based virtual tool for the electromagnetic wave scattering from a perfectly reflecting wedge. *IEEE Antennas and Propagation Magazine 53*, 6 (2011), 234–243.

[25] HOSOYA, K., PRASAD, N., RAMACHANDRAN, K., ORIHASHI, N., KISHIMOTO, S., RANGARAJAN, S., AND MARUHASHI, K. Multiple sector id capture (midc): A novel beamforming technique for 60-ghz band multi-gbps wlan/pan systems. *IEEE Transactions on Antennas and Propagation 63*, 1 (2015), 81–96.

[26] HUANG, D., NANDAKUMAR, R., AND GOLLAKOTA, S. Feasibility and limits of Wi-Fi imaging. In *Proc. of SenSys* (2014).

[27] IEEE 802.11 Task Group AD. http://www.ieee802.org/11/Reports/tgad_update.htm.

[28] IHRKE, I., KUTULAKOS, K. N., LENSCH, H., MAGNOR, M., AND HEIDRICH, W. Transparent and specular object reconstruction. *Computer Graphics Forum 29*, 8 (2010).

[29] KUMAR, S., GIL, S., KATABI, D., AND RUS, D. Accurate indoor localization with zero start-up cost. In *Proc. of MobiCom* (2014).

[30] LAMBERT, F. Understanding the fatal Tesla accident on autopilot and the NHTSA probe. Electrek, July 2016.

[31] LANGEN, B., LOBER, G., AND HERZIG, W. Reflection and transmission behavior of building materials at 60ghz. In *Proc. of PIMRC* (1994).

[32] LANZISERA, S., LIN, D. T., AND PISTER, K. S. J. RF time of flight ranging for wireless sensor network localization. In *Proc. of WISES* (2006).

[33] LIPTAK, A. 7-eleven just made the first commercial delivery by drone. The Verge, July 2016.

[34] LIU, K., WANG, X., SAMARABANDU, J., AND AKHTAR, A. Monostatic airborne sar using license exempt wimax transceivers. In *VTC* (2014).

[35] LOHR, S. A lesson of tesla crashes? Computer vision can't do it all yet. The New York Times, September 2016.

[36] MAMANDIPOOR, B., MALYSA, G., ARBABIAN, A., MADHOW, U., AND NOUJEIM, K. 60 GHz synthetic aperture radar for short-range imaging: Theory and experiments. In *Proc. of ASILOMAR* (2014).

[37] MOLERÓN, M., AND DARAIO, C. Acoustic metamaterial for subwavelength edge detection. *Nature Communications 6*, 8037 (2015).

[38] NANDAKUMAR, R., GOLLAKOTA, S., AND WATSON, N. Contactless sleep apnea detection on smartphones. In *MobiSys* (2015).

[39] NEWMAN, P., BOSSE, M., AND LEONARD, L. Autonomous feature-based exploration. In *Proc. of ICRA* (2003).

[40] ORALKAN, O., ERGUN, A. S., JOHNSON, J. A., KARAMAN, M., DEMIRCI, U., KAVIANI, K., LEE, T. H., AND KHURI-YAKUB, B. T. Capacitive micromachined ultrasonic transducers: Next-generation arrays for acoustic imaging? *IEEE transactions on ultrasonics, ferroelectrics, and frequency control 49*, 11 (2002), 1596–1610.

[41] PU, Q., GUPTA, S., GOLLAKOTA, S., AND PATEL, S. Whole-home gesture recognition using wireless signals. In *Proc. of MobiCom* (2013).

[42] SE, S., LOWE, D., AND LITTLE, J. Vision-based mobile robot localization and mapping using scale-invariant features. In *Proc. of ICRA* (2001).

[43] SE, S., LOWE, D. G., AND LITTLE, J. J. Vision-based global localization and mapping for mobile robots. *IEEE Transactions on Robotics 21*, 3 (2005), 364–375.

[44] SMITH, R. C., AND CHEESEMAN, P. On the representation and estimation of spatial uncertainty. *The International Journal of Robotics Research 5*, 4 (1986), 56–68.

[45] SOLON, O. Lidar: the self-driving technology that could help tesla avoid another tragedy. The Guardian, July 2016.

[46] SOUMEKH, M. *Synthetic aperture radar signal processing*. New York: Wiley, 1999.

[47] SUN, L., SEN, S., KOUTSONIKOLAS, D., AND KIM, K. Widraw: Enabling handsfree drawing in the air on commodity wifi devices. In *Proc. of MobiCom* (2015).

[48] SUR, S., VENKATESWARAN, V., ZHANG, X., AND RAMANATHAN, P. 60 ghz indoor networking through flexible beams: A link-level profiling. In *SIGMETRICS* (2015).

[49] TAN, S., AND YANG, J. Wifinger: Leveraging commodity wifi for fine-grained finger gesture recognition. In *MobiHoc* (2016).

[50] THRUN, S., BURGARD, W., AND FOX, D. *Probabilistic robotics*. MIT press, 2005.

[51] VALDES-GARCIA, A., REYNOLDS, S., NATARAJAN, A., KAM, D., LIU, D., LAI, J.-W., HUANG, Y.-L., CHEN, P.-Y., TSAI, M.-D., ZHAN, J.-H., NICOLSON, S., AND FLOYD, B. Single-element and phased-array transceiver chipsets for 60-GHz Gb/s communications. *IEEE Communications Magazine 49*, 4 (April 2011), 120 –131.

[52] WANG, J., ZHAO, K., ZHANG, X., AND PENG, C. Ubiquitous keyboard for small mobile devices: Harnessing multipath fading for fine-grained keystroke localization. In *MobiSys* (2014).

[53] WEI, T., AND ZHANG, X. mTrack: High-precision passive tracking using millimeter wave radios. In *Proc. of MobiCom* (2015).

[54] ZHENG, J. Y., AND MURATA, A. Acquiring a complete 3d model from specular motion under the illumination of circular-shaped light sources. *IEEE Transactions on Pattern Analysis and Machine Intelligence 22*, 8 (2000).

[55] ZHU, Y., ET AL. Demystifying 60GHz outdoor picocells. In *Proc. of MobiCom* (2014).

[56] ZHU, Y., ZHU, Y., ZHANG, Z., ZHAO, B. Y., AND ZHENG, H. 60GHz mobile imaging radar. In *Proc. of HotMobile* (2015).

[57] ZHU, Y., ZHU, Y., ZHAO, B. Y., AND ZHENG, H. Reusing 60GHz radios for mobile radar imaging. In *Proc. of MobiCom* (2015).

BreathPrint: Breathing Acoustics-based User Authentication

Jagmohan Chauhan [†*], Yining Hu [†*], Suranga Seneviratne [†⊥]
Archan Misra [‡], Aruna Seneviratne [†*], Youngki Lee [‡]

[†]Data61, CSIRO; [*]School of EET, UNSW, Australia; [⊥] School of CSE, UNSW, Australia;
[‡] School of Information Systems, SMU, Singapore

ABSTRACT

We propose *BreathPrint*, a new behavioural biometric signature based on audio features derived from an individual's commonplace breathing gestures. Specifically, *BreathPrint* uses the audio signatures associated with the three individual gestures: sniff, normal, and deep breathing, which are sufficiently different across individuals. Using these three breathing gestures, we develop the processing pipeline that identifies users via the microphone sensor on smartphones and wearable devices. In *BreathPrint*, a user performs breathing gestures while holding the device very close to their nose. Using off-the-shelf hardware, we experimentally evaluate the *BreathPrint* prototype with 10 users, observed over seven days. We show that users can be authenticated reliably with an accuracy of over 94% for all the three breathing gestures in intra-sessions and deep breathing gesture provides the best overall balance between true positives (successful authentication) and false positives (resiliency to directed impersonation and replay attacks). Moreover, we show that this breathing sound based biometric is also robust to some typical changes in both physiological and environmental context, and that it can be applied on multiple smartphone platforms. Early results suggest that breathing based biometrics show promise as either to be used as a secondary authentication modality in a multimodal biometric authentication system or as a user disambiguation technique for some daily lifestyle scenarios.

Keywords

Security, Usability, Authentication, Breathing Gestures

1. INTRODUCTION

Robust user authentication on small form-factor personal devices, such as smartphones and wearables, remains an important problem, especially as such devices increasingly become stores of sensitive personal data, such as daily digital payment traces, health/wellness records, or contact e-mails.

Permission to make digital or hard copies of all or part of this work for personal or classroom use is granted without fee provided that copies are not made or distributed for profit or commercial advantage and that copies bear this notice and the full citation on the first page. Copyrights for components of this work owned by others than ACM must be honored. Abstracting with credit is permitted. To copy otherwise, or republish, to post on servers or to redistribute to lists, requires prior specific permission and/or a fee. Request permissions from permissions@acm.org.

MobiSys '17, June 19–23, 2017, Niagara Falls, NY, USA.

© 2017 ACM. ISBN 978-1-4503-4928-4/17/06...$15.00

DOI: http://dx.doi.org/10.1145/3081333.3081355

Ensuring that the authentication mechanisms remain secure and user-friendly will be even more important with the upcoming surge in IoT-rich environments, where everyday objects such as coffee makers, cabinet doors, and pantries are embedded with sensing and actuation capabilities.

User authentication approaches are broadly organized according to three principles: (i) "what you know" approaches, such as PINs, passwords or memorable questions that leverage secret information that only you should be privy to, and have well known usability challenges (ii) "what you have" approaches, such as the use of smart tokens, that rely on hardware-generated temporary credentials that only the possessor of the device has access to, and are susceptible to device theft, and (iii) "what you are" approaches that utilize personal traits (biometrics) of an individual that are hard to reproduce or mimic. Within the "what you are" category, there are two classes of methods: *physiological biometrics* (such as fingerprints or iris scans) and *behavioural biometrics* (such as gait or heart rate measurements [75]).

In this paper, we introduce a new modality of behavioural biometrics based authentication called *BreathPrint*: it uses the sounds generated by a user's *breathing behavior*, as captured by a microphone sensor in close proximity to the user's nose. If the biometrics of "breathing sounds" are indeed *unique* (i.e., it can distinguish among multiple users) and *persistent* (i.e., an individual's signature remains relatively unchanged over time), then *BreathPrint* can provide a compelling mode of authentication. Among other advantages, (i) it is universal: all living users need to breathe!, whereas touch or gait-based biometrics pose challenges for people with hand or foot disabilities; (ii) it is highly usable: breathing is a naturally-occurring reflex activity that requires no additional cognitive or physical effort; (iii) it has low observability: the breathing sounds are essentially inaudible even to an observer that is 10–20 cms away, and (iv) it avoids specialized hardware: unlike past work which needed chest straps [42] or flow sensors [64] to monitor breathing, a commodity microphone sensor is almost universally available on mobile devices.

Key Research Questions and Contributions: Using a set of real world studies (10 users observed over a period of seven days), we first demonstrate that breathing gestures can indeed provide an individual specific fingerprint. We then develop the analytics pipeline on a microphone sensor based system (8 kHz sampling, placed 1–2 cm below the nose) that can extract and use such a fingerprint for practical authentication.

Our key challenges and contributions are:

- **What Natural Breathing Gestures Constitute a Fingerprint?** We develop an authentication approach that uses three distinct, natural breathing gestures: *sniff*, *normal* breathing and *deep* breathing. We show that users have distinctive differences in the amplitude and frequency components of the sound signals for these three breathing gestures, and that each individual breathing gesture achieves over 94% accuracy for user authentication (among 10 users).
- **What is the Processing Pipeline for Breathing-based Authentication?** We develop a classification pipeline that uses Gammatone Frequency Cepstral Coefficients (GFCC) as features as part of a GMM (Gaussian Mixture Model) based classifier. We describe how *BreathPrint* uses a segmentation technique to isolate individual breathing gestures, and how the selection of an appropriate number of GMM components helps the classifier achieve both high authentication accuracy and low false positive rates.
- **Is the Authentication Accurate & Resilient?** We show that *BreathPrint* is able to achieve between 90%–100% true positive rates (*TPR*) for different breathing gestures, especially by changing the number of GMM components. More importantly, we show that this approach is resilient to both impersonation (where an attacker hears the breathing audio records and tries to manually mimic the user) and replay attacks (where an attacker eavesdrops on the sounds from a short distance). The false positive rates (*FPR*) due to *impersonation* and *audio replay* attacks are less than 2%, and 0% respectively. This is lower than the FPR of comparable audio based authentication systems.
- **Are Breathing Biometrics Persistent?** Using studies that trained the classifier models on 50 samples of breathing data, we show that, when users attempt to authenticate 2–3 days later, the classification accuracy degrades somewhat for deep (8%) and sniff (6%) breathing gestures, with the drop being noticeably higher (23%) for normal breaths. To counteract these medium time-scale changes, we develop a simple online unsupervised learning technique to *continually* update the GMM-based classifier. This approach partially solves the persistency challenge – the breathing gesture classification accuracy increases by 3%. Note that the TPR for deep and sniff breathing gestures between the initial sessions and the session done after 2–3 days did not drop using the evolutionary technique, when the number of GMM components is small. *BreathPrint's* robustness to longer-term variation remains an open question.
- **Is the Authentication Robust to Contextual Changes?** *BreathPrint* appears to be robust to changes in the user's breathing pattern caused by selected natural daily activities: TPR remains high (over 80%) even after the episodes of walking for all the breathing gestures except the normal breathing gesture. Similarly, the microphone-based sensor is robust to background noise. TPR drops by only 4% when the noise level measured by a smartphone is 50 dB.

Overall, we believe that our work is the first to demonstrate the promise of a robust and non-intrusive breathing-based authentication mechanism. Besides enabling explicit user authentication (e.g., where a user breathes into a smartwatch or smartphone), our work opens up the possibility of continuous user authentication, perhaps by incorporating other breathing related features, e.g., the heatmap of breaths captured by an infra-red sensor embedded in a smartglass.

2. BACKGROUND

We start our exploration by providing a short background on the physiology of breathing, how it varies across different demographic segments and why we believe that breathing can act as a distinguishing behavioural biometric. Lastly, we describe three breathing gestures: *sniff*, *normal*, and *deep*.

2.1 Breathing Mechanics

Breathing occurs naturally, and a healthy adult takes around 12–20 breaths per minute. Normal breathing has two phases: inhalation (taking air in) and exhalation (pushing air out), and involves three major parts of the body: trachea, lung, and diaphragm. Air enters and leaves the body through the nose and reaches the lungs through the trachea. A large dome-shaped muscle under the lungs, called the diaphragm, aids the process. During inhalation, the diaphragm contracts, creating a vacuum that lowers the pressure in the lungs; consequently, air is sucked into the lungs. The reverse happens during exhalation: the diaphragm relaxes upwards, compressing the lungs and increasing the air pressure there, forcing air out through the trachea. Normally breathing occurs through the nose. We exclude the scenarios where breathing occurs from the mouth - e.g., when people are suffering from some medical condition.

Extensive medical and physiological research exists on respiratory sounds [45] and the effect of demographic attributes, such as age [46], weight [60], height [55], and gender [25] on respiration. These papers studied sounds coming from the lung and trachea, as measured either over the chest wall, at the suprasternal notch (hollow between the neck and the collarbone) or the lateral neck. Lung sound's amplitude differs between persons and different locations on the chest surface, and primarily varies with airflow in the lungs [23]. Moreover, as shown by Pasterkamp et al. [47], the spectral shape of tracheal sounds is highly variable across subjects.

Pasterkamp et al. [46] studied the properties of normal respiratory lung sounds and how they differ between children and adults. Authors showed that infants had higher median frequencies present, compared to older children and adults, and concluded that this was due to the presence of less power in low-frequency regions (small lungs and thin chest walls) among infants. However, the roll-off in the power of higher frequency components was similar at all ages. Sanchez et al. [55] found that tracheal sounds of children have higher cut-off frequency (the frequency after which the audio signal's power drops sharply) than adults due to shorter tracheal length. Sharp et al. [60] reported that the pressure, volume and air flow is very different between a normal and an obese person. The difference has mainly been attributed to the different efforts needed to move the ponderous thoracic wall (lungs, diaphragm) and abdomen during breathing. Gross et al. [25] found that the ratio of power between two frequency bands (60–330 Hz and 330–600 Hz) is very distinct between males and females for lung sounds.

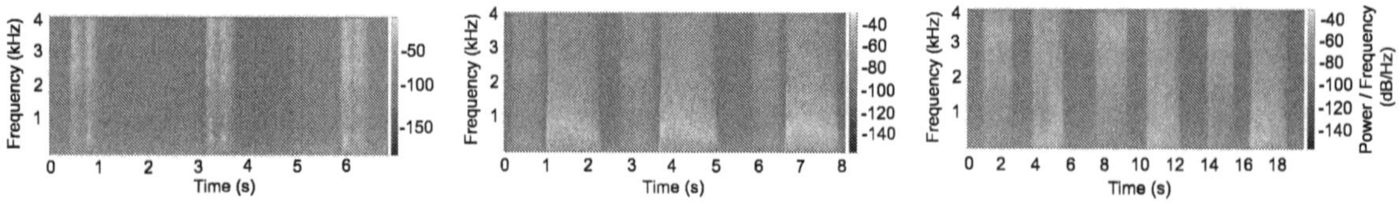

(a) Sniff (b) Normal breathing (c) Deep breathing

Figure 1: Spectrograms for the three breathing gestures

The role of the diaphragm is studied by Mead et al. [43], where they demonstrated that the volume change in lungs during breathing is influenced more by the diaphragm than the rib cage. More recently, breathing-related parameters have been used to detect different medical conditions [22, 6, 28, 61]. Sinues et al. [61] used mass spectrometry to analyze the composition of the exhaled breath. They found that individual signatures of breath composition exist, implying that analysis of breathing can be used for metabolic studies. We believe that we are the first to utilize the audio signal of breathing to authenticate an individual.

2.2 Breathing Gestures

In our proposed approach, we focus on audio generated by three distinct breathing gestures: *Sniff*, *Normal*, and *Deep*. We have deliberately restricted ourselves to these three gestures, because they occur "naturally" and can thus be easily performed by a healthy person. In fact, we initially also considered a few additional more complex breathing gestures, such as "two quick inhales followed by an exhale" and vice versa, and "one quick exhale followed by two quick inhales" and vice versa. However, during initial exploratory studies, our participants indicated that they found such breathing gestures too cumbersome to perform and too difficult to remember. Such complex breathing gestures were thus excluded from deeper analysis.

Figure 1 shows the spectrograms for three breathing gestures: Sniff, Normal, and Deep. Each spectrogram contains three samples of each breathing gesture. The figure is obtained using data collected during our experiments with 10 participants (see Section 3). Sniff breathing gesture has the shortest duration of less than a second and consists of two successive quick inhalations. Normal breathing gesture lasts around 2–3 seconds and comprises an inhalation, followed by an exhalation. Deep breathing gesture has longer inhalation and exhalation phases than normal breathing gesture, and lasts around 4–5 seconds.

Motivated by the aforementioned research findings over respiratory sounds, we hypothesized that acoustic features derived from different breathing patterns, measured by a microphone sensor, should provide an effective approach for authenticating people. However, we needed to discover the key features (e.g., amount of air, forcefulness, time duration of inhalation and exhalation, etc.) that can both be detected through audio signal analysis and provide high discriminatory power across individuals.

3. DATASET

In this section, we describe the data collection process, including the experimental setup and user demographics. We also present results to show what makes user's breathing behaviour different across the three breathing gestures.

3.1 Data Collection

We recruited 10 volunteers (two females and eight males, aged between 20 and 35) to perform three types of breathing gestures: *sniff (two quick consecutive inhalations)*, *normal breathing*, and *deep breathing*. The participants were employees and postgraduate students affiliated with Data61, CSIRO. The user study was approved by the CSIRO Human Research Ethics Committee under Ref. No. 085/16 and was performed in a closed office room of size 1.7m (w) x 3.8m (l) x 2.7m (h). The hardware used for the data collection was a wired iPhone 6 earphone attached to a Dell XPS 13-9343 laptop running Windows 10 (see Figure 2a). We used the free version of Gold Wave software[1] to capture the acoustic signal generated by different breathing gestures.

Each user held the microphone of the earphone 1–2 *cm* below their nose and repeated each breathing gesture multiple times, while remaining seated. We used an 8000 Hz sampling rate to capture the generated acoustic signals and store them as *.wav* files. We repeated the experiment on three days; the first day (Session 1), 3–4 days after the first day (Session 2), and 6–7 days after the first day (Session 3). In the first two experiment sessions, the participants repeated 30 instances of each breathing gesture. During the third session, participants repeated 10 instances of each breathing gesture. They also performed impersonation attacks by trying to mimic a target user breathing gestures after listening to an audio recording. Additionally, to perform replay attacks, we also recorded the user's breathing sounds via a smartphone placed close to the user.

The acoustics of the breathing signal depends on various physical conditions. Also, our data acquisition process may be affected by ambient noise. To understand the effect of such factors, we carried out additional "contextual" experiments with three users (two of whom are part of the original pool of 10 participants). For these users, we captured the acoustic signal for the three breathing gestures in multiple scenarios: *i) normal experiment conditions (while sitting without background noise), ii) while standing, iii) after 2-3 min of walking, iv) after 2-3 min of going up and down the staircases, v) while sitting under three levels of ambient noise, and vi) while keeping the microphone at different distances from the user's nose.* The contextual experiments are only carried out once (one session) for each user. More details about the attacks performed and the different contextual experiments are presented later in Section 5.

[1]https://www.goldwave.com

We also evaluated the proposed biometrics on two smartphones: iPhone 6 and Nexus 6P, by asking the same three users to perform breathing gestures on the two devices. We used the smartphone's microphone to record the breathing gestures. We did not use the headphone mic, as it has a built-in AGC (Automatic Gain Control) function that we could not disable. Experimental setups: (a) of a laptop with an earphone and (b) smartphones only are shown in Figure 2.

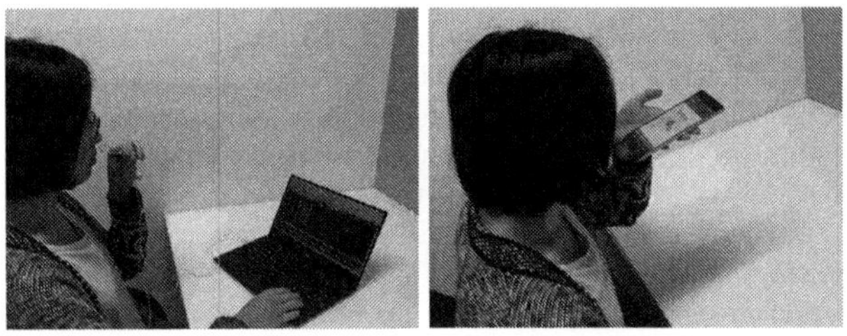

(a) Laptop - Earphone (b) Smartphone

Figure 2: Experimental Setups

3.2 Breathing Gesture Characteristics

Here we discuss the characteristics of different breathing gestures and why they are different across individuals. Table 1 shows the statistics about the average, minimum, and maximum length of different breathing gestures obtained from the dataset. Sniff breathing gesture is the shortest in length with an average duration of less than a second. Normal breathing gesture length varies between 1.7–4.3 seconds, while deep breathing gesture is the longest gesture with an average duration of approximately 5 seconds.

Table 1: Breathing Gesture Lengths (Seconds)

Gesture Type	Average	Minimum	Maximum
Snifff	0.55	0.42	0.71
Normal	2.83	1.79	4.28
Deep	4.8	3.74	6.53

Figure 3 shows the spectrograms of the same breathing gesture from two users. We can see that the spectrograms are different across the two users. The energy for a sniff breathing gesture lies mostly in the higher frequency range; conversely, for normal breathing gesture, most of the energy lies in the low frequency range. Also, more power exists in the exhalation phase than the inhalation phase. The same is true for deep breathing gesture, except that the energy distribution across the inhalation and exhalation phases is more evenly distributed.

To get a clearer picture of why different people might have different breathing signatures, we plot the root mean square of the amplitude of the breathing signal and the power present in different frequency bands for all the three breathing gestures for all the participants. The frequency bands are chosen according to the Gammatone filterbank frequency ranges, described later in Section 4. The results are shown in Figure 4. The Root Mean Square (RMS) of the breathing signal for all the users is distinctive. Also, the frequencies, which separate the users in case of a sniff breathing gesture, lie in the high frequency range (2000–4000 Hz). On the other hand, the separating frequency range for normal and deep breathing gestures lies in lower frequency ranges, specifically normal breathing gesture between 100–1300 Hz and deep breathing gesture between 100–1600 Hz.

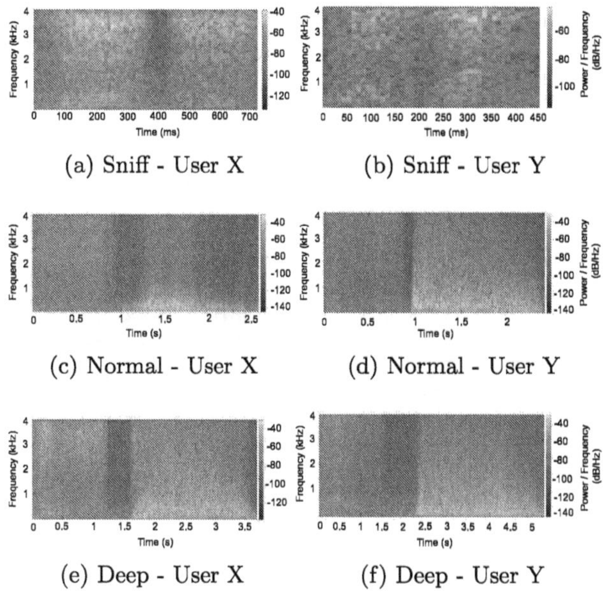

(a) Sniff - User X (b) Sniff - User Y

(c) Normal - User X (d) Normal - User Y

(e) Deep - User X (f) Deep - User Y

Figure 3: Spectrograms for Two Users

Inter-gesture correlation: We also investigated the correlation, in the average RMS value of the breathing signal across different users, for each breathing gesture pair. We found that this correlation was negligible (in the range of [-0.27, 0.17]) between sniff and normal breathing gesture or between sniff and deep breathing gesture. The correlation was highly significant (0.75) between normal and deep breathing gestures. These results on correlation, along with the robustness studies performed in Section 5.4, suggest that "sniff" and "deep" are the two distinct, independent breathing gestures that provide *BreathPrint* the highest discriminatory power.

4. THE BREATHPRINT PIPELINE

We first describe the overall design of *BreathPrint*, showing its different components. Next, we explain the feature extraction process we used to represent the acoustic signals in a form that can be fed into an appropriate classifier, which determines whether the presented acoustic signal was from a specific individual or not. The classifier input is a discrete breathing gesture. Finally, we present a segmentation algorithm that automatically extracts episodes of individual breathing gestures from an underlying continuous sequence of audio sensor data.

4.1 Overall System

In this subsection, we describe the general working mechanism of *BreathPrint*. Figure 5 provides a schematic overview of the system setup used to generate our empirical results. The user breathes into a microphone, mounted near his/her nose. The acoustic signal from the microphone first goes through the segmentation algorithm that separates out each breathing gesture and also removes leading and trailing silence periods. After this step, the audio signal of the breath-

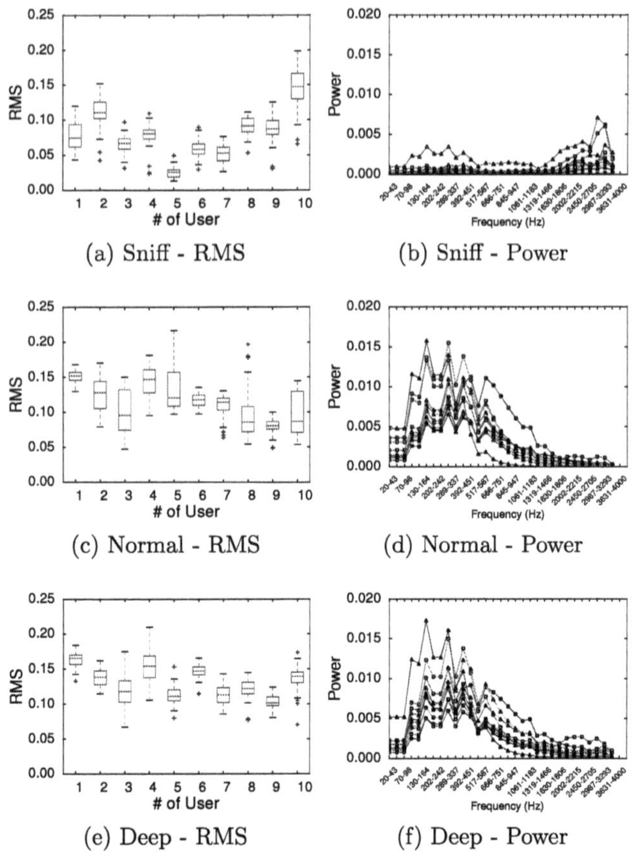

(a) Sniff - RMS (b) Sniff - Power

(c) Normal - RMS (d) Normal - Power

(e) Deep - RMS (f) Deep - Power

Figure 4: RMS and Power-Frequency Distribution

ing gesture is divided into non-overlapping frames of 10 ms. Acoustic feature vectors (described shortly in Section 4.2) are extracted from each frame. The feature vectors are then fed into both GMM_{user} model and GMM_{others} model to obtain two different log likelihood values: LL_{user} and LL_{other}. The resulting log likelihood ratio ($\frac{LL_{user}}{LL_{other}}$) is derived for each frame. Subsequently, we compute the average of this ratio across all the frames constituting the gesture, and accept (authenticate) the user only if this average ratio is greater than one. In case the value of average ratio is less than one, the user is not allowed to access the system.

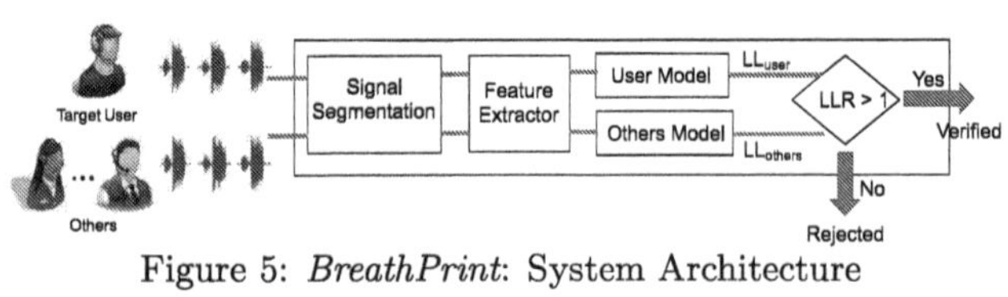

Figure 5: *BreathPrint*: System Architecture

4.2 Feature Extraction

We utilize the Gammatone Frequency Cepstral Coefficients (GFCC) as features, which are based on signal power in a set of frequency bands. While Mel Frequency Cepstral Coefficients (MFCC) is more widely used as features in audio signal processing, especially for human speech analysis, recent research [56, 66, 31] has shown that Gammatone filterbanks [2] can offer higher accuracy than Mel filterbanks. The major reason why GFCC is more accurate than MFCC is because GFCC provides finer resolution at low frequencies than MFCC, making GFCC not only more robust in the presence of noise [77], but also better suited for detecting low frequency sounds. Given that a single breath is barely audible at larger distances, we anticipate that breathing has its dominant energy at lower frequencies.

Generally, a filterbank divides the frequency spectrum of the signal into multiple overlapping bands (adjustable) called filters and then calculates the log-energy (weighted sum of the FFT magnitudes) for each filter. As, the final step in calculating the cepstral coefficients, the Discrete Cosine Transformation (DCT) is applied to each of the log-energy. This yields number of cepstral coefficients equal to the number of filters. DCT is a standard orthogonal transformation technique; the most important information about the spectrum is typically embedded in the lower order DCT coefficients. Note that the DCT coefficients capture the energy variation across the entire spectrum; for example, the first DCT coefficient is the sum of all the log-energies. For our purpose, we used the GFCC implementation by Zhao et al. [76]. We extracted 32 GFCC as features using a 32-Gammatone filterbank, in which each filter is defined by a center frequency, f and a bandwidth, b. We also used GFCC *delta* and GFCC *double delta* as features, which capture the rate of change between two consecutive GFCC and GFCC delta coefficients respectively. In total, we used 96 features. For GFCC, the filterbank centre frequencies are distributed across frequency in proportion to their bandwidth, known as the ERB (Equivalent Rectangular Bandwidth) scale [24]. ERB scale provides an approximation as how the bandwidths of the filters should be divided. The center frequencies we used are in the range of 20–4000 Hz. The bandwidth B of each Gammatone filter is given by 1.019 ERB, where ERB is calculated as: $24.7*(4.37*0.001*f+1)$, where f being the filter's center frequency. For comparison purposes, we also implemented our classifier using MFCC. Similar to GFCC, we used MFCC, its delta and double delta as features.

4.3 Classifier

We used GMM (Gaussian Mixtures Model) as a classifier as it has been shown to perform better than DTW (Dynamic Time Warping) or supervised learning methods such as SVM for speech recognition classification tasks [33, 51]. GMM is a probabilistic model, which assumes that all the data points in a dataset are generated from a mixture of a finite number of Gaussian distributions. Each Gaussian distribution has its own mean and covariance and is represented as a component in the GMM based model.

By adjusting the number of components and the type of covariance matrix, one can attempt to represent a set of data points. We tried with 5, 10, 15, 20, 25, and 30 as the number of components in the classifier. We stopped at 30, as the classifier's accuracy drops below 50% beyond 30 components (as we shall see in Section 5). Moreover, larger volumes of training data are also needed to train a model with a higher number of GMM components. For example, speech recognition systems typically include 256–1024 GMM components, as they usually utilize hours of speech data [51]. In our case, we seek to train classifiers with only limited training data (at most a few minutes of human effort). Given such limited training data, the use of a greater number of GMM components is likely to lead to overfitting.

The other parameter of the GMM, called covariance matrix type, can be chosen from four options: *full, tied, diagonal,* and *spherical. Full* covariance matrix means that each component has its own general covariance matrix, whereas *diagonal* implies that each component has its own diagonal covariance matrix. In this work, we used the *diagonal* option, as estimating the parameters of a full covariance GMM requires more training data and is more computationally expensive. Moreover, past empirical evidence suggests that diagonal matrix GMMs outperform full matrix GMMs [52].

To train the classifier, we first created two GMM models for each user. The first model GMM_{user} is constructed only using the breathing audio samples from the target user. The second model GMM_{others} is constructed using the samples from all other users (i.e. excluding the target user samples). Each audio sample was divided into $10\,ms$ frames with no overlap. 10–30 ms is the preferred choice of frames in audio processing tasks [70]. For each frame, a feature vector of GFCC is extracted and fed to the training module, which uses the well known Expectation Maximization (EM) technique to compute the GMM components. During the test phase, the incoming audio sample is divided into 10 ms frames, features are extracted and a log likelihood ratio, $LLR = LL_{user}/LL_{other}$ is calculated by classifying the incoming feature vectors with both GMM_{user} and GMM_{others} models.

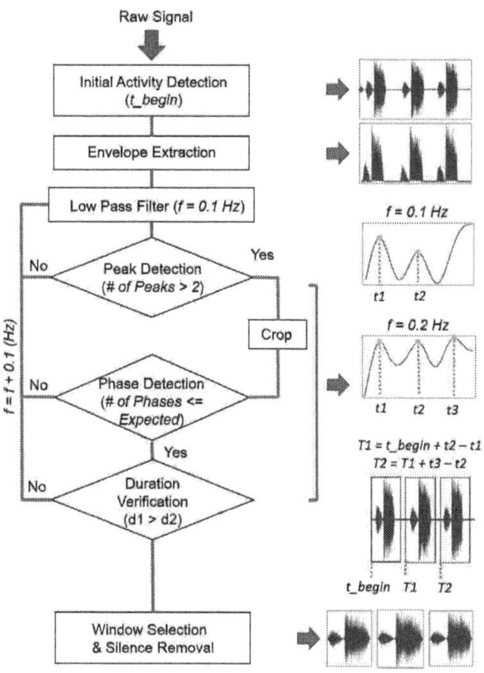

Figure 6: Segmentation Algorithm

4.4 Segmentation Algorithm

To automate the feature extraction process, we designed a waveform segmentation algorithm. While inspired by existing work, our segmentation algorithm is specially tuned to isolate the (start, stop) duration of each individual breath. In contrast, the majority of the respiration monitoring works focus only on breathing rate estimation [14, 7, 71] - e.g., reliably isolating the peak of each breath. In addition, segmentation in speech recognition is threshold based and is used to separate speech vs. non-speech frames [32, 38] – such approaches do not directly work in our case as the thresholds need to be different for different frames, over the full breathing gesture signal. When a raw recording is given to the algorithm, it calculates the breathing rate (number of breathing cycles per unit time), a suitable window size (for each breathing gesture), and the starting points of each window. The steps of segmentation algorithm are illustrated in Figure 6.

i) Initial activity detection - To identify the start of the activity (i.e. where a user starts performing repeated breathing gestures), we use a simple threshold method. The raw signal is separated into frames of $10\,ms$. If five consecutive frames (i.e., $50\,ms$) each have signal power higher than an empirically predetermined threshold, the starting point of the first frame t_{begin} is considered as the starting point.

ii) Envelope extraction - We then extract the envelope of the acoustic signal by applying Hilbert transformation. For acoustic signals, applying Hilbert transformation smooths the signal and eliminates negative values.

iii) Low pass filter - The signal envelope is then passed through a low-pass Butterworth filter as suggested in [14] to get the fundamental frequency of the signal; i.e. the breathing rate. The starting frequency (f) is set to be $0.1Hz$ (as the corresponding window size of $10s$ is sufficient for any breathing gesture) and is iteratively incremented by $0.1Hz$ until three criterion are met: (a) *Number of peaks*, (b) *Number of phases*, and (c) *Duration.*

a) Peak detection - When f is close enough to the fundamental frequency, peaks on the filtered envelope are uniformly distributed; otherwise, the filtered signal is irregular in shape without clear peaks. Thus, when the *number of peaks* criterion is met, the algorithm determines that it has correctly estimated the breathing rate. Once this criterion is met, the window length is calculated as the average distance between adjacent peaks and the starting points of the windows are estimated by adding t_{begin} to the distance between the target peak to the first peak. The raw signal is then cropped into distinct windows using the average window length and window locations.

b) Phase detection - A segment detection method is used to check the *Number of phases.* A phase in a breathing cycle corresponds to either inhalation or exhalation. Therefore, the number of expected phases for normal breathing, deep breathing, and sniffing breathing gestures are two, two, and one respectively. Note that since sniffing breathing gesture is two quick inhalations it does not have two phases, as there is no significant time gap between the two inhalations. The algorithm compares the number of phases inside each window and if most windows contain more phases than expected, the window size is shortened by increasing f (which indirectly decreases the distance between adjacent peaks).

c) Duration verification - For some users, we observe that the inhalation phase for normal or deep breathing gesture is weak and hence buried in the noise. For such users, for breathing gestures with two expected phases, two exhalations belonging to two adjacent but separate breathing cycles may be cropped into one window. To avoid such fusion of multiple breathing gestures, the algorithm performs

an additional *duration verification* step. The *duration verification* step compares the duration $d1$ of each detected phase and the distance $d2$ between the two phases inside a window. If $d1 < d2$, then it implies that the two breathing cycles are incorrectly grouped together and the window size is shortened by increasing f.
iv) Window selection and silence removal - To ensure that there is only one complete breathing gesture inside each window, the algorithm selects windows with silence periods at both the beginning and at the end. This is based on the assumption that the user brings the microphone close to his/her nose only during the authentication step and otherwise usually the microphone is sufficiently away from the nose at other times. A frame level, threshold based method is used to eliminate windows with consecutive high power frames on the sides and the silence periods (that occur due to the pauses between the breathing gestures) of the selected windows are later removed.

Segmentation Performance: To study the performance of the segmentation algorithm, we fed it five waveforms containing a total of 100 individual breathing gesture instances (counted manually). For sniff, normal breathing, and deep breathing gestures the segmentation algorithm was able to correctly segment 95%, 93%, and 84% respectively, of the manually annotated individual gesture instances. A segment generated by the algorithm was considered correct if it contains a one complete (individual) breathing gesture when manually inspected. The segmentation process applied to continuous breathing activity does not relate to the accuracy of authentication of individual breathing gestures. Even though our segmentation method cannot capture all breathing cycles, a user can simply repeat the breathing gesture until a correct segment is extracted.

5. RESULTS

As discussed in Section 3.1, we collected the data from 10 volunteers for the three breathing gestures in three sessions: first day (Session 1), 3–4 days after the first day (Session 2), and 6–7 days after the first day (Session 3). Each user held the microphone of the earphone 1–2 *cm* below their nose. We collected 30 instances of each breathing gesture in the first two sessions and 10 instances in the last session. In the last session, the volunteers were also asked to do impersonation attacks for a target user 10 times for each breathing gesture. Three volunteers were picked to perform data collection (out of which two were from the initial pool of 10 participants) for an additional set of "contextual" experiments, and to test robustness of BreathPrint on two additional smartphones.

5.1 Baseline: Intra-Session User Verification

We first used all the 30 samples from Session 1 and first 20 samples from Session 2 to train the classifier for each user and each breathing gesture. To create the "others" model, 50 samples from each other user were taken (total, 9*50=450 samples per breathing gesture). The rest of the 10 samples from Session 2 were used as the testing set (total, 10*10=100 samples per breathing gesture). We report the values of performances metrics – *TPR* and *FPR* – achieved by the *BreathPrint* classifier. Note that TPR in this context is the percentage of instances where a user is correctly verified (i.e. calculated based on 100 predictions where each user's 10 samples are fed into their corresponding GMM). FPR is the percentage of instances where a classifier misclassifies other user's samples as the legitimate (actual) user's sample (i.e. calculated based on 900 predictions where all other users' samples are fed into one user's GMM). In the context of user verification, by True Positive we mean how many times a genuine user was correctly verified to be the claimed user on the basis of some threshold to get legitimate access to the system. While, False Positive means how many times an illegitimate user gets access to the genuine user's account because the system fails to detect the fraudulent access. We compare the performance of *BreathPrint's* classifier, built with GFCC, against an alternative built using the MFCC.

Figure 7 shows the results, as the number of GMM components is varied between 5 to 30, in increments of 5. For all the breathing gestures, TPR varies between 90% and 99% when GFCC are used. MFCC perform worse than GFCC as the TPR drops to 50%. For GFCC, FPR is between 0.4% and 6.4% and for MFCC, it is between 0% and 5.2%. Although, MFCC provides a slightly better FPR than GFCC, it comes at the cost of dropped TPR. We attribute this notable performance difference to the fact that GFCC provides finer resolution at low frequencies where most of the energy of the breathing signal is located. The performance of the classifier is promising and comparable to the other forms of behavioural biometrics as discussed in Section 7.

Figure 7 also shows that number of GMM components (M) plays a significant role in classification accuracy. TPR and FPR both decrease with the number of GMM components. TPR drops as M increases; 2%–7% for GFCC and 7%–40% for MFCC. This might be due to overfitting. As the number of components increases, the ability of the classifier to correctly classify the actual user diminishes. However, the affect is more drastic for MFCC than GFCC. Overall, the experimental results suggests that GFCC provide a better balance, compared to MFCC, between the usability and security of the system.

Until now, we have presented results to verify a user based on the prediction of a single test sample. We also increase the number of testing samples at the time of user verification from one to three and used a majority voting based decision to check how it affects the accuracy of the system, in terms of TPR and FPR for GFCC based classifier only as GFCC provided better results than MFCC. We pick three random test samples out of 10 at each iteration and successfully authenticate a user if the classifier verifies at least two of the three test samples correctly. We run 10 such iterations for each user. Referring back to Figure 7, we can see that majority voting (GFCC-TPR-MV) increases the TPR for deep breathing by 1.5% (average) across all the components while for the other two breathing gestures it has a minimal impact. For FPR (GFCC-FPR-MV), we a see a drop of 0.6%, 0.9% and 1.2% on average against GFCC-FPR across all components for sniff, normal and deep breathing gestures.

The running time for building a classifier for all the 10 users using GFCC varied between 32-47 seconds, 110-275 seconds, and 165–435 seconds for sniff, normal, and deep breathing gestures respectively across different GMM components we tested. The time taken for testing a sample was 2 seconds for any of the three breathing gestures irrespective of the number of GMM components. The time was calculated on a laptop running Mac OS X (Sierra version) with 2.6 GHz Intel Core i5 processor and 8 GB of RAM.

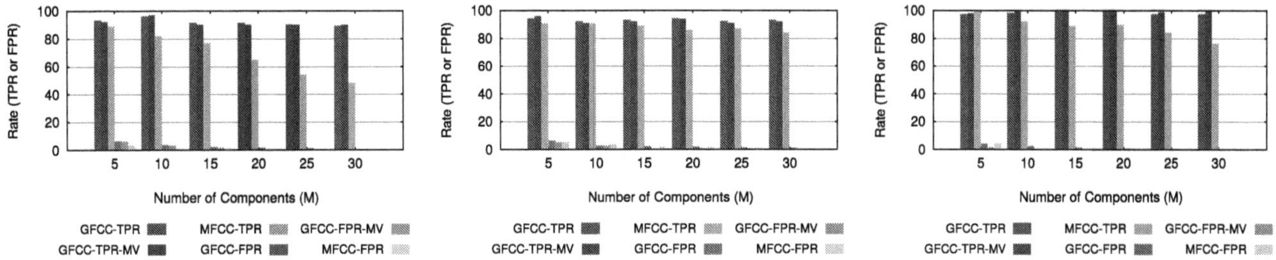

(a) Sniff (b) Normal (c) Deep

Figure 7: TPR and FPR for the three breathing gestures

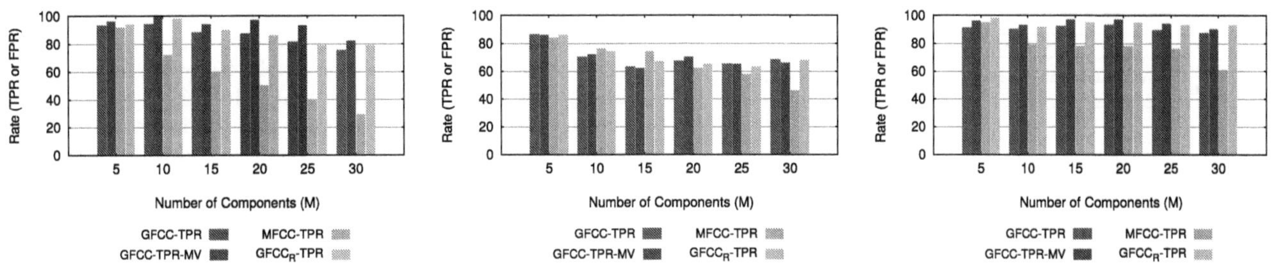

(a) Sniff (b) Normal (c) Deep

Figure 8: TPR and FPR for the three breathing gestures - Evolution

5.2 Evolution: Inter-Session User Verification

We tested the classifier performance (built using Session 1 and Session 2 data) on 10 samples collected on Session 3 (i.e. 6-7 days after Session 1). The results are shown in Figure 8 in the form of TPR and FPR similar to Section 5.1. As Figure 8 shows the TPR varies between 75%–93%, 68%–86%, and 87%–91% for sniff, normal, and deep breathing gestures respectively. Compared to the intra-session TPR, there is an average 8%, 23%, and 6% drop in inter-session TPR for sniff, normal, and deep breathing gestures respectively. This can be ascribed to temporal factors such as user's physiological condition and activity levels. More notably, if the number of components M=5, the TPR for sniffing does not drop while it drops only by 8% and 6% for the normal and deep breathing gestures. Lower TPR for the normal breathing gesture was due to the presence of a single *outlier* user, for whom none of the 10 breathing gestures were correctly authenticated.

To counteract these medium scale temporal changes, we develop a simple online unsupervised learning technique to continually update the GMM-based classifier. We replaced the first 10 samples belonging to Session 1 from the user's model with the 10 testing samples from Session 2. The results are labeled as $GFCC_R$. This approach partially solves the persistency issues as it improves the authentication accuracy by 3%. The TPR for deep and sniff breathing gestures did not drop using the technique, when the number of GMM components is small.

We also performed majority voting for inter-session user verification. As we can see from Figure 8, majority voting increases the TPR for all three breathing gestures: 7% for sniff, 0.3% for normal, and 4% for deep on an average across all the components. Overall, majority voting improves the accuracy of the system by decreasing the FPR while having slight increase in the TPR.

5.3 Security Evaluation: Attacks

We evaluated the security of the breathing based biometrics system under three different types of attacks; i) *random attacks*, ii) *impersonation attacks*, and iii) *audio replay attacks*. In random attacks, an attacker does not know how a target user performs a certain breathing gesture. To simulate random attacks, we used last 10 samples from Session 2 of each user against a target user's classifier and obtained the FPR at different GMM components. This is exactly the process that is used to calculate the FPR in Section 5.1. FPR is in the range of 0.4%–2% when the number of GMM components is between 15–30 indicating that the proposed biometrics is safe against random attacks.

Recall that in the final session (c.f. Section 3.1), all the users were asked to act as an attacker by trying to *impersonate* a target user. The attackers had to listen to the audio recording of the target user breathing gesture and then attempt to mimic the breathing gesture 10 times. The attacker could play the audio recordings any number of times. We collected 10 impersonation attack samples from each user and in total 100 samples for each breathing gesture.

To simulate *audio replay attacks*, we placed a smartphone near the laptop at a distance of 40-50 cm. The smartphone was recording the breathing gestures. In total, 100 samples for each breathing gesture were collected for audio replay attacks. These samples were then replayed on the microphone of the earphone so that the system thinks that an actual user is performing the breathing gesture. One can argue that recording breathing sounds from a smaller distance (4–5 cm) will increase the likelihood of a successful attack against a target user. However, launching attacks from smaller distances will be easily observable to the target user and hence would be difficult to be launched successfully.

Table 2 shows the results. For impersonation attacks, the number of successful attacks is: 7% for sniff breathing gesture and more than 10% for normal and deep breathing gestures. However, as the number of components increases the successful impersonation attacks drop to less than 4% across all the breathing gestures. The same is true for audio replay attacks. The successful attacks go to 0% across all the breathing gestures when using GFCC. More replay attacks on sniff and deep breathing gestures are successful because sniff and deep breathing gestures contain higher energy than a normal breathing gesture, which makes them audible at a larger distance compared to a normal breathing gesture.

Table 2: Results of Attack Scenarios

Gesture Type	M*	GFCC Imper.	GFCC Replay	MFCC Imper.	MFCC Replay
Sniff	5	7	7	7	12
	10	3	0	0	10
	15	1	0	0	7
	20	2	0	0	5
	25	1	0	0	4
	30	0	0	0	0
Normal	5	16	10	19	0
	10	3	1	9	0
	15	3	1	9	0
	20	2	1	8	0
	25	2	1	6	0
	30	2	0	3	0
Deep	5	18	19	26	10
	10	6	0	7	10
	15	9	0	6	10
	20	3	0	4	10
	25	2	0	6	10
	30	2	0	1	10

(M* - Number of GMM components)

To summarize, our results show that highest TPR is achieved when the number of GMM components (M) is 5. However, the system also becomes more prone to impersonation and audio replay attacks at lower values of M. When the number of GMM components is 30, the exact opposite is true. The TPR is too low for a usable system but very high security (low FPR) can be achieved by the system. Nonetheless, *BreathPrint* can achieve a good balance between security and usability by using GFCC and a GMM classifier with 15–20 components. The number of components can be increased at the expense of collecting more training data. Our results suggest that the *deep* breathing gesture provides the best balance between TPR and FPR while preventing targeted attacks. The deep breathing gesture also has the highest TPR rate during evolution. For the rest of this section, we use GFCC for classification purposes as they perform better than MFCC.

5.4 Contextual Results

We check the accuracy of the classifier in following scenarios: (a) having the user perform some physical activity, (b) having the user stand, (c) increasing distance between the user (3–5 cm and 6–8 cm) and the microphone of the earphone, and (d) increasing the level of ambient noise. These results are obtained using data from three users (c.f. Section 3). 30 samples are collected for training from each user for each breathing gesture under normal experiment conditions (sitting without background noise). Then 10 samples are collected for each breathing gesture under eight different scenarios. The physical activity scenarios include: (a) walking for 2-3 minutes and (b) going up and down the staircase for 2-3 minutes. The ambient noise is generated by playing music from a smartphone at three levels. We chose music because playing a recorded audio can be done repeatedly easily for all the participants. The noise levels are achieved by dividing the maximum volume of the smartphone speaker into three equal parts. The average decibel values measured from the user device side are 50 dB, 54 dB, 66 dB for Level 1, Level 2, and Level 3 respectively. 50–55 dB is equivalent to general activities in a business office. 65 dB corresponds to average road traffic heard at a distance of 25 m.

Table 3 shows the results. We can clearly see that the accuracy of the classifier only lies between 40%–60% in most of the cases across breathing gestures for 3–5 cm. For 6–8 cm, the accuracy hovers around 33%. This implies that the microphone needs to be really close (0–2 cm) to the user's nose for *BreathPrint* to perform well. However, on the other hand, this very disadvantage makes breathing gestures extremely safe against audio replay and similar attacks. With respect to ambient noise, the breathing gestures are quite resilient at Level 1 and Level 2 except the normal breathing gestures for which accuracy ranges between 40%–60%. This is due to the fact that more energy is present in sniff and deep breathing gestures, thereby making them highly unsusceptible to the ambient noise. The standing posture also has relatively low impact on the accuracy of the classifier.

For activity scenarios, we find that the *after stairs climbing* results are worse than after walking scenario. Naturally, walking puts less strain on the user body and hence the chances of breathing gestures being changed are less compared to the stairs scenario. We also observe better results for deep and sniff breathing gestures compared to normal breathing gesture, which suggests that normal breathing is affected more compared to the other two gestures after a physical activity is performed by a person. We expected the accuracy of the classifier to go down with physical activity scenarios. We leave increasing the accuracy of our system in different physiological contexts as future work.

5.5 Multi Platform Results

We tested the feasibility of using breathing gestures on two other devices: an iPhone 6 and a Google Nexus 6P Android smartphone. The three users who participated in contextual experimental scenarios performed each breathing gesture 30 times on both the smartphones. The first 20 samples are used for training and the remaining 10 are used for testing. The TPR of the classifier is 100% on both the devices for all the breathing gestures across all the GMM components. However, we used a different threshold to remove silence from the segmented breathing gestures in case of iPhone 6 compared to Android smartphone breathing samples. For samples collected using iPhone, we used 0.1 times the threshold value being used for samples collected using Android phone. The samples collected using Android phone used the same threshold as used for the earphones.

6. RELATED WORK

We divide related work into i) detecting non-speech body sounds and their applications, ii) breath control for interactive gaming, iii) breath monitoring for respiratory disorder detection, and iv) behavioural biometrics for authentication.

Table 3: Contextual Results (TPR)

Gesture Type	M*	Distance		Ambient Noise			User Activity		
		3-5cm	6-8cm	Level 1	Level 2	Level 3	After Stairs	After Walking	Standing Idle
Sniff	5	70	66	100	73	76	73	83	96
	10	50	33	96	56	60	46	83	86
	15	43	33	93	60	46	46	83	90
	20	43	33	96	90	46	43	83	83
	25	36	33	96	83	40	43	83	76
	30	40	33	90	76	40	50	80	73
Normal	5	63	23	100	63	36	63	53	76
	10	63	20	100	43	36	43	33	56
	15	60	30	100	53	36	50	33	66
	20	56	16	100	50	40	46	26	76
	25	56	36	100	43	40	53	36	73
	30	66	20	96	43	40	50	33	76
Deep	5	43	33	100	96	36	66	86	100
	10	40	50	100	96	36	63	83	100
	15	43	33	100	96	33	66	90	100
	20	43	36	100	100	36	66	96	100
	25	43	43	100	100	33	66	93	100
	30	43	43	100	100	33	66	90	100

(M* - Number of GMM components)

i) Non-speech body sounds: Bodybeat [49], SymDetector [62], BodyScope [74], CoughSense [35], iSleep [26], Woosh [50], UbiBreathe [1], Zephyr [4], and ApneaApp [44], are some of the earlier works on detecting various types of body sounds for applications under different contexts. BodyBeat [49] is a mobile sensing platform that captures and recognizes four different types of non-speech body sounds: eating, drinking, breathing, and coughing using a custom-built piezoelectric microphone placed near the user's throat. Such a system can be used for food journaling and detecting illness conditions like coughing. SymDetector [62] detects multiple respiratory sounds such as coughing, sneezing, sniffling, and throat clearing with a smartphone microphone. It handles users' privacy and reduces power consumption to record users' respiratory symptoms for a longer duration of time.

BodyScope [74] aims at detecting sounds produced in a user's throat area, such as eating, drinking, speaking, laughing, and coughing using a special sensor working at 22 kHz. A similar mobile system named CoughSense [35] aims at detecting cough sounds with high accuracy while maintaining the users' privacy using a smartphone worn around the user's neck or placed in a shirt pocket. Woosh [50] relies on air blown from the mouth as a way to interact with smartwatches. UbiBreathe [1] uses WiFi RSS (Received Signal Strength) patterns to enable ubiquitous and non-invasive respiratory rate estimation. ApneaApp [44] monitors the minute movements in chest and abdomen caused by breathing on smartphones to detect sleep apnea. Our research is different compared to the earlier works because we are interested in using different type of breathing sounds for user authentication on commodity hardware (an earphone or a smartphone) using a microphone placed near the user's nose.

iii) Breath control for interactive gaming: Breath can be used to control a wide range of gaming applications [42, 64]. Marshall et al. [42] demonstrated the feasibility and benefits of breath control over thrill rides. Breathing phases including inhaling, exhaling, and holding the breath were detected by a chest strap and directly mapped to the horizontal rotation of a thrill chair. Tennent et al. [64] examined breath control via a gas mask embedded with flow sensors. Five customized games were chosen to investigate breath as a mechanism to control them. Besides the aforementioned breathing phases, breathing frequency was used as an additional control mechanism. Instead our primary focus is to use breathing gestures as a means for user authentication.

iii) Breath monitoring for respiratory disorder detection: Auscultation of body sounds has long been an important part in both sleep and breathing related studies. Many systems were proposed to continuously monitor and detect abnormal breathing activities such as wheezes [63, 29], crackles [40, 58], and snores [5, 73]. Azarbarzin et al. [5] devloped a snoring detection algorithm for breathing sounds captured by two microphones, one over the tracheal and the other one in the air. A vertical box method was applied to detect activity episodes and frame level features were then extracted in each episode. Using an unsupervised fuzzy C-means clustering algorithm, episodes with snoring activities were labeled. A similar segmentation method was also used by Yadollahi et al. [73] to study sleep apnea detection. Jain et al. [29] developed a wheeze detection method using frame-level FFT on 50 ms Hamming windows. A frame was selected if a frequency peak is detected and subsequent frames have frequency peaks within the 30 Hz range. A continuity check was performed to find episodes with more than 250 ms of duration.

In our case, one recording only contains one periodically repetitive pattern and no classification is needed for the initial cropping stage. Therefore instead of using moving windows and comparing signal powers across the whole original recording, our cropping algorithm simply cuts the recording into pieces according to the detected frequency.

iv) Behavioural biometrics for user authentication: Acoustic features from user speech have been used to design systems for speaker recognition [19, 57, 52, 10, 17, 8]. However, voice can be easily spoofed, especially using replay [39] (27.3% and 70.0% FPR), text to speech [16], and voice conversion attacks [48, 34]. Various works [20, 37, 59, 54, 72, 11] have used touch gestures such as taps, swipes, and multiple fingers for user authentication on touchscreen devices. These works report a very low EER (Equal Error Rate) in the range of 1%-5%. However, all these works fail to test the security of touch gestures in the presence of sophisticated attacks such as shoulder surfing or video based observation

Table 4: Comparison Between Different Systems
(x – Not Applicable)

Work	Modality	Hardware	Application	FPR (Random)	FPR (Targeted)	TPR
Woosh [50]	Blow air (mouth)	Commodity	Gesture Recognition	x	x	x
Tennet et al. [64]	Breath Flow	Specialized	Game Control	x	x	x
Zhao et al. [75]	ECG	Specialized	Authentication	8.7	x	91.3
Venugopalan et al. [67]	EMG	Specialized	Authentication	10.0	x	97.3
Eberz et al. [18]	Eye Movements	Specialized	Authentication	4.0	x	96.0
Shahzad et al. [59]	Swipes	Commodity	Authentication	4.0	2.1	94.6
Gafurov et al. [21]	Gait	Commodity	Authentication	13.0	15.0	87.0
Hautamaki et al. [27]	Audio	Commodity	Authentication	9.0	11.6	91.0
Ours	Breathing Gestures	Commodity	Authentication	0.5	2.0	98.0

attacks. Recently, a study from Khan et al. [30] pointed out that touch gestures are highly susceptible to such attacks. The way a person walks (gait) has also been proposed in the literature [41, 65, 78] for user authentication. The EER achieved with gait in these works varied between 4%-9%. However, gait based biometrics are vulnerable to sophisticated attackers [21]. Additionally, a person has to walk in order to be authenticated.

Behavioural biometrics based on heart rate (ECG) [75], electrical activity of skeleton muscles (EMG) [9], eye movements [18], and electrical activity of the brain (EEG) [13] have been proposed in the literature. All of these methods require special apparatus to be attached to the body of the person. On the contrary, the major advantage of our proposed modality is its pervasive nature: a simple smartphone-embedded microphone is more widely available and ubiquitously usable than specialized hardware (fingerprint sensor, or heart rate sensor), which can achieve higher accuracy but often needs to be mounted on specific body locations (e.g., on the chest). Table 4 shows the comparison between our work and some of the existing works. For our work we show the results of deep breathing gesture as it provides the best balance between TPR and FPR while preventing targeted attacks.

Complementing the earlier works, we have introduced a new behavioural biometric, which is usable, easily deployable, accessible, highly resilient to several kind of attacks and can be combined with other modalities to provide highly secure multimodal biometric authentication systems.

7. DISCUSSION AND LIMITATIONS

Additional Attack Modalities: We have demonstrated that our proposed biometric is resilient to basic impersonation and audio replay attacks. However, we have not considered more sophisticated attacks, such as the voice conversion attack (well-known in speaker recognition systems). In this attack, an expert attacker can perform fine-grained manipulation of the frequency components and amplitude of audio samples. In another example, a sophisticated attacker equipped with a large directional array of sensitive microphones and good signal processing skills can pick up the signal from a considerable distance (a microphone array could be built using tightly time synchronized discrete units rather than a large visible physical array of antenna). We believe that although such attacks are possible, they require highly motivated attackers with significant time and resources at their disposal. Also, as breathing-based authentication involves both frequencies, as well as temporal, components (the duration of breathing gestures), it may prove more resilient to such attacks. Nonetheless, they need to be investigated. Techniques from speech verification systems to counter replay attacks [68, 69] and voice conversion attacks [3] can be borrowed to prevent such attacks in any acoustics based authentication system.

Physiological Context: Our studies in Section 5.4 demonstrate the robustness of the system under certain short-term *extrinsic* contextual factors, such as physical activity. However, breathing-related features are also likely to exhibit longer timescale changes, due to *intrinsic* physiological changes, such as aging and decrease in the lung capacity. Longitudinal studies are needed to establish how sensitive *BreathPrint* is to such changes. We also did not study *BreathPrint's* sensitivity to short-term intrinsic context, such as when someone is sick or has breathing difficulties. Such sensitivity is common to other biometrics-based authentication approaches as well. For example, fingerprint-based authentication is known to fail if there is a severe cut on the user's finger. Additionally, to understand other possible unexpected context related deficiencies, we need to perform an extensive longitudinal study, which involves collecting data from a large number of users. We are developing a smartphone app to enable such large-scale, longitudinal data collection. As collecting data for all possible contexts is challenging, we plan to also use data augmentation techniques [53, 36] to synthesize new data.

Intermittent vs. Continuous Authentication: Our canonical usage model has involved the use of *deliberate* breathing gestures, performed solely for authentication purposes–e.g., the user breathing into the microphone of a smartphone. Given the non-stop nature of breathing, future possibilities include the use of one or more microphones that provide continuous, breathing-based authentication of a user in a non-intrusive way. *A particularly exciting case might be that of a smartglass*: a microphone embedded in the lower rim of the glass should be able to pick up the natural breathing sounds. Such breathing-based authentication and interaction might be especially appealing in assisted-living environments, where breathing gestures may be used to control lights, turn on/off appliances etc.

Realizing this vision will require additional advances, such as (i) Improved segmentation: our current pipeline segments breathing gestures based on the knowledge that the user is deliberately performing one of the three predefined breathing gestures. This does not apply to the case of continuous, natural breathing; and (ii) Energy efficiency: Microphones on wearable platforms typically incur high energy overhead and cannot be operated continuously. However, it may be possible to design special-purpose microphones, operating at low duty cycles and low sampling frequency for detecting the low-frequency breathing-based features.

Multimodal Sensing and Authentication: *BreathPrint* currently uses only audio sensing of selected breathing gestures. There is a body of work that uses additional sensor data as an attestation mechanism–e.g., the use of motion estimates, based on inertial sensing to provide greater resiliency to 2-D face authentication systems against photo/video attacks [12]. Similar approaches can be applied to breathing gestures as well, especially if additional sensors are placed at locations that can sense the breathing-related motion artifacts (e.g., inertial sensing on a smartglass).

Device-independence: In this study, we primarily evaluated the model using the data collected from same hardware (either a laptop or a smartphone). To explore the device-dependence of such models, we need to verify: i) Is it possible to train the model on one device and test on another device?, and ii) what parameters need to be adjusted to make cross device transferability viable? Robust cross-device models may prove to be widely deployable in emerging IoT-rich smart environments. To this end we are considering to use transfer learning methods [15] to create cross device adaptive models.

8. CONCLUSION

We have proposed a new authentication mechanism, called *BreathPrint*, for mobile and wearable devices. *BreathPrint* requires the user to perform three distinct, but commonplace, breathing gestures: sniff, normal, and deep, and uses audio captured by a microphone sensor to authenticate individuals. *BreathPrint* offers several advantages, such as accessibility, usability, deployability, and security. We show that *BreathPrint* has TPR rates of over 94% across all three gestures and also incurs very low FPR ($< 2\%$), even under directed *replay* and *impersonation* attacks. The authentication pipeline also proves to be quite robust to a selected set of artifacts, such as user activity and background noise. While larger, longer-lasting user studies are necessary, *BreathPrint* shows promise as a pervasive and novel method for identifying users in a variety of settings – e.g., in disambiguating between two sleeping individuals. We believe that *BreathPrint*, in tandem with other sensor modalities, can also prove to be an easy to use and robust mechanism for continuous authentication in future wearable and IoT platforms.

9. ACKNOWLEDGMENTS

The authors would like to thank the anonymous reviewers and the shepherd Mary Baker (HP Labs) for constructive feedback on preparation of the final version of this paper.

This research is supported partially by Singapore Ministry of Education Academic Research Fund Tier 2 under research grant MOE2014-T2-1063, and by the National Research Foundation, Prime Ministers Office, Singapore under its IDM Futures Funding Initiative. All findings and recommendations are those of the authors and do not necessarily reflect the views of the granting agency, or SMU.

10. REFERENCES

[1] H. Abdelnasser, K. A. Harras, and M. Youssef. Ubibreathe: A ubiquitous non-invasive wifi-based breathing estimator. In *MobiHoc*, pages 277–286. ACM, 2015.

[2] A. Aertsen, P. Johannesma, and D. Hermes. Spectro-temporal receptive fields of auditory neurons in the grassfrog. *Biological Cybernetics*, 38(4):235–248, 1980.

[3] F. Alegre, A. Amehraye, and N. Evans. Spoofing countermeasures to protect automatic speaker verification from voice conversion. In *ICASSP*, pages 3068–3072. IEEE, 2013.

[4] H. Aly and M. Youssef. Zephyr: Ubiquitous accurate multi-sensor fusion-based respiratory rate estimation using smartphones. In *INFOCOM*, pages 1–9. IEEE, 2016.

[5] A. Azarbarzin and Z. M. Moussavi. Automatic and unsupervised snore sound extraction from respiratory sound signals. *IEEE Transactions on Biomedical Engineering*, 58(5):1156–1162, 2011.

[6] A. Bajtarevic, C. Ager, M. Pienz, M. Klieber, K. Schwarz, M. Ligor, T. Ligor, W. Filipiak, H. Denz, M. Fiegl, et al. Noninvasive detection of lung cancer by analysis of exhaled breath. *BMC cancer*, 9(1):1, 2009.

[7] L. Boccanfuso and J. M. O'Kane. Remote measurement of breathing rate in real time using a high precision, single-point infrared temperature sensor. In *Biomedical Robotics and Biomechatronics*, pages 1704–1709. IEEE, 2012.

[8] W. M. Campbell, D. E. Sturim, and D. A. Reynolds. Support vector machines using gmm supervectors for speaker verification. *IEEE signal processing letters*, 13(5):308–311, 2006.

[9] J. Cannan and H. Hu. Automatic user identification by using forearm biometrics. In *Advanced Intelligent Mechatronics*, pages 710–715. IEEE, 2013.

[10] M. J. Carey, E. S. Parris, and J. S. Bridle. A speaker verification system using alpha-nets. In *ICASSP*, pages 397–400. IEEE, 1991.

[11] J. Chauhan, H. J. Asghar, M. A. Kaafar, and A. Mahanti. Gesture-based Continuous Authentication for Wearable Devices: The Smart Glasses Use Case. In *ACNS*, pages 648–665. Springer, 2016.

[12] S. Chen, A. Pande, and P. Mohapatra. Sensor-assisted facial recognition: an enhanced biometric authentication system for smartphones. In *MobiSys*, pages 109–122. ACM, 2014.

[13] J. Chuang, H. Nguyen, C. Wang, and B. Johnson. I think, therefore i am: Usability and security of authentication using brainwaves. In *FC*, pages 1–16. Springer, 2013.

[14] P. Corbishley and E. Rodríguez-Villegas. Breathing detection: towards a miniaturized, wearable, battery-operated monitoring system. *IEEE Transactions on Biomedical Engineering*, 55(1):196–204, 2008.

[15] W. Dai, Y. Chen, G.-R. Xue, Q. Yang, and Y. Yu. Translated learning: Transfer learning across different feature spaces. In *NIPS*, pages 353–360, 2008.

[16] P. L. De Leon, M. Pucher, J. Yamagishi, I. Hernaez, and I. Saratxaga. Evaluation of speaker verification security and detection of hmm-based synthetic speech. *IEEE Transactions on Audio, Speech, and Language Processing*, 20(8):2280–2290, 2012.

[17] N. Dehak, P. J. Kenny, R. Dehak, P. Dumouchel, and P. Ouellet. Front-end factor analysis for speaker

verification. *IEEE Transactions on Audio, Speech, and Language Processing*, 19(4):788–798, 2011.

[18] S. Eberz, K. B. Rasmussen, V. Lenders, and I. Martinovic. Preventing lunchtime attacks: Fighting insider threats with eye movement biometrics. In *NDSS*. Internet Society, 2015.

[19] K. R. Farrell, R. J. Mammone, and K. T. Assaleh. Speaker recognition using neural networks and conventional classifiers. *IEEE Transactions on speech and audio processing*, 2(1):194–205, 1994.

[20] M. Frank, R. Biedert, E. Ma, I. Martinovic, and D. Song. Touchalytics: On the Applicability of Touchscreen Input as a Behavioral Biometric for Continuous Authentication. *IEEE TIFS*, 8(1):136–148, 2013.

[21] D. Gafurov, E. Snekkenes, and P. Bours. Spoof attacks on gait authentication system. *IEEE TIFS*, 2(3):491–502, 2007.

[22] G. Gamez, L. Zhu, A. Disko, H. Chen, V. Azov, K. Chingin, G. Krämer, and R. Zenobi. Real-time, in vivo monitoring and pharmacokinetics of valproic acid via a novel biomarker in exhaled breath. *Chemical Communications*, 47(17):4884–4886, 2011.

[23] N. Gavriely, M. Nissan, A. Rubin, and D. W. Cugell. Spectral characteristics of chest wall breath sounds in normal subjects. *Thorax*, 50(12):1292–1300, 1995.

[24] B. R. Glasberg and B. C. Moore. Derivation of auditory filter shapes from notched-noise data. *Hearing research*, 47(1-2):103–138, 1990.

[25] V. Gross, A. Dittmar, T. Penzel, F. Schuttler, and P. Von Wichert. The relationship between normal lung sounds, age, and gender. *American journal of respiratory and critical care medicine*, 162(3):905–909, 2000.

[26] T. Hao, G. Xing, and G. Zhou. isleep: unobtrusive sleep quality monitoring using smartphones. In *SenSys*, page 4. ACM, 2013.

[27] R. G. Hautamäki, T. Kinnunen, V. Hautamäki, T. Leino, and A.-M. Laukkanen. I-vectors meet imitators: on vulnerability of speaker verification systems against voice mimicry. In *INTERSPEECH*, pages 930–934. Citeseer, 2013.

[28] J. He, P. M.-L. Sinues, M. Hollmén, X. Li, M. Detmar, and R. Zenobi. Fingerprinting breast cancer vs. normal mammary cells by mass spectrometric analysis of volatiles. *Scientific reports*, 4, 2014.

[29] A. Jain and J. Vepa. Lung sound analysis for wheeze episode detection. In *Engineering in Medicine and Biology Society*, pages 2582–2585. IEEE, 2008.

[30] H. Khan, U. Hengartner, and D. Vogel. Targeted Mimicry Attacks on Touch Input Based Implicit Authentication Schemes. In *MobiSys '16*, pages 387–398. ACM, 2016.

[31] C. Kim and R. M. Stern. Power-normalized cepstral coefficients (pncc) for robust speech recognition. In *ICASSP*, pages 4101–4104. IEEE, 2012.

[32] T. Kinnunen, E. Karpov, and P. Franti. Real-time speaker identification and verification. *IEEE Transactions on Audio, Speech, and Language Processing*, 14(1):277–288, 2006.

[33] T. Kinnunen and H. Li. An overview of text-independent speaker recognition: From features to supervectors. *Speech communication*, 52(1):12–40, 2010.

[34] T. Kinnunen, Z.-Z. Wu, K. A. Lee, F. Sedlak, E. S. Chng, and H. Li. Vulnerability of speaker verification systems against voice conversion spoofing attacks: The case of telephone speech. In *ICASSP*, pages 4401–4404. IEEE, 2012.

[35] E. C. Larson, T. Lee, S. Liu, M. Rosenfeld, and S. N. Patel. Accurate and privacy preserving cough sensing using a low-cost microphone. In *UbiComp*, pages 375–384. ACM, 2011.

[36] H. Lee, P. Pham, Y. Largman, and A. Y. Ng. Unsupervised feature learning for audio classification using convolutional deep belief networks. In *NIPS*, pages 1096–1104, 2009.

[37] L. Li, X. Zhao, and G. Xue. Unobservable Re-authentication for Smartphones. In *NDSS*. Internet Society, 2013.

[38] Q. Li, J. Zheng, A. Tsai, and Q. Zhou. Robust endpoint detection and energy normalization for real-time speech and speaker recognition. *IEEE Transactions on Speech and Audio Processing*, 10(3):146–157, 2002.

[39] J. Lindberg, M. Blomberg, et al. Vulnerability in speaker verification-a study of technical impostor techniques. In *Eurospeech*, volume 99, pages 1211–1214, 1999.

[40] X. Lu and M. Bahoura. An automatic system for crackles detection and classification. In *Canadian Conference on Electrical and Computer Engineering*, pages 725–729. IEEE, 2006.

[41] J. Mantyjarvi, M. Lindholm, E. Vildjiounaite, S.-M. Makela, and H. Ailisto. Identifying users of portable devices from gait pattern with accelerometers. In *ICASSP.*, volume 2, pages 973–976. IEEE, 2005.

[42] J. Marshall, D. Rowland, S. Rennick Egglestone, S. Benford, B. Walker, and D. McAuley. Breath control of amusement rides. In *CHI*, pages 73–82. ACM, 2011.

[43] J. Mead and S. H. Loring. Analysis of volume displacement and length changes of the diaphragm during breathing. *Journal of Applied Physiology*, 53(3):750–755, 1982.

[44] R. Nandakumar, S. Gollakota, and N. Watson. Contactless sleep apnea detection on smartphones. In *MobiSys*, pages 45–57. ACM, 2015.

[45] H. Pasterkamp, S. S. Kraman, and G. R. Wodicka. Respiratory sounds: advances beyond the stethoscope. *American journal of respiratory and critical care medicine*, 156(3):974–987, 1997.

[46] H. Pasterkamp, R. E. Powell, and I. Sanchez. Lung sound spectra at standardized air flow in normal infants, children, and adults. *American journal of respiratory and critical care medicine*, 154(2):424–430, 1996.

[47] H. Pasterkamp, J. Schafer, and G. R. Wodicka. Posture-dependent change of tracheal sounds at standardized flows in patients with obstructive sleep apnea. *CHEST Journal*, 110(6):1493–1498, 1996.

[48] P. Perrot, G. Aversano, R. Blouet, M. Charbit, and G. Chollet. Voice forgery using alisp: Indexation in a client memory. In *ICASSP*, pages 17–20. IEEE, 2005.

[49] T. Rahman, A. T. Adams, M. Zhang, E. Cherry, B. Zhou, H. Peng, and T. Choudhury. Bodybeat: A mobile system for sensing non-speech body sounds. In *MobiSys*, pages 2–13. ACM, 2014.

[50] G. Reyes, D. Zhang, S. Ghosh, P. Shah, J. Wu, A. Parnami, B. Bercik, T. Starner, G. D. Abowd, and W. K. Edwards. Whoosh: non-voice acoustics for low-cost, hands-free, and rapid input on smartwatches. In *ISWC*, pages 120–127. ACM, 2016.

[51] D. Reynolds. An overview of automatic speaker recognition. In *ICASSP*, pages 4072–407. IEEE, 2002.

[52] D. A. Reynolds and R. C. Rose. Robust text-independent speaker identification using gaussian mixture speaker models. *IEEE transactions on speech and audio processing*, 3(1):72–83, 1995.

[53] G. Rogez and C. Schmid. Mocap-guided data augmentation for 3d pose estimation in the wild. In *NIPS*, pages 3108–3116, 2016.

[54] N. Sae-Bae, K. Ahmed, K. Isbister, and N. Memon. Biometric-rich gestures: A novel approach to authentication on multi-touch devices. In *CHI*, pages 977–986. ACM, 2012.

[55] I. Sanchez and H. Pasterkamp. Tracheal sound spectra depend on body height. *American Review of Respiratory Disease*, 148:1083–1083, 1993.

[56] R. Schluter, I. Bezrukov, H. Wagner, and H. Ney. Gammatone features and feature combination for large vocabulary speech recognition. In *ICASSP*, volume 4, pages 649–652. IEEE, 2007.

[57] M. Schmidt and H. Gish. Speaker identification via support vector classifiers. In *ICASSP*, volume 1, pages 105–108. IEEE, 1996.

[58] G. Serbes, C. O. Sakar, Y. P. Kahya, and N. Aydin. Effect of different window and wavelet types on the performance of a novel crackle detection algorithm. In *International Conference on Hybrid Information Technology*, pages 575–581. Springer, 2011.

[59] M. Shahzad, A. X. Liu, and A. Samuel. Secure Unlocking of Mobile Touch Screen Devices by Simple Gestures: You Can See It but You Can Not Do It. In *MobiCom*, pages 39–50. ACM, 2013.

[60] J. Sharp, J. Henry, S. Sweany, W. Meadows, and R. Pietras. The total work of breathing in normal and obese men. *Journal of Clinical Investigation*, 43(4):728, 1964.

[61] P. M.-L. Sinues, M. Kohler, and R. Zenobi. Human breath analysis may support the existence of individual metabolic phenotypes. *PloS one*, 8(4):e59909, 2013.

[62] X. Sun, Z. Lu, W. Hu, and G. Cao. Symdetector: Detecting sound-related respiratory symptoms using smartphones. In *UbiComp*, pages 97–108. ACM, 2015.

[63] S. A. Taplidou and L. J. Hadjileontiadis. Wheeze detection based on time-frequency analysis of breath sounds. *Computers in biology and medicine*, 37(8):1073–1083, 2007.

[64] P. Tennent, D. Rowland, J. Marshall, S. R. Egglestone, A. Harrison, Z. Jaime, B. Walker, and S. Benford. Breathalising games: understanding the potential of breath control in game interfaces. In *International Conference on Advances in Computer Entertainment Technology*, page 58. ACM, 2011.

[65] H. M. Thang, V. Q. Viet, N. D. Thuc, and D. Choi. Gait identification using accelerometer on mobile phone. In *ICCAIS*, pages 344–348. IEEE, 2012.

[66] X. Valero and F. Alias. Gammatone cepstral coefficients: Biologically inspired features for non-speech audio classification. *IEEE Transactions on Multimedia*, 14(6):1684–1689, 2012.

[67] S. Venugopalan, F. Juefei-Xu, B. Cowley, and M. Savvides. Electromyograph and keystroke dynamics for spoof-resistant biometric authentication. In *CVPR Workshops*, pages 109–118. IEEE, 2015.

[68] J. Villalba and E. Lleida. Detecting replay attacks from far-field recordings on speaker verification systems. In *European Workshop on Biometrics and Identity Management*, pages 274–285. Springer, 2011.

[69] J. Villalba and E. Lleida. Preventing replay attacks on speaker verification systems. In *ICCST*, pages 1–8. IEEE, 2011.

[70] L. Weisi, D. Tao, J. Kacprzyk, Z. Li, E. Izquierdo, and H. Wang. *Multimedia analysis, processing and communications*, volume 346. Springer Science & Business Media, 2011.

[71] D. Wertheim, C. Olden, E. Savage, and P. Seddon. Extracting respiratory data from pulse oximeter plethysmogram traces in newborn infants. *Archives of Disease in Childhood-Fetal and Neonatal Edition*, 94(4):F301–F303, 2009.

[72] H. Xu, Y. Zhou, and M. R. Lyu. Towards Continuous and Passive Authentication via Touch Biometrics: An Experimental Study on Smartphones. In *SOUPS*, pages 187–198. ACM, 2014.

[73] A. Yadollahi, E. Giannouli, and Z. Moussavi. Sleep apnea monitoring and diagnosis based on pulse oximetery and tracheal sound signals. *Medical & biological engineering & computing*, 48(11):1087–1097, 2010.

[74] K. Yatani and K. N. Truong. Bodyscope: A wearable acoustic sensor for activity recognition. In *UbiComp*, pages 341–350. ACM, 2012.

[75] C. X. Zhao, T. Wysocki, F. Agrafioti, and D. Hatzinakos. Securing handheld devices and fingerprint readers with ecg biometrics. In *BTAS*, pages 150–155. IEEE, 2012.

[76] X. Zhao, Y. Shao, and D. Wang. Casa-based robust speaker identification. *IEEE Transactions on Audio, Speech, and Language Processing*, 20(5):1608–1616, 2012.

[77] X. Zhao and D. Wang. Analyzing noise robustness of MFCC and GFCC features in speaker identification. In *ICASSP*, pages 7204–7208. IEEE, 2013.

[78] Y. Zhong, Y. Deng, and G. Meltzner. Pace independent mobile gait biometrics. In *BTAS*, pages 1–8. IEEE, 2015.

Glimpse: A Programmable Early-Discard Camera Architecture for Continuous Mobile Vision

Saman Naderiparizi
Microsoft
U. of Washington

Pengyu Zhang
Microsoft
U. of Massachusetts Amherst

Matthai Philipose
Microsoft

Bodhi Priyantha
Microsoft

Jie Liu
Microsoft

Deepak Ganesan
U. of Massachusetts Amherst

ABSTRACT

We consider the problem of continuous computer-vision based analysis of video streams from mobile cameras over extended periods. Given high computational demands, general visual processing must currently be offloaded to the cloud. To reduce mobile battery and bandwidth consumption, recent proposals offload only "interesting" video frames, discarding the rest. However, determining what to discard is itself typically a power-hungry computer vision calculation, very often well beyond what most mobile devices can afford on a continuous basis. We present the Glimpse system, a redesign of the conventional mobile video processing pipeline to support such "early discard" flexibly, efficiently and accurately. Glimpse is a novel architecture that gates wearable vision using low-power vision modalities. Our proposed architecture adds novel sensing, processing, algorithmic and programming-system components to the camera pipeline to this end. We present a complete implementation and evaluation of our design. In common settings, Glimpse reduces mobile power and data usage by more than one order of magnitude relative to earlier designs, and moves continuous vision on lightweight wearables to the realm of the practical.

Keywords

Continuous mobile vision; low-power early discard; low-power vision modalities; energy efficient wearable vision system

(a)

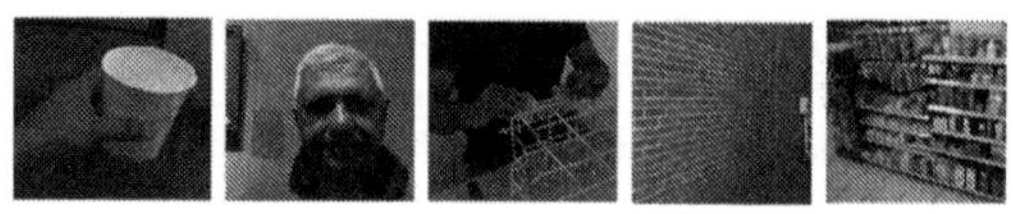

(b)

Figure 1: **Glimpse prototype and its applicability.** (a) Glimpse prototype board (size 5 × 8cm) (b) Entities of interest to applications: the wearer's hands [41], their conversational partners' faces [25], their partners' limbs [7], nearby walls [8, 47] and indoor places [44].

1. INTRODUCTION

Continuous visual analysis of video from wearable devices has the potential to enable many applications beyond those based on conventional wearable sensors such as accelerometers and GPS [4, 14, 24, 30, 43]. However, modern computer vision techniques, such as those based on Deep Neural Networks, have resource demands that require cloud-based servers rather than mobile processors [16]. The obvious solution, off-loading all computer vision to the cloud, drains the typical mobile battery within two hours, motivating a solution that can inexpensively select a few frames for cloud processing. To our knowledge, no mobile-battery-based solution to date is able to run continuously for a 10-hour day while allowing flexible selection of informative frames. In this paper, we present Glimpse, a hardware-software add-on to the traditional mobile imaging pipeline that allows frames to be selected for processing *efficiently*, averaging under 100mW over a 10-hour day, and *flexibly*, allowing safe application-level extension.

For continuous functioning, a frame-selection subsystem must address the *resource-accuracy tradeoff* between resource usage, i.e., restricting the execution cost of rejection so it can run for extended periods, and accuracy, i.e., rejecting as many uninteresting frames as possible while preserving the interesting ones. A traditional solution to this problem is to use low-power sensors such as inertial, light [21], time [22] and even skin conductance [19] to trigger frame selection. These techniques score high on the resource-usage axis, since these sensors usually consume orders of magnitude less power than the image processing pipeline. However, in terms

Permission to make digital or hard copies of all or part of this work for personal or classroom use is granted without fee provided that copies are not made or distributed for profit or commercial advantage and that copies bear this notice and the full citation on the first page. Copyrights for components of this work owned by others than ACM must be honored. Abstracting with credit is permitted. To copy otherwise, or republish, to post on servers or to redistribute to lists, requires prior specific permission and/or a fee. Request permissions from permissions@acm.org.

MobiSys'17, June 19-23, 2017, Niagara Falls, NY, USA
© 2017 ACM. ISBN 978-1-4503-4928-4/17/06...$15.00
DOI: http://dx.doi.org/10.1145/3081333.3081347

of accuracy, i.e. detecting all events of interest, they are limited: many situations of interest are simply not detectable using low-datarate sensors.

At the other end of the spectrum are approaches that use (less expensive) visual processing to trigger more expensive visual processing. Such vision-based triggers can be quite rich relative to sensors, and include, e.g., those based on pixel values (e.g., faces [25]), depth values (e.g., foreground [8]) or temporal variation (e.g., "change" detection [9]). However, because they re-use existing machinery (imagers, algorithms and processors) for visual processing, these approaches are limited by the design assumptions baked into these components:

- **Imagers** The quality of imaging necessary for selection is often much less then that for recognition. E.g., face detection works well at 25×25 grayscale [49] pixel resolution; recognition requires 200×200 color [40].
- **Algorithms** Particular selection tasks often require much less precision than general algorithms provide. E.g., detecting a camera-wearer's hand may only require checking if a pixel is within 1m, whereas a stereo depth system may return cm-level depth for every pixel.
- **Processors** Standard mobile application processors may be energy inefficient because of the mismatch between highly parallelizable image computations and the inherently sequential nature of CPUs. For example, temporal frame differencing for change detection can easily keep a mobile applications processor busy [9], impractical for day-long processing.

To avoid the overhead of reusing the standard vision pipeline while preserving the benefits of vision-based frame selection, we advocate that **vision-based frame selection be treated as a first-class design goal, with a corresponding dedicated hardware/software subsystem in a mobile device**. To this end, we present Glimpse, a system dedicated to discarding uninteresting frames by itself performing coarse visual processing at very low power. Glimpse combines several novel components in a novel way: An array of *gating sensors and imagers* (including a thermal imager and a stereo pair) draws substantially lower power than the primary imager, and is adequate for many selection (but possibly, not deeper analysis) tasks. A suite of *coarse image processing* algorithms is optimized for common early rejection sub-tasks using the gating imagers. A dedicated efficient *gating computation fabric*, comprising of a low-power microcontroller and an FPGA, with efficient access to the gating imagers, is designed to execute (coarse) vision algorithms more efficiently than the standard CPU/DRAM model. A simple programming model, based on *rejection cascades*, allows applications to combine the output of gating sensors into efficient, customized frame-selection classifiers.

Glimpse is fully implemented as a modular circuit board (Figure 1a) and embedded software. We tested its frame selection abilities by wearing it for 15 hours over 3 days and programming it to select frames where a new person entered the personal space of the wearer (as a front end for social assistance [25, 33]), and those where the wearer's hand came in the field of view (as a front end for activity tracking applications [41, 50]). Glimpse is able to detect frames representing events of interest over 87% (100%) of the time for visual

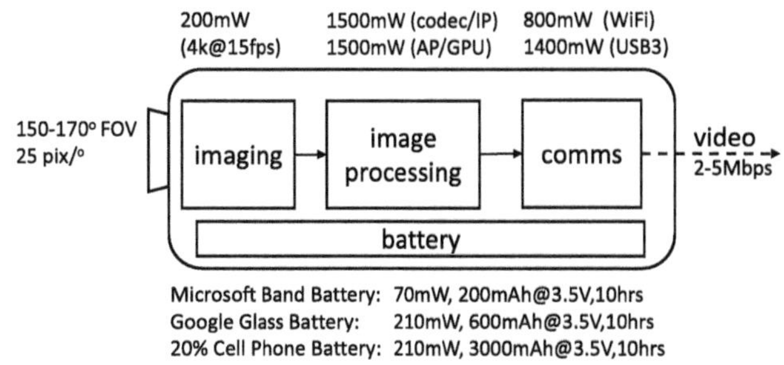

Figure 2: **Wearable camera pipeline.** Day-long continuous operation off a band/wearable-sized battery is infeasible with the conventional wearable camera systems pipeline.

events longer than 1s (3s) while drawing roughly 41-54mW for frame selection and 43-153mW in total. These represent a 10-20× improvement over state-of-the-art mobile application processor based implementations. We believe our work is a significant step toward day-long, programmable, continuous vision on wearable-device energy budgets.

2. BACKGROUND AND MOTIVATION

Figure 2 illustrates the structure and key performance characteristics of a wearable camera pipeline comprised of state-of-the art components. The basic pipeline consists of a high-resolution, large field of view color imager[1] feeding into a compression and/or image processing subsystem. The resulting video stream is either stored on board (not shown) or transmitted using either wireless or wired communications ("comms") module. In the figure, we detail the power *consumption* of each component above the camera, and also specify the average power *budget* of the entire camera, under varying battery assumptions, below the camera.

We now consider two configurations. In the "full offload" model, we could compress the resulting frames into a video stream and offload it to, e.g., the cloud. Compression, via a codec/image processor (IP) combination, would require at least another 1.5W on top of about 200mW high-resolution camera power consumption [1], and the resulting stream would require a steady 800mW or more to offload via WiFi (and considerably more via WWAN). In the "selective offload" model, we could use an application processor (AP) to detect and transmit frames of interest. Keeping up with high-resolution 15fps would easily require multiple cores, including GPU support [28], and consume 1.5W or more. In this latter model, we would hopefully need to transmit frames only a small fraction of the time (e.g., 10% of the time), so that transmission power in this case would be lower, say 10% of 800mW, say 80mW. In either model, average power draw from the camera would exceed 2W. These numbers are in line with recent reported mobile vision systems [9].

This level of power consumption is problematic for two reasons. First, as the lower part of Figure 2 shows, most reasonable battery configurations will only yield at most roughly 200mW. Thus, if the wearable device is to be powered by either a compact battery (a la Google Glass) or by a fraction of a cell-phone battery (a generous 20% of the battery), a constant power draw of 2W is roughly 10× more than is sustainable. Second, for wearable devices of the Glass

[1] A large field of view is critical to wearable devices because interesting events occur in a wide area in front of the user.

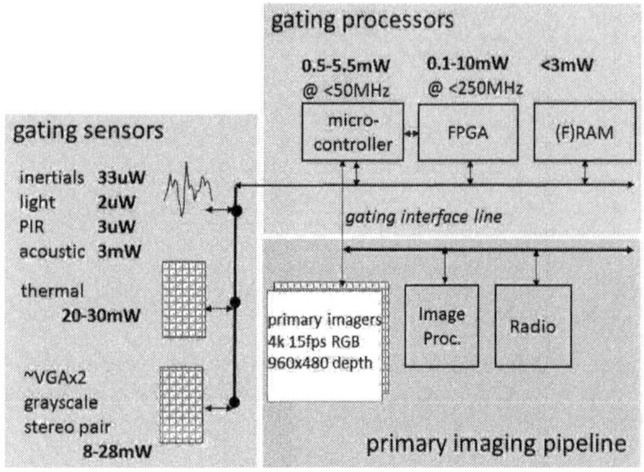

Figure 3: **The Glimpse hardware architecture.**

form factor, a reasonable rule of thumb is that each Watt of power dissipated raises the temperature of the device by 10°C [28] above its surroundings. The resulting 20°C (36°F) temperature rise is quite noticeable and potentially unpleasant for wearable devices. Thus even if it is feasible to power the entire camera via a wire connected to a large battery pack, e.g., police cameras (this is the "USB" transmit option in the figure), significantly reducing device power draw may be important.

3. SYSTEM ARCHITECTURE

We now present the hardware and software architecture of Glimpse.

3.1 Hardware Architecture

The primary imaging pipeline, as outlined in Section Section 2 and colored gray in Figure 3, will typically contain high-power imaging, computation and communications components that consume an order of magnitude more power than budgeted. Glimpse duty-cycles this pipeline so that aggregate power consumption is below budget, implying a duty cycle of 10% or less.

The design philosophy of Glimpse is to provide a variety of low-power sensing (crucially, including a variety of imaging options) and processing capabilities that can be combined in a flexible manner to select frames inexpensively for a given application. Glimpse therefore has two primary subsystems (green and orange in Figure 3). *Gating sensors* run at relatively high duty cycle compared to the primary imagers and must consume relatively little power. *Gating processors* initialize sensors, control communication with sensors, run application extensions on sensed data, and coordinate task execution with other processors.

Sensors typically run in the 1uW to tens of mW range. These sensors are selected such that, for many applications, they can (individually or collectively) predict whether the primary imagers are likely to detect events of interest to the application at any given time. Note that, crucially, gating sensors are not required to detect the interesting events themselves. Thus, for example:

The **inertial sensor** (accelerometer and gyroscope) may indicate that the velocity of the camera is high enough that motion blur will make it unlikely that faces, or other specific objects, can be detected or recognized.

The **light sensor** may indicate that light levels are not adequate for detection or recognition.

The **passive-infrared** sensor, which is triggered when the thermal signature of the field of view changes, may indicate that it is unlikely that people or their parts are close to the camera in the field of view.

The **microphone**, with accompanying custom analog spectral decomposer for sub-mW acoustic feature extraction, may indicate, based on acoustic activity, that the wearer is in an uninteresting activity state (e.g., driving), or social context (e.g., not in conversation).

The **thermal (or far-infrared/FIR) imager**, which reports the temperature of every pixel in the field of view at 9 fps, may identify the *parts* of the field of view that are unlikely to contain people, vehicles, lights, monitors, etc as per their temperature.

The **VGA grayscale imager pair**, a pair of synchronized low-resolution grayscale imagers, from which a depth map of the field of view may be derived, may indicate that a part or whole of the field of view is too far/close to be of interest.

In every case, these sensors act as gatekeepers to the primary imagers, hence the term "gating" sensors. Good gating sensors have a few key characteristics:

1. Low power draw relative to the primary imager.
2. High information content in terms of predicting, for a variety of applications, the required behavior of the primary imaging pipeline *with high recall*: the gating sensor must seldom falsely imply that the primary imager need not wake up.
3. Low latency in making the prediction, since the primary imagers then need to be turned on to analyze the detected image.

The gating calculations themselves, which determine if a certain application is likely to find the current primary-imager frame interesting, are performed on the *gating processors*. These calculations range from simple digital IO checks (e.g., on motion detection using passive IR sensors) to lightweight computer vision algorithms (e.g., depth from stereo on the grayscale pair and object tracking on a thermal image). Gating processors must run at substantially lower power than the primary imaging pipeline. Glimpse achieves this by providing a very low-power microcontroller for simple calculations and user-friendly interface and a low power FPGA to handle the vision algorithms, with a small amount (e.g., 1 MB) of static RAM for buffering. The FPGA is also responsible for reading data from gating imagers, which allows FPGA-based vision algorithms to process pixels in a "streaming" manner as they are read off the imager *with no intermediate memory accesses*.

In summary, two aspects of the Glimpse hardware architecture are especially worth noting. First, it advocates the use of multiple possibly unconventional imaging technologies (e.g., thermal imager, low-power grayscale imager and stereo pair) dedicated to frame selection. Second, it incorporates dedicated programmable hardware (i.e., FPGAs) tightly coupled with these imagers for computations related to selection.

3.2 Software Architecture

The Glimpse software architecture is designed to allow applications to specify custom frame selection criteria in a sim-

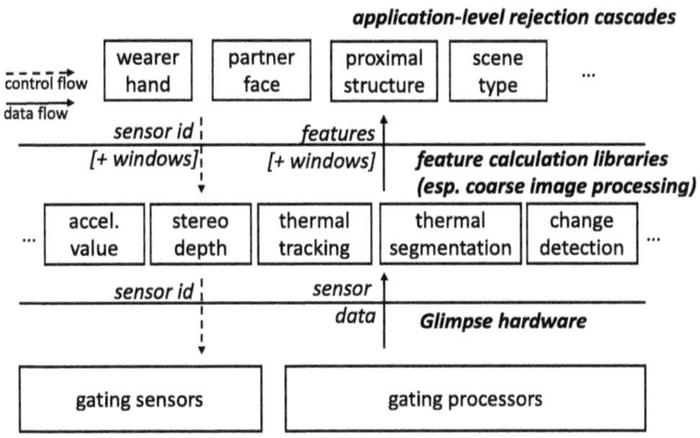

Figure 4: **The Glimpse software architecture.**

ple, expressive and safe manner. Several applications should be able to simultaneously register interest in frames, based on a rich range of conditions without interfering with each other, and without having to write Glimpse microcontroller or FPGA code.

Glimpse takes the perspective that frame selectors are essentially *cost-sensitive classification cascades* [49, 51]. As such, they can be divided into relatively heavyweight *feature calculation libraries* and lightweight *rejection cascades* (Figure 4), which applications can safely chain together to make increasingly expressive but efficient classifiers as described below.

3.2.1 Feature calculation libraries

Feature calculation is performed exclusively by optimized native libraries. Features range from simple wrappers around sensors like accelerometers to versions of visual primitives such as depth estimation, tracking, segmentation and change detection. Only feature calculators are allowed to interact directly with sensors. Feature calculation is optimized both via the design of new "coarse" versions of vision algorithms (discussed in Section 4), and also via careful implementation of these algorithms that, for instance, exploits the underlying hardware such as the FPGA.

Each feature calculation function is required to take as input a set of windows partitioning the field of view of the primary imager and return a set of windows, each annotated with a vector of values. For instance the "accelerometer" value feature calculator may ignore the contents of its input window and simply annotate it with system acceleration. On the other hand, the thermal segmentation function, given a window, returns a set of sub-windows along with the temperature for each window. The depth estimator annotates each of its input windows with the (coarse) depth of that window.

3.2.2 Interpreting rejection cascades

Applications are allowed to define *rejection cascades*, small programs that define classifiers. Glimpse provides a simple embedded *cascade interpreter* to execute the cascade and notify the primary imaging pipeline.

A cascade is a list of triples $(f_i, \hat{w}_i, t_i)$. Each triple consists of a reference f to a feature calculator, a vector $\hat{w}$ of linear-classification weights and a single scalar threshold value t. Given a set X_{i-1} of windows from the previous step of the cascade (the first step always starts with a single window that encompasses the entire field of view of the primary imager), the interpreter applies feature calculator f_i to produce a new set $X'_i = f(X_{i-1})$ of candidate windows and corresponding feature vectors V_i. For each candidate window $x'_{ij} \in X'_i$ and corresponding feature vector $\hat{v}_{ij} \in V_i$, the interpreter includes window x'_{ij} in set X_i for processing in the next cascade step if $t_i > \hat{v}_{ij}\hat{w}_i$, and rejects it otherwise. If, at any step, no windows remain to be forwarded, the interpreter stops. After the final stage of the cascade, if any (non-rejected) windows remain, the interpreter notifies the primary imaging pipeline to select a frame.

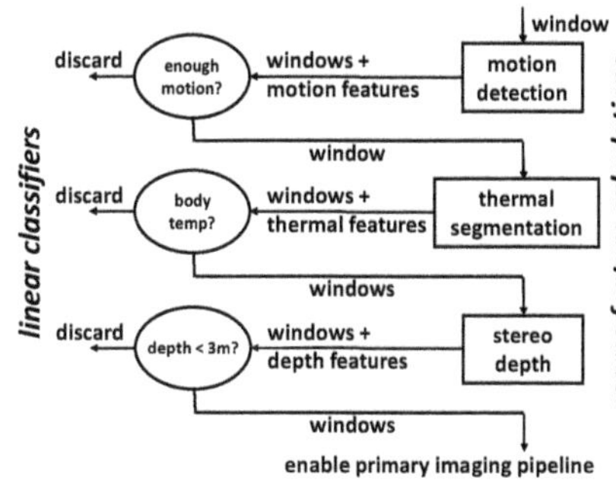

(a) Human + hand detection

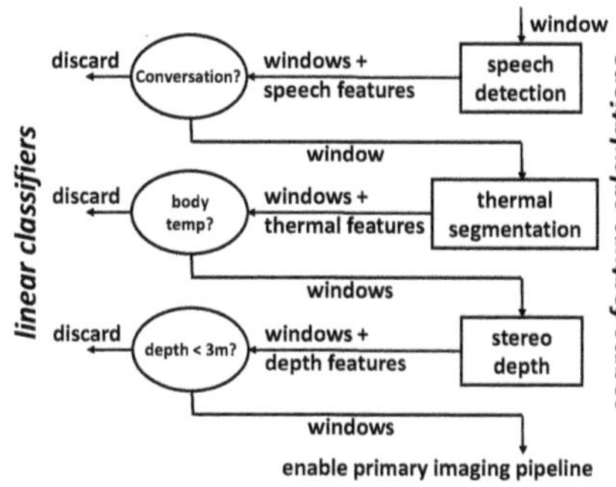

(b) Conversation partner detection

Figure 5: **Sample cascades.** 5a shows a cascade that detetcts if the wearer is either interacting with a human or with an object in his hand. 5b shows a cascade that triggers whenever the wearer is in conversation with another person.

In Figure 4, solid arrows represent data flow, and dashed lines control flow, during interpreter execution.

3.2.3 Sample cascades

Figure 5 illustrates two rejection cascades. Figure 5a shows a cascade that triggers whenever either the wearer is interacting with a human or an object in his hand. This requires existence of human body parts closer than a certain distance (here set to 3m) from the wearer. It checks a motion-detector (typically passive infrared based) to check for adequate thermal activity in the field of view (either due to background or the wearer motion). If not, it discards the frame. If so, it uses thermal imager output to look for sub-windows in the frame that are at body temperature; if none are found, it rejects the frame. Finally, it checks the depth of the surviving sub-windows, retains any within 3 meters of distance and rejects the rest. If any windows survive, the primary imaging pipeline is enabled. Feature extractors that are inexpensive are expected earlier in the cascade, and more informative, and usually more expensive ones, later.

Changing the depth threshold from 3 meters to 1 meter will configure Glimpse to trigger only when the wearer's hand is in the field of view (e.g., detecting if the wearer is manipulating objects). These two cascades are evaluated in Section 7.

Similarly, Figure 5b illustrates another cascade that programs Glimpse to trigger whenever the wearer is in a conversation with another human. The steps are identical to the first cascade except here we replace "motion detection" step with "audio detection" which uses a low-power microphone and a microcontroller to detect if there is a conversation happening. A noteworthy point about this cascade is that the "speech detection" feature calculation library function consists of a simple linear classifier coupled with a hardware implementation of spectral features suitable for voice classification tasks [11, 32], yielding useful classification at the 1-mW power level.

We believe the Glimpse architecture attains a useful balance of simplicity, flexibility and safety. By providing optimized libraries that perform most of the heavy lifting, Glimpse makes programming simple. By allowing applications to nevertheless combine a variety of feature libraries in different orders, and by allowing early exits from processing these libraries, Glimpse programs stay expressive and fast. Finally, since applications can only specify linear orderings in which features may be calculated, it is relatively simple to bound the runtime cost of execution of cascades. In particular, because rejection cascades contain no application-level loops, their safety is relatively easy to ensure.

4. COARSE IMAGE PROCESSING

Early-discard systems such as Glimpse have different accuracy requirements from primary imaging pipelines. In particular, primary imagers must discriminate between several classes of interest, and achieve low false-positive *and* false-negative rates for each class. Early-discard systems, on the other hand, typically discriminate between a "background" or "uninteresting" class and interesting ones, often a task requiring less discriminatory power. More importantly, because the primary pipeline will re-process their results, they are only required to have low false negative rates (i.e., they should rarely reject interesting frames) and are allowed modest false-positive rates: as long as they let through only a small number of frames, it is acceptable for some large fraction of those frames to be uninteresting.

Glimpse exploits these less-stringent accuracy requirements by providing, via feature calculation libraries, *coarse* variants of several vision algorithms that are optimized for low false-negative but modest false-positive classification. We have found that *it is feasible to approximate many existing vision algorithms by systematically relaxing traditional computer vision design choices* such as distance metrics, accuracy, data representation bitwidth, output precision, trading off global for local search and "giving up" conservatively on hard cases. In the other words, we show that our approximated algorithms are not only more power efficient than their fine-grained variants, but they also provide satisfactory accuracy when coarser levels of granularity are sufficient. Below, we present two detailed case studies where we use such coarsening techniques, stereo-based depth estimation, and tracking in thermal video. We validate our design choices via measurement studies in Section 6.

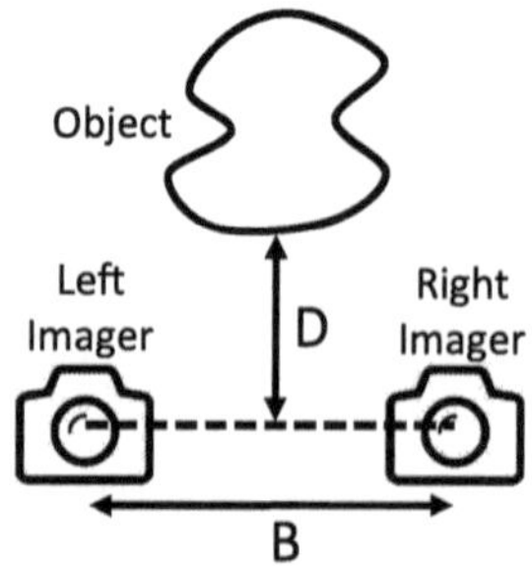

Figure 6: **Stereo vision setup.** An object at distance D in front of a stereo pair of cameras.

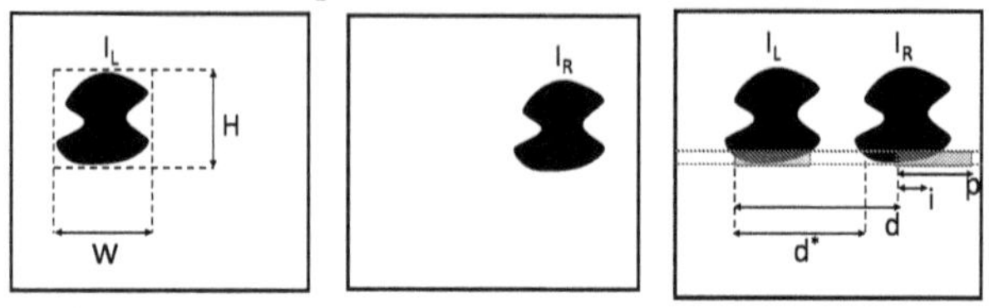

(a) left image (b) right image (c) superimposed

Figure 7: **Components of stereo matching.**

4.1 Coarse Stereo on FPGA

As illustrated in Figure 7, traditional stereo takes as input a pair of synchronized images ("left" and "right" images, Figures 7a and 7b) captured by two aligned imagers ("Left Imager" and "Right Imager" in Figure 6) at a fixed baseline distance B from each other. When the left and right images are superimposed (Figure 7c), the image I_L of a given rigid object in the left image is displaced from its image I_R by an x-distance of d^* pixels. The actual depth D of the object is inversely proportional to d^*, so that finding the displacement d^* between corresponding patches in an image (the "correspondence problem") is the central computation in stereo vision [18].

For each original patch at pixel (x, y) in the left image, say the gray length-p patch in Figure 7c, the check is performed by iterating over every length-p *candidate* patch in the corresponding row of the right image (say the relative offset, or *disparity* of the new patch is d pixels), calculating a patch difference metric Δ between the candidate patch (e.g., the green one in Figure 7c) and the original one, and finding disparity d^* that minimizes Δ:

$$d^*(x,y) = \arg\min_d \Delta(I_L(x : x+p, y), I_R(x+d : x+d+p, y)) \tag{1}$$

We optimize this calculation in several ways to reduce power and real-estate consumption on our FPGA. Our goal is a *coarse* depth algorithm that (a) only reports a few discrete depth levels (e.g., 1m, 3m and ∞), and (b) only detects objects greater than a minimum size up to a minimum distance (e.g., size 10cm up to 3m).

4.1.1 Relaxed Distance Metric

Glimpse relaxes the distance measure Δ. The standard measure sum-of-squares (SOS). We instead use the sum of absolute difference (SAD) [26]:

$$\Delta(I_L(x : x+p, y), I_R(x+d : x+d+p, y)) = \sum_{i=1}^{p} |I_L(x+i, y) - I_R((x+i+d), y)| \tag{2}$$

SAD can be implemented in FPGA fabric using a subtrac-

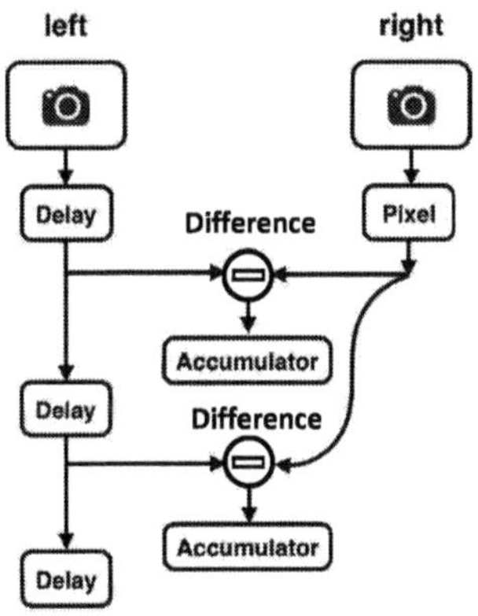

Figure 8: **Microarchitectural support for buffer-free disparity checking.**

tion followed by a comparison, and is significantly less complex than SOS, which requires multiplications.

4.1.2 *Buffer-Free Microarchitecture*

Most imagers output the pixels of each frame row-by-row. Traditional stereo algorithms read the entire frame out to memory (typically DRAM) and then iterate on this buffered data when solving Equation 1. Such a buffered implementation requires almost continuous access to on-board DRAM, adding a significant overhead to the stereo subsystem power draw. To eliminate the overhead of buffering in memory, we implement the correspondence algorithm in a streaming fashion.

The key observation is that finding the correspondence between two rows of spatially separated pixels translates to finding the correspondence between delayed variants of the pixels as they stream out from the imagers. Figure 8 shows the hardware architecture of the depth calculator design. This is composed of three HW building blocks: delay, computing absolute difference between pixels, and accumulator, which adds in and stores the running sum.

Delays are used to shift the pixel stream coming from the left image sensor by the various disparity levels d we wish to try. The delayed pixels from the left image are differenced with the pixels from the right image. Each accumulator then aggregates the results and outputs the measure of similarity for the two image windows associated with a particular delay length. The optimal disparity for a particular window is the delay value which minimizes the similarity measure.

An important implication of the above design is that every iteration of the minimization loop over d in Equation 1 has corresponding circuitry on the FPGA (i.e., the loop is unrolled). Further, within the accumulator, the area of SAD circuitry itself is proportional to the bitwidth of the pixel values being SAD'ed. In addition to avoid buffers, this design has the advantage that these operations can be parallelized, but poses the challenge of requiring additional real-estate.

4.1.3 *Low-Bitwidth Pixel Representation*

Most off-the-shelf cameras use 7 or 8 bits to represent monochrome pixels. We hypothesize that *if only coarse depth estimates are required,* it is possible to truncate the least significant bits (LSB) of the pixels $I(x, y)$ while introducing little error. Note that a few bits of truncation makes the resulting picture indistinguishable to the human eyes from the original. On the other hand, in an FPGA implementation, reducing the bitwidth of numbers manipulated in the innermost loop yields roughly proportional reductions in gate count and power at little reduction in accuracy of coarse depth estimation (Sections 6.1 and 6.2).

4.1.4 *Sparse Disparity Checking*

Equation 1 moves the candidate patch to every possible disparity d with respect to the original patch. In our subsampled VGA image, we must consider $n_d = 60$ different disparity values. The power consumption (and in our FPGA implementation, the circuit size) is directly proportional to n_d. Reducing n_d could therefore substantially improve matching cost.

The intuition behind considering every possible disparity d is to find the d^* that absolutely minimizes the patch difference Δ. However, if we are willing to settle for a difference d^+ that is "close enough" to d^*, we could possibly get away with testing fewer disparities. An initial try may be to shift the candidate patch by $k > 1$ (instead of $k = 1$) pixels when searching for d^+. This brings up the question of how big k can be. If it is too big, we run the risk of not detecting objects smaller than k in image space. If too small, we lose efficiency.

Our approach is to require only that objects of width $\geq W_{min}$ will be detected. For instance, we may specify that the object must be at least the size of a face, e.g., $W_{min} =$ 25cm. It is well known [18] (and simple to verify via high-school geometry) that the width in pixels W_D of an object's image is linearly related to the disparity d^* between its left and right images: $W_D = ad^* + b$ for constants a and b. Intuitively, the closer the object to the stereo pair, the larger the disparity d^*, and the larger the size of the image, so that the disparity and image size vary together. Now if we only require that the candidate patch *overlaps* by a factor of ω to its corresponding image from the other imager, as d increases, the patch expands linearly so that the set of pixels at which the candidate patch can be placed expands: the gap k between positions of the candidate patch (i.e., values of d) can increase with d instead of remaining fixed.

In Glimpse, we fit the values of k greedily using data "labeled" by the brute-force $k = 1$ algorithm. Instead of checking 60 disparities for every original patch, we settle on checking 18 disparities d: $\{1, 2, 3, 4, 5, 6, 7, 8, 9, 11, 13, 15, 17, 20, 23, 26, 30, 34, 39, 44, 50, 57\}$ (thus k increases from 1 to 7), a 70% reduction in matching overhead and circuitry. We require overlap $\omega = 0.95$, and require faces to be detectable: $W_{min} =$ 25cm. Section 6.1 shows that sparse checking is accurate when applied to coarse depth estimation.

4.1.5 *Depth Quantization*

Coarse stereo introduces noticeable error in depth estimates. This is problematic if applications rely on the coarse depth estimation module for fine-grained depth information. For instance, assume coarse depth estimation may introduce an error of 0.3m when the object is about 5m away. If an application were only interested in objects in a band 5.0-5.1m away, using coarse depth to select frames for this purpose could result in mistakenly ignored objects.

To remain conservative, i.e., to maintain good recall, Glimpse's coarse depth API only reports depth in a limited number of bins (e.g., less than 1m, 1-3m, 3-10m and beyond 10m). Given disparity d^+ we derive the corresponding object depth D^+ and quantize it into these bins. The additional quantization circuitry is minimal. The big impact, as we show in our evaluation (Section 6.1) is that although the optimizations described in the previous subsection introduce noticeable error in *raw* depth estimation, they are usually well within the slack provided by the *quantized* bins.

4.2 Coarse FIR-Based Tracking

We now turn to functionality based on the thermal (or Far Infra-Red (FIR)) imager, a sensor not broadly available on camera platforms. FIR imagers have lower resolution (16×16-80×80 pixels are common) than RGB, but provide temperature at every pixel. In principle, therefore, they can often directly detect the presence of exceptionally cool or warm bodies (e.g., humans, vehicles, machines, monitors, lighting fixtures) in the environment. One simple but useful feature calculator based on the thermal sensor that Glimpse therefore provides, is a (time-averaged) temperature-based segmentation module, which detects boxes in the field of view with temperature above or below a specified threshold.

In this section, however, we present a related feature calculator, a *tracker*, implemented on the Glimpse microcontroller, given the relatively small volume of data from the FIR imager, that detects and tracks across frames objects in a particular temperature range. Tracking is especially important in early-discard systems such as Glimpse because for many applications, once an object of interest is detected in the field of view, it ceases being of interest. For instance, an application may wish to be notified of a new face coming into the field of view (it may capture a high-resolution frame of the face using the primary imager for further analysis), but once the face is identified it may wish to ignore it.

Glimpse allows high-level applications to notify it to ignore the entity in a particular window. Glimpse does so by tracking the window and not enabling the primary imager on re-detecting it, even if it is otherwise interesting. Prior work [9] has noted a similar benefit in tracking on mobile devices to avoid uploading to the cloud.

4.2.1 Traditional Tracking in RGB

At a high level, tracking in RGB video works as follows [17, 38, 42]. Suppose a window w_t of frame f_t is to be tracked. Given the next frame f_{t+1}, the goal is to calculate window w_{t+1} in f_{t+1}, such that w_{t+1} matches w_t in appearance and dynamics. To perform this match, the tracker may recursively maintain velocity v_t of w_t, hypothesize that the new location of the window is $w'_{t+1} = w_t + v_t$, and search the vicinity of w'_{t+1} for the window w_{t+1} with the best appearance match to w_t. Then the velocity gets updated and the whole process repeated with the next frame, f_{t+2}.

A key design choice is the manner in which the search for the window with the best appearance match is performed. Typically (e.g., [38]), the tracker identifies a set of *keypoints* (locations) in w_t. Each keypoint is associated with a *descriptor* that encodes its surroundings in an illumination (and often scale) invariant manner. The tracker then identifies all keypoints and associated descriptors in f_{t+1}, and matches the old descriptors to a subset of the new ones to determine an appearance match to w_t. Keypoints and related descriptors are relatively computationally intensive to find because they require scanning an entire (relatively) high-resolution image, and need to be illumination invariant since illumination can change significantly across frames in RGB video.

A second choice that adds to the computational over-

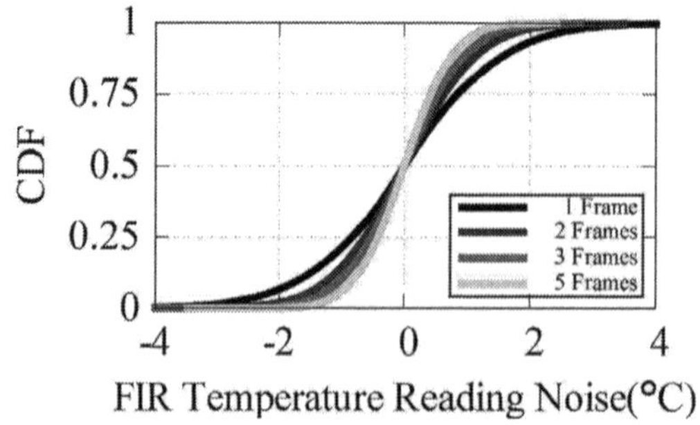

Figure 9: **White noise on the FIR camera's pixel reading.** CDF of noise at each pixel of FIR camera for different frame averaging lengths.

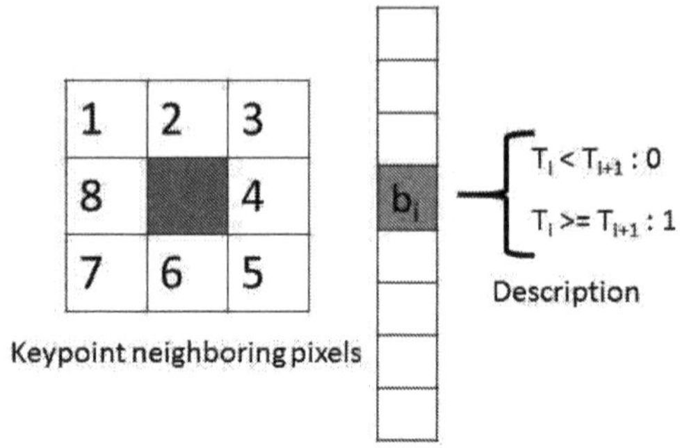

Figure 10: **8-bit binary spiral descriptor.**

head of conventional tracking is the manner in which multiple possible matches are resolved, especially when tracking multiple objects. Resolving this ambiguity usually requires some amount of global reasoning [42] possibly including geometry-based consensus [38]. Below, we describe designs for temperature-based keypoints; descriptors that are simple, but fast and adequately accurate by conservatively and quickly handle ambiguities in matching.

4.2.2 Temperature-Thresholded Keypoints

An advantage of FIR imaging is that it is fairly robust to the environment, unlike RGB imaging. The measured temperature of a point does not change due to change in direction of viewing, illumination sources in the environment, shadows, etc. Given that the tracker is intended for use to track objects that have temperature T significantly different from the background, Glimpse therefore uses the "raw" temperature to find candidate locations for keypoints: all pixels in some temperature range $T \pm \delta$ (we pick $\delta = 3°C$ currently) are considered potentially matching keypoints. Given that the FIR imager has only 1024 pixels (significantly less pixels than a regular RGB camera), keypoint generation is extremely fast.

One complication is that FIR imagers are prone to (zero-mean Gaussian) white noise [12]. We therefore average across $n = 3$ frames to reduce the temperature variance. Figure 9 shows CDF of pixel reading noise from a fixed scene when averaged over frame sub-sequences of varying lengths. It is clear that no averaging (black curve) will result in about $\pm 4°C$ of noise, but a moving average over three consecutive frames will reduce the generated noise to about $\pm 2°C$. Although averaging over five frames reduces the noise even further, the resulting blur is unacceptable for our purposes.

4.2.3 Temperature-Spiral Descriptors

Given keypoints, we seek to associate descriptors with them

in order to determine which, if any, match with descriptors from the previous frame. To ensure illumination, rotation and scale invariance, traditional descriptors are fairly computationally intensive, involving multiple rounds of gradient, histogram and multi-scale smoothing calculations [10, 31].

For our descriptors, we simply choose an encoding of the temperature values around the keypoint arranged in a spiral. We present four different encodings/descriptors here and evaluate their performance later in this paper. The descriptors, detailed below, are **1.** 8-bit binary **2.** 24-bit binary **3.** 8-point absolute temperature and **4.** 24-point absolute temperature.

Figure 10 shows the 8-bit binary descriptor. The keypoint (red pixel) and its neighboring pixels are shown in the Figure 10. This descriptor is an 8-bit number such that each of its bits (b_i) represent the logical result of comparing temperature at pixel i and $i+1$. Similarly, 24-bit binary descriptor follows the same procedure with the difference that we consider two layers of circular neighboring pixels around the keypoint instead of just one. The 8 and 24-points absolute temperature descriptors are similar to the binary versions with the difference that the ith element of the descriptor vector is the temperature of the ith neighboring pixel of the corresponding keypoint.

Finding the best match is standard: we use the sum of absolute differences to compare absolute temperature descriptors and using bitwise-xor for binary descriptors.

4.2.4 Losing Track Conservatively

A limitation of FIR imaging is that its resolution is low, and different instances of objects often have indistinguishable thermal signatures. For instance, it is infeasible (for even humans) to tell one person from another using currently available low-power thermal imagers. The problem of resolving ambiguities between descriptors from multiple objects is therefore especially challenging in FIR tracking.

Our solution is simply to be conservative about matching. Applications will be notified if there is a potential break in the track and it is up to the application to stitch together tracks, potentially using higher level information such as RGB pixels.

To implement conservative matching, at each time step, Glimpse first expands each keypoint in the new frame f_{t+1} into a "blob" (i.e., connected component of similar temperature values) surrounding it by iteratively thresholding on pixel values, a simplified version of Otsu's segmentation method [39]. If any pair of blobs in the new frame are "too close to each other", we terminate the track.We determine if two blobs are close to each other by dilating them by a single pixel [2] and checking if the blobs merged. Given that iterative thresholding, connected components and dilation are fast operations, the implementation is fast.

5. HARDWARE IMPLEMENTATION

Glimpse is fully implemented as a modular add-on board (1a) called the "Glimpse Gating Board" (GGB). The board is designed to run autonomously for a day on a 200mAh battery. Any primary imaging system that has an "image enable" line can be connected to Glimpse via a control line and can communicate with it via a 2 Mbps SPI bus.

[2]Note that at 32×32 resolution, a single pixel represents several degrees of spatial separation.

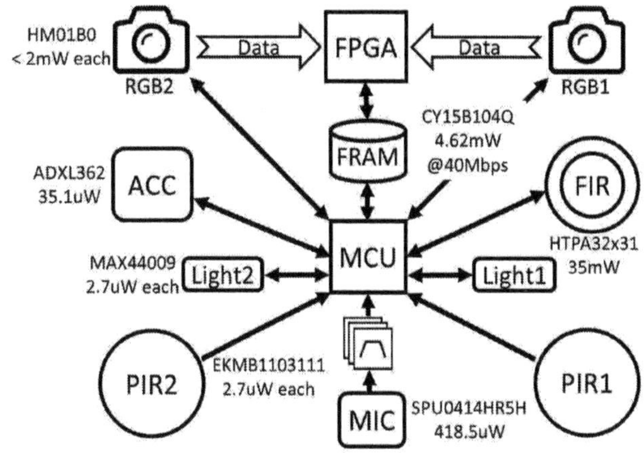

Figure 11: **Glimpse gating board implementation block diagram.**

Figure 11 shows the block diagram for GGB. Given our small power budget, all components are selected to balance low power while providing adequate performance for coarse, cascaded algorithms. Both the (Ti MSP430) microcontroller and the (AGLN250 Igloo Nano) FPGA are some of the lowest-power parts available in their category. Even a careful implementation of coarse stereo matching (along with video readout circuitry for the two imagers), for instance, consumes half the FPGA. In many cases, power consumption of components will reduce significantly in the near future, tracking advances in commercially available parts. For instance, that the highest power consumer is the (relatively low-resolution) thermal FIR imager, a part ripe for improvement.

6. EVALUATING COARSE VISION

We wish to answer three questions about the coarse vision (depth estimation and stereo tracking) algorithms introduced in Section 4:

- What is their accuracy?
- What is their resource consumption?
- How do these vary with our design choices?

We use data collected under controlled conditions in these experiments. We restrict detailed experimental evaluation to the low-bitwidth representation, sparse disparity checking and depth quantization optimizations of Section 4. With respect to the other optimizations, briefly: 1. Using SAD instead of SOS for distance measure (Section 4.1.1) yields a depth measurement circuit that uses 42% fewer gates[3], and 2. Buffer-free implementation of stereo (Section 4.1.2) saves 13% in average power draw over the buffered version.

6.1 Coarse Stereo: Accuracy

What is the impact of reducing the number of bits used to represent pixels (Section 4.1.3) on precision of depth measurement? To answer this question, we placed the Glimpse camera in front of a textured wall and moved the camera between 0.5m to 3.9m from the wall, by 0.3m increments. For a set of patches of varying sizes $s \times s$ (s selected from 20, 40, 60 and 100pixels) in the field of view, we calculated

[3]Power reductions should be similar. The SOS-based circuit is too large for implementation on our FPGA, so we cannot report measured power gains.

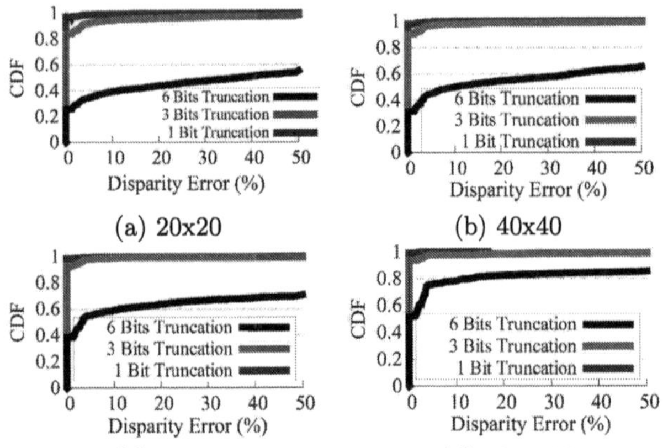

(a) 20x20 (b) 40x40 (c) 60x60 (d) 100x100

Figure 12: **Disparity error versus truncation length.**

the pixel disparity d^* while varying the number b of bits used to represent the captured stereo pairs. We used $b = 7, 6, 4$ and 1, corresponding to 0, 1, 3 and 6-bit truncation. Figure 12 reports the CDF of error in disparity d^* relative to the disparity measured from the un-truncated stereo-pair version.

Two points are worth noting. First, relative error with a 3-bit truncation (i.e., b=4) is quite acceptable, whereas going down to 6-bit truncation introduces a significant amount of error in disparity estimation. We therefore use 3-bit truncation in Glimpse. Second, although the error depends to some extent on the size of the patch being matched (larger patches contain more visual information and thus less matching error), even small patches can be matched with quite small error with 3 bits truncated. Even with $s = 20$-sized patches, relative disparity is zero 82% of the time (red line in 12(a)) and 94% of the time, it is less than 9%. With $s = 60$, disparity is zero over 93% of the time.

We now study the impact of quantized depth levels on the accuracy of depth estimation Section 4.1.5. Suppose that instead of estimating depth as precisely as possible, we are only interested in knowing which of four bins the depth belongs to: bin_0:0-1m, bin_1: 1-2m, bin_2: 2-3m or bin_3: 3-∞m. We focus now on the challenging 20×20 patches and quantize the results of the above experiment into these bins. In other words, we convert the pixel disparity for each measurement into the actual depth then instead of basing our analysis on the actual depth, we measure the bin index in which it falls into. Figure 13 shows the results when 1 to 6 bits are truncated. For each truncation level, the bar shows the distribution of the *bin error*. The bin error is simply the absolute value of the difference between bin index calculated using the truncated and un-truncated data. Focusing on the 3-bit truncation case, we see that *at the bin level*, 96% of the measurements have zero bin error, and almost all the rest are off by just one bin. We also note in passing that even for 6-bit truncation (i.e., just black and white pixels), quantized accuracy is encouraging: ~60% of measurements are binned correctly.

In the above algorithms, we calculated the optimal disparity d^* by exhaustively checking all 60 possible disparities. We now evaluate *sparse disparity checking* (from Section 4.1.4), assuming that a) we are only interested in depth of objects wider than 25cm, and b) we are only interested in bin-level precision. We recomputed bin-level results as in the previous experiment, but now require the algorithm to

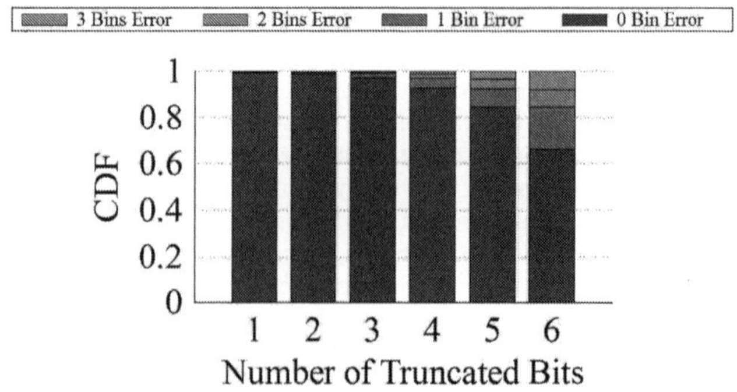

Figure 13: **Bin-level depth error vs. truncation.**

use just $n \in \{7, 17, 22, 37, 41, 50\}$ different disparity checks, using fixed bitwidth $b = 4$ (i.e., truncation length 3). We compare the binning error relative to using all 60 checks. Figure 14 shows results for patches of sizes $s = 20$ and 100. The upshot is that $n \approx 37$ checks are enough for excellent bin-level accuracy over all patch sizes. In Glimpse, because our patches tend toward being larger, we use just $n = 22$ disparity checks.

6.2 Coarse Stereo: Resource Consumption

How does resource consumption vary with our approximate implementation of depth detection? Our primary target FPGA is the Igloo Nano AGLN250. However the AGLN250 is not big enough to handle stereo depth detection with full disparity checks and un-truncated pixels. For comparison purposes, we therefore consider the more powerful (and power-hungry) AGL400 and M1AGL1000 FPGAs as well.

In our first experiment, we fixed bitwidth at 7, increased the total number of allowed disparity checks until the AGLN250 ran out of resources, switched to AGL400 and continued increasing the number of disparity checks until it ran out of resources too and finally switched to M1AGL1000. At each point we let the FPGA calculate the depth map over the entire VGA frame which is computationally the most demanding version of our depth detection algorithm. We then simulate power consumption and resource utilization of the FPGA using Microsemi Libero SoC software. Figure 15a shows power consumption and Figure 15b shows resource utilization (i.e. fraction of all available logic elements on the FPGA used) of the three FPGAs under different pixel disparities. As shown in the figures, the power consumption increases generally as the number of disparity checks increases. Also the utilization of a particular FPGA increases as the number of disparity checks increases.

Figure 16 examines the power draw and utilization impact of different bit truncation. These experiments are performed with $n = 22$ disparity checks. Resource use drops almost linearly with optimization level (truncation length in this case). Comparing with Figure 13 and Figure 14, we see

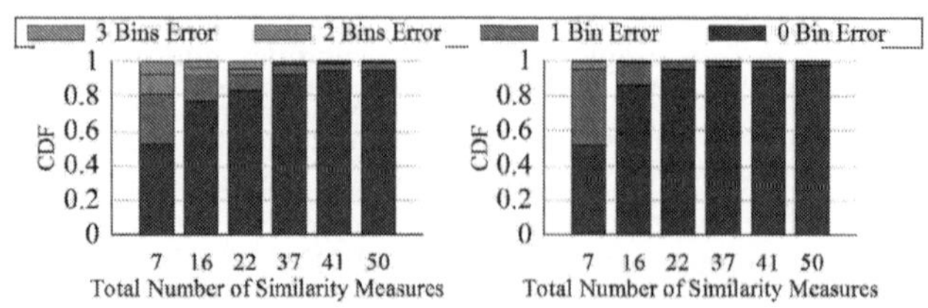

(b) 20x20 (c) 100x100

Figure 14: **Bin-level error vs. no. of disparity checks.**

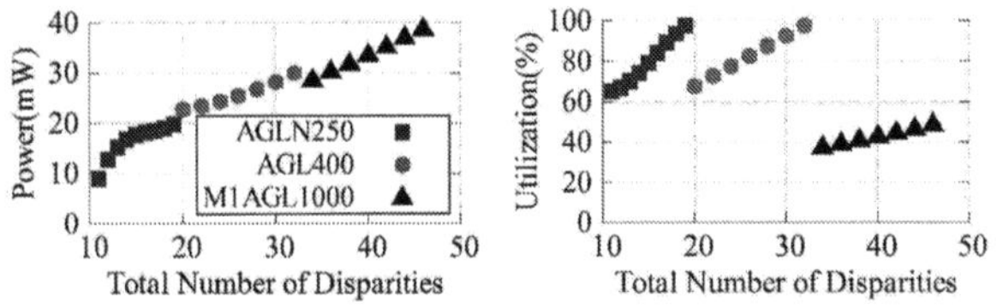

(a) Power Consumption (b) Gate Utilization

Figure 15: **Resource use versus disparity checks.**

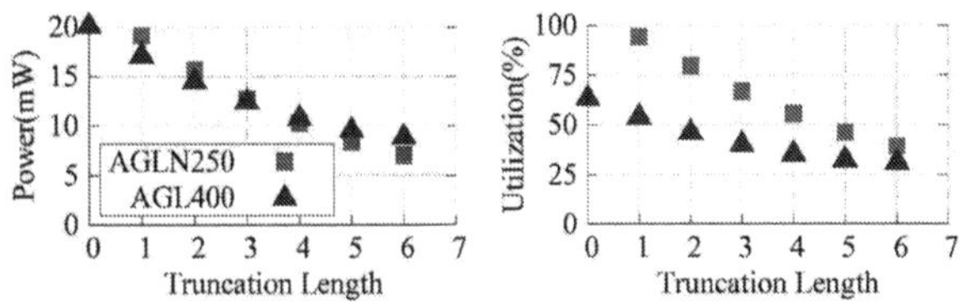

(a) Power Consumption (b) Resource Utilization

Figure 16: **Resource use versus pixel truncation.**

that 3-bit truncation and 22 disparity checks is likely the accuracy/power sweet spot, yielding 95%+ accuracy on size-60 patches at a stereo-computation draw of $\sim 12mW$ while using less than 75% of the AGLN250 logic elements.

6.3 FIR Tracking

We now evaluate the coarse FIR tracking algorithm. We try to answer three questions: 1. **Accuracy:** How well does the algorithm keep track? 2. **Resource use:** How much energy does the algorithm consume? 3. **Design choices:** How well do the various spiral descriptors work?

To answer these questions, we performed the following experiment. We pointed Glimpse into an empty office room and asked two human subjects to enter and interact in the field of view in a scripted manner for up to 25 seconds per interaction. We collected 7 versions of the interaction where subjects were moving at "slow" (leisurely strolling with stops), "medium" (walking) and "fast" (brisk walking, almost running) speeds. We manually annotated the tracks i.e., added distinct boxes surrounding each subject in the video and compared these "ground-truth" tracks to those returned by (variants of) our algorithm.

Figure 17a shows how the average fraction of properly tracked frames over total available frames varies with the speed of movement and the various descriptors (in the "no descriptor" case, just the temperature of the central pixel is used as descriptor). The noteworthy points are: First, absolute temperature descriptors are much better than the binary ones; the absolute value of the temperature is clearly a lot more informative than a single bit representation *temperature change* at each pixel. Second, the difference in tracking quality between the 8-point and 24-point descriptors is relatively small, encouraging the use of 8-point descriptors due to their lower computational complexity. Third, given the absolute descriptors, the tracker does an acceptable job of tracking: it maintains track for 60-90% of tracks on average, depending on whether subjects are moving fast or slow. Fourth (Figure 17b), we applied a tuned state-of-the-art RGB tracker [38] to the FIR videos to evaluate the importance of FIR-specific descriptors. 17b shows that the FIR-specific tracker clearly does better; we found that standard RGB descriptors do not fare well with low- resolution thermal footage.

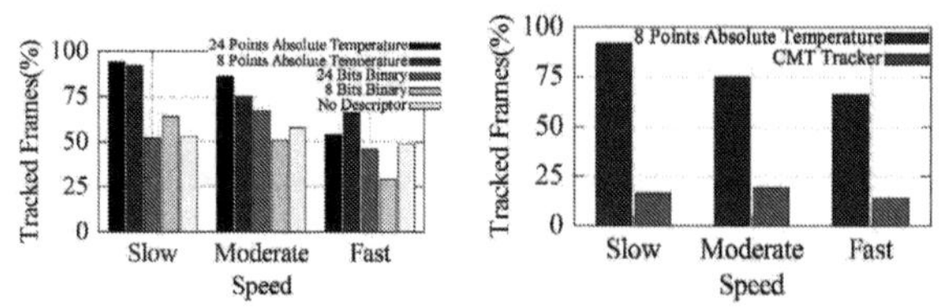

(a) Comparison of descriptors (b) FIR vs RGB tracker

Figure 17: **FIR tracking evaluation.** 17a shows for how many frames our FIR tracker can contiuously track an object given different descriptors, and 17b compares the track length of our FIR tracking algorithm vs a well-known object tracking algorithm when applied to a theremal video.

Scenario	PIR	FIR	Depth	Total	Precision
Driving	0.96	0.30	0.43	0.12	31%
Corridor	0.94	0.00	0.33	0.00	100%
Monitor	0.83	0.07	0.34	0.02	8%
Outdoor	0.99	0.23	0.20	0.04	1.7%
Lunch	0.99	0.50	0.34	0.17	42%
Meeting	0.97	0.13	0.23	0.03	12%
1 to 1	0.99	0.09	0.31	0.03	36%

Table 1: **Glimpse pass-through rates and precision.**

7. END TO END EVALUATION

Finally, we wish to understand how well suited the Glimpse system is to its primary role of supporting day-long wearable vision. One of the authors wore a Glimpse-based camera for 15 hours over three days of daily activity (roughly 3, 7 and 5 hours each) while running a cascade (Figure 5a) on Glimpse. Glimpse produced a high-resolution 30-frame video snippet every time a person came within 3 meters from the wearer (typically a conversation partner) or the wearer's hand entered the Glimpse's field of view. The rejection cascade used is similar to that in 5a, except that the thermal segmentation module was replaced by an FIR tracker as in Section 4.2. The analysis of another cascade that triggers the primary imager only when the wearer's hand appeared in the field of view is presented in Section 7.3.

All video produced by the primary imager was offloaded via wireless to a mobile device. In this experiment we did not attempt off-board analysis of the video. Common activities performed by the wearer included but were not limited to, *driving*, *going for lunch with friends*, *one-to-one meeting*, *group meeting*, *playing ping-pong*, *corridor walking*, *outdoor walking*, and *working in front of a monitor*.

We paired up a Glimpse Gating Board (GGB) with a Raspberry Pi 3 board (which we call *Gated Pi* below) as the primary imager, via a trigger wire. The Pi has an 8MP imager. For the mobile device, the wearer carried a WiFi connected laptop in a backpack; a production system would likely use a mobile phone instead. To collect ground truth, we added a second Raspberry Pi (the *Continuous Pi*) that recorded *all* video in the field of view. Both Pis offloaded data to the laptop via WiFi, one sporadically, the other continuously. We logged *real-time* power draw of the GGB, the Gated Pi and its components to the laptop via a National Instrument data acquisition system in the backpack.

Event Duration, d (s)	$d \geq 3$	$3 > d \geq 2$	$2 > d \geq 1$
Recall Rate (%)	100	96	86.5

Table 2: **Glimpse recall rate vs event duration.**

7.1 Gating Accuracy

The primary job of Glimpse is to reject many uninteresting frames while letting through almost all interesting ones. In daily use, what fraction ("pass-through rate") of frames did it allow to pass through? What fraction of these truly should have passed through ("precision")? What fraction of all interesting events actually went through ("recall")? We answer these questions in this section.

Our detailed power measurements allowed us to monitor in real time when each component of each cascade triggered, and whether or not the Gated Pi was finally triggered. We were therefore able to measure the pass-through rate of each stage of the rejection cascades, and of the two cascades as a whole. Table 1 reports the results, broken down per scenario. For each cascade stage, we report the fraction of *its* input passed through.

Overall, total pass-through rates range from 0 to 17%, with an average (not shown) of roughly 6%. The ultra-low-power PIR can reject 1-17% of input: it is especially good at detecting inactivity when sitting roughly still in front of the monitor. Both FIR and Depth are highly effective gates. When walking in the corridor on these three days, the wearer encountered just two persons, for which the FIR stage let through 3 frames, which rounds off to a 0.00% pass-through. The Depth system allowed one of these frames, for a 1/3 pass-through rate.

We inspected all passed through frames manually to determine what fraction had wearer hands or nearby people i.e., the precision. As the "Precision" column shows, Glimpse's precision is modest. Again, since the one frame let through in the corridor was indeed a person, precision is 100%, even though the overall pass-through rate rounds to 0.00.

Measuring recall is harder, since we need to inspect roughly 1.6M frames from Continuous Pi to determine if we missed any events. We looked through the video manually and counted instances where a hand or person appeared in the field of view for duration d seconds, such that $d \geq 3$, $3 > d \geq 2$ and $2 > d \geq 1$. We found the shorter the event, the more episodes there were when the object moved so fast through the field of view that GGS, at 10FPS, was unable to detect it. For events of modest (e.g., > 2s) length, however, Glimpse has excellent recall (Table 2).

7.2 Resource Usage

What is Glimpse's average power and wireless bandwidth consumption? The low overall pass-through rate (6%) indicates that power consumed by the primary imaging pipeline, and data sent by it, should be correspondingly low. Further, by design, the Glimpse board itself should have low power draw. How do these play out in practice?

Scenario	Total	Primary	GGS	Depth	FIR
Driving	116	67	49	6	38
Corridor	43	0.6	42	0.2	37
Monitor	80	39	41	1.4	33
Outdoor	80	30	50	5.1	40
Lunch	153	99	54	10	39
Meeting	85	39	46	2.8	38
1 to 1	73	26	47	2.2	39

Table 3: **Glimpse power consumption (mW).**

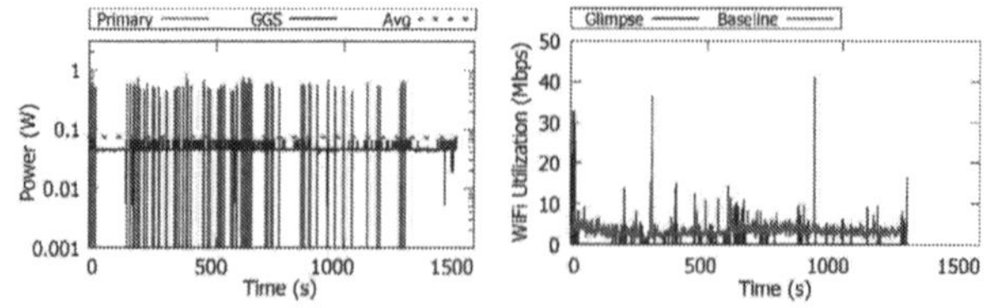

(a) Real-time Power Consumption (b) Real-time WiFi Utilization

Figure 18: **Real-time Power and WiFi Utilization.** Power consumption and WiFi transmissions of a primary imager become bursty when it is being gated by Glimpse system during an example one-to-one meeting scenario.

Table 3 shows the average power (mW) breakdown for the major components of GGS, that of Gated Pi and their sum. Overall average for the total power consumption (not shown in the table) was roughly **112mW**. 18a shows the real-time power traces for Glimpse system in blue, Gated Pi in green, and their overall power consumption in red. This curve illustrates that power consumption of the Gated Pi becomes bursty in the existence of Glimpse system in a sample scenario of one-to-one. For comparison, the average power draw of Continuous Pi, which off-boards all data is **1016mW**. A few points are worth noting. First, Glimpse *total* power consumption is low both in absolute and relative terms. In relative terms, it is **7x** to **25x** lower than pure offloading, depending on the scenario. In absolute terms, its *worst-case* 153mW draw will allow it to run for over 5 hours on a tiny 200mAh battery; the average of 112mW would allow almost 7 hours. Second, the gating board itself (average draw 55mW) can easily be powered by a 200mAh battery through a day. Third, the FIR sensor and tracker is a power bottleneck, with the sensor itself averaging well over 20mW.

Finally Table 4 shows savings in bandwidth utilization. Figure 18b shows intermittent WiFi transmissions of Gated Pi when triggered by Glimpse system in a sample scenario of one-to-one meeting. Even when Gated Pi transmits a one-second burst of video every time it is triggered, it still sends 4× to 16× less data. Our measurements show that if it only sent one frame each time it was triggered, data sent would reduce by another 3.2×. Overall, therefore, Glimpse clearly has the potential to reduce data transmitted by roughly 12-50× relative to pure offloading. Of course, all these reductions are predicated on the application only being interested in a sparse set of frames.

7.3 Glimpse Programmability

Here we run a cascade on the Glimpse similar to Figure 5a except the depth threshold is set to 1 meter. The goal here is to trigger the primary imager whenever the wearer's hand enters the field of view, indicating that the wearer is probably interacting with an object. Here we ask the Glimpse wearer to interact with objects in hand while standing in an office setting with background thermal activities. In each experiment we varied the temperature threshold from 33°C to

Scenario	Gated BW(Mbps)	Baseline BW(Mbps)
Driving	1.01	5.90
Corridor	0	5.15
Monitor	0.58	8.72
Outdoor	2.46	10.56
Lunch	2.61	8.25
Meeting	0.14	1.58
1 to 1	0.24	3.14

Table 4: **Glimpse WiFi bandwidth consumption.**

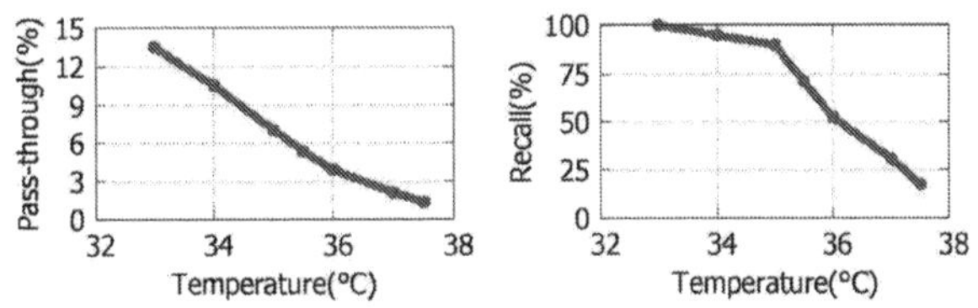

(a) Pass-through vs Temperature (b) Recall vs Temperature

Figure 19: **Recall vs pass-through rate trade-off.** Recall and trigger dependence on the temperature threshold for hand detection cascade.

$37.5°C$ and measured the recall and the pass-through rates of the detected frames.

Figure 19 shows the recall and pass-through rates versus the threshold temperature on two separate graphs. The key observation is that as the temperature threshold increases the pass-through rate decreases which helps lowering the power consumption but it decreases the recall rate as well. There is a clear trade-off between the total power consumption (pass-through rates) and the resulting recall rate, which can be controlled straightforwardly via the corresponding parameter in the rejection cascade.

8. RELATED WORK

Glimpse is built based on previous research on continuous mobile vision, ultra-low power depth sensing, and FarIR tracking. However, our system differs from previous work from multiple perspectives.

Continuous mobile vision: Prior work investigates various layers across the vision processing pipeline to identify the power bottleneck of each layer. Traditional off-the-shelf image sensors' power consumption is not proportional to their frame rate and resolution, thus it is not feasible to trade quality with power consumption using them. [23] [27] [5] tune hardware parameters of an image sensor to achieve proportional energy consumption to the number of pixels sensed. [29] leverages shared intermediate results within a vision processing software framework to reduce redundant computational overhead. [15] and [6] look at the benefit of using low-power accelerometers to gate the operation of the image sensor. Perhaps the biggest difference between our work and these is our advocacy for a *dedicated* hardware/software subsystem that, perhaps paradoxically, includes imagers, that applications can use in a *programmable* manner to control the computer vision costs they would incur by using the primary imaging pipeline.

Sensing depth at low power: Sensing depth at low power is hard in general. Several depth sensors [2] can operate at low power and high resolution. However, these sensors just report the depth of a single pixel. Other sensors [3, 34, 46, 48, 52, 53] can compute the depth of a wide field of view with high resolution. However, their power consumption is high. Our primary insight is that *for purposes of early discard*, it is often adequate to have depth estimated in subsets of the field of view and at coarse resolution. By identifying corresponding relaxations in the algorithm design, we deliver useful depth estimation at a few mW.

FarIR tracking at low-power: Prior works use FarIR sensors to detect the presence of objects of interests for Heating, Ventilation, Air Conditioning, (HVAC) and lighting control of building [13]. [20] also looks at the opportunity of using FarIR sensors for objects tracking. Different from these work, our FarIR subsystem is a customized design that can run on a microcontroller at low-power consumption.

Battery-free cameras: Work parallel to ours has shown battery-free cameras that harvest energy from ambient Radio Frequency (RF) signal sources and capture and transmit images on a forced duty-cycled basis [36] [45] [37]. These devices reduce the maintenance costs of camera systems by eliminating the battery, but due to their constrained energy budget, they suffer from limited computational capabilities required for on-board complex machine vision operations [35]. Although the vision algorithm presented here cannot be applied to those such energy constrained devices, the idea of application-specific cascaded operation for gating a high-power sensor using low-power sensors and algorithms (such as the use of motion detectors) seems a feasible approach to enable battery-free devices with more continuous operation.

9. CONCLUSION

In this work we designed, implemented and evaluated Glimpse, a programmable embedded system designed to detect at low power events worthy of further processing. Key innovations include a low-power imager array and computational fabric dedicated to image-discard calculations, a safe but expressive programming model for applications and coarse variants of conventional stereo depth and tracking algorithms suited for the discard pipeline. Combining Glimpse with a high-power imaging pipeline system allows the high-power pipeline to process less than 10% of the frames it would have processed otherwise, while drawing about 100mW of overall power. Correspondingly, the amount of video data transmitted for further processing is also lower by an order of magnitude. Based on these results, we believe that Glimpse moves continuous vision on lightweight wearables to the realm of the practical.

References

[1] Ambarella a9 ultra hd 4k camera soc product brief. http://www.ambarella.com/uploads/docs/A9-product-brief.pdf.

[2] Long distance measuring sensor datasheet. http://www.sharp-world.com/products/device/lineup/data/pdf/datasheet/gp2y0a02yk_e.pdf. Accessed: May 2017.

[3] Stereographic depth mapping on an fpga. https://courses.cit.cornell.edu/ece576/FinalProjects/f2010/pfk5_jk459/pfk5_jk459/index.html.

[4] S. Agarwal, M. Philipose, and P. Bahl. Vision: The case for cellular small cells for cloudlets. In *International Workshop on Mobile Cloud Computing and Services*, 2014.

[5] S. U. Ay. A 1.32 pw/frameÂě pixel 1.2 v cmos energy-harvesting and imaging (ehi) aps imager. In *Solid-State Circuits Conference Digest of Technical Papers (ISSCC), 2011 IEEE International*, pages 116–118. IEEE, 2011.

[6] P. Bahl, M. Philipose, and L. Zhong. Vision: cloud-powered sight for all: showing the cloud what you see. In *Proceedings of the third ACM workshop on Mobile cloud computing and services*, pages 53–60. ACM, 2012.

[7] S. Bambach, J. M. Franchak, D. J. Crandall, and C. Yu. Detecting hands in childrenâĂŹs egocentric views to understand embodied attention during social interaction. *Proceedings of the 36th Annual Conference of the Cognitive Science Society (pp. 134-139). Quebec City, Canda: Cognitive Science Society*, pages 134–139, 2014.

[8] S. Blessenohl, C. Morrison, A. Criminisi, and J. Shotton. Improving indoor mobility of the visually impaired with depth-based spatial sound. In *ICCV-ACVR workshop*, December 2015.

[9] T. Y. Chen, L. Ravindranath, S. Deng, P. Bahl, and H. Balakrishnan. Glimpse: Continuous, real-time object recognition on mobile devices. In *Proceedings of the 13th ACM Conference on Embedded Networked Sensor Systems, SenSys 2015, Seoul, South Korea, November 1-4, 2015*, pages 155–168, 2015.

[10] N. Dalal and B. Triggs. Histograms of oriented gradients for human detection. In *In CVPR*, pages 886–893, 2005.

[11] Y. Deng, S. Chakrabartty, and G. Cauwenberghs. Analog auditory perception model for robust speech recognition. In *IEEE International Joint Conference on Neural Networks*, 2004.

[12] E. L. Dereniak and G. D. Boreman. *Infared Detectors and Systems.* Wiley, second edition, 1996.

[13] V. L. Erickson, A. Beltran, D. A. Winkler, N. P. Esfahani, J. R. Lusby, and A. E. Cerpa. Toss: Thermal occupancy sensing system. In *Proceedings of the 5th ACM Workshop on Embedded Systems For Energy-Efficient Buildings*, pages 1–2. ACM, 2013.

[14] K. Ha, Z. Chen, W. Hu, W. Richter, P. Pillai, and M. Satyanarayanan. Towards wearable cognitive assistance. In *MobiSys*, 2014.

[15] S. Han, R. Nandakumar, M. Philipose, A. Krishnamurthy, and D. Wetherall. Glimpsedata: Towards continuous vision-based personal analytics. In *Proceedings of the 2014 workshop on physical analytics*, pages 31–36. ACM, 2014.

[16] S. Han, H. Shen, M. Philipose, S. Agarwal, A. Wolman, and A. Krishnamurthy. MCDNN:An Approximation-Based Execution Framework for Deep Stream Processing Under Resource Constraints. In *Proceedings of the 14th International Conference on Mobile Systems, Applications, and Services (MobiSys)*. ACM, 2016.

[17] S. Hare, S. Golodetz, A. Saffari, V. Vineet, M. M. Cheng, S. L. Hicks, and P. H. S. Torr. Struck: Structured output tracking with kernels. *IEEE Transactions on Pattern Analysis and Machine Intelligence*, 38(10):2096–2109, Oct 2016.

[18] R. I. Hartley and A. Zisserman. *Multiple View Geometry in Computer Vision.* Cambridge University Press, ISBN: 0521540518, second edition, 2004.

[19] J. Healey and R. W. Picard. Startlecam: A cybernetic wearable camera. In *Second International Symposium on Wearable Computers (ISWC 1998)*, pages 42–49, 1998.

[20] P. Hevesi, S. Wille, G. Pirkl, N. Wehn, and P. Lukowicz. Monitoring household activities and user location with a cheap, unobtrusive thermal sensor array. In *Proceedings of the 2014 ACM International Joint Conference on Pervasive and Ubiquitous Computing*, pages 141–145. ACM, 2014.

[21] S. Hodges, L. Williams, E. Berry, S. Izadi, J. Srinivasan, A. Butler, G. Smyth, N. Kapur, and K. R. Wood. Sensecam: A retrospective memory aid. In *UbiComp 2006*, pages 177–193, 2006.

[22] J. Hoisko. Context triggered visual episodic memory prosthesis. In *Fourth International Symposium on Wearable Computers (ISWC200.*

[23] K. Kagawau, S. Shishido, M. Nunoshita, and J. Ohta. A 3.6 pw/frameâ· pixel 1.35 v pwm cmos imager with dynamic pixel readout and no static bias current. In *Solid-State Circuits Conference, 2008. ISSCC 2008. Digest of Technical Papers. IEEE International*, pages 54–595. IEEE, 2008.

[24] T. Kanade and M. Hebert. First-person vision. *Proceedings of the IEEE*, 100(8):2442–2453, 2012.

[25] S. Krishna, G. Little, J. Black, and S. Panchanathan. A wearable face recognition system for individuals with visual impairments. In *Proceedings of the 7th International ACM SIGACCESS Conference on Computers and Accessibility*, Assets '05, pages 106–113, New York, NY, USA, 2005. ACM.

[26] N. Lazaros, G. C. Sirakoulis, and A. Gasteratos. Review of stereo vision algorithms: From software to hardware. *International Journal of Optomechatronics*, 2(4):435–462, 2008.

[27] R. LiKamWa, B. Priyantha, M. Philipose, L. Zhong, and P. Bahl. Energy characterization and optimization of image sensing toward continuous mobile vision. In *Proceeding of the 11th annual international conference on Mobile systems, applications, and services*, pages 69–82. ACM, 2013.

[28] R. LiKamWa, Z. Wang, A. Carroll, F. X. Lin, and L. Zhong. Draining our glass: An energy and heat characterization of google glass. *arXiv preprint arXiv:1404.1320*, 2014.

[29] R. LiKamWa and L. Zhong. Starfish: Efficient concurrency support for computer vision applications. In *Proceedings of the 13th Annual International Conference on Mobile Systems, Applications, and Services*, pages 213–226. ACM, 2015.

[30] H. Liu, M. Philipose, M. Pettersson, and M.-T. Sun. Recognizing object manipulation activities using depth and visual cues. *Journal of Visual Communication and Image Representation*, 25(4):719–726, 2014.

[31] D. G. Lowe. Object recognition from local scale-invariant features. In *Proceedings of the Seventh IEEE International Conference on Computer Vision*, volume 2, pages 1150–1157 vol.2, 1999.

[32] H. Lu, A. B. Brush, B. Priyantha, A. K. Karlson, and J. Liu. Speakersense: Energy efficient unobtrusive speaker identification on mobile phones. In *International Conference on Pervasive Computing*, pages 188–205. Springer, 2011.

[33] B. Mandal, S. Chia, L. Li, V. Chandrasekhar, C. Tan, and J. Lim. A wearable face recognition system on google glass for assisting social interactions. In *Computer Vision - ACCV 2014 Workshops - Singapore, Singapore, November 1-2, 2014, Revised Selected Papers, Part III*, pages 419–433, 2014.

[34] C. Murphy, D. Lindquist, A. M. Rynning, T. Cecil, S. Leavitt, and M. L. Chang. Low-cost stereo vision on an fpga. In *Field-Programmable Custom Computing Machines, 2007. FCCM 2007. 15th Annual IEEE Symposium on*, pages 333–334. IEEE, 2007.

[35] S. Naderiparizi, Z. Kapetanovic, and J. R. Smith. Wispcam: An rf-powered smart camera for machine vision applications. In *Proceedings of the 4th International Workshop on Energy Harvesting and Energy-Neutral Sensing Systems*, pages 19–22. ACM, 2016.

[36] S. Naderiparizi, A. N. Parks, Z. Kapetanovic, B. Ransford, and J. R. Smith. Wispcam: A battery-free rfid camera. In *RFID (RFID), 2015 IEEE International Conference on*, pages 166–173. IEEE, 2015.

[37] S. Naderiparizi, Y. Zhao, J. Youngquist, A. P. Sample, and J. R. Smith. Self-localizing battery-free cameras. In *Proceedings of the 2015 ACM International Joint Conference on Pervasive and Ubiquitous Computing*, pages 445–449. ACM, 2015.

[38] G. Nebehay and R. Pflugfelder. Consensus-based matching and tracking of keypoints for object tracking. In *Applications of Computer Vision (WACV), 2014 IEEE Winter Conference on*, pages 862–869, March 2014.

[39] N. Otsu. A threshold selection method from gray-level histograms. *IEEE Transactions on Systems, Man, and Cybernetics*, 9(1):62–66, Jan 1979.

[40] O. M. Parkhi, A. Vedaldi, and A. Zisserman. Deep face recognition. In *BMVC*, 2015.

[41] H. Pirsiavash and D. Ramanan. Detecting activities of daily living in first-person camera views. In *Computer Vision and Pattern Recognition (CVPR), 2012 IEEE Conference on*, pages 2847–2854. IEEE, 2012.

[42] H. Pirsiavash, D. Ramanan, and C. C. Fowlkes. Globally-optimal greedy algorithms for tracking a variable number of objects. In *Computer Vision and Pattern Recognition (CVPR), 2011 IEEE Conference on*, pages 1201–1208. IEEE, 2011.

[43] M.-R. Ra, A. Sheth, L. Mummert, P. Pillai, D. Wetherall, and R. Govindan. Odessa: Enabling interactive perception applications on mobile devices. In *Mobisys*, 2011.

[44] S. Rallapalli, A. Ganesan, K. Chintalapudi, V. N. Padmanabhan, and L. Qiu. Enabling physical analytics in retail stores using smart glasses. In *Proceedings of the 20th annual international conference on Mobile computing and networking*, pages 115–126. ACM, 2014.

[45] V. Talla, B. Kellogg, B. Ransford, S. Naderiparizi, S. Gollakota, and J. R. Smith. Powering the next billion devices with wi-fi. In *Proceedings of the 11th ACM Conference on Emerging Networking Experiments and Technologies*, page 4. ACM, 2015.

[46] N. H. Tan, N. H. Hamid, P. Sebastian, and Y. V. Voon. Resource minimization in a real-time depth-map processing system on fpga. In *TENCON 2011-2011 IEEE Region 10 Conference*, pages 706–710. IEEE, 2011.

[47] R. Tapu, B. Mocanu, and T. B. Zaharia. ALICE: A smartphone assistant used to increase the mobility of visual impaired people. *JAISE*, 7(5):659–678, 2015.

[48] R. Y. Tsai. A versatile camera calibration technique for high-accuracy 3d machine vision metrology using off-the-shelf tv cameras and lenses. *Robotics and Automation, IEEE Journal of*, 3(4):323–344, 1987.

[49] P. Viola and M. J. Jones. Robust real-time face detection. *International journal of computer vision*, 57(2):137–154, 2004.

[50] J. Wu, A. Osuntogun, T. Choudhury, M. Philipose, and J. M. Rehg. A scalable approach to activity recognition based on object use. In *2007 IEEE 11th International Conference on Computer Vision*, pages 1–8, 2007.

[51] Z. Xu, M. Kusner, M. Chen, and K. Q. Weinberger. Cost-sensitive tree of classifiers. In *ICML*, 2013.

[52] Z. Zhang. A flexible new technique for camera calibration. *Pattern Analysis and Machine Intelligence, IEEE Transactions on*, 22(11):1330–1334, 2000.

[53] Z. Zhang. Camera calibration with one-dimensional objects. *Pattern Analysis and Machine Intelligence, IEEE Transactions on*, 26(7):892–899, 2004.

Accelerating Mobile Audio Sensing Algorithms through On-Chip GPU Offloading

Petko Georgiev[§], Nicholas D. Lane[†*], Cecilia Mascolo[§], David Chu[‡]
[§]University of Cambridge, [†]University College London, [*]Nokia Bell Labs, [‡]Google

ABSTRACT

GPUs have recently enjoyed increased popularity as general purpose software accelerators in multiple application domains including computer vision and natural language processing. However, there has been little exploration into the performance and energy trade-offs mobile GPUs can deliver for the increasingly popular workload of deep-inference audio sensing tasks, such as, spoken keyword spotting in energy-constrained smartphones and wearables. In this paper, we study these trade-offs and introduce an optimization engine that leverages a series of structural and memory access optimization techniques that allow audio algorithm performance to be automatically tuned as a function of GPU device specifications and model semantics. We find that parameter optimized audio routines obtain inferences an order of magnitude faster than sequential CPU implementations, and up to 6.5x times faster than cloud offloading with good connectivity, while critically consuming 3-4x less energy than the CPU. Under our optimized GPU, conventional wisdom about how to use the cloud and low power chips is broken. Unless the network has a throughput of at least 20Mbps (and a RTT of 25 ms or less), with only about 10 to 20 seconds of buffering audio data for batched execution, the optimized GPU audio sensing apps begin to consume less energy than cloud offloading. Under such conditions we find the optimized GPU can provide energy benefits comparable to low-power reference DSP implementations with some preliminary level of optimization; in addition to the GPU always winning with lower latency.

1. INTRODUCTION

Graphics Processing Units (GPUs) are the method of choice for executing high computational loads and accelerating compute-intensive applications in domains such as computer vision [57, 23, 36] and deep learning [16, 17]. But GPUs like any complex processor architecture need to be used smartly to maximize their throughput and efficiency. There have been extensive studies for graphics and games [57, 36, 57, 50] including mobile [23], but the analysis has largely evaded other general-purpose GPU computations on a mobile device such as audio applications that rely on the power-hungry microphone sensor. Examples of audio sensing apps are personal digital assistants such as Apple's Siri [2] or Google Now [5], as well as a plethora of behavior monitoring apps that recognize emotions from voice [52, 46], or perform conversation analysis [45, 58, 48]. These applications are capable of deep inferences about user behavior, often require continuous sensor monitoring, and boast highly sophisticated inference algorithms that easily strain scarce mobile resources(battery, memory and computation) [41]. As a result, computational offloading to cloud [24] or low-power co-processors [27, 45] has often been the solution applied to keep these apps functional on the mobile device, but no study has been done on the feasibility of GPU offloading for this data-intensive workload.

In the mobile landscape where energy is the biggest limiting factor, it is not immediately obvious whether accelerating these sensing applications via GPU offloading will result in energy-justified performance boosts compared to the above mentioned alternatives (cloud and low-power co-processors). Questions that we investigate in this paper are: What trade-offs do we get in terms of speed and energy if we express audio sensing algorithms in a GPU-compliant manner? How can we best take advantage of the general-purpose computing capabilities of mobile GPUs to offload audio processing? When should we prefer GPU computation to cloud? Can we obtain energy efficiency on a scale comparable to a low-power Digital Signal Processor (DSP)?

In this work, we show that the GPU performance of audio sensing algorithms is sensitive to two key control-flow parameters such as the frame fan-out (total number of frame processing GPU threads) and per-thread compute factors (amount of computation relative to memory accesses). We present a GPU offloading engine that leverages parallel optimization techniques that allow us to control these parameters and auto-tune the performance of audio routines. Without such optimization, naively parameterized GPU implementations may be up to 1.5x slower than multi-threaded CPU alternatives, and consume more than 2x the energy of cloud offloading.

Through extensive evaluation we find that *for time-sensitive audio apps, and when energy is less of a concern, there is no better option than using GPU optimized audio routines*. Algorithms tuned for the GPU can deliver inferences an order of magnitude faster than a sequential CPU deployment, and 3.1x or 6.5x faster than cloud offloading with good connectivity for deep audio inferences such as speaker identification and keyword spotting, respectively. At the same time, the energy consumed is 3-4x lower than when using the CPU. Perhaps more surprising, *for tasks that are more continuous but tolerate short delays (of 10-20 secs) GPU is also a top choice*. When raw data is accumulated for batched processing, algorithms optimized for the GPU begin to consume less energy than cloud offloading with fast connections. Further, the optimized GPU can deliver energy efficiency levels in ranges comparable to what can be achieved by low-power DSP implementations

Permission to make digital or hard copies of all or part of this work for personal or classroom use is granted without fee provided that copies are not made or distributed for profit or commercial advantage and that copies bear this notice and the full citation on the first page. Copyrights for components of this work owned by others than ACM must be honored. Abstracting with credit is permitted. To copy otherwise, or republish, to post on servers or to redistribute to lists, requires prior specific permission and/or a fee. Request permissions from permissions@acm.org.

MobiSys '17, June 19–23, 2017, Niagara Falls, NY, USA

© 2017 ACM. ISBN 978-1-4503-4928-4/17/06...$15.00

DOI: http://dx.doi.org/10.1145/3081333.3081358

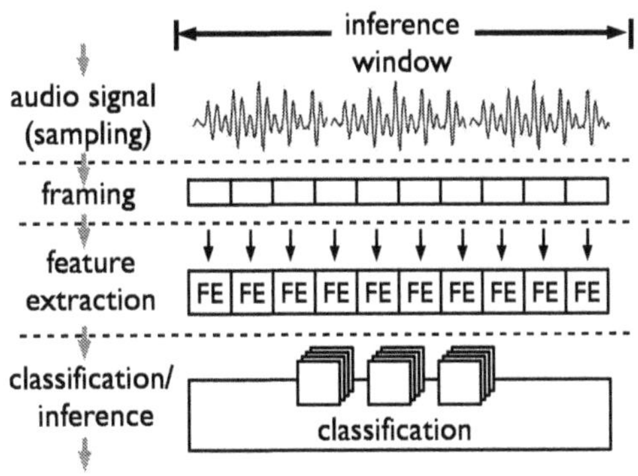

Figure 1: Audio pipeline structure.

with some preliminary optimization. The batching delays required for the benefits to appear are sufficiently short to support the operation of not only life-logging style behavior monitoring applications that tolerate large delays, but also apps that deliver context aware services and notifications such as conversation analysis [58, 43].

The contributions of our work are:

- A detailed study of the trade-offs of using mobile system-on-a-chip GPUs for audio sensing workloads.
- An optimization engine that uses key structural and memory access parallel patterns applicable to popular algorithm building blocks used in numerous audio sensing apps available commercially and in the literature. These patterns allow us to automatically tune the GPU performance boost of audio pipelines: they 1) increase the data parallelism by allowing a larger number of threads to work independently on smaller portions of the audio input stream; and 2) strategically place data needed by the threads into GPU memory caches where access latency is lower and the data can be reused.
- A comprehensive proof-of-concept OpenCL [11] implementation of widely used audio sensing algorithms built on a smartphone development board [15]. Our prototype includes a library of sensing components for feature extraction and classification (including DNNs [34], GMMs [18] etc.) needed for common forms of context inference. These components serve as the building blocks for numerous apps from the audio processing literature – as a demonstration, we implement 3 recently proposed application pipelines (e.g., emotion recognition, speaker identification and spoken keyword spotting).

To the best of our knowledge, we are the first to identify generalizable GPU parallel optimizations that are *applicable across multiple algorithms* used in the unique workloads required by audio sensing. Previous efforts [60, 29] have focused on different workload scenarios (e.g., automated speech recognition) where processing requirements differ from those imposed by audio sensing: continuous background monitoring of coarse sound classes supported by offline-trained models that can operate entirely cloud-free.

2. AUDIO SENSING MEETS THE GPU

In this section, we detail the operation of typical microphone-based sensor apps, elaborate on the GPU execution model and highlight some of the challenges it presents for audio sensing.

2.1 Audio Sensing Primer

Audio sensing apps are characterized by their ability to sample and process microphone data – they include specialized audio processing code that is distinctly different from the app specific logic (e.g., activating services based on detected audio context). The dataflow of sensor processing within these apps share many similarities which we illustrate in Figure 1. The execution begins with the sampling of the microphone where raw data is typically accumulated over a short time window (hundreds of milliseconds up to a few seconds) sufficient to capture distinctive characteristics of sounds and utterances. The audio signal is then subdivided into much shorter (e.g., 30ms) segments called *frames* which are subject to preprocessing and feature extraction. The aim of the features is to summarize the collected data in a way that describes the differences between targeted behavior or context (e.g., sounds, words, or speaker identity). Identifying which activity or context is observed in the sensor data in the analyzed time window requires the use of one or more classification models. Models are usually built offline prior to deploying a sensor app based on examples of different activities and often the classification (i.e., model evaluation applied to the whole window of stacked frame feature data) is a bottleneck stage of the audio pipeline [27]. Example audio apps with their execution properties are listed in Table 1.

2.2 Example Audio Applications

Two most widely used classification models in the audio sensing domain are Gaussian Mixture Models (GMMs) and Deep Neural Networks (DNNs). Table 2 gives instances of their near ubiquitous usage. Here we describe the operational semantics of 3 representative data-intensive deep-inference examples built on these models. However, we note that the techniques we develop are applicable to any other audio sensing application from Table 2 that uses these models as a building block.

Speaker Identification (GMM based). The pipeline is introduced by Rachuri et al. [52]. Gaussian Mixture Model classifiers are trained using speech from 23 speakers. Each of the speakers is represented by a speaker-specific GMM built by performing Maximum a Posteriori (MAP) adaptation of a 128-component background GMM representative of all speakers. The GMM evaluates the probability with which certain acoustic observations match the model and in our case these observations are 32 Perceptual Linear Prediction (PLP) coefficients [32] extracted from 30-ms frames over 5 seconds of recorded audio. At runtime, the likelihood of the audio sequence is calculated given each speaker model and the speaker with the highest likelihood is predicted.

Emotion Recognition (GMM based). Structurally, the pipeline is identical to the Speaker Identification. The difference comes from the parameters of the GMMs which are trained on a different dataset (the Emotional Prosody Speech and Transcripts library [44]) so that each GMM represents an emotional category [52].

Keyword Spotting (DNN based). The application is based on the small-footprint implementation of Chen et al. [22], and its aim is to detect a hot phrase spoken by a nearby speaker. The example application is trained to detect an "Ok, Google" command. The audio analysis is performed by segmenting the input signal into frames of length 25ms with an offset of 10ms, i.e. the frames overlap. Filter-bank energies (40 coefficients) are extracted from each frame and accumulated into a group of 40 frames. The features from these frames serve as the input layer to a DNN with as many output layer nodes as there are target keywords (plus an additional sink node to capture other words). The DNN is fully connected and has 3 hidden layers with 128 nodes each. The output of the DNN is raw posterior probabilities of encountering each of the keywords over the last second of data. The DNN feed forwarding is performed in a sliding window with every new frame, resulting in 100 propagations per second (once every 10 ms).

Application	Purpose	Main Features	Inference Model	Frame	Window
Emotion Recognition* [52]	emotion recognition	PLP* [32]	14 Gaussian Mixture Models* [18]	30ms	5s
Speaker Identification* [52]	speaker identification	PLP*	23 Gaussian Mixture Models*	30ms	5s
Keyword Spotting* [22]	hotphrase recognition	Filterbank Energies*	Deep Neural Network* [34]	25ms	1s
Stress Detection [46]	stress from voice	MFCC [26], TEO-CB-AutoEnv [61]	2 Gaussian Mixture Models*	32ms	1.28s
Speaker Count [58]	speaker counting	MFCC, pitch [25]	Unsupervised Clustering	32ms	3s
Ambient Sound Classification [47]	sound recognition	MFCC, Time Domain Features	Gaussian Mixture Models*	64ms	1.28s

Table 1: Example audio sensing applications and their properties. *Apps and models implemented in OpenCL.

Classifier	Applications
GMM	emotion recognition [52], speaker identification [52, 45], ambient sound classification [47], stress detection [46]
DNN	keyword spotting [22], emotion recognition [30], speech recognition [33], sound event classification [49]

Table 2: Categorization of audio sensing applications based on classification model.

Pattern	Type	Applicability
fan-out	structural	GMM, DNN, feature extraction sub-phases
vectorization	memory access	ubiquitous
sliding window	memory access	DNN, pre-emphasis
tiling	memory access	GMM, filter banks

Table 3: Parallel optimization patterns taxonomy.

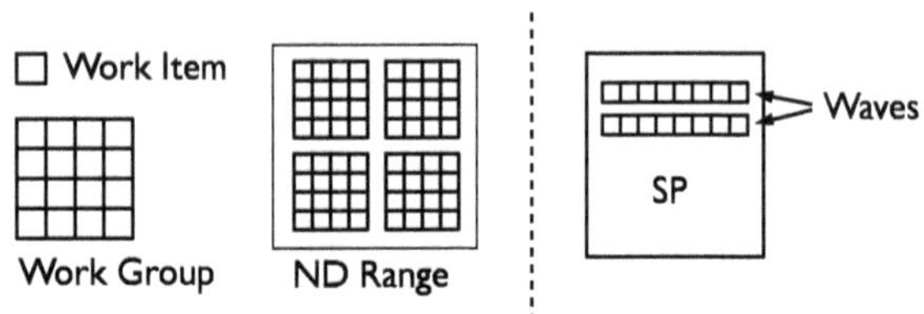

Figure 2: OpenCL thread model and a GPU Shader Processor. The SP features 2 waves of 8 work items each, it can run 16 threads in total simultaneously. The work items of one work group are executed on a single SP.

2.3 GPU Execution Model and Challenges

We use OpenCL's terminology [11] and Qualcomm Adreno GPU [12] as an example for GPU architecture and programming model, but our discussion and conclusions apply equally to other GPU platforms, such as NVIDIA with CUDA [9]. To an OpenCL programmer, a computing system consists of a *host* that is traditionally a CPU, such as the Snapdragon 800 Krait CPU, and one or more *devices* (GPU) that communicate with the host to perform parallel computation. Programs written in OpenCL consist of host code (C API extensions) and device code (OpenCL C kernel language) – communication between the two is performed by issuing commands to a command queue through the host program space. Example commands are copying data from host to device memory, or launching a *kernel* for execution on the device. Kernels specify the data-parallel part of the program that will be executed by the GPU threads. When a kernel is launched, all the threads execute the same code but on different parts of the data.

Thread Model and Compute Granularity. All the threads generated when the kernel function is called are collectively known as a grid (or ND Range) and are organized in a two-level hierarchy independently from the underlying device architecture. Figure 2 illustrates this organization. The grid consists of *work groups* each containing a set of threads known as *work items*. The exact thread scheduling on the GPU is decoupled from the work groups and is vendor specific although it shares a lot of similarities among GPU varieties. Switching from a group of work items to another occurs when there is a data dependency (read/write) that must be completed before proceeding and is done to mask these IO latencies.

One of the challenges of implementing GPU-friendly algorithms is providing the right level of work item granularity. If the GPU threads are too few, the GPU will struggle with hiding memory access latency due to not being able to switch between compute-ready threads while others are stalled on a memory transaction. Audio sensing algorithm execution revolves around the analysis of frames, and a natural candidate for data parallelization is to let each work item/thread analyze a frame. However, the number of frames in an inference window is on the order of tens to hundreds, whereas the GPU typically requires thousands of threads for any meaningful speedups to begin to appear. A challenge is organizing the audio algorithm execution in a way that allows more work items to perform computation.

Managing Memory-Bound Audio Kernels. Work items have access to different memory types (global, constant, local/shared, or private) each of which provides various size vs. access latency trade-offs. Global memory is the largest but also the slowest among the memories. Private memory is exclusive to each work item and is very limited in size, whereas the shared memory is larger and accessible by all work items in a group. Often, a *compute to global memory access (CGMA) ratio* is used as an indicator of the kernel efficiency – the higher the ratio is, the more work the kernel can perform per global memory access, the higher the performance.

Typical algorithms used in audio sensing need to read a large number of model parameters which they apply to the frame data, but the number of floating point operations per read is relatively low making audio kernels *memory-bound*. In order to squeeze maximum performance out of the mobile GPU (highest speed and thus lowest energy consumed), algorithms will need to reduce the global memory traffic by intelligently leveraging the smaller but lower access latency memories (shared and private). The challenge is enabling appropriate memory optimization strategies that keep the CGMA ratio high while maintaining a suitable level of granularity for the work items.

Summary. GPUs are a powerful platform for general-purpose computing programmed by language abstractions such as OpenCL and CUDA. An unanswered challenge is how and what performance control techniques we can leverage that depend on the algorithm semantics rather than a concrete hardware configuration.

3. OPTIMIZATION ENGINE OVERVIEW

To address the GPU deployment challenges presented in the previous section, we build a library of OpenCL auto-tunable audio routines that form the narrow waist of audio processing pipelines found in the mobile sensing literature (e.g., filter bank feature extraction, Gaussian Mixture Model, Deep Neural Network inference). This library builds upon a set of structural and memory access techniques that expose a set of tunable audio model-dependent *control-flow parameters* which we can control in a pre-deployment step

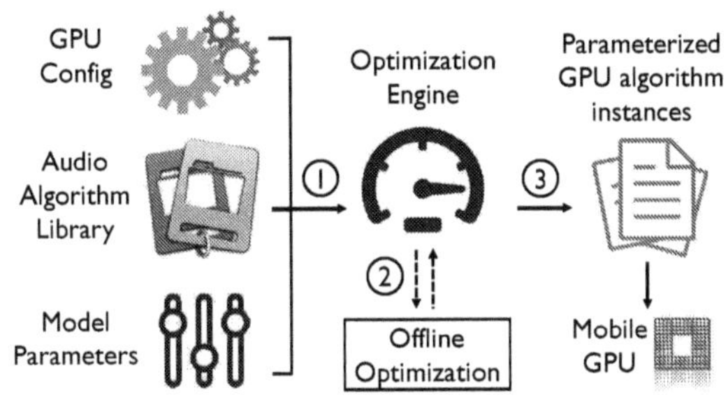

Figure 3: High-level optimization engine workflow.

with an optimization engine. The goal of this engine is to provide the best match between the domain-specific library implementation and mobile GPU hardware constraints. The engine helps to avoid cumbersome hand tuning, instead automatically finds optimal parameters for the audio kernel routines with large performance boosts for some of the algorithms. This requires *zero* change in the kernel code itself, the parameters are passed through OpenCL commands as kernel arguments at runtime. A high-level workflow is illustrated in Figure 3.

The pre-deployment step is a three-staged process, where the engine first loads as input audio model parameters such as the DNN layout and queries the GPU device specification (e.g., GPU shared cache size) in order to be able to estimate optimum values for the GPU algorithm control-flow parameters. In the second stage, the engine performs the optimization step by solving a series of linear and quadratic equations and outputs a configuration file with GPU-kernel parameter values required by our audio library. The third stage is loading the values from the locally persisted config file to parameterize the audio algorithms upon initialization of concrete sensor apps.

To provide high-performance parallel implementations, we build the techniques listed in Table 3 that enable control over the following parameters. Empirically we found that for memory-bound audio kernels, these provide a sweet spot of tunable but not too complex parameters with a key impact on mobile GPU performance:

- **frame fan-out factor** (ϕ) – defined as the total number of audio frame processing GPU threads. A higher value results in an increase in the number of concurrent threads that can work independently.
- **per-thread compute factor** (κ) – defined as the number of computed output values per GPU thread. By optimizing this the engine attempts to maximize the number of computations each thread can perform relative to its memory reads and writes (favoring compute-bound operation instead of memory-bound).

Manipulating the first parameter is achieved in our library through *the frame fan-out* structural optimization pattern. The core idea behind it is to split the audio analysis so that each GPU thread can work on a subset of the output values extracted from an audio frame. The second parameter is tightly related to a set of memory access patterns that reduce expensive global memory traffic and increase the per-thread compute factor. These techniques are: 1) *Vectorization* that consolidates slow global memory reads into a single load operation which is possible thanks to the sequential nature of accessing values from the audio stream. In our examples, the engine selects larger read batches and can fetch into the thread registers up to x values from memory, where x is vendor specific (for Qualcomm Adreno $x = 16$, for NVidia Tegra X1 $x = 4$ [10]). 2) *Memory Sliding Window* and *Memory Tiling*: the techniques allow threads to collaboratively load data into shared memory where this data can be subsequently reused with lower latency to produce multiple output values. These are critical optimizations since global memory access is arguably the most prominent bottleneck we observe in the widely used audio classification and feature extraction algorithms.

4. PARALLEL CONTROL-FLOW OPTIMIZATION

In this section, we detail the structural and memory access parallel patterns that enable the optimization engine to parameterize the audio routines in our library.

4.1 Inter- and Intra- Frame Fan-Out

This pattern controls the level of data parallelism by allowing a larger number of concurrent threads to perform independent computations on the input data. We can support such a mode of operation thanks to the way audio pipelines process frames – repeatedly mixing the frame samples/coefficient with multiple parameters (GMM mixtures, DNN network weights). Independent computations are performed not only among different frames but also within a single frame as well, a phenomenon which we call the *frame fan-out*. This allows the total amount of threads, or *fan-out factor* (ϕ), to be relatively high. It can be computed as follows: $\phi = \frac{n*\nu}{\kappa}$ where n is the number of frames, ν is the total number of output values per frame, and κ is the number of computed values per GPU thread (*per-thread compute factor*). This structural optimization is applicable across both feature extraction (filter bank computation) and classification phases. The next two examples illustrate how this pattern can be applied:

GMM Fan-Out. The input for this classification phase is the extracted feature coefficients from all frames. In the Speaker Identification pipeline there are 32 PLP frame features and a total of $n = 500$ frames per inference window (one frame every 10ms for 5s). Each GMM has $\nu = 128$ mixtures each of which computes a probability score by mixing the 32 PLP coefficients from a frame with the parameters (mean and variance) of 32 Gaussian distributions. With a per-thread compute factor of $\kappa = 1$, we could let each OpenCL work item estimate the probability score for one mixture per frame resulting in a fan-out factor of $\phi = 500 \times 128$. We enable the kernel to generate this massive number of work items by letting them write intermediate scores to global memory and a separate kernel is launched to sum the scores.

DNN Fan-Out. Similarly, the input data for the keyword spotting DNN classification is the extracted filter bank energies from the frames. In a 1-second inference window there are a total of $n = 100$ network propagations (one per new frame every 10ms). A DNN kernel computes partial results across all input frames by performing the feed forward propagation for one layer across the frames simultaneously. Multiple kernels are launched each of which computes the node activation values for the next layer. With $\nu = 128$ nodes in the hidden layers we could let each OpenCL work item compute the activation for one node per frame offset ($\kappa = 1$) resulting in a fan-out factor of $\phi = 100 \times 128$.

The role of the optimization engine is to provide optimum values for the control-flow parameters ϕ and κ. n and ν are determined directly by the audio model specification, whereas the final value of ϕ depends on κ, or the amount of work each GPU thread is assigned. The engine tunes the per-thread compute factor κ since we observe that *maximum GPU performance may not necessarily be reached when parallelism is highest.* The fan-out factor ϕ reaches its maximum when its denominator (κ) has its lowest value ($\kappa = 1$), i.e.

Algorithm 1 Shared Memory Use Kernel Template

```
Input: (i) Pointer to input buffer (in), (ii) Pointer to output
  buffer (out), (iii) Thread local id (lid), (iv) Thread group id
  (gid), (v) Shared memory maximum size (max_s).
                                        ▷ Collaborative data load:
loadOffset ← compute_load_offset(lid)
inputOffset ← compute_input_offset(gid, lid)
__shared floatN data[max_s]     ▷ shared memory declaration
if loadOffset < max_s then
    data[loadOffset] ← vloadN(0, &in[inputOffset])     ▷ vectorized
barrier(CLK_LOCAL_MEM_FENCE)  ▷ wait for all threads
  to finish loading data
                                        ▷ Shared data processing:
for (i = 0; i < x; ++i) do
    localDataOffset ← compute_local_offset(lid, i)
    result ← process(&data[localDataOffset])
    outputOffset ← compute_output_offset(gid, lid, i)
    out[outputOffset] ← result
```

when there are more threads performing less work. The memory access patterns in the following subsection enable each GPU thread to perform more computation ($\kappa > 1$) relative to the number of its memory reads and writes: the total count of threads decreases but they can make a more efficient use of memory.

4.2 Memory Access Control

Tuning audio kernel performance with the per-thread compute factor κ is closely related to how memory access is managed by the threads in a work group. Increasing the number of computations per thread per global memory access and thus finding optimum values for κ depends on maximum exploitation of the faster but limited in size GPU memories. We discuss several key strategies, enabled by the specifics of digital signal processing, to lower the number of global memory operations. These strategies either 1) batch global memory transactions into fewer operations, or 2) let the *threads in a work group collaboratively load data needed by all of them into shared memory where access latency is lower*.

Vectorization. When kernels read the input data features or parameters, for instance, they access all the adjacent values in a frame. As a result, the memory access can be vectorized and consolidated with vector load operations that fetch multiple neighboring values at once from global to private memory. For example, when a thread requires the 32 PLP coefficients from a frame, it can use the OpenCL *vloadx* operation to issue 2 reads with 16 values (*vload16*) fetched simultaneously instead of performing 32 reads for each coefficient separately.

Shared Memory Sliding Window. Often the input raw audio or feature stream is processed in sliding window steps, i.e. the input is divided into overlapping frames over which identical computations are performed. Example scenarios where this type of processing is commonly applied are the feature extraction (PLP, MFCC [26]), or the classification of the feature stream into observed phenomena (as is the case for the DNN keyword spotting, see Figure 4). The data overlap is usually quite substantial – the feature extraction phase for the Speaker Identification pipeline, for instance, uses 30ms frames (240 samples at a sampling rate of 8kHz) with a 10ms frame rate (an offset of 80 samples) resulting in a 66% data overlap between subsequent frames. We can exploit this property of the audio stream processing to let the threads in a work group collaboratively load a larger chunk from the input spanning samples from multiple frames into shared memory (where access latency is lower), and let each thread reuse its loaded parameters by applying them against several offsets from the input. The higher the data overlap for adjacent frames, the larger the opportunity the threads have to load more adjacent regions with fewer read operations, and the more computation they can perform per global memory read. The pattern enables the control of the per-thread compute factor κ by increasing the CGMA ratio of the kernel operation.

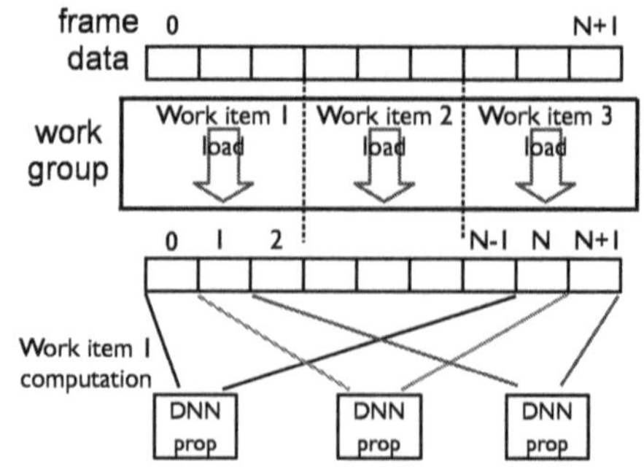

Figure 4: Sliding window example. The DNN activation of one node in the first layer (denoted by DNN prop) is performed by each work item in a work group. The required data for one such computation is N frames. The figure explicitly shows the computation for work item 1 which is performed for 3 frame offsets from the accumulated frame input data (0 to $N-1$, 1 to N, and 2 to $N+1$). Each work item in a group can load a part of the data needed for the DNN layer activation, but will use all data loaded by the peers in the group, as work item 1 does. A work item computes the activation for one node in a layer (DNN prop), but since more data is accessible from the collaborative loading, the item can reuse its parameters to compute the activation for the same node for 3 different frame offsets.

Algorithm 1 shows example kernel pseudo code where the work items cooperate to load data into shared memory. The key advantage is that each thread can use a single vectorized fetch which is only a small proportion of the actual data needed from global memory. Collectively, however, all threads are able to load the data needed by their peers in the work group. The number of adjacent input regions x over which the threads in a work group perform computations are limited by the maximum size of the shared memory reserved to a work group. For Adreno 330 that size is 8KB. The optimization engine estimates the maximum x as a function of the model size and shared memory constraints, the pattern exposes x as the per-thread compute factor ($\kappa = x$).

Shared Memory Tiling. As discussed in the description of the frame fan-out in §4.1, when audio processing pipelines work on a frame they usually produce multiple output values (e.g., feature coefficients or probability scores) by combining the frame data with multiple parameters. The procedure can be treated as *generalized dense matrix-matrix multiplication* with the two matrices being: 1) an input matrix $I_{(n,d)}$ with n input frames each of which has d elements (samples/coefficients); and 2) a parameter matrix $P_{(k,d)}$ with k parameters each of which has dimensionality d. The result of the combination of the two matrices is a matrix $O_{(n,k)} = I_{(n,d)} \bigotimes P^T_{(k,d)}$ where $\bigotimes$ can be a generalized operation that performs a reduction over d elements from the two matrices (a row from O and a column from P^T). Prominent applications of this operation can be found in the computation of the filter bank coefficients, the GMM mixture probability estimation, and the DNN network propagation. An example reduction $\bigotimes$ used in the GMM classification stage is shown in the following equation:

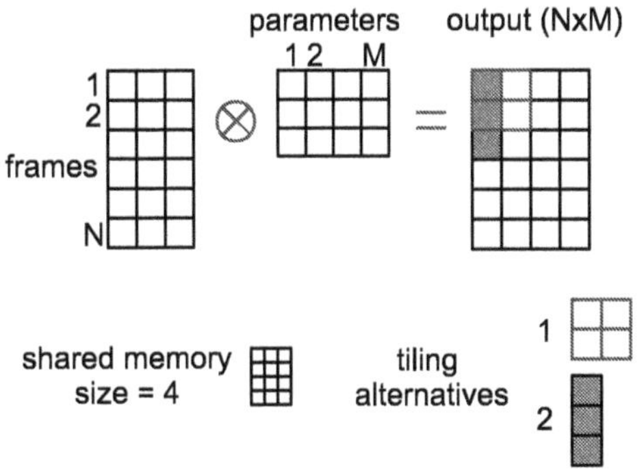

Figure 5: Tiling example. There are N frame data rows and M parameter columns that can be combined to yield N×M output values. The shared memory size of a work group is limited to 4 frame rows or parameter columns in total. There are 2 tiling alternatives. Alternative 1 fills shared memory by loading data for 2 frames and 2 parameters leading to 4 computed values in total from the work group. Alternative 2 loads data for 3 frames and 1 parameter leading to 3 computed values in total.

$$o_{ij} = -\frac{1}{2}(g_j + \sum_{0 \leq s < d} (x_{is} - m_{js})^2 v_{js}) \qquad (1)$$

where o_{ij} is one element from the output matrix; m_j, v_j, and g_j are the Gaussian parameters of a mixture component; and x_i are feature values from frame i.

The straightforward implementation of a GPU kernel to compute matrix O would be to let each thread compute one output value o_{ij} and load independently an input row i and a parameter column j. However, a strategy for reducing global memory traffic is to introduce a model-specific version of *tiled algorithms* used in matrix-matrix multiplication [39]. The core idea is to let the work groups of a kernel partition the output matrix into *tiles* so that the total data for each tile fits into shared memory. Our goal is to have the threads in a work group collaboratively load both input data and parameters into shared memory in a way that maximizes the number of computations per global memory read. This can be achieved if the number of computed values ({number of frames} N_f × {number of parameters} N_p) per loaded data is as large as possible for the entire work group. Figure 5 illustrates the pattern in operation.

4.3 Parameter Estimation

We calculate key optimization parameters as described below.

Vector size x. The engine selects the vector size for batched memory reads by querying with OpenCL commands whether the audio kernel can successfully be compiled with the given value for x. The engine enumerates the possible values for x in descending order and picks the highest value under which the kernel successfully compiles. Compilation may fail when the size of the vectorized loads exhausts the thread register space.

Memory sliding κ. Optimizing this parameter involves solving a linear equation with respect to the GPU shared memory size, and input model parameters. If S_M is the total number of values the shared memory can accommodate, S_F is the input region size, and r is the frame offset in number of input values, then the maximum κ is computed in the following manner: $\kappa = \left\lfloor \frac{S_M - S_F}{r} \right\rfloor + 1$.

Memory tiling κ. The optimization engine makes a two-staged decision: whether to activate this pattern and if activated how to best parameterize it. The decision is based on the type of the model used for audio analysis (filter banks, GMM, or DNN), input model dimensions (size of the model parameters), maximum work group size, and shared memory size. The optimization engine estimates the work group size and an optimum number of output matrix values each thread in the work group should compute so that global memory accesses are minimized. This is implemented by solving a quadratic equation with respect to N_f and N_p under the shared memory constraints. In our examples, the pattern would be activated for the filter banks and GMM computation, but not for the DNN where the size of the network is prohibitively large for any meaningful subset to be effectively exploited from shared memory.

Frame fan-out ϕ and work group size. The engine estimates the fan-out factor in a final step by reading the specified audio model parameters (e.g., number of frames) and having κ determined in a prior step. We strive to select the largest work group size possible. Similarly to vectorization, this can be done by exhaustively trying to compile the kernels with values up to the maximum size allowed. Sizes are enumerated in multiples of the *preferred group multiple parameter* (queried from the GPU with OpenCL).

5. IMPLEMENTATION

We briefly summarize the details of the software artifacts used in this work.

Hardware and APIs. We prototype the audio sensing algorithms on a Snapdragon 800 Mobile Development Platform for Smartphones (MDP) [15] with an Android 4.3 Jelly Bean OS featuring Adreno 330 GPU present in mobile phones such Samsung Galaxy S5 and LG G Pro2. All GPGPU development is done with OpenCL 1.1 Embedded Profile and we reuse utilities for initializing and querying the GPU from the Adreno SDK that is openly available [12]. In addition, we prototype baseline versions of the audio sensing pipelines for the Qualcomm Hexagon DSP [13] with the Hexagon C SDK v1.0 [14]. The DSP has 3 hardware threads and we use the *dspCV* thread pool library shipped with the Hexgagon SDK to build multithreaded versions of the algorithms for the DSP. The CPU sequential baselines reuse the C code built for the DSP and are accessed by interfacing with the Android Native Development Kit (NDK). Multithreaded CPU versions are built by using C++11 threads – we leverage the 4 cores available to the Snapdragon Krait CPU. Note, our implementation does not explicitly leverage, nor is structured for the use of, SIMD instructions (like NEON) as available in the Krait CPU. Although we take advantage of Qualcomm SDK primitives and other best practices (described next) that enhance the performance of the CPU and DSP in the Snapdragon. Power measurements are performed with a Monsoon Power Monitor [8] attached to the MDP. Classifier models are trained with the HTK toolkit [6] for the Speaker/Emotion Recognition and the Theano python library [17] for the Keyword Spotting.

DSP Baseline Implementation. We implement basic DSP benchmarks as a ballpark reference on energy consumption and a first indication of latency when machine learning algorithms found in audio sensing are executed on a low-power chip. As stated above, we use the Qualcomm Hexagon SDK to tailor implementations to the DSP which are not a direct compilation of CPU-based code. The DSP C language features are a subset of the standard C distributions [27], which is why without significant modifications most CPU algorithms cannot be directly executed on the Hexagon DSP. Instead, we build our baselines to match the requirements and conventions of the Hexagon Elite SDK for audio processing, our basis is DSP-targeted code which has been modified to be executed on the CPU as well. Although we have yet to take advantage of the more advanced VLIW (Very Long Instruction Word) instructions available to the DSP everywhere in our code, our DSP implementations are not naive CPU-variants as we reuse some of the optimized DSP processing routines coming readily with the DSP SDK (such as FFT computation): these already come with VLIW optimized instructions and intrinsics. The algorithms that are not included in these DSP libraries we have implemented ourselves following the guidelines provided by the Elite audio processing SDK (e.g., for memory allocation). We acknowledge additional research is needed to find the most optimal DSP implementations, however we do leverage optimized algorithmic primitives distributed with the SDK to give some reference numbers on the amount of energy required to process machine learning algorithms found in audio sensing.

Kernel Compilation. Building the OpenCL kernels can be done either via reading the sources from a string and compiling them at runtime or by pre-compiling the source into a binary. We use pre-compiled binaries that drastically reduce the kernel load time and that need to be produced once per deployment.

6. EVALUATION

In this section, we provide an extensive evaluation of the parallel optimizations under representative audio sensing algorithms when deployed on a mobile GPU. The main findings are:

- Optimizing the control-flow parameters is critical – naively parameterized GPU implementations may be up to 1.5x slower than multithreaded CPU baselines and consume more than 2x the energy of offloading batched computation to the cloud.
- The total speedup against a sequential CPU implementation for an optimized GMM-based and a DNN-based pipeline running entirely on the GPU is 8.2x and 13.5x respectively, making the GPU the processing unit of choice for fast real-time feedback. The optimized GPU is also 3-4x more energy efficient than sequential CPU implementations, but can consume up to 3.2x more energy than a low-power DSP.
- After a certain batching threshold (10 to 20 seconds) of computing multiple inferences in one go, optimized GPU algorithms begin to consume less energy than cloud offloading with good throughput (5Mbps and 10Mbps), in addition to obtaining inferences 3.1x and 6.5x times faster for the GMM and DNN-based pipelines respectively.
- The total energy consumption under batching scenarios is in ranges comparable to those delivered by reference low-power DSP implementations with some basic optimization.

6.1 Experimental Setup

Experiments are performed with the display off and the algorithms are executing in the background, as is typical for sensing apps to operate in such mode. We denote with *Audio Optimized GPU (a-GPU)* the output from the optimization engine as described in §3. Throughout the section we use the following baselines.

- *DSP sequential (DSP).* Our DSP baselines are implemented as specified in Section 5 via the Hexagon DSP in DSP- compatible C. We reuse optimized built-in primitives for FFT computation, memory allocation and follow the conventions of the Elite SDK for audio processing. Our implementations are meant to be used as a ballpark reference on the energy efficiency that can be supported by low-power units but do not claim they are the most efficient that can be achieved through advanced hardware optimizations applied rigorously throughout the code base.

Computation	Parameters	Speed-up Gain
GMM	$x = 1, \kappa = \nu$	3.6x
	$x = 16, \kappa = \nu$	12.8x
	$x = 16, \kappa = 1$	15.6x
	$\mathbf{x = 16, \kappa = 4}$ (tiling)	**16.2x**
DNN	$x = 1, \kappa = \nu$	1.8x
	$x = 16, \kappa = \nu$	4.8x
	$x = 16, \kappa = 1$	13x
	$\mathbf{x = 16, \kappa = 5}$ (sliding window)	**21.3x**
Filter banks	$x = 1, \kappa = \nu$	1.7x
	$x = 16, \kappa = \nu$	4x
	$x = 16, \kappa = 1$	6x
	$\mathbf{x = 16, \kappa = 2}$ (tiling)	**6.6x**

Table 4: Parameter configuration speed-ups vs. CPU sequential implementation. Lines in bold show the optimal parameter values found by the optimization engine.

- *CPU sequential (CPU).* Our implementations have a sequential workflow that follows the DSP code structure but reimplements some of the routines that require DSP-specific VLIW instructions (e.g., FFT computation). The baselines are based on DSP-compatible C.
- *CPU multi-threaded (CPU-m).* We implement variants of the pipeline algorithms where the bottleneck classification stage of the audio pipeline (occupying $> 90\%$ of the runtime in our examples) is parallelized across multiple threads. The GMM classification is restructured so that each GMM model probability is the unit of work for a separate thread. We maintain a pool of 4 threads which equals the number of physical cores of the Snapdragon Krait CPU – adding more threads did not lead to any performance benefits. The DNN classification is restructured so that the network propagation step is performed in parallel: each thread processes the activation of one node in a layer.
- *DSP multi-threaded (DSP-m).* Similarly to the multi-threaded CPU versions of the algorithms, we adopt DSP alternatives that parallelize the pipeline classification. The parallel DSP variants have logically the same threading model as the CPU one, with the difference that the DSP thread pool size is 3, i.e. it equals the number of hardware threads. We use the worker pool utility library *dspCV* which speeds up the execution for Computer Vision algorithms on the DSP.
- *Naive GPU (n-GPU).* We add the most naively parameterized GPU implementations as explicit baselines in addition to showing different parameter configurations. For all algorithmic building blocks (GMM, DNN, and features) in this naive baseline category we set the vectorized load factor $x = 1$, and the per-frame compute factor to be $\kappa = \nu$ which results in a frame fan-out factor of $\phi = n$.

Energy Measurements. All energy measurements are taken with a Monsoon Power Monitor attached to our MDP device. By default, the experiments were performed with a display off, with no services running in the background except system processes. This reflects the case when GPU offloading is done in the background, as in a continuous sensing scenario. The power evaluation setup closely matches the one reported by LEO [28]. Each application is profiled separately for energy consumption by averaging power over multiple runs on the CPU, DSP and GPU.

6.2 Pattern Optimization Benchmarks

In this subsection, we study how the application and parameterization of the various optimization techniques presented in §4

	GMM full pipeline	GMM classification	DNN full pipeline	DNN classification
DSP	-8.8x	-8.6x	-4.5x	-4.0x
DSP-m	-3.2x	2.5x	-2.1x	-1.5x
CPU (runtime)	1.0x (1573 ms)	1.0x (1472 ms)	1.0x (501 ms)	1.0x (490 ms)
CPU-m	3.0x	3.4x	2.8x	2.9x
n-GPU	3.1x	3.6x	1.8x	1.8x
a-GPU	**8.2x**	**16.2x**	**13.5x**	**21.3x**

Table 5: Speedup factors for one run of the various pipeline implementations compared against the sequential CPU baseline. Negative numbers for the DSP variants show that the runtime is that amount of time slower than the CPU baseline. CPU average runtime in ms is given for reference in brackets. Note that the DSP numbers are provided by our reference implementation under the conditions specified in the baseline definition. A highly optimized DSP implementation might challenge the CPU latency-wise in certain scenarios. We still expect the a-GPU to be the lead given its current massive speed-ups.

affect the GPU kernel runtime performance. Table 4 shows different points in the parameter space compared to the engine optimized configuration.

Pattern Speedups. A first observation is that using vectorization with larger batches ($x = 16$) provides a significant boost across all algorithms. The speedup of the most naïve GMM kernels jumps from 3.6x to 12.8x, the DNN ones – from 1.8x to 4.8, and the filter banks – from 1.7x to 4x. The success of this simple technique can be attributed to the fact that the mobile GPU is optimized to efficiently access multiple items with a single instruction.

Another observation is that increasing the fan-out factor ϕ by setting $\kappa = 1$ provides tangible runtime boosts. As illustrated, speedups increase from 12.8x to 15.6x for the GMM, and from 4.8x to 13x for the DNN. Interestingly, the higher fan-out provides benefits even though the number of global memory accesses is raised by issuing writes of intermediate values to a scratch memory. The reason for this is that the fan-out pattern prominently increases the total number of work items and as a consequence there are more opportunities for the GPU to hide memory access latencies – whenever a group of threads is stalled on a memory read or write operation, with a higher probability the GPU can find another group that can perform computation while the former waits.

Last but not least, the more advanced tiling and sliding window techniques tuned by the optimization engine provide noticeable speedup improvements over the straightforward use of shared memory. The sliding window optimization boosts the second best DNN kernel speedup from 13x to 21.3x, which is also the highest cumulative gain observed across all algorithms. Optimally parameterized tiling, on the other hand, brings the overall GMM speedup to 16.2x and filter banks to 6.6x. In these cases, increasing κ further results in suboptimal use of shared memory – since its size is limited, the work items can fetch only a proportion of the total data they need, the rest needs to be loaded from the slower global memory into thread registers.

Summary. The engine optimized kernels allow GPU computation to exhibit much higher performance than naively parameterized baselines. The optimization techniques can be ubiquitously applied across multiple stages of the pipelines.

6.3 GPU Pipeline Runtime and Energy

We compare our engine optimized GPU pipelines against the baselines listed in §6.1. Table 5 shows the runtime for running the pipelines on the various processing units. The most prominent observation is that the optimized GPU implementation is the fastest one. For instance, the full GMM and DNN pipelines are 8.2x and 13.5x times faster than a sequential CPU implementation respectively, an order of magnitude faster. In comparison, the CPU multi-threaded alternatives are around 3x times faster only. If the GPU is not carefully utilized, the naively parameterized GPU implementations may be up to 1.5x slower than the multicore variants (e.g., DNN pipeline). The reason why the audio-optimized GPU fares so much better than both multicore CPU and naive GPU alternatives is because massive data parallelism is enabled by the parallel techniques – the hundreds of cores on the GPU can work on multiple small independent tasks simultaneously and hide memory access latency. This is especially true for the classification tasks that are 16.2x (GMM) and 21.3x (DNN) faster than their sequential CPU counterparts.

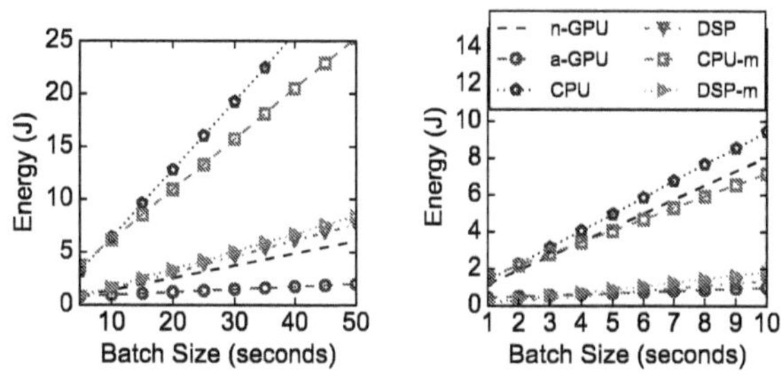

(a) GMM pipeline (b) DNN pipeline

Figure 6: Energy (J) as a function of the audio processing batch size in seconds. Legend is shared, axis scales are different.

In Figure 6 we plot the energy needed by the various units to execute the pipeline logic repeatedly on batched audio data. For one-off computations the cheapest alternative energy-wise is the DSP which can be up to 3.2x more energy efficient than the optimized *a-GPU* for the DNN pipeline. Yet, the a-GPU is between 3x and 4x times more energy efficient than the sequential CPU for both applications. *If high performance is of utmost priority for an application, the GPU is the method of choice for on-device real-time feedback* – when optimized, GPU offloading will obtain inferences much faster and significantly reduce energy compared to the CPU.

A notable observation is that as the size of the buffered audio data increases, the a-GPU begins to deliver energy efficiency in the ranges provided by the low-power DSP. For instance, with batch sizes of 10 and 6 seconds for the GMM and DNN pipeline respectively, the a-GPU provides comparable energy while being multiple times faster (> 50x compared to our reference baselines). If applications can tolerate small delays in obtaining inferences, batched GPU computation will save amounts of energy similarly to a low-power DSP and at the same time obtain results faster. We note that a heavily optimized DSP implementation will be the best option energy-wise; here we show that contrary to conventional wisdom, there is a scenario in which the GPU can be used to save energy on a scale that is much closer to what a low-power unit can achieve.

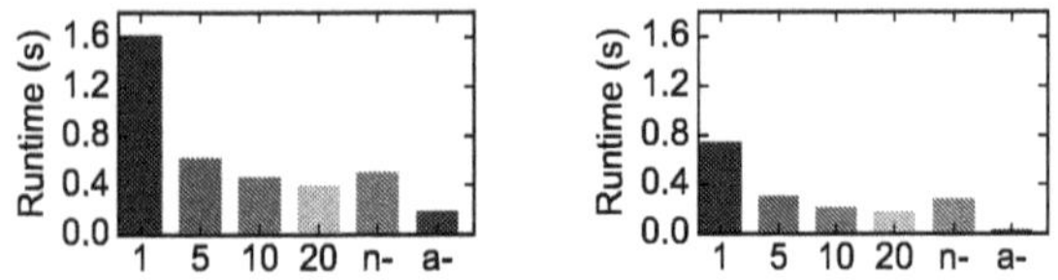

(a) GMM (b) DNN

Figure 7: End-to-end latency for computing the audio pipelines on the GPU vs cloud. Numbers on the x axis show throughput in Mbps, and n- and a- refer to n-GPU and a-GPU.

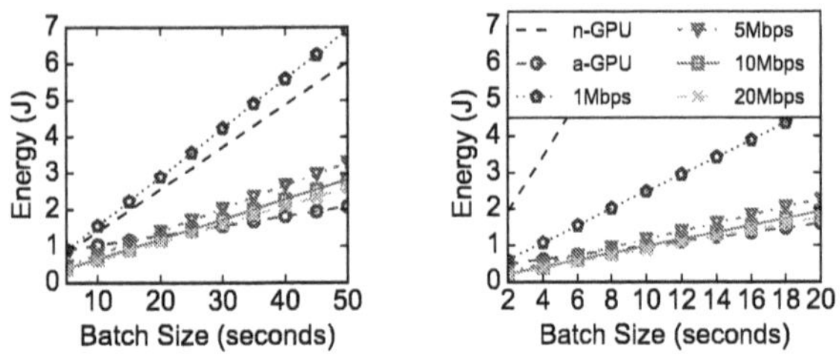

(a) GMM (b) DNN

Figure 8: End-to-end energy as a function of the batch computation size for running the audio pipelines on the GPU vs cloud offloading. Legend is shared.

6.4 GPU Sensing vs Cloud Offloading

Cloud baselines. We compare the performance of the sensing algorithms on the GPU against the best performing cloud alternatives. For the DNN-style Keyword Spotting application, the cheapest alternative is to send the raw data directly for processing to the cloud because the application generates as many features as the size of the raw input data. For the GMM-style Speaker Identification pipeline, the cheapest alternative is to compute the features on the DSP and send them for classification to the cloud. However, this variant is > 10 times slower than computing the features on the CPU. Further, we find that when sending the features to the cloud, establishing the connection and transferring the data dominate the energy needed to compute features on the CPU. For this reason, the GMM cloud baseline in our experiments computes features on the CPU and sends them for classification to a remote server.

Latency Results. In Figure 7 we plot the end-to-end time needed to offload one pipeline computation to the cloud and compare it against the total time required by the GPU to do the processing (including the GPU kernel set-up and memory transfers). We assume a window size of 64KB and vary the network RTT so that the throughput ranges from 1 to 20Mbps. Given this, the a-GPU implementation is 3.1x and 6.5x faster than the good 5Mbps cloud alternative for the GMM and DNN pipelines respectively. This comes at the expense of a 1.6x and 1.4x increase in the energy for a one-off computation for the two pipeline types respectively. The takeaway is that *if speed is favoured over energy, the GPU should be used for local processing because it will deliver inference results several times faster than cloud offloading even with good connectivity.*

Energy Results. In Figure 8 we plot the total energy required to offload batched pipeline computations to the cloud as a function of the batch size in seconds for which raw audio data is queued for processing. The most notable outcome is that *the a-GPU competes energy-wise with good connectivity cloud offloading in addition to being multiple times faster.* After a certain batching threshold, the total processing with the optimized a-GPU consumes even less energy. For instance, unless the network has a throughput of 20Mbps (and an RTT of 25 ms) the GMM-style pipeline starts getting cheaper than the faster connections after 20 seconds of buffered audio, and the DNN Keyword Spotting pipeline – after only 10 seconds of audio data. The reason for this phenomenon (batched processing is less expensive than cloud and one-off computation is not) is that the initial kernel set-up and memory transfer costs are high, but once paid, the a-GPU offers better energy per second for audio sensing.

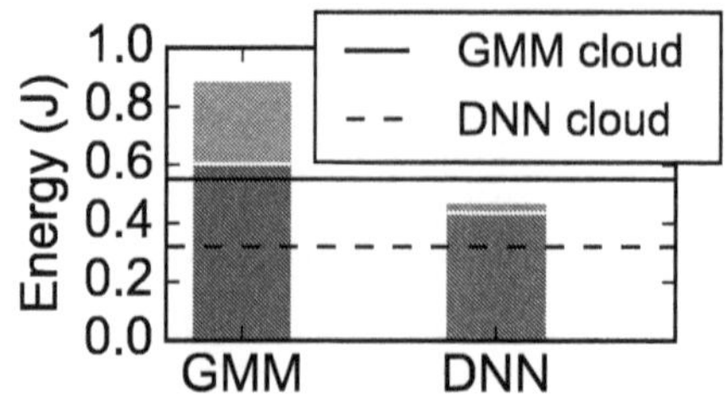

Figure 9: Energy consumed for one-off computation for the GMM- and DNN-based audio apps. Lighter shaded bars show energy spent for processing, the rest is GPU tail energy. Lines show the total energy consumed by cloud offloading for the two apps for a network connection with an RTT of 104 ms.

In Figure 9 we plot a breakdown of the energy for a one-time run of the audio apps on the GPU to quantify the GPU setup overhead. Overall, the amount of energy spent in the GPU tail states is over 65% of the total consumption for both applications which confirms the prohibitively high setup/tear-down GPU costs. With a network that has an average RTT of 104ms (translating to $\approx$ 5Mbps throughput), the energy spent by cloud offloading is less than the GPU setup cost. Unless the audio app is highly sensitive to the runtime, cloud offloading may provide a desirable trade-off between energy and latency.

Another critical result is that optimizing GPU execution is crucial – the naive n-GPU is more expensive ($>$ 2x) energy-wise than almost all types of cloud offloading when batching. With the better but still unoptimized baselines with highest fan-out ($\kappa = 1$), the batching threshold for preferring GPU execution over cloud is higher (e.g., $\approx$ 14 seconds for the DNN algorithm), delaying the application response time further than what could be achieved with the engine optimized version.

Summary. While cloud offloading has a significant computational lead over mobile, the GPU now provides advantages that makes local processing highly desirable – it is faster, less susceptible to privacy leaks as execution is entirely local, works regardless of connection speed, and even competes with cloud in terms of energy.

6.5 GPGPU and Graphics Workloads

Here we investigate how GPGPU computations interfere with other GPU workloads such as those used for graphics processing – *will the background GPU computation affect negatively the user experience?* We schedule the execution of the audio sensing pipelines (either Speaker Identification or Keyword Spotting) to run continuously for a minute on the GPU while the mobile user is interacting with other applications that are known to strain the GPU resources, i.e. games. We pick 5 hugely popular Android games with multi-

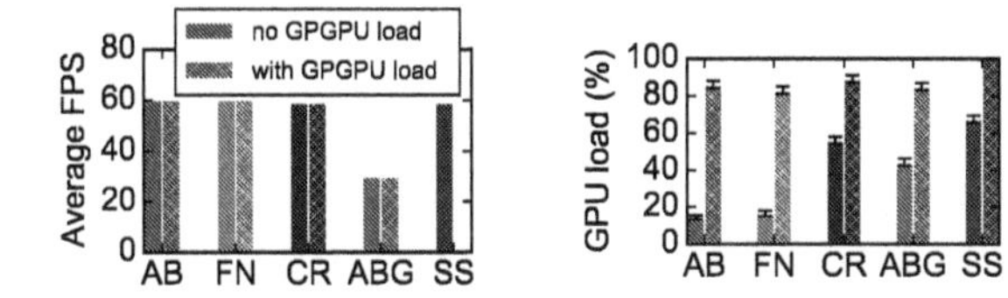

(a) Frame rate (FPS)

(b) total GPU load

Figure 10: Average frame rate and GPU load when the games run without and with additional GPGPU load. Games in the experiment are Angry Birds (AB), Fruit Ninja (FN), Crossy Road (CR), Angry Birds GO (ABG), and Subway Surfers (SS). Legend is shared.

million downloads and different play styles (Angry Birds, Fruit Ninja, Crossy Road, Angry Birds GO, and Subway Surfers), and observe the effect GPGPU computation has on the perceived gameplay quality. To quantify this we measure the average frame rate (frames per second (FPS)) with GameBench [3] during gameplay over 5 1-minute long runs.

In Figure 10 we show the aggregate results from the experiments. *For all games except Subway Surfers the GPGPU computation does not change the original frame rates of the games, although the total GPU load substantially increases.* For instance, the render-heavy racing Angry Birds GO maintains an average frame rate of 30 FPS both with and without the added audio sensing workload, even though the total GPU load jumps from 44% to 85%. For this and the other three games with similar behavior (Angry Birds, Fruit Ninja, Crossy Road), the effect can be explained by the facts that 1) the original load the games place on the GPU is not too high, 2) GPU rendering is time-shared with GPGPU computation, and 3) the audio sensing kernels are short-duration (a single kernel execution never exceeds tens of milliseconds). With the endless runner Subway Surfers, however, the original average GPU load is already very high ($\approx 70\%$), and adding the GPGPU computation results in a screen freeze so that the game becomes unresponsive. This can be attributed to the fact that the OS does not treat the GPU as a shared resource and there is a lack of isolation of the various GPU workloads. One way to approach this is introduce OS-level abstractions that provide performance guarantees [53].

7. DISCUSSION AND IMPLICATIONS

Here we survey key scenarios and issues related to the applicability of the GPU parallel optimizations for audio sensing.

Targeted Scenarios. There are many chains of audio workloads that we envisage are relevant to GPU offloading with delayed cloud-free batch processing. Examples are continuous low latency audio tasks (hot key word recognition) followed by a much heavier processing that is more tolerant to the delays offered by GPU acceleration – all types of analysis possible on human voice fall into this category. There are numerous such examples of behavior monitoring in the audio sensing literature: conversation analysis [48], speaker counting [58], speaker identification [45], emotion recognition [52], and ambient scene analysis [47] to name a few. Context monitoring through sounds and triggering notifications (e.g., detect conversation to mute the speaker) is another key functionality that can be supported with this type of offloading: delayed cloud-free batch processing with entirely offline trained models, or models that need to be only infrequently updated. GPU offloading will be a crucial part of more complicated scheduling schemes that involve other processing units as well (e.g., [28]) and possibly cloud. In that case hybrid solutions that use multiple processing units and cloud can reap the benefits of GPU execution, and more applications including those that need cloud support such as Shazam can take advantage of the more advanced local processing (e.g., to extract the features necessary to discriminate the encountered songs).

7.1 Implications

We believe the results presented in this work provide insights of value to the following areas.

Privacy. Our findings suggest that algorithms optimized for embedded-class GPUs can bring the much coveted privacy guarantees to devices such as Amazon Echo [1] and Google Home [4], if the operation remains entirely on the device itself. These assistants respond to simple home user requests (such as, "turn on the light"), but are known to heavily exploit cloud offloading. With the help of our techniques doing the processing locally on the GPU can be done faster than cloud offloading, and without exposing sensitive information to untrusted third parties.

Servicing multi-app workloads. GPUs will play a crucial role in offloading the sensing workloads of digital assistants as they cannot be serviced by the DSP capabilities alone. Amazon Echo, for instance, performs multiple audio sensing tasks on a continuously processed audio stream, including: 1) detect the presence of speech vs other sounds; 2) perform spoken keyword spotting (as all commands are triggered by the same starting word); and, 3) speech recognition, along with additional dialog system analysis that allows it to understand and react to the command. These tasks collectively are well beyond the DSP processing and memory capabilities [27], in such multi-app audio sensing scenarios approaching the mobile GPU with routines that maximize runtime performance and minimize energy consumption is critical.

Energy reductions. Audio sensing algorithms are notorious for their continuous monitoring of the sensor stream. Whereas DSP offloading is massively adopted as the go-to power reduction approach for applications such as hot keyword spotting, with the increase in number of concurrent audio sensing services mobile users adopt (e.g., Google Now, Auto Shazam), the DSP will have to selectively process a subset of the algorithm stages. In multi-app scenarios, optimally using the GPU as we have done in this work will be instrumental in keeping the power-hungry CPU or privacy-invading cloud offloading at bay.

7.2 Discussion

Our design, and its results, also highlight the following issues.

Performance on other mobile GPU varieties. Although it is highly likely there will be a difference in the exact values for the performance boosts on other GPU models (such as NVIDIA's Tegra), we expect qualitatively similar results when deploying the pipelines there. For example, speedups from the GPU data parallelism will be sufficiently high to deliver real-time performance for applications that can afford the energy costs. This is because our proposed optimizations can be generalized to any OpenCL-compliant GPU architecture, and do not rely on vendor-specific features.

Parallelizing other sensor processing algorithms. The core mechanics behind the optimization patterns can be applied to other classifiers such as Support Vector Machines (SVM), and deep learning network topologies such as Convolutional Neural Networks (CNN). This is because the patterns depend on how the classification is applied to the audio data stream (in sliding windows, combining model parameters with frame data independently to different frame offsets), rather than fully depend on the concrete algorithm implementation. We believe the broader lessons learned from this work on using the GPU will promote further research into how it can be used to accelerate algorithms in other application domains (e.g., alternative sensor processing from accelerometer, or GPS).

GPU vs. multicore CPUs. As single-thread performance for microprocessor technology is leveling off, multiple cores will become major drivers for increased performance [19] (e.g., up to 61 for Intel Xeon Phi [7]). Developers will likely be faced with similar data parallel challenges – increasing the total number of concurrent tasks for better utilization, and efficiently leveraging memory caches to mask access latency. As OpenCL manages heterogeneous parallel algorithms transparently from the underlying multicore architecture, the developed OpenCL-compliant optimization techniques will prove valuable to multicore CPUs as well.

GPU programmability. GPUs are notoriously difficult to program – even if the algorithm exhibits data parallelism, restructuring it to benefit from GPU computation often requires in-depth knowledge about the algorithm mechanics. In fact, automated conversion of sequential to parallel code has been an active area of research [21, 20], but fully automating the parallelization process still remains a big challenge. We provide a portable OpenCL library of parallel implementations for key audio sensing algorithms (e.g., GMMs, DNNs) and expect developers will either compose pipelines by reusing the OpenCL host and kernel code, or by applying the insights from our optimization patterns to their implementations.

We acknowledge that currently programming GPUs requires skillful development. We hope that through our library we can simplify the pure GPU kernel development by providing optimized machine learning primitives developers can reuse. Without them, developers will mostly likely encounter the problems we uncovered while designing our library (e.g., memory-bound processing) in order to incorporate GPU processing into their audio application. We do not fully automate the process, a potential direction for future research is designing or reusing a simpler high-level declarative language that can be used to specify pipeline processing. In the case that all algorithmic components are covered by our library, this can greatly simplify the developer burden. This compiler component can be built on top of CUDA/OpenCL or industrial strength GPU APIs.

8. RELATED WORK

Our work is touches most closely the following areas of research related to efficient sensing and efforts to optimize GPU usage.

Sensor Processing Acceleration and Efficiency. A large body of research has been devoted to the use of heterogeneous computation via low-power co-processors [51, 45, 27, 40, 42, 54] and custom-built peripheral devices [56] to accelerate or sustain power efficient processing for extended periods of time. Little Rock [51] and SpeakerSense [45] are among the first to propose the offloading of sensor sampling and early stages of audio sensing pipelines to low-power co-processors – the processing enabled by such early units is extremely energy efficient but limited by their compute capabilities to relatively simple tasks such as feature extraction. DSP.Ear [27] and Shen et al. [54] study more complex inference algorithms for continuous operation on DSPs but demonstrate such units can be easily overwhelmed and often the energy efficiency comes at the price of increased inference latency.

LEO [28] is a low-power scheduler that dynamically distributes computation across heterogeneous resources, including the GPU as a possible resource, and lowers the overall energy consumption for concurrent sensor apps. However, it does not investigate the trade-offs of GPU offloading in detail, nor does it show what is required to optimally utilize such a processing unit. We believe the optimizations we designed complement sensor scheduling, and are critically needed to allow frameworks to maximize GPU usage.

General-Purpose GPU Computing. GPUs have been used as general-purpose accelerators for a range of tasks, the most popular applications being computer vision [57, 23, 36] and image processing [55, 50]. Object removal [57] and face recognition [23] on mobile GPUs have been showcased to offer massive speedups via a set of carefully selected optimization techniques. Although the techniques found in the graphics community as well as in the field of speech processing (fast spoken query detection [60]) address similar data parallel challenges to what we identify (increasing thread throughput, careful memory management), these techniques remain specific to the presented use cases.

The GPU implementation of automatic speech recognition based on GMMs [29], for example, proposes optimizations that are related to the specifics of a more complex speech recognition pipeline. Instead, we target a different workload scenario emerging from a growing number of coarse-sound classification applications that require processing that can happen entirely cloud-free. For this distinctly different workload, we introduce general techniques that are applied at the level of the machine learning model, or the level of organization related to multiple algorithms for processing audio data. As such, the insights drawn from our work are directly applicable to a class of algorithms that build upon commonly adopted machine learning models in audio sensing.

Packet routing [31] and SSL encryption [37] leverage GPUs to increase processing throughput via batching of computations, but none of these works is focused on studying energy efficiency aspects which are critical for battery-powered devices.

GPU Resource Management. PTask [53] is an OS-level abstraction that attempts to introduce system-level guarantees such as fairness and performance isolation, since GPUs are not treated as a shared system resource and concurrent workloads interfere with each other. The relative difficulty in manually expressing algorithms in a data parallel manner may lead to missed optimization opportunities – works such as those of Zhang et al. [59] and Jog et al. [38] attempt to streamline the optimization process. The former improves GPU memory utilization and control flow by automatically removing data access irregularities, whereas the latter addresses problems with memory access latency at the thread scheduling level. Both types of optimizations are complementary to our work – we optimize the general structure of the parallel audio processing algorithms, while the mentioned frameworks tune parallel behavior of already built implementations. Last but not least, Sponge [35] provides a compiler framework that builds portable CUDA programs from a high-level streaming language. Instead, we study the trade-offs mobile GPUs provide for sensing, and build on top of OpenCL which together with the Qualcomm Adreno GPU dominates the mobile market.

9. CONCLUSION

In this paper we have studied the trade-offs of using a mobile GPU for audio sensing. We devised an optimization engine that leverages a set of structural and memory access parallel patterns to auto-tune GPU audio pipelines – optimized GPU routines are an order of magnitude faster than sequential CPU implementations, and up to 6.5x faster than cloud offloading (5Mbps throughput). With just 10-20 seconds of batched audio data, the optimized GPU begins to consume less energy than cloud offloading and in the range typical for low-power DSPs. The insights drawn can help towards the growth of the next-generation mobile sensing apps that leverage GPU capabilities for extreme runtime and energy performance.

10. ACKNOWLEDGMENTS

This work was supported by Microsoft Research through its PhD Scholarship Program. We thank the anonymous reviewers and our shepherd (Lin Zhong) for their valued comments and suggestions.

11. REFERENCES

[1] Amazon Echo. http://www.amazon.com/Amazon-Echo-Bluetooth-Speaker-with-WiFi-Alexa/dp/B00X4WHP5E.

[2] Apple Siri. https://www.apple.com/uk/ios/siri/.

[3] GameBench. https://www.gamebench.net/.

[4] Google Home. https://home.google.com/.

[5] Google Now. http://www.google.co.uk/landing/now/.

[6] HTK Speech Recognition Toolkit. http://htk.eng.cam.ac.uk/.

[7] Intel Xeon Phi. http://www.intel.com/content/www/us/en/processors/xeon/xeon-phi-detail.html.

[8] Monsoon Power Monitor. http://www.msoon.com/LabEquipment/PowerMonitor/.

[9] NVIDIA CUDA. http://www.nvidia.com/object/cuda_home_new.html.

[10] NVidia Tegra X1. http://www.nvidia.com/object/tegra-x1-processor.html.

[11] OpenCL. https://www.khronos.org/opencl/.

[12] Qualcomm Adreno GPU. https://developer.qualcomm.com/software/adreno-gpu-sdk/gpu.

[13] Qualcomm Hexagon DSP. https://developer.qualcomm.com/mobile-development/maximize-hardware/multimedia-optimization-hexagon-sdk/hexagon-dsp-processor.

[14] Qualcomm Hexagon SDK. https://developer.qualcomm.com/mobile-development/maximize-hardware/multimedia-optimization-hexagon-sdk.

[15] Qualcomm Snapdragon 800 MDP. http://goo.gl/ySfCFl.

[16] TensorFlow. https://www.tensorflow.org/.

[17] Theano. http://deeplearning.net/software/theano/.

[18] C. M. Bishop. *Pattern Recognition and Machine Learning (Information Science and Statistics)*. Springer-Verlag New York, Inc., Secaucus, NJ, USA, 2006.

[19] S. Borkar and A. A. Chien. The future of microprocessors. *Commun. ACM*, 54(5):67–77, May 2011.

[20] S. Campanoni, K. Brownell, S. Kanev, T. M. Jones, G.-Y. Wei, and D. Brooks. Helix-rc: An architecture-compiler co-design for automatic parallelization of irregular programs. In *Proceeding of the 41st Annual International Symposium on Computer Architecuture*, ISCA '14, pages 217–228, Piscataway, NJ, USA, 2014. IEEE Press.

[21] S. Campanoni, T. M. Jones, G. H. Holloway, G.-Y. Wei, and D. M. Brooks. Helix: Making the extraction of thread-level parallelism mainstream. *IEEE Micro*, 32(4):8–18, 2012.

[22] G. Chen, C. Parada, and G. Heigold. Small-footprint keyword spotting using deep neural networks. In *IEEE International Conference on Acoustics, Speech, and Signal Processing*, ICASSP'14, 2014.

[23] K. T. Cheng and Y. C. Wang. Using mobile gpu for general-purpose computing – a case study of face recognition on smartphones. In *VLSI Design, Automation and Test (VLSI-DAT), 2011 International Symposium on*, pages 1–4, April 2011.

[24] D. Chu, N. D. Lane, T. T.-T. Lai, C. Pang, X. Meng, Q. Guo, F. Li, and F. Zhao. Balancing energy, latency and accuracy for mobile sensor data classification. In *Proceedings of the 9th ACM Conference on Embedded Networked Sensor Systems*, SenSys '11, pages 54–67, New York, NY, USA, 2011. ACM.

[25] A. de Cheveigné and H. Kawahara. YIN, a fundamental frequency estimator for speech and music. *The Journal of the Acoustical Society of America*, 111(4):1917–1930, 2002.

[26] Z. Fang, Z. Guoliang, and S. Zhanjiang. Comparison of different implementations of mfcc. *J. Comput. Sci. Technol.*, 16(6):582–589, Nov. 2001.

[27] P. Georgiev, N. D. Lane, K. K. Rachuri, and C. Mascolo. DSP.Ear: leveraging co-processor support for continuous audio sensing on smartphones. In *Proceedings of the 12th ACM Conference on Embedded Network Sensor Systems*, SenSys '14, New York, NY, USA, 2014. ACM.

[28] P. Georgiev, N. D. Lane, K. K. Rachuri, and C. Mascolo. Leo: Scheduling sensor inference algorithms across heterogeneous mobile processors and network resources. In *Proceedings of the 22Nd Annual International Conference on Mobile Computing and Networking*, MobiCom '16, pages 320–333, New York, NY, USA, 2016. ACM.

[29] K. Gupta and J. D. Owens. Compute & memory optimizations for high-quality speech recognition on low-end gpu processors. In *Proceedings of the 2011 18th International Conference on High Performance Computing*, HIPC '11, pages 1–10, Washington, DC, USA, 2011. IEEE Computer Society.

[30] K. Han, D. Yu, and I. Tashev. Speech emotion recognition using deep neural network and extreme learning machine. In *Fifteenth Annual Conference of the International Speech Communication Association*, 2014.

[31] S. Han, K. Jang, K. Park, and S. Moon. Packetshader: A gpu-accelerated software router. In *Proceedings of the ACM SIGCOMM 2010 Conference*, SIGCOMM '10, pages 195–206, New York, NY, USA, 2010. ACM.

[32] H. Hermansky. Perceptual linear predictive (PLP) analysis of speech. *J. Acoust. Soc. Am.*, 57(4):1738–52, Apr. 1990.

[33] G. Hinton, L. Deng, D. Yu, G. Dahl, A. rahman Mohamed, N. Jaitly, A. Senior, V. Vanhoucke, P. Nguyen, T. Sainath, and B. Kingsbury. Deep neural networks for acoustic modeling in speech recognition. *Signal Processing Magazine*, 2012.

[34] G. Hinton, L. Deng, D. Yu, A. rahman Mohamed, N. Jaitly, A. Senior, V. Vanhoucke, P. Nguyen, T. S. G. Dahl, and B. Kingsbury. Deep neural networks for acoustic modeling in speech recognition. *IEEE Signal Processing Magazine*, 29(6):82–97, November 2012.

[35] A. H. Hormati, M. Samadi, M. Woh, T. Mudge, and S. Mahlke. Sponge: Portable stream programming on graphics engines. In *Proceedings of the Sixteenth International Conference on Architectural Support for Programming Languages and Operating Systems*, ASPLOS XVI, pages 381–392, New York, NY, USA, 2011. ACM.

[36] A. Huqqani, E. Schikuta, S. Yea, and P. Chena. Multicore and gpu parallelization of neural networks for face recognition. In *International Conference on Computational Science, ICCS*, Procedia Computer Science, pages 349–358, London, UK, June 2013. Elsevier.

[37] K. Jang, S. Han, S. Han, S. Moon, and K. Park. Sslshader: Cheap ssl acceleration with commodity processors. In *Proceedings of the 8th USENIX Conference on Networked*

Systems Design and Implementation, NSDI'11, pages 1–14, Berkeley, CA, USA, 2011. USENIX Association.

[38] A. Jog, O. Kayiran, N. Chidambaram Nachiappan, A. K. Mishra, M. T. Kandemir, O. Mutlu, R. Iyer, and C. R. Das. Owl: Cooperative thread array aware scheduling techniques for improving gpgpu performance. In *Proceedings of the Eighteenth International Conference on Architectural Support for Programming Languages and Operating Systems*, ASPLOS '13, pages 395–406, New York, NY, USA, 2013. ACM.

[39] D. B. Kirk and W.-m. W. Hwu. *Programming Massively Parallel Processors: A Hands-on Approach*. Morgan Kaufmann Publishers Inc., San Francisco, CA, USA, 1st edition, 2010.

[40] N. D. Lane, S. Bhattacharya, P. Georgiev, C. Forlivesi, L. Jiao, L. Qendro, and F. Kawsar. Deepx: A software accelerator for low-power deep learning inference on mobile devices. In *2016 15th ACM/IEEE International Conference on Information Processing in Sensor Networks (IPSN)*, pages 1–12, April 2016.

[41] N. D. Lane, S. Bhattacharya, P. Georgiev, C. Forlivesi, and F. Kawsar. An early resource characterization of deep learning on wearables, smartphones and internet-of-things devices. In *Proceedings of the 2015 International Workshop on Internet of Things Towards Applications*, IoT-App '15, pages 7–12, New York, NY, USA, 2015. ACM.

[42] N. D. Lane, P. Georgiev, and L. Qendro. Deepear: Robust smartphone audio sensing in unconstrained acoustic environments using deep learning. In *Proceedings of the 2015 ACM International Joint Conference on Pervasive and Ubiquitous Computing*, UbiComp '15, pages 283–294, New York, NY, USA, 2015. ACM.

[43] Y. Lee, C. Min, C. Hwang, J. L. 0001, I. Hwang, Y. Ju, C. Yoo, M. Moon, U. Lee, and J. Song. Sociophone: everyday face-to-face interaction monitoring platform using multi-phone sensor fusion. In H.-H. Chu, P. Huang, R. R. Choudhury, and F. Zhao, editors, *MobiSys*, pages 499–500. ACM, 2013.

[44] M. Liberman, K. Davis, M. Grossman, N. Martey, and J. Bell. Emotional prosody speech and transcripts. 2002.

[45] H. Lu, A. J. B. Brush, B. Priyantha, A. K. Karlson, and J. Liu. Speakersense: Energy efficient unobtrusive speaker identification on mobile phones. In *Proceedings of the 9th International Conference on Pervasive Computing*, Pervasive'11, pages 188–205, Berlin, Heidelberg, 2011. Springer-Verlag.

[46] H. Lu, D. Frauendorfer, M. Rabbi, M. S. Mast, G. T. Chittaranjan, A. T. Campbell, D. Gatica-Perez, and T. Choudhury. Stresssense: Detecting stress in unconstrained acoustic environments using smartphones. In *Proceedings of the 2012 ACM Conference on Ubiquitous Computing*, UbiComp '12, pages 351–360, New York, NY, USA, 2012. ACM.

[47] H. Lu, J. Yang, Z. Liu, N. D. Lane, T. Choudhury, and A. T. Campbell. The jigsaw continuous sensing engine for mobile phone applications. In *Proceedings of the 8th ACM Conference on Embedded Networked Sensor Systems*, SenSys '10, pages 71–84, New York, NY, USA, 2010. ACM.

[48] C. Luo and M. C. Chan. Socialweaver: Collaborative inference of human conversation networks using smartphones. In *Proceedings of the 11th ACM Conference on Embedded Networked Sensor Systems*, SenSys '13, pages 20:1–20:14, New York, NY, USA, 2013. ACM.

[49] I. McLoughlin, H. Zhang, Z. Xie, Y. Song, and W. Xiao. Robust sound event classification using deep neural networks. *Trans. Audio, Speech and Lang. Proc.*, 23(3):540–552, Mar. 2015.

[50] I. K. Park, N. Singhal, M. H. Lee, S. Cho, and C. Kim. Design and performance evaluation of image processing algorithms on gpus. *IEEE Trans. Parallel Distrib. Syst.*, 22(1):91–104, Jan. 2011.

[51] B. Priyantha, D. Lymberopoulos, and J. Liu. Littlerock: Enabling energy-efficient continuous sensing on mobile phones. *IEEE Pervasive Computing*, 10(2):12–15, 2011.

[52] K. K. Rachuri, M. Musolesi, C. Mascolo, P. J. Rentfrow, C. Longworth, and A. Aucinas. Emotionsense: A mobile phones based adaptive platform for experimental social psychology research. In *Proceedings of the 12th ACM International Conference on Ubiquitous Computing*, Ubicomp '10, pages 281–290, New York, NY, USA, 2010. ACM.

[53] C. J. Rossbach, J. Currey, M. Silberstein, B. Ray, and E. Witchel. Ptask: Operating system abstractions to manage gpus as compute devices. In *Proceedings of the Twenty-Third ACM Symposium on Operating Systems Principles*, SOSP '11, pages 233–248, New York, NY, USA, 2011. ACM.

[54] C. Shen, S. Chakraborty, K. R. Raghavan, H. Choi, and M. B. Srivastava. Exploiting processor heterogeneity for energy efficient context inference on mobile phones. In *Proceedings of the Workshop on Power-Aware Computing and Systems*, HotPower '13, pages 9:1–9:5, New York, NY, USA, 2013. ACM.

[55] N. Singhal, I. K. Park, and S. Cho. Implementation and optimization of image processing algorithms on handheld gpu. In *Image Processing (ICIP), 2010 17th IEEE International Conference on*, pages 4481–4484, Sept 2010.

[56] S. Verma, A. Robinson, and P. Dutta. Audiodaq: Turning the mobile phone's ubiquitous headset port into a universal data acquisition interface. In *Proceedings of the 10th ACM Conference on Embedded Network Sensor Systems*, SenSys '12, pages 197–210, New York, NY, USA, 2012. ACM.

[57] G. Wang, Y. Xiong, J. Yun, and J. R. Cavallaro. Accelerating computer vision algorithms using opencl framework on the mobile gpu - a case study. In *ICASSP*, pages 2629–2633. IEEE, 2013.

[58] C. Xu, S. Li, G. Liu, Y. Zhang, E. Miluzzo, Y.-F. Chen, J. Li, and B. Firner. Crowd++: Unsupervised speaker count with smartphones. In *Proceedings of the 2013 ACM International Joint Conference on Pervasive and Ubiquitous Computing*, UbiComp '13, pages 43–52, New York, NY, USA, 2013. ACM.

[59] E. Z. Zhang, Y. Jiang, Z. Guo, K. Tian, and X. Shen. On-the-fly elimination of dynamic irregularities for gpu computing. In *Proceedings of the Sixteenth International Conference on Architectural Support for Programming Languages and Operating Systems*, ASPLOS XVI, pages 369–380, New York, NY, USA, 2011. ACM.

[60] Y. Zhang, K. Adl, and J. Glass. Fast spoken query detection using lower-bound dynamic time warping on graphical processing units. In *In Proc. ICASSP*, pages 5173–5176, 2012.

[61] G. Zhou, J. H. L. Hansen, and J. F. Kaiser. Nonlinear feature based classification of speech under stress. *IEEE Transactions on Speech and Audio Processing*, 9(3):201–216, 2001.

Enabling Cross-ISA Offloading for COTS Binaries

Wenwen Wang, Pen-Chung Yew,
Antonia Zhai, and Stephen McCamant
University of Minnesota, Twin Cities
{wenwang, yew, zhai,
mccamant}@cs.umn.edu

Youfeng Wu and Jayaram Bobba
Intel Labs
{youfeng.wu,
jayaram.bobba}@intel.com

ABSTRACT

Work offloading allows a mobile device, i.e., the client, to execute its computation-intensive code remotely on a more powerful server to improve its performance and to extend its battery life. However, the difference in instruction set architectures (ISAs) between the client and the server poses a great challenge to work offloading. Most of the existing solutions rely on language-level virtual machines to hide such differences. Therefore, they have to tie closely to the specific programming languages. Other approaches try to recompile the mobile applications to achieve the specific goal of offloading, so their applicability is limited to the availability of the source code.

To overcome the above limitations, we propose to extend the capability of dynamic binary translation across clients and servers to offload the identified computation-intensive binary code regions automatically to the server at runtime. With this approach, the native binaries on the client can be offloaded to the server seamlessly without the limitations mentioned above. A prototype has been implemented using an existing retargetable dynamic binary translator. Experimental results show that our system achieves 1.93X speedup with 48.66% reduction in energy consumption for six real-world applications, and 1.62X speedup with 42.4% reduction in energy consumption for SPEC CINT2006 benchmarks.

Keywords

Computation Offloading; Dynamic Binary Translation; Dynamic Binary Optimization; Offloading Target Selection

1. INTRODUCTION

Mobile devices, such as smart phones and tablets, have become ubiquitous nowadays, and the trend seems likely to continue in the foreseeable future. People increasingly rely on their smart phones and tablets to accomplish more and more heavy tasks, e.g., image and voice processing, 3D games and even virtual reality. However, most mobile devices suffer from low computing capability (due to their power constraints) and limited battery life compared to their desktop and server counterparts. A recent study [29] shows that a mobile device is more than 5 times slower than a desktop computer when used to play the same chess game. Therefore, users have to put up with longer waiting time while playing the same game on mobile devices.

Some recent survey [10] conducted on 1000 individuals showed that 89% rated long battery life was among the top features they considered when buying a new smart phone. This result indicates that battery life is crucial to the commercial success of mobile devices. However, increasingly heavy workloads on mobile devices could shorten battery life and curtail good user experiences.

Previous research work [22, 29, 41, 31, 38, 18, 43, 20, 30, 42, 27, 19, 35, 26] has shown that work offloading is an effective way to improve performance and to prolong battery life of mobile devices. In a work offloading system, the computation-intensive tasks on a mobile device, i.e., the *client*, are sent to a more powerful *server* and executed remotely. After the server completes the work, the results are sent back to the client. With much more powerful computing capability of the server, the performance of the offloaded application can be improved, and the battery energy is conserved because of the work offloading and the shortened execution time.

One of the biggest obstacles to an offloading system is the difference in instruction set architectures (ISAs) between the client and the server, e.g., ARM on a mobile device and Intel x86-64 on a server. To overcome such difficulties, some existing offloading systems [22, 18, 26, 27, 42] rely on language-level virtual machines (VMs) such as Dalvik JVM and the Microsoft .NET Common Language Runtime (CLR) to hide the ISA differences with strong runtime support. However, such approaches often tie closely to the specific programming languages and their runtime systems, and the trend for such VMs is to incorporate more native code, e.g., Java Native Interface (JNI) libraries, so that they can be more adaptive to the native environment and/or to meet the performance requirements, e.g., Android ART runtime [1]. Basically, many of the JNI libraries are developed by third party developers, and the source code is usually not available to VM developers to build the x86-64 version for the server. With more native binaries integrated into such VM systems, their portability across ISAs is significantly hampered. A recent study [29] shows that one third of the top 20 open source Android applications contain more than 50% native code and spend more than 20% of the execution time in native mode.

Permission to make digital or hard copies of all or part of this work for personal or classroom use is granted without fee provided that copies are not made or distributed for profit or commercial advantage and that copies bear this notice and the full citation on the first page. Copyrights for components of this work owned by others than ACM must be honored. Abstracting with credit is permitted. To copy otherwise, or republish, to post on servers or to redistribute to lists, requires prior specific permission and/or a fee. Request permissions from permissions@acm.org.

MobiSys'17, June 19 - 23, 2017, Niagara Falls, NY, USA

© 2017 ACM. ISBN 978-1-4503-4928-4/17/06...$15.00

DOI: http://dx.doi.org/10.1145/3081333.3081337

Some other offloading systems [30, 38, 29, 41, 31] rebuild/recompile mobile applications with the specific goal of offloading at runtime. To make optimal partition of the code between the client and the server, these offloading systems statically analyze the source code using different static performance estimators and cost models. Due to the complexity of the source programs, some static analyzers [30, 38, 41, 31] are limited to applications with simple structures such as media encoding and decoding programs, or requiring annotations in the source code from the developers for assistance. A recent approach [29] allows more general-purpose native applications. However, its applicability is still limited to the availability of the source code, which is usually unavailable in practice due to commercial reasons.

To overcome the above limitations, we propose to extend the capability of dynamic binary translation across the client and server boundary, and automatically offload the identified computation-intensive binary code regions and their related memory data at runtime. An *offline profiler* using dynamic binary instrumentation is used to select *offloading targets*, i.e., hot code regions that can be offloaded to the server. At runtime, a *dynamic binary optimizer* is employed on the client to facilitate the migration of offloading targets to the server. In addition, an enhanced *dynamic binary translator/optimizer* is used to retarget, re-optimize and emulate the client binaries on the server.

Since most existing dynamic binary translation systems only run on a single physical machine, we need to address several critical issues in order to support the new client/server environment, e.g., the handling of required I/O operations and system calls across the client/server boundaries, managing the amount of data transferred between the client and the server to minize the communication overhead, and the maintenance of the necessary data/memory consistency between the two.

In our offloading system, client's virtual addresses are mapped to the server virtual address space by the translator. The I/O operations performed in the offloading targets are also supported in our system by sending them back to the client. Using this approach, native binary applications can be offloaded seamlessly to a server without the limitations mentioned above.

A prototype has been implemented using an existing retargetable dynamic binary translation system HQEMU [24], which is based on QEMU with an LLVM backend for optimization purpose. Experimental results show that our offloading system achieves 1.93X performance speedup with 48.66% reduction in energy consumption for six real-world applications, and 1.62X performance speedup with 42.4% reduction in energy consumption for SPEC CINT2006 benchmarks on an ARM-based client and an Intel Xeon Ivy Bridge server.

In summary, we made the following contributions:

- We propose a cross-ISA offloading system for COTS binaries on a mobile client to a remote server. This approach is not limited to specific programming languages, runtime systems, nor the availability of application source code. *To the best of our knowledge, this is the first attempt to allow native binary applications to be offloaded across ISAs.*
- A prototype for such an offloading system has been implemented. It includes three parts: an offline profiler and a dynamic optimizer using dynamic binary instrumentation/rewriting to support the migration of binary code regions from client to server, and an enhanced dynamic binary translator/optimization system based on HQEMU to work with the client on the server.
- A number of experiments are conducted to demonstrate the effectiveness of the proposed approach on an ARM-based client and an Intel Ivy Bridge server. On average, 1.93X speedup with 48.66% reduction in energy consumption are observed on six real-world applications that include games and a JavaScript engine, and 1.62X speedup with 42.4% reduction in energy consumption on industry standard benchmark SPEC CINT2006.

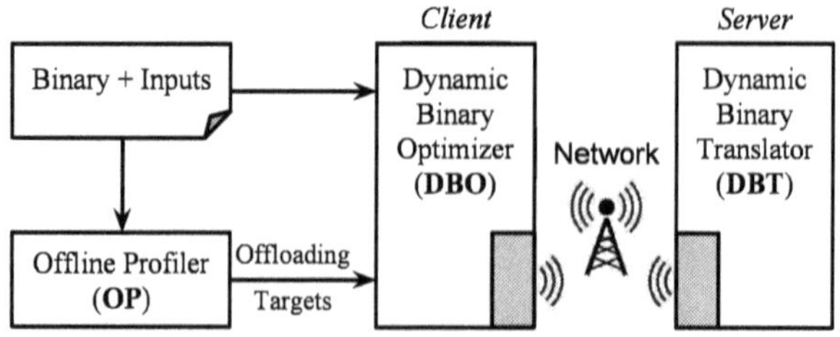

Figure 1: The framework of our offloading system.

The rest of this paper is organized as follows. Section 2 presents an overview of our offloading system. Section 3 describes some of its design issues. Section 4 presents the implementation details. Section 5 shows some experimental results. Section 6 discusses related work. And Section 7 concludes the paper.

2. SYSTEM OVERVIEW

Figure 1 shows the framework of our proposed offloading system. The system is composed of two subsystems, one on the client and the other on the server.

On the client side, the subsystem includes an *offline profiler* (OP) and a *dynamic binary optimizer* (DBO). The OP profiles the mobile application binaries offline on the client with some available inputs. It dynamically instruments the binary code to collect profiling information for offloading target selection. An *offloading target* (or *target* for short) is a binary code region offloaded to the server. The granularity of a target can be a basic block, a code trace, a code region that includes a loop, or a function. In our prototype system, the granularity is set at the *function* level. Determining the best granularity for an offloading target is beyond the scope of this paper.

For each profiled function, the OP records its execution time, the amount of live-in/live-out data accessed and I/O activities that can impact the communication overhead between the client and the server. Using a heuristic target selection algorithm, the OP performs target selection as described in Section 3.1. Generally, the most time-consuming functions are selected as targets in our prototype system.

After the offloading targets are identified, the DBO on the client can automatically offload the targets to the server at runtime. The DBO takes over the control of a mobile application immediately after the mobile application is launched.

The DBO tries to connect the client to the server via existing wireless network and checks the availability of the server. If the server is temporarily unavailable, no offloading is carried out and the execution proceeds as a native execution on the client. Otherwise, the DBO rewrites the beginning instructions of the target to redirect its execution to a *jump stub*, which is a code block that helps to offload the target to the server. After the target is offloaded, the DBO waits for the results to be returned from the server and resumes the execution of the mobile application.

In a jump stub, it saves the current execution state of the application including the content of its registers, and then sends the offloading request to the server. Each offloading request contains the saved execution state and the *beginning* and the *ending* addresses of the offloading target. After the request is sent, the DBO enters a wait mode for the results to come back from the server. In the wait mode, the DBO still needs to respond to the requests from the target running on the server, e.g., memory pages needed and/or the system calls from the target. More details are presented in Sections 3.2 and 3.3. When the server completes its emulation of the target, the DBO recovers the execution state of the application and resumes its execution until the next target is encountered.

Figure 1 also shows an enhanced *dynamic binary translator* (DBT) deployed on the server side, which receives and processes offloading requests from the client. Typically, a cross-ISA DBT system can dynamically translate *guest* binary code in one ISA to a different *host* ISA, and emulate the guest binary on the host machine by executing the generated host code [36]. In our offloading scenario, the client is the guest and the server is the host.

When an offloading request is received from the client via the wireless network, the DBT on the server initializes its internal emulation state according to the received execution state of the target. After the initialization, the DBT starts the emulation of the offloaded target. A memory page request is sent to the client if the page is not included in the initial execution state of the target. More details are presented in Section 3.2. The DBT terminates the emulation when the ending address of the target is encountered. Then it sends back the results together with the emulation state to the client, and then enters a wait mode for the next request from the client.

Figure 2 shows an example from a real-world application, GNU Chess [3], which is a chess-playing game. In this example, the OP first identifies that around 97.3% of the execution time is spent in the function **_ZN6engine6searchEv**, which is invoked at the address *0x2b778*. This particular function evaluates all potential moves and determines the best move among them. Thus, it is selected as an offloading target.

The DBO then replaces the beginning instruction of this target, i.e., the instruction at *0x2b778*, with a branch instruction and directs its execution to a jump stub as shown in the figure. When the execution reaches *0x2b778*, the jump stub is executed and an offloading request is sent to the server. Once the request is received, the DBT on the server starts its emulation from the address *0x2b778*. The emulation of the function **_ZN6engine6searchEv** terminates at the address *0x2b77c*, which is the return address of the function call. The DBT then sends back the emulation results to the client, and the client resumes its execution from *0x2b77c*. In this way, the function **_ZN6engine6searchEv** is offloaded to the server seamlessly.

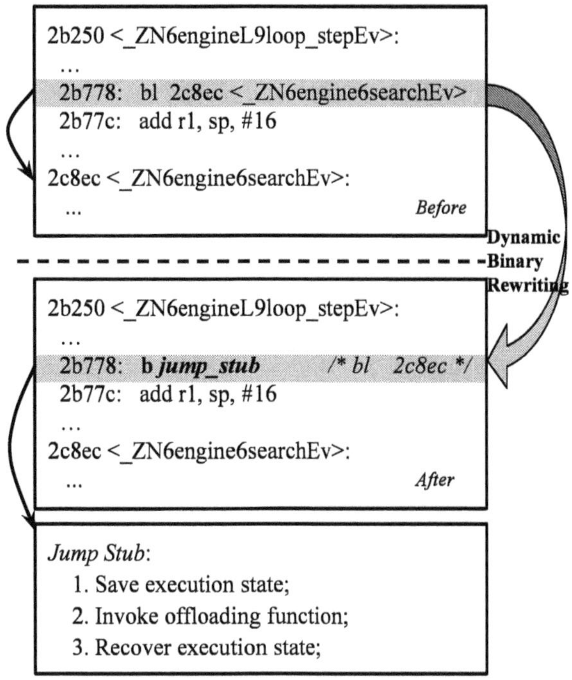

Figure 2: A real-world example from GNU Chess, with its binary code before and after dynamic binary rewriting, and the jump stub.

3. SYSTEM DESIGN ISSUES

As mentioned earlier, there are two main phases on the client, i.e., target selection (offline) and target offloading. The first phase is realized by the OP using a heuristic target selection algorithm. Target offloading in the second phase is achieved by the DBO using a dynamic binary rewriting technique.

The DBT on the server is responsible for receiving and processing the offloading requests from the client. During the DBT's emulation, data transfer may be required between the DBT (server) and the DBO (client). It is implemented in a way similar to demand paging. I/O operations and some system calls during the emulation also need to be handled between the DBT and the DBO. The following sections discuss these design issues in more details.

3.1 Target Selection for Offloading

We can avoid the target selection problem by sending the entire binary code that includes the application's binary and its shared libraries to the server, and asking the server to emulate the entire execution from the start. Although this simplifies the target selection problem, it has three fundamental limitations.

First, the communication overhead between the client and the server will increase substantially due to the large sizes of the application binaries and the shared libraries. Table 1 shows the sizes of the top 10 free applications from Google Play store [9] after their installation on a Google Nexus 6P smart phone. As shown in the table, up to 6 applications have more than 50 MB of executable binaries (including Java

Application	Category	Version	Size (MB)
Slither.io	Game	1.1.2	**43.35**
Messenger	Communication	69.0.0	**122**
Snapchat	Social	9.29.3	**109**
Facebook	Social	74.0.0	**249**
Pandora	Music & Audio	7.1	**46.16**
Instagram	Social	7.21.1	**48.15**
Clean Master	Tool	5.12.1	**70.42**
Color Switch	Game	2.4.0	**51.17**
Kika Emoji	Tool	3.4.148	**38.2**
Spotify Music	Music & Audio	5.2.0	**79.47**

Table 1: Application size of the top 10 free applications from Google Play store after their installation on a Google Nexus 6P smart phone.

bytecode). The largest application, i.e., Facebook, even approaches 250 MB.

Second, the performance benefit of offloading can be substantially reduced by the overhead of dynamic binary translation if there are too many infrequently executed code regions. Generally, a dynamic binary translator emulates a guest binary by translating it into host binary first [36]. For the *cold* code regions, i.e., the code regions that are rarely executed, the cost of translation often cannot be amortized during the application's lifetime. Previous work [34, 40] shows that almost 90% of the emulation time can be contributed to the translation overhead of cold code regions in graphical user interface (GUI) applications.

Third, it is hard for a client to recover from unexpected network failures if the entire execution is offloaded to the server. For example, suppose a chess playing game on the client is offloaded to the server. After several moves played, it encounters occasional connection disruptions, which means the client loses the connection to the server and cannot send/receive any data to/from the server. If the entire execution was offloaded to the server, the client would not be able to resume the execution because most of the intermediate data is on the server.

To overcome such limitations, our offloading system uses profiling to identify only *hot* code regions as offloading targets. The profiling information is gathered at the *function* level for simplicity. For each executed function, the following information is collected:

Execution Time The execution time is used to identify major time-consuming functions. The total execution time of a function is calculated by adding its own execution time and the time of all its callee functions.

Dynamic Memory Allocation and Deallocation Dynamic memory allocation and free operations are monitored to collect the starting address, the size, and other relevant information of the allocated memory region. The *time stamp* at the time of a dynamic memory allocation is assigned to the allocated memory region as its unique ID for future references.

Memory Access and I/O Operation Each memory access in a function is instrumented to collect the information such as its memory address, the size, and the ID of the accessed memory region. The I/O operations are also tracked to estimate the communication overhead.

Calling Context The calling context is the call path from the `main` function to the current function, which can be used

Algorithm 1: Target Selection for Offloading

Input: (1) a ranked linked list F of hot functions based on hotness, i.e. execution time
(2) a DCG graph $G = (V, E)$

Output: a final set S of selected offloading targets

```
S ← ∅;
f ← HEAD(F);
while f ≠ NULL do
    // Step 1
    if f ∉ S and f is not invoked during the execution of
      any function in S then
        // Step 2
        T_f ← total execution time of f;
        I_f ← total data size of I/O in f;
        if I_f / T_f < M then
            S ← S + {f};
            // Step 3
            foreach v ∈ V do
                if e : v -n-> f ∈ E or e : f -n-> v ∈ E then
                    if n > N and v ∉ S and v is not
                      invoked during the execution of any
                      function in S then
                        T_v ← total execution time of v;
                        I_v ← total data size of I/O in v;
                        if I_v / T_v < M then
                            S ← S + {v};
    f ← f → next;
return S;
```

by the OP to backtrack the location where the function is invoked and to distinguish different contexts of the same function.

Based on the collected profiled information, the OP then proceeds with offloading target selection. Intuitively, the most time-consuming functions should be included in the *initial target set*. But, the execution time is not the only concern because some of these targets may have very large live-in and/or live-out data sets and extensive I/O activities, which can incur a large communication overhead and offset the benefit of work offloading.

Take GNU Chess [3] discussed in Section 2 as an example. There is a huge memory region (around 256 MB) that is frequently accessed in the hot function **`_ZN6engine6searchEv`**. This memory region is allocated and initialized dynamically in another function **`_ZN6engine11trans_allocEPNS_5transE`**, which is not a time-consuming function and, hence, will not be included in the initial target set. However, if this function is not offloaded and stays on the client, a huge amount of data has to be transferred through the network to the server when the function **`_ZN6engine6searchEv`** is being emulated on the server. To reduce this kind of excessive communication overhead, the OP heuristically extends the initial target set to include the functions that generate (or consume) large live-in/live-out data sets used (or produced) by the functions in the initial target set. It may also exclude the targets in the initial target set that have excessive I/O activities to avoid excessive communication overhead.

To simplify the target selection process, if a function is selected as an offloading target, all of its callee functions are also selected for offloading. A directed data communication graph (DCG) $G = (V, E)$ is constructed to facilitate the selection process. Each node $v \in V$ represents a function, and an edge $e : v_1 \xrightarrow{n} v_2 \in E$ connects the functions v_1 and v_2 if there are n memory pages produced in v_1 and accessed in v_2 at runtime. Thus, if v_2 is offloaded to the server and v_1 stays on the client, these memory pages need to be transferred from the client to the server over the network.

The initial target set is determined based on the *hotness* of each function, i.e., the total execution time including its callee functions. Algorithm 1 shows the target selection process. The input F is the ranked list of hot functions in the initial target set based on the hotness. The output S is the final selected target set by OP. For each target $f \in F$, there are three steps in the algorithm.

In the first step, the OP checks if f has been included in S, or called during the execution of any function in S. If yes, the OP skips f and goes to next target in F. Otherwise, the OP moves to the second step.

In the second step, the OP examines the I/O operations in f (including its callee functions) to see if they are excessive in f. If they are not excessive, f is included into S and the OP moves to the third step.

In the third step, the OP traverses each node $v \in V$ in G that is connected with f, i.e., $e : v \xrightarrow{n} f \in E$ or $e : f \xrightarrow{n} v \in E$. If the value of n is large, it indicates that function v should be offloaded together with f to reduce the communication overhead. The OP also examines the I/O operations in v to further check if it is suitable for offloading. If yes, v can be included into S. The selection process iterates until all of the functions are examined.

For each target in S, we need to locate all of its call sites in the collected calling context and their corresponding return locations, i.e., the instructions that follow the call instructions, which are referred to as the *beginning* and the *ending* instructions of this offloading target, respectively. The DBO on the client replaces the beginning instruction by a branch instruction to a jump stub that enables the offloading of this target. Similarly, the DBT on the server uses the ending instruction to terminate the emulation of the offloaded target. Here, we did not use the entry and exit points of a function because there are often multiple exit points, i.e., return instructions, in a function and it is not easy to locate all of them in the binary. Besides, this choice of beginning and ending instructions can be extended easily to other types of offloading targets with different granularities, such as hot loops or traces, without additional work required.

3.2 Memory Mapping

To guarantee the correct execution of the offloaded targets, the data must be maintained coherent between the client and the server. To meet this requirement, the relevant memory regions in the virtual address space of an offloaded application on the client are mapped to their corresponding memory regions in the virtual address space of DBT on the server, as shown in Figure 3. This means the application and the DBT can see the same memory layout. Here, we only focus on offloading from a 32-bit or 64-bit client to a 64-bit server, where we can take advantage of a larger or equal address space available. Offloading from a 64-bit client to a 32-bit server is quite rare, and DBT on such systems is still an open research issue [16].

To simplify the memory mapping between the client and the server, it is done at the *page* level. We can take advantage of the access permission mechanism provided in modern operating systems. Figure 4 shows some details of the memory mapping between the mobile application on the client and the DBT on the server.

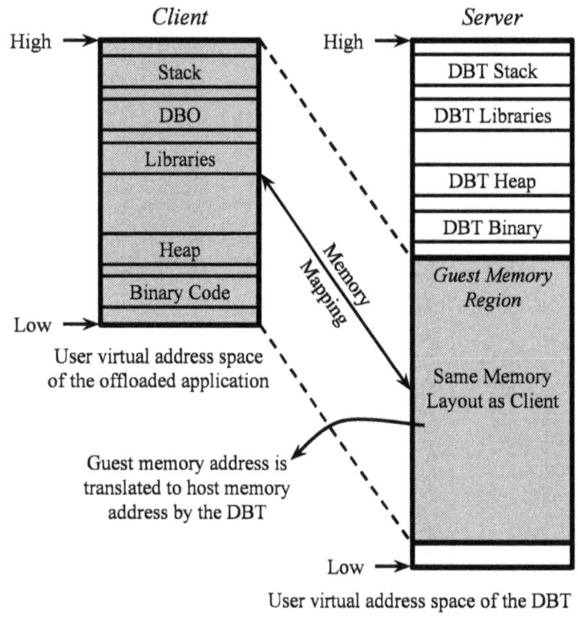

Figure 3: Memory address mapping between the offloaded application and the guest memory region in the DBT.

Initially, the DBT on the server allocates a guest memory region, but leaves it uninitialized. After receiving an offloading request from the client, the DBT initializes the guest memory region with the memory layout encapsulated in the offloading request. This initialization only organizes the guest memory region according to the memory layout in the offloading request. The actual data may still be on the client side, and is brought to the server at the page level when needed.

During the emulation of the offloaded target in the DBT, the first access to any memory page in the guest memory region will trigger a page access exception. The exception handler then sends a memory page request to the client, as shown in Figure 4. The DBO on the client responds to the request with the content of the requested page, and marks this page inaccessible on the client. Then the DBT loads the received page content to its corresponding page in the guest memory region, and marks it accessible. After the DBT finishes the emulation of the offloaded target, the DBO resumes the execution on the client with the received results as shown in Figure 4. A page transfer from the DBT to the DBO is triggered by an access to an inaccessible page on the client, and then this page is marked as inaccessible in the DBT.

To guarantee the same memory layout after the target is offloaded to the server, each time when a new memory region is dynamically allocated or an old memory region is deallocated on one side, the other side is informed to perform the same operation to maintain the same memory layout.

The memory mapping mechanism might be complicated by multi-threaded applications when some threads are offloaded to the server while others are remained on the client. The offloaded threads and the threads on the client can then

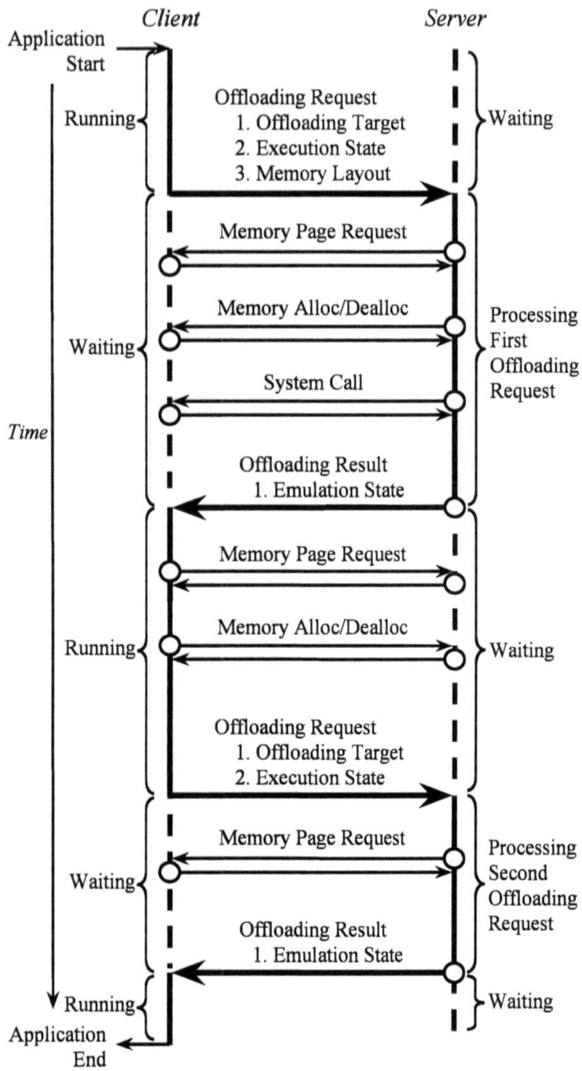

Figure 4: The detailed network communication between the client and the server.

synchronize via memory, e.g., through locks. In that case, our OP can be extended to collect synchronization information (e.g., `lock()`/`unlock()`) for each function and take them into consideration when selecting offloading targets.

3.3 I/O and System Calls

One significant limitation of most existing offloading systems is to avoid offloading code regions with I/O operations [22, 29]. However, it is very common in mobile applications to have I/O operations in hot code regions, e.g., reading or writing a file. In most mobile applications, the I/O operations are realized by invoking system calls provided by the operating system. To offload code regions with system calls, our offloading system classifies guest system calls into three categories, each of which is handled in a different way.

In the first category, the guest system calls can be emulated directly with similar system calls on the server, e.g., **gettimeofday**, **clock_gettime** and the like. System calls in this category are usually used to acquire generic information such as time and date. The execution results of such system calls are generally same/similar on both client and server[1]. The DBT can invoke these system calls on the server directly without going back to the client.

In the second category, the guest system calls need to be sent back to the client, e.g., **open**, **read**, **write** and **unlink**. These system calls are typically related to I/O operations, and thus the results of these system calls are system specific. For example, the **open** system call should open the file on the client, not on the server. The DBT sends the parameters of such system calls back to the client for execution, as shown in Figure 4. The DBO on the client executes received system call and sends the results back to the server.

In the last category, the guest system calls are required to be executed on both the server and the client, e.g., **brk**, **mmap**, **mremap** and **munmap**. These system calls are usually related to dynamic memory allocation and deallocation. Thus, these system calls might modify the memory layout of both virtual address spaces. To guarantee the same memory layout between the client and the server system calls in this category are executed in both DBT and DBO.

By classifying system calls into above three categories, our system can offload code regions that include I/O and other system calls. However, if the amount of I/O and system calls is too excessive, the network latency can significantly increase the execution time because each I/O operation requires two connections between the server and the client. Such targets may have to be excluded from the target set as mentioned earlier, and remain on client.

To reduce the communication overhead involved in I/O operations, the DBT will buffer the results of several output I/O operations on the server until they have to be sent back to the client for execution in one communication session. Similarly, for input I/O operations, the DBO will also try to buffer as much data as possible and send the data to the server in as few communication sessions as possible. In this way, the number of communication sessions between the server and the client required for I/O operations can be reduced substantially.

3.4 Network Failure Recovery

Typically, unexpected network disruptions and failures are caused by lost or closed network connections between the client and the server. To tolerate these occasional network failures, the client should be able to recover the execution when it loses response from the server during the offloaded execution. Our offloading system tries to support such recovery with minimal effort. Basically, the point of execution when the client sends an offloading request to the server is considered as a *nominal checkpoint*. If there is a network failure after the client sends an offloading request to the server, e.g., no response to this request from the server, the client can resume the execution from the nominal checkpoint by disabling the offloading function. Note that there is no additional work required at the nominal checkpoint (i.e., there is no need to save machine states) because the client halts its execution and waits for a response from the server at the nominal checkpoint.

To support a network failure recovery, the server needs to track modified guest memory pages when processing an

[1]Here, we assume the server has the same system time as the client. This is reasonable in practice because two connected computers can synchronize their system times with each other.

offloading request from the client. This can be easily done by marking the guest memory region in the DBT as read-only before the server starts to process each offloading request. After an offloading request is finished, the modified guest memory pages are sent back to the client. The client can then update corresponding memory pages before resume its execution. In addition, the client needs to record the results of each system call executed during the offloaded execution. These recorded system call results could be reused during a recovery execution when there is a network failure. With these extensions, the client can recover the execution from an unexpected network failure with minimal overhead.

4. IMPLEMENTATION

A prototype of the proposed offloading system has been implemented with three major components: OP, DBO and DBT. In our implementation, the client is an ARM-32 development board and the server is an Intel Xeon Ivy Bridge. Also, both the client and the server have a memory page size of 4KB.

The OP component is implemented using DynamoRIO [14], which is a dynamic binary instrumentation framework. DynamoRIO exports an interface for users to build user-defined program instrumentation tools. In our implementation, several DynamoRIO tools are used to gather profiling information. Each function call/return is instrumented to collect execution time information at runtime. Memory loads, stores, and system calls are also instrumented to gather data accesses to memory and I/O operations. In addition, the information on the calling context of each function is collected based on the calling context encoding method [37].

The DBO is implemented as a shared library on the client. It intercepts the `__libc_start_main` function via the environment variable `LD_PRELOAD`. In this way, the DBO can perform binary rewriting on the mobile application before its `main` function is executed. Alternatively, the DBO can be implemented as a lightweight dynamic binary instrumentation system to support statically linked applications.

A jump stub is generated for each offloading target. To accommodate these jump stubs, a memory page is created on the application heap. The page is marked as read-only and executable after the generation of the jump stubs. The original binary code is saved for future reference before it is rewritten and replaced by a branch instruction to the jump stub. If the offset from the original binary code to the jump stub is too large, e.g., more than 2^{25} in ARM-32, a load instruction to load the program counter: `ldr pc, [pc, -4]` is employed to perform the branch operation instead, and the absolute address of the jump stub is stored immediately after the load instruction.

In the first offloading request, the current memory layout on the client is included and sent to the server. This is done in the DBO by reading the file located at `/proc/self/maps`, which contains the detailed information about the available memory regions in the current process. In our implementation, the system call `mprotect` from Linux is used to set different access permissions of a virtual memory page. A signal handler is registered for the signal SIGSEGV, which is the signal received from the operating system when a protected page is accessed. Some applications might have registered their signal handlers as well. In that case, the original signal handler is saved in the DBO. If the received SIGSEGV signal is not caused by our offloading system, the original signal handler is invoked from our signal handler in the DBO. In addition, to track dynamic memory allocation and free operations on the client, the DBO also wraps related library functions, e.g., `mmap` and `munmap`, in `libc.so.6`. The original library functions are invoked from our wrapper functions.

The DBT is implemented within an existing retargetable dynamic binary translation system, HQEMU [24], which is based on QEMU [11]. HQEMU leverages LLVM [28] to generate more optimized code for the hot code regions. To amortize additional performance overhead introduced by LLVM, HQEMU spawns helper threads to perform the translation and optimization. In our implementation, helper threads are also enabled for performance consideration.

To implement memory mapping in HQEMU, `mprotect` is used to change the access permission of guest memory pages. HQEMU has its own signal handler for the signal SIGSEGV. Thus, we keep the original signal handler and insert our signal processing function at the beginning of the original handler. Each time when a SIGSEGV signal is received, our signal processing function is invoked first, and it checks the fault memory address to see if it is in the guest memory space or not. If yes, a memory page fetching request is triggered and sent to the client for the real content of the page. Otherwise, our signal processing function returns to the original signal handler and no request will be generated. The SIGSEGV signal is then handled by the original signal handler in HQEMU.

One special case in this signal handling process is from the dynamically generated binary in the offloaded target, e.g., the offloaded target is a JavaScript engine that includes a JIT compiler, which can dynamically generate and optimize guest binary at runtime. To maintain the consistency between the original guest binary code generated by the JavaScript engine and the translated host code, HQEMU (also QEMU) marks each guest binary page generated by the JavaScript engine read-only when the binary code in this page is being translated [11]. Thus HQEMU can detect the code changes on this page when a write event to this page occurs, e.g., by the JavaScript engine itself. This kind of page exceptions should be handled by the original signal handler in HQEMU. Our signal processing function ignores such page exceptions by checking if the page is a read-only page marked by HQEMU before sending a memory page fetching request to the client.

5. EVALUATION

Table 2 shows some characteristics of the applications evaluated in our experiments. We did not use most of the mobile applications listed in Table 1 because our implemented prototype system is constrained by the capability of HQEMU, which does not support those mobile applications but only desktop applications. HQEMU could be extended to emulate mobile applications, e.g., Android apps, which is left as part of our future work. We instead used two different types of applications to evaluate the effectiveness of the system. They include six real-world applications and the industry standard benchmark SPEC CINT2006. Among the six real-world applications, GNU Go [4] is a go game engine using the territorial effect values to find the best move. Free Awale [2] is a hole-and-seed game based on a min-max Von Neuman's algorithm. GNU Chess [3] is a chess engine using the classical principal variation search (PVS) algorithm

Application	Lang.	LoC (K)	Description	Size (MB)	Time (S)	#MemPage		#SystemCall		Comm. (KB)	
						C2S	S2C	OnC	OnS	C2S	S2C
GNU Go	C	229.5	Go Game	8.51	629.06	963	232	0	837	4223.92	979.26
Free Awale	C	9.7	Hole and Seed Game	0.05	243.54	13	4	0	0	53.04	40.69
GNU Chess	C++	48.1	Chess Game	1.27	325.88	216	91	1292	27594	890.81	481.71
Natch	C	21	Game Solver	0.32	250.63	116	12	738	1162	468.43	89.70
Sudoku	C	0.8	Puzzle Game	0.03	238.91	30	6	0	0	157.22	32.80
SpiderMonkey	C/C++	336	JavaScript Engine	108.97	677.62	1016	19	507	6986	5479.75	113.81
400.perlbench	C	128	Perl Interpreter	3.67	177.57	1564	50	8310	2318	20167.62	639.3
401.bzip2	C	5.7	Compression	0.21	340.85	307	21	77	83	62312.82	117.06
403.gcc	C	385.7	C Compiler	11.04	7.75	840	9	52	172	3444.21	230.11
429.mcf	C	1.6	Vehicle Scheduling	0.07	244.62	90	7	613	12	2605.42	123.8
445.gobmk	C	157.7	Go Game	5.85	554.4	7891	80	1729	292	35650.42	554.82
456.hmmer	C	40.7	Gene Sequence	1.01	322.06	184	10	63	39	815.63	90.47
458.sjeng	C	10.5	Chess Game	0.45	806.14	725	7	1515	6	2938.73	92.96
462.libquantum	C	2.6	Quantum Computing	0.15	15	121	9	3	54	486.94	46.29
464.h264ref	C	36	Video Compression	1.77	562.4	266	9	904	757	5539.08	82.71
471.omnetpp	C++	26.7	Event Simulation	4.17	413.26	302	202	517	701	1229.15	1014.02
473.astar	C++	4.3	Path Finding	0.23	558.19	314	26	104	2284	5105.09	128.73
483.xalancbmk	C++	266.9	XML Processing	47.2	442.68	621	16	80543	932	42316.02	40959.39

Table 2: Applications evaluated in our experiments. **Lang.**: programming language, **LoC (K)**: thousand lines of source code, **Size (MB)**: size of the application binary, **Time (S)**: execution time on the client in seconds, **#MemPage**: number of memory pages transferred, **C2S**: from the client to the server, **S2C**: from the server to the client, **#SystemCall**: number of system calls invoked during the emulation, **OnC**: executed on the client, **OnS**: emulated on the server, **Comm. (KB)**: the amount of data transferred between the client and the server.

with iterative deepening. Natch [7] is a proof game solver used to find the shortest moves to a given position. Sudoku [8] is a puzzle game generator with a difficulty level estimator. SpiderMonkey [6] is a JavaScript engine from Mozilla, which has been deployed in various Mozilla products including Firefox. These applications are quite representative and their stripped-down versions could also be found on smart mobile devices. For SPEC CINT2006, the *train* input set (instead of the larger *reference* input set) is purposely used to reflect the fact that most mobile applications are predominantly smaller and shorter applications with short execution times, which make them more sensitive to DBT overheads. Benchmarks with more than one input under the train input set are tested with all inputs covered.

To evaluate those real-world applications, we played 5 steps for the games against a computer, i.e., GNU Go, Free Awale, and GNU Chess. For Natch, a given position is solved for 16 moves. Sudoku is evaluated to generate and solve 6 puzzles. SpiderMonkey is evaluated on Google Octane [5], which is a benchmark suite used to measure a JavaScript engine's performance by running a series of test applications. Our evaluation covers 11 of 15 applications in Octane because HQEMU failed to emulate 3 of the applications and produced random emulation errors for the remaining application.

Our evaluation platform includes a client and a server. The client is an ARM development board equipped with a Quad-Core Cortex-A7 running at 1.3 GHz with a 2-GB main memory and the operating system is Linaro-14.04 with Linux-3.4.39. The server is equipped with a 16-Core Intel Xeon E5-2650 Ivy Bridge running at 2.60 GHz with Hyper-threading enabled. It also has a 64-GB main memory running Ubuntu-14.04 with Linux-3.13. Both the client and the server are connected to a public 802.11g WiFi network.

To collect the energy consumption data, the ARM development board is powered with an external 4V battery. During the measurements, there is no other task running on the board. The Linux command line tool `powerstat` is used to measure the power consumption on the board. `powerstat` can collect the whole-system power statistics in a user-specified sampling time interval. In our measurements, the sampling interval is set at 1 second, which is the minimum sampling interval supported by `powerstat`. In addition, to reduce the influence of random factors, each application is run three times, and the arithmetic mean of the three runs is used as the final result.

5.1 Performance Improvement

The first benefit of work offloading is the performance improvement because of the significant performance gap between the client and the server. Assume P_{Server} and P_{Client} are the performance of a mobile application running on the server and the client, respectively. The overhead introduced by the network communication is $O_{Network}$. Considering that the offloaded binary code is emulated by HQEMU instead of running natively on the server because of the need of DBT, we assume the overhead introduced by HQEMU is O_{HQEMU}. The performance improvement, I, that can be

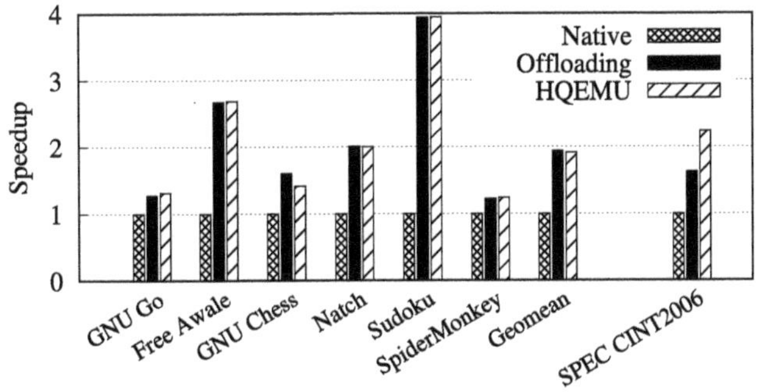

Figure 5: Performance speedup. The baseline is the native execution on the client without offloading. The HQEMU performance is from the emulation of a benchmark on original HQEMU (running entirely on server). SPEC CINT2006 is aggregated using the geometric mean.

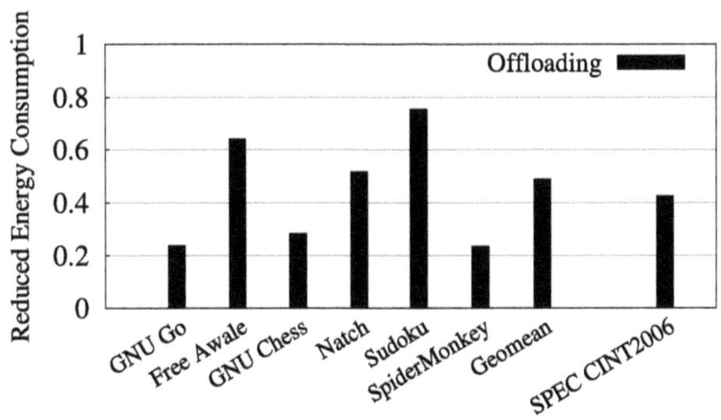

Figure 6: Reduced energy consumption of all benchmarks. The baseline is the amount of energy consumed during the native execution on the client without offloading. The results of SPEC CINT2006 are aggregated using the geometric mean.

achieved on our offloading system is shown in the following equation:

$$I \approx P_{Server} - P_{Client} - O_{Network} - O_{HQEMU} \quad (1)$$

Figure 5 shows the speedups on our offloading system. The baseline is the native execution on the client without offloading. The performance of original HQEMU running only on the server is also presented for comparison. The performance results of SPEC CINT2006 is aggregated using the geometric mean, and presented separately to avoid skewing the overall speedup because of its large number of programs in the benchmark suite and most of them are computation intensive.

As shown in Figure 5, our system can achieve good performance improvement for all of the applications. For most of the evaluated applications, our offloading system achieves similar performance as HQEMU emulating them on server, i.e., they are approaching the server performance with DBT.

An interesting anomaly is observed on GNU Chess. It achieves a 1.6X speedup with offloading, while the emulation using HQEMU on the server only gains 1.41X speedup. After studying this application, we found it is a multi-threaded application and the best move searching function is only invoked by one thread. Thus, only this thread is offloaded to the server in our offloading system with good speedup. However, HQEMU emulates multi-threaded guest applications sequentially, which degrades its overall performance. On average, 1.93X performance speedup can be observed for the real-world applications with our offloading system, compared with 1.91X performance speedup of original HQEMU.

For SPEC CINT2006 benchmark suite, our offloading system gains an overall speedup of 1.62X, while the emulation on HQEMU can achieve a 2.24X speedup. The performance difference comes from two sources. The first is from some extremely short running applications, such as 403.gcc. These applications complete their execution in only a few seconds. Due to the short running time, the network communication becomes a dominant overhead even if the communication volume is small. The second is from the large amount of data transferred from client to server in some benchmarks. The last two columns in Table 2 show the amount of data transfer between the client and the server. For 483.xalancbmk, it requires 41.32 MB of data from the client to the server, and 40 MB of data from the server to the client because this application processes a huge XML file and writes the processed result to another file. Similarly, 60.85 MB of data needs to be transferred from the client to the server for 401.bzip2 because it applies compression on this file.

5.2 Energy Efficiency

In general, the energy consumption of an application should be consistent with its performance improvement because the battery usage is proportionate to the execution time. Suppose W_{Native} is the average power consumption of the native execution on the client without offloading, and T_{Native} is the execution time. Correspondingly, $W_{Offloading}$ and $T_{Offloading}$ are the average power consumption and the execution time with offloading, respectively. The energy consumption reduced by offloading S can be represented by the following equation:

$$\begin{aligned} S &= W_{Native} \times T_{Native} - W_{Offloading} \times T_{Offloading} \\ &= W_{Native} \times (T_{Native} - T_{Offloading}) + \\ &\quad (W_{Native} - W_{Offloading}) \times T_{Offloading} \\ &= W_{Native} \times I + W_{\Delta} \times T_{Offloading} \quad (2) \end{aligned}$$

The reduced energy consumption comes mainly from two sources, i.e., $W_{Native} \times I$ and $W_{\Delta} \times T_{Offloading}$, where W_{Δ} is the reduced power consumption due to offloading.

Figure 6 illustrates the energy consumption on the client reduced by our offloading system. Here the baseline is the energy consumed in the native execution on the client without offloading. As shown in the figure, our offloading system successfully reduces the energy consumption for all of the evaluated applications. Even when the performance improvement of GNU Go and SpiderMonkey is not as much as other applications after offloading to server, they can still achieve 26.62% and 23.26% energy reduction, respectively. On average, 48.66% and 42.4% energy consumption is reduced, respectively, for the real-world applications and SPEC CINT2006.

Figure 7 shows some detailed power consumption behavior in the first 500 seconds on our offloading system compared to the native execution without offloading on the client. As shown in the figure, our offloading system exhibits peak power consumption in the initial stage due to the network activity between the client and the server for the required

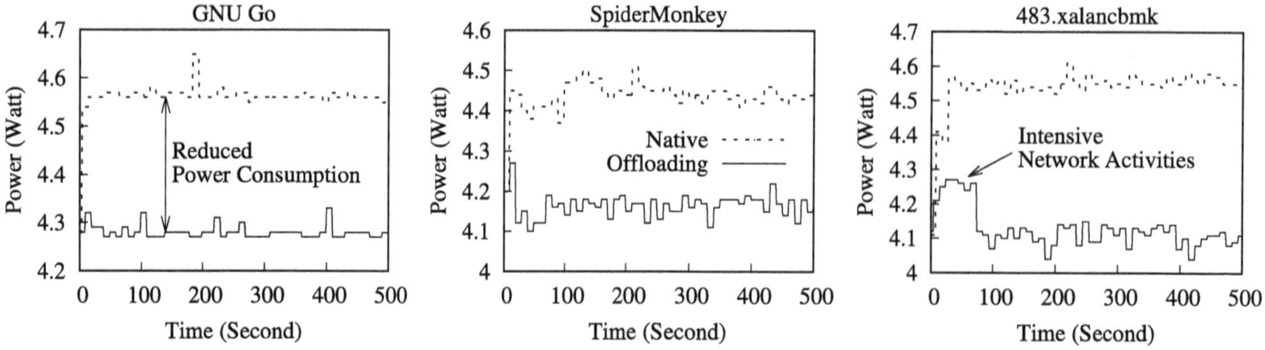

Figure 7: Power consumption in the first 500 seconds of the execution with and without offloading.

data transfer. The heavy power consumption is observed for 483.xalancbmk in the first 74 seconds due to the large input file transferred from the client to the server. However, in most cases, the client then settles into the wait mode, and the power consumption reduced to a level similar to the system standby state.

Even though we aim to reduce the power consumption of an application by offloading the computation-intensive code regions to the server side, it is probable that the power consumption might actually increase due to the potential fluctuation in the network communication overheads between the client and the server. It is generally hard to detect such scenarios [18, 22]. In that case, the benefit of computation offloading might come only from the performance improvement.

5.3 Network Sensitivity

To study the performance sensitivity to the network latency, we also tried to simulate real-world network environments by inserting randomized delays to each connection between the server and the client. The delay is implemented using `usleep` system call from Linux, which suspends the execution of the calling thread for an interval in microseconds specified by the parameter. To emulate different network environments, the parameter of `usleep` is generated using the expression: `random()` mod $(m + 1)$, where m is the maximum network delay in microseconds. Since our target client/server environments are those with short network latencies such as fog computing, the maximum network delay for each connection is set to 10^5 microseconds in this network sensitivity study.

Figure 8 shows the performance results of the 6 real-world applications with different values of m. As expected, the performance speedup achieved by our offloading system decreases as the network delay between the client and the server increases. The reason is obvious, because the increased network latency lowers the performance benefit of work offloading.

However, one interesting phenomenon that can be observed from this figure is that the decrease in speedup is rather slow relative to the increase in network latency for most of applications, i.e., the speedup is quite insensitive to the network delay until the maximum delay approaches 10^5 microseconds, at which point the performance drops suddenly for some applications, e.g., GNU Chess and SpiderMonkey. This demonstrates the capability of our offloading

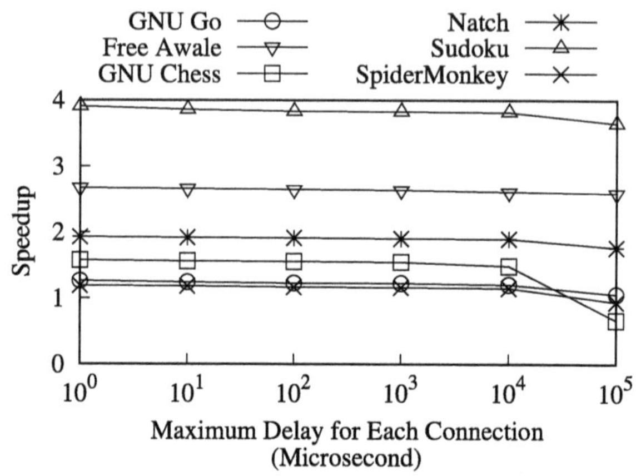

Figure 8: Network sensitivity with randomized delay for each connection between the client and the server.

system to tolerate reasonable network latency, which makes the work offloading quite robust in practice.

6. RELATED WORK

A significant amount of previous research work [17, 30, 18, 43, 22, 29, 33, 31, 20, 42, 19, 41, 23, 38, 35, 27, 26, 21] has demonstrated that computation offloading is an effective approach to improve the performance of mobile devices and prolong their battery life.

MAUI [18], ThinkAir [27], and COMET [22] are representative offloading systems using language-level virtual machines such as JVM and the Microsoft .NET CLR. MAUI and ThinkAir recompile mobile applications to enable their offloading features, i.e., they rely on the availability of the source code. Furthermore, they require specific annotations in mobile applications from expert programmers to enable their offloading targets. COMET offloads mobile applications in Java bytecode without the recompilation requirement, but it needs Dalvik JVM support to hide the differences in the underlying ISAs with strong runtime support. Tango [21] replicates a mobile application and executes it on both the client and the server. It allows either replica to lead the execution because either of the client or the server execution may be faster during different phases of the application. Besides, it also leverages techniques from deterministic replay to synchronize the two replicas. However, Tango still relies on Dalvik JVM to tackle the cross-ISA issue between the client and the server and cannot offload mobile applications using native libraries. Additionally, similar offloading systems include CloneCloud [17], Cuckoo [26], HELVM [31], JESSCIA2 [43] and the system described in [42].

Compared with these offloading systems, the main difference of our system is that our system works directly on native binary code across different ISAs. Thus there is no requirement on the availability of the source code, which is usually unavailable due to commercial reasons in practice, and there is no required support from the programming languages or runtime systems. The OP in our system automatically selects offloading targets based on the collected profiling information. So no programmer annotation is required. Besides, there is also no specific constraint on the native code regions to have I/O and system calls, which is usually avoided in most offloading systems mentioned above.

Paranoid Android [33] offloads computation-intensive security checks from mobile devices to the cloud. In Paranoid Android, a tracer is placed on the client to dynamically record the execution trace of each executed mobile application. Once the execution gets completed, the generated trace is transmitted to the server over the network. Then the server can replay the execution using a system level virtual machine and the computation-intensive security checks are applied during this process. Different with Paranoid Android, our system offloads the computation from the client to the server on the fly, which avoids the requirement of the record-replay support. In addition, our system uses a lightweight process level dynamic binary translator on the server instead of a system level virtual machine, which can substantially reduce the resource usage on the server and improve the offloading throughput.

Some new programming language features have been designed to facilitate offloading. Network Objects [12] specify an object whose methods can be invoked over a network. Obliq [15] allows computation roaming over the network. Emerald [25] supports fine-grained object mobility such as arrays, records, and integers. Instead of extending a programming language, our system offloads mobile applications written in existing languages with no need to rewrite the applications.

Some schemes [30, 38, 41, 31] use static analysis techniques to partition mobile applications into tasks that can run on mobile devices and on servers separately. To minimize the communication overhead, various partitioning algorithms and cost analysis are proposed. However, most of those algorithms are limited to mobile applications with simple structures, e.g., media encoding and decoding applications, due to conservative pointer alias analysis. To offload general-purpose applications, Native Offloader [29] leverages offline profiling and performance estimator to select offloading targets, which is similar to our offloading system. But, code regions that include assembly code, system calls, or unknown external library calls are not allowed to be offloaded in Native Offloader, while there is no such limitation in our approach. The applicability of Native Offloader is also dependent on the availability of the source code, which is often unavailable in practice.

Some other offloading systems optimize task offloading for cloud environments, e.g., managing cloud resources to support offloading requests from various mobile devices [35], making offloading decisions with the consideration of cloud parameters and related rules [20, 19], and offloading with an intelligent selection of partitioning policy adaptively [23]. Our offloading system can work effectively with such systems. In addition, our offloading system can also benefit from various optimization techniques for DBT systems [34, 13, 32, 39, 40].

7. CONCLUSION

In this paper, we present a cross-ISA offloading system for native binary applications on mobile devices. The system offloads the identified computation-intensive binary code regions and their related data from the client to the server at runtime. The client leverages a dynamic binary optimizer to rewrite the binaries and to send offloading requests. An enhanced dynamic binary translator is employed on the server to retarget and re-optimize the client binaries to server ISA. With this approach, the native binary applications on the client can be offloaded to the server with a different ISA seamlessly. A prototype has been implemented using an existing retargetable dynamic binary translation system HQEMU. Experimental results show that our offloading system can achieve 1.93X performance speedup with 48.66% reduction in energy consumption for six real-world applications and 1.62X performance speedup with 42.4% reduction in energy consumption for SPEC CINT2006 benchmarks on an ARM-based client and an Intel Xeon Ivy Bridge server.

8. ACKNOWLEDGEMENTS

We would like to thank Gang Shi and Minjun Wu for their help in setting up the experimental environment and collecting the experimental results. We are also very grateful to Geoffrey Challen and the anonymous reviewers for their valuable comments and feedback. This work is supported in part by the National Science Foundation under the grant number CNS-1514444.

9. REFERENCES

[1] ART and Dalvik. https://source.android.com/devices/tech/dalvik/index.html.

[2] Free Awale. http://www.nongnu.org/awale.

[3] GNU Chess. https://www.gnu.org/software/chess.

[4] GNU Go. https://www.gnu.org/software/gnugo.

[5] Google Octane. https://developers.google.com/octane.

[6] Mozilla SpiderMonkey. https://developer.mozilla.org/en-US/docs/Mozilla/Projects/SpiderMonkey.

[7] Natch. http://natch.free.fr/Natch.html.

[8] Sudoku. http://dlbeer.co.nz/articles/sudoku.html.

[9] Top 10 free Android applications from Google Play store. https://play.google.com/store/apps/collection/topselling_free.

[10] Your smartphone's best app? Battery life, say 89% of Britons. https://www.theguardian.com/technology/2014/may/21/your-smartphones-best-app-battery-life-say-89-of-britons.

[11] F. Bellard. QEMU, a Fast and Portable Dynamic Translator. In *Proceedings of the Annual Conference on USENIX Annual Technical Conference*, ATC '05, pages 41–41, Berkeley, CA, USA, 2005. USENIX Association.

[12] A. Birrell, G. Nelson, S. Owicki, and E. Wobber. Network objects. In *Proceedings of the Fourteenth ACM Symposium on Operating Systems Principles*, SOSP '93, pages 217–230, New York, NY, USA, 1993. ACM.

[13] D. Bruening and V. Kiriansky. Process-shared and Persistent Code Caches. In *Proceedings of the Fourth ACM SIGPLAN/SIGOPS International Conference on Virtual Execution Environments*, VEE '08, pages 61–70, New York, NY, USA, 2008. ACM.

[14] D. L. Bruening. *Efficient, Transparent, and Comprehensive Runtime Code Manipulation.* PhD thesis, Cambridge, MA, USA, 2004. AAI0807735.

[15] L. Cardelli. A language with distributed scope. In *Proceedings of the 22Nd ACM SIGPLAN-SIGACT Symposium on Principles of Programming Languages*, POPL '95, pages 286–297, New York, NY, USA, 1995. ACM.

[16] C.-J. Chang, J.-J. Wu, W.-C. Hsu, P. Liu, and P.-C. Yew. Efficient memory virtualization for cross-isa system mode emulation. In *Proceedings of the 10th ACM SIGPLAN/SIGOPS International Conference on Virtual Execution Environments*, VEE '14, pages 117–128, New York, NY, USA, 2014. ACM.

[17] B.-G. Chun, S. Ihm, P. Maniatis, M. Naik, and A. Patti. Clonecloud: Elastic execution between mobile device and cloud. In *Proceedings of the Sixth Conference on Computer Systems*, EuroSys '11, pages 301–314, New York, NY, USA, 2011. ACM.

[18] E. Cuervo, A. Balasubramanian, D.-k. Cho, A. Wolman, S. Saroiu, R. Chandra, and P. Bahl. Maui: Making smartphones last longer with code offload. In *Proceedings of the 8th International Conference on Mobile Systems, Applications, and Services*, MobiSys '10, pages 49–62, New York, NY, USA, 2010. ACM.

[19] H. Flores and S. Srirama. Adaptive code offloading for mobile cloud applications: Exploiting fuzzy sets and evidence-based learning. In *Proceeding of the Fourth ACM Workshop on Mobile Cloud Computing and Services*, MCS '13, pages 9–16, New York, NY, USA, 2013. ACM.

[20] H. Flores and S. Srirama. Mobile code offloading: Should it be a local decision or global inference? In *Proceeding of the 11th Annual International Conference on Mobile Systems, Applications, and Services*, MobiSys '13, pages 539–540, New York, NY, USA, 2013. ACM.

[21] M. S. Gordon, D. K. Hong, P. M. Chen, J. Flinn, S. Mahlke, and Z. M. Mao. Accelerating mobile applications through flip-flop replication. In *Proceedings of the 13th Annual International Conference on Mobile Systems, Applications, and Services*, MobiSys '15, pages 137–150, New York, NY, USA, 2015. ACM.

[22] M. S. Gordon, D. A. Jamshidi, S. Mahlke, Z. M. Mao, and X. Chen. Comet: Code offload by migrating execution transparently. In *Proceedings of the 10th USENIX Conference on Operating Systems Design and Implementation*, OSDI'12, pages 93–106, Berkeley, CA, USA, 2012. USENIX Association.

[23] X. Gu, K. Nahrstedt, A. Messer, I. Greenberg, and D. Milojicic. Adaptive offloading inference for delivering applications in pervasive computing environments. In *Proceedings of the First IEEE International Conference on Pervasive Computing and Communications*, PERCOM '03, pages 107–114, Washington, DC, USA, 2003. IEEE Computer Society.

[24] D.-Y. Hong, C.-C. Hsu, P.-C. Yew, J.-J. Wu, W.-C. Hsu, P. Liu, C.-M. Wang, and Y.-C. Chung. HQEMU: A Multi-threaded and Retargetable Dynamic Binary Translator on Multicores. In *Proceedings of the Tenth International Symposium on Code Generation and Optimization*, CGO '12, pages 104–113, New York, NY, USA, 2012. ACM. `http://itanium.iis.sinica.edu.tw/hqemu/`.

[25] E. Jul, H. Levy, N. Hutchinson, and A. Black. Fine-grained mobility in the emerald system. *ACM Trans. Comput. Syst.*, 6(1):109–133, Feb. 1988.

[26] R. Kemp, N. Palmer, T. Kielmann, and H. Bal. *Mobile Computing, Applications, and Services: Second International ICST Conference, MobiCASE 2010, Santa Clara, CA, USA, October 25-28, 2010, Revised Selected Papers*, chapter Cuckoo: A Computation Offloading Framework for Smartphones, pages 59–79. Springer Berlin Heidelberg, Berlin, Heidelberg, 2012.

[27] S. Kosta, A. Aucinas, P. Hui, R. Mortier, and X. Zhang. Thinkair: Dynamic resource allocation and parallel execution in the cloud for mobile code offloading. In *Proceedings of the 31st Annual IEEE International Conference on Computer Communications*, INFOCOM '12, pages 945–953, Washington, DC, USA, 2012. IEEE Computer Society.

[28] C. Lattner. LLVM: An Infrastructure for Multi-Stage Optimization. Master's thesis, Computer Science Dept., University of Illinois at Urbana-Champaign, Urbana, IL, Dec 2002. `http://llvm.org`.

[29] G. Lee, H. Park, S. Heo, K.-A. Chang, H. Lee, and H. Kim. Architecture-aware automatic computation offload for native applications. In *Proceedings of the 48th International Symposium on Microarchitecture*, MICRO-48, pages 521–532, New York, NY, USA, 2015. ACM.

[30] Z. Li, C. Wang, and R. Xu. Computation offloading to save energy on handheld devices: A partition scheme. In *Proceedings of the 2001 International Conference on Compilers, Architecture, and Synthesis for Embedded Systems*, CASES '01, pages 238–246, New York, NY, USA, 2001. ACM.

[31] S. Ou, K. Yang, and A. 'Liotta. An adaptive multi-constraint partitioning algorithm for offloading in pervasive systems. In *Proceedings of the Fourth Annual IEEE International Conference on Pervasive Computing and Communications*, PERCOM '06, pages 116–125, Washington, DC, USA, 2006. IEEE Computer Society.

[32] J. a. Porto, G. Araujo, E. Borin, and Y. Wu. Trace Execution Automata in Dynamic Binary Translation. In *Proceedings of the 2010 International Conference on Computer Architecture*, ISCA'10, pages 99–116, Berlin, Heidelberg, 2012. Springer-Verlag.

[33] G. Portokalidis, P. Homburg, K. Anagnostakis, and H. Bos. Paranoid android: Versatile protection for smartphones. In *Proceedings of the 26th Annual*

Computer Security Applications Conference, ACSAC '10, pages 347–356, New York, NY, USA, 2010. ACM.

[34] V. J. Reddi, D. Connors, R. Cohn, and M. D. Smith. Persistent code caching: Exploiting code reuse across executions and applications. In *Proceedings of the International Symposium on Code Generation and Optimization*, CGO '07, pages 74–88, Washington, DC, USA, 2007. IEEE Computer Society.

[35] C. Shi, K. Habak, P. Pandurangan, M. Ammar, M. Naik, and E. Zegura. Cosmos: Computation offloading as a service for mobile devices. In *Proceedings of the 15th ACM International Symposium on Mobile Ad Hoc Networking and Computing*, MobiHoc '14, pages 287–296, New York, NY, USA, 2014. ACM.

[36] J. Smith and R. Nair. *Virtual Machines: Versatile Platforms for Systems and Processes (The Morgan Kaufmann Series in Computer Architecture and Design)*. Morgan Kaufmann Publishers Inc., San Francisco, CA, USA, 2005.

[37] W. N. Sumner, Y. Zheng, D. Weeratunge, and X. Zhang. Precise calling context encoding. In *Proceedings of the 32Nd ACM/IEEE International Conference on Software Engineering - Volume 1*, ICSE '10, pages 525–534, New York, NY, USA, 2010. ACM.

[38] C. Wang and Z. Li. Parametric analysis for adaptive computation offloading. In *Proceedings of the ACM SIGPLAN 2004 Conference on Programming Language Design and Implementation*, PLDI '04, pages 119–130, New York, NY, USA, 2004. ACM.

[39] W. Wang, C. Wu, T. Bai, Z. Wang, X. Yuan, and H. Cui. A pattern translation method for flags in binary translation. *Journal of Computer Research and Development*, 51(10):2336–2347, 2014.

[40] W. Wang, P.-C. Yew, A. Zhai, and S. McCamant. A general persistent code caching framework for dynamic binary translation (dbt). In *2016 USENIX Annual Technical Conference (USENIX ATC 16)*, pages 591–603, Denver, CO, June 2016. USENIX Association.

[41] C. Xian, Y.-H. Lu, and Z. Li. Adaptive computation offloading for energy conservation on battery-powered systems. In *Proceedings of the 13th International Conference on Parallel and Distributed Systems - Volume 01*, ICPADS '07, pages 1–8, Washington, DC, USA, 2007. IEEE Computer Society.

[42] K. Yang, S. Ou, and H.-H. Chen. On effective offloading services for resource-constrained mobile devices running heavier mobile internet applications. *Comm. Mag.*, 46(1):56–63, Jan. 2008.

[43] W. Zhu, C.-L. Wang, and F. C. M. Lau. Jessica2: A distributed java virtual machine with transparent thread migration support. In *Proceedings of the IEEE International Conference on Cluster Computing*, CLUSTER '02, pages 381–388, Washington, DC, USA, 2002. IEEE Computer Society.

Mobile Plus: Multi-device Mobile Platform for Cross-device Functionality Sharing

Sangeun Oh, Hyuck Yoo, Dae R. Jeong, Duc Hoang Bui, and Insik Shin
School of Computing, KAIST
Daejeon, Republic of Korea
{ohsang1213, yoohuck12, dragon812, ducbuihoang, insik.shin}@kaist.ac.kr

ABSTRACT

In recent years, the explosion of diverse smart devices such as mobile phones, TVs, watches, and even cars, has completely changed our lives. We communicate with friends through social network services (SNSs) whenever we want, buy stuff without visiting shops, and enjoy multimedia wherever we are, thanks to these devices. However, these smart devices cannot simply interact with each other even though they are right next to each other. For example, when you want to read a PDF stored on a smartphone on a larger TV screen, you need to do complicated work or plug in a bunch of cables. In this paper, we introduce M+, an extension of Android that supports cross-device functionality sharing in a transparent manner. As a platform-level solution, M+ enables unmodified Android applications to utilize not only application functionalities but also system functionalities across devices, as if they were to utilize them inside the same device. In addition to secure connection setup, M+ also allows performing of permission checks for remote applications in the same way as for local. Our experimental results show that M+ enables transparent cross-device sharing for various functionalities and achieves performance close to that of within-device sharing unless a large amount of data is transferred.

CCS Concepts

•**General and reference** → **Design;** •**Human-centered computing** → **Mobile computing; Mobile devices;** *Collaborative interaction;* •**Software and its engineering** → *Operating systems; Communications management;*

Keywords

Multi-device Mobile Platform; Functionality Sharing; Remote Procedure Call; Inter-Process Communication;

Permission to make digital or hard copies of all or part of this work for personal or classroom use is granted without fee provided that copies are not made or distributed for profit or commercial advantage and that copies bear this notice and the full citation on the first page. Copyrights for components of this work owned by others than ACM must be honored. Abstracting with credit is permitted. To copy otherwise, or republish, to post on servers or to redistribute to lists, requires prior specific permission and/or a fee. Request permissions from permissions@acm.org.

MobiSys'17, June 19-23, 2017, Niagara Falls, NY, USA

© 2017 ACM. ISBN 978-1-4503-4928-4/17/06...$15.00

DOI: http://dx.doi.org/10.1145/3081333.3081348

1. INTRODUCTION

The mobile app ecosystem continues to grow and mature rapidly, and offers a wide variety of services, such as SNS, shopping, entertainment, and healthcare. Mobile applications have become complex and diverse, and they have come to use the *functionalities*[1] of other applications or system services. At the same time, users own multiple mobile devices. A recent survey reported an average of more than three devices per person [1], and users are easily tempted to use on each device the functionalities available on other devices.

Such trends present exciting opportunities for multiple smart devices to be used together, including (1) video conferencing on a camera-less smart TV using a smartphone's camera, (2) secure internet shopping on an unsecured public device using payment service from one's own private smartphone, (3) replying to an email on a smartphone while scrolling through its attached documents on a tablet, and doing copy and paste between the two devices, and (4) playing sensor-based games on a tablet while using sensors from a smartphone, which can provide a more convenient method to control them.

Many solutions have been proposed to enable this exciting opportunity. First, many interesting studies have been done to use the resources of other devices through the cooperation of applications. Many apps [26, 32, 6, 7, 15, 31] are available for sharing specific resources, including screen casting, cameras, and sensors. However, their applicability is quite limited, because they work with their own custom applications but do not support unmodified applications. This imposes a great burden on those wanting to develop and deploy such applications for each individual resource or functionality. Second, a great deal of work [39, 14, 27, 37, 22, 23, 13, 21, 4, 42] has been done to develop a cross-device platform that enables unmodified applications to use the resources of other devices. However, these mainly focus on utilizing system resources such as sensors and cameras but do not support application functionalities such as in-app payment and SNS login.

Here, we present a novel platform M+ (Mobile Plus). The main goal of M+ is to allow unmodified applications to share a wide range of functionalities across devices. That is, our system is intended to be insensitive to the type of func-

[1]In this paper, we define functionality as a collection of services, features, content, and resources. We classify functionalities into two categories according to their providers: *application* functionalities offered by applications, and *system* functionalities by Android system services.

tionality, and with no extra burden of application development. To achieve the design goal, M+ extends the existing remote procedure call (RPC) scheme and its underlying binder inter-process communication (IPC) mechanism to multi-device environments. In other words, our key idea is to intercept RPC messages (binder parcels) from a client device and forward them to a server device to execute RPC function logic. This approach suits our design goal for two reasons. First, to the best of our knowledge, all existing applications are using RPCs to utilize the functionalities of other applications or system services. Therefore, extending the RPC scheme will naturally enable support of both application and system functionalities in the multi-device environment. Second, RPC is transparent to the application layer because it is supported at the platform layer. Therefore, the RPC extension does not require modification of applications.

M+ should address several fundamental challenges in extending within-device RPC to cross devices because Android is designed under the assumption that client and server processes run on the same device. (i) Android allows passage of various type of references or handles as RPC parameters, including shared memories, sockets, binders, and files, for better performance. However, passing RPC arguments in a call-by-reference manner does not work properly across different devices. M+ detects reference-type arguments in a functionality-agnostic way and makes their values available transparently between devices. (ii) Android app management logic will not work properly in the multi-device environment: it cannot manage execution context and semantics (e.g., app lifecycles, caller-callee information) of app beyond the device boundary. Hence, M+ addresses this unprecedented issue based on the concept of *virtual activity* to enable unmodified applications to execute on different devices without having their interaction semantics violated, while incurring little change to Android system services. (iii) The Android assumption that there is only one instance of an application will not hold. Because each device can have its own resident app, there could exist multiple instances of the same app when multiple devices are joined for functionality sharing. For this reason, M+ leverages the notion of *remote app registration* to manage multiple instances properly for correct security checks and communication support.

We proved the M+ concept with a prototype using Nexus 6 (smartphone) and Nexus 10 (tablet)[2]. It was demonstrated that M+ allows existing applications on different devices to successfully share functionalities such as Facebook Login, Google Market Payment, Android Contacts, and PDF Viewer; as well as system features (camera, sensor, notification and clipboard). Interestingly, all these sharing processes do not incur significant performance overhead and behave almost like sharing within the same device in most cases, unless they require transfer of a large amount of data. The details about the experiment will be discussed in later sections. In addition, it is worth noting that even if heterogeneous types of devices interact with each other, M+ can easily support the interaction if the devices have just the same RPC interfaces. This is possible because our system is designed to provide functionality sharing via cross-device RPC regardless the type of device.

[2]See http://cps.kaist.ac.kr/mobileplus for our demo video illustrating the interaction between Nexus 6 and Nexus 10.

2. USE CASES

Service sharing: login, payment, and notification. M+ can change the way people utilize services across devices in many places. With M+, one could dispatch certain services to designated devices or users for various reasons. For example, a user might want to log into an SNS app (e.g., Instagram) on a public device such as a free rental tablet in a public library or a smart TV in her hotel room. This comes with a risk to privacy (e.g., social media account hijacking) because public devices could have malware or keystroke-logging software secretly installed. With M+, she can log into the SNS app securely using her Facebook login on her own smartphone. Moreover, a kid might feel an impulse to purchase in-game items after failing to move on to the next round in a mobile game. With M+, her mother can be prompted to deal with the purchase order via PayPal or Google Play on her smartphone. With M+, a user could receive notifications or alarms (e.g., incoming calls, SMS messages, and low battery alarms) forwarded from a smartphone and displayed on a TV.

Contents sharing: file, contact, and calendar. M+ can facilitate the way users access and interact with information between devices. When checking emails on a smartphone, a user might want to view an attached PDF document on a larger-screen device, such as a tablet. With M+, this could be done right away with a single tap on the PDF icon on a smart watch, rather than go through a cloud storage service (e.g., Dropbox) or use an email client app on the tablet. Interestingly, she could work on both devices at the same time: write an email reply on a smartphone and scroll through the attached documents on a tablet simultaneously. In this case, the user could also copy any part of the attached document on the tablet and paste it on the smartphone. With M+, a user could run video conferencing or daily briefing apps on a TV, while accessing contact and calendar data on her smartphone.

I/O sharing: camera. The digital world is now shifting from 2D to 3D, and one great example is the success of 3D selfie camera applications. However, in order to render 3D images from a single camera, the camera must take multiple images from different angles. Apparently, this condition puts critical restrictions on development of many creative uses. Instead, applications seek to construct 3D images using multiple cameras. In this context, M+ provides a platform-level I/O sharing so that those applications can use remote cameras easily.

3. ANDROID BACKGROUND

Application components. Each functionality in Android is implemented as one of four application components: activity, service, content provider, or broadcast receiver. an activity represents the user interface of an application, allowing interaction between the application and the user. Everything a user sees in an application is provided by activities. For example, Facebook login activity provides a UI to allow users to enter ID and password. a service is designed to perform long-running operations in the background. For example, I/O functionalities, such as camera and sensor, are provided with system services. a content provider gives an interface for storing and sharing data using a relational database (e.g. SQLite database). For instance, contact lists and calendar information are managed by content providers.

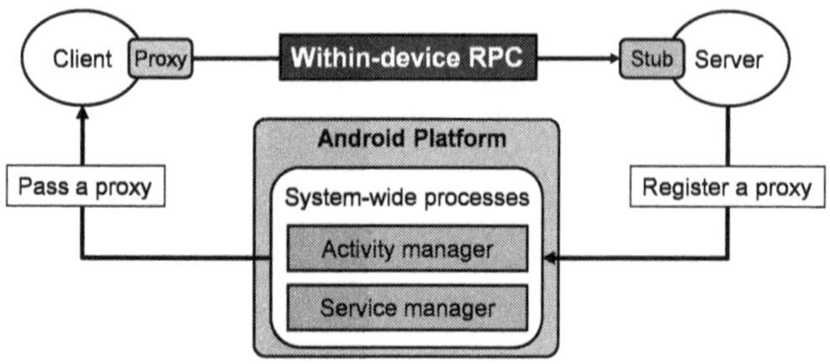

Figure 1: Within-device RPC in Android

a broadcast receiver is for receiving system-wide messages. For example, low battery level warning is broadcast and applications save their states to prevent any data loss.

Functionality sharing in Android. Android is designed to allow applications (processes) to share their functionalities through remote procedure calls (RPCs). Suppose that a client application tries to use a functionality of a server application. Here, function sharing is achieved between them if the client invokes RPC functions for the functionality to the server. The invocation procedure typically consists of two steps. The client first forwards a message (called *parcel*) for calling a RPC function to the server. Upon receiving the parcel, the server executes the RPC function and passes the parcel containing its result to the client.

The Android RPC employs the inter-process communication (IPC) mechanism managed by the binder driver, because it is achieved across the process boundary. To deliver parcels from the client to the server, the binder driver creates a binder connection: a route between the two processes for the parcels. This procedure is called *binding*. Here, the source and target endpoints of a binder connection are a proxy and a stub. RPC invocations are always made in one direction: from proxy to stub.

Figure 1 shows how binding works between client and server processes. A client first requests a proxy to Android system services; then it asks the service manager to share a system functionality or asks the activity manager to share an application functionality. We note that each individual server has registered its proxy to the service/activity manager when it is initiated. When the client obtains the proxy from the server/activity manager, binding is completed in one of two ways depending on the component type of server functionality. The client binds to the server's component directly if the component is a service or content provider, or indirectly via the activity manager if the component is an activity. The latter allows the activity manager to mediate interaction between the client and server activities according to their own interaction semantics. We will describe this in more detail in Section 6.

4. SYSTEM DESIGN OVERVIEW

The main goal of M+ is to allow transparent sharing of both application and system functionalities across multiple mobile devices. To this end, M+ should be oblivious to the type of functionality without incurring any extra burden of application development. M+ extends the within-device RPC scheme across different devices to achieve this goal. Figure 2 shows an overview of M+ consisting of these main components: cross-device IPC connection, cross-device RPC execution, and security management.

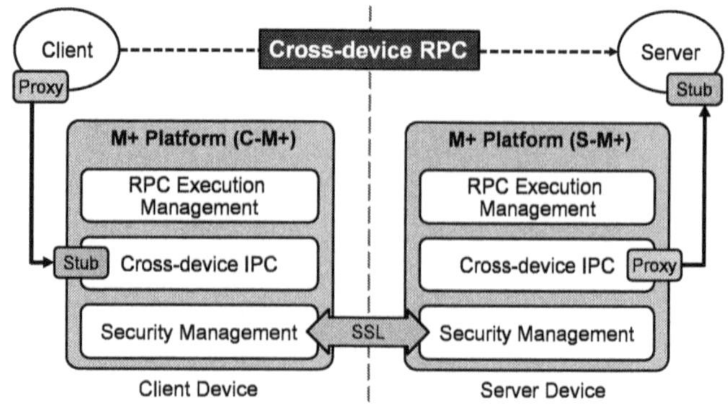

Figure 2: M+ design overview

Cross-device IPC connection. Towards transparent cross-device RPC execution, M+ first seeks to deliver RPC function calls to server processes on different devices without requiring modifications to applications. To this end, M+ extends the existing binder IPC mechanism to create a cross-device binder connection, yet offers the illusion of a within-device IPC. We describe this in detail in Section 5.

Cross-device RPC execution. M+ aims to create an environment in which RPC functions can be executed correctly on remote devices. Many RPC functions may not execute properly across different devices, because Android is designed to support RPC execution within a single device. This gap engenders a different set of challenges which has not previously been addressed to support cross-device RPC. For example, M+ should manage execution context and semantics properly across multiple devices when supporting transparent cross-device RPC execution, because Android does it only within the device boundary. As another example, servers may request information about clients while executing RPC functions. M+ should make such information available on server devices in a transparent manner. In Section 6, we explain which challenges M+ faces and how it addresses them.

Security management. As M+ allows multiple devices to cooperate over the network, various security issues arise. For example, M+ needs to distinguish multiple application instances in multi-device environments in order to perform permission checks accurately. In addition, the existence of various kinds of attacks through the network threaten the security of M+. Thus, M+ establishes a secure connection between the two devices via the SSL protocol. We explain how M+ addresses security concerns in Section 7.

5. CROSS-DEVICE IPC CONNECTION

We first need to extend the binder IPC mechanism to support cross-device RPC, addressing several issues. First, we determine the right place to intercept binder parcels without modifying applications. Second, we need to intercept the smallest set of parcels to minimize an interception overhead. Third, unmodified applications should be able to reach their destinations across devices. This section explains how to address such issues to establish an efficient cross-device binder connection for unmodified applications.

5.1 Binder Parcel Interception

First, we need to intercept parcels from applications to create a cross-device IPC channel transparently. One important decision to make is how to determine the right place to intercept parcels, to support a broad range of functionalities without any modification of existing applications. As shown in Figure 3, a parcel goes through a number of binder layers. The first layer, which is the interface layer, is designed to provide the same function interfaces to both client and server applications. In most cases, the function interfaces are generated in application code through an interface language, called Android interface description language (AIDL). If the parcels were to be intercepted in the interface layer (as done in [25]), function interfaces in existing applications must be modified through recompilation; this is not an adequate solution for our goal.

All the layers below the interface layer belong to the Android platform. These layers are not included in application code, but are dynamically linked during application's runtime. Therefore, in order to support existing applications without modifications, parcels have to be intercepted at one of these layers. M+ determines the parcel intercept point as *BpBinder*, a binder object at the native IPC layer. Because a BpBinder object is placed at the native IPC layer, all Android applications (with either Java or native source codes) should pass through this object for binder IPC. This means that M+ can intercept any parcels at this layer to create cross-device IPC channels for various types of functionalities, no matter whether functionalities are based on either Java or native source codes.

Another important issue is which parcels to intercept. It would impose a considerable overhead if all the parcels should be intercepted. Instead, M+ intercepts the smallest set of parcels, which we call *seed* parcels, that initiate interactions with other applications. Specifically, it intercepts parcels to invoke some specific methods of `ActivityManager` and `ServiceManager`, which fall into two categories: (i) ones to establish a new binder IPC channel such as `getService()` of `ServiceManager`, `bindService()` and `getContentProvider()` of `ActivityManager`, and (ii) others to launch new application components such as `startActivity()` of `ActivityManager`. In this way, M+ narrows down a set of parcels to intercept to the minimum, without having to identify which parcels belong to which functionalities.

5.2 Cross-device Binder IPC

A binder IPC channel is established when a client obtains a (binder) proxy object for a server's (binder) stub, as described in Section 3. One design principle that is important for cross-device binder channels is to provide transparency to both client and server processes. In other words, it should provide the illusion to them that they are interacting within the same device. To achieve this, client and server processes are logically connected via three intermediate connections with two M+ components (see Figure 2). For ease of presentation, we often distinguish the roles of client-side M+ (C-M+) and server-side M+ (S-M+). That is, client and server processes perform binding locally with C-M+ and S-M+, respectively; while C-M+ and S-M+ communicate through a network connection.

Specifically, the binding procedure in the cross-device environment takes place as follows. First, a seed parcel is intercepted and passed to C-M+. It then prompts a window,

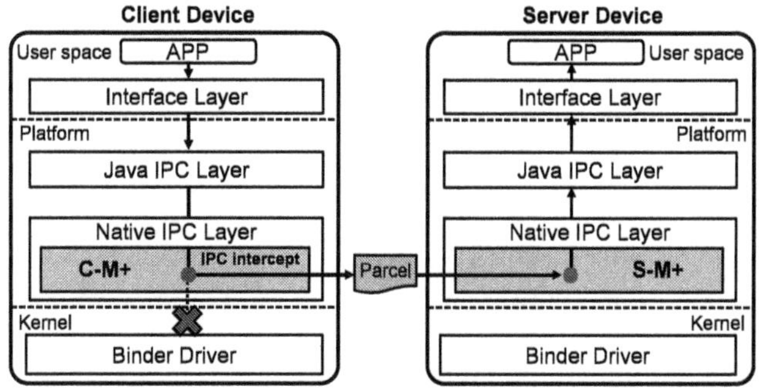

Figure 3: Binder IPC interception point

allowing the client user to decide which server applications to use for the functionality of interest, if there are multiple candidates, including remote ones. When the user decides to use a remote device's functionality, then C-M+ forwards the parcel to S-M+, which passes it to the activity/service manager on the server device. S-M+ obtains a proxy object for the server's stub when the binder driver creates a local binder channel between S-M+ and the server process. The proxy object is then passed back to C-M+. However, this proxy is not valid on the client device, because it is device-specific. So, C-M+ creates a new stub and provides its proxy to the client process, establishing a local binder channel between them. After that, C-M+ and S-M+ maintain the mapping for the two local binder channels by bridging them with a TCP network connection. With the procedure complete, the client recognizes C-M+ as the server and sends all the parcels related to the functionality of interest directly to C-M+. These are then delivered to the server through the cross-device binder connection.

6. CROSS-DEVICE RPC SUPPORT

As explained in Section 5, M+ supports transparent cross-device binder connections, allowing a client to invoke a RPC call on a remote server. Yet, there are many issues to address in supporting cross-device RPC successfully. First, Android applications often pass reference arguments for RPC calls (call-by-reference) to improve efficiency within a single device. Second, client and server applications generally access information about their counterpart in order to perform interaction properly, assuming the information is available on the same device. Third, Android is designed to manage the execution of a client and a server while preserving their interaction semantics mainly for a single device. Each of the above issues makes it impossible for unmodified applications to perform RPC interaction correctly across different devices, if proper support is not provided. In this section, we explain how M+ addresses each individual issue.

6.1 RPC Argument Handling

Android, designed for a single device, allows client and server to pass RPC arguments under call-by-reference semantics to achieve efficiency. For instance, when client or server wants to make an extra binder connection, then they send a proxy as an argument. In addition, when a client wants to share some files (such as photos or PDF documents) with other applications, the client passes either uniform resource identifiers (URIs) or file descriptors. File descriptors for shared memory and Unix domain socket (UDS) also can be used as RPC arguments to share a large amount of data (e.g., camera frames) and to transfer data streams (e.g., sensor readings), respectively.

To support cross-device RPC transparently, M+ needs to identify all reference arguments used in each RPC call and make the value of each reference available on the server device, without incurring any modifications to both client and server applications. In addition, M+ should address such issues in a functionality-oblivious manner, because a great deal of effort is required to examine each individual functionality to determine which reference arguments are involved.

We categorize the reference arguments into four types depending on which IPC channels they are associated with: binder proxy, URI, UDS, and shared memory. For each type, we will explain how M+ detects reference arguments within parcels and deals with them for cross-device RPC. In addition, we will also explain how to resolve synchronization issues for shared memory.

Binder proxy: M+ is able to detect binder proxy objects easily, if included in parcels, since the parcels include metadata in reference to the proxy objects. Upon detecting a proxy object, M+ creates a new binder IPC connection as described in Section 5.

URI: Unlike the proxy object, parcels do not have any information about URI. So, we re-design the parcel structure so that it contains metadata in reference to the URI. We rewrote the `writeToParcel()` function of Android `Uri` class, which is one of the most commonly used URI transmission methods, so that the URI can be easily found in the parcel. If a URI is found, S-M+ stores a copy of the corresponding file on the internal storage of the server device, preventing other processes from accessing it without proper permissions. S-M+ then creates a new URI for the location and replaces the original URI with the new URI before passing the parcel to the server.

UDS and shared memory: UDS and shared memory are stored in parcels in the form of file descriptor, and the parcels contain metadata about file descriptors. Thus, M+ can detect file descriptors easily within parcels. Then, C-M+ refers to the `proc` file system to identify the type of file descriptor exactly. If the file descriptor is found to be UDS, S-M+ creates a new UDS; then passes it to the server. When this comes to shared memory in Android, it is further divided into anonymous shared memory (ASHMEM) and ION memory. S-M+ allocates corresponding shared memory and sends the file descriptor to the server. When allocating memory, it should use the same on both devices. In the case of ASHMEM, C-M+ finds it easily with `ashmem_get_size_region()`, which is provided by the ASHMEM device driver. However, in the case of ION, its device driver does not expose an API function that returns the size of an allocated memory. So, instead of using such a function, M+ obtains it by parsing parameters of the RPC function that is used to allocate an ION memory (i.e., `dequeueBuffer()` of `IGraphicBufferProducer`). It will be easier to solve the issue if the ION device driver can provide proper API functions like ASHMEM.

Unlike other IPC connections, shared memory requires synchronization, because either client or server can make modifications to its own copy. To be synchronized correctly, M+ must know when the memory begins to be modified and when it ends. Android uses some RPC functions related to lock protocols for ION memory (e.g., `requestBuffer()`, `queueBuffer()` of `IGraphicBufferProducer`), and we resolve synchronization issues by using them. Typically, when `requestBuffer()` is called to acquire a lock before modifying the memory, M+ prepares the ION memory where data will be written. Similarly, when `queueBuffer()` is invoked to release the lock after finishing the modification, M+ copies the modified memory back to the remote device. We note that synchronization issues are not considered for ASHMEM, because it tends to be utilized as a one-shot memory to transfer a large amount of data to another process unlike ION. For example, a content provider uses ASHMEM to deliver results for database queries sent by other process.[3] After that, the allocated ASHMEM is not used again by the content providers, and only the receiving process accesses and utilizes the shared memory. This means that M+ does not have to care about its synchronization. We will discuss more about ASHMEM in Section 10.

6.2 Remote App Registration

Client and server processes typically require some information (so-called *app metadata*) about their counterpart application when they begin to interact with one another. For example, upon receiving a RPC request from a client, a server process often requires information about the client application to ensure that the client is eligible for the requested functionality by checking its permissions and/or that the client is authentic by checking its application signature.

On Android, each application comes with a configuration file, called a *manifest*, that describes its metadata, such as its components, package name, permissions, and application signature. Upon the installation of an application, the package manager, which is one of the system-wide processes in Android, stores and maintains its metadata. Then, applications and system services access the metadata of their counterpart applications via the package manager.

Problems arise when a server process asks the package manager to provide metadata of a client application running on a different device. A simple solution is to intercept such a request, forward it to the client device, and bring the metadata over the network. However, this solution will be inefficient when such requests are made several times.

For this reason, M+ performs what we call *(remote) app registration* to make app metadata available between different devices. During app registration, the package manager brings the metadata of an application from a different device, where the application was installed. The package manager is then able to store and manage the metadata of the remote application, providing it to local applications on the same device. We note that an application can be installed once on a home device and may be registered remotely to any different device.

Client and server applications are remotely registered at different times. Upon device discovery and secure channel setup, two devices exchange a list of their own server applications and server applications are registered to the other device. On the other hand, a client application is registered to a different server device when it makes the first RPC request to a server device. App registration requires user agreement to proceed, the same as app installations do. This is explained further in Section 7.

[3]As another example, ASHMEM is also used to manage Dalvik machines, but it is beyond the scope of this paper.

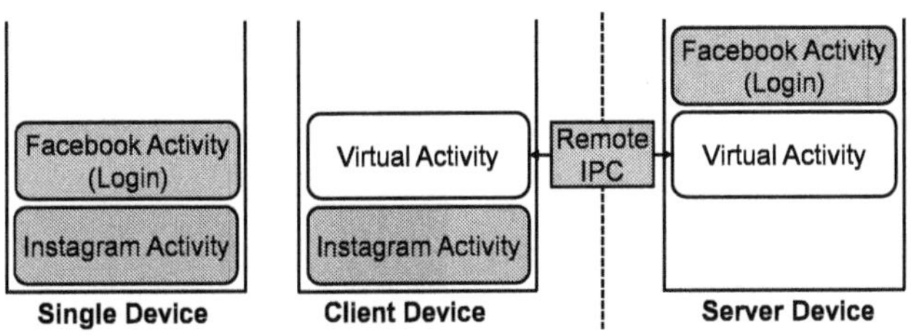

(a) Single-device (b) Multi-device

Figure 4: Android back stack example: Instagram launches Facebook login activity.

6.3 Cross-device Execution Management

In many cases, client applications launch server activities when executing server functionalities. Here, a new execution context is generated, and it should be managed properly according to the execution semantics.

One of the most important kinds of context information is the caller-callee relationship. This information is particularly useful for many reasons. The callee typically wants to identify and verify who is making a request in order to ensure it is legitimate and to pass the RPC results to the caller correctly. In order to maintain such a caller-callee relationship, the activity manager in Android uses a stack (the back stack) to arrange a sequence of activities in the order in which each activity is launched. Figure 4(a) shows an example, where an activity of Instagram launches the Login activity of Facebook on the same device. In addition to the caller-callee relationship, the stack is also useful for indicating which activities are currently active or paused; the activity at the top of the stack is active, and all the others below it are paused.

Execution semantics can broadly fall into two categories: sequential and concurrent executions. While the former indicates a situation where caller and callee activities should be executed one by one synchronously to guarantee correct behavior, the latter allows a situation where caller and callee can execute concurrently. It is important to preserve such execution semantics when supporting cross-device RPC execution.

In the case of sequential execution, when a new activity is launched on the same device, it belongs to the same back stack, as shown in Figure 4(a). When it comes to multiple devices, however, caller and callee activities are placed in separate stacks across different devices. For example, the Instagram activity remains in the stack on a client device, and the Facebook Login activity is placed onto a new stack on a server device. This causes a couple of problems. First, the two back stacks of the client and server devices are independent, and they do not capture the caller-callee relationship. Second, the Instagram activity remains at the top of the stack, and the activity manager considers it to be active. That is, the Instagram activity will not be paused but will continue to execute even before receiving a login result from the Facebook activity. This may yield incorrect execution behavior. One solution is to re-design the activity managers in a way that they collaborate each other by exchanging execution contexts across devices. However, this requires a significant amount of modifications to existing activity managers, which is not good for ease of deployment.

For these reasons, M+ employs the concept of *virtual activity* to address the above problems, while incurring little change to activity managers. A virtual activity is an artificial activity to maintain the caller-callee relationship under the sequential execution semantics across different devices. As shown in Figure 4(b), virtual activities are added to each back stack of the client and server devices. Here, virtual activities play two major roles. First, a virtual activity is pushed to the top of the Instagram activity to keep the Instagram activity in the paused state. This allows the Instagram activity to wait to receive a login result from the Facebook activity. Second, it builds a chain of caller-callee relations across the two devices. In this chain, the virtual activity on the server side has identifier information about the client activity (Instagram). Thus, the Facebook activity can identify what has been launched. In addition, through this chain, the Facebook activity can send login results to the Instagram activity. That is, the Facebook activity sends a return value to a virtual activity on the server side, which forwards the value to S-M+ such that it is finally forwarded to the client device.

On the other hand, in the concurrent execution case, users can execute caller and callee activities independently. The activity manager puts the callee activity into a new separate back stack, which its focus is set to. This causes the callee activity to be active, while all activities in the other stacks remain paused. The user can switch the focus to the caller activity manually by pushing the menu button. This way, the user can alternate the execution between caller and callee activities on a single device. However, in multi-device environments, M+ is able to run caller and callee activities truly concurrently across different devices. As an example, consider a user reading an email on a smartphone. The user can launch the activity of a PDF Viewer on a tablet to open a PDF file attached to the email. She can then continue scrolling through the email for further reading and/or start writing an email reply on the smartphone while reading through the PDF file on the tablet at the same time. In this way, M+ offers a new user experience through an unprecedented way of using unmodified applications over multiple devices.

7. ENHANCING CROSS-DEVICE SECURITY

In this section, we discuss a fundamental difference between M+ vs. Android from the permission system point of view and describe how to extend it to close the difference. In addition, because M+ uses the network as the medium for data transmission, we describe what kind of new threats are introduced and how M+ mitigates the vulnerability derived from the network.

7.1 Cross-device Permission Check

Android uses a permission-based security mechanism to restrict the types of operations (or functionalities) that each application is allowed to perform, and so do many other popular mobile operating systems, including iOS and Windows Phone. Because each Android application operates in a process sandbox, applications must acquire the permissions for additional capabilities needed to share resources and data beyond the sandbox boundary. Because the Android permission system is designed for a single device environment, M+ extends it to a multi-device environment.

In Android, a client process is normally trusted when accessing the resource provided by another process. This is because the same stakeholder is responsible for the client process imposing a risk of misusing or abusing the resource, and is exposed to the risk. In M+, however, the client process is no longer be fully trusted when accessing resources across devices. The user of a server device can be vulnerable to the risk while little information is available about the client process.

During app registration, M+ determines whether or not to allow the client's permission request at the discretion of server device users. When a remote client appears to utilize server functionality for the first time, M+ prompts the server device user for consent. M+ informs the user of the remote server process, including what kind of application it is and which device it comes from; then asks the user to grant the permissions that the client application requires. For backward compatibility, M+ considers the client application to require the same set of permissions as the one it required when installed on its local device; such permissions are declared in a configuration file, called a manifest file.

Once a client application is registered to a server device, M+ allows server processes to carry out permission checks for the client application as if it were a local application installed on the server device. In the Android permission system, upon receiving a request from a client application for a particular functionality, a server process may ask the package manager to get further information about the client application. For example, Android system services (e.g., camera service) will check the package manager the relevant permissions of the client applications before allowing them to use the functionalities. Server applications (e.g., Facebook for Login) may also ask the package manager to get the relevant information about client applications, such as application signatures. In M+, both existing Android applications and system services can ask the package manager the relevant permissions or information about remote client applications in the same way as the above, while no modification is required to both client and local processes.

One of the key differences between Android and M+ is that M+ allows applications to register to remote server devices. This makes it possible for a single server process to interact with multiple instances of the same application, while each instance is either installed or registered to the server device. Because each instance can be individually granted or not granted during its installation or registration, it is important to distinguish each instance properly to do the permission check correctly. Because M+ assigns a unique UID to each individual application instance at its installation or registration, server processes can successfully identify individual application instances by calling `getCallingUID()`, which returns the UID of the caller process. Because the binder driver was in charge of returning the UID, we slightly modified Android `Parcel` class and `getCallingUID()` to deliver the remote client's UID instead of M+'s UID.

It is worthwhile to mention that some existing Android applications recognize applications by their package names. This works successfully in the Android single-device environment, because two or more instances of the same application cannot be installed on the same device. However, package names are no longer distinct identifiers in the M+ multi-device environment. Thus, some applications may have to change their logic to use UID for identifying application instances in the M+ multi-device environment. To this end, M+ provides an additional API, `getCallingActivityUID()`, that returns the UID of a client (caller) activity.

7.2 Network Security

Because M+ uses the network as the medium for communication and data transmission, the network can be a source of vulnerability. Therefore, various network-based attacks have presented as challenges. Packet sniffing attacks capture the wireless traffic and export sensitive data (i.e., phone number, ID and password). Man-in-the-middle attacks (MitM) [17] can eavesdrop or possibly change the communication between a client and server believed to be communicating with each other. Also, adversary can operate the server device maliciously by a packet replay attack [16] that repeatedly transmit valid data. M+ has to be safe against attacks such as these.

M+ leverages the popular Secure Sockets Layer (SSL) protocol [11] to mitigate the vulnerability derived from the network. It is a challenge to establish an SSL channel without requiring public key infrastructures (PKI) and public key servers. Therefore, we use a pre-shared password for device authentication and secure public key exchange. Although we can simply transmit data encrypted by the shared password, SSL provides advanced security features such as Perfect Forward Secrecy [5, 30]. With the pre-shared password, M+ provides security channels similar to WiFi Protected Access with advanced encryption standard (AES) encryption [41].

To establish an SSL channel, a client device needs to know the network address of its server device. Here, we assume that the client has already discovered the server and knows its address. As described in Section 10, this assumption makes sense, because device discovery can be easily done with existing technologies.

8. EVALUATION

We implemented an M+ prototype in Android and demonstrated its complete operation of functionality sharing for unmodified applications across multiple devices. M+ seamlessly enables Android applications to share a wide range of functionalities. For compatibility, the prototype was tested to see whether it works between different versions of Android.

We measured the performance and power consumption of M+. The M+ implementation used for our measurements was based on Google Nexus 6 with the Android open source project (AOSP) version 5.0.1, unless otherwise stated. During the measurements, we enabled all cores to run at the maximum CPU frequency (2.65 GHz), and all devices were connected to the same Wi-Fi access point. This connection had a throughput of 24.9 Mbps and a round-trip time (RTT) with the median, average, and standard deviation of (61.55, 62.80, and 37.69) ms, respectively.

8.1 Functionality Coverage

We first explore how broad a range of functionalities M+ can support unmodified applications. We installed and ran twenty-seven different applications from the listing of top free Android applications from Google Play, including Facebook, the top social media application.

Type		Client ↔ Server	Functionality	Coverage	Max parcel size (bytes)
Activity		Instagram ↔ Facebook	Login	○	2,180
		Candy crush ↔ Facebook	Login	○	2,196
		Line Ranger ↔ Line	Login	△	604
		Gmail ↔ Adobe Acrobat Reader	PDF file viewing	○	680
		SMS ↔ Browser	Web page browsing	○	588
		Browser ↔ Android System UI	Web page sharing	○	190,372
		Gallery ↔ Facebook	Photo sharing	○	1,160
Service	Application service	Real racing 3 ↔ Google play store	Payment	○	39,316
		Candy crush ↔ Google play store	Payment	○	10,352
	I/O system service	Real racing 3 ↔ Sensor service	Game control	○	5,228
		Ladybug ↔ Sensor service	Game control	○	5,228
		Camera2Basic ↔ Camera service	Camera preview	○	15,512
		Body messager ↔ Vibrator service	Vibration	○	204
	Non-I/O system service	Chrome ↔ Clipboard service	Copy & Paste	○	1,540
		SMS ↔ Notification service	Message notification	○	1,500
		Clock ↔ Notification service	Alarm notification	○	4,324
Content Provider		Google drive ↔ Downloads	File download	○	1,956
		Dropbox ↔ Downloads	File download	△	2,528
		True phone ↔ Contacts	Contacts management	○	1,936
		Simple contacts ↔ Contacts	Contacts management	○	1,936
		Google messenger ↔ Telephony	SMS management	○	1,500
		ZeroSMS ↔ Telephony	SMS management	○	1,500

Table 1: Use case list for the functionality coverage test. Coverage is marked with ○ if M+ supports the use case correctly or △ if it does so with user's proper choice.

Table 1 shows a list of use cases, where client applications utilize various functionalities from server applications or Android services on different devices. The fourth column (labeled "Coverage") shows whether M+ supports each use case. As shown in the table, M+ successfully supports cross-device functionality sharing for a wide range of functionalities, except the two use cases marked with triangles (△).

Those two use cases employ multiple independent binder connections while sharing a single functionality. Line, one of Japan's popular messengers, returns an access token as a login result through a separate binder connection that it initiates with a new seed parcel. Dropbox also uses two binder connections initiated by two seed parcels, one for downloading a file and the other for naming the file. Those two binder connections should be made between the same client and server pair for correct operation. When a new binder connection is requested with a seed parcel, a user is prompted to select the right destination if there are multiple candidates. Confusion may arise when there are multiple instances of the same app across several devices. For example, when Line initiates a new binder connection to pass an access token in response to Line Ranger's login request, the user of the Line device may be asked to select the right instance of Line Ranger among multiple across different devices. If the user makes the right choice, M+ can work correctly. However, if the user makes a wrong decision, such a use case would not work properly. We will discuss possible solutions in Section 10.

8.2 Performance and Power Consumption

We quantitatively evaluate performance and power consumption of M+ in supporting cross-device functionality sharing. We generated four types of micro-benchmarks depending on which IPC connections are used: binder, URI, Unix domain socket (UDS), and ION memory. In each micro-benchmark, a client utilizes the functionality of a server through one of the IPC connections. We ran each micro-benchmark within a single device (labeled "LOCAL") and across two devices with M+ (labeled "M+ "). Unless otherwise stated, we repeated each experiment ten times and herein report the average and standard deviation of these measurements. We also report the overhead from using the SSL connection.

8.2.1 Performance

Interception overhead: The time to intercept a parcel for decision making can be considered as *interception overhead*, if the destination of the parcel is a server process on the same device. In order to measure such overhead, we wrote a micro-benchmark program that repeated launch of a simple activity via the `startActivity` method 100 times. Our experiment results show that it takes 17.79 ms on average (standard deviation of 8.99 ms) to run the simple activity on stock Android, and 20.23 ms on average (with a standard deviation of 19.51 ms) with M+. Thus, the interception overhead of M+ is 2.44 ms on average. Though such an overhead is not negligible, its impact on the overall sys-

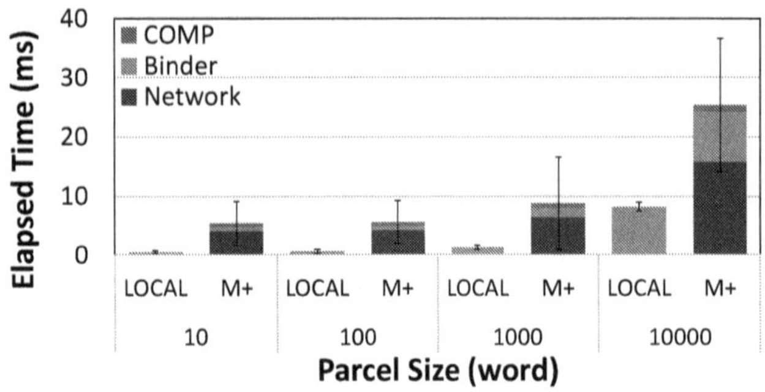

Figure 5: Performance of binder communication. The X axis is size of a parcel in words; each is four bytes in Android.

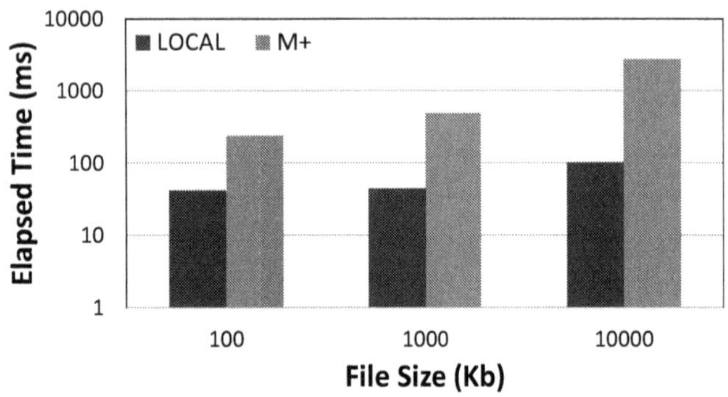

Figure 6: Performance of communication using URI for file. Note that the Y axis is log-scaled.

tem performance is quite limited since M+ intercepts only seed parcels, which occupy a very small portion of the whole parcel communication.

Binder: Figure 5 shows the time between when a client sends a binder parcel to a server and when the client receives a return signal from the server, as a function of the amount of data included in the parcel. It also shows the percentage breakdown of average elapsed times. We broke down the time into three stages: (1) "COMP " involves spending time in C-M+ and S-M+ to intercept and determine its destination, (2) "binder" involves the time spent in the binder communication between Java applications and the binder driver, including the time to copy data to the server's memory space, and (3) "network" involves the time spent on cross-device communication via M+. The figure shows that it takes longer to send a larger amount of data through binder and network, while network delays are the most significant factor. It is also shown in the figure that M+ does not impose much computation overhead. We note Table 1 shows the maximum parcel size of each use case.

File: Figure 6 shows the average time between when a client sends a uniform resource identifier (URI) to share a file and when the client receives a return signal from the server, including the time for the server to read the file. As the file size increases, the performance gap between LOCAL and M+ increases due to file transfer costs. Given that the performance of file sharing is bound by the network bandwidth, it will continually improve as wireless technologies evolve. Similar performance characteristics are observed for anonymous shared memory (ASHMEM).

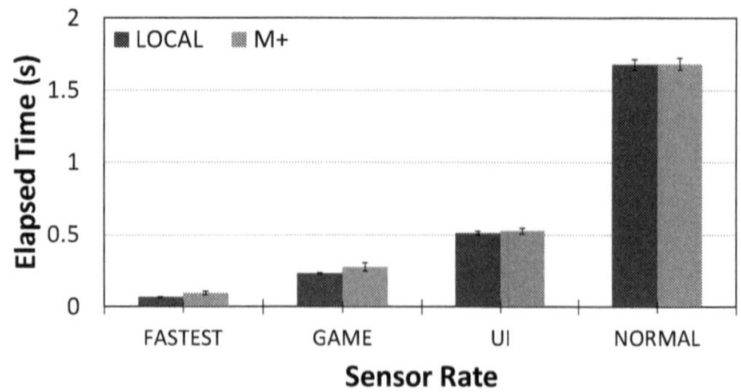

Figure 7: Performance of streaming accelerometer sensor data. X axis shows the registration type declared in Android Sensor Manager. M+ has sufficient throughput (maximum of 90 Hz).

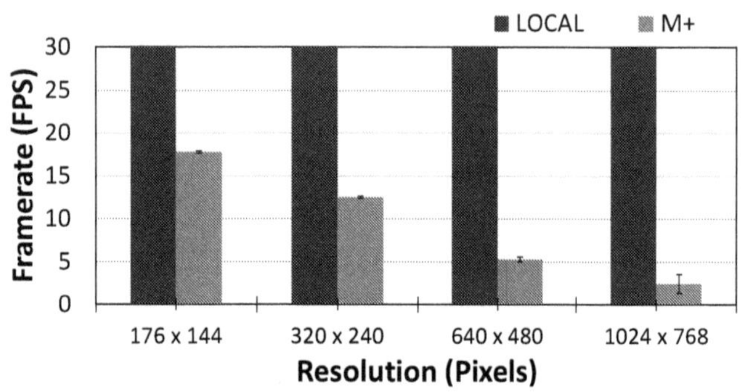

Figure 8: Performance of a real-time streaming camera preview with a 24.9 Mbps wireless LAN connection between the client and server. As the wireless network speeds up, performance will improve without requiring changes to M+.

UDS: To evaluate the performance of M+ when using UDS, we selected a sensor service that uses UDS internally to transfer sensor data streaming. We measured the average time it took for a client to obtain the first 10 sensor readings since sensor callback is registered. We registered accelerometer sensor callbacks at four different sensor rates, which are pre-defined in Android Sensor Manager: FASTEST, GAME, UI, and NORMAL. Each of them has a target sensor delay of (0, 20, 60, and 200) ms, respectively. Figure 7 shows the elapsed time according to the sensor rate. M+ was shown to have comparable performance with the single-device case, except when the sensor rate is FASTEST.

ION memory: We evaluated the performance of M+ when using ION memory. We wrote a camera microbenchmark that uses a real-time streaming camera preview. In each experiment, we measured the average frame rate (frames per second) that could be achieved during the first 1000 frames, excluding the first 50 frames to avoid the effect of camera initialization. Figure 8 shows M+ can achieve acceptable performance (i.e., > 13 FPS) at low resolutions (i.e., 176×144 and 320×240). At higher resolutions, however, M+ exhibited performance degradation. To maintain 15 FPS for the NTSC (i.e., 720×480) or higher resolution, it requires at least 89 Mbps of network throughput to transmit more than 760 KB of data per frame. We expect that M+ will support 15 FPS for HD resolutions (i.e., 1280×720 and 1920×1080) by taking advantage of future wireless net-

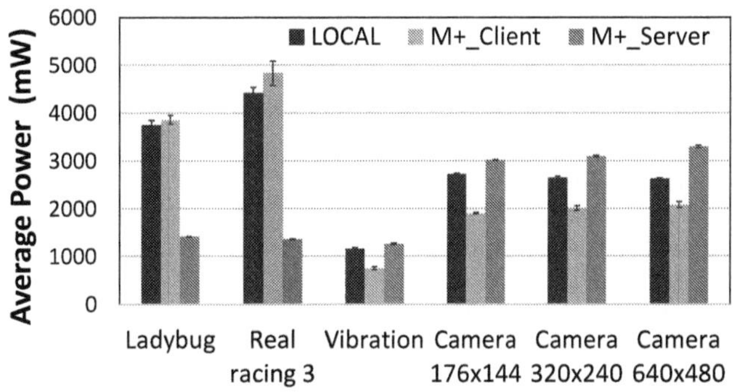

Figure 9: Average system power consumption of when sensor, vibrator, and camera (for preview streaming) are used remotely with M+ and LOCAL. Note that the numbers below **Camera** represent resolution.

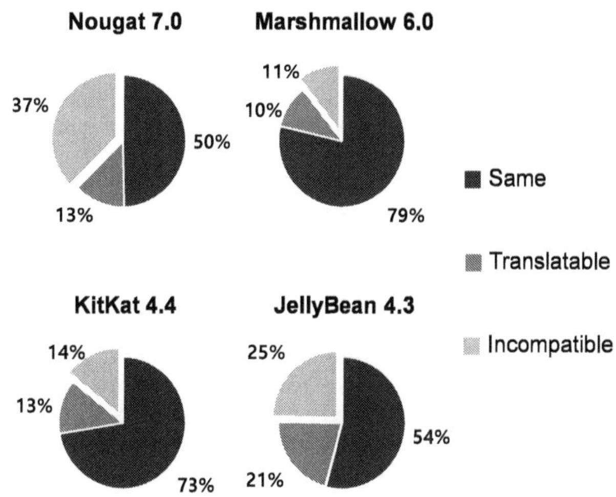

Figure 10: Compatibility study between Android Lollipop 5.0.1 and other latest Android versions. We compared the RPC APIs used by the functionalities shown in Table 1.

working standards. For example, 802.11ad can reach around 7 Gbps of throughput. In addition, M+ can be further extended to maintain acceptable FPS on high resolutions by incorporating video encoding/compression techniques.

8.2.2 *Power Consumption*

We evaluated the power consumption of M+ compared to a single-device case. For proper evaluation, we selected only the I/O system services shown in Table 1. This is because applications typically utilize such I/O system services continuously consuming a significant amount of energy while the other use cases utilize functionalities only once in a while, and incurring negligible additional power consumption. We ran each experiment for one minute and measured the average power consumption of a mobile device using the Monsoon Power Monitor [8][4]. During each experiment, we turned on the display of all the devices and set the brightness to 50% which consumed 819 mW on average.

Figure 9 compares the power consumption of different applications on three different devices: a single device with stock Android, a client device with M+, and a server device with M+. It is shown that M+ consumes 1.5× to 2× the power consumption by the local device, depending on which functionality to use. The first two applications, Ladybug and Real racing 3, are 3D game applications that make use of continuous sensor readings. Those clients perform heavy computation (e.g., 3D image rendering) and consume a little more energy with M+, mostly for additional cross-device communication, while incurring much less power consumption on servers. On the other hand, other client applications, such as Vibration and Camera, are shown to impose even slightly more power consumption on servers than on the local device. This is because some computation, such as camera preview encoding, takes place on servers.

8.2.3 *SSL Overheads*

As explained in Section 7.2, M+ is able to establish a secure SSL connection between client and server devices. Here, we evaluate the overheads of using the SSL connection in terms of performance and power consumption. Using the SSL connections incurs overheads in encrypting and decrypting data to transfer. During our experiments, using SSL connections degraded performance by 3.1%, 6.8%, 4.5%, and 51.7%, when using binder, file, sensor, and camera, respectively. On average, the client uses 7.3% more energy and the server consumes 5.9% more energy when using SSL connections, compared to the case of using M+ without SSL.

8.3 Compatibility Study

In this subsection, we discuss the compatibility of M+ with different versions of Android. Because M+ allows client applications to utilize the functionalities of server processes through cross-device RPC, the compatibility of M+ depends solely upon that of RPC application programming interfaces (APIs) between different Android versions. To explore such compatibility, we conducted a comparison of the five latest Android versions for the RPC APIs used by all the functionalities shown in Table 1. Specifically, we investigated 173 RPC functions in 16 RPC interfaces, including **IServiceManager** and **IActivityManager**, to study the compatibility of Android Lollipop 5.0.1 with the four other latest versions.

Figure 10 shows the compatibility of the RPC APIs between different Android versions, reporting 50% to 79% of identical RPC APIs. We used the **diff** tool to examine how many RPC functions have exactly the same APIs between different Android versions. The figure shows that more than 70% of the RPC functions examined have identical function names and arguments between Lollipop and its closest versions (KitKat and Marshmallow), and the numbers drop to 50% when they are two versions away.

Figure 10 also shows that the compatibility increases by 10% to 21% with a trivial effort. We analyzed the RPC functions of non-identical APIs to see whether they can be translated in a trivial way. For example, we can use zero or null for any additional arguments or combine multiple arguments into a single argument without violating the semantics. We translated such RPC arguments and verified

[4]We note that since Nexus 6 and its battery are integrated, it is not trivial to use the Monsoon tool for measurement. We thus measured the power as follows. We first disconnected the battery by breaking the two pins corresponding to (+) and (-) terminals on the circuit. We then soldered wires to pads on the circuit that are connected to the (+) and (-) terminals and connected the wires to the Monsoon.

that they worked correctly between different Android versions; and then classified them as *translatable*. The figure shows that Lollipop is easily compatible with other Android versions with an average of 78.25% of the RPC APIs, when including translatable ones. Some RPC APIs are inherently incompatible, because some functionalities are available only on newer or older Android versions or do not support backward compatibility with older versions.

In addition, we ran each individual use case shown in Table 1 while client and server devices ran on Lollipop and Nougat, respectively. All use cases but three successfully worked between different Android versions. The three did not work when they utilized camera and notification services through the RPC interfaces of `ICameraServer`, `ICameraDeviceUser`, and `INotificationManager`. Nougat came with a number of new camera RPC interfaces and significant changes to notification RPC interfaces with new user interface.

It is worth noting that the compatibility of application functionality does not depend on the Android version. Applications are compatible without problems if they are all up-to-date versions via the Google Store. Note that even a client cannot use a server's functionality on a single device if the RPC interface between client and server is different.

9. RELATED WORK

Multi-device mobile platform: Support of mobile applications in multi-device environments has been receiving increasing attention. One theme in the literature is seamless migration of execution of a single app between devices. There have been several studies such as MAUI [19], CloneCloud [18], Odessa [35], COMET [20], ColPhone [38] and Lee et al. [28]. The focus of these papers is on automatic execution partitioning and migration of applications onto nearby smartphones and cloud servers to save energy and improve performance. Recently, Flux [42] leverages app migration to switch from a mobile device to another. Sapphire [43] provide a framework that supports distributed execution of the same app on different mobile devices. However, all the aforementioned studies do not consider supporting an app running on one device to utilize functionalities on another device.

Another recent theme is cross-device functionality sharing. There are many pieces of work that support remote I/O resource access for a specific class of I/O, such as remote file systems [14, 27, 37], network USB [22, 23, 13, 21], sensors [24, 40], and remote printers [4]. Rio [39] is the closest work to ours, and allows sharing of various I/O resources across devices by virtualization at device file layer with distributed shared memory. Compared to Rio, M+ provides a platform-layer solution for cross-device functionality sharing, with the following differences: (i) it supports a wider range of functionalities for cross-device sharing, including application functionality and Non-I/O system services, (ii) it extends single device execution management logic to cross-device, and (iii) it provides a cross-device permission check.

Android RPC: AndroidRMI [25] considers extending Android binder IPC to support remote method invocation. Yet, its solution requires modifying existing applications by extending their Android interface definition language (AIDL) interface description. Compared to AndroidRMI, M+ handles reference types for RPC arguments and extends execution management logic so that unmodified applications can still use RPC interactions across different devices. Thus, M+ supports a much wider range of applications. Nakao et al. [33] proposes an extension to the intent class for remote service invocation at the application layer in Android, while supporting screen sharing only by using VNC remote screen sharing middleware [3].

App-level I/O resource sharing: Many apps are available for sharing specific I/O resources, including IP Webcam [26] for camera, WiFi Speaker [32] for audio, and MightyText [6] for SMS and MMS messages. Several apps support screen sharing, such as Miracast [7], by allowing streaming a screen from one device to another. VNC [15] and Microsoft Remote Desktop Services [31] employ thin client solutions instead of resource sharing. The above approaches develop cross-device sharing atop low-level APIs, coming with high development cost. On the other hand, M+ provides a platform that reduces the burden of developing applications for I/O resource sharing across multiple devices. This extends app capabilities to provide novel user experience.

10. DISCUSSION

Device discovery: In this paper, devices are assumed to know the addresses of others. We can leverage existing techniques to relax this assumption. The DNS-SD [2] protocol uses multicast DNS [9, 10] that performs DNS queries over IP multicast on a local area network with no conventional DNS server installed. When there is no common local WiFi network around, WiFi Direct [12] can be used to facilitate device discovery and data transmission. Using these techniques, M+ can easily find out the address of the device to which it wants to connect.

Mitigating compromised M+: In this work, we assume that M+ is not compromised. If so, privacy-sensitive data can be leaked to unauthorized parties. One may check the integrity of M+ through remote attestation [34, 36] to avoid interaction with compromised devices. This will be a topic of future work.

Supporting ASHMEM reuse: We could not find any case such that ASHMEM is reused while experimenting for twenty-seven different applications (in Section 8.1). If there are some applications that reuse ASHMEM under their custom synchronization protocols, the current prototype of M+ cannot handle them. However, if M+ uses a distributed shared memory (DSM) technique as Rio [39] does, it is possible to support ASHMEM reuse in the future.

Non-standard way of cross-device interaction: The design of M+ cannot support apps across devices if they interact with each other through private channels rather than using the standard binder IPC. For example, apps may communicate over a shared file (such as a common data file in *tmp* directory). However, in our experience, such communication is not popular because it requires tight coupling between the apps which are typically developed independently.

Multiple seed parcels: As discussed in Section 8.1, applications can share a single functionality with multiple binder connections each of which is initiated by an individual seed parcel. In this paper, M+ assumes that users, when prompted, will determine the right destination in the presence of multiple instances of the same application across several devices. There are two possible solutions. M+ will be able to address such a case correctly without relying on users, if (i) application developers provide information about the dependency between seed parcels, or (ii) applications distinguish different app instances individually by device IDs and package names.

Applying M+ to other mobile platforms: Although M+ is specialized for Android, the general design of M+ is applicable to other mobile platforms. M+ was designed under the key assumption that applications utilize the functionalities of other processes through RPC over well-defined IPC mechanisms. This assumption is a common mobile platform design paradigm (e.g., XPC and Mach messages in iOS [29]). Supporting transparent cross-device functionality sharing over such mobile platforms will face the following three challenges; it must i) extend execution management logic, ii) handle multiple instances of the same application, iii) extend the single-device IPC mechanism to cross-device. For the first challenge, the design of M+ will be typically applicable in managing execution context and semantics across multiple devices. For the second, the concept of remote app registration will be helpful to manage multiple app instances. For the third, M+ employs a functionality-agnostic approach leveraging the following three binder characteristics. Binding is made through a proxy and a stub, new binder connections are generated through seed parcels, and there are some standard reference types for RPC arguments. If such characteristics are not provided, engineering effort can be made to address the challenge in a functionality-aware manner.

11. CONCLUSION

We presented M+, an extension of Android that supports a range of cross-device functionality sharing. With M+, unmodified applications can utilize application and system functionalities across devices, when they use RPC based on the binder IPC mechanism. M+ also provides secure connection and performs cross-device permission check for both local and remote applications in the same way. In addition, M+ distinguishes multiple instances of applications, which has not been considered in existing mobile platforms. Our experiment with the M+ prototype demonstrated that it achieves performance close to local unless data transfer is large. We expect the cross-device sharing (M+) platform to accelerate development of creative and useful applications to provide novel user experience.

Acknowledgements

This work was supported in part by BSRP (NRF-2015R1D1A1A01058713), IITP (B0101-15-0557), and NRF(2015M3A9A7067220) funded by the Korea Government (MEST/MSIP/MOTIE). We also thank our anonymous reviewers for their insightful and constructive comments that helped us improve this paper.

12. REFERENCES

[1] A number of connected devices in 2016. https://www.globalwebindex.net/blog/digital-consumers-own-3.64-connected-devices.

[2] DNS-Based Service Discovery. https://tools.ietf.org/html/rfc6763.

[3] Droid VNC Server. https://github.com/oNaiPs/droidVncServer.

[4] Epson Remote Print. http://goo.gl/f7EdUh.

[5] Forward Secrecy. https://en.wikipedia.org/wiki/Forward_secrecy.

[6] MightyText: SMS Text Messaging. https://goo.gl/oLXH0T.

[7] Miracast. http://www.wi-fi.org/wi-fi-certified-miracast.

[8] Monsoon power monitor. https://www.msoon.com/LabEquipment/PowerMonitor/.

[9] Multicast DNS. http://www.ietf.org/rfc/rfc6762.txt.

[10] NsdManager. http://developer.android.com/reference/android/net/nsd/NsdManager.html.

[11] The transport layer security (tls) protocol version 1.2. https://tools.ietf.org/html/rfc5246.

[12] Wi-Fi Direct. http://www.wi-fi.org/discover-wi-fi/wi-fi-direct.

[13] Wireless USB. http://www.usb.org/developers/wusb/.

[14] Network file system (nfs) version 4 protocol. *IFTF Network Working Group RFC Draft*, 2003.

[15] T. R. andQ. Stafford-Fraser, K. R. Wood, and A. Hopper. Virtual network computing. *IEEE Internet Computing*, 1998.

[16] D. Bruschi, L. Cavallaro, A. Lanzi, and M. Monga. Replay attack in tcg specification and solution. In *21st Annual Computer Security Applications Conference (ACSAC'05)*, pages 11–pp. IEEE, 2005.

[17] F. Callegati, W. Cerroni, and M. Ramilli. Man-in-the-middle attack to the https protocol. *IEEE Security and Privacy*, 7(1):78–81, 2009.

[18] B. Chun, S. Ihm, P. Maniatis, M. Naik, and A. Patti. CloneCloud: Elastic Execution between Mobile Device and Cloud. In *Proc. ACM EuroSys*, 2011.

[19] E. Cuervo and A. Balasubramanian. MAUI: Making Smartphones Last Longer with Code Offload. In *Proc. ACM MobiSys*, 2010.

[20] M. S. Gordon, D. A. Jamshidi, S. Mahlke, Z. M. Mao, and X. Chen. COMET: Code Offload by Migrating Execution Transparently. In *Proc. USENIX OSDI*, 2012.

[21] A. Hari, M. Jaitly, Y. Chang, and A. Francini. The Swiss Army Smartphone: Cloud-Based Delivery of USB Services. In *Proc. ACM MobiHeld*, 2011.

[22] D. International. AnywhereUSB. http://www.digi.com/products/usb/anywhereusb.jsp.

[23] D. International. USB Over IP. http://usbip.sourceforge.net/.

[24] Y.-W. Jong, P.-C. Hsiu, S.-W. Cheng, and T.-W. Kuo. A semantics-aware design for mounting remote sensors on mobile systems. In *Proceedings of the 53rd Annual Design Automation Conference*, page 140. ACM, 2016.

[25] H. Kang, K. Jeong, K. Lee, S. Park, and Y. Kim. Android RMI: A User-Level Remote Method Invocation Mechanism between Android Devices. *The Journal of Supercomputing*, 2015.

[26] P. Khlebovich. IP Webcam. https://goo.gl/FQgQst.

[27] P. J. Leach and D. Naik. A common internet file system (cifs/1.0) protocol. *IFTF Network Working Group RFC Draft*, 1997.

[28] G. Lee, H. Park, S. Heo, K.-A. Chang, H. Lee, and H. Kim. Architecture-aware automatic computation offload for native applications. In *Proceedings of the*

48th International Symposium on Microarchitecture, pages 521–532. ACM, 2015.

[29] J. Levin. *Mac OS X and iOS Internals: To the Apple's Core*. Wrox, 2012.

[30] A. J. Menezes, P. C. van Oorschot, and S. A. Vanstone. *Handbook of Applied Cryptography*. CRC Press, 2001.

[31] Microsoft. Remote Desktop Services. https://technet.microsoft.com/en-us/windowsserver/ee236407.aspx.

[32] W. Morrison. WiFi Speaker. https://goo.gl/N128Ar.

[33] K. Nakao and Y. Nakamoto. Toward Remote Service Invocation in Android. In *Proc. Ubiquitous Intelligence & Computing/Autonomic & Trusted Computing*, 2012.

[34] M. Nauman, S. Khan, X. Zhang, and J.-P. Seifert. Beyond kernel-level integrity measurement: enabling remote attestation for the android platform. In *Proceedings of International Conference on Trust and Trustworthy Computing*, 2010.

[35] M. Ra, A. Sheth, L. Mummert, P. Pillai, d. Wetherall, and R. Govidan. Odessa: Enabling Interactive Perception Applications on Mobile Devices. In *Proc. ACM MobiSys*, 2011.

[36] H. Raj, S. Saroiu, A. Wolman, R. Aigner, J. Cox, P. England, C. Fenner, K. Kinshumann, J. Loeser, D. Mattoon, et al. fTPM: A firmware-based tpm 2.0 implementation. Microsoft Research Technical Report (MSR-TR-2015-84), 2015.

[37] A. P. Rifkin, M. P. Forbes, R. L. Hamilton, M. Sabrio, S. Shah, and K. Yueh. RFS Architectural Overview. In *Proc. USENIX Conference*, 1986.

[38] A. Salem and T. Nadeem. ColPhone: a smartphone is just a piece of the puzzle. In *Proc. ACM MobiCom*, 2014.

[39] A. A. Sani, K. Boos, M. H. Yun, and L. Zhong. Rio: A System Solution for Sharing I/O between Mobile Systems. In *Proc. ACM MobiSys*, 2014.

[40] C. Shen, R. P. Singh, A. Phanishayee, A. Kansal, and R. Mahajan. Beam: Ending monolithic applications for connected devices. In *2016 USENIX Annual Technical Conference (USENIX ATC 16)*. USENIX Association, 2016.

[41] I. Standards. *IEEE 802.11i-2004: Amendment 6: Medium Access Control (MAC) Security Enhancements*. 2003.

[42] A. Van't Hof, H. Jamjoom, J. Nieh, and D. Williams. Flux: Multi-surface computing in android. In *Proceedings of the Tenth European Conference on Computer Systems*, page 24. ACM, 2015.

[43] I. Zhang, A. Szekeres, D. V. Aken, I. Ackerman, S. D. Gribble, A. Krishnamurthy, and H. M. Levy. Customizable and Extensible Deployment for Mobile/Cloud Applications. In *Proc. USENIX OSDI*, 2014.

Indoor Follow Me Drone

Wenguang Mao, Zaiwei Zhang, Lili Qiu, Jian He, Yuchen Cui, and Sangki Yun[†]
The University of Texas at Austin, [†] Hewlett Packard Labs
{wmao,zaiwei92,lili,jianhe,yuchen93}@cs.utexas.edu, [†] sangki.yun@hpe.com

ABSTRACT

Professional video taping is a costly and time consuming process. With the availability of inexpensive and powerful drones, it is possible to let drones automatically follow a user for video taping. This can not only reduce cost, but also support video taping in situations where otherwise not possible (*e.g.*, during private moments or at inconvenient locations like indoor rock climbing). While there have been many follow-me drones on the market for outdoors, which rely on GPS, enabling indoor follow-me function is more challenging due to the lack of an effective approach to track users in indoor environments.

To this end, we develop a holistic system that lets a mobile phone carried by a user accurately track the drone's relative location and control it to maintain a specified distance and orientation for automatic video taping. We develop a series of techniques to (i) track a drone's location using acoustic signals with sub-centimeter errors even under strong propeller noise from the drone and complicated multipath in indoor environments, and (ii) solve practical challenges in applying model predictive control (MPC) framework to control the drone. The latter consists of developing measurement-based flight models, designing measurement techniques to provide feedback to the controller, and predicting the user's movement. We implement our system on AR Drone 2.0 and Samsung S7. The extensive evaluation shows that our drone can follow a user effectively and maintain a specified following distance and orientation within 2-3 cm and 1-3 degree errors, respectively. The videos taped by the drone during flight are smooth according to the jerk metric.

Keywords

Drone; Tracking; Acoustic signals; FMCW; MUSIC; MPC

1. INTRODUCTION

Motivation: The global drone industry has grown rapidly in the past few years. It reached $8 billion in 2015, and is expected to reach $12 billion by 2021 [14]. It has a long list of applications in agriculture, energy, news media, and film production. In particular, one attractive application of drones is to follow a subject for autonomous video taping. This is motivated by the fact that professional video taping has been a costly and time-consuming process, and sometimes not even possible, such as during private moments or at dangerous locations. The wide availability of powerful and inexpensive drones makes it possible for low-cost autonomous video taping via drones.

Inspired by this vision, lots of commercial products are becoming available on the market. [18] lists top 10 drones with the follow-me mode, which are designed for the outdoor usage. They rely on GPS to follow the subject. Their typical follow-me distances are from tens of meters to a few kilometers [19]. In this case, meter-level variation on the following distance has negligible impact on the video quality. However, in indoor environments, the follow-me distance is only up to a few meters, and meter- or even decimeter-level distance variation can significantly degrade the video quality. Therefore realizing the follow-me mode indoors poses several new challenges: (i) How to accurately and efficiently track the user indoors without GPS signals. This requires accurate distance and orientation estimation. (ii) How to control the drone to accurately maintain a specified following distance and orientation from the user for high-quality video taping.

Tracking: When GPS is not available, computer vision (*CV*) is commonly used for a drone to track a user [21, 30, 35, 43, 8, 22, 36]. However, the accuracy of current CV-based tracking is usually limited because the vibration of a drone during flight may blur the captured images and degrade tracking accuracy. CV-based tracking also degrades in a busy background [8, 22]. As a result, the error of follow-me distance for CV-based approaches is decimeter- to meter-level [35, 43, 8, 36], which is insufficient for our purpose. Moreover, CV-based methods tend to be too expensive for mobile devices [25].

In addition to CV-based methods, there are other tracking techniques, including RF-based localization (*e.g.*, [54, 56, 5, 4]), acoustic-based tracking (*e.g.*, [37, 61, 39, 62, 55]), and coarse movement tracking using depth sensors and infrared cameras (*e.g.*, [1, 2, 33]). We find that acoustic based tracking is attractive because (i) its slow propagation speed makes it possible to achieve high tracking accuracy, (ii) it can be generated and received using widely available speakers and microphones on mobile devices, and (iii) it can be efficiently processed in software without any extra hardware. Therefore, we mount multiple speakers on a drone to send special acoustic signals to a mobile device (*e.g.*, a smartphone or a smart watch) carried by a user. The mobile device processes the received signals to track the drone's position in real-time.

While there have been several accurate acoustic-based motion tracking systems proposed recently, tracking in the context of a drone poses several new challenges. First, there can be many objects in indoor environments, which results in significant multipath

Permission to make digital or hard copies of all or part of this work for personal or classroom use is granted without fee provided that copies are not made or distributed for profit or commercial advantage and that copies bear this notice and the full citation on the first page. Copyrights for components of this work owned by others than ACM must be honored. Abstracting with credit is permitted. To copy otherwise, or republish, to post on servers or to redistribute to lists, requires prior specific permission and/or a fee. Request permissions from permissions@acm.org.

MobiSys '17, June 19–23, 2017, Niagara Falls, NY, USA.

© 2017 ACM. ISBN 978-1-4503-4928-4/17/06. . . $15.00

DOI: http://dx.doi.org/10.1145/3081333.3081362

between the drone and mobile device. Moreover, these paths are all changing since both the drone and user are moving. Therefore the acoustic-based tracking schemes developed in [39] and [55] are not applicable because they assume the tracking target is the only moving object in the environment and all other paths are static. Second, some paths may have similar lengths to that of the direct path, which causes signals traversing these paths to interfere and leads to large distance estimation error. This issue degrades [37], a state-of-the-art acoustic-based tracking. Therefore, we need to develop a motion tracking that has high resolution to separate the paths with similar lengths. Third, when a drone is flying, the propellers on a drone generate large noise over a wide spectrum, which may interfere with the acoustic signals used for tracking. The existing acoustic-based tracking approaches use different frequency from the background noise and do not need to explicitly handle noise. Fourth, tracking must be performed efficiently in real-time on a mobile device.

Motivated by these challenges, we develop a **R**obust **A**coustic-**B**ased **I**ndoor **T**racking system, called Rabbit. It is based on distributed Frequency Modulated Continuous Wave (FMCW) [37] for estimating the distance between the drone and mobile. Furthermore, it applies MUltiple SIgnal Classification (MUSIC) during FMCW detection to significantly improve the capability of resolving multiple paths and enhance distance estimation. This is very different from the traditional use of MUSIC for deriving the Angle-of-Arrival (AoA) using multiple antennas [51, 58, 32], which is not feasible in our setup due to the lack of a microphone array.

Recently, a few work [60, 3, 28] explore applying MUSIC in frequency domain for distance estimation. Compared to these work, our approach enables accurate and efficient acoustic tracking under strong propeller noise and complicated multipath due to four unique designs. First, since MUSIC is a model-based parameter estimation method, which is sensitive to distortion, we develop an effective method to calibrate and compensate for the speaker distortion in acoustic signals. Second, multipath causes multiple frequency peaks during FMCW detection and strong noise from a drone may generate false peaks that do not correspond to any real propagation path. We develop an effective mechanism to select the correct frequency peak corresponding to the direct path for distance estimation. Third, MUSIC needs eigenvalue decomposition, which is expensive, so we develop an effective subsampling to improve the efficiency without compromising accuracy. Finally, we fuse the distance and velocity estimation using Kalman filter to improve the accuracy under propeller noise. While this paper uses Rabbit to track a drone, its robustness and efficiency make it suitable for *other* applications (*e.g.*, gaming, augmented reality/virtual reality, and remote control for IoT devices).

Control design: To address the second challenge, we apply control theory. Despite a variety of control algorithms available, there are several important practical issues. (i) Which control algorithm is appropriate to accurately control low-end drones? (ii) How can we capture the unique dynamics of our drone to maximize effectiveness? (iii) How to measure the deviation from the desired distance and orientation, which will be used as feedback to the controller ? (iv) How to predict a user's movement and leverage this information to enhance the control performance?

Motivated by these questions, we conduct systematic measurement between the control inputs to the drone (*e.g.*, pitch, yaw, and roll) and its actual movement. We find that pitch and yaw have predictable impact on the forward and rotation movement, whereas the relationship between the roll and lateral movement has high variability in the range of interest. We develop measurement-based models for the first two dimensions by applying aerodynamics principles and compensating nonlinear system behaviors, and using model predictive control (MPC) to control movement along these dimensions. We apply Proportional Integral Derivative (PID), which does not require a model, to control the lateral movement, since MPC does not work well when the model accuracy is low. Moreover, our acoustic-based tracking is applied to measure the distances from the mobile to multiple speakers mounted on the drone. Based on the measurements, we use geometry methods to derive the distance and orientation between the user and drone, which serve as feedback to our controller. Finally, based on the Doppler shift of acoustic signals, we develop a simple yet effective way to predict a user's movement so that the controller can respond in advance to optimize the follow-me performance. This paper is a pioneering work that realizes an indoor follow-me drone based on MPC framework. Our procedure and insights are valuable for realizing other important drone functionalities in the future.

System: We develop a follow-me drone for indoor use, called DroneTrack, on top of Rabbit. As shown in Figure 1, Rabbit processes the received signals to estimate the distances between the mobile and speakers on the drone. The observer derives the relative location of the drone with respect to the user, and the predictor estimates the user's movement in the near future. The controller computes the command to move the drone in an appropriate direction. We implement a prototype on AR drone 2.0 and Samsung Galaxy S7, and evaluate it in real indoor environments by either holding the mobile in hand or putting it in a bag. The evaluation shows our system measures the distance between the drone and user with a median error within 1 cm, and maintains the specified following distance and orientation within 2-3 cm and 1-3 degree errors, respectively. Also, our system is robust to various interference including propeller noise, human voices, and music. The processing delay for the tracking part and the whole system is 9 ms and 13 ms, respectively, and the corresponding CPU usage is 13% and 42%, respectively. Moreover, the videos taped by the drone during flight are stable according to the jerk metric [16].

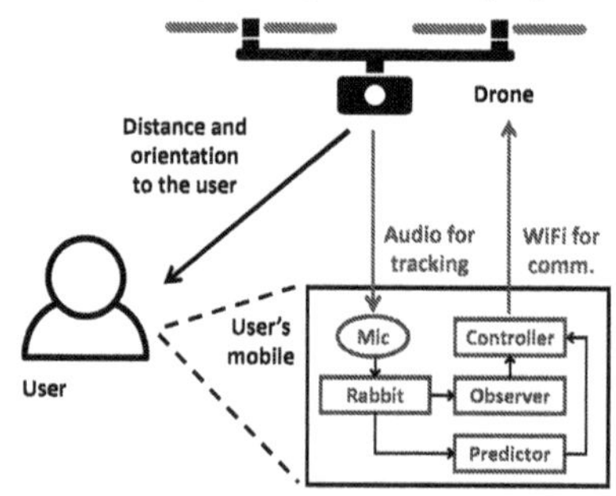

Figure 1: System diagram.

Summary: Our main contributions include (i) developing an accurate, robust, and efficient acoustic-based tracking system on mobile devices (Section 2), (ii) a holistic design of a follow-me drone based on the MPC framework, which includes developing measurement based models, continuously estimating deviation from the specified distance and orientation, and predicting the user's movement (Section 3), and (iii) a prototype system and extensive evaluation that demonstrate the effectiveness of our approaches (Section 4 and Section 5).

2. ROBUST ACOUSTIC TRACKING

In this section, we first review existing approaches for estimating velocity and distance, and identify the limitations for distance estimation. Then we present Rabbit – our approach to enhance robustness of tracking by (i) developing an efficient and robust distance estimation approach based on FMCW and MUSIC, and (ii) fusing distance and velocity measurements using Kalman filter to further improve the accuracy. These techniques are not only useful under environments with significant multipath, but also help tolerate strong noise from a drone.

2.1 Overview of Existing Approaches

Estimating velocity based on Doppler shift: The Doppler shift is a well known phenomenon where the frequency changes with the relative velocity between the sender and receiver as $F^s=(v/c)F$, where F is the original frequency, F^s is the amount of frequency shift, v is the receiver's speed towards the sender, and c is the speed of sound waves. Therefore, we can estimate the receiver's velocity by measuring the amount of frequency shift.

According to [61], we use the following steps to estimate the relative velocity between the drone and mobile : (i) The speaker on the drone continuously transmits sine waves at frequency F. (ii) The mobile applies Fast Fourier Transform (FFT) to extract the spectrum of the received signals. We use 1764 acoustic samples in a period of 40 ms to compute FFT. Then, we find a peak frequency and compare it with F. The difference between the two is the frequency shift F^s. (iii) We compute the velocity based on the estimated frequency shift using $v=(F^s/F)c$.

Estimating distance based on distributed FMCW: FMCW is an effective way to estimate the distance traveled by acoustic signals. Compared to phase-based approaches [55], FMCW is more robust to multipath. Compared to pulse-based methods [62], FMCW achieves higher accuracy using the same amount of bandwidth.

We first review FMCW for a synchronized sender and receiver, and then describe how to support an unsynchronized sender and receiver. In FMCW, a speaker transmits periodic chirp signals, whose frequency linearly increases over time as $f=f_{min}+\frac{Bt}{T}$ in each period, where B is the signal bandwidth and T is the duration of a period. Thus, the transmitted signal in the k-th period is given by $v_t=\cos(2\pi f_{min}t'+\frac{\pi B t'^2}{T})$, where $t'=t-kT$, and the received signal is $v_r=\alpha\cos(2\pi f_{min}(t'-t_d)+\frac{\pi B(t'-t_d)^2}{T})$, where α is the attenuation factor and t_d is the propagation delay. The receiver mixes (*i.e.*, multiplies) the received signal with the transmitted signal. After passing a low-pass filter, the mixed signal is given by

$$v_m(t)=\alpha\cos(2\pi f_{min}t_d+\frac{\pi B(2t't_d-t_d^2)}{T}). \quad (1)$$

Then we can derive the propagation delay t_d by finding the peak frequency in the spectrum of the mixed signal (called *FMCW peak frequency*), and estimate the distance based on $c{\cdot}t_d$. Traditional FMCW works for a co-located sender and receiver with a shared clock. To support a separate and unsynchronized sender and receiver as in our context, we apply a distributed FMCW approach developed in [37]. It first estimates the initial distance and then determines the current distance based on the distance change from the initial position as follow: $R_k=(f_k^p-\frac{f_{min}v_k}{c}-\frac{Bv_k}{c}-f_1^p)\frac{cT}{B}+R_1$, where R_k is the distance between the sender and receiver at the k-th period, f_1^p and f_k^p are FMCW peak frequencies in the first and k-th periods, v_k is the velocity measured by Doppler shift, and R_1 is the initial distance.

2.2 Limitations of Existing FMCW

Traditionally, Fast Fourier Transform (FFT) is used to detect the FMCW peak frequency, which is then used to estimate the distance, as discussed above. However, multipath can result in multiple peaks in the spectrum of mixed signals. In this case, we need to locate the first peak, which corresponds to the direct path. When there exist some paths close to the direct path, the peaks for these paths may merge together due to limited frequency resolution of FFT-based FMCW [31]. This will cause erroneous peak detection.

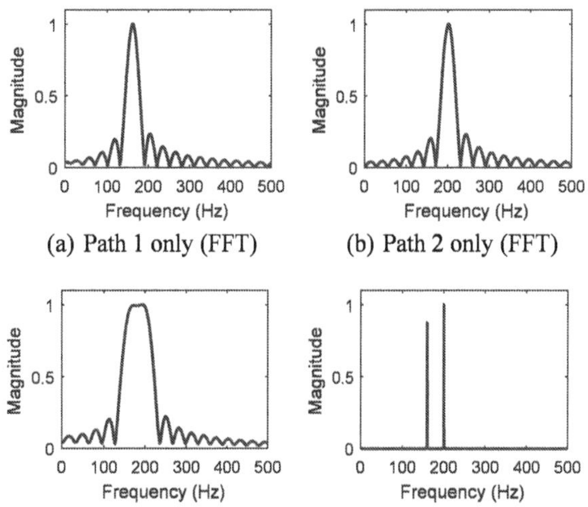

(a) Path 1 only (FFT) (b) Path 2 only (FFT)
(c) Two Paths (FFT) (d) Two Paths (MUSIC)

Figure 2: Peak merging in FFT-based FMCW.

Figure 2 illustrates an example. We generate two paths in simulation, where the first and second paths are 0.8m and 1m long, respectively. The two paths have the same magnitude, and their phase difference is π. There is no noise in the received signals. All other settings are the same as those we used for experiments. When the signals from the two paths naturally add up at the receiver, we can only detect one peak using FFT-based FMCW as shown in Figure 2(c). The peak occurs at 194 Hz, corresponding to a distance estimation of 0.96m, which gives an estimation error of 16 cm. When there is ambient noise (*e.g.*, from drone's propellers), the error of FFT-based FMCW detection can be even larger.

The limited resolution of FMCW comes from the Fourier transform [31]. When applying the transform to time-domain signals with finite duration, the frequency-domain representation of the signals will spread out. This degrades the ability to differentiate signals at different frequencies. MUltiple SIgnal Classification (MUSIC) [48] is a potential solution for this problem. It is a super-resolution parameter estimation algorithm and widely used in radar and localization applications for determining angle-of-arrival (AoA). According to Equation 1, the mixed signals can be expressed as a sum of cosines when multiple paths are present. This model is the same as that used for AoA detection [48]. Thus, we can apply MUSIC to determine the frequency components in the mixed signals to enhance the ability of resolving multipath and improve the distance estimation with FMCW. In our previous example, if we apply MUSIC to derive a pseudo-spectrum of the mixed signals, we can clearly see the two peaks corresponding to the two paths, as shown in Figure 2(d).

2.3 Enhancing Robustness of FMCW

The simulation results in the previous section shows the promise of MUSIC. However, there are several challenges in applying MUSIC to our context. First, in real environments, the signals suffer from various distortions, which make them deviate from the ideal model required by MUSIC (*i.e.*, a sum of cosines). These distortions significantly degrade the resolution of the algorithm. Second, the distortion and strong noise from the drone may cause the peak frequencies derived by MUSIC not to correspond to a real propagation path. We need to carefully filter out these false peaks and select the true peak corresponding to the direct path between the sender and receiver. Third, MUSIC requires eigenvalue decomposition, which is computationally expensive. To run MUSIC on smartphones, we need to significantly improve its efficiency. Below, we first review MUSIC, and then present our approaches to enhance the robustness and efficiency of MUSIC.

Basics of MUSIC: Based on Equation 1, the mixed signals under multipath propagation becomes

$$v_n=\sum_{i=1}^{M_p}\cos(2\pi f_i n t_s+\phi_i), \tag{2}$$

where M_p is the number of paths, n is the sample index, t_s is the sample interval, and t' in Equation 1 is replaced by nt_s. f_i is the frequency for the i-th cosine wave, and it is proportional to the propagation delay of the i-th path. ϕ_i is the phase in Equation 1. This expression follows the model required by MUSIC [48].

To apply MUSIC, we calculate the auto-correlation matrix R for the mixed signals v as $V^H V$, where V is the Toeplitz matrix of v with the size $(N-M+1)\times M$. M is the *order* of the auto-correlation matrix (*i.e.*, R has the size $M\times M$) and N is the number of samples in mixed signals. The i-th column of V is given by $[v_{M+1-i},v_{M+2-i},\ldots,v_{N+1-i}]^T$. Following that, we apply eigenvalue decomposition to R, and sort the eigenvectors in a descending order in terms of the magnitude of corresponding eigenvalues. The space spanned by the first M_p eigenvectors are called *signal space*, and the space spanned by the other eigenvectors are called *noise space*. Let R_N denote the noise space matrix, whose i-th column is the i-th eigenvector for the noise space. It can be shown [48] that

$$R_N^H \cdot s(f_i)=0, \tag{3}$$

for any f_i in Equation 2, where $s(f)$ is a *steering vector* defined as

$$[1,e^{j2\pi f t_s},\ldots,e^{j2\pi f(M-1)t_s}]^T. \tag{4}$$

Based on this property, we can define a pseudo-spectrum of the mixed signals as

$$p(f)=\frac{1}{s(f)^H R_N R_N^H s(f)}. \tag{5}$$

We find f_i by locating peaks in the pseudo-spectrum as shown in Figure 2(d). Alternatively, we can determine f_i using a variant of MUSIC called *Root-MUSIC* [45]. Based on Equation 3, it can be shown that the complex number $e^{j2\pi f_i t_s}$ is the root for *the characteristic polynomial* $\sum_{l=-M+1}^{M-1}(\sum_{j-k=l} r_{kj})z^l$ [45], where r_{kj} is an entry in the matrix $R_N R_N^H$. Root-MUSIC is equivalent to MUSIC except that it directly computes the solution whereas MUSIC searches for f that gives the highest $p(f)$. Therefore, Root-MUSIC is more efficient, and we use Root-MUSIC in our implementation. However, for the ease of visualization, we use MUSIC to generate the pseudo-spectrum plots to help explain our design.

Frequency response compensation: MUSIC is a model-based approach. Its performance is determined by how accurately the signals follow the model. A major source of distortion in the acoustic channel is non-flat frequency response of the speaker. Figure 3 shows the speaker gain decreases with the frequency. The non-flat frequency response is common for inaudible bands (*e.g.*, above 16 KHz), which we use for transmission, because general purpose speakers are not optimized for these bands. The non-flat frequency response distorts the transmitted chirps, which causes the mixed signals to deviate from the model in Equation 2. When applying MUSIC to these signals, the peak becomes less sharp, which degrades the resolution of MUSIC.

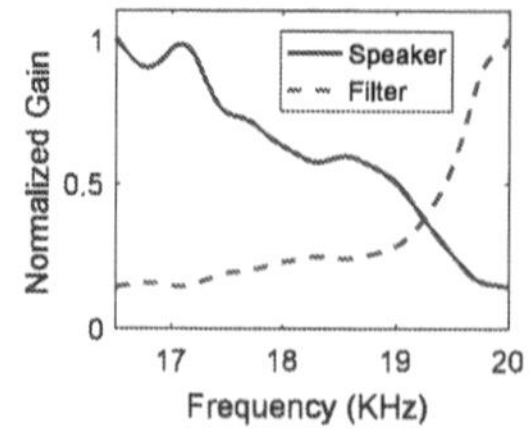

Figure 3: The frequency response of the speaker and filter.

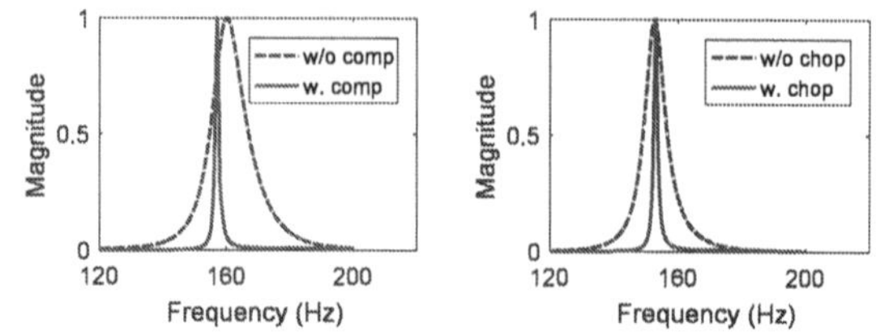

(a) Compensation (b) Chopping

Figure 4: The sharpness of peaks: (a) applying signal chopping and comparing the performance with/without frequency response compensation; (b) applying response compensation and comparing the performance with/without signal chopping.

To minimize the impact of non-flat frequency response of the speaker, we measure the response and compensate its effect. We apply the gated frequency response measurement (*i.e.*, extracting multipath-free samples to derive the response) as [20]. The advantage of this method is that we do not need any special environment (*e.g.*, an anechoic room), and the impact of multipath can be minimized effectively. Once the speaker response is measured, we implement a digital filter whose frequency response is the reciprocal of the measured response, as shown in Figure 3. The transmitted samples need to pass this digital filter before forwarding to the speaker. As a result, the acoustic signals coming out of the speaker have a flat gain at all frequencies in the interested band. To eliminate overhead for users, the speakers sold together with the drone can be calibrated in advance before shipping and compensated chirp signals are saved in a file so that a user can simply play it as usual. From our experience, speakers of the same model experience similar distortion and do not need to calibrated individually. Figure 4(a) shows that the peaks in the pseudo-spectrum derived by MUSIC become much sharper after frequency response compensation. The peak width (the difference between frequencies where the magnitude is half of the maximum) reduces from 14 Hz to 1.2 Hz, which significantly improves the resolution.

Chopping the mixed signals: Another distortion on the mixed signals occurs at their boundary (*i.e.*, the first and last few samples) due to the following two reasons. First, the mixed signals are the product of a transmitted chirp and received chirp, but the boundary of a chirp has discontinuity in frequency. As a result, the boundary of the mixed signals suffer from distortion caused by the discontinuity. Second, in FMCW detection, a low pass filter is applied to the mixed signals before performing MUSIC, and the low pass filter distorts the samples at the beginning [26].

Based on these insights, we chop the mixed signals before applying MUSIC to minimize the impact of distortion. In our scheme, the mixed signals for each period contain 1764 samples (corresponding to 40 ms), and we discard the first 140 samples and the last 100 samples. As shown in Figure 4(b), the peak in the pseudo-spectrum becomes much sharper after chopping.

Peak frequency selection: By applying MUSIC, we can determine f_i in Equation 2. Each f_i corresponds to a propagation path

Matrix order	20	30	40	60	90	120
Time (ms)	1.6	2.9	4.5	11	22	39

Table 1: MUSIC Running time.

between the speaker and microphone, and its value is proportional to the path length. Without noise, the minimum among f_i, denoted by $f_{\min}$, corresponds to the direct path. However, this may not be true under strong noise in our context. In fact, we need to determine the signal space and noise space in the MUSIC derivation. When strong noise is present, some eigenvectors in the noise space may have larger eigenvalues than certain eigenvectors for the signal space. Because we sort the eigenvectors based on the magnitude of the corresponding eigenvalues, some eigenvectors in the noise space will be treated as eigenvectors in the signal space. In this case, when applying MUSIC, we may find some peak frequencies do not correspond to any real propagation path. It is possible that such false frequency peaks occur before the peak corresponding to the direct path. To address the issue, we leverage the following two properties to filter out false peak frequencies:

- Root magnitude: As mentioned, we use Root-MUSIC to find peak frequency f_i. Based on each root of the characteristic polynomial, we can derive a peak frequency. The root corresponding to a true peak frequency has a magnitude close to 1 [45]. Therefore, we remove roots whose magnitude is larger than b_u or smaller than b_l. Based on our experiments, we select b_u as 1.03 and b_l as 0.97.
- Temporal continuity: we track the distance between the speaker and microphone every 40 ms. During this period, the distance will not change too much. As a result, $f_{\min}$ in consecutive periods should be close to each other. Thus, we only consider peak frequencies falling into $[f_{\min}^p-\delta f, f_{\min}^p+\delta f]$, where $f_{\min}^p$ is the frequency corresponding to the direct path detected in the previous period. Based on experiments, we select δf as 25 Hz. 25 Hz corresponds to 12.46 cm movement in 40 ms (*i.e.*, over 3 m/s), which is a loose bound that can tolerate errors in the previous measurement.

Then, we select the minimum peak frequency among the remaining unfiltered frequencies.

Sub-sampling for mobile implementation: The high computation cost of MUSIC makes it challenging to implement on a mobile. As mentioned above, we need to perform eigenvalue decomposition on the auto correlation matrix R. The computation time rapidly increases with the matrix size. Table 1 shows the time of running Root-MUSIC under different M. The test is performed on Samsung Galaxy S7. The algorithm implementation is based on Android NDK to maximize the performance. We use the *eigen* function provided by OpenCV package [41] to perform eigenvalue decomposition. When M is 120, the running time for Root-MUSIC is almost equal to our tracking period (*i.e.*, 40 ms). In this case, the processing speed cannot catch up with incoming samples, and the delay will accumulate over time.

Simply choosing a small M reduces the computation time, but also degrades the resolution. When M becomes smaller, the difference between the steering vectors for a peak frequency f and its nearby frequency $f+\delta f$ is also smaller according to Equation 4. As a result, the pseudo-spectrum magnitude at f and $f+\delta f$ (*i.e.*, $p(f)$ and $p(f+\delta f)$) becomes similar based on Equation 5. In this case, the peak around f becomes less sharp, which results in degraded resolution.

To reduce the computation cost without compromising the performance, we apply sub-sampling on the mixed signals v by a factor K. The sub-sampling gives us a series of sub-sequences $v_K^i = [v_i, v_{i+K}, \cdots, v_{i+lK}]$, where $i \in [1, K]$ and $l = \lfloor (N-K)/K \rfloor$. Then the auto-correlation matrix R_{sub} is estimated by $R_{\text{sub}} = \frac{1}{K}\sum_i V_i^H V_i$, where V_i is the Toeplitz matrix of v_K^i. Following that we apply the remaining steps of MUSIC to R_{sub}. It can be shown that for any f_i in Equation 2, there is a corresponding peak in the pseudo-spectrum generated based on R_{sub}. Moreover, since sub-sampling is applied, the effective sampling interval becomes Kt_s. Thus, the steering vector in this case is given by $[1, e^{j2\pi f K t_s}, \ldots, e^{j2\pi f (M_s-1) K t_s}]^T$, where M_s is the order of R_{sub}. Therefore, with sub-sampling, we can select a small M_s to reduce computation cost while achieving similar resolution as choosing $M = (M_s - 1)K$ in the case without sub-sampling. Based on our experiments, we set the sub-sampling factor $K = 25$ and the matrix order $M_s = 25$.

Multipath resolution: MUSIC algorithm has infinite resolution when the signals perfectly follow the required model (*i.e.*, a sum of cosines) and no noise is present [63]. In this case, our approach can always separate the direct path from other paths. In practice, there are noise and distortion that make the signals deviate from the ideal model. To determine the resolution of our approach, we place a cardboard near the direct path between the speaker and microphone to create a reflected path whose length is close to the direct one. When the length difference between these two paths is 5 cm, we can still separate them in the pseudo-spectrum generated by MUSIC. Thus, the resolution of our approach is 5 cm.

2.4 Kalman Filter

To filter out noise and further improve the accuracy of the distance estimation, we combine distance and velocity measurements using a Kalman filter as follows. Let x_k denote the actual distance between the speaker and microphone in the k-th period, t denote the period duration, v_k denote the measured Doppler velocity, n_k capture the error in Doppler measurements, y_k denote the measured distance, and w_k denote the distance measurement error. These variables have the following relationship:

$$\begin{aligned} x_k &= x_{k-1} + v_k \cdot t + n_k \\ y_k &= x_k + w_k, \end{aligned}$$

Note that y_k and v_k are given by distance and velocity measurements, respectively. Large noise from the propellers degrades the accuracy of these measurements. The basic idea of Kalman filter is to exploit the redundancy between these two measurements to reduce the impact of noise. According to [17], the optimal distance estimation $\hat{x}_k$ is given by

$$\hat{x}_k = \hat{x}_{k-1} + v_k t + \frac{\hat{p}_{k-1} + q_k}{\hat{p}_{k-1} + q_k + r_k}(y_k - \hat{x}_{k-1} - v_k t),$$

where $\hat{p}_k = \frac{r_k(\hat{p}_{k-1}+q_k)}{\hat{p}_{k-1}+q_k+r_k}$. q_k and r_k are the standard deviation for n_k and w_k, respectively. Based on our experiments, we set q_k and r_k to 0.0005 and 0.01, respectively.

3. CONTROL DESIGN

In this section, we describe the control system for our indoor follow-me drone.

3.1 Primer for Control Approaches

Controller: For many applications, we need to ensure that the system output takes its desired value. To this end, we add a controller to the system as shown in Figure 5. The controller manipulates the system input to drive the output to its desired value. Thus, in a controlled system, the input is called *manipulated variable*, while

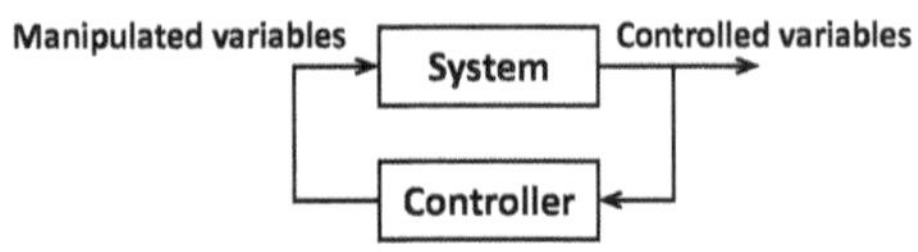

Figure 5: The system with a controller

	Manipulated var.	Controlled var.	Method
1	pitch	drone-to-user dist.	MPC
2	yaw	drone orientation	MPC
3	roll	lateral velocity	PID

Table 2: Controllers in our system.

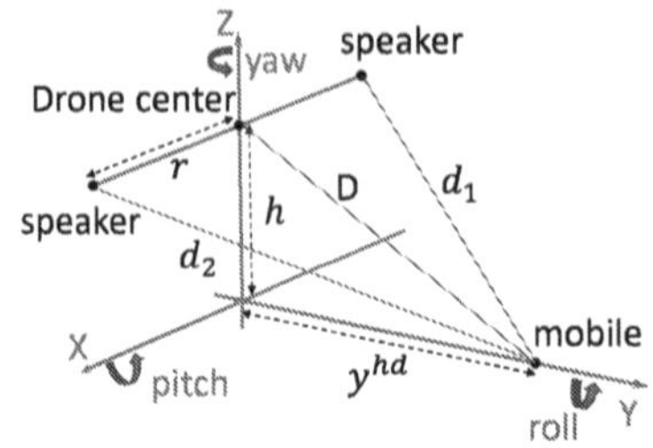

Figure 6: System 3D view. y^{hd} is the drone-to-user distance. d_1 and d_2 are the distances between the speakers and microphone. r is the drone's radius. h is the altitude difference between the drone and mobile.

the output is called *controlled variable*. The relationship between the input and output is called *system model*. In some systems, such a relationship is known. A straightforward way to control these systems is to derive the input for the desired output based on the system model. However, this approach is sensitive to disturbance and modeling error. To solve this issue, many controllers exploit *feedback*, *i.e.*, the mechanism that adjusts the input based on the current measurement of the output.

Primer for PID Control: Proportional Integral Derivative (PID) controllers have been widely used in industrial control systems for its simplicity. It computes the manipulated variable based on the error of the controlled variable as $u(t)=K_p e(t)+K_i\int_0^t e(\tau)d\tau+K_d\frac{de(t)}{dt}$, where $u(t)$ is the manipulated variable and $e(t)$ is the error of the controlled variable, which is computed as the difference between its measured value and desired value. K_p, K_i and K_d are non-negative coefficients of the proportional, integral, and derivative terms, respectively. The main advantage of PID is that it does not require knowledge of the system and can control the output simply based on the error $e(t)$. However, the lack of knowledge of the system does not come for free, and may affect the stability and convergence rate of the control system.

Primer on MPC: Model Predictive control (MPC) is a model-based control framework that works as follows [50]:

1. **Build the system model:** Determine controlled variables and manipulated variables, and build a system model to capture their relationship.
2. **Predict the future output:** Based on the system model, the future values of the controlled variable can be predicted in terms of the manipulated variable. Let $\mathbf{u}$ denote the values of the manipulated variable, where the i-th element stands for the value in the i-th period of the future. Let $\mathbf{y}_p(\mathbf{u})$ denote the controlled variable in the next N_p periods predicted based on the model, where N_p is called *prediction horizon*.
3. **Correct the prediction with feedback:** $\hat{\mathbf{y}}_p(\mathbf{u})=\mathbf{y}_p(\mathbf{u})+m-y_0$, where $\hat{\mathbf{y}}_p(\mathbf{u})$ is the corrected prediction, m and y_0 are the measured and predicted controlled variable during the current period, respectively. $m-y_0$ captures the prediction error (*e.g.*, coming from modeling error).
4. **Find the optimal input for the next period:** Let $\mathbf{y}_e(\mathbf{u})$ denote the difference between $\hat{\mathbf{y}}_p(\mathbf{u})$ and the desired values of the controlled variable in the next N_p periods. MPC minimizes the objective $|\mathbf{y}_e(\mathbf{u})|^2+w_u|\Delta\mathbf{u}|^2$, where w_u is a regularization parameter and $\Delta\mathbf{u}$ is the variation of the manipulated variable. The regularization term in the objective is to avoid significant variation in the manipulated variable, which can cause instability. Let $\mathbf{u}^*$ denote the optimal solution for the objective function. In the next period, the manipulated variable is set to the first element of $\mathbf{u}^*$.

The steps 2-4 are repeated every control period. We select MPC due to its following advantages. First, the controller can take action in advance by leveraging prediction, which is greatly helpful to improve convergence rate and avoid fluctuation of controlled variables. This is critical for high quality video taping. Second, MPC has well-understood tuning parameters, such as the prediction horizon and regularization parameter, which allows us to easily tune the controller for the optimal performance.

3.2 Control Design

To make a drone follow the user for high-quality video taping, we need to ensure (i) the drone-to-user distance is maintained at the desired value, (ii) the camera on the drone is facing the user, (iii) there is no random swing in the direction perpendicular to the forward motion of the drone (random swing along the forward direction is already captured in (i)). Thus, the controlled variables in our system are the drone-to-user distance, drone's orientation, and lateral velocity, as shown in Table 2.

Our goal is to adjust the manipulated variables to make the controlled variables close to the desired values. The manipulated variables in most commercial drones are pitch, yaw, and roll. As shown in Figure 6, pitch captures a rotation angle along the x-axis and determines the forward velocity; yaw captures an angle along the z-axis and determines how the drone's orientation is changed over time; and roll captures rotation along the y-axis and determines the lateral velocity.

We develop three controllers to maintain the drone-to-user distance, drone's orientation, and lateral velocity at their desired values using pitch, yaw, and roll, respectively. As shown in Table 2, we use MPC for pitch and yaw since we can accurately model the relationship between the manipulated and controlled variables. We use PID for roll since the relationship between the lateral velocity and roll has large variability in the range of interest and a simple PID, which does not require a model, works better.

In order to apply MPC to our system, we should address several major challenges. First, MPC requires modeling the relationship between the manipulated and controlled variables, as mentioned in Section 3.1 (Step 1 in MPC). Every drone is different (*e.g.*, different weight). We need a simple method to model the drones. Second, one of the controlled variables in our system is the drone-to-user distance, which requires us to predict not only the drone movement but also the user movement (Step 2 in MPC). Third, we should accurately measure the controlled variables so that we can use the measured values as the feedback to our controllers to improve the robustness against modeling errors and disturbance (Step 3 in MPC). Below we address these challenges by (i) developing measurement-based models, (ii) measuring the controlled variables using Rabbit, and (iii) predicting a user's movement.

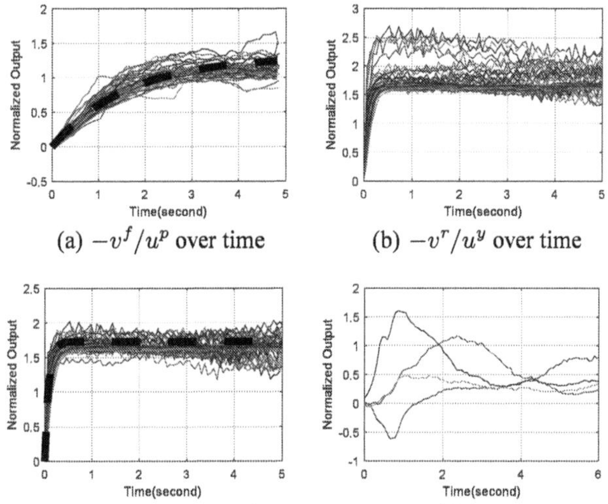

(a) $-v^f/u^p$ over time (b) $-v^r/u^y$ over time

(c) Compensated $-v^r/u^y$ (d) $-v^l/u^r$ over time

Figure 7: Model measurements

3.3 Measurement-based Models

First, we conduct extensive measurements to develop system models that describe the relationship between our manipulated and controlled variables.

Drone forward movement vs. pitch: We build a model between the forward displacement of the drone and the pitch as follows.

1. **Find the relationship between forward velocity (v^f) and pitch (u^p).** Based on the aerodynamic principle [12], their relationship over time can be expressed as

$$v^f(t) = -\frac{\alpha}{\beta}(1-e^{-\beta t})u^p(t), \quad (6)$$

where t denotes time, and α and β are unknown constants and need to be determined.

2. **Determine the parameters in Equation 6 based on measurements.** To this end, we choose different values for the pitch, and measure the forward velocity of the drone over time. The velocity is estimated by the camera on the bottom of the drone using optical flow [12]. For each value of pitch, we plot a line representing $-v^f/u^p$ over time, as shown in Figure 7(a). Based on Equation 6, we know that all these lines follow the expression $\frac{\alpha}{\beta}(1-e^{-\beta t})$. Thus, we find α and β that fit these measurements best by minimizing the mean squared fitting error.

3. **Integrate Equation 6.** After integrating speed over time, we get the relationship between the forward displacement and pitch.

Drone orientation vs. yaw: We build a model between the drone orientation and yaw (u^y) using similar steps as above. We first find the expression for the rotation rate (v^r) in terms of u^y, then integrate the expression to obtain the model between the orientation and u^y. However, when we determine the relationship between v^r and u^y using an equation similar to Equation 6, we observe discrepancy in the collected data as shown in Figure 7(b). The stable value of $-v^r/u^y$ for small yaw (u^y) is higher than that for large u^y. As a result, we cannot find coefficients α and β in Equation 6 that fit all measurements.

To solve this problem, we design a compensator to reduce the discrepancy for different yaw (u^y) values. When we set $u^y{=}x$, we actually specify the yaw value $x/(1+e^{-cx})$ to the drone, where c is a constant. If x is small, the compensation gain $1/(1+e^{-cx})$ is smaller than 1, which reduces the rotation rate (v^r) compared to the

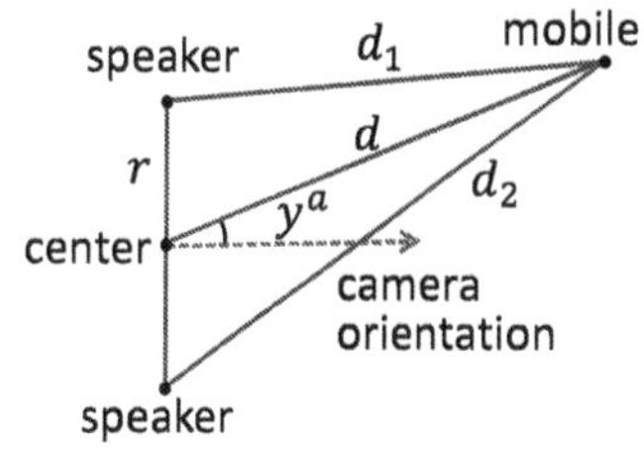

Figure 8: System top-down view.

uncompensated case. If x is large, $1/(1+e^{-cx})$ is close to 1, and v^r remains the same as the uncompensated case. As a result, $-v^r/u^y$ for small u^y is reduced, while that for larger u^y remains the same. We can tune the parameter c to make $-v^r/u^y$ for different u^y agree with each other as much as possible. Based on experiments, we set $c{=}15$. The values of $-v^r/u^y$ over time after compensation are shown in Figure 7(c). We see that the discrepancy among collected data is significantly reduced, and we are able to find a curve (*i.e.*, the dashed line) to fit all measurements.

Drone lateral velocity vs. roll: We try to model the relationship between the lateral velocity (v^l) and roll (u^r) using a similar procedure as above. Since we want to maintain the lateral velocity close to zero (so that there is no side-to-side swing), we focus on small lateral velocity. However, in this case, the relationship has large unpredictability and cannot be accurately modeled as shown in Figure 7(d). Without an accurate model, the effectiveness of MPC degrades. A simpler PID, which does not require any model, performs better. Thus, we use PID to stabilize the lateral velocity to zero. Our implementation uses $K_p{=}4$, $K_i{=}0.4$, $K_d{=}0.1$ based on our experiments.

3.4 Measuring Controlled Variables

Both MPC and PID need feedback to improve robustness against disturbance or model inaccuracy. Introducing feedback requires measuring the controlled variables (*i.e.*, the drone-to-user distance, drone's orientation, and lateral velocity) so that we can compare them with the desired values and adjust the system accordingly. For this purpose, we attach two speakers at each side of the drone and use Rabbit developed in Section 2 to derive the drone-to-user distance and drone's orientation as follows. For lateral velocity, we use the measurement provided by the drone as feedback [12].

Drone-to-user distance: The drone-to-user distance y^{hd} is defined as the horizontal distance between them as shown in Figure 6, while Rabbit measures the distance between the speakers and mobile (d_1 and d_2). To determine y^{hd}, we first calculate the distance from the mobile to the line defined by two speakers, denoted by D. Based on simple geometry, we can derive $D^2{=}d_2^2{-}(\frac{4r^2+d_2^2-d_1^2}{4r})^2$, where r is the drone's radius and can be easily measured. Let h denote the altitude difference between the drone and mobile. It is easy to see $y^{hd}{=}\sqrt{D^2{-}h^2}$. The drone can measure its altitude using the ultrasound transceiver on its bottom [12] and the mobile's altitude can be approximated based on the user's height. Moreover, we find y^{hd} mainly depends on d_1 and d_2, and is robust to the estimation error in h: it sees little difference even when h has 10 cm error.

Drone orientation As shown in Figure 8, the orientation of the drone with respect to the user, *i.e.*, y^a, can be derived based on the distances between speakers and microphone (*i.e.*, d_1 and d_2). Using simple geometry, we obtain $y^a{=}\arcsin(\frac{d_2^2-d_1^2}{4r\sqrt{\frac{d_1^2+d_2^2-2r^2}{2}}})$.

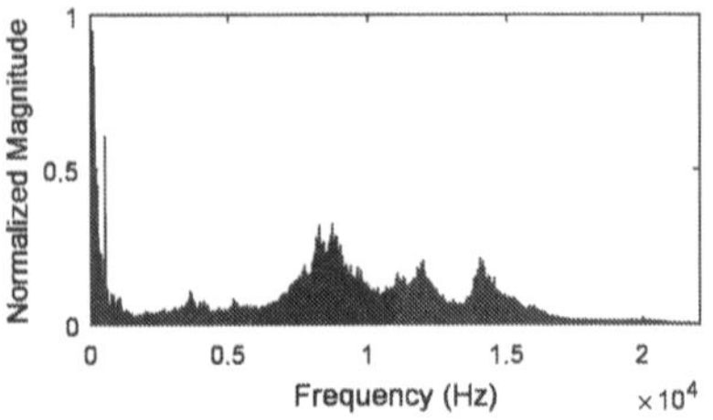

Figure 9: The spectrum of propeller noise.

3.5 Predicting a User's Movement

Standard MPC predicts the controlled variable using the future manipulated variable value and their relationship. However, in our system, certain controlled variable (*e.g.*, drone-to-user distance) depends not only on the manipulated variable (*e.g.*, pitch) but also on the user's movement. Therefore, to predict such controlled variables and apply MPC, we need to predict the user's movement.

We predict drone-to-user distance $y^{hd}(t)$ as $(t-t_0)v^h-y^d(t)+m$, where t denotes the time in the near future and t_0 is the current time. y^d is the displacement of the drone from t_0 to t, which can be predicted based on the model in Section 3.3. m is the currently measured drone-to-user distance. v^h is the user's moving speed and assumed to be constant during the prediction horizon (*i.e.*, how far future we need to predict), which is 1 s in our implementation.

Predicting y^{hd} requires the knowledge of v_h. We estimate it based on Doppler shift of acoustic signals, which provides the relative velocity between the user and drone. From Figure 6, it can be shown:

$$-v^{D,1} = (v^h-v^d)\frac{y^{hd}}{d_1}+v^z\frac{h}{d_1}-v^l\frac{r}{d_1}$$
$$-v^{D,2} = (v^h-v^d)\frac{y^{hd}}{d_2}+v^z\frac{h}{d_2}+v^l\frac{r}{d_2}$$

where v^l, v^d, v^z are the drone velocities in the x, y, and z axes, respectively, and $v^{D,1}$ and $v^{D,2}$ are Doppler velocities with respect to the two speakers. In our system, y^{hd} is controlled to its desired value y_0^{hd}, and d_1 and d_2 are maintained equal to each other so that the camera on the drone perfectly faces the user. In this case, d_1 and d_2 are given by $d_0=\sqrt{(y_0^{hd})^2+h^2+r^2}$ as shown in Figure 6. Moreover, since the drone flies at a constant altitude, v^z is zero. Thus, v^h can be estimated by $v^h=v^d-\frac{d_0}{2y_0^{hd}}(v^{D,1}+v^{D,2})$, where $v^{D,1}$ and $v^{D,2}$ are measured by Rabbit, while v^d is measured by the drone [12]. In addition, when we detect the user does not move using accelerometer readings, we directly set v^h=0. This improves stability when the user is stationary as shown in our experiments (Section 5).

3.6 Important Parameters

We need to determine two parameters for MPC: (i) prediction horizon N_p, which represents how many control periods to predict in advance, and (ii) regularization parameter w_u, which determines if large variation of the manipulated variables is favored. We select these parameters based on experiments in Section 5.

4. IMPLEMENTATION

We implement our system on *A.R. Drone 2.0* and Samsung Galaxy S7. To support our scheme, we attach two speakers on the left and right sides of the drone, along with an audio amplifier board (Sure Electronics AA-AB32231). To power the amplifier and the speakers, we add a light-weight li-ion battery (EBL 6F22) in the drone's battery compartments. Altogether we add 140 grams to the drone.

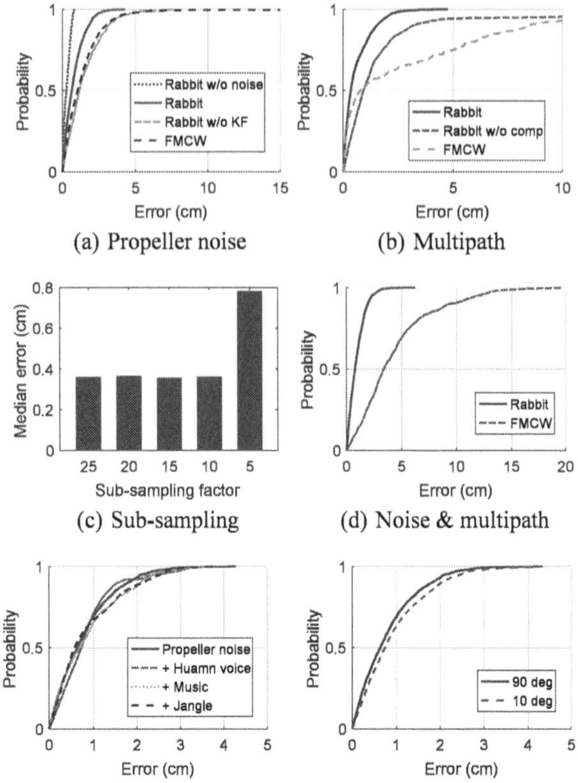

(a) Propeller noise (b) Multipath

(c) Sub-sampling (d) Noise & multipath

(e) Environment noise (f) Mic orientation

Figure 10: Distance estimation accuracy.

We use Galaxy S7 for tracking and controlling. It runs Android 6.0.1. We develop an application including all modules presented in the paper. The tracking part is implemented on Android NDK for efficiency, and other parts are based on Android SDK. We use the speakers on the drone to send chirp signals and sinusoid signals for distance and velocity measurements, respectively. The smartphone app analyzes the received signals to track the drone and derives control instructions. Then it uses APIs provided by Javadrone [27] to send instructions to the drone through Wi-Fi.

Figure 9 shows the spectrum of the propeller noise of our drone during flight. In the spectrum above 10 KHz, there is a dip between 13 KHz and 13.5 KHz. Also, the noise strength reduces noticeably beyond 17 KHz. Therefore, we use 17 - 19.5 KHz to send chirp signals for distance estimation. We also generate sinusoid signals at 13 KHz and 13.3 KHz for Doppler shift estimation. Signals around 13 KHz are audible, but they are not noticeable due to large noise from the propellers.

5. EVALUATION

We evaluate Rabbit and DroneTrack in this section.

5.1 Distance Estimation

To evaluate the performance of distance estimation using Rabbit, we use a multi-camera 3D positioning system [44] to measure the distance between the speakers on the drone and the microphone on the mobile during the experiments. The positioning error of the system is less than 1mm. The camera measurements serve as the ground truth. In the experiments, the user holds a mobile, and faces its microphone towards the drone. The distance between the microphone and speakers is 1.5m. We collect 2000 distance measurements for each scheme in an experiment.

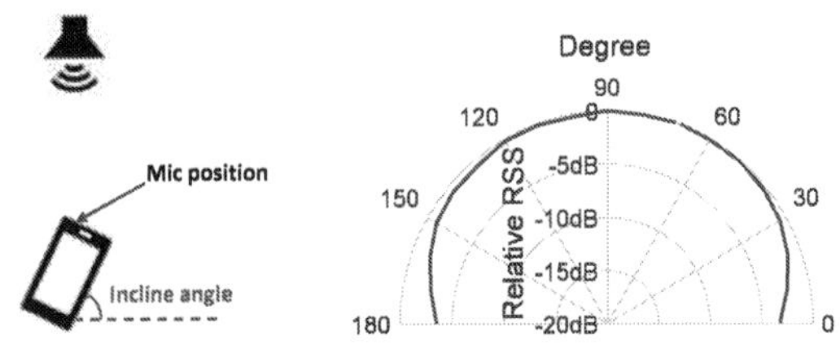

(a) Mic orientation (b) Receiving beam pattern

Figure 11: Sensitivity of microphone orientation.

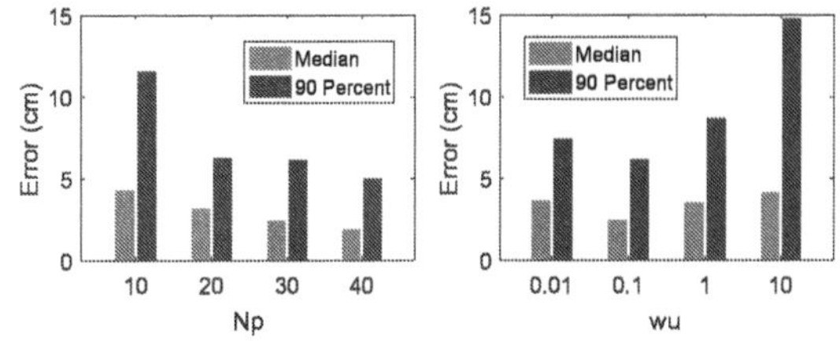

Figure 12: Errors on drone-to-user distance.

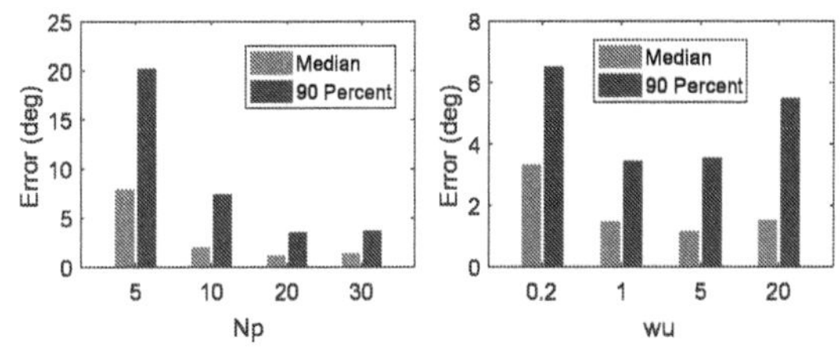

Figure 13: Errors on drone orientation.

Performance under propeller noise: We evaluate the performance of distance estimation under propeller noise by having the drone hover in the air. Figure 10(a) compares three schemes: (i) Rabbit, (ii) Rabbit without Kalman filter, and (iii) distributed FMCW [37]. We also compare with Rabbit without propeller noise to understand the impact of the noise. We use [37] to estimate the initial distance required by these schemes. It has 6 mm error, which is not included in the figure. In our application, a small constant error has no impact on the user experience. A user only needs the drone to follow him at a constant distance for stable video taping, and does not care if the constant is a few millimeter away from the specified value. Among these schemes, Rabbit performs best with a median error of 0.63 cm. When the Kalman filter is disabled, Rabbit and distributed FMCW have similar performance. Kalman filter reduces the median error of Rabbit from 1.1 cm to 0.63 cm.

Performance under multipath: Next, we evaluate Rabbit under multipath. To exclude the impact of propeller noise, we put the drone on a stand instead of having it fly. As discussed in Section 2.2, the major interference caused by multipath comes from the paths that have similar lengths to the direct path. Therefore, we put a large cardboard near the direct path between the speaker and microphone, and move it during the experiment to generate interfering paths with varying lengths. We compare three schemes: Rabbit, Rabbit without compensating speaker distortion, and distributed FMCW. As shown in Figure 10 (b), Rabbit has 0.36 cm median error, which is much smaller than Rabbit without compensation. Rabbit also outperforms FMCW by using MUSIC since MUSIC is better at resolving multipath.

Performance of sub-sampling: We use the raw acoustic signals recorded from the above experiment to evaluate the impact of sub-sampling offline. We use different sub-sampling factors K but keep KM to 640 for fair comparison, where M is the order of the auto-correlation matrix. Figure 10(c) shows the median errors as K varies. For most K, the performance does not change. However, when K is small, the performance degrades because we need to use a large M for a small K and the eigenvalue decomposition for a large matrix has much larger numerical errors [46]. Thus, sub-sampling not only improves efficiency, but also enhances the accuracy of eigenvalue decomposition.

Performance under noise and multipath: We evaluate Rabbit under both propeller noise and multipath. As shown in Figure 10(d), Rabbit continues to perform well with a median error of 0.78 cm, and significantly outperforms FMCW.

Performance under environment noise: We evaluate Rabbit under both propeller noise and environment noise. We consider three types of environment noise: 1) human voices: two people continuously talk during the experiment; 2) music: different genres of music (Jazz, Pop, and Classic) are played together using the same volume as that for our tracking signals; 3) jangles generated by continuously jangling metal keys. These noise sources are 1m away from the microphone. As shown in Figure 10(e), the performance under both propeller noise and environment noise is close to that with only propeller noise, because 1) the frequency of environment noise, such as human voices and music, is mostly below 10 KHz [38], while our tracking signals are higher than 13 KHz, and 2) the environment noise is much weaker than that of propeller noise.

Sensitivity of Mic orientation: To evaluate the sensitivity of the microphone orientation, we vary the inclination angle of the mobile from 0 to 180 degree, as shown in Figure 11(a). We record the received signal strength (RSS) for different inclination angles. When the angle is 90 degree, the microphone perfectly aligns with the speaker and RSS is maximized. We plot RSS at different angles relative to that at 90 degree in a polar coordinate system as shown in Figure 11(b), where the angular coordinate stands for the inclination angle and the radical coordinate represents the relative RSS. The RSS at the inclination angles of 10 or 170 degrees is only 3dB weaker. Thus, 3-dB beam width of the microphone is 160 degree. Figure 10(f) compares the distance estimation accuracy when the inclination angle is 10 and 90 degrees. The results indicate that Rabbit is not sensitive to microphone orientation.

5.2 System Evaluation

In this section, we evaluate the performance of DroneTrack system. The user holds a mobile in hand, and faces the microphone towards the drone. Since 3-dB beam width of the microphone is 160 degree, it does not need to align with the speakers perfectly. We use DroneTrack to make the drone follow the user with a desired distance of 1.5m. We quantify the user following performance using three metrics: the drone-to-user distance, the drone's orientation with respect to the user, and the drone's lateral velocity. To evaluate the following performance, we record the difference between their measured and desired values over time. We define the difference as *following errors*. We measure these metrics using Rabbit, whose accuracy is established in the previous section. We do not use the multi-camera system, because it only covers a 2m×3m area, but we fly the drone across tens of meters. It is too expensive to deploy 3D camera systems over such a large area.

Parameter study: We first study the impact of the MPC parameters on the control performance. There are two critical parameters: prediction horizon N_p and regularization parameter w_u.

For the drone-to-user distance control, the user moves along a 15 m straight line three times with a regular walking speed. Figure 12 compares the following errors as we vary N_p and w_u. We see that the following errors reduce as N_p increases. However, further

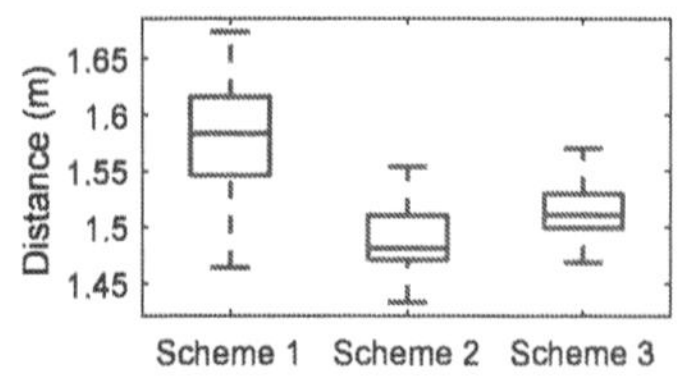

Figure 14: Stability of the drone.

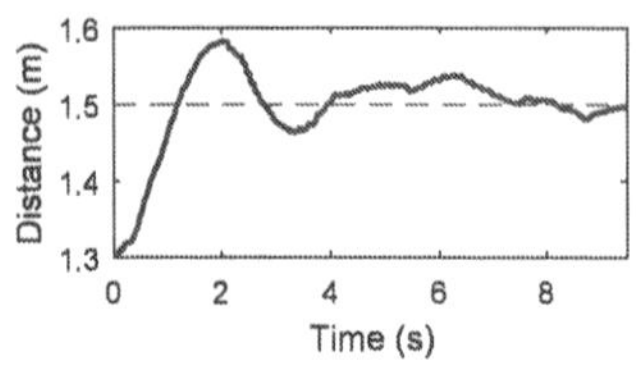

(a) Drone-to-user distance

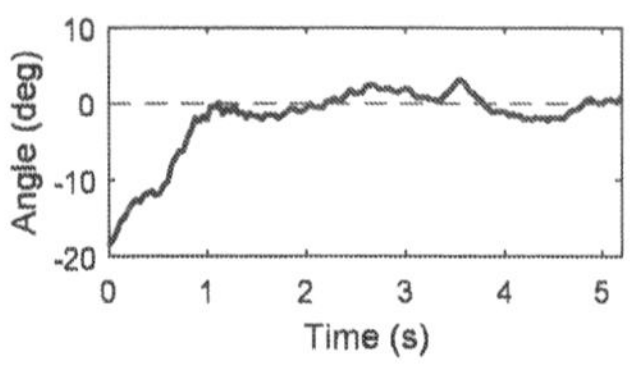

(b) Drone orientation

Figure 15: Convergence behavior.

increasing N_p beyond 40 helps little, because it is challenging to accurately predict far into the future and increasing the prediction error degrades the effectiveness of MPC. Our results show N_p=40 and w_u=0.1 yield the best performance. In this case, the median error of the drone-to-user distance is 1.9 cm.

For the drone orientation control, the user moves along a circle with the radius equal to 1.5m three times . Figure 13 shows the following errors as N_p and w_u vary. Under the most favorable setting (N_p=20 and w_u=5), the median following error is 1.1 degree.

Below we use the parameters that yield the best performance. For the distance control, N_p=40 and w_u=0.1. For the orientation control, N_p=20 and w_u=5.

Stationary scenario: We study the stability of DroneTrack when the user does not move. We compare three schemes: (i) hovering mode: a built-in function of our drone, which makes the drone stay at the same position; (ii) DroneTrack without detecting if the user is stationary; (iii) DroneTrack, which detects when the user is stationary and sets v^h=0 whenever the user is stationary. To evaluate these schemes, we measure the drone-to-user distance over one minute. Figure 14 shows the results with the box-plot. The span (in y-direction) of each box reflects the fluctuation in the distance. Rabbit, which detects the stationary user performs the best due to the smaller prediction error when it knows the user is stationary.

Convergence behavior: To evaluate how fast drone-to-user distance converges to its desired value, the user stands at 1.3 m from the drone and does not move. Then we let the drone follow the user. We record the distance over time. As shown in Figure 15(a), it takes 4 s to converge to the desired distance. We conduct a similar experiment to evaluate the convergence behavior of drone orientation. As shown in Figure 15(b), given a 20-degree disturbance, it takes less than 1 s to converge to the desired orientation. These results show that our system can quickly respond to sudden changes.

Impact of user movement speeds: We let a user move along a 15 m straight line at various speeds (3 times for each speed), and measure the drone-to-user distance error. For slow, normal, and fast walking, the speeds are 0.4 m/s, 1 m/s, and 2 m/s, respectively.

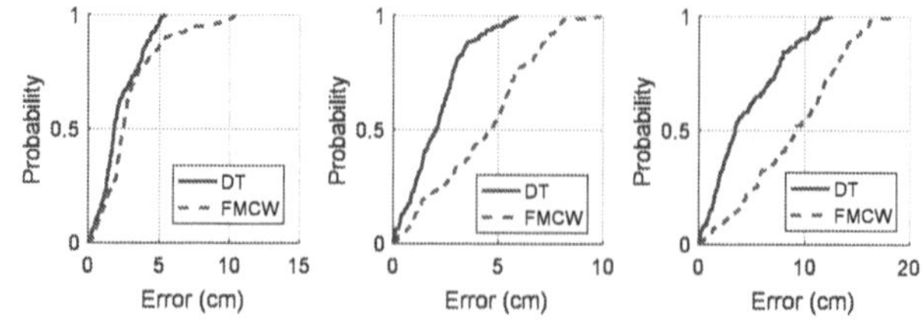

(a) Slow speed (b) Normal speed (c) Fast speed

Figure 16: Performance under various user speeds.

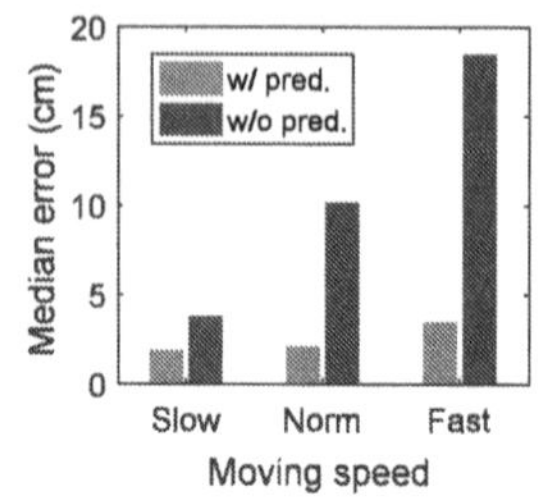

Figure 17: The impact of user movement prediction.

Figure 16 shows the performance of DroneTrack (denoted by "DT") under various speeds. For comparison, we replace Rabbit with distributed FMCW (denoted by "FMCW") in DroneTrack and evaluate its performance. DroneTrack is accurate across different speeds: the 90-percentage error for slow and norm speeds is 4 cm, and that for fast movement is 10 cm. In comparison, distributed FMCW has much larger error. The improvement of DroneTrack over distributed FMCW is higher for faster speeds. FMCW may have a large tracking error due to multiple nearby propagation paths (*e.g.*, caused by tables, chairs, or walls), which results in a large following error. When the user moves faster, a large tracking error makes it harder to converge to the desired distance.

Impact of user movement prediction: Next we compare the performance with and without predicting user movement using the same setup as the previous experiment. As Figure 17 shows, removing prediction significantly increases the median error of drone-to-user distance by 106%, 391%, and 438% for slow, normal, and fast moving speeds, respectively. In comparison, prediction helps to reduce the performance gap between the fast and slow movement since the drone is able to take actions in advance and maintain a constant distance to the user.

Impact of following distances: We evaluate DroneTrack by varying the desired distances between the drone and user. For each distance, we let a user move along a 15 m straight line for three times. Figure 18 shows that the median following error only marginally increases from 2 cm to 3 cm as the desired distance increases from 2 m to 5 m. As the distance increases, both the signals used for tracking and propeller noise attenuate. Thus the SINR does not change significantly, and the accuracy of distance estimation remains similar.

Video taping experiment: Next we let a user move along a fixed

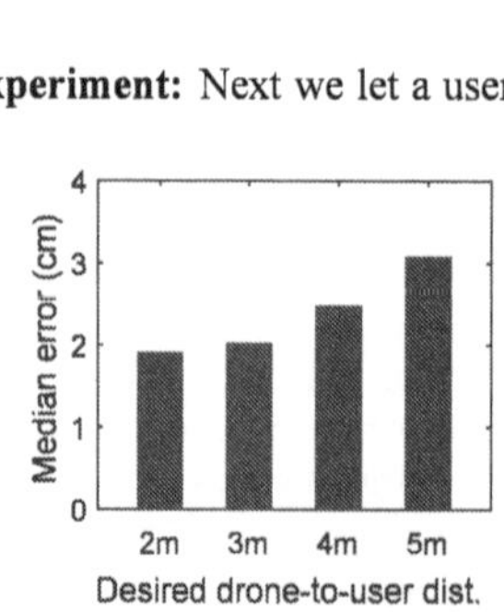

Figure 18: The impact of following distances.

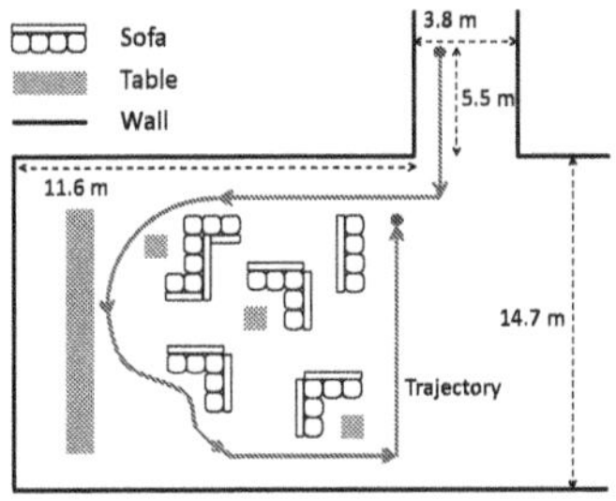

Figure 19: The trajectory for video experiments.

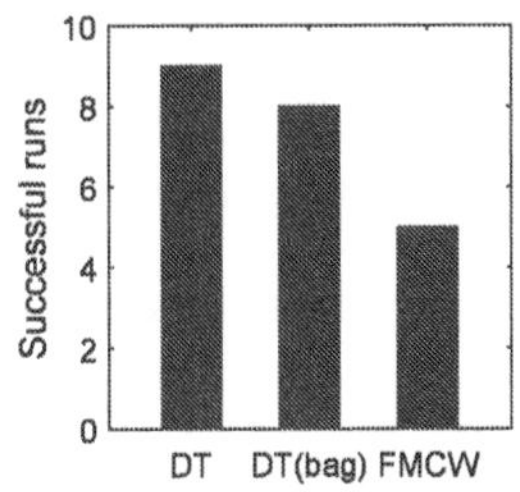

Figure 20: Successful runs.

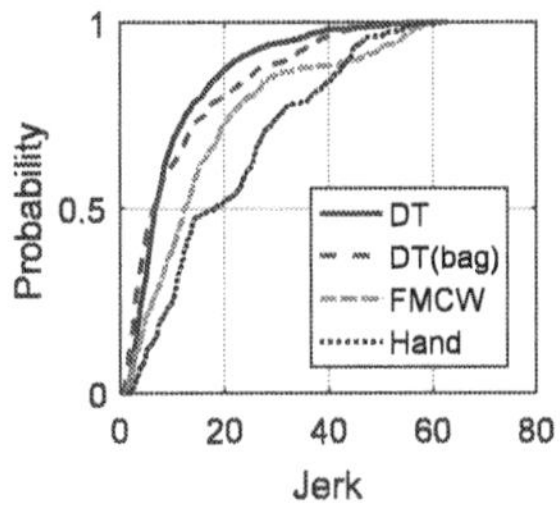

Figure 21: Video stability.

trajectory in our department building as shown in Figure 19. We use the fixed trajectory for fair comparison across different schemes. The trajectory includes various natural walking patterns, such as straight paths, curved paths, and left and right turns. There are furniture (*e.g.*, tables and sofa) and walls along the trajectory. When the user walks, the drone follows him and the camera on it is used to record videos. We compare the performance of three schemes: 1) DroneTrack where the user holds the mobile in hand (denoted by "DT"); 2) DroneTrack where the mobile is placed in a PC sleeve with its microphone facing the drone and the user carries the case (denoted by "DT (bag)"); 3) using distributed FMCW for distance estimation instead of Rabbit (denoted by "FMCW"). As the baseline, we let a person follow the user and take videos with a camera held in his hand (denoted by "Hand"). For each scheme, we conduct experiments along the trajectory for 10 times. An experiment is considered as a failure if the user is outside the view at any point in the video. This may happen due to inaccurate distance estimation or significant WiFi delay which leads to the loss of control instructions.

Figure 20 compares the number of successful runs across different schemes. As we can see, DroneTrack in hand yields the best performance, closely followed by DroneTrack in bag. The gap between the two is small, which demonstrates the robustness of DroneTrack. In comparison, distributed FMCW based approach succeeds only 50% since it cannot effectively resolve multipath.

Figure 21 and Figure 22 compare the video stability and the following errors of the successful runs for each scheme, respectively. For video stability, we use the standard jerk metric [16], which captures the smoothness between two consecutive frames in the video. The lower the jerk metric, the more stable the videos. As we can see, DroneTrack with the mobile in hand performs the best and followed by DroneTrack with the mobile in bag. The hand-held video taping performs the worst due to hand vibration during walking and there is no optical-image-stabilization system on our camera. From Figure 22, we can observe that DroneTrack performs well: the median drone-to-user distance error is 2.5 cm (in hand) and 2.6 cm (in bag); the median drone orientation error is 1.5 deg (in hand) and 2.3 deg (in bag); and the lateral velocity error is 1.6 cm/s (in hand) and 1.8 cm/s (in bag). Note that the lateral velocity control does not depend on the performance of distance estimation, and thus different schemes perform similarly.

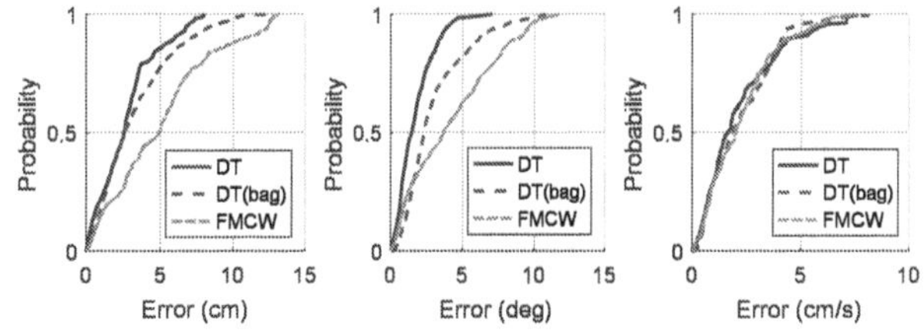

(a) Drone-user dist. (b) Drone orientation (c) Lateral velocity

Figure 22: Following errors.

5.3 Computation cost

Finally, we quantify the computation cost. Table 3 summarizes the mean CPU usage and processing delay of DroneTrack running on Galaxy S7. We use *adb shell top* command to sample the CPU usage every second during a 200-second period. As we can see, the CPU usage for tracking is only 13%, and that for the whole system is 42%. Tracking takes 9 ms to process, and the whole system takes 13 ms. Also, we observe the battery of Galaxy S7 (3000 mAh) drops from 100% to 97% after 10-minute running of DroneTrack with the screen off. We plan to further improve the energy efficiency by porting more codes from Android SDK to NDK.

	CPU Usage (%)	Delay (ms)
Tracking	13	9
Overall	42	13

Table 3: Computation cost.

6. DISCUSSION

Loss of direct path signals: Our approach estimates the distance between the drone and user by extracting the signals propagated through the direct path between them. Since acoustic signals can penetrate through some materials, such as clothes, our system continues to work when the mobile is in a bag.

However, there are a few cases where the received signals via the direct path are too weak to detect. This can occur when the microphone is completely opposite to the speaker. Note that we can still easily detect signals from the direct path when the incline angle of the mobile is within 180 degree as shown in Figure 11(a). This is easy to satisfy in most cases since our control algorithm can automatically adjust the drone's orientation when the user makes turns. The direct path may also be blocked by obstacles, which acoustic signals cannot penetrate, such as human body and concrete pillars. If blocking is temporary, it can be handled by extrapolation using the recent past measurements. Long-term blocking is more challenging and may require using other signals in addition to acoustic signals for tracking. We plan to explore it in future.

7. RELATED WORK

Our work is related to the following research areas: (i) tracking and localization, (ii) drone control and modeling, and (iii) autonomous user following with a drone.

Tracking and localization: Acoustic signals are attractive for localization and tracking due to their potential to achieve high accuracy and widely available speakers and microphones. Several acoustic-based tracking systems are developed. [61] uses Doppler shifts of acoustic signals for tracking and achieves 1.4 cm median tracking error. [39] develops a device-free tracking based on cross correlation of acoustic signals and OFDM, while [55] uses the phase change of acoustic signals. Both [39] and [55] assume that the target to be tracked is the only moving object in the environment. However, in our case the drone and mobile are both moving and all paths can change over time. [42] estimates the distance between two phones by having them transmit and receive the beeps to cancel out the processing delay and clock difference. [62] further improves [42] for mobile gaming applications. [37] proposes a distributed FMCW-based approach to support distance estimation between a separate sender and receiver, and combines various measurements to achieve 6 mm tracking error. We apply the distributed FMCW in [37], but make several important improvements: 1) compensate for the speaker distortion and use MUSIC to process FMCW to achieve better resolution of resolving multiple paths, 2) use velocity measurements and Kalman filter to reduce noise in distance estimation.

RF signals are also widely used for tracking and localization. [59] uses an array of RF antennas to achieve 23 cm median error. [53] uses multiple frequency bands for localization with a single AP point. Its median distance estimation error is 14.1 cm in light-of-sight (LOS) and 20.7 cm in non-LOS case. [54] relies on multiple RFID antennas and angle-of-arrival (AoA) estimation to achieve 3.7 cm tracking error. [5] and [4] use RF-based FMCW signals to localize a person with 11.7 cm error. [56] achieves 0.8 cm tracking error using highly directional and steerable 60 GHz antennas.

MUSIC is used to derive AoA using multiple antennas. Combined with propagation delay measurements (*e.g.*, using FMCW [57, 7, 49, 13]) or channel state information (*e.g.*, [51, 58, 32]), the target can be localized. However, since smartphones do not have a microphone array, our acoustic tracking system cannot derive AoA using MUSIC. [60] applies MUSIC in the frequency domain to estimate the propagation delay, and combines multiple frequency bands to improve the estimation accuracy. In [3, 28], MUSIC is applied to enhance the resolution of FMCW-based propagation delay measurement. Our tracking system also leverages this idea, but significantly improves the performance by (i) calibrating and compensating for the speaker distortion, (ii) improving the peak selection under strong propeller noise, (iii) improving the efficiency for mobile implementation, and (iv) combining Doppler measurements using Kalman filter.

Drone control and modeling: There have been significant works on controlling drones [47, 40, 52, 15, 6, 29, 10, 24]. We can broadly classify them into three categories: 1) stabilize a drone at a target location, 2) make a drone follow a pre-defined path, 3) make a drone reach a set of positions at specified time. In all these works, the target positions or paths are given in advance, which is different from our application, where the drone is required to follow a user, whose movement is not known in advance.

Many algorithms have been applied to control drones, such as PID [47], nonlinear guidance low [52], MPC [24], vector field control [40], and gain-scheduled control [29]. Among them, we find MPC best suits our need due to its predictive power. We address practical challenges in applying MPC to our context, including building the system models for the drone, measuring the distance and orientation between the drone and user as the control feedback, and predicting the user movement.

Several research papers model drone dynamics. [9, 34, 11] model the relationship between the drone movement and its rotor thrusts. However, we do not have access to the low-level attributes like rotor thrusts. Instead, we model the relationship between the drone displacement and its inclination angles. Our modeling procedures are closer to [23, 12], but differ from these works in that we find the non-linear behavior of the drone, and apply the compensation to address the issue.

User following: There have been some works that let a drone automatically follow a user [18, 21, 30, 35, 43, 8, 22, 36, 53]. Most off-the-shelf drones rely on GPS [18] to enable follow-me. GPS-based approaches are only feasible outdoors. When GPS is not available, computer vision (CV) is most widely used for tracking a user [21, 30, 35, 43, 8, 22, 36]. However, CV has a few limitations. First, the accuracy of CV-based tracking is limited due to two main reasons: 1) A drone vibrates during flight due to air disturbance. The vibration blurs the images captured by the drone, which significantly degrades the tracking performance. 2) CV based tracking needs depth information. Depth sensors or multiple cameras are required to get the depth information, but they are not available on most drones. Therefore, existing works use the relative size of a target in the image for tracking [30, 43, 8, 36]. However, such an approach is not accurate and sensitive to target deformation and view angle variation. Due to these facts, the error for CV-based user following is typically decimeters or higher (*e.g.*, [35, 43, 8, 36]). Second, CV based approaches are sensitive to visual interference, and its performance degrades in a busy background [8]. As a result, state-of-the-art CV approaches can successfully detect the target for only 67% - 88% [22]. Our acoustic based indoor follow-me drone is not affected by visual interference. To avoid acoustic interference, we use frequencies higher than 13 KHz, which are different from noise in the environment, such as human voices and music, whose frequency is mostly below 10 KHz [38]. We also develop several mechanisms to combat with noise generated by the propellers. Thus, our system is robust to the interference. In addition, the computation of CV based approaches is too heavy for mobile devices. [35, 8, 22] use sophisticated CV approaches, which are more accurate and robust than simple CV methods, such as color filtering, but require extracting and matching image descriptors for the target. These operations take from 30 ms to 3 s for each image when running on a mobile device [25]. In contrast, our tracking approach takes 9 ms for processing 40 ms acoustic samples, and the CPU usage during this period is only 13%.

[53] develops a novel tracking approach using WiFi signals to achieve decimeter-level tracking, and uses one experiment to show their tracking can be applied to follow-me drones. We believe an effective control algorithm is essential to enable follow-me drones under general user movement. Our paper advances [53] by significantly improving the tracking accuracy, designing a holistic system including both tracking and control, and extensively evaluating user-following performance.

Remarks: In short, our work complements existing work by enhancing the tracking accuracy and efficiency and developing a practical control system to allow a drone to follow a user with desired following distance and orientation.

8. CONCLUSION

This paper presents a novel design and implementation of a system that accurately tracks the drone and controls its movement to maintain a specified distance and orientation to the user. Our tracking approach (Rabbit) advances existing tracking technologies by improving robustness under multipath and has applications beyond drones. We further build a holistic follow-me drone system (DroneTrack) on top of Rabbit for low-end drones to achieve high following accuracy in indoor environments through measurement-based modeling, deriving accurate feedback using Rabbit, and predicting user movement.

9. REFERENCES

[1] Microsoft X-box Kinect. http://xbox.com.

[2] Nintendo Wii. http://www.nintendo.com/wii.

[3] M. Abou-Khousa, D. Simms, S. Kharkovsky, and R. Zoughi. High-resolution short-range wideband FMCW radar measurements based on MUSIC algorithm. In *IEEE Instrumentation and Measurement Technology Conference*, page I2MTC, 2009.

[4] F. Adib, Z. Kabelac, and D. Katabi. Multi-person localization via RF body reflections. In *12th USENIX Symposium on Networked Systems Design and Implementation (NSDI 15)*, pages 279–292, 2015.

[5] F. Adib, Z. Kabelac, D. Katabi, and R. Miller. WiTrack: motion tracking via radio reflections off the body. In *Proc. of NSDI*, 2014.

[6] A. P. Aguiar, J. P. Hespanha, et al. Trajectory-tracking and path-following of underactuated autonomous vehicles with parametric modeling uncertainty. *IEEE Transactions on Automatic Control*, 52(8):1362–1379, 2007.

[7] F. Belfiori, W. van Rossum, and P. Hoogeboom. 2D-MUSIC technique applied to a coherent FMCW MIMO radar. In *Radar Systems (Radar 2012), IET International Conference on*, pages 1–6. IET, 2012.

[8] V. Bevilacqua and A. Di Maio. A computer vision and control algorithm to follow a human target in a generic environment using a drone. In *International Conference on Intelligent Computing*, pages 192–202. Springer, 2016.

[9] P. Bouffard. On-board model predictive control of a quadrotor helicopter: Design, implementation, and experiments. Technical report, DTIC Document, 2012.

[10] E. Bregu, N. Casamassima, D. Cantoni, L. Mottola, and K. Whitehouse. Reactive control of autonomous drones. MOBISYS, 2016.

[11] T. Bresciani. Modelling, identification and control of a quadrotor helicopter. *MSc Theses*, 2008.

[12] P.-J. Bristeau, F. Callou, D. Vissiere, N. Petit, et al. The navigation and control technology inside the AR. Drone micro UAV. In *18th IFAC world congress*, volume 18, pages 1477–1484, 2011.

[13] J. Choi, J. Park, and D. Yeom. High angular resolution estimation methods for vehicle FMCW radar. In *Proceedings of 2011 IEEE CIE International Conference on Radar*, volume 2, pages 1868–1871. IEEE, 2011.

[14] The drones report: market forecasts, regulatory barriers, top vendors, and leading commercial applications. http://www.businessinsider.com/uav-or-commercial-drone-market-forecast-2015-2.

[15] P. Encarnação and A. Pascoal. Combined trajectory tracking and path following: an application to the coordinated control of autonomous marine craft. In *Decision and Control, 2001. Proceedings of the 40th IEEE Conference on*, volume 1, pages 964–969. IEEE, 2001.

[16] F. D. et al. Time-optimal path following for robots with trajectory jerk constraints using sequential convex programming. 2013.

[17] R. Faragher et al. Understanding the basis of the Kalman filter via a simple and intuitive derivation. *IEEE Signal processing magazine*, 29(5):128–132, 2012.

[18] Top 10 drones with follow me mode in 2016. http://www.top10drone.com/top-10-drones-follow-me-mode/.

[19] 12 best follow me drones and follow me technology reviewed. https://www.dronezon.com/drone-reviews/best-follow-me-gps-mode-drone-technology-reviewed/.

[20] Making gated-impulse frequency measurements using ARTA. http://opencv.org/.

[21] J.-E. Gomez-Balderas, G. Flores, L. G. Carrillo, and R. Lozano. Tracking a ground moving target with a quadrotor using switching control. *Journal of Intelligent & Robotic Systems*, 70(1-4):65–78, 2013.

[22] K. Haag, S. Dotenco, and F. Gallwitz. Correlation filter based visual trackers for person pursuit using a low-cost quadrotor. In *Innovations for Community Services (I4CS), 2015 15th International Conference on*, pages 1–8. IEEE, 2015.

[23] A. Hernandez, C. Copot, R. De Keyser, T. Vlas, and I. Nascu. Identification and path following control of an AR. Drone quadrotor. In *System Theory, Control and Computing (ICSTCC), 2013 17th International Conference*, pages 583–588. IEEE, 2013.

[24] A. Hernandez, H. Murcia, C. Copot, and R. De Keyser. Model predictive path-following control of an AR. Drone quadrotor. In *Proceedings of the XVI Latin American Control Conference (CLCAÂŠ14), Cancun, Quintana Roo, Mexico*, pages 14–17, 2014.

[25] M. A. Hudelist, C. Cobârzan, and K. Schoeffmann. Opencv performance measurements on mobile devices. In *Proceedings of International Conference on Multimedia Retrieval*, page 479. ACM, 2014.

[26] V. K. Ingle and J. G. Proakis. *Digital signal processing using MATLAB*. Cengage Learning, 2016.

[27] Javadrone. https://github.com/codeminders/javadrone.

[28] W. Jiang, S. Pennock, and P. Shepherd. A novel w-MUSIC algorithm for GPR target detection in noisy and distorted signals. In *2009 IEEE Radar Conference*, pages 1–6. IEEE, 2009.

[29] I. Kaminer, A. Pascoal, E. Hallberg, and C. Silvestre. Trajectory tracking for autonomous vehicles: An integrated approach to guidance and control. *Journal of Guidance, Control, and Dynamics*, 21(1):29–38, 1998.

[30] J. Kim and D. H. Shim. A vision-based target tracking control system of a quadrotor by using a tablet computer. In *Unmanned Aircraft Systems (ICUAS), 2013 International Conference on*, pages 1165–1172. IEEE, 2013.

[31] H.-H. Ko, K.-W. Cheng, and H.-J. Su. Range resolution improvement for FMCW radars. In *Radar Conference, 2008. EuRAD 2008. European*, pages 352–355. IEEE, 2008.

[32] M. Kotaru, K. Joshi, D. Bharadia, and S. Katti. Spotfi: Decimeter level localization using WiFi. In *ACM SIGCOMM Computer Communication Review*, volume 45, pages 269–282. ACM, 2015.

[33] Leap motion. https://www.leapmotion.com/.

[34] T. Lee, M. Leoky, and N. H. McClamroch. Geometric tracking control of a quadrotor UAV on SE (3). In *49th IEEE conference on decision and control (CDC)*, pages 5420–5425. IEEE, 2010.

[35] F. Lin, X. Dong, B. M. Chen, K.-Y. Lum, and T. H. Lee. A robust real-time embedded vision system on an unmanned rotorcraft for ground target following. *IEEE Transactions on Industrial Electronics*, 59(2):1038–1049, 2012.

[36] J. J. Lugo and A. Zell. Framework for autonomous on-board navigation with the AR. Drone. *Journal of Intelligent & Robotic Systems*, 73(1-4):401–412, 2014.

[37] W. Mao, J. He, and L. Qiu. CAT: high-precision acoustic motion tracking. In *Proc. of ACM MobiCom*, 2016.

[38] The frequency spectrum, instrument ranges, and EQ tips. http://www.guitarbuilding.org/wp-content/uploads/2014/06/Instrument-Sound-EQ-Chart.pdf.

[39] R. Nandakumar, V. Iyer, D. Tan, and S. Gollakota. FingerIO: Using active sonar for fine-grained finger tracking. In *Proc. of ACM CHI*, pages 1515–1525, 2016.

[40] D. R. Nelson, D. B. Barber, T. W. McLain, and R. W. Beard. Vector field path following for miniature air vehicles. *IEEE Transactions on Robotics*, 23(3):519–529, 2007.

[41] Opencv. http://audio.claub.net/tutorials/FR%20measurement%20using%20ARTA.pdf.

[42] C. Peng, G. Shen, Y. Zhang, Y. Li, and K. Tan. BeepBeep: a high accuracy acoustic ranging system using COTS mobile devices. In *Proc. of ACM SenSys*, 2007.

[43] J. Pestana, J. L. Sanchez-Lopez, S. Saripalli, and P. Campoy. Computer vision based general object following for GPS-denied multirotor unmanned vehicles. In *2014 American Control Conference*, pages 1886–1891. IEEE, 2014.

[44] Phasespace motion capture. http://www.phasespace.com/impulse-motion-capture.html.

[45] B. D. Rao and K. Hari. Performance analysis of root-MUSIC. *IEEE Transactions on Acoustics, Speech, and Signal Processing*, 37(12):1939–1949, 1989.

[46] H. Ren. On the error analysis and implementation of some eigenvalue decomposition and singular value decomposition. 1996.

[47] R. Rysdyk. UAV path following for constant line-of-sight. In *2th AIAA Unmanned Unlimited. Conf. and Workshop and Exhibit, San Diego, CA*, 2003.

[48] R. O. Schmidt. A signal subspace approach to multiple emitter location spectral estimation. *Ph. D. Thesis, Stanford University*, 1981.

[49] M. Schoor and B. Yang. High-resolution angle estimation for an automotive FMCW radar sensor. In *Proc. of Intern. Radar Symposium (IRS), Cologne, Germany*, 2007.

[50] D. E. Seborg, D. A. Mellichamp, T. F. Edgar, and F. J. Doyle III. *Process dynamics and control*. John Wiley & Sons, 2010.

[51] S. Sen, J. Lee, K.-H. Kim, and P. Congdon. Avoiding multipath to revive inbuilding WiFi localization. In *Proceeding of the 11th annual international conference on Mobile systems, applications, and services*, pages 249–262. ACM, 2013.

[52] P. Sujit, S. Saripalli, and J. B. Sousa. Unmanned aerial vehicle path following: A survey and analysis of algorithms for fixed-wing unmanned aerial vehicless. *IEEE Control Systems*, 34(1):42–59, 2014.

[53] D. Vasisht, S. Kumar, and D. Katabi. Decimeter-level localization with a single WiFi access point. In *13th USENIX Symposium on Networked Systems Design and Implementation (NSDI 16)*, pages 165–178, 2016.

[54] J. Wang, D. Vasisht, and D. Katabi. RF-IDraw: virtual touch screen in the air using RF signals. In *Proc. of ACM SIGCOMM*, 2014.

[55] W. Wang, A. X. Liu, and K. Sun. Device-free gesture tracking using acoustic signals. In *Proceedings of the 22nd Annual International Conference on Mobile Computing and Networking*, pages 82–94. ACM, 2016.

[56] T. Wei and X. Zhang. mTrack: high precision passive tracking using millimeter wave radios. In *Proc. of ACM MobiCom*, 2015.

[57] P. Wenig, M. Schoor, O. Gunther, B. Yang, and R. Weigel. System design of a 77 ghz automotive radar sensor with superresolution DOA estimation. In *2007 International Symposium on Signals, Systems and Electronics*, pages 537–540. IEEE, 2007.

[58] Y. Xie, Z. Li, and M. Li. Precise power delay profiling with commodity WiFi. In *Proceedings of the 21st Annual International Conference on Mobile Computing and Networking*, pages 53–64. ACM, 2015.

[59] J. Xiong and K. Jamieson. Arraytrack: A fine-grained indoor location system. In *Proc. of NSDI*, pages 71–84, 2013.

[60] J. Xiong, K. Sundaresan, and K. Jamieson. Tonetrack: Leveraging frequency-agile radios for time-based indoor wireless localization. In *Proceedings of the 21st Annual International Conference on Mobile Computing and Networking*, pages 537–549. ACM, 2015.

[61] S. Yun, Y. chao Chen, and L. Qiu. Turning a mobile device into a mouse in the air. In *Proc. of ACM MobiSys*, May 2015.

[62] Z. Zhang, D. Chu, X. Chen, and T. Moscibroda. Swordfight: Enabling a new class of phone-to-phone action games on commodity phones. In *Proc. of ACM MobiSys*, 2012.

[63] C. Zhou, F. Haber, and D. L. Jaggard. A resolution measure for the MUSIC algorithm and its application to plane wave arrivals contaminated by coherent interference. *IEEE Transactions on signal processing*, 39(2):454–463, 1991.

iBlink: Smart Glasses for Facial Paralysis Patients

Sijie Xiong†, Sujie Zhu†, Yisheng Ji†, Binyao Jiang†, Xiaohua Tian†,
Xuesheng Zheng‡, Xinbing Wang†
†School of Electronic, Info. & Electrical Engineering, Shanghai Jiao Tong University, China
‡Xin Hua Hospital Affiliated to Shanghai Jiao Tong University School of Medicine, China
†{qq420778733, zhusujie, acetanil, emberspirit, xtian, xwang8}@sjtu.edu.cn,
‡pheiphei@126.com

ABSTRACT

Facial paralysis makes patients lose their facial movements, which can incur eye damage even blindness since patients are incapable of blinking. The paralysis usually occurs on just one side of the face, and clinical trials show that electrical stimulation could trigger blink. Based on such observations, we design and implement a pair of smart glasses *iBlink* to assist facial paralysis patients to blink. The basic idea is to monitor the normal side of the face with a camera and stimulate the paralysed side, so that the blink of the both eyes become symmetric. To the best of our knowledge, this is the first piece of wearable device for facial paralysis therapy.

Our contributions are: First, we propose an eye-blink detection mechanism based on deep convolutional neural network (CNN), which can detect asymmetric blinks of patients under various illumination conditions with an accuracy above 99%. Our eye-image library for training CNN models is published online for further related studies, which contains more than 30,000 eye images. Second, we design and implement an automatic stimulation circuits to generate electrical impulse for stimulating the patient's facial nerve branches, which can configure operational parameters in a self-adaptive manner for different patients. Third, we implement the entire *iBlink* system, which integrates the two functions above and a communication function module for tele-medicine applications. Moreover, we conduct clinical trials in a hospital, in order to obtain the design basis and verify effectiveness of our device.

CCS Concepts

•**Computer systems organization** → *Sensors and actuators;*

Keywords

Smart glasses; facial paralysis vfill

Permission to make digital or hard copies of all or part of this work for personal or classroom use is granted without fee provided that copies are not made or distributed for profit or commercial advantage and that copies bear this notice and the full citation on the first page. Copyrights for components of this work owned by others than ACM must be honored. Abstracting with credit is permitted. To copy otherwise, or republish, to post on servers or to redistribute to lists, requires prior specific permission and/or a fee. Request permissions from permissions@acm.org.

MobiSys'17, June 19-23, 2017, Niagara Falls, NY, USA
© 2017 ACM. ISBN 978-1-4503-4928-4/17/06...$15.00
DOI: http://dx.doi.org/10.1145/3081333.3081343

1. INTRODUCTION

Facial paralysis is a disease making people losing facial movements, which is caused by nerve damage. People suffering from facial paralysis usually have muscles on one side of the face noticeably droop, which seriously impacts the person's quality of life. What is worse, facial paralysis can incur eye damage even blindness, because the eyelid on the affected side can not fully close, which makes the eye dry and infected by debris. The most common form of facial paralysis is known as Bell's palsy, which impacts 40,000 people in U.S. each year, where the typical symptom is the muscle dysfunction on one side of the face [1,27].

Most Bell's palsy patients will completely recover in around 6 months with or without medical treatment; however, a few cases of facial paralysis patients could never completely return to normal. The current treatments for Bell's palsy include drugs and surgery, which is of side effect and controversial, respectively [1].

Efforts have been dedicated to find the cause of Bell's palsy; however, the exact cause is still unknown [1]. To the best of scientists' knowledge, the paralysis is due to the pressure incurred by infection in the tunnel containing main trunk of facial nerves, where the tunnel is inside of the people's head termed as the *Facial canal.* An interesting phenomenon corroborating the theory is: using electric current of $3 - 11mA$ to stimulate the facial nerve branches could make the eye closing for most of patients, which indicates that the facial muscle and nerve branches are still working.

In this paper, we propose to use wearable device to improve the facial paralysis patient's quality of life. In particular, we design and implement a pair of smart glasses *iBlink* to assist facial paralysis patients to blink. To the best of our knowledge, this is the first piece of wearable device for facial paralysis therapy. The basic idea of *iBlink* is to monitor the normal side of the face with a camera and stimulate the paralysed side, so that the blink of both sides of the face could become symmetric. As wearable devices such as Google glass are widely accepted, wearing *iBlink* could conceal the patient's defect and help them live like a normal people. Our contributions are as following:

First, we propose an eye-blink detection mechanism based on convolutional neural network (CNN), which can detect not only movements of eyes such as closing, opening and blink but also asymmetric blinks of facial paralysis patients under various lighting conditions even at night (§4.2). We collected more than 26,000 eye images under different illumination conditions and more than 7,750 images under infrared (IR) lights from 12 different people to train the CNN models. The detection accuracies for daytime and nighttime are both above 99%. We publish the image library to support further related studies on facial paralysis [2].

Second, we design and implement an automatic stimulation circuits to generate electrical impulse for stimulating the user's facial nerve branches (§5). The circuits are controlled by a self-adaptive control mechanism, which accommodates individual and environment diversity. In particular, the circuit can elevate stimulation level incrementally until an appropriate level is found for a specific user. We also implement a pain control protection scheme, so that the possible pain incurred by over stimulation can be avoided (§6.1); moreover, the circuits can also automatically switch to different modes according to illumination conditions (§6.1). Further, we develop an approach to derive a person's blink frequency, so that the sampling frequency for anomaly detection can be adjusted for power saving (§6.2). Experiments show that the iBlink system could continuously work in the highest power consumption level for at least 10 hours with a lithium battery pack.

Third, we implement the entire *iBlink* system, which integrates the mechanism mentioned above and a communication function module for tele-medicine applications (§7). The related computing and control mechanisms are hosted in a Raspberry PI Zero [35] platform, which connects other hardware components such as camera and stimulation circuits. We conduct clinical trials in a hospital with our device, which enables us to obtain the design basis of *iBlink* and verify the effectiveness of our device (§9.4).

2. BACKGROUND AND MOTIVATION

Facial paralysis. A person's facial muscles are controlled by facial nerves, and a facial paralysis sufferer has a dysfunction in the facial nerve system, thus loses the facial movements. The left part of Fig. 1 shows a man with Bell's palsy on his right side of the face tries to raise his eyebrows and show his teeth [3]. It is clear that the facial muscles on his right side of face cannot move. The right part of Fig. 1 shows the anatomy of facial nerves based on [4]. The yellow and orange curves represent facial nerves of the left and right side of the face, respectively. The lesions typically occur at or beyond the stylomastoid foramen to the facial canal, which is a canal between the stylomastoid foramen and the internal acoustic meatus as shown in the right part of Fig. 1. Facial nerve branches are usually still working.

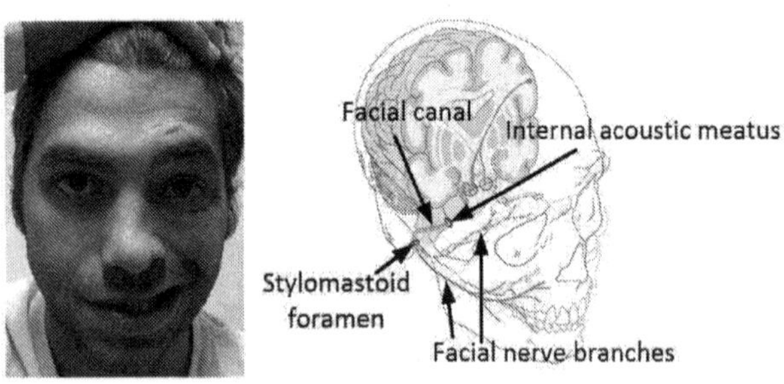

Figure 1: Anatomy of facial nerves.

The basic aim of facial rehabilitation is facial symmetry at rest and when facial expressions are performed [21]. Eye protection plays a crucial role, since patients could not blink, which makes the eye lack of moisture and protection. The incurred complications such as corneal ulcer and lagophthalmos could further cause blindness. In clinical cases, doctors provide different treatments especially towards eye care based on an individual's expectation for recovery, degree of risk to the cornea and eye weakness [1,9,22].

Since a majority of Bell's palsy patients will completely recover in around 6 months, they normally take *supportive measures*, which include lubrication with artificial tears, ocular ointments and taping of the eyelid [30]. However, moisture chemicals has high risk of surface toxicity and tapes may touch the cornea or conjunctiva, which incur further trauma. *Static or dynamic surgical procedures* could be operated on prolonged and permanent paralysis sufferers. Nevertheless, such procedures involve complicated medical techniques and complications, which increase pain of patients [24,28,29,31].

Electrical stimulation. Transcutaneous electrical stimulation (TENS) is taken by physiotherapists as an option for enhancing recovery in patients with facial paralysis [6,7,10], which is to apply electrical stimulation to facial nerves without breaking the facial skin. The electrical stimulation has been proved safe and does not interfere with recovery [6,11,25].

An interesting observation of electrical stimulation is: the appropriate electrical stimulation could make people blink if the facial nerve branches are not damaged. We conduct an experiment in a hospital to verify the effect, as shown in Fig. 2. The device in the left sub-figure is a Medtronic Keypoint electromyography (EMG) workstation [8], which is used to evaluate and record the electrical activity produced by skeletal muscles. The EMG workstation can generate electric current impulses, which can be directed to the person's facial skin through a pair of electrodes as shown in the middle sub-figure. By appropriately configure the strength, width and frequency of the impulse, the impulse can induce a person with functional facial nerve branches to blink as shown in the right sub-figure, where the right eye of the person is smaller than the left one as the right eye is to blink when the picture is taken.

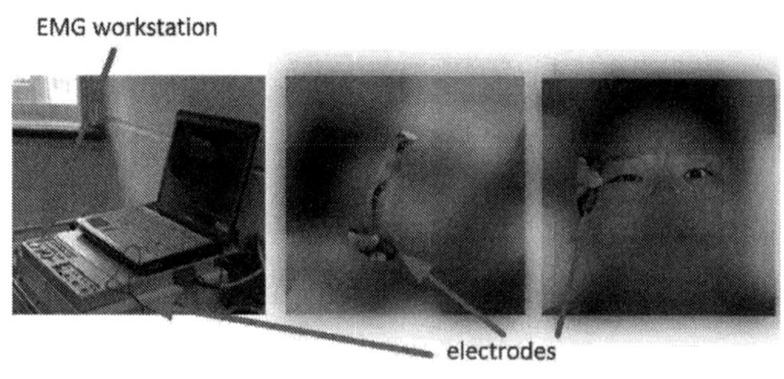

Figure 2: Electrical stimulation induced blink.

Motivation. Our work in this paper is motivated by the electrical stimulation approach for facial paralysis treatment, and the observations of facial paralysis' characteristics. Since paralysis usually occurs in one side of the face and the facial nerve branches are usually functioning, we could use electrical stimulation to make the paralyzed side to move accordingly to make the both sides of the face symmetric. In particular, the electrodes could be applied to nerve branches controlling blinks, so that the eye damage could be avoided. These functions could be implemented in a wearable smart glasses for the user's convenience, which could improve their quality of life before the paralysis goes away completely. Moreover, the electrical stimulation approach is non-invasive, thus the device could be considered as health care products as facemasks according to the FDA regulations [5], which avoids the all-consuming license application procedures for implanting devices.

3. DESIGN AND CHALLENGES

The architecture design of *iBlink* is shown in Fig. 3, which includes hardware and software function modules.

Hardware. A camera is installed in front of the eyes to monitor blinks in real time. The eye camera captures images of both eyes and send them to the Raspberry PI Zero platform, which also monitors the ambient lighting condition. The Raspberry PI Zero and stimulation circuits are located on the patient's paralyzed side of the face. In particular, the Raspberry PI Zero and stimulation circuits are in the outer side of the glass frame, and two stimulating electrodes are in the inner side of the frame pressing on the patient's facial skin. The Raspberry PI Zero has Wi-Fi and Bluetooth interfaces which can be utilized for communication with smartphones. A power unit supports both the processing platform and the stimulation circuits. Our circuits also contain a potentiometer as the pain switch, which could fine-tuning the automatic stimulation level control scheme. This is to accommodate individual diversity in case of discomfort.

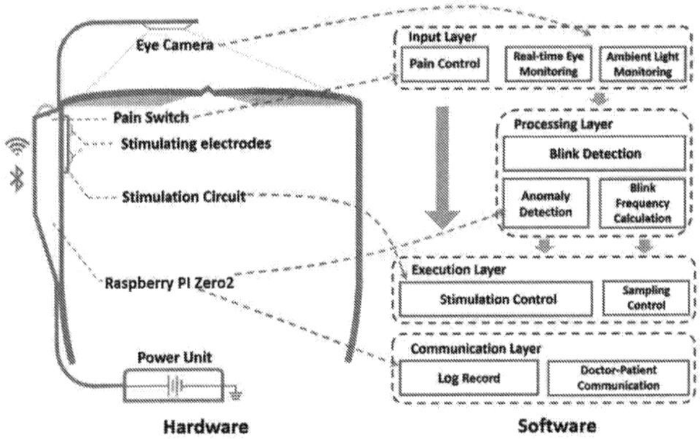

Figure 3: Design of the iBlink system

Software. The software consists of four layers: input layer, processing layer, execution layer and communication layer. The input layer receives the input images and ambient illumination data from the camera and pain control action from the pain switch. The images and illumination data are sent to the processing layer for operation model selection, blink detection, anomaly detection and blink frequency calculation. The execution layer contains stimulation control and sampling control. The stimulation control takes in the result of detections and calculations from the processing layer to adjust the electric stimulation parameters for the patient automatically. It also responds to patients' actions on the pain switch. The sampling control takes in results from the processing layer and adjusts the sampling frequency of the camera. When a doctor needs to acquire the patient's pathology data or the patient needs to report the pathology records, they can transmit data via the communication layer. The communication layer can support both Wi-Fi and Bluetooth transmissions.

Challenges. First, the system has to accommodate individual diversity. The EMG clinical trials show that different patients require different configurations of the stimulation impulse to enable blinking. The blink frequencies of different people also vary, which makes efficient blinking detection difficult. Moreover, the paralysis could make muscles around the eye droop in different degrees for different patients, which also incurs difficulties for detecting asymmetric blinks.

Second, the system has to accommodate environment changing. The patient's current conditions are monitored by the camera, thus illumination conditions could significantly influence the accuracy of the detection layer; however, the illumination conditions could change due to people's mobility and time changing. Such an un-static factor also imposes the challenge to facial expression detection.

Third, the system has to be power efficient. This is the challenge for all mobile devices. In our case, we need to lower the frequency of the power-consuming electrical impulses as much as possible. The stimulation circuits generate electrical impulses at the frequency of blink detection, while the camera has to monitor movements of the eyes at a high sampling rate to avoid information loss, which makes the sampling control a difficult trade-off and the power saving a noticeable challenge.

4. FACIAL IMAGE PROCESSING

4.1 Working Procedure

Facial image processing provides basis for blink detection, anomaly detection and blink frequency calculation, where the procedure is shown in Fig. 4. The system needs to detect whether an eye is blinking. The event that the healthy eye is blinking and the other eye is not can be detected by the anomaly detection module, which initiates the stimulation circuits. By analyzing the sequence of blink detection, the system could estimate the patient's blink frequency, so that an appropriate sampling frequency for the camera could be obtained.

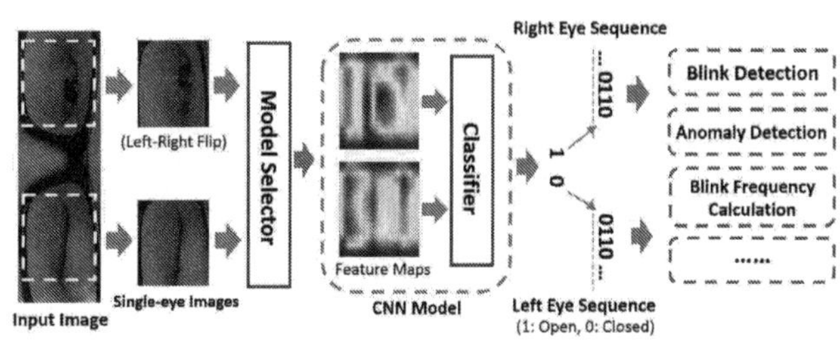

Figure 4: Workflow of facial image processing

In particular, we use two fixed windows to cut the single-eye images from the camera input for each image frame captured by the eye camera. We train the CNN model with images of the left eye and the right-to-left flip of the right eye, so that we could use just one CNN model to detect status of two eyes. Considering different illumination conditions, we train two CNN models for daytime and night-time with IR scenarios. The model selector is to decide the images are to be processed by the model for which illumination condition. We find the threshold of model selection through experiments, which are to be introduced in Section 9 in detail. With the extracted CNN features, we implement a classifier acting as a solver of the two-class classification problem, which labels 0 as eye closure and 1 as eye opening. A sequence of such labels could be used for detecting different events.

4.2 Deep Convolutional Neural Network

We use deep learning for image processing due to its robustness. Facial paralysis patients' eyes could sometimes be half-way open, slanted or in other more complicated shapes, thus eye images with the same 'open' label can vary greatly. Moreover, illumination, personal difference and expression can add diversity to eye images, making labeling eye images more difficult. Since high precision for our medical device is a must, we need a robust model to achieve high accuracy and high computation efficiency with different persons and under different conditions. Considering such requirements, we choose deep convolutions neural network (CNN) [17]. The details of our CNN network structure is shown in Fig. 5. We train our CNN using the deep learning framework Caffe [14].

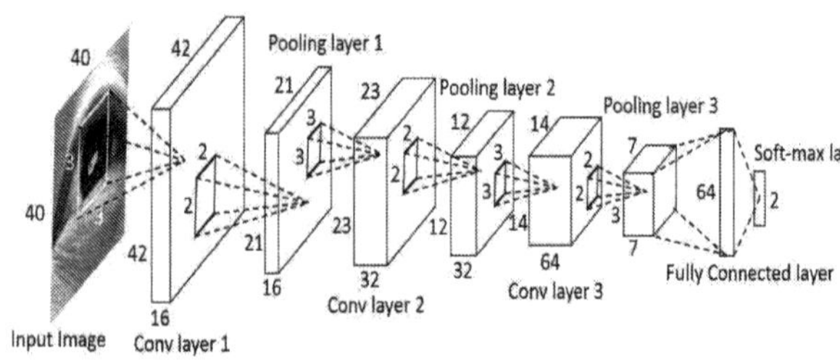

Figure 5: CNN structure

Our CNN consists of three convolutional layers and one fully connected layer. Each convolutional layer is followed by a max-pooling layer. For each convolutional layer we extract the convolved feature of previous layer's output with a linear filter. We apply multiple filters with weights W^k and bias b^k to obtain multiple feature maps. For each feature map F^k at layer k, its values are obtained by:

$$F_{ij}^k = \sigma(W^k \times x_{ij} + b^k), \quad (1)$$

where σ is a non-linear operator and x_{ij} is the input. After the convolutional layer, each feature map is sampled by the pooling layer to lower the dimension. We use the max-pooling with a non-overlapping manner. We also use ReLU [15] layers after every convolutional layer and dropout [16] layer after the third convolutional layer to improve the performance. After extracting robust features, the Softmax Loss layer computes the probability vector for classifying the images. The input for our CNN is 40×40 single-eye images.

In order to reduce the effect of local expression and personal difference in eye shapes, and to cover different illumination conditions the patients will encounter in different daily scenarios, we collected 16,951 eye images under different daylight condition and 5,750 images under IR lights from 12 different people to train the CNN models. Due to the facial symmetry, we mirrored the eye images to augment the dataset and yield 33,902 training images. We used 10% of the training data for cross validation and the other 90% for training the deep convolutional neural networks. The training accuracies for daytime and nighttime model are 99.5% and 99.1%, respectively. We also collected another 12,000 eye images under 6 different illumination conditions for testing the two CNN models. The testing accuracies will be shown in the performance evaluation section.

4.3 Blink Detection and Anomaly Detection

After we have the eye status sequence, we define a blink sequence as a short status sequence in the form of '1,0,1', which means the eye opens, then closes and opens again. Since a normal blink takes about 200ms to 400ms and our sampling rate is 20 to 30 frames per second, there could be multiple frames captured in a normal blink process. Multiple 1s and 0s can appear in a blink sequence, e.g., '1100011'. The adjustable sampling rate of iBlink ensures that there will be at least three consecutive 0s in a normal blink sequence. Since there could be false detection on the eye status, we introduce a polling method to correctly identify a blink action. For each detection we take N_p sampling results in the eye status sequence in a sliding-window manner. If 0s are the majority in the poll, a blink will be identified. The polling method makes our system tolerant of detection exceptions in the eye status. The value of N_p is empirically set to 3 in our system.

The blink detection will be applied to both left and right eye sequences simultaneously. In most cases, people close and open their eyes at the same time, while a facial paralysis patient usually cannot close their eye on the ill-side. Consequently, if the blink detection gives a different result on two eye status sequences, we define it as an anomaly. Once an anomaly is detected, iBlink will give the patient an electrical stimulation through sending out a signal through GPIO interface of the Raspberry PI Zero.

5. STIMULATION CIRCUITS

The stimulation circuits are consisted of an amplifying circuit and a level control circuit. The amplifying circuit takes in pulse width modulation (PWM) waves from the Raspberry Pi Zero and amplifies them to generate the stimulation output on the stimulating electrodes. The level control circuit implements 16 different output stimulation levels on the stimulating electrodes by adjusting the power level of the amplified PWM waves according to the control signals from the Raspberry Pi Zero and the input from the pain switch. The working procedure of the stimulation circuits is shown in Fig. 6.

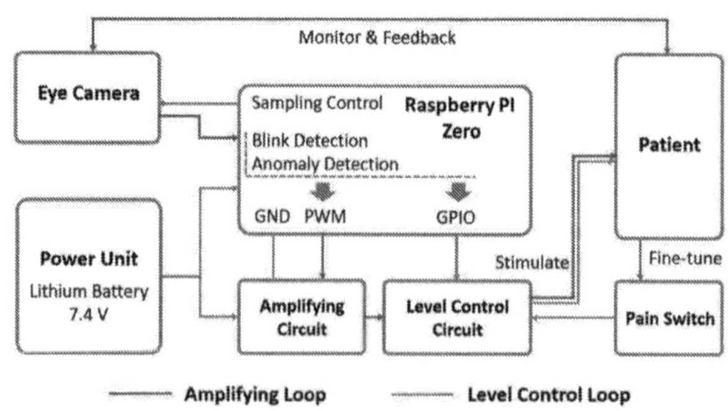

Figure 6: Workflow of the stimulation module.

The amplifying circuit takes in 3.3V PWM waves from the Raspberry PI Zero and 7.4V power input from the power unit. In the red amplifying loop, the camera monitors the feedback of the patient after every stimulation. The Raspberry PI Zero sends out the PWM waves according to the result of blink detection and anomaly detection. And the amplifying circuit amplifies the PWM waves to output between 100V to 200V on the stimulating electrodes. The level control circuit takes in the GPIO signals and the fine-tuned pain switch input to adjust the level of the stimulation, which is shown in the level control loop.

Amplifying circuit. The amplifying circuit contains three bipolar junction transistors (BJTs), one transformer and several resistances to amplify the PWM waves from the Raspberry PI Zero. The lithium battery pack provides 7.4V power supply to the circuit, and a pair of finely placed stimulating electrodes are used to stimulate the patient's facial nerve branches. The implementation of the amplifying circuit is shown in the left part of Fig. 7.

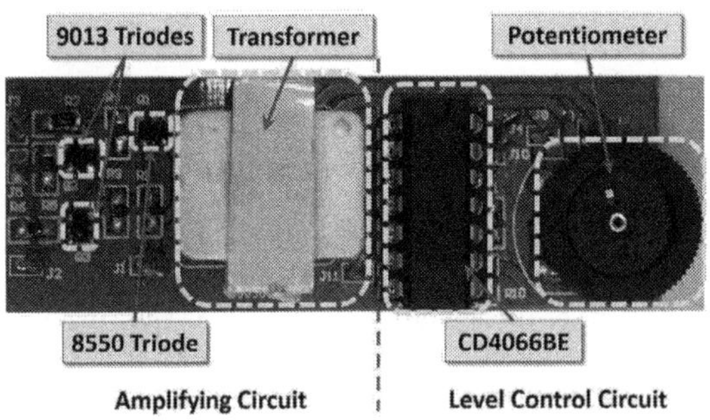

Figure 7: Circuit implementation.

We use 9013 NPN BJT triode [32] in the circuit, which is a kind of NPN low power triode mainly used for audio amplification and radio 1W push-pull output. The type of the PNP BJT is 8550 [33], which is characterized by small signal, low voltage and high current and is mainly used in switches and RF amplification. The transformer amplifies the 3.3V PWM waves to about 200V output. Altough the instantaneous voltage is very high, the stimulation is safe since the high voltage lasts only in about 3 ms. For stimulating electrodes, we use electrodes made of conductive ointment, which can be finely attached to human skin and have good electrical conductivity. The distance between the two stimulating electrodes is set to be 3.3 cm, which is chosen empirically from our experiments and clinical trials to invoke the best stimulation reactions. Those conductive ointment electrodes can be easily changed for maintenance purpose on a regular basis.

Level control circuit. The level control circuit is shown in the right part of Fig. 7. It consists of a bilateral switch chip CD4066BE [34] and a potentiometer. The bilateral switch chip takes in GPIO control signals from Raspberry PI Zero and changes the output voltage level of the stimulating electrodes by switching resistances to different values. In our circuit, we implement 16 stimulation levels for the output. We also use a potentiometer as a pain switch to allow patients to adjust the output voltage manually. The potentiometer is designed to adjust the voltage only within one stimulation level in case of misoperation.

Due to unpredictable factors such as temperature, humidity and shape of human skin, conductivity of the skin varies not only among different people but also in different time and places. It is impossible to accurately set the stimulation intensity to a fixed value; our level control circuit provides both automatic stimulation level selection and manual fine-tuning capabilities.

6. AUTOMATIC CONTROL MECHANISM

6.1 Stimulation Control

Requirements analysis. First, the conductivity of human skin varies in different situations as mentioned in the previous section, so people can have different thresholds for stimulation. We conduct clinical experiments on 5 volunteers in a hospital with the EMG workstation. The equipment we use in the hospital measures the stimulation intensity by electric current. Table. 1 shows the critical points for stimulation reactions of different patients. The values of the electric current thresholds are found by manually increasing the value by a stride of 0.1 mA, which is inconvenient and inefficient. There is a need of a mechanism that can automatically and efficiently find patients' critical points of stimulation.

Table 1: Measurement of critical points on different people

Label	Gender	Age	Critical Point (mA)
1	Female	42	5.7
2	Male	19	10.6
3	Male	35	7.0
4	Male	28	6.4
5	Female	22	4.5

Second, patients wear the iBlink on a daily basis, where the electric stimulations are applied to the patients according to the result of real-time image processing. Since the status of a human body and the surrounding environment can be changing in different times of a day, dynamically adjusting the stimulation parameters is a practical need.

Third, since human facial skin is very sensitive, in case of discomfort or pain, the iBlink needs to adjust the stimulation parameters in time according to the real-time feedback from the patients. Thus, automatic stimulation control is a must for our medical device.

Mechanism design and implementation. We define four working modes for the iBlink system:

- **Startup Mode:** When the patient wears the device for the first time and turns on the system, the iBlink automatically searches for a lowest stimulation level that can invoke an eye-closing reaction. The corresponding stimulation voltage is recorded for future use.
- **Daytime Mode:** The iBlink works in this mode when the illumination condition is good. This is the basic mode that runs in majority time of a day.
- **Nighttime Mode:** When the illumination intensity is low, iBlink starts the infrared lights and use the nighttime CNN for image processing.
- **Pain Control Mode:** This mode runs concurrently with the other four modes. Once receives the patient's signal, the iBlink automatically decreases the stimulation level to avoid pain by over stimulating.

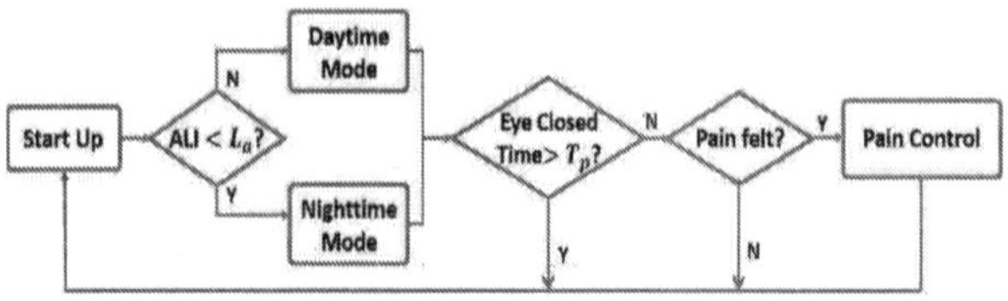

Figure 8: Working flow of automatic control mechanism.

Figure. 8 shows the workflow of the automatic stimulation control, where ALI means ambient light intensity, T_p is the pain threshold. The automatic stimulation control mechanism relies mainly on the input of illumination data and blink detection results. In the startup mode, the stimulation level starts from 0 and increases incrementally. The eye camera monitors the feedback of the patient's eyes. If there is no blink resulting from the stimulation, the stimulation level continues to rise, until it reaches the level that causes an eye-closing reaction. The eye camera also monitors the illumination data, with which a model selector can switch between daytime mode and nighttime mode. In the nighttime mode, the infrared lights are turned on automatically. The infrared component emits the invisible light, which however reports no sense of uncomfort either in the test on our own or in the experiments on volunteers. In case of discomfort or pain, which means there exists an over stimulating situation, the patient can give a signal by closing the healthy-side eye for a certain length of time. This triggers the pain control mode and the stimulation level starts dropping, until a new critical level is found. The pain control algorithm is shown in Algorithm 1.

Algorithm 1 Pain Control Algorithm

Require: Control Threshold $\mathbf{C_T}$;Test times $\mathbf{k}$;
Minimum Level $\mathbf{Level_{min}}$;
Initial Level $\mathbf{Level_{init}}$;
Ensure: Level series changing with time **Level[]**

$\mathbf{k} \leftarrow 1$, $\mathbf{Level[k]} \leftarrow \mathbf{Level_{init}}$
$\mathbf{t_1} \leftarrow getSystemTime()$, $\mathbf{s_1} \leftarrow getEyeStatus()$
while True **do**
  $\mathbf{k} \leftarrow \mathbf{k}+1$
  $\mathbf{t_2} \leftarrow getSystemTime()$, $\mathbf{s_2} \leftarrow getEyeStatus()$
  if $\mathbf{s_2}$=Open **then**
    $\mathbf{s_1} \leftarrow \mathbf{s_2}$
    $\mathbf{Level[k]} \leftarrow \mathbf{Level[k-1]}$
  else
    if $\mathbf{s_1}$=Open **then**
      $\mathbf{t_1} \leftarrow \mathbf{t_2}$
      $\mathbf{s_1} \leftarrow Closed$
      $\mathbf{Level[k]} \leftarrow \mathbf{Level[k-1]}$
    else
      if $\mathbf{t_2} - \mathbf{t_1} > \mathbf{C_T}$ **then**
        $\mathbf{t_1} \leftarrow \mathbf{t_2}$
        $\mathbf{Level[k]} \leftarrow \mathbf{Level[k-1]} - 1$
        if $\mathbf{Level[k]} < \mathbf{Level_{min}}$ **then**
          $\mathbf{Level[k]} \leftarrow \mathbf{Level_{min}}$
        end if
      end if
    end if
  end if
end while

6.2 Sampling Control

Normally, people can keep their eyes open for about 2 seconds to 8 seconds and then close their eyes for about 0.2 seconds to 0.4 seconds. To capture the exact movement of patients' eyes, the camera sampling frequency should be neither over low to lose useful information nor over high to consume much power. In this section, we describe our adaptive sampling algorithm which automatically adjusts the system's sampling frequency.

Upper and lower bounds of sampling interval. We set the upper bound of sampling interval B_U to be 0.05 seconds, which ensures there will be at least 3 eye-closing images captured by the camera. Since the fastest sampling frequency of our camera is 30Hz, the lower bound of the sampling interval B_L is 0.033 seconds.

Adaptive sampling algorithm. Suppose the sampling interval is τ_s, it can be expressed as

$$\tau_s = B_L + (B_U - B_L)r, \quad (2)$$

where r is a factor with $0 < r < 1$. We calculate the blink interval τ_b by averaging the time of all neighboring points of the same status in the blink graph and aggregate them into one point. The blink graph is derived by applying the polling method to the eye status sequences during blink detection. In this way, all neighboring points on blink graph are of different status. The blink interval is the time interval between two neighboring points when the eye is open. The definition of the blink interval is defined in Fig. 9.

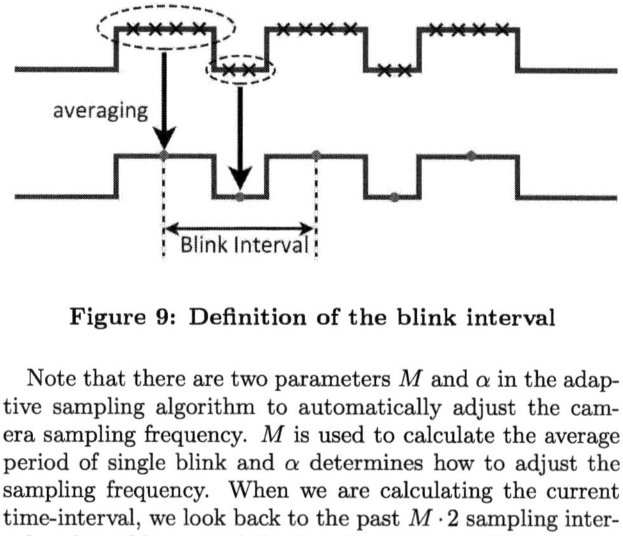

Figure 9: Definition of the blink interval

Note that there are two parameters M and α in the adaptive sampling algorithm to automatically adjust the camera sampling frequency. M is used to calculate the average period of single blink and α determines how to adjust the sampling frequency. When we are calculating the current time-interval, we look back to the past $M \cdot 2$ sampling intervals, where M is a predefined positive integer. We calculate the average of the early M blink intervals as $\bar{\tau_b^1}$ and the average of the other M intervals as $\bar{\tau_b^2}$. We set a empirical threshold τ_T and compare $\bar{\tau_b^1}$ with $\bar{\tau_b^2}$. Different events can be defined according to the comparison result:

- Advance Event: $\bar{\tau_b^2} - \bar{\tau_b^1} > \tau_T$, i.e., the increment of blink interval is larger than the threshold.
- Back-off Event: $\bar{\tau_b^1} - \bar{\tau_b^2} > \tau_T$, i.e., the decrement of blink interval is larger than the threshold.
- Stable Event: $|\bar{\tau_b^1} - \bar{\tau_b^2}| < \tau_T$, i.e., the change of blink interval is within the threshold.

If the Advance Event is detected, the iBlink increases the sampling frequency as the patient has the tendency to increase their blink frequency. If the Back-off Event is detected, the iBlink decreases the sampling frequency.

The new r under Advance Event can be calculated as

$$r = \hat{r} - \alpha_D \hat{r}, \tag{3}$$

where $0 < \alpha_D < 1$, $\hat{r}$ is the previous r and α_D is a constant factor controlling the rate at which r decreases.

The new r under Back-off Event can be calculated as

$$r = \hat{r} + \alpha_I (1 - \hat{r}), \tag{4}$$

where $0 < \alpha_I < 1$ and α_I is a constant factor controlling the rate at which r decreases.

The design of the formula makes r decrease slower and increase faster when it is small and increase slower and decrease faster when it is big. The parameter r will change the sampling interval accordingly. We set the initial value of r to be 0.5, which is empirically suitable for most of patients. The adaptive sampling algorithm is shown in Algorithm 2.

Algorithm 2 Adaptive Sampling Algorithm

Require: Lower bound of sampling interval $\mathbf{B_L}$;
Upper bound of sampling interval $\mathbf{B_U}$;
Parameter of sampling interval $\mathbf{r}$;
Increasing factor $\alpha_\mathbf{I}$; Decreasing factor $\alpha_\mathbf{D}$;
Turn count $\mathbf{t}$; Average window $\mathbf{M}$.
Ensure: All sample time $\mathbf{S}[]$;

$\mathbf{t} \leftarrow 1$, $\mathbf{r} \leftarrow 0.5$
$\tau_\mathbf{s} \leftarrow \mathbf{B_L} + (\mathbf{B_U} - \mathbf{B_L})\mathbf{r}$
$\mathbf{S[0]} \leftarrow 0$, $\mathbf{S[t]} \leftarrow \mathbf{S[t-1]} + \tau_\mathbf{s}$
while True **do**
  if t $geq2 \cdot M$ **then**
    $\tau_\mathbf{s}^\mathbf{1} \leftarrow 0$, $\tau_\mathbf{s}^\mathbf{2} \leftarrow 0$
    for $i = 0 \rightarrow M$ **do**
      $\tau_\mathbf{s}^\mathbf{1} \leftarrow \tau_\mathbf{s}^\mathbf{1} + S[t - 2M + i] - S[t - 2M + i - 1]$
      $\tau_\mathbf{s}^\mathbf{2} \leftarrow \tau_\mathbf{s}^\mathbf{2} + S[t - M + i] - S[t - M + i - 1]$
    end for
    $\bar{\tau_\mathbf{s}^\mathbf{1}} \leftarrow \tau_\mathbf{s}^\mathbf{1}/M$, $\bar{\tau_\mathbf{s}^\mathbf{2}} \leftarrow \tau_\mathbf{s}^\mathbf{2}/M$
    if $\bar{\tau_\mathbf{s}^\mathbf{2}} - \bar{\tau_\mathbf{s}^\mathbf{1}} > \tau_T$ **then**
      $\mathbf{r} \leftarrow \mathbf{r} - \alpha_\mathbf{D}\mathbf{r}$
    else if $\bar{\tau_\mathbf{s}^\mathbf{1}} - \bar{\tau_\mathbf{s}^\mathbf{2}} > \tau_T$ **then**
      $\mathbf{r} \leftarrow \mathbf{r} + \alpha_\mathbf{I}(1 - \mathbf{r})$
    end if
  end if
  $\tau_\mathbf{s} \leftarrow \mathbf{B_L} + (\mathbf{B_U} - \mathbf{B_L})\mathbf{r}$
  $\mathbf{t} \leftarrow \mathbf{t} + 1$
  $\mathbf{S[t]} \leftarrow \mathbf{S[t-1]} + \tau_\mathbf{s}$
end while

7. COMMUNICATION BETWEEN THE PATIENT AND THE DOCTOR

We develop an APP to enable the iBlink system to be linked to the smart phone. The APP could collect and analyze data of the patients and send the derived information to the doctor. The doctor can request different analyzed data from the patients' devices. The communication module leverages the Wi-Fi interface of Raspberry PI Zero. The screenshots of the APP is shown in Fig. 10, from left to right is the data request page, data analysis page and its zoomed in view.

The three buttons on the data request page stand for three ways to transmit data. The "Hour" button starts a thread to request all the current day's saved data from the patient, stores them in a file and append newly collected data to the file every hour. The "Day" button will request the previous day's data and save them in a file. The "All" button will request all the data on the server and save them in files identified by date.

The data analysis page shows the blink data in a blink graph and gives data analysis result, *e.g.* blink times per day, minimum blink interval and maximum blink interval. The data are recorded to help doctors to better study the patients' pathology features.

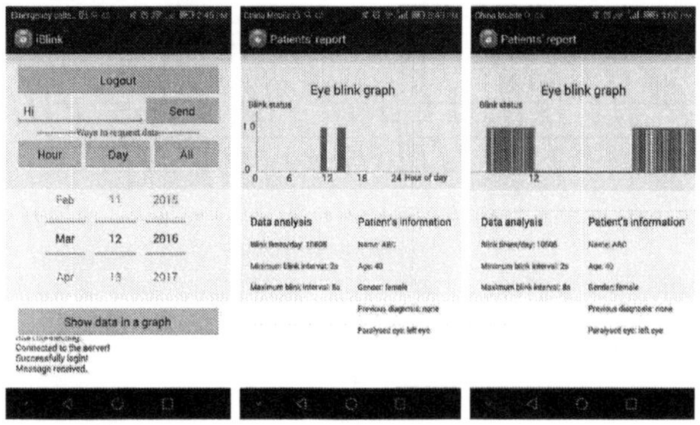

(a) (b) (c)

Figure 10: (a) Data request page. (b) Data analysis page. (c) Data analysis page (Zoomed in).

Since sometimes intervals of blinks can be useless, like when the eye is closed due to sleep or rest for a long time, we devise a way to detect effective time interval during a day. If any time interval between two blinks is longer than a predefined value, that interval will be discarded and not be stored in the record. The process is illustrated in Fig. 11. The predefined value is empirically chosen to be 10 seconds.

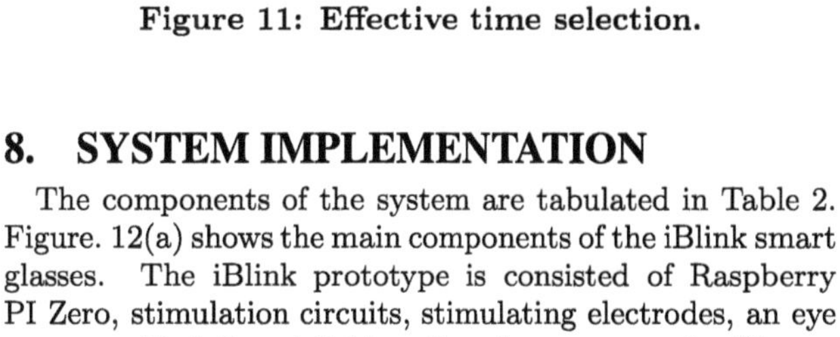

Figure 11: Effective time selection.

8. SYSTEM IMPLEMENTATION

The components of the system are tabulated in Table 2. Figure. 12(a) shows the main components of the iBlink smart glasses. The iBlink prototype is consisted of Raspberry PI Zero, stimulation circuits, stimulating electrodes, an eye camera with infrared light unit and a power unit. We use Raspberry PI Zero as the main processor. The infrared light unit is installed on the USB eye camera and powered by the GPIO output from Raspberry PI Zero. We design our own stimulation circuits with amplifying and level control circuit embedded. The pain switch is implemented by a potentiometer to fine-tune the voltage output on the stimulating electrodes. The power unit is a 7.4V lithium battery pack and the adjustable regulator converts 7.4V to 5V to supply the Raspberry PI Zero. For wearing comfort and convenience, we design our own spectacles frame using the state-of-art 3D print machine to eliminate the complex structure of traditional frame. The components can easily be attached to the designed spectacles frame. Figure. 12(b) shows our wearable prototype.

Table 2: Components of the system

Component	Properties
Raspberry Pi Zero 2	1GHz CPU, 512MB RAM
Eye Camera	640 * 480, 30fps
CD4066BE	$-0.5V$ to $20V$, $\pm 10mA$
9013 triode	NPN, $I_{max} = 0.5A$, $625mW$
8550 triode	PNP, $I_{max} = 0.5A$, $625mW$

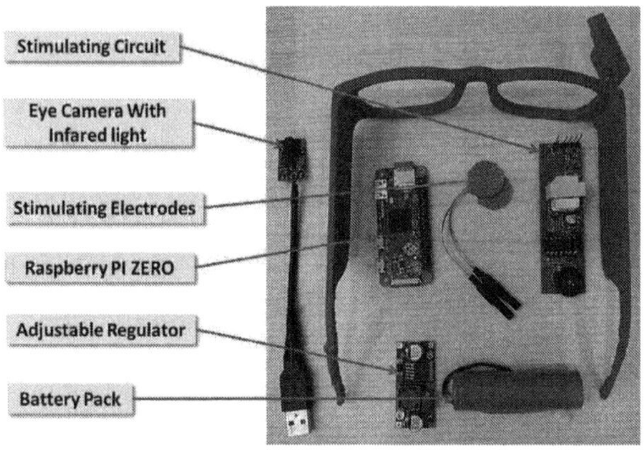

(a)

(b)

Figure 12: (a) The main components of iBlink. (b) The wearable prototype.

9. PERFORMANCE EVALUATION

9.1 Eye Status Detection

We first visualize the convolved feature maps for eye images with different status and illumination conditions, and then evaluate the performance of eye status detection by measuring the accuracy of the two CNN models.

Figure 13 shows open and closed eye images under different illumination conditions and the convolved feature maps for each image. Row (a) shows the open eye images in different scenarios and row (b) contains the convolved feature maps after the third convolutional layer in CNN. The closed eye images and their corresponding feature maps after the third convolutional layer of CNN are shown in row (c) and row (d). The six columns demonstrate 6 different scenarios under different illumination conditions. From left to right the average illumination intensities are: less than $10lx$, $10lx$, $20lx$, $50lx$, $100lx$ and more than $1500lx$. These illumination intensities corresponds to six major scenarios a patient will encounter in daily life. Column 1 corresponds to the night-time scenario and column 6 represents the outdoor scenario. Column 2-5 represent four different light condition in indoor scenarios: dark indoor spot, indoor on a cloudy day, room with dim light and indoor on a sunny day. For those different illumination conditions, we trained two CNN models, daytime and nighttime. The daytime model is used in outdoor scenario and indoor scenarios with sufficient light. The nighttime model is used at night and in some dark indoor scenarios with little illumination. The input images for the nighttime model are captured with the infrared lights on.

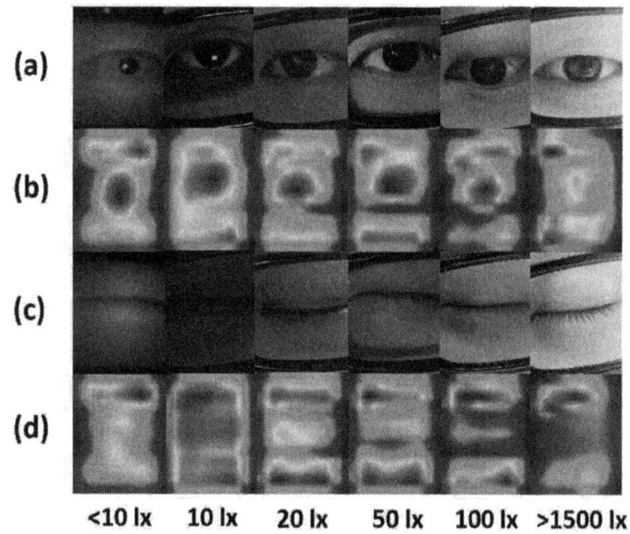

Figure 13: Eye images and convolved feature maps after the third convolutional layer.

In Fig. 13, the feature maps of open eye images in row (b) all have a circle-sized hot spot in the middle, which indicates the appearance of an eyeball, while in row (d) the closed eyes are indicated by a line figure in the feature maps.

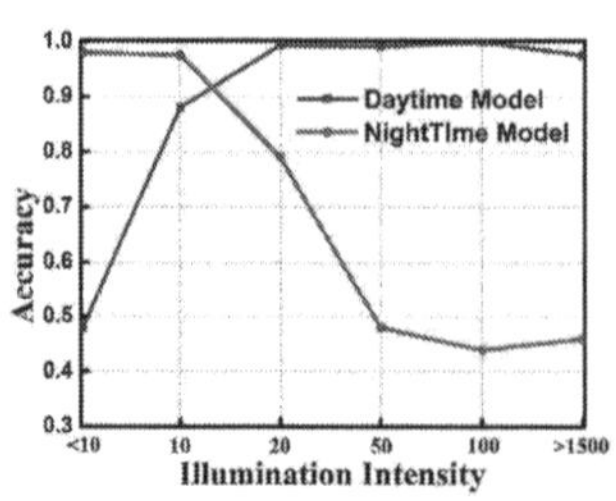

Figure 14: Eye status detection.

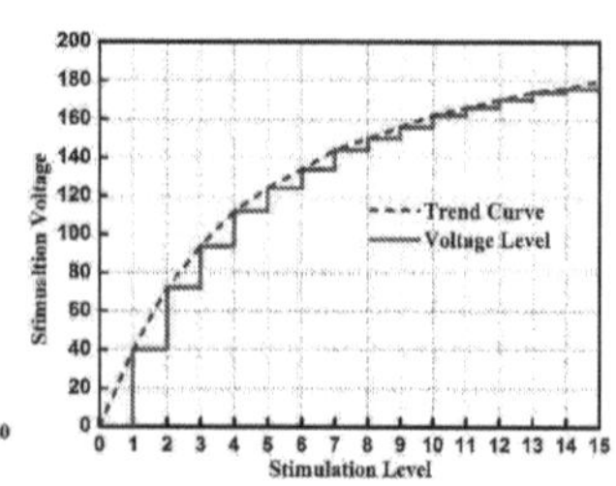

Figure 15: Voltage - Stimulation Level.

Note that in column 2 most values of the closed eye image's feature map are high, which can result in lower accuracy in the classification step. This is caused by low illumination intensity. To avoid the low accuracy, we set a threshold of $15lx$. Scenarios with lower than $15lx$ illumination intensity will be processed by the nighttime model.

Illumination is the main environment factor that influences our system's performance. We conduct experiments both in the laboratory and in the wild under different illumination conditions. The eye status detection accuracies of daytime model and nighttime model are shown in Fig. 14. We collected 500 open eye images and 500 closed eye images for each illumination condition in both normal and infrared version from 5 different people as the test data (12000 in total). With the illumination intensity over $20lx$, the daytime model's accuracy is very close to 100%. When the illumination condition reaches more than $1500lx$, the accuracy slightly drops due to the existence of some extreme cases, i.e., the illumination intensity reaches more than $10000lx$. Since those extreme cases are rare and unlikely, our daytime model satisfies patients' needs in daily scenarios. When the illumination intensity drops to under $20lx$, the nighttime model performs much better than the daytime model. In scenarios like dark indoor corners or corridors, the nighttime model can achieve an accuracy higher than 98%, which is 10% more than the daytime model. Due to the accuracy drop, we set a $15lx$ threshold for the model selector to ensure a high accuracy in different scenarios.

9.2 Automatic Stimulation Control

According to the clinical trial, a voltage between $100V$ to $200V$ can induce an eye-closing reaction. We divide the output voltage into 16 levels in our circuits, ranging from 0 to 184V. Figure 15 shows the output voltage for each stimulation level and the trend curve of the levels. In our circuit the stimulation levels do not divide the voltage range equally. The trend curve's slope tend to decrease when the stimulating level rises. We choose this level distribution since we need those levels with high voltages to increase slowly in case of discomfort or pain, while those with low voltages to increase fast to reach the critical point.

To test our stimulation control method in practice, we record the change of stimulation level by measuring the output voltage of the stimulating electrodes. Figure 16 shows the output stimulation level change we recorded. Our test covers all the scenarios we considered in the stimulation control. From time unit 0 to 12 is the startup phase. The stimulation level continues to rise according to the feedback from the eye camera. When it reaches the lowest level that can cause an eye-closing reaction, i.e., a critical point, the rising procedure stops and the voltage stabilizes on that stimulation level. Starting from time unit 13 to 18 is the first pain control phase. It is when the patient feels a mild pain and needs to fine-tune the voltage output. Note that the fine-tuning can increase or decrease the voltage in at most half range of the current stimulation level. The stimulation level eventually stabilizes on a voltage that is slightly smaller than the voltage of level 12.

At the 50th time unit the second pain control starts. In this pain control phase the patient feels a relatively strong pain and triggers the close-eye method. When iBlink detects the patient closes his eye for more than 3 seconds, the stimulation level starts dropping and stops at the first level that cannot invoke the eye-closing reaction. Then the level rises back by one to the new critical level that can cause the close eye reaction. The patient then fine-tunes the voltage by the pain switch. After time unit 100, the patient simulates falling asleep. The close-eye method is again triggered. The stimulation control attempts to drop the stimulation level every several time units. When the attempted stimulation level causes an eye-closing reaction, the voltage stabilizes at the lower level. By this method, the stimulation level is always kept on the lowest level that can cause a close-eye action.

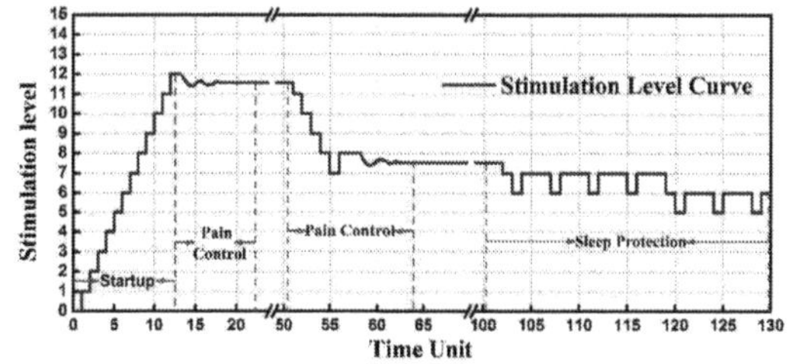

Figure 16: The change of stimulation level

9.3 Power Consumption

Power consumption is the crux of wearable devices and this also applies to iBlink. Our system uses a 7.4V lithium battery pack as the power unit, which provides power supply for both blink detection and stimulation subsystems. A natural question to ask is: how long the battery pack could support operations of the entire system. To answer this question, we conduct power consumption experiments and measure the voltage of the battery pack during the device's usage. In the experiment process, we activate the CNN based blink detection mechanisms all the time and set the highest stimulation level for the stimulation circuits. The voltage of the battery pack is measured every 10 minutes. The purpose of such a setup is to make the system operate in the highest power consumption level so that the worst case scenario can be examined. The experimental results are shown in Fig. 17, which presents how the voltage of the battery pack changes as the time goes on. It indicates that the 7.4 V lithium battery pack can support the system's operation in the worst power consumption scenario for at least 10 hours, which is sufficient for a patient's daytime use.

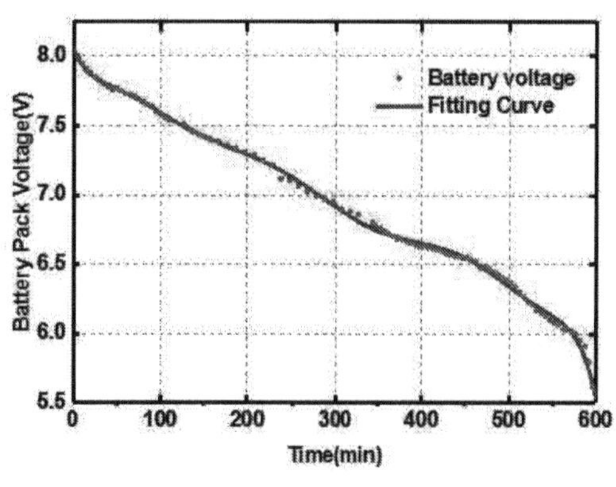

Figure 17: Power consumption.

(a)

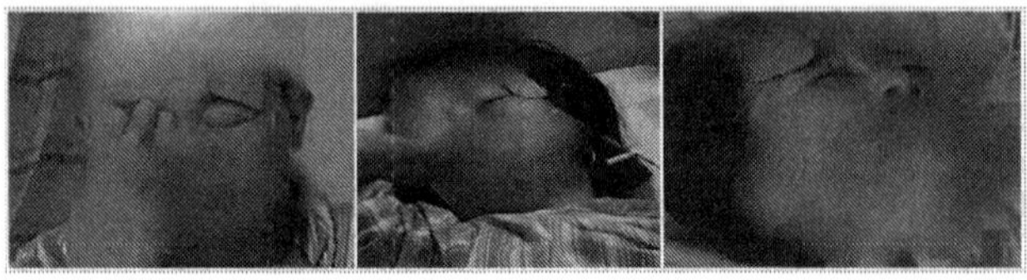

(b)

Figure 18: (a) Before stimulation. (b) After stimulation.

9.4 Experiments on Volunteers

We conduct experiments on volunteers in a hospital to verify the function of our system under the doctor's supervision. There are six volunteers testing the stimulation circuits. We illustrate the testing snapshots of some of the patients with their permission in Fig. 18 and Fig. 19. In the process as shown in Fig. 18, the donator sticks the brown ointment electrodes to the facial nerve branches near the abnormal eye as shown in Fig. 18(a). We increase the stimulation level gradually to manually simulate the Startup Mode until the eye is stimulated to close as shown in Fig. 18(b). Table. 3 shows the critical level for stimulation of corresponding patients. All of the six patients report no feeling of pain during the whole test and only the 43-aged female volunteer mentions a slight sense of tingling. All volunteer patients appreciate our work and believe the product is useful for facial paralysis patients.

Table 3: Critical stimulation levels of different patients

Label	Gender	Age	Critical stimulation level
1	Male	21	12
2	Male	22	13
3	Female	30	7
4	Male	35	7
5	Female	43	9
6	Female	59	11

Another middle-aged female patient volunteers to try our prototype as shown in Fig. 19. The left image in Fig. 19 is the patient's normal eye status. The camera is installed on the health left side of face and the electrodes are on the right side of her face, which is the paralyzed side. We can see that her right eye opens a little wider than the healthy side eye. The middle image is when the patient is closing her left eye while her right eye cannot be closed. This is when the iBlink sends out the stimulation signals. The right image in Fig. 19 is when the electric stimulation invokes an eye-closing reaction and the patient is able to close both of her eyes. The result of this trial proves that our device can satisfy the patient's requirement. Note that our iBlink prototype has updated after the clinical trials in the hospital. In Fig. 19 is the previous version of the iBlink and it is used for testing and data collection purpose. We upgraded the iBlink to the one as shown in Fig. 12.

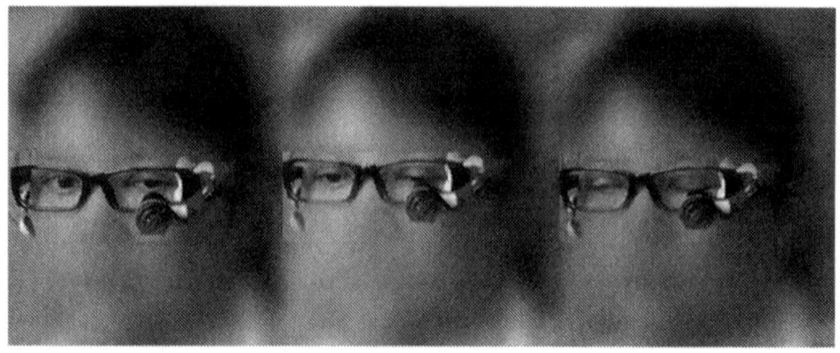

Figure 19: Experiment on Volunteers

10. RELATED WORK

Kim *et al.* propose to use smart phones to diagnose facial paralysis [26], where the 'asymmetric index' is proposed to evaluate the degree of asymmetry of both sides of the face. Through measuring the asymmetric index during different expressions like resting, eye-brow raising and smiling, the smartphone could help determine if the facial paralysis happens to the person. However, the diagnosis accuracy reaches only 89%, which still needs significant improvement. In contrast to the work just propose an approach to facilitate diagnosis of facial paralysis, we implement a wearable device to provide eye protection for paralysis patients.

Wearable computing devices such as Google glasses have been attracting much attention in recent years. Efforts have been dedicated to not only design and implement new types of glasses with interesting functions, but also utilize existing equipment to carry out jobs like data collection and analysis. *iGaze*[19] and *iShadow*[18] are representatives of smart glasses proposed recently. *iGaze* establishes person-to-person as well as person-objects communication by recognizing eye gaze action. Mayberry *et al.* propose *iShadow*, where the power consumption of real-time sensing is dramatically reduced. Rallapalli *et al.* realize physical analysis in retail stores based on customer behaviors collected from smart glasses. Although smart glasses are prevailing nowadays, most existing devices just focus on entertainment. Our work in this paper focuses on eye protection for facial paralysis patients, which is an urgent requirements for a considerable group of people.

11. LIMITATIONS AND FUTURE WORK

Although the current iBlink system can realize the basic blink triggering function, considerable efforts are still needed before it can be practically deployed. The major issue of the current version of iBlink system is that the weight of the device is higher than the ordinary glasses, which makes it uncomfortable for long-time wearing. There is a need to remove some unnecessary components from the frame. Our tentative plan for the next version is to remove the Raspberry PI Zero and the eye camera from the frame and just keep the stimulation circuits and stimulating electrodes. The motivation of this revision is the observation that nowadays people spend much time watching the smartphone. We could develop a smartphone APP to learn the pattern of the user's blink actions in the background, and the APP can send the stimulation commands to the stimulation circuits. The circuits will be enhanced with a bluetooth low energy (BLE) module to receive commands from the smartphone and generate stimulating impulses. In this manner, the Raspberry platform and the eye camera could be removed, and it is easier to develop a graceful appearance design for the frame with remained components. In particular, the wiring overhead, and the power supply need could also be reduced, which will lay the foundation to improve the current clunky design.

12. CONCLUSION

We have designed and implemented iBlink, a pair of smart glasses to provide eye protection for facial paralysis patients. We have proposed an eye-movements detection mechanism based on deep convolutional neural network (CNN), which can detect asymmetric eye-movements of patients under various illumination conditions with an accuracy above 99%. Our library for training CNN models has been published online for further related studies, which contains more than 30,000 eye images. Moreover, we have designed and implemented an automatic stimulation circuits to generate electrical impulse for the patient's facial nerve branches stimulation, which can configure operational parameters in a self-adaptive manner for different patients. Further, we have implemented the entire *iBlink* system, which integrates the two functions above and a communication function module for tele-medicine applications. We have conducted comprehensive clinical trials in a hospital, in order to obtain the design basis and verify effectiveness of our device.

13. ACKNOWLEDGEMENTS

We sincerely appreciate our shepherd Dr. Pengyu Zhang for iteratively assisting in improving our paper. We would also like to thank the anonymous reviewers for their valuable feedback. This work is supported by National Natural Science Foundation of China (No. 61532012, 61572319, U1405251).

14. REFERENCES

[1] National institute of neurological disorders and stroke, "Bell's Palsy Fact Sheet," Online:http://www.ninds.nih.gov/disorders/bells/detail_bells.htm

[2] Eye image library, Online: https://www.dropbox.com/s/vgrk4mfkpjmc0jo/EyeData.zip?dl=0.

[3] Picture of a Bell's palsy patient from wikepedia, Online: https://en.wikipedia.org/wiki/Bell\%27s_palsy#/media/File:Bellspalsy.JPG.

[4] Figure of anatomy of facial nerves, Online: https://en.wikipedia.org/wiki/Stylomastoid_foramen#/media/File:Facial_canal.png.

[5] FDA regulations on facemasks, Online: http://www.fda.gov/MedicalDevices/ProductsandMedicalProcedures/GeneralHospitalDevicesandSupplies/PersonalProtectiveEquipment/ucm055977.htm.

[6] P. Alakram and T. Puckree,"Effects of electrical stimulation in early Bell's palsy on facial disability index scores," SA Journal of Physiotherapy, vol. 67, no. 2, pp. 35–40, 2011.

[7] S. M. Sandeep and V. N. Jayprakash, "Effect of electrical stimulation on facial grading system in subjects with early facial palsy," National Journal of Integrated Research in Medicine, vol. 4, pp. 29–32, 2013.

[8] Electromyography, Online: https://en.wikipedia.org/wiki/Electromyography.

[9] J. Cole, S. Zimmerman and S. Gerson, "Nonsurgical neuromuscular rehabilitation of facial muscle paresis,"*Rubin LR (ed): The Paralyzed Face*, pp. 107-122, 1991.

[10] D. J. Farragher, "Electrical stimulation: A method of treatment for facial paralysis," *Rose FC, Jones R, Vrbova G (eds): Neuromuscular Stimulation: Basic Concepts and Clinical Implications.*, vol. 3, pp. 303-306, 1989.

[11] C. S. Cohan and S. B. Kater, "Suppression of neurite elongation and growth cone motility by electrical activity,"*Science*, pp. 232:1638-1640, 1986.

[12] M. C. Brown and R. L. Holland, "A central role for denervated tissues in causing nerve sprouting,"*Nature*, pp. 282:724, 1979.

[13] D. Prutchi and M. Norris, "Design and development of medical electronic instrumentation: a practical perspective of the design, construction, and test of medical devices," 2005

[14] Y. Jia, E. Shelhamer, J. Donahue, S. Karayev, J. Long and , R. Girshick, S. Guadarrama and T. Darrell, "Caffe: Convolutional architecture for fast feature embedding,"*in Proc. of the ACM International Conference on Multimedia*, pp. 675-678, 2014.

[15] V. Nair and G. E. Hinton, "Rectified linear units improve restricted boltzmann machines,"*in Proc. of ICML*, pp. 807-814, 2010.

[16] G. E. Hinton, N. Srivastava, A. Krizhevsky, I. Sutskever and R. R. Salakhutdinov, "Improving neural networks by preventing co-adaptation of feature detectors,"*arXiv preprint arXiv:1207.0580*, pp. 1988-1996, 2012.

[17] A. Krizhevsky, I. Sutskever and G. E. Hinton, "Imagenet classification with deep convolutional neural networks,"*NIPS*, pp. 1097-1105, 2012.

[18] A. Mayberry, P. Hu, B. Marlin, C. Salthouse and D. Ganesan, "iShadow: design of a wearable, real-time mobile gaze tracker,"*in Proc. of MobiSys*, pp. 82-94, 2014.

[19] L. Zhang, X. Li, W. Huang, K. Liu, S. Zong, X. Jian, P. Feng, T. Jung, Taeho and Y. Liu, "It starts with igaze: Visual attention driven networking with smart glasses,"*in Proc. of ACM/IEEE MobiCom*, pp. 91-102, 2014.

[20] Z. Zhu and Q. Ji, "Robust real-time eye detection and tracking under variable lighting conditions and various face orientations,"*Computer Vision and Image Understanding*, vol. 98, no. 1, pp. 124-154, 2005.

[21] I. Mavrikakis, "Facial nerve palsy: anatomy, etiology, evaluation, and management,"*Orbit*, vol. 27, no. 6, pp. 466-474, 2008.

[22] U. S. Rao, J. Poll and M. T. Yen, "Prognosis for recovery vital to facial nerve palsy management,"*Ophthalmology Times*, vol. 34, no. 19, pp. 24-26, 2009.

[23] S. L. Spruance, "Bell palsy and herpes simplex

virus,"*Annals of Internal Medicine*, vol. 120, no. 12, pp. 1045, 1994.

[24] A. K. Das, K. Sabarigirish and R. C. Kashyap, "Facial nerve paralysis: A three year retrospective study,"*Indian Journal of Otolaryngology and Head and Neck Surgery*, vol. 58, no. 3, pp. 225-228, 2006.

[25] P. Alakram and T. Puckree, "Effects of electrical stimulation on house-brackmann scores in early bells palsy,"*Physiotherapy theory and practice*, vol. 26, no. 3, pp. 160-166, 2010.

[26] H. Kim, S. Kim, Y. Kim and K. Park, "A smartphone-based automatic diagnosis system for facial nerve palsy,"*Sensors*, vol. 15, no. 10, pp. 26756-26768, 2015.

[27] H. Kim, S. Kim, Y. Kim and K. Park, "What Is Bell's Palsy?"*Harvard Women's Health Watch*, vol. 8, no. 10, pp. 8, 2001.

[28] V. Gelder, S. Ronald and L. Gelder, "Facial expression and speech: Neuroanatomical considerations,"*International journal of psychology*, vol. 25, no. 10, pp. 141-155, 1990.

[29] H. Arion, "Dynamic closure of the lids in paralysis of the orbicularis muscle,"*Plastic and Reconstructive Surgery*, vol. 50, no. 6, pp. 629, 1972.

[30] D. Moral-Fatio and J. Laiardrie, "Palliative surgical treatment of facial paralysis. The palpebral spring,"*Plastic and reconstructive surgery*, vol. 33, no. 5, pp. 446-456, 1964.

[31] F. Masters, D. Robinson and J. Simons, "Temporalis transfer for lagopthalmos due to seventh nerve palsy,"*The American Journal of Surgery*, vol. 110, no. 4, pp. 607-611, 1965.

[32] Datasheet of 9013, Online:http://datasheet.eeworld.com.cn/pdf/WINGS/66397_9013.pdf

[33] Datasheet of 8550, Online:http://datasheet.eeworld.com.cn/pdf/142482_STANSON_8550.html

[34] Datasheet of CD4066BE, Online:http://www.ti.com/lit/ds/symlink/cd4066b-mil.pdf

[35] Raspberry Pi user guide, Online:https://www.raspberrypi.org/blog/raspberry-pi-user-guide-2nd-edition/

BigRoad: Scaling Road Data Acquisition for Dependable Self-Driving

Luyang Liu[♮], Hongyu Li[♮], Jian Liu[§], Cagdas Karatas[♮],
Yan Wang[◇], Marco Gruteser[♮], Yingying Chen[§], Richard P. Martin[♮]
(The first two authors are co-primary student authors.)
[♮]WINLAB, Rutgers University, North Brunswick, NJ, USA
[♮]{luyang, hongyuli, cagdas, gruteser, rmartin}@winlab.rutgers.edu
[§]Stevens Institute of Technology, Hoboken, NJ, USA
[§]{jliu28,yingying.chen}@stevens.edu
[◇]Binghamton University, Binghamton, NY, USA
[◇]yanwang@binghamton.edu

ABSTRACT

Advanced driver assistance systems and, in particular automated driving offers an unprecedented opportunity to transform the safety, efficiency, and comfort of road travel. Developing such safety technologies requires an understanding of not just common highway and city traffic situations but also a plethora of widely different unusual events (e.g., object on the road way and pedestrian crossing highway, etc.). While each such event may be rare, in aggregate they represent a significant risk that technology must address to develop truly dependable automated driving and traffic safety technologies. By developing technology to scale road data acquisition to a large number of vehicles, this paper introduces a low-cost yet reliable solution, BigRoad, that can derive internal driver inputs (i.e., steering wheel angles, driving speed and acceleration) and external perceptions of road environments (i.e., road conditions and front-view video) using a smartphone and an IMU mounted in a vehicle. We evaluate the accuracy of collected internal and external data using over 140 real-driving trips collected in a 3-month time period. Results show that BigRoad can accurately estimate the steering wheel angle with 0.69° median error, and derive the vehicle speed with 0.65 km/h deviation. The system is also able to determine binary road conditions with 95% accuracy by capturing a small number of brakes. We further validate the usability of BigRoad by pushing the collected video feed and steering wheel angle to a deep neural network steering wheel angle predictor, showing the potential of massive data acquisition for training self-driving system using BigRoad.

Keywords

Self-Driving, Road data acquisition, Smartphone, IMU

Permission to make digital or hard copies of all or part of this work for personal or classroom use is granted without fee provided that copies are not made or distributed for profit or commercial advantage and that copies bear this notice and the full citation on the first page. Copyrights for components of this work owned by others than ACM must be honored. Abstracting with credit is permitted. To copy otherwise, or republish, to post on servers or to redistribute to lists, requires prior specific permission and/or a fee. Request permissions from permissions@acm.org.

MobiSys '17, June 19–23, 2017, Niagara Falls, NY, USA.

© 2017 ACM. ISBN 978-1-4503-4928-4/17/06...$15.00

DOI: http://dx.doi.org/10.1145/3081333.3081344

1. INTRODUCTION

Advanced driver assistance systems and, in particular, automated driving offer an unprecedented opportunity to transform the safety, efficiency, comfort, and economics of road travel. This has led many organizations in the computing and transportation domains to focusing on self-driving technology research. While this has resulted in a number of prototypes with impressive performance, it remains widely recognized that ensuring dependability under varied traffic conditions remains a key challenge [1, 2, 3].

Self-driving vehicles have to operate safely even under unusual or rare traffic events that are challenging to address and could lead to potential accidents. Developing such technology therefore requires an understanding of not just common highway and city traffic situations but also a plethora of widely different unusual events (e.g., objects on the roadway, pedestrian crossing highway, deer standing next to the road, etc.). While each such event may be rare, in aggregate they represent a significant risk that technology must address to develop truly dependable automated driving and traffic safety technologies. The average human driver achieves on the order of almost 100 million vehicle miles traveled per fatality [4]. Demonstrating driving performance at an above-average, advanced human driver level will therefore require successfully avoiding fatalities with unusual events that might be encountered within a billion miles of driving. This motivates the need for scaling road dataset to billions of miles of driving so that they contain a representative set of such unusual and rare events.

Most existing efforts to collect driving data build on a small fleet of tens of highly instrumented vehicles that are continuously operated with test drivers [5, 6, 7]. In terms of miles recorded, it is challenging to accumulate a sufficiently large dataset with this approach. From the tidbits of published information, we know, for example, that Google's fleet has completed about 2 million testing miles [5]—impressive but still far off from a billion miles. On the other hand, since many existing efforts to develop automated driving technology are proprietary, the data obtained is usually closely guarded. It is not easy for individuals outside vehicle industry to collect driving inputs such as steering wheel angle and pedal operations. The OpenPilot [8] project reverse engineers the OBD-II data from two vehicle models of Hondas and Acuras, and uses the collected data to train the CNN based Adaptive Cruise Control (ACC) and Lane Keeping Assist System (LKAS). However, this solution can only be deployed in specific vehicle models, which makes it harder to recruit very large numbers of vehicles. Government-sponsored naturalistic driving studies have produced similar datasets, such as the UMTRI Naturalistic Driving Data [9] or the 100-vehicle VTTI Naturalistic Driving Study [10] that reached 2 million miles. These studies are more focused on human driving behaviors and still far below the target scope for supporting robust self-driving.

To address this challenge, this paper asks whether data useful for self-driving can be gathered with only minimal instrumentation of vehicles. Such a minimal vehicle instrumentation approach would enable scaling by capturing events from tens of thousands of vehicles rather than only attempting to collect data with a few highly instrumented vehicles or certain vehicle models, as is common practice. A key challenge in creating such minimal instrumentation is the heterogeneity of vehicle designs and the proprietary nature of in-vehicle systems. To be useful for driver assistance and automated driving applications, the dataset must capture the surrounding traffic situation of the vehicle and how the vehicle was driven through this traffic scenario (i.e., it's precise trajectory and the necessary driver input). The latter is especially important for approaches relying on machine learning, which is increasingly used in such systems [11]. Here, the driver input data provides important positive and negative training examples that allow the system to learn how to react to traffic situations. It is also useful for system validation, since it allows automated comparisons of the response of automated driving algorithms with those of a human driver. Any significant deviations can then be more closely examined.

The primary technical challenge is to obtain accurate vehicle movements without extensive instrumentation of the vehicle. While vehicles contain internal sensors to track steering and pedal inputs, the specific sensors vary among models and car makers use different proprietary data formats, if the information is exposed through the OBD-II port at all [12]. This heterogeneity renders scaling to many different vehicles difficult. Global Positioning System tracking of vehicles does not always capture fine-grained steering and speed changes, particularly in urban canyons. Gathering information about the surrounding traffic situation is more straightforward—in most situations, a front-facing camera can provide rich information. It is worthwhile complementing this information, however, in darkness and other situations where visual information may be insufficient.

BigRoad, as shown in Figure 1, aims to minimize instrumentation of vehicles by relying on low-cost inertial sensors that can be affixed to the vehicle. An inertial sensor in a dash-cam or windshield mounted smartphone enhances speed estimation, particularly in low-speed scenarios, therefore providing an indirect measurement of acceleration and braking inputs. A second steering wheel sensor gathers angle information, which allows a much more precise measurement of vehicle turning. To achieve this, BigRoad incorporates algorithms that isolate steering and vehicle movements from other forces acting on the vehicle. It also compensates for unknown orientations of the devices.

To understand whether such data can be useful for self-driving research, we study the performance of a key self-driving component, a self-steering algorithm. When trained with our data, this deep neural network-based algorithm takes road video as input and outputs the desired steering angle.

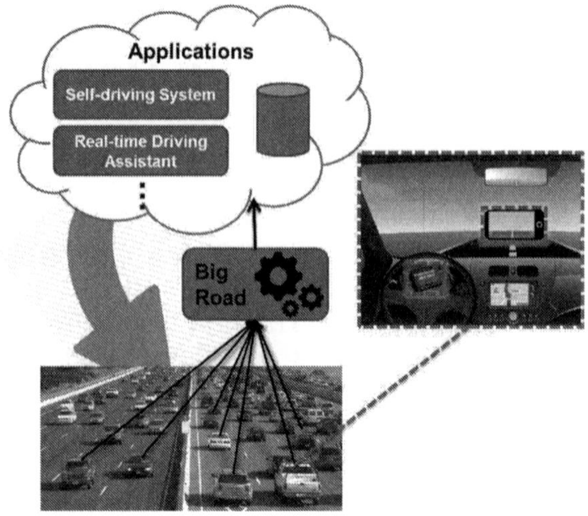

Figure 1: Illustration of BigRoad containing a smartphone and an IMU sensor: scaling road data acquisition.

The contributions of this work can be summarized as follows:

- To our knowledge, this study is the first to analyze whether driving data useful for self-driving research can be collect with a minimal set of inertial and video add-on devices, in contrast to the existing work with significant instrumentation for scaling data acquisition.
- Developing steering wheel angle estimation algorithms by leveraging low-cost sensing devices (i.e., inertial measurement units (IMUs) and smartphones). The key novelty of this approach is that it extracts steering wheel rotation by eliminating vehicle movement from the steering-wheel-mounted sensor measurements.
- Designing robust vehicle speed sensing algorithms that combine GPS with speed delay shifting, and an acceleration based complementary filter.
- Devising an acceleration-based road condition estimator to enhance road condition awareness under poor lighting conditions and to illustrate further uses of the sensed data.
- Collecting and analyzing 40 hours of driving data to determine the accuracy of the estimation techniques and to demonstrate that the fine-grained driving data provided by the proposed framework achieves comparable performance in an automated vehicle steering algorithm.

2. MOTIVATION & APPLICATIONS

Road and driving data are not only useful for constructing validation scenarios but can also support driving algorithm development. Automated vehicles increasingly rely on machine learning. Learning can be employed for specific subsystems such as recognition of traffic signs or traffic participants

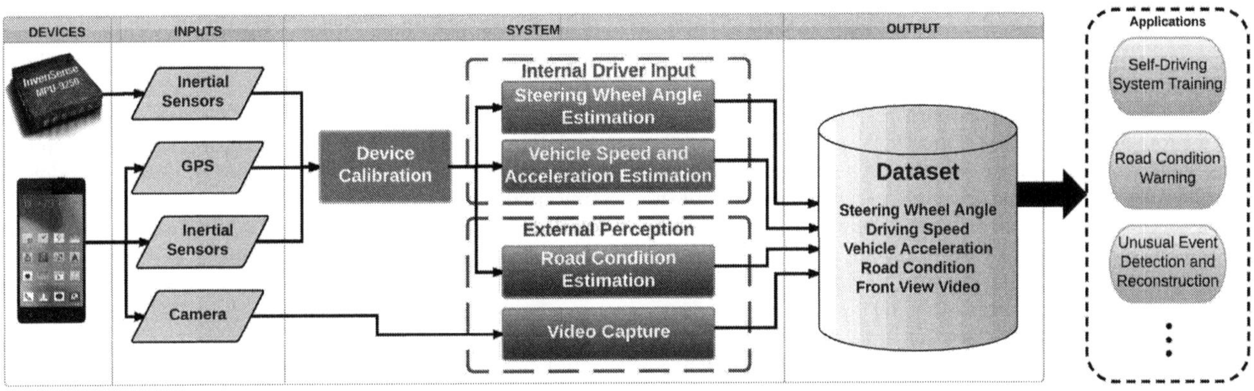

Figure 2: BigRoad system overview.

from video data. Learning is also increasingly explored for vehicle control. In fact, recent research [11] demonstrated how a deep neural network can support end-to-end automated steering. The network takes as input raw video data, without using a separate feature extraction step, and converts this into a steering control signal. Such approaches rely on an extensive dataset for training the network with both video and steering inputs from a human driver.

Furthermore, the massive road data could also support various real-time driving assistant applications. BigRoad can speed up innovation by providing an open large-scale datasets of unusual traffic events, which can be utilized to understand the various scenarios that driver-less vehicles need to be trained and tested on. For example, detecting bad weather conditions or adverse road situations and then adapting the driving parameters accordingly is an important task in self-driving cars. The data collected in BigRoad could serve as a training set for dealing with bad weather conditions and adverse road situations, thereby contributing to faster development of robust and reliable autonomous driving environments. When it rains or snows, not only does slick asphalt pose control issues that a vehicle has to deal with but the vehicle will also need to deal with reckless and negligent drivers who could be more dangerous under adverse road conditions. To help prevent and avoid collisions under adverse road conditions, the self-driving vehicle needs to make corresponding actions such as reducing the turning speed, braking gently and slowly, etc.

In particular, in order to take advantage of the driver inputs and road information collected from BigRoad, we design a crowd sourcing based application associated with BigRoad that can warn the driver with the waiting time of traffic light, as well as the road condition in front. The users of this application can contribute their driving input and traces through BigRoad to our server in real-time, and will in turns benefit from the drivers who uploaded data previously. Previous works demonstrate that the traffic light schedule can be trained based on the crowd sourcing video feed of the front facing camera [13] or the GPS data [14] from vehicles passing through the traffic light. We adopt the second method, which utilizes the crowd sourcing inertial sensor and GPS readings from the smartphone of multiple drivers to predict the schedule of each traffic light. For each end user, the application runs a stop detection and analyzes the vehicle facing direction based on the GPS location and bearing. Through Google Map API, the application could determine whether the driver is stopped for a traffic light and which light the driving is waiting for, then provide the predicted traffic light waiting time. In the same way, drivers could receive the road condition warning through the road condition model which is trained by the crowdsourcing driving data as introduced in Section 5.2.

3. SYSTEM DESIGN

The main goal of BigRoad is to provide a light-weight automated data logging system dedicated to crowdsourcing fine-grained driving data, which can facilitate extensive research in self-driving vehicles and driving safety monitoring. By installing very few off-the-shelf sensing devices (i.e., a smartphone and an IMU) in a vehicle, the system can track vehicles' dynamics, drivers' driving behaviors, and road environments in real time. In addition to logging raw sensing data (i.e., GPS locations, motion sensor readings, and vehicles' front-view video), BigRoad devises novel approaches to derive various fine-grained driving data (i.e., steering wheel angles, vehicle speeds, and vehicle accelerations) by fusing the measurements from various sensors.

The major advantage of BigRoad is that it provides a minimum-effort solution for self-driving companies and researchers, who want to collect large datasets of ready-to-use driving data in real world without concerns of different vehicle types and driving behaviors. Traditional data logging systems only provide coarse-grained sensing data without recording the ground truth. Our system leverages various sensing technology in smartphones and IMUs to provide fine-grained measurements and experimental ground truth in the context of real driving. The information generated by BigRoad is two-fold: 1) The estimated steering wheel angles (directly from drivers), vehicle speeds and accelerations (indirectly from drivers) are considered to be *Internal Driver Input* to reconstruct vehicles' motions and driving behaviors in a fine-grained manner. 2) The estimated road conditions and videos captured by the cameras of smartphones are considered to be *External Perception* that can capture driving environments and provide experimental ground truth.

BigRoad is realized with five main sub-tasks: *Device Calibration, Steering Wheel Angle Reconstruction, Vehicle Speed and Acceleration Estimation, Road Condition Estimation,* and *Time-stamped Video Capture*. Figure 2 shows the system overview of BigRoad. To participate, the user needs to install a smartphone on the dashboard and an IMU on the center of the steering wheel as illustrated in Figure 1. The system takes measurements of inertial sensors (i.e., acceleration and rotation rate in both the IMU and smartphone) as inputs to *Device Calibration*, which derives the rotation matrices that can calibrate the sensing measurements from both devices to the vehicle's coordinate system, disregarding vehicle models, steering wheel positions and IMU placements. The components of Internal Driver Input including *Steering Wheel Angle Estimation* and *Driving Speed and Acceleration Estimation* fuse GPS location and calibrated sensing measurements from inertial sensors to derive steering wheel angles, vehicle speeds, and accelerations. The components of External Perception including *Road Condition Estimation* and *Time-stamped Video Capture* utilize video camera and inertial sensors to capture critical information in the driving environment (i.e., traffics, road conditions, etc.). Road conditions in inclement weather can severely affect traffic demands, roadway capacity and increase risks of having traffic crashes [15].

The insight of our steering wheel angle estimation is that after applying the *Device Calibration*, which is discussed in Section 6, the rotation angles of the IMU aligned to the steering wheel plane could be used to estimate steering wheel angles. However, accurately estimating the steering wheel angles involves several challenges. First, steering motions from human usually happen in a sudden and change all the time, which makes them extremely hard to be captured by the IMU's inertial sensors. Second, the measurements from the inertial sensors of the IMU are contaminated by motions of the vehicle, such as turning and braking. Third, although the IMU's position on the steering wheel is stable, it is unknown and could be different from time to time. To harness these challenges, We obtain the rotation of the steering wheel based on IMU's sensor readings and uses the smartphone's acceleration to remove the error caused by vehicle motion during driving.

Besides, BigRoad fuses GPS and acceleration from smartphone to predict accurate vehicle driving speed. Since road conditions in inclement weather can severely affect traffic demands, roadway capacity and increase risks of having traffic crashes [15], we propose to use real-time normalized traction force derived from inertial sensor readings during brakes activities to identify binary road conditions (i.e., dry or wet). Moreover, the *Time-stamped Video Capture* utilizes cameras of smartphones to provide the front-view video of the vehicle together with millisecond-granularity time stamps, which serves as the ready-to-use training datasets for various applications such as self-driving system training, road condition warning, and dangerous event detection and recommendation.

4. INTERNAL DRIVER INPUT

Let us now consider the specific techniques to improve the accuracy of estimating human driver inputs such as steering wheel angle and vehicle speed from generic IMU and smartphone sensors that can be widely deployed across vehicle models.

4.1 Steering Wheel Angle Estimation

As one of the most important driver inputs, steering wheel operations play a critical role in self-driving systems. Compared to vehicle speed that is openly available via a standard OBD-II interface, steering wheel operations (i.e., rotation angles) are usually harder to access since it can be carried on separate buses or encoded in proprietary formats only known to the vehicle manufacturers. In order to obtain drivers' steering inputs irrespective of vehicle models with minimal instrumentation, we propose two sensor-based approaches to estimate steering wheel angles: 1) steering wheel IMU based estimation and 2) phone based estimation. The difference between these two approaches is that the former requires an inertial measurement unit (IMU) attached to the steering wheel together with the smartphone in the vehicle, while the latter only needs one smartphone with its internal inertial sensors.

In particular, the steering wheel IMU based estimation includes three steps: 1) the system fuses steering wheel angles estimated based on different inertial sensors in the IMU by using a complementary filter; 2) it removes the angle errors caused by vehicle motions from the sensor measurements; 3) the system calculates the angle biases from the coordinate alignment, and further calibrates the estimated steering wheel angle by removing the biases. Next, we first introduce the three steps for the steering wheel IMU based estimation in section 4.1.1, 4.1.2 and 4.1.3, then we discuss the phone based estimation in section 4.1.4.

4.1.1 IMU Sensor Fusion

After coordinate alignment using the device calibration algorithms described in section 6, measurements from the inertial sensors in the IMU are aligned to the steering wheel's two-dimensional plane. Intuitively, we could estimate changes in the steering wheel angle by accumulating the angular velocities (ω) from the IMU's gyroscope. The angle change from time t_1 to t_2 ($\Delta\theta_{gyro}^{t_2|t_1}$) is equal to the integration of the ω readings in this period, as shown in $\Delta\theta_{gyro}^{t_2|t_1} = \int_{t_1}^{t_2} \omega dt$. While the gyroscope measures rotation changes precisely, the integration process suffers from accumulating errors and results in large drifts over time. We can also estimate steering wheel angles based on the angular changes derived from the gravity projected onto the different axis from the IMU's accelerometer (θ_a), but the accelerometer readings show significant vibration noise, which causes large dynamic errors. [1]

To address these limitations in both approaches, we devise a complementary filter [16] to fuse the estimated steering wheel angles based on the measurements from the IMU's accelerometer and gyroscope. The design of the complementary filter is shown with the following equation that applies both high-pass and low-pass filters:

$$\theta^{t|t-1} = cc * (\theta^{t-1} + \Delta\theta_{gyro}^{t|t-1}) + (1 - cc) * \theta_a, \qquad (1)$$

where $\theta^{t|t-1}$ is the estimated steering wheel angle at time t based on the angle estimated at time $t-1$ denoted as θ^{t-1}, $\Delta\theta_{gyro}^{t|t-1}$ is the estimated steering wheel angle change obtained by accumulating the IMU's gyroscope measurements around the axis of rotation from time t to $t-1$, θ_a is the steering wheel angle derived from the accelerometer's measurements, and *cc* is a variable that determines the time scale

[1] We have also considered exploiting magnetometer based approaches, but they are significantly affected by the surrounding magnetic field, which is usually unstable in urban environments.

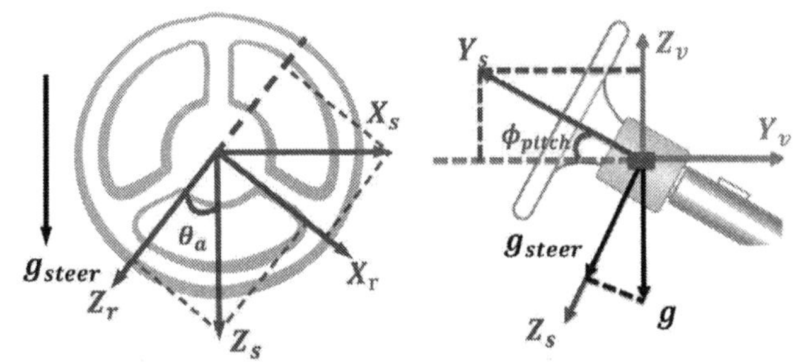

(a) Steering wheel and rotated steering wheel coordinate system.

(b) Steering wheel and vehicle coordinate system.

Figure 3: Several coordinate systems and angle estimation.

of the high and low-pass filters, which is set to 0.9 empirically. Since the gyroscope integration process is relatively straightforward, we will put more emphasis on the derivation of θ_a.

Steering Wheel Angle Estimation based on Accelerations. We first consider the scenario when the vehicle is static, e.g., the vehicle is parked, in which gravity is the only force applied to the steering wheel. We examine the IMU's accelerations on the two dimensional steering wheel plane as illustrated in Figure 3(a). In the plane, we define two sub-coordinate systems: 1) X_s and Z_s denote the x and z-axis of the *steering wheel coordinate system*, and 2) X_r and Z_r denote the same in the *rotated steering wheel coordinate system.* We assume Z_s points to the the same direction with the gravity projection (g_{steer}) on this plane and y-axis of both sub-coordinate are perpendicular to this surface as shown in Figure 3(b). Note that the *steering wheel coordinate system* is fixed but the *rotated steering wheel coordinate system* changes with the rotation of the steering wheel and IMU. Therefore, the problem becomes how to determine the angle between two coordinate systems.

Intuitively, when there is only gravity acceleration in the static scenario, the steering wheel angle θ_a can be estimated by first calculating the arc-tangent over the projection of the gravity acceleration on X_r and Z_r as shown in $\theta_{static} = atan2(a_{X_r}, a_{Z_r})$, where a_{X_r} and a_{Z_r} can be derived from the IMU's acceleration readings aligned from its own coordinate system to the *rotated steering wheel coordinate system*, which is discussed in in the Device Calibration section. $atan2(x, y)$ is the arc-tangent function that can calculate the angle in all four quadrants. The output of $atan2(x, y)$ ranges from -180° to 180°. Because the steering wheel angle may overflow this range, we find all possible angles by adding multiples of 360° to the θ_{static}, and use the one closest to the last estimation as the estimated steering wheel angle θ_a.

4.1.2 Vehicle Motion Removal

The above steering wheel angle estimation is obtained when the vehicle is static. To have a better understanding of how the motions of vehicles affect θ_a, we revisit Figure 3(a) for driving scenarios. When the vehicle is moving, the inertial sensors in the IMU and smartphone capture other accelerations (e.g., accelerations caused by turning, accelerating, and braking) in addition to the gravity force. Thus the accelerations projected to the X_r and Z_r axes can be derived as:

$$\begin{aligned} a_{X_r} &= sin(\theta_a) * a_{Z_s} + cos(\theta_a) * a_{X_s}, \\ a_{Z_r} &= cos(\theta_a) * a_{Z_s} - sin(\theta_a) * a_{X_s}, \end{aligned} \quad (2)$$

where a_{X_s} and a_{Z_s} are the accelerations aligned to the x- and z-axes of the *steering wheel coordinate system.* By combining two equations, we further derive the steering wheel angle in moving scenarios as below:

$$\begin{aligned} tan(\theta_a) &= \frac{tan(\theta_{static}) - a_{X_s}/a_{Z_s}}{1 + a_{X_s}/a_{Z_s} * tan(\theta_{static})}, \\ &= tan(\theta_{static} + atan(a_{X_s}/a_{Z_s})), \\ \Rightarrow \theta_a &= \theta_{static} - atan(a_{X_s}/a_{Z_s}), \\ &= \theta_{static} - \theta_{error}. \end{aligned} \quad (3)$$

We note that the estimated steering wheel angle in Equation 3 can be considered as the angle estimated in the static scenario (i.e., θ_{static}) calibrated by removing an angular error (i.e., θ_{error}), which is determined by the accelerations in the *steering wheel coordinate system* and independent of the poses of the steering wheel and IMU.

In order to obtain a_{X_s} and a_{Z_s} in Equation 3, we examine the relationship between the *steering wheel coordinate system* and the *vehicle coordinate system* as illustrated in Figure 3(b). We find that a_{X_s} is the same as the vehicle's acceleration on the x-axis of its own coordinate system (a_{X_v}), which can be easily obtained by aligning the measurements of the smartphone's accelerometer to the *vehicle coordinate system* in the Device Calibration. In addition, we find that the steering wheel always has a pitch angle (ϕ_{pitch}) to the y-axis of the vehicle coordinate system. Therefore, a_{Z_s} is the combination of the gravity acceleration and the vehicle's acceleration projecting to the z-axis of the *steering wheel coordinate system* as shown below:

$$a_{Z_s} = g * sin(\phi_{pitch}) - a_{Y_v} * sin(\phi_{pitch}). \quad (4)$$

Finally, the complementary filter is still used to estimate the steering wheel angle by fusing the estimated steering wheel angle based on accelerations (θ_a) and angular velocity derived from IMU's y-axis gyroscope reading after aligned to the *rotated steering wheel coordinate system.*

4.1.3 Angle Bias Removal

The constant rotation of steering wheel makes error existing in the coordinate alignment during Device Calibration, resulting in a bias in the estimated steering wheel angle. To remove this angle bias, our system calibrates itself by examining the average estimated steering wheel angle when the vehicle is driving straight. The intuition is that the ideally estimated steering wheel angle should be zero degrees when driving straight, therefore any non-zero average estimated steering wheel angle found when driving straight is the angle bias that we should remove.

In particular, our system keeps collecting the angular velocity on the z-axis of the *vehicle coordinate system* from the gyroscope of the smartphone ($gyro_{Z_v}$) and that on the y-axis of the *steering wheel coordinate system* from the gyroscope of the IMU ($gyro_{Y_s}$) since the start of each trip. If the angular velocities from both sources are less than a threshold (e.g., $0.01 rad/s$ and $0.1 rad/s$ for $gyro_{Z_v}$ and $gyro_{Y_s}$, respectively), the system considers that the vehicle is driving straight and pushes the estimated steering wheel angle into a sample pool. The average of the samples in the pool is considered as the angle bias to be removed from all the steering

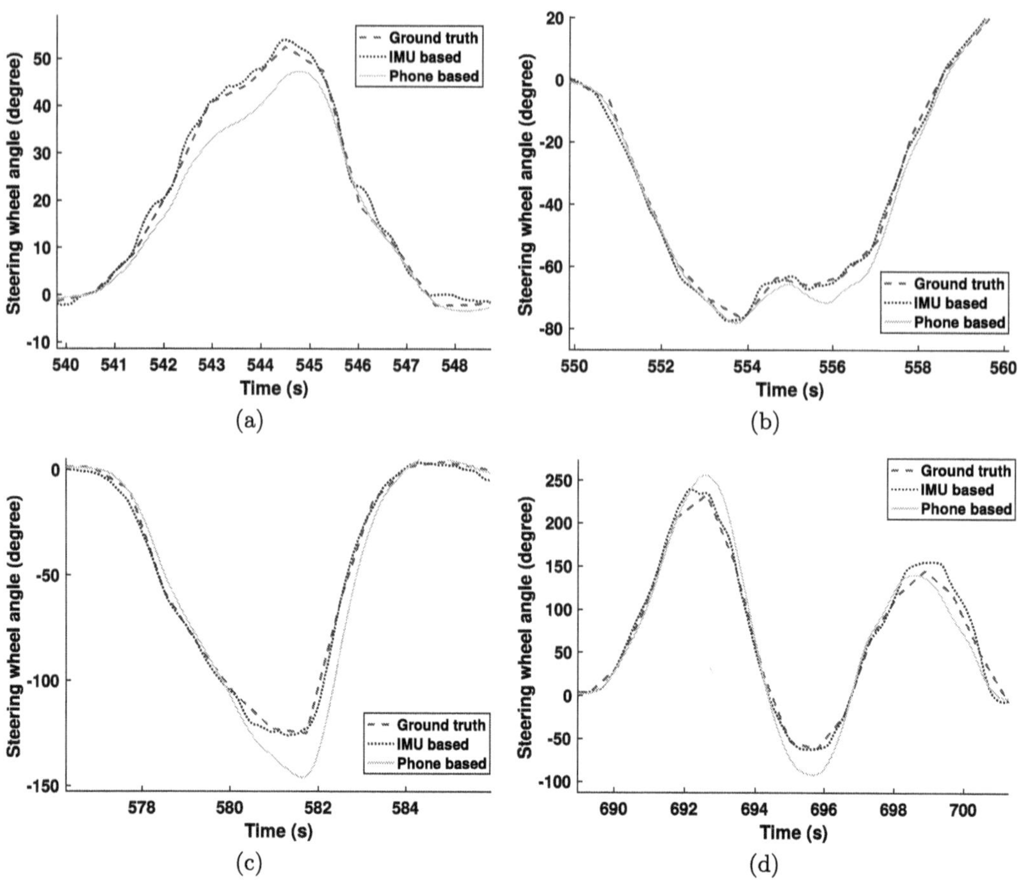

Figure 4: Compare the steering wheel angle estimation results of steering-wheel based and phone based approach.

wheel angles estimated in the rest of the trip. The size of the sample pool depends on the time needed to collect enough samples that can confidently determine the angle bias in every trip. In our experiments, we find that our system can successfully find and remove this angle bias within the first one minute of typical daily commute trips.

4.1.4 Phone Based Steering Wheel Angle Estimation

An alternative approach in BigRoad is not to fix the sensor on the steering wheel. Instead, we can just employ the available smartphone inside the vehicle to accomplish the steering wheel angle estimation task. This method can be adapted to any inertial sensors, but we use the smartphone sensor here to minimize the infrastructure needs. Instead of explaining bunches of complex mathematical equations, we simplify the model as shown in Figure 5, in which we assume the turning angle of the two front tires is the same. For common vehicles, the steering wheel angle $\theta_{steering}$ is equal to the front tire's turning angle θ_{tire} multiply the vehicle's steering ratio k. And if the turning radius r and wheelbase l of the testing vehicle are known, θ_{tire} can be calculated in real time:

$$\theta_{steering} = k * \theta_{tire} = k * asin\frac{l}{r},$$
$$r = \frac{v}{\omega} = \frac{v}{gyroz_v}. \tag{5}$$

The vehicle turning radius r can be obtained as shown in Equation 5 based on the physics phenomenon inherited from

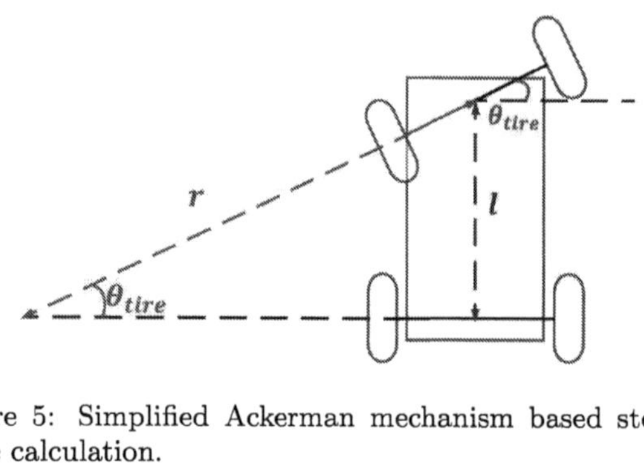

Figure 5: Simplified Ackerman mechanism based steering angle calculation.

inertial sensor readings. Here v stands for the vehicle speed, which we can get from the vehicle speed estimation module presented in section 4.2. ω represents the angular velocity of the vehicle, which can be replaced by the gyroscope reading on the z-axis of the *vehicle's coordinate system*($gyroz_v$). Thus, we can calculate the vehicle turning radius, and then get θ_{tire} leveraging only a smartphone. However, the steering ratios(k) of most commercial vehicles are proprietary. To obtain the steering ratio of our testing vehicle, we apply linear regression on the steering wheel angle ground truth and estimated tire angle from part of our collected dataset, and use the ratio to evaluate the remaining part of the dataset.

To compare these two steering wheel angle estimation approaches, the phone based approach utilize less infrastructures, but it needs more vehicle information such as steering ratio and wheelbase. The steering-wheel IMU based approach can estimate steering wheel angle of any vehicle model without extra information by exploiting the additional IMU sensor on the steering wheel. Figure 4 demonstrates the estimation result of two approaches and compare them with ground truth. We will show that the performance of steering-wheel IMU sensor based approach is better than the phone based approach in section 7.

4.2 Driving Acceleration and Speed Estimation

In addition to steering wheel angles, driving accelerations and speed are also critical inputs for self-driving research and thus part of the system's outputs. The driving acceleration is the smartphone's acceleration projected to the driving direction when the smartphone is fixed in the vehicle for video recording. Therefore the acceleration can be obtained after the smartphone's measurements are aligned to the vehicle's coordinate system. An intuitive way to obtain the driving speed is exploiting the location service in smartphones' operating systems. However, we found the speed information to deviate on average by more than 1 km/h from the internal vehicle speed. To improve the accuracy, we propose to (i) shift the speed measurements from the system with an average delay and (ii) apply an acceleration-based complementary filter to compensate for large speed changes.

4.2.1 *Speed Delay Shifting*

The speed information provided by smartphones' operating systems are derived by fusing the GPS, WiFi and cellular network information. Compared with the speedometer reading of vehicles logged on the same smartphone from the OBD port, the smartphone speed readings showed a delay. We observed this on a Nexus 5 with Android 5.1 as well as a Nexus 6 and a Nexus 6P with Android 6.1. This delay may be due to specific processing and filtering methods employed in the GPS and Android positioning system. Since this delay appears reasonably similar for the same smartphones across different trips, the system corrects for this delay by adjusting the GPS speed log time stamps. Figure 6 illustrates the time delay between OBD readings and the GPS readings from a Nexus 5 with Android 5.1, and its consistency in a single trip. Based on this observation, we determine the time delay τ by minimizing the average absolute errors between the speed measurements from the OBD and smartphone's GPS through a segment of data of m samples as shown in the following equation:

$$\underset{\tau}{\text{argmin}} \sum_{i=1}^{m} \frac{1}{m} |V_i^{obd} - V_{i+\tau}^{gps}|, \qquad (6)$$

where V_i^{obd} and $V_{i+\tau}^{gps}$ are i^{th} speed measurement from OBD and GPS, respectively. The time delay τ will then be applied to shift all speed measurements from the smartphone's GPS.

4.2.2 *Acceleration based Complementary Filter*

The speed reading shifting is able to largely reduce the error from delay, but the speed obtained from a smartphone is still less accurate during rapid acceleration or deceleration, because the update rate of the GPS receiver is as low as one update per second. To capture rapid changes in speed, we fuse inertial acceleration measurements with the speed

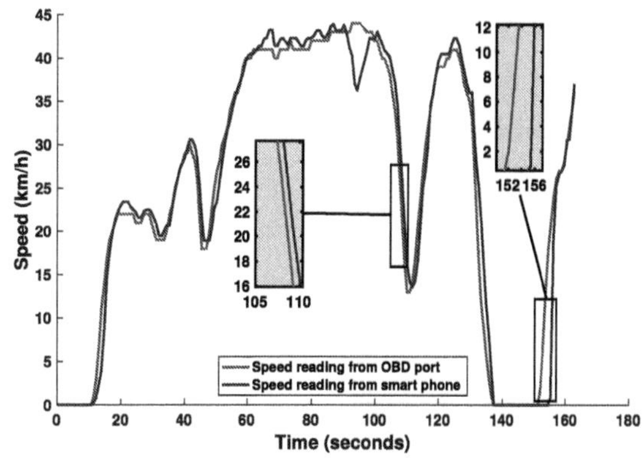

Figure 6: Speed readings from OBD-II and smartphone.

obtained from the GPS. In particular, we estimate the driving speed by using a complementary filter as shown in the following equation:

$$V_t^E = \alpha * (V_{t-1}^E + \Delta V_t) + (1 - \alpha) * V_t^P, \qquad (7)$$

where V_t^E and V_{t-1}^E denote the speed of the vehicle at time t and $t-1$, ΔV_t is the speed change between t to $t-1$ derived from the accumulated accelerations of the vehicle, V_t^P is the speed from the GPS, and α is a variable controlling the balance between two speed sources. The acceleration of the vehicle is available from the smartphone's accelerometer measurements after the coordinate alignment procedure described in section 6. Some advanced GPS chipsets [17] integrated accelerometers for tracking speed, while our method is able to improve the accuracy of speed logged by commodity smartphones after an automatic device calibration, which are only equipped with standalone GPS module.

5. EXTERNAL PERCEPTION RECORDING

In addition to driver inputs, the external environment should be acquired in order to provide a perception for self-driving vehicle studies. We focus on cameras and provide a synchronization mechanism in the next subsection since cameras have become the key low-cost sensor for monitoring the external environment. Beyond the visual perception, better knowledge of road surface conditions can also be useful. In section 5.2, we introduce methods to distinguish wet and dry road conditions .

5.1 Time-stamped Video Capture

The most intuitive external perception provided by BigRoad is the real-time front-view video feed from smartphones' rear cameras that capture everything happening on the road in front of the vehicle. The desire of such directly visual information is tremendous, as it has been exploited in many vehicle applications, including self-driving, traffic crowdsourcing, etc. Most of these applications need to synchronize the video frames to sensor data at millisecond granularity for training or evaluation. To this end, BigRoad can record video frames with a list of time stamps for each frame using the smartphone's system current time at millisecond granularity. The fine-grained time information provided by BigRoad can facilitate many vehicle applications. For instance, the steering wheel angle output can be interpolated to match the time stamp of each frame, and used to train automated steering systems.

5.2 Road Condition Estimation

Next, we introduce how BigRoad provides the estimation of road conditions (i.e., dry or wet) based on sensors integrated in smartphones.

5.2.1 *Intuition*

In advanced driving assistance and automated driving systems, the awareness of road conditions is one of the critical parameters for adjusting speed and turning angles to ensure the safety of passengers. Most existing studies identify factors that affect the road's friction coefficient by using vehicle-mounted specialized sensors (e.g., optical fibers [18], stereo camera [19], 24-GHz automotive radar [20] and voice recorder [21, 22]), which require either extra cost and installation effort or visibility/lighting environments. Our approach is thus challenging as we do not use any additional sensors (e.g., camera, automotive radar) to directly sense the road's condition. In contrast, we analyze the statistics of braking events captured by phones' inertial sensors through crowdsourcing and estimate road conditions, which is low-cost and easy to deploy.

In particular, we develop a proof-of-concept estimation framework to determine binary road conditions (i.e., dry or wet) by examining inertial sensors measurements in vehicles' brake activities from BigRoad. The intuition is two-fold: First, different road conditions have different maximum friction coefficients, which are usually defined by the following equation [23]:

$$\mu_{max} = max(|\frac{F_x}{F_z}|), \tag{8}$$

where F_x is the longitudinal traction force and F_z is the normal force acting on the tire. By defining the normalized traction force (NTF) of the vehicle as $\rho = \frac{F_x}{F_z}$, the μ_{max} can be represented by the $max(\rho)$, which can be obtained by a smartphone's inertial sensors when the vehicle is experiencing a hard brake. Because dry roads always have much larger μ_{max} than wet roads have, the $max(\rho)$ of a vehicle in dry road conditions should be larger than those in wet road conditions.

Second, in order to avoid skids on wet roads, most drivers would brake earlier and more gently [24] than they do on dry roads, resulting in relatively smaller ρ in normal braking activities. Since drivers usually perform multiple braking activities in each trip due to the stop signs, traffic lights, traffics, and etc, it is possible to crowdsource NTFs in braking activities from a large number of vehicles and drivers to accurately estimate road conditions. We note that video camera in BigRoad is another sensor that we can use to estimate road conditions by using image processing techniques, but it highly depends on the visibility and lighting environments. Therefore, we focus on using the inertial sensors based approach in this paper.

5.2.2 *Per-brake NTF Derivation*

In order to derive the NTF ρ during each brake, we first detect and segment the braking events using the acceleration readings collected by the smartphone in BigRoad. Specifically, we examine the standard deviation of accelerations on three axes to determine the vehicle's stop period using a threshold-based approach. We then extract six-second measurements before the starting point of the stop period as the segment data in a braking event.

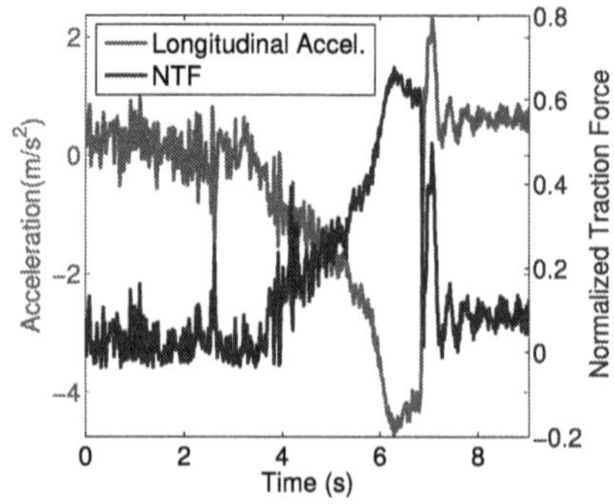

Figure 7: Example of longitudinal acceleration and normalized traction force during a brake.

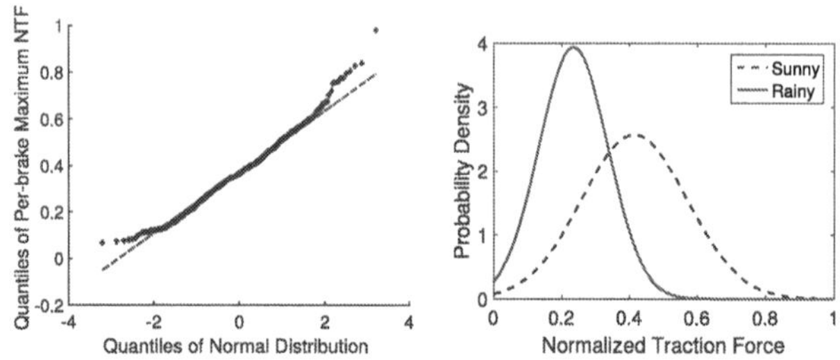

(a) QQ-plot (vs. normal distribution). (b) Probability density functions.

Figure 8: QQ-plot and probability density functions of maximum per-brake NTFs.

Next, we calculate the NTF in each brake event using the longitudinal acceleration, which can be obtained by the Device Calibration (Section 6). To simply the problem, we consider a bicycle-type vehicle model [23], where the difference between left and right tires is ignored. If we ignore the effects caused by winds and road gradient, the longitudinal force during a brake can be obtained by:

$$F_x = m|a_x| - |F_r|, \tag{9}$$

where m is the total mass of the vehicle, a_x is the longitudinal acceleration and F_r is rolling resistance force which is usually between $0.015mg$ and $0.02mg$.

In addition, the normal forces on the front and rear tires can be calculated as:

$$F_{zf} = \frac{mgL_r - ma_x h}{L}; F_{zr} = \frac{mgL_f + ma_x h}{L}, \tag{10}$$

where L_f and L_r are the distances from the center of gravity to the front and rear axles respectively. h is the distance from the center of gravity to the road surface and L is the wheel base (i.e., $L = L_f + L_r$). Note that we can use either F_{zf} or F_{rf} to calculate the vehicle's NTF ρ depending on the form of the vehicle's drivetrain (i.e., front-wheel drive or rear-wheel drive). Finally, the NTF can be derived using the vehicle's longitudinal acceleration during each brake and a few of the vehicle's basic information. Figure 7 shows an example of the longitudinal acceleration and its corresponding NTF during a brake.

5.2.3 *Crowd-sourcing-based Road Condition Estimation*

The instant NTF derived from each brake can be exploited to estimate road-conditions by being compared to different road-condition models. Such models are nothing but the distributions of NTFs abstracted from a large number of NTFs crowd-sourced from vehicles driving in different road conditions. The crowdsourced data used for building general models should cover different braking types, driving behaviors, etc., so that the models can be resilient to these different situations. Additionally, we empirically observe that the maximum NTF in each brake (e.g., the peak value of the NTF in Figure 7) fits normal distributions. The Quantile-Quantile plot in Figure 8(a) compares over 700 maximum NTFs from 40 daily trips of 5 drivers with normal distribution and verifies this observation. We thus use the least-squares based approach to fit the maximum NTFs collected from brakes in sunny days (i.e., dry condition) and rainy days (i.e., wet condition) to two road-condition models, which are two probability density function following normal distributions, namely pdf_d and pdf_w. Figure 8(b) shows an example of pdf_d and pdf_w generated by a training dataset (i.e., 350 brakes in sunny days and 100 brakes in rainy days) collected by BigRoad from 5 users at different locations. The figure also verifies that drivers brake more gently in rainy days as we expected.

It is important to note that determining the road condition based on the NTF information of only a single braking action is difficult, because the two distributions shown in Figure 8(b) are largely overlapping with each other. BigRoad takes advantage of crowdsourcing techniques and collects a large number of braking events with different braking types and driving behaviors from various on-road vehicles in a specific driving area. The system eventually can respectively calculate the joint probability of all these brakes performed on dry or wet roads, and determine the road conditions accordingly.

Specifically, we can estimate the road condition by comparing the instant maximum NTF with the abstracted road condition models as shown in the following equations:

$$\begin{cases} \text{Road is dry, if} \prod_{i=1}^{N} pdf_d(\hat{\rho}_i) \geqslant \prod_{i=1}^{N} pdf_w(\hat{\rho}_i) \\ \text{Road is wet, if} \prod_{i=1}^{N} pdf_d(\hat{\rho}_i) < \prod_{i=1}^{N} pdf_w(\hat{\rho}_i), \end{cases} \quad (11)$$

where $\hat{\rho}_i$ is the maximum NTF of the ith collected brake, N is the total number of brakes being used.

6. DEVICE CALIBRATION & SYSTEM IMPLEMENTATION

In order to ensure BigRoad work with most vehicle models, the system should be able to calibrate itself to different steering wheel positions, sensor placements, and vehicle models. The main challenge is that both the smartphone and IMU have their own coordinate systems, and the sensor measurements from both devices need to be aligned to a fixed coordinate system (e.g., the vehicle coordinate system) before they are useful.

We develop two modules to automatically align measurements from smartphone and IMU to the *vehicle coordinate system*(X_p, Y_p, Z_p) and *rotated steering wheel coordinate system*(X_r, Y_r, Z_r) when driving, namely *Smartphone Calibration* and *IMU Calibration*. The relationship between the two coordinate systems is shown in Figure 9.

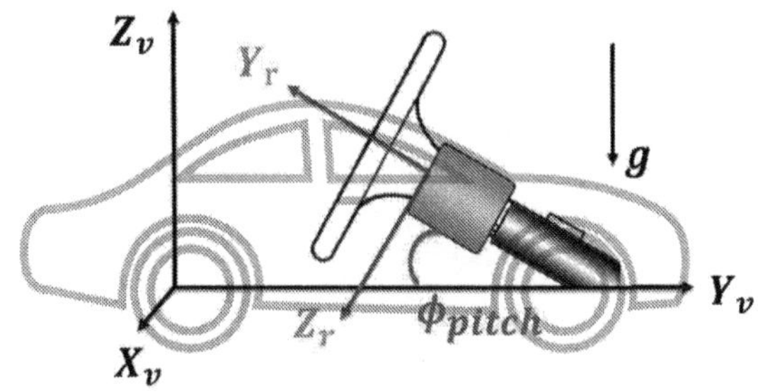

Figure 9: Vehicle coordinate system and rotated steering wheel coordinate system.

6.1 Smartphone Calibration

We implement the coordinate alignment algorithm to align sensor measurements from the smartphone to the *vehicle coordinate system* based on an existing work [25]. Specifically, it utilizes the smartphone's accelerometer and gyroscope measurements when the vehicle brakes while driving straight to derive the corresponding rotation matrix.

6.2 IMU Calibration

The coordinate alignment for IMU is challenging, because the IMU's orientation is subject to the rotation of the steering wheel, IMU's position, and vehicle models. The IMU Configuration adopts two steps to align the sensor measurements from the IMU to the *steering wheel coordinate system*: First, the system aligns the sensor measurements to the *vehicle coordinate system* when vehicle is driving straight using the same approach introduced in the Smartphone Calibration. Since we perform this alignment while driving straight, aligned IMU's coordinate system will depart the *vehicle coordinate system* when steering wheel turns, but its x-axis is always identical to the *rotated steering wheel coordinate system*. Second, the system calculates the steering wheel pitch angle (ϕ_{pitch}) and further rotate other two axes to the *rotated steering wheel coordinate system*.

As shown in Figure 9, ϕ_{pitch} is the angle between Y_v's negative direction and Y_r's positive direction, which is usually adjustable by the driver. And this angle also exists between negative direction y-axis of the aligned IMU and Y_r's positive direction. Thus, ϕ_{pitch} can be derived from the angular velocity projection on aligned IMU's coordinate system's y- and z-axis, as shown in equation 12:

$$\phi_{pitch} = atan(\frac{-gyro_{Y_i}}{gyro_{Z_i}}), \quad (12)$$

where $gyro_{Y_i}$ and $gyro_{Z_i}$ are the gyroscope reading's on IMU's y- and z- axes after aligned to *vehicle coordinate system*. The system automatically picks twenty samples from a steering motion and calculate ϕ_{pitch} based on Equation 12. Then, IMU's measurements can be rotated to the *rotated steering wheel coordinate system* by rotating around x-axis for $(180 - \phi_{pitch})^{\circ}$. Besides, BigRoad also includes a data synchronization module to remove the delay of IMU data caused by Bluetooth transmission. This module uses the same brake segment used in smartphone coordinate alignment and runs cross correlation on smartphone and IMU acceleration trace to find the delay.

6.3 Implementation

In summary, two components are required in BigRoad:

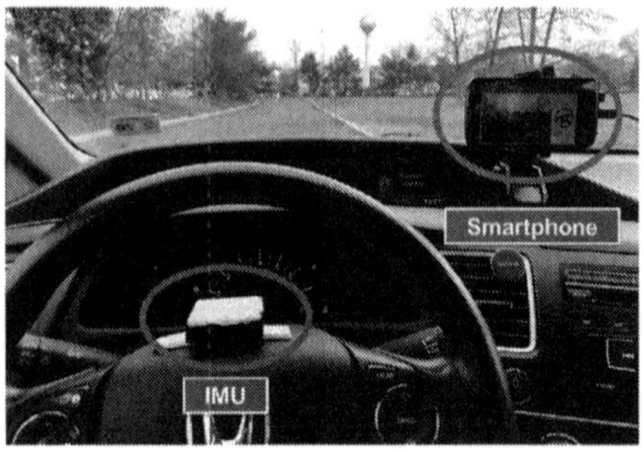

Figure 10: BigRoad setup.

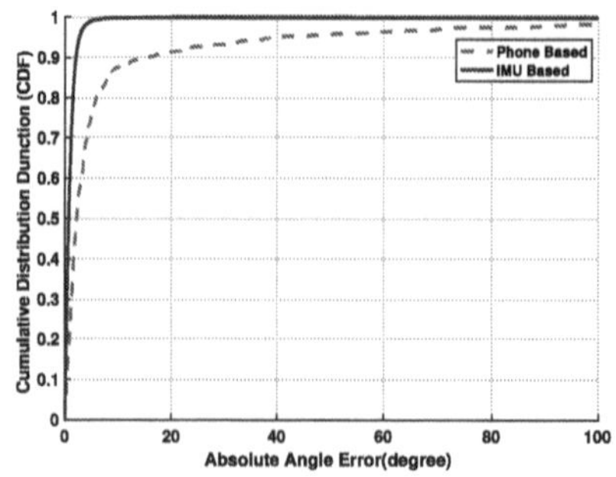

Figure 11: CDF of steering wheel angle absolute error.

an IMU and a smartphone, which are mounted on top of the steering wheel and a phone holder respectively as shown in Figure 10. Specifically, the smartphone is equipped with inertial sensors, a camera and a GPS receiver. The IMU contains inertial sensors and periodically sends sensor data to the smartphone via Bluetooth. In our implementation, we use the Invensense MPU-9150 9-axis motion sensor as the IMU. We implement the BigRoad as an app on Android 4.1, which is applicable to any major brand of Android smartphones. All the data collected by BigRoad will be synchronized to the smartphone's system clock, and could be automatically uploaded to the cloud server via WiFi or cellular network.

7. PERFORMANCE EVALUATION

In this section, we evaluate our system with respect to (i) the accuracy of internal driver input information it provides, (ii) the accuracy of external perception monitoring, and (iii) the usefulness of our collected data, namely whether our collected data could allow training of self-driving system components.

7.1 Experiment Setup

We conduct driving experiments with BigRoad to evaluate its performance. Our experiments include six vehicle models and 7 drivers driving on various types of roads for their daily commute in two states. In total, we collect 143 trips in a 3-month period. During these trips we used different experiment configurations to allow studying different questions as follows:

Internal Driver Inputs Accuracy. We collect 84 trips from three vehicles (i.e., 2015 Honda Civic, 2016 Chevrolet Impala, and 2016 Chevrolet Equinox) and five drivers to evaluate the accuracy of the collected driver inputs. We used these vehicles because we were able to gain access to ground truth steering wheel angle data reported by an internal sensor (for two of the vehicles a carmaker provided us with a specialized device and for one vehicle we were able to reverse engineer the data format of messages captured with a standard OBD-II/CAN interface). We also recorded driving speed from the internal vehicle bus, which is openly available as part of the OBD-II standard. We were able to sample the data from the Honda Civic, Chevrolet Impala and Equinox at 1.43Hz, 100Hz and 10Hz, respectively.

External Perception Accuracy. We evaluate the performance of road condition estimation based on 59 trips from four vehicles (i.e., 2008 Nissan Rogue, 2010 Honda Civic, 2015 Mazda CX-5 and 2015 Mercedes-Benz GLC 350) and five drivers. The ground truth of the road condition and weather for each trip was manually labeled by the drivers.

Data Usefulness. We use 5 trips from three different drivers driving the 2015 Honda Civic on highways to evaluate the usability of BigRoad's video output. The dataset includes about 1.5 hours of video at 30 frames per second and steering wheel angle ground truth from the OBD interface at 100Hz. We were able to achieve a higher sampling rate of 100Hz here, because we do not simultaneously capture vehicle speed information in these experiments.

7.2 Accuracy of Driver Input

Steering Wheel Angle Estimation. We first evaluate the performance of our steering-wheel estimation approaches based on IMU and phone sensing to quantify the accuracy-complexity trade-off (how accuracy degrades when only phone sensors are used) and to understand whether the accuracy with phone sensors is still sufficient for self-driving data collection. In particular, we measure the absolute error[2] of the estimated steering wheel angle for both approaches by reporting the difference between the estimated value and the ground truth from the OBD readers. Figure 11 shows the CDFs of the steering wheel angle estimation errors of our two approaches.

We observe that the IMU-based approach performs similarly to the tolerances reported for a built-in steering wheel sensor. In particular, the mean error of the steering-wheel IMU based approach is 0.96° with the median of 0.69° and 90-percentile of 1.99°. This compares to 1.5° accuracy reported for an internal steering angle sensor [26].

We also observe that the overall errors of the steering-wheel IMU based approach are much smaller than those of the phone based approach. The mean error of the phone based approach is 7.53°, with the median at 2.19° and the 90-percentile at 15.05°.

We further study the impact of the driving speed and steering wheel angle on the estimation accuracy. Figure 12(a) presents the error distribution of the IMU based and phone based steering-wheel estimation approaches with respect to 13 bins of driving speed between 0 to 60km/h. From the figure, we can tell that the steering-wheel IMU based approach has consistently low errors across all driving speeds. The phone based approach, however, shows larger errors in the lower speed range (i.e., between 5-30km/h). We believe this is because the error of the driving speed and angular velocity becomes more obvious in low speed, so the phone

[2]The errors used in the rest of the paper are all absolute error, unless stated otherwise.

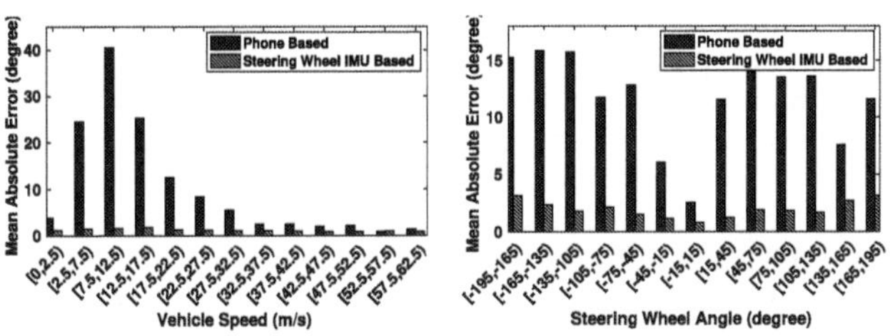

(a) Error distribution with respect to vehicle speed.

(b) Error distribution with respect to steering angle.

Figure 12: Error distribution with respect to speed and steering angle.

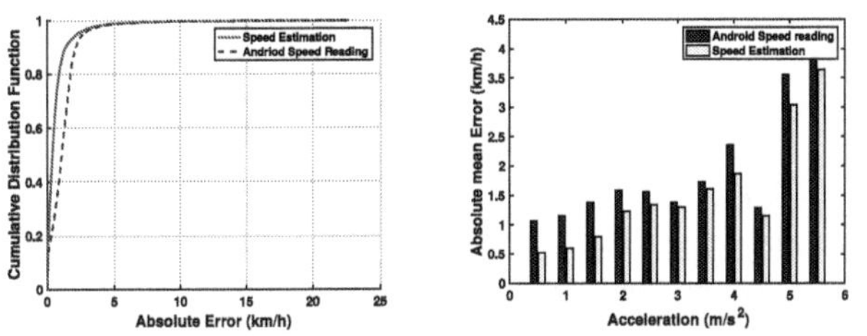

(a) CDF of speed estimation absolute error.

(b) Error distribution with respect to acceleration.

Figure 13: CDF of speed estimation absolute error.

based approach cannot accurately measure vehicle turning radius based on equation 5.. Figure 12(b) presents the error distribution of the two approaches with respect to 13 bins of steering wheel angle ranging from $-180°$ to $180°$. We find that the estimation error of the phone based approach increases significantly for larger steering wheel angles, while the steering-wheel IMU based approach shows comparatively low errors across steering wheel angles. Note that larger steering wheel angles are normally correlated with lower vehicle speeds.

Driving Speed Estimation. Next, we evaluate the performance of the driving speed estimation component of BigRoad by respectively comparing the deviation of the estimated driving speed and the driving speed directly obtained from Android with the internal vehicle speed obtained from OBD-II in Figure 13(a). The smartphones we used in this experiment include a Nexus 5 with Android 5.1, and a Nexus 6 and a Nexus 6P with Android 6.1. From the figure we can observe that BigRoad can achieve much lower deviations than the smartphone-reported speed. In particular, the smartphone driving speeds from the Android location service have an average deviation of 1.17 km/h, while that of BigRoad is only 0.65 km/h. The 90-percentile deviation of the estimated speeds from Android and BigRoad are 2.11 km/h and 1.37 km/h, respectively, which indicate that the delay shifting and complementary filtering techniques in BigRoad can effectively reduce deviations.

To further explore the limitation of our speed estimation method, we plot the mean deviation of the estimated speed from Android and BigRoad with respect to the y-axis absolute acceleration of the vehicle in Figure 13(b). We find that the speed estimation errors of both approaches generally increase with the accelerations of the vehicle although BigRoad

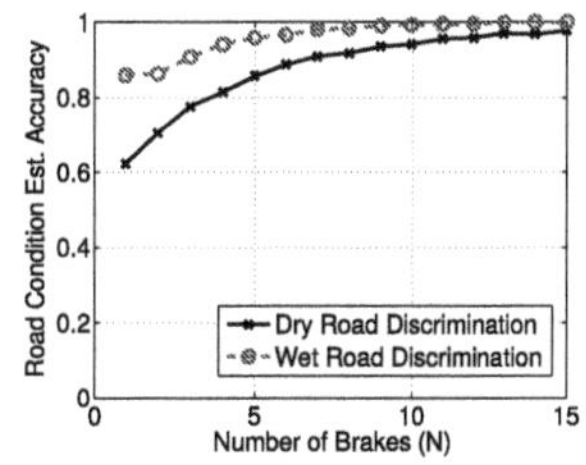

Figure 14: Discrimination accuracy of the road condition estimation.

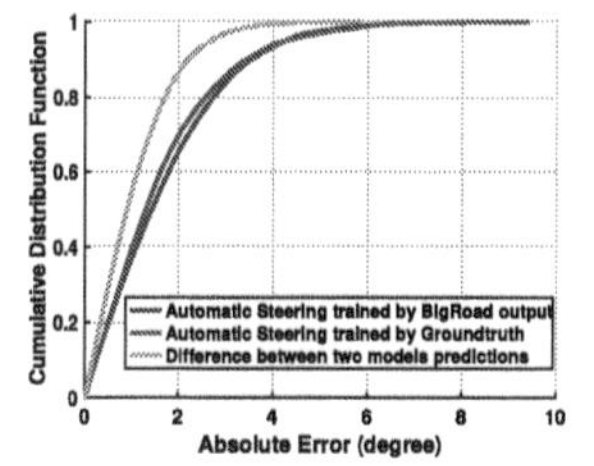

Figure 15: CDF of two trained Automatic Steering Algorithms and their comparison.

can achieve lower errors. We believe this is because both approaches rely on the location updates from GPS, which have a low refresh rate and cannot capture speed changes between two samples.

7.3 Accuracy of External Perception

As the main part of external perception, we mainly evaluate the performance of road condition estimation in this section. As discussed in Section 7.1, we distribute BigRoad systems to 5 users to collect driving data in their daily commutes. In total, we collected 737 braking events from 43 trips in sunny days and 193 braking events from 16 driving trips on rainy days. We use 50% of the braking data for training the road condition models (i.e., pdf_d and pdf_w) and use the rest of the data for the testing purpose.

Specifically, we can identify the road conditions by using the NTF statistics from N collected braking events according to equation 11. Figure 14 shows the road condition discrimination accuracy with a different number of events N. We observe that BigRoad can achieve high accuracy to determine the road's condition (i.e., dry or wet) by only using the normal braking events from crowdsourced driving data. And the system only needs a small number of braking events (e.g., 15) from the vehicles to achieve over 95% discrimination accuracy.

7.4 Usefulness of BigRoad Output

To explore the usefulness of data collected with the proposed BigData approach, in this work we implemented an automatic steering algorithm, which represents an important component of a self-driving system. The automatic steering algorithm is constructed through an end-to-end learning approach that forgoes feature extraction and trains a deep convolutional neural network to directly map raw pixels from a single front facing camera to steering commands, which has recently been demonstrated [11]. The neural network is implemented based on the open source code from [27] with 5 layers, including three convolutional layers and two fully connected layers. To feed the collected data into the deep neural network, we developed a few strategies including synchronizing each video frame with the recorded steering wheel angle and speed for training purposes and video rescaling and cropping. In particular, a Nvidia Quadro K5000 is used to train the network, and the trained network takes $3ms$ to process each input frame. The trained neural network shall have the capability to output the intended steering angle solely based on the front camera view.

We demonstrate the usefulness of BigRoad's outputs by

comparing the results of our automatic steering application when using two different pairs of driving data: the front-view video together with either (i) the estimated steering wheel angles from BigRoad or (ii) the ground truth from the OBD port. We use about 1.3 hours of real-road driving data to train the deep neural network in the application, and use the remaining 0.2 hours of the data for testing. The comparison of the results is shown in Figure 7.4, in which we regard the OBD port steering angle of human drivers as the ground truth. We observe that the median errors of the application are 1.30° and 1.42° for using the steering wheel angles provided by the OBD and BigRoad, respectively. Moreover, we plot the CDF of the sample-to-sample difference between the prediction results from the two scenarios in Figure 7.4. We observe that the median difference between using these two inputs is 0.90°. These small differences suggest that this self-steering application can effectively be trained by using the data from BigRoad.

Furthermore, we find that the state-of-the-art end to end self-steering work based on CNNs [11] does not directly use the driver's steering angle obtained from steering sensors as a training label because the driver's input may not be perfect. It applies a computer vision based calibration to slightly correct the driver's steering angles. We note that such a calibration could also be applied to BigRoad outputs before using them to train the self-steering network, which presumably results in even smaller performance differences.

8. RELATED WORK

There has been extensive work on vehicular sensing and self-driving that BigRoad can contribute to [11, 13, 28, 29, 30, 31, 32, 33, 34]. Machine learning methods are primarily chosen due to the complexity the problem. Pomerleau's pioneering work [33] estimates the vehicle's steering direction from the camera images and a laser rangefinder. [29, 30, 31] incorporate high-resolution video and laser data to track trajectory, obstacle, terrain roughness, etc. Some other studies used only a camera to solve self-driving vehicle problems. [34] and [11] developed an adaptive cruise control and steering systems, respectively. Brubaker et.al. [28] use visual odometry and road maps for a real-time self-localization system. [13] and [32] extract traffic light states from the camera to help route planning and increase energy efficiency. Developing these systems need an enormous amount of data which can be facilitated by BigRoad with minimum infrastructure.

Most existing efforts to collect driving data build on a small fleet of tens of highly instrumented vehicles that are continuously operated with test drivers [5, 6, 7, 8]. Traditional vehicle manufacturers [6, 7] are testing their autonomous driving technologies on redesigned cars. Google's parent company, Waymo [5], has accumulated 2 millions miles of testing drives with their self-driving cars. Comma.ai's project OpenPilot [8] reverse engineering the OBD-II data from two vehicle models of Hondas and Acuras, and uses the collected data to train CNN based self-driving systems. However, limited by the vehicle numbers and models, it is challenging to accumulate a sufficiently large dataset with these approaches.

Smartphones are also used to monitor the vehicle and the driver [25, 35, 36, 37, 38]. Wang et.al. [25] utilize smartphone sensors and OBD device to capture vehicle dynamics. Bo et.al. [35] detect texting and driving using smartphones. Dai et.al. [36] and Johnson et.al. [37] propose driving behavior monitoring systems to track other risky driving events. Chen et.al. [39] introduce a middleware to sense a vehicle's steering using smartphone sensors. However, this work only limits to high-level steering motion, such as lane change. Other approaches [40, 41] track steering wheel usage and angle leveraging smart watches. Different from these studies, which use only the gyroscope measurements, BigRoad fuses the accelerometer and gyroscope readings from both the IMU and smartphone to achieve the fine-grained steering wheel angle estimation. Besides, these studies suffer from the hand-over-hand problem and have relatively low accuracy.

Another body of work focuses on crowdsourcing data for driving applications. CrowdITS and Waze [42, 43] utilized crowd's feedback to gather the traffic conditions. Chen et. al. [44] proposed a semi-automated approach to tag parking spots from speed and driver feedback. SmartRoad [45] locates traffic signals and stop signs from vehicle speed. Finally, Li et. al. [14] predict traffic light state based on observed wait times.

9. CONCLUSION

In this paper, we seek a low-cost yet reliable solution to collect fine-grained driving data that can support developing dependable automated driving and traffic safety technologies. We present BigRoad, a light-weight sensing and driving data logging system that can derive internal driver inputs (i.e., steering wheel angle, driving speed and acceleration) and external perceptions of road environments (i.e., road conditions and front-view video) using very few off-the-shelf sensing devices (i.e., a smartphone and an IMU), which are not dependent on vehicle types. The system uses advanced coordinate alignment techniques to enable driving data acquisition independent of sensor orientation in heterogeneous driving scenarios across different vehicle models and drivers. We develop estimation algorithms based on complementary filtering to derive accurate steering wheel angle, driving speed and acceleration. By crowdsourcing real driving data, we model binary road conditions (i.e., dry and wet) based on the distributions of vehicle's accelerations and use them for real-time road condition estimation. In addition, BigRoad captures front-view videos with millisecond granularity time stamps to facilitate various vehicle applications and research that need to synchronize video frames with high-sampling-rate sensing data. Over 140 trips from six different vehicles and seven drivers show that the system can generate steering wheel angle with 0.69°median error, driving speed with 0.65km/h deviation, and determine binary road conditions with 95% accuracy. We further develop train an automatic steering angle predictor to demonstrate that data from such light-weight sensors can be used without significant performance degradation. We hope that these techniques will allow larger-scale driving data collection and facilitate the development of advanced driver assistance and automated driving technologies.

Acknowledgments

We sincerely thank our shepherd Dr. Souvik Sen and the reviewers for their insightful comments. This material is based in part upon work supported by the National Science Foundation under Grant Nos. CNS-1329939, CNS-1409767, CNS-1409811, and CNS-1566455.

10. REFERENCES

[1] Tom Krisher and Joan Lowy. Tesla driver killed in crash while using car's 'autopilot'. *ASSOCIATED PRESS(June 30, 2016)*.

[2] Chris Urmson. Google Self-Driving Car Project. https://www.transportation.gov/sites/dot.gov/files/docs/AV%20policy%20guidance%20PDF.pdf. Talk at SXSW Interactive 2016.

[3] National Highway Traffic Safety Administration. Federal Automated Vehicles Policy. https://www.transportation.gov/sites/dot.gov/files/docs/AV%20policy%20guidance%20PDF.pdf.

[4] National Highway Traffic Safety Administration. Fatality Analysis Reporting System. https://www.transportation.gov/sites/dot.gov/files/docs/AV%20policy%20guidance%20PDF.pdf. Talk at SXSW Interactive 2016.

[5] Waymo: Google's parent company on self-driving. https://waymo.com/.

[6] Kirsten Korosec. GM's Cruise Automation Is Testing Self-Driving Chevy Bolts in Arizona. http://fortune.com/2016/08/09/cruise-automation-arizona-gm/.

[7] Mercedes-Benz Research & Development, Autonomous Driving. http://mbrdna.com/divisions/autonomous-driving/.

[8] Openpilot. https://github.com/commaai/openpilot.

[9] UMTRI Naturalistic Driving Data. http://www.umtri.umich.edu/our-focus/naturalistic-driving-data.

[10] VTTI Naturalistic Driving Study. http://www.vtti.vt.edu/impact/index.html.

[11] Mariusz Bojarski, Davide Del Testa, Daniel Dworakowski, Bernhard Firner, Beat Flepp, Prasoon Goyal, Lawrence D Jackel, Mathew Monfort, Urs Muller, Jiakai Zhang, et al. End to end learning for self-driving cars. *arXiv preprint arXiv:1604.07316*, 2016.

[12] The OpenXC platform. http://openxcplatform.com/.

[13] Emmanouil Koukoumidis, Li-Shiuan Peh, and Margaret Rose Martonosi. Signalguru: leveraging mobile phones for collaborative traffic signal schedule advisory. In *Proceedings of the 9th international conference on Mobile systems, applications, and services*, pages 127–140. ACM, 2011.

[14] Hongyu Li, Luyang Liu, Cagdas Karatas, Jian Liu, Marco Gruteser, Yingying Chen, Yan Wang, Richard P Martin, and Jie Yang. Towards safer texting while driving through stop time prediction. In *Proceedings of the First ACM International Workshop on Smart, Autonomous, and Connected Vehicular Systems and Services*, pages 14–21. ACM, 2016.

[15] Thomas Maze, Manish Agarwai, and Garrett Burchett. Whether weather matters to traffic demand, traffic safety, and traffic operations and flow. *Transportation research record: Journal of the transportation research board*, (1948):170–176, 2006.

[16] Hyung Gi Min and Eun Tae Jeung. Complementary filter design for angle estimation using mems accelerometer and gyroscope. *Department of Control and Instrumentation, Changwon National University, Changwon, Korea*, pages 641–773, 2015.

[17] LS20126 GPS Receiver. https://www.sparkfun.com/products/retired/9838.

[18] Johan Casselgren, Mikael Sjödahl, and James LeBlanc. Angular spectral response from covered asphalt. *Applied optics*, 46(20):4277–4288, 2007.

[19] Youngmin Kim, Namcheol Baik, and Jonghun Kim. A study on development of mobile road surface condition detection system utilizing probe car. *Journal of Emerging Trends in Computing and Information Sciences*, 4(10), 2013.

[20] Ville V Viikari, Timo Varpula, and Mikko Kantanen. Road-condition recognition using 24-ghz automotive radar. *IEEE transactions on intelligent transportation systems*, 10(4):639–648, 2009.

[21] D Gailius and S Jačenas. Iec detection on a road by analyzing tire to road friction ultrasonic noise. *Ultragarsas*, 62(2):17–20, 2007.

[22] Yunha Kim, Sehoon Oh, and Yoichi Hori. Road condition estimation using acoustic method for electric vehicles. In *The 10th FISITA Student Congress*, pages 30–6, 2010.

[23] Rajesh Rajamani. *Vehicle dynamics and control*. Springer Science & Business Media, 2011.

[24] Lin Zhang and P Prevedouros. Motorist perceptions on the impact of rainy conditions on driver behavior and accident risk. In *Proceedings of the 84th Annual Meeting of the Transportation Research Board, Washington, DC*, 2005.

[25] Yan Wang, Jie Yang, Hongbo Liu, Yingying Chen, Marco Gruteser, and Richard P Martin. Sensing vehicle dynamics for determining driver phone use. In *Proceeding of the 11th annual international conference on Mobile systems, applications, and services*, pages 41–54. ACM, 2013.

[26] Methode Electronic Steering Wheel Angle Sensor. http://www.methode.com/Documents/TechnicalLibrary/Steering_Angle_Sensor_Data_Sheet.pdf.

[27] Eder Santana and George Hotz. Learning a driving simulator. *arXiv preprint arXiv:1608.01230*, 2016.

[28] Marcus A Brubaker, Andreas Geiger, and Raquel Urtasun. Lost! leveraging the crowd for probabilistic visual self-localization. In *Proceedings of the IEEE Conference on Computer Vision and Pattern Recognition*, pages 3057–3064, 2013.

[29] Hendrik Dahlkamp, Adrian Kaehler, David Stavens, Sebastian Thrun, and Gary R Bradski. Self-supervised monocular road detection in desert terrain. In *Robotics: science and systems*, volume 38. Philadelphia, 2006.

[30] David Held, Jesse Levinson, Sebastian Thrun, and Silvio Savarese. Combining 3d shape, color, and motion for robust anytime tracking. *Proceedings of the 2014 Robotics: Science and Systems, Berkeley, CA, USA*, 1216, 2014.

[31] Jesse Levinson, Jake Askeland, Jan Becker, Jennifer Dolson, David Held, Soeren Kammel, J Zico Kolter, Dirk Langer, Oliver Pink, Vaughan Pratt, et al. Towards fully autonomous driving: Systems and algorithms. In *Intelligent Vehicles Symposium (IV), 2011 IEEE*, pages 163–168. IEEE, 2011.

[32] Jesse Levinson, Jake Askeland, Jennifer Dolson, and

Sebastian Thrun. Traffic light mapping, localization, and state detection for autonomous vehicles. In *Robotics and Automation (ICRA), 2011 IEEE International Conference on*, pages 5784–5791. IEEE, 2011.

[33] Dean A Pomerleau. Alvinn: An autonomous land vehicle in a neural network. Technical report, DTIC Document, 1989.

[34] Gideon P Stein, Ofer Mano, and Amnon Shashua. Vision-based acc with a single camera: bounds on range and range rate accuracy. In *Intelligent vehicles symposium, 2003. Proceedings. IEEE*, pages 120–125. IEEE, 2003.

[35] Cheng Bo, Xuesi Jian, Xiang-Yang Li, Xufei Mao, Yu Wang, and Fan Li. You're driving and texting: detecting drivers using personal smart phones by leveraging inertial sensors. In *Proceedings of the 19th annual international conference on Mobile computing & networking*, pages 199–202. ACM, 2013.

[36] Jiangpeng Dai, Jin Teng, Xiaole Bai, Zhaohui Shen, and Dong Xuan. Mobile phone based drunk driving detection. In *PervasiveHealth*, 2010.

[37] Derick A Johnson and Mohan M Trivedi. Driving style recognition using a smartphone as a sensor platform. In *IEEE ITSC*, pages 1609–1615, 2011.

[38] Yan Wang, Yingying Jennifer Chen, Jie Yang, Marco Gruteser, Richard P Martin, Hongbo Liu, Luyang Liu, and Cagdas Karatas. Determining driver phone use by exploiting smartphone integrated sensors. *IEEE Transactions on Mobile Computing*, 15(8):1965–1981, 2016.

[39] Dongyao Chen, Kyong-Tak Cho, Sihui Han, Zhizhuo Jin, and Kang G Shin. Invisible sensing of vehicle steering with smartphones. In *Proceedings of the 13th Annual International Conference on Mobile Systems, Applications, and Services*, pages 1–13. ACM, 2015.

[40] C. Karatas, L. Liu, H. Li, J. Liu, Y. Wang, S. Tan, J. Yang, Y. Chen, M. Gruteser, and R. Martin. Leveraging wearables for steering and driver tracking. In *IEEE INFOCOM 2016 - The 35th Annual IEEE International Conference on Computer Communications*, pages 1–9, April 2016.

[41] Luyang Liu, Cagdas Karatas, Hongyu Li, Sheng Tan, Marco Gruteser, Jie Yang, Yingying Chen, and Richard P Martin. Toward detection of unsafe driving with wearables. In *Proceedings of the 2015 workshop on Wearable Systems and Applications*, pages 27–32. ACM, 2015.

[42] Kashif Ali, Dina Al-Yaseen, Ali Ejaz, Tayyab Javed, and Hossam S Hassanein. Crowdits: Crowdsourcing in intelligent transportation systems. In *2012 IEEE Wireless Communications and Networking Conference (WCNC)*, pages 3307–3311. IEEE, 2012.

[43] WAZE. https://www.waze.com/.

[44] Xiao Chen, Elizeu Santos-Neto, and Matei Ripeanu. Crowd-based smart parking: A case study for mobile crowdsourcing. In *International Conference on Mobile Wireless Middleware, Operating Systems, and Applications*, pages 16–30. Springer, 2012.

[45] Shaohan Hu, Lu Su, Hengchang Liu, Hongyan Wang, and Tarek F Abdelzaher. Smartroad: a crowd-sourced traffic regulator detection and identification system. In *Information Processing in Sensor Networks (IPSN), 2013 ACM/IEEE International Conference on*, pages 331–332. IEEE, 2013.

Characterizing Smartwatch Usage In The Wild

Xing Liu[1] Tianyu Chen[1] Feng Qian[1]
Zhixiu Guo[23] Felix Xiaozhu Lin[4] Xiaofeng Wang[1] Kai Chen[25]

[1]Indiana University Bloomington
[2]SKLOIS, Institute of Information Engineering, Chinese Academy of Sciences
[3]Beijing Jiaotong University [4]Purdue ECE
[5]School of Cyber Security, University of Chinese Academy of Sciences

ABSTRACT

Smartwatch has become one of the most popular wearable computers on the market. We conduct an IRB-approved measurement study involving 27 Android smartwatch users. Using a 106-day dataset collected from our participants, we perform in-depth characterization of three key aspects of smartwatch usage "in the wild": usage patterns, energy consumption, and network traffic. Based on our findings, we identify key aspects of the smartwatch ecosystem that can be further improved, propose recommendations, and point out future research directions.

CCS Concepts

•Human-centered computing → Ubiquitous and mobile devices;

1. INTRODUCTION

Wearable devices are weaving computing into our daily lives. Among diverse wearables, smartwatches are probably one of the most popular gadgets. According to a recent CNET article [10], smartwatch sales are expected to jump from 30 million in 2015 to 50 million in 2016 and then to 67 million in 2017. Smartwatches offer great convenience to end users through a wide range of features such as receiving push notifications, issuing voice control, monitoring fitness, and interacting with 3rd-party apps. Despite their popularity, smartwatches are still relatively new to the commercial mobile device family, and the research community lacks a thorough understanding of the smartwatch ecosystem.

This paper bridges the above gap by conducting an IRB-approved crowd-sourced measurement study of smartwatches involving 27 users. We first demonstrate it is feasible to build a self-contained and comprehensive measurement data collector on today's off-the-shelf Android smartwatches. The collector transparently collects a wide range of usage data, network traffic, and system events in realistic usage scenarios, with very low runtime and energy overhead incurred (§3). We then provide each of the 27 users with a state-of-the-art smartwatch instrumented with the data collector. Using a 106-day dataset collected from our participants, we conduct an in-depth characterization of three key aspects of smartwatch usage "in the wild": usage patterns, energy consumption, and network traffic characteristics. This is to our knowledge the most comprehensive and in-depth crowd-sourced study of smartwatches. Our key measurement results consist of the following.

Permission to make digital or hard copies of all or part of this work for personal or classroom use is granted without fee provided that copies are not made or distributed for profit or commercial advantage and that copies bear this notice and the full citation on the first page. Copyrights for components of this work owned by others than ACM must be honored. Abstracting with credit is permitted. To copy otherwise, or republish, to post on servers or to redistribute to lists, requires prior specific permission and/or a fee. Request permissions from permissions@acm.org.

MobiSys'17, June 19-23, 2017, Niagara Falls, NY, USA
© 2017 ACM. ISBN 978-1-4503-4928-4/17/06...$15.00
DOI: http://dx.doi.org/10.1145/3081333.3081351

• We characterize the smartwatch usage patterns. An Android watch can stay in one of the four states with diverse power characteristics: fully awake, dozing (with dimmed watch face display and restricted system activity), sleeping (screen further turned off), and charging. We find that smartwatch's wake-up period accounts for only 2% of the overall usage period among the four states. The wake-up sessions are not only short, but also frequent (72 times per day on average). We then analyze their triggering factors, which help us identify key usage scenarios of a watch: short "flick and look" sessions (the most common interaction type that the OS needs to be optimized for), push notifications, longer interaction sessions, and unintended wake-up (§4.1).

• A key usage scenario of smartwatches is to receive push notifications. In our dataset, more than 200 apps send push notifications to the watch through either the OS-provided Android Wear service or custom data channels between phone-side and watch-side apps. Push notifications are dominated by instant messaging and emails. Despite a potential lack of long-term predictability, push notifications' arrival exhibits a strong bursty pattern, with a median inter-arrival time of only 49 seconds. Also there is room for the OS to improve push notification delivery, by strategically determining whether to push and how to push (§4.2).

• We also investigate how smartwatch applications (apps) behave. We find smartwatch app execution is dominated by short but frequent background services, whose total duration is more than 50 times longer than that of full-screen activities, which users seldom launch due to a watch's small form factor making full-fledged interaction challenging. The services, together with the OS infrastructures (*e.g.*, the push notification and card management subsystems) should therefore be the optimization focus for OS and app developers (§4.3).

• We derive comprehensive and accurate power models for two popular Android smartwatches (§5.1). We then apply the power models to the user study data to quantify the energy consumption of smartwatches in the wild. We made several interesting observations. More than half of the smartwatch energy is consumed by the dozing state (56%) due to its long duration. Meanwhile, the awake state also plays an important role in energy consumption (27%) despite its very short usage duration (2%). Due to the

§	Topic	Key Results
§4.1	Device states	Dozing dominates the usage (50.6%); wake-up accounts for 2% of usage period; wake-up sessions are short but frequent (72 per day on average) with various root causes such as "flick and look" and push notifications.
§4.2	Push notifications	Push notifications are used by 200+ apps, dominated by IM/emails, and exhibiting bursty arrival patterns.
§4.3	Smartwatch apps	A wide spectrum of watch apps are observed; their execution is dominated by short background services.
§5.1	Power models	Accurate and comprehensive power models for two popular watches. The models have error rates <6%.
§5.2	Energy utilization	Dozing and wake-up account for 56% and 27% of overall energy respectively. At component level, CPU (29%) and display (30%) dominate the energy consumption. Network consumes only 3.4% of the energy.
§5.3	Energy optimization	"What-if" analysis over real data for improving energy efficiency; impact of state machine on battery drain.
§6	Network traffic	Watches are paired with phones during 84% of the daytime; most flows are small, short, slow, and bursty.

Table 1: Key results and findings of our study.

big power consumption gap between awake and dozing/sleeping, a small increase of the wake-up duration will be "amplified" from the battery draining perspective, thus shortening the standby time of the watch. The top-2 energy-hungry components on smartwatches are the same as those on smartphones: CPU and display. Despite smartwatches' small screen sizes, display still contributes to 30.2% of the overall energy. CPU accounts for 29.3% of the overall smartwatch energy. Network interfaces, however, consume a very small fraction of energy on smartwatches without a cellular interface (§5.2).

• We investigate how to make smartwatches more energy-efficient using combined approaches of trace-driven "what-if" analysis and controlled in-lab experiments. Our results suggest that the energy efficiency can be further improved through a wide range of optimization strategies such as optimizing the display, bundling delay-tolerant push notifications, and dynamically configuring CPU's online cores and frequencies. Also the watch's state machine (Figure 1) and its associated timers affect the energy consumption and need to be strategically determined, as demonstrated by our "what-if" analysis (§5.3).

• We conduct a first measurement study of smartwatch network traffic. We find that watches are paired with phones during 84% of the day time, making Bluetooth traffic account for 91% of the overall smartwatch traffic. Smartwatch traffic is dominated by downlink traffic (from phone/Internet to the watch). The vast majority of network flows are small, short, slow, and bursty, with the flow size and rate being very well correlated. Our characterizations provide hints and knowledge for improving the network protocol stack for future wearable devices (§6).

Overall, our findings suggest that in many aspects (user behaviors, app execution patterns, energy consumption, network traffic, *etc.*), smartwatches exhibit characteristics that are different from those of smartphones, which have been extensively studied in the literature. Our quantitative measurement results complement the qualitative smartwatch app design guidelines published by major vendors [4, 11, 8]. Our key findings are summarized in Table 1. To summarize, our contributions consist of the following.

• We develop a self-contained and lightweight measurement data collection system for Android Wear smartwatches, and conduct a real deployment on 27 users.

• We derive accurate and comprehensive power models for two commodity Android Wear watches.

• We perform systematic measurements of smartwatches' usage patterns, energy consumption profiles, and network traffic characteristics using a 106-day dataset collected from 27 users. Based on our findings, we identify key aspects in the smartwatch ecosystems that can be further improved, and propose recommendations and future research directions.

2. RELATED WORK

Understanding Mobile Devices "in the Wild". Researchers have carried out numerous crowd-sourced measurements of smartphones [28, 20, 52, 7, 46, 49, 39, 14]. While they partially motivate our user trial, much fewer efforts have been made for wearable devices. Among them, Gouveia *et al.* studied how users engage with activity trackers [22]. Lazar *et al.* interviewed 17 participants to study the incentives of using and abandoning smart devices [29]. Lyons studied usage practices of traditional dumb watches by conducting a user survey [34]. Min *et al.* characterized smartwatch battery use based on online survey and a user study involving 17 users [37]. They studied users' satisfaction toward smartwatch life, charging behaviors, and interaction patterns. In a recent extended abstract [44], Poyraz *et al.* also described their smartwatch user study involving 32 users for 70 days. Using the collected data, they analyzed the watches' power consumption and characterized user activities. While the detailed data collection and measurement methodologies were not fully documented, many of their findings such as the active state's high energy contribution compared to its short usage duration are qualitatively similar to ours. Compared to [37] and [44], we instead investigate a much wider spectrum of characteristics such as push notification, app usage, and network traffic by leveraging a much richer set of data items collected in Table 2. We also make our power models publicly available.

Wearable System, Energy, and Applications. LiKamWa *et al.* characterized the energy consumption of Google Glass [30]. Huang *et al.* proposed a fast storage system for wearables based on battery-backed RAM and offloading [25]. Santagati *et al.* designed an ultrasonic networking framework for wearable medical devices [50]. Miao *et al.* investigated the implications of smartwatches' circular display on resource usage [36]. Ham *et al.* proposed a novel display energy conservation scheme for wearables [24]. There also exists a large body of work from the mobile computing, sensing, and HCI community. These studies focus on novel wearable applications [51, 40, 35], wearable user interface design [15, 43], and wearable security [53, 33]. In contrast, our measurement focuses on characterizing wearable user behavior, application usage, energy consumption, and network traffic – all in the wild.

Characterizing Android Wear OS. Recently, Liu *et al.* analyzed the execution of Android Wear OS and presented a series of inefficiencies and OS implications [32, 31]. Compared to its in-lab, controlled experiments, this paper contributes the understanding of real-world wearable usage as well as the entailed design implications – backed by more solid evidence. Furthermore, our study characterizes key system aspects that were missing in the prior work, most notably power modeling and network behaviors.

Collected Data Item	Method*	Source
Wi-Fi packet trace	E	tcpdump
Bluetooth packet trace	E	BT Snoop Logger
User input events	E	/dev/input/
Voice control input event	E	Android Wear log
Device wakeup/doze/sleep	E	Android Wear log
Device charging	E	Android Wear API
Card post	E	Android Wear API
App activity/service state	E	atrace
Installed apps list	P (1 hour)	/data/app/
Screenshot	P (30 sec)	screencap
CPU utilization	P (1 sec)	/proc/stat
Screen brightness level	P (5 sec)	Android Wear API

*E = event triggered callback; P (interval) = periodical polling

Table 2: Types of data collected in the user study.

3. THE SMARTWATCH USER TRIAL

We launched an IRB-approved user study at Indiana University Bloomington. We made the study open to students, faculty, and staff members on our campus, and recruited 27 participants from more than 200 applicants. In our selection process, we tried to maximize the participants' diversity in terms of the occupation (student vs. non-student), gender, age, *etc.* An eligible participant must have an Android smartphone that can be paired with the watch. The selected voluntary participants consisted of 18 students (6 Ph.D. and 12 master students), 4 IU faculty members, and 5 staff members. 7 out of the 27 participants were female. Each user was provided with an LG Urbane watch, a high-end smartwatch as of early 2016 (cost ~$250 USD). It is equipped with a quad-core Cortex A7 processor, 4GB storage, 512MB memory, Wi-Fi, Bluetooth, and various sensors. The watch runs Android Wear OS 1.3, which is based on Android 5.1.1. Android Wear is a version of Android OS tailored to small-screen wearable devices. Compared to an Android smartphone app, an Android Wear app has a different UI, but its developers still largely follow Android's programming paradigm. The wearable apps are written in Java and run on top of the managed Android Runtime [32]. Note that although our data is collected from Android Wear 1.3, when presenting the results, we do consider relevant new features to be added to Android Wear 2.0, the next version Android Wear (in its development preview stage at the time when this paper was written).

We face two challenges in deploying the study. The first challenge is, despite being very familiar with smartphones and conventional watches, many users had no or limited experience of using smartwatches. Ideally we do not want to collect data from a user who is still learning to use her smartwatch. We took two measures to address this. First, all users were required to attend an orientation session where we walked through all features of the watch and demonstrated popular smartwatch apps. Second, we started the actual data collection for this study at least two months *after* giving the watches to the users. This gives more than enough time for users to learn the watch usage and to develop their usage habits.

The second challenge is to build for the watches a data collector that is reliable, lightweight, and energy-efficient. Despite several mobile data collection systems having been developed in the literature [28, 20, 52, 46, 14], none of them was designed for smartwatches and was able to collect smartwatch-specific data such as card posts and push notifications. We therefore developed our own, which collects a wide range of data listed in Table 2 in the background. The data collector was written in Java and native C/C++ with about 6,500 LoC. Note the collector only runs at the watch side (the watch is rooted) and does not require any change on users' smartphones (which are usually not rooted). The collected data is automatically uploaded to our secure server over Wi-Fi at night when the watch is being charged. The data collection and upload processes are completely transparent to users. As listed in Table 2, most data items are collected using event-triggered callbacks, including network traffic (both packet header and payload), user input, card post[1], device status, application states, *etc.* In addition, the data collector performs periodic polling for a limited amount of other information, with the polling intervals being carefully chosen to balance between the runtime overhead and data collection frequency.

The data collector incurs very low runtime and energy overhead. We have measured that in common usage scenarios, its CPU and energy overhead (measured using Monsoon power monitor [5]) are less than 3%. The low overhead can be explained by several reasons. Although the collector captures many types of data, most types have low data rate and low arrival frequency. In particular, as to be measured in §6, the data rate of the network traffic is very low. We also strategically perform various system-level optimizations and polling interval tuning to reduce the collector's resource and computational footprint. It is also worth mentioning that compared to regular Android, the Android Wear OS enforces more aggressive sleeping policy for battery saving. During most of the time, the watch stays in "dozing" or "sleeping" mode where network and CPU-intensive services are suspended (see §4 for details). Therefore, our data collector is largely paused by the OS when the watch is dozing/sleeping so no periodical data is collected during that time. This brings little impact on the completeness of our data, because most data items collected periodically in Table 2 largely remain unchanged when the watch is dozing/sleeping. Meanwhile, the aggressive sleeping policy ensures the data collector incurs almost zero overhead during most of the time. Also the CPU periodically wakes up during the dozing/sleeping states and its utilization will be captured by the collector during that time.

We launched incremental deployment of the user study in spring 2016. Due to the incremental nature of our deployment, different users had different learning periods (at least two months) before we started the actual data collection. In this paper we analyze a 106-day dataset collected from 8/17/2016 to 11/30/2016. About 37 GB of data was collected during this period.

4. SMARTWATCH USAGE PATTERNS

In this section, we leverage our dataset to study how real users interact with the watch. We first provide some background of different states of an Android smartwatch. As shown in Figure 1, a watch can be in one of four states: dozing, sleeping, awake, and charging. During most of the time when a user wears a watch, the watch stays in the dozing state where user applications are suspended [6]. The user only sees a simplified watch face (*e.g.*, without the *second* hand) with low brightness, thus incurring very low power consumption (§5). Periodically, the watch exits dozing for a very short period of time (called "maintenance window") to let apps complete their deferred activities. The transition from awake to dozing is usually through an inactivity timer of a fixed duration (measured to be 5 seconds by default). The transition from dozing to awake is triggered by either user interaction or other external events (*e.g.*, the reception of a push notification). Also, if the watch is not worn (*e.g.*, left on a desk), it will enter from dozing to sleeping after a long timeout (measured to be about 35 minutes). In the sleeping mode, the display is further turned off. Note the watch does not sleep when it is worn unless the battery level is

[1]A *card* is a UI element in Android Wear. It shows a piece of information (*e.g.*, an incoming text message) to the user.

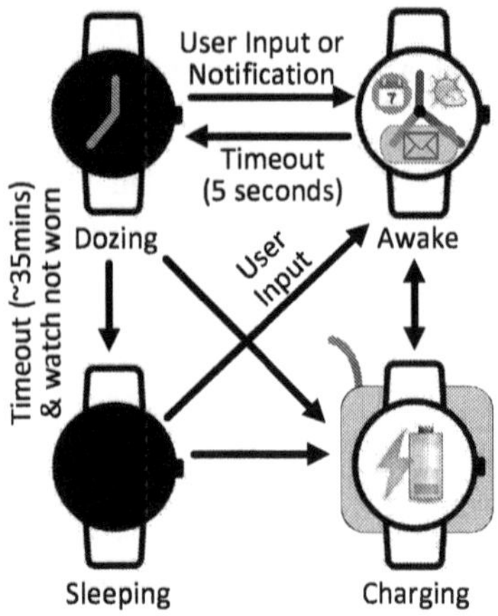

Figure 1: Device states for an Android smartwatch.

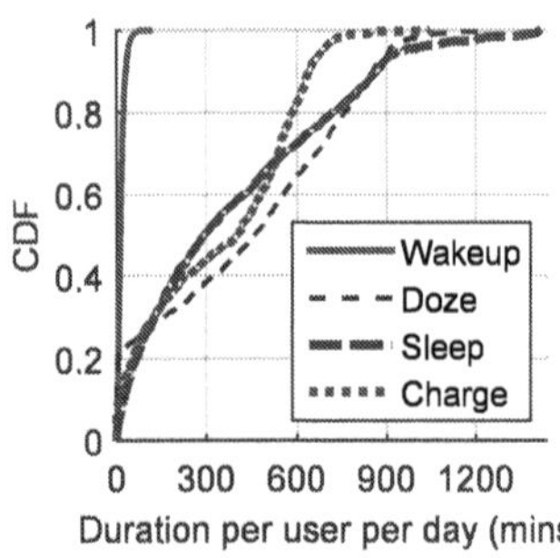

Figure 2: Distributions of the total daily duration of the four states that a watch stays at.

critically low. The transition to (from) the charging state is done by attaching the watch to (detaching it from) the charging dock.

4.1 Watch States and Basic Usage Patterns

We begin with understanding how long a watch stays at each state depicted in Figure 1. We calculate the daily awake/dozing/sleeping/charging duration across 24 hours starting from every midnight. As shown in Figure 2, the 25-th, 50-th, and 75-th percentiles of daily wake-up duration are 5.1, 11.6, and 19.6 minutes, respectively. In sharp contrast, the daily dozing duration tends to be much longer, with the 25-th, 50-th, and 75-th percentiles being 89, 460, and 711 minutes, respectively. The daily sleeping and charging time are also long. Table 3 shows the overall time breakdown for the four states. For half of the time, the watch is dozing while the wake-up time only accounts for 2% of the overall usage period. Despite this, the awake state is still very important due to two reasons. First, it is the key state where the user is actively interacting with the watch so providing good user experience is critical. Second, as shown in Table 3, the awake state contributes 27.2% of the overall energy consumption (to be characterized in §5), making its energy optimization also important.

Characteristics of Wake-up Sessions. Figure 3 plots the distribution of wake-up session duration across all users. A *wake-up session* starts when the watch wakes up, and ends when it dozes. As shown, the vast majority of wake-up sessions are short. The 5-second duration corresponds to the default inactivity timer for dimming the screen. We find that the wake-up sessions are not only short, but also frequent: the 25-th, 50-th, and 75-th percentiles of the number of wake-up sessions per user per day are 34, 72, and 120, respectively. As to be studied shortly, wake-ups are triggered by different reasons and not all of them are noticed by the user. Note that prior measurements indicate smartphone interaction sessions are much longer: tens of seconds reported by [20] and even longer as measured recently by [48]. Such a striking difference between watches and phones can be explained not only by smartwatches' wearable nature enabling easy and ubiquitous access for users, but also by their tight coupling with smartphones that may frequently push notifications (chat, email, *etc.*) to watches. A recent study involving 17 smartwatch users also found that people interact with their watches very frequently but for a short time [37]. Despite their qualitatively similar findings, their reported numbers are a bit different from ours: in [37], users interact for an average of 20.6 minutes per day and the average session lasts for 13.0 seconds. Several factors such as users, watch type, and timeout settings may contribute to such quantitative differences.

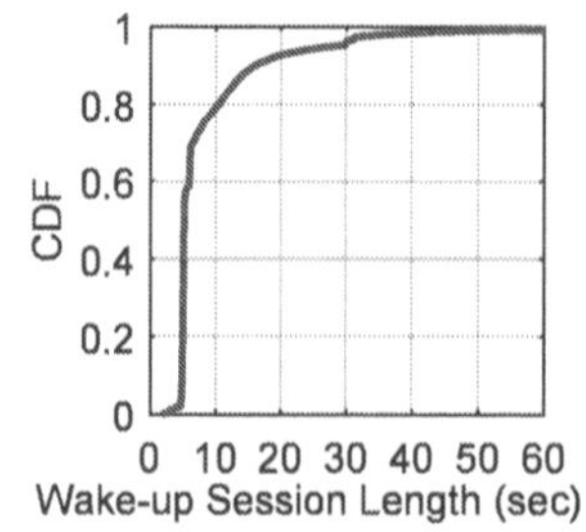

Figure 3: Wake-up session length distribution.

State	Awake	Dozing	Sleeping	Charging
Duration	2.0%	50.6%	24.7%	22.8%
Energy	27.2%	56.0%	16.8%	N/A

Table 3: Overall usage duration and energy breakdown. The energy breakdown will be discussed in §5.

Wake-up Root Cause Analysis. We next investigate which factors trigger a watch's wake-up by correlating each wake-up event w with an external event e, which can be either a user input event (*e.g.*, gesture, screen touch, side-button press) or notification event. Doing so can help identify the watch's key usage scenarios. Let $T(x)$ be the timestamp when event x occurs. If $T(w) - \delta \leq T(e) \leq T(w)$, then we assume w is triggered by e. Based on controlled experiments, we set the detection window size δ to 1000ms while changing it to 500ms and 750ms yields qualitatively similar results. As shown in Table 4, 26.3% of wake-up sessions are triggered at the sleeping state when the watch is not worn. Such wake-ups are likely not seen by the user. For the remaining 73.7% of the sessions triggered at the dozing state (recall that at the dozing state, the watch is worn except during the 35-minute timeout), we classify all wake-up sessions into three categories. Category (a) consists of sessions that are triggered by user input and have the same session length as the timeout period (we use 6s instead of 5s to tolerate the duration of the user input itself). In other words, the user takes no further action after waking up the watch. Accounting for 43.5% of all sessions, this category corresponds to the watch's major usage scenario. We find such short sessions are mostly triggered by the "flick and look" action: 80.3% of sessions within Category (a) (35% of all sessions) are triggered by wrist gesture (as opposed to other user input types): when the user turns the watch toward herself to look at the watch face, the watch will wake up. It is likely that these short sessions are for a simple usage scenario: users take a quick glance at the watch to see the time, to

Type	%	Median Len (sec)
Triggered when sleeping	26.3%	5.0
Triggered when dozing	73.7%	
.... (a) by user interaction, duration < 6s	.... 43.5%	5.0
.... by wrist gesture	.... 35.0%	5.0
.... by other user input types	.... 8.5%	5.0
.... (b) by user interaction, duration ≥ 6s	.... 19.7%	11.9
.... (c) by notification	.... 10.5%	6.1

Table 4: Breakdown of wake-up sessions.

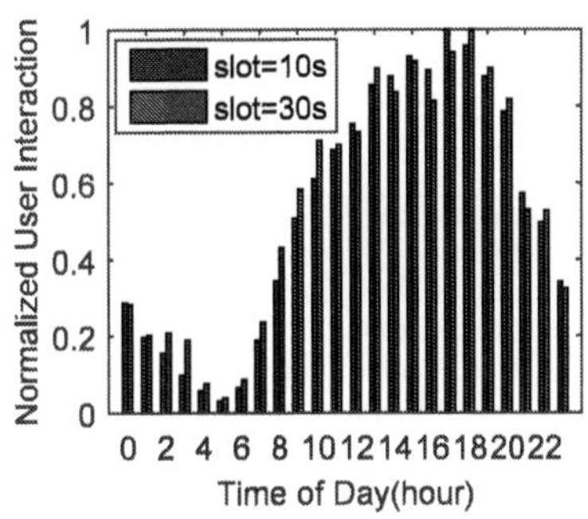

Figure 4: User interaction level during different hours.

Category	%
Instant messenging	43.3%
Email	25.6%
Google Search box	15.0%
Social media	2.5%
Text message	3.9%
Other	9.8%

Table 5: Application breakdown of push notifications.

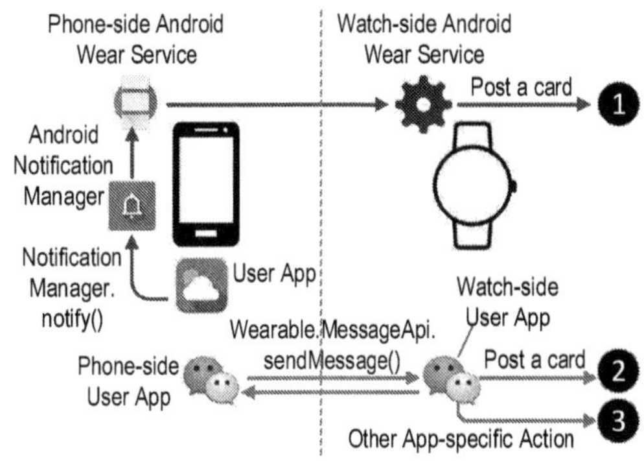

Figure 5: Communication between phone and watch.

check for notifications that she might have missed, or to see other information (*e.g.,* weather, temperature, or fitness records) that is directly displayed on the watch face (Figure 14). Also, although difficult to quantify, based on users' feedback, some of such "flick and look" sessions are unintended *i.e.,* due to the inaccuracy of the gesture sensing algorithm.

Category (b) in Table 4 consists of user-triggered sessions that are longer than the timeout period. Typical examples include browsing cards (recall a card is an Android Wear UI element), voice control, and interacting with smartwatch apps, which will be characterized in §4.3. Category (c) are those triggered by notifications. Upon the reception of a notification, the watch wakes up and pops up a card (Figure 9 left). We analyze push notifications in §4.2.

Diurnal Usage Pattern. We also investigate when our participants use the watch. The methodology is as follows: for each user, we discretize the timeline using fixed-length slots (*e.g.,* 10 seconds), and mark a slot if at least one user input event (touch, gesture, or voice) occurs within that slot. Figure 4 plots the user interaction level in terms of the normalized number of marked slots during different hours, across all users. As shown in Figure 4, despite the apparent diurnal pattern, there still exist some differences from smartphones' diurnal usage pattern. During daytime (9am to 9pm), the smartwatch usage is more uniformly distributed compared to that of smartphones [54, 20]. This is again explained by smartwatches' wearable and ubiquitous nature, as well as their function as an "on-wrist extension" of the phone.

4.2 Push Notification

This section characterizes push notification, an important application on smartwatches. We begin with explaining how an Android watch communicates with its paired phone. There are two ways as explained in Figure 5. For a smartphone app that does not have its watch version, when the app posts a notification[2], the phone-side Android Wear service will automatically and transparently push this notification to the watch-side service. Since at the time when this paper was written, most smartphone apps do not have their watch versions, this (the red arrows in Figure 5) is a common way for allowing *one-way* communication from the phone to its paired watch. If a phone app has its watch version, they can leverage Android Wear APIs [9] to perform *two-way* communication by exchanging arbitrary data, as illustrated by the green arrows. When the watch-side Android Wear service receives a notification, it will post a card and wake up the watch (❶ in Figure 5). The watch-side app may either post a card (❷) or take other app-specific actions (❸). Note the above scheme works over both BT and Wi-Fi. When using Wi-Fi, the watch and phone communicate through Google's servers.

We define push notifications as those that trigger ❶ and ❷ in Figure 5. A challenge we face is that they cannot be directly collected so we develop a robust method of extracting them from our data. Recall in Table 2 that we capture all card posts. However, not all cards correspond to push notifications. To capture ❶, we correlate each card posted by the Android Wear service with the network traffic by searching for a specific signature in the traffic that we reverse engineered from controlled experiments. To capture ❷, we also correlate each card posted by a watch-side app with network traffic. This may incur some false positives but we expect the error rate to be very low.

We now describe the results. Table 5 breaks down all push notifications into six categories. As shown, notifications are dominated by instant messaging (IM) and email. We identify more than 10 IM apps and 3 email client apps in the dataset. In particular, *WhatsApp*, a popular IM app, accounts for 23.8% of all notifications. Also, the *Google Quick Search Box* app pushes various notifications such as weather, traffic, news, and stock to the watch. Other apps performing pushes include social media, text message, phone calls, calendar, news, maps, *etc.* Overall, we observe that 230 apps create notifications that are pushed to the watch. Among them, most apps (196 out of 230) do not have a watch-side version (*i.e.,* belong to ❶).

[2]In Android, a *notification* is a message that can be displayed outside of an app's normal UI. It first appears as an icon in the phone's notification area. The user can find its details in the *notification drawer* [1].

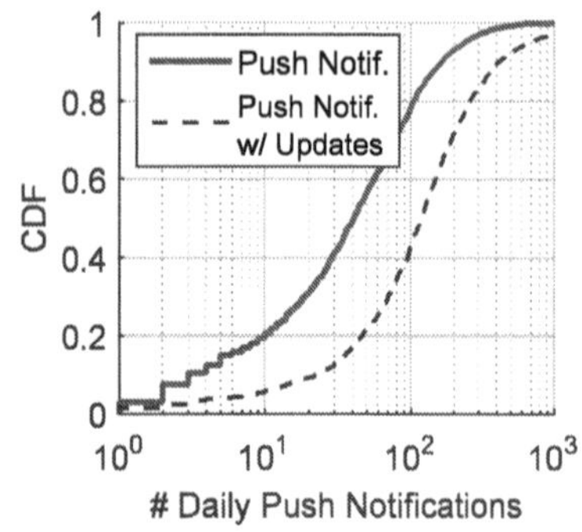

Figure 6: The number of a user's daily received notifications.

The solid curve in Figure 6 plots the distribution of the number of notifications received daily by each user. The number of received notifications are diverse with the 25-th, 50-th, and 75-th percentiles being 14, 41, and 91, respectively. We observe high variation both across users and for the same user across different days. To illustrate this, we compute for each user the average number (μ) and standard deviation (σ) of notifications across days. Across users, μ ranges from 10 to 256, and σ spans between 13 and 342. This implies the potential challenge for predicting notifications in the long-term. Despite this, we do observe that the arrival of notifications exhibits very strong bursty pattern: the median inter-arrival time of notifications across all users is only 49 seconds, implying potentially good short-term predictability for notifications. This can be explained by the bursty pattern of instant messages that dominate the push notifications. We further observe that if a posted notification card is not removed, it may be constantly updated by the phone-side app. A representative example is turn-by-turn navigation in Google Maps. If such updates are also included in notification counting, the total number will increase by 2.4x, as plotted in the dashed curve in Figure 6.

We have also identified two possible improvements for notifications. First, notifications are often delay-tolerant. Delaying their push and piggybacking them with other notifications or watch wake-up events can lead to significant energy savings, as will be demonstrated in our controlled experiments in §5.3. Second, we find that most (if not all) phone apps today employ very simple logic to determine *whether or not* to push a notification. For example, in its vehicular navigation mode, *Google Maps* keeps sending turn-by-turn updates to the watch – this is unnecessary and may distract the driver if the phone is already mounted to the dashboard for navigation. In another example, *WhatsApp* performs push if and only if the phone-side chat window is not in the foreground. This however may cause both false positives (*i.e.,* the user is interacting with the phone but the message is still pushed to watch[3]) and false negatives (*e.g.,* the user leaves the phone on her desk with the chat window open but the message is not pushed to watch). Ideally, in most use cases, an app should perform pushes only when the user is not interacting with the phone. One possible improvement is thus to introduce an API that intelligently determines whether to push or not to push by leveraging diverse types of information sources such as the user interaction level, the application type, and even the physical distance between the watch and the phone.

[3]The phone will always show the message in its notification area so if the user is looking at the phone, usually there is no need to push.

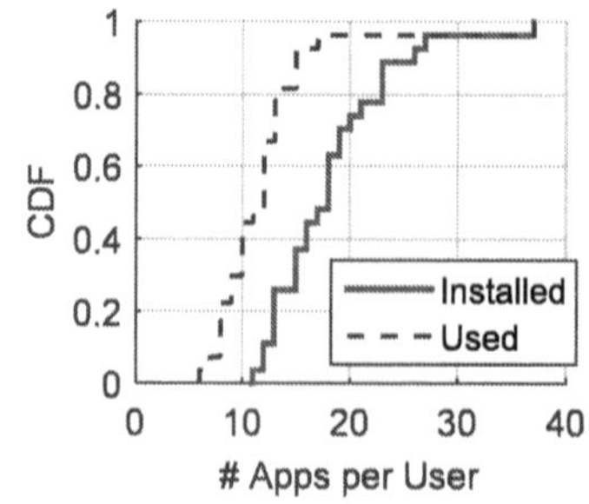

Figure 7: The number of installed vs. used apps per user, across all users.

Apk Name	Description
com.google.android.keep	Note taking
com.tencent.mm	WeChat messenger
com.google.android.deskclock	Clock
com.google.android.apps.fitness	Fitness tracker
com.google.android.apps.maps	Map
com.callpod.android_apps.keeper	Passwd manager
com.appfour.wearmessages	Messenger
com.appfour.wearmail	Email

Table 6: A list of popular apps in our dataset (based on their overall execution duration).

4.3 Application Usage

Compared to a traditional watch, a unique feature of a smartwatch is its capability of running diverse 3rd-party applications ("apps"). We first note that as for now, smartwatch apps are still much less popular than smartphone apps: in 10/2016, we crawled the top-500 free and paid apps on Google Play Store, and found only 2.8% of free apps and 3.4% of paid apps have their watch versions. Despite this, a trend we believe is that more and more apps will be shipped with their wearable stubs giving the increasing maturity of the wearable ecosystem [10].

The solid line in Figure 7 plots the distribution of installed apps across users (as of 11/14/2016). An average user has 18 apps installed on her watch. We include built-in apps such as Google Maps but exclude system processes that users cannot interact with. Within the installed apps, how many of them are actually used? The dashed line in Figure 7 plots the distributions of the apps that have been used at least twice. We find that users do use diverse apps on their watches: Table 6 lists the most popular used apps in our dataset; they include messengers, email clients, maps, activity trackers, and note taking software.

Figure 7 also reveals that many installed apps are almost *never* used on watch. This is because a smartwatch app usually has its smartphone counterpart, and both versions (phone-side and watch-side) are bundled together in a single installation package. When the phone version is installed, the watch version will be automatically pushed to and installed on the watch. As a result, a user may only use the app on the phone despite its watch version being automatically installed. We noticed that this issue is addressed in the Developer Preview version of Android Wear 2.0 where the user can choose to only install either the phone-side or the watch-side app [3].

Activity and Service are two important components of Android apps. An *activity* represents a visible user interface, whereas a *service* runs in the background without a user interface. Almost all smartphone apps contain one or more activities, and some may run services. Figure 8 plots ranked total running time of activities and services for each watch app in our dataset. We make two

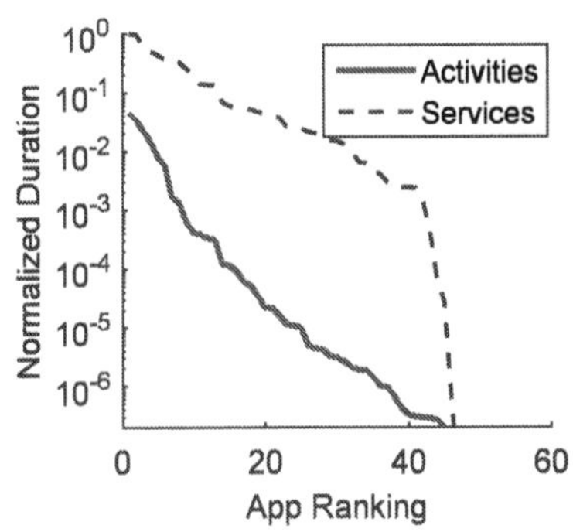

Figure 8: Activities and services ranked by their overall execution duration.

Duration	$d \leq 1s$	$1 < d \leq 10s$	$10 < d \leq 60s$	$d > 60s$
% Services	71.8%	12.7%	5.3%	10.1%

Table 7: Distribution of services' duration.

observations. First, despite a large number of lightly used apps, a small fraction of apps (*e.g.,* those listed in Table 6) dominate the usage, a phenomenon also observed for smartphone apps [54]. Second, a more unexpected finding is that the background service execution is 55.8 times longer that of full-screen activities (we filtered out core OS services and the service of our data collector). One may explain this using the common sense that services may continuously run in the background for a long time, as is often the case for smartphone apps. This is however not always the case on Android watches. Table 7 shows the distribution of the lifetime of services. The vast majority of them are very short (less than 1s).

Overall, we find that short but frequent background service executions dominate the Android watch app usage. Based on our controlled experiments, we find many short services are caused by push notification or short message exchanges between watch and phone. We use *WeChat*, a popular instant messenger app, as an example. When the phone pushes a notification containing a new message to the watch, the watch will be woken up, and a notification card will be displayed (Figure 9 left, following ❷ in Figure 5). There are several possible actions that a user can then take: *(a)* take a glance of the message and ignore it; *(b)* open the *WeChat* app on her phone to reply to the message; and *(c)* directly reply to the message on her watch by swiping the card and tapping "reply"; in that case the watch version of the *WeChat* app (with an activity) will be launched. As indicated by the short notification-triggered wake-up session duration shown in Table 4, users seldom take Action *(c)*, very likely due to the watch's small form factor making full-fledged user interaction difficult. As shown in the right side of Figure 9, The watch version of *WeChat* only allows replying to a message by voice, sticker icons, or pre-defined text. On the other hand, Action *(a)* and *(b)* only involve short-lived services. For each notification of *WeChat*, we observe three ephemeral services invoked by *WeChat* and some other short-lived services started by the system processes managing the card and push notification. We observe similar patterns for other popular apps.

5. ENERGY CONSUMPTION

Smartwatches have very limited battery capacity. Our LG Urbane watch has a battery of only 410 mAh, much smaller than that of a typical smartphone battery (2K to 3K mAh). Charging a watch requires special charging dock making it difficult for users to charge the watches during the day. Understanding watches' battery usage can greatly facilitate the development of new power management solutions.

Figure 9: **Left**: a WeChat card showing at the bottom of the screen. **Right**: reply to a message using the WeChat app on watch.

5.1 Smartwatch Power Models

A prerequisite for fine-grained energy analysis is a *power model*, which is a function $E(\vec{A})$ that maps $\vec{A}$, system activities and events directly measurable on the device, to their incurred energy and power consumption. In the literature, numerous studies have derived energy models for smartphones [55, 47, 26, 42, 41, 38, 16]. Nevertheless, to our knowledge, no power model is publicly available for smartwatches whose energy consumption profiles are quite different. To fill this gap, we empirically derive accurate power models for today's off-the-shelf smartwatches.

To measure the watch's energy, we extract a compatible battery interface, which is used as a connector between the watch and the Monsoon power monitor [5], from a same-vendor smartphone. Our modeling approach follows the high-level methodology for smartphone power modeling [55, 16, 38]. When measuring a component, we keep other components offline (*e.g.,* Wi-Fi, BT, display) or at a steady power state (*e.g.,* CPU) whose power consumption is then subtracted from measured power value. For components involving parameters (*e.g.,* CPU utilization), we programmatically change them and use regression to derive an empirical model as a function of the parameters. We repeat each experiment 10 times and use the average power for modeling. The overall watch power is then estimated as the sum all components' power consumption.

We study two commercial smartwatches: LG Urbane (used in our user study) and LG Watch R. LG Watch R has a similar configuration compared to LG Urbane except that it does not have built-in Wi-Fi. Table 8 presents our derived power models for the two watches. We first highlight our findings for the LG Urbane watch. The power consumption of each state (awake, dozing, and sleeping) consists of an almost-constant base power plus power consumption of other components such as CPU, display, and network interfaces. (1) At the dozing state, the overall device power consumption is low (24.3 mW). The watch face display power accounts for about half of the overall dozing power. Since the watch face display has low brightness and mostly dark colors, its power can be modeled using a constant value (about 12.2 mW). (2) At the sleeping state, the power consumption is even lower since the display is turned off. Also note that the watch is equipped with a low-power movement sensor and a microphone, whose power consumption is included in the base power. Since they run in an "ambient" manner (*i.e.,* always-on), it is difficult for us to separate their individual power contributions. (3) The watch is equipped with a 1.3 inch 320x320 P-OLED display, whose power is determined by the brightness level and the pixel colors [17, 19] when the watch is awake. We find that blue is the most energy-consuming color component, followed by green and then red. Note our model does take into account the circular shape of

Component	Power Consumption (mW)	
	LG Urbane (user study)	LG Watch R
Dozing base + display	24.3 (base 12.1 + display 12.2)	22.7 (base 10.7 + display 12.0)
Sleeping base	14.5	17.6
Wake-up base	47.1	54.9
CPU	$214.0u$, $u \in (0,1]$: CPU util.	$216.2u$, $u \in (0,1]$
Wake-up display power = $\sum(c_r \cdot r + c_g \cdot g + c_b \cdot b + C)/K$, Per-pixel $r, g, b \in [0, 255]$, K = 320*320. Values of $\{c_r, c_g, c_b, C\}$ are listed below.		
Wake-up brightness 1	{.023, .060, .084, 67.2}	{.014, .036, .092, 60.6}
Wake-up brightness 2	{.034, .071, .129, 67.2}	{.027, .060, .126, 60.6}
Wake-up brightness 3	{.041, .092, .167, 67.2}	{.029, .077, .159, 60.6}
Wake-up brightness 4	{.055, .120, .201, 67.2}	{.044, .096, .210, 60.6}
Wake-up brightness 5	{.058, .144, .236, 67.2}	{.065, .127, .255, 60.6}
Wake-up brightness 6	{.076, .179, .303, 67.2}	{.077, .163, .325, 60.6}
BT Tail	4.77 sec, Power: 34.1	4.00 sec, Power: 13.88
BT Data ($\sim$ 0.5m)	Tx: 111.5, Rx: 117.2	Tx: 103.0, Rx: 104.6
BT Data ($\sim$ 5m)	Tx: 132.9, Rx: 116.2	Tx: 121.5, Rx: 97.3
BT Data ($\sim$ 10m)	Tx: 130.8, Rx: 113.9	Tx: 120.9, Rx: 98.2
BT Scan	146.0	155.1
Screen touch/swipe	198.9	182.3

Table 8: Derived power models for LG Watch Urbane and LG Watch R.

Component	Power (mW)
Wi-Fi Tail	0.18 sec, Power: 121.2
Wi-Fi Promotion	0.30 sec, Power: 242.5
Wi-Fi Data (-42 dBm)	Tx: 669.1, Rx: 378.5
Wi-Fi Data (-55 dBm)	Tx: 672.8, Rx: 343.0
Wi-Fi Data (-65 dBm)	Tx: 840.7, Rx: 341.8
Wi-Fi Scan	252.3

Table 9: Wi-Fi power model for LG Urbane.

Use Case	Trace Length	Energy Consumption (μAh)		
		Measure	Model	Err.
Check time	11 sec	206	196	4.7%
Google map over BT	60 sec	1881	1792	4.7%
Fitness tracking	30 sec	773	730	5.5%
Web browsing over Wi-Fi	60 sec	2407	2513	4.4%
Hangout Chat over BT	30 sec	893	876	1.9%
Push notify. over BT	65 sec	1378	1437	4.3%
Push notify. over Wi-Fi	65 sec	1933	1920	0.7%

Table 10: Power model validation for LG Urbane.

the watch display [36] since only the displayed pixels are counted. (4) The CPU power is determined by three factors: the number of online cores, the frequency of each core, and the utilization of each core. The LG Urbane watch is equipped with a quad-core Qualcomm Cortex A7 processor. However, three of the cores are forced to be offline by the OS, and the clock of the only online core is fixed at 787 Mhz. This is a common practice on Android smartwatches [32]. Therefore, the only factor affecting the power is the CPU utilization, and we find both are linearly correlated. (5) The Bluetooth state machine consists of an idle and an active state. The state promotion takes negligible time, while the demotion from the active to the idle state is triggered by an inactivity timer ("tail time") of 4.77s. (6) We find that the capacitive touch input also incurs non-negligible power consumption. (7) Table 9 measures the Wi-Fi power model for LG Urbane. The Wi-Fi state machine is similar to that of smartphones [16, 38], except that we observe a non-trivial state promotion delay of 0.3s. Also, we find when the RSSI is lower than -70dBm, likely due to its small built-in antenna, the watch has difficulty associating with the AP. For LG Watch R, as shown in Table 8, its power model is qualitatively similar to that of LG Urbane except that it does not have a Wi-Fi interface.

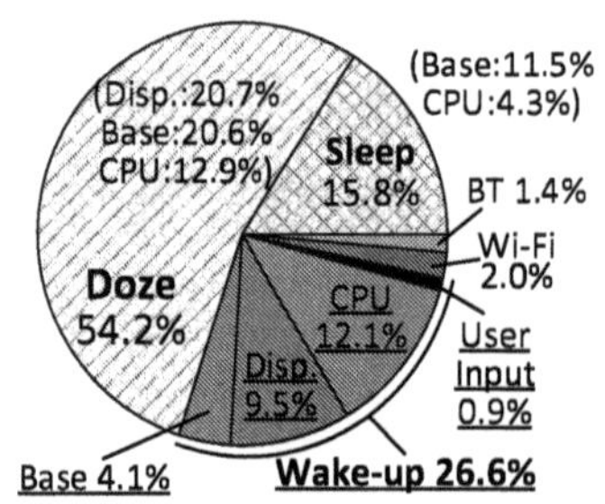

Figure 10: Component-level energy breakdown across all users.

Power Model Validation. We conduct thorough validation for our models for both watches at the component level and device level. Table 10 shows the in-lab device-level validation results for LG Urbane. We study seven diverse use cases. The "measure" and "model" columns correspond to the device-level energy consumption measured from the power monitor and computed from our model, respectively. The error rates, defined as $|E(\text{Model}) - E(\text{Measure})|/E(\text{Measure})$, are less than 6%. For LG Watch R, the device-level error rates are less than 5% for these usage scenarios (table not shown).

5.2 Energy Consumption in the Wild

We now apply the LG Urbane power model to our user study dataset, to quantify the energy consumption of smartwatches in realistic settings. Our dataset contains all information needed by the power model except the following limitations. First, we are not able to obtain the BT signal strength using Android Wear API, so we use the 0.5m BT power model. Second, to ensure the data collector itself incurs very low overhead, we capture a screenshot every 30 seconds (§3). Such an interval may lead to less accurate display energy estimation (in our validation we use an interval of 1 second). Note this is already more accurate than prior smartphone display modeling approaches that do not consider the displayed content [14] or sample the pixels every several minutes [55]. We also want to remind readers that the results below are relevant to the specific brand of the watch used in our study (LG Urbane), and other types of watches may possibly exhibit different energy consumption profiles.

Recall that Table 3 shows the energy breakdown among the three states: awake, dozing, and sleeping. More than half of the overall energy is consumed by the dozing state due to its long duration despite its low power. But somewhat unexpectedly, despite the very short duration of the awake state (2%), its energy contribution is as high as 27.2%. Figure 10 shows a more fine-grained energy breakdown. Within the dozing state, the energy consumed by the base, display, and CPU are roughly 1.6:1.6:1. Despite its low brightness, display is still a key factor of battery drain when the watch is dozing. The dozing CPU energy comes from the maintenance window (§4) that periodically wakes up the CPU. Within the awake state, display and CPU also dominate the energy consumption, accounting for 34.9% and 44.5% of the wake-up energy, respectively (or 9.5% and 12.1% of the overall energy respectively). The network incurs very small energy footprint (3.4%). About 22% of the Wi-Fi energy and 9% of the Bluetooth energy are spent at the awake state (not shown in Figure 10).

From Table 8 and Figure 10, we compute the average power consumption at the wakeup, dozing, and sleeping state to be 309.8mW, 31.9mW, and 14.5mW, respectively, across all users. Note that the average dozing power (31.9mW) includes the base, the display, and the CPU power. By weighing them using the usage duration breakdown listed in Table 3, we can further compute the smartwatch's average power consumption to be 25.9mW across all states and users. Assuming that, a fully charged watch (with a battery capacity of 410 mAh for LG Urbane) can last for about 41.7 hours.

Comparison with Smartphone. We next compare our results with smartphone energy consumption profiles reported in the literature. We pick [14], a recent crowd-sourced smartphone energy study, to facilitate the discussion. We highlight three observations. First, the authors of [14] report that on a smartphone, the top two energy consumers are CPU (30.6%) and display (27.4%). This is also true for smartwatches: CPU accounts for 29.3% of the overall energy; more interestingly, despite smartwatches' small screen sizes, display still contributes to 30.2% of the overall energy. Second, networking is very power-hungry on smartphones: cellular and Wi-Fi consume 26.4% and 8% of the overall energy, respectively. But networking (Wi-Fi and Bluetooth) is responsible for only 3.4% of the overall smartwatch energy. Besides an apparent reason that most watches do not have a cellular interface, such a disparity is also caused by the different traffic patterns between a watch and phone as well as the fact that Bluetooth dominates the smartwatch network usage, as to be studied in §6. Third, [14] reports that an average smartphone spends about 2 hours every day on the screen-on state, which incurs about 59% of the overall energy consumption. The smartwatch case is very different: an average user's watch wakes up for only about 10 minutes every day, corresponding to about 27% of the energy (Table 3). Meanwhile, smartwatches are more energy-efficient in non-awake (*i.e.*, dozing and sleeping) states where user application and system activities are strictly restricted (§4).

Diversity across Users. We equally divide the 27 users into three groups: light ("L"), medium ("M"), and heavy users ("H"), based on users' average daily awake duration. The left side of Figure 11 plots the duration breakdown for each group where "W", "S+D", and "C" correspond to awake, sleeping/dozing, and charging, respectively. The three groups exhibit similar patterns except that the heavy users spend a little more time on the awake and charging states. The right side of Figure 11 plots the corresponding energy breakdown, where the wake-up energy consumption is significantly higher for heavy users. The results again indicate that smartwatch's active usage time is unanimously short across users. However, due to the big power consumption gap between awake and dozing/sleeping, a small increase of the

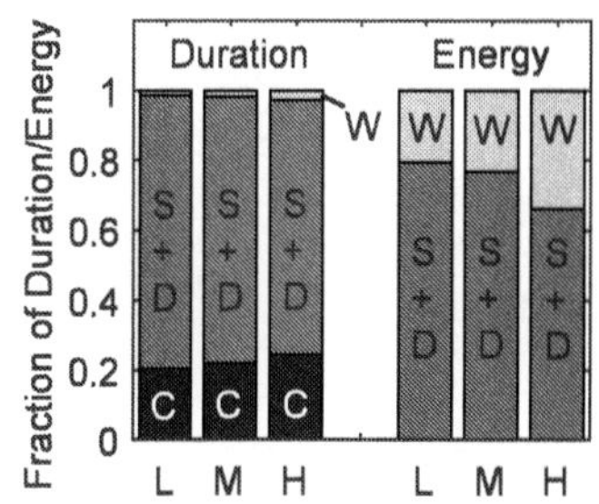

Figure 11: Usage duration and energy consumption diversity across three user groups: **L**ight, **M**edium, and **H**eavy users.

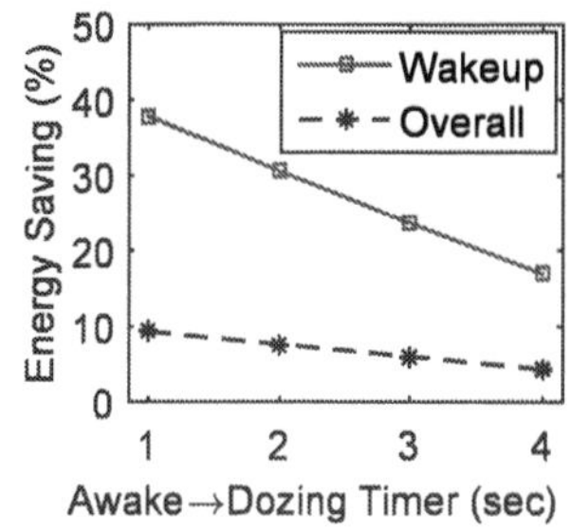

Figure 12: Tuning the Awake → Dozing Timer.

wake-up duration will be "amplified" from the battery draining perspective, thus shortening the overall standby time of the watch.

5.3 Improving Smartwatch Energy Efficiency

We study five methods for improving the smartwatch energy efficiency. Note that although some of them have been applied to smartphones, our contributions here are two-fold: we study them in the context of smartwatches; we also perform "what-if" analysis on our dataset to reveal their impact on real smartwatch workloads (or doing controlled experiments if a trace-driven analysis is not feasible).

1. Tuning the Awake→Dozing Timer. We consider tuning the inactivity timer that controls the transition from awake to dozing. Recall in Figure 1 that its default value is 5 seconds. We develop a trace-driven simulator that takes as input the original user study trace, the smartwatch power model, and a new timer setting. The simulator computes the energy consumption in the new setting: if the timer is reduced to $x < 5$ seconds, we turn the last $5-x$ seconds within an original wake-up session into dozing by changing its power consumption accordingly. Figure 12 plots the energy reduction in the "what-if" scenario where the timer is set to 1 to 4 seconds. Doing so leads to energy savings between 17% and 38% for the awake state. The overall energy saving, however, ranges from only 4% to 9%, which is equivalent to 1.7 to 3.8 hours of average usage time (assuming 41.7 hours of battery capacity as computed in §5.2). Note that a more intelligent approach the OS may take is to dynamically determine when to doze. This has already been partially implemented in Android Wear 2.0, which uses user's gesture (*i.e.*, moving the wrist away) as a signal to dim the watch in addition to using a regular timer. Although more sensing techniques can be developed (*e.g.*, dimming the watch when it is covered by a sleeve), the overall energy saving brought by this scheme is limited.

2. Improving the Dozing→Sleeping Mechanism. Recall in Figure 1 that the current policy adopted by Android Wear is to enter the sleeping state after an idle period of 35 minutes only when the watch is not worn. We consider a more energy-efficient scheme

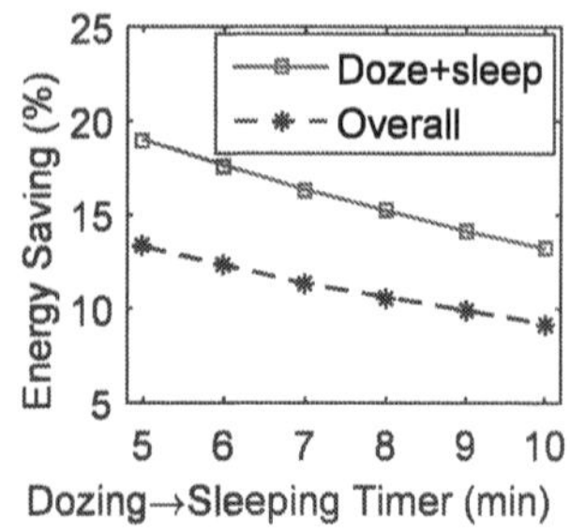

Figure 13: Sleep after a timeout even when the watch is worn.

Figure 14: An example of power-saving color transformation.

where even when the watch is worn, it enters the sleeping state after a timeout. Our dataset suggests that almost all (98%) dozing sessions (including those when the watch is worn) are shorter than 35 minutes, implying the current timeout is too conservative if applied to our scheme. In Figure 13, we simulate our new scheme by applying a shorter dozing→sleeping timer (regardless of whether the watch is worn or not) to our dataset. On one hand, changing the timeout to 5 to 10 minutes brings no effect on most (80% to 88%) dozing sessions, so the impact on the user experience is marginal: when the user looks at the watch face, it is still on as before. On the other hand, this very simple tuning leads to a decent amount of energy savings: 13% to 19% of the non-awake energy or 9% to 13% of the global energy (equivalent to 3.8 to 5.4 hours of average watch usage time).

3. Power-saving Color Transformation. A wide range of smartwatches today use OLED display where different colors incur different power consumption. We apply the power-saving color transformation technique that was proposed in [18] and was applied to smartphone web browsing in [19]. Its high-level idea is to map a display's color histogram to a more energy-efficient one while satisfying human perception constraints in a color space (CIELAB) designed to mimic human vision. We apply the algorithm (using the "Color64" scheme in [18]) to all wake-up screenshots in our dataset, and find that for most screens, the algorithm yields recognizable display despite the colors becoming less perceptually pleasing to humans (an inherent limitation of this approach as illustrated in Figure 14). Nevertheless, color transformation results in 41.4% reduction of the overall wake-up display energy across all users. This provides incentives to develop energy-efficient user interfaces for wearables with OLED display.

4. Bundling Delay-tolerant Push Notifications. Recall in §4.2 that many push notifications are delay-tolerant. We conduct controlled experiments to quantify how much energy can be potentially saved when delay-tolerant notifications are bundled together. We wrote a phone-side app that performs push using Method ❶ in Figure 5. The app employs three schemes (S_1 to S_3) to push n notifications, each containing a short message, in t=5 minutes: in S_1, the notifications are equally spaced with inter-arrival time (IAT) of $t/(n-1)$; (2) in S_2, they are pushed one-by-one with an IAT of 3 seconds to allow the user to read each message; (3) in S_3, all messages are packed into a single notification pushed to the watch. Table 11 lists the normalized overall energy consumption for the three push schemes with n set to 5, 10, and 20. The results suggest that bundling effectively decreases the energy consumption by reducing the overall wake-up period. Designing a full-fledged delay-tolerant-aware push notification system for wearables is our future work.

	S_1	S_2	S_3
$n = 5$	100%	74%	46%
$n = 10$	100%	66%	34%
$n = 20$	100%	58%	19%

Table 11: Normalized energy consumption when bundling delay-tolerant push notifications. n is the number of notifications and S_1 to S_3 are three delivery schemes.

CPU Config.	C_1	C_2	C_3	C_4
# Cores	1	1	2	2
Freq. each core	787 Mhz	384 Mhz	787 Mhz	384 Mhz
W_1: app launch	265, 7.6s	278, 9.8s	175, 4.4s	161, 4.5s
W_2: push notif.	46, 1.8s	64, 2.9s	61, 1.8s	49, 1.9s

Table 12: Balancing the energy-QoE tradeoff for two workloads using four CPU configurations. In each cell, the first number is the energy consumption (in μAh), and the second number is the QoE. All cells are averaged over 3 runs with standard deviation < 10%.

5. Workload-aware CPU Configuration. Recall in §5.1 that on a quad-core watch, Android Wear forces three cores offline and fixes the frequency of the only online core. We conduct controlled measurements to explore the performance-energy tradeoff incurred by different CPU configurations under diverse workloads. We consider four CPU configurations: C_1 uses one core at the default frequency (787 Mhz); C_2 employs one core at a lower frequency (384 Mhz); C_3 and C_4 use two cores at 787 Mhz and 384 Mhz, respectively. We study their performance under two common workloads: W_1 for launching the *Google Maps* app and W_2 for receiving/posting a push notification. Table 12 measures the (Energy, QoE) for the 8 combinations of CPU configuration and workload. The energy consumption is measured by the power monitor at the device level, and the QoE metric depends on the workload: app launch time for W_1 and the notification delivery time for W_2 (from the reception of the first byte to the notification being posted). As shown, the CPU configuration yielding the best energy-QoE tradeoff depends on the workload: C_4 for W_1 and C_1 for W_2. The results imply that using multiple cores can potentially improve both the QoE and the energy efficiency for common smartwatch workloads such as app launching.

6. NETWORK TRAFFIC

Many smartwatches (including our user study watches) are equipped with Bluetooth and Wi-Fi interfaces. Per Android Wear OS, if the watch is paired with a phone over Bluetooth (BT), Wi-Fi is turned off for saving energy and the watch uses the phone as a "gateway" to access the Internet. If the phone is not present, the watch can directly access the Internet using TCP/IP over Wi-Fi. We now provide a first-of-its-kind measurement of smartwatch traffic. Our characterizations provide hints for improving the network stack for future wearable devices.

We first answer an important question: how often does the watch pair with a phone? Using our dataset, we find that during most of the time (80%), the watch and phone are paired. This is somewhat expected as we usually carry phones with us. During

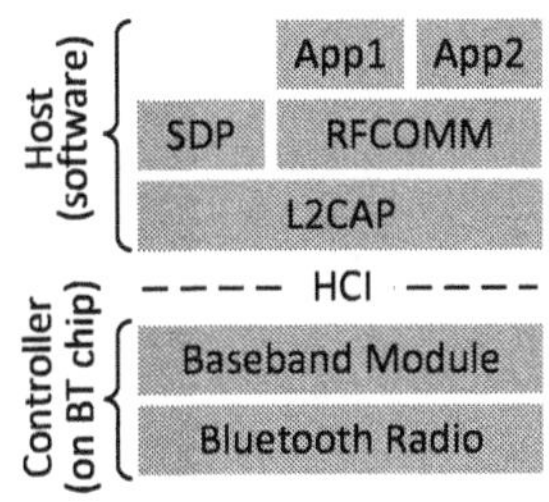

Figure 15: The BT protocol stack of Android smartwatch.

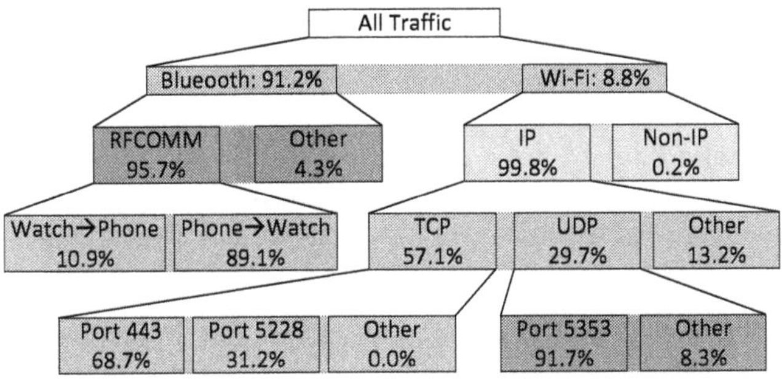

Figure 16: Smartwatch traffic volume breakdown.

the daytime (9am to 9pm), the percentage is slightly higher (84%), likely because some users turn off their phones at night.

Before presenting detailed characterization, we give some background of the BT protocol stack used by Android smartwatches[4] shown in Figure 15 [23, 13]. The *controller* resides on a BT chip, which performs lower-layer functions such as (de)modulation, physical channel management, and peer discovery. The *host* realizes higher-layer protocols in software (OS or device driver). The Logical Link Control and Adaptation Protocol (L2CAP) provides multiplexing of upper layer protocols such as SDP and RFCOMM. The Service Discovery Protocol (SDP) allows to discover services provided by nearby BT devices. RFCOMM [12] is the data-plane protocol allowing multiple application streams to be multiplexed. Between the controller and host lies the Host-Controller Interface (HCI), which is our data collection point. We build a tool (in ~1,300 LoC) that processes the collected BT traces. It parses HCI signaling messages and L2CAP/SDP/RFCOMM packets, and outputs assembled and demultiplexed RFCOMM streams carrying the application data. Note non-smartwatch devices may use different upper-layer protocols over BT.

BT Traffic. Figure 16 shows the overall traffic volume breakdown. Since smartwatches are usually paired with phones, the vast majority (91.2%) of bytes are delivered over BT. Most BT traffic belongs to the RFCOMM protocol that carries user data. Also downlink BT traffic (from phone to watch) overweighs the uplink, as a smartwatch is mostly a consumer device that receives data from the phone.

We next investigate three key characteristics of BT traffic: flow size, duration, and rate, which are known to be the most important metrics for Internet flows [56, 45]. One issue we need to address is how to define a *flow* for BT. Since RFCOMM streams are usually persistent and long-lived (they may last for tens of minutes or even hours), we employ an idle period threshold i to split a (demultiplexed) RFCOMM stream into segments, such that the packet inter-arrival time (IAT) within a segment is shorter than i

[4]We verified three Android watches: LG Urbane, LG Watch R, and Samsung Gear. They all use the same protocol stack in Figure 15.

Idle gap threshold i	5 sec	10 sec	20 sec
1. Flows initiated by phone	72.8%	68.4%	71.0%
2. Flows initiated by watch w/o UI	24.7%	28.0%	26.0%
3. Flows initiated by watch w/ UI	2.5%	3.6%	3.0%

Table 13: Origin of BT traffic (breakdown by bytes).

and IAT across segments is at least i. We then regard each segment to be a user flow.

Figure 17 and 18 plot the distributions of BT flow size and duration, respectively. The vast majority of flows are very small and short compared to smartphone traffic [20, 27]: when the idle threshold i=10 sec, 76.8% of the flows are smaller than 10KB, and 53.1% of the flows are shorter than 1 sec. Only 0.4% of the flows are considered to be indeed large (> 1MB), and only 0.1% are indeed long-lived (> 100 sec). Based on manual inspection of the payload of these "heavy-hitter" flows, we identify some of their semantics to be the following: app download, web browsing (some users do use the on-watch browser to surf the Internet), continuous data download (*e.g.,* map tiles), and synchronization of other large data. Figure 17 and 18 also indicate that the selection of the idle threshold i has very small impact on the measured distributions.

Figure 19 measures the BT flow rate, defined as flow size divided by duration, using i=10 sec. In order for the computed rate to be meaningful, we only include flows whose duration is at least $d \in \{0.5, 1.0 \text{ sec}\}$. Also downlink (phone to watch) and uplink (watch to phone) rates are measured separately. As shown, the vast majority of flows are slow, and uplink flows are even slower than downlink: only 3.5% (21.5%) of uplink (downlink) flows are faster than 100kbps. We also find that flow sizes and rates are highly correlated. When d=1 sec, the Pearson Correlation Coefficient between log(size) and log(rate) is 0.84 and 0.88 for uplink and downlink, respectively, much higher than those for Internet flows [45].

We next investigate the origin of BT traffic by answering the following question: how much BT traffic is triggered by a user? We break down all BT flows into three categories: (1) a flow is initiated from the phone side, as indicated by the downlink direction of the first data packet within the flow, (2) a flow is initiated from the watch side, as indicated by the uplink direction of the first packet, and the network activity is *not* triggered by user interaction[5], and (3) a flow is initiated from the watch side by user interaction. As shown in Table 13, most of BT traffic belongs to Category 1 (*e.g.,* data/notification push); a small fraction of the traffic belongs to Category 2 (*e.g.,* periodical fitness data upload), and only a tiny fraction of traffic falls into Category 3 (*e.g.,* user touches the watch and triggers some traffic). Note within Category 1, we are not able to tell the fraction of traffic initiated by a user interacting with the *phone*. Nevertheless we expect that fraction to be low, because most of the pushes and background sync are indeed "spontaneously" incurred.

Wi-Fi Traffic plays a less important role in smartwatch. As shown in Figure 16, more than half of the Wi-Fi traffic is TCP, which is dominated by server port 443 and 5228. For port 443, most server IPs point to Google that provides various services such as push notification. Port 5228 is used by Google Play Store. Surprisingly, due to Google's "HTTPS everywhere" principle, we do not observe any port 80 traffic, which still prevails in the smartphone world today. It is therefore difficult for a middlebox to use DPI-based approach to identify Android

[5]We use a 2-second window [t_0-2, t_0] to detect user interaction right before a flow where t_0 is the timestamp of the first data packet of a flow. Different window sizes yield qualitatively similar results.

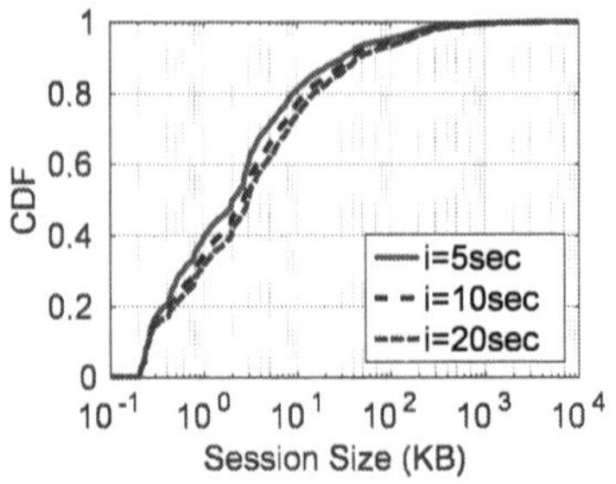

Figure 17: BT flow size distributions.

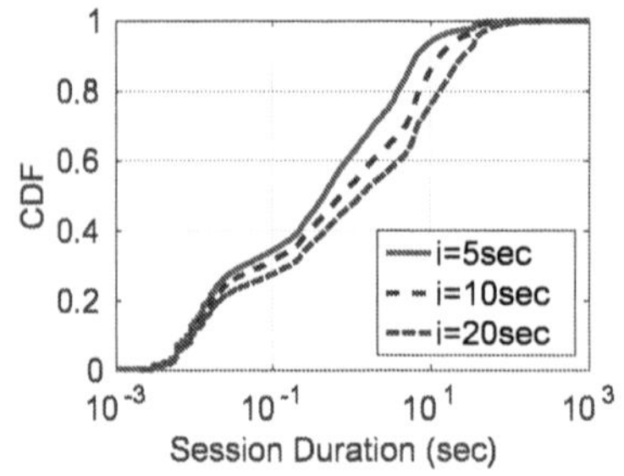

Figure 18: BT flow duration distributions.

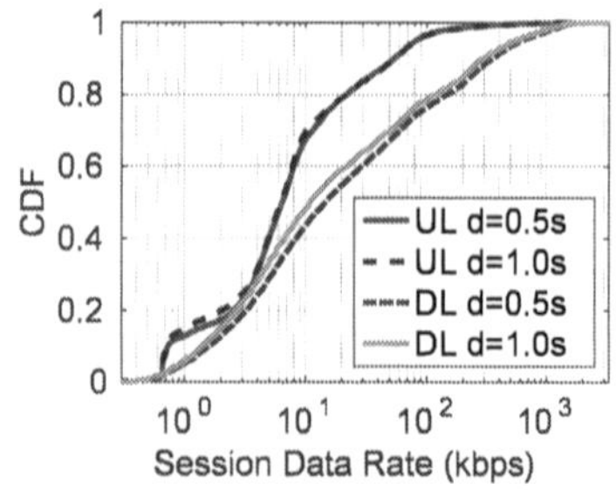

Figure 19: BT flow rate distributions (i=10s).

smartwatch traffic. Regarding UDP, more than 90% of the UDP traffic is for name resolution (port 53/5355/5353), and the remaining UDP traffic mostly relates to DHCP (port 67) and SSDP (port 1900). Virtually no UDP traffic carries application data. Wi-Fi flows exhibit characteristics similar to those of BT flows observed in Figure 17, 18, and 19.

Handover between BT and Wi-Fi. Dual networks are common on mobile devices. We are interested in how smartwatches handle the handover between BT and Wi-Fi, a common use case that needs to be supported when the watch moves out of or into the phone's BT coverage. We find that many smartwatch apps do support handover, but oftentimes a handover takes a long time (more than 5 seconds). This may be unacceptable for real-time streaming between the watch and phone (*e.g.,* Samsung Gear S3 Frontier has a speaker, making it possible to answer phone calls or to do VoIP on the watch). Researchers have proposed robust and transparent handover solutions such as Multipath TCP (MPTCP [21]). However, since BT by default does not speak TCP/IP, it is difficult to directly apply MPTCP on smartwatches. The potentially excessive power consumption of maintaining multiple interfaces simultaneously is also a concern. More research needs to be done in this direction.

7. DISCUSSION

Limitations. We discuss several limitations of our current user study deployment.

- First, our study lacks device diversity since all participants use the same type of watch. Although we use a popular commodity watch (LG Urbane) with state-of-the-art hardware, we admit that smartwatches are diverse, from basic ones with black-and-white display (*e.g.,* Pebble Classic) to advanced models with built-in GPS and cellular (*e.g.,* Samsung Gear S3 Frontier). Additional hardware components such as GPS and cellular bring in new applications, and may thus change user behaviors and energy consumption profiles of smartwatches. We however believe that due to the very nature of smartwatches (wearable, small form factors, *etc.*), the basic usage patterns such as short "flick and look" wake-up sessions and key applications such as push notification reception tend to remain the same.

- Second, as mentioned in §4, the participants in our study have limited diversity (faculty, students, and staff members at Indiana University). We plan to further increase the user base and its diversity in our future deployment.

- Third, there are other factors that might impact the user behavior and thus the measurement results. For example, our participants do not own the watches (in contrast, in [44], users used their personal smartwatches). In another example, the participants were given similar orientation sessions making them "equally" familiar with the device. The distribution of feature usages may possibly be different for "untrained" users than a set of users who had a good orientation.

- Lastly, since all our data collection is performed on the watch, we are not able to obtain information that is only collectible on the phone. For example, it is impossible for us to tell how a smartwatch impacts the smartphone usage, or to quantify the impact of a watch on its paired phone's energy consumption. We plan to expand the data collector to phones in our future work.

Other Smartwatch OSes. The OS also plays an important role in determining the resource consumption [32]. In this study we focus on Android Wear Version 1.3 while other wearable OSes such as Apple watchOS and Tizen exist. We are in particular interested in Android Wear 2.0 that was in its developer preview stage when this paper was written. Android Wear 2.0 provides several new features that enhance the usability and energy-efficiency of wearable devices. To name a few, it supports standalone wearable apps that do not require their smartphone counterparts and that have direct Internet access through Wi-Fi or cellular; it allows the transition to the dozing state through a dynamic timer; it introduces "Complications API [2]" to allow 3rd-party apps to show custom data on a watch face; it also has new input methods including built-in virtual keyboards. We plan to conduct an in-depth study of Android Wear 2.0 in our future work.

8. CONCLUDING REMARKS

Through an IRB-approved user study involving 27 users for 106 days, we conducted an in-depth analysis of smartwatch usage in the wild by answering several key research questions such as how users interact with the watch, how smartwatch apps behave, how push notifications look like on watches, how smartwatch energy is consumed, and what key characteristics of smartwatch traffic are. Our findings shed light on improving the design for wearable systems, which indeed requires cross-layer efforts and involves multiple entities in the wearable ecosystem.

Acknowledgements

We would like to thank the smartwatch users at Indiana University Bloomington who voluntarily participated in our user study. The user study devices were sponsored by Indiana University Bloomington. We also thank the MobiSys reviewers and especially Elizabeth M. Belding for shepherding the paper. Feng Qian's research was supported in part by NSF Award #1629347. Felix Xiaozhu Lin was supported in part by NSF Award #1464357 and a Google Faculty Award. Kai Chen was supported in part by NSFC U1536106, 61100226, Youth Innovation Promotion Association CAS, and strategic priority research program of CAS (XDA06010701).

9. REFERENCES

[1] Android Notifications. https://developer.android.com/guide/topics/ui/notifiers/notifications.html.

[2] Android Watch Face Complications. https://developer.android.com/wear/preview/features/complications.html.

[3] Android wear 2.0 developer preview 3: Play store and more. http://android-developers.blogspot.com/2016/09/android-wear-2-0-developer-preview-3-play-store-and-more.html.

[4] Apple watch human interface guidelines. https://developer.apple.com/watchos/human-interface-guidelines/overview/.

[5] Monsoon Power Monitor. https://www.msoon.com/LabEquipment/PowerMonitor/.

[6] Optimizing for Doze and App Standby. https://developer.android.com/training/monitoring-device-state/doze-standby.html.

[7] PhoneLab: A Smartphone Platform Testbed. https://phone-lab.org/.

[8] Samsung Gear Application Programming Guide. http://img-developer.samsung.com/contents/cmm/Samsung_Gear_Application_Programming_Guide_1.0.pdf.

[9] Sending and Syncing Data with Watch. https://developer.android.com/training/wearables/data-layer/index.html.

[10] Smartwatches now more popular than Swiss watches. https://www.cnet.com/news/smartwatches-now-more-popular-than-swiss-watches-thanks-largely-to-apple/.

[11] UI patterns for android wear. https://developer.android.com/design/wear/patterns.html.

[12] RFCOMM WITH TS 07.10. https://www.bluetooth.org/docman/handlers/DownloadDoc.ashx?doc_id=40909, 2012.

[13] Specification of the Bluetooth System (Core Specification). https://www.bluetooth.com/specifications/adopted-specifications, 2014.

[14] Chen, X., Ding, N., Jindal, A., Hu, Y. C., Gupta, M., and Vannithamby, R. Smartphone Energy Drain in the Wild: Analysis and Implications. In *SIGMETRICS* (2015).

[15] Chen, X., Grossman, T., Wigdor, D., and Fitzmaurice, G. Duet: Exploring joint interactions on a smart phone and a smart watch. In *ACM CHI* (2014).

[16] Chen, X., Jindal, A., Ding, N., Hu, Y. C., Gupta, M., and Vannithamby, R. Smartphone Background Activities in the Wild: Origin, Energy Drain, and Optimization. In *MobiCom* (2015).

[17] Dong, M., Choi, Y.-S. K., and Zhong, L. Power Modeling of Graphical User Interfaces on OLED Displays. In *DAC* (2009).

[18] Dong, M., Choi, Y.-S. K., and Zhong, L. Power-Saving Color Transformation of Mobile Graphical User Interfaces on OLED-based Displays. In *ISLPED* (2009).

[19] Dong, M., and Zhong, L. Chameleon: A Color-Adaptive Web Browser for Mobile OLED Displays. In *MobiSys* (2011).

[20] Falaki, H., Mahajan, R., Kandula, S., Lymberopoulos, D., and Estrin, R. G. D. Diversity in Smartphone Usage. In *Mobisys* (2010).

[21] Ford, A., Raiciu, C., Handley, M., and Bonaventure, O. TCP Extensions for Multipath Operation with Multiple Addresses. RFC 6824, 2013.

[22] Gouveia, R., Karapanos, E., and Hassenzahl, M. How do we engage with activity trackers? a longitudinal study of habito. In *UbiComp* (2015).

[23] Gupta, N. Inside Bluetooth Low Energy. Arech House, 2013.

[24] Ham, M., Dae, I., and Choi, C. Lpd: Low power display mechanism for mobile and wearable devices. In *Usenix ATC* (2015).

[25] Huang, J., Badam, A., Chandra, R., and Nightingale, E. B. Weardrive: Fast and energy-efficient storage for wearables. In *USENIX ATC* (2015).

[26] Huang, J., Qian, F., Gerber, A., Mao, Z. M., Sen, S., and Spatscheck, O. A Close Examination of Performance and Power Characteristics of 4G LTE Networks. In *Mobisys* (2012).

[27] Huang, J., Qian, F., Guo, Y., Zhou, Y., Xu, Q., Mao, Z. M., Sen, S., and Spatscheck, O. An In-depth Study of LTE: Effect of Network Protocol and Application Behavior on Performance. In *SIGCOMM* (2013).

[28] Huang, J., Xu, Q., Tiwana, B., Mao, Z. M., Zhang, M., and Bahl, P. Anatomizing Application Performance Differences on Smartphones. In *Proc. ACM MobiSys* (2010).

[29] Lazar, A., Koehler, C., Tanenbaum, J., and Nguyen, D. H. Why we use and abandon smart devices. In *UbiComp* (2015).

[30] LiKamWa, R., Wang, Z., Carroll, A., Lin, F. X., and Zhong, L. Draining our glass: An energy and heat characterization of google glass. In *APSys* (2014).

[31] Liu, R., Jiang, L., Jiang, N., and Lin, F. X. Anatomizing System Activities on Interactive Wearable Devices. In *APSys* (2015).

[32] Liu, R., and Lin, F. X. Understanding the Characteristics of Android Wear OS. In *MobiSys* (2016).

[33] Liu, X., Zhou, Z., Diao, W., Li, Z., and Zhang, K. When good becomes evil: Keystroke inference with smartwatch. In *CCS* (2015).

[34] Lyons, K. What can a dumb watch teach a smartwatch? informing the design of smartwatches. In *ISWC* (2015).

[35] Mayberry, A., Hu, P., Marlin, B., Salthouse, C., and Ganesan, D. ishadow: Design of a wearable, real-time mobile gaze tracker. In *MobiSys* (2014).

[36] Miao, H., and Lin, F. X. Tell your graphics stack that the display is circular. In *HotMobile* (2016).

[37] Min, C., Kang, S., Yoo, C., Cha, J., Choi, S., Oh, Y., and Song, J. Exploring current practices for battery use and management of smartwatches. In *ISWC* (2015).

[38] Nika, A., Zhu, Y., Ding, N., Jindal, A., Hu, Y. C., Zhou, X., Zhao, B. Y., and Zheng, H. Energy and Performance of Smartphone Radio Bundling in Outdoor Environments. In *WWW* (2015).

[39] Nikravesh, A., Yao, H., Xu, S., Choffnes, D., and Mao, Z. M. Mobilyzer: An Open Platform for Controllable Mobile Network Measurements. In *Mobisys* (2015).

[40] Nirjon, S., Gummeson, J., Gelb, D., and Kim, K.-H. Typingring: A wearable ring platform for text input. In *MobiSys* (2015).

[41] Pathak, A., Hu, Y. C., and Zhang, M. Where is the energy spent inside my app?: fine grained energy accounting on smartphones with Eprof. In *EuroSys* (2012).

[42] Pathak, A., Hu, Y. C., Zhang, M., Bahl, P., and Wang, Y.-M. Fine-grained power modeling for smartphones using system call tracing. In *EuroSys* (2011).

[43] Plaumann, K., Muller, M., and Rukzio, E. Circularselection: Optimizing list selection for smartwatches. In *ISWC* (2016).

[44] Poyraz, E., and Memik, G. Analyzing power consumption and characterizing user activities on smartwatches: Summary. In *IEEE International Symposium on Workload Characterization (IISWC)* (2016).

[45] Qian, F., Gerber, A., Mao, Z. M., Sen, S., Spatscheck, O., and Willinger, W. TCP Revisited: A Fresh Look at TCP in the Wild. In *IMC* (2009).

[46] Qian, F., Quah, K. S., Huang, J., Erman, J., Gerber, A., Mao, Z. M., Sen, S., and Spatscheck, O. Web Caching on Smartphones: Ideal vs. Reality. In *Mobisys* (2012).

[47] Qian, F., Wang, Z., Gerber, A., Mao, Z. M., Sen, S., and Spatscheck, O. Profiling Resource Usage for Mobile Applications: a Cross-layer Approach. In *Mobisys* (2011).

[48] Rahmati, A., and Zhong, L. Studying smartphone usage: Lessons from a four-month field study. *IEEE Transactions on Mobile Computing 12*, 7 (2013).

[49] Rosen, S., Nikravesh, A., Guo, Y., Mao, Z. M., Qian, F., and Sen, S. Revisiting Network Energy Efficiency of Mobile Apps: Performance in the Wild. In *Proc. ACM IMC* (2015).

[50] Santagati, G. E., and Melodia, T. U-Wear: Software-Defined Ultrasonic Networking for Wearable Devices. In *MobiSys* (2015).

[51] Shen, S., Wang, H., and Choudhury, R. R. I am a smartwatch and i can track my user's arm. In *MobiSys* (2016).

[52] Shepard, C., Rahmati, A., Tossell, C., Zhong, L., and Kortum, P. LiveLab: Measuring Wireless Networks and Smartphone Users in the Field. In *HotMetrics* (2010).

[53] Wang, H., Lai, T. T., and Choudhury, R. R. Mole: Motion leaks through smartwatch sensors. In *MobiCom* (2015).

[54] Xu, Q., Erman, J., Gerber, A., Mao, Z. M., Pang, J., and Venkataraman, S. Identifying Diverse Usage Behaviors of Smartphone Apps. In *IMC* (2011).

[55] Zhang, L., Tiwana, B., Qian, Z., Wang, Z., Dick, R., Mao, Z. M., and Yang, L. Accurate Online Power Estimation and Automatic Battery Behavior Based Power Model Generation for Smartphones. In *CODES+ISSS* (2010).

[56] Zhang, Y., Breslau, L., Paxson, V., and Shenker, S. On the Characteristics and Origins of Internet Flow Rates. In *Proc. ACM SIGCOMM* (2002).

Reptor: Enabling API Virtualization on Android for Platform Openness

Taeyeon Ki, Alexander Simeonov, Bhavika Pravin Jain, Chang Min Park,
Keshav Sharma, Karthik Dantu, Steven Y. Ko, Lukasz Ziarek
Department of Computer Science and Engineering
University at Buffalo, The State University of New York
{tki, agsimeon, bhavikap, cpark22, keshavsh, kdantu, stevko, lziarek}@buffalo.edu

ABSTRACT

This paper proposes a new technique that enables open innovation in mobile platforms. Our technique allows third-party developers to modify, instrument, or extend platform API calls and deploy their modifications seamlessly. The uniqueness of our technique is that it enables modifications *completely at the app layer* without requiring any platform-level changes. This allows practical openness—third parties can easily distribute their modifications for a platform without the need to update the entire platform. To demonstrate the benefits of our technique, we have developed a prototype on Android called *Reptor* and used it to instrument real-world apps with novel functionality. Our evaluation in realistic scenarios shows that Reptor has little overhead in performance and energy, and only modest overhead in memory usage that ranges from 0.6% to 10% for the observed worst cases.

Keywords

API virtualization; Android app instrumentation; Android platform instrumentation; platform openness

1. INTRODUCTION

Openness drives innovation. There are numerous examples in computer systems where openness has led to an explosion of new advances. Perhaps the most recent example is Software-Defined Networking (SDN) [23], which has unlocked the control interface of commodity routers and switches. This has enabled third-party developers to easily write and deploy software controllers for networking hardware. Many other examples exist [8, 26, 29, 5, 9], where openness has enabled realization of novel ideas.

By openness we broadly mean two properties—(1) *extensibility*, i.e., the ability for third-party developers to *modify, instrument, or extend* an existing platform, and (2) *deployability*, i.e., the ability for end users to *easily deploy* third-party platform modifications. Previously, extensibility on desktop platforms has been studied extensively at all layers, i.e., the kernel (e.g., Kprobes [8]), system libraries (e.g., Detours [26]), and the application layer (e.g., AspectJ [29]). It has also been studied across different subsystems, e.g.,

Permission to make digital or hard copies of all or part of this work for personal or classroom use is granted without fee provided that copies are not made or distributed for profit or commercial advantage and that copies bear this notice and the full citation on the first page. Copyrights for components of this work owned by others than ACM must be honored. Abstracting with credit is permitted. To copy otherwise, or republish, to post on servers or to redistribute to lists, requires prior specific permission and/or a fee. Request permissions from permissions@acm.org.

MobiSys '17, June 19–23, 2017, Niagara Falls, NY, USA.

© 2017 ACM. ISBN 978-1-4503-4928-4/17/06...$15.00

DOI: http://dx.doi.org/10.1145/3081333.3081341

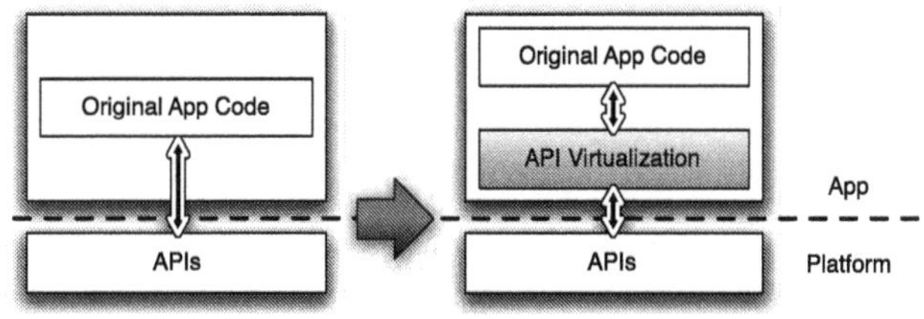

Figure 1: App Transformation with API Virtualization

FUSE [5] for filesystems and NetFilter [9] for networking. On the other hand, deployability for end users has not been studied in detail as it is less of a concern in desktop environments. End users have low-level access (such as shell or root access) which allows them to easily download and deploy third-party platform modifications. For example, FUSE allows an end user to download a new filesystem such as SSHFS [12] and deploy it easily.

However, this is not the case in modern mobile platforms. Deployability is severely restricted, and regular end users cannot easily use any third-party platform modifications. The default interaction available between a regular user and an off-the-shelf mobile platform is installing and using apps downloaded from online stores (such as Google Play). Platform modifications typically require a vendor-controlled update mechanism (such as Google's Over-The-Air), low-level system access to overwrite system files, or an ability to recompile and install a new platform image—none of which is realistic to expect for a regular user.

Given this constraint, deploying third-party platform modifications on a mobile platform requires an *app-layer* approach, where all platform modifications are contained *in an app* and those modifications are embedded in the app *statically*. This way, we can achieve both extensibility and deployability—we can use existing app distribution mechanisms (such as Google Play) to disseminate third-party platform modifications, without requiring any other form of access to user devices. This app-layer approach has an additional benefit that per-app customizations are possible, i.e., different apps can use different platform modifications on a single mobile device.

This observation brings us to the central idea of this paper—enabling openness through *API virtualization*. We introduce a shim layer between an app and its platform (Figure 1), where we allow third parties to customize platform API call behavior and add new functionality. We then statically inject this virtualization layer into an app for ease of deployment, leveraging bytecode instrumentation. Example use cases could be automatically augmenting local storage read/write calls to enable seamless cloud backup [20], improving energy efficiency for always-on sensing [36], or seamless HTTP-to-HTTPS migration and vendor-specific library switching as we describe in Section 4.

To concretely demonstrate the benefits of our idea, we have developed a prototype called *Reptor* on Android. The primary challenge we address is *correctly enforcing* an app to use our API virtualization layer. The exact description of this challenge entails an involved discussion, which we defer to Sections 2 and 3. Briefly, the challenge stems from the constraint that all platform modifications should occur in an app, coupled with the need to comply with a rich set of features in Android and its default language, Java, such as sub-typing, polymorphism, and callbacks. To the best of our knowledge, this challenge of correct enforcement has not been addressed in the literature. As we detail in Section 2, previous instrumentation systems (e.g., SIF [24] and RetroSkeleton [21]) as well as systems that leverage instrumentation (e.g., AppInsight [33], VanarSena [32], and MobileHub [36]) do not provide techniques for correct enforcement.

We make three contributions. First, we show that an app-layer approach to platform openness is *feasible* by designing and implementing a mechanism that enables it on Android (Section 3). Second, we show that our approach is *useful* by implementing three use cases as well as discussing how our approach could improve previously-proposed systems (Section 4). Third, we show that our approach is *practical* by evaluating our prototype with our own micro-benchmark apps as well as 1,200 real apps downloaded from Google Play (Section 5). Our prototype has correctly processed about 234.8M lines of code to produce the results presented in this paper, and shows modest overhead—for real apps we see almost no difference in performance, 0.6% to 10% increase in memory usage for the observed worst cases, and no statistically significant overhead in energy usage.

2. API VIRTUALIZATION CHALLENGES

Our goal in enabling API virtualization on Android is to allow third-party developers to provide *alternative platform API implementations with novel functionality*. For example, if a third-party developer has an implementation for a novel gesture recognition algorithm, we want to be able to provide that as an alternative to the default gesture recognition provided by Android.

We target Android platform APIs for extensibility because all functionality of Android is provided by the platform APIs for an app—they provide traditional OS service APIs (e.g., file system operations), APIs to access system resources (e.g., sensors), sensor data analytics APIs (e.g., gesture recognition APIs), high-level app support APIs (e.g., HTTP APIs), and convenient data structure APIs from standard Java (e.g., hash maps). Conceptually, they are analogous to the system call interface for a traditional OS. Thus, allowing alternate implementations for the platform APIs enables extensibility of the platform.

However, when designing an extensibility mechanism for Android, we need to be conscious about deployability as discussed in Section 1. Many existing techniques cannot be adopted easily because they fall short in this regard. Examples include library overloading using `LD_PRELOAD`, Java class loaders, syscall library hooks, Java VM hooks, proxies [28], AspectJ [29], etc. These techniques require either low-level access or modifications to the underlying platform, resulting in limited deployability for Android.

Thus, we devise an *app-layer* approach that provides both extensibility and deployability where (1) we *statically inject* an alternative third-party API implementation into an app, and (2) we make sure that the app *correctly* uses the injected API implementation instead of the original API implementation from Android. Consequently, there are two challenges we need to address: (1) injecting a third-party platform API implementation into an existing app, and (2) correctly enforcing the app to use the injected code. Among

```
1  public class MyStream extends FileOutputStream {
2    public void write(int b) {
3      // Overriding
4    }
5  }
6  public class Main {
7    public void main(String args[]){
8      MyStream obj1 = new MyStream("/tmp/test");
9      mainWrite(obj1, 10);
10   }
11   public void mainWrite(
12                FileOutputStream obj, int b) {
13     obj.write(b);
14   }
15 }
```

Figure 2: Sub-Typing Example

these, the first challenge (code injection) is a solved problem and can be done by Java bytecode rewriting [37, 21, 24].

While code injection can easily be solved, correctly enforcing the use of injected code is not. To illustrate this challenge, suppose an app calls `FileOutputStream.write()`, a platform API method. Also suppose that we want to replace it with a third-party `write()` implementation that augments the original `write()`. For example, it could perform a local write as well as a remote write for seamless cloud backup.

At first glance, it may seem that all we need to do is *call replacement* that consists of two steps—(1) search every occurrence of `obj.write()`, where `obj` is of type `FileOutputStream`, and (2) replace it with a call to the third party's `write()` implementation. This, however, can easily result in incorrect behavior as shown in Figure 2.

In the code, there are two classes, `MyStream` and `Main`. `MyStream` extends a platform class `FileOutputStream` and overrides `write()`. `Main` initializes a `MyStream` object (in line 8) and calls `mainWrite()` (in line 9). `mainWrite()`, in turn, calls `write()` to perform a file write (in line 13).

Note that `mainWrite()` (line 11) takes `FileOutputStream` as a parameter, and not `MyStream`. In `Main.main()`, `MyStream` is passed as an argument to `mainWrite()` (line 9). This is possible because of sub-typing, i.e., `MyStream` can be cast to `FileOutputStream`.

Now suppose that we want to extend the example code to use a third-party implementation of `FileOutputStream.write()` by searching and replacing objects of type `FileOutputStream` on which we call the `write()` method (i.e., using the call replacement approach as described earlier). In the example code, there is only one such place, line 13. However, replacing this call is *incorrect*; at run time, line 9 passes `MyStream` to `mainWrite()`, and replacing line 13 means replacing `MyStream.write()`, not `FileOutputStream.write()`. We note that this is *not* an isolated problem; in general, it is not difficult to construct various examples where call replacement produces incorrect behavior.

Unfortunately, previous systems such as SIF [24] and RetroSkeleton [21] only allow call replacement and cannot enforce an app to use a third-party API implementation correctly. Moreover, many recent systems, e.g., AppInsight [33], VanarSena [32], and MobileHub [36], instrument API calls to enable selective logging, fuzzy testing, and sensor call replacement, respectively. Their instrumentation requires correct replacement of API calls but only uses call replacement that does not produce correct program behavior.

In Section 7, we further discuss previous techniques and their limitations. In general, prior work falls into two broad categories, each with a major limitation—techniques with limited deployabil-

```
1  public class NewFOS {
2    public void write(int b) {
3      // A reimplementation goes here.
4    }
5  }
6  public class MyStream extends NewFOS {
7    public void write(int b) {
8      // Overriding
9    }
10 }
11 public class Main {
12   public void main(String args[]) {
13     MyStream obj1 = new MyStream("/tmp/test");
14     mainWrite(obj1, 10);
15   }
16   public void mainWrite(NewFOS obj, int b) {
17     obj.write(b);
18   }
19 }
```

Figure 3: Class Replacement Example

ity (e.g., LD_PRELOAD, Java class loaders, Java VM hooks, proxies [28], AspectJ [29], etc.), and techniques that only support call replacement (e.g., SIF, RetroSkeleton, etc.).

3. API VIRTUALIZATION ON ANDROID

The above discussion reveals that using method calls as the unit of replacement is fundamentally incorrect, as there are many class-level features that determine method-level behavior. Consequently, our approach uses a more natural unit of replacement—*classes*. This means that (1) a third party writes a *replacement class* for a platform API class that has a new implementation of the platform class, and (2) our approach replaces all uses of the platform class in an app with this replacement class. Effectively, our API virtualization layer becomes a set of replacement classes that modify or reimplement Android platform APIs, and are injected into an app. Since a class is a natural abstraction for modular implementation, it is also well-suited as a programming interface for third-party developers.

Figure 3 extends the previous example and illustrates our use of a replacement class. In the example, there is a new class `NewFOS` that replaces `FileOutputStream` and reimplements `write()`. It is injected into the app's bytecode (we show the source for illustrative purposes). In the app classes (`MyStream` and `Main`), `NewFOS` is used instead of the original class, `FileOutputStream`. This is shown in line 6 and line 16, which are the only places where `FileOutputStream` is used in the original app code. Essentially, `NewFOS` replaces all uses of `FileOutputStream` in the app. This correctly solves the sub-typing problem described earlier as line 17 uses `MyStream`, not `NewFOS`.

Unfortunately, we cannot rely on simple examples such as Figure 3 to determine whether or not class replacement is the right approach. We must examine all possible uses of a platform class in app code, and make sure that we can correctly replace a platform class with a replacement class provided by a third party. Thus, we start our solution discussion by presenting our classification of platform class uses. We then discuss how we handle the different uses.

3.1 Platform Class Uses on Android

In order to determine all possible uses of a platform class in app code on Android, we have examined every feature described in the Android API documentation [15] as well as the Java specification [7]. We have then classified the uses of platform classes into the categories shown in Table 1. For simplicity of presentation, we use the term *class* to refer to all class-level constructs, i.e., interfaces, abstract classes, and enums, unless otherwise specified.

Our categorization achieves two purposes. First, it concisely summarizes the vast list of platform class uses. Since Java and Android have many features that enable a wide range of platform class uses, it is infeasible for us to discuss every single use in the space given for this paper. Our categorization allows us to capture sufficient details without going into each and every use. Second, our categorization shows our findings that (1) there are a few major challenges we need to address for class replacement, (2) each category represents one such major challenge, and (3) these challenges are inter-related, and it is best to *avoid* solving them individually in isolation. Initially, we came up with point solutions for different categories but had much difficulty integrating them together since our individual solutions ended up being logically incompatible. After some iterations, we have realized that *addressing the categories progressively in the order we present in Table 1* allows us to arrive at a coherent design in the end. The rest of this section discusses this progression.

There are many engineering challenges that we address in the implementation of our design. However, since these only require mechanical solutions, we refrain from discussing those in detail and only briefly mention them when needed. To prove that we have indeed addressed other engineering challenges not discussed in this paper, we take a pragmatic approach where we use 1,200 real apps downloaded from Google Play as test cases. In Sections 4 and 5, we show that these apps work correctly after our transformation, and the total lines of code we have processed is more than 234.8M. In Section 6, we further discuss the experiences and implications of our evaluation strategy with real apps.

3.2 Handling Basic Uses of Platform Classes

We first discuss the most basic uses of platform classes, i.e., (both local and class) variables, parameters, and return types. Together, they pose a challenge for class replacement due to a dependency problem they raise. To illustrate this, consider one method in a platform class, `AtomicFile`:

```
void finishWrite(FileOutputStream str)
```

As shown, `FileOutputStream` is used as a parameter in `finishWrite()`. Using this, the following code shows variable and parameter uses of `FileOutputStream`:

```
FileOutputStream fos = new FileOutputStream(...);
AtomicFile af = new AtomicFile(...);
af.finishWrite(fos);
```

Now suppose that we are replacing `FileOutputStream` with `NewFOS` as done before in Figure 3. The code becomes:

```
NewFOS fos = new NewFOS(...);
AtomicFile af = new AtomicFile(...);
af.finishWrite(fos); // does not work
```

However, this code does not work; `finishWrite()` expects `FileOutputStream`, not `NewFOS`. To make this work, the first thing one could try might be modifying `finishWrite()` to use `NewFOS`. However, we cannot do this—`AtomicFile` is a platform class provided by one of the Android system libraries, which we cannot modify.

Although the above code only shows variable and parameter uses of a platform class, the same problem occurs with return types as well. The broader challenge is that replacing a platform class has a dependency problem, since a platform class we want to replace can

Category	Description	Discussion
Basic	Uses of platform classes in variables, parameters, and return types	Section 3.2
Class hierarchy	Uses of platform classes in inheritance, `super` calls, and type-casting	Section 3.3
Callback	Uses of platform classes in Android lifecycle callbacks, and event (UI, sensor, etc.) callbacks	Section 3.4
Interface return	Uses of platform interfaces returned by platform calls	Section 3.5
Runtime	Dynamic uses of platform classes, i.e., reflection, `synchronized`, reference access, and `instanceof`	Section 3.6
Exception	Uses of platform exception classes	Section 3.6
JNI	Uses of JNI	Section 3.6

Table 1: Platform Class Use Categories

```
1  public class DummyAtomicFile {
2    AtomicFile realObj;
3    // Constructor
4    public DummyAtomicFile() {
5      realObj = new AtomicFile();
6    }
7    // Wraps the original method
8    public void finishWrite(NewFOS str) {
9      Object realStr = str.getRealObj();
10     return realObj.finishWrite(realStr);
11   }
12   // Returns the instance of the original type
13   public Object getRealObj() {
14     return realObj;
15   }
16 }
```

Figure 4: Dummy Class Example

be used as a parameter or return type in other platform classes that we cannot modify.

Solution—Dummy Classes: We solve the above problem by creating an additional set of replacement classes called *dummy* classes. Using them, we replace the target platform class we want to replace as well as other platform classes that use the target platform class as parameters and/or return types. This is inevitable as we cannot modify other platform classes.

Essentially, a dummy class is a simple wrapper around a platform class and uses replacement classes as parameters and return types. Figure 4 shows an example dummy class that replaces `AtomicFile`. As shown in line 8, `finishWrite()` is a simple wrapper over the original, but uses `NewFOS` instead of `FileOutputStream`. All other methods also simply wrap the original methods. For this wrapping to work, it holds a reference to an instance of the original class (line 2).

The following code snippet shows how the dependency problem illustrated above is solved with dummy classes:

```
NewFOS fos = new NewFOS(...);
DummyAtomicFile af = new DummyAtomicFile(...);
af.finishWrite(fos);
```

It works correctly as expected.

A dummy class (such as `DummyAtomicFile`) and an actual replacement class (such as `NewFOS`) share the same code structure in our design. They all wrap original methods and hold a reference to an instance of the original type. The only difference is that an actual replacement class contains third-party's reimplementation for some or all of the methods; if a third party does not reimplement a method, it simply calls its corresponding original method.

Now, it is not difficult to see that there is a rippling effect—replacing `AtomicFile` with `DummyAtomicFile` affects other platform classes that use `AtomicFile` as parameters or return types, just as `NewFOS` affects `AtomicFile`. That is, if we use a dummy class as described above, it leads us to create even more dummy classes.

Our initial idea was to track this rippling effect and determine the exact set of platform classes that need dummy classes, in a hope that we would minimize the number of new classes we create. However, we observed that most real apps require us to create dummy classes for almost the entire set of platform classes. Thus, we have decided to just create a dummy class for *each and every* platform class. Effectively, this means that our API virtualization layer is a layer that consists of dummy and actual replacement classes.

This approach may seem to incur potentially large overhead. However, compilers are very good at eliminating dead code as well as inlining small methods—our implementation in fact performs basic dead code elimination. Further, using dummy classes paves the way for the rest of the refinements, i.e., if we use dummy classes, most of the other refinements logically follow. The runtime overhead of these dummy classes is modest in terms of latency, energy, and memory, which we show in Section 5. Nevertheless, there is an inevitable static cost of code size increase, which we also show in Section 5.

For the simplicity of presentation, we will simply use "a replacement class" to refer to either a dummy or an actual replacement class in the rest of the paper.

3.3 Handling Class Hierarchy Uses

Our second category is platform class uses related to Java's class hierarchy. This comes second in our category list for a reason, since addressing the previous category gives us a natural starting point of addressing this category.

In Java, every class is part of one large class hierarchy, where `java.lang.Object` is the root. This enables many convenient features of object-oriention: (1) *inheritance*—a class inherits all its parent class's methods and fields without defining or implementing them, (2) *super calls*—even if a class overrides a parent class's method, it can still call the parent class's implementation of the method by calling it with the keyword `super`, and (3) *type casting*—a class can be cast to any of the classes up in the hierarchy and vice versa. A platform class can be used in all these cases.

Ideally, a replacement class for a platform class should be a *complete* replacement in the class hierarchy as well, seamlessly enabling all features of the hierarchy such as inheritance, super calls, and type casting. Otherwise, we need to devise ad-hoc solutions for point cases, which is not a principled way of solving the problem at hand.

Unfortunately simply replacing a platform class does not achieve complete replacement in the class hierarchy. To illustrate this, suppose we have a replacement class `NewStream` that has a reimplementation of `OutputStream`, a platform class. Figure 5 shows the original class hierarchy on the left. Now, consider the following code snippet:

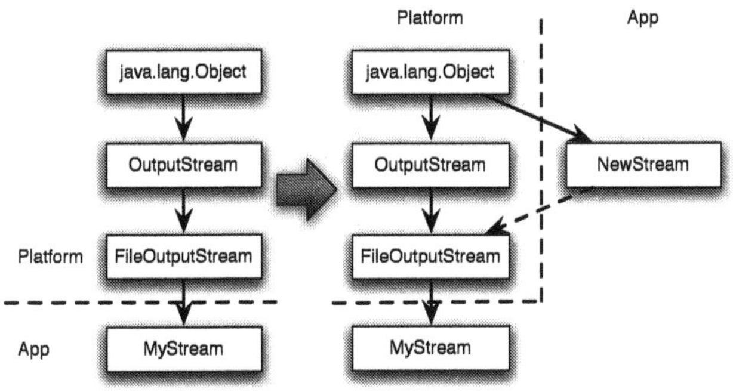

Figure 5: Class Hierarchy Comparison

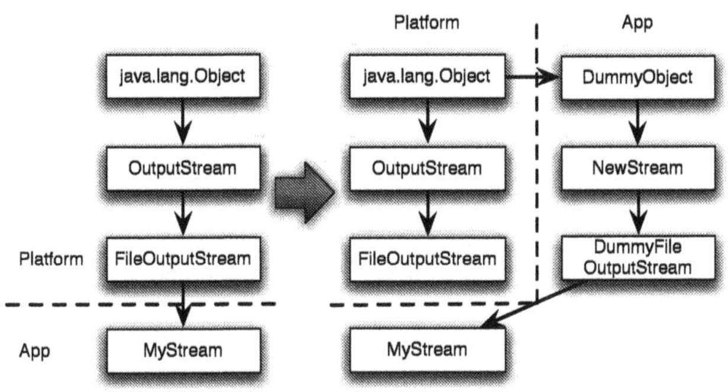

Figure 6: New Mirrored Class Hierarchy

```
MyStream ms = new MyStream();
FileOutputStream fos = (FileOutputStream) ms;
OutputStream os = (OutputStream) fos;
```

Simply replacing `OutputStream` with `NewStream` would produce:

```
MyStream ms = new MyStream();
FileOutputStream fos = (FileOutputStream) ms;
NewStream os = (NewStream) fos; // does not work
```

However, the type casting done in the last line does not work; unlike `OutputStream`, `NewStream` is not a parent class of `FileOutputStream`.

To make this code work, it may seem that we only need to make `FileOutputStream` a subclass of `NewStream`. However, we cannot do this since `FileOutputStream` is once again a platform class, which we cannot modify. Figure 5 gives a different view on this using two class hierarchies—the original class hierarchy on the left and the new hierarchy in question on the right. As shown by the dotted arrow, in order to make `NewStream` a drop-in replacement for `OutputStream` in the class hierarchy, we need to make `FileOutputStream` a subclass of `NewStream` instead of `OutputStream`, which we cannot.

Solution—Class Hierarchy Mirroring: To address the above problem, we use *class hierarchy mirroring* that exactly replicates the original *platform-side* class hierarchy in the *app side*. This is possible since we create replacement classes for all platform classes anyway, and we can mirror the entire platform class hierarchy by connecting the replacement classes the same way. Figure 6 illustrates this.

With this class hierarchy mirroring, we can correctly address the problem described above; in addition to `NewStream` replacing `OutputStream`, we have `DummyFileOutputStream` replacing `FileOutputStream`. These replacement classes mirror the original hierarchy in the app side, and correctly make the code work as follows:

```
MyStream ms = new MyStream();
DummyFileOutputStream fos =
    (DummyFileOutputStream) ms;
NewStream os = (NewStream) fos;
```

```
// This is the original.
public class MyActivity extends Activity {
  protected void onCreate(Bundle savedState) {
    super.onCreate(savedState);
  }
}
// After using replacement classes
public class MyActivity extends ActivityRep {
  protected void onCreate(DummyBundle savedState) {
    super.onCreate(savedState);
  }
}
```

Figure 7: Callback Method Example

3.4 Handling Callback Uses

Our third category is callbacks, one of the prominent ways of using platform classes on Android. Callbacks require app developers to create subclasses of callback-defining platform classes, and implement them. They are critical in Android apps since they are used in essential functions such as handling app lifecycle and UI events.

We present this category after discussing the previous two categories for a reason—we cannot consider callback uses of platform classes in isolation since they are tied together with basic and class hierarchy uses. Figure 7 illustrates this with two versions of code. The top one shows original app code, which is in fact a much-used code structure in Android; `MyActivity` (an app class) extends `Activity` (a platform class), and implements `onCreate()` (a callback), which expects `Bundle` (a platform class) as a parameter. This means that basic, class hierarchy, and callback uses of platform classes are all occurring together. This also demonstrates that we cannot consider individual categories separately.

Now, the bottom code is a version that uses our design described so far. It assumes that `ActivityRep` is a replacement class provided by a third party, and replaces `Activity` with `ActivityRep` and `Bundle` with `DummyBundle`.

However, this causes two problems for callbacks. First, we now break the relationship between `MyActivity` and `Activity`; `MyActivity` is now a subclass of `ActivityRep` instead of `Activity`. This is a problem as it violates the callback semantics of Android—`MyActivity` must be a subclass of `Activity`, either directly or indirectly. This is the only way for Android to correctly recognize it as a class that implements callbacks defined in `Activity`.

The second problem is that `onCreate()` now has a different method signature from the original one, since it accepts `DummyBundle` instead of `Bundle`. This is another violation of the callback semantics; Android passes a `Bundle` object, not a `DummyBundle` object when it calls `onCreate()`.

Solution—Compiler-Driven Selective Code Rewriting: To preserve Android's callback semantics, we *need* to retain the relationship between a callback-defining platform class and any app class that implements it. But as illustrated above, this conflicts with our current design.

To resolve this conflict, we devise a strategy where we retain all callback relationships, while still incorporating the uses of replacement classes. Figure 8 demonstrates how we retain callback

```
1  // After handling callbacks
2  public class MyActivity extends SuperRep {
3    protected void onCreate(Bundle savedState) {
4      DummyBundle dBd = new DummyBundle(savedState):
5      this.onCreateWrapped(dBd);
6    }
7    protected void onCreateWrapped(DummyBundle dBd) {
8      super.onCreate(dBd);
9    }
10 }
```

Figure 8: Wrapped Callback Example

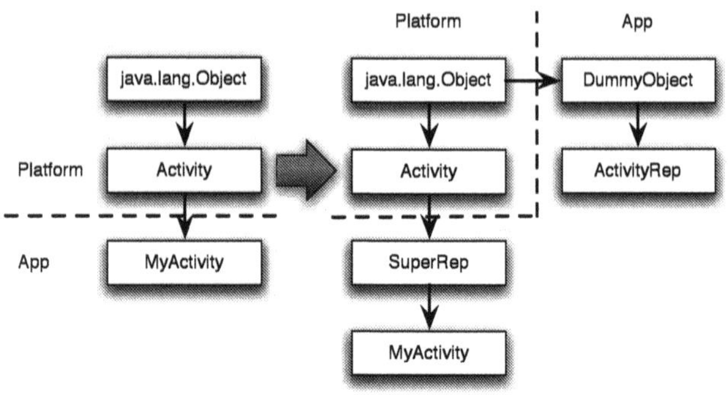

Figure 9: New Class Hierarchy for Callbacks

relationships by extending the previous example in Figure 7. Line 3 shows that `MyActivity` still implements `onCreate()` defined in `Activity`, without modifying the signature. In addition, we make `MyActivity` an indirect subclass of `Activity` as shown in line 2 (`MyActivity` extends `SuperRep`, which extends `Activity`; we discuss `SuperRep` later). In other words, it functions as a proper callback-implementing class.

We then use three techniques that *selectively rewrite* app code to incorporate the uses of replacement classes. The first technique incorporates the basic uses of platform classes, i.e., variable, parameter, and return type uses. The second technique incorporates two of the class hierarchy uses, inheritance and `super` call uses. The third technique incorporates the last of the class hierarchy uses, type casting uses. In implementing these techniques, we leverage a compiler (Soot [37]) to identify places where rewriting needs to occur. This is not difficult as it only needs to detect callback class uses in app code.

Our first technique is *callback wrapping*, as demonstrated in lines 4-5 and lines 7-9 in Figure 8. `onCreate()` calls a new method `onCreateWrapped()`, which wraps the original `onCreate()` code with replacement classes. This callback wrapping allows us to keep original callback signatures so that Android can correctly invoke callbacks, while using replacement classes in actual callback handling code.

Our second technique is to introduce a new type of replacement class called *super replacement class*. We show an example (`SuperRep`) in Figure 9. We insert this super replacement class between `MyActivity` and `Activity` to correctly handle two of the three features of the Java class hierarchy—`super` calls and inheritance. Since `SuperRep` is now a parent class of `MyActivity`, it intercepts all invocations of `super` calls and inherited method calls. This means that we can put third-party code that replaces `Activity` *inside* of `SuperRep`, so that all inherited calls and `super` calls in `MyActivity` use the third-party code correctly.

However, there are two subtleties involved further. First, there are now two replacement classes for a single third-party reimplementation for a platform class, e.g., `SuperRep` and `ActivityRep` for `Activity`. In order for both replacement classes to use the same third-party code, we ask developers to write static methods, as described in Section 3.7. Both replacement classes call these static methods to use the same code. We note that a super replacement class exists only for a callback-defining platform class, and as part of the class hierarchy.

Another subtle issue is that we cannot override `final` methods in a super replacement class to replace them. For example, in `SuperRep` we cannot override `final` methods defined in `Activity`, which prevents us from replacing them. In order to overcome this issue, we add a common suffix to all `final` methods when we put them in a super replacement class. We then rewrite all call sites that make inherited or super calls to `final` methods.

Our final technique for incorporating replacement classes is *explicit casting* between an app class and a platform class. This enables the remaining feature of the Java class hierarchy (type casting) with callbacks. To illustrate this strategy, consider once again the class hierarchy example in Figure 9. If an app originally casted `MyActivity` to `Activity` in its code, our design described so far would try casting `MyActivity` to `ActivityRep` since we replace `Activity` with `ActivityRep`. However, this casting does not work since there is no subclass relationship between the two classes.

Thus, we *explicitly* create an instance of the corresponding replacement class and rewrite the casting statement as follows (we assume `myAtv` is of type `MyActivity`):

```
// Original
Activity atv = (Activity) myAtv;

// After API virtualization
ActivityRep atv = new ActivityRep(myAtv);
```

Conversely, when it gets cast back to the original type, we use the `getRealObj()` method in the replacement class to get the original object as follows:

```
// Original
MyActivity myAtv = (MyActivity) atv;

// After API virtualization
MyActivity myAtv = (MyActivity) atv.getRealObj();
```

Technically, explicit casting could be used in general cases, i.e., we could use explicit casting instead of mirroring the platform-side class hierarchy. However, this incurs unnecessary overhead of creating a new replacement class instance whenever there is casting. Thus, we still mirror the class hierarchy and only use explicit casting in a limited fashion.

3.5 Handling Interface Return Type Uses

Our fourth category is related to interfaces, another feature of Java used for polymorphism that only contain class and method definitions. An interface must be implemented by a concrete class, and one cannot instantiate an interface. This poses a challenge for class replacement, since the return type of a method in a platform class can be an interface.

For example, a platform class `Context` has `getSharedPreferences()` that returns a platform interface `SharedPreferences`. `SharedPreferences` is a popular data storage option provided by Android. If we create a replacement class for `Context`, it will be:

```
public class DummyContext {
  DummySharedPreferences getSharedPreferences(...){
```

```
    SharedPreferences sp =
        realObj.getSharedPreferences(...);
    return new DummySharedPreferences(sp);
  }
}
```

However, this code does not work as is; `SharedPreferences` is an interface and we need to make its corresponding `DummySharedPreferences` also an interface to mirror the class hierarchy. This means that we cannot instantiate `DummySharedPreferences` as it is done above.

Solution—Using Concrete Dummy Classes: In order to solve the problem, whenever we mirror an interface with a replacement interface, we also create a concrete class that implements it. For example, for `DummySharedPreferences`, we create `ConcreteDummySharedPreferences` class that implements it. The only case where a concrete class is used is when a platform method returns an interface. For example, the replacement class for `Context` becomes:

```
public class DummyContext {
  DummySharedPreferences getSharedPreferences(...){
    SharedPreferences sp =
        realObj.getSharedPreferences(...);
    return new ConcreteDummySharedPreferences(sp);
  }
}
```

This way, we can correctly use a replacement class even when a platform class method returns an interface. We note that `abstract` platform classes have a similar problem, but the solution is much simpler—for each replacement class of an `abstract` platform class, we simply make it a concrete class so we can instantiate it.

3.6 Runtime, Exception, and JNI Uses

The remaining categories we handle are runtime, exception, and JNI uses of platform classes. Among these, the runtime use category includes reflection, `synchronized`, reference access, and `instanceof`. For reflection, we leverage the fact that a reflection call uses a plain string to identify which class to reflect on. We add extra code that, at run time replaces a class string with the string for the corresponding replacement class. The following (simplified) code demonstrates this:

```
// Original (a call to java.lang.System.exit())
String str0 = "java.";
String str1 = "lang.System";
Class c = Class.forName(str0+str1);
Object t = c.newInstance();
Method m = c.getDeclaredMethod("exit", ...);
Object o = m.invoke(t, ...);

// After API virtualization
// Assume that str0 and str1 are replaced already
DummyClass c = DummyClass.forName(str0+str1);
DummyObject t = c.newInstance();
DummyMethod m = c.getDeclaredMethod("exit", ...);
DummyObject o = m.invoke(t, ...);
```

In our `DummyClass.forName()`, we implement logic that replaces a passed-down string (e.g., `str0+str1`) with its replacement class string. Since there are only a few prefixes for platform API classes (e.g., `android.`, `java.`, etc.), we can easily identify at run time if a string is for a platform class. In our implementation, all replacement classes use the same prefix (`reptor.`), and we simply prepend our prefix. We emphasize that this is different from statically replacing a string with another string. There are many ways to compose a string dynamically (e.g., as shown in the example above), and it is generally difficult to infer a string statically. We are able to handle reflection gracefully, since we replace and instrument reflection classes.

For all other runtime uses, i.e., `synchronized`, reference access (e.g., using == or != to compare object references), and `instanceof`, we call `getRealObj()` to use the actual instance and the original type. This way, we preserve the semantics of app code.

We also wrap all exceptions, but use original exceptions whenever necessary to preserve Java exception semantics. This means that when app code has a try-catch block, we do not change the catch statement, but add extra code to wrap the caught exception before it is used in the rest of the code. On the other hand, when app code throws an exception, we use `getRealObj()` to throw the actual exception. The following code demonstrates this:

```
// Original
try {
  ...
} catch (IOException e) {
  e.printStackTrace();
  throw e;
}

// After API virtualization
try {
  ...
} catch (IOException e) {
  DummyIOException de = new DummyIOException(e);
  de.printStackTrace();
  throw de.getRealObj();
}
```

For JNI calls, we still wrap them from the Java side but do not touch native code. We do this since Android is primarily a Java platform, and our focus is virtualizing the Java APIs of Android. Other techniques exist that give the ability to intercept native API calls [38, 17, 39], and we could potentially leverage those as well.

3.7 Implementation

Our prototype called *Reptor* implements our design. It uses Soot [37] for injecting replacement classes and rewriting bytecode. There are two noteworthy features of our prototype. First, it asks a third-party developer to provide a reimplementation for an API method as a static method, for which we provide a template. For example, a third-party developer replaces `Activity.onCreate()` by filling the following template:

```
public class ActivityTemplate {
  static void onCreate(Activity is, DummyBundle b){
    // Third-party code
  }
}
```

This static method is called within both a regular replacement class and a super replacement class as discussed in Section 3.4. The first parameter is always a reference to a real object of the original type (e.g., `Activity`), so that a third-party developer can call the original method if necessary. The rest of the parameters use replacement classes, and third-party developers can use both replacement and original types in their code as they see fit. One limitation is that since we inject a third-party reimplementation into an app, it cannot perform any privileged operation; however, this is inevitable for an app-only approach.

The second noteworthy feature of our prototype is that it sometimes generates multiple DEX files. DEX is a bytecode format that Android uses, and has a limitation—it only allows 64K methods to be included in a single DEX file. Since we create replacement classes, sometimes we go over this limit. If that happens, we generate multiple DEX files [3].

4. USE CASES

We demonstrate the extensibility Reptor affords by implementing three use cases, and discussing how we can improve the correctness of previous systems. We acknowledge that these use cases can be developed independently; thus, our primary purpose of the use cases is showcasing that Reptor is a general tool that makes it easy, correct, and complete for a third party to add new platform-level functionality.

4.1 Vendor-Tied Library Switching

There is a growing concern that Google has started to offer critical functionality *not* as part of stock Android but as part of a proprietary, closed-source library called "Google Play Services," in order to maintain their competitive edge [16]. It provides important features such as location services (maps), search, in-app purchasing, etc. Although it is installed as a separate system app, it works much like built-in platform APIs—a large number of popular Android apps do not work if Google Play Services is not installed. Even worse, it does not work on non-Google-approved devices such as Amazon Fire. If an app is developed with it, the app does not run on Amazon devices. To alleviate this, a few vendors such as To alleviate this, a few vendors such as Amazon and Samsung offer compatible, alternate libraries. However, a developer now has the burden of implementing the use of multiple libraries.

Given this status quo, our first use case is to automatically transform an app developed with Google's library to use Amazon's library. It even allows a *user* with an Amazon device, without any help from original developers, to download an app that uses Google's library, transform it to make the app use Amazon's library instead, and run it on the user's Amazon device. To demonstrate this, we have implemented a mechanism that replaces Google Maps APIs with Amazon Maps APIs. Although Amazon Maps APIs provide matching classes for Google Maps classes, switching from Google's to Amazon's is not a simple matter of replacing Google API calls with Amazon API calls; in order to use Google Maps, an app must not only make API calls, but also provide callbacks to receive location updates—this is done by extending `abstract` classes or implementing interfaces defined in the Google APIs. Thus, proper replacement of all classes is necessary.

Our test app for this use case is Airbnb and we have posted a video [1] that demonstrates this use case. The original Airbnb app was not developed to use Amazon Maps, but our instrumented Airbnb app uses Amazon Maps on an Amazon Fire HD tablet.

4.2 Runtime Permission

We have implemented a runtime permission mechanism that asks a user to grant a permission to an app at run time, mirroring the iOS permission model. Recent versions of Android have added a similar runtime permission mechanism, introduced from version 6.0 [11]. Using Reptor we can enable such a mechanism for apps running on older Android versions. Google reports that the market share of Android 6.0 is 24% as of November 2016 [4], which means that the majority of devices do not benefit from runtime permissions.

With Reptor, we can replace sensitive API calls, wrap them with a permission-asking dialog, and ask a user for a permission. We have posted a video [14] that demonstrates this use case using Twitter app running on Android 4.4. Our instrumented Twitter app asks a user to grant a permission to access the Internet at login, unlike the original version that does not ask for any runtime permission.

To enable this, we have mainly replaced `URLConnection.connect()`, even though typical apps (including Twitter) often use `HttpURLConnection.connect()` to access the Internet. We do this because, (1) `HttpURLConnection` inherits `connect()` from `URLConnection` and (2) other classes such as `HttpsURLConnection` (used for HTTPS) also inherit `connect()` from `URLConnection`. Since Reptor correctly handles inheritance, we can uniformly enforce the runtime permission for both HTTP and HTTPS by replacing `URLConnection.connect()`.

4.3 HTTP-to-HTTPS Translator

Most web browsers such as Firefox, Chrome, and Opera provide an extension that automatically switches many major websites from HTTP to HTTPS for more secure browsing. However, Android platform does not provide such functionality for Android apps. Thus, we have implemented an HTTP-to-HTTPS translator, which automatically makes apps use HTTPS instead of HTTP if HTTPS is available on a requested URL. To implement this, we replace `URL` class so that it returns an HTTPS object instead of an HTTP object. Although previous work [21] introduces this use case, it in fact requires correct API replacement. We have posted a video for this as well [6].

4.4 Improving Previous Systems

As mentioned in Section 2, previous systems [33, 32, 36] use call replacement to augment certain API calls. Using Reptor, these systems can automatically get correct augmentation. In addition, previous instrumentation tools for Android [24, 21] discuss use cases where in fact correct API replacement is necessary. These include an API call timing profiler, an ad blocker, etc. Reptor can provide correct API replacement for these use cases as well. Lastly, BlueMountain [20] discusses a vision of replacing file system API calls to automatically add advanced storage functionality. An example can be automatic cloud integration as mentioned earlier, where local storage read/write calls are augmented to perform not only local operations but also cloud operations. Reptor can replace storage APIs for BlueMountain.

5. EVALUATION

This section characterizes the overhead of Reptor with microbenchmark apps of our own as well as 1,200 real apps downloaded from Google Play. Since our approach creates replacement classes for all platform classes, we have an extra layer that wraps the Android APIs and creates extra objects of replacement class types. Thus, we primarily measure the raw overhead of this extra layering, i.e., the overhead of passing all API calls through our API virtualization layer that does not implement any extra functionality.

We use Samsung Galaxy Nexus (1GB RAM, 64MB per-app heap size unless otherwise mentioned) running Android 4.4 to measure our run-time overhead. This is an older version of Android, and we detail our reasons for using this in Section 6. For our app instrumentation, we run Reptor on a desktop PC with a 3.10 GHz Intel Core i5-2400 CPU, 16GB of RAM, and a single 7200 RPM hard disk. We have measured all our instrumentation-time overhead in this setting.

Reptor has processed roughly 234.8M lines of code to produce the results presented in this section. We have verified that the runtime behavior is correct for every app Reptor transforms for our

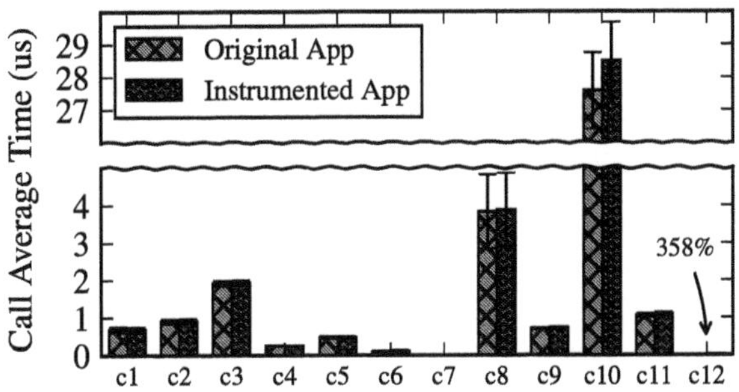

Figure 10: Call Latency for Regular Platform Calls

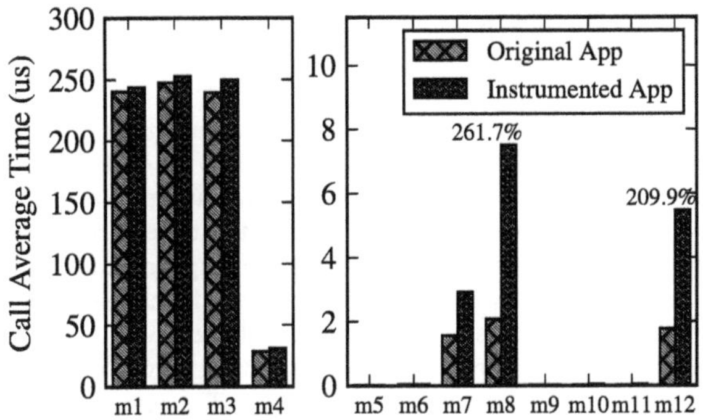

Figure 11: Call Latency for Memory Operations

evaluation, using our automated UI testing system described in Section 5.4 as well as deep manual code introspection.

5.1 Latency Overhead Characterization

We first characterize our latency overhead with a suite of micro-benchmark apps. There are two types of calls we measure—regular platform API calls that just go through our replacement classes, and API calls that involve memory operations.

Latency for Regular Platform Calls: For measuring the overhead of regular API calls, we have written an app that calls eleven platform methods from five categories: device information, network, sensing (GPS), storage, and reflection. Figure 10 shows the result. The methods in the device information category are `getLine1Number` (c1) and `getDeviceID` (c2). The methods in the network category are `getCellLocation` (c3) and `isWifiConnected` (c4). The method in the sensing category is `getLastKnownLocation` (c5). The methods in the storage category are `putValueInPreference` (c6), `getValueFromPreference` (c7), `putValueInFile` (c8), `getValueFromFile` (c9), `putValueInSQLite` (c10), and `getValueFromSQLite` (c11). The method in the reflection category is `forName` (c12). Since the time consumed by an individual call is too small to measure, we make 1K invocations of each method, and consider this an atomic unit of measurement. We perform 1K such measurements for a total of 1M invocations of each method. Most calls do not show any noticeable overhead except SQLite write (c10; 3.3%) and reflection class lookup (c12; 358%). The reflection class lookup (`forName`) has the overhead of string comparison and translation as mentioned in Section 3.6. Regardless, since all the calls add less than 1 μs per call, we believe that our approach would still be feasible in practice.

Call Latency for Memory Operations: The next micro-benchmark app measures memory-related calls, including creating, initializing, and retrieving data from two data structures—an array and a `HashMap`. The app uses an integer array, a string array, and an `Object` array as well as a `HashMap`. There are twelve methods we use: `createIntArray` (m1), `createStringArray` (m2), `createObjectArray` (m3), `createHashMap` (m4), `initializeIntArray` (m5), `initializeStringArray` (m6), `initializeObjectArray` (m7), `putValueInHashMap` (m8), `retrieveIntArray` (m9), `retrieveStringArray` (m10), `retrieveObjectArray` (m11), and `getValueFromHashMap` (m12).

Since these method calls also take very little time, we combine 100 method calls as a unit of measurement, and repeat each measurement 10K times for a total of 1M calls. While the overhead for creating the data structures is negligible (the left plot in Figure 11), there is higher overhead involved in creating object arrays, and to put/get values in/from `HashMap` (the right plot in Figure 11)). Our manual analysis has revealed that the overhead for `HashMap` is because Reptor also virtualizes the key and value classes used by `HashMap`, resulting in nested levels of indirection. This is inevitable as it is necessary for the correct functioning of the data structure. While the percentage overhead seems high, we note that the overhead in absolute time is very little (4-6 μs per call on average) leading us to believe that this would also be feasible in practice. Common compiler optimization techniques, e.g., method inlining, will likely help as well.

5.2 Memory Overhead Characterization

Since our approach creates extra objects for replacement classes, it adds to the memory requirements of an app. Thus, we study the increase in memory requirements for three types of workload—compute-intensive, basic memory, and memory-intensive.

Memory Performance on the Compute-Intensive App: For the compute-intensive workload, we have written an app that calculates π to n decimal place as a result of the infinite series:
$\pi = 4*(1-1/3+1/5-1/7+1/9...+1/(2n-1)-1/(2n+1))$
For our tests, we set $n = 100000000$.

We then conduct heap size variation tests. This is performed by changing the heap size given to the app during execution. As shown in Figure 12 (a), we vary the heap size from 1MB to 64MB for both the original and the instrumented versions. The purpose is to measure how execution time varies depending on available memory. Unlike the memory-related apps discussed below, our compute-intensive app does not require a large amount of memory, hence does not exhibit much difference in performance across different heap sizes.

Memory Performance for the Basic Memory App: For the basic memory workload, we use the same micro-benchmark app from the second part of Section 5.1, which creates, initializes, and retrieves data from four data structures—an integer array, a string array, an `Object` array, and a `HashMap`.

Figure 12 (b) shows the performance of the instrumented and non-instrumented versions with varying the heap size from 8MB to 64MB. Under the heap size of 8MB, our app throws an out-of-memory exception, and we could not collect any data point. As shown, smaller heap sizes require much longer execution times to finish. This is due to the activities of the garbage collector; it gets frequently invoked to reclaim the heap. However, both versions exhibit similar overall behavior in terms of memory usage.

Memory Performance for the Memory-Intensive App: For the memory-intensive workload, we have written an app that creates a `HashMap` array with 10,000 elements, copies even elements to odd elements, deletes all even elements, creates 5,000 elements again, and assigns them to even elements. The app repeats this process 100 times. We emphasize that this has been done to create a rather *extreme case* where we comprehensively stress-test all memory-

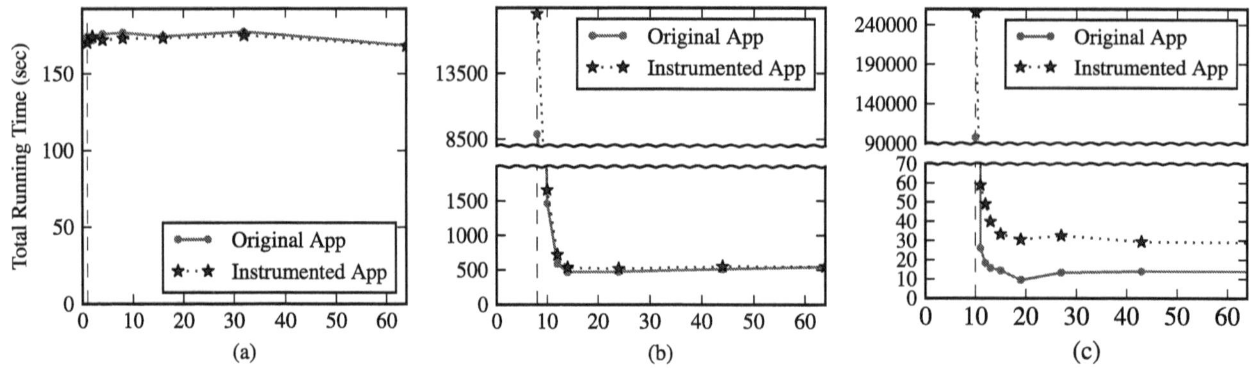

Figure 12: Heap Size Variation (X-axis: size in MB)

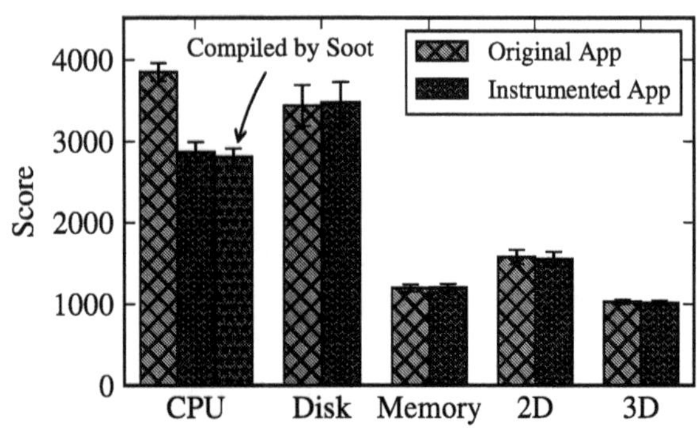

Figure 13: PassMark Benchmark App Results

related operations such as allocation, reading, writing, and deallocation. This kind of memory usage is unrealistic, but effectively fragments the memory and creates pressure on the garbage collector—it triggers the garbage collector to frequently scan the heap to keep track of live objects with active references.

Figure 12 (c) shows the results. We vary the heap size from 10MB to 64MB. Our app throws an out-of-memory exception below 10MB, which means that 10MB is roughly the minimum heap size required to run the app. Besides this, we make two observations. First, the original version takes ~98,000 seconds at 10MB; we can extrapolate that the instrumented version roughly requires 10.5 MB of heap to finish within the same amount of time. This means that there is a slight increase in the minimum heap size requirement to maintain the same performance. Second, both the original and the instrumented versions start to stabilize at 13 MB, and the instrumented version takes approximately three times longer to finish at steady state. This is not too surprising as we have created an extreme case that intentionally stresses the memory in various ways.

5.3 Benchmark App Performance

In addition to our own micro-benchmark apps, we have downloaded and instrumented a benchmark app called PassMark [10] from Google Play. We have chosen this app since it uses Java for benchmarking code. PassMark has 19 benchmarks in 5 categories—CPU, Disk, Memory, 2D, and 3D. We show average scores based on 10 runs.

Figure 13 shows that most of the benchmarks report similar numbers except CPU. The reason is that there are six benchmarks in CPU, and three of them (random string sort, encryption, and compression) have shown a performance decrease by 40%-70%. To determine the root cause of the overhead, we have manually examined the code and determined that it is due to a difference between Android's compiler and Soot, the baseline compiler we use to implement Reptor—they produce distinct bytecode that gives different performance results. To prove this point, we have used Soot to just decompile and recompile PassMark without any of our Reptor implementation, and tested the performance. The extra third bar in Figure 13 shows the result. We can see that the CPU performance numbers are similar between the second and the third bars.

5.4 Stock App Performance

Although micro-benchmarks provide a way to gauge different types of overhead under very specific conditions, they do not necessarily mirror real-world considerations. To demonstrate the feasibility of Reptor in the real world, we have instrumented apps downloaded from Google Play, verified the correctness of our instrumentation, and characterized the instrumentation performance as well as the run-time performance. We have chosen 1,200 popular and representative apps from Google Play. Below, we first discuss our strategy for verifying instrumentation correctness. We then discuss our overhead results.

Instrumentation Correctness: With 1,200 real apps, we have verified the instrumentation correctness of Reptor. Our verification consists of two steps—instrumentation-time validation and run-time testing. First, after we instrument an app through Reptor, we pass the instrumented app through a *validator* that we have developed. Our validator checks static properties of app code, such as type matching, local variable declaration correctness, method declaration correctness, etc. In the end, this static validator makes sure that the Java bytecode produced by our instrumentation for an app is not malformed (to the best it can).

Second, we verify the run-time correctness of an instrumented app by using an *automated UI testing system* that we have also developed. Our UI testing system leverages Android's UI Automator [2] which can inspect all UI elements and their hierarchy for an app running on a device. Using this information, it generates random UI events, such as button clicks and text input, and tests the run-time behavior of an app. It also captures all logs that an app generates during testing using `adb` (Android Debugging Bridge).

With this UI testing system, we run an app both with and without Reptor's instrumentation. After that, we compare the logs produced by the instrumented version of the app to the logs produced by the original version. If we find that an instrumented app has finished its execution without crashing and has not produced any extra ex-

Category	Examples	Inst. Time Avg. (Min./Max.)	APK Size Avg. (Min./Max.)	APK Size Increase Avg. (Min./Max.)	LoC Avg. (Min./Max.)	Loc Increase Avg. (Min./Max.)
Game	Farm Heroes Saga, Glow Hockey, Turbo Driving Racing 3D	85.7s (22.5s/248.1s)	24.5M (6.2M/99.7M)	160.7K (31.0K/1.3M)	220.4K (2.0K/681.0K)	330.3K (77.0K/888.0K)
Entertainment	Xbox 360 SmartGlass, Roku, TWC TV	79.9s (22.5s/308.5s)	9.0M (655.4K/54.2M)	410.0K (5.0K/2.3M)	210.7K (4.0K/802.0K)	346.3K (102.0K/839.0K)
Media	SiriusXM, Marvel Unlimited, Merriam-Webster	60.6s (12.0s/212.9s)	6.7M (38.3K/49.8M)	366.0K (74.0K/2.0M)	149.2K (1.0K/595.0K)	266.0K (67.0K/745.0K)
Education	NeuroNation, NASA, Mobile Learn (Blackboard)	63.7s (13.1s/192.3s)	8.4M (1014.7K/45.0M)	307.2K (475.0K/1.1M)	153.2K (1.0K/591.0K)	279.4K (72.0K/803.0K)
Personalization	Backgrounds HD, Twemoji, XFINITY home	53.3s (12.4s/303.2s)	5.9M (128.8K/54.7M)	311.6K (89.0K/1.0M)	120.5K (1.0K/683.0K)	234.1K (68.0K/821.0K)
Productivity	Wunderlist, Google Now Launcher, Microsoft Office Mobile	60.9s (13.4s/228.6s)	3.4M (336.7K/27.3M)	409.0K (390.0K/1.8M)	143.2K (1.0K/804.0K)	263.2K (82.0K/772.0K)
Business	Mint, Chase Mobile, Microsoft Remote Desktop	68.4s (13.1s/247.8s)	6.5M (397.9K/46.2M)	386.3K (19.0K/1.8M)	174.9K (2.0K/735.0K)	315.6K (76.0K/902.0K)
Social	WordPress, GasBuddy, Pixlr	87.7s (18.9s/312.4s)	10.3M (892.3K/48.4M)	340.4K (64.0K/1.5M)	242.0K (2.0K/714.0K)	372.4K (96.0K/826.0K)
Total	N/A	70.0s (12.0s/312.4s)	9.4M (38.3K/99.7M)	336.4K (5.0K/2.3M)	176.8K (1.2K/804.2K)	300.9K (67.0K/902.0K)

Table 2: Instrumentation Results for 1200 Popular Apps (150 apps in each category)

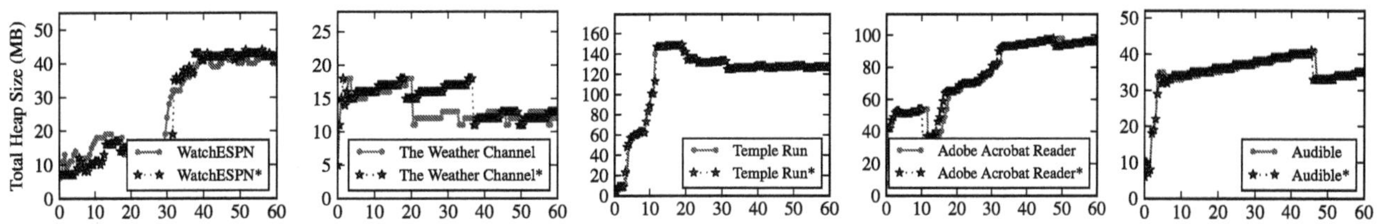

Figure 14: Heap Usage (*Instrumented apps): The x-axis shows elapsed time in seconds.

ception compared to the original, we mark that the verification has passed successfully for the app.

Using these verification steps, we have first verified that all 1,200 apps have passed our validator after instrumentation. In addition, we have verified that no instrumented app crashed during our UI testing and there is no extra exception thrown by an instrumented app compared to its original version. We have run each of 1,200 apps 10 times for 30 seconds, both with and without Reptor instrumentation. The total testing time is 100 hours.

Instrumentation Overhead: Table 2 shows our instrumentation overhead results. We have re-categorized 1,200 apps into eight categories based on Google's categorization to concisely present our results. Each category contains 150 apps. We show average, maximum, and minimum values for instrumentation times, original APK sizes, APK size increases after instrumentation, original lines of code (LoC), and LoC increases after instrumentation. We observe that the instrumentation time for each app is modest and finishes in 6 minutes or less. However, since our design generates replacement classes, there is an inevitable cost of static code size increase. On average, the APK size increases by 21.8% and the LoC by 538.9%. The large percentage increase in average LoC is partly because we have many small apps that have a far fewer number of app classes compared to the platform classes they use. In general, we expect that other standard compiler optimization techniques will help reduce our code size.

Heap Usage and Energy Consumption Overhead: For more realistic evaluation, we have manually used five apps and measured two aspects—heap usage and energy consumption. The apps are WatchESPN, The Weather Channel (TWC), Temple Run, Adobe Acrobat Reader, and Audible. We have played video clips on WatchESPN, looked up weather on TWC, played a game on Temple Run, viewed PDF files on Adobe Acrobat Reader, and played audio books on Audible.

App Name	Average (J)	Std Dev (J)
WatchESPN	781.5	20.0
WatchESPN*	790.3	17.4
The Weather Channel	170.2	13.6
The Weather Channel*	181.4	8.9
Temple Run	991.5	29.5
Temple Run*	993.0	22.3
Adobe Acrobat Reader	838.3	8.9
Adobe Acrobat Reader*	850.0	10.1
Audible	787.5	18.5
Audible*	778.0	8.9

Table 3: Energy Consumption (*Instrumented apps)

Shown in Figure 14 is the heap usage over time. We use Android tools to record heap allocation sizes every 0.3s while we run each app for 60s. While the heap usage is slightly higher for the instrumented apps, both versions show similar behavior across the five apps. At steady state (typically around 40s $\sim$ 50s), the worst-case heap usage increase we observe is 4.2% for WatchESPN, 9.5% for TWC, 0.6% for Temple Run, 8.4% for Adobe Acrobat Reader, and 0.6% for Audible.

For energy measurement, we have used a Monsoon Power Monitor and run the five apps for ten minutes five times. Table 3 shows the results. All the averages are within statistical deviations of each other indicating that there is no significant energy overhead added by our instrumentation.

We have also created a video [13] of two users playing Temple Run side-by-side. The game was instrumented to display notifications whenever a touch event occurred. We have observed that there is no noticeable delays in game play, even though we use a Galaxy Nexus released five years ago.

6. DISCUSSION

Security: A potential concern for any instrumentation tool including Reptor is that it can be abused to inject malicious code. While we acknowledge that we do not improve the status quo, we argue that malicious actors do not need Reptor to inject malicious code. There are many tools available already for creating malicious apps as evidenced by the massive quantity of malicious repackaged apps [40]. Using these tools, malicious actors are already downloading paid apps, injecting malicious code to the apps, and publishing them on online stores as free versions.

Ethics: Another common concern that instrumentation tools raise is whether or not it is ethical (or even legal) to modify apps that other developers have published. For this, we envision a new ecosystem where there are two different types of developers that *cooperate* to provide better experiences for end users—app developers and extension developers. App developers write and distribute apps, and extension developers write and distribute new platform API extensions. In this ecosystem, Reptor becomes a tool that integrates extensions and apps.

Experience with Real Apps: In the early stage of our development, we hand-crafted app code that implements common uses of platform classes, and made Reptor work correctly with it. Our hope was that by doing so, we would eventually be able to transform at least a small set of real apps. However, it turns out that real apps, even when their code sizes are small, are often non-trivial and use platform classes in a wide variety of ways. Thus, it was *required* for us to thoroughly examine the Android documentation and the Java specification to determine what we need to address—it was impossible to transform real apps until we did it.

Formal Correctness: A formal proof is the most rigorous way to show Reptor's correctness and completeness. However, it is an extremely difficult task since we essentially need a formal proof of our implementation against two highly complex systems, Java and Android. Thus, we take a more pragmatic approach and show the correctness and completeness of Reptor empirically by instrumenting over a thousand apps and two hundred million lines of code. The apps we instrument are non-trivial, real-world apps that contain complex code. By instrumenting large bodies of code we have a good estimation of completeness across Java features and Android constructs.

API 19 (Android 4.4): We started our development with API 19 roughly two and a half years ago when it was the latest release, and have not changed the version since. This is because API 19 is still a popular version and we want to keep our development environment stable. The biggest difference in recent versions is the new VM (ART), but our basic idea of using replacement classes do not have any dependency on specific VMs or versions. This is because we generate a list of all platform classes automatically by leveraging a compiler (Soot), and from the list, we create corresponding replacement classes. This can be done on any Android API version. It is our future work to transition to the latest version.

7. RELATED WORK

Traditional techniques that allow extensibility in desktop environments do not provide good deployability on mobile platforms, since they require low-level system access. These include library overloading (using `LD_PRELOAD` or Java class loaders), and syscall library or Java VM hooks. Other techniques, such as Java bytecode rewriting [37, 35, 19], I-ARM-Droid [22], SIF [24], RetroSkeleton [21], `mach_inject` [34], Detours [26], and Windows Hooks [30], enable general instrumentation specific to a language, a platform, or a combination of them. Reptor addresses a different set of challenges previously not addressed by these techniques, i.e., how to replace a platform class with an app-level replacement class on Android. In addition, Reptor provides a more general form of proxy objects (e.g. [28]) and is able to handle the situation where certain classes (e.g., platform classes in Android) are not allowed to be proxied. Aspects (e.g., AspectJ [29]) provides an ability to instrument, but requires access to all target classes to instrument them.

Aurasium [38] and Boxify [17] have proposed app-level techniques for access control and sandboxing. Aurasium intercepts the Global Offset Table (GOT) of a process, and redirects `libc` calls; Boxify monitors and intercepts inter-process communication channels and system calls. These approaches are complementary to Reptor as they provide different capabilities for intercepting native API calls.

Reference Hijacking [39] has recently proposed an app-level technique that allows an app to load custom system libraries. It intercepts the launch sequence of an Android app, loads custom system libraries, and restarts the app with the newly-loaded libraries. However, this approach has a few limitations compared to Reptor. First, system libraries are customized for and specific to vendors (e.g., Google, Amazon, or Samsung), Android versions, target devices, or some combinations of them. It is difficult, if not impossible, for a third party to keep track of the dependencies and generate their own custom system libraries for each and every dependency. Second, their technique can only be applied to system libraries, thus cannot handle Google Play Services which is installed as a system app, not a library. Third, there is also memory and storage overhead since a modified system library needs to be distributed in its entirety. Fourth, the technique relies on the particular app launch sequence of Android, and is difficult to generalize even conceptually.

Many previous systems leverage app instrumentation as a tool to achieve different goals, such as UI automation [25], performance monitoring [33], mobile network control [31], and privacy [27, 18]. These systems further prove the applicability of app instrumentation, and Reptor provides a general way of replacing API classes.

8. CONCLUSIONS

In this paper, we have proposed a new system called Reptor that enables API virtualization on Android for practical openness. Reptor allows third-party developers to modify, instrument, or extend Android platform API call behavior as needed and deploy their modifications seamlessly. The practicality of Reptor comes from the fact that it takes an app-layer approach; it does not require any platform-level changes. Reptor combines many techniques to address the challenges specific to Android, including the use of replacement classes, super replacement classes, concrete classes for interfaces, class hierarchy mirroring, as well as selective code rewriting. Using various micro-benchmarks and real apps from Google Play, our evaluation proves that Reptor incurs minimal overhead in performance and energy consumption, and only modest overhead in terms of memory.

9. ACKNOWLEDGMENTS

We would like to thank the anonymous reviewers and our shepherd, Aruna Balasubramanian, for their valuable feedback. We are also grateful to Feng Shen, Kyungho Jeon, Farshad Ghanei, and Sharath Chandrashekhara for their insightful comments. This work was supported in part by the generous funding from the National Science Foundation, CNS-1350883 (CAREER) and CNS-1618531.

10. REFERENCES

[1] Airbnb Demo. https://goo.gl/tyVoQX.

[2] Android UI Automator. https://developer.android.com/topic/libraries/testing-support-library/index.html#UIAutomator.

[3] Building Apps with Over 64K Methods. http://developer.android.com/tools/building/multidex.html.

[4] Dashboards. http://developer.android.com/about/dashboards/index.html.

[5] FUSE. http://fuse.sourceforge.net/.

[6] HTTP-to-HTTPS Translator Demo. https://goo.gl/GpW21u.

[7] Java Language and Virtual Machine Specifications. https://docs.oracle.com/javase/specs/.

[8] Kernel Probes (KProbes). https://www.kernel.org/doc/Documentation/kprobes.txt.

[9] NetFilter. http://www.netfilter.org/.

[10] PassMark Performance Test. https://play.google.com/store/apps/details?id=com.passmark.pt_mobile&hl=en.

[11] Requesting Permissions at Run Time. http://developer.android.com/training/permissions/requesting.html.

[12] SSHFS. https://github.com/libfuse/sshfs.

[13] TempleRun Demo. https://goo.gl/2kYMgh.

[14] Twitter Demo. https://goo.gl/05IEIC.

[15] G. Android. Android API Guides. http://developer.android.com/guide/index.html.

[16] ArsTechnica. Google's Iron Grip on Android: Controlling Open Source by Any Means Necessary. http://goo.gl/c7VhN5.

[17] M. Backes, S. Bugiel, C. Hammer, O. Schranz, and P. von Styp-Rekowsky. Boxify: Full-fledged App Sandboxing for Stock Android. In *Proceedings of the 24th USENIX Security Symposium*, USENIX Security '15, 2015.

[18] A. R. Beresford, A. Rice, N. Skehin, and R. Sohan. MockDroid: Trading Privacy for Application Functionality on Smartphones. In *Proceedings of the 12th Workshop on Mobile Computing Systems and Applications*, HotMobile '11, 2011.

[19] A. Chander, J. Mitchell, and I. Shin. Mobile Code Security by Java Bytecode Instrumentation. In *DARPA Information Survivability Conference and Exposition II, 2001. DISCEX '01. Proceedings*, volume 2, pages 27–40, 2001.

[20] S. Chandrashekhara, K. Marcus, R. G. M. Subramanya, H. S. Karve, K. Dantu, and S. Y. Ko. Enabling Automated, Rich, and Versatile Data Management for Android Apps with BlueMountain. In *Proceedings of the 7th USENIX Workshop on Hot Topics in Storage and File Systems*, HotStorage '15, 2015.

[21] B. Davis and H. Chen. RetroSkeleton: Retrofitting Android Apps. In *Proceeding of the 11th Annual International Conference on Mobile Systems, Applications, and Services*, MobiSys '13, 2013.

[22] B. Davis, B. Sanders, A. Khodaverdian, and H. Chen. I-ARM-Droid: A Rewriting Framework for In-App Reference Monitors for Android Applications. In *Proceedings of the IEEE Mobile Security Technologies*, MoST '12, 2012.

[23] N. Feamster, J. Rexford, and E. Zegura. The Road to SDN: An Intellectual History of Programmable Networks. *SIGCOMM Comput. Commun. Rev.*, 44(2), Apr. 2014.

[24] S. Hao, D. Li, W. G. Halfond, and R. Govindan. SIF: A Selective Instrumentation Framework for Mobile Applications. In *Proceeding of the 11th Annual International Conference on Mobile Systems, Applications, and Services*, MobiSys '13, 2013.

[25] S. Hao, B. Liu, S. Nath, W. G. Halfond, and R. Govindan. PUMA: Programmable UI-Automation for Large-scale Dynamic Analysis of Mobile Apps. In *Proceedings of the 12th Annual International Conference on Mobile Systems, Applications, and Services*, MobiSys '14, 2014.

[26] G. Hunt and D. Brubacher. Detours: Binary Interception of Win32 Functions. In *Proceedings of the 3rd Conference on USENIX Windows NT Symposium - Volume 3*, WINSYM '99, 1999.

[27] J. Jeon, K. K. Micinski, J. A. Vaughan, A. Fogel, N. Reddy, J. S. Foster, and T. Millstein. Dr. Android and Mr. Hide: Fine-grained Permissions in Android Applications. In *Proceedings of the Second ACM Workshop on Security and Privacy in Smartphones and Mobile Devices*, SPSM '12, 2012.

[28] M. Keil, S. N. Guria, A. Schlegel, M. Geffken, and P. Thiemann. Transparent Object Proxies in JavaScript. In *29th European Conference on Object-Oriented Programming*, ECOOP '15, 2015.

[29] R. Laddad. *AspectJ in Action*. Manning Publications, 2nd edition, 2009.

[30] Microsoft. Windows Hooks. http://goo.gl/r32d7B.

[31] L. Ravindranath, S. Agarwal, J. Padhye, and C. Riederer. Procrastinator: Pacing Mobile Apps' Usage of the Network. In *Proceedings of the 12th Annual International Conference on Mobile Systems, Applications, and Services*, MobiSys '14, 2014.

[32] L. Ravindranath, S. Nath, J. Padhye, and H. Balakrishnan. Automatic and Scalable Fault Detection for Mobile Applications. In *Proceedings of the 12th Annual International Conference on Mobile Systems, Applications, and Services*, MobiSys '14, 2014.

[33] L. Ravindranath, J. Padhye, S. Agarwal, R. Mahajan, I. Obermiller, and S. Shayandeh. AppInsight: Mobile App Performance Monitoring in the Wild. In *Proceedings of the 10th USENIX Conference on Operating Systems Design and Implementation*, OSDI '12, 2012.

[34] J. Rentzsch. mach_inject. http://goo.gl/SnOZQW.

[35] A. Rudys and D. S. Wallach. Enforcing Java Run-time Properties Using Bytecode Rewriting. In *Proceedings of the 2002 Mext-NSF-JSPS International Conference on Software Security: Theories and Systems*, ISSS '02, 2003.

[36] H. Shen, A. Balasubramanian, A. LaMarca, and D. Wetherall. Enhancing Mobile Apps to Use Sensor Hubs Without Programmer Effort. In *Proceedings of the 2015 ACM International Joint Conference on Pervasive and Ubiquitous Computing*, UbiComp '15, 2015.

[37] R. Vallée-Rai, P. Co, E. Gagnon, L. Hendren, P. Lam, and V. Sundaresan. Soot - a Java bytecode Optimization Framework. In *Proceedings of the 1999 Conference of the Centre for Advanced Studies on Collaborative Research*, CASCON '99, 1999.

[38] R. Xu, H. Saïdi, and R. Anderson. Aurasium: Practical Policy Enforcement for Android Applications. In *Proceedings of the 21st USENIX Conference on Security Symposium*, Security '12, 2012.

[39] W. You, B. Liang, W. Shi, S. Zhu, P. Wang, S. Xie, and X. Zhang. Reference Hijacking: Patching, Protecting and Analyzing on Unmodified and Non-rooted Android Devices.

In *Proceedings of the 38th International Conference on Software Engineering*, ICSE '16, 2016.

[40] Y. Zhou and X. Jiang. Dissecting Android Malware: Characterization and Evolution. In *Proceedings of the 2012 IEEE Symposium on Security and Privacy*, SP '12, pages 95–109, Washington, DC, USA, 2012. IEEE Computer Society.

iCharge: User-Interactive Charging of Mobile Devices

Liang He
University of Michigan
2260 Hayward St.
Ann Arbor, MI, 48109
lianghe@umich.edu

Yu-Chih Tung
University of Michigan
2260 Hayward St.
Ann Arbor, MI, 48109
yctung@umich.edu

Kang G. Shin
University of Michigan
2260 Hayward St.
Ann Arbor, MI, 48109
kgshin@umich.edu

ABSTRACT

Charging mobile devices "fast" has been the focus of both industry and academia, leading to the deployment of various fast charging technologies. However, existing fast charging solutions are agnostic of users' available time for charging their devices, causing early termination of the intended/planned charging. This, in turn, accelerates the capacity fading of device battery and thus shortens the device operation. In this paper, we propose a novel user-interactive charging paradigm, called `iCharge`, that tailors the device charging to the user's real-time availability and need. The core of `iCharge` is a relaxation-aware (`R-Aware`) charging algorithm that maximizes the charged capacity within the user's available time and slows down the battery's capacity fading. `iCharge` also integrates `R-Aware` with existing fast charging algorithms via a user-interactive interface, allowing users to choose a charging method based on their availability and need. We evaluate `iCharge` via extensive laboratory experiments and field-tests on Android phones, as well as user studies. `R-Aware` is shown to slow down the battery fading by more than 36% on average, and up to 60% in extreme cases, when compared to existing fast charging algorithms. This slowdown of capacity fading translates to, for instance, an up to 2-hour extension of the LTE time for a Nexus 5X phone after its use for 2 years, according to our trace-driven analysis of 976 device charging cases of 7 users over 3 months.

Keywords

Mobile devices; battery fading; user-interactive charging; battery relaxation

1. INTRODUCTION

The limited operation time of mobile devices, such as smartphones, tablets, and laptops, has become the main gripe of user experience, especially with their increasing functionalities and computation demands [6,28]. Moreover, batteries become weaker with usage, known as *capacity fading* [26,34,38,46], shortening the device operation time [14]. For example, an over 50% capacity fading of a 14-month-old Galaxy S4 battery was reported [12]; our measurements with a Galaxy S6 Edge phone show a 14% battery capacity fading over 4 months of real-life usage.[1] Also, our user study with 146 participants shows that 89% of them noticed their device operation time shortened under normal usage patterns and 70% of them view it as crucial.

Charging mobile devices "fast" alleviates the users' concern on the limited device operation time by replenishing the devices with energy faster. This has been the focus of both industry and academia, developing and deploying various fast charging technologies, such as Quick Charge 3.0 by Qualcomm [5], TurboPower by Motorola [10], VOOC Flash Charge by OPPO [11], to name a few.

Fast charging, unfortunately, accelerates the capacity fading of device battery owing to, besides the high charging rate [14], the joint effects of two properties they share: the basic principle of *Constant Current, Constant Voltage* (CCCV) charge and *user-agnosia*. State-of-the-art fast charging technologies, in general, follow the classical CCCV charging for Li-ion batteries [12,42] — a two-phase charging process consisting of (i) Constant-Current Charge (CC-Chg) and (ii) Constant-Voltage Charge (CV-Chg). Also, these fast charging technologies are agnostic of users' time availability for charging their devices. Implicitly assuming the availability of sufficient charging time, they blindly try to fully charge the devices, resulting in premature termination of the planned charging if users only have limited time. This, in turn, leads to an incomplete or even skipping the CV-Chg phase. Our empirical measurements, however, reveal that *CV-Chg relaxes the batteries and slows down their capacity fading by up to* 80% — an incomplete CV-Chg shortens the battery life faster!

This limitation of fast charging motivated us to design `iCharge`, a novel user-interactive charging paradigm that tailors the device charging to the users' availability and need.[2] At the core of `iCharge` is a relaxation-aware (`R-Aware`) charging algorithm that plans the device charging based on the users' available time. `R-Aware` maximizes the charged capacity while ensuring the use of CV-Chg to relax the battery, thus improving battery health and device

Permission to make digital or hard copies of all or part of this work for personal or classroom use is granted without fee provided that copies are not made or distributed for profit or commercial advantage and that copies bear this notice and the full citation on the first page. Copyrights for components of this work owned by others than ACM must be honored. Abstracting with credit is permitted. To copy otherwise, or republish, to post on servers or to redistribute to lists, requires prior specific permission and/or a fee. Request permissions from permissions@acm.org.

MobiSys'17, June 19-23, 2017, Niagara Falls, NY, USA

© 2017 ACM. ISBN 978-1-4503-4928-4/17/06...$15.00

DOI: http://dx.doi.org/10.1145/3081333.3081350

[1]The capacity fading rate depends on the device-usage pattern.

[2]`iCharge` applies to any battery-powered systems, including electric vehicles where the batteries are a significant portion of their weight and cost.

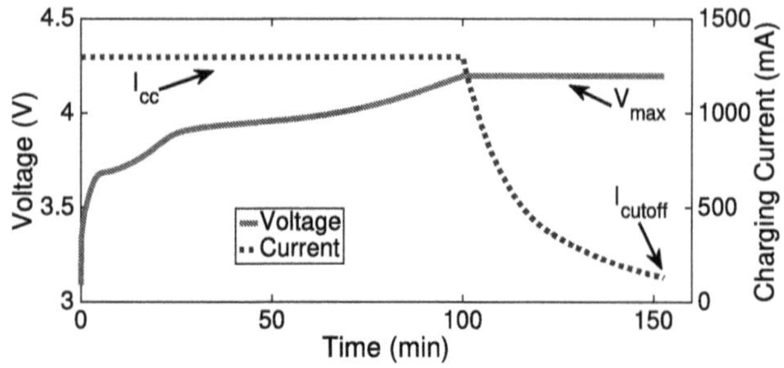

Figure 1: CCCV-based charging process: the battery is first charged with CC-Chg and then CV-Chg.

operation time in the long run. Note that CV-Chg is slow in charging the device, thus limiting the power of charging devices. To remedy this problem, **R-Aware** shortens and triggers the CV-Chg phase earlier than the original CCCV by introducing a new control knob to CCCV and determining the proper charging profiles based on the user's available time. We have evaluated **R-Aware** via laboratory experiments over 15 months with advanced battery testing systems, discovering a more than 36% slowdown of battery capacity fading. These experimental results, coupled with real-life user traces of more than 20 months, show **R-Aware** extends the LTE time of a Nexus 5X phone by up to 2 hours over 2 years.[3] We have also implemented **R-Aware** as a system component on various Android devices, corroborating its compatibility with commodity devices.

R-Aware offers an attractive alternative to keep the device battery healthier at the expense of a slower charging rate. To preserve user experience when a high charging rate is required, **iCharge** also integrates/combines **R-Aware** with fast charging via easy-to-use interactions between users and the charger. Specifically, **iCharge** allows the users to specify their available charging time, displays the charged capacity if **R-Aware** or fast charging is used, and adopts the user's selection of a charging method in the charging plan.

This paper makes the following contributions:

- Discovery and demonstration of CV-Chg's slowdown of battery capacity fading, and absence of its use in state-of-the-art charging of mobile devices (Sec. 2);
- Development of a novel charging paradigm for mobile devices, **iCharge**, that slows down their battery fading with a novel charging algorithm, **R-Aware**, and allows the users to interactively choose a method for tailoring their device charging to their availability and need (Sec. 3);
- Extensive evaluation of **iCharge** via laboratory experiments (Sec. 4), implementation on commodity Android phones (Sec. 5), and user-studies (Sec. 6).

The paper is organized as follows. Sec. 2 motivates the design of **iCharge**, while Sec. 3 provides its details. **iCharge** is evaluated extensively in Secs. 4–6. Further issues relevant to **iCharge** are discussed in Sec. 7. Sec. 8 reviews the related literature, and the paper concludes in Sec. 9.

[3]A new Nexus 5X is reported to have an 8-hour LTE time [3].

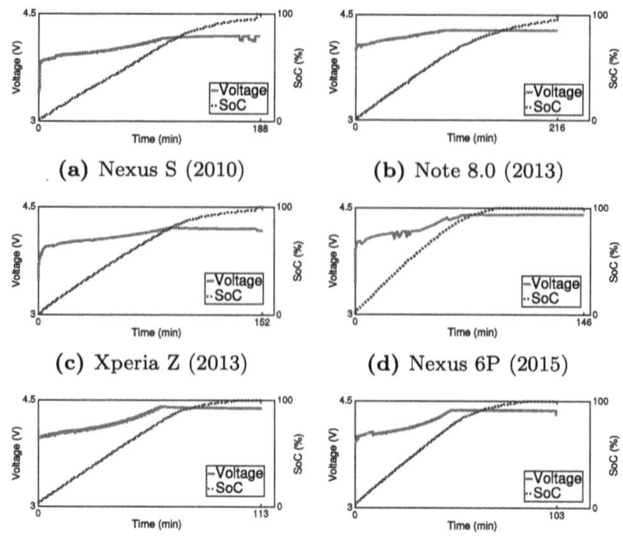

(a) Nexus S (2010) (b) Note 8.0 (2013) (c) Xperia Z (2013) (d) Nexus 6P (2015) (e) Galaxy S5 (2014) (f) Galaxy S6 Edge (2015)

Figure 2: Charging mobile devices with respective chargers, showing (i) shortened charging time with the advancement of charging technologies, (ii) CCCV charging in principle, and (iii) CV-Chg takes long and is slow in charging.

2. CHARGING AFFECTS FADING

Batteries get weakened over usage, shortening their device operation time [8]. For example, an over 50% capacity fading of a 14-month-old Galaxy S4 battery is reported in [12], shortening device operation time by over 4 hours. The capacity fading of device batteries becomes more critical as mobile devices with non-replaceable batteries — such as iPhones and Galaxy S6 and their descendants — are becoming a new trend.

The capacity fading of batteries is inevitable due to their intrinsic electrochemical characteristics, e.g., loss of active materials over usage [26,34,38,46]. Their fading rates, however, depend on their usage pattern. In this paper, we focus on how the charging of mobile devices affects the fading of their battery capacity.

2.1 Fast Charging

Various fast charging technologies have been developed and deployed to improve user experience. These technologies can be viewed as various extensions of the classical two-phase CCCV charging of Li-ion batteries, described by

$$< I_{cc},\ V_{max},\ I_{cutoff} >_{cccv} . \quad (1)$$

First, the battery is charged with a large and constant current I_{cc} (normally 0.5–1C) until its voltage reaches the fully-charged level V_{max} (e.g., 4.25V), i.e., Constant-Current Charge (CC-Chg), during which its state-of-charge (SoC) increases quickly.[4] Then, the battery is charged further by a constant voltage V_{max} until the charging current decreases to a pre-defined cutoff level I_{cutoff} (normally 0.025–0.05C), fully charging the battery. This second phase is called the *Constant-Voltage Charge* (CV-Chg). Fig. 1 plots our empirically collected data of CCCV-based charging of a Li-ion battery.

[4]The charging (and discharging) currents of batteries are often expressed in *C-rate*. For example, in case of discharging, a 1 C-rate means that the current drains the battery completely in 1 hour, i.e., 3,100mA for 3,100mAh batteries.

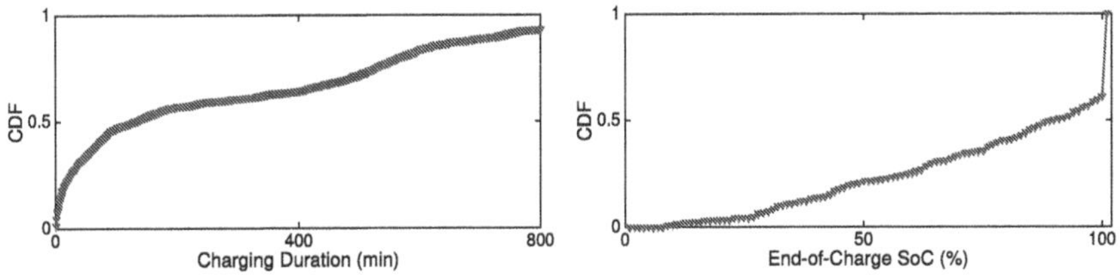

(a) Charging duration (b) End-of-Charge SoC

Figure 3: Users' charging behavior (only the first 800 minutes of the charging process are shown for clarity): device charging is likely to be prematurely terminated.

Figure 4: Experiment bench.

Table 1: Statistics of users' charging behavior.

User	#1	#2	#3	#4	#5	#6	#7
Incomp. Ratio	0.93	0.69	0.60	0.51	0.63	0.14	0.80
# Charges / Day	2.05	2.41	1.40	2.28	1.57	1.76	3.79

To examine how this CCCV principle is implemented in commodity devices, we record the charging processes of 6 mobile devices as shown in Fig. 2 — from depleted to fully charged and with their respective chargers — and make the following three key observations.

1. The time to fully charge these devices has been shortened with the advancement of charging technologies, e.g., from 188 minutes for Nexus S released in 2010 to 113 minutes for the 2014 Galaxy S5, but it still takes about 100 minutes to fully charge even for the fastest charging Galaxy S6 Edge.
2. All of these charging processes, in principle, follow the CCCV charging — the devices are charged quickly during the first phase until their batteries reach about 4.25–4.4V, after which a constant voltage is applied until they become fully charged.
3. CC-Chg is the major phase to charge devices. In contrast, CV-Chg is slow and takes long in charging the device batteries, e.g., CV-Chg for Galaxy S6 Edge takes ≈55% of the total time to charge the last 20% capacity.

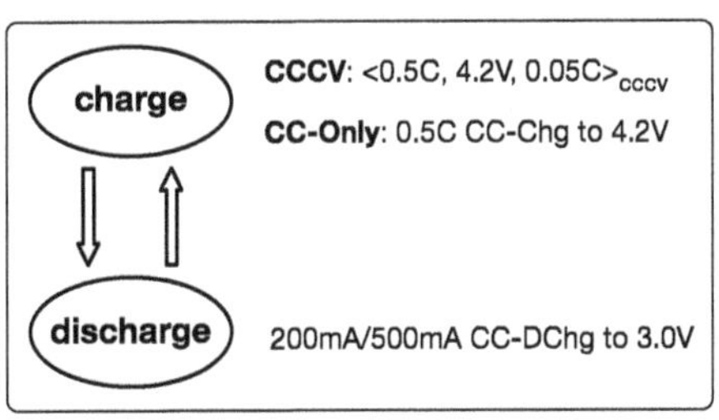

Figure 5: Cycling test methodology.

2.2 Users' Charging Behavior

To see how these charging technologies are used in real-life, we plot in Fig. 3(a) the charging time distributions of 976 cases collected from 7 users over 3 months.[5] About 50% of the charging is observed to last less than 2 hours, representing the device charging during daytime [24]. Comparison of this with Fig. 2 indicates that these short charging durations may not be enough to fully charge the devices. To validate this, we record the battery SoC (State-of-Charge) — an indicator of battery's remaining capacity in percentage (0% = empty; 100% = full) — when the charging is terminated, and plot their distributions in Fig. 3(b). As expected, the device charging is prematurely terminated, leading to an incomplete CV-Chg with a 61% probability. Table 1 shows the details of the individual users' charging behavior. Moreover, 80% SoC is considered as the threshold for the charging to switch from CC-Chg to CV-Chg, which is roughly the case shown in Fig. 2. This way, we find about 41% of charging cases terminated prematurely without CV-Chg at all.

[5]One of the user-traces was collected from our data-collection campaign and the other six traces were obtained from the sample dataset of Device Analyzer from Cambridge University [44].

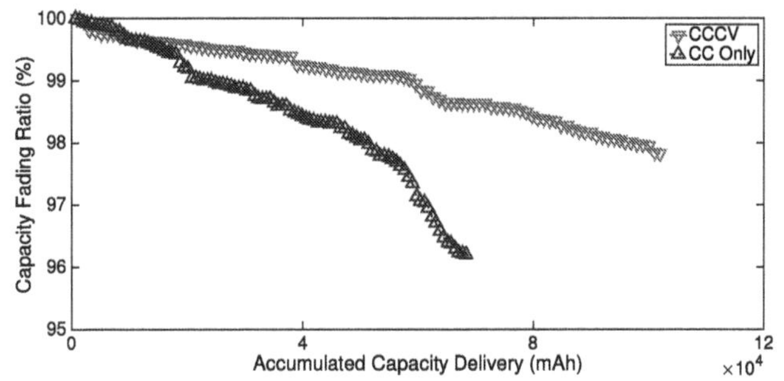

Figure 6: Capacity fading of the Nexus S battery over 100 cycles.

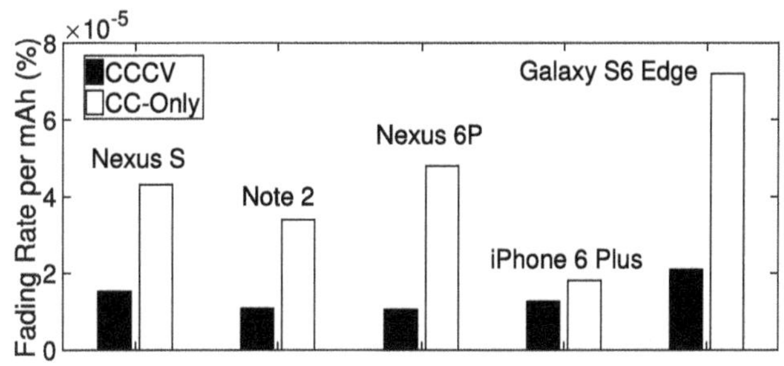

Figure 7: Capacity fading of 5 phone batteries over 100 cycles, showing the slow-down of capacity fading with CV-Chg.

2.3 CV-Chg Slows Down Capacity Fading

Skipping the slow and long CV-Chg does not reduce the charged capacity much. However, *CV-Chg slows down the capacity fading of batteries and thus improves their lifetime* — a new discovery from our measurement study.

We conducted cycling tests with the batteries of Nexus S, Note 2, Nexus 6P, iPhone 6 Plus, and Galaxy S6 Edge to corroborate this finding. The 8-channel NEWARE battery testers are used as both the charger and the load, with which the battery charging and discharging can be programmed with error $\leq 0.05\%$ and logged at frequency up to 10Hz. Fig. 4 shows our lab bench for these experiments. We charge and discharge the batteries 100 times/cycles with completed CCCV (i.e., ensuring the use of CV-Chg) and CC-Chg only (i.e., skipping CV-Chg), respectively, as illustrated in Fig. 5. We record the batteries' capacity delivery during each discharging to calculate their capacity fading ratio — the ratio of the delivered capacity during the i-th cycle to that during the first cycle. Fig. 6 illustrates the degradation of the Nexus S battery during the measurement. Fig. 7 plots the batteries' fading ratios after these cycling tests, showing that CV-Chg reduces battery fading by 0.00003% per-delivered-capacity — an averaged slowdown of 62.35% and up to 80% in some extreme cases, e.g., for the Nexus 6P battery.

2.4 Why Does CV-Chg Help?

Li-ion batteries operate according to the principle of intercalation: during charging, Li-ions is extracted from the lattice of the active materials at the cathode, and then inserted at the anode; the process is reversed for discharging. The insertion of Li-ions causes volume expansion of the materials' lattice structure, while extraction causes contraction. The expansion and contraction are pronounced with large currents and their frequency depends on the switching between charging and discharging. High magnitude and frequency of expansion/contraction accelerate the fracture of lattice structure, leading to permanent loss of active materials and thus capacity fading of Li-ion batteries [2, 34]. Gradually decreasing CV-Chg current allows the anode's (cathode's) lattice volume to equilibrate after the intensive expansion (contraction) caused by CC-Chg and before its contraction (expansion) during the following discharging, relaxing the active materials. This slows down the fracture of lattice structure and thus battery fading. The decreasing current also reduces battery heating, another key contributor to battery degradation.

Note that both the insertion and extraction of Li-ions are achieved via chemical reactions requiring certain time, which could fail if the current is terminated before their completion. For battery charging, this is reflected by a battery voltage drop upon the current termination, a key consideration in our design (Sec. 3.3).

3. USER-INTERACTIVE CHARGING

The user-agnosia of existing charging solutions motivated us to design `iCharge`, which integrates existing fast charging with a novel relaxation-aware (`R-Aware`) charging algorithm via user interactions, providing users customized device charging.

Fig. 8 presents an overview of `iCharge`. Upon connection of the charger, a user interface — consisting of a seekbar and two buttons — prompts. The seekbar allows the user to specify his available time for device charging and the buttons show the charging results with `R-Aware` and fast charging, respectively. The user chooses his preferred charging profile — how long to charge with which method — based on his availability and need simply by clicking the corresponding button, and then the device will be charged accordingly.

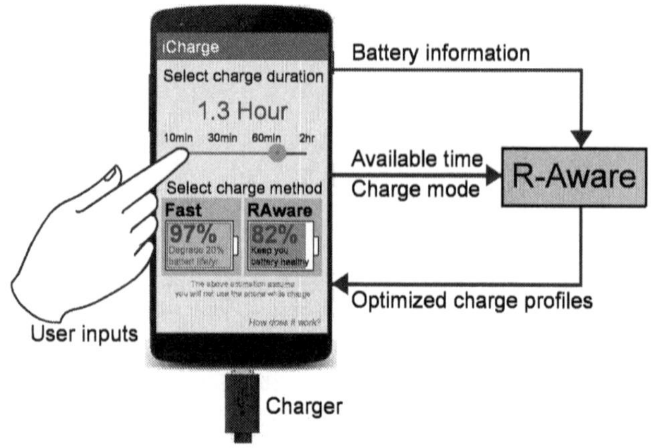

Figure 8: `iCharge` overview: tailoring the device charging to the user's available time and selection of charging method.

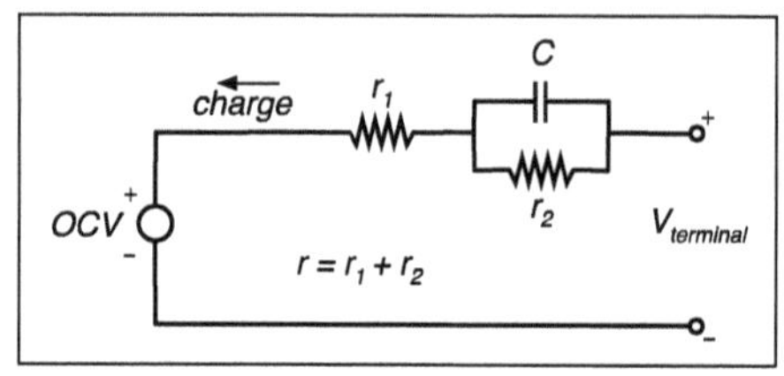

Figure 9: Battery circuit model.

3.1 Background

To facilitate the understanding of `iCharge`, we first introduce the necessary background on battery charging.

3.1.1 *Open-Circuit and Terminal Voltages*

Battery voltage plays a key in its charging. The open-circuit voltage (OCV) of a battery is the voltage between its terminals without connecting load, which becomes the terminal voltage of the battery when load is connected. In other words, OCV is an inherent battery property and the terminal voltage is what is measured in practice. Fig. 9 shows the commonly used battery circuit model, from which we get

$$V_{\text{terminal}} = OCV + I \cdot (r_1 + r_2), \tag{2}$$

where I is the current charging the battery, and r_1 and r_2 are the battery's ohmic and capacitive resistance, respectively. We use the term "voltage" for convenience to mean the terminal voltage, and define $r = r_1 + r_2$.

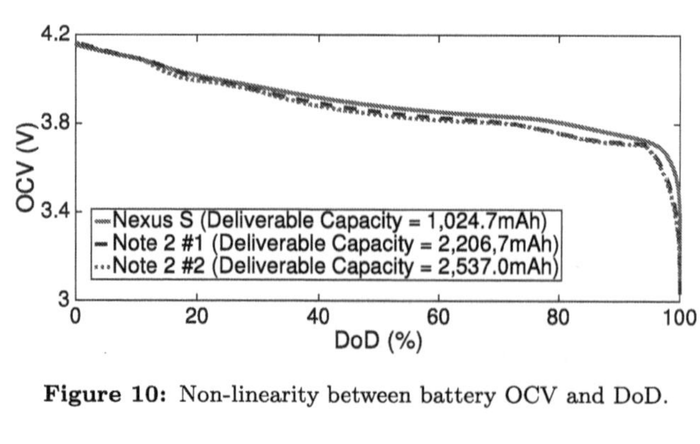

Figure 10: Non-linearity between battery OCV and DoD.

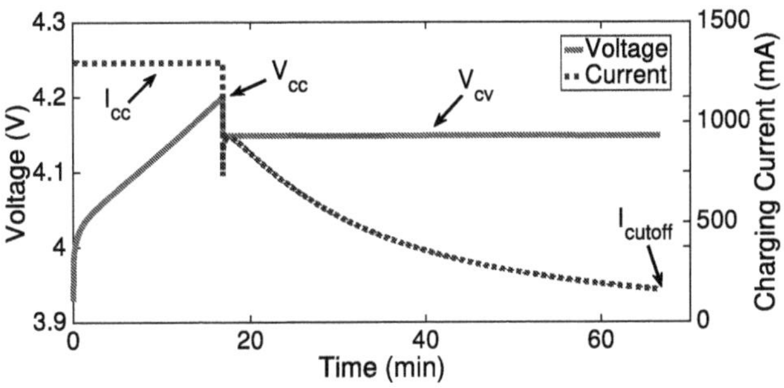

Figure 11: **R-Aware**-based charging process.

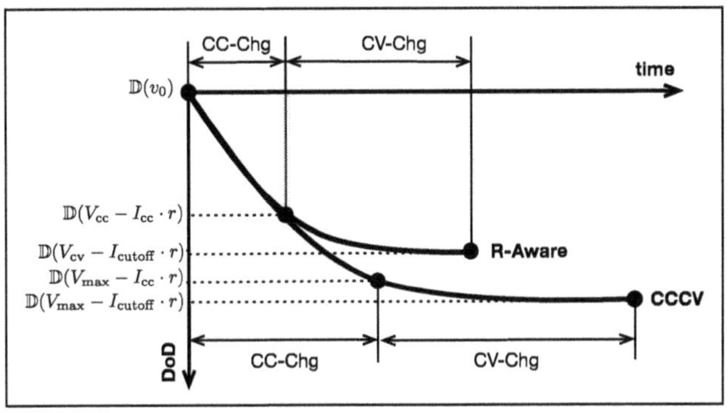

Figure 12: Comparison between **R-Aware** and CCCV: **R-Aware** initiates CV-Chg earlier and makes it shorter.

3.1.2 *Non-Linearity between OCV and DoD*

Batteries exhibit a monotonic relationship between their OCVs and DoDs (Depth-of-Discharge).[6] This relation is stable for batteries of the same chemistry and does not vary much with manufacturers (e.g., <5mV variances in OCV with given DoD [1]). Fig. 10 plots our empirically collected OCV–DoD curves with one Nexus S battery and two Note 2 batteries. Although these batteries are different in both rated and deliverable capacities, their OCV–DoD curves are close to each other, thus validating the stable OCV–DoD relation. We will in Sec. 4.1 elaborate on how the curves in Fig. 10 are obtained. This monotonic OCV–DoD relation allows the mapping between them, denoted as $\mathbb{D}(v)$ and $\mathbb{O}(d)$, respectively, in the rest of the paper.

Fig. 10 also shows that the OCV–DoD relation is not linear — the OCVs are more sensitive to DoDs when the batteries are nearly fully charged (e.g., below 20% DoD) or completely discharged (e.g., approaching 100% DoD), but are not very sensitive in certain middle ranges, e.g., between 40–80% DoD. This non-linearity plays a crucial role in battery charging, as we shall see later.

3.2 Design Overview

As the core of **iCharge**, **R-Aware** offers an alternative to fast charging when fast charging is not strictly required. **R-Aware** takes the user's available time and other battery information such as its OCV–DoD table and initial OCV v_0 as input, and then plans the charging process to maximize the charged capacity while ensuring the use of CV-Chg.

[6]DoD describes the battery capacity that has been discharged as the percentage of its maximum capacity, i.e., the inverse of SoC (100% = empty; 0% = full).

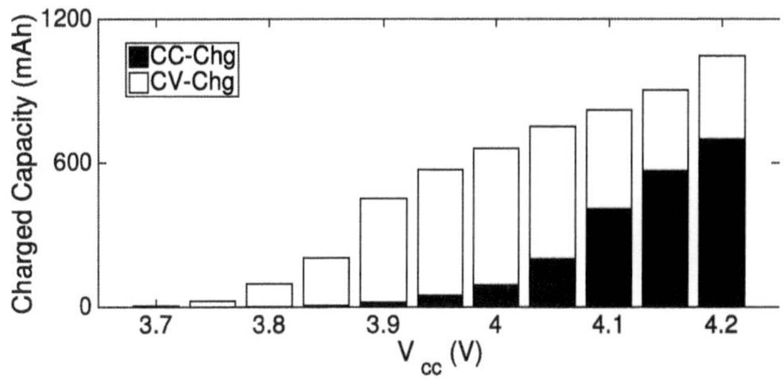

(a) V_{cc} w.r.t. charged capacity

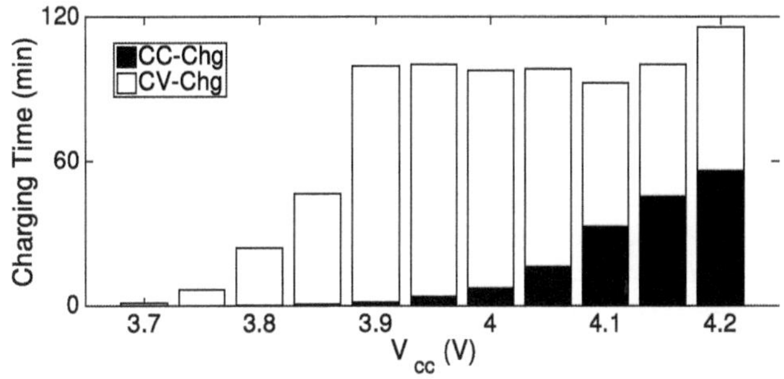

(b) V_{cc} w.r.t. charging time

Figure 13: A smaller V_{cc} leads to less charged capacity but not necessarily shorter charging time.

R-Aware is also an extended CCCV, i.e., a two-phase charging algorithm described by four control knobs

$$< I_{cc}, V_{cc}, V_{cv}, I_{cutoff} >_{\texttt{R-Aware}} \quad (V_{cv} \le V_{cc} \le V_{max}). \quad (3)$$

The **R-Aware**-based charging process starts with CC-Chg with current I_{cc} until the battery voltage rises to V_{cc}, and then the battery is charged with CV-Chg with voltage V_{cv} until the current falls to I_{cutoff}, as illustrated in Fig. 11. This way, the key to **R-Aware** is identifying a proper combination of the four control knobs in (3).

3.2.1 *Earlier and Shorter CV-Chg by R-Aware*

CV-Chg takes long and is slow in charging rate, hence limiting the charged capacity within the available time. **R-Aware** remedies this problem by initiating it earlier and making it shorter. This is illustrated in Fig. 12 which shows the battery's DoD trace during the **R-Aware**-based charging process and compares it with that of the original CCCV.

R-Aware first extends CCCV by reducing V_{max} to V_{cc}. This way, CC-Chg charges the battery to the OCV of $V_{cc} - I_{cc} \cdot r$, which is smaller than the original CCCV (i.e., $V_{max} - I_{cc} \cdot r$), leading to shorter CC-Chg and thus triggering CV-Chg earlier.

Triggering CV-Chg earlier alone, however, may lead to a longer CV-Chg. This also leads to an interesting finding that, when the use of a complete CV-Chg is required, charging less capacity does not necessarily result in a shorter charging time.

To demonstrate this, we use the profiles of $<0.5C, V_{cc}, 0.05C>_{cccv}$ to charge a Nexus S battery with various V_{cc} from 3.7V to 4.2V. Fig. 13 compares the charged capacity and the charging durations, showing that a smaller V_{cc} leads to less charged capacity but not necessarily a shorter charging time. This discrepancy between charged capacity and charging time is due to the nonlinearity between the

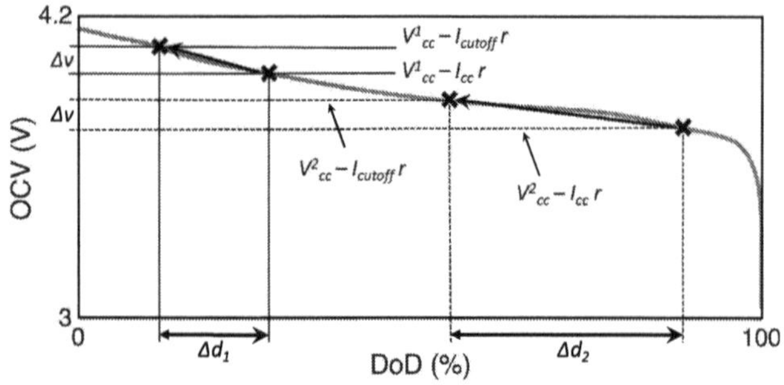

Figure 14: Same magnitude of OCV change may lead to significantly different magnitudes of DoD changes.

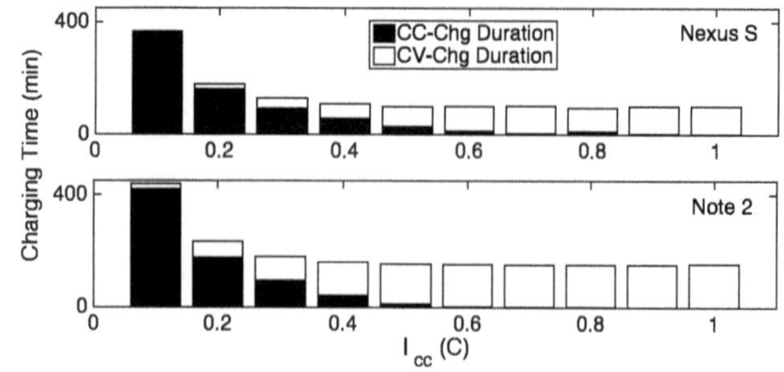

Figure 15: Over-large I_{cc} cannot further shorten the charging process.

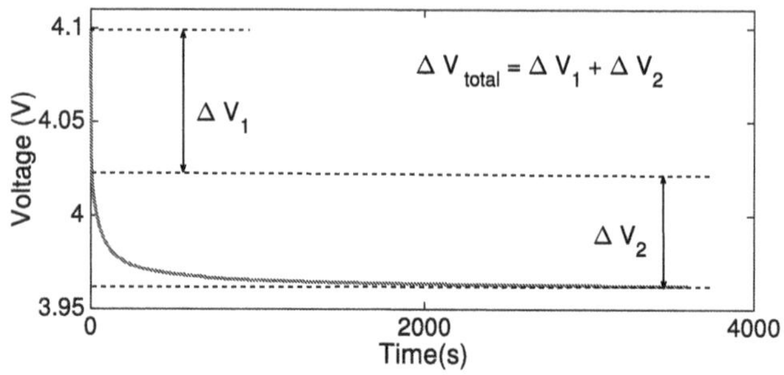

Figure 16: Two-phase voltage drop after terminating the charging current.

battery's OCV and DoD. Let's consider the case when reducing V_{cc} from V_{cc}^1 to V_{cc}^2 ($V_{cc}^1 > V_{cc}^2$). From Fig. 12, we know the OCV range within which CC-Chg applies shrinks from $[v_0,\ V_{cc}^1 - I_{cc} \cdot r]$ to $[v_0,\ V_{cc}^2 - I_{cc} \cdot r]$, leading to shorter CC-Chg. However, the OCV ranges for which CV-Chg is responsible are $[V_{cc}^1 - I_{cc} \cdot r,\ V_{cc}^1 - I_{cutoff} \cdot r]$ and $[V_{cc}^2 - I_{cc} \cdot r,\ V_{cc}^2 - I_{cutoff} \cdot r]$ before and after the change, respectively. These OCV ranges may map to different DoD intervals (and thus to-be-charged capacities) because of the nonlinear OCV–DoD table, albeit sharing the same OCV gap of $(I_{cc} - I_{cutoff}) \cdot r$. Fig. 14 illustrates the case in which the same magnitude of OCV change (i.e., Δv) results in significantly different magnitudes of DoD changes (i.e., $\Delta d_1 << \Delta d_2$). Thus, a smaller V_{cc} shortens CC-Chg, but may lead to longer CV-Chg — the overall charging time is not necessarily reduced.

`R-Aware` further extends CCCV by providing another control knob $V_{cv}(V_{cv} \leq V_{cc})$ to reduce the OCV range of CV-Chg from $[V_{cc} - I_{cc} \cdot r,\ V_{cc} - I_{cutoff} \cdot r]$ to $[V_{cc} - I_{cc} \cdot r,\ V_{cv} - I_{cutoff} \cdot r]$, making CV-Chg shorter.

3.2.2 *Algorithm Overview*

Alg. 1 provides an overview of `R-Aware`, which will be detailed later. `R-Aware` adopts I_{cc} as in the fast charging implementation of the corresponding device (line 1), and then identifies I_{cutoff} that offers sufficient relaxation to the battery (line 2–3). The two control knobs on voltages are identified by searching down the potential voltage range with a granularity of δ_v (line 4–9). `R-Aware` has a complexity of $\mathcal{O}(log(\frac{V_{max}-v_0}{\delta_v}))$ when using binary search in the **for** loop.

Algorithm 1 `R-Aware` Charging.

1: set I_{cc} as in fast charging;
2: estimate r_1 and r_2 by (4) and (6);
3: determine I_{cutoff} by (5);
4: **for** $V_{cc} = V_{max} : -\delta_v : v_0$ **do**
5: $\quad V_{cv} = V_{cc} - I_{cc} \cdot r_1$ (as in (7));
6: $\quad$ estimate C_{total}, C_{cc} and C_{cv} by (8), (9), and (11);
7: $\quad$ estimate T_{cc} and T_{cv} by (10) and (13);
8: $\quad$ **if** $T_{cc} + T_{cv} \leq T_{available}$ **then**
9: $\quad\quad$ **break;**
10: $\quad$ **end if**
11: **end for**
12: **return** $<I_{cc}, V_{cc}, V_{cv}, I_{cutoff}>_{\texttt{R-Aware}}$;

3.3 Design Details

We now discuss how to determine the four control knobs in `R-Aware`.

3.3.1 *Identifying I_{cc}*

Intuitively, a larger I_{cc} shortens the charging process. An over-large current, however, has a diminishing effect on further reduction of the charging time, as shown in Fig. 15 where Nexus S and Note 2 batteries are charged with I_{cc} that varies from 0.1C to 1.0C. This is because CC-Chg charges the battery to $(V_{cc} - I_{cc} \cdot r)$, and CV-Chg further charges it to $(V_{cv} - I_{cutoff} \cdot r)$. All things being equal, a larger I_{cc} completes CC-Chg faster but extends the OCV range of CV-Chg. Whether or not the overall charging process is shortened is unclear.

Also, a larger charging current leads to a faster temperature rise of the battery, due to the heating of its internal resistance. The charging current has to be reduced to cool the battery once its temperature rises to a pre-defined safety threshold [39], e.g., 45°C for Nexus 5X. This, again, indicates that a larger I_{cc} may not always be good.

As a result, instead of employing larger charging currents, `R-Aware` uses the same I_{cc} as in the fast charging implementation of the corresponding device.

3.3.2 *Identifying I_{cutoff}*

CV-Chg slows down the battery fading by allowing it to equilibrate, but is slow in charging the battery. `R-Aware` ensures a CV-Chg to be only long enough for equilibration, which is, in turn, indicated by the battery's voltage-drop after terminating the charging current. Fig. 16 plots the battery voltage during a 1-hour idle period after terminating the charging current. The voltage drops instantly by a certain level (i.e., ΔV_1) upon current termination, then it decreases gradually by another level (i.e., ΔV_2). This can be explained with the battery circuit model in Fig. 9 — the instantaneous drop ΔV_1 is due to the immediate disappearance of voltage across r_1 upon current termination, and the

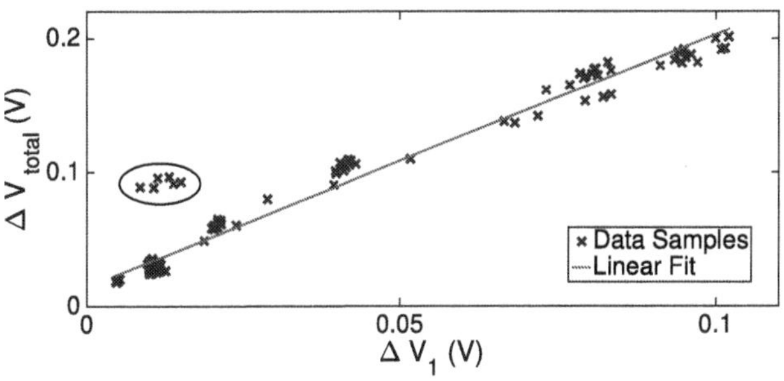

Figure 17: Linearity between instant voltage drop (ΔV_1) and total drop (ΔV_{total}).

Table 2: Measurement settings to validate $\Delta V_{\text{total}} = a \cdot \Delta V_1 + b$.

# Batt.	Ini. V.	I_{cc}	V_{cc}	V_{cv}	I_{cutoff}
7	3.0–3.24V	0.19–1C	3.8–4.2V	3.8–4.2V	0.025–0.4C

following gradual drop ΔV_2 is due to the gradual effect of r_2, thanks to the parallel capacitor. Fuller *et al.* [25] have shown that ΔV_2 is the result of relaxation and a smaller V_2 indicates a closer equilibrium. This way, **R-Aware** uses I_{cutoff} that ensures small enough ΔV_2, e.g., 0.02V.

We estimate ΔV_2 with given I_{cutoff} based on an empirical finding that ΔV_1 is linear in $\Delta V_{\text{total}} = \Delta V_1 + \Delta V_2$, i.e., $\Delta V_{\text{total}} = a \cdot \Delta V_1 + b$ for certain coefficients a and b, and thus linear in ΔV_2 as well. Fig. 17 shows such a plot based on 152 voltage-drop traces after charging batteries with profiles summarized in Table 2. Most of these data samples follow a linear relation well, e.g., the linear fit shown in Fig. 17 has a mean-squared error of 1.77e-04. Outliers, however, exist as highlighted. A closer examination reveals a common feature in them that there is no CV-Chg in their corresponding charging traces. This linear relation allows us to estimate ΔV_2 if we can (i) identify the linear coefficients, (ii) estimate ΔV_1, and (iii) ensure CV-Chg is used during charging.

R-Aware learns these linear coefficients by collecting the voltage-drop traces of idle batteries from a device-charging history, and linear fitting ΔV_1s and ΔV_{total}s therein. This is feasible because of the separated power paths of mobile devices as shown in Fig. 18 [16]. The charger power is separated into two flows to power the device and charge the battery, allowing the battery to rest and thus collecting its voltage-drop traces, e.g., by keeping the charger connected after fully charging the battery during night-time. To verify this, we kept the charger connected after fully charging a Nexus 6P phone and recorded its battery voltage and current, as shown in Fig. 19. The battery current reduces to, and stays at 0mA after the charging is completed, and its voltage drops first instantly and then gradually, agreeing with Fig. 16.[7]

Next let's consider the estimation of ΔV_1. According to the basic physics, $\Delta V_1 = I_{\text{cutoff}} \cdot r_1$ for any charging process ending with I_{cutoff}, so the question transforms to the estimation of r_1 after the charging completion. **R-Aware** estimates r_1 by applying a current pulse I to the battery before charging it, and monitoring its instant voltage response Δv, i.e.,

$$r_1 = \frac{\Delta v}{I}. \tag{4}$$

However, this before-charge r_1 may differ from the after-charge r_1, because battery resistance varies over time [32]. Again, we show via measurements that r_1 does not vary much over a single charge of batteries. Fig. 20 compares r_1 measured before and after charging the batteries based on 115 empirically collected traces. The fact that most samples fall along the line of $y = x$ supports **R-Aware** to use the before-charge r_1 to estimate that after charging. This way, we can compute ΔV_1 via $\Delta V_1 = I_{\text{cutoff}} \cdot r_1$, and thus $\Delta V_{\text{total}} = a \cdot (I_{\text{cutoff}} \cdot r_1) + b$. **R-Aware** determines the desired I_{cutoff} as

$$\Delta V_2 \le \theta \quad \Leftrightarrow \quad I_{\text{cutoff}} \le \frac{\theta - b}{(a-1) \cdot r_1}. \tag{5}$$

We can also estimate r_2 by

$$r_2 = \frac{\Delta V_{\text{total}} - \Delta V_1}{I_{\text{cutoff}}}. \tag{6}$$

Knowing how to determine the proper I_{cutoff} when CV-Chg is used during charging, we must now explore how to ensure its usage by identifying a proper V_{cv}.

3.3.3 *Identifying* V_{cv}

A voltage higher than the battery voltage is required to charge it, i.e., V_{cv} must be higher than the battery voltage when switching from CC-Chg to CV-Chg. From the circuit model in Fig. 9, we know the battery voltage would drop to $(V_{\text{cc}} - I_{\text{cc}} \cdot r_1)$ instantly when CC-Chg is terminated without starting CV-Chg, such that

$$V_{\text{cv}} \ge V_{\text{cc}} - I_{\text{cc}} \cdot r_1.$$

On the other hand, Fig. 12 shows that a larger V_{cv} extends the OCV range for charging the battery with CV-Chg, indicating that a small V_{cv} is desired to shorten the CV-Chg period. The combination of these two observations makes **R-Aware** set V_{cv} as

$$V_{\text{cv}} = V_{\text{cc}} - I_{\text{cc}} \cdot r_1. \tag{7}$$

3.3.4 *Identifying* V_{cc}

The last step is to identify V_{cc}, which, together with the above-identified control knobs, maximizes the charged capacity within the user's available time $T_{\text{available}}$. The total charged capacity with **R-Aware** is

[7]Certain mobile devices use trickle charging to keep their batteries fully charged after reaching 100% SoC, which prevents batteries to stay resting. Relaxing sub-traces, however, can still be observed and collected.

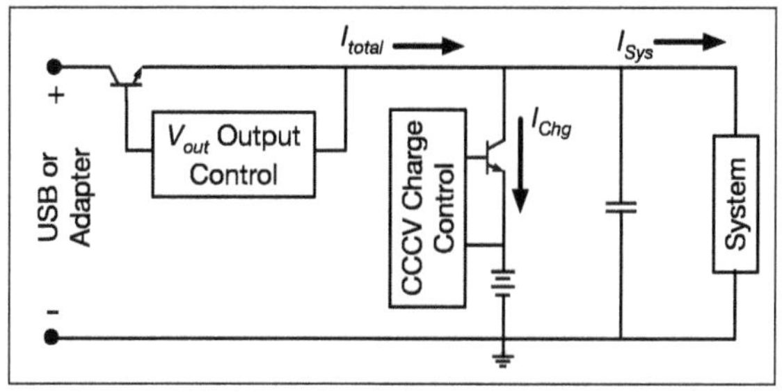

Figure 18: Separate power paths from the charger to the battery and the system, allowing the battery to rest after being fully charged [16].

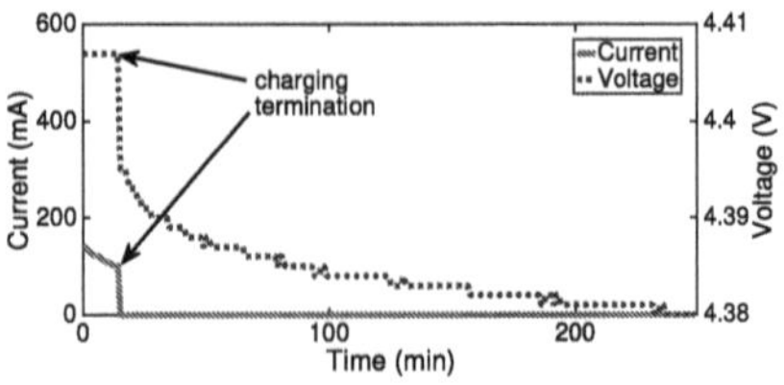

Figure 19: Resting a Nexus 6P battery after fully charging it.

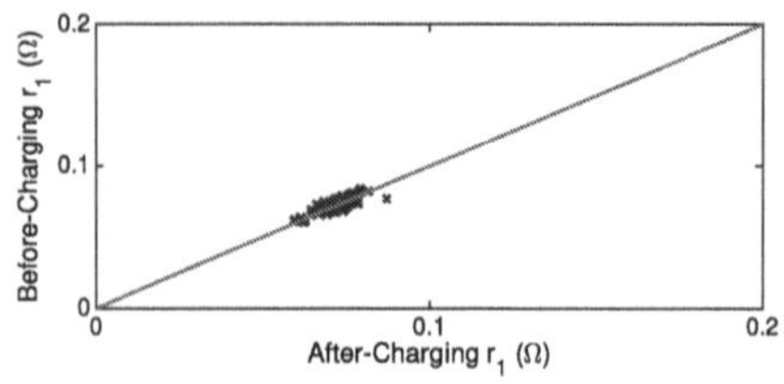

Figure 20: The ohmic resistance r_1 is stable before and after charging.

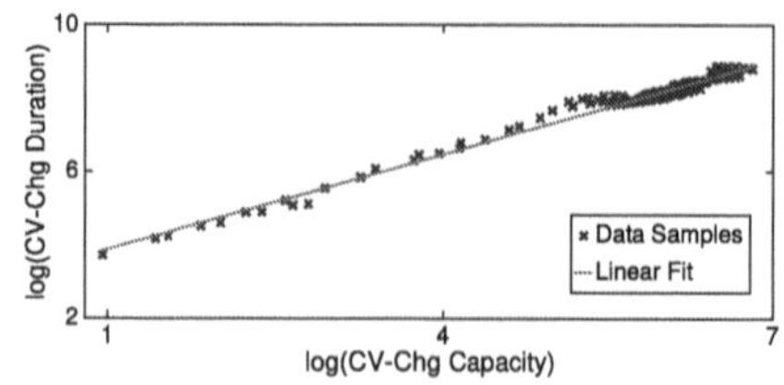

Figure 21: Log-log plot of T_{cv} and C_{cv} demonstrates a linear relation.

Table 3: Measurement settings to validate $log(T_{cv}) = c \cdot log(C_{cv}) + d$.

# Batt.	Ini. OCV	I_{cc}	V_{cc}	V_{cv}	I_{cutoff}
4	3.36–3.74V	0.5–1C	3.90–4.20V	3.89–4.19V	0.05–0.1C

Table 4: Collected charging traces to validate R-Aware's accuracy.

# of Batt.	Ini. OCV	I_{cc}	V_{cc}	V_{cv}	I_{cutoff}
8 × 2,600mAh	3.37 – 3.81V	0.5 – 1C	3.9 – 4.2V	3.85 – 4.2V	0.05 – 0.1C

Table 5: Experimental settings.

Cases	Ava. Time	Ini. OCV	θ
I	100min	3.120V	0.02V
II	90min	3.232V	0.02V
III	70min	3.866	0.02V
IV	70min	3.853	0.02V
V	60min	3.200V	0.02V
VI	60min	3.878V	0.02V
VII	55min	3.869V	0.02V
VIII	30min	3.505V	0.02V

$$C_{\text{total}} = \frac{C_0 \cdot (\mathbb{D}(v_0) - \mathbb{D}(V_{cv} - I_{\text{cutoff}} \cdot r))}{100} = \frac{C_0 \cdot (\mathbb{D}(v_0) - \mathbb{D}(V_{cc} - I_{cc} \cdot r_1 - I_{\text{cutoff}} \cdot r))}{100} \quad (8)$$

where C_0 is the total battery capacity when it is fully charged, e.g., 1024.7mAh for the Nexus S battery as shown in Fig. 10.

All things being equal, a larger V_{cc} leads to a larger C_{total} since $\mathbb{D}(v)$ monotonically decreases with v. So, we search down the potential ranges of V_{cc} and return the first charging profile that completes within $T_{\text{available}}$, which charges the device to the maximum capacity. This, however, requires estimation of the charging duration with a given R-Aware-based charging profile: the CC-Chg duration T_{cc} and the CV-Chg duration T_{cv}.

The charged capacity and the charging time of R-Aware-based CC-Chg can be computed by

$$C_{cc} = \frac{C_0(\mathbb{D}(v_0) - \mathbb{D}(V_{cc} - I_{cc} \cdot r))}{100} \quad (9)$$

$$T_{cc} = \frac{C_{cc}}{I_{cc}}. \quad (10)$$

So, we can estimate C_{cv} based on (8) and (9) by

$$C_{cv} = C_{\text{total}} - C_{cc}. \quad (11)$$

Moreover, our measurements show T_{cv} and C_{cv} to be log-log-linear to each other, i.e., $log(T_{cv}) = c \cdot log(C_{cv}) + d$, based on which T_{cv} can be estimated. To demonstrate this, Fig. 21 shows the log-log plot of T_{cv} and C_{cv} from 174 charging traces, along with their corresponding linear fit $log(T_{cv}) = 0.8648 \cdot log(C_{cv}) + 3.0024$, which has a mean-squared error of 0.0162. The details of these traces are summarized in Table 3. The log-log-linearity holds because the current trace of CV-Chg conforms to the shape of $I_{cv}(t) = A \cdot t^B$, as illustrated in Fig. 11. This way, we know

$$C_{cv} = \int_0^{T_{cv}} I_{cv}(t)dt = \frac{A}{B+1} T_{cv}^{B+1}, \quad (12)$$

and thus $\log(T_{cv}) = \frac{1}{B+1}\log(C_{cv}) - \frac{1}{B+1}\log(\frac{B+1}{A})$, demonstrating a log-log-linear relation. Again, we learn these linear coefficients from the device-charging history and estimate T_{cv} as

$$T_{cv} = e^{c \cdot log(C_{cv})} + d. \quad (13)$$

4. LABORATORY EXPERIMENTS

Real-life evaluation of R-Aware's effectiveness in slowing down battery capacity fading is challenging owing to its dependency on user behavior. This is just as challenging as for Apple or Samsung to specify the operation time of their phones, in which case only the operation time under simplified conditions is provided, e.g., an up to 14-hour talk time on 3G for iPhone 6 without user interactions. In this section, we first detail our in-lab evaluation of the accuracy of R-Aware in predicting the charging process and its effectiveness in slowing down battery capacity fading. We then analyze its real-life effectiveness based on these experimental results as well as real-life user traces.

4.1 Collection of OCV–DoD Data

R-Aware needs the battery OCV–DoD table to plan the charging process. We use the battery tester as shown in Fig. 4 to charge the battery with 200mA current and sample the process at 1Hz, observing the relation between the battery terminal voltage and its DoD. We then perform resistance compensation on the thus-collected traces based on (2) to derive the OCV–DoD table. The small charging current is to reduce the $I \cdot r$ voltage and thus improve the accuracy of the derived OCD–DoD table. Likewise, we obtain the OCV–DoD curves in Fig. 10.

4.2 Accuracy in Charging Estimation

The accuracy in estimating the charging duration and charged capacity with a given profile is key to R-Aware. We collected 115 R-Aware-based charging traces with various charging profiles as summarized in Table 4. R-Aware takes these profiles as input to estimate the corresponding charging processes, which are then compared with the empirical traces to verify its estimation accuracy. Fig. 22 summarizes the estimation errors. The estimation errors in charged capacity are within 60mAh for 96% of the traces, with only 5 traces slightly off at 60.2mAh, 61.4mAh, 69.3mAh, 67.8mAh, and 61.0mAh. These errors correspond to a ratio of about $\frac{60}{2,600} \times 100\% = 2.3\%$ of the rated battery capacity. The error

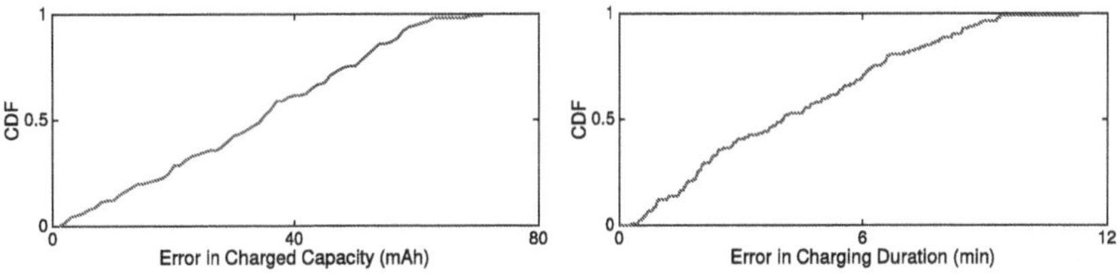

(a) Error in charged capacity (b) Error in charging duration

Figure 22: Accuracy of **R-Aware** in predicting the charging process.

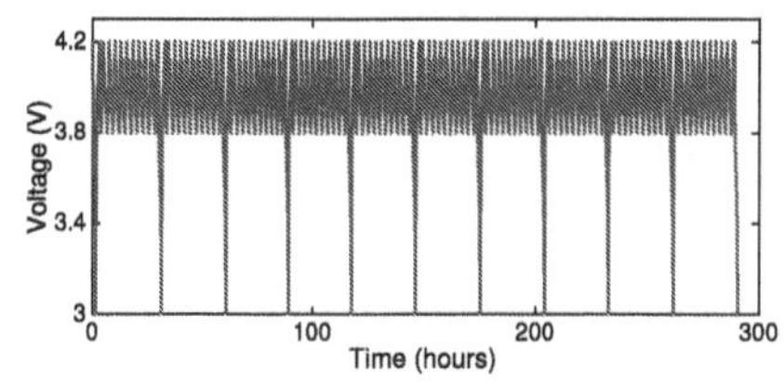

Figure 23: Voltage traces during one cycling measurements.

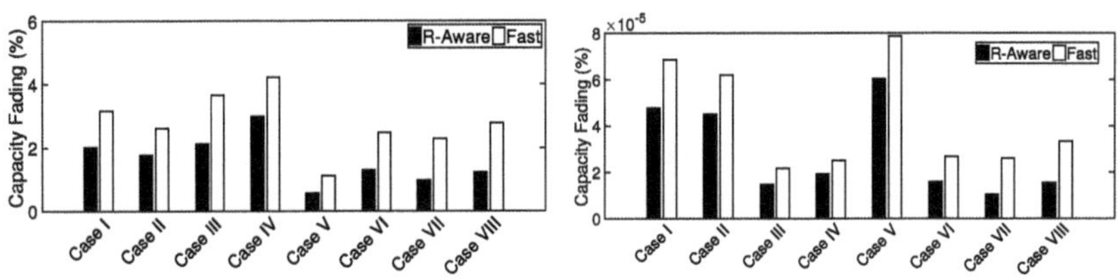

(a) Fading over the 100 cycles (b) Fading per delivered-capacity

Figure 24: **R-Aware** slows down battery capacity fading by up to 60%.

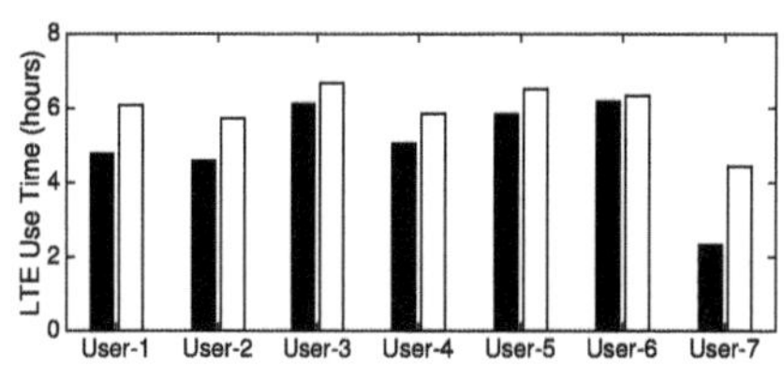

Figure 25: LTE time after 2-year usage

in estimating the charging duration is within 10 minutes for all traces with only an exception at 11.3 minute. This corresponds to an averaged ratio of 5.5% of their total charging durations.

4.3 Slowdown of Capacity Fading

We evaluate the effectiveness of **R-Aware** in slowing down the battery capacity fading. We conducted experiments with 8 batteries which are charged with both **R-Aware** and fast charging as summarized in Table 5. To study the capacity fading due to charge/discharge cycling, we discharged the charged batteries with a 500mA current until their OCVs decreased to the initial levels, and repeated the charge/discharge cycle 100 times. We fully charged and discharged the batteries every 10 such cycles to collect their total deliverable capacities. Each of these measurements lasts up to 16 days. Fig. 23 plots the voltage traces during one of these cycling tests as an illustration. Note that the fast charging process was terminated before batteries were fully charged due to the limited time available for charging. Fig. 24(a) shows the total capacity fading after these cycling measurements. The batteries fade 0.5–2% when charged with **R-Aware**, while those with fast charging fade 1–4.2%, showing a 43.9% slowdown of capacity fading on average. Averaging the capacity fading over the total capacity delivery during the measurements, Fig. 24(b) shows the batteries' fading rates per delivered-capacity. **R-Aware** shows the slowdown of capacity fading by 36.5% on average, and by up to 60% in certain extreme cases (e.g., Case-VII).

4.4 Trace-Driven Analysis

We also analyze the effectiveness of **iCharge** in real life based on the user-traces as shown in Fig. 3 (and Table 1) and the experimental results in Fig. 24 — what if **iCharge** is widely used in real life?

Fig. 24 shows an average capacity fading rate of 0.0161% and 0.0279% per cycle when the device is charged with **R-Aware** and incomplete fast charging, respectively. We further assume a 0.0161% fading rate when the device is charged completely with fast charging, which is reasonable because enough relaxation is applied to its battery as with **R-Aware**. We adopt the following linear model to estimate the fading rate in real life.

$$[0.0279\cdot(1-p)(1-q)+(0.0161\cdot(1-(1-p)(1-q))]\% \text{ / cycle}, \quad (14)$$

when the user chooses **R-Aware** to charge his device with probability p, and there is enough time to complete the charging with probability q if fast charging is selected.

Let's consider the following users' charging patterns.

- *Always-Fast:* Users always charge their devices with fast charging regardless of their available time, i.e., $p = 0$ in (14). This is the state-of-the-art mobile device charging.
- *Fast+R-Aware:* Under this mixed charging pattern, users charge their devices with fast charging if there is enough time for full charging; otherwise, they use **R-Aware** to keep their battery healthier, i.e., $q = 1$ in (14).

Nexus 5X is reported to have an initial 8-hour LTE use time [3], which gets shortened over usage due to capacity fading. Fig. 25 plots the estimated LTE time over a 2-year period for these 7 users when they charge the devices with the two patterns. The devices operate longer by up to 2.1 hours under the mixed charging pattern after 2 years when **iCharge** is equipped in them. Also, user behavior significantly affects device operation: higher chance of incomplete charging and higher frequency of charging make **iCharge** more effective in slowing down battery fading.

5. SMARTPHONE IMPLEMENTATION

We also implemented **R-Aware** on commodity Android phones to verify its feasibility and deployability.

5.1 Circuit Logic of R-Aware

Fig. 26 shows the circuit logic of **R-Aware** and compares it with the CCCV-based charging, such as fast charging. For CCCV, the current source outputs I_{cc} and the voltage source supplies V_{max}. The switch selects CC-Chg or CV-Chg based

Table 6: Phone-based case-study results.

Cases	Device	Available Time	Initial SoC	Charging Time (min) Estimated	Charging Time (min) Ground Truth	Charging Time (min) Error	End-of-Charge SoC (%) Estimated	End-of-Charge SoC (%) Ground Truth	End-of-Charge SoC (%) Error
I	Nexus 5X	90min	29%	84.79	93.00	-8.21	62	68	-4
II	Nexus 5X	80min	50%	69.11	78.67	-9.56	76	78	-2
III	Nexus 5X	45min	6%	44.96	42.00	+2.96	14	15	-1
IV	Nexus 5X	45min	4%	42.32	39.00	+3.32	11	10	+1
V	Nexus 6P	60min	56%	59.72	63.00	-3.28	77	82	-5

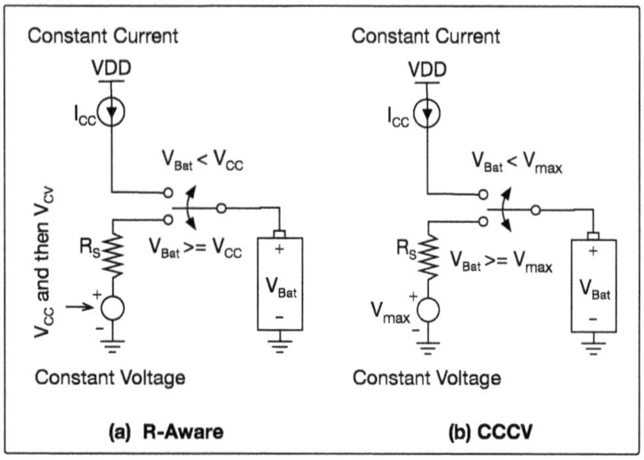

Figure 26: Circuit logic for R-Aware and CCCV: R-Aware does not require support of an additional circuit.

on real-time feedback of the battery voltage. On top of this CCCV implementation, R-Aware poses only one additional requirement for the voltage source to supply V_{cc} first and then V_{cv} — an evolution from one single voltage threshold to two voltage thresholds sequentially. This way, R-Aware does not require any additional circuit beyond existing CCCV implementation — all we need to do is to change the *soft* charging configuration.

5.2 Implementation Details

To implement R-Aware on mobile devices, we need (i) the ability to actively configure the charging profile, (ii) the OCV–DoD table of device battery, and (iii) the initial SoC of the device before charging.

Existing charger drivers on mobile devices support the active configuration of charging profile. In the case of Nexus 6P, for example, its battery charger driver defines the interfaces shown in Fig. 27 to configure the charging process. Specifically, the *qpnp_chg_ibatterm_set()* function allows for setting the terminating current I_{cutoff}, the maximum charging current can be set with *qpnp_chg_ibatmax_set()*, and V_{cc} and V_{cv} can be configured with the last two functions. Similar interfaces can be found in the kernels of other devices, such as Nexus 5X, Xperia Z, and Galaxy S6 Edge. The corresponding inputs to these interfaces can be accessed from the directory of /sys/class/power_supply/battery/. For example, V_{cc} and V_{cv} can be set by writing proper values to */sys/class/power_supply/battery/voltage_max*.

Similarly, writing a small current to file *current_max* facilitates to collect the OCV–DoD table of the device battery with high accuracy, similarly to the discussion in Sec. 4.1. Fig. 28 shows the thus-collected OCV–DoD curves of Nexus 5X and Nexus 6P phones with a maximum charging current of 300mA and 500mA, respectively.

Last but not the least, the real-time SoC of device batteries can be obtained using BatteryManager in Android, which also provides real-time battery voltage, allowing the logging of the charging process.

5.3 Validation of R-Aware's Implementation

We implemented R-Aware on Nexus 5X and 6P, and evaluated its performance via 5 case-studies, as summarized in Table 6. The errors of R-Aware in estimating the charging duration are within the range of $(-10, +4)$ minutes and those in the charged capacity are in the range of $(-5, +1)\%$. Fig. 29 shows the charging process in Case-I as an illustration, where $\times$ is the estimated charging results by iCharge. Another interesting observation is that there are two valleys in the voltage trace as highlighted. They occur because the battery temperature has risen to a pre-defined threshold of 45°C, forcing the charging current to be reduced (and thus the voltage to drop) for cooling. This, in turn, supports R-Aware that does not push for larger I_{cc}, as explained in Sec. 3.3.

6. USER STUDY

We have also conducted a user study to collect the detailed users' feedback on iCharge, such as whether users are willing to have their device battery equipped with additional interactive operations, and whether users want to use R-Aware for its extension of their device life despite its slower charging rate. The users study consists of two parts: a questionnaire-based survey and a conceptual app of iCharge users used in real-life.

6.1 User Survey

We surveyed 146 users to collect their charging behavior and opinions on iCharge. These participants are from 5 countries (US, Canada, Korea, Singapore, and China), aged from 15 to 40, and have various occupations such as government and commercial company employees, self-employers, school teachers, university faculties and students. The survey results corroborate the motivation of iCharge— i.e., slowing down the capacity fading of mobile device batteries is crucial — and demonstrate its attractiveness to users. Specifically,

- 80% of participants were aware that device charging affects battery fading;
- 89% of participants noticed the degradation of their device batteries over time;
- 70% of them regard it as crucial;
- 77% of them will use iCharge if available.

Moreover, with state-of-the-art charging solutions, 94% of the participants frequently prematurely terminated their

```
static int qpnp_chg_ibatterm_set(struct qpnp_chg_chip *chip,  int term_current){...};
static int qpnp_chg_ibatmax_set(struct qpnp_chg_chip *chip, int chg_current){...};
static int qpnp_chg_vddmax_and_trim_set(struct qpnp_chg_chip *chip, int voltage, in trim_mv){...};
static void qpnp_chg_adjust_vddmax(struct qpnp_chg_chip *chip, int vbat_mv){...};
```

Figure 27: Driver interfaces to configure the charging profile in Android kernel.

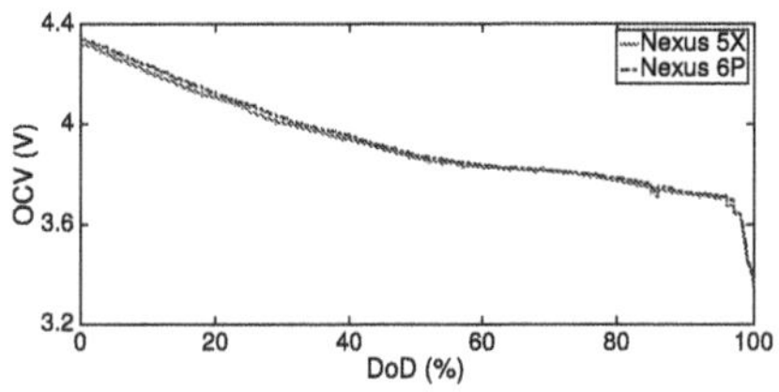

Figure 28: OCV–DoD curves collected from Nexus 5X and Nexus 6P.

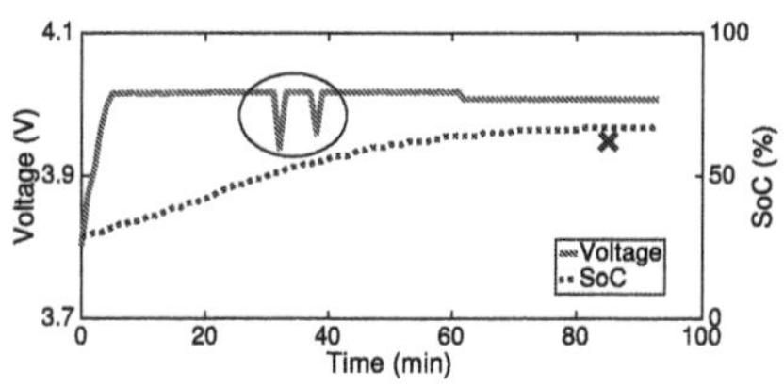

Figure 29: `R-Aware`-based charging process in Case-I on Nexus 5X.

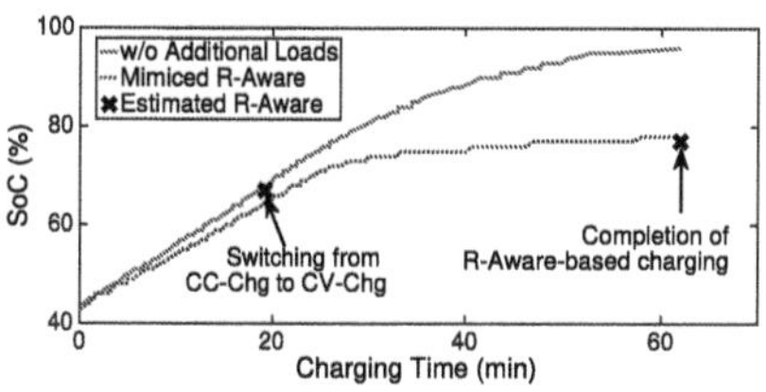

Figure 30: Mimicked `R-Aware`-based charging in the conceptual app of `iCharge`.

device charging, leading to incomplete CV-Chg; 52% of them charge their devices more than twice a day; less than 16% of them tried to charge only when they have enough time for fully charging the devices. These indicate a large room for improvement by `iCharge`.

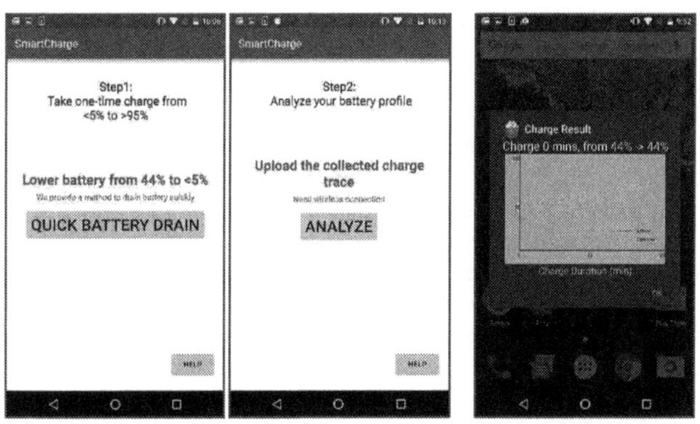

(a) Guide to finish initial training (b) Charge result

Figure 31: Conceptual app of `iCharge`. The user does one-time charging from below 5% to 95% or higher for the conceptual app to learn the battery. This charging process is displayed to the user after each charging.

6.2 Field Test with a Conceptual App

We further recruited 13 participants (6 females and 7 males) to use a conceptual Android app of `iCharge` in real-life. These participants are recruited from a user-study campaign posted online or at our university students center. None of them had prior knowledge of our research. After they agreed to participate in our user study, we sent them the conceptual app of `iCharge`, a short user manual, and a survey questionnaire regarding their opinion about `iCharge`. This user study was ruled by our university to be IRB non-regulated since it does not intrude user privacy nor records private information.

We refer this app to as *conceptual* because the system-level implementation of `R-Aware` introduced in Sec. 5 needs root permission of the device, which is not a feasible requirement for the user study participants. Instead, we "achieve" the same charging results as with `R-Aware`, but take a different approach.

Table 7: Controlling device power consumption to mimic `R-Aware`-based charging (Galaxy Note 4 as an example).

Level	Methodology	Load (mW)
1	WiFi scan every 500ms	508
2	WiFi scan every 250ms	635
3	Enable GPS Location Sensing	741
4	WiFi scan continuously	2,017
5	Math calculation every 500ms	2,824
6	Enable Microphone	2,853
7	Math calculation every 250ms	2,904
8	Enable inertial sensors	3,027
9	Math calculation continuously	5,554
10	Bluetooth scan	5,662

As explained in Fig. 18, the charger power is separated into two flows to charge the battery and power the device, respectively. Also, the charger's maximum output power is limited, e.g., 5V at 3A for Nexus 5X. This way, we can indirectly control the charging process by adjusting the power consumption of devices in the Android userspace, mimicking a `R-Aware`-based charging process. Specifically, the conceptual app uses 10 levels of cumulative power consumptions as summarized in Table 7 to regulate the charging process as if `R-Aware` were implemented. Our user-study verified these power consumption levels to be high enough to regulate the charging process. Fig. 30 shows one of thus-mimicked `R-Aware`-based charging process, which is slowed down to the estimated levels of `R-Aware` by adaptively adjusting the additional power consumptions.

A one-time training is required for the conceptual app to collect the basic information of device battery, such as its OCV–DoD table and resistance, by draining the battery to below 5% and then charging it to higher than 95%. Fig. 31 displays the user-interface to guide users to finish this initial training. This conceptual app records the user's input of available time and selection of a charging method, logs the charging process, and uploads the collected data to our server when a WiFi connection is available.

The conceptual app uses fast charging as default if no user input is collected from the UI within 5 minutes after the device plugged in a charger. The device will be continuously charged with I_{cutoff} if the user chooses `R-Aware` for charging but keeps the charger connected after the specified charging time elapsed, preserving the established equilibration. Also, users may disconnect the charger before their specified charging time elapses. Although `iCharge` cannot prevent such cases, it would not cause additional fading when compared to the case where only fast charging is provided.

We have monitored the charging behavior of these 13 participants over an accumulated period of 28 weeks, collecting 319 charging cases of which

- 49% were day-time charging that lasts less than 2 hours, agreeing with the statistics shown in Fig. 3;
- 36% used `R-Aware` (up to 65% for certain specific users), showing users' willingness to care for their device batteries at the costs of slower charging rate and some user interactions;
- users completed their input on the available time and choose their preferred charging method within a medium of 8 seconds, validating the user-friendliness of `iCharge`; this interaction time decreases as users become more familiar with the UI.

7. EXTENSIONS AND IMPROVEMENTS

`iCharge` can be extended/improved in various ways some of which are discussed below.

7.1 iCharge as a Portable Charger

We have implemented `iCharge` on Android devices as a system component to control their charging process. An interactive portable charger would be another implementation choice. Actually, a few of the survey participants expressed their stronger preference to use `iCharge` if provided as a portable charger. To meet this need, we are now building a portable version of `iCharge` based on the programmable CCCV charger in [4].

7.2 iCharge for Electric Vehicles

Capacity fading exists in all battery-powered systems, including electric vehicles (EVs). In fact, `iCharge` is not only applicable to mobile devices, but also desperately needed for EVs for two reasons. First, the battery packs of EVs are expensive, e.g., replacing the 70kWh battery pack of Tesla Roadster costs as high as $29,000 [7]. Slowdown of battery fading means reduced operating cost for users. It is also attractive to EV manufacturers as a slower fading rate reduces the battery pack size with the same warranty period, thus reducing the capital cost for users and increasing the competitiveness of products for manufacturers. Second, the available charging time would always be limited for certain types of EVs, e.g., taxis [9], causing pronounced capacity fading due to the early-termination of CV-Chg. This, on the other hand, offers more room for improvement with `iCharge`.

7.3 Enhancing iCharge with User Behaviors

`R-Aware`, the core of `iCharge`, needs users' available time as input to plan the charging, which is provided via a user-interactive interface. Yet, this incurs overhead to users (e.g., seconds of interaction time) and the users may not always follow their input (e.g., early disconnection of the charger before the specified time or keeping the connection after the charging time elapsed), both of which have been reflected in our user study introduced in Sec. 6.2. Another choice is to predict users' available charging time and needed power in real time by learning their usage behavior. This way, no additional user actions are required and the new charging paradigm offered by `iCharge` would be automatically triggered upon connecting the charger. The challenge, however, is to ensure high prediction accuracy so as not to degrade user experience. It is also possible to further improve the accuracy of `R-Aware` in predicting the charging process based on the user's charging history.

8. RELATED WORK

Existing efforts improve the limited operation time of mobile devices from two aspects: optimizing their energy consumption [15,17,21–23,30,33,37] and enhancing their energy-supply by charging faster [5,10,11].

Fast charging of batteries has been explored at different layers of abstraction, including algorithms [19,20,29,36], circuit topology [18], and specially-designed batteries [45]. For example, a variable frequency pulse charging system was proposed in [19] and a fuzzy-controlled charging design was presented in [29]. Boostcharging [36] advocates charging with large current by directly charging drained batteries in the CV mode. A grey predication-based charging algorithm was developed in [20]. A circuit topology for battery charging was proposed in [18], demonstrating the advantage of phase-locked loop. A unique type of Li-ion battery that can be charged in a few minutes was proposed in [45].

On the other hand, batteries get weakened over usage due to the loss of active materials [26, 27, 34, 38, 46], known as capacity fading. Efforts have been made to model the fading process [26,35], revealing that it is roughly linear [13,31,41, 46] and affected by various factors, such as current [32,35], temperature [26,43], DoD [35], etc.

In this paper, we discovered that CV-Chg slows down the capacity fading of batteries by allowing them to relax, corroborating the reported finding that relaxation after discharge helps improve the cycle life of batteries [40,41]. Also, we demonstrated that existing fast charging solutions may lead to incomplete CV-Chg due to their user-agnosia, thus accelerating the capacity fading of device batteries. To solve this problem, we proposed `iCharge` which customizes the device charging based on users' availability and need, and hence slows down the battery fading, opening a new charging paradigm for mobile devices.

9. CONCLUSIONS

We have and evaluated proposed a novel charging paradigm for mobile devices, called `iCharge`, that customizes the device charging based on users' real-time needs. At the core of `iCharge` is a relaxation-aware (`R-Aware`) charging algorithm that plans the device charging based on the user's available time, maximizing the charged capacity while ensuring the use of CV-Chg to relax the battery and thus slow down its capacity fading. `iCharge` also integrates `R-Aware` with fast charging via its interactions with users, allowing the users to choose a charging method based on their real-time needs. We have extensively evaluated `iCharge` via laboratory experiments, implementation on commodity phones, and user studies, all of which demonstrate the salient features of `iCharge`. Particularly, `iCharge` is shown to slow down the battery fading by 36% on average and up to 60% in certain extreme cases.

10. ACKNOWLEDGMENTS

The work reported in this paper was supported by NSF under Grant CNS-1446117.

11. REFERENCES

[1] Battery Monitoring Basics. https://training.ti.com/sites/default/files/BatteryMonitoringBasics.ppt.

[2] Lengthening the Life of Lithium-Ion Batteries. https://www.asme.org/engineering-topics/articles/energy/lengthening-life-of-lithiumion-batteries.

[3] Nexus 5X. https://store.google.com/product/nexus_5x.

[4] Programmable CCCV Charger. http://www.ti.com/tool/pmp8955.

[5] Quick Charge 3.0. http://www.droid-life.com/2015/09/14/qualcomm-quick-charge-3-0/.

[6] Survey shows battery life to be the single main gripe of today's mobile phone user. http://www.phonearena.com/news/Survey-shows-battery-life-to-be-the-single-main-gripe-of-todays-mobile-phone-user_id49818.

[7] Tesla Roadster battery pack replacement will cost $29,000. http://www.autoblog.com/2015/09/01/tesla-roadster-battery-pack-replacement/.

[8] The Care and Feeding of Lithium Polymer Batteries. http://forums.androidcentral.com/ambassador-guides-tips-how-s/500054-guide-care-feeding-lithium-polymer-batteries.html.

[9] The case for EV taxi. http://newyork.thecityatlas.org/lifestyle/the-case-for-the-electric-taxi/.

[10] TurboPower Charger. https://www.motorola.com/us/TurboPower/turbopower.html.

[11] VOOC Flash Charge. http://www.oppo.com/en/technology/vooc/.

[12] H. M. A. and T. Sasu. Understanding smartphone state of charge anomaly. In *HotPower'15*, 2015.

[13] L. Ahmadi, M. Fowler, S. B. Young, R. A. Fraser, B. Gaffney, and S. B. Walker. Energy efficiency of Li-ion battery packs re-used in stationary power applications. *Sustainable Energy Technologies and Assessments*, 8:9–17, 2014.

[14] A. Badam, R. Chandra, J. Dutra, A. Ferrese, S. Hodges, P. Hu, J. Meinershagen, T. Moscibroda, B. Priyantha, and E. Skiani. Software defined batteries. In *SOSP'15*, 2015.

[15] N. Balasubramanian, A. Balasubramanian, and A. Venkataramani. Energy consumption in mobile phones: a measurement study and implications for network applications. In *IMC'09*, 2009.

[16] Y. Barsukov and J. Qian. Battery power management for portable devices. *Artech House*, page 67, 2013.

[17] A. Carroll and G. Heiser. An analysis of power consumption in a smartphone. In *USENIXATC'10*, 2010.

[18] L.-R. Chen. PLL-based battery charge circuit topology. *Journal of Power Sources*, 51(6):1344–1346, 2004.

[19] L.-R. Chen. A design of an optimal battery pulse charge system by frequency-varied technique. *IEEE Transactions on Industrial Electronics*, 54(1):398–405, 2007.

[20] L.-R. Chen, R. C. Hsu, and C.-S. Liu. A design of a grey-predicted Li-ion battery charge system. *IEEE Transactions on Industrial Electronics*, 55(10):3692–3701, 2008.

[21] E. Cuervo, A. Balasubramanian, D. ki Cho, A. Wolman, S. Saroiu, R. Chandra, and P. Bahl. Maui: making smartphones last longer with code offload. In *MobiSys'10*, 2010.

[22] N. Ding, D. Wagner, X. Chen, A. Pathak, Y. C. Hu, and A. Rice. Characterizing and modeling the impact of wireless signal strength on smartphone battery drain. In *SIGMETRICS'13*, 2013.

[23] M. Dong, T. Lan, and L. Zhong. Rethink energy accounting with cooperative game theory. In *MobiCom'14*, 2014.

[24] D. Ferreira, A. K. Dey, and V. Kostakos. Understanding human-smartphone concerns: A study of battery life. In *Pervasive'11*, 2011.

[25] T. F. Fuller, M. Doyle, and J. Newman. Relaxation Phenomena in Lithium-Ion-Insertion Cells Thomas. *Journal of The Electrochemical Society*, 141(4):982–990, 1994.

[26] S. Grolleau, A. Delaille, H. Gualous, P. Gyan, R. Revel, J. Bernard, E. Redondo-Iglesias, and J. Peter. Calendar aging of commercial graphite/$LiFePO_4$ cell – Predicting capacity fade under time dependent storage conditions. *Journal of Power Sources*, 225:450–458, 2014.

[27] L. He, E. Kim, K. G. Shin, G. Meng, and T. He. Battery state-of-health estimation for mobile devices. In *ICCPS'17*, 2017.

[28] L. He, G. Meng, Y. Gu, C. Liu, J. Sun, T. Zhu, Y. Liu, and K. G. Shin. Battery-aware mobile data service. *IEEE Transactions on Mobile Computing*, 16(6):1544–1558, 2017.

[29] G.-C. Hsieh, L.-R. Chen, and K.-S. Huang. Fuzzy-controlled Li-ion battery charge system with active state-of-charge controller. *IEEE Transactions on Industrial Electronics*, 48(3):585–593, 2001.

[30] J. Huang, F. Qian, A. Gerber, Z. M. Mao, S. Sen, and O. Spatscheck. A close examination of performance and power characteristics of 4G LTE networks. In *MobiSys'12*, 2012.

[31] L. Lam and P. Bauer. Practical Capacity Fading Model for Li-Ion Battery Cells in Electric Vehicles. *IEEE Transactions on Power Electronics*, 28(12):5910–5918, 2013.

[32] B. Y. Liaw, E. P. Roth, R. G. Jungst, G. Nagasubramanian, H. L. Case, and D. H. Doughty. Correlation of Arrhenius behaviors in power and capacity fades with cell impedance and heat generation in cylindrical lithium-ion cells. *Journal of Power Sources*, 119(121):874–886, 2003.

[33] R. Mittal, A. Kansal, and R. Chandra. Empowering developers to estimate App energy consumption. In *MobiCom'12*, 2012.

[34] G. Ning, B. Haran, and B. N. Popov. Capacity fade study of lithium-ion batteries cycled at high discharge rates. *Journal of Power Sources*, 117:160–169, 2003.

[35] G. Ning and B. N. Popov. Cycle Life Modeling of Lithium-Ion Batteries. *Journal of The Electrochemical Society*, 151(10):A1584–A1591, 2004.

[36] P. Notten, J. O. het Veld, and J. van Beek. Boostcharging Li-ion batteries: A challenging new

charging concept. *Journal of Power Sources*, 145:89–94, 2005.

[37] A. Pathak, Y. C. Hu, and M. Zhang. Fine grained energy accounting on smartphones with Eprof. In *EuroSys'12*, 2012.

[38] M. B. Pinson and M. Z. Bazant. Theory of SEI Formation in Rechargeable Batteries: Capacity Fade, Accelerated Aging and Lifetime Prediction. *arXiv:1210.3672*, 2012.

[39] J. Qian. Li-ion battery-charger solutions for JEITA compliance. *Analog Applications Journal*, pages 8–11, 2010.

[40] M. Rashid and A. Gupta. Effect of relaxation periods over cycling performance of a Li-ion battery. *Journal of The Electrochemical Society*, 162(2):A3145–A3153, 2015.

[41] B. Saha and K. Goebel. Modeling Li-ion Battery Capacity Depletion in a Particle Filtering Framework. In *PHM'09*, 2009.

[42] A. Sanpei. Charging Method for Secondary Battery. US Patent, 5,237,259, 1993.

[43] H. Song, Z. Cao, X. Chen, H. Lu, M. Jia, Z. Zhang, Y. Lai, J. Li, and Y. Liu. Capacity fade of $LiFePO_4$/graphite cell at elevated temperature. *Journal of Solid State Electrochem*, 17:599–605, 2013.

[44] D. Wagner, A. Rice, and A. Beresford. Device analyzer: Understanding smartphone usage. In *MOBIQUITOUS'13*, 2013.

[45] K. Zaghib, M. Dontigny, A. Guerfi, P. Charest, I. Rodrigues, A. Mauger, and C. Julien. Safe and fast-charging Li-ion battery with long shelf life for power applications. *Journal of Power Sources*, 196:3949–3954, 2011.

[46] Y. Zhang and C.-Y. Wang. Cycle-Life Characterization of Automotive Lithium-Ion Batteries with $LiNiO_2$ Cathode. *Journal of The Electrochemical Society*, 156(7):A527–A535, 2009.

Accelerating Mobile Web Loading Using Cellular Link Information

Xiufeng Xie
University of Wisconsin-Madison
xiufeng@ece.wisc.edu

Xinyu Zhang
University of Wisconsin-Madison
xyzhang@ece.wisc.edu

Shilin Zhu
University of Wisconsin-Madison
szhu@ece.wisc.edu

ABSTRACT

Despite the 4G LTE's 10× capacity improvement over 3G, mobile Web loading latency remains a major issue that hampers user experience. The root cause lies in the inefficient transport-layer that underutilizes LTE capacity, due to high channel dynamics, wireless link losses, and insufficient application traffic to propel the bandwidth probing. In this paper, we propose Cellular Link-Aware Web loading (CLAW), which boosts mobile Web loading using a physical-layer informed transport protocol. CLAW harnesses the limited PHY-layer statistics available on LTE phones to quantitatively model the LTE channel resource utilization, which is then translated into a transport window that best fits the bandwidth. Consequently, CLAW can estimate and fully utilize the available bandwidth almost within one RTT. In addition, CLAW can precisely differentiate LTE wireless loss from congestion loss, and identify the rare cases when the wireline backhaul becomes the bottleneck. We have prototyped CLAW on commodity LTE phones. Across a wide range of experimental settings, CLAW consistently reduces Web loading latency by more than 30%, compared to classical TCP variants and state-of-the-art congestion controls for cellular networks.

1. INTRODUCTION

Web access has become a main portal of content consumption on mobile devices, and user-perceived Web performance becomes a vital metric for network services. In online shopping, for example, merely 100ms increase in Web loading latency leads to 1% profit loss [1]. Over the past years, wireless service providers have strived to improve the cellular network performance to match the demanding Web access. However, the mobile Web loading performance does not match up to the infrastructure upgrade. Nation-wide 4G vs. 3G speed tests in the US showed 10× throughput improvement [2], but the typical Web latency only decreases by around half [3]. Given the typical mobile Web size of below 1.5 MB, and median 4G LTE throughput of 12 Mbps [2–4], one would expect the Web loading latency to be well below 1 second. In reality, most mobile webpages take 2 to 9 seconds to be loaded over LTE [3].

The disappointing mobile Web performance roots in the poor interaction between HTTP–the application-layer protocol for the Web, and TCP–the underlying transport-layer protocol. It is well established that TCP performs best when there is a steady stream of data packets and returning ACKs to keep the network pipeline full. This is because TCP implicitly uses the data packets to probe the network, and it takes time to gradually ramp up the data load towards the network's available bandwidth. Since HTTP generates short, bursty flows, TCP lacks time to converge, thus severely underutilizing the network capacity. Such laggy responses are exacerbated in cellular networks with relatively long RTT and dynamically changing bandwidth. In addition, existing TCP protocols use packet delay or loss as congestion indicators to facilitate bandwidth probing. However, the unstable RTT makes the delay metric unreliable and vulnerable to spurious timeout [3]. The loss metric, on the other hand, tends to overreact to wireless link losses, and is insensitive to real congestion because of the deep buffers at LTE basestations [5–7].

Given the mismatch between TCP's continuous packet flow requirement and HTTP's bursty traffic pattern, we propose to replace TCP's probing mechanism with a direct estimate of bandwidth from the LTE physical layer. This principle builds on several observations: *(i)* The end-to-end path for most cellular connections is bottlenecked by the last hop [8], particularly because content delivery networks (CDN) and Web caches shorten the wireline path. Hence it suffices to track the cellular link bandwidth, and gracefully detect and handle the corner cases when the wireline backbone becomes the bottleneck. *(ii)* Since an LTE basestation (BS) itself already enforces fair scheduling [9], the transport-layer protocol should focus on fully utilizing the available physical bandwidth. *(iii)* LTE BS's available frequency/time resources are shared among clients. Thus, it is feasible for a client to estimate the resource utilization within the shared medium from its PHY layer signaling with the basestation.

We realize these principles through a novel system design called Cellular Link-Aware Web loading (CLAW). CLAW accelerates mobile Web loading using a bandwidth exploration mechanism facilitated by cellular link statistics available on commodity smartphones. It replaces TCP's AIMD-style rate control with a PHY-layer informed scheme that can estimate available bandwidth almost within one RTT, without relying on the application traffic pattern. The key challenge here lies in the limited PHY information available to clients. Ideally a client would need a global view of the BS's resource usage, so as to estimate the amount of resources and hence bandwidth available to it. But the PHY signaling channel is encrypted and each user equipment (UE) can only observe the resource allocated to itself [10,11]. Although the BS could separate a dedicated control channel to broadcast the resource usage as public

Permission to make digital or hard copies of all or part of this work for personal or classroom use is granted without fee provided that copies are not made or distributed for profit or commercial advantage and that copies bear this notice and the full citation on the first page. Copyrights for components of this work owned by others than ACM must be honored. Abstracting with credit is permitted. To copy otherwise, or republish, to post on servers or to redistribute to lists, requires prior specific permission and/or a fee. Request permissions from permissions@acm.org.

MobiSys '17, June 19–23, 2017, Niagara Falls, NY, USA.

© 2017 ACM. ISBN 978-1-4503-4928-4/17/06...$15.00

DOI: http://dx.doi.org/10.1145/3081333.3081367

information, this requires non-trivial update to the LTE MAC/PHY stack and causes huge compatibility issue.

To overcome the constraints, we design a cellular load analyzer incorporating a quantitative model that allows an LTE phone to extrapolate cell-wide resource utilization, by leveraging public PHY statistics of the downlink channel. Prior work in LTE resource analysis needs fine-grained per-subcarrier channel information [10, 11], which can be obtained only through a software-radio monitor. Even if such information eventually becomes available, it entails non-trivial signaling overhead when streamed in real-time from the LTE modem and to user space. In contrast, our model enables accurate cell load analysis even with abstracted diagnostic information (*e.g.*, average signal power and modulation level), which is readily available on commodity LTE phones.

Given the estimation of available frequency/time on the PHY layer, CLAW further translates it into usable bandwidth, and feeds it back to facilitate rate control at the TCP sender (*i.e.*, Web server). Unlike prior LTE resource analyzers [10–12], CLAW can estimate both cell-wide and individual client's resource usage, enabling more informed rate control under competing traffic. Moreover, a CLAW client harnesses its link-layer retransmission and queue overflow statistics to discriminate wireless loss from real congestion, preventing unnecessary sender rate fallback.

In addition, CLAW incorporates a simple bottleneck detector, which identifies the rare cases of wireline bottleneck, through a consistency check between the PHY resource utilization and transport-layer window evolution. The detection does not require any dedicated probing traffic and can complete within a few RTTs. When a wireline bottleneck occurs, CLAW falls back to an AIMD-style bandwidth exploration, which resembles legacy TCP but still harnesses certain PHY information such as packet losses and usable PHY resources.

We have implemented CLAW on an Android client that executes the idle resource estimation and bottleneck identification, and an HTTP server that replaces legacy TCP's rate control with CLAW's cellular-informed rate control. We benchmark CLAW's performance against conventional TCP variants, along with two state-of-the-art transport protocols, CQIC [12] and Verus [13], which are designed for cellular networks. A thorough evaluation demonstrates that CLAW can quickly track the available bandwidth resource, leading to 27% to 66% latency reduction across a wide range of websites and network conditions. We also observe that loss/delay based TCP protocols often lead to large performance variation, and CLAW reduces the worst-case latency (which is likely to be the bottleneck to user experience) by up to 73%.

To our knowledge, CLAW represents the first work to quantitatively model the relation between LTE's resource utilization and the PHY-layer statistics on commodity cellphones. The model can be adapted by a broader range of wireless protocols, including not only web loading, but also video streaming [10], background traffic scheduling [14], *etc.* CLAW is also the first to achieve zero-overhead bottleneck detection and explicit loss differentiation over LTE. The CLAW design relies on PHY information, but entails no PHY-layer modification and is readily deployable on current LTE devices.

2. BACKGROUND AND RELATED WORK

Web loading is a sophisticated procedure involving both networking and computation. In general, it begins by downloading an HTML page which refers to the objects (*e.g.*, images) within the requested webpage, the browser then iteratively parses the HTML file while downloading the referred objects. In parallel with the downloading process, the client device progressively renders the retrieved objects on its display. Page loading time (PLT) is typically used as the performance metric, which accounts for both object downloading and processing time, and directly impacts end-user experience. Optimizations for both the downloading and computation are vital to enhancing the mobile Web performance. This paper focus on the networking part, we further discuss about this in §7.

HTTP has been the de facto vehicle protocol to deliver Web content, accounting for more than 82% of the traffic that ends at mobile devices [15]. Many of today's Web services adopt HTTP 1.1, which use short-lived TCP connections to deliver objects, one connection per object. This inevitably incurs long latency as modern Web sites contain tens to hundred level objects. The HTTP/2, inspired by Google's SPDY [3] and ratified by the IETF in 2015 [16], optimized the data transfer paradigms, allowing multiple outstanding object requests through one TCP connection. To date, HTTP/2 has been supported by all main-stream mobile browsers and content providers. However, recent measurement studies revealed disappointing HTTP/2 performance in cellular networks [3], due to *poor interaction between TCP, HTTP and the radio link layer*. In particular, TCP cannot track the high RTT variations and often treats an RTT surge as timeout, which in turn leads to spurious retransmissions and extended Web loading time.

Parallel to the protocol evolution, Web caching has been widely deployed through CDNs at the network edge. Browsers and intermediate DNS servers employ caching/prefetching to reduce DNS lookup latency, with up to 80% hit rate [17]. In addition, LTE cellular networks have widely adopted middleboxes that take over the TCP establishment and termination to reduce TCP's handshake latency [6]. All of these optimizations amortize the HTTP initialization latency and signifies the importance of reducing actual downloading time.

Our CLAW design builds on prior measurement insights which revealed that mobile Webs' performance bottleneck lies in the long RTT [18]. Since cellular networks' long RTT roots in the legacy infrastructure [19], the key to accelerating Web download is to reduce the number of RTTs needed to retrieve the objects.

The key to cutting the Web loading round-trips lies in the underlying transport layer, *e.g.*, HTTP/2 adopts the innovation to reuse a conventional TCP connection. However, conventional TCP protocols treat the network path as a black box, and attempt to infer network congestion from end-to-end metrics like delay and loss, which have to be generated through trial-and-error probing across many round-trips and hence lack responsiveness. In effect, most Web loading sessions are short and finish well before TCP converges to the network bandwidth [20]. Explicit congestion control protocols [21, 22] advocate more informed rate adaptation based on router's feedback. But the deployment is rare to date, as they require new router hardware and sophisticated queue management. CLAW can be considered as providing a better-informed explicit congestion feedback that quantitatively characterizes how much more traffic load can be added before it congests the network. Yet it is much easier to deploy, as it harnesses the cellular bottleneck, and only requires the client to act as a single-point rate estimator.

Recently, the new challenges in cellular networks like buffer bloat [7] and high link dynamics triggered a revisit of the transport protocol design. Sprout [5] uses a stochastic model estimated from throughput probing to forecast network bandwidth. Verus [13] adapts the sending rate following a delay-to-bandwidth mapping learned from a training phase. PCC [23] directly tests a wide range of sending rates and then picks the rate with the best measured performance. Although these model-driven protocols showed high throughput for bulk data transfer, they are unsuitable for mobile Web applications, because the short HTTP flows preclude building/updating/reusing an empirical model.

A vast body of research has touched upon cross-layer transport protocols for wireless networks [24, 25], but most built on abstract models. Recently, CQIC [12] built a transport protocol atop UDP, which adapts rate by estimating link capacity in HSPA+ cellular networks. However, a CQIC client cannot perform bandwidth exploration – it essentially estimates the bit-rate supported by the fraction of channel time it is *currently allocated*, but is blind to the idle time/frequency resources that it can further *explore*, which results in an over-conservative bandwidth estimation. LoadSense [14] takes PHY layer metrics at coarse time granularity (5 per second) as input, and empirically classify the cell load as a binary "busy" or "idle" using a support vector machine. It then sneaks traffic into the idle period to improve energy efficiency. CLAW, on the other hand, models the cell load quantitatively and at millisecond resolution. piStream [10] uses a software-radio board to monitor the LTE BS's resource usage which in turn guides video applications' rate adaptation. In contrast, CLAW works for commodity LTE phones, and develops a new model to estimate the resource usage based on the limited PHY information available on LTE phones' diagnostic interface. Eventually, the per-subcarrier channel information needed in the piStream model may become available just as in certain WiFi chipset, but streaming such information from the LTE modem to the user space at the granularity of LTE frames still entails non-trivial overhead. Moreover, piStream cannot discriminate a client's own resource usage from competing users, leaving fairness an open issue (Sec. 4.3.1).

Cellular last-mile typically bottlenecks the end-to-end connection. However, in some corner cases, the bottleneck may appear in the wireline path and the server can adapt correspondingly for performance optimization [26]. State-of-the-art bottleneck identification schemes like Qprobe [27] require massive dedicated probing packets, which makes them infeasible in short-flow applications as the probing traffic itself overshadows data transmissions. In contrast, CLAW employs a bottleneck detector facilitated by the awareness of cellular network load, which bears zero overhead, can run in parallel with Web data transfer and discriminate between wireline and cellular bottlenecks in real time.

3. CHALLENGES FOR WEB OVER LTE

In this section, we present the root causes to the unsatisfactory mobile Web performance in LTE networks, and highlight the challenges in resolving these issues.

The large and unstable RTTs mislead TCP adaptation. Although LTE adopts a more flattened network architecture and reduced the number of gateways compared with 3G, its 70ms average TCP handshake RTT remains much longer than wireline networks and even WiFi [2], and the RTT over LTE quickly inflates with the number of bytes in flight (it easily exceeds 100ms with only 100KB data in flight). In addition, LTE links often experience large RTT variation due to link-layer packet retransmission/reordering, channel quality change, and traffic dynamics of competing LTE clients. The RTT's standard deviation is typically $3\times$ to $4\times$ of the mean for static LTE nodes, and even larger for mobile ones [19]. Such large RTT variations lead to the poor performance of conventional TCP during mobile Web loading (Sec. 6), which falsely treats a temporary RTT surge as packet timeout caused by network congestion.

Fig. 1 shows one case study, where we load the same static webpage 50 times on an LTE phone (detailed page hosting setup is in Sec. 6). The loading events scatter sparsely across the day to include various network conditions. The server uses the default TCP Cubic, and each page loading involves around 2700 packet

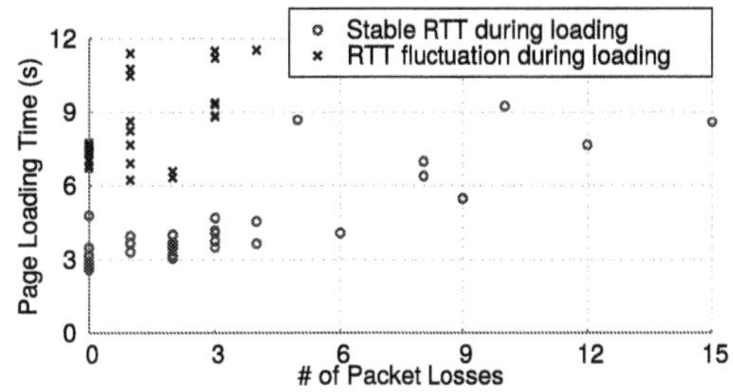

Figure 1: Page loading latency over LTE is affected by both RTT and packet losses.

transfers. From the results, we observe that packet losses are rare over LTE networks. However, even a small number of lost packets can significantly slow down the Web loading, which is consistent with existing observations [1]. Furthermore, under few or no packet losses, sometimes the Web latency still surges due to TCP's aforementioned sensitivity to RTT variations: a temporary RTT surge misleads the server to assume a network congestion/timeout and exit TCP slow start early, even when its current sending rate is still far below the optimum. To minimize such negative effects caused by cellular RTTs, *an efficient transport protocol should be able to quickly converge to the network bandwidth, with least number of round-trip probes.* Quick convergence also enables accurate adaptation to LTE channel dynamics, preventing bandwidth underutilization (due to underestimation) and self-inflicted congestion (due to bandwidth overestimation).

TCP overreacts to LTE link losses. Although LTE's link-level retransmission improves reliability, packet losses are still unavoidable, and even a few losses across an entire Web loading session can substantially increase latency [28]. This is because TCP protocols typically treat packet loss as a congestion indicator, and multiplicatively reduce the sending rate even when the loss is caused by fluctuations of wireless link quality rather than a network congestion, resulting in poor bandwidth utilization and hence slower flows. As shown in Fig. 1, across the experiments, we observed very low packet loss rate, less than 1% even in the worst case. But we found even a few more packet losses lead to explosive growth of latency, which echoes the large-scale measurements in [28]. Moreover, due to unpredictable wireless losses, the Web latency becomes very unstable across runs. The worst-case latency can be extremely high and ruin the user experience, as the users are sensitive to performance degradations.

The short mobile Web flows hinders the sending rate from quick convergence to the network bandwidth. TCP's bandwidth exploration is propelled by application traffic. Its congestion window size accumulates as more packets are acknowledged over previous round-trip transmissions. This property fares poorly with HTTP that creates sparsely distributed packet bursts — measurements studies showed that 90% of Web flows finish within TCP's slow start phase [20], *i.e.*, well before it converges to network bandwidth.

To showcase the problem, we load a static HTTP/2 webpage on an LTE phone for 5 times consecutively with small time interval. Fig. 2 plots the loading time and evolution of TCP congestion window (`cwnd`) size. In the 1st trial, due to the slow start mechanism, TCP aggressively increases the `cwnd` by one upon receiving each ACK (acknowledgement) packet. The `cwnd` ideally doubles per RTT if it were for bulk transfer, but in fact accumulates slowly due to lack of sufficient HTTP data to fill in the window. In the following trials, since HTTP/2 reuses the TCP connection, the `cwnd` gradually accumulates and the 5th trial's latency almost reduces to $1/3$ of the 1st one. Obviously, TCP fails to fully explore the avail-

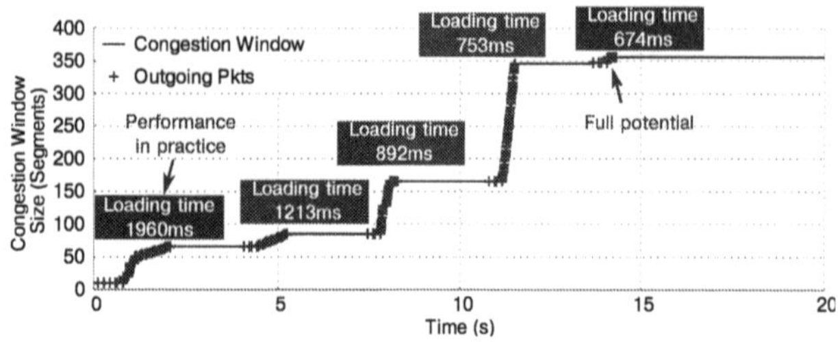

Figure 2: A snapshot of TCP sender cwnd for 5 back-to-back loading events visiting the same static HTTP/2 webpage (with browser cache disabled).

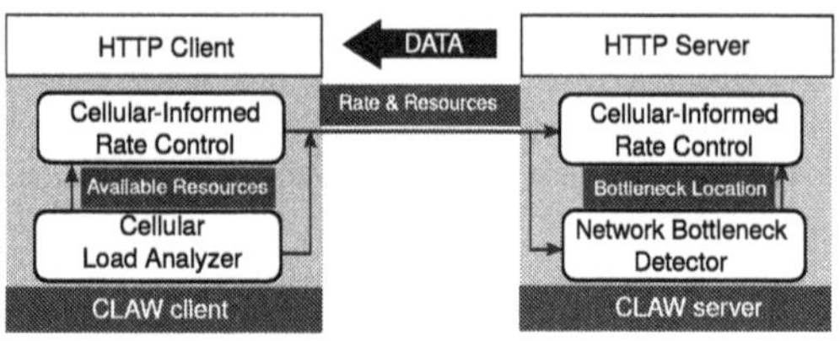

Figure 3: CLAW system architecture.

able bandwidth as mobile Web traffic lacks sufficient data to drive TCP's self-clocked rate adaptation. Thus, *an efficient rate control algorithm for mobile Web should be able to estimate the network bandwidth regardless of the source bit-rate.*

4. CLAW DESIGN

We propose Cellular-Link-Aware Web-loading (CLAW), which harnesses LTE's PHY-layer statistics, including signal energy, packet loss and modulation schemes, to accelerate the network bandwidth exploration for mobile Web traffic. CLAW aims to approach a design ideal that makes TCP converge to network bandwidth within one RTT. Below we outline CLAW's operations and components that work towards the design goal. CLAW consists of three mechanisms running on the HTTP client (*i.e.*, LTE phone) and server (Fig. 3). The CLAW client runs a *cellular load analyzer* that models the cell-wide downlink traffic load on BS and estimates available resources, based on the real-time PHY statistics locally available from the phone's diagnostic interface. The client then performs *cellular-informed rate control* to map available resources into additional traffic that can be carried over the network path, and accordingly optimizes the congestion window size to be fed back to the CLAW server. Meanwhile, the client employs a *cellular bottleneck identifier* to detect and adapt to the rare cases with wireline rather than LTE link being the network bottleneck. In what follows, we introduce CLAW's design components in detail.

4.1 A Primer on LTE Resource Structure

LTE BS allocates radio resources to clients in the unit of time and frequency blocks (Fig. 4). In time domain, the channel is divided into *frames* of 10ms length, each comprising 10 *subframes* of 1ms length. A subframe can be further divided into two 0.5ms *slots*. In frequency domain, LTE further uses the OFDM modulation to divide an entire spectrum band (5MHz or 10MHz) into small units. *Resource Element* (RE) is the smallest resource unit, which spans one OFDM symbol (66.7μs) in time and one OFDM subcarrier (15kHz) in frequency. *Resource Block* (RB) is the smallest *allocatable* resource unit. Typically, each RB contains 7 $\times$ 12 REs as it spans across 7 time-domain symbols (total 0.5ms, or one slot) and 12 frequency-domain subcarriers (total 180kHz).

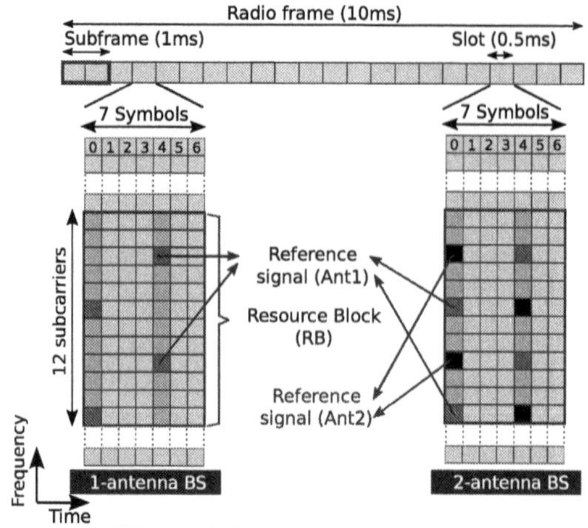

Figure 4: LTE downlink resource structure.

LTE clients can access the following cellular link statistics which characterize the quality of PHY resources:

Receive Strength Signal Indicator (RSSI): the total received power across the entire downlink frequency band, which is measured from the OFDM symbols carrying *reference signals* (symbol 0 & 4 as shown in Fig. 4).

Reference Signal Received Power (RSRP): average per-RE received power on the REs carrying reference signals, *i.e.*, the sum power of all reference REs divided by the number of reference REs.

Reference Signal Received Quality (RSRQ): the ratio between RSRP and RSSI, *i.e.*,

$$Q = N_{rb}P/I \tag{1}$$

where Q, P and I denote RSRQ, RSRP, and RSSI, respectively. N_{rb} is the number of RBs across the downlink spectrum band, specified to $N_{rb} = 25$ and 50, for 5MHz and 10MHz downlink band, respectively [29].

Modulation and Coding Scheme (MCS): an index to the combination of modulation type, coding rate and number of spatial streams (for MIMO transmission), which can be translated into bit-rate through a look-up table.

In addition, each client can read the BS's configuration parameters, such as frequency bandwidth and the number of antennas N_{ant}, from a shared control channel.

4.2 Cellular Load Analyzer

Instead of relying on the irresponsive network congestion indicators like packet delay/loss to probe the network capacity, CLAW can quantitatively assess the gap between current traffic rate and the network capacity based on the *cell load*, *i.e.*, the volume of allocated radio resources (time/frequency) on the downlink channel. It then translates the load estimation into a proper sending rate for the server that fully utilizes the network resource without causing congestion.

Ideally, the BS knows the cell load and can pass such information to all clients. But such a new signaling channel requires modifications to the LTE MAC/PHY standard. Alternatively, cell load information may be obtained if a client can decode the BS's downlink control channel which specifies the resource allocation. But the BS logically isolates the control channel among different clients [11], so that the standard LTE clients are blind to each other's resource usage. More specifically, on commodity smartphones, although the diagnostic interface can expose the per-subframe resource allocation statistics to the user space, it only shows the resource allo-

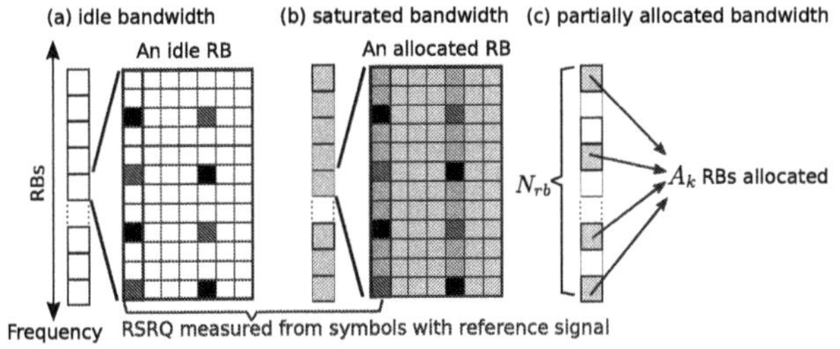

Figure 5: LTE reference signal under different resource allocation status (example shows a 2-antenna BS).

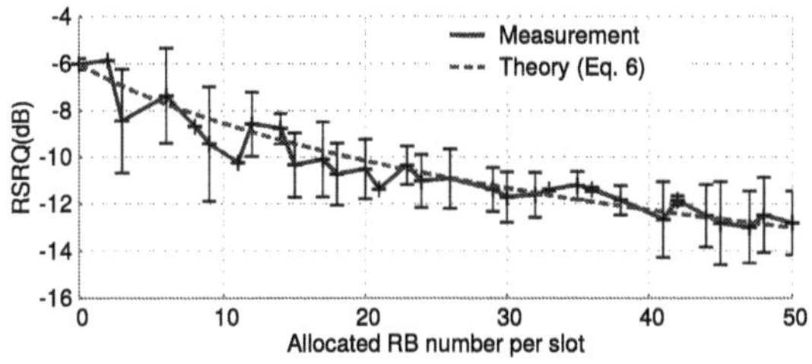

Figure 6: CLAW models LTE downlink resource allocation using a phone's locally sensed RSRQ metric. This figure compares the model with measurement (error bars show std.).

cated to the phone itself, while the cell-wide resource utilization information remains unavailable. Substantial hardware modifications or external sniffers [10,30] are needed to enable an LTE client to decode the downlink control channel dedicated for other clients. The aim of CLAW's cellular load monitor is to make precise cell load estimation by harnessing the PHY metrics available on unmodified commodity phones.

Quantitative cell load estimation based on RSRQ. The RSRQ metric is originally provided to LTE clients to assist local decisions like handoff and bit-rate adaptation. By digging deep into the LTE resource structure, CLAW repurposes RSRQ and quantitatively maps it to the cell load, *i.e.*, a BS' cell-wide downlink resource allocation. In what follows, we describe the analytical model for the mapping.

(i) When the downlink channel is idle, the client only receives reference signals, and thus the total received power over one RB is $N_{ref}P$, where N_{ref} is the number of REs occupied by reference signals in one RB, and P is the RSRP. Meanwhile, the RSSI is measured within the OFDM symbols carrying reference signals. Since the OFDM symbols span the entire bandwidth or N_{rb} RBs, the resulting RSSI is:

$$I_{idle} = N_{rb} N_{ref} P \tag{2}$$

Per LTE specification, $N_{ref} = 2$ and 4, for $N_{ant} = 1$ and 2, respectively, where N_{ant} denotes the number of antennas on the BS. Combining Eq. (1) and (2), the corresponding RSRQ equals $1/N_{ref}$, *i.e.*, 1/2 and 1/4 (or -3 dB and -6 dB), respectively.

(ii) Now we analyze a saturated downlink channel with full resource utilization. The reference signals from different BS antennas do not overlap [29], so the received power of an RE carrying reference signal still equals P, whereas the power on an RE carrying data becomes $N_{ant}P$. As one RB spans across $N_{subc}^{rb} = 12$ REs, the power of one RB equals $N_{ref}P + (N_{subc}^{rb} - N_{ref})N_{ant}P$, and the RSSI over the fully occupied bandwidth is:

$$I_{full} = N_{rb}\big(N_{ref} + (N_{subc}^{rb} - N_{ref})N_{ant}\big) \cdot P \tag{3}$$

From Eq. (1) and (3), we infer that on a saturated LTE channel, RSRQ$= 1/12 \approx -11dB$ and RSRQ$= 1/20 \approx -13dB$ for BS with $N_{ant} = 1$ and 2, respectively.

(iii) For a downlink channel with intermediate traffic load, consider a subframe k with A_k out of the total N_{rb} RBs allocated, the corresponding RSSI consists of the power over the A_k occupied RBs and $(N_{rb} - A_k)$ idle RBs:

$$I_k = A_k I_{full} + (N_{rb} - A_k) I_{idle} \tag{4}$$

Combining with Eq. (1), we have the RSRQ:

$$Q_k = \frac{N_{rb} P}{A_k I_{full} + (N_{rb} - A_k) I_{idle}} \tag{5}$$

Given I_{idle} from Eq. (2) and I_{full} from Eq. (3), we can derive the relation between Q_k, the RSRQ, and k, the number of allocated RBs in this subframe:

$$Q_k = \frac{1}{A_k(N_{subc}^{rb} - N_{ref})N_{ant}/N_{rb} + N_{ref}} \tag{6}$$

To validate this model, we record the number of allocated RBs for each subframe with an RSRQ measurement when performing web loading over LTE. Our result combines records from multiple BSs in our area, all of which have 10MHz bandwidth ($N_{rb} = 50$) and 2 antennas. Fig. 6 plots the average RSRQ value for each subframe-level RB allocation number. We can observe that the measurement results match the theoretical computation well. As a result, the fraction of allocated RBs in a time window, or cell load, can be reliably estimated based on the LTE-frame level RSRQ measurements following Eq. (6), which is the foundation of CLAW design.

Estimating available resources for a client. Following the model in Eq. (6), CLAW computes the instantaneous resource utilization, *i.e.*, fraction of allocated RBs in a subframe, as:

$$r_k = A_k/N_{rb} = \frac{Q_k^{-1} - N_{ref}}{(N_{subc}^{rb} - N_{ref})N_{ant}} \tag{7}$$

In practice, CLAW reads Q_k, N_{ant} from the phone's diagnostic interface, and all other parameters in Eq. (7) can be derived from the LTE standard, following our foregoing analysis.

To combat the burstiness in network traffic and the model variance shown in Fig. 6, CLAW accesses the current cell load L by averaging r_k across all K samples of RSRQ collected during a sliding *time window* of length T:

$$L = (\sum_{k=1}^{K} r_k)/K \tag{8}$$

An interesting fact is that if we set the window size T as the round-trip time (RTT), the traffic capacity of the currently unused radio resources in this window is exactly the gap between current TCP congestion window and its target value — the bandwidth-delay product. Therefore, CLAW uses RTT as its time window size T.

Given the cell load L, a CLAW client can gauge the *number of RBs allocated to all clients* within this time window T, as $N_a = N_t L$, where N_t denotes the total number of RBs within T. N_t can be easily obtained following the LTE specification: Since each subframe lasts for 1ms, the number of subframes in a time window equals its length T in milliseconds. Also, one subframe consists of two time slots, each containing N_{rb} RBs, so the total number of RBs within T equals $N_t = 2N_{rb}T$. Then the client can obtain N_I, the *number of idle RBs* within T:

$$N_I = N_t - N_a = 2N_{rb}T(1 - L) \tag{9}$$

Algorithm 1 Cellular-Informed Rate Control.

Input: $\overline{\text{MCS}}$ – Average MCS in sliding time window
N_a – Sum number of RBs allocated to all clients
N_t – Total amount of RBs in the sliding time window
N_f – The number of RBs available to this CLAW client
$\mathcal{P}$ – Bottleneck location (0 is cellular bottleneck)
Output: `cwnd` – to be used by server
/*CLAW Client*/
Slide forward RTT-sized time window by one subframe
Estimate BDP $\hat{B}$ based on $\overline{\text{MCS}}$ and N_f following Eq. (12)
The optimal congestion window $W_{claw} = \hat{B}$
Feedback W_{claw} to the CLAW server
Repeat the steps above
/*CLAW Server*/
On receiving a new W_{claw}
if ($\mathcal{P} == 0$) **then** /*Cellular bottleneck*/
    if $N_a/N_t < 1$ **then**
        /*Cellular-Informed BW Exploration*/
        `cwnd` $= W_{claw}$
    else/*On saturated channel, act as aggressive as Cubic*/
        `cwnd` $= max(W_{cubic}, W_{claw})$
else /*Wireline bottleneck*/
    `cwnd` $= W_{cubic}$

Denote the *number of RBs allocated to the client itself* as S_k, which can be read from the phone's diagnostic interface for every scheduled LTE subframe. At the end of a time window T, the client obtains N_s, the sum number of RBs allocated to itself within T:

$$N_s = \sum_{k=1}^{T} S_k \tag{10}$$

Finally, CLAW estimates N_f, the number of *available* RBs in this time window T, which consists of its currently consumed RBs and additional idle RBs it can leverage:

$$N_f = N_s + N_I \tag{11}$$

4.3 Cellular-Informed Rate Control

Given the estimation of currently available radio resources, CLAW performs cellular-informed rate control to shape the traffic bit-rate to the optimum by adapting the transport-layer congestion window (`cwnd`) size. Algorithm 1 outlines our design and we provide more details in what follows.

4.3.1 Cellular-Informed Bandwidth Exploration

Quick bandwidth convergence facilitated by cellular link statistics. During bandwidth exploration stage, CLAW boosts the server's sending rate to network capacity based on available radio resources. After estimating the volume of available RBs (N_f) in current RTT-sized time window T_i, the CLAW client translates N_f into the congestion window size matching the potential network capacity. Specifically, from the phone's diagnostic port, the CLAW client reads the Modulation and Coding Scheme (MCS) for every allocated LTE subframe. It then estimates the cellular link capacity $\hat{B}$ that can be supported by the N_f RBs under average MCS in current time window:

$$\hat{B} = T_i F(N_f/T_i, \overline{\text{MCS}}) \tag{12}$$

where the mapping rule $F(\cdot)$ is specified in the LTE standard [31, Table 7.1.7.1 and 7.1.7.2], which maps the MCS and the number of RBs per subframe (N_f/T_i) to the *Transport Block Size*, *i.e.*, the number of bytes that can be carried over a subframe. This size

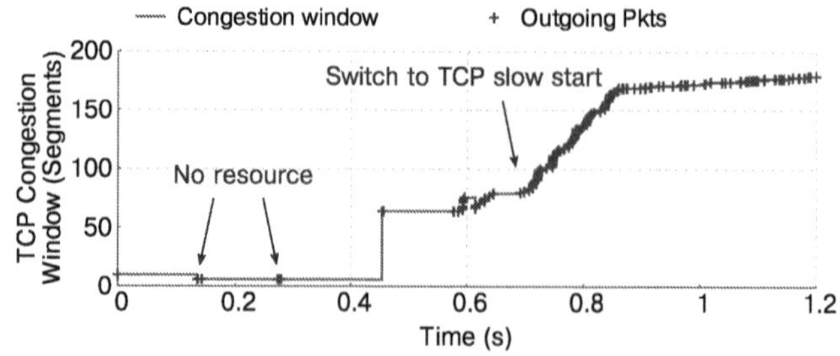

Figure 7: A running instance of the cellular-informed hybrid bandwidth exploration over an LTE channel saturated by existing users.

$F(N_f/T_i, \overline{\text{MCS}})$ is further multiplied by T_i, the number of subframes in a time window, to obtain the potential capacity $\hat{B}$. Since CLAW uses RTT as the time window length (§4.2), $\hat{B}$ essentially equals the bandwidth-delay-product, *i.e.*, the ideal congestion window size W_{claw} that best fits current network condition. W_{claw} is updated every time the sliding time window T moves forward, it is then fed back to the server, which sets W_{claw} as the congestion window (`cwnd`).

CLAW's cellular-informed bandwidth exploration design essentially addresses the conflict between the sparse Web traffic and the data-driven network capacity probing mechanism discussed in §3. Even with a small volume of traffic, CLAW can still instantaneously *converge to the available LTE bandwidth in one RTT*.

Hybrid bandwidth exploration mode. Note that a fully utilized LTE downlink channel does not necessarily imply the client has converged to its fair-share bandwidth. For instance, when the cellular downlink is saturated and all PHY resources are fully exploited, a new CLAW user that just joined the cell will keep estimating $W_{claw} = 0$, thus failing to explore the network bandwidth. To handle such situations, CLAW employs a *hybrid bandwidth exploration* mechanism, in which the sender maintains another window size W_{cubic} following the legacy TCP Cubic algorithm, and finally selects the larger one between W_{claw} and W_{cubic} as the actual `cwnd`. To avoid the false alarm of channel saturation caused by the traffic burstiness, we allow CLAW to switch to TCP Cubic only after it keeps detecting no idle resources for two consecutive RTTs, and then compensate it for the window size it could have increased in these two RTTs when it performs the mode switching. This hybrid bandwidth exploration design ensures that even over a saturated cellular link, the newly joined CLAW clients can still compete for the bandwidth as aggressively as the legacy TCP flows.

To demonstrate its effectiveness, we showcase a running instance of the hybrid bandwidth exploration in Fig. 7. We plot the server's `cwnd` and mark the sending time of each outgoing packet during a Web loading session over a saturated LTE channel. We see that the CLAW sending rate freezes in the beginning since there are no idle resource to explore. But after the 2-RTT inertia, mode switching is triggered: it first has a steep `cwnd` increase which follows the aforementioned window size compensation, and then ramps up with TCP Cubic's slow start operations.

Multi-user fairness. CLAW's cellular load awareness enables a client to detect the activities of competing downlink clients in the same cell, which allows it to explicitly achieve multi-user fairness. In contrast, conventional TCP is blind to competing clients and can slowly approach fair-share only for long-lived flows based on probing-and-trial. Specifically, CLAW design ensures fairness no matter when coexisting with conventional TCP flows or other CLAW flows: *(i)* When the LTE downlink channel is partially utilized by existing TCP Cubic or CLAW clients, a CLAW flow only takes its currently allocated resources plus idle resources. It does not attempt to preempt the resources currently occupied by other clients. *(ii)* Under a saturated LTE channel, CLAW's hybrid bandwidth exploration mode (Sec. 4.3.1) ensures it to be as fair as legacy TCP Cubic when competing for its fair share of bandwidth. *(iii)* When existing CLAW flows have fully exploited the downlink resources and other TCP Cubic/CLAW clients join later, the LTE BS will allocate less resources to existing flows based on its built-in fairness scheduling algorithm (proportional fairness for typical BS), thus an existing CLAW flow can promptly scale down its traffic rate following the reduced W_{claw} after detecting less fraction of resources allocated to itself, so as to prevent a potential network congestion. Then it falls back to TCP Cubic to guarantee the fairness afterwards. As a result, *CLAW achieves better fairness than conventional TCP since its resource awareness enables its rate adaptation to explicitly follow the BS's resource scheduling.*

4.3.2 Discriminating Link Loss from Congestion

Packet losses over cellular links, though infrequent, can severely disturb conventional TCP's congestion estimation, and lead to slow and unstable Web loading (§3). CLAW overcomes this fundamental limitation by discriminating the wireless loss and congestion loss using cellular link statistics available on commodity phones. LTE's RLC (Radio Link Control) layer handles the packet retransmission process on the downlink channel. The RLC layer statistics are available through the phone's diagnostic port, which include the number of packet losses, number of retransmitted packets and an overflow indicator for the RLC-layer packet queue. The CLAW client reports the RLC-layer loss events to the server, which then compare this information with the transport-layer packet losses. For instance, if a transport-layer loss happens along with RLC-layer losses caused by poor channel quality, the server notices it is not a congestion loss, and thus refrains from reducing the sending rate (congestion window). In contrast, the server will slow down immediately if the reported reason of packet loss is the buffer overflow at the LTE BS.

To facilitate the loss information feedback, CLAW marks the reserved bits in the header of the TCP ACK packets to represent different type of RLC loss events, so that the server can distinguish the wireless loss and congestion loss by reading these marks in the duplicate ACKs triggered by losses. §5 introduces how we implement this ACK flagging in the Android OS.

4.4 Network Bottleneck Detector

CLAW's cellular-informed rate control mechanism essentially boosts the traffic bit-rate to fit the client's share of cellular network capacity. However, in some corner cases, the network bottleneck may appear at the wireline path rather than the cellular link, and sending the traffic at the cellular capacity will lead to congestion at the bottleneck. To achieve a robust design, CLAW needs to detect and adapt to the rare scenarios where wireline bottlenecks the network.

Online bottleneck detection. CLAW's network bottleneck detector builds on a simple principle originating from its bandwidth exploration mechanism – If CLAW boosts the sending rate to harness currently unallocated resources, but the client's resource usage does not increase correspondingly, then there should be a bottleneck along the wireline path between the server and the BS.

To demonstrate the feasibility of this principle, we record the LTE resource allocation when loading the same Website, across a wireline bottleneck and cellular bottleneck, respectively (detailed

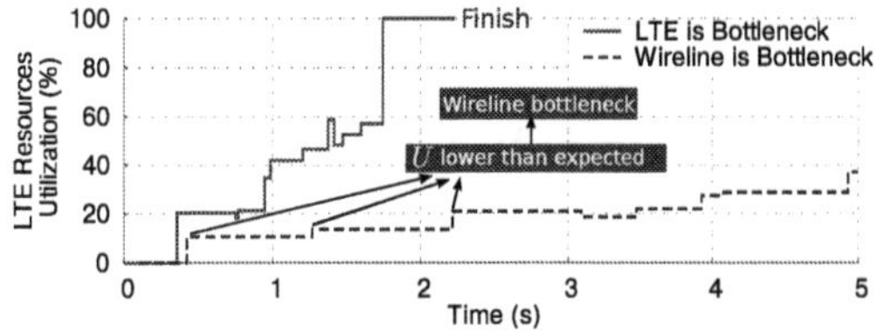

Figure 8: CLAW detects wireline bottleneck based on resource allocation pattern during bandwidth exploration.

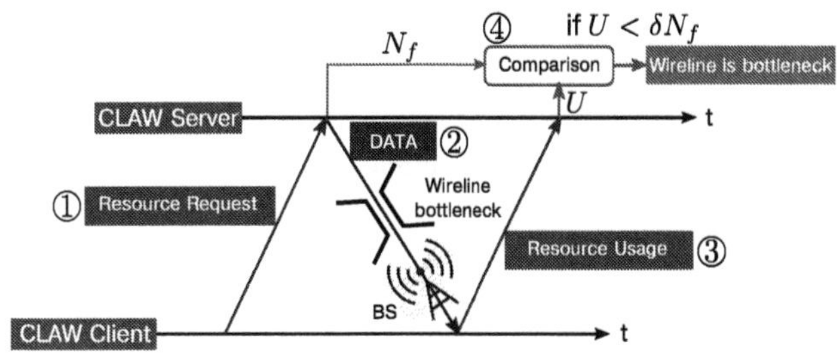

Figure 9: The network bottleneck detector in CLAW.

implementation in § 6.1). The results in Fig. 8 contrast the resource allocation patterns in the two cases, which show clear distinction.

Following this principle, the workflow of the network bottleneck detector design is outlined in Fig. 9. It runs in parallel with the cellular-informed rate control, at a time granularity of RTT level. Specifically, our design compares the volume of resources (N_f) available to a client, and its consequently allocated amount of resources (U) after one RTT. If $U < \delta N_f$, the detector declares a wireline bottleneck, otherwise a cellular bottleneck. The multiplicative factor $0 < \delta < 1$ controls the safe margin to accommodate for the RTT variations that can occasionally make U less than expected due to some delayed packets. We empirically set δ to 0.8. To further combat the network variations, the bottleneck is asserted only after consistent observations over a sliding window of 3 RTTs.

We emphasize that the bottleneck detector should be used as a sanity check. In most common cases, the wireless and wireline bottlenecks should have a non-trivial gap, even under channel variations, cross traffic disturbances, *etc.* So even a coarse check suffices. If these two happen alternately and inconsistently for a client, then they may be comparable and CLAW should degrade to the conventional TCP to avoid unnecessary oscillation.

Adapting to wireline bottleneck. After detecting a wireline bottleneck, CLAW falls back to TCP-style rate control. However, we emphasize that this fallback mode is still superior over conventional TCP, as it can still use cellular link statistics to discriminate wireless losses from congestion losses. Since the capability to discriminate between wireline and cellular bottlenecks is essentially a byproduct of the cellular-informed rate control and incurs zero overhead, CLAW client can run it in the background in parallel with web loading. Since it takes 3 RTTs to detect a wireline bottleneck, to avoid this latency, the client can also cache the decision based on server's IP address and reuse it for later sessions.

5. CLAW IMPLEMENTATION

Client side. Our implementation reads the logs containing the cellular link statistics from the diagnostic interface available on most cellphone models with Qualcomm chipsets. In Android system, the logs are passed to user space through `/dev/diag`, following the implementation of MobileInsight [32]. From such logs, we decode the RSRQ, MCS, PHY resource (RB) allocation, subframe index, and other statistics in real time with LTE subframe

(1ms) granularity. The output logs of the Qualcomm chipsets rearrange the cellular link statistics into obscure formats that can be decoded only by Qualcomm's QCAT, a proprietary software tool that parses the logs offline. To automate the real-time decoding, we reverse-engineer the log format by matching the raw HEX payload and QCAT's decoding results. We timestamp each decoded cellular link statistics based on which subframe it comes from, *e.g.*, the 7th subframe within the frame with System Frame Number (SFN) 100 has timestamp 107 (the elapsed milliseconds since the SFN counting started). Since the SFN cycles between 0 to 1023, we unwrap this value to avoid ambiguity. The decoded cellular link statistics are then fed to CLAW's cellular load analyzer implemented in the client's user space to facilitate the estimation of available resources following our model in § 4.2, and the estimation of the optimal congestion window size best fitting current network capacity following the algorithm in § 4.3.

In addition, the HTTP traffic pattern occasionally causes long idle durations, *e.g.*, when waiting for the response of HTTP GET, in which no downlink LTE traffic arrives. In such circumstances, the phone's radio enters the idle state and measures the downlink channel infrequently to save energy (only 5 RSRQ measurements per second), and hence is largely blind to the background traffic. Fortunately, since there is no traffic at all, the CLAW flow does not need to update the TCP congestion window. Therefore, the CLAW algorithm is frozen in such idle durations and takes effect only when a TCP connection is activated. In contrast, LoadSense [14] attempts to estimate the background traffic load before the client cuts into the cellular channel, where the radio is still in idle state and listens to the channel infrequently for every 200ms. Hence LoadSense can only get a rough correlation between the RSRQ and cell load, and a binary cell load estimation of "idle" or "busy". As a result, the on-the-fly operation of CLAW guarantees its more accurate cell load estimation over existing works.

For prototyping purpose, our current CLAW client implementation uses a UDP path to carry the optimal congestion window size for every 100 ms from the client to the server. Our future implementation will substitute this out-of-band feedback with an in-band signaling using the TCP Option field which can be more responsive. In addition, the client should also feedback the cellular-related packet loss events caused by BS buffer overflow or poor wireless channel (Sec. 4.3). To precisely synchronize the RLC-layer loss events reported by the diagnostic interface and the corresponding TCP packet loss, CLAW piggybacks the feedback in the TCP header like ECN-based TCP variants. To keep compatibility with current packet format, we use two of the 6 reserved bits in the TCP ACK's packet header (`th->res1`), one as the flag for the wireless channel loss, the other for the BS buffer overflow. To implement such a feedback channel in the TCP packet header, we modified `tcp_input.c` of the Android kernel to mark the wireless loss and buffer overflow notification bits, and `tcp_output.c` of the server kernel to extract these bits. We also add a customized `sysctl` variable to the Android kernel so that the CLAW application running in the user space can pass the identified loss & overflow events to the kernel.

Server side. We setup our test websites using an Apache HTTP/2 server [33] on an Amazon EC2 instance which also acts as the CLAW sender. At the server side, we tune the Linux TCP buffer size to guarantee the performance over high-speed networks like LTE. Besides, we set `net.ipv4.tcp_no_metrics_save` to 1 to ensure each Web loading test will not be affected by previous tests. To guarantee the performance of HTTP/2 which reuses TCP connection, `net.ipv4.tcp_slow_start_after_idle` is set to 0 as suggested in the HTTP/2 Wiki [34]. Upon receiving feedback containing the client's estimated `cwnd` size, the server passes it to CLAW's cellular informed rate control algorithm (Sec. 4.3), which runs in the user space and writes its `cwnd` size decision to the kernel via a customized `sysctl` interface. The new window takes effect by superseding the legacy TCP window just before the `cwnd` value is used for rate throttling within the packet transmission function `tcp_write_xmit()`. Such simple retrofitting allows flexible fallback to legacy TCP when CLAW identifies a wireline bottleneck (Sec. 4.4). For evaluation purpose, our modified server kernel also logs the packet losses, retransmissions, ACKs and behaviors of CLAW in real time. Since running CLAW implementation may change the TCP state parameters and HTTP/2 reuses TCP connection, to minimize the impact of the previous test to current Web loading, we reinitialize the TCP congest control state parameters by calling `tcp_init_congestion_control(sk)` in the TCP output engine at the end of each CLAW test. Overall, the majority of CLAW implementation lies in the client's user-space, and it only involves 41 lines of kernel patch at the server side.

6. EVALUATION

Experiment setup. We benchmark CLAW's performance against both classic TCP variants and state-of-the-art congestion control schemes for cellular networks, including CQIC [12] and Verus [13] which showed superior performance over alternatives (*e.g.*, Sprout [5]). Following [12], the CQIC implementation takes the LTE TBS (Sec. 4.3) controlled by the BS's MCS adaptation and resource allocation as the PHY capacity estimation. This essentially upgrades the original CQIC from HSPA+ to LTE [12]. We implement Verus in the server's Linux kernel following the source code (UDP-based) [35]. The original Verus updates `cwnd` every 5s, longer than a typical Web session. We thus reduce the time granularity to 500ms. Verus's bandwidth-delay profile is built during the slow start phase as suggested in [13]. For fair comparison, the tests with different schemes are conducted back-to-back to ensure similar channel conditions, and we employ the kernel's `sysctl` interface to enable fast and flexible switch between the algorithms.

Webpages and PLT measurement. We download and host a list of the Alexa top sites on an Amazon EC2 server that runs the HTTP/2 and CLAW's sender implementation. Following [4], the server hosts all Web objects of a website, including the dynamic objects generated by JavaScript, to avoid the clash between domain sharding and HTTP/2. More details about the sites we used can be found in §6.2.1. Our evaluation uses page loading time (PLT) as the primary performance metric, which directly impacts end-user experience. We use Chrome Developer Tools [36] which are widely adopted in Web loading related studies [37–39] to measure the PLT of a webpage over Android phones. The phones run the Chrome browser, with cache disabled to isolate individual Web loading tests.

Configurations for the phone. The smartphones used in our implementation are rooted so that the application layer can access and read from the diagnosis interface. We emphasize that no hardware modification is required, which is a big advantage over software-radio based cross-layer solutions like piStream [10]. Sometimes the phone may switch between LTE and HSPA when both networks are available, especially in the mobility experiments. Since the CLAW design is customized for LTE, we select "LTE Only" as the preferred network type inside the diagnostic and general setting mode of Android system to prevent unexpected network switching.

6.1 Micro-benchmarks of the CLAW design

Validating the cellular load analyzer. We first evaluate the ac-

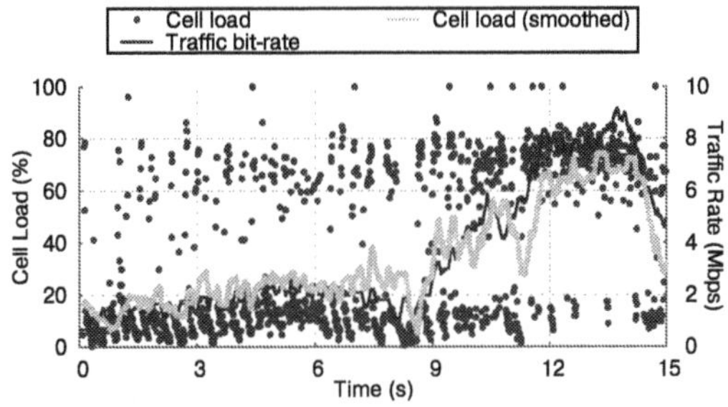

Figure 10: A microscopic demonstration of how CLAW's cell load analyzer can reliably track the cell load.

curacy of the cellular load analyzer and its real-time cell load tracking capability. We generate an `iperf` TCP traffic stream with bit-rate increasing linearly by 0.5 Mbps per second, between the server and LTE phone. The experiment runs in late night isolate the interference from background traffic. Figure 10 plots the raw cell load (frame-level granularity) as scattered points, the smoothed cell load curve using a $200ms$ (approximately RTT sized) sliding window following Eq. (8), and the network layer traffic pattern measured at the phone using `tcpdump`. The results show that the raw cell load vary drastically over time, with a polarized resource allocation pattern – the BS either allocates most RBs in a subframe or leave it empty, implying that it enforces frame aggregation. After smoothing, we can observe a high consistency between the PHY-layer cell load estimated following §4.2 and the corresponding network layer traffic intensity, which verifies the accuracy of the cellular load analyzer design. In addition, this result demonstrates the feasibility of tracking cell load in real time using the phone's diagnostic interface.

Validating the cellular-informed rate control. To demonstrate the effectiveness of *Cellular-Informed Rate Control* in CLAW design, we load the same webpage using CLAW and TCP Cubic, the most widely deployed TCP variant. For fair comparison, we run the two experiments consecutively over the same idle LTE channel.

Fig. 11a plots the sender's `cwnd` over time. We see that CLAW explores the network bandwidth much faster than TCP Cubic. Once the data transfer starts, it first quickly maps the PHY resource to a close-to-optimum `cwnd`[1], and then keeps adapting the `cwnd` based on channel quality. Its downloading finishes early at 1.7s due to effective utilization of the bandwidth. In contrast, TCP Cubic can only gradually explore the bandwidth first via slow start, and then overshoots the bandwidth and jams the LTE downlink, because its congestion indicator, packet loss, is always masked by the large LTE buffer [40]. With queue building up at the BS, the RTT surges up and eventually exceeds RTO (Retransmission Timeout), which in turn causes multiplicative rate decrease. Such trial-based probing operations lead to long PLT (2.6s). Fig. 11a also plots one additional experiment that shows a case when Cubic's slow start fails due to RTT variation (§ 3), which causes early termination of slow start and hence even longer PLT (3.2s).

Fig. 11b further compares the corresponding resource utilization reported from the client. We can observe that the BS's PHY resource allocation follows the sender's traffic intensity, and CLAW exploits LTE resources much more efficiently than TCP Cubic.

To inspect CLAW's bandwidth utilization in comparison with other Linux TCP variants, we create a bare-bones HTML page with

[1]The sender side `cwnd` surge happens at around t=500ms, which exceeds one RTT. This issue is caused by the overhead to read the diagnostic interface, and process & feedback the computed `cwnd` in the application layer. A more refined implementation can further reduce such overhead and improve the responsiveness.

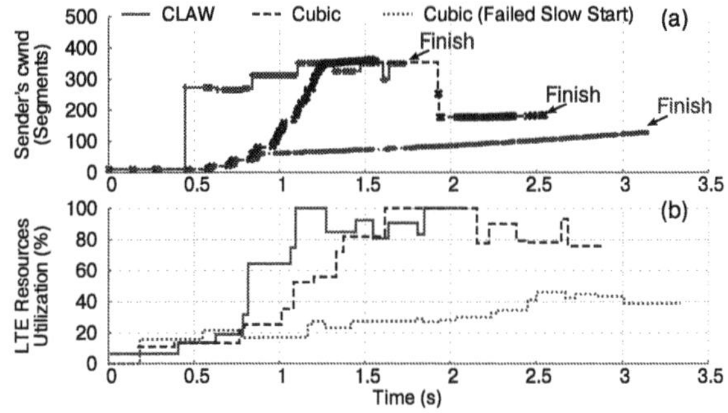

Figure 11: (a) CLAW server explores the network bandwidth faster than TCP Cubic (b) CLAW client is thus allocated more LTE PHY resources than TCP Cubic.

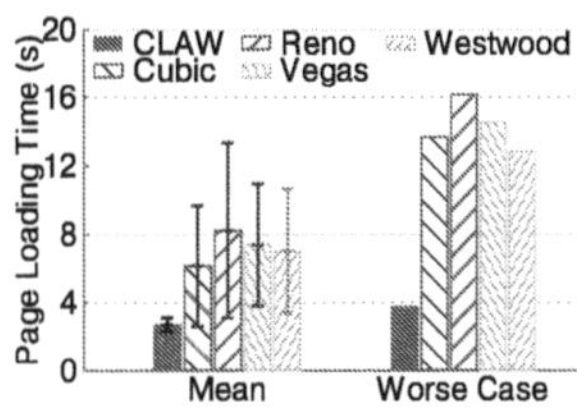

Figure 12: Web loading latency for a bare-bone Web page with a 2MB image.

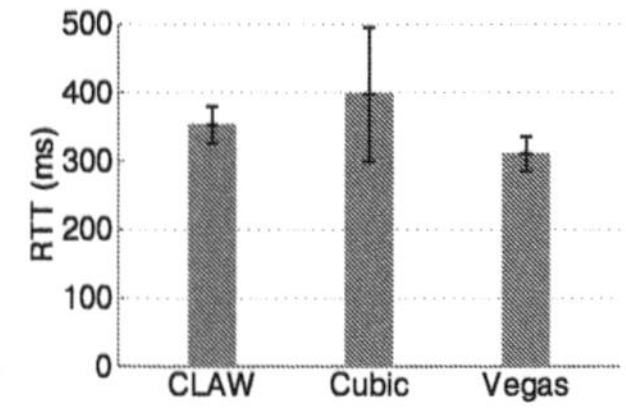

Figure 13: Packet latency (RTT) during loading Web page with a 2MB image

a single 2MB image, and load the page 20 consecutive times using each algorithm. Fig. 12 plots the average PLT and its standard deviation across 20 trials. CLAW obviously outperforms all the TCP variants and, compared to the runner-up algorithm TCP Cubic, it reduces the average PLT by 3.44s (56%). Remarkably, it also significantly reduces the PLT variance, reducing the worst case PLT by 9.92s (73%) compared with Cubic.

Fig. 13 further shows a microscopic inspection for the *packet-level* RTT of CLAW, along with the loss-based (Cubic) delay-based (Vegas) TCP. Since Vegas throttles rate on high RTT, it shows 48ms (15%) smaller mean RTT than CLAW, whereas interestingly its PLT is 2.2× longer! This is because Vegas often overreacts to delay spikes, resulting in extremely small queues and leaving the LTE BS barely anything to send. On the other hand, the BS's deep buffer makes Cubic insensitive to queue build up, misleading it to send at a high rate which causes self-inflicted congestion [5] and hence large RTT.

Effectiveness of CLAW's bottleneck detector. Since wireline bottleneck rarely occurs, to evaluate the bottleneck detector, we manually throttle the Web server's network interface at 30 Kbps using the `Dummynet` kernel module [41]. We run the same bare-bones page downloading experiment as above. Fig. 14 shows that, without the bottleneck detector, CLAW's performance becomes comparable to Cubic, because attempts to leverage the idle resources on

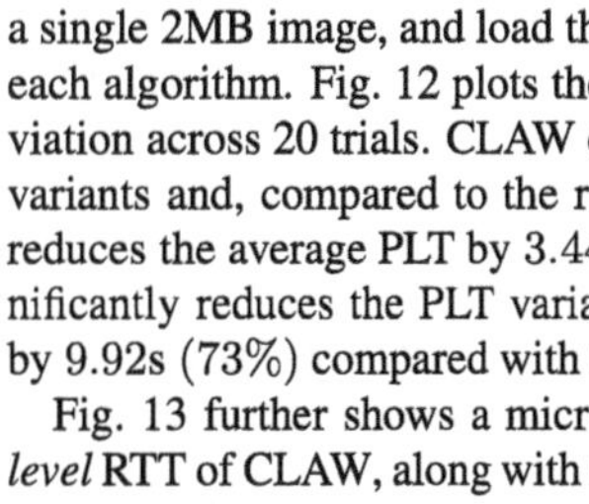

Figure 14: CLAW's bottleneck detector handles the rare wireline bottleneck.

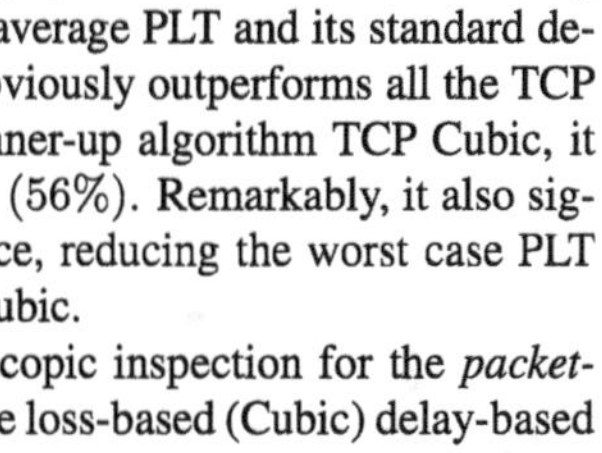

Figure 15: Profiling Alexa top 200 Website sizes.

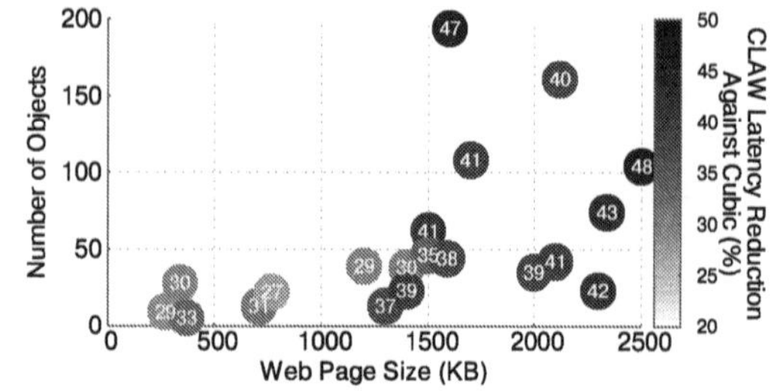

Figure 16: CLAW over different websites (number in circle is the percentage of latency reduction over Cubic).

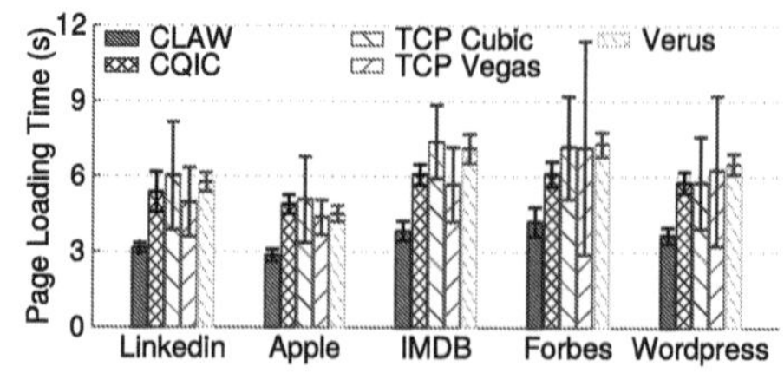

Figure 17: PLT under different transport protocols.

the LTE channel when its sending rate already exceeds the wireline bottleneck capacity, which causes high RTT, packet loss or retransmission timeout. In contrast, we can see 2.3s (20%) latency reduction after turning on CLAW's bottleneck detector and fallback mechanism, which is also slightly better than the TCP Cubic performance since CLAW's fallback mode can still distinguish wireless losses. This experiment verifies that the bottleneck detector can effectively guarantee CLAW's performance in the rare case of wireline bottleneck.

6.2 System Level Test

In this section, we perform a system level test that compares CLAW's PLT against other transport protocols, across various Websites and network conditions. To control the experiment environment, unless otherwise stated, all tests load identical webpages on the same remote server. Each test loads the page for 20 times consecutively. The interval between adjacent tests is around 10s, long enough to ensure isolation and prevent HTTP/2 from reusing the previous `cwnd`.

6.2.1 CLAW with Different Websites

We conduct experiments with popular webpages selected from the top 200 Alexa list [42]. Fig. 15 plots the CDFs for both the page size and number of objects.

What kind of Webpages benefit the most from CLAW? We first evaluate CLAW's performance on 20 selected webpages that cover a wide spectrum of size and object number. To rule out the influence of other factors, we experiment on the idle LTE channel during late night at a static location, with other settings following the default configuration discussed at the beginning of this section. The scatter plot in Fig. 16 shows CLAW's PLT reduction *w.r.t.* TCP Cubic (in percentage) of each tested Website. Note that it is unlikely to have a page with small size but large number of objects, thus the upper-left corner of Fig. 16 remains blank.

We can observe that *(i)* CLAW reduces PLT by 27% to 48% compared with Cubic. *(ii)* CLAW's performance gain increases with larger page size or larger number of objects. Since CLAW accelerates page loading by faster downloading, it can save more time if the content downloading time accounts for more across the entire page loading process (Sec. 2). In addition, with more data packets, conventional TCP is more likely to experience at least one outage event, *e.g.*, overreacting to loss/RTT (§ 3), which causes extended PLT.

PLT under different transport protocols. We further compare CLAW and other benchmark protocols over 5 randomly selected popular webpages. From the results in Fig. 17, we can observe that *(i)* CLAW achieves the minimum latency and CQIC is always the runner-up. CQIC has around 50% higher PLT than CLAW because CQIC restricts itself to the currently allocated PHY resource, whereas CLAW effectively estimates the BS's remaining resources that it can exploit. *(ii)* Among the two delay-based congestion controls, Verus's PLT is even worse than TCP Vegas, because it is designed for long-lived flows, and cannot reliably learn the bandwidth-delay profile within the short HTTP flow.

6.2.2 CLAW under various network conditions

In the following set of experiments, we evaluate the impact of various network conditions to the page loading performance of CLAW and benchmark protocols. To isolate the influence of webpage size and object number, we test the same typical LinkdIn profile webpage (that people may need to frequently check over mobile phones) across the following experiment sets.

Under different LTE cell loads. To evaluate the impact of cell loads, we run the Web loading test at different time of the day – noon for a congested LTE cell, and late night for an idle cell. We used CLAW's cellular load analyzer to inspect the cell load before the tests and found that the background cell load is around 70% during the noon and close to 0% during late night.

From the results in Fig. 18a, we make the following observations: *(i)* CLAW achieves the lowest PLT under different cell loads. For the idle channel, it reduces the latency by 5.06s (66%) against TCP Cubic and 1.63s (38%) against the performance runner-up, CQIC, while on the busy channel the reduction becomes 6.63s (59%) and 4.87s (51%), respectively. *(ii)* A CQIC client can only estimate the cellular link capacity supported by the fraction of resources allocated to itself [12], because it is unable to sense and harness the unallocated radio resources. This unfairly penalizes itself under a busy channel, leading to a sharp latency growth of 5.21s (55%) compared with the idle case. *(iii)* The delay-based TCP Vegas performs poorly over busy channel (mean PLT 8.04s), due to its well-known conservative rate control when coexisting with loss-based protocols [43]. Verus suffers from a similar problem, worsen by its inability to acquire a reliable bandwidth-delay profile.

Under different LTE channel qualities. We evaluate how the LTE channel quality affects the PLT by running tests at places with high (12dB SINR) and low (5dB SINR) channel quality reported by the phone. The results in Fig. 18b show that the PLT increases under lower channel quality for all schemes since the throughput unavoidably degrades and translates into longer downloading time. Yet, CLAW always achieves the lowest latency: it reduces the latency by 2.2s (44%) against the widely-deployed TCP Cubic and 1.04s (27%) against the performance runner-up, CQIC. Similar to CLAW, CQIC can also adjust the downstream rate following the channel quality, but it is incapable of exploiting unallocated idle resources (Sec. 2) and hence its performance always falls behind CLAW. Besides, lower channel quality tends to increase packet loss, but CLAW's PLT only increases by 0.76s, smaller than all other schemes, due to its capability of explicit loss differentiation (§ 4.3.2).

Under different outdoor mobility scenarios. We further run the tests in a moving vehicle under three outdoor mobility scenarios: *(i) slow driving* with around 10 mph within a university campus, *(ii) city driving* with around 20 mph in an urban area and *(iii) fast driving* with around 50 mph in a suburban highway. We care-

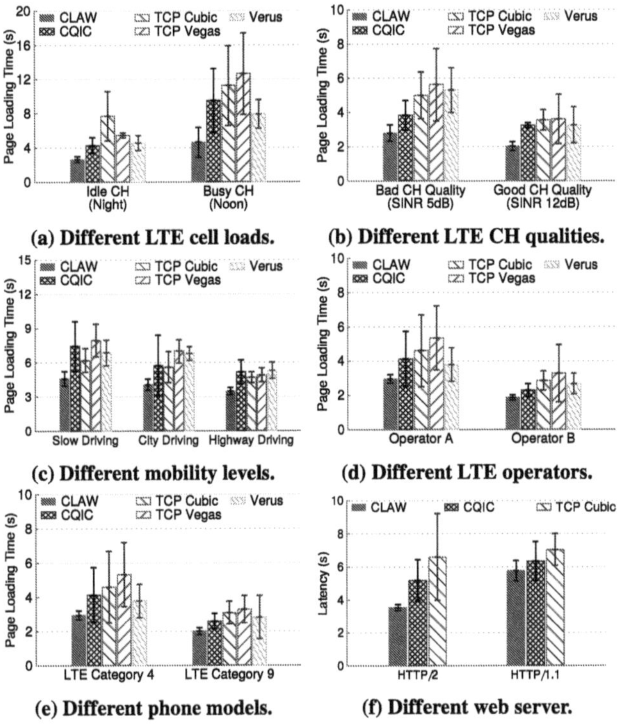

(a) **Different LTE cell loads.** (b) **Different LTE CH qualities.**

(c) **Different mobility levels.** (d) **Different LTE operators.**

(e) **Different phone models.** (f) **Different web server.**

Figure 18: CLAW outperforms benchmark schemes under various scenarios.

fully choose the spots on the route to perform Web loading so that the cross-cell handoff does not happen during a web loading.

From the results (Fig. 18c), we can observe that CLAW again achieves the lowest PLT across all the mobility scenarios. This proves that CLAW's cellular congestion monitor and rate controller perform consistently well even under very high channel dynamics. It may be counter-intuitive that the PLT decreases with the mobility level. We found the reason lies in the channel quality: the slow driving mode crosses routes between tall buildings which severely blocks the LTE signal; city driving partially suffers from similar effect; the highway driving occurs in relatively empty space with plenty of line-of-sights between the client and BS, resulting in extremely high link quality – our congestion monitor shows the corresponding TBS size is almost 3× higher than the slow driving case.

Over different cellular operators. As a cross-validation, we run CLAW on the same phone supporting two operators possibly with different resource allocation policies. Fig. 18d shows that, despite the different average PLT due to different channel conditions, CLAW shows similar fraction of PLT reduction across the two operators, compared with alternative schemes. In particular, compared to TCP Cubic, CLAW reduces the page loading time by 1.6s (36%) for Operator A and 1.0s (35%) for Operator B. We also observe that Operator B provides better performance for all algorithms under the same channel quality, which owes to Operator B's BS scheduling algorithm that schedules the LTE client with shorter interval to propel the TCP self-clock. Regardless of the BSs used by different operators, CLAW achieves consistent performance gain over TCP Cubic since the BS's scheduling strategy equally impacts them. Due to lack of phone hardware, we are unable to test a wider range of operators. But we believe the experiment hints to the fact that the CLAW's design is not limited to a certain cellular operator.

Over different LTE hardware. To demonstrate that CLAW can always accelerate Web loading regardless of the peak LTE data rate

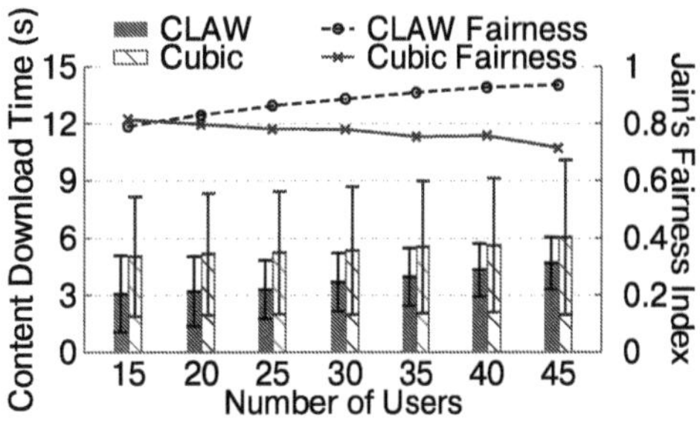

Figure 19: Scalability test.

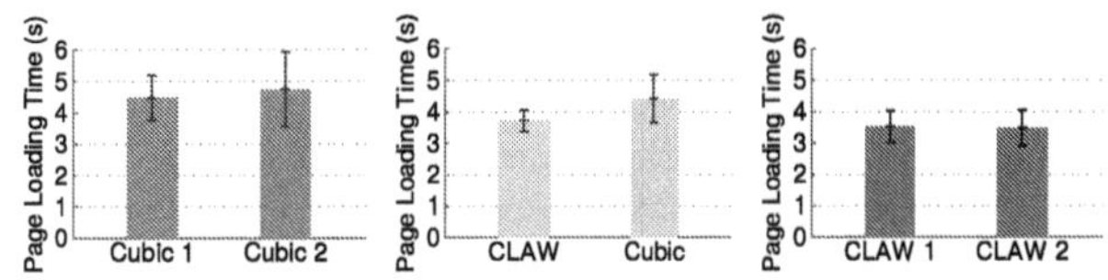

(a) **Two Cubic user load concurrently.** (b) **CLAW&Cubic load concurrently.** (c) **Two CLAW user load concurrently.**

Figure 20: TCP coexistence and multi-user scenarios.

and processing power supported by the hardware, we cross-validate CLAW over two mainstream phone models: Nexus 5 with category [44] 4 LTE and Nexus 5X with category 9 LTE chipset, supporting 150 Mbps [45] and 450 Mbps peak downlink rate [46], respectively. The newer Nexus 5X is also equipped with more powerful hardware, *e.g.*, CPU, that accelerates the network stack and OS services. From Fig. 18e, we observe that the latter can significant accelerate page loading, due to higher PHY bit-rate and more powerful hardware. CLAW again shows consistent performance gain over both phone models. Interestingly, CLAW's latency reduction over TCP Cubic is around 35% for both Nexus 5 and Nexus 5X. In fact, although the low-end phones like Nexus 5 may lack proecessing power hence suffer from higher computational time, they typically have LTE hardware with lower category number or data rate. Therefore, reducing the network latency is still crucial for mobile Web acceleration.

With HTTP/1.1 and HTTP/2. Although CLAW is designed with HTTP/2 in mind, we have conducted experiments to verify its backward compatibility with HTTP/1.1. The same server is used to test different HTTP versions to isolate the influence of server hardware and the network path to the server. We switch the server between different HTTP versions by enabling/disabling the `http2` module of the Apache server. The results in Fig. 18f show worse performance for all tested algorithms when degrading the server from HTTP/2 to HTTP/1.1. In addition, compared to TCP Cubic, CLAW reduces the page loading time by 3.05s (46%) over HTTP/2 and a smaller 1.28s 18% over HTTP/1.1. This is because even though the network bandwidth explored by CLAW allows the Web contents to be downloaded all at once, without the multiplexing feature of HTTP/2, CLAW can only download the Web contents sequentially under HTTP/1.1, which raises the latency and reduces CLAW's performance gain.

6.2.3 TCP friendliness and multi-user cases

We conduct a microscopic examination of CLAW's TCP friendliness, by concurrently tapping the reload buttons of the same webpage on two phones of the same model, so as to create the worse-case traffic overlapping. We evaluate 3 configures with different combinations as shown in Fig. 20. By comparing Fig. 20a and Fig. 20b, we see that CLAW is as fair as TCP Cubic itself: when coexisting with CLAW, TCP Cubic achieves similar level of latency compared to when coexisting with another TCP Cubic flow.

Note that in the CLAW-Cubic coexisting scenarios, CLAW will not sacrifice its own performance for Cubic, rendering similar performance to the CLAW-CLAW coexisting scenarios in Fig. 20c, which owes to CLAW's gentle aggression – it exploits the idle resources without touching the resource occupied by other users, until the idle resources are drained off (§4.3).

Due to lack of LTE phones, we were unable to test a large number of CLAW users concurrently. Instead, we develop a simulator to simulate a network with LTE bottleneck. The BS uses a simple round-robin scheduler, and the PHY parameters, RTT, loss rate, are configured to be consistent with our empirical measurements. We implement and run CLAW and Cubic separately. Each of our experiments lasts for 30s with up to 45 users, wherein each user starts a 750KB page loading at a random time. The result (Fig. 19) shows that, the CLAW users consistently outperform Cubic even under a heavily loaded network. As the network saturates, CLAW's benefit diminishes as it has less idle resource to explore and falls back to the hybrid bandwidth exploration most of the time. Consistent with our reasoning in Sec. 4.3.1, CLAW shows a higher level of fairness (in Jain's index) than Cubic.

7. DISCUSSION

Comparison with BS-based solutions. CLAW works with commodity phones and existing LTE infrastructure, which makes it readily deployable. In contrast, redesigning the BS to explicitly convey bandwidth information, as suggested in [47], requires fundamental modifications to the LTE infrastructure, phone hardware and MAC/PHY standard. Furthermore, such solutions require close cooperation between content providers and the cellular operators, whereas a software-based solution like CLAW is more feasible for the vast majority of Web services like online retailers.

CLAW's design is also transferable to future-generation cellular networks, as long as the clients can collect certain PHY statistics as CLAW does for 4G LTE networks. Furthermore, future cellular networks may deploy more TCP proxies and caching servers to optimize the Web latency. CLAW could be the perfect match for these servers as the cellular link is almost surely the bottleneck in such scenarios.

Computational latency vs. networking latency. Recent research [48, 49] reveals that the computational time also plays an important role in the Web loading latency. However, even under the extreme cases with a tiny RTT of 5ms, the content downloading time still accounts for more than 40% of the total latency [49], and starts to dominate under higher RTT of 150ms. We emphasize that the RTT quickly inflates during data transfer due to network queuing [2, 5, 7, 13], and can easily exceed 150ms with only 200KB data in flight [2], which further justifies CLAW's strategy of accelerating the bandwidth convergence with fewer round-trips.

Generations of smartphones have been embracing escalating CPU power to minimize the computational latency, which always outpaces the network upgrades. In addition, to catch up with the rapid growth of phone screen size/resolution, the Web content sizes will scale accordingly to offer better user experience, which further elevates the networking latency. We believe that CLAW's data transport protocol can better prepare the mobile networks for future demands. It can certainly be combined with page optimization [50] and better object fetching strategies [37] to further cut the PLT.

Remarkably, with shorter PLT, a CLAW user's radio interface stays in the energy-hungry active state for shorter duration, which directly translates into energy saving. We also plan to explore this benefit in our future work.

8. CONCLUSION

In this paper, we have presented the design, implementation and evaluation of CLAW, which accelerates mobile Web loading through a physical-layer informed transport protocol. CLAW extracts the LTE cell load, packet loss and bit-rate information based on the PHY statistics available locally on a smartphone. By exposing such fine-grained information, CLAW unleashes the transport-layer from data-driven bandwidth probing, and enables judicious rate control under channel dynamics and losses. CLAW improves mobile Web performance remarkably, in terms of both average latency and stability. We believe its PHY-informed design can benefit a broader range of mobile protocols and applications.

Acknowledgement

We appreciate the anonymous reviewers for their insightful comments. This research was supported in part by the NSF under Grant CNS-1343363, CNS-1350039, CNS-1506657 and CNS-1518728.

9. REFERENCES

[1] T. Flach, N. Dukkipati, A. Terzis, B. Raghavan, N. Cardwell, Y. Cheng, A. Jain, S. Hao, E. Katz-Bassett, and R. Govindan, "Reducing Web Latency: The Virtue of Gentle Aggression," in *ACM SIGCOMM*, 2013.

[2] J. Huang, F. Qian, Y. Guo, Y. Zhou, Q. Xu, Z. M. Mao, S. Sen, and O. Spatscheck, "An In-depth Study of LTE: Effect of Network Protocol and Application Behavior on Performance," in *ACM SIGCOMM*, 2013.

[3] J. Erman, V. Gopalakrishnan, R. Jana, and K. K. Ramakrishnan, "Towards a SPDY'Ier Mobile Web?" in *ACM CoNEXT*, 2013.

[4] X. S. Wang, A. Balasubramanian, A. Krishnamurthy, and D. Wetherall, "How Speedy is SPDY?" in *USENIX NSDI*, 2014.

[5] K. Winstein, A. Sivaraman, and H. Balakrishnan, "Stochastic Forecasts Achieve High Throughput and Low Delay Over Cellular Networks," in *NSDI*, 2013.

[6] N. Becker, A. Rizk, and M. Fidler, "A Measurement Study on the Application-Level Performance of LTE," in *IFIP Networking Conference*, 2014.

[7] H. Jiang, Y. Wang, K. Lee, and I. Rhee, "Tackling Bufferbloat in 3G/4G Networks," in *ACM IMC*, 2012.

[8] Y. Zhang, A. Arvidsson, M. Siekkinen, and G. Urvoy-Keller, "Understanding HTTP flow rates in cellular networks," in *IFIP Networking Conference*, 2014.

[9] K. I. Pedersen, T. E. Kolding, F. Frederiksen, I. Z. Kovacs, D. Laselva, and P. E. Mogensen, "An Overview of Downlink Radio Resource Management for UTRAN Long-term Evolution," *IEEE Communications Magazine*, 2009.

[10] X. Xie, X. Zhang, S. Kumar, and L. E. Li, "piStream: Physical Layer Informed Adaptive Video Streaming Over LTE," in *ACM MobiCom*, 2015.

[11] S. Kumar, E. Hamed, D. Katabi, and L. Erran Li, "LTE Radio Analytics Made Easy and Accessible," in *ACM SIGCOMM*, 2014.

[12] F. Lu, H. Du, A. Jain, G. M. Voelker, A. C. Snoeren, and A. Terzis, "CQIC: Revisiting Cross-Layer Congestion Control for Cellular Networks," in *ACM HotMobile*, 2015.

[13] Y. Zaki, T. Pötsch, J. Chen, L. Subramanian, and C. Görg, "Adaptive Congestion Control for Unpredictable Cellular Networks," in *ACM SIGCOMM*, 2015.

[14] A. Chakraborty, V. Navda, V. N. Padmanabhan, and R. Ramjee, "Coordinating Cellular Background Transfers Using Loadsense," in *ACM MobiCom*, 2013.

[15] J. Erman, A. Gerber, M. Hajiaghayi, D. Pei, S. Sen, and O. Spatscheck, "To Cache or Not to Cache: The 3G Case," *IEEE Internet Computing*, vol. 15, no. 2, 2011.

[16] IETF, "Hypertext Transfer Protocol Version 2 (HTTP/2)," https://tools.ietf.org/html/rfc7540/, 2015.

[17] S. Sundaresan, N. Feamster, R. Teixeira, and N. Magharei, "Measuring and Mitigating Web Performance Bottlenecks in Broadband Access Networks," in *Proc. of Internet Measurement Conference*, 2013.

[18] Z. Wang, F. X. Lin, L. Zhong, and M. Chishtie, "Why are web browsers slow on smartphones?" in *Proc. of the Workshop on Mobile Computing Systems and Applications (HotMobile)*, 2011.

[19] N. Larson, D. Baltrunas, A. Kvalbein, A. Dhamdhere, k. claffy, and A. Elmokashfi, "Investigating Excessive Delays in Mobile Broadband Networks," in *Proc. of the Workshop on All Things Cellular (AllThingsCellular)*, 2015.

[20] P. Sun, M. Yu, M. J. Freedman, and J. Rexford, "Identifying Performance Bottlenecks in CDNs Through TCP-level Monitoring," in *Proc. ACM SIGCOMM Workshop on Measurements Up the Stack (W-MUST)*, 2011.

[21] D. Katabi, M. Handley, and C. Rohrs, "Congestion Control for High Bandwidth-Delay Product Networks," *ACM SIGCOMM Computer Communication Review*, 2002.

[22] M. Caesar, D. Caldwell, N. Feamster, J. Rexford, A. Shaikh, and J. van der Merwe, "Design and Implementation of a Routing Control Platform," in *USENIX NSDI*, 2005.

[23] M. Dong, Q. Li, D. Zarchy, P. B. Godfrey, and M. Schapira, "PCC: Re-architecting Congestion Control for Consistent High Performance," in *NSDI*, 2015.

[24] V. Srivastava and M. Motani, "Cross-layer Design: A Survey and the Road Ahead," *IEEE Communication Magazine*, vol. 43, no. 12, 2005.

[25] B. Fu, Y. Xiao, H. J. Deng, and H. Zeng, "A Survey of Cross-Layer Designs in Wireless Networks," *IEEE Communications Surveys Tutorials*, vol. 16, no. 1, 2014.

[26] R. Kateja, N. Baranasuriya, V. Navda, and V. N. Padmanabhan, "DiversiFi: Robust Multi-Link Interactive Streaming," in *ACM CoNEXT*. ACM, 2015.

[27] N. Baranasuriya, V. Navda, V. N. Padmanabhan, and S. Gilbert, "QProbe: Locating the Bottleneck in Cellular Communication," in *CoNEXT*, 2015.

[28] T. Flach, N. Dukkipati, A. Terzis, B. Raghavan, N. Cardwell, Y. Cheng, A. Jain, S. Hao, E. Katz-Bassett, and R. Govindan, "Reducing Web Latency: The Virtue of Gentle Aggression," in *ACM SIGCOMM*, 2013.

[29] 3GPP, "LTE: Evolved Universal Terrestrial Radio Access (E-UTRA); Physical channels and modulation," *TS 36.211 version 12.3.0 Release 12*, 2014.

[30] N. Bui and J. Widmer, "OWL: A Reliable Online Watcher for LTE Control Channel Measurements," in *Proceedings of the 5th Workshop on All Things Cellular: Operations, Applications and Challenges*, 2016.

[31] 3GPP, "LTE: Evolved Universal Terrestrial Radio Access (E-UTRA); Physical layer procedures," *TS 36.213 version 12.4.0 Release 12*, 2015.

[32] Y. Li, C. Peng, Z. Yuan, J. Li, H. Deng, and T. Wang, "MobileInsight: Extracting and Analyzing Cellular Network Information on Smartphones," in *ACM MobiCom*, 2016.

[33] "The Apache HTTP Server Project." [Online]. Available: https://httpd.apache.org/

[34] IETF HTTP Working Group, "HTTP/2 Wiki." [Online]. Available: https://github.com/http2/http2-spec/wiki/Ops

[35] Yasir Zaki, "Verus Source Code on GitHub." [Online]. Available: https://github.com/yzaki/verus/

[36] Google, "Remote Debugging Android Devices." [Online]. Available: https://developers.google.com/web/tools/chrome-devtools/debug/remote-debugging/remote-debugging?hl=en

[37] R. Netravali, A. Goyal, J. Mickens, and H. Balakrishnan, "Polaris: Faster Page Loads Using Fine-grained Dependency Tracking," in *USENIX NSDI*, 2016.

[38] Y. Zhu, M. Halpern, and V. J. Reddi, "Event-Based Scheduling for Energy-Efficient qos (eqos) in Mobile Web Applications," in *2015 IEEE 21st International Symposium on High Performance Computer Architecture (HPCA)*. IEEE, 2015.

[39] X. Li and Z. Bao, "Performance Characterization of Web Applications with HTML5 Enhancements," in *Dependable, Autonomic and Secure Computing (DASC), 2014 IEEE 12th International Conference on*. IEEE, 2014.

[40] J. Gettys and K. Nichols, "Bufferbloat: Dark Buffers in the Internet," *Communications of the ACM*, vol. 55, no. 1, 2012.

[41] M. Carbone and L. Rizzo, "Dummynet revisited," in *ACM SIGCOMM Computer Communication Review*, 2010.

[42] Alexa. [Online]. Available: http://www.alexa.com/

[43] U. Hengartner, J. Bolliger, and T. Gross, "TCP Vegas Revisited," in *INFOCOM 2000*, 2000.

[44] 3GPP, "LTE UE-Category." [Online]. Available: http://www.3gpp.org/keywords-acronyms/1612-ue-category

[45] Qualcomm, "Snapdragon 800 Processor." [Online]. Available: https://www.qualcomm.com/products/snapdragon/processors/800

[46] ——, "Snapdragon 808 Processor." [Online]. Available: https://www.qualcomm.com/products/snapdragon/processors/808

[47] A. Jain, A. Terzis, N. Sprecher, S. Arunachalam, K. Smith, and G. Klas, "Requirements and reference architecture for Mobile Throughput Guidance Exposure," 2015. [Online]. Available: https://tools.ietf.org/html/draft-flinck-mobile-throughput-guidance-03

[48] J. Huang, F. Qian, A. Gerber, Z. M. Mao, S. Sen, and O. Spatscheck, "A close examination of performance and power characteristics of 4g lte networks," in *ACM MobiSys*, 2012.

[49] J. Nejati and A. Balasubramanian, "An In-Depth Study of Mobile Browser Performance," in *Proceedings of the 25th International Conference on World Wide Web*. International World Wide Web Conferences Steering Committee, 2016.

[50] Google, "Accelerated Mobile Pages (AMP)," 2016. [Online]. Available: https://www.ampproject.org

Open Data Kit 2.0: A Services-Based Application Framework for Disconnected Data Management

Waylon Brunette, Samuel Sudar, Mitchell Sundt, Clarice Larson, Jeffrey Beorse, Richard Anderson
Department of Computer Science and Engineering
University of Washington
Box 352350, Seattle, WA 98195
{wrb, sudars, msundt, clarice, jbeorse, anderson}@cse.uw.edu

ABSTRACT

In resource-constrained communities, organizations often use information and communication technologies to amplify their limited resources to improve education, health, and economic opportunity. Over two-thirds of the world's population have mobile phones, yet less than half are connected to the Internet [23]. Organizations helping disadvantaged populations often rely on mobile devices as their primary computing resource because of their availability in resource-constrained contexts. However, to reach under-served populations, mobile applications often operate in areas with no connectivity or challenged network environments. Unfortunately, many mobile application frameworks are generally not well-suited for long periods of disconnected data collection and management. Furthermore, mobile application frameworks are generally aimed at users with significant technical skills and resources. In this paper, we discuss our experiences building, deploying, and refining the Open Data Kit (ODK) 2.0 tool suite. ODK 2.0 is a modular application framework that facilitates organizations with limited technical capacity to build application-specific information services for use in disconnected environments. We discuss ODK 2.0's flexible abstractions that enable users of varying technical skill levels to create customizable mobile data management solutions. We present ODK 2.0 case studies involving multiple organizations and discuss lessons learned from building a service-based mobile application framework for disconnected data management.

Keywords

Open Data Kit; ICTD; mobile application framework; disconnected operation; mobile databases; mobile data management

1. INTRODUCTION

Organizations focused on improving education, health, and economic opportunity in under-served communities often operate in areas with limited resources, power, connectivity, and infrastructure. According to a 2016 World Bank report, over 90% of the world's population live within mobile network coverage [23] making mobile computing technologies one of the few technologies well suited for use in global development interventions. Therefore, organizations often rely on the mobile phone as their primary computing device. While over two-thirds of the world's population have mobile phones, less than half the world's population are connected to the Internet [23]. This scenario where billions of people have mobile phones but lack consistent Internet connectivity will likely continue for years. Thus, organizations helping disadvantaged populations need to rely on mobile applications that can operate in disconnected environments.

Various research projects focus on improving Internet connectivity by extending infrastructures (e.g., long distance WiFi, village base stations). However, a parallel approach is needed that focuses on creating abstractions and frameworks for mobile applications to operate in challenged network environments until affordable, universal connectivity is a reality. Unfortunately, many mobile application frameworks are generally designed for relatively short periods of disconnected operation as they often only include basic offline features with limited caching. Furthermore, existing mobile application frameworks generally require programming skills and focus on features for programmers, such as platform independence across multiple mobile operating systems (e.g., iOS, Android). However, in resource-limited settings there is often a shortage of qualified programmers and limited funds to hire consultants.

Open Data Kit (ODK) [9, 20] is a mobile tools suite that operates in disconnected environments with abstractions that lower technical barriers. ODK enables governments, organizations, and individuals to use technology to "magnify their human resources" and has experienced widespread adoption. ODK's website has received over 700,000 unique visitors from 232 different countries/territories and averages over 30,000 hits a month. ODK's 1.x toolkit [20] is a successful data collection platform enabling users to collect millions of data points for a diverse set of domains (e.g., health, election monitoring, disaster response). Over 210,000 users have installed ODK Collect according to Google Play (excludes ODK derivative apps distributed by other companies or installations directly from the ODK website). Analytics reports ODK Collect is used daily by thousands of users in over 130 distinct countries. However, ODK 1.x's uni-directional data flow, linear navigation, and limited data types of Java-Rosa's XForm standard constrained its applicability to certain categories of use cases. While ODK 1.x was designed to enhance and replace paper-based data collection, the focus on simplicity left certain requirements unmet. The 2.0 tool suite [9] expanded ODK features to include two-way data synchronization, a local database for disconnected operation, runtime modifiable user interfaces, and a platform for customizable user applications.

Based on feedback from ODK 2.0 pilot deployments in over 18 countries by a variety of organizations, the 2.0 tool suite went through a significant redesign from the original ODK 2.0 vision [9].

This work is licensed under a Creative Commons Attribution International 4.0 License.

MobiSys'17 June 19-23, 2017, Niagara Falls, NY, USA
© 2017 Copyright held by the owner/author(s).
ACM ISBN 978-1-4503-4928-4/17/06.
DOI: http://dx.doi.org/10.1145/3081333.3081365

This paper summarizes the constraints and feedback that drove the revision. ODK 2.0 was redesigned as a modular service-oriented architecture, comprised of six tools, with framework abstractions that were flexible enough to empower users of varying technical skill levels to build mobile data management applications tailored to their specific use cases. ODK 2.0 aims to create a *data management platform* for resource-constrained environments that provides greater functionality than the ODK 1.x's *data collection platform.*

This paper discusses ODK 2.0's revised framework and presents the design considerations that led to its evolved modular service-based architecture for disconnected data management. We describe how system design decisions were influenced by the challenged network environments and resource-constrained contexts. We examine the implications of the revised architecture and show it had relatively minimal impact on performance. We also share feedback from multiple organizations that experienced limitations with 1.x and participated in ODK 2.0 pilots and discuss how the revised framework has better met their deployment requirements.

2. DESIGN CONSIDERATIONS

The ODK 2.0 tool suite provides an Android application framework that reduces the complexity organizations face when creating a mobile data management application. Organizations in resource-constrained environments often lack the technical personnel or resources to build and customize information systems. Instead, organizations commonly use productivity software (e.g., Excel, Word) to create solutions customized to their domain and context. Microsoft Office is an example of software that is adaptable to multiple domains by users with no programming expertise. Unfortunately, productivity software is often designed for conventional personal computers which are usually poorly suited to resource-constrained environments. While personal-computer-based productivity applications generally have a broad focus for domain utility, mobile apps (Android native executable applications that will be referred to as 'apps' for the scope of this paper) tend to reduce their scope to a single task (e.g., calendar, maps, email) and often lack customization features.

ODK 2.0 enables creation and customization of domain independent mobile applications that address organization's needs within constraints imposed by Android. ODK 2.0's synchronization protocols and structures are designed to be adaptable in extreme mobile networking conditions, such as long periods of disconnection or low bandwidth and high latency. ODK 2.0 replicates data to the mobile devices, enabling the framework to preserve full functionality in disconnected environments.

ODK takes a multi-perspective approach to the creation of customizable abstractions for varying contexts [10]. The *platform perspective* incorporates the device and operating system perspective on aspects such as connectivity, power, features, and mobility. The *application developer perspective* encompasses the features and functionality of an 'app' that executes on a specific platform. It also incorporates the perspective of the software developer who writes the 'app'. The developer's choices about what functionality and platform features to expose constrain how the 'app' can be used. Unfortunately, developers likely do not fully understand how future users will want to deploy the framework in different contexts with varying connectivity, budgets, laws, data policies, user education level, etc. Therefore, ODK focuses on creating frameworks that give flexibility to a *deployment architect* who has an *application deployment perspective* that encompasses issues relating to contextual deployment requirements that are often dynamic.

We identify the *deployment architect* as the non-programmer or programmer with limited technical skills who adapts an ensemble of off-the-shelf software (e.g., ODK 2.0) to create a data management application. Unlike standard reusable model-view-controllers, ODK attempts to create abstractions usable by *deployment architects* emulating productivity software that targets non-software developers. In addition to *deployment architect*, other ODK *users* are often site managers, supervisors, and data collectors that use the configured data management platform to complete their tasks. For an organization to successfully implement a mobile application in a resource-constrained context, *deployment architects* must be able to scale their applications. ODK tool suites leverage commercial cloud offerings and Android's common APIs to simplify an organization's ability to scale. Building on Android OS enables organizations to easily purchase a diverse set of commercially available smartphones and tablets with varying form factors, battery life, ruggedness, and prices. While there is a notion that the cloud "effortlessly scales," in reality there are complex technical issues handled by an army of software engineers at cloud companies (e.g., Amazon, Microsoft). ODK 2.0's cloud-based components leverage this army and work in concert with ODK's Android application framework with non-programmer abstractions to insulate the *deployment architect* from technical details so that organizations can "effortlessly scale" their mobile data management applications.

2.1 Limitations of ODK 1.x

The ODK 1.x tool suite is a successful data collection platform used by many organizations to digitize their data collection in the field. The system design focuses on collecting data via digital surveys that are then aggregated in the cloud or on a PC for analysis. However, ODK 1.x's purposeful simplicity to enable a *deployment architect* to replace paper data collection with mobile data collection meant the tool suite lacked features for certain use cases.

To illustrate, consider the common scenario in which organizations use previously collected data to influence their next action when revisiting a specific location. Examples of such a scenario include logistics management, patient follow-up in medical care, and environmental monitoring. In these scenarios, users often return to locations and reference previously collected data that they either verify or update. Each visit may require field workers to complete multiple forms, produce multiple data records, and/or require multiple review steps. Each phase may draw upon data collected during any other phase or data found in supporting information tables, this data needs to be available even when disconnected. Revisiting data from previous surveys is not supported in ODK 1.x.

The multi-visit scenario requires bidirectional synchronization of data, support for complex workflows, references or updates to previously collected data, and security and data isolation for specific users. Working with partner organizations, we constructed a list of common requirements that were not met by the 1.x tools. These were discovered both through initial design sessions as well as lessons learned from field deployments. Some key requirements for ODK 2.0 that were beyond the scope of ODK 1.x include:

- Complex / Non-Linear Workflows
- Linking Longitudinal Data to Collected Data
- Data Security and User Permissions
- Reuse of Data Fields across Forms
- Bidirectional Synchronization
- Customizable Form Presentation
- Custom Apps Built with a Runtime Language (JavaScript)
- Sensor Integration
- Paper Digitization
- Custom Data Types that Update Multiple Fields in a Single User Action

To meet these requirements, ODK 2.0 expands its scope from ODK 1.x's *data collection platform* to a *data management platform*. A mobile "data management application" (designated as an 'application' to delineate from the previously defined 'app') is the customized set of activities created by an organization to perform its data collection and management workflows to accomplish its business objective.

2.2 Design Principles & Features

The ODK 2.0 tool suite is a parallel effort (not a replacement) to the ODK 1.x tool suite; it provides the general-purpose tools for a virtually unlimited set of use cases and enables organizations in resource-constrained environments to build, deploy, maintain, and ultimately own mobile data management applications and business logic. While many of the details have evolved, the four design principles that were outlined in the ODK 2.0 vision paper [9] for refinement and expansion of ODK remain the same:

1. *when possible, UI elements should be designed using a more widely understood runtime language instead of a compile time language, thereby making it easier for individuals with limited programming experience to make customizations;*
2. *the basic data structures should be easily expressible in a single row, and nested structures should be avoided when data is in display, transmission, or storage states;*
3. *data should be stored in a database that can be shared across devices and can be easily extractable to a variety of common data formats;*
4. *new sensors, data input methods and data types should be easy to incorporate into the data collection pipeline by individuals with limited technical experience.*

Expanding on these basic design principles, a larger list of features were generated based on specific use case requirements. For example, dynamic value checking based on previous data was required to improve data integrity which is seen as a key benefit of digital data collection. Consider agricultural longitudinal studies: agricultural extension workers visit crops multiple times during a growing season. They track the progress of the crop to compare growing conditions and try to improve crop yields. However, the validation logic in ODK 1.x uses static formulas so it has an absolute min and max that would differ early in the season from later in the season. Thus, to better support this type of longitudinal study, ODK 2.0 should allow its *data management applications* to access previous crop heights and use dynamic calculations to catch data anomalies. The following includes a more detailed view of some of the key design goals of the ODK 2.0 framework.

- Workflow navigation should use intuitive procedural constructs, function independent of data validation, and allow for user-directed navigation of the form.
- The presentation layer must be independent of the navigation and validation logic.
- The presentation layer must be customizable without recompiling the Android apps via HTML, JavaScript, and CSS.
- Partial validation of collected data should be possible and the validation logic should be able to be dynamic.
- Local storage should be robust and performant for data curation and for longitudinal survey workflows using a relational data model.
- Multiple data collection forms should be able to modify data within a single, shared, data table.
- Foreground and background sensors should be supported for data collection.
- Disconnected operation should be assumed as data must be able to be collected, queried, and stored without a reliable Internet connection. When the Internet becomes available, the framework and cloud components should efficiently replicate data across all devices.
- User and group permissions are needed to limit data access.
- Cloud components should be able to fully configure the data management application remotely as well preserve a change log of all collected data.

3. RELATED WORK

A variety of existing solutions and application frameworks attempt to solve varied issues; however, ODK focuses on a certain class of problems. What distinguishes ODK 2.0 from other solutions is its focus on providing a suite of inter-operable tools that work together to provide base functionality for a flexible information management system. For example, Apache Cordova [1] (the open-source version of Adobe's PhoneGap) is a popular open-source framework for building mobile applications with HTML and JavaScript. It provides a native plugin-framework to access hardware features of the mobile device. Many mobile application frameworks wrap and augment Cordova in other products, such as Ionic [3] and Intel XDK [2]. Similar to ODK, Cordova uses a custom native SQLite library; however, Cordova and ODK have different overall focuses. Cordova, designed for programmers, helps solve the problem of cross compatibility for different OSes (e.g., iOS, Android, Windows, BlackBerry, Ubuntu, FireOS) to let programmers write code once and deploy it on multiple platforms. ODK 2.0 instead focuses on making it simpler for non-programmers to create mobile applications specifically for the Android platform. ODK focuses solely on Android compatible devices because these devices come in a variety of form factors with different price points, making Android devices popular in economically constrained environments, unlike more expensive iOS devices (Android had more than 87% world smartphone market share in Q2 2016 [4]).

Computing for global development research has produced multiple mobile application framework research projects. CAM [21], one of the earliest mobile application frameworks for resource-constrained environments, used J2ME phones with a custom scripting language and barcodes to augment paper forms and trigger custom prompts for manual data entry. Unfortunately, CAM was tied to a specific phone model, and while hooks were exposed for customization, the custom scripting language was seen as a barrier to entry as it was a new skill someone had to acquire. In comparison, ODK 2.0 exposed JavaScript as its customization language to allow the tools to have a pre-existing base of trained programmers. Another early example was the E-IMCI project [15], which used PDAs as the mobile computing device in resource-constrained environments to encode complex medical workflows. While E-IMCI was not customizable, it provided an early example of how mobile computing platforms could improve an organization's workflow in remote locations. The Uju project [22] focused on making it easier to create database-centric applications for SMS, but, unlike ODK 2.0, it was not designed to integrate with multiple tools that obtain data from various inputs (e.g., sensors, paper forms). The CommCare framework with CaseXML [16] has design goals similar to ODK; it enables organizations to customize their field worker's digital workflows. CommCare operates on both J2ME and Android devices and uses *Collect* (an ODK 1.x tool) as the base for the CommCare Android app by adding custom features to work with CaseXML. CaseXML lets organizations specify an application workflow and data exchange, enabling health workers to share 'cases' through synchronization of atomic transaction in an XForm. While CommCare has been a successful platform for organizations with field healthcare workers, other organizations reported problems adapting CaseXML to other domains. The limitations reported by organizations with CaseXML contributed to the decision to abandon XForms entirely in the ODK 2.0 design.

Several research projects have tried to simplify mobile development by providing abstracted table APIs that assist mobile app programmers with data management. Two examples of such projects that build database-table-like schematics are Izzy [19] and Mobius [12]. Like ODK, Izzy tries to make application development easier by providing a simple API to access database tables; however, these APIs are targeted at programmers. Mobius takes a different approach and presents logical table extractions but uses a unified messaging scheme for updates. This approach becomes problematic for long periods of disconnected operation, which are expected to be experienced by ODK 2.0 users.

4. MOBILE FRAMEWORK

The ODK 2.0 tool suite (individual tool names are italicized) provides a platform for organizations to create customized data management applications on Android devices. Based on feedback from multiple pilot deployments (some are described in section 5), the ODK 2.0 architecture went through a significant redesign to address multiple issues. In the first iteration of the architecture, the modular mobile tools were designed as completely independent applications that directly accessed a single shared Android database. The basic concept was that all applications would individually read and write data directly into a shared database, thereby enabling data sharing and consistency. Unfortunately, the simplistic design led to database contention problems, security issues, performance issues, and limited code reuse. This section presents how the Android applications in the ODK 2.0 tool suite have been re-architected to follow a services-based architecture running on the Android device. Key aspects of the architecture are: 1) Modular Design – individual Android tools designed for particular tasks that, used in concert, can achieve complex behaviors, 2) Data and Configuration Management – the storage, sharing and protection of configuration and data across mobile devices and cloud components, 3) Synchronization Protocol – designed to adaptable in extreme networking conditions, 4) Services Architecture – common functionality consolidated into a unifying services layer.

4.1 Modular Design

The ODK 2.0 framework seeks to satisfy an organization's specific usage scenario through the composition of narrowly focused tools rather than a single monolithic app. An app that tries to provide abstractions for every usage scenario can be overwhelming, so ODK tools focus on a singular task and are designed to smoothly transition between one another to give the feel of unified application. The six apps shown in Figure 1 each contribute abstractions to specific areas: *Scan* the paper digitization framework, *Tables* the data curation framework, *Survey* the question rendering and constraint verification framework, *Sensors* the device connection framework, *Services* the common data services framework, and *Submit* the communication framework. To fulfill complex requirements, the deployment architect uses the necessary subset of tools in concert to build a customized data management application.

4.1.1 Services

The Android *Services* app contains common services that are used by all ODK 2.0 apps running on the mobile device. One of the key components of *Services* is the database service that abstracts database access to a single shared interface that enables the enforcement of consistency semantics and data-access restrictions. *Services* also exposes interfaces to other shared functionality, including a lightweight web server, user authentication, framework preferences, and the cloud synchronization protocol. The ODK 2.0 the synchronization protocol is discussed in Section 4.3 and the service-oriented architecture is discussed in detail in Section 4.4.

4.1.2 Survey

Survey focuses on data collection through the use of questions. Users progress through question prompts as they capture data, similar to the flow of an ODK 1.x form. However, departing from the 1.x model, JavaScript and HTML are used to define a suite of prompt widgets and to encapsulate the rendering, event handling, and form navigation logic required for data collection. The presentation layer can be easily customized by revising *Survey's* templates and CSS style sheets to create an organization-specific look-and-feel. To simplify survey design, the XLSForm syntax from ODK 1.x was restructured to reduce the number of spreadsheet columns and move complex programming syntax into a single column. The aim is to make it easier for users to initially learn the simpler *Survey* definition structure and then ramp up their knowledge as they require more advanced features. To help users keep complex workflows organized, the concept of 'sections' was added to enable logical groupings of questions. The concept of 'repeats' is replaced by the concept of 'subforms' to give users the full power of an independent survey definition when dealing with repeated input sets.

Survey increases an organization's ability to customize an application by implementing the user interface with a run-time scripting language that allows for customizing without recompiling. The entire flow of *Survey*, from the opening screen to the outline/index view of a form, can be redefined or extended, thereby enabling more customization than XForm syntax of ODK 1.x's Collect tool. Organizations can extend standard widgets at runtime to: change the rendering or workflow logic itself (e.g., complex types, value constraints), customize event handling, or define new question widgets. *Survey* has several new features that improve ODK's malleability to various application domains. Since the question widgets are all modifiable at runtime, organizations can now define custom question types with multiple input values but with a single question prompt (e.g., blood pressure, pulse/oxygen) instead of being limited to the one-question/one-value model of ODK 1.x's JavaRosa XForm. Furthermore, users can use the new complex commands to express non-linear workflow logic using 'gotos' in the survey definition. Buttons can be specified in *Survey* to perform user-directed form navigation expressed, effectively, as computed 'goto' (switch-like) statements. Users are also no longer limited to using one form to edit a row of data. *Survey* allows multiple forms to edit a row of collected data, which can assist in a variety of situations including longitudinal studies.

4.1.3 Tables

While *Survey* focuses on collecting and editing data, *Tables* focuses on displaying collected data to the user [8]. *Survey* serves as the primary tool to manipulate an individual row, while *Tables* provides functionality to display and interact with the entire data set. *Tables* serves as a platform to host what is essentially a webpage, allowing customizations via HTML, CSS, and JavaScript. Views of the data can be both tabular or graphical depending on the context and what is appropriate for an end user's task. Views can also link to other views or launch other ODK apps.

The flexibility provided by *Tables* greatly increases the usability of the 2.0 tool suite. Deployment architects can capture complex workflows and decision logic in *Tables*. For example, consider a

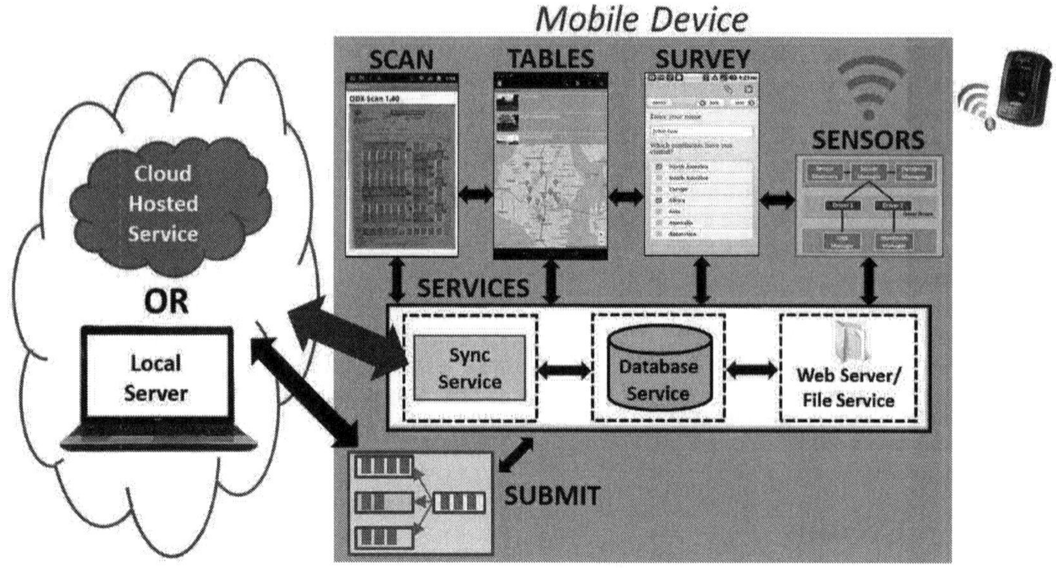

Figure 1: ODK 2.0 modular framework's five mobile tools are used in concert to create customizable *mobile data management* applications. The five ODK mobile 'apps' that comprise the framework are *Services*, *Survey*, *Tables*, *Scan*, *Sensors*, and *Submit*.

longitudinal study that needs to revisit subjects at multiple time points within a deployment. The data collector might be expected to follow different steps or complete a different set of forms when enrolling new subjects than when following up with existing ones. In an ODK 1.x deployment, the correct procedure must be imparted to a data collector through training. As a workflow becomes more complex, the training and support materials (e.g., flow charts) must increase as well. With *Tables*, however, the correct logic can be encoded in the app, both lowering the training burden and increasing compliance to the study protocol. Upon opening *Tables*, a collector would be presented with an HTML page with options to enroll or revisit a subject. When selecting the correct option, a new page would be opened that contains instructions and the set of forms required. Selecting one of these forms would then open *Survey* to permit data collection. While *Tables* apps will typically reference files (web content) stored on the device and synchronized via *Services* (in support of disconnected operations), deployment architects can also choose to issue network requests.

4.1.4 Scan

Scan bridges the gap between paper and digital data collection without forcing organizations to wholly adopt either scheme [13]. Paper remains an integral component in the workflows and data management processes of many development organizations, filling niches where digital systems are not currently appropriate [14]. *Scan* provides these organizations with a tool to quickly and easily digitize their paper forms in disconnected environments. Paper forms are adapted by adding *Scan*-compatible data input components, which include QR codes, multiple choice bubbles and checkboxes, structured hand-written number boxes, and free-form hand-written text boxes. Both digital and physical versions of this form are generated: a *Survey* form definition and a JPEG image file that can be used to print and distribute the *Scan*-compatible form. *Scan* can digitize completed forms in the field by taking a picture with the device's camera. Computer vision algorithms, running on the device, process and segment the form image into snippets corresponding to the individual data components [13]. These snippets (excluding free-form, hand-written text boxes that *Scan* cannot digitize programmatically) are then fed into classifiers that digitize the respective values. The digitized values can be reviewed and free-form, hand-written text values transcribed by viewing the form instance in *Survey* or *Tables*. All image processing is performed on the device without the need for an Internet connection. Form images can be processed in real time, typically requiring less than one minute per form, or saved and batch processed at a later time.

4.1.5 Sensors

Sensors simplifies the task of integrating external hardware sensors into an organization's data collection and management workflow [7]. For example, a medical application might use a pulse-oximeter during screening, or a vaccine refrigerator might need to report its temperature for regular audits. To address these requirements, *Sensors* provides a modular framework for organizations to implement drivers and user-level applications for third-party sensors that integrate into the ODK 2.0 ecosystem. The driver-level implementation and the user application are developed independently, and *Sensors* provides a common interface that abstracts communication channels between the two domains. This lets framework software programmers develop sensor drivers that can be reused by multiple user applications, while deployment architects can abstract sensor particulars and focus on their particular usage scenario needs. The *Sensors* app integrates with *Services* database directly, providing easy integration of sensors into complex data collection and management workflows.

4.1.6 Submit

The ODK 2.0 framework is built with performance in disconnected environments as a core tenant of its design philosophy. However, the synchronization service provided in *Services* requires Internet connectivity before data can be shared among devices. Despite growing access to cell coverage throughout the world, sufficient bandwidth to share the megabytes and gigabytes of data generated by data management applications is not always available, convenient, or cost efficient. *Submit* provides a framework for organizations to adapt their applications to share data using appropriate technologies for their various network conditions and data communication needs [10]. A variety of networking and data transfer technologies are exposed, ranging from peer-to-peer communications technologies (e.g., Bluetooth, WiFi Direct) to more traditional cellular and WiFi access. Deployment architects can prioritize which data should be shared using which technologies under what circumstances. For example, a clinic might share patient records over Bluetooth connections, schedule high-priority case files to be uploaded to the cloud over cell service as it becomes available, and perform regularly scheduled full synchronizations at Internet cafes. *Submit* separates networking implementations from application logic by exposing a service API with which to schedule data transfers or receive notifications about changing conditions.

4.2 Data and Configuration Management

ODK 2.0 data management applications consist of survey definitions, web content, configuration files, data tables, and data rows. These are consumed by the framework to define the control flow, user interface, schema, data validation logic, and business logic of the application. Departing from the ODK 1.x framework, which uses an XForm-based hierarchical document model, the ODK 2.0 framework stores data in a relational database on the Android device. The presentation layer can execute arbitrarily complex SQL queries (e.g., joins, unions), vastly increasing the expressive capability of the 2.0 framework. This expressiveness is required for complex workflow decisions, such as the disaster response case study in Section 5.4 that requires queries of previously collected beneficiary data to determine future distributions. Relational databases also permit more complex relationships between data sets. Dependent data sets, similar to ODK 1.x's 'repeat groups' concept, that were previously store in the same document are now stored in a separate data table allowing the deployment architect to define business logic to maintain their linkage with other data sets.

The ODK 2.0 framework uses a cloud component to provide robust permanent storage of data and configuration information. The data management application interacts with the cloud component through RESTful interfaces. The ODK 2.0 cloud component manages the 1) user permissions (user authentication and group membership), 2) slowly changing configuration (configuration files, form definitions, data table definitions), and 3) frequently changing data (content of the data tables and associated row-level media attachments). To support disconnected operations *Services* uses the ODK 2.0 synchronization protocol to maintain a filtered snapshot of the user permissions and a full snapshot of its configuration and data onto each mobile device. Upon connecting to the Internet, the mobile device initiates the synchronization protocol to reconcile changes and update its local state to a new, reconciled snapshot of the cloud component's content.

On the device, a user's identity is established via a successful login to an ODK cloud component. Thereafter, the user's identity and permissions are cached until the user resets his or her credentials or until the device is next synchronized with the cloud component. During this disconnected period of operation, successfully unlocking the device is considered sufficient to re-confirm a user's identity. There are 4 classes of users: (1) anonymous and/or unauthenticated users, (2) authenticated *unprivileged users* with permissions to read and modify a subset of the data, (3) authenticated *superusers* with permissions to read and modify all data, (4) authenticated *administrators* can read and modify all data, update user permissions, and change the configuration files that specify the data management application. Administrators and superusers can manage which authenticated users can see or modify which rows. Unprivileged users may be given access and modification rights to individual rows that unauthenticated or anonymous users cannot access and/or modify.

4.3 Synchronization Protocol

The ODK 2.0 data synchronization protocol is designed to be adaptable in extreme networking environments with high latencies, low bandwidths, and long periods of disconnected operation. To accommodate these varying conditions, the synchronization protocol was designed to use a small granularity of change-tracking to enable smaller data transmission and simplify conflict resolution. A single database row was chosen as the base unit of the synchronization protocol to follow the design principles of ODK 2.0 outlined in Section 2.2. Tracking synchronization state at the data-row-level ensures the efficiency of the synchronization protocol by using a reasonably small unit of data. A common use case for ODK 2.0 entails multiple enumerators collecting longitudinal data over the span of many days with no network connectivity. Based on feedback from partners, off-the-shelf file-based solutions (e.g., Dropbox, OneDrive) are not sufficient as the probability of having multiple enumerators edit the same file during long periods of disconnected operation is very high. In these file-based solutions, resolving conflicts once connectivity is re-established is challenging. These issues are avoided with a row-based solution because the probability that multiple enumerators touch the same rows (e.g., visit the same sites) decreases; thus, less conflicts are generated.

Data rows use globally unique primary keys to track the data stored at the row level. If any data in the row changes, an new ETAG (a universally unique identifier) is generated to identify that changes have been made to the row. By tracking changes at the row level, the bulk of the database content on the device can stay in sync with the server without any communication overhead. Names of any files attached to these data rows are also globally unique, thus only a single instance needs to be transmitted for multiple rows to reference it. The files themselves are stored on the device's file system and treated as immutable once referenced by a data row. The server maintains a manifest of the application-level files, their hashes, and their size. It computes a unique ETAG from this manifest content. If the ETAG of the last application-level file manifest on the device does not match the corresponding ETAG on the server, then the application-level files have changed. In this case, the device then scans its folders to confirm that its local copies match those in the server manifest, resolving any conflicts. A similar interaction is repeated for table-level files.

The server assigns a schema ETAG and a version ETAG to each data table when it is created. This lets the device verify that its table schemas match those on the server and, if a version ETAG differs but the schema ETAGs match, the client knows that the device's copy of the rows are out of sync with the server. Every row is tracked with a version ETAG and a synchronization state: 'synced', 'new_row', 'changed', 'deleted', 'in_conflict', or 'synced_pending_files'. For each table, the rows in the 'new_row', 'changed', and 'deleted' states are processed. If these rows do not have conflicting changes on the server, the device's synchronization state for these data rows transitions into the 'synced_pending_files' state (or are removed, for those formerly in the 'deleted' state). Finally, for each data table, the data rows in the 'synced_pending_files' state are processed. Before beginning a synchronization, the user can choose whether to perform a possibly bandwidth intensive upload and/or download file attachments from the server. The choice enables users to optimize their use cases for the currently-available communication bandwidth and cost. If bandwidth is low or cost is high, they may elect to do nothing, leaving the rows in the 'synced _pending_files.' This recognizes that transmission of files over lower-bandwidth communications channels is generally both time- and cost- prohibitive. However, users in extremely remote locations may decided that the few times they reach Internet connectivity it is worth the cost to perform a full synchronization based on their business requirements. The change-tracking design enables the synchronization protocol to adapt to currently-available communication bandwidths and costs.

When a row change on the device conflicts with a row change on the server, the change on the server is pulled down to the mobile device and the data row is marked as 'in_conflict'. The user must then resolve the conflict by either taking the server's change, the local change, or mix of the local change and the server change. If the user does not take the server's change, the synchronization state of the data row is updated to either 'changed' or 'deleted'. On the next synchronization, the local updates will then update the state on the server resolving the conflict.

4.4 Services Architecture

In the first iteration of ODK 2.0, tools were designed as completely independent Android apps that directly accessed a single shared Android database. The shared database presented users with a seamless data management application experience by smoothly transitioning between the tools (e.g., from *Tables* to *Survey* and back). The tools evolved to each include their own logic for accessing the database. From within the WebKit, the shared Android database was directly accessed via WebSQL. Stress tests of ODK app transitions exposed an instability between the WebKit and the Java layer's Android UI lifecycle[1]. Interleaving multiple Android UI lifecycle events during transactions resulted in deadlock if the outgoing activity did not release the transaction. The rate of deadlock occurrences varied by device model and OS version.

To resolve the deadlock issue the tools were re-architected to access the database through *Services*. The *Services* app provides a centralized database service that facilitates 1) an enhancement of initialization with automatic pre-population of tables with data rows from configuration files and 2) a reduction in overhead when opening an already-initialized database since *Services* maintains knowledge of the database state. After creating the database service we uncovered deficiencies within the Android database implementation including reference counting issues, database locking, and the database connection object being stored in thread local storage. These concerns led us to use a custom build of the SQLite database with a Java wrapper to eliminate the need to address behavioral differences across Android OS levels, 2) enable direct management of connections, 3) speed up opening of connections, 4) enable use of write-ahead-logging, and 5) enable changes to the native interface to minimize memory allocations.

While *Services* exposes content providers for a few basic static queries, the primary access to stored data is through the database service. The database service presents a restrictive API that does not expose database transactions or cursors. Instead, it exposes atomic-update primitives and queries that return snapshot-in-time result sets. This atomicity eliminates the possibility of a misbehaving client causing deadlock or leaking cursor resources. We chose a service over a content provider because 1) insert/update/delete operations would not capture the atomic update primitives used to simplify database management, 2) the full capabilities of a SQL query cannot be exposed without introducing our own expression language embedded within that URL as opposed to a service API, and 3) the ability to apply row-level access control cannot be expressed through a single content provider. To use a content provider would require a custom defined URL parser for SQL syntax. This would introduce custom non-standardized parsers causing a future pain point similar to the custom JavaRosa XForm definition and parser in ODK 1.x. Android Services have a 1 MB size limit on remote-procedure calls which is insufficient for large result sets. We implemented a primitive transport-level chunking interface using a client-side proxy to re-assemble chunks and only expose a higher-level abstraction to the tools. The client-side proxy provided additional benefits, such as caching and typed exception throwing across processes.

To create a unified user experience, all application-level settings were consolidated into the *Services* app. Additionally, the local web service and the synchronization service were centralized into *Services*. By placing the synchronization service within the same trusted layer as the database service, we could maintain a chain of custody for the authenticated user identity gained through the interactions with the cloud component. This authenticated user could then be used when enforcing row-level and table-level permissions inside the database service. More specifically, it enabled us to: 1) verify the active user's identity, 2) fetch that user's permissions from the cloud component, and 3) cache the user's identity and permissions within this trusted services layer where those permissions could be used within the database service to enforce the visibility and modification constraints on the data tables.

Services also simplifies tool updates. By effectively consolidating persistent state behind this service layer, individual tools can be upgraded in a rolling-update fashion without affecting persistent state. If the data representation (schema) needed to change, only a single update of the *Services* tool is required. Other benefits include defining our own service APIs makes it easier to port ODK software to other platforms and increased code reuse allows for improved testing and stability.

4.5 Experiments

To evaluate the revised architecture, six different variants of ODK 2.0 'apps' were created to compare performance timings. The builds differed by type of database, whether an Android service was used, and whether the logic was separated into two different APKs or combined into one. We performed the tests on three different Android devices, across a spectrum of performance capabilities: a ~$40 Vodaphone purchased in Kenya, a Nexus 7 tablet (a device commonly used by our partners), and a Nexus 6 phone. We used Android OS versions commonly found in our target regions.

The setup used to evaluate performance consisted of an ODK 2.0 data management application and automated Android UI tests. The application queried 200 rows of a 3000-row data set in succession until 100 iterations had been performed. A timestamp was recorded by the application before the query was issued, when the query results returned, and when the application had finished rendering the UI elements on the screen. Table 1 presents the average query turnaround time, the average WebKit rendering time, and the overall (Full RTT) times. It compares queries performed through the service API with the service and caller residing in separate APKs (the standard ODK 2.0 configuration), queries performed through the service API with the service and caller bundled into the same APK, and queries performed directly against the database without any service intermediary. These tests show that restructuring our tools to use a service-oriented architecture (SOA) did not incur prohibitive performance penalties. Comparing the *SOA Multi APKs* timings and the *Direct DB Access* timings showed a ~150 ms overhead with SOA; which is well below the 940 ms rendering time incurred by the WebKit and is below the limit of perceivable delay.

An alternative architecture combines all tools (e.g., *Tables*, *Services*) required for a particular usage scenario into a single large multi-dex APK. The timings results in Table 1 (comparing *SOA Multi APKs* timings and *SOA Single APK*) shows that there was a performance penalty, perhaps due to the increased proportion of available memory consumed by application code within a single APK. Combining only *Tables* and *Services* incurred a 25-50 ms penalty on a high-end device. If this penalty were driven by appli-

[1]The WebKit performs synchronous calls to the Java layer, but only asynchronous calls from the Java layer to the WebKit are provided. Android lifecycle event handlers are synchronous and provide no mechanism for asynchronous resumption of lifecycle transitions.

Table 1: Database Query Timing Comparison of Different Implementations on three different Android Devices. Service-Oriented Architecture in Multiple APKs, vs Service-Oriented Architecture in Single APK, vs Direct Database Access.

Device & Operating System	*Architecture*	*Database Type*	*Query Avg. (ms)*	*Query Std. Dev*	*Webkit Render Avg. (ms)*	*Full RTT Avg. (ms)*	*Full RTT Coeff. of Var.*
Vodafone v4.4.2	SOA Multi APKs	custom	2572	60	1474	4046	2.98
Vodafone v4.4.2	SOA Single APK	custom	2635	222	1475	4110	6.81
Vodafone v4.4.2	Direct DB Access	custom	2518	62	1446	3964	3.21
Vodafone v4.4.2	SOA Multi APKs	default	2685	56	1509	4194	2.75
Vodafone v4.4.2	SOA Single APK	default	2692	74	1539	4231	3.28
Vodafone v4.4.2	Direct DB Access	default	2631	76	1504	4135	3.17
Nexus 7 v4.4.4	SOA Multi APKs	custom	881	102	1049	1930	8.02
Nexus 7 v4.4.4	SOA Single APK	custom	821	80	1063	1884	7.86
Nexus 7 v4.4.4	Direct DB Access	custom	613	77	974	1587	8.58
Nexus 7 v4.4.4	SOA Multi APKs	default	993	92	1047	2040	6.78
Nexus 7 v4.4.4	SOA Single APK	default	1083	106	1067	2150	7.75
Nexus 7 v4.4.4	Direct DB Access	default	1358	209	1043	2400	9.89
Nexus 6 v5.1	SOA Multi APKs	custom	402	52	944	1347	17.63
Nexus 6 v5.1	SOA Single APK	custom	425	53	968	1393	16.61
Nexus 6 v5.1	Direct DB Access	custom	261	34	942	1202	17.87
Nexus 6 v5.1	SOA Multi APKs	default	615	84	956	1571	14.54
Nexus 6 v5.1	SOA Single APK	default	663	101	995	1658	13.36
Nexus 6 v5.1	Direct DB Access	default	386	41	942	1328	14.52

cation code size, then an SOA would be more performant than a monolithic APK should the six ODK 2.0 tools be combined. Tests to determine how the SOA scales given changing database query sizes were also performed. For this round of tests, the test setup again consisted of an ODK 2.0 data management application and automated Android UI tests. The application repeatedly queried a 3000-row data set with a fixed query size (one of 2, 20, 200 or 2000 rows) until 100 iterations had been performed via the Android UI tests. In this case, no UI elements were rendered after the query results were returned. The application recorded a timestamp before the query was issued and when query results returned. Table 2 shows the average round-trip time and standard deviation for the database queries. Table 2 shows the times for a Nexus 6 running the 5.1 version of the Android OS and a Vodafone running the 4.4.2 version of the Android OS. These results show that our query times scale as expected with a lower end device taking proportionately longer than a more powerful device.

Table 2: Avg Database Query RTT vs Number of Rows Queried

Rows	*Nexus 6 Avg. RTT (ms)*	*Nexus 6 Std. Dev (ms)*	*Vodafone Avg. RTT (ms)*	*Vodafone Std. Dev (ms)*
2	207	48	483	46
20	233	56	549	46
200	402	61	975	66
2000	2156	87	6008	139

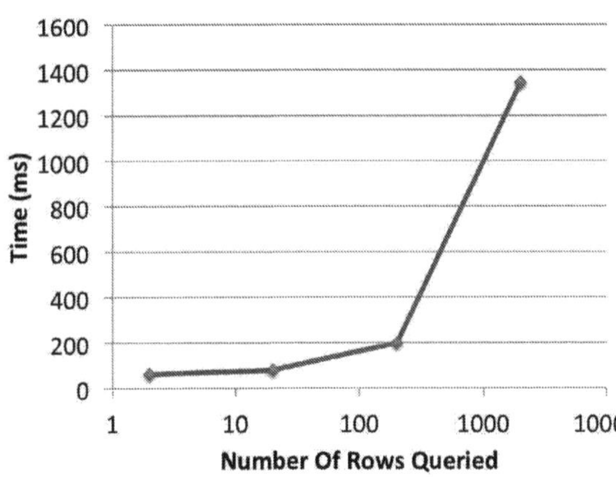

Figure 2: Nexus 6 5.1 Average Java To JavaScript Transfer Time vs. Number Of Rows Queried

Finally, the amount of time spent marshaling database query results between the Java layer and the JavaScript layer was measured. To determine the transfer time between these layers, an ODK 2.0 application and automated suite of Android UI tests were used with the 3000-row data set. A timestamp was recorded in a log file when the Java layer obtained the query result and when the JavaScript layer received the query result. Figure 2 shows the average time difference between when the database query result was available in the Java layer to when the database query result was returned to the JavaScript layer for 100 test iterations. This data shows that the transfer time from the Java to JavaScript layer did not have a major performance impact.

5. CASE STUDIES

A guiding principle of ODK has been to work with field partners during technology development to validate the suitability of the tool suite in resource-constrained environments. This section presents case studies from partners working in global health, disaster management, and other areas to demonstrate and verify the reuse, flexibility, and extensibility of ODK 2.0 application framework, as well as to report key lessons learned. We enumerate requirements for each case study in Table 3 that were identified as necessary in the ODK 2.0 framework but are not fulfilled by the ODK 1.x tools.

5.1 Childhood Pneumonia

The mPneumonia project is a partnership with PATH, a non-government global health organization, that supports health workers in low-resource environments. PATH sought to create a mobile application to improve health care providers' diagnosis and management of childhood pneumonia, a leading cause of disease deaths for children under 5 [17]. The resulting diagnosis and treatment application assisted lightly trained healthcare workers with screening

Table 3: Case Study ODK 2.0 Feature Requirement Summary

	Childhood Pneumonia	*Chimpanzee Behavior Tracking*	*HIV Clinical Trial*	*Disaster Response*	*Mosquito Infection Tracking*	*Tuberculosis Patient Records*
Complex / Non-Linear Workflows	X	X	X	X	X	
Link Longitudinal Data To Collected Data	X		X	X	X	X
Data Security and User Permissions	X		X	X	X	X
Reuse of Data Fields Across Forms			X	X		
Bidirectional Synchronization	X		X	X	X	X
Customizable Form Presentation	X		X	X		
Custom JavaScript Apps		X	X	X	X	X
Sensor Integration	X					
Paper Digitization						X
Custom Data Types Update Multiple Fields in a Single User Action	X	X		X	X	

tasks. *Survey* was used to digitize complex medical workflows and customize their form presentation, while *Sensors* was used to integrate a USB sensor to record a patient's oxygen saturation.

Previous projects found that digitizing the World Health Organization's Integrated Management of Childhood Illness (IMCI) protocol on PDAs led to increased adherence while maintaining examination time [15]. However, when other organizations tried to re-implement IMCI using ODK 1.x, they struggled to map IMCI's complex medical workflow to XForms. ODK 2.0 addressed the complexity with *Survey*, which allowed a non-programmer global health intern to digitize the IMCI protocol using an Excel workflow description format. Furthermore, the layout, styling, and presentation of each prompt in the form was customized to meet the specific needs of the mPneumonia project. These customizations were simplified by making changes to HTML and CSS, which enabled a rapid iterative design process.

The mPneumonia project added a pulse and a blood oxygen saturation reading from the patient to IMCI. The *Sensors* framework connected the pulse-ox sensor to the mobile device, allowing sensor readings to be written directly to the patient record. ODK 1.x only allows a single value to be recorded to the data model for an individual user action. A pulse-ox sensor reads two values at a time, requiring updates to two database columns. ODK 2.0 allows the specification of custom data types with multiple database columns enabling the pulse-ox data to be recorded in a single action.

To evaluate usability, feasibility and acceptability, PATH conducted studies in Ghana and India. They interviewed 8 health administrators, 30 health care providers, and 30 caregivers. PATH found that mPneumonia was feasible to integrate into rural healthcare workers workflow and had the potential to improve patient care. Interviewees reported mPneumonia was "easy to use" and lent confidence to their diagnosis and treatments [18].

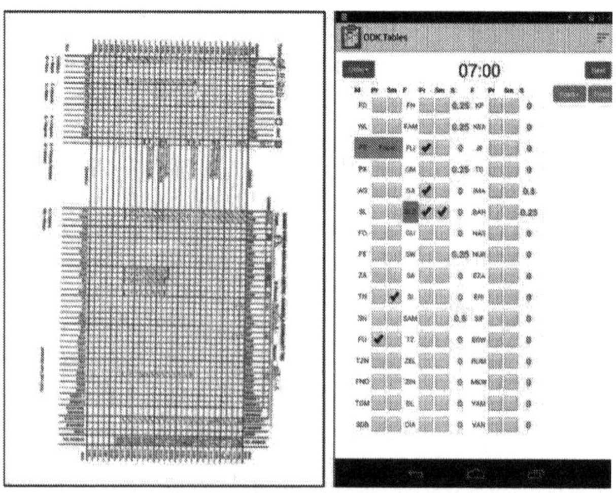

Figure 3: The paper version of JGI's chimpanzee behavior tracking form (left) compared to *Tables* digital version (right)

5.2 Chimpanzee Behavior Tracking

The Jane Goodall Institute (JGI), an early adopter of ODK 1.x, successfully replaced multiple existing paper data forms with ODK 1.x. However, after several attempts, they were unable to digitize one of their most important data collection efforts and needed an alternative to form-based data entry to be able to track chimpanzee behavior in real time. In this scenario, park rangers follow troupes of chimpanzees through the jungle with a clipboard and a paper form. The paper form is organized into a grid format, with names of chimpanzees and boxes indicating presence or absence, proximity to the group leader, and estrus state. A new form is completed every 15 minutes, and at the end of the day the information is transcribed and added to a database. There was no way to enforce internal consistency or data quality when using paper. However, the paper form's grid structure prevented the conversion to an ODK 1.x question based workflow. An example of the paper form is shown in Figure 3. Maintaining the format of the data collected is very significant to the organization, since it has been used for years and the rangers feel comfortable with it.

Conceptualizing the workflow as a series of webpages let the form be converted to an ODK 2.0 *Tables* application. The grid, created using an HTML table, represents a database row that associates the current time and the chimp ID. Edits to the data update the corresponding database row. Additional value is added by pre-populating information from the previous time point, lowering the burden on the ranger by reducing the duplicate effort of re-entering data every 15 minutes.

While more complex than other examples, this application was able to written with a much smaller codebase than would be required using native Android. The database is defined declaratively using CSV files. The application consists of a single page of HTML and roughly 1200 lines of JavaScript. While this approach requires some basic programming knowledge, to do the same task in Android programming constructs would require extensive knowledge of the Android persistence APIs, familiarity with the Android UI framework, an understanding of Android's activity lifecycle. A *Tables*-based approach allowed developers to leverage ODK 2.0 framework for most functionality and focus on solely on the UI to create an encapsulated and manageable mobile application.

5.3 HIV Clinical Trial

Adaptive Strategies for Preventing and Treating Lapses of Retention in Care (AdaPT-R) is a multi-year University of California San Francisco (UCSF) study that tracks HIV patient clinic visits. The AdaPT-R case study demonstrates ODK 2.0's applicability to medical trials that are longitudinal and require patient follow-ups at specific locations. The study requires daily synchronization of a field worker's mobile device so that the medical workflows and study parameters can be updated appropriately.

AdaPT-R is deployed in three clinics in Kisumu County, Kenya and two clinics in Migori County, Kenya that combined serve approximately 65,000 patients. It is a randomized control trial studying 1,745 enrolled patients of the approximately 17,000 HIV patients. The non-linear workflow needed to ensure protocol adherence along with historical data to track lapses in care required the flexibility of ODK 2.0. The project also required an ODK 2.0 application to integrate with their existing medical records systems. The UCSF team uses the ODK 2.0 tool suite to collect and synchronize patient data daily to an ODK Aggregate server. Once the data has been synchronized, it is combined with information from a separate medical records systems to determine patient status. The patient information is then synchronized to the field worker's phone, where it can be used during data collection the next day.

The AdaPT-R study has 18 employees using 17 Android devices to interact with patients. Research assistants were provided 1-2 hours of initial training and receive two ~30 min refresher trainings a year. Additional one-on-one training is provided by AdaPT-R's data manager in Kenya on an as-needed basis. Examples of one-on-one training include: 30-60 min trainings to familiarize site leads with ODK update process, and ~20-30 min to teach zipping files and logs from devices to send to manager for troubleshooting.

Early in the study, field workers experienced issues such as periodic application freezes because of database locking issues and sluggish navigation. The AdaPT-R workflow required users to move back and forth between *Tables* and *Survey*, thereby increasing the probability of database locking due to Android life cycle issues. The revised ODK 2.0's SOA, discussed in section 4.4, was built in response to some of the problems experienced by the AdaPT-R study. The AdaPT-R team deployed ODK's revised framework to one site initially and after experiencing immediate positive results decided to expedited the upgrade of the remaining sites.

Having all study participants available on the mobile device let the AdaPT-R team move devices between clinics without reconfiguring them (or physically moving paper files). This was helpful when devices broke or when the AdaPT-R team needed to reallocate a device to another clinic if one site had a higher volume of data entry compared to another. Additionally, AdaPT-R has research assistants who cover tasks for more than one clinic; having the data for multiple locations on a single device lets these employees use the same device for data entry at all locations.

When asked why they chose to use ODK 2.0, the co-primary investigator of the randomized control trial noted *"We needed a solution for capturing data from multiple forms and that would allow longitudinal follow-up of individual patients. We had experience with earlier versions of ODK, so the new features of 2.0 made it the only option for us if we wanted phone-based longitudinal form completion. Would definitely recommend ODK 2.0!"*

5.4 Disaster Response

The International Federation of Red Cross and Red Crescent (IFRC) is the world's largest humanitarian and development network that has millions of volunteers in 190 member National Societies. The diversity of use cases and business requirements of the National Societies demonstrate the need for a flexible, customizable system like ODK 2.0. A disaster response platform used by volunteers on the ground needs to be easily adaptable by a deployment architect since time is critical under these circumstances.

Figure 4: Red Cross enumerator using ODK to distribute goods in Belize after Hurricane Earl

The IFRC created prototype disaster response software using ODK 1.x for beneficiary registration and custom software for distributions. The IFRC then contacted us to figure out how ODK could be used to create a single mobile application to handle both registrations and distributions. ODK 1.x was not suited to the task due to missing features (Section 2.1). Bidirectional synchronization is required to maintain a consistent database of beneficiaries and delivered distributions across all devices and distribution centers to prevent fraud, enable auditing, etc. User permissions are required to ensure that field workers see only the appropriate list of beneficiaries relevant to their work and cannot update data fields beyond the scope of their responsibilities. Their complex workflow that reuses certain data fields requires a more robust interface than basic form based navigation provided by ODK 1.x.

We worked with the IFRC to prototype a solution using a combination of *Survey* forms a *Tables* data navigation. The IFRC's goal to build a reference disaster response/recovery and crisis management application that leverages ODK 2.0 to handle common data collection and field management tasks. This reference application could then be adapted to the diverse use cases of its 190 member societies. The IFRC conducted an initial field feasibility study using ODK 2.0 to distribute disaster-aid cash at two locations in Jamaica involving 93 participants. The initial study had positive results, and the IFRC plans to conduct deployment pilots during actual disaster responses in the next few months to further evaluate ODK 2.0 usage for cash distributions during emergencies. ODK 2.0's customizable workflow, user permissions, rule and adherence enforcement, disconnected operations, and eventual data synchronization were critical features to successfully coordinate distribution of cash and supplies.

5.5 Mosquito Infection Tracking

Led by Monash University, 'Eliminate Dengue' is an international research collaboration focused on reducing the spread of Dengue, Chikungunya, and Zika. The program operates across a variety of countries, languages, terrains, and worker skill levels. Currently, Eliminate Dengue ODK 2.0 application is deployed in Brazil, Columbia, Indonesia, Australia, and Vietnam. Their operational workflow requires ODK 2.0's bidirectional sync protocol to provide historical as well as timely data to their field workers during site visits to remote environments.

The Eliminate Dengue program is developing a method to reduce the spread of dengue by introducing the naturally occurring Wolbachia bacteria into local mosquito populations. This bacteria reduces the ability of mosquitoes to transmit dengue between people. Workers monitor mosquito reproduction at field sites until the bacteria is established in a critical mass of the local population and propagation is self sustaining. This requires repeated weekly visits to field collection sites. The ODK 2.0 framework is used to provide workers with an interactive map of site locations, historical data about each site, individualized instructions on what tasks to perform at which sites, and a data capture application.

The Eliminate Dengue team designed and developed their own custom ODK 2.0 *Tables* application using consultants specializing in web development. They decided to use *Tables* because *"developers don't like to be restricted,"* and *Tables* gave them the flexibility to customize their solution to their needs without being in *Survey's* question rendering framework. Furthermore, *Tables* let them *"focus on web dev"* rather than worry about editing Android code, as would have been necessary with an ODK 1.x solution. An example of a customization is their eschewing the provided Google Maps library for a runtime library called Leaflet.js[2] to serve their own map files from ODK 2.0's framework. This let them provide more accurate and customized maps to their workers in disconnected settings.

A key component of the program is regular visits to multiple sites over a period of weeks and months. These visits require historical data to be available to field workers, who may not be the only workers visiting the same site. This requirement was the driving factor in the Eliminate Dengue team's decision to use ODK 2.0 over ODK 1.x: when describing ODK 2.0's benefits, they said, *"we needed two-way synchronization"* and that all other benefits were discovered and leveraged later: *"we had a requirement to send data to the devices as well as receive from them."*

The greatest challenge to the team has been logistical: the velocity with which they are developing and deploying requires frequent changes to the data model. Neither ODK 1.x nor ODK 2.0 is well suited to this type of change. The Eliminate Dengue team is using JSON objects in the database to work around the issue, but in general changing data models remain an open problem in the ODK 2.0 framework. The trade-offs between a document based model storage vs row based storage is further discussed in section 6. However, the program manager reports *"the app is scaling quite well"* and that ODK 2.0 apps are *"quite easy to use and we haven't had any acceptance issues."*

5.6 Tuberculosis Patient Records

Mercy Corps' effort to combat tuberculosis in Pakistan provides a case study for the ODK 2.0 framework's ability to serve rural medical facilities that maintain paper workflows. This project explored how to incorporate less expensive paper collection methods into a hybrid workflow to reduce data collection and aggregation times in disconnected environments. The large data sets generated by these facilities, coupled with their unreliable Internet connectivity, provided scalability tests for the ODK 2.0 framework's service architecture and synchronization capabilities.

Mercy Corps maintains paper based patient records in local clinics, which are subsequently aggregated and used to generate reports for administrators. Paper records are valuable in this environment since they are cheap, trusted, and easily understood. However, shipping paper records to central facilities and transcribing data from paper to digital systems hinders reporting efforts with significant time delays and financial burdens [5]. We partnered with Mercy Corps to pilot ODK 2.0 effectiveness at streamlining the digitization and validation of their patient records and providing basic reporting to clinicians in the field. The pilot ran for three months with four field workers in two districts in Pakistan working with 122 patients. Mercy Corps' health register was converted to a *Scan*-compatible format. Their register had 39 data input fields, which expanded into 121 user data columns in the ODK database when factoring in metadata and image snippets for each field. Field workers used *Scan* to digitize patient records as they were filled in at the clinics, then validated the digitization with *Survey* at the point of capture. Additionally, a data reporting mechanism was developed on *Tables* for field workers to track overdue patient visits.

When Internet connectivity became available, usually at an Internet cafe, new data would be synchronized and used to generate administrative reports. The wide rows and extensive metadata for each patient caused the database size to grow, and with the spotty connectivity offered by Internet cafes, health workers struggled to upload the thousands of files generated each day. Our responses to these challenges are discussed in Sections 4.3 and 4.4.

The custom data management application built on *Tables* provided health workers with a summary of patient data and reminders of upcoming appointments. This required disconnected historical queries of patients under the care of the health care worker using the device. Additionally, workers would often delay their validation of transcribed records until after a visit was complete, sometimes validating an entire day's worth of visits in a single batch. In this case it was essential that they had disconnected access only to their own patients to prevent them from mistakenly altering records of other patients. To address this issue of filtering the database based on the context of the user, user and group permissions were developed, as discussed in Section 4.2.

At the conclusion of the pilot, Mercy Corps interviewed its field workers about their experience and performed timing comparisons between workflows. The interviews discussed by Ali [5] revealed that workers were particularly enthused about the reporting on the device, with one stating *"follow up visit report has revolutionized our work. Now, we will never miss out any patient."* Data collection was slowed by the need to validate transcribed data, but the transfer process was reduced from days via courier to minutes via connected synchronization [5]. The pilot showed that ODK 2.0 is robust enough to handle large datasets in disconnected environments and that organizations unable to fully adopt direct-to-digital workflows can benefit from field digitization.

6. DISCUSSION

For computing technology to solve global problems, researchers need to push not only the boundaries of technology, but also the boundaries of how the technology can be applied in various environments with differing constraints. Two-thirds of the world's population have access to mobile phones; however, technical limitations prevent billions of users from adopting some of the revolutionary capabilities of these mobile devices [6, 23]. The concept of "applied computer science research" is needed to extend the reach of technology to include the billions of people in the world that currently have limited access to it. To address this, research is needed to answer: "what are the proper abstractions and frameworks for mobile devices that are appropriate for a broader range of technical skills and familiarity?" In resource-constrained environments common assumptions used by designers and developers (e.g., connectivity and power availability) can vary significantly between contexts. For example, the availability of power can vary from an

[2]JavaScript mapping library: http://leafletjs.com/

always-on grid connection, to sporadic grid connections, to having to pay someone to use a generator or car battery to charge a mobile device. Depending on your location in the world, mobile devices move from disconnected environments to connected environments with dramatically different bandwidths and latencies.

The ODK research project seeks to identify appropriate technologies for resource-constrained environments and identify barriers that prevent existing solutions in high-resource contexts from being similarly adopted in these settings. ODK 2.0 was created to address the limitations uncovered through the widespread adoption of ODK 1.x. Field experience with real organizations is needed to understand the problems that prevent adoption of mobile data management solutions. Conceptually akin to testbeds (e.g., PlanetLab [11]), by working with organizations to build real systems that are deployed in regions with challenging constraints, we were able to test ODK 2.0 in a way that far extends beyond the lab environment. Deploying at scale reveals different classes of problems. ODK 2.0 has been piloted or is deployed in over 18 countries by more than 15 organizations. By listening to our partners and understanding their needs, we addressed limitations of ODK 1.x. To understand the contextual limitations, we developed and maintained a suite of tools and gave them to non-programmers to use in their mobile applications. While ODK is designed to operate in extremely diverse environments, the lessons learned can be applied generally to system design to make mobile system platforms more resilient to adverse and varying conditions.

A problem that has not been fully solved by the ODK 2.0 is how to handle frequent changes to the data model, as experienced by Eliminate Dengue (Section 5.5). Initial design discussions for ODK 2.0 pitted a document-based data model against a row-based model. The document-based model allows for easier updates to the data model, but extracting results and generating reports after multiple data models have been used becomes difficult and often requires hiring a programmer to write code to merge the data and perform data cleaning. The row-based model employed by ODK requires organizations to establish a schema before deploying, front-loading the costs, and is difficult to update if the schema must be altered, but it makes reporting simple. Ultimately, the row-based model was chosen because organizations have more existing expertise in understanding their business workflow and making a flexible schema requires less programming knowledge than dealing with data merging and cleaning issues. However, a scenario like Eliminate Dengue's, in which rapidly changing needs on the ground require frequent changes confirmed that if you have programming resources to handle the data merging and cleaning then a document-based model can make for easier iterative design.

ODK 2.0 focuses on scale and adaptability instead of a novel single purpose application useful only for limited cases. Through the generalizable application framework, ODK 2.0 allows users of varying technical skill levels to create custom solutions that support a wide range of scenarios. ODK 2.0 aims to create base APIs, standards, and free reusable libraries to minimize the start-up costs for organizations, researchers, and companies seeking to participate in the space. To create an ecosystem, ODK uses the permissive Apache 2 open-source to enable free use and encapsulation of the technology. This empowers companies to have business models based around both creating products with additional features or providing consulting assistance to global aid workers.

7. FUTURE WORK

Future expansion of the ODK 2.0 framework will focus on security and usability improvements. Currently, the local database contains a full copy of the data since the authenticated user may change and have different access privileges. However, for sensitive information it would be preferable to have a data wipe feature, where on a user authentication the previously synchronized data on the device would be deleted to increase security. This poses a trade off between bandwidth to continually re-download the subset of data versus data security. As ODK's 2.0 framework's abstractions mature from more successful deployments and the user base grows, we plan to start creating additional graphical tools to further reduce the skills needed to build and customize mobile data management applications. For example, we are working on a PC-based tool called "Application Designer" for creating, customizing and previewing forms. It will include a theme generator to help novice users graphically select basic styles and colors which will then automatically generated into a basic CSS style file. Similarly, the "Application Designer" will include a help wizard to generate basic *Table* views that will auto generate the corresponding HTML and JavaScript files.

8. CONCLUSION

ODK 2.0 provides development organizations with a new mobile framework to build data collection and management services for resource-constrained environments. This paper presents lessons learned from creating an application framework that makes mobile devices more useful in contexts where high-income countries' engineering assumptions do not necessarily match the infrastructure realities in resource-constrained communities.

Building a real system used by development organizations in differing domains shows the general applicability of the mobile framework. By piloting with these organizations and incorporating their needs and feedback into the development process, the ODK 2.0 framework was made robust to a variety of challenges met in the field including extreme mobile networking conditions such as low bandwidth, high latencies, and long periods of disconnected activity. ODK 2.0 provides a generalizable application framework for users with varying technical skill levels to create customizable mobile data management solutions that address global problems in resource-constrained environments. Implementing ODK 2.0's framework as an SOA yielded benefits in the areas of upgradability, security enforcement, management of global state, and future portability, without incurring a significant performance cost. ODK 2.0 provides a second, complementary, open-source toolkit to the ODK 1.x framework, that is targeted at *deployment architects* and is easy to use and easy to scale. By expanding the variety of use cases that ODK technology can be adapted to, the ODK 2.0 tool suite helps to achieve ODK's goal of "magnifying human resources through technology."

9. ACKNOWLEDGEMENTS

Both ODK 1.x and 2.0 were ideas of ODK visionary Gaetano Borriello. ODK has been a team effort that involved many people at the University of Washington. We would like to acknowledge Rohit Chaudhri, Nicola Dell, Joshua Fan, Ori Levari, Shahar Levari, Li Lin, Luyi Lu, Madhav Murthy, and Sang-Wha Sien for their work on ODK 2.0. We also thank Adam Rea, Sandy Kaplan, and Kurtis Heimerl for their insightful feedback on this paper. Additionally, we would like to thank all the organizations (e.g., PATH, JGI, ADAPT, IFRC, Eliminate Dengue, Village Reach, Mercy Corps) who used ODK and provided feedback. Finally, we thank our anonymous reviewers and our shepherd Rajesh Balan, for their guidance and suggestions. The material in this paper is based upon work supported by Bill and Melinda Gates Foundation Grant No. OPP-1132099 and USAID Agreement AID-OAA-A-13-00002.

10. REFERENCES

[1] Apache Cordova. https://cordova.apache.org/, Dec 2016.

[2] Intel XDK. https://software.intel.com/intel-xdk, Dec 2016.

[3] Ionic Framework. http://ionicframework.com/, Dec 2016.

[4] Sartphone OS Market Share, 2016 Q2. https://www.idc.com/prodserv/smartphone-os-market-share.jsp, Dec 2016.

[5] S. Ali, R. Powers, J. Beorse, A. Noor, F. Naureen, N. Anjum, M. Ishaq, J. Aamir, and R. Anderson. Odk scan: Digitizing data collection and impacting data management processes in pakistan's tuberculosis control program. *Future Internet*, 8(4):51, 2016.

[6] E. Brewer, M. Demmer, B. Du, M. Ho, M. Kam, S. Nedevschi, J. Pal, R. Patra, S. Surana, and K. Fall. The case for technology in developing regions. *Computer*, 38(6):25–38, 2005.

[7] W. Brunette, R. Sodt, R. Chaudhri, M. Goel, M. Falcone, J. Van Orden, and G. Borriello. Open data kit sensors: A sensor integration framework for android at the application-level. In *Proceedings of the 10th International Conference on Mobile Systems, Applications, and Services*, MobiSys '12, pages 351–364, New York, NY, USA, 2012. ACM.

[8] W. Brunette, S. Sudar, N. Worden, D. Price, R. Anderson, and G. Borriello. Odk tables: Building easily customizable information applications on android devices. In *Proceedings of the 3rd ACM Symposium on Computing for Development*, ACM DEV '13, pages 12:1–12:10, New York, NY, USA, 2013. ACM.

[9] W. Brunette, M. Sundt, N. Dell, R. Chaudhri, N. Breit, and G. Borriello. Open Data Kit 2.0: Expanding and Refining Information Services for Developing Regions. In *Proceedings of the 14th Workshop on Mobile Computing Systems and Applications*, HotMobile '13, pages 1–6, 2013.

[10] W. Brunette, M. Vigil, F. Pervaiz, S. Levari, G. Borriello, and R. Anderson. Optimizing mobile application communication for challenged network environments. In *Proceedings of the 2015 Annual Symposium on Computing for Development*, 2830644, 2015. ACM.

[11] B. Chun, D. Culler, T. Roscoe, A. Bavier, L. Peterson, M. Wawrzoniak, and M. Bowman. Planetlab: an overlay testbed for broad-coverage services. *SIGCOMM Comput. Commun. Rev.*, 33(3):3–12, 2003.

[12] B.-G. Chun, C. Curino, R. Sears, A. Shraer, S. Madden, and R. Ramakrishnan. Mobius: unified messaging and data serving for mobile apps. In *Proceedings of the 10th international conference on Mobile systems, applications, and services*, pages 141–154, 2307650, 2012. ACM.

[13] N. Dell, N. Breit, T. Chaluco, J. Crawford, and G. Borriello. Digitizing paper forms with mobile imaging technologies. In *Proceedings of the 2nd ACM Symposium on Computing for Development*, 2160604, 2012. ACM.

[14] N. Dell, T. Perrier, N. Kumar, M. Lee, R. Powers, and G. Borriello. Paper-digital workflows in global development organizations. In *Proceedings of the 18th ACM Conference on Computer Supported Cooperative Work and Social Computing*, pages 1659–1669, 2675145, 2015. ACM.

[15] B. DeRenzi, N. Lesh, T. Parikh, C. Sims, W. Maokla, M. Chemba, Y. Hamisi, D. S. hellenberg, M. Mitchell, and G. Borriello. e-imci: improving pediatric health care in low-income countries. In *Proceedings of the SIGCHI Conference on Human Factors in Computing Systems*, pages 753–762, 1357174, 2008. ACM.

[16] B. DeRenzi, C. Sims, J. Jackson, G. Borriello, and N. Lesh. A framework for case-based community health information systems. In *2011 IEEE Global Humanitarian Technology Conference*, pages 377–382, Oct 2011.

[17] A. S. Ginsburg, J. Delarosa, W. Brunette, S. Levari, M. Sundt, C. Larson, C. Tawiah Agyemang, S. Newton, G. Borriello, and R. Anderson. mpneumonia: Development of an innovative mhealth application for diagnosing and treating childhood pneumonia and other childhood illnesses in low-resource settings. *PloS one*, 10(10), 2015.

[18] A. S. Ginsburg, C. Tawiah Agyemang, G. Ambler, J. Delarosa, W. Brunette, S. Levari, C. Larson, M. Sundt, S. Newton, G. Borriello, and R. Anderson. mpneumonia, an innovation for diagnosing and treating childhood pneumonia in low-resource settings: A feasibility, usability and acceptability study in ghana. *PLOS ONE*, 11(10), 2016.

[19] S. Hao, N. Agrawal, A. Aranya, and C. Ungureanu. Building a delay-tolerant cloud for mobile data. In *2013 IEEE 14th International Conference on Mobile Data Management*, volume 1, pages 293–300, 2013.

[20] C. Hartung, Y. Anokwa, W. Brunette, A. Lerer, C. Tseng, and G. Borriello. Open Data Kit: Tools to Build Information Services for Developing Regions. In *Proceedings of the 4th ACM/IEEE International Conference on Information and Communication Technologies and Development*, ICTD '10, pages 1–12, 2010.

[21] T. S. Parikh, P. Javid, S. K., K. Ghosh, and K. Toyama. Mobile phones and paper documents: evaluating a new approach for capturing microfinance data in rural india. In *Proceedings of the SIGCHI Conference on Human Factors in Computing Systems*, pages 551–560, 1124857, 2006. ACM.

[22] L. Wei-Chih, M. Tierney, J. Chen, F. Kazi, A. Hubard, J. G. Pasquel, L. Subramanian, and B. Rao. Uju: Sms-based applications made easy. In *Proceedings of the First ACM Symposium on Computing for Development*, pages 1–11, 1926200, 2010. ACM.

[23] World Bank Group. *World Development Report 2016: Digital Dividends*. International Bank for Reconstruction and Development (World Bank), 1818 H Street NW, Washington DC, 20433, 2016.

Heimdall: A Privacy-Respecting Implicit Preference Collection Framework

Amir Rahmati
University of Michigan
rahmati@umich.edu

Earlence Fernandes
University of Michigan
earlence@umich.edu

Kevin Eykholt
University of Michigan
keykholt@umich.edu

Xinheng Chen
University of Michigan
xinheng@umich.edu

Atul Prakash
University of Michigan
aprakash@umich.edu

ABSTRACT

Many of the everyday decisions a user makes rely on the suggestions of online recommendation systems. These systems amass implicit (*e.g.,* location, purchase history, browsing history) and explicit (*e.g.,* reviews, ratings) feedback from multiple users, produce a general consensus, and provide suggestions based on that consensus. However, due to privacy concerns, users are uncomfortable with implicit data collection, thus requiring recommendation systems to be overly dependent on explicit feedback. Unfortunately, users do not frequently provide explicit feedback. This hampers the ability of recommendation systems to provide high-quality suggestions.

We introduce Heimdall, the first privacy-respecting implicit preference collection framework that enables recommendation systems to extract user preferences from their activities in a privacy respecting manner. The key insight is to enable recommendation systems to run a *collector* on a user's device and precisely control the information a collector transmits to the recommendation system back-end. Heimdall introduces *immutable blobs* as a mechanism to guarantee this property. We implemented Heimdall on the Android platform and wrote three example collectors to enhance recommendation systems with implicit feedback. Our performance results suggest that the overhead of immutable blobs is minimal, and a user study of 166 participants indicates that privacy concerns are significantly less when collectors record only specific information—a property that Heimdall enables.

Keywords

Privacy; Recommendation Systems; Implicit Feedback; Internet of Things

1. INTRODUCTION

Recommendations play an integral role in everyday decisions such as food and book choices. Online recommendation systems specialize in providing suggestions to help make these decisions, and often suggest new choices based on prior choices of an individual user or a large group. These systems have grown to greatly influence user decisions. A one-star increase in rating for the restaurant recommendation service Yelp, which draws more than 80 million unique visitors from the United States every month, has been shown to result in a $5-9\%$ increase in revenue [6, 27].

However, despite the influence of these systems, users are increasingly concerned about sharing sensitive data, especially on mobile devices [14]. This concern stems from the numerous intentional or unintentional privacy breaches that has happened in recent years [15]. Breaches can result from an over-claim of permissions [16], an overuse of permissions [37], or an outright misuse of permissions [16] by applications. To address user privacy concerns, recommendation systems utilize explicit feedback mechanisms, which provide users control over what data is shared.

Unfortunately, the amount of explicit feedback received is usually very small compared to the amount of feedback required for quality recommendations [8, 46]. This is especially true for recommendation systems that are not owned by the platform vendor (*e.g.,* Yelp app running on Android). Explicit feedback also requires extra effort from the user ranging from short interactions (*e.g.,* clicking on "check-in," "like," "up and down vote") to long interactions (*e.g.,* writing an in-depth review). Furthermore, users are more likely to provide this kind of explicit feedback after an extreme experience [7]. These combined factors result in sparse feedback data and hence lower-quality recommendations. This makes it difficult for current recommendation systems to accurately answer simple questions such as "What is the most popular theater in the area?" or "What time is the gym least crowded?" Previous research has hinted at implicit inference using user data as a possible solution to this problem [46].

To address user privacy concerns and data sparsity, we introduce Heimdall, the first preference collection framework that allows recommendation systems to extract implicit user preferences, while giving users control over how and where their data and identity is shared. Our design enforces that the user must explicitly consent to sharing any implicitly collected feedback before it is shared with the recommendation system back-end. We note that Heimdall does not provide any privacy guarantees once data is shared with the back-end—§5 contains a discussion of future work that might enable such a guarantee.

Heimdall allows third-parties to develop preference *collectors* for smartphone and smart home environments. A collector is a piece of code that accesses sensitive implicit data sources, performs pre-processing, and submits that data to its recommendation system back-end. Within Heimdall, collectors can access user data and are able to query trusted knowledge-base services (*e.g.,* Google Map) through Heimdall's secure API. Heimdall depends on the APIs hav-

Permission to make digital or hard copies of all or part of this work for personal or classroom use is granted without fee provided that copies are not made or distributed for profit or commercial advantage and that copies bear this notice and the full citation on the first page. Copyrights for components of this work owned by others than the author(s) must be honored. Abstracting with credit is permitted. To copy otherwise, or republish, to post on servers or to redistribute to lists, requires prior specific permission and/or a fee. Request permissions from permissions@acm.org.

MobiSys'17, June 19-23, 2017, Niagara Falls, NY, USA

© 2017 Copyright held by the owner/author(s). Publication rights licensed to ACM.

ISBN 978-1-4503-4928-4/17/06...$15.00

DOI: http://dx.doi.org/10.1145/3081333.3081334

ing known structures (*e.g.,* JSON, XML, YAML)—an API, by definition, must publicly declare the data format it uses. To share user preferences, collectors must declare in their manifest the type (*e.g.,* location) and granularity (*e.g.,* restaurant name) of the shared data, and the sources used to compute these preferences. Users have control over what data is shared and whether the submission should be anonymous or not.

Consider a restaurant recommendation collector. It continuously monitors a user's location, performs a reverse geocode on the GPS co-ordinates using an online service such as Google Places API, gets back a JSON object representing the address corresponding to the location. This JSON object has a known structure—it contains a field that represents the kind of location whose values might be "Restaurant," or "Drug Store." Heimdall requires collectors to declare the data they will disclose to the recommendation system cloud back-end. This declaration is expressed in terms of the structure and contents of the JSON data—the collector will declare that it will expose the JSON object only if the kind of location is "Restaurant." To ensure that the collector does not manipulate the other fields of the JSON object, Heimdall introduces *immutable blobs* as a security primitive. Any return value from a sensitive data source is immutable. Therefore, even if the collector accesses other sensitive data sources when determining what the most popular restaurant for a particular user is, the output value is guaranteed to not contain information from any of these sources due to immutability. Furthermore, Heimdall provides a secure API to expose immutable blobs, and it ensures that the collector adheres to its manifest by inspecting the structure and contents of the blobs.

Therefore, Heimdall enforces strict privacy guarantees on implicit data collection, thus easing user privacy concerns. Furthermore, recommendation systems do not always require user-identifiable data to provide a general consensus. For example, questions such as "what is the most popular sushi bar in this area?" can be answered without knowing the identity of the visitors to each location. Heimdall allows for such data collection by enabling anonymous submission of preferences.

By granting controlled access to user data and device sensors, Heimdall enables recommendation systems to access implicit preferences, removing their sole reliance on explicit user interactions to measure user preferences. Implicit feedback can be used to measure user interest regarding a particular item, thus addressing the data sparsity problem.

Our Contributions:

- We conduct a study of five online systems with recommendation capability (Goodreads, Yelp, Google Play, IMDB, and Youtube) and analyze the level of user engagement in them. Based on our findings, we distill a set of desired features for collectors and users. (Section 2)

- We develop a prototype of Heimdall on the Android platform (Section 3) and implement a sample set of data collectors spanning the smartphone and smart home environments. These collectors represent the versatility of the Heimdall framework. We perform a thorough evaluation of Heimdall from three perspectives:

  - We perform a series of microbenchmarks that evaluate immutable blob generation time, call latency, and storage overhead of Heimdall. Our results show that API calls in Heimdall impose a $2.3ms$ overhead. An immutable blob of size $1KB$ takes less than $0.3ms$ to generate and only imposes $32B$ of storage overhead. (Section 4.1)
  - We implement three collectors using our framework and discuss developer effort, data collected by the collectors using Heimdall, and the privacy guarantees provided by our system. (Section 4.2)
  - We perform a user study of 166 Amazon Mechanical Turkers to examine the privacy benefits of Heimdall. Our results suggest that the purpose-specific data collection of Heimdall (*e.g.,* recording the name of a restaurant vs. recording fine-grained location information) significantly reduces user concerns.(Section 4.3)

Therefore, in designing Heimdall, we achieve a balance between a user's need for privacy and the need for richer and better recommendations.

2. RECOMMENDATION SYSTEMS: CHALLENGES & OPPORTUNITIES

Online recommendations play a large role in consumer decisions and selections. The number of consumers who search for products online has risen from 41% in 2010 to 50% in 2012 and this number is only expected to increase [30]. With the increased dependence of users on online reviews, services such as Yelp, IMDB, TripAdvisor, and Goodreads aggregate user reviews of various items to produce a general consensus. The reviews that products or locations receive greatly influence their sales and number of user visits—a one-star increase in Yelp reviews of a restaurant increases revenues for that restaurant by $5 - 9\%$ [27].

Although online recommendations and reviews have a large influence over consumers decisions, recommendation systems still suffer posses numerous shortcomings:

- ***Data Collection, Data Breach, and User Privacy:*** Large amounts of data, or big data, provides significant competitive advantages to companies [22] and are correlated with a company's growth and productivity [41]. This is especially true for recommendation systems whose business relies on analyzing user feedback to provide better recommendations and personalization. One major obstacle in collecting and analyzing mass user data is the privacy concerns of users who are worried about abuse of their data and potential tracking of their activities.

  There are multiple dimensions to these users concerns. Data collection in applications happens opaquely with minimal communication to the user about the kind and extent of data [10]. Applications often excessively collect data that is unnecessary for their function [2, 19]. Furthermore, such data collection creates a gold mine of user-identifiable data that is an attractive target for hackers and state-level attackers who regularly steal such confidential information [20]. The Identity Theft Resource Center reported 783 breaches in 2014, which exposed $85,611,528$ user records [12].

- ***Sparsity of Explicit Feedback:*** User feedback is often too few to accurately produce a consensus that reflects the general user opinion. This is especially true for items that are not in the digital or electronics categories [30]. We studied 5 different online recommendation services (Table 1) and compared the number of products (*e.g.,* books, restaurants, movies) to the number of user ratings (*i.e.,* rating bar value) received (Figure 1). We observe that a majority of products do not have even a single user rating, and the products that have ratings contain too few to produce a representative characterization of user opinion. For instance, 70% of products

Source	Type	# of Samples	Definition of Interaction
Goodreads	Books	500	Rating (1-5 stars)
Yelp	Restaurants	10,000	Rating (1-5 stars)
Google Play	Applications	10,000	Rating (1-5 stars)
IMDB	Movies	500	Rating (0.5-5 stars)
Youtube	Videos	500	Up/down vote

Table 1: Data used for evaluating user interaction with different services. Samples were collected at random from each service.

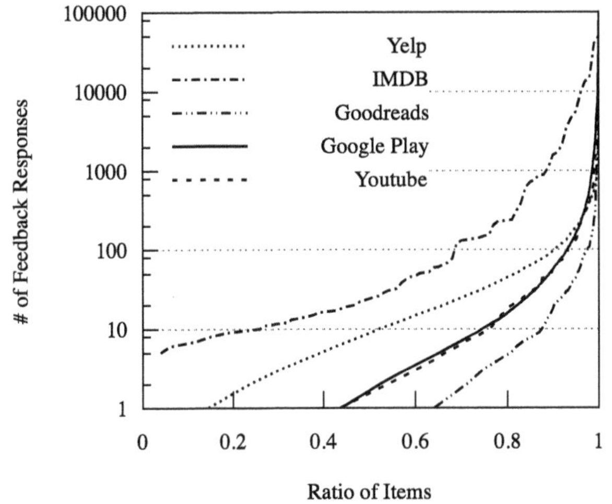

Figure 1: Explicit user feedback (rating bar values) is sparse in general for products from 5 different recommendation systems.

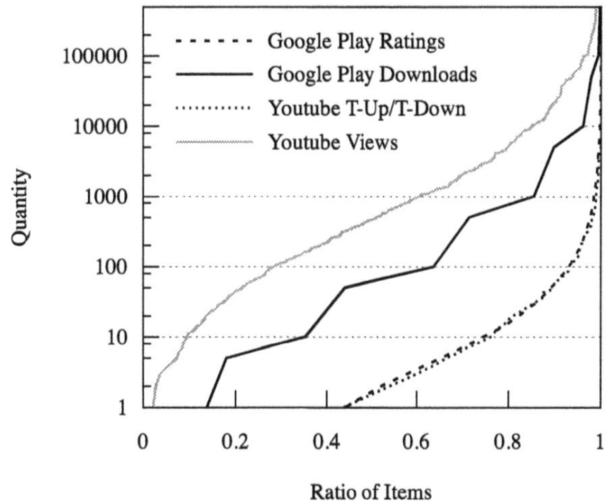

Figure 2: In both Youtube and Google Play store, more than 70% of items have less than 10 reviews. This data suggests that while utilization of products is high, the feedback is still sparse. The Y-axis is interpreted based on the line under consideration. For example, if we consider Google Play ratings, then the Y-axis is the number of ratings, and if we consider Google Play downloads, the the Y-axis is number of downloads. We note that the Google Play ratings and YouTube T-Up/Down lines are slightly different, even though they look visually the same.

on Google Play have fewer than 10 ratings. Recommendation systems recognize this problem, and encourage users to provide more explicit feedback using incentives such as providing discount codes and points-based rewards to those who elect to provide feedback. These techniques have been shown to have limited positive effect [21].

- ***Discrepancy between utilization and feedback:*** One of the reasons for sparse explicit user feedback in the data shown in Figure 1 might be because consumers are not using the majority of products we studied. To confirm that this is not the case, we also measured consumer utilization using approximate metrics appropriate to the type of product. For example, an approximate utilization metric for software on Google Play is the number of downloads,[1] and an approximate metric for video consumption on Youtube is the number of views. Figure 2 shows a CDF for these two utilization metrics for $10,000$ randomly selected apps on Google Play and 500 randomly selected videos on Youtube. We observe that utilization is high but feedback is still low, validating our earlier observation that explicit user feedback fundamentally leads to sparse data. Most of the applications have orders of magnitude fewer reviews than downloads. For applications downloaded at least 1000 times, more than 55% of them have fewer than 100 reviews. Figure 2 also shows the potential to counter data sparsity using implicit feedback. Heimdall unlocks this potential using privacy-respecting implicit feedback collection.

[1]Google Play only provides a range for number of downloads and does not provide exact numbers. In our analysis we conservatively consider the minimum number of downloads.

3. HEIMDALL DESIGN

Heimdall is a framework that enables recommendation systems to build collectors that execute on a user's smartphone or smart home hub. A collector records implicit feedback by observing user activity. Heimdall provides strong privacy guarantees on the type and granularity of data that a collector exposes to the recommendation service cloud back-end, and provides users control over this process. Heimdall directly addresses the fundamental challenge discussed in §2—feedback sparsity, by augmenting explicit feedback with implicit feedback. We design Heimdall to provide these guarantees under the following threat model:

Threat Model. We assume that the Heimdall framework and its underlying operating system are not exploited. This is not a strong assumption as an adversary who has compromised the operating system can freely access data and sensor readings and transfer them regardless of Heimdall. We assume that collectors are untrusted and do not place any restrictions on the kinds of algorithms they run to extract user preferences—they are free to access data existing on the device, from sensors in the built environment, or from knowledge-bases such as Google Maps. Our goal is to prevent collectors from leaking any data that has not been previously approved by the user. We consider addressing side- and covert-channels to be out of scope of the current paper, but we discuss approaches to mitigate them in §5.

The information a collector submits to its recommendation system could implicitly encode additional characteristics. For example, sending a restaurant name implicitly means that the exact GPS co-ordinates of the user are sent out. However, we observe that a GPS co-ordinate does not add information about the activities of the user that cannot be gleaned from the restaurant name itself. That is, it does not add new information. In some cases, new information can be added. For example, if a collector transmits power consumption of devices, then an attacker could use a model of typical consumption of various devices to learn about the kind of device that generated the power data. In a home setting, this means that an attacker can learn whether a user has a specific type of washing machine (or more generally, a specific kind of appliance). However, such home device information is arguably less privacy sensitive than the actual power consumption data. Nevertheless, we envision that k-anonymity [39] techniques could be adapted to further reduce the privacy loss with such kind of implicit information leakage.

Heimdall does not provide any guarantees on whether the recommendation system (back-end of the collectors) leaks information to third-parties. We leave this end-to-end privacy problem to future work.

3.1 Heimdall Programming Model

Consider the example data collector described in §1 that uses GPS co-ordinates and the Google Places API to infer the restaurants a user visits, and then sends that information to its cloud back-end. The collector requires Internet access to function. Under current smartphone or smart home permission models, use of the collector is tied to an inherent risk of the collector leaking fine-grained location data for tracking a user's movements. Heimdall, however, allows a user to use the collect without such risk.

Listing 1 presents pseudo-code for a minimalistic restaurant collector and Listing 2 presents the associated manifest. Line 2 calls a secure location API that returns the location data as an *immutable blob* (IB). An immutable blob can only be created as the return value from a secure API that Heimdall provides. Once created, it cannot be modified. At Line 3, the collector passes the location immutable blob to the Google Places API that only accepts immutable blob types as arguments. This call returns another IB that represents a reverse geocode of the raw location data. The collector checks if the blob is of the restaurant type, and submits the name value of the blob to the collector's cloud back-end.

Whenever a collector attempts to submit a value, Heimdall will first verify that the value being submitted is a valid immutable blob, and then it will ensure that the submission adheres to the collector's manifest (Listing 2). The manifest provides the user fine-grained control over what data is read and submitted by the collector. In our example, the manifest is expressed in terms of the structure of the return value of the Google Places API. That is, Heimdall leverages the known structure of data objects to support fine-grained policies. Our design formats immutable blobs as JSON strings because they are widely used in RESTful webservices, and are easy to parse. Listing 3 shows example immutable blobs used in our restaurant collector.

We note that the goal of our work is to contribute a mechanism that requires the recommendation collectors to declare the kind of data they release to the recommendation system. In our implementation, this choice is presented to the user during the collector's installation. An interesting question is determining how these choices should be presented to the user and the granularity of the manifest prompt—should we present an all-or-nothing choice to the user while installing a collector, or should we provide more fine-grained control over the kind of data that is released? We envision a user study to determine the appropriate granularity of control, and we leave this to future work.

Collectors run in sandboxes that Heimdall provides. The sandboxes precisely control the data that flows into and out of the collectors within. Whenever a collector tries to submit data to its cloud back-end, it must use a secure API that Heimdall provides that au-

Listing 1 Pseudocode for a simple restaurant visit collector. The application collects user's location; uses Google Places API to get data on the location and submits it if it is of type restaurant. A more advanced collector can use a more complex combination of signals to reduce false reports.

```
1 def visitCollector:
2     IB loc = location_service.getloc()
3     IB p = googleapis.place.search(loc[lat],loc[lng])
4     for result in p[results]:
5         if result[types]=="restaurant":
6             submit result[name]
```

Listing 2 Example data collector manifest. The collector uses GPS location and Google geocoding API to collect name of locations of type location.

```
#Sources:
    FINE_LOCATION
    googleapis:place

#Collects:
    @anonymized
    if(googleapis:place:results:types=="restaurant"):
        submit(googleapis:place:results:name,"Link")
```

tomatically checks the manifest of the collector. Our example collector is obviously very basic, but our goal is to simply provide a high-level picture of the abilities of Heimdall. A real collector may use various other data (*e.g.,* time of the day, past visits, credit card charges) to create an arbitrarily complex model to understand user activity.

A collector may set the @anonymized decorator in its manifest. This activates anonymous submissions so that the recommendation system cloud back-end cannot associate the submitted data with any single user's identity. Unless marked for anonymous submission in the manifest, submitted data is transmitted to the collectors' cloud back-end along with the device advertising ID [1]. However, there are many cases where the user is uncomfortable with tying their identity to the submitted data. In some cases, data might be of a sensitive nature (*e.g.,* health related) or users themselves may have higher privacy expectations. In these cases, anonymous submission of data can still provide useful aggregate information on a population's preferences. For example, a collector can reliably extract which physician in your area is more popular with anonymous visit data.

The key primitive providing the desired privacy guarantees in Heimdall is the immutable blob. Listing 4 presents four examples of how Heimdall prevents a collector from accessing or submitting data outside its pre-defined limits:

- The collector is denied access to a resource that has not been requested in its manifest (Line 3-4).
- The collector cannot submit a value that has not been approved in its manifest (Line 8-9).
- The collector cannot pass a parameter that is not of type IB (Line 11-12). All parameters are either an IB or come from a list of static values pre-defined in the API.
- The collector cannot submit a value that does not meet the conditions defined in its manifest (Line 18-19).

These qualities ensure that data entering and leaving a collector always meet the strong type-checking defined in the collector's manifest.

Listing 3 Structure of location and Google Places immutable blobs. Heimdall provides access to sensor and user data (*e.g.*, location, contacts). Web services RESTful APIs naturally produce JSON structures that are stable and well documented. Heimdall defines standard libraries for trusted services (*e.g.*, Google Maps) on top of these APIs.

```
"Location"
{
    "lat": 40.7155809802915,
    "lng": -73.9599399197085,
    "time": "2012-04-23T18:25:43.511Z"
}

"googleapis:place"
{
    "results":[
        { "name":"Subway",
          "types":["restaurant"],
          ... }
        ...
    ]
}
```

Listing 4 Sample of possible malicious activities a collector may attempt and how they are blocked in Heimdall.

```
def malicious visitCollector:

    IB call_history = phone_service.getcalls()
    #Error: Access to phone_service is denied.

    IB loc = location_service.getloc()

    submit loc
    #Error: Location is not one of the approved data
  ↪  types for collection.

    IB p = googleapis.place.search(38.8977,77.0365)
    #Error: Parameters are not of type
  ↪  IB:Location:lat and IB:Location:lng

    IB p = googleapis.place.search(loc[lat],loc[lng])

    for result in p[results]:
        if result[types]=="doctor":
            submit result[name]
    #Error: googleapis:place:results:name does not
  ↪  meet the required conditions for collection.
```

3.2 Heimdall Framework

As discussed above, collectors enable recommendation systems to record implicit user preferences in a privacy-respecting way. From a framework perspective, Heimdall uses two mechanisms that enable useful and secure collector construction (Figure 3): (1) Sandboxes in which collectors execute; (2) a trusted service that makes sensitive resources available to sandboxed collectors using immutable blobs. A collector in a sandbox can only communicate with the trusted service. Furthermore, the trusted service ensures that only immutable blobs cross sandbox boundaries.

We discuss the design of these components in the context of the Android OS. We choose Android because the availability of source code and ease of access to a wide variety of user data. Basing our design on Android also allows Heimdall to be applicable to smart home environments through Android variants such as Brillo [3] and Google Weave [4].

Collectors and Immutable Blobs. Developers write collectors for Heimdall in Java. A collector runs inside a sandbox that controls its communication with the outside world. A collector may only

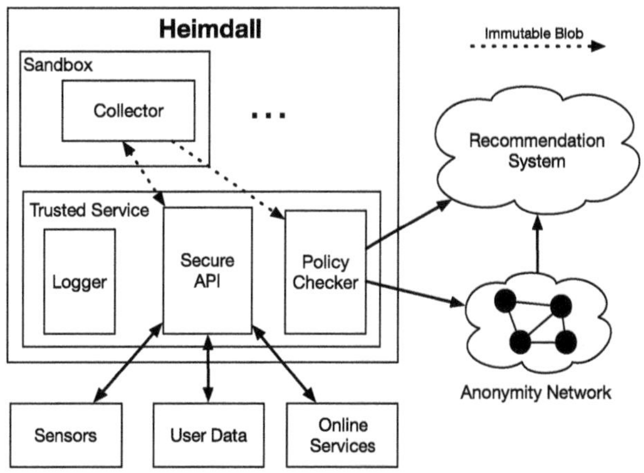

Figure 3: Design overview of Heimdall. Collector can gain access to sensor, user data, and online services through Heimdall secure API. Submission to recommendation system can happen in two ways: 1) Direct submission which includes the device advertisement ID, or 2) Anonymous submission which is sent through an anonymity network (*i.e.*, TOR)

access sensors, user data, and communication methods (*e.g.*, methods to transmit data to the cloud) using a secure API that Heimdall provides. Furthermore, these secure API calls only use immutable blobs. Each immutable blob is a tuple: $< D, P, Sig >$, where D is a JSON structure containing sensitive data, P is a path inside D and is used when the collector wants to refer to a specific item in D, and Sig is a SHA256 HMAC of D generated by the trusted service. Any parameters used to invoke API calls by the collector are in form of immutable blobs. The trusted service verifies the Sig whenever the collector attempts to transmit an immutable blob outside the sandbox boundaries (*e.g.*, either for submission to the cloud back-end or as parameters to call other APIs). This ensures that any data leaving the sandbox is known and verified by the trusted service.

Secure API. The secure API enables collectors to access sensitive data. The API falls into two categories:

- ***Local API:*** provides access to local data (*e.g.*, browsing history, contacts), sensors (*e.g.*, gps, camera), and devices for smart home environments (*e.g.*, door lock, switch) . To keep the structures of immutable blobs uniform, the secure API converts data into pre-defined JSON structures similar to the structure presented for location in Listing 3.

- ***Online Services API:*** provides access to selected online services that Heimdall trusts (*e.g.*, Google Places, Weather Channel). A collector cannot query these services with arbitrary parameters. The parameters used to call the online services can only come from immutable blobs that have been obtained from local sensors or queries previously run on these online services. As these systems use REST APIs with parameters whose structure is known, they automatically supply a JSON response that can be signed and transferred as an immutable blob by the trusted service to the collector.

Policy Checker. A collector can only submit data to its corresponding online recommendation service through a submit function provided by the trusted service. On submission of data, the policy checker will compare the submitted immutable blob against the approved list of submissions in the collector's manifest and verify that it meets the required constraints. In Listing 2, on submission of an immutable blob, the policy checker first verifies the signature Sig. Next it verifies that the path P inside the blob matches the legal submission types defined in the manifest (*i.e.,* `googleapis:place:result:name` and the JSON structure meets the conditions defined in the manifest (*i.e.,* `googleapis:place:results:types =="restaurant"`). Our implementation at this time supports relation constraints (*e.g.,* IF, AND, OR). If these conditions are met, the policy checker will transmit the data to the submission link that is pre-defined in the collector's manifest. If the anonymization flag is active, the transmission will be conducted through the TOR network to anonymize the sender's identity. Otherwise, the submission will include a unique device identifier associated with the device running Heimdall. Any other attempt to leak an identifier has to be declared in the collector's manifest and will be detectable to the user.

Logger. Heimdall provides transparency about the activities of collectors by providing a detailed log of every interaction a collector has with the trusted service. Logging dissuades malicious collectors from using side-channels as a signaling method and also enables auditing of collectors. Future work could also provide a potential platform for anomaly detection to impede side-channels. Creating such a detector, however, is outside of scope of this work and we leave it for future work.

4. IMPLEMENTATION AND EVALUATION

We implemented Heimdall on a smartphone running Android 4.1 and performed the evaluations on a Nexus 4 device. Heimdall creates the sandboxes with the isolatedProcess flag set. Setting the isolatedProcess flag causes Android to activate a combination of restrictive user IDs, IPC limitations, and strict SELinux policies. These restrictions prevent isolated processes from communicating with the outside world, except via an IPC interface connected to the Trusted Service. The Trusted Service provides an API through which collectors can access sensors and data on the device. It also generates and validates immutable blob signatures on API calls or submission. To give Heimdall access to smart switches, we developed a simple application on the Samsung SmartThings platform that reports the status of all smart switches connected to the SmartThings hub. We use this app as a source in our framework.

We evaluate Heimdall from multiple perspectives. First, we run a series of microbenchmarks to study the blob generation and storage overhead, and the latency for calling a secure API. We find that Heimdall adds modest overhead: A blob of size $1K$ bytes takes $282\mu s$ to generate and takes an additional 256 bits to store. A parameter-less API call by a collector has $2.3ms$ overhead on average.

Second, we developed three simple collectors and integrated them with Heimdall. For each collector, we evaluated the data collection capability, the privacy guarantees, and the development effort of the app. Our results show that Heimdall allows recommendation systems to collect the implicit data required and provides privacy guarantees regarding the data collected. Our collectors are on average 194 lines of code.

Finally, we conducted a user study with 166 participants on Amazon Mechanical Turk.[2] We evaluated the effect of Heimdall on decreasing the privacy concerns of users for a restaurant recommendation system. Our results suggest that use of Heimdall significantly lowers users' concerns on sharing their location and browser history data.

[2]We received exemption from our institution's IRB under title 45 CFR 46.101.(b). Survey data was collected anonymously and did not include any user-identifiable or sensitive information about the participants.

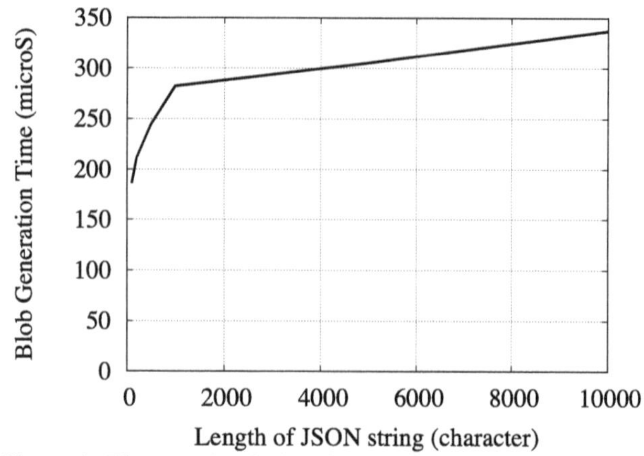

Figure 4: Time overhead of blob generation based on the JSON string size.

4.1 Microbenchmarks

Blob Generation Time. We recorded and averaged 10000 blob generations with data size varying from 100 to 10000 bytes in length. We note that a Google Places API response is $\sim 5KB$ long so our experiments should cover most API response sizes. Figure 4 presents the results of this experiment. The blob generation time increases as the size of the JSON string increases. Note that even when the blob contains $10KB$ bytes, the generation time does not exceed $340\mu s$. This delay does not have a significant negative effect on a collector's functionality as the IPC mechanism used in the operating system has an order of magnitude more latency.

Storage Overhead. A Heimdall collector does not impose a significant memory overhead compared to a collector written outside of the framework. A Heimdall collector only needs to store additional HMACs received for any data that will be submitted to the recommendation system. A SHA256 HMAC is $32B$ in length. As storage/memory space is plentiful in modern phones, this is a very modest overhead.

Call Latency Overhead. We varied the number of parameters of a secure API from 0 to 10. We used immutable blobs with 1000 bytes data length as our parameters and repeated the experiment 100 times for each data point. We observed that as the number of parameters for the secure API increased, the latency increased from $2.3ms$ to $4.2ms$. These measurements include additional latency caused by the IPC and immutable blob verification. This latency is comparable to standard IPC call and is acceptable for collectors' functions.

4.2 Macrobenchmarks

We developed three collector applications for Heimdall framework to evaluate the impact on their capability to collect implicit data from user activities, their privacy guarantees, and the required developer effort. Table 2 presents an overview of these applications. The RestaurantCollector can be used to augment restaurant recommendation services such as Yelp. It tracks and analyses user location and reports the name of the restaurant user have visited to the recommendation system. Using this data, restaurant recommen-

Name / Category	Description	Privacy Risk	Implicit Signal	LoC
RestaurantCollector / Smartphone	Monitors location of smartphone device, infers when the device is at a restaurant, submits name of restaurant to cloud back-end. This helps generate restaurant recommendations.	Can track user's location.	Fine-Grained GPS	359
NewsCollector / Smartphone	Reads user browsing history, detects web pages belonging to news organizations, transmits news items to cloud back-end. This help generate list of most popular news articles.	Sensitive browser history can be leaked to attackers.	Browser History	64
EnergySaver / Smart Home	Monitors power status of devices around the home. Transmits usage of only certain types of high-wattage devices (*e.g.,* oven) if they are used at peak-hour. This helps generate energy saving recommendations.	Can track activity in the home (also, can detect whether the home is occupied or not).	Power state of physical devices	157

Table 2: Example Collectors built using Heimdall.

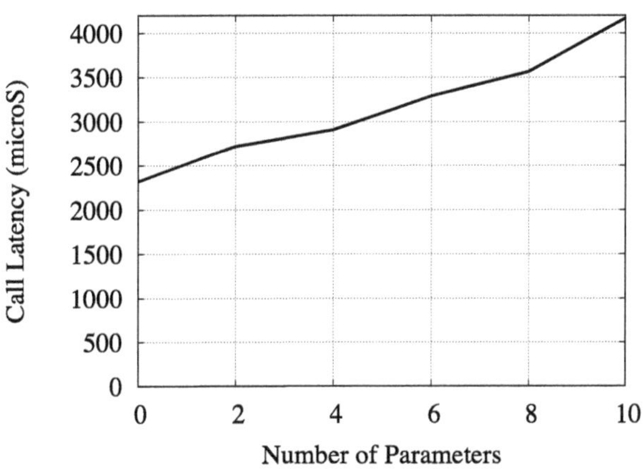

Figure 5: Secure API call latency for different number of parameters. Each Parameter is an immutable blob with $1KB$ JSON data length.

dation system can gain insight into the popularity of each restaurant and how busy they are during different times of day. This application can also potentially use other data such as browsing history (*e.g.,* which restaurant website the user viewed) and purchase history (*e.g.,* how much money the user spent in a restaurant) as additional signals.

NewsCollector can be used by news aggregators such as Digg, Reddit, or feedly. It tracks the browsing history of the user and sends the urls associated with news articles to the recommendation system. Using this collector allows news aggregators to gain insight into popularity of each article in a privacy-respecting manner. This application can be augmented with data such as how much time is spent on each article and subscriptions user has to newsletters for more insight.

Finally, the EnergySaver collector gains access to the status of smart switches in a smart home environment to understand the pattern of energy usage during the day. An application can potentially use this data to provide the user with energy saving suggestions. These three collectors present a diverse set of data that can be gained by relying on implicit user feedbacks.

Data Collection & Privacy. We discuss the data privacy risk that each of the three collectors pose when running on existing platform and examine how Heimdall eliminates those risks successfully.

- *RestaurantCollector:* The collector can potentially track all user movement and misuse this data. Using Heimdall, the collector can still use the location data to extract the restaurants user has visited, but it can only transmit their name to the recommendation system.
- *NewsCollector:* This collector can leak all user browsing history to an attacker. Using Heimdall, the collector is limited to reporting the urls from news organization domains. It cannot report any other urls in an attempt to leak the user's browsing history.
- *EnergySaver:* It has the potential to leak data on all devices usage in a smart home environment. Using Heimdall, the collector can only report certain types of high-wattage devices if they are being used at peak hours.

Developer Effort. Developing collectors for Heimdall does not impose a significant burden over implementing the collector as a regular app in the Android environment. Table 2 provides the number of lines of codes it took to write each collector. When developing a collector in Heimdall, the developer is limited to using Heimdall provided API for accessing user data. These APIs return their results in form of immutable blobs. Much of the extra code developers is required to develop is to maintain and use the immutable blob structure. We envision that with appropriate tool support, many boiler plate tasks for maintaining these blobs can be automated.

4.3 User Study

To evaluate whether Heimdall is a step towards reducing user privacy concerns, we conducted a user study with 166 Amazon Mechanical Turk users. We asked the participants how comfortable they are about a restaurant recommendation service accessing various private data and asked them to rate their level of concern (Likert Scale). We provided the participants with the following description and choices:

> *We are building a restaurant recommendation app for Android and iOS. For it to provide good recommendations, we need to access various kinds of information*

Implicit Signal	Question	Avg. Level of Concern (1-5 Range)
Fine-Grained GPS	[Q1] The recommendation app records and transmits your exact location all the time to its cloud service	3.31
	[Q2] The recommendation app records and transmits your exact location to its cloud service only when you are using the app	2.68
	[Q3] The recommendation app records and transmits only the name of the restaurants you visit to its cloud service	2.41
Purchase History	[Q4] The recommendation app records and transmits your purchase history to its cloud service	3.15
	[Q5] The recommendation app records and transmits how much you spend on meals to its cloud service	3.03
Browser History	[Q6] The recommendation app records and transmits your browsing history to its cloud service	3.42
	[Q7] The recommendation app records and transmits only restaurant websites you visit using your browser to its cloud service	2.61

Table 3: The seven questions in our user study of 166 MTurk participants. All questions concern a restaurant recommendation collector. After filtering for random clickers, we averaged the level of concern users reported for 150 participants. The level of concern is encoded as 1 = not concerned, 5 = would not allow this data collection to happen. We see a significant reduction in concern between Q1 and Q3, and between Q6 and Q7. We did not see a significant reduction in concern between Q4 and Q5, partly due to the general sensitivity of purchase history. Q3, Q5, and Q7 represent the behavior of a Heimdall collector.

about you from your smartphone. In what follows, we will describe type of information being collected. This collected information is transmitted to our recommendation system cloud service. Your task is to rate your feelings towards such collection based on the following scale:

1. ***Not Concerned*** *- Select this option if you are not concerned about sharing the specified data with third parties.*
2. ***Mildly Concerned*** *- Select this option if you are mildly concerned about sharing the specified data with third parties.*
3. ***Concerned*** *- Select this option if you are concerned about sharing the specified data with third parties.*
4. ***Very Concerned*** *- Select this option if you are very concerned about sharing the specified data with third parties.*
5. ***Would Not Allow*** *- Select this option if you would not allow the specified data to be shared with third parties.*

After filtering for random clickers with the help of responses to trap questions [29], we were left with 150 filtered responses. Table 3 contains the survey questions and the average level of concern that users reported. Q1, Q2, Q4, and Q5 represent the behavior of current collectors. Q3, Q5 and Q7 represent the behavior of Heimdall collectors. We conducted a paired t-test for Q1 and Q3 (see Table 3) and found a significantly reduced level of concern ($p < 0.05$) when the recommendation app only collected fine-grained and relevant information (*i.e.,* a location value only when it is a restaurant). A t-test for Q2 and Q3 indicated a significant effect ($p < 0.05$)—even if data is being collected only when the app is being used, users are significantly less concerned when Heimdall informs them that only restaurant names are sent out.

We conducted another paired t-test for Q4 and Q5, but did not find a significant effect ($p > 0.05$). We believe the reason for no significant reduction in level of concern is probably because of the generally sensitive nature of purchase data—be it specific to a kind of item or generic purchase data. Finally, we conducted a paired t-test for Q6 and Q7 and observed a significant effect ($p < 0.05$) suggesting a reduced level of concern. As Q3, Q5, and Q7 represent the behavior of Heimdall collectors, these results suggest that users are possibly more comfortable with purpose-specific data collection that Heimdall enables as compared to the current state of the art where no restrictions exist on how and what data recommendation systems can implicitly record. Although this brief user survey suggests that Heimdall is a step in the right direction, our results do have limitations.

User Study Limitations. Our survey questions were presented in the same specific order to all participants—questions relating to how collectors function today followed by questions relating to how collectors function in Heimdall. This ordering is a potential source of option bias.

Even though Heimdall collectors do not arbitrarily collect sensitive information, our study suggests that users are still mildly concerned about data collection. We believe that this level of concern can be further reduced by coupling Heimdall with a mechanism that enforces data-use policies on the recommendation system backend, to gain an end-to-end privacy guarantee that collected data is only used for recommendation purposes. We elaborate further on this aspect in §5.

Our survey does not determine whether users would stop giving explicit feedback because they (possibly erroneously) assume that implicit feedback is sufficient. This is an interesting side-effect of privacy-respecting implicit feedback collection, and we envision a future survey that is designed to study this aspect.

5. DISCUSSION

Implicit vs Explicit Feedback. Heimdall does not replace explicit feedback, but rather augments it with implicit feedback. Use of implicit feedback only allows a collector to infer a user's interest and preferences; it does not replace user experiences reflected in textual reviews or explicit ratings in scoring systems. Heimdall, however, gives a voice to the vast majority of users who do not provide any feedback on their experiences when using recommendation systems.

Targeted Explicit Feedback. Currently, recommendation systems solicit explicit feedback on all products and services irrespective of whether these products and services are relevant to users. Using implicit feedback that Heimdall enables, a recommendation system can personalize how it solicits explicit feedback. For example, if a recommendation system learns that a user has visited two restaurants very frequently in the past month, the system can dynamically generate explicit feedback UI for only *those* two restaurants, that are arguably more relevant to a user than all the other restaurants. We believe that this can incentivize users to provide explicit feedback. We leave it to future work to design such a system.

Pluggable Secure APIs. Although our current prototype supports a limited set of secure APIs, we envision a pluggable architecture (*e.g.,* using dynamic code loading) where modules containing new secure APIs can be connected to the basic Heimdall framework. Open source developers can build and vet such plugin-based secure APIs to extend the functionality of the Heimdall framework.

Limitations. Heimdall allows recommendation systems to access a wide variety of user's implicit signals that they can use to infer user preferences, thus improving the quality of recommendations. In Heimdall, collectors can use arbitrarily complex models to extract user preference from their data (*e.g.,* This user likes California sushi roll). Collectors, however, are not designed to create digests of these preferences. Questions such as "How many times the user has eaten out this month?" cannot be answered by a collector directly because of the limitations imposed by immutable blobs, but they can be answered on the recommendation system by collecting data on user's restaurant visits.

The recommendation system itself can possibly misuse data that collectors submit (*e.g.,* leak user behavior to third parties). Our design currently does not provide any guarantees on the behavior of the recommendation system. Information flow control approaches are a promising step in providing end-to-end privacy guarantees [36], including recent work on structuring code to make flows explicit [17]. Nevertheless, Heimdall collectors are a first step towards achieving the end-to-end privacy goal, and is the focus of this work. Another promising direction to obtain end-to-end guarantees is the notion of policy-carrying data [34]. A collector could attach a policy before submitting to the recommendation system. Then, the recommendation system can only access the submitted data if it publicly acknowledges (in an unforgeable way) that it will follow the rules of the associated policy. If it deviates from the policy, then either technical mechanisms or legal instruments could be used to address the privacy breach.

Side/Covert Channels. Heimdall controls the data that collectors gather by enforcing fine-grained data type tracking through immutable blobs that contain multiple data fields (*e.g.,* type of location, name of location, value of sensor). However, it is possible for a malicious collector to transmit information through side and covert channels, such as encoding data within timing, frequency, or pattern of data submissions. While we don't address these challenges, many of the techniques proposed in the literature (*e.g.,* creating a delay before any submission to protect against timing side channels) are applicable to Heimdall [44,45]. Furthermore, providing an accurate log of collector's activities allows for auditing and anomaly detection.

6. RELATED WORK

Recommendation Systems. As discussed in §1, recommendation systems suffer from three shortcomings: (1) users have privacy concerns while sharing preferences [9,42,43], (2) users must take extra steps to provide explicit feedback by interacting with review-related UI elements like rating bars, and (3) users often leave feedback only after an extreme experience [8,26]. Our key insight in Heimdall is that all of these problems can be solved if recommendation systems could collect implicit preferences in a privacy-respecting manner. Therefore, Heimdall is design with this goal in mind. Heimdall enables recommendation systems to construct collectors that *augment* explicit preferences with a user's implicit preferences.

Automatically collecting implicit preferences can increase the privacy concerns of the user if they do not have control of the process or are unaware that such collection occurs. Heimdall forces implicit preference collectors to declare what data is exported to the recommendation system's back-end. Therefore, users are informed that data collection is occurring and can choose to block undesired collection. Zhang *et al.* showed that adding privacy control mechanisms to implicit data input addressed user privacy concerns [43].

There is a body of work discussing privacy attacks on recommendation services. Calandrino *et al.* leverage temporal changes in the public output of a recommendation service to infer information about a specific customer's transactions with only a small amount of auxiliary information [11]. Ramakrishnan *et al.* discuss how information on the existence of customers with eclectic preferences in products, or straddlers, can be used to reveal personal details of other customers with similar preferences [33]. These are attacks on the algorithm the recommendation system uses to produce recommendations. In contrast, our work is concerned with privately leveraging implicit signals to improve the quality of recommendations. Preventing attacks on the recommendation algorithm are orthogonal to our goals.

Implicit Preference Collection. A recent class of systems are emerging that perform entity recognition and task extraction directly on data that appears on smartphone UI. For instance, Fernandes *et al.* built Appstract [18], and Chandramouli *et al.* built Insider [13]. These systems extract structured data from smartphone app UI and associate semantics to that data. Such extraction creates a rich data source that recommendation systems can use for implicit preference collection. However, these systems leave designing proper security controls for third-party access to this data as future work. We believe that Heimdall is a suitable framework that enables recommendation systems to leverage this rich source of semantically labeled data in a privacy-respecting manner.

Information Flow Tracking. JFlow and Jif are security-typed languages where developers must learn a new type-system to gain security benefits [5, 31]. Heimdall draws on ideas from such languages, but it simplifies the type-system to only include a single new security-oriented type—immutable blobs. A collector may only sink specific immutable blobs declared in its manifest.

FlowFence is a general-purpose information flow control system aims at Internet of Things apps [17] that only allows data to flow from a source to a sink if the data policy permits. In contrast, Heimdall does not monitor data flows from a source to a sink. Instead, it simply ensures that data exported at a sink has been declared in a collector's manifest and has been approved by the user. However, a system like FlowFence, which supports information flow control as a first-class primitive (as opposed to bolt-on approaches discussed below), can be used on the recommendation system itself to obtain end-to-end privacy guarantees that limit the misuse of data submitted by collectors.

A large body of work deals with dynamic and static taint analyses that track how data flow of a program affects the contents of variables containing sensitive information [36]. These techniques, which introduce large performance overheads, are generally applied in non-adversarial settings such as test generation and integrity protection, where the attacker does not control the code that is being taint checked. Within an adversarial setting, attackers can defeat current taint analysis techniques using control flows and concurrency [35]. Heimdall does not use taint tracking to achieve its privacy goals because the application area is very specific and does not require tracking data and control flow—a collector's only function is to sink an immutable blob whose contents, by definition, cannot be changed by data or control flow of the collector's code.

Linkability & K-Anonymity. Heimdall enables users to anonymize their submissions to the recommendation system using an anonymity network such as TOR. While this approach removes any direct link between different data submissions of an individual, it does not provide an unlinkability guarantee. Prior work such as Narayanan *et al.* [32] has shown how large sparse datasets of recommendations can get deanonymized by collusion between different sources. Providing such guarantees fall outside our threat model, but has been extensively studied in K-Anonymity literature [23–25, 28, 38, 40] .

7. CONCLUSION

Many users today rely on online recommendation systems (*e.g.,* Yelp, Goodreads, IMDB) to better inform their decisions about whether or not to use a certain product or service. These systems seek to aggregate large amounts of implicit (*e.g.,* GPS data, purchase history, browsing history) and explicit (*e.g.,* written reviews, ratings) user feedback in order to produce high quality recommendations. However, due to user privacy concerns, these systems are not given access to implicit data sources, and thus must rely on explicit feedback, which most users do not provide. We have proposed Heimdall, a practical privacy-respecting preference collection framework that allows recommendation systems to collect implicit feedback. Implicit preference collectors declare the type (*e.g.,* location) and granularity (*e.g.,* restaurant name) of data they share. Users approve or reject these requests to share data and Heimdall ensures that the collectors behave in accordance with their declared data accesses and the user's decision. Heimdall introduces immutable blobs as a mechanism to help provide these guarantees. We built Heimdall for Android (and also interfaced it with Samsung SmartThings). Our evaluation indicates that performance overhead is minimal—generating immutable blobs adds a $340\mu s$ delay to IPCs that transfer data into a collector. We conducted a user study with 166 MTurk participants to determine whether Heimdall collectors decrease privacy concerns. We find that users are significantly less concerned with data collection when they have control over the collection process and when the nature of the collected data is made explicit (*e.g.,* collecting fine-grained location vs. using location to only collect restaurant names).

Acknowledgements

We thank Chunyi Peng, our shepherd, and the anonymous reviewers for their insightful feedback. This material is based upon work supported by the National Science Foundation under Grant No. 1318722. Any opinions, findings, and conclusions or recommendations expressed in this material are those of the author(s) and do not necessarily reflect the views of the National Science Foundation.

8. REFERENCES

[1] Advertising id. https://support.google.com/googleplay/android-developer/answer/6048248.

[2] Apple Q&A on location data - April 27, 2011. http://www.apple.com/pr/library/2011/04/27Apple-Q-A-on-Location-Data.html.

[3] Google Brillo OS for IoT. https://developers.google.com/brillo/.

[4] Google Weave for IoT. https://developers.google.com/weave/.

[5] JIF. http://www.cs.cornell.edu/jif/.

[6] Quantcast number of visitors ranking. https://www.quantcast.com/top-sites/US/1.

[7] Why Do Consumers Leave Reviews? https://www.getfivestars.com/blog/survey-why-do-consumers-leave-reviews/.

[8] G. Adomavicius and A. Tuzhilin. Toward the next generation of recommender systems: A survey of the state-of-the-art and possible extensions. *Knowledge and Data Engineering, IEEE Transactions on*, 17(6):734–749, 2005.

[9] N. F. Awad and M. S. Krishnan. The personalization privacy paradox: An empirical evaluation of information transparency and the willingness to be profiled online for personalization. *MIS Q.*, 30(1):13–28, Mar. 2006.

[10] J. L. Boyles, A. Smith, and M. Madden. Privacy and data management on mobile devices. *Pew Internet & American Life Project*, 4, 2012.

[11] J. A. Calandrino, A. Kilzer, A. Narayanan, E. W. Felten, and V. Shmatikov. "you might also like: " privacy risks of collaborative filtering. In *Proceedings of the 2011 IEEE Symposium on Security and Privacy*, SP '11, pages 231–246, Washington, DC, USA, 2011. IEEE Computer Society.

[12] I. T. R. Center. Breach report 2014. 2014.

[13] V. Chandramouli, V. N. Abhijnan Chakraborty, S. Guha, V. Padmanabhan, and R. Ramjee. Insider: Towards breaking down mobile app silos. In *TRIOS Workshop held in conjunction with the SIGOPS SOSP 2015*, September 2015.

[14] E. Chin, A. P. Felt, V. Sekar, and D. Wagner. Measuring user confidence in smartphone security and privacy. In *Proceedings of the Eighth Symposium on Usable Privacy and Security*, page 1. ACM, 2012.

[15] Z. Fang, W. Han, and Y. Li. Permission based android security: Issues and countermeasures. *computers & security*, 43:205–218, 2014.

[16] A. P. Felt, K. Greenwood, and D. Wagner. The effectiveness of application permissions. In *Proceedings of the 2nd USENIX conference on Web application development*, pages 7–7, 2011.

[17] E. Fernandes, J. Paupore, A. Rahmati, D. Simionato, M. Conti, and A. Prakash. Flowfence: Practical data protection for emerging iot application frameworks. In *25th USENIX Security Symposium (USENIX Security 16)*, pages 531–548, Austin, TX, Aug. 2016. USENIX Association.

[18] E. Fernandes, O. Riva, and S. Nath. Appstract: On-the-fly app content semantics with better privacy. In *Proceedings of the 22Nd Annual International Conference on Mobile*

Computing and Networking, MobiCom '16, pages 361–374, New York, NY, USA, 2016. ACM.

[19] N. Geri and Y. Geri. The information age measurement paradox: Collecting too much data. *Informing Science: the International Journal of an Emerging Transdiscipline*, 14:47–59, 2011.

[20] G. Greenwald. *No Place to Hide: Edward Snowden, the NSA, and the U.S. Surveillance State*. Metropolitan Books, May 2014.

[21] J. Hamari, J. Koivisto, and H. Sarsa. Does gamification work?–a literature review of empirical studies on gamification. In *System Sciences (HICSS), 2014 47th Hawaii International Conference on*, pages 3025–3034. IEEE, 2014.

[22] E. Junqué de Fortuny, D. Martens, and F. Provost. Predictive modeling with big data: is bigger really better? *Big Data*, 1(4):215–226, 2013.

[23] K. LeFevre, D. J. DeWitt, and R. Ramakrishnan. Incognito: Efficient full-domain k-anonymity. In *Proceedings of the 2005 ACM SIGMOD international conference on Management of data*, pages 49–60. ACM, 2005.

[24] K. LeFevre, D. J. DeWitt, and R. Ramakrishnan. Mondrian multidimensional k-anonymity. In *Data Engineering, 2006. ICDE'06. Proceedings of the 22nd International Conference on*, pages 25–25. IEEE, 2006.

[25] N. Li, T. Li, and S. Venkatasubramanian. t-closeness: Privacy beyond k-anonymity and l-diversity. In *Data Engineering, 2007. ICDE 2007. IEEE 23rd International Conference on*, pages 106–115. IEEE, 2007.

[26] X. Li and L. M. Hitt. Self-selection and information role of online product reviews. *Information Systems Research*, 2008.

[27] M. Luca. Reviews, reputation, and revenue: The case of yelp. com. *Com (September 16, 2011). Harvard Business School NOM Unit Working Paper*, (12-016), 2011.

[28] A. Machanavajjhala, D. Kifer, J. Gehrke, and M. Venkitasubramaniam. l-diversity: Privacy beyond k-anonymity. *ACM Transactions on Knowledge Discovery from Data (TKDD)*, 1(1):3, 2007.

[29] W. Mason and S. Suri. Conducting behavioral research on amazon's mechanical turk. *Behavior Research Methods*, 44(1):1–23, 2012.

[30] McKinsey&Company. Telecommunications, media, technology - iconsumers: Life online. 2013.

[31] A. C. Myers. Jflow: Practical mostly-static information flow control. In *Proceedings of the 26th ACM SIGPLAN-SIGACT Symposium on Principles of Programming Languages*, POPL '99, pages 228–241, New York, NY, USA, 1999. ACM.

[32] A. Narayanan and V. Shmatikov. Robust de-anonymization of large sparse datasets. In *Security and Privacy, 2008. SP 2008. IEEE Symposium on*, pages 111–125. IEEE, 2008.

[33] N. Ramakrishnan, B. J. Keller, B. J. Mirza, A. Y. Grama, and G. Karypis. Privacy risks in recommender systems. *IEEE Internet Computing*, 5(6):54–62, Nov. 2001.

[34] S. Saroiu, A. Wolman, and S. Agarwal. Policy-carrying data: A privacy abstraction for attaching terms of service to mobile data. In *Proceedings of the 16th International Workshop on Mobile Computing Systems and Applications*, HotMobile '15, pages 129–134, New York, NY, USA, 2015. ACM.

[35] G. Sarwar, O. Mehani, R. Boreli, and D. Kaafar. On the effectiveness of dynamic taint analysis for protecting against private information leaks on android-based devices. In *SECRYPT 2013, 10th International Conference on Security and Cryptography*, pages 461–467, ReykjÃąvik, Iceland, jul 2013. SciTePress.

[36] E. J. Schwartz, T. Avgerinos, and D. Brumley. All you ever wanted to know about dynamic taint analysis and forward symbolic execution (but might have been afraid to ask). In *Proceedings of the 2010 IEEE Symposium on Security and Privacy*, SP '10, pages 317–331, Washington, DC, USA, 2010. IEEE Computer Society.

[37] M. Sheppard. Smartphone apps, permissions and privacy. In *Office of the Privacy Commissioner of Canada*, 2013.

[38] L. Sweeney. Achieving k-anonymity privacy protection using generalization and suppression. *International Journal of Uncertainty, Fuzziness and Knowledge-Based Systems*, 10(05):571–588, 2002.

[39] L. Sweeney. k-anonymity: A model for protecting privacy. *International Journal of Uncertainty, Fuzziness and Knowledge-Based Systems*, 10(05):557–570, 2002.

[40] L. Sweeney. k-anonymity: A model for protecting privacy. *International Journal of Uncertainty, Fuzziness and Knowledge-Based Systems*, 10(05):557–570, 2002.

[41] P. Tambe. Big data investment, skills, and firm value. *Management Science*, 60(6):1452–1469, 2014.

[42] E. Toch, Y. Wang, and L. F. Cranor. Personalization and privacy: A survey of privacy risks and remedies in personalization-based systems. *User Modeling and User-Adapted Interaction*, 22(1-2):203–220, Apr. 2012.

[43] B. Zhang, N. Wang, and H. Jin. Privacy concerns in online recommender systems: Influences of control and user data input. pages 159–173. USENIX Association, 9999.

[44] D. Zhang, A. Askarov, and A. C. Myers. Predictive mitigation of timing channels in interactive systems. In *Proceedings of the 18th ACM Conference on Computer and Communications Security*, CCS '11, pages 563–574, New York, NY, USA, 2011. ACM.

[45] D. Zhang, A. Askarov, and A. C. Myers. Language-based control and mitigation of timing channels. In *Proceedings of the 33rd ACM SIGPLAN Conference on Programming Language Design and Implementation*, PLDI '12, pages 99–110, New York, NY, USA, 2012. ACM.

[46] H. Zhang, K. E. Nejad, A. Rahmati, and H. V. Madhyastha. Towards comprehensive repositories of opinions. In *Proceedings of the 15th ACM Workshop on Hot Topics in Networks*, HotNets '16, pages 15–21, New York, NY, USA, 2016. ACM.

Trust but Verify: Auditing the Secure Internet of Things

Judson Wilson, Riad S. Wahby, Henry Corrigan-Gibbs, Dan Boneh, Philip Levis, Keith Winstein
{judsonw, rsw, henrycg, dabo, pal, keithw}@cs.stanford.edu
Stanford University

ABSTRACT

Internet-of-Things devices often collect and transmit sensitive information like camera footage, health monitoring data, or whether someone is home. These devices protect data in transit with end-to-end encryption, typically using TLS connections between devices and associated cloud services.

But these TLS connections also prevent device owners from observing what their own devices are saying about them. Unlike in traditional Internet applications, where the end user controls one end of a connection (e.g., their web browser) and can observe its communication, Internet-of-Things vendors typically control the software in both the device and the cloud. As a result, owners have no way to audit the behavior of their own devices, leaving them little choice but to hope that these devices are transmitting only what they should.

This paper presents TLS–Rotate and Release (TLS-RaR), a system that allows device owners (e.g., consumers, security researchers, and consumer watchdogs) to authorize devices, called auditors, to decrypt and verify recent TLS traffic without compromising future traffic. Unlike prior work, TLS-RaR requires no changes to TLS's wire format or cipher suites, and it allows the device's owner to conduct a surprise inspection of recent traffic, without prior notice to the device that its communications will be audited.

1. INTRODUCTION

The Internet of Things (IoT) is notoriously insecure [34,65]. Recent exploits have shown a drone flying by a building to take control of its lights [56], and tens of thousands of compromised webcams were behind recent denial-of-service attacks against PayPal, Twitter, Netflix, and other prominent sites [14]. A recent study by HP Labs found that cleartext data, insecure firmware updates, and poor cryptographic practices mean that a substantial majority of devices had exploitable security flaws [38].

One well-accepted way to improve IoT security is to use Transport Layer Security (TLS). Products from Nest [3] and Samsung SmartThings, for example, use TLS to connect to their respective cloud services. TLS provides useful guarantees: message integrity and confidentiality, and mutual authentication of devices and servers.

However, the use of strong encryption on a locked-down consumer device has a worrisome effect for privacy: you, the device owner, cannot tell what your own devices are reporting about you. For example, if you install a Nest thermostat or camera in your home, you cannot observe the contents of its traffic to verify that it's only sending data of the kind the vendor has promised.

Internet-of-Things applications pose new security and privacy concerns because *both* ends of a secure connection are controlled by a single party: the vendor. While a Nest thermostat runs Linux, the owner cannot log in to it or otherwise control its operation. Because you cannot modify the thermostat's firmware, trace its applications, or intercept its unencrypted traffic, you cannot see what a device is reporting about you and your home.

The IoT therefore marks a break from the tradition, essentially as old as the Internet, of end users being able to inspect their own communications. Web browsers generally have a developer interface that lets end users see the contents of network traffic. And with local control of the operating system, one can look inside TLS streams by installing the public key of a trusted middlebox as a root certificate. IoT devices generally do not allow these.

While it may be rare that any given consumer will want to inspect the contents of their apps' encrypted traffic, the *ability* to do so has allowed consumer watchdogs and security researchers to uncover undisclosed exposures of personal information [5,15,25,34,67], and by reporting or publicizing these exposures, cause manufacturers to fix them.

At the same time, IoT manufacturers are understandably reluctant to provide a means to weaken a device's security by installing a new root certificate, which allows the holder to act as a man-in-the-middle between the device and the cloud, modifying traffic or impersonating one to the other. Manufacturers have also shown little interest in proposals, such as mcTLS [45], that diverge from the TLS protocol by adding additional keys and message-authentication codes to allow "read-only" middleboxes. These modified protocols are not supported by TLS terminators and load balancers in the cloud, which are often out of a vendor's control.

In this paper, we present a mechanism, TLS-Rotate and Release (TLS-RaR), which allows device owners to audit their devices' traffic without compromising application integrity, and without modifying the TLS format on the wire. Using

Permission to make digital or hard copies of all or part of this work for personal or classroom use is granted without fee provided that copies are not made or distributed for profit or commercial advantage and that copies bear this notice and the full citation on the first page. Copyrights for components of this work owned by others than the author(s) must be honored. Abstracting with credit is permitted. To copy otherwise, or republish, to post on servers or to redistribute to lists, requires prior specific permission and/or a fee. Request permissions from permissions@acm.org.

MobiSys '17, June 19–23, 2017, Niagara Falls, NY, USA.

© 2017 Copyright held by the owner/author(s). Publication rights licensed to ACM.

ISBN 978-1-4503-4928-4/17/06...$15.00

DOI: http://dx.doi.org/10.1145/3081333.3081342

TLS-RaR, TLS connections between an IoT device and the cloud retain their end-to-end integrity and remain encrypted as before, but an owner can optionally install any number of read-only, in-home **auditors**, low-cost devices on the owner's home network that passively sniff the ciphertext of TLS sessions.

TLS-RaR's key idea is that at any moment, the user can log in to the cloud service and instruct the device to *rotate* a TLS connection's symmetric encryption keys. Once the device is certain that both it and the server will no longer use the old keys, it securely *releases* the superseded keys to the user or the user's designated auditor. Using these keys, the auditor decrypts and verifies its cache of past ciphertext. As a result, the auditor receives delayed access to the same session keys as the TLS endpoints, and therefore the same integrity-protected plaintext, even from before the endpoints were informed about the auditor's existence; but the auditor cannot forge data or masquerade as either party.

Compared with approaches like mcTLS, TLS-RaR is simpler and more deployable. TLS-RaR requires no modifications to TLS's wire format, state machines, or the server-side TLS endpoint. This last point is beneficial because large-scale TLS deployments often offload server-side TLS termination to middleboxes or specialized hardware. Changing TLS software or hardware on the server side is difficult, and existing systems may be architected such that the TLS and application layers are independent. We found (§5.3) that TLS-RaR can already be used today with most TLS servers in the wild.

TLS-RaR differs in other respects from previous proposals to audit encrypted communications. It works with passive auditors that do not have to act as men-in-the-middle. Auditors are guaranteed to see the same payloads and perform the same integrity checks as the TLS endpoints. Endpoints cannot send a different stream to auditors than they do to each other, in order to conceal malicious traffic. Multiple auditors can observe encrypted streams in parallel, without being able to confuse one another.

TLS-RaR also carries major limitations. First, auditors only learn the plaintext after some delay. TLS-RaR cannot be used to detect and prevent compromise in real time. Second, TLS-RaR simply allows an auditor to see inside the encrypted stream provided by TLS. TLS-RaR does not, by itself, detect or defeat additional layers of encryption or covert channels within a TLS stream. Finally, TLS-RaR of course requires the vendor's cooperation. Manufacturers who are not interested in subjecting their devices' communications to independent audits are unlikely to implement TLS-RaR.

Nonetheless, we believe the benefits of IoT audits would be considerable. We envision independent watchdogs (e.g., Consumer Reporters, Underwriters Laboratories, security firms, independent researchers, and academics) purchasing a random sample of popular devices off the shelf, and using TLS-RaR to verify that they communicate as they should.

For example, Amazon states that its Alexa devices listen to audio all the time, but only transmit recordings that are made while the light is on (and shortly before the light turned on) [1]. Is this statement true? Can it be independently verified, and monitored, as the software on these devices is updated over time? We believe that IoT manufacturers ought to welcome the idea of independent audits to verify that their devices are communicating as advertised, just as they allow financial auditors to inspect their warehouses and financial statements. In both cases, such audits build confidence and allow consumers or shareholders to separate good products—and companies—from bad ones.

This paper makes these contributions:

1. The design of TLS-RaR, including secure protocols for key rotation and for key release.
2. Measurements of TLS-RaR's existing support across a survey of popular websites.
3. Measurements of the communications of 5 IoT devices.
4. An evaluation of TLS-RaR's effect on application traffic using an implementation of TLS-RaR based on OpenSSL 1.0.2 running on embedded hardware, and an auditor based on tshark.

The rest of this paper is structured as follows. Section 2 describes requirements for IoT auditing. Section 3 gives an overview of TLS-RaR's operating model and approach. Sections 4.1 and 4.2 present the TLS-RaR protocols for rotation and release, respectively. Section 5 evaluates TLS-RaR's compatibility with existing servers, the performance of a prototype implementation, and the behavior of existing IoT devices. An auditor may have significant ethical and surveillance implications; we discuss these in Section 6, and limitations of the approach in Section 7. Section 8 surveys related work.

2. AUDITING IOT DEVICES

TLS-RaR's goal is to enable *auditing*—after-the-fact inspection of traffic—without modifying TLS or giving auditors man-in-the-middle access to encrypted channels. To that end, this section defines four requirements for a secure and practical IoT auditing system: past auditability, present-moment integrity, audit robustness, and compatibility with TLS. It also describes the threat model against which the security notions are defined, and discusses limitations.

We use the following notation for a TLS session when describing these requirements. A TLS session uses a set of symmetric *session keys* for its ciphers; the number and size of keys is determined by the TLS cipher suite, which is chosen by the the client and server endpoints independent of the auditing system. We refer to keys and their lifetime in terms of *epochs*. In an epoch t, a client and server communicate using session keys k_t. TLS allows the client and server to generate new keys, whereupon epoch $t+1$ begins. In practice, the client and server can generate new keys asynchronously, so the endpoints' notions of the current epoch may differ transiently. This means that epochs are defined with respect to a sequence of TLS records rather than with respect to wall-clock time.

2.1 Requirements

In this section, we outline four requirements for an IoT auditing system. The first three, past auditability, present-moment integrity, and audit robustness, are security properties; we define the corresponding threat model in Section 2.2. The fourth requirement, TLS compatibility, responds to the practical realities of deploying new protocols using existing infrastructure.

Past Auditability. The primary goal of an IoT auditing system is allowing the owner of an IoT device to empower one or more *auditors* to decrypt and verify past traffic to and from that IoT device. Informally, auditors should be able to examine the plaintext sent through a TLS connection after some delay, provided that the auditor captured the encrypted traffic from the network.

More formally, if a TLS session is in epoch t, an auditor with all of the encrypted records in each of the epochs $T \subseteq \{0, \ldots, t-1\}$ will either recover the exact sequence of plaintext bytes sent for all epochs $t' \in T$ (after some delay; §2.3), or the auditor will output "failure."

Present-Moment Integrity. An auditor should not violate the integrity of communication between device and server: the auditor must not add, drop, or modify TLS traffic without detection. This ensures that an auditor cannot mount attacks against the device or the server. This protection serves two purposes. First, it prevents the owner of an IoT device from disrupting the device's proper functioning (for example, by falsifying water metering information). Second, it means that a compromised auditor cannot be used to attack devices, their owners, or their manufacturers (e.g., by spoofing an unlock command to a smart door lock).

Formally, if a device believes the current epoch to be t_d and the server believes it to be t_s, then an auditor cannot produce a valid TLS record for any epoch t' such that $t' \geq \min\{t_c, t_s\}$. Note that auditors can forge records for past epochs, but the device and server will ignore these.

Audit Robustness. The data produced by an audit whose output is not "failure" should be correct: no adversary can cause an auditor to output plaintext that differs from what was sent between the device and server. This ensures that malicious third parties, including compromised auditors, cannot falsely implicate IoT devices, and that endpoints cannot persuade auditors to accept incorrect plaintexts.

Formally, if an auditor has the all of the keys released by the device for epochs $T \subseteq \{0 \ldots t\}$ (but not necessarily the corresponding TLS records), a third party cannot produce any TLS record r such that the auditor falsely believes that the device or server sent r in epoch $t' \in T$ when the device or server did not do so.

TLS Compatibility. To be practically deployable, an auditing system should be deployable using existing infrastructure. This means that the system should not require changes to the TLS protocol or wire format: the former risks introducing security vulnerabilities, while the latter might cause incompatibility with middleboxes. More generally, the system should not require changes to the server's implementation, because many deployments use special-purpose hardware to terminate the server's end of TLS connections (say, to accelerate expensive cryptographic operations). On the other hand, the client is an IoT device controlled by the manufacturer, so changes to its software (provided they comply with the above) are acceptable.

Finally, the auditing system must maintain the forward-secrecy properties [39] of the TLS cipher suite that the client and server negotiate. (Roughly speaking, a session has forward secrecy if future key compromises do not reveal past plaintext.)

Non-Requirement: Real-Time Auditing. As a consequence of satisfying these four requirements, TLS-RaR does not give auditors the ability to decrypt and verify traffic in real time. Doing so using unmodified TLS ciphersuites (required for TLS compatibility) would require giving an auditor the current traffic keys (which would violate present-moment integrity). Compared with real-time monitoring, past auditability is weaker, but still sufficient to detect improper behavior. The auditor can choose when—and how often—to ask the device to rotate keys and release them to the auditor, but even if the auditor asks for a rotation and receives keys every second, it will always be slightly behind.

2.2 Threat and Network Model

As in a standard TLS session, there are two endpoints (an IoT device and a server). We assume that the endpoints cooperate to realize the same security as TLS against all parties other than auditors, which can audit past epochs as specified above; we discuss auditors below. Endpoints may attempt to undermine past auditability, but we consider some attacks out of scope (see §2.3).

We make standard cryptographic assumptions, and assume all of the standard threats against TLS. The network, may drop, delay, or reorder packets, even adversarially. Attackers may use passive or active attacks.

Auditors distrust the TLS endpoints they are auditing, and they distrust other auditors—either may attempt to undermine audit robustness. Other than allowing auditors to observe past epochs' plaintext, TLS endpoints distrust auditors. Auditors may attempt to undermine present-moment integrity or audit robustness, except that we do not consider denial of service attacks. Device owners and auditor manufacturers may attempt to disrupt or corrupt IoT applications via auditors (i.e. by attempting to undermine present-moment integrity), except that auditors divulging plaintext from past epochs is out of scope.

2.3 Limitations of the Auditing Model

Auditing is a useful means of detecting incorrect, insecure, or undesirable operation. For example, devices may be compromised; being able to audit their traffic provides a limited but useful check on their behavior. And while auditing does not protect devices from compromise, it may indirectly improve their security by obviating man-in-the-middle proxies.

On the other hand, auditing is not a panacea. Being able to audit TLS traffic does not ensure that a device's owner can see all data sent by that device, or that a device's manufacturer acts in good faith. As examples, a device's manufacturer could use steganography to hide data in innocent-looking exchanges or even install a hidden wireless modem in the device. These *covert channels* are a broad and complementary issue; we leave defending against covert-channel attacks [11, 31, 36, 40, 47, 60] out of scope. Likewise, a device might refuse to allow auditing—though an auditor can detect (and should report) missed audits.

Finally, as mentioned in Section 2.2, users trust auditors with their private information. Auditors might divulge this information or use it for mischief. For example, an auditor might spoof a device's application-layer credentials if those credentials are not resistant to replay attacks. Applications can address this issue, e.g., by using TLS client certificates.

3. SYSTEM OVERVIEW

This section considers three straw man proposals for providing the four properties described in Section 2 and describes a high-level overview of TLS-RaR, including relevant parts of the TLS key exchange protocol.

3.1 Straw Man: TLS Inside TLS

One straw man approach is to tunnel one TLS session inside another. In this arrangement, the outer TLS session provides both confidentiality and integrity, while the inner session uses an integrity-only cipher suite (i.e., anyone can read the plaintext, but it cannot be modified without a key). Then, an auditor can act as a man in the middle for the outer TLS session, but not the inner one. Since the auditor is acting as a man in the middle for the outer session, it can read the plaintext of the inner session, but because only the client and server have the keys to the inner session, the auditor cannot forge or modify data.

This approach has three major flaws. First, it imposes a significant overhead in message size and connection setup, which is a major concern for some IoT devices. More significantly, integrity-only cipher suites are being removed from TLS 1.3, and they have limited support even today. Supporting this approach in the future would require modifications to the TLS specification. Finally, TLS-inside-TLS may break compatibility with some servers and middleboxes, e.g., TLS terminators.

3.2 Straw Man: Application Layer MAC

A second possibility is simply to add application-layer authentication in the form of a MAC. An auditor acting as a man-in-the-middle at the TLS layer can decrypt and inspect traffic, but because it does does not have the application-layer MAC key, it cannot modify this traffic.

This approach has the major issue that safe auditing requires modifications to *all* application-layer protocols in use—each one essentially reimplementing a subset of TLS (key exchange, etc.), in the process inheriting the attendant difficulty of correctly designing and implementing such protocols.

3.3 Straw Man: Separate TLS Channel

A third straw man approach is for clients to log everything they send and receive to each auditor over a separate TLS channel. This approach also has two major problems. First, it requires each device to send copies of all traffic to every auditor; for low-power or embedded IoT devices, this increase in traffic might present an unacceptable energy cost. Second, in this scheme, a device can equivocate by exfiltrating private data to the manufacturer while sending a benign-looking stream of traffic to the auditors. Barring careless mistakes (e.g., data size differences) on the part of the device, auditors would have no way of detecting this misbehavior.

3.4 TLS-RaR

Our approach, which we call TLS-RaR, is illustrated in Figure 1. A person owns one or more networked *devices* that use a local-area network under that person's control, where they can install auditors that passively observe all traffic. An owner cannot modify the software or security credentials of devices. Each device communicates with its manufacturer or other *servers* outside the LAN. These communication channels, which we call *main channels*, are secured using TLS with standard cipher suites.

In addition to communicating with servers, a device allows *auditors* to establish *key release channels*. Key release channels can either be directly with the device, or with an agreed-upon third party, such as the application's cloud service. Key release channels require that an auditor authenticate that it is allowed to decrypt traffic. The choice of authentication mechanism is outside the scope of this paper; possibilities include passwords, public-key infrastructure, or whatever the user already uses to authenticate to the cloud service's website.

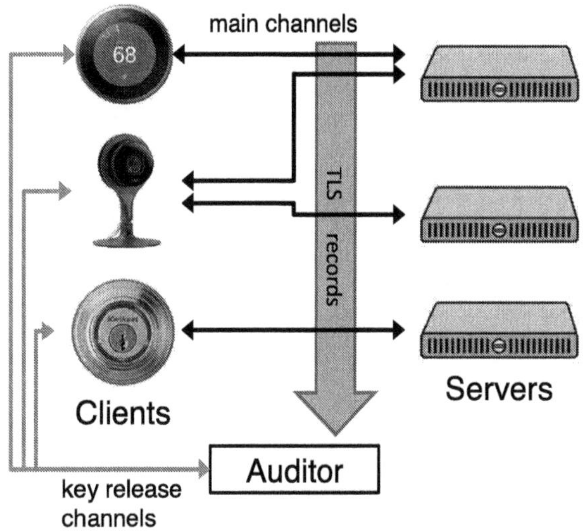

Figure 1: TLS-RaR architecture. Both the main client-server channels and the auxiliary key-release channels use TLS. An auditor passively collects TLS records from the client-server channel. After a key rotation has been fully consummated, clients share the old session key with the auditors. Several independent auditors may operate in tandem.

Auditors buffer encrypted TLS records to and from devices. Initially, the auditors do not have the keys used to encrypt these records and so cannot view the underlying cleartext. Upon a request by the user or auditor, the device *rotates* the TLS connections of their main channels to use new keys. This request may come as an impromptu "surprise inspection"—the cloud service and device may not know of the presence of the auditor until receiving this request.

Once a device is certain that both it and the server have retired the old keys, it uses its key release channel to *release* the old keys to auditors. The auditors use these keys to authenticate and decrypt the saved ciphertext.

Withholding keys from auditors while they passively monitor and buffer encrypted TLS records to and from devices meets the present-moment integrity requirement, while releasing only expired keys meets the past auditability requirement. Meeting the audit robustness and requiring no TLS changes depends on exactly how the key rotation and release protocols are implemented, which the next two sections describe.

4. KEY ROTATION AND RELEASE

TLS-RaR has two protocols, rotation and release. The *rotation* protocol advances a TLS session to a new epoch by using new symmetric keys and retiring the old ones. The *release* protocol gives auditors the keys from a prior epoch which it is sure have been safely retired.

4.1 Key Rotation

To rotate keys, TLS-RaR generates new keying material for the session and *retires* the old keys, meaning that the device and server will discard any further TLS records using

TLS mechanism	*auth-ack?*	*RTT*	*version*
KeyUpdate	✗	1	1.3
KeyUpdate + Heartbeat	✓	1	1.3
KeyUpdate + `OPTIONS`	✓	1	1.3
Resume	✗	1	≤ 1.2
Resume + Heartbeat	✓	1	≤ 1.2
Resume + `OPTIONS`	✓	1	≤ 1.2
Renegotiate	✓	2	≤ 1.2
Reconnect	?	4	any

Table 1: Mechanisms for rotating keys (§4.1).

the old keys. If the old keys are not retired, an attacker with the key can violate present-moment integrity. For example, suppose a device releases the TLS session keys immediately after closing the TCP stream and without verifiably shutting down the TLS session. An attacker who prevents the device's `FIN` from reaching the server and spoofs the server's `FIN/ACK` response could use the released keys to continue the TLS session and masquerade as the device. This broken straw man protocol illustrates the following necessary condition for secure key rotation:

Authenticated Key-Retirement ACK (auth-ack): For a device to securely rotate keys, it must first receive an authenticated acknowledgment that the server has retired the keys.

The TLS standards define several mechanisms for a TLS session to choose new symmetric keys, but most require an extra step to have an authenticated key-retirement ACK. Table 1 lists these mechanisms; below, we briefly describe each.

KeyUpdate. The TLS 1.3 draft standard [53] introduces a mechanism called KeyUpdate that causes both TLS endpoints to generate new session keys. KeyUpdate is asynchronous, may be initiated by either side of the connection, and imposes no blocking and almost no overhead.

Unfortunately, KeyUpdate is not sufficient for an auth-ack because it is possible for either endpoint to send KeyUpdate on its own initiative. As a result, a device that sends and then receives a KeyUpdate message does not know if the server was responding to the device's KeyUpdate or if the server initiated a KeyUpdate on its own. To distinguish these two cases, a device must send a message after initiating KeyUpdate and then wait for the server to respond to that message.

The simplest mechanism for the required request-response exchange is a TLS heartbeat [52]. In this approach, the device sends a heartbeat request after initiating KeyUpdate; the corresponding heartbeat response serves as authenticated acknowledgment that the server has received and acted upon the request. This mechanism is efficient: the device can send this heartbeat message immediately after sending a KeyUpdate. The entire rotation takes one round trip and doesn't block traffic at any point.

Because of security concerns in the wake of the Heartbleed bug [19], TLS heartbeat is an optional feature that is often disabled. When heartbeat is not available, a device can instead send an application-layer request. For example, devices communicating with an HTTP server can send an `OPTIONS` request [28], which elicits a short response and has no effect on the HTTP session.

Resume. TLS standards prior to 1.3 [22,23,24] allow clients to resume a prior session with a server using a session ID or session ticket [57]. While this causes a key rotation, the device does not immediately learn that the server has changed its keys: because the device speaks last in a session resumption, it does not know that its final message arrived until it receives more traffic from the server. Like KeyUpdate, pairing Resume with a heartbeat or an application-layer request-response gives an auth-ack.

Renegotiate. TLS standards prior to 1.3 allow endpoints to renegotiate an existing TLS session, meaning that they repeat the TLS handshake over the existing connection and then continue communicating using new keys. The server sends the final message in a renegotiation exchange, and this message serves as an auth-ack. The major drawback of renegotiation is its cost: it requires computationally expensive public key cryptographic operations.

Reconnect. The final rotation approach is for a device to disconnect a TLS session by sending a TLS `close_notify` message and waiting for a corresponding TLS `close_notify` from the server. After receiving the `close_notify`, the device knows the server has retired the session's keys. The device starts the next epoch by initiating a new connection. Like KeyUpdate, disconnection can be initiated asynchronously by either side, but TLS implementations can nevertheless give an auth-ack by discarding all incoming traffic after sending or receiving a `close_notify` message. Implementations that close a session's underlying TCP connection immediately upon receiving a `close_notify` without sending a response do not provide an auth-ack.

TLS Session Termination. Except for reconnection, the above protocols obtain an auth-ack by assuming that a device will continue communicating after rotation: this post-rotation traffic provides authenticated acknowledgment of an epoch's end because it uses new keys. When a TLS session terminates, however, there are no new keys or messages that serve as an auth-ack, meaning that a device cannot safely release the session's final keys and auditors cannot examine the session's final plaintext.

The reconnection protocol above can provide an auth-ack at session termination when paired with a TLS implementation that discards all incoming traffic after sending or receiving a `close_notify`. Alternatively, the application can use a session tracking mechanism at the application layer and invalidate that session before terminating the TLS connection. If an attacker attempts to append data, the server will ignore it because the application session has terminated.

4.2 Key Release

Once a TLS-RaR device has safely rotated keys, it releases the old keys to auditors. The release protocol must maintain the auditability and robustness properties of Section 2. In particular, it must prevent falsifying the plaintext of an epoch, and it must prevent devices from equivocating about that content. For example, a device that broadcasts keys to several auditors does not give audit robustness: if one auditor fails to receive the keys, an attacker with the keys can falsify additional TLS records. When that auditor finally receives the keys, it will be convinced that the forged traffic is real.

To safely release keys, TLS-RaR uses a *Sealed-History Release* protocol. Devices compute cryptographic hashes of all TLS records sent and received. After a device rotates keys and is ready to release the keys k_t for epoch t, it signs and discloses to the auditors a message:

$$\left(\texttt{release}, t, k_t, \text{Hash}(r_1^d, \ldots, r_n^d), \text{Hash}(r_1^s, \ldots, r_n^s)\right)$$

where $(r_1^d, \ldots, r_n^d)$ and $(r_1^s, \ldots, r_n^s)$ are the TLS records sent by device and server, respectively, in epoch t.

Providing a sealed history prevents falsified content. While an attacker can delay a key release message's arrival at another auditor, it cannot forge a new one (because devices and auditors communicate over an authenticated key release channel). Meanwhile, for a given key-release message, an attacker cannot forge new records because doing so requires finding a hash collision. To participate, the device must compute a cryptographic hash of the messages sent and received during each key epoch. This may be computed incrementally.

A remaining concern is that a malicious device might attempt to evade audit using *deniable encryption* [12], allowing the device to equivocate between an inappropriate plaintext (sent to the server) and an innocuous one (decrypted by the auditor). Specifically, the device could release a key $\hat{k}_t$ that seems to decrypt and authenticate data correctly, but the device and server know of another key k_t that decrypts and authenticates a different, valid plaintext TLS transcript. Sealed-History Release prevents deniable encryption from producing valid plaintext by requiring auditors to check that the structure of every decrypted TLS record is valid. Under reasonable assumptions about the security of modern AEAD ciphers (such as `AES_GCM` [43]), finding two different keys that correctly authenticate this header content but yield different records is infeasible. With overwhelming probability, no such pair of keys exists.

5. EVALUATION

To evaluate how the key rotation protocols affect performance, we implemented TLS-RaR on our own IoT device and web service, along with a prototype auditor.

Our IoT device is a temperature sensor built on the Raspberry Pi 3 platform with 4 × 1.2 GHz ARM Cortex-A53 cores. The web service consists of web servers built on the Python Twisted Web library. The device periodically uploads JSON objects encoding timestamped temperature readings. The device owner can view the readings from a web interface.

We implemented a "surprise" auditing interface on the website, where a user can click a button to request keys for auditing. Upon clicking the button, the server requests a key rotation and release from the device. The device then initiates a key rotation by TLS Renegotiate or Resume on its TLS connections. After a key rotation is complete, the device signs the superseded keys and traffic hashes and submits them to the web server, where the user can view and download them.

Because TLS 1.3 is not fully specified or implemented in current software and libraries our implementation communicates using TLS 1.2 with help from the OpenSSL 1.0.2 library. Implementing the TLS-RaR client required making only one modification to OpenSSL: we added a callback that releases the TLS session keys to the application after a rotation.

We also implemented a prototype auditor, built on `libpcap` and `tshark`, that captures TLS streams. After a rotation-and-release, our auditor reads the signed key-release message, verifies the signature and hashes, and decrypts the captured ciphertext.

	(CPU seconds / GiB)
Baseline TLS (encrypt/send)	9.8
TLS-RaR (encrypt/hash/send)	11.9
Mean CPU overhead per byte:	22%

Table 2: Ongoing CPU overhead. The extra SHA-256 hashing required by TLS-RaR imposes about 22% CPU overhead on an ARM Cortex-A53 processor, versus baseline TLS using AES-128.

	(CPU milliseconds)
Rotate by Renegotiation	46
Rotate by Resume + heartbeat	1.2
Release	0.7

Table 3: Rotation/release overhead. It takes less than two milliseconds of total CPU time on the ARM Cortex-A53 for TLS-RaR to rotate keys (using the Resume + heartbeat method) and prepare a signed release.

	(transport bytes)
Rotate by Renegotiation	3004
Rotate by Resume + heartbeat	573
Release	900

Table 4: Network overhead. Each time the user requests a key rotation-and-release, TLS-RaR will need to send roughly 1.5 kilobytes over the wire (using the Resume + heartbeat method).

5.1 Performance

We used our IoT temperature sensor as a platform for analyzing the costs of TLS-RaR. Tables 2, 3, and 4 show the ongoing CPU overhead, the CPU cost of each rotate/release event, and the IO cost of each rotate/release event, as measured on the Cortex-A53 processor using standard TLS 1.2 with the AES-128 cipher.

In summary, TLS-RaR imposes an ongoing CPU overhead of roughly 22%, compared with baseline TLS. This is attributable to the ongoing hashing required to be able to prepare a Sealed-History Release if the device is eventually audited. This ongoing overhead would decrease on IoT devices with hardware support for SHA-256 or another secure hash algorithm. By contrast, the CPU and network costs associated with rotating and releasing keys are minimal.

The values from the tables can be used to estimate the cost of rotation in relation to TLS traffic encryption. Rotation by Renegotiation, the most computationally expensive method, reaches parity with the traffic encryption and hashing cost at approximately 4 MiB of plaintext per epoch, and it reduces to approximately 10% of the overall CPU cost of TLS at approximately 36 MiB of plaintext per epoch. At 36 MiB per epoch, Rotation by Renegotiation increases the amount of bytes transferred by less than 0.01%, but data transfer will be interrupted by 2 round trips.

Rotation by Resume and Heartbeat is approximately 1/20 of the CPU cost of Rotation by Renegotiation. At approximately 1.5 MiB per epoch, rotations consume 10% of overall TLS CPU time while placing less than 0.04% extra bytes on the wire, and interrupting transfer for 1 round trip.

Rotation by a TLS 1.3 KeyUpdate will consume an amount of CPU similar to a Resume, and will not interrupt data transfer at all.

5.2 IoT Communications Survey

To put TLS-RaR in the context of real-world IoT systems, we recorded and inspected the traffic from commercially available devices: a Nest Protect smoke detector, a Nest Cam, a Samsung SmartThings hub with a SmarthThings Outlet, and a Vizio TV.

We connected the devices to the Internet through a Wi-Fi base station that itself was connected through a desktop PC with two Ethernet interfaces. The PC recorded the IoT devices' traffic using tcpdump for several weeks. We observed the following communication characteristics:

1. The Nest Cam makes a single long-lived HTTPS connection to subdomains of dropcam.com that resolve to Amazon EC2 hosts, and uploads video continuously at a rate of approximately 200 kilobits/s.

2. The Nest Protect makes a TCP connection to an Amazon EC2 server about every six hours. The traffic doesn't appear to be TLS; we believe it is using Nest's Weave protocol. The TCP connections last between 3 and 12 seconds, and the device sends between 1 kilobyte and 45 kilobytes, and receives between 1 kilobyte and 6 kilobytes, each time. (This is with the device idle and no fires happening.)

3. The Samsung SmartThings Hub, with a SmartThings Outlet connected to it, maintains one long-lived HTTPS connection to an Amazon EC2 host. It exchanges about 50 bytes every 30 seconds. Every five minutes, the device makes an HTTPS connection to another Amazon EC2 host, sending approximately 550 bytes and receiving about 2000 bytes each time.

4. Every 24 hours, the Vizio TV made a series of brief HTTPS and HTTP connections to hosts on Amazon EC2, uploading tens of kilobytes and receiving up to a megabyte each time.

These flow lengths and durations, combined with the performance measurements from the previous section, suggest that the overheads of deploying TLS-RaR in the context of these IoT devices would be reasonable—even if the user wished to audit their devices' traffic every minute. Even at that frequency, the overall cost would be dominated by the ongoing cost of computing the hashed history, not of rotating and releasing keys.

5.3 Survey: Server Compatibility

TLS-RaR requires no changes to the TLS protocol, but it does require a server that supports certain TLS features. To test the compatibility of TLS-RaR with real-world servers, we surveyed the subset of the Alexa Top 1,000,000 sites [2] that support long-lived HTTPS connections [29]. Table 5 gives an overview of the results.

	Fraction of Servers
Rotation by Reconnect	54.2%
Rotation by Renegotiate	12.2%
Rotation by Resume	0.5%
TLS 1.3 KeyUpdate	*0% at time of survey*

Table 5: Survey of the top 1,000,000 websites, conducted in early 2016. Most existing server-side TLS implementations support at least one method of key rotation and could be used with TLS-RaR today. As TLS 1.3 is deployed, we expect close to 100% of updated servers to support rotation by KeyUpdate.

Most of the servers in our sample are compatible with Rotate by Reconnection (assuming they stop receiving data before sending `close_notify`; §4.1). The remaining servers are incompatible because they do not reply to `close_notify` correctly; incompatible servers simply close the underlying TCP connection without sending a `close_notify`.

Full reconnection of a TLS session, however, is an expensive way to rotate a key. Of the lighter-weight methods, about 12% of servers in our sample support Rotate by Renegotiation, while only a small fraction (0.5%) support Rotate by Resume.

Because the TLS 1.3 specification is still in draft form, we were unable to test Rotation by KeyUpdate, but expect support to become ubiquitous when TLS 1.3 is deployed because KeyUpdate is a mandatory part of the draft specification.

6. ETHICAL CONSIDERATIONS

This paper arose out of our personal concerns about the privacy implications of IoT devices. As everyday users, we would like to know exactly what our devices are saying about us. Though the motivation for this work is to empower the consumer, there is a risk that businesses or governments could deploy TLS-RaR in a way that would harm the privacy or agency of end users. Recent disclosures of vast and sophisticated surveillance by state-sponsored actors [13,26,30,33,44,49,54,58,62,63] have brought new focus to the ethical implications of computer-security systems [55]. Understanding the ethical status of TLS-RaR requires a weighing of the potential social risks and rewards of the scheme.

In terms of risks, it is possible that the comparably benign nature of TLS-RaR—in that it allows only read-only auditing—might permit an employer or government to more easily compel its use. Even so, we expect that corporations or governments with the power to force their employees or citizens to use TLS-RaR would almost certainly prefer to deploy a full man-in-the-middle proxy to skirt the limitations on the auditor that TLS-RaR imposes. Indeed, employers already exert considerable control over their employees' devices, and workplace policies requiring man-in-the-middle proxies are already widespread [37]. We find it unlikely that the existence of TLS-RaR would change the calculus of those engaging in network surveillance in a meaningful way.

One of the design goals of TLS-RaR was to enable auditing of TLS traffic even for devices that are cryptographically bound to communicate only with their manufacturers' servers (e.g., via certificate pinning [27]). This raises another potential ethical qualm: by providing a means to audit IoT device traffic, TLS-RaR could make it more acceptable for manufacturers to sell "locked down" devices. We appreciate that some users value the ability to redirect their devices' traffic to a user-controlled server, but business realities mean that the sale of locked devices will likely continue. With TLS-RaR, manufacturers will be able to produce locked devices that still allow their owners to audit the traffic the devices send.

With these potential risks in mind, we now recall the social benefits of TLS-RaR. We find the fact that today's IoT devices are unaccountable to their owners troubling, and we view it as socially unwise to grant manufacturers unbridled control over devices placed inside private homes—a place "strongly guarded by every holy feeling" [16]. From the perspective of those who wish to combat inappropriate surveillance, the fact that TLS-RaR enables device owners and security researchers to learn what information their devices are sending back to the manufacturer has considerable social value.

While TLS-RaR allows anyone to audit their IoT devices, its benefits come even if only a handful of people do. Watchdog groups will be able to verify manufacturers' claims about their devices' behaviors (as they can for Web browser [32] and ISP behaviors [35]) and consumers will gain confidence in manufacturers' privacy polices, or avoid products that behave unfavorably.

7. LIMITATIONS AND DISCUSSION

TLS-RaR allows device owners (including consumer watchdogs and security researchers) to audit the traffic of their IoT devices. It achieves this without modifying the TLS protocol or compromising the integrity of the device-cloud connection. This model, while valuable, has some limitations, which we discuss here.

First, TLS-RaR assumes that IoT application vendors are willing to share their traffic with device owners. Our initial responses from numerous vendors across many application domains (home automation, insurance, automotive, industrial automation, smart appliances) has been unanimously positive. The most common concern we have heard is that owners may react irrationally to raw data. For example, the owner of a carbon monoxide sensor reporting a concentration of 2 parts per million might be alarmed even though this is well below the recommended safe limit, 9 ppm. On the whole, the vendors we have spoken with said that the benefits of transparency would likely outweigh its costs.

Second, TLS-RaR provides auditors with delayed access to an encrypted stream and so does not support systems that require real-time access to encrypted traffic, such as intrusion-prevention systems that seek to interdict harmful traffic before it reaches an endpoint. To our knowledge this is a necessary tradeoff to simultaneously provide present-moment integrity and past auditability while maintaining backwards compatibility with existing TLS implementations and infrastructure.

Third, as we discuss in Section 2, TLS-RaR does not prevent a device from intentionally hiding communication from an auditor. A deceptive manufacturer—or a compromised device—can leak private data by encrypting it again (within the TLS stream) or by using steganography, a hidden wireless modem, or another covert channel. A complementary system might attempt to frustrate, or at least detect, likely covert channels.

Fourth, the primary benefits of auditing can be achieved even if only a small fraction of devices are ever audited. A device does not know it is being audited until *after* it has sent the traffic. Only a few audits by consumer watchdogs or security researchers will benefit everyone, encouraging device engineers to respect owner privacy and influencing them to fix flaws when discovered.

Finally, there are several alternative or complementary approaches to TLS-RaR; we discuss related work more fully in the next section.

8. RELATED WORK

The idea of allowing trusted third parties to inspect the contents of encrypted communications has a considerable literature. In this section, we compare TLS-RaR with related work and systems.

Man-in-the-Middle TLS Proxies. The standard way to give middleboxes access to the plaintext of a TLS stream is to install the middlebox's public key as a root certificate on end-users' devices [37,59], allowing the middlebox to act as a man-in-the-middle. This technique carries risk. A recent survey [21] found that 75% of the man-in-the-middle TLS proxies tested exposed the client behind the proxy to MITM attacks by adversaries on the Internet (i.e., not the proxy). These middleboxes become another point of failure for the client's security, and any vulnerability in the middlebox can become a vulnerability for the client (e.g. [18,20]).

Multi-Context TLS [45] is a recent proposal that allows endpoints to grant middleboxes read-only or read-write access to parts of a TLS stream. In brief, mcTLS augments the TLS protocol with three keyed message-authentication codes that control access to encrypted data. Endpoints hold one key, the second is shared with middleboxes with read/write access, and the third is shared with middleboxes with read-only access.

Unlike mcTLS, TLS-RaR maintains compatibility with the TLS protocol (and with some existing endpoint implementations, §5.3). Avoiding changes and extensions to the TLS protocol is desirable both for ease of deployment and for security: TLS is a subtle protocol [7,8,9], and making changes risks introducing new vulnerabilities. On the server side, TLS is commonly implemented by hardware TLS terminators and load balancers, which the vendor may not be able to modify.

Further, TLS-RaR ensures that auditors see the same byte stream that the TLS recipient does (§2). In contrast, mcTLS's use of separate keying material held by endpoints and by different kinds of middleboxes opens the door to mischief. Finally, TLS-RaR allows auditors to begin auditing "impromptu" in the middle of a long-running TLS session. In contrast, mcTLS requires participation by all middleboxes when the TLS session is being negotiated, meaning that existing connections cannot be audited, and devices might choose to behave honestly only when under an auditor's gaze.

mcTLS has several capabilities that TLS-RaR does not. mcTLS allows for read-write middleboxes (e.g., a transparent Web cache), and for real-time read-only middleboxes (e.g., an intrusion-prevention system that immediately interdicts harmful traffic). TLS-RaR only supports applications that audit traffic after the fact.

BlindBox [61] is another proposed system for granting middleboxes restricted access to TLS traffic. BlindBox allows middleboxes to search for substrings in TLS-encrypted traffic. To do so, the BlindBox endpoints use a secondary connection to the middlebox, and on that connection, send the same traffic with a *searchable encryption* scheme [4, 6, 10, 17, 64] that allows the middlebox to determine if a particular substring appears in the TLS traffic without learning the full contents. BlindBox requires the endpoints to faithfully execute the protocol by providing an accurate version of their communications on the secondary stream, so that the middlebox can see if an intrusion-signature substring was sent. This differs from the goals of TLS-RaR: we wish to allow the auditor to see everything that the device transmits, and do not trust the vendor that controls both endpoints.

Proposed TLS Proxy Support. In parallel to the academic work on inspecting TLS traffic, a number of protocol designers have proposed extensions or modifications to TLS. One theme in this line of work is to enable a way for a TLS client to specify an explicit proxy with the privileges to decrypt and modify the TLS stream [41, 42, 46, 48]. TLS-RaR differs from these proposals in that it never allows the auditor to modify the TLS stream and does not require changes to TLS.

Another approach is to make changes at the application layer rather than at the transport layer. QoS2 enables HTTP caching middleboxes while providing TLS-strength integrity and authenticity guarantees [68]. When deployed in tandem with QoS2, TLS-RaR could allow a device owner to audit their device's QoS2 sessions.

Computing on Encrypted Data. A substantial literature has developed about systems that compute on encrypted data [50, 51, 61, 66]. In these systems, the client is trusted but the server isn't. From a privacy perspective, such protocols are preferable to ones that reveal sensitive information to the server, but the trust model differs from that of the IoT, where both the device and server are under the control of the same vendor and may not faithfully execute the protocol. We regard this work as complementary. A privacy-preserving IoT system might use both mechanisms in concert: the protocol would prevent sensitive information from being shared with the cloud, *and* auditors would verify that the device faithfully executed that protocol.

9. CONCLUSION

Owners of IoT devices should have the right to listen in on what their own devices are saying about them. Towards this goal, we have proposed TLS-RaR, a system that allows device owners, consumer watchdogs, and security researchers to inspect TLS streams with the cooperation of the device. TLS-RaR is compatible with some existing TLS servers, makes no changes to the TLS protocol, and does not allow the auditor to man-in-the-middle TLS connections. In this way, TLS-RaR reconciles the desire for end-to-end encryption with the ability to see what our devices are saying about us.

10. ACKNOWLEDGMENTS

We would like to thank our shepherd, Lin Zhong, and the anonymous reviewers for helpful feedback. We are grateful to Eric Rescorla, Adam Langley, and David Benjamin for discussions about this proposal. This work was supported in part by Intel/NSF CPS Security grant #1505728, with additional support from an NDSEG Fellowship, the Simons Foundation, VMware, Qualcomm, Analog Devices, Google, Amazon, and the Secure Internet of Things Project.

11. REFERENCES

[1] Alexa and Alexa device FAQs. Amazon.com. https://www.amazon.com/gp/help/customer/display.html?nodeId=201602230. Accessed: 2017-04-25.

[2] Top 1,000,000 sites (updated daily). Alexa Internet Inc., 2009-2016. http://s3.amazonaws.com/alexa-static/top-1m.csv.zip. Accessed: 2016-01-18.

[3] Keeping data safe at Nest. Nest Labs, Dec. 2016. https://nest.com/security/.

[4] M. Abdalla, M. Bellare, D. Catalano, E. Kiltz, T. Kohno, T. Lange, J. Malone-Lee, G. Neven, P. Paillier, and H. Shi. Searchable encryption revisited: Consistency properties, relation to anonymous IBE, and extensions. In *Advances in Cryptology – CRYPTO 2005: 25th Annual International Cryptology Conference, Santa Barbara, California, USA, August 14-18, 2005. Proceedings*, pages 205–222, Berlin, Heidelberg, 2005. Springer Berlin Heidelberg.

[5] J. Angwin and J. Valentino-Devries. Google's iPhone tracking: Web giant, others bypassed Apple browser settings for guarding privacy. The Wall Street Journal, Feb. 17, 2012. http://www.wsj.com/articles/SB10001424052970204880404577225380456599176.

[6] M. Bellare, A. Boldyreva, and A. O'Neill. Deterministic and efficiently searchable encryption. In *Proceedings of the 27th Annual International Cryptology Conference on Advances in Cryptology*, CRYPTO'07, pages 535–552. Springer-Verlag, Berlin, Heidelberg, 2007.

[7] B. Beurdouche, K. Bhargavan, A. Delignat-Lavaud, C. Fournet, M. Kohlweiss, A. Pironti, P.-Y. Strub, and J. K. Zinzindohoue. A messy state of the union: Taming the composite state machines of TLS. In *IEEE Symposium on Security & Privacy 2015*, San Jose, United States, May 2015. IEEE.

[8] K. Bhargavan, A. D. Lavaud, C. Fournet, A. Pironti, and P. Y. Strub. Triple handshakes and cookie cutters: Breaking and fixing authentication over TLS. In *Proceedings of the 2014 IEEE Symposium on Security and Privacy*, SP '14, pages 98–113, Washington, DC, USA, 2014. IEEE Computer Society.

[9] K. Bhargavan and G. Leurent. Transcript collision attacks: Breaking authentication in TLS, IKE, and SSH. In *23nd Annual Network and Distributed System Security Symposium 2016, NDSS 2016*, Feb. 2016.

[10] D. Boneh, G. Di Crescenzo, R. Ostrovsky, and G. Persiano. Public key encryption with keyword search. In *Advances in Cryptology - EUROCRYPT 2004: International Conference on the Theory and Applications of Cryptographic Techniques, Interlaken, Switzerland, May 2-6, 2004. Proceedings*, pages 506–522, Berlin, Heidelberg, 2004. Springer Berlin Heidelberg.

[11] S. Cabuk, C. E. Brodley, and C. Shields. IP covert timing channels: design and detection. In *Proceedings of the 11th ACM Conference on Computer and Communications Security*, CCS '04, pages 178–187, New York, NY, USA, 2004. ACM.

[12] R. Canetti, C. Dwork, M. Naor, and R. Ostrovsky. Deniable encryption. In *Annual International Cryptology Conference*, CRYPTO '97, Aug. 1997.

[13] L. Cauley. NSA has massive database of Americans' phone calls; 3 telecoms help government collect billions

of domestic records. USA Today, May 11, 2006. http://usatoday30.usatoday.com/news/washington/2006-05-10-nsa_x.htm.

[14] E. Chiel. Here are the sites you can't access because someone took the internet down. Fusion, October 20 2016. http://fusion.net/story/360952/which-sites-affected-ddos-attack/.

[15] R. Chirgwin. Internet of Things 'smart' devices are dumb by design. The Register, Jan. 19, 2016. https://www.theregister.co.uk/2016/01/19/iot_smart_devices_are_dumb/.

[16] Cicero. *Ad Pontifices*, XLI., 109, translated by Harbottle, Dictionary of Quotations (Classical) (Sonnenschein 1906).

[17] R. Curtmola, J. Garay, S. Kamara, and R. Ostrovsky. Searchable symmetric encryption: Improved definitions and efficient constructions. In *Proceedings of the 13th ACM Conference on Computer and Communications Security*, CCS '06, pages 79–88, New York, NY, USA, 2006. ACM.

[18] CVE-2012-3372: Vulnerability in Cyberoam DPI devices. Common Vulnerabilities and Exposures List, June 30, 2012. https://cve.mitre.org/cgi-bin/cvename.cgi?name=CVE-2012-3372.

[19] CVE-2014-0160: OpenSSL 'Heartbleed' Vulnerability. Common Vulnerabilites and Exposures List, Apr. 2014. https://cve.mitre.org/cgi-bin/cvename.cgi?name=CVE-2014-0160.

[20] CVE-2016-1280: Self-signed certificate with spoofed trusted issuer cn accepted as valid. Common Vulnerabilites and Exposures List, July 2016. https://cve.mitre.org/cgi-bin/cvename.cgi?name=CVE-2016-1280.

[21] X. d. C. de Carnavalet and M. Mannan. Killed by proxy: Analyzing client-end tls interception software. In *23nd Annual Network and Distributed System Security Symposium 2016, NDSS 2016*, Feb. 2016.

[22] T. Dierks and C. Allen. The TLS protocol version 1.0. IETF, 1999. RFC 2246.

[23] T. Dierks and E. Rescorla. The transport-layer security (TLS) protocol, version 1.1. IETF, 2006. RFC 4346.

[24] T. Dierks and E. Rescorla. The transport layer security (TLS) protocol version 1.2. IETF, 2008. RFC 5246.

[25] B. Donohue. Dozens of popular Android apps leak sensitive user data. Kaspersky Lab official blog, Sept. 18, 2016. https://blog.kaspersky.com/privacy_holes_in_popular_android_apps/6047/.

[26] R. Ensafi, D. Fifield, P. Winter, N. Feamster, N. Weaver, and V. Paxson. Examining how the Great Firewall discovers hidden circumvention servers. In *Proceedings of the 2015 Internet Measurement Conference*, IMC '15, pages 445–458, New York, NY, USA, 2015. ACM.

[27] S. Fahl, M. Harbach, H. Perl, M. Koetter, and M. Smith. Rethinking SSL development in an appified world. In *Proceedings of the 2013 ACM SIGSAC Conference on Computer and Communications Security*, CCS '13, pages 49–60, New York, NY, USA, 2013. ACM.

[28] R. Fielding, J. Gettys, J. Mogul, H. Frystyk, L. Masinter, P. Leach, and T. Berners-Lee. Hypertext transfer protocol—HTTP/1.1. IETF, 1999. RFC 2616.

[29] R. Fielding and J. Reschke. Hypertext transfer protocol (HTTP/1.1): Message syntax and routing. IETF, 2014. RFC 7230.

[30] J. Follorou and F. Johannès. Révélations sur le Big Brother français [revelations about the French Big Brother]. Le Monde, July 4, 2013. http://www.lemonde.fr/societe/article/2013/07/04/revelations-sur-le-big-brother-francais_3441973_3224.html.

[31] S. Gianvecchio and H. Wang. Detecting covert timing channels: An entropy-based approach. In *Proceedings of the 14th ACM Conference on Computer and Communications Security*, CCS '07, pages 307–316, New York, NY, USA, 2007. ACM.

[32] M. Godbe. Google deceptively tracks students' internet browsing, EFF says in FTC complaint. Electronic Frontier Foundation, December 1, 2015. https://www.eff.org/press/releases/google-deceptively-tracks-students-internet-browsing-eff-says-complaint-federal-trade.

[33] G. Greenwald. *No Place to Hide: Edward Snowden, the NSA, and the U.S. Surveillance State*. Metropolitan Books, 2014.

[34] S. Grover and N. Feamster. The internet of unpatched things. In *PrivacyCon*, Jan. 2016.

[35] J. Hoffman-Andrews. Ad network turn will suspend zombie cookie program. when will verizon? Electronic Frontier Foundation, January 16, 2015. https://www.eff.org/deeplinks/2015/01/ad-network-turn-will-suspend-zombie-cookie-program-when-will-verizon.

[36] A. Houmansadr and N. Borisov. CoCo: Coding-based covert timing channels for network flows. In *Proceedings of the 13th International Conference on Information Hiding*, IH'11, pages 314–328, Berlin, Heidelberg, 2011. Springer-Verlag.

[37] L. S. Huang, A. Rice, E. Ellingsen, and C. Jackson. Analyzing forged SSL certificates in the wild. In *Proceedings of the 2014 IEEE Symposium on Security and Privacy*, SP '14, pages 83–97, Washington, DC, USA, 2014. IEEE Computer Society.

[38] Internet of things research study, 2015 report. Hewlett Packard. http://www8.hp.com/h20195/V2/GetPDF.aspx/4AA5-4759ENW.pdf.

[39] H. Krawczyk. Perfect forward secrecy. In *Encyclopedia of Cryptography and Security*, pages 457–458. Springer, 2005.

[40] Y. Liu, D. Ghosal, F. Armknecht, A.-R. Sadeghi, S. Schulz, and S. Katzenbeisser. Hide and seek in time: Robust covert timing channels. In *Proceedings of the 14th European Conference on Research in Computer Security*, ESORICS'09, pages 120–135, Berlin, Heidelberg, 2009. Springer-Verlag.

[41] S. Loreto, J. Mattsson, R. Skog, H. Spaak, G. Gus, D. Druta, and M. Hafeez. Explicit trusted proxy in HTTP/2.0. IETF HTTPBis Working Group Internet-Draft `draft-loreto-httpbis-trusted-proxy20-01`, February 14, 2014.

[42] D. McGrew, D. Wing, Y. Nir, and P. Gladstone. TLS

proxy server extension. IETF TLS Internet-Draft `draft-mcgrew-tls-proxy-server-01`, July 16, 2012.
[43] D. A. McGrew and J. Viega. The Galois/counter mode of operation (GCM), May 31, 2005. http://csrc.nist.gov/groups/ST/toolkit/BCM/documents/proposedmodes/gcm/gcm-spec.pdf.
[44] E. Nakashima. Chinese hackers who breached Google gained access to sensitive data, U.S. officials say. The Washington Post, May 20, 2013. https://www.washingtonpost.com/51330428-be34-11e2-89c9-3be8095fe767_story.html.
[45] D. Naylor, K. Schomp, M. Varvello, I. Leontiadis, J. Blackburn, D. R. López, K. Papagiannaki, P. Rodriguez Rodriguez, and P. Steenkiste. Multi-context TLS (mcTLS): Enabling secure in-network functionality in TLS. In *Proceedings of the 2015 ACM Conference on Special Interest Group on Data Communication*, SIGCOMM '15, pages 199–212, New York, NY, USA, 2015. ACM.
[46] Y. Nir. A method for sharing record protocol keys with a middlebox in TLS. IETF TLS Working Group Internet-Draft `draft-nir-tls-keyshare-02`, March 26, 2012.
[47] V. Paxson, M. Christodorescu, M. Javed, J. R. Rao, R. Sailer, D. L. Schales, M. P. Stoecklin, K. Thomas, W. Venema, and N. Weaver. Practical comprehensive bounds on surreptitious communication over DNS. In *Proceedings of the 22nd USENIX Security Symposium*, USENIX-SS'17, pages 17–32. USENIX Association, Aug. 2013.
[48] R. Peon. Explicit proxies for HTTP/2.0. IETF Network Working Group Internet-Draft `draft-rpeon-httpbis-exproxy-00`, June 8, 2012.
[49] A. Peterson. How the NSA may be using games to encourage digital snooping. The Washington Post, June 18, 2014. https://www.washingtonpost.com/news/the-switch/wp/2014/06/18/how-the-nsa-may-have-used-games-to-encourage-digital-snooping/.
[50] R. A. Popa, C. M. S. Redfield, N. Zeldovich, and H. Balakrishnan. CryptDB: Protecting confidentiality with encrypted query processing. In *Proceedings of the Twenty-Third ACM Symposium on Operating Systems Principles*, SOSP '11, pages 85–100, New York, NY, USA, 2011. ACM.
[51] R. A. Popa, E. Stark, J. Helfer, S. Valdez, N. Zeldovich, M. F. Kaashoek, and H. Balakrishnan. Building web applications on top of encrypted data using Mylar. In *Proceedings of the 11th USENIX Conference on Networked Systems Design and Implementation*, NSDI'14, pages 157–172, Berkeley, CA, USA, 2014. USENIX Association.
[52] M. W. R. Seggelmann, M. Tuexen. Transport layer security (TLS) and datagram transport layer security (DTLS) heartbeat extension. IETF, 2012. RFC 6520.
[53] E. Rescorla. The transport layer security (TLS) protocol version 1.3. IETF, 2017. draft-ietf-tls-tls13-19.
[54] J. Risen and E. Lichtblau. Bush lets U.S. spy on callers without courts. The New York Times, December 16, 2005. https://www.nytimes.com/2005/12/16/politics/bush-lets-us-spy-on-callers-without-courts.html.
[55] P. Rogaway. The moral character of cryptographic work. Cryptology ePrint Archive, Report 2015/1162, 2015. http://eprint.iacr.org/2015/1162.
[56] E. Ronen, C. O'Flynn, A. Shamir, and A. Weingarten. IoT Goes Nuclear: Creating a ZigBee Chain Reaction, Preliminary Draft Version 0.93, Nov. 2016. http://iotworm.eyalro.net/iotworm.pdf.
[57] J. Salowey, H. Zhou, P. Eronen, and H. Tschofenig. Transport layer security (TLS) session resumption without server-side state. IETF, 2008. RFC 5077.
[58] D. E. Sanger and J. H. Davis. Hacking linked to China exposes millions of U.S. workers. The New York Times, June 4, 2015. https://www.nytimes.com/2015/06/05/us/breach-in-a-federal-computer-system-exposes-personnel-data.html.
[59] S. Schultze. How the Nokia browser decrypts SSL traffic: A "man in the client". Freedom To Tinker Blog, January 11, 2013. https://freedom-to-tinker.com/blog/sjs/how-the-nokia-browser-decrypts-ssl-traffic-a-man-in-the-client/.
[60] G. Shah, A. Molina, and M. Blaze. Keyboards and covert channels. In *Proceedings of the 15th Conference on USENIX Security Symposium - Volume 15*, USENIX-SS'06, Berkeley, CA, USA, 2006. USENIX Association.
[61] J. Sherry, C. Lan, R. A. Popa, and S. Ratnasamy. BlindBox: Deep packet inspection over encrypted traffic. In *Proceedings of the 2015 ACM Conference on Special Interest Group on Data Communication*, SIGCOMM '15, pages 213–226, New York, NY, USA, 2015. ACM.
[62] G. R. Simpson. Treasury tracks financial data in secret program. The Wall Street Journal, June 23, 2006. http://www.wsj.com/articles/SB115101988281688182.
[63] R. Singel. Whistle-blower outs NSA spy room. Wired, April 7, 2006. https://archive.wired.com/science/discoveries/news/2006/04/70619.
[64] D. X. Song, D. Wagner, and A. Perrig. Practical techniques for searches on encrypted data. In *Proceedings of the 2000 IEEE Symposium on Security and Privacy*, SP '00, pages 44–55, Washington, DC, USA, 2000. IEEE Computer Society.
[65] Vulnerability note VU#792004. CERT Vulnerability Notes Database. https://www.kb.cert.org/vuls/id/792004.
[66] F. Wang, J. Mickens, N. Zeldovich, and V. Vaikuntanathan. Sieve: Cryptographically enforced access control for user data in untrusted clouds. In *Proceedings of the 13th Usenix Conference on Networked Systems Design and Implementation*, NSDI'16, pages 611–626, Berkeley, CA, USA, 2016. USENIX Association.
[67] C. Wisniewski. Smart meter hacking can disclose which TV shows and movies you watch. naked security by SOPHOS, Jan. 8, 2012. https://nakedsecurity.sophos.com/2012/01/08/28c3-smart-meter-hacking-can-disclose-which-tv-shows-and-movies-you-watch/.
[68] Z. Zhou and T. Benson. Towards a safe playground for HTTPS and middle boxes with QoS2. In *Proceedings of the 2015 ACM SIGCOMM Workshop on Hot Topics in Middleboxes and Network Function Virtualization*, HotMiddlebox '15, pages 7–12, New York, NY, USA, 2015. ACM.

Techu: Open and Privacy-Preserving Crowdsourced GPS for the Masses

Ioannis Agadakos
Dept. of Computer Science
Stevens Institute
of Technology
iagadako@stevens.edu

Jason Polakis
Dept. of Computer Science
University of Illinois
at Chicago
polakis@uic.edu

Georgios Portokalidis
Dept. of Computer Science
Stevens Institute
of Technology
gportoka@stevens.edu

ABSTRACT

The proliferation of mobile devices, equipped with numerous sensors and Internet connectivity, has laid the foundation for the emergence of a diverse set of crowdsourcing services. By leveraging the multitude, geographical dispersion, and technical abilities of smartphones, these services tackle challenging tasks by harnessing the *power of the crowd*. One such service, Crowd GPS, has gained traction in the industry and research community alike, materializing as a class of systems that track lost objects or individuals (e.g., children or elders). While these systems can have significant impact, they suffer from major privacy threats.

In this paper, we highlight the inherent risks to users from the centralized designs adopted by such services and demonstrate how adversaries can trivially misuse one of the most popular crowd GPS services to track their users. As an alternative, we present Techu, a privacy-preserving crowd GPS service for tracking Bluetooth tags. Our architecture follows a hybrid decentralized approach, where an *untrusted* server acts as a bulletin board that collects reports of tags observed by the crowd, while observers store the location information locally and only disclose it upon proof of ownership of the tag. Techu does not require user authentication, allowing users to remain anonymous. Our security analysis highlights the privacy offered by Techu, and details how our design prevents adversaries from tracking or identifying users. Finally, our experimental evaluation demonstrates that Techu has negligible impact on power consumption, and achieves superior effectiveness to previously proposed systems while offering stronger privacy guarantees.

Keywords

Crowd GPS, BLE Tags, Location-based Services, User Tracking, Location Privacy, Privacy-Preserving Protocol

CCS Concepts

•Security and privacy → Domain-specific security and privacy architectures; *Embedded systems security;* **•Networks → Location based services;**

Permission to make digital or hard copies of all or part of this work for personal or classroom use is granted without fee provided that copies are not made or distributed for profit or commercial advantage and that copies bear this notice and the full citation on the first page. Copyrights for components of this work owned by others than ACM must be honored. Abstracting with credit is permitted. To copy otherwise, or republish, to post on servers or to redistribute to lists, requires prior specific permission and/or a fee. Request permissions from permissions@acm.org.

MobiSys '17, June 19–23, 2017, Niagara Falls, NY, USA.

© 2017 ACM. ISBN 978-1-4503-4928-4/17/06. . . $15.00

DOI: http://dx.doi.org/10.1145/3081333.3081345

1. INTRODUCTION

The widespread adoption of smartphone devices has transformed many aspects of everyday life, and led to the emergence of a plethora of novel services that range from the menial to critical. This availability of a massive number of geographically dispersed mobile devices with internet connectivity has lent significant traction to the crowdsourcing paradigm and numerous incarnations have surfaced, from collecting real-time traffic data [56] to providing early warning for earthquakes [26].

Crowd GPS is one such type of service that utilizes a network of users, *a crowd*, to locate lost or misplaced objects, or monitor the location of pets [8] and "vulnerable" individuals like children [46] and elders [16]. It has taken off after the release of Bluetooth Low Energy (BLE), which allows near-range communication with a significantly reduced power consumption [31], as it facilitated the creation of small, battery-powered, BLE-enabled tags that can be easily attached to objects, or worn by people and pets. The loss or misplacement of an item is a problem that has tormented many. In 2013 alone, 26,000 articles were forgotten in New York's transportation system [13] and a survey [3] found that one in five people lose or misplace an item every week. This has lead to the rapid growth of crowd GPS, with services such as TrackR boasting over 5 million users.

Despite the obvious benefits of crowd GPS, the designs of existing systems suffer from various drawbacks. Most notably, the location of personal items, and consequently of the user, is collected centrally by the crowd GPS service, which is frequently run by the vendors offering BLE tags for sale. This poses a significant privacy threat, as a large body of research on location privacy in other applications has also highlighted [12,36,58,65]. Second, the ecosystem is fragmented, forming disjoint crowds of users based on the vendor they have purchased tags from. Crowd sourcing performance improves as the size of the crowd grows, hence, this fragmentation limits the effectiveness of current systems.

In this work, we first audit TrackR, one of the most popular crowd GPS services, and expose a vulnerability that enables the misuse of the service for tracking the location of *any* tag owned by a customer. Our findings highlight a critical risk of crowd GPS; *current centralized designs expose a single-point of failure, where vulnerabilities can result in the exfiltration of the location of users.*

Previous works on locating lost or stolen Bluetooth-enabled tags suffer several shortcomings. First, and foremost, they present privacy threats to participating users; in [22,70] users can be trivially tracked by any member of the crowd by supplying the tag's identifier, while in [70] the service also possesses coarse-grained location data that can lead to deanonymization [24]. Second, [28,70] follow a "search after the fact" approach, where the crowd searches for a tag *after* the query is issued, i.e., participants do not maintain information of recently seen tags; this can severely limit the effectiveness of the system, especially in areas with few users.

To ameliorate the aforementioned drawbacks, we propose Techu[1], an open crowd GPS system designed to overcome the above issues and ensure the privacy of users participating in the crowd. In Techu we follow a hybrid decentralized architecture, where reports about tag observation events are kept in an untrusted public server, while the actual location information is stored in a distributed manner. In a nutshell, Techu works as follows. Users participating in our system download a client side app and pair their smartphones with their BLE tags they want to keep track of. The app periodically creates a randomly generated secret for each paired tag, and stores it on the tag as the `DeviceName`, which is advertised by the tag. Participants log the `DeviceName` of all the tags in range that belong to other users, and create observation reports that contains an identifier derived by the `DeviceName`, a timestamp, and their unlinkable communication pseudonym (`ObserverID`). Reports are periodically uploaded in batches to a centralized *untrusted* database that serves as a bulletin board. If a tag is lost, the owner initiates the object-discovery process, and uses the last generated `DeviceName` to retrieve the most recent observation reports for that tag from the server. The owner then uses the `ObserverID` to communicate with the observer over an ephemeral communication channel, through the Google Cloud Messaging (GCM) infrastructure [33]; after proving ownership of the tag, the observer discloses the location at which the tag was seen. By maintaining reports of recently observed tags, Techu allows for the tracking of tags even in sparsely populated areas; it is sufficient for a single user to have been in range of the tag at some point in time, for the owner to obtain information about the tag's location.

We conduct an extensive experimental evaluation of our system, and quantify performance in terms of storage requirements, power consumption, communication costs, and query overhead. As the prevailing role for participants is that of the observer, the overhead introduced by our protocol is of key importance. Apart from the baseline cost of BLE scanning, which is shared by all crowd GPS systems, under "typical" mobility patterns our system requires less than 30 seconds of client-side computation per day (for all the required calculations plus the time required to report to the Techu service) and client storage requirements are less than 55KB. Storage requirements for the bulletin board are very moderate, reaching approximately 23 TB for 12 million participating users with typical mobility patterns. Our system's impact on the battery lifetime of tags is negligible, with less than a 2% reduction. Finally, the cost for owners to locate lost tags is very low, as the relevant observation records that have to be fetched are ~2MB and the communication protocol with an observer is completed within a few seconds. Overall, our system introduces minimal overhead while offering significant privacy properties compared to existing services or proposed solutions.

The key contributions of our work are the following:

- We conduct a security analysis of TrackR, a prominent crowd GPS service, and discover a vulnerability that enables adversaries to misuse the service, effectively turning the participants into a *malnet* [44] that can track the location of any user through time.
- We present Techu, a crowdsourced GPS system designed to effectively locate BLE tags, while guaranteeing the location privacy of participants. Our system is built around an *untrusted* server that can be adopted by vendors or used as a public bulletin board, and it does not require user enrollment or authentication, allowing users to anonymously participate in the crowd.
- We present a series of extensions to our basic design, and analyze the tradeoff between the security guarantees of our system and performance overhead.
- We experimentally evaluate Techu, and find that our client-side and server-side requirements and overhead are minimal, while our protocol allows users to efficiently obtain the required information while preserving their privacy. Techu achieves its goals while reducing the operating costs and without the implications of proprietary "security through obscurity" approaches, enabling the deployment of our system either as community effort or by a tag-selling vendor.

[1]Named after the Egyptian god of record-keeping.

The remainder of the paper is structured as follows. Section 2 provides the necessary background information and privacy risks of existing crowd GPS services, while Section 3 presents our security analysis of a prominent service. In Section 4 we describe our system design and privacy extensions, while Sections 5 and 6 outline the security guarantees and implementation details of our system, respectively. We continue with the experimental evaluation of Techu in Section 7, and discuss limitations and future work in Section 8. Finally, we present related work in Section 9 and conclude in Section 10.

2. BACKGROUND

Here we provide background information on crowd GPS and discuss the privacy risks of its current instantiations.

2.1 Crowd GPS

In crowd GPS the location of objects is established through crowd sourcing, i.e., by enlisting the services of a number of individuals that form a network, referred to as a *crowd*, typically through the Internet. This model is appropriate for tracking objects and devices that do not, or cannot, feature a GPS sensor and Internet connectivity to report their location to their owners. Instead, the objects can be sensed, typically through wireless sensors, by the individuals participating in the crowd, who can establish their location and, hence, help locate the objects.

This is an instantiation of *crowd sensing*, where user devices become part of a network collecting locally observable information through their sensors and uploading it to the cloud, to be aggregated and analyzed at a large scale. This is usually achieved through dedicated client-side apps running on devices carried by users, such as smartphones. Crowd sensing may require different levels of user participation [51], ranging from active participation (*participatory crowd sensing*) [40] to a completely transparent process for end users (*opportunistic crowd sensing*) [55]. A detailed taxonomy of crowd sensing can be found in [38].

Crowd GPS has gained a lot of traction since the introduction and proliferation of BLE, a low-energy Bluetooth network technology. There are multiple vendors (e.g., Tile [41] and TrackR [42]) offering BLE tags, or beacons, that can be attached on objects (e.g., keys and backpacks) or come in the form of bracelets that can be worn by vulnerable individuals [16, 46]. Users that purchase such tags become part of a vendor-maintained crowd by installing an app on their smartphone. The app automatically reports the location of sensed tags and enables users to query the vendor to locate the tags. Most apps, like TrackR and Tile, only track and report their own tags and users are only allowed to query the tags they have already paired, through conventional Bluetooth, with their smartphone. Other services, such as Locus Pocus [21], are device-agnostic and enable the user to track any BLE device and tag. Locus Pocus, instead, monetizes the offered service by charging a fee for querying the location of tags. Besides general purpose tags that can be attached to different objects, BLE beacons are also being incorporated in various commercial products, like luggage [2], for tracking purposes. Automotive companies have also started deploying vehicles with support for such functionality, with Land Rover integrating support for Tile [52].

The success of services that build on crowd GPS mainly depends on two factors: battery life and user base. BLE tags are powered by small batteries, so energy efficiency is critical to keep the maintenance cost of battery replacement low, while the number of people participating in a crowd GPS crowd determines its coverage. Consequently, the existence of multiple, disjoint GPS crowds, created by different vendors hampers their effectiveness. As Techu is not tied to a specific type of tag and is built around a public server, our approach can reduce the segmentation of the user base.

2.2 Privacy Threats of Crowd GPS

Despite the unprecedented opportunities offered by the paradigm of crowd sensing, which can have significant societal impact in critical scenarios, these technologies do not come without risks for participants. Alarmingly, in scenarios where users frequently expose their location to the service, that information can be leveraged for inferring sensitive information [54] (e.g., medical conditions, religious beliefs, sexual orientation) or deanonymizing the user [49]. In the context of object-discovery services, the privacy of users is also threatened by the periodic broadcasting of information from the tags, which are usually carried by the users, as it can lead to tracking [45]. Since the utility of many services stem from the aggregation and processing of location-aware data from users, in practice, participants can be subjected to tracking. This can be catalytic in deterring users from participating. For example, both TrackR and Locus Pocus mention that the collected data, including location, may be shared with third parties. The latter also explicitly states that data may be shared with law enforcement agencies.

The current state of *fragmentation*, with each tag vendor deploying a platform for their own set of tags, significantly reduces the effectiveness that could be achieved by a vendor-agnostic platform that unifies all disparate crowds into a single mass. Furthermore, the existence of multiple centralized proprietary services also increases the chances of misuse. Given the frequency of security breaches and theft of user data [5, 6], centrally-stored user location information poses a significant privacy risk. As we demonstrate in § 3, the security flaws of TrackR enable the tracking of their users.

Our goal is to highlight the privacy and security concerns that stem from device tracking in this emerging ecosystem, which motivates our design of a decentralized public crowd GPS platform, that in not bound to any specific type of tag and *does not require any manufacturer modification.*

3. A SECURITY ANALYSIS OF TRACKR

Here we present our security analysis of TrackR, one of the most popular crowd GPS services, which has also partnered with Amazon [7]. While claims of being the "largest Crowd GPS network in the world" [9] cannot be verified, the reported number of over 5 million users across the USA and Europe renders TrackR a suitable candidate for highlighting the significant privacy risks of crowd GPS.

We obtained the official TrackR app for Android from the Google Play store and decompiled it, following an established procedure. This involved unzipping the .apk file, using `dex2jar` to convert the extracted .dex files to class files in a .jar archive, and finally decompiling the jar file using `jd-gui`. The retrieved code was readable almost in its entirety. Review of the app's code revealed that the app communicates with TrackR servers through `REST`ful calls. As expected, the TrackR app scans for BLE beacons of the vendor and uploads their IDs (i.e., their Bluetooth MAC addresses) to TrackR servers along with the GPS coordinates where they were seen. The apps looks for TrackR's manufacturer ID in the received BLE packets, so the crowd only tracks beacons of the vendor. To search for a lost tag, the app issues a call to the service using the following URL:

https://phonehalocloud.appspot.com/rest/tracker/[tracker-id]

The tracker-id is not the beacon's MAC address (BSSID), but a value derived from it, which is calculated by appending the string representation of BSSID, least-significant byte first, to '0000'.

For instance, a tag that has the address `01:23:45:67:8a:bc:ef` will have the tracker-id `0000efbc-8a67452301`. The service responds with a JSON object, similar to the one shown in Listing 1, containing information about the most recent observation of the tag, including a timestamp, coordinates, and its battery level.

```
{"lastTimeUpdated": 1460751872294,
"timeUpdatedDiff": 256354145,
"lastKnownLocation": {
"longitude":-73.98,"latitude":40.75},
"trackerId": "0000EFBC-8A67452301"}
```

Listing 1: Example response of tag tracking API call at the time of disclosure (April 2016).

```
{"lastTimeUpdated":1467043953079,
"timeUpdatedDiff":3307969283,
"lastKnownLocation":{"longitude":-74.03,"latitude":40.74}
"friendlyName":"**","locationName":"***"
"trackerId":"0000EFBC-8A67452301"}
```

Listing 2: Example response of tag tracking API call at a later time (August 2016), leaking additonal information.

Tracking Vulnerability. While most of API calls of the TrackR service require authentication (e.g., an OAUTH token), the URL above, used to search for lost tags *does not.* As such, *anyone* can at *anytime* query about *any* tracker they have encountered at least once. As a result, unauthorized parties can locate tags and track the owner. By periodically obtaining this information adversaries can reconstruct user trajectories, which can lead to their identification [24, 32] and the inference of sensitive information.

Ethical Considerations. Upon discovering this vulnerability in April 2016, we immediately disclosed it to the vendor and offered a detailed report of our analysis. Some might argue that disclosing an attack against a popular service raises ethical concerns, as this attack can be deployed in practice by malicious individuals. However, we believe that it is crucial to raise the public's awareness and expedite patching, as millions of users are already participating in such services, and numbers are expected to grow even more in the near future. Nonetheless, we have followed the widely accepted practice of responsible disclosure, and offered a detailed report of our analysis to the vendor in an effort to help improve their system.

As a final note, it is important to highlight that despite the straightforward nature of the attack and the corresponding fix, it took TrackR more than 9 months (December 2016) to address this issue. To make matters worse, in the meantime, they introduced new attributes in the returned `JSON` message that leaked more information as can

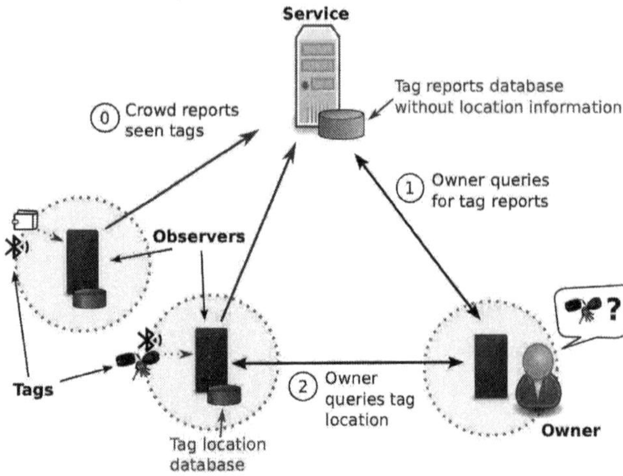

Figure 1: Design overview. The crowd regularly sends reports of observed *tags* (without location information) to the *server* ⓪. When tagged property is lost, the *owner* queries the server to learn who *observed* the tag ①, and contacts them to obtain the corresponding locations ②.

be seen in Listing 2; the one denoted as "friendlyName" reveals the user-supplied nature of the tagged item.

4. TECHU: CROWD GPS

Threat Model. To better capture the privacy threats that crowd-sourced GPS systems face, we consider the server component to be untrusted and assume a "*malicious but cautious*" behavior, which has been proposed for cloud computing providers [20]. In this model, the server can actively attempt to learn or deduce information from incoming reports and queries, but will try to appear legitimate by returning the appropriate results to queries, as users could easily identify records being tampered with. We do not require users to register or exchange any keys with the server, and assume that they can obtain a non-tampered version of our app, e.g., through the official app store.

Our threat model captures two orthogonal adversarial behaviors that target complimentary aspects of Techu. In the first case, the adversary's goal is to compromise the privacy offered by design, and obtain sensitive information about the user(s). This may include tracking a user's location through time, or inferring sensitive information and uncovering the user's identity by obtaining location data (e.g., home or work address [30]). In the second case, the adversary is driven by economic incentives, and monitors the information available so as to identify lost tags and attempt to recover them. We assume that adversaries have access to all information contained in the bulletin board, can deploy a *limited* number of physical "agents" within the crowd, and even report fake events to the system. Furthermore, the adversary can monitor traffic incoming to the server, and has significant computational resources at his disposal, thus, is able to perform brute force attacks against information encrypted with low entropy. As is the case with all crowd-sourcing services [11], our system is susceptible to users reporting fake data (e.g., spoofing their location [59]).

4.1 System Design

We designed Techu as a decentralized privacy-preserving crowd GPS system that addresses the privacy risks of existing vendor-based solutions and services proposed in the literature. Our design was motivated by the inherent risks of collecting location data centrally, including data leaks, cryptanalysis attacks against encryption algorithms, and weak keys. We further discuss the security advantages of our approach over a centralized design in § 5. Our system consists of four entities: the *tags*, the *owners* of the tags, the *observers* that form the crowd, and the *service* that collects reports from observers and accepts queries from owners.

A high-level overview of our design is depicted in Figure 1. Owners store an ephemeral ID on each of their tags, which is unique for each of their tags and is periodically updated when in range. Tag IDs are broadcast to nearby observers through BLE advertisement packets and become part of the reports observers send to the service for nearby tags (step ⓪). Reports do not include location data, but contain sufficient information for owners to identify the reports that correspond to their tags and contact the observer that issued them. When a tag is lost, owners first retrieve the corresponding reports for a desired time range from the service (step ①) and then proceed to contact observers and retrieve the location where a tag was seen, after proving to them that they are the tag owner (step ②). Below, we elaborate on the various phases of our system's functionality.

Generating tag IDs. For each tag, owners periodically generate a key pair (pk_i, sk_i) using an asymmetric-encryption algorithm, such as ElGamal, Elliptic Curve techniques, or RSA, with the public key, pk_i, acting as the tag's ID, t_i:

$$t_i \equiv pk_i$$

t_i is stored on the tag using a writable BLE attribute, which is accessible only to the owner after pairing with it. Unauthorized users should not be able to overwrite it, as, among other issues, it would disrupt the operation of the system. To make it observable to the crowd, t_i is included in the advertisement packet periodically transmitted by the tag to announce its presence. In commercially available tags this can be done by storing t_i into the `Device Name` attribute. Tag IDs are *ephemeral* and *unlinkable*, that is, we periodically update them and each ID is independent of the others. As such, an ID t_i is only associated with a tag for a limited amount of time, preventing long-term tracking of the tags, since third-parties cannot guess t_{i+1}. Techu does not use MAC addresses to track tags. Instead, we assume that tags are using private MAC addresses [18] (further discussed in § 8) to avoid tracking from malicious observers [45].

Reporting observed tags. Each observer in the crowd is identified by $observerID_k$, an ephemeral client ID in a messaging service, like Google's Cloud Messaging (GCM), which the owners use to contact them. For each tag observed, they upload a report r_j to the service, where:

$$r_j = ts_j \mid E_{pk_i}(observerID_k) \mid \hat{t_i}, \quad \hat{t_i} = H(t_i)$$

Report r_j includes the timestamp (ts_j), the observer's ID encrypted with the public key pk_i (i.e., the tag ID t_i), and the secure hash digest of t_i $(\hat{t_i})$. The encryption function E actually creates a digital envelope utilizing a secret-key algorithm and message authentication to provide confidentiality and integrity. This ensures that only the tag owner can obtain the observer's ID from a report, and only the owner or an observer of a tag can identify the reports associated with a particular tag, because they can generate $\hat{t_i}$.

Storing tag locations. The actual location of the observation is stored locally by observers, as tuples of:

$$\{ts,\ t_i,\ location\}$$

We assume that the service has enough storage to store reports for a few days or even weeks to facilitate the recovery of lost property. On the other hand, the storage required by observers can be bound by discarding old observations, keeping only the most recent entry for each tag, or even probabilistically dropping certain entries.

Querying lost tags. To retrieve information for a lost tag, the owner issues a query requesting all the reports corresponding to

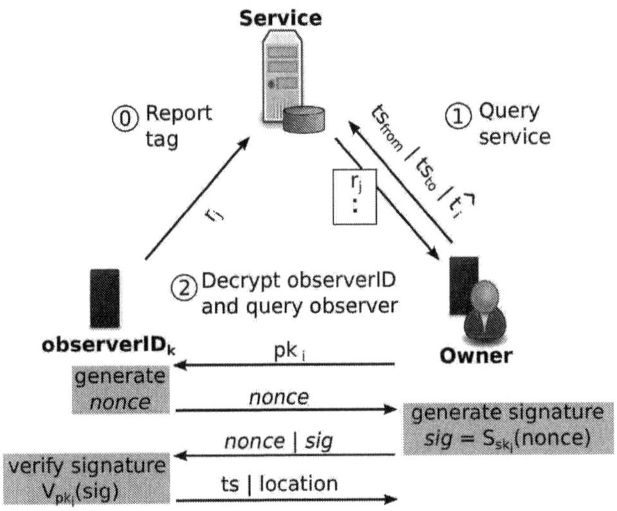

Figure 2: Messages involved in tracking tags and querying for lost tags.

a tag's $\hat{t}_i$ for a time range (ts_{from} : ts_{to}), which are returned by the service , as shown in step ① of Figure 2. Since queries are performed based on $\hat{t}_i$ and a time range, they are lightweight. By choosing a hash function like SHA-3, collisions are highly improbable and the returned reports will most likely correspond to the owner's tag.

For each returned report r_j, the owner decrypts the observer ID information, using the tag's secret key sk_i. The owner then communicates with observers over a channel that ensures confidentiality, e.g., over TLS, to prove ownership of the tag and obtain the location information. Various techniques can be used to achieve this, but we employ the well-established technique of digital signing, as shown in Figure 2 (step ②). The protocol is as follows: the observer generates a random number *nonce*, which it transmits as a challenge to the owner. The owner signs the nonce using function S and the appropriate private key and sends it to the observer. The observer can verify the validity of the signature using function V and the public key of the tag t_i. If verification succeeds, the location information can be sent to the owner. pk_i is used to search the locally-stored data and, in the case of a match, respond with the timestamped location of the tag.

4.2 Privacy Extensions

In this section, we present two extensions to our basic design that trade performance for improved security and privacy properties. We evaluate the tradeoffs in § 7.

4.2.1 Decoy Queries

We introduce the use of *decoy* lost-tag queries, which are sent to observers so as to obfuscate actual incidents of owners searching for lost tags. This creates "uncertainty" which deters malicious observers from reasoning about tags being lost, as the received query could be a decoy. Owners initiate the process at random intervals emulating the loss of one of their objects and its tag. The whole process needs to be indistinguishable from a real tag discovery event, so it follows the exact same steps, i.e., the owner retrieves the most recent reports from the service (e.g., the ones sent in the last hour) and it issues queries to the corresponding observers.

We choose to generate decoys at random intervals, even though, one might argue that in the real world it is unlikely for inquiries to occur during the night, when most users are asleep. That would allow malicious observers to infer that a request received at night has a higher probability of being a genuine one. In other words, maximum uncertainty is achieved when all events are equally likely to happen [64]. To generate decoys, each owner periodically (with period T) decides to initiate a decoy event with probability p.

Security improvements. Observers that receive queries from owners are now uncertain of whether the query corresponds to an object that was actually lost. In particular, if an owner initiates on average X decoy lost-tag events per hour, where $X = T \times p$, and an observer has reported N tags belonging to different owners, then the observer will receive $X \times N$ decoy queries per hour. The probability of an observer receiving a real tag discovery query is probabilistically very small; our goal is to hinder malicious observers from "scavenging" for lost items they receive queries for. Essentially, we aim to maximize $X \times N$ without overburdening benevolent observers, which could lead them to blocking owner queries or abandoning the system. For the same reason, which tags are queried in the decoys is not of importance and could be selected randomly. This extension allows owners to insert a configurable amount of noise in the system that will render scavenging unprofitable.

4.2.2 Salted Tag IDs

Tag tracking. We can replace the hashed tag ID $\hat{t}_i$ that is sent to the service, with a salted version $\dot{t}_i$. For each report, we generate a random number, $salt_j$, and hash it with t_i:

$$\dot{t}_j = H(salt_j \mid t_i)$$

To facilitate querying the server, we generate a "color" value c_j consisting of the b least-significant bits of the unsalted hash value $\hat{t}_i$. Since we only keep a few bits of the hash, c_j is not a unique value, and reports for different tags will share the same color. So given a function LSB that keeps the b least-significant bits, the color is produced as:

$$c_i = LSB_b(\hat{t}_i)$$

The report $\dot{r}_j$ is extended to include the salt and color:

$$\dot{r}_j = ts \mid o_i \mid \dot{t}_j \mid salt_j \mid c_i$$

As before, an HMAC code is appended to the report.

Querying lost tags. The owner uses t_i to produce a c_i to query the service. Since different tags will be colored the same way, reports referring to other tags will also be returned. A time range (ts_{from} : ts_{to}), which remains part of the query, can be used to reduce the number of reports retrieved from the service. For each report $\dot{r}_j$, the tag owner uses the tag's t_i and the salt ($salt_j$) contained within the report to produce $\dot{t}_j$ and compare it to the one in the report. Matching reports correspond to the owner's tag, and are used to query the observer for the tag's location as before.

5. SECURITY ANALYSIS

Techu is designed to ensure the location privacy of the crowd's participants, while offering more effective object tracking as opposed to other proposed systems [28, 70] that attempt to locate the tags after the issues are queried. Here we present threats that affect crowd GPS systems, and outline the privacy guarantees that are attained by core aspects of Techu's basic design (§ 4.1) and privacy extensions (§ 4.2).

Untrusted Server: owner privacy. In our design, the service cannot obtain any information regarding the location of tags, as that information is stored locally by the observers. As that information is only disclosed to the owner *after proof of ownership* through the private key *pk*, the server cannot trick the observers into divulging the information.

Untrusted server: observer privacy. The service cannot learn anything about observers because their IDs are encrypted using t_i, which is never disclosed to the service by the owner nor any observers. The service could potentially try to estimate an observer's IP-based geolocation. However, previous work has demonstrated that geolocating IP addresses that belong to cellular networks cannot achieve accurate results; using geolocation databases results in errors in the order of tens of kilometers [72], while measuring application-level latencies can only be used to distinguish cities [14]. As such, both of these techniques would fail to offer any useful location information to an adversary.

Malicious Observers: *direct* tag tracking. By using ephemeral IDs for the tags, we ensure that observers cannot continuously track tags based on their t_i. In the case of observers colluding and forming a malicious crowd, such as a malnet [44], observers can track the tag after they observe it for the remaining time window (e.g., a few minutes), until the generation of the next t_i [2]. This is not long enough to reconstruct a trajectory of the user's whereabouts, and is the same trade-off faced by existing privacy-oriented mechanisms like private MAC addresses. Thus, Techu offers significant location privacy guarantees over previous systems that were susceptible to user tracking [22, 70].

Malicious observers: *indirect* tag tracking. After logging a device, observers can use the tag's ID to query the service and obtain the observation events generated by other observers for that ID while it was active. However, observers cannot obtain location information from other observers because they do not possess the secret key sk, thus, lack the ability to prove ownership.

Malicious observers: co-observer privacy. The observation events uploaded to the service contain the observer's ID encrypted using t_i. This prevents users from discovering the IDs of other observers that reported the tag in their vicinity. Furthermore, these IDs for communicating with apps over Google's GCM are in no way linked to the user's actual identity, and do not disclose any actual information about the user. Moreover, these IDs are periodically changed, to prevent third parties from linking the same observer across different observation entries.

Malicious observers: scavenging lost tags. Observers in our system may (try to) infer that a tag was lost, and attempt to retrieve/steal the lost property the tag corresponds to.

Tag discovery query. When observers receive a discovery query from the tag's owner, they can directly infer that the tag has been lost. We address this threat with our *decoy query* privacy extension. Observers that receive queries from owners are now uncertain of whether the query corresponds to an object that was actually lost. The goal is to maximize the number of decoy queries without introducing a significant overhead for observers in terms of battery consumption, which could result in users abandoning the system. While introducing noise in the system results in uncertainty and renders scavenging unprofitable, nonetheless, in practice attackers could still attempt to physically recover any tags for which they received queries (including potential decoys).

Tag ID persistence. Owners periodically change their tags' name to prevent observers from being able to track their location. As a side-effect, once a tag is separated from its owner it will retain the same t_i for a longer period of time, allowing observers and the service to infer that a tag may have been lost (or purposefully left behind by the owner). While the time window is configurable, thus allowing each user to tweak the tradeoff between privacy and power consumption based on their own requirements, our system sets an upper bound of 10 minutes to ensure the privacy of participants.

[2] Users can configure the time window to be arbitrarily short.

5.1 Alternate Design Analysis

Here, we present an alternative centralized design and the inherent risks it suffers from. While such a centralized approach simplifies the design and reduces the overhead, it also introduces significant privacy risks. Insider threats [15], the interest of intelligence agencies in tracking users [10], the precedence of law enforcement agencies issuing subpoenas to access user data [67], and the frequency of data breaches [5], all highlight the risks of centralized crowd GPS systems.

Design. In the centralized design, observers upload reports containing a timestamp (ts), the observed tag's location encrypted with t_i as the public key, and the secure hash digest of t_i. Owner's then simply fetch the most recent reports with a hash digest that corresponds to their tag's ID, and decrypt the location using their private key.

Cryptanalysis. All reports uploaded to the server can be trivially collected and stored by adversaries. Even though the sensitive information (i.e., the *location*) is encrypted, previous work has extensively explored the risks of archiving encrypted sensitive information and the need for long term secrecy (e.g., [15, 68, 69]). Specifically, Storer et al. [69] argued: *an adversary who can compromise an archive need only wait for cryptanalysis techniques to catch up to the encryption algorithm used at the time of the compromise in order to obtain "secure" data.* In this case, there is no need for compromising the archive, as it is publicly available online.

To make matters worse, the hardware restrictions of BLE tags limit the potential key sizes, further increasing the risks of storing the sensitive information on the server. While current recommendations call for minimum key sizes of 256 bits in Elliptic Curve cryptography [1] (which has already been deprecated by the NSA), BLE advertisement are restricted to 248 bits per the BLE specification which allows a maximum of 31 bytes used as data payload [17]. This size restriction naturally leads to the use of elliptic curves instead of other public key techniques like RSA. While more data can be transferred through a scan response packet, that would incur a massive overhead as it would require an extra packet sent for each device in the tag's vicinity. Furthermore, as the size of the advertisement payload impacts the tag's battery life [62], further increasing the advertisement packet size could have undesirable implications, given the low energy consumption tenet of BLE technology. Finally, notable cryptographers have expressed concerns regarding the robustness of elliptic curves against potential advancements by the NSA [35, 48]. Assuming that the adversary decrypts the encrypted locations in the report, we describe two attack scenarios that can recreate users' location traces.

Attack 1: observer tracking. A malicious but curious (or compromised) server can link observer reports uploaded from a specific IP address. As users typically connect over a cellular network when on the move, attackers could recreate a user's daily commute and identify the user [30], and infer sensitive data from other visited locations. To gauge how persistent cellular IP addresses are, we conducted an experiment over the duration of one week with 3 devices, that belong to the authors, connected to a major US cellular provider. We found that the IP address changes when the cellular connection is switched off (e.g., switch to WiFi, turn off device) or if the cellular signal is lost due to bad reception; in our experiments IP addresses remained unchanged for 3-62 hours when the connection was not manually switched, demonstrating the practicality of such an attack.

Attack 2: tag tracking. While the ephemeral tag IDs used in Techu prevent the straightforward tracking of tags, a malicious server could potentially link successive ephemeral IDs. Figure 3, presents an example scenario where four participants are in the same area.

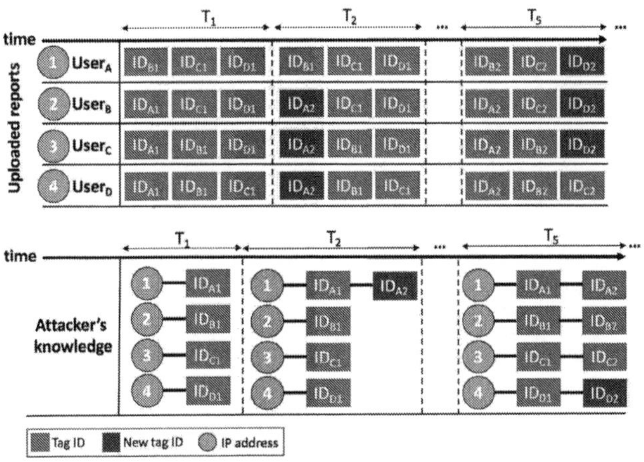

Figure 3: Example scenario with 4 co-located users, outlining an attack that links users' consecutive tag IDs.

Note that the different time windows T_i do not have the same duration, but only represent the time window within which all tag IDs remain the same. For instance, during T_1 every observer uploads reports regarding the remaining 3 tags in the vicinity. Based on the IP address of the observer uploading each report, the adversary learns which tag belongs to the user behind each IP address. Now, suppose that the first user's tag gets a new ID assigned, which means that we are now in T_2; since the first user will report observations for the same tags as in T_1, while all other users will report 2 identical tags from before plus the new tag, the attacker can now associate the new tag ID_{A2} with tag ID_{A1}. This can similarly be done for all the tags. Its important to note that this is a hypothetical scenario that assumes that the set of users remains constant for some time, and in practice this assumption may not hold true. The dynamic nature of user mobility and scenarios where large crowds of users momentarily coincide may introduce significant complexity that hinders the practicality of this attack. As such, while various settings seem suitable for such an attack (e.g., mass transportation rides between stops), further exploration is required for evaluating the feasibility and effectiveness of the attack under realistic conditions.

Motivation. All these issues motivated the *decentralized* design of Techu where location information is *temporarily* stored by observers and shared only upon *proof of ownership*, thus, nullifying the threat of these attacks.

6. IMPLEMENTATION

In this section, we present details regarding our prototype implementation, and discuss aspects of BLE, the more energy-efficient version of Bluetooth; BLE was developed for communicating with devices with limited resources, and presents constraints that guided the design of Techu.

We implemented a prototype for the client-side software of observers and owners on the Android platform, and built a service for collecting the data from observers as a web application over JBoss AS 6.3. The clients handle BLE devices following the Bluetooth specification v4.2, which defines that advertising packets can have a payload of 6 to 37 bytes. The first 6 bytes are reserved for the device's advertisement address (i.e., the Bluetooth MAC address). The remaining 31 bytes can be used by developers to store the data that will be advertised by the beacon to the other devices. More information on how those bytes are broken down into commonly used data types can be found in the specification [18].

Due to the limitations of the Bluetooth specification, we can advertise tag IDs of up to 248 bits through the advertisement packets. We used AES-128 for symmetric crypto, SHA3-224 as a secure hash-function, and elliptic-curve ElGamal with 224-bit public keys for PK-encryption. We used the security providers[3] bundled with our device when available, and the Bouncy Castle[4] library v1.54 for ECC.

For owners to communicate with observers that have reported seeing their tags, we utilize the Google Cloud Message (GCM) service. Our design deviates from the common GCM architecture as our app registers 2 different IDs and runs both as a server and a client; one serves as the user's `ObserverID`, and the other is used for sending tag-discovery queries to other users (preventing observers from learning a tag owner's `ObserverID`). Crowd clients communicate by pushing XMPP messages to the GCM service. Clients periodically (e.g., every few days) may obtain new IDs by creating new instances and re-registering with the GCM service; this enables the ephemeral nature of observer IDs. While new observations will be reported under the newly acquired ID, by keeping the older instances alive, up to a given time, observers can receive queries for tags reported with the previous `ObserverID`. As this is not the intended use of GCM, in the future it could be modified to invalidate the old IDs, or limit the amount of instances each client may register. While this would prevent the use of ephemeral observer IDs, the privacy offered by our system would remain. We would like to emphasize that there is no app or user registration server in Techu, which could be potentially breached.

TrackR's Bravo tags expose a writable `NAME` attribute that we use for storing the tag's ID t_i, as its contents are placed in the payload of the advertisement packet. This behavior is typical for BLE devices. For example, we also tested Jawbone UP3 fitness wearables and found they expose a name attribute which can be written and is advertised.

Experiment Location	Duration	tags per hour	
		Average (std.dev.)	Max
Large US city metropolitan area	41 days	57.33 (52.73)	491
Large US city center	4 hours	274.67 (162.59)	549

Table 1: Results from two experiments where BLE tags were collected in the wild.

7. EVALUATION

We evaluate Techu in terms of the overhead it imposes on owner and observer smartphones, and estimate the storage requirements for the server. For our experiments, we used TrackR Bravo tags, and two stock, low-to-midrange smartphones as observers and owners: an Asus Zenphone and a BLU Studio Energy 2, both running Android 5.0.

Tag density. The effectiveness of crowd GPS systems depends on the size of the crowd. While there are projections for an explosion in the number of BLE devices [73], to the best of our knowledge, there have not been any studies about the number of devices that can be currently found in the wild. To help us establish the parameters and quantify the overhead of our system if deployed today, we performed two experiments collecting tags. We present the summary of their results in Table 1.

[3]I.e., the classes extending the java.security.provider class.
[4]https://www.bouncycastle.org

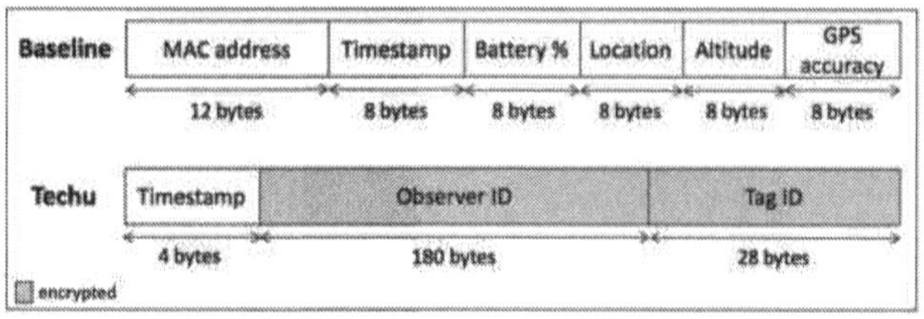

Figure 4: Comparison of reports sent by a baseline crowd GPS and Techu's tag observations.

	Average	Std. dev.	Median
Baseline	564ms	134ms	524ms
Techu	1025ms	140ms	1011ms

Table 2: Report transmission times including required cryptographic operations, for batches of 50 reports (based on tags/hour observed in mid-density area).

In the first experiment, we continuously collected BLE tags using the smartphone of one of the authors for 41 days, in the broader metropolitan area of a city; the majority of measurements were collected in a mid-sized town where one author works (Hoboken, NJ), including occasional trips to the city (New York City, NY). The dataset includes measurements from workdays as well as weekends. In the second experiment, we included measurements from a four hour period (4-8pm) collected during a weekday in the busiest center of a major metropolitan area (Manhattan, NY). In both cases, we took measurements every 5 minutes and identified unique BLE devices using their MAC addresses. Unsurprisingly, the results show that in a *high-density* area (e.g., the city center during peak hours), we observed significantly more BLE tags on average, than in a *mid-density* area. We use these observation rates to frame the remaining experiments.

Reporting overhead. Reporting the observed tags imposes an overhead on observers in terms of both storage and battery consumption. In this section, we evaluate the overhead of Techu compared with a commercial crowd GPS service such as TrackR, referred to as the baseline. Figure 4 compares the reports sent by Techu with the baseline. Even though we do not transmit location information to the service, due to the size of the *encrypted* observer ID (180 B), we need to transmit about four times more data for each reported tag. Transmitting these reports to the service is not four times slower though, because even when batching reports together the overhead of establishing a connection over SSL dominates the cost. Table 2 shows the time needed to transmit 50 reports (the average tags/hour observed in a mid-density area) over WiFi to the service.

	High-density Area		Mid-density Area	
	Rows	Size (KB)	Rows	Size (KB)
Hour	275.00	10.00	57.00	2.20
Day	6,592.00	258.00	1,368.00	53.40
Week	46,1447.00	1,803.00	9,576.00	374.10

Table 3: Estimated size of client database when retaining data for different time periods.

Techu stores the location of recently observed tags on the client side. In Table 3, we show the number of reports and amount of storage required for retaining location information for an hour, day, and week, for high and mid-density areas. Our prototype requires 40 bytes per report (tag ID, timestamp, location), resulting in negligible storage requirements, even when retaining reports for a week.

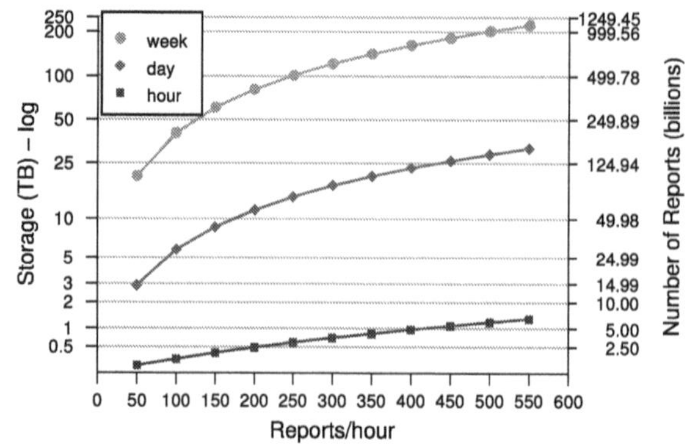

Figure 5: Storage requirements per data retention period, based on the reports/hour generated by observers, under an extreme scenario of 12 million users in a city.

Battery overhead. Preparing and transmitting the reports to the service also consumes energy. For Techu this includes all cryptographic operations and transmissions. For the baseline crowd GPS, we simply transmit reports to the service. As both the baseline and Techu need to activate the BLE adapter to receive advertisement packets, we focused our experiment on the differentiating aspects of our approach. We measure the impact on the battery by sending 1000 reports to the service, which results in a 3% drop in the battery level for Techu, compared to 1% for the baseline. While the relative overhead seems non-negligible, we should emphasize that if we periodically send reports to the service every hour, 30, 5, and 1 minutes, 1000 reports will be sent in 41.6, 20.8, 3.5, and 0.7 days respectively.

Service overhead. Figure 5 shows the server's storage requirements. We plot the estimated size versus the reports/hour generated by observers, using a broad range that captures both mid and high-density areas. We assume a city size of 12 million users (significantly larger than New York, the most populous city in the US), who are all part of Techu and continuously report at the same rate. Assuming typical mobility behavior, our system will require 23 TB of storage for retaining the reports of the past week. At the most extreme scenario where the entire population forms high-density clusters, storage may surpass 200 TB. That, however, is an unrealistic scenario and in practice requirements will be significantly lower than 23 TB even for major cities.

Querying lost tag. While this operation is infrequent and only occurs when an owner attempts to locate a lost tag, it is critical since a high latency between querying for a tag and receiving an answer might render our system ineffective. We tested three different connection setups to evaluate performance over all possible connection combinations between the owner querying about the tag and the observer that holds the location data. We issued 1000 requests from a device acting as the owner to a device acting as the observer, and measured the time required to receive the location information for the observed tag. As shown in Figure 6 the cost is less than 2 seconds in the worst case scenario, which occurs when both the owner and observer connect over 3G.

Overhead on tag. Our design periodically writes a new tag ID to the BLE tags, and this additional operation may impact the tag's battery life. Experimental measurements from other sources [47, 62] and the BLE specification indicate that the cost of a write operation is on par with the transmission cost of an advertisement

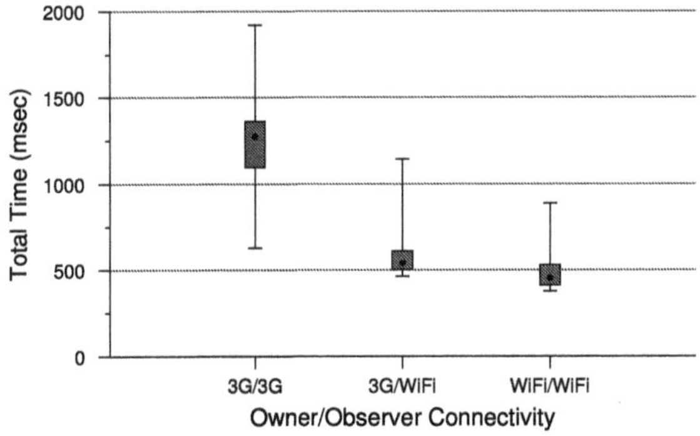

Figure 6: Time required to query the location of a tag from an observer, depending on type of connectivity. Median denoted by the "dot" commonly reffered as Q2, the bottom side of the box is Q1 (lower median), the upper side of the box is Q3 (upper median), the whiskers show the min and max value respectively.

Write Period (min)	Lifetime (days)	Lifetime Reduction (%)
1	35.82	8.83
5	38.54	1.90
10	38.91	0.96
20	39.10	0.48
30	39.16	0.32
60	39.22	0.16
120	39.25	0.08

Table 4: Tag battery lifetime reduction due to frequency of writing new IDs (normal lifetime is 39.29 days).

package for small payloads. Since our design writes the tag at a frequency that is as least two orders of magnitude *lower* than the frequency of broadcasting advertisement packets (e.g., once a minute vs 100-500ms), we did not expect a considerable impact on battery life.

We experimentally verified our expectations by performing over 100,000 writes to a TrackR tag over the course of a week. Simultaneously we activated a second tag as a control tag. We then measured the battery voltage of both and used the manufacturer's data sheet [53] to estimate the remaining mAh. Using our control tag we calculated the difference due to our write operations, as:

$$\Delta(C_{control} - C_{test})/C_{full}$$

where the nominator is the difference in remaining charge between control and test tag and the denominator is the capacity of a brand new battery. The battery model was CR1616 with a charge of 55mAh when full. The results for different frequency updates are shown in Table 4. Even for tag generation periods as small as 5 minutes, our system reduces the lifetime of the battery by less than 2%, which is negligible compared to the privacy benefits obtained.

Salted tag IDs extension. When using salted tag IDs (see § 4.2.2), the owner needs to fetch a larger part of the database, which is determined by the color c_i of the tag. Once those reports are obtained, the owner much check each returned report to determine if it corresponds to the desired tag. This requires calculating a hash for each report using the salt contained in the report and the tag's ID. The number of bits used for c_i, along with the time range used in the query, determine the number of entries returned to the owner.

In Table 5, we show the number and size of reports returned to the user, along with the time required to produce a hash for each report, when using different numbers of bits for c_i and querying for data from the last hour, day, and week. We notice that by using 16 bits (out of 28) of the tag ID as color, an owner querying for a tag

c_i size (bits)	Query Range	Downloaded Reports		Generating Hashes (sec)
		Size (MB)	# (in thousands)	
8	Hour	5,630.40	25,781.00	3,532.21
	Day	135,129.69	618,750.00	84,773.08
	Week	945,907.83	4,331,250.00	593,411.57
16	Hour	22.09	101.00	13.80
	Day	530.16	2,417.00	331.14
	Week	3,711.09	16,919.00	2,318.01
24	Hour	0.09	0.39	0.05
	Day	2.08	9.44	1.29
	Week	14.56	66.09	9.05

Table 5: Size and processing effort for discovering location of lost tag when using salted hashes, for maximum number of generated reports/hour (taken from Table 1).

	Basic	Salted IDs (Color bits)		
		24	16	8
Mid-density	0.01 MB	0.02 MB	3.61 MB	938.40 MB
High-density	0.07 MB	0.09 MB	22.09 MB	5,630.40 MB

Table 6: Data fetched from service for query targeting one hour time window, under different configurations.

lost in the last hour will need to download approximately 22 MB of reports and spend less than 15 seconds processing them. When using a 24 bit color, even for a query window spanning an entire day, the owner would only need to fetch about 2 MB. Note that the reports stored in the service now include an additional 8-byte salt and a color value of variable size.

Decoy queries extension. Decoy queries (see § 4.2.1) defend from malicious observers that wish to identify and steal lost objects. However, a high number of decoys introduces overhead. To quantify this, we consider a scenario where $N+1$ users all own one tag and, within a certain time window, all observe every other tag[5]. Each user has two roles:

- *Owner:* randomly decides to issue decoy query to each of the N observers of his tag.
- *Observer*: receives N decoy queries for observed tags.

If every member decides to issue one decoy query within the time window, each user will need to query the service once and participate in $2 \times N$ queries, as an owner or observer.

Table 6 shows the amount of data (in MB) that need to be fetched by owners for various configurations of Techu in the two tag-density scenarios we have been considering. We notice that, when using salted IDs, unless we use a large color value, decoy queries become expensive for tag owners.

In order to calculate the average energy cost of performing a single query, we configured our testbed smartphones to exchange messages over 3G and performed 1000 queries. Our experiments show that the cost of issuing and responding to query are the same, hence, the overhead is mostly affected by the frequency decoys are generated at.

Figure 7 shows the number of queries/hour that would be generated by a user, for different decoy-generation frequencies in the mid and high-density areas. It also shows the battery consumption inflicted on the user, who acts both as an owner and observer (i.e., both sends and responds to decoy queries). If owners issue one decoy query per hour on average, in the medium-density area an observer receives and issues 57 decoy queries every hour. Our results indicate that we should adapt the frequency decoys are gen-

[5]Obviously this offers an extreme upper bound and, in practice, the introduced overhead would be orders of magnitude lower.

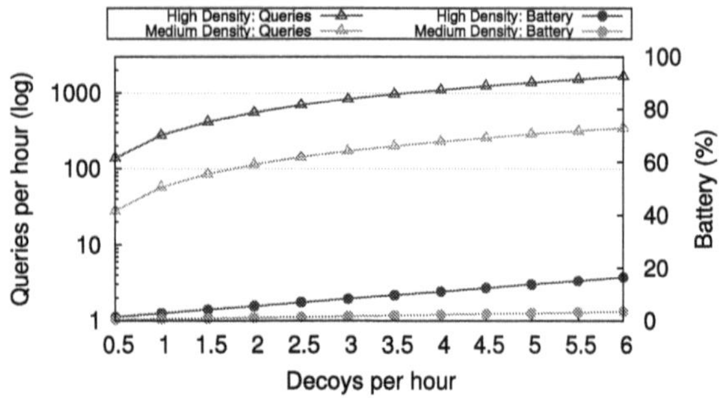

Figure 7: Cost of decoy queries extension for the two different population density datasets.

erated at based on the density of the area, as it could otherwise lead to a large number of decoy requests and significant overhead.

8. DISCUSSION AND FUTURE WORK

Geolocation. As aforementioned, IP-based geolocation techniques for cellular connections do not offer enough accuracy to pose a risk for users. If that changed, users could employ Tor [25] or VPNs for hiding their IP address; that, however, would impact the usability and adoption of Techu.

Beacon Sampling. Our experimental evaluation revealed the moderate storage requirements of the server, even when deployed for major metropolitan areas. As we envision Techu being deployed as part of community effort and not by a private vendor, maintaining state-wide "instances" of our service may require significantly more storage, which could potentially hinder such initiatives. Since in high-density areas many of the reports are overlapping (i.e., concern the same tag), we can reduce the volume of reports by probabilistically sampling the beacons to be reported. We leave the analysis of such an approach as part of our future work.

Silent Zones. An adversary with significant physical resources, could distribute a large number of malicious tags, and attempt to track users through their observer IDs. Alternatively, adversaries that have collected the reports over a long period of time and manage to decrypt them, may try to infer very coarse-grained information regarding a tag's location, based on the number or frequency of observation reports for specific tags. Through empirical measurements, adversaries could potentially differentiate locations based on the density of observers at specific locations. This could allow the adversary to reconstruct a user's trajectory and infer the user's work and home locations; previous work has shown how that information can lead to the identification of the user [30]. Our *salted tag ID* privacy extension significantly increases the difficulty of such an attack, as the adversary would have to decrypt a large number of reports (if not all), to obtain correct number/frequency information per tag.

While these attacks would require significant physical resources, nonetheless, users can configure *silent zones* within which the Techu app will not search for tags or create observation reports. These areas need not be large, which could also impact Techu's effectiveness, but would merely contain the two city blocks containing their workplace and home. Silent zones could potentially pose a privacy threat if the user's whereabouts are tracked over a very long period of time and the user visits every neighborhood in the city; then a heatmap could expose the silent zones. This is prevented by periodically changing observer IDs.

Random MAC. The Bluetooth specification defines private addresses [17] as resolvable or non-resolvable. Techu is designed to be coupled with non-resolvable private addresses, where all the address bits are random and change based on a timer. Simply relying on these private addresses would break the functionality of a crowd GPS system, as the tag would keep changing addresses after being lost, and the owner would not be able to query for it; we solve this by using a tag attribute to store our ephemeral identifier t_i.

Eddystone. Google's Eddystone framework uses ephemeral IDs to improve privacy [34]; they are time-based and generated by the tag based on a shared secret with the owner. These would allow us to prevent attackers inferring lost devices without using decoy queries, but may significantly increase battery consumption. As part of our future work we will explore how too modify Techu for incorporating these tags without incurring the overhead. Also, since EIDs are time-based and clocks will not be synchronized, the owner may need to query the service for multiple IDs.

BLE 5.0. Early reports [66] for the upcoming BLE 5.0 specification call, among other things, for extending the advertisement packet length. One could argue that this will allow for stronger keys, thus, enabling a design where observers encrypt and store the user's location in the public server, as the concern for forward privacy would be mitigated due to the use of keys of higher sizes. However, this may not be a viable solution, since extensive experimentation [62] has shown that the energy required for packet transmission is *directly* correlated to the payload size; in conjunction with the de-facto high transmission rate of the advertisement packets, this would undermine the tags usability by significantly reducing the battery lifespan.

Business model. As crowd GPS services are becoming increasingly popular, we envision that the low operational costs of Techu could enable the deployment of our system as a community effort by volunteers. Given how such a service could potentially be of use in critical scenarios (e.g., elderly getting lost, children being abducted) and the emergence of relevant services, local Techu instantiations could also be supported by government organizations. Nonetheless, our approach can be readily adopted and deployed as a profitable alternative architecture by tag vendors, as it efficiently addresses the CrowdGps tracker market, while also offering attractive economic benefits by removing the operational and liability costs that stem from safeguarding user-data.

9. RELATED WORK

Crowd GPS. Frank et al. [28] presented a system for locating objects through mobile phones, where other users attempt to locate objects within a predefined defined time window which will result in failure if the object is not within range of users during that time. On the other hand, our design allows owners to obtain the most recent sightings of the device, even if no observer is within range at that moment in time. Furthermore, the heuristic-based selection of potential observers may result in the selection of nodes that have not been in proximity to the lost device, while Techu reports information by *any* member of the crowd.

Recently, Sun et al. proposed SecureFind [70], a system for locating lost objects. One of the design goals of their system is to offer object security, i.e., to prevent the service provider from identifying which objects have actually been lost or infer which users have the device in their vicinity. To achieve that, some participating nodes also return dummy locations as responses to the query. However, this introduces false positives that can mislead the device's owner to wrong locations. Furthermore, as per their threat model of an honest but curious service, they argue that they ensure user privacy as the service only knows the general area of each user (areas are configured to match the granularity that cellular service providers have based on which tower the user is connected to). However, previous work has demonstrated how users can be deanonymized using location traces of such coarse granularity [24]. Furthermore, their protocol requires proximity of observers to the lost object at the time of the query, while our approach allows the location of objects even in sparsely-populated areas, as we provide information on observations even after the observes leave the object's range, by returning the most recent sightings. Finally, in their system users can issue queries for obtaining location information for tags of other users, effectively being able to track them. While this threat is not part of their threat model, it is a critical threat nonetheless, as their system can effectively be transformed into a malnet, as we demonstrated with the TrackR service.

Cornelius et al. [22] proposed a framework for creating privacy-preserving opportunistic sensing tasks. One of their example test cases was the implementation of the Object Finder service. However, their system has significant privacy drawbacks, as it is vulnerable to user tracking; since the MAC addresses of the objects never change, adversaries can issue queries for the user's device and obtain the user's location. Furthermore, anyone in the crowd can see the requests for specific devices (i.e., everyone knows which devices are lost), and can issue a query for locating those devices.

These systems build upon a centralized service, which requires considerable infrastructure, rendering their deployment as a public service improbable. Thus, users either have to pay for the service, or have their data used for revenue [4]. Techu only needs a public bulletin board as the server, rendering it ideal for a community-driven deployment.

Ho et al. [71] presented a framework that leverages differential privacy for protecting the location privacy of workers during the assignment of tasks in spatial crowdsourcing services. Wang et al. [74] demonstrated how Sybil attacks could impact Waze, a real-time crowdsourced map, by reporting fake incidents such as accidents or congestion.

Device tracking. Ristenpart et al. proposed Adeona [61], a system for locating lost (or stolen) devices. The core of their system is based on the ability of the device to periodically upload reports, i.e., it only works for internet-enabled devices with considerably higher storage capacities, while our system is designed for BLE tags that have limited storage and no internet connectivity, and relies on the *power of the crowd* for locating devices. Furthermore, their system employs round-trip time measurements of known hosts (landmarks) for estimating the geo-location of the device, and potentially requiring communication with the ISP; apart from the impracticality of requiring such communication, these geo-locating techniques [37, 43] achieve very coarse-grained estimations (e.g., within a large metropolitan area) and are, thus, not suitable for this type of functionality. An interesting aspect of their system is that it is built over a Distributed Hash Table, enabling the use of public infrastructure without the need of a trusted central service. As this matches our motivation behind the use of a public server that serves as a bulletin board, we could modify our approach to similarly employ OpenDHT [60] for storing the observation events.

Bluetooth tracking. The issue of location tracking using ubiquitous devices has been extensively studied in the past. Jakobsson and Wetzel [45] discussed, among other attacks, how the location of users could be tracked by an adversary that had deployed or compromised Bluetooth-enabled devices distributed over a (large) area. In this paper, we demonstrated how adversaries can leverage an existing popular crowdsourcing service for deploying such an attack. Following that work a plethora of researchers have explored this issue both for WiFi and Bluetooth devices [39, 61, 63]. Das et al. [23] showed how the network traffic of BLE wearables could lead to the inference of user activities, or identification of the user within a small group through the user's gait.

Location privacy. A lot of research has focused on location privacy for applications where a user's location needs to be sent to a third party [29, 50]. Many of these studies focus on services that provide location-specific information and, as such, propose solutions that add noise or perturb the user's location [12, 19, 27] or employ cryptographic primitives [57]. These approaches are not suitable for many crowd GPS systems, as accuracy is of prime importance and tags have limited computational power. Also, recent work demonstrated how attackers can accurately pinpoint a user's location in popular services, despite the noise they introduce [58].

10. CONCLUSIONS

As the saying goes, *"there is strength in numbers"*. While the crowd's power can be harnessed for tackling significant tasks, with several examples of crowd sourced platforms demonstrating important results, it can also be misused with dire implications. To motivate this discussion, we demonstrated how a very popular service could be trivially misused as a distributed surveillance system, effectively tracking the whereabouts of any user within the system. To proactively prevent such incidents, we designed Techu to offer strong security guarantees, and ensure the location privacy and anonymity of participants from other users, as well as the service itself. In the security analysis of our system we outlined how users are protected against a wide range of attacks, and discussed the tradeoff between privacy and performance overhead. Furthermore, our experiments showed that our system has negligible impact on the user's device in terms of computational overhead and power consumption. Thus, the low operational costs and privacy-preserving nature of Techu can incentivize vendors to adopt our system design. Nonetheless, if crowdsourced GPS services continue to gain traction for critical tasks (e.g., locating missing elderly or children), one could envision the deployment of Techu by volunteers or as a government-led operation.

Acknowledgments

We want to thank the reviewers for their valuable feedback. Special thanks to our shepherd Morley Mao for all her help. This work is based upon research supported in part by the U.S. Office of Naval Research under award number N00014-16-1-2261.

11. REFERENCES

[1] Cryptographic key length recommendation. https://www.keylength.com/en/.

[2] Daily mail - samsonite set to install tracking beacons. http://www.dailymail.co.uk/sciencetech/article-3540967/Now-lost-luggage-tell-Samsonite-set-install/tracking-beacons-new-cases-using-smartphone-app.html.

[3] Daily news - lost items cost americans $5,591: survey. http://www.nydailynews.com/news/national/lost-items-cost-americans-5-591-survey-article-1.2237244.

[4] Forbes - if you're not paying for it, you become the product. http://www.forbes.com/sites/marketshare/2012/03/05/if-youre-not-paying-for-it-you-become-the-product/.

[5] Identity theft resource center - 2015 data breaches. http://www.idtheftcenter.org/ITRC-Surveys-Studies/2015databreaches.html.

[6] Network world - biggest data breaches of 2015. http://www.networkworld.com/article/3011103/security/biggest-data-breaches-of-2015.html.

[7] Reuters - amazon bolsters voice based-platform alexa with investment in trackr. http://www.reuters.com/article/us-amazon-com-alexa-trackr-idUSKCN0XT1GB.

[8] Trackr - pets. http://support.thetrackr.com/hc/en-us/articles/210902166-Can-I-Use-TrackR-On-My-Pet-.

[9] https://www.indiegogo.com/projects/trackr-bravo-the-thinnest-tracking-device-ever--2#/.

[10] Washington post - nsa tracking cellphone locations worldwide, snowden documents show. https://www.washingtonpost.com/world/national-security/nsa-tracking-cellphone-locations-worldwide-snowden-documents-show/2013/12/04/5492873a-5cf2-11e3-bc56-c6ca94801fac_story.html.

[11] M. Allahbakhsh, B. Benatallah, A. Ignjatovic, H. R. Motahari-Nezhad, E. Bertino, and S. Dustdar. Quality control in crowdsourcing systems: Issues and directions. *IEEE Internet Computing*, 17(2), 2013.

[12] M. E. Andrés, N. E. Bordenabe, K. Chatzikokolakis, and C. Palamidessi. Geo-indistinguishability: Differential privacy for location-based systems. In *Proceedings of the 2013 ACM SIGSAC conference on Computer & communications security*, pages 901–914. ACM, 2013.

[13] Associated Press. NYC transit hubs handle flood of lost items. Crain's New York Business, Dec 2013. http://www.crainsnewyork.com/article/20131227/TRANSPORTATION/131229942/nyc-transit-hubs-handle-flood-of-lost-items.

[14] M. Balakrishnan, I. Mohomed, and V. Ramasubramanian. Where's that phone?: Geolocating ip addresses on 3g networks. In *Proceedings of the 9th ACM SIGCOMM conference on Internet measurement conference*, pages 293–300. ACM, 2009.

[15] A. Bessani, M. Correia, B. Quaresma, F. André, and P. Sousa. Depsky: Dependable and secure storage in a cloud-of-clouds. *ACM Transactions on Storage (TOS)*, 9(4):12, 2013.

[16] K. Bishop. Growth business: GPS tracking the elderly. CNBC. http://www.cnbc.com/2014/03/11/growth-business-gps-tracking-the-elderly.html.

[17] Bluetooth SIG. Specification of the Bluetooth system, 2010. https://www.bluetooth.org/docman/handlers/downloaddoc.ashx?doc_id=229737.

[18] Bluetooth Special Interest Group. *Bluetooth Specification*, 4.2 edition, 2014.

[19] N. E. Bordenabe, K. Chatzikokolakis, and C. Palamidessi. Optimal geo-indistinguishable mechanisms for location privacy. In *Proceedings of the 2014 ACM SIGSAC Conference on Computer and Communications Security*, pages 251–262. ACM, 2014.

[20] V. Cheval, S. Delaune, and M. Ryan. Tests for establishing security properties. In *International Symposium on Trustworthy Global Computing*, pages 82–96. Springer, 2014.

[21] S. Cohen. Locus pocus can track all your bluetooth devices – and other people's, too. VentureBeat, 2015. http://venturebeat.com/2015/06/06/locus-pocus-can-track-all-your-bluetooth-devices-and-other-peoples-too/.

[22] C. Cornelius, A. Kapadia, D. Kotz, D. Peebles, M. Shin, and N. Triandopoulos. Anonysense: Privacy-aware people-centric sensing. In *Proceedings of the 6th international conference on Mobile systems, applications, and services*, pages 211–224. ACM, 2008.

[23] A. K. Das, P. H. Pathak, C.-N. Chuah, and P. Mohapatra. Uncovering privacy leakage in ble network traffic of wearable fitness trackers. In *Proceedings of the 17th International Workshop on Mobile Computing Systems and Applications*, pages 99–104. ACM, 2016.

[24] Y.-A. de Montjoye, C. A. Hidalgo, M. Verleysen, and V. D. Blondel. Unique in the crowd: The privacy bounds of human mobility. *Nature Scientific Reports*, 3, 2013.

[25] R. Dingledine, N. Mathewson, and P. Syverson. Tor: The second-generation onion router. Technical report, DTIC Document, 2004.

[26] M. Faulkner, M. Olson, R. Chandy, J. Krause, K. M. Chandy, and A. Krause. The next big one: Detecting earthquakes and other rare events from community-based sensors. In *Information Processing in Sensor Networks (IPSN)*, 2011.

[27] K. Fawaz and K. G. Shin. Location privacy protection for smartphone users. In *Proceedings of the 2014 ACM SIGSAC Conference on Computer and Communications Security*, pages 239–250. ACM, 2014.

[28] C. Frank, P. Bolliger, C. Roduner, and W. Kellerer. Objects calling home: Locating objects using mobile phones. *Pervasive computing*, pages 351–368, 2007.

[29] G. Ghinita. Privacy for location-based services. *Synthesis Lectures on Information Security, Privacy, and Trust*, 4(1), 2013.

[30] P. Golle and K. Partridge. On the anonymity of home/work location pairs. *Pervasive Computing, Springer*, pages 390–397, 2009.

[31] C. Gomez, J. Oller, and J. Paradells. Overview and evaluation of bluetooth low energy: An emerging low-power wireless technology. *Sensors*, 12(9):11734–11753, 2012.

[32] M. C. Gonzalez, C. A. Hidalgo, and A.-L. Barabasi. Understanding individual human mobility patterns. *Nature*, 453(7196), 2008.

[33] Google. Google cloud messaging. https://developers.google.com/cloud-messaging/.

[34] Google. Growing Eddystone with ephemeral identifiers: A privacy aware & secure open beacon format, 2016. https://developers.googleblog.com/2016/04/growing-eddystone-with-ephemeral-identifiers.html.

[35] M. Green. A riddle wrapped in a curve. https://blog.cryptographyengineering.com/2015/10/22/a-riddle-wrapped-in-curve/.

[36] M. Gruteser and D. Grunwald. Anonymous usage of location-based services through spatial and temporal cloaking. In *Proceedings of the 1st international conference on Mobile systems, applications and services*, pages 31–42. ACM, 2003.

[37] B. Gueye, A. Ziviani, M. Crovella, and S. Fdida. Constraint-based geolocation of internet hosts. *IEEE/ACM Transactions on Networking*, 14(6):1219–1232, 2006.

[38] B. Guo, Z. Wang, Z. Yu, Y. Wang, N. Y. Yen, R. Huang, and X. Zhou. Mobile crowd sensing and computing: The review of an emerging human-powered sensing paradigm. *ACM Comput. Surv.*, 48(1), 2015.

[39] M. Haase, M. Handy, et al. Bluetrack–imperceptible tracking of bluetooth devices. In *Ubicomp Poster Proceedings*. Citeseer, 2004.

[40] K. Han, E. A. Graham, D. Vassallo, and D. Estrin. Enhancing motivation in a mobile participatory sensing project through gaming. In *Privacy, Security, Risk and Trust (PASSAT) and*

2011 IEEE Third Inernational Conference on Social Computing (SocialCom), 2011 IEEE Third International Conference on, pages 1443–1448. IEEE, 2011.

[41] https://www.thetileapp.com/. Tilebeacon.

[42] https://www.thetrackr.com/. Trackr.

[43] Z. Hu, J. Heidemann, and Y. Pradkin. Towards geolocation of millions of ip addresses. In *Proceedings of the 2012 ACM conference on Internet measurement conference*, pages 123–130. ACM, 2012.

[44] N. Husted and S. Myers. Mobile location tracking in metro areas: Malnets and others. In *Proceedings of the 17th ACM conference on Computer and communications security*, pages 85–96. ACM, 2010.

[45] M. Jakobsson and S. Wetzel. Security weaknesses in bluetooth. In *Cryptographers' Track at the RSA Conference*, pages 176–191. Springer, 2001.

[46] C. Jones. 10 wearable safety and GPS devices for kids. The SafeWise Report, 2015. http://www.safewise.com/blog/10-wearable-safety-gps-devices-kids/.

[47] P. Kindt, D. Yunge, R. Diemer, and S. Chakraborty. Precise energy modeling for the bluetooth low energy protocol. *arXiv preprint arXiv:1403.2919*, 2014.

[48] N. Koblitz, Alfred, and J. Menezes. A riddle wrapped in an enigma. Security and Privacy, 2015.

[49] J. Krumm. Inference attacks on location tracks. *Pervasive computing*, pages 127–143, 2007.

[50] J. Krumm. A survey of computational location privacy. *Personal Ubiquitous Comput.*, 13(6), 2009.

[51] N. D. Lane, S. B. Eisenman, M. Musolesi, E. Miluzzo, and A. T. Campbell. Urban sensing systems: opportunistic or participatory? In *Proceedings of the 9th workshop on Mobile computing systems and applications*, pages 11–16. ACM, 2008.

[52] R. Lawler. Land Rover puts Tile's stuff-finding Bluetooth tech in an SUV. engadget, 2016. https://www.engadget.com/2016/04/26/land-rover-puts-tiles-stuff-finding-bluetooth-tech-in-an-suv/.

[53] Maxell. Cr1616 battery datasheet. http://www.maxell.com.tw/images/uploads/2014/10/CR1616_DataSheet_e.pdf.

[54] K. Minami and N. Borisov. Protecting location privacy against inference attacks. In *Proceedings of the 9th annual ACM workshop on Privacy in the electronic society*, pages 123–126. ACM, 2010.

[55] P. Mohan, V. Padmanabhan, and R. Ramjee. Nericell: Rich monitoring of road and traffic conditions using mobile smartphones. In *ACM Sensys '08*, 2008.

[56] B. Pan, Y. Zheng, D. Wilkie, and C. Shahabi. Crowd sensing of traffic anomalies based on human mobility and social media. In *Proceedings of the 21st ACM SIGSPATIAL International Conference on Advances in Geographic Information Systems*, pages 344–353. ACM, 2013.

[57] S. Papadopoulos, S. Bakiras, and D. Papadias. Nearest neighbor search with strong location privacy. *Proc. VLDB Endow.*, 3(1-2), 2010.

[58] I. Polakis, G. Argyros, T. Petsios, S. Sivakorn, and A. D. Keromytis. Where's Wally? Precise user discovery attacks in location proximity services. In *Proceedings of the 22nd ACM SIGSAC Conference on Computer and Communications Security*, pages 817–828. ACM, 2015.

[59] I. Polakis, S. Volanis, E. Athanasopoulos, and E. P. Markatos. The man who *was* there: validating check-ins in location-based services. In *Proceedings of the 29th Annual Computer Security Applications Conference*, pages 19–28. ACM, 2013.

[60] S. C. Rhea. *Opendht: A Public Dht Service*. PhD thesis, 2005.

[61] T. Ristenpart, G. Maganis, A. Krishnamurthy, and T. Kohno. Privacy-preserving location tracking of lost or stolen devices: Cryptographic techniques and replacing trusted third parties with dhts. In *Usenix Security Symposium*, pages 275–290, 2008.

[62] J. L. Sandeep Kamath. Measuring bluetooth® low energy power consumption, application note an092.

[63] T. S. Saponas, J. Lester, C. Hartung, S. Agarwal, T. Kohno, et al. Devices that tell on you: Privacy trends in consumer ubiquitous computing. In *Usenix Security*, volume 3, 2007.

[64] C. E. Shannon. A mathematical theory of communication. *The Bell System Technical Journal*, 27:379–423, 623–656, 1948.

[65] R. Shokri, G. Theodorakopoulos, C. Troncoso, J.-P. Hubaux, and J.-Y. Le Boudec. Protecting location privacy: Optimal strategy against localization attacks. In *Proceedings of the ACM Conference on Computer and Communications Security*, pages 617–627. ACM, 2012.

[66] B. S. I. G. (SIG). Bluetooth®5 quadruples range, doubles speed, increases data broadcasting capacity by 800%. PRESS RELEASE, 2016. https://www.bluetooth.com/news/pressreleases/2016/06/16/-bluetooth5-quadruples-rangedoubles-speedincreases-data-broadcasting-capacity-by-800.

[67] S. W. Smith. Gagged, sealed & delivered: Reforming ecpa's secret docket. *Harvard Law & Policy Review*, 6, 2012.

[68] M. W. Storer, K. Greenan, and E. L. Miller. Long-term threats to secure archives. In *Proceedings of the Second ACM Workshop on Storage Security and Survivability*, StorageSS '06.

[69] M. W. Storer, K. M. Greenan, E. L. Miller, and K. Voruganti. Potshards—a secure, recoverable, long-term archival storage system. *ACM Transactions on Storage*, 5(2), 2009.

[70] J. Sun, R. Zhang, X. Jin, and Y. Zhang. Securefind: Secure and privacy-preserving object finding via mobile crowdsourcing. *IEEE Transactions on Wireless Communications*, 15(3):1716–1728, 2016.

[71] H. To, G. Ghinita, and C. Shahabi. A framework for protecting worker location privacy in spatial crowdsourcing. *Proc. VLDB Endow.*, 7, 2014.

[72] S. Triukose, S. Ardon, A. Mahanti, and A. Seth. Geolocating ip addresses in cellular data networks. In *International Conference on Passive and Active Network Measurement*, pages 158–167. Springer, 2012.

[73] Unacast. Beacons on track to hit 400M deployed by 2020 reports Unacast. BusinessWire. http://www.businesswire.com/news/home/20160126005779/en/Beacons-Track-Hit-400M-Deployed-2020-Reports.

[74] G. Wang, B. Wang, T. Wang, A. Nika, H. Zheng, and B. Y. Zhao. Defending against sybil devices in crowdsourced mapping services. In *Proceedings of the 14th Annual International Conference on Mobile Systems, Applications, and Services*, pages 179–191. ACM, 2016.

TrustShadow: Secure Execution of Unmodified Applications with ARM TrustZone

Le Guan*, Peng Liu*, Xinyu Xing*, Xinyang Ge#, Shengzhi Zhang†, Meng Yu‡, Trent Jaeger*
*Pennsylvania State University
{lug14, pliu, xxing}@ist.psu.edu, {tjaeger}@cse.psu.edu
#Microsoft Research
{xing}@microsoft.com
†Florida Institute of Technology
{zhangs}@cs.fit.edu
‡University of Texas at San Antonio
{meng.yu}@utsa.edu

ABSTRACT

The rapid evolution of Internet-of-Things (IoT) technologies has led to an emerging need to make them smarter. A variety of applications now run simultaneously on an ARM-based processor. For example, devices on the edge of the Internet are provided with higher horsepower to be entrusted with storing, processing and analyzing data collected from IoT devices. This significantly improves efficiency and reduces the amount of data that needs to be transported to the cloud for data processing, analysis and storage. However, commodity OSes are prone to compromise. Once they are exploited, attackers can access the data on these devices. Since the data stored and processed on the devices can be sensitive, left untackled, this is particularly disconcerting.

In this paper, we propose a new system, `TrustShadow` that shields legacy applications from untrusted OSes. `TrustShadow` takes advantage of ARM TrustZone technology and partitions resources into the secure and normal worlds. In the secure world, `TrustShadow` constructs a trusted execution environment for security-critical applications. This trusted environment is maintained by a lightweight runtime system that coordinates the communication between applications and the ordinary OS running in the normal world. The runtime system does not provide system services itself. Rather, it forwards requests for system services to the ordinary OS, and verifies the correctness of the responses. To demonstrate the efficiency of this design, we prototyped `TrustShadow` on a real chip board with ARM TrustZone support, and evaluated its performance using both microbenchmarks and real-world applications. We showed `TrustShadow` introduces only negligible overhead to real-world applications.

Permission to make digital or hard copies of all or part of this work for personal or classroom use is granted without fee provided that copies are not made or distributed for profit or commercial advantage and that copies bear this notice and the full citation on the first page. Copyrights for components of this work owned by others than ACM must be honored. Abstracting with credit is permitted. To copy otherwise, or republish, to post on servers or to redistribute to lists, requires prior specific permission and/or a fee. Request permissions from permissions@acm.org.

MobiSys '17, June 19–23, 2017, Niagara Falls, NY, USA.

© 2017 ACM. ISBN 978-1-4503-4928-4/17/06...$15.00

DOI: http://dx.doi.org/10.1145/3081333.3081349

Keywords

Malicious Operating Systems; ARM TrustZone; IoT; Trusted Execution

1. INTRODUCTION

The emerging Internet of Things (IoT) technologies have enabled more and more isolated "things" to collect, process, analyze, and exchange data. To become smart, IoT devices tend to be built atop ARM-based multi-programming platforms, in which multiple programs run simultaneously on commodity Operating Systems (OSes). This allows them to install product-ready applications and saves effort and budget in application development.

For example, edge computing [9, 8] is a decentralized computing infrastructure that connects IoT devices to process their data on other, more powerful devices that are on – or close to – the network edge. Examples of such edge devices include industrial controllers, smart gateway and routers, embedded servers, and even automotive in-vehicle infotainment etc. Compared to a central data center in the cloud, edge devices are geographically closer to the IoT devices. Thus, they can respond to IoT devices more quickly, making them more suitable to environments where operations are time-critical or Internet connectivity is poor. In telemedicine scenarios, edge devices could run sophisticated analytics and turn around results in real time [15]. As another example, a smart 3D-printer [19] can directly download an STL (STereoLithography) file from the "MakerBot Digital Store" [19], convert it into `GCODE` by running a slicer program, and feed the `GCODE` to the actuator.

Unfortunately, the security provided by commodity OSes in the multi-programming platforms is often inadequate. Once an OS is compromised, attackers gain complete access to the data on a system. Since these devices may often deal with confidential data, possibly subject to laws and regulations, this is particularly disconcerting.

To address this problem, a straightforward reaction is to safeguard applications against the OSes potentially vulnerable to exploitable bugs or misconfiguration. Prior efforts on this explore executing applications that handle sensitive data in separate virtual machines (e.g., [13, 26, 43]), taking advantage of hardware features (e.g., [6, 34, 33]) or retrofitting commodity OSes (e.g. [16]). Unfortunately, these solutions are not applicable to the aforementioned IoT multi-programming platforms.

First, these devices do not have the hardware features typically available on PCs. To be energy efficient, these devices generally incorporate ARM Cortex-A processors, making the techniques that rely on unique hardware completely futile (e.g., Haven [6] based on Intel SGX). Second, these devices do not have abundant computational resources in comparison with PCs or a data center in the cloud. Thus, it is not realistic to adopt to these devices those techniques specifically designed for PCs or data centers. Last but not least, some techniques previously proposed require radical changes to applications and OSes, which poses a substantial barrier to their adoption. This is especially true in the scenario where device manufacturers would like to retain compatibility with existing applications.

In this paper, we address the aforementioned issues by developing `TrustShadow`. `TrustShadow` is a system that shields legacy applications from a compromised OS. By taking advantage of ARM TrustZone technology [4], our system constructs a trusted execution environment for security-critical applications. Different from some existing techniques, `TrustShadow` does not radically change existing OSes. Rather, it utilizes a lightweight runtime system to coordinate communications between applications and untrusted OSes. As such, `TrustShadow` requires no changes to existing applications either.

More specifically, we develop `TrustShadow` with a runtime system running in the TrustZone of an ARM processor. The runtime manages the page tables for applications locally in an isolated secure environment, and ensures their virtual memory cannot be accessed by an untrusted OS running outside the environment. To accommodate the execution of applications in a lightweight manner, the runtime does not incorporate complicated system services. Rather, it forwards application requests for system services to the untrusted OS, similar to Proxos [43]. To guarantee security, the runtime verifies return values from system services to defeat Iago attacks [11], and interposes context switches between the applications and the untrusted OS. Considering an application might interact with file I/O, the runtime system also encrypts the data before revealing it to the untrusted OS for storing.

With the design above, `TrustShadow` protects legacy applications from the untrusted OSes running them. As a result, developers no longer need to re-engineer applications in order to run them on IoT devices. Since `TrustShadow` does not implement system services itself, the complexity of Trusted Computing Base (TCB) is reduced, making `TrustShadow` less vulnerable to exploits. To the best of our knowledge, `TrustShadow` is the first solution on ARM-based IoT devices that allows an unmodified application to run protected from attacks from untrusted OSes

In summary, this paper makes the following contributions.

- We propose a system – `TrustShadow`– for ARM-based multi-programming platforms. It can protect security-critical applications from untrusted OSes without the requirement of re-engineering the applications.

- We introduce a runtime system within `TrustShadow`. It accommodates the execution of Linux applications with a lightweight forwarding-and-verifying mechanism.

- We implemented `TrustShadow` on a real chip (SoC) board with the ARM TrustZone support with only about 5.3K lines of code (LOC) in the secure world, and 300 LOC in the normal world. Using microbenchmarks and real world software, we showed that `TrustShadow` imposes only negligible performance overhead.

The rest of the paper is organized as follows. Section 2 and 3 present related work and the background of TrustZone, respectively. Section 4 discusses our threat model. Section 5 describes the overview of `TrustShadow`. Section 6 and 7 introduce our design and prototype implementation in detail. We present the evaluation of `TrustShadow` in Section 8, followed by some discussion in Section 9. Finally, we conclude the paper in Section 10.

2. RELATED WORK

As is described in Section 1, prior research primarily focuses on taking advantage of virtual machines, hardware features and radical code re-engineering to protect applications from compromised OSes. In this section, we summarize these works and describe why they are not suitable for IoT devices with more details.

Hypervisors and Virtual Machines. To protect an application from a compromised OS, one research effort focuses on utilizing hypervisor to construct trusted execution environment for applications. Systems following this design principle include **Overshadow** [13], **CHAOS** [12], **SP**^{3} [46], **Inktag** [26], etc. They encrypt address space for an application under protection through a hypervisor, so that a compromised OS can only view the address space of the application in ciphertext. Using the hypervisor, they also verify the integrity of memory contents, and thus ensure a compromised OS cannot jeopardize the execution of the application. Similar to these techniques, another research effort focuses on escalating protection with virtual machines. For example, **Terra** [21] and **Proxos** [43] allocate a dedicated VM for an application, making it resistant to a malicious OS.

While these systems have been shown to be effective in shielding applications, they are an overkill for resource-constrained IoT devices, and sometimes cannot be adopted by IoT devices. First, deploying a hypervisor-based system cannot provide the best (native) performance for the already performance-hungry IoT devices [20]. Second, virtualization extension used in **InkTag** etc., is a new hardware feature for the ARM platform, and is missing for many existing ARM devices[1]. Third, ARM has recently released the new IoT-oriented Cortex-M processor series which incorporate TrustZone extension, not virtualization extension [3]. This meets our speculation that virtualization is not suitable for resource-constrained IoT devices.

From the security perspective, hypervisor or virtual machine based solutions relies on hypervisor, which is already struggling with its own security problems due to increasing TCB size [18, 17]. In this work, `TrustShadow` harnesses TrustZone technology to mediate communication between OS and applications, which eliminates complex, error-prone resource allocation in a hypervisor.

Hardware Features. Research in the past also explores using various hardware features to protect applications from

[1]ARM released virtualization extension in the year 2010 [2].

untrusted OSes. For example, `Haven` [6] takes advantage of Intel Software Guard eXtension (SGX) [35] to safeguard applications. More specifically, it harnesses SGX to instantiate a secure region of address space, and then protects execution of applications within that region from malicious privilege code. In addition to Intel SGX, Trusted Platform Module (TPM) is also used for shielding applications from a potentially malicious OS. For example, both `Flicker` [34] and `TrustVisor` [33] utilize TPM to isolate the execution of sensitive code. As is described in Section 1, IoT devices generally incorporate ARM Cortex-A processors which do not have the aforementioned hardware features. As a result, previous techniques based on those cannot be applicable.

Trusted Language Runtime (`TLR`) [39], `VeriUI` [32] and `TrustOTP` [42] utilize ARM TrustZone technology for shielding applications. `TLR` implement a small runtime capable of interpreting .NET managed code inside the secure world. By splitting mobile application into secure part and non-secure part, the secure part of the app is never exposed to the untrusted OSes. `VeriUI` utilizes TrustZone to provide a trustworthy setting for handling passwords. `TrustOTP` harnesses TrustZone to protect the confidentiality of the One-Time-Password against a malicious mobile OS. While these works take advantage of TrustZone, they require modifications to applications in order to be under protected. This poses a substantial barrier to their adoptions.

Code Instrumentation. `Virtual Ghost` [16] is another research endeavor on protecting applications from a hostile OS. Different from those techniques discussed above, it uses compiler techniques and run-time checking to implement a mechanism similar to `InkTag` within the OS kernel. Since the compiler instrumentation and run-time checking introduce more privilege code to kernel, not only does it increase TCB of a computer system but also imposes performance overhead, making it not suitable to energy-efficient, computation-lightweight IoT devices.

3. TRUSTZONE

In this section, we present the background of ARM TrustZone technology. To be more specific, we briefly describe its architecture, address space controller and memory management unit (MMU).

3.1 Architecture

ARM TrustZone partitions all of the System-on-Chip (SoC) hardware and software resources in one of two worlds - the secure world for the security subsystem, and the normal world for everything else. With this partition, a single physical processor core can safely and efficiently execute code from both the normal world and the secure world in a time-sliced fashion. When the processor executes code in the normal world, it enters a non-secure state in which the processor can only access resources in the normal world. Otherwise, it is in a secure state in which the processor can access resources resided in both worlds.

To determine whether program execution is in the secure or normal world, ARM TrustZone extends a Non-Secure bit (NS-bit) on the AMBA Advanced eXtensble Interface (AXI) bus. With this NS-bit, the processor can check permissions on the access. To manage switches to and from the secure world, TrustZone provides *monitor mode software* which ensures the state of the world that the processor is leaving is safely saved, and the state of the world the processor is switching to is correctly restored. The secure world entry to the monitor mode can be achieved by an explicit call via an `smc` instruction.

3.2 Address Space Controller

TrustZone Address Space Controller (TZASC) is an Advanced Microcontroller Bus Architecture (AMBA) compliant SoC peripheral. It allows a TrustZone system to configure security access permissions for each address region. In TrustZone, the access permissions are managed by a group of registers, the access to which must be from the secure world. In addition, TZASC controls data transfer between an ARM processor and Dynamic Memory Controller (DMC). To permit data transfer, it examines whether NS-bit matches the security settings of the memory region. Given a memory region set to *secure access only*, for example, an attempt to read returns all zeros and that to write has no change to the contents in that region.

3.3 Memory Management Unit

An ARM processor also provides MMU to perform the translation of virtual memory addresses to physical addresses. Since TrustZone partitions memory space into secure and normal worlds, a processor with TrustZone enabled provides two separated virtual MMUs which allow each world to map virtual addresses to physical addresses independently.

In the normal world, a process can only access physical memory in the non-secure state. In the secure world, it however can specify how to access physical memory by tuning NS-bit. For example, it could adjust the NS field in the first-level page table, and access the memory in either the secure or non-secure state. This flexibility augments a TrustZone system with an ability to efficiently share memory across the worlds.

4. THREAT MODEL

`TrustShadow` shields a trustworthy application from a hostile OS. We consider a completely compromised OS, which means the attacker can execute arbitrary hostile code with system privilege to interfere with the memory and registers of a process. For example, it may read/write any memory in victim process's address space, through either load/store instructions or Direct Memory Access [7, 27], causing memory disclosure and code injection attacks. As another example, OS could modify interrupted process state (e.g., the `PC` register) during exception handling and resume the execution from an arbitrary instruction to change the program execution's control flow.

In addition, the OS could change victim process's behavior by hijacking system services (e.g., forging system call responses), leading to Iago attacks [11]. Recent study shows that an adversary can infer data by observing a program's page fault patterns [45]. This kind of controlled channel attack is also covered in this work.

Availability is out of scope in this paper. In fact, a compromised OS could simply refuse to boot, or decline the time slices of an HAP to launch Denial-of-Service (DoS) attacks. Side channel attacks such as timing and power analysis are out of scope in this paper. We assume the runtime system running in the TrustZone is trusted. Throughout our design of `TrustShadow`, we keep its functionality simple and its code

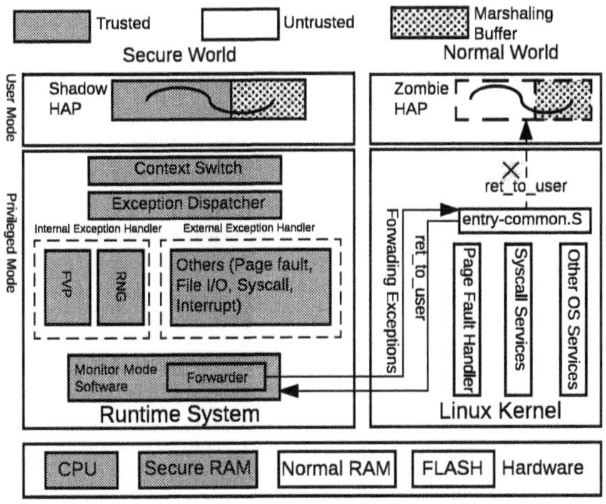

Figure 1: The architecture of TrustShadow.

base minimal. This makes it easier to ensure its correctness through formal verification [41] or manual review.

5. OVERVIEW

Figure 1 illustrates the architecture of TrustShadow, where the runtime system and Linux kernel run in the secure and normal world, respectively. Within the secure world, the runtime system shields the execution of a High-Assurance Process (HAP), and all the trusted modules shown in the figure cannot be accessed by the ordinary Linux running in the normal world.

To be resistant to a hostile OS, an application needs to be initialized through a customized system call, which creates a "zombie" HAP and its "shadow" counterpart. In our design, the zombie HAP represents the application running in the normal world. However, it *never* gets scheduled to run. Rather, TrustShadow runs its "shadow" counterpart residing in the secure world. To support the execution of the shadow HAP, TrustShadow introduces a lightweight runtime system to the secure world.

The runtime system does not provide system services for shadow HAPs. Instead, it intercepts exceptions and forwards them to the Linux OS running in the normal world. In this way, the runtime system can maintain a trusted execution environment for HAPs without introducing a large amount of code to the secure world. To enable cross-world communications, TrustShadow introduces data structure **task_shared** to share data between the runtime system and the OS. In addition, TrustShadow sets aside data structure **task_private** to store sensitive metadata for shadow HAPs. In our design, this data structure can only be accessed by the runtime system.

To accommodate the execution of HAPs and coordinate communications across two worlds, the runtime system is designed with various modules (see Figure 1). Serving as the gateway for all exceptions and their returns, the context switch module maintains the CPU hardware context for each HAP, and restores/clears general-purpose registers accordingly. It allows the runtime system to coordinate the execution of an HAP and avoid leaking sensitive data to the OS running in the normal world.

As is shown in Figure 1, the runtime system also implements an internal exception handler module – indicated by FVP and RNG. They are designed to handle floating point computation and random number requests locally, for the reasons that cryptographic operation must rely upon trustworthy random number generation, and floating point computation necessarily exposes floating registers if TrustShadow relies upon the Linux OS for handling this exception. In Section 6.5, we describe this internal exception handler in detail.

In our design, the runtime system handles exceptions using three modules, including exception dispatcher, external exception handler, and forwarder. The exception dispatcher is responsible for dispatching exceptions to corresponding handlers. Except for floating point exception and random number requests, this module dispatches all the exceptions to the external exception handler which further redirects the exceptions to the forwarder module. To accommodate exception forwarding in a transparent manner, the forwarder module *emulates* an exception context for the normal world, pretending that exception is trigger by the zombie HAP. After receiving exceptions, the Linux OS handles them and returns results through **task_shared**. The external exception handler verifies the return results before reflecting them to the execution environment of the corresponding HAP. In Section 6.2, 6.3 and 6.4, we describe how the three modules coordinate and perform external exception handling.

Since the normal OS does not have the privilege to access a shadow HAP, TrustShadow also introduces a world-shared buffer, indicated as the marshaling buffer in Figure 1. Through this buffer, not only does TrustShadow share the parameters of system calls with the ordinary OS but also retrieves the returns of the system calls. To retrieve the return value of a system call, TrustShadow copies the data in the buffer to the memory region corresponding to the system call, provided that the verifier module marks it valid.

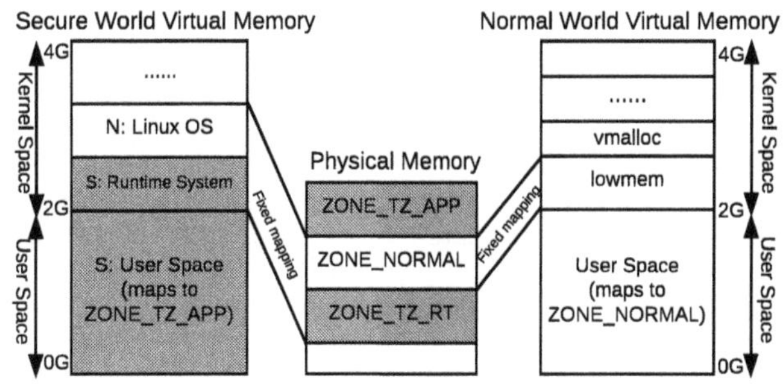

Figure 2: Physical memory partition vs. virtual memory layout.

6. RUNTIME SYSTEM

In this section, we detail the runtime system illustrated in Figure 1. We begin with memory management for security. Then, we discuss how the aforementioned modules coordinate HAP execution. More specific, we describe how they forward exceptions, handle page faults and intervene system calls. Last, we present internal exception handling.

6.1 Memory Management

Here, we describe how we partition physical memory regions, and specify the design of virtual memory system.

Physical Memory Partition. Using TZASC, TrustShadow creates three distinct physical memory regions. They are non-secure region ZONE_TZ_APP as well as secure regions ZONE_TZ_RT and ZONE_TZ_APP. The non-secure region can be accessed by both the normal and secure worlds, whereas the secure regions have to be accessed through the secure world. In our design, we designate secure region ZONE_TZ_APP for shadow HAPs, ZONE_TZ_RT for the runtime system and non-secure region ZONE_NORMAL for holding the Linux OS and other ordinary processes. We illustrate these three regions in Figure 2. With the partition above, the runtime, HAPs and Linux OS are all physically isolated, which provides the essential support for safeguarding the HAPs.

Virtual Memory Layout. TrustShadow supports executing legacy Linux code in the secure world. As a result, we design the virtual address of the secure world to follow the same user/kernel memory split as that in the Linux OS. With this design, legacy code can be offloaded to execute in the secure world without any code relocation. In our current design, both Linux OS and the runtime system maintain a 2G/2G virtual address split, as shown in Figure 2.

In the kernel space of secure world, in addition to mapping itself to ZONE_TZ_RT, the runtime system maps the physical memory holding the Linux OS (ZONE_NORMAL) in the virtual address space. With this mapping, the runtime system can efficiently locate shared data from the OS (such as task_shared) by adding a corresponding offset.

6.2 Forwarding Exceptions

In general, a program is not self-contained. During execution, it might be trapped into the OS (e.g., calling a system service, encountering a page fault or interrupt). In the ARM architecture, system calls are requested by issuing the svc instruction which traps the processor into privileged SVC mode to accomplish the system services. Likewise, other exceptions during execution would trap the processor into the corresponding privileged modes.

As is described in Section 5, except for float point computation and random number generation, the runtime system intercepts exceptions and redirects them to the Linux running in the normal world. Here, we describe how TrustShadow performs exception forwarding.

ARM processors utilize current program status register (cpsr) to hold the current working mode of a processor (e.g., USR or SVC). When an exception is taken, a processor enters the target mode by performing the following operations. First, register pc points to the corresponding offset in the exception vector table. Then, the processor stores the value of previous cpsr to saved program status register (spsr) before setting cpsr to indicate the current working mode (i.e., the target mode). In the ARM architecture, spsr is a banked register and thus each processor mode has its own copy. Based on the value of spsr, an exception handler could get information about the pre-exception processor mode.

Since the monitor mode software can access resources in both worlds, the runtime system can *re-produce* an exception as follows. Here, we take forwarding a SVC exception as an example. (i) The runtime system sets spsr in monitor mode to represent the target mode (SVC). (ii) It sets the target mode's spsr to represent user mode (USR). (iii) It issues movs instruction to jump to the target exception handler (0xFFFF0008). Here, movs is an exception return instruction. In addition to jumping to the target address, it copies spsr in the current mode (SVC, which is set in Step i) to cpsr in the target mode. As a result, the OS kernel catches the exception at the correct address (0xFFFF0008) in the right mode (SVC), with spsr indicating that the exception comes from user mode (set in Step ii). We provide a code snippet to demonstrate this implementation in Appendix A. Forwarding other types of exception can be implemented in a similar way.

6.3 Handling Page Fault

A page fault is one type of exception resulting from the failure of fetching an instruction or accessing data. In the ARM architecture, a page fault is also called an abort exception, raised by MMU, indicating that the memory accessed does not have a page table entry set properly. After such an exception is taken, an OS invokes its page fault handler which assigns an appropriate physical page and updates the page table entry accordingly. Typically, a page table entry includes the virtual-to-physical address mapping and the access permissions of the virtual memory.

In general, an OS maintains page tables for applications. However, considering that an OS might be hostile and can tamper with the page tables for applications, we isolate these page tables from the OS by placing them in the secure world. The runtime system updates their entries by taking advantage of the page fault handler provided by Linux OS.

To harness the page fault handler, we modify the existing on-demand page fault handing mechanism in Linux. In particular, we hook the page fault handler so that it can store the context of page fault handling in the aforementioned shared memory, task_shared[2]. After retrieving the updating information and before installing a page table entry, the runtime system validated the returned information. In the following, we provide more details on this procedure.

6.3.1 Basic Page Table Update

A page fault occurs in various situations, and TrustShadow handles page faults differently. The most simple situation is accessing anonymous memory, in which case the page table entries in the Linux OS and the runtime system point to the same secure page $\mathbb{S}$. Besides duplicating the page table entry retrieved from task_shared, the run time system must first make sure that the mapped page is within the memory region defined in ZONE_TZ_APP. We illustrate this basic page fault handling in Figure 3a.

6.3.2 Page Table Update with Integrity Check

Different from anonymous memory, accessing memory backed by a file needs assistance from the OS to load the file contents to memory. As the OS may be hostile, besides ensuring that the translated pages are within the range of ZONE_TZ_APP, the runtime system also verifies the integrity of loaded contents. This section describes page fault handling on the memory regions backed by executable images.

We take loading a code page as an example in Figure 3b. When a prefetch abort happens, the Linux page fault handler will eventually call do_read_fault, which lo-

[2]In our design, task_shared carries the updated page table entry value (which contains the address of the translated physical memory page), the influenced virtual address, and additional contextual information.

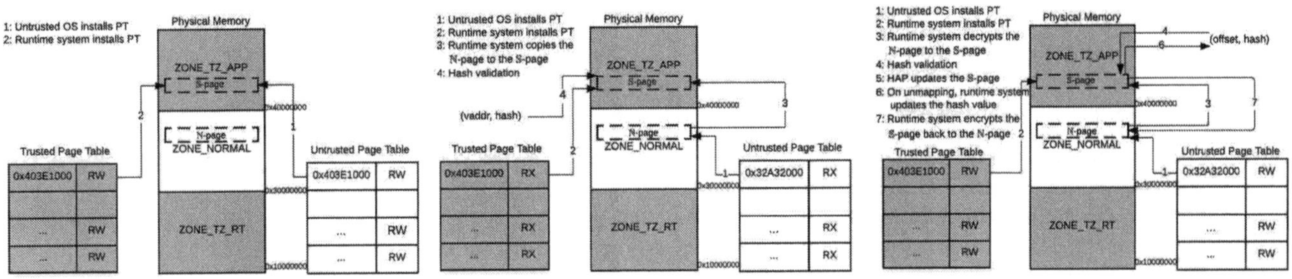

(a) Basic Page Table Update.

(b) Page Table Update with Integrity Checking.

(c) Page Table Update for Protected Files.

Figure 3: Page Table Update.

cates the physical page ℕ caching the corresponding code page (Step 1). In this context, a new secure world page 𝕊 from **ZONE_TZ_APP** is allocated, and the physical addresses of both ℕ and 𝕊 pages are saved in **task_shared**. With this shared information, the runtime system first ensures that 𝕊 page is actually a fresh page from **ZONE_TZ_APP**. Then, the runtime system installs a new page table entry in the trusted page table (Step 2), copies the ℕ page to the 𝕊 page (Step 3) and verifies the integrity of the copied page (Step 4). Note that verification is performed on 𝕊 pages, therefore, **TrustShadow** is resilient to **TOCTTOU** (Time Of Check To Time Of Use) attacks.

The described page table update with integrity check is the low level primitive for ensuring *load time program integrity*. **TrustShadow** enforces such checking on all the memory segments of type **PT_LOAD** in the ELF program images, including executable and dynamic libraries. In the following, we provide details on verifying the integrity of program images.

Verifying Executable Integrity. The Runtime system maintains a list of hash values in the format of **(vaddr, hash)**, which is initialized according to the bundled manifest (see Section 6.6). Once a page fault occurs in the covered range, the runtime system installs a secure page table entry as mentioned above. If validation is failed, the runtime system immediately terminates the process by sending an **_exit** system call to the OS. We note that such validation is a one-time effort, so it does not influence execution performance at run time when the program is warmed up.

Verifying Shared Library Integrity. Different from executables, shared libraries are position independent. To verify pages loaded for shared libraries, the runtime system maintains a system wide **(offset, hash)** list for all shared libraries frequently used. When a shared library image is mapped in the address space, the runtime system obtains the loaded base address **baseAddr** by monitoring the return value of the **mmap** system call. Then, the integrity of the loaded page is verified at address **(baseAddr + offset)**.

6.3.3 *Page Table Update for Protected Files*

This section describes page fault handling of data files. Different from executable image, the purpose of protecting data file is to prevent OS from accessing clear-text contents. Therefore, the runtime system further employs encryption technique in handling this type of page fault. **TrustShadow** allows developers to differentiate data files based on their the sensitivity levels. Only sensitive files that are specified in a manifest bundled with the application (see Section 6.6 for details) are protected.

Before elaborating page fault handling when accessing protected files, we first describe how **TrustShadow** manages them at high level. All the operations accessing these files are transparently transformed into memory mapped I/O. To correctly map file descriptor offsets to virtual addresses, preceding pages of a file are reserved for meta-data. This includes the real file length, time stamp of the last access, along with hash values of the real data pages. These preceding meta pages are protected by a per-application AES key that is provided by the manifest.

As shown in Figure 3c, when accessing a non-present page of a protected file, the runtime system decrypts the ciphertext ℕ page loaded by the OS, and writes it into a secure 𝕊 page (Step 3), which is also allocated by the OS and verified by the runtime system. After that, the hash value of the page is calculated and validated (Step 4). When unmapping this page, the runtime system recalculates and stores the hash value of the updated 𝕊 page (Step 6), and then encrypts it into the original ℕ page (Step 7), which is finally written to the permanent storage by the OS. The encryption key, again, is the per-application AES key that comes with the manifest.

6.4 Intervening System Calls

Two problems are raised when a system call is forwarded to the OS. First, due to isolation, the OS kernel cannot access the address space of a shadow HAP, while some system call services rely on input data from user space. Second, the results returned by the OS are not trusted, which may lead to potential attacks. The runtime system coordinates the intervention between an HAP and the OS, provides the OS with essential service request data, and verifies the responses from an untrusted OS. For critical system services that cannot be served by the OS (e.g., random number generator), the runtime system implements them inside the secure world, which is discussed in Section 6.5.

6.4.1 *Adapting System Calls*

Memory isolation changes the way that the OS manages and accesses the memory of an HAP. Without the runtime system acting as an intermediator, it is impossible for the OS to access application data containing system call requests. We follow existing marshaling techniques available on x86 platform, in which system call parameters are adapted in a world-shared buffer. This allows the OS to have temporary access to system call parameters. Besides this, there still remains challenges that are specific to our design. This section briefly reviews existing marshaling technique, and then describes our specifics.

Parameter Marshaling. Most system call parameters are scalar in that they contain values instead of pointers to memory, for instance, `close`, `getpid`, and `_exit`. The runtime system forwards them directly without any modification.

However, complex system calls allow a process to pass in a pointer so the kernel can read data from or write result to a user space buffer. For example, the `open` system call passes in a buffer containing the file path as a pointer. As the OS cannot access user space data, the runtime system marshals them into a world-shared buffer, and adjusts the parameters accordingly. The system call service works on the marshaling buffer. After it completes, the runtime system copies back the results into the original user buffer if necessary. More complex system calls, such as `ioctl` and `fcntl`, have different behaviors according to subcommands. A marshaling code for each request/cmd must be prepared separately according to the specifications of the subcommands.

Signal. In signal handling, a signal delivery allows an untrusted OS to resume user space code at arbitrary location, thus compromising control flow integrity of a shadow HAP. In addition, `setup_frame` needs to manipulate the process's stack to craft signal information and return code, while the OS has no privilege to do so.

`TrustShadow` addresses these problems by both hacking the OS code and supporting in the runtime system. Specifically, when a signal is registered, the runtime system inserts the handler address into the `task_private` structure of the shadow HAP. When a signal is caught by the OS, a reserved page in the marshaling buffer is used by `setup_frame` to set up a separate user mode stack specifically for signal handling. At the same time, the intended return address for signal handler is placed in `task_shared`. When the runtime system resumes, it first verifies that the address has been registered and that the `pretcode` on the signal stack is correct[3]. If so, the signal stack is copied to an unused virtual address backed by a secure page[4]. Then the hardware context of the normal control flow is saved in a temporary structure in `task_private`, and is replaced with the signal's hardware context. When the signal handler returns by issuing the `rt_sigreturn` system call, the hardware context of the normal control flow is restored.

Futex. Fast userspace mutex (futex) is another interesting kernel service that conflicts with process isolation. In Linux, a futex is identified by a four-bytes memory shared among processes or threads. It acts as a building block for many higher-level locking abstractions such as semaphores, POSIX mutexes, and barriers. If a thread fails to acquire a lock, it passes the lock's address along with its current value to a `futex` wait operation. This `futex` operation will block the thread if and only if the value in lock's address still matches the value it received. The blocked thread resumes when another thread releases the lock by issuing a `futex` wake operation, which unblocks all the threads waiting on a specific lock. Obviously, the `futex` system call needs to read the value of the lock which is in the user space of an HAP.

We observe that a thread never waits for more than one futex at a time[5]. Therefore, we hack the `futex` system call to always read from a fixed memory location in the marshaling buffer. Each time a `futex` wait operation is issued, the runtime system synchronizes the current futex value to that fixed address. In `TrustShadow`, we further handle a futex shared across processes by maintaining a system wide map that keeps physical addresses of involved memories. The runtime system queries this map to synchronize futex updates to different processes.

6.4.2 *Defeating Iago Attack*

As disclosed in [11], a compromised OS could subvert an HAP by manipulating the return values of system calls, thus leading to Iago attacks. For example, when an HAP requests a new memory region through the `mmap` system call, it expects that the returned region is disjoint with any existing mapping in the process's address space. However, a compromised OS could return an address that overlaps with the process's stack. Without proper checking on the return values, the following write on the new region would smash the stack and the process can be coerced into executing a return-oriented program [10].

With the runtime system sitting in-between the shadow HAP and the untrusted OS, it is straightforward to address known Iago attacks by interposing the system call interface and checking their results. For a known Iago attack, we need a specification for that particular system service. Here, we take the `mmap` system call as an example. Every return address of the `mmap` or `brk` system system call is compared with the current memory mapping. If an overlap is found, the HAP is immediately killed. The runtime system collects current memory mapping in three ways. First, the range of stack is obtained from current `sp`, because the stack spans from `sp` to the top of user space virtual memory. Second, heap limit can be monitored by examining return values of the `brk` system calls. Finally, the return value of each successful `mmap/munmap` system call is recorded.

6.5 Internal Exception Handling

In this section, we list security-critical exceptions that are handled directly inside the runtime system. Forwarding them to the OS would leak user data or lead to security breach.

Floating Point Computation. ARM architecture supports hardware floating point calculation by Vector Floating-Point (VFP) architecture extension. VFP introduces a set of registers and instructions specific for floating point calculations. The access to them is controlled by a privileged register `FPEXC`. In Linux, when a program accesses VFP for the first time, an `UNDEFINED` exception is raised and the kernel is responsible for enabling VFP support for this program. To support multiple processes accessing VFP concurrently, the kernel maintains a VFP context for each process in its kernel stack. This design obviously leaks user data contained in VFP registers to kernel. In `TrustShadow`, the

[3]`pretcode` points to a piece of code calling the `rt_sigreturn` system call on sigpage. This piece of code is common to all the processes.

[4]`TrustShadow` reserves configurable number of secure pages specifically for this purpose.

[5]A blocked thread can never issue another `futex` wait operation.

```
{
  .executable = "nginx",
  .key = {0xef, 0xe2, ... },
  .imageHash = {
    {
      .vaddr = 0x10000,
      .hash = {0x36, 0x3f, ...},
    },
    ...
  }
  .protectedFile = {"/opt/nginx/private.key",0},
  .digest = {0x32, 0x34, ...}
}
```

Figure 4: A sample manifest. Note that **`protectedFile`** specifies the file names that `TrustShadow` needs to protect; **`digest`** indicates the signature of this manifest.

runtime system duplicates the code handling VFP from the Linux OS. More specifically, the runtime system maintains a VFP context in the secure memory for each HAP that requires VFP calculation, and clears VFP registers whenever switching to the ordinary OS.

Random Number Generator. The Linux pseudo-Random Number Generator (LRNG) is the main source of randomness for many cryptographic applications, such as OpenSSL. Linux provides LRNG service by exposing `/dev/(u)random` devices to applications. Since using weak random values is a catastrophe for cryptographic systems, and an untrusted OS should not know the key materials used in the application, `TrustShadow` provides a trusted RNG service in the secure world. Specifically, the runtime system maintains a list of file descriptors that correspond to opened `/dev/(u)random` devices. Read operations on these descriptors are intercepted such that trusted random values are directly provided. The runtime system readily utilizes the on-board hardware random number generator RNG4 to generate strong random numbers.

6.6 Manifest Design

As mentioned in prior sections, each HAP is bundled with a manifest that provides metadata for the security features. We design a manifest to contain the following – a per-application secret key, the integrity metadata of the application (i.e., the `(vaddr, hash)` list), and a list of file names that should be cryptographically protected.

Since the manifest is stored on a local persistent storage which can be accessed by the OS, we design two mechanisms to ensure its security. First, we encrypt the per-application secret key using a per-device public key. Therefore, only the runtime system which has access to the per-device private key is able to decrypt it. Second, to ensure the integrity of the manifest, we append a digital signature calculated on the content of the manifest using a per-device private key. In a real deployment, we note that per-device public/private key pairs used for encryption and signature should be separated. In the presentation of this paper, we refer to them as a single key pair for simplicity. Figure 4 shows a C-data-structure-equivalent of a sample manifest we used to safeguard the Nginx web server.

7. IMPLEMENTATION

We have implemented `TrustShadow` on a `Freescale` `i.MX6q` ARM development board that integrates an ARM Cortex-A9 MPCore processor, 1GB DDR3 DRAM and 256KB iRAM. As is discussed in the section above, `TrustShadow` involves operations on both the normal and secure worlds. In this section, we therefore describe our implementation details in turn.

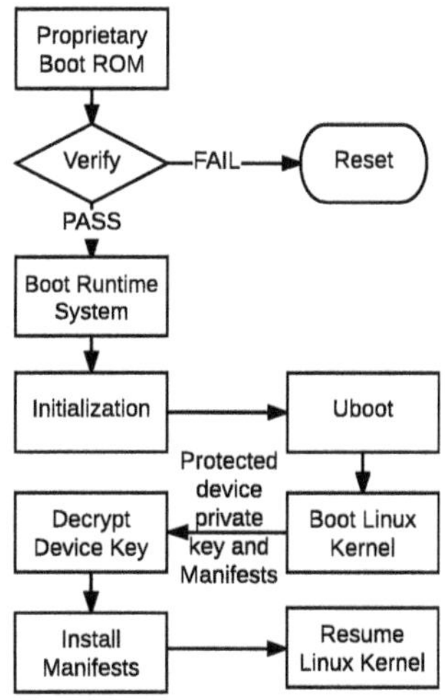

Figure 5: The boot sequence of `TrustShadow`. The components on the left and right indicate the operations in the secure and normal world, respectively.

7.1 Normal World

In the normal world, we made the following changes to a Linux OS distribution with kernel version 3.18.24. (i) We added kernel parameter **`tz_mem=size@start`** which indicates the memory region used for HAPs, i.e., `ZONE_TZ_APP`. (ii) We changed zone-based allocator to ensure that the pages designated to shadow HAPs must be from the memory region indicated by **`tz_mem=size@start`**. (iii) We added a **`tz`** flag to **`task_struct`** in order to make the OS capable of distinguishing HAPs. (iv) We implemented a new system call **`tz_execve`** in order to start an HAP in Linux. (v) We changed the control flow of **`ret_to_user`** and **`ret_fast_syscall`**, so that the Linux OS can pass the execution back to a corresponding shadow HAP instead of a zombie HAP. (vi) We hooked the page fault handler so that it can prepare page table update information for the runtime system. (vii) We modified the code handling signals in order to set up a signal stack in the marshaling buffer and make it ready for an HAP. In total, these changes introduce about 300 LOC to the Linux kernel.

7.2 Secure World

In the secure world, we implemented the aforementioned runtime system with about 4.5K LOC of ANSI C and 0.8K LOC of assembly. In addition, we implemented a secure boot mechanism to guarantee the integrity of **`TrustShadow`**. Figure 5 describes how we implemented a secure boot for **`TrustShadow`**.

Using High Assurance Boot (HAB), a proprietary boot ROM first loads the image of the runtime system. Then, it performs a verification and examines the integrity of the image. After passing the integrity check, the runtime system starts, using TZASC to configure the access policy of mem-

Test case	Latency (μs)		Overhead		
	Linux	Trust Shadow	Trust Shadow	InkTag	Virtual Ghost
null syscall	0.7989	1.6048	2.01x	55.80x	3.90x
open/close	29.2168	40.7886	1.40x	4.83x	7.95x
mmap (64m)	559.0000	784.0000	1.40x	4.70x	9.94x
pagefault	4.7989	7.9764	1.66x	1.15x	7.50x
signal handler install	1.6257	3.8294	2.36x	3.24x	-
signal handler delivery	51.6111	57.0349	1.11x	1.61x	-
fork+exit	987.0000	2328.6000	2.36x	4.40x	5.74x
fork+exec	1060.3333	2509.0000	2.37x	4.20x	3.04x
select (200fd)	15.0707	18.8649	1.25x	3.40x	-
ctxsw 2p/0k	30.3700	32.7100	1.08x	-	1.41x

Table 1: LMbench micro-benchmark results.

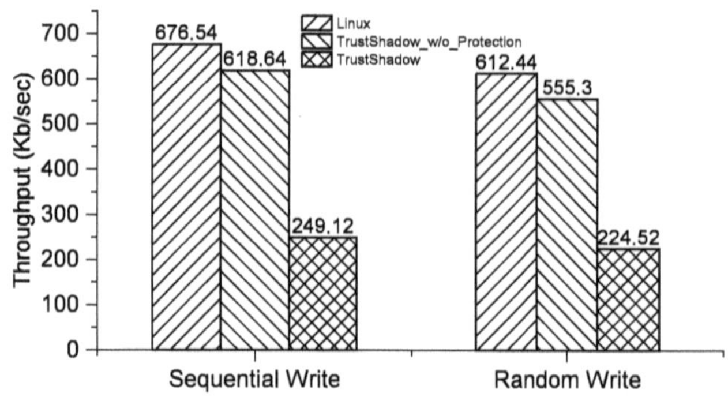

Figure 6: File I/O performance as measured by sequential and random write.

ory regions ZONE_TZ_RT, ZONE_NORMAL, and ZONE_TZ_APP. To guarantee the policy cannot be maliciously altered, the runtime locks the configuration. As a result, further modifications to the policy requires system reboot.

After the success of initialization, the runtime system loads uboot binary [44] which further boots the Linux system implemented above. The Linux system runs in the normal world where it retrieves the manifest as well as the public/private key pair stored on the persistent storage. Note that, our implementation encrypts the public/private key pair in advance using the 256-bit Zeroizable Master Key (ZMK) stored on Freescale i.MX6q board. This ensures the key pair is not disclosed to the Linux in plaintext. We believe this implementation is a common practice for many device manufacturers [38].

To facilitate the secure boot, the Linux system passes the manifest and public/private key pair to the runtime system which further decrypts the key pair and installs the manifest. With this process completion, the runtime passes the execution back to the Linux system.

8. EVALUATION

In this section, we evaluate TrustShadow by conducting extensive experiments. Using microbenchmarks, we first explore the impact of TrustShadow upon primitive OS operations. Second, we quantify the overhead of I/O operations imposed by TrustShadow. Last, we run real world applications and study the overall performance overhead introduced by our system. We conducted the aforementioned experiments on a Freescale i.MX6q board running both native Linux and our TrustShadow. We treated the performance observed from native Linux as our baseline and compared it with that observed from TrustShadow.

8.1 Microbenchmarks

Using LMBench [36], we study the overhead imposed to basic OS operations. More specifically, we ran various system services present in Table 1 against both native Linux and TrustShadow. To minimize the noise involved during our experiment, we ran each benchmark with 1,000 iterations and took the average as our measures. We also compared the overhead imposed by TrustShadow with that introduced by InkTag [26] and VirtualGhost [16]. This is because both share the same goal with our system although they are designed specifically for x86 architecture and not applicable to IoT devices typically embedded with ARM processors.

Table 1 shows the results indicating the overhead that TrustShadow imposes to various system services. In addition, it presents the overhead introduced by InkTag and VirtualGhost. Note that we did not run experiments on these two systems. Rather, we obtained their overhead measures from the articles previously published in [26, 16].

First, we observe that TrustShadow introduces considerable overheads to individual operations. Most notably are fork+exit, fork+exec and signal handler install, all of which increase overhead by about 2.36x. The high overhead introduced by the first two services is mainly due to the fact that TrustShadow optimizes the OS to populate all the marshaling buffer in one go when creating a new thread. And, the high overhead imposed by signal handler install results from copying a signal stack from the page in the normal world to one in the secure world.

Second, across most test cases shown in Table 1, we observe that the overhead imposed by TrustShadow are relatively lower than that introduced by InkTag and VirtualGhost. The reason is, InkTag and VirtualGhost require additional CPU cycles to communicate with Virtual Machine (VM) or execute the code instrumented to kernel, whereas TrustShadow does not rely on VM nor instrument large amount of code to kernel. Compared with InkTag, we also observe that TrustShadow imposes high overhead to system service pagefault. This is because TrustShadow needs to perform additional page copy or zeroization, which is not required for InkTag.

While the overhead shown in the table appears large, it should be noted that, this does not imply that TrustShadow jeopardizes the performance of applications under protection. In fact, applications are significantly less sensitive to system services. As we will show later in the section, TrustShadow imposes only negligible performance overhead to application execution.

8.2 File Operations

To quantify the overhead imposed to I/O throughput, we conducted an experiment by using Sysbench [29] in different modes. As is discussed earlier, TrustShadow allows developers to designate whether or not to protect a particular file. Thus, we did this experiment with and without file protection enabled.

We prepared 128 files, each of which has 8Mb, and tested both sequential write and random write. To minimize cache effects and best reflect the actual I/O performance, we con-

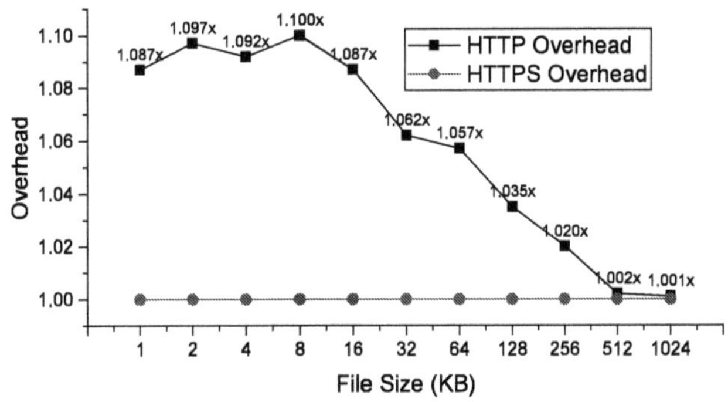

Figure 7: Throughput overhead imposed by TrustShadow across HTML responses in different sizes.

ducted experiments with write-through mode, and forced a call to `fsync()` after each write operation.

Figure 6 shows the results. Because caching is disabled, sequential write did not exhibit significant advantage over random write. In both cases, the slowdown introduced by TrustShadow without file protection is about 1.09x, while the slowdown by TrustShadow with file protection is about 2.71x. This is due to the fact that TrustShadow with file protection enabled involves heavy encryption and hashing computations when it synchronizes pages to persistent storage. Note that the difference between TrustShadow with and without file protection solely results from cryptographic operations. As a result, employing a more efficient cryptographic engine is a straightforward way of improving file I/O performance.

8.3 Embedded Web Server

To study the impact of TrustShadow upon real-world applications, we mimic an embedded web server running on an IoT device. More specifically, we ran the Nginx web server with version 1.9.15 on our testbed against both native Linux and TrustShadow. We configured Nginx to respond with HTML file in different sizes through both HTTP and HTTPs. To quantify the server throughput, we utilized the Apache benchmark [1] on another machine to connect to the server. We configured the benchmark program to create 10 connections simultaneously sending 10,000 HTTP requests. This experiment setting allows us to overwhelm the server and thus compare the throughput variation from the viewpoint of an end user.

Figure 7 shows the throughput overhead of Nginx. Regarding to the requests through HTTP, we observe that, TrustShadow downgrades the server throughput by about 6% $\sim$ 10% when a client requests a file in a relatively small size. However, this throughput downgrade is alleviated when the requested file increases. As is shown in Figure 7, the server throughput drops only by 2% when a client requests a file with a size more than 256 KB. Regarding latency, we measured the 95% percentile in each experiment, and found almost no latency overhead. The raw HTTP performance measurements can be found in Appendix B. In addition, we discover TrustShadow introduces nearly no overhead regardless of whether the size of the file requested varies when HTTP traffic is carried through TLS. The reason behind these observations is that the overhead imposed by TrustShadow is overwhelmed by intensive I/O and computationally intensive cryptographic operations, respectively.

8.4 Data Analytics

We also evaluate the performance overhead when performing data analysis using machine learning techniques. This kind of applications is popular for many edge computing platforms. To evaluate the impact of TrustShadow upon such applications, we chose two data analytic applications to emulate face recognition and image classification. To be more specific, we ran an DLIB image classification program [28] powered by deep neural networks against 60,000 images from the MNIST database [30], as well as a face recognition program against 10 images with human faces from the DLIB toolkits.

In the first experiment, we observed that TrustShadow classifies 60,000 images in 998 seconds, which is only 4 seconds higher than performing the same classification on native Linux. In the second experiment, we observed that TrustShadow recognizes faces in 163.271 seconds, whereas native Linux finishes the same task in 162.591 seconds. The observations from both experiments again indicate TrustShadow introduces only negligible overhead to IoT devices.

9. DISCUSSION AND FUTURE WORK

In this section, we first summarize how TrustShadow defeats OS level attacks to an HAP. Then, we analyze the security of TrustShadow, quantify its TCB, and discuss the remaining attack surface. Finally, we discuss future work.

HAP Security. TrustShadow protects an application from three aspects. (1) With a mechanism to verify the integrity of a program image, an attacker cannot manipulate application code/data at *load time*. (2) With the isolation of resources and introspection mechanism, an attacker cannot interfere with HAP execution at *run time*. The only user memory that the OS can access is the marshaling buffer. (3) With a cryptographic mechanism encrypting files and signing meta data, attackers can no longer read a file under protection or make any modification to it.

Runtime System Security. The protection above is established on the basis of the correctness and robustness of the runtime system. Our design guarantees the security of the runtime system from three aspects. First, our design ensures the integrity of the runtime system at load time because the hash of the verification public key is burned in the chip's fuses and HAB uses this key to verify the signature of the runtime system image before loading it. Second, our design reduces the attack surface of the runtime system because the runtime system itself is loaded into a secure physical region which the ordinary OS cannot manipulate. Third, our design raises the bar for exploiting the runtime system. This is due to three reasons. (1) An application must undergo critical security reviews before being authorized to run as an HAP (i.e., providing it with a manifest with manufacture signature). (2) Even if an HAP has vulnerabilities that may be exploited to execute arbitrary code, it only runs with user privilege. (3) The interface exposed by the runtime system is narrow, because it simply forwards most exceptions to the OS. Also, the small code base of runtime system makes it possible for formal verification.

TCB Size. To demonstrate the security of `TrustShadow` quantitatively, we identify the TCB of our system, and compare its size with x86 alternatives.

Ultimately, all the code in the user's TCB must be trusted. Therefore, like all the other works in this line, user application is included in the TCB. The size of user application is highly dependent on its functionality and complexity. We rely on code review to achieve trust for this part of TCB.

The runtime system maintains the execution environment for an HAP, and thus must be included in the TCB. As mentioned earlier, our runtime system has only about 5.3K LOC, which we believe is small enough for manual review or formal verification. In comparison, previous x86 works have their own privileged code that must be trusted. Hypervisor-based solutions [13, 12, 46, 26] include the whole hypervisor in its TCB, bloating their TCBs by several hundreds of thousands of lines of code. Although thinner hypervisors exist [33], we are not aware of any similar system built on top of them. Haven [6] includes LibOS, a large subset of Windows in its TCB, resulting a TCB of millions LOC. VirtualGhost [16] includes about 5.3K LOC for their run-time system and LLVM passes. This is the only solution that has comparable TCB with `TrustShadow`.

Remaining Attack Surface. To minimizes TCB, the runtime system does not implement system services itself, but relies on the OS. With full control of process scheduling, the OS can easily launch DoS attacks to an HAP. Similarly, to start an HAP, the OS may choose to invoke the normal `execve` system call instead of `tz_execve`. However, the process is executed in the normal world, so it cannot access cryptographically protected files.

Another concern is the manipulation of manifest files. If a manifest file can be forged, integrity checking of the corresponding executable image is bypassed. As a result, arbitrary code can be loaded in the secure world. We address this problem by signing the manifests using a per-device private key. When a vulnerable program is updated, the corresponding manifest should be updated as well. A roll-back attack happens when an attacker executes the vulnerable version of the program with an older manifest. To prevent this from happening, one of our future work is to add a version number field in the manifest, and periodically communicate a list showing the updated version numbers of trusted programs between the runtime system and a remote server.

Last but not least, side channel attacks have been developed to extract information across processes in an OS, or even virtual machines [47, 49, 24, 31]. For example, in [24], the authors introduced a cache storage channel that exploits the inconsistence of cache and physical memory data, and infers victim's behaviors in TrustZone by checking if the constructed inconsistence has been destroyed. `TrustShadow`'s current design may be subject to this line of side channel attacks. However, we can adopt existing techniques to mitigate such attacks. For example, contemporary cryptographic libraries such as OpenSSL have already been designed to resist some side channel attacks [40].

Future Work. Many IoT devices, such as cyber-physical systems, are sometimes deployed in an unmonitored environment. As a result, secret data stored in the DRAM chip is subject to inexpensive physical attacks, such as cold-boot attack [25, 37], bus monitoring [23], and DMA attacks [7, 27]. In [14, 48], the authors proposed to process confidential data within SoC components such as cache and iRAM, because it is considered much harder to compromise a SoC component. In `TrustShadow`, we can simply configure the region `ZONE_TZ_APP` to be within the range of iRAM to make HAPs immune to physical attacks.

We have tested this idea on our experiment board, which integrates a 256KB iRAM. We successfully ran a small program that generates a 2048-bit RSA key-pair with OpenSSL. As the capacity of iRAM is usually limited, this enhanced security feature could only be activated for low footprint programs. One of our future work is to "extend" iRAM by introducing another level of virtual memory – utilizing DRAM as a backup storage for encrypted iRAM pages.

Although hypervisor-based solutions are not applicable to shield trusted applications in ARM platform as discussed in Section 2, the idea of cloaking memory with a privileged layer has long been studied. With a hypervisor, trusted applications can run in the normal world, which could greatly reduce the risk in the presence of a vulnerable runtime system. While TrustZone is not designed to provide features such as shadow page table that a standard hypervisor could provide, some existing work, such as TZ-RKP [5] and Sprobes [22], has the potential to emulate these features in the secure world. Integrating the technique of across worlds hypervision with existing shielding mechanisms remains another topic for our future work.

10. CONCLUSION

In this paper, we have presented `TrustShadow` that utilizes a carefully designed runtime system to shield applications running on multi-programming IoT devices. With `TrustShadow`, security-critical applications on these devices can be comprehensively protected even in the face of total OS compromise. Unlike techniques previously proposed, the design of `TrustShadow` does not require modification to applications. As a result, security can be guaranteed without the requirement of re-engineering applications. Since `TrustShadow` imposes only negligible – and occasionally moderate – overhead to IoT devices, the protection of an application can be achieved in a lightweight manner. With an increasing number of IoT devices developed, we expect the design of `TrustShadow` could inspire more research in the area of IoT computing.

11. ACKNOWLEDGMENTS

We would like to thank the anonymous reviewers for their insightful feedback and our shepherd, Ardalan Amiri Sani, for his valuable comments on revision of this paper. This work was supported by U.S. Army Research Office award W911NF-13-1-0421 (MURI), NSF under Grant No. CNS-1422594, CNS-1505664, CNS-1634441, CNS-1422355, CNS-1408880, SBE-1422215, and the Penn State Institute for CyberScience (ICS) Seed Funding Initiative grant. Any opinions, findings, and conclusions or recommendations expressed in this material are those of the authors and do not necessarily reflect the views of the National Science Foundation and U.S. Army Research Office.

12. REFERENCES

[1] Apache Software Foundation. Apache HTTP server benchmarking tool. http://httpd.apache.org/docs/2.4/programs/ab.html.

[2] ARM Architecture Group. Virtualization Extensions Architecture Specification, 2010. https://www.arm.com/products/processors/technologies/virtualization-extensions.php.

[3] ARM Architecture Group. ARMv8-M Architecture Simplifies Security for Smart Embedded Devices, 2015. https://www.arm.com/about/newsroom/armv8-m-architecture-simplifies-security-for-smart-embedded-devices.php.

[4] ARM Ltd. Security technology building a secure system using trustzone technology (white paper). 2009.

[5] A. M. Azab, P. Ning, J. Shah, Q. Chen, R. Bhutkar, G. Ganesh, J. Ma, and W. Shen. Hypervision across worlds: Real-time kernel protection from the arm trustzone secure world. In *ACM CCS'14, 2014*, pages 90–102. ACM, 2014.

[6] A. Baumann, M. Peinado, and G. Hunt. Shielding applications from an untrusted cloud with haven. In *OSDI'14, 2014*, pages 267–283, Broomfield, CO, Oct. 2014. USENIX Association.

[7] M. Becher, M. Dornseif, and C. Klein. Firewire: All your memory are belong to us. In *6th Annual CanSecWest Conference*, 2005.

[8] F. Bonomi, R. Milito, P. Natarajan, and J. Zhu. Fog computing: A platform for internet of things and analytics. In *Big Data and Internet of Things: A Roadmap for Smart Environments*, pages 169–186. Springer, 2014.

[9] F. Bonomi, R. Milito, J. Zhu, and S. Addepalli. Fog computing and its role in the internet of things. In *Proceedings of the First Edition of the MCC Workshop on Mobile Cloud Computing*, MCC '12, pages 13–16, New York, NY, USA, 2012. ACM.

[10] S. Checkoway, L. Davi, A. Dmitrienko, A.-R. Sadeghi, H. Shacham, and M. Winandy. Return-oriented programming without returns. In *ACM CCS'10, 2010*, pages 559–572. ACM, 2010.

[11] S. Checkoway and H. Shacham. Iago attacks: Why the system call api is a bad untrusted rpc interface. In *ASPLOS'13, 2013*, pages 253–264, New York, NY, USA, 2013. ACM.

[12] H. Chen, F. Zhang, C. Chen, Z. Yang, R. Chen, B. Zang, P.-c. Yew, and W. Mao. Tamper-resistant execution in an untrusted operating system using a virtual machine monitor. Technical Report FDUPPITR-2007-0801, Parallel Processing Institute, Fudan University, August 2007.

[13] X. Chen, T. Garfinkel, E. C. Lewis, P. Subrahmanyam, C. A. Waldspurger, D. Boneh, J. Dwoskin, and D. R. Ports. Overshadow: A virtualization-based approach to retrofitting protection in commodity operating systems. In *ASPLOS'08, 2008*, pages 2–13, New York, NY, USA, 2008. ACM.

[14] P. Colp, J. Zhang, J. Gleeson, S. Suneja, E. de Lara, H. Raj, S. Saroiu, and A. Wolman. Protecting data on smartphones and tablets from memory attacks. In *ASPLOS'15, 2015*, pages 177–189, New York, NY, USA, 2015. ACM.

[15] N. Constant, D. Borthakur, M. Abtahi, H. Dubey, and K. Mankodiya. Fog-assisted wiot: A smart fog gateway for end-to-end analytics in wearable internet of things. *CoRR*, abs/1701.08680, 2017.

[16] J. Criswell, N. Dautenhahn, and V. Adve. Virtual ghost: Protecting applications from hostile operating systems. In *ASPLOS'14, 2014*, pages 81–96, New York, NY, USA, 2014. ACM.

[17] CVEdetails.com. Vmware: Vulnerability statistics. http://www.cvedetails.com/vendor/252/Vmware.html.

[18] CVEdetails.com. Xen: Vulnerability statistics. http://www.cvedetails.com/vendor/6276/XEN.html.

[19] Eric Brown. First linux-based 3d printers hit the market. http://hackerboards.com/first-linux-based-3d-printers-hit-the-market/.

[20] Felix Baum. Why you don't necessarily need a hypervisor, 2014. http://embedded-computing.com/guest-blogs/why-you-dont-necessarily-need-a-hypervisor/.

[21] T. Garfinkel, B. Pfaff, J. Chow, M. Rosenblum, and D. Boneh. Terra: A virtual machine-based platform for trusted computing. In *SOSP'03, 2003*, pages 193–206, New York, NY, USA, 2003. ACM.

[22] X. Ge, H. Vijayakumar, and T. Jaeger. Sprobes: Enforcing kernel code integrity on the trustzone architecture. 2014.

[23] G. Gogniat, T. Wolf, W. Burleson, J.-P. Diguet, L. Bossuet, and R. Vaslin. Reconfigurable hardware for high-security/high-performance embedded systems: the safes perspective. *Very Large Scale Integration (VLSI) Systems, IEEE Transactions on*, 16(2):144–155, 2008.

[24] R. Guanciale, H. Nemati, C. Baumann, and M. Dam. Cache Storage Channels: Alias-Driven Attacks and Verified Countermeasures. In *The 37th IEEE Symposium on Security and Privacy (S&P)*, SAN JOSE, CA, May 23-25 2016. IEEE.

[25] J. Halderman, S. Schoen, N. Heninger, W. Clarkson, W. Paul, J. Calandrino, A. Feldman, J. Appelbaum, and E. Felten. Lest We Remember: Cold Boot Attacks on Encryption Keys. In *17th USENIX Security Symposium*, pages 45–60, 2008.

[26] O. S. Hofmann, S. Kim, A. M. Dunn, M. Z. Lee, and E. Witchel. Inktag: Secure applications on an untrusted operating system. In *ASPLOS'13, 2013*, pages 265–278, New York, NY, USA, 2013. ACM.

[27] D. Hulton. Cardbus bus-mastering: 0wning the laptop. In *Annual ShmooCon Convention*, 2006.

[28] D. E. King. Dlib-ml: A machine learning toolkit. *J. Mach. Learn. Res.*, 10:1755–1758, Dec. 2009.

[29] A. Kopytov. SysBench: A System Performance Benchmark, 2004. https://github.com/akopytov/sysbench.

[30] Y. LeCun, C. Cortes, and C. J. Burges. The mnist database of handwritten digits, 1998. http://yann.lecun.com/exdb/mnist/.

[31] M. Lipp, D. Gruss, R. Spreitzer, C. Maurice, and S. Mangard. Armageddon: Cache attacks on mobile devices. In *25th USENIX Security Symposium (USENIX Security 16)*, pages 549–564, Austin, TX, Aug. 2016. USENIX Association.

[32] D. Liu and L. P. Cox. Veriui: Attested login for

mobile devices. In *Proceedings of the 15th Workshop on Mobile Computing Systems and Applications*, page 7. ACM, 2014.

[33] J. M. McCune, Y. Li, N. Qu, Z. Zhou, A. Datta, V. Gligor, and A. Perrig. Trustvisor: Efficient tcb reduction and attestation. In *2010 IEEE Symposium on Security and Privacy*, pages 143–158, May 2010.

[34] J. M. McCune, B. J. Parno, A. Perrig, M. K. Reiter, and H. Isozaki. Flicker: An execution infrastructure for tcb minimization. *SIGOPS Oper. Syst. Rev.*, 42(4):315–328, Apr. 2008.

[35] F. McKeen, I. Alexandrovich, A. Berenzon, C. V. Rozas, H. Shafi, V. Shanbhogue, and U. R. Savagaonkar. Innovative instructions and software model for isolated execution. In *Proceedings of the 2Nd International Workshop on Hardware and Architectural Support for Security and Privacy*, HASP '13, pages 10:1–10:1, New York, NY, USA, 2013. ACM.

[36] L. McVoy and C. Staelin. Lmbench: Portable tools for performance analysis. In *Proceedings of the 1996 Annual Conference on USENIX Annual Technical Conference*, ATEC '96, pages 23–23, Berkeley, CA, USA, 1996. USENIX Association.

[37] T. Müller, M. Spreitzenbarth, and F. Freiling. FROST: Forensic recovery of scrambled telephones. In *11th International Conference on Applied Cryptography and Network Security*, pages 373–388, 2013.

[38] Samsung Electronics. The KNOX Workspace Technical Details. https://www.samsungknox.com/en/products/knox-workspace/technical.

[39] N. Santos, H. Raj, S. Saroiu, and A. Wolman. Using arm trustzone to build a trusted language runtime for mobile applications. In *ASPLOS'14, 2014*, pages 67–80, New York, NY, USA, 2014. ACM.

[40] P. Schwabe. Eliminating Timing Side-Channels. A Tutorial, 2015.

[41] V. D. Silva, D. Kroening, and G. Weissenbacher. A survey of automated techniques for formal software verification. *Computer-Aided Design of Integrated Circuits and Systems, IEEE Transactions on*, 27(7):1165–1178, 2008.

[42] H. Sun, K. Sun, Y. Wang, and J. Jing. Trustotp: Transforming smartphones into secure one-time password tokens. In *ACM CCS'15, 2015*, pages 976–988. ACM, 2015.

[43] R. Ta-Min, L. Litty, and D. Lie. Splitting interfaces: Making trust between applications and operating systems configurable. In *OSDI'06, 2006*, pages 279–292. USENIX Association, 2006.

[44] Wolfgang Denk. Das U-Boot – the Universal Boot Loader. http://www.denx.de/wiki/U-Boot/WebHome.

[45] Y. Xu, W. Cui, and M. Peinado. Controlled-channel attacks: Deterministic side channels for untrusted operating systems. In *2015 IEEE Symposium on Security and Privacy*, pages 640–656, May 2015.

[46] J. Yang and K. G. Shin. Using hypervisor to provide data secrecy for user applications on a per-page basis. In *Proceedings of the Fourth ACM SIGPLAN/SIGOPS International Conference on Virtual Execution Environments*, VEE '08, pages 71–80, New York, NY, USA, 2008. ACM.

[47] Y. Yarom and K. Falkner. FLUSH+RELOAD: A High Resolution, Low Noise, L3 Cache Side-Channel Attack. In *USENIX Security'14, 2014*, pages 719–732, San Diego, CA, Aug. 2014. USENIX Association.

[48] N. Zhang, K. Sun, W. Lou, and T. Hou. Case: Cache-assisted secure execution on arm processors. In *The 37th IEEE Symposium on Security and Privacy (S&P)*, SAN JOSE, CA, May 23-25 2016. IEEE.

[49] Y. Zhang, A. Juels, M. K. Reiter, and T. Ristenpart. Cross-tenant side-channel attacks in paas clouds. In *ACM CCS '14, 2014*, New York, NY, USA, 2014. ACM.

APPENDIX

A. CODE SNIPPET OF EXCEPTION FORWARDING

```
forward_syscall:
@ we start at monitor mode
@ spsr is set to SVC, which is the target
    mode
mov     r0, #(MODE_SVC | I_BIT | F_BIT)
msr     spsr_cxsf, r0

@ load r0 with the address of user space
    CPU_context
ldr     r0, =uregs
ldr     r0, [r0]

@ switch to SVC mode to set target mode's
    registers
cpsid   if, #MODE_SVC
ldr     r1, [r0, #CPSR]
msr     spsr_cxsf, r1

@ restore critical registers required by
    normal OS in SVC, ATB and IRQ modes
ldr     r1, =svc_sp
ldr     sp, [r1]
cpsid   if, #MODE_ABT
ldr     r1, =abt_sp
ldr     sp, [r1]
cpsid   if, #MODE_IRQ
ldr     r1, =irq_sp
ldr     sp, [r1]

@ back to monitor mode
cpsid       if, #MODE_MON

@ restore syscall arguments. r0-r6 for
    arguments, r7 for syscall number
...
@ before switching to normal OS, change
    securiry state to non-secure
pop     {r4}
eor     r4, r4, #NS_BIT @ Toggle NS bit
mcr     p15, 0, r4, c1, c1, 0
isb

@ branch to 0xFFFF0008, which is the
    offset for the SVC exception handler
mov     r8, #0x8
movt    r8, #0xFFFF
movs    pc, r8
```

Listing 1: Code snippet that forwards SVC exception to the normal OS.

B. RAW HTTP PERFORMANCE MEASUREMENTS

File size	Throughput (Requests/second)		95% Percentile (ms)	
	Linux	TrustShadow	Linux	TrustShadow
1KB	652.50	600.46	17	17
2KB	622.83	567.96	18	18
4KB	621.72	569.37	16	18
8KB	603.75	548.74	17	19
16KB	531.15	488.64	19	21
32KB	433.68	408.25	24	25
64KB	316.64	299.57	33	36
128KB	220.73	213.25	48	49
256KB	133.26	130.58	84	85
512KB	75.85	75.69	158	158
1024KB	42.68	42.64	307	309

Author Index

NOTES

9 781450 355964

www.ingramcontent.com/pod-product-compliance
Ingram Content Group UK Ltd.
Pitfield, Milton Keynes, MK11 3LW, UK
UKHW051415290926
15471UKWH00009B/1616

9 781450 355964